Chapter 8 (Variance Analysis) (continued)

Market share variance	Actual market size $\times$ (Actual market share $-$ Budgeted market share) $\times$ Budgeted unit contribution margin
Market size variance	(Actual market size $-$ Budgeted market size) $\times$ Budgeted market share $\times$ Budgeted unit contribution margin
Sales mix variance	Actual total sales $\times$ ($\text{WUCM}_{\text{flexible budget}} - \text{WUCM}_{\text{master budget}}$)
Sales price variance	(Actual sales price $-$ Budgeted sales price) $\times$ Actual sales quantity
Sales quantity variance	(Actual total sales $-$ Budgeted total sales) $\times \text{WUCM}_{\text{master budget}}$
Sales volume variance	Flexible budget profit $-$ Master budget profit (Actual sales quantity $-$ Budgeted sales quantity) $\times$ Budgeted unit contribution margin
Total profit variance	Actual profit $-$ Master budget profit

Chapter 11 (Capital Budgeting)

Accounting rate of return	Average annual income/Average annual investment
Depreciation tax shield	Depreciation expense $\times$ Tax rate
Future value of $1	$(1 + r)^n$
Future value of an annuity of $1 in arrears	$\dfrac{(1 + r)^n - 1}{r}$
Present value of $1	$1/(1 + r)^n$
Present value of an annuity of $1 in arrears	$\dfrac{1 - (1 + r)^{-n}}{r}$

Chapter 12 (Performance Evaluation)

Asset turnover	Sales/Investment
Economic value added (EVA)	Net operating profit after taxes $-$ [Weighted average cost of capital $\times$ (Invested capital $-$ Current liabilities)]
Profit margin	$1 - $ (Operating expenses/Sales)
Residual income (RI)	Profit $-$ (Required return $\times$ Investment)
Return on investment (ROI)	Profit/Investment
Minumum transfer price acceptable to selling division (TP_{MIN})	Variable cost of transfer $+$ Selling division's opportunity cost of capacity
Maximum transfer price the buying divisions is willing to pay (TP_{MIN})	Buying division's opportunity cost

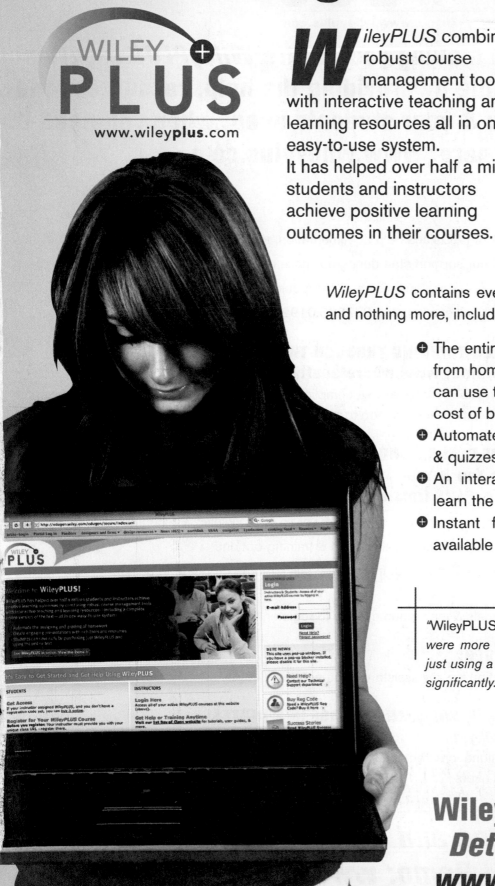

WILEY PLUS

www.wileyplus.com

Wiley is committed to making your entire *WileyPLUS* experience productive & enjoyable by providing the help, resources, and personal support you & your students need, when you need it. It's all here: www.wileyplus.com –

TECHNICAL SUPPORT:

⊕ A fully searchable knowledge base of FAQs and help documentation, available 24/7

⊕ Live chat with a trained member of our support staff during business hours

⊕ A form to fill out and submit online to ask any question and get a quick response

⊕ **Instructor-only** phone line during business hours: 1.877.586.0192

FACULTY-LED TRAINING THROUGH THE WILEY FACULTY NETWORK: Register online: www.wherefacultyconnect.com

Connect with your colleagues in a complimentary virtual seminar, with a personal mentor in your field, or at a live workshop to share best practices for teaching with technology.

1ST DAY OF CLASS...AND BEYOND! Resources You & Your Students Need to Get Started & Use *WileyPLUS* from the first day forward.

⊕ 2-Minute Tutorials on how to set up & maintain your *WileyPLUS* course

⊕ User guides, links to technical support & training options

⊕ ***WileyPLUS for Dummies***: Instructors' quick reference guide to using *WileyPLUS*

⊕ Student tutorials & instruction on how to register, buy, and use *WileyPLUS*

YOUR *WileyPLUS* ACCOUNT MANAGER:

Your personal *WileyPLUS* connection for any assistance you need!

SET UP YOUR *WileyPLUS* COURSE IN MINUTES!

Selected *WileyPLUS* courses with QuickStart contain pre-loaded assignments & presentations created by subject matter experts who are also experienced *WileyPLUS* users.

Interested? See and try WileyPLUS *in action!* Details and Demo: www.wileyplus.com

MANAGERIAL ACCOUNTING

MANAGERIAL ACCOUNTING

RAMJI BALAKRISHNAN

The University of Iowa

K. SIVARAMAKRISHNAN

University of Houston

GEOFFREY B. SPRINKLE

Indiana University

John Wiley & Sons, Inc

PUBLISHER	George Hoffman
ASSOCIATE PUBLISHER	Christopher DeJohn
SENIOR ACQUISITIONS EDITOR	Jeff Howard
SENIOR MARKETING MANAGER	Julia Flohr
SENIOR PRODUCTION EDITOR	William A. Murray
SENIOR DESIGNER	Kevin Murphy
SENIOR ILLUSTRATION EDITOR	Sandra Rigby
EDITORIAL ASSISTANT	Kara Taylor
ASSOCIATE PHOTO EDITOR	Sheena Goldstein
SENIOR MEDIA EDITOR	Allie K. Morris
INTERIOR DESIGN	Nancy Field
COVER DESIGN	David Levy
COVER PHOTO	Tyler Stableford/Getty Images

This book was set in New Baskerville Regular by GGS Book Services PMG and printed and bound by R.R. Donnelley.

This book is printed on acid free paper. ∞

To order books or for customer service please call 1-800-CALL WILEY (225-5945).

Library of Congress Cataloging-in-Publication Data
Balakrishnan, Ramji.
    Managerial accounting/Ramji Balakrishnan, K. Sivaramakrishnan, Geoffrey B. Sprinkle.
        p. cm.
    Includes index.
    ISBN 978-0-471-46785-4 (cloth)
    1. Managerial accounting. I. Sivaramakrishnan, K. (Konduru) II. Sprinkle, Geoffrey B.
    III. Title.
    HF5657.4.B34 2009   2008039519
    658.15'11—dc22

Printed in the United States of America
10 9 8 7 6 5 4 3 2 1

Dedication

Ramji Balakrishnan

To my parents, Usha, Vasu and Uma

K. Sivaramakrishnan

To my father, my sisters Viji and Parvathi, my wife Devika,
my daughter Vidya, and in loving memory of my mother

Geoffrey B. Sprinkle

To Shari, Jason, Jack, and Scott

About the Authors

Ramji Balakrishnan is the Carlson-KPMG Professor of Accounting and the Director of the RSM McGladrey Institute for Accounting Research and Education at the University of Iowa. Dr. Balakrishnan has a B.Sc. in Statistics from the University of Madras in 1977, an MBA from the Indian Institute of Management, Ahmedabad in 1979, and a Ph.D. from Columbia University in 1986. He is a Certified Management Accountant and is a recipient of the Robert Beyer Bronze Medal. He joined the University of Iowa in 1986 and has been there since except for a year at Georgia State University. A top-rated teacher and researcher, Dr. Balakrishnan has published his research in premier journals such as *The Accounting Review, Journal of Accounting Research, Contemporary Accounting Research, Management Science, Journal of Management Accounting Research* and *Accounting Horizons*. Along with Dr. Sivaramakrishnan, he won the 2003 Best Paper award for notable contribution to the management accounting literature. Dr. Balakrishnan serves on several Editorial Boards and has served as Associate Editor. He has taught managerial accounting at the undergraduate, graduate, and doctoral levels, and has published several teaching cases. He was the President of the Management Accounting Section of the AAA for 2005-2006.

Konduru "Shiva" Sivaramakrishnan is currently a Professor and C.T. Bauer Endowed Chair in Accounting at the C.T. Bauer College of Business, University of Houston. He received his BTech in Engineering from the Indian Institute of Technology, Madras in 1977, an MBA from Xavier Institute, Jamshedpur, India, in 1982, and a Ph.D. in Accounting and Information Systems from the Kellogg Graduate School of Management at Northwestern University in 1989. Prior to his current position, he was a tenured Associate Professor at the Graduate School of Industrial Administration, Carnegie Mellon University, and Professor and Philip Ljungdahl Chair in Accounting at Texas A&M University. Dr. Sivaramakrishnan has significant research and teaching accomplishments. His research has appeared in premier journals such as *The Accounting Review, Journal of Accounting Research, Contemporary Accounting Research, Management Science, Journal of Management Accounting Research, Accounting Horizons, Journal of Accounting and Economics, and Review of Financial Studies*. Along with Dr. Ramji Balakrishnan, he won the 2003 Best Paper award for notable contribution to the management accounting literature. Shiva serves on several editorial boards, and is currently an Associate Editor of the *Journal of Management Accounting Research*. He has won numerous awards for teaching excellence at both undergraduate and graduate levels.

Geoffrey B. Sprinkle is an Associate Professor, Whirlpool Faculty Fellow, and Chair of the Honors Program at the Kelley School of Business at Indiana University. Dr. Sprinkle has both B.S. and M.S. degrees in Accounting from Arizona State University, and his Ph.D. from The University of Iowa. He is a Certified Public Accountant, earning the Gold Medal in the state of Arizona on the May, 1989 CPA exam and the Elijah Watts Sells award nationally. He primarily teaches managerial accounting to undergraduates and is the recipient of numerous school-wide and university-level teaching awards. Dr. Sprinkle's writings focus on motivation and coordination problems within organizations, including performance-evaluation and reward systems. His work has been published in journals such as *The Accounting Review, The American Economic Review, Accounting, Organizations and Society, Journal of Accounting Research, Behavioral Research in Accounting, Issues in Accounting Education, and The Journal of Management Accounting Research*. He also currently serves on the Editorial Boards of *The Accounting Review, The British Accounting Review, Accounting, Organizations and Society*, and *The Journal of Management Accounting Research*.

Preface

Executive Summary

Compared to existing books on the market, we believe our book offers several advantages and unique features. Below, we summarize the key attributes of our text. In the pages following the summary, we provide a richer discussion of our approach and pedagogy.

- We provide an easy to understand **integrated framework** that links topics into a seamless whole. In the early chapters, we introduce two ideas: More costs and benefits become relevant as a decision's horizon expands, and all decisions involve a cycle of planning and control. We implement the first idea by organizing the text into modules corresponding to short-term and long-term decisions. We then address planning and control decisions within each horizon. We are pleased to report that our colleagues and we have received outstanding student feedback on the tightly integrated nature of our text— students and instructors report that chapters follow naturally from one to the next, with everything "fitting" together.

- Both the overall structure of the book and individual chapters emphasize **using accounting information for decision making.** Across chapters, we use the time-based template to emphasize the links among the various decisions that managers make, enabling students to see the linkages among seemingly unrelated decisions. Before each module, we use a part-opener to remind students about the relations among organizational decisions, and to place forthcoming topics in the appropriate context. Within each chapter, we maintain the focus on decision making by

exploring a specific business problem. Each chapter also uses the same four-step approach to solving business problems.

- Both the chapter text and end-of-chapter materials provide a **balanced coverage** of manufacturing and service sectors. Examples considered in the chapters include a gym, a caterer, a hospital, a consulting firm, a copy center, and a call center. Moreover, every chapter contains numerous exercises and problems relating to service and nonprofit settings. We have received rave reviews from instructors and students about both the breadth and depth of our end-of-chapter materials.

- The book is **student friendly.** Our initial drafts used a conversational tone and everyday examples to illustrate concepts. We then subjected these drafts to several rounds of review by English editors, undergraduate students, and faculty to increase accessibility and impact. In addition to the standard exhibits, we include "*Check It!*" boxes of mini-worksheets that students can use to verify and fine-tune their understanding of the material.

- We maintain the integrity of the framework while allowing instructors the **flexibility** to modify coverage to best suit their individual needs. We help instructors by presenting several sample syllabi that show alternate sequencing of topics (please see Section 5 in this Preface for further details). The primary flexibility lies in whether, after covering basic terminology and cost flows, instructors choose to cover product costing or to plunge directly into short-term decisions.

1. Introduction

Managerial accounting facilitates planning and control decisions. Planning decisions relate to choices about acquiring and using resources to deliver products and services to customers (e.g., which products and services to offer, their prices, and the resources needed, such as materials, labor, and equipment). Control decisions concern how much to delegate, as well as how to motivate, measure, evaluate, and reward performance.

Current managerial accounting textbooks generally group product costing, cost management (ABC/ABM), short-term decisions, and performance evaluation practices into four separate modules. This grouping allows students to gain a working knowledge of current managerial accounting practices. However, while each book may provide solid coverage on one or more important dimensions, none offers a satisfactory, overarching theme. The average student walks away with a collection of concepts and techniques but with little idea of why things work the way they do. Armed with only the "what" and the "how" but not the "why," students have no *framework* that lets them see the principles that drive practice or helps them adapt to novel or changing circumstances.

We provide instructors and students with a unifying, problem-solving framework. We believe that the framework itself must be the key takeaway from any introductory managerial accounting course. By virtue of its logic and internal consistency, the framework allows students to:

- Understand the big picture.
- Examine new ideas and concepts and their relation to existing practice.
- See how accounting information helps manage a complex entity.

At the core of our framework is the one feature common to all decisions—*every decision involves a cost-benefit trade-off.* The decision could be personal (should I eat out or make dinner?) or organizational (should we continue using traditional performance measures or switch to the balanced scorecard?). The decision could relate to planning (how should we price this product?) or control (where should we set the sales quota?). The theme of systematically measuring costs and benefits to make effective decisions runs throughout our text.

The first outgrowth of this theme, indicated by the titles of the modules, is our emphasis on a decision's horizon. Time influences whether a cost or benefit is relevant for decision. The costs of the production plant and equipment are not relevant to many short-term decisions. Thus, there is no need to allocate these fixed costs to make effective short-term decisions. In the long term, however, a firm can manage capacity costs by shrinking or expanding its investment in plant and equipment. Thus, to make effective long-term decisions, a firm needs to identify variations in resource consumption patterns and create allocation mechanisms that capture the cost impact of these variations. Ultimately, when confronted with a decision problem, the successful manager knows what costs and benefits to include in the decision, and how to measure these costs and benefits.

A second important aspect of our framework is an integrated treatment of planning and control decisions. Planning and control are two sides of the same coin. Diagnostic and feedback measures inform organizations of how well they implemented the plan, thereby providing input for the next plan. Similarly, performance evaluation and incentive schemes arise in response to strategic aspects of the planning process. An integrated treatment highlights these links, permitting students to perceive planning and control decisions as part of the same framework.

PEDAGOGY

Students learn best from simple examples. Once students understand the basic issues at an intuitive level, it is easier for them to understand similar issues in other business contexts. We therefore begin each chapter with an example that students can readily comprehend and to which they could relate. We then walk students through the issues and use the vignette as a springboard to more advanced settings.

In addition to linking topics across chapters, we tightly integrate topics within a chapter. To this end, each chapter tells a story. The opening vignette serves to raise pertinent questions, and the chapter answers these questions. In this fashion, the student perceives the concepts as being interrelated and not disjointed.

We note three other important features:

- We made a strategic decision to collaborate on one chapter at a time; although more time-consuming, this team-based approach ensures that we choose the best among the many ways of presenting the same material. This approach ensures that the book speaks with one voice.

- We have tried to make the text extremely accessible. This allows instructors, after ensuring that students understand the basics, to devote some class time to higher-order learning and explore conceptual and qualitative issues. As detailed in Section 4, the end-of-chapter materials contain thought questions that instructors can use to initiate such discussions.

- We hope to surprise you with both the breadth and depth of our end-of-chapter materials. We have devoted substantial efforts to ensuring that the problems and solutions are of the highest quality.

2. Audience

The typical student has limited exposure to business, even though she may have taken courses in financial accounting and microeconomics. Accordingly, the key task is both to explain the many kinds of decisions needed to operate a successful business and to communicate how managers use cost information in these decisions. It is not enough to know prevalent practice. It is vital that the student understand whether and why a certain practice has merit in a given situation. This understanding requires a sound framework. In line with the adage about teaching a man to fish, we believe that the average student will appreciate our framework for decision making.

The focus on using cost data for decision making makes our book well suited for a course that employs a user-perspective. We believe that such a user-focus is particularly appropriate for the introductory course. It also is consistent with the widespread move to change the curriculum from a technical-accounting perspective to a business-oriented, or process, perspective.

3. Organization of Content

Module I: INTRODUCTION AND FRAMEWORK

Our first module contains three chapters. In Chapter 1, we illustrate a four-step framework for decision making, and we distinguish how individuals make decisions from how organizations make decisions. We next introduce two important classes of organizational decisions—planning decisions and control decisions. We then discuss how organizations use managerial accounting information for both planning and control. We conclude Chapter 1 by examining the role of ethics in decision making, and discussing how societal and professional standards shape organizational decisions.

Making a decision requires that we identify what costs and benefits to measure, and then estimate them. Chapters 2 focuses on the principles that help us accomplish these two tasks. We begin with two principles, controllability and relevance, that determine *which costs and benefits to measure.* Using these principles, we offer an approach for grouping business decisions per their horizon. This grouping of decisions forms the basis for the modular approach that unfolds. We next discuss the principles that are fundamental to estimating costs and benefits: variability and traceability. Finally, we extend the principle of variability to develop a hierarchy of costs, which helps to increase the accuracy of estimated costs.

We conclude this introductory module with a chapter on cost terminology and an overview of how accounting systems record the flow of costs. This chapter begins by discussing cost flows in a service environment such as a health club, where the accounting and cost flows are somewhat intuitive. We next move to cost flows in merchandising firms to introduce the concept of an inventory account. Finally, we consider manufacturing organizations.

Module II: SHORT-TERM PLANNING AND CONTROL: MAXIMIZING CONTRIBUTION

We define the short term as a period over which organizations cannot change capacity costs arising from long-term commitments related to property, plant, equipment, and personnel. These costs, which we often term fixed costs, are therefore not relevant for short-term decisions. Accordingly, the goal for short-term decisions is to maximize contribution margin, which is revenue less variable costs.

We begin Module II with a discussion of how to estimate relevant costs for short-term decisions. The key here is to identify fixed and variable costs, leading us to discuss techniques such as account classification, the high-low method, and regression analysis. We end this chapter by showing how a contribution margin statement helps managers organize the resulting information to make effective short-term decisions.

We devote Chapters 5 and 6 to planning decisions. In Chapter 5, we introduce Cost-Volume-Profit (CVP) analysis, a natural outgrowth of the contribution margin statement studied in the previous chapter. The CVP relations among costs, volume, and profit provide a convenient tool for profit planning. Following this, we apply the CVP relation to evaluate decision options and, in the process, illustrate how managers could use the CVP relations to evaluate operating risk.

While CVP analysis is useful for overall profit planning, it is not suitable for many localized decision problems that arise because of the temporary mismatch between the supply and demand for capacity resources. Specifically, most organizations invest in capacity resources such as plant, equipment, and personnel based on expectations of long-term demand. Actual demand rarely equals anticipated demand, however. In some periods, actual demand falls short of expectations, meaning that managers must find ways to utilize idle resources gainfully. At other times, actual demand exceeds available capacity, changing the manager's problem to one of extracting the maximum benefit from available resources. In either instance, organizations cannot fix the mismatch by changing capacity because they cannot control capacity levels and costs in the short term. In Chapter 6, we discuss two approaches—the incremental and totals—to frame and solve such decision problems. We illustrate these approaches in several contexts such as make-or-buy, accepting a special order, and allocating a scarce resource.

Chapter 7 examines operating budgets. Budgets incorporate planning decisions on how and where to use resources. Budgets also serve as the benchmark for evaluating actual results, a control decision. In this way, budgets bridge the planning and control dimensions. We emphasize the tension between the planning and control roles for budgets in our discussion of both the mechanics of budgeting and the budgeting process.

Chapter 8 focuses on short-term control decisions. We begin by introducing the concept of a variance, which is the deviation between a budgeted and actual result. We then present the mechanics of variance analysis, with a focus on using variances to reconcile budgeted and actual profit. Finally, we emphasize the link back to planning decisions by discussing how to construct and interpret a profit reconciliation statement to determine possible corrective actions.

Module III: PLANNING AND CONTROL OVER THE LONG TERM: MAXIMIZING PROFIT

Over the long term, organizations can control most costs considered fixed in the short term. That is, organizations can alter capacity levels over this horizon. Thus, the goal for long-term decisions is to maximize profit, which is revenue less variable costs less capacity costs. However, it often is difficult to estimate the controllable costs for many long-term decisions that pertain to individual products or customers. The difficulty arises because products and customers typically share capacity resources, meaning that organizations cannot trace capacity costs to individual products and customers. In the language of Chapter 2, capacity costs are indirect costs. Consequently, while performing a detailed account analysis to estimate controllable capacity costs is the economically correct approach, it is not cost effective. Thus, as a practical matter, firms use cost allocations to approximate the change in capacity costs.

We devote Chapter 9 to cost allocations, a tool that firms employ to estimate costs over the long term. We begin by describing how a firm might use allocations in a common decision problem—setting prices. We note that firms allocate costs not just for decision making but for other reasons as well, including reporting income to external parties such as shareholders and the IRS, justifying cost-based reimbursements, and influencing behavior within the organization. Accordingly, we discuss these uses of cost allocations and how an allocation's intended purpose guides the choice of an allocation procedure. In this way, the chapter provides an integrated discussion of the various demands for cost allocations within an organization.

We focus Chapter 10 on activity-based costing (ABC) and management. At its core, ABC is a refined methodology for allocating capacity costs. We examine how ABC can lead to better decisions by improving estimates of controllable capacity costs. We then discuss the steps associated with designing product-costing systems and symptoms that might help organizations decide if they need to update the current costing system. We end by highlighting some of the costs and benefits of implementing ABC. ABC exploits the linkages among resources, activities, and products to provide more accurate measures of product profitability than traditional allocation systems do. Thus, after describing the mechanics of ABC, we discuss how to use ABC data to improve profitability by managing products, customers, and resources. Customer Profitability Analysis allows organizations to identify profitable and unprofitable customers, and suggests ways to increase profit by managing customer relationships. We refer to this and other uses of activity-based costing information to manage profit as activity-based management, or ABM.

Despite their widespread use, allocations have two limitations when used to make decisions: (1) They do not consider the time value of money; and (2) they do not consider the lumpy nature of capacity resources. These limitations are of particular concern when the firm is considering a large expenditure on a long-lived resource. For such expenditures, organizations routinely engage in capital budgeting, the focus of Chapter 11. As operational budgets do for short-term decisions, capital budgets provide the link between long-term planning and control decisions. In particular, capital budgets provide an economic basis for analyzing expenditures on capacity resources, and control decisions focus on the effective use of these resources.

Chapter 12 examines control decisions over the long term. Most organizations delegate decisions over the use of resources to managers lower in the organizational hierarchy. Decentralization leads to a conflict arising from the lack of goal congruence among different levels in the organization. Accordingly, we begin the chapter by discussing the benefits and costs associated with decentralizing decision making. We describe common forms of decentralization in organizations and highlight the critical role of performance evaluation systems in these environments. We discuss the principles that govern performance measurement in organizations, and apply them to measure and evaluate the performance of different responsibility centers.

In Chapter 13, we discuss how an organization's strategy affects its cost structure and defines the business and operational constructs that require measurement. We also introduce and present the balanced scorecard as a means of effectively integrating an organization's strategy with its control system. We begin with value chain analysis and strategic planning. We introduce strategy and, using real-world examples, highlight the critical linkages between the value chain, strategy, and cost structure. We next discuss the impact of strategy on key organizational processes. In each instance, our aim is to show why the process configuration follows naturally from the strategic choice and provides a competitive advantage. This approach allows us to discuss how to measure whether a process actually is yielding the desired advantage and how to motivate employees to stay focused on strategic objectives. We then illustrate how the balanced scorecard can help in this regard. Our discussion underscores how the scorecard categories flow naturally from the organization's strategy. We emphasize the choice among metrics and the importance of linking the metrics both within and across categories. We conclude with a brief discussion of implementation issues.

Module IV: COST ACCOUNTING SYSTEMS

This module explores the mechanics of cost accounting systems. Chapters 14 and 15, respectively, introduce students to two basic cost accounting systems: job and process costing. Both of these systems use allocations to value inventory and compute the cost of goods sold in accordance with GAAP. As such, these chapters distinguish between cost accounting (computing product costs) and managerial accounting (providing information for decision making). In the context of job costing, we introduce the notion of a predetermined overhead rate, and we discuss how to deal with under- or over-applied overhead. In the process-costing chapter, we explain the concept of an equivalent unit and discuss how to apply process costing to settings with many cost pools and opening inventory.

Chapter 16 presents two refinements that could help organizations increase the accuracy of cost systems: dual-rate systems and accounting for interactions among departments (service department allocations). We discuss how these refinements arise from the organization's desire to improve the accuracy in reported product costs. Because many might wish to skip or skim these topics, we adopt a modular presentation to give instructors flexibility in the depth of coverage.

We put the "traditional" cost accounting topics into separate chapters in a stand-alone module. This placement provides instructors flexibility in coverage. One can cover one or more of these chapters immediately after Chapter 3, after Chapter 9, or even skip this material entirely without interrupting the flow of the text.

4. Chapter Template

PART OPENER

Each module begins with a one- to two-page overview of the module. Part openers refer to a template for organizing business decisions and explain how the topics in the module fit within the framework. The goal is to provide a "road map" for the module.

Each chapter has the following features:

LEARNING OBJECTIVES

Learning objectives are useful because they prime students' thinking and focus their attention on the big picture both before and after delving into the details. Our goal is to have an average of four to five learning objectives per chapter. Each learning objective has its own section within the chapter. Common terminology and margin notes alert students to these linkages between learning objectives and sections. The summary discusses each of the learning objectives and reiterates the key concepts.

OPENING VIGNETTE

We open each chapter with a simple "story" of a business facing a decision problem. Vignettes include a story about a gym dealing with new competition, a catering business deciding whether to accept an engagement, and a cabinet-maker expanding his product line. These vignettes help us link different sections in the chapter logically. A few vignettes continue across chapters to show linkages among the topics.

BODY OF THE CHAPTER

Each chapter begins with an intuitive discussion of the issues in the opening vignette. Rather than providing a solution, we focus the discussion on sharpening the relevant questions and identifying pertinent costs and benefits. Following this discussion, we proceed as per the list of learning objectives. We use numerical examples, graphs, and additional everyday examples to make the concepts resonate with students. Our goal is to tell a story rather than present disjointed techniques.

As mentioned earlier, one of our main goals is to provide an integrated framework for using accounting information to make effective decisions. Two features help us deliver on this goal.

- **Apply the Decision Framework!** In Chapter 1, we provide four steps for effective decision making:

(1) Specify the decision problem, including the decision maker's goals, (2) identify options, (3) measure costs and benefits to determine the value of each option, and (4) make the decision, choosing the option with the highest value. At the beginning of each chapter, we summarize the vignette in this sequence, "solving" it by the end of the chapter. This feature serves to underscore our text's emphasis on introducing every concept in the context of a specific decision and then generalizing the idea.

- **Chapter Connections** For every chapter, we have boxes that show how the concept under discussion builds on concepts from prior chapters, and how the current topic is the foundation is the material discussed in later chapters. For instance, we link the discussion of CVP analysis (Chapter 5) back to identifying fixed and variable costs (Chapter 4). We also note that while CVP analysis is useful for profit planning and short-term decisions that pertain to the firm as a whole, it can be difficult to adapt CVP analysis to more localized short-term decision problems. Accordingly, we consider such decisions in Chapter 6.

In the spirit of active learning, we induce students to work along with the text.

- **Check-It!** These exercises and mini-worksheets ask students to verify some numbers or computations in the text. The objective is to confirm that the student is following the material and is not lost. There usually are four to six such boxes per chapter. (We provide solutions at the end of each chapter to help the student verify that they have mastered the concept.)

Finally, we show application to current business.

- **Connecting to Practice: (Description of decision context).** We have three to five such "call-out" boxes per chapter. Each call-out box discusses a relevant and recent phenomenon, drawing from business publications such as the *Wall Street Journal, Business Week,* or the *New York Times.*

SUMMARY

Our summary section links directly back to our learning objectives. The opening paragraph in the summary section discusses the general theme of the chapter. We then provide a transition to the next chapter.

RAPID REVIEW

We present this summary of key points at the end of the chapter. There are four to six summary observations that distill the take-away points for each learning objective (section). The intent is to cement the student's understanding and to provide a ready review prior to an examination.

REVIEW (SELF-STUDY) PROBLEM

Each chapter has one or two integrated self-study problems with solutions. These problems assist students in working through the concepts presented in the chapter and also ready students for the end-of-chapter material.

GLOSSARY

Key terms—that is, terms that are novel to the student and require definition—are boldfaced and defined in the chapter. We repeat these terms, with their accompanying definition, in a section immediately following the summary section.

END OF CHAPTER MATERIALS

We hope to surprise you with the quality of the end-of-chapter materials. We note the following points:

- We wrote both the questions and the solutions manual. We also developed the materials concurrently with the text to ensure tight linkages between chapter content and the end-of-chapter materials. Our extremely detailed solutions go well beyond providing the calculations. By discussing the application in detail, the solutions manual serves to reinforce student understanding.
- We consider examples in both the manufacturing and the service sectors. We also provide a range of problems that apply the concepts to not-for-profit entities.
- Many questions raise ethical and social issues. These issues arise not as stand-alone topics but as part of the decision-making process.
- We provide spreadsheet and graphing templates, where appropriate.

We provide two sets of qualitative questions, with the aim of verifying student preparation and as a basis for class discussion. These are:

- **Review Questions.** These 10 to 15 questions test definitions and comprehension of key concepts. The goal is to verify that the student has read the chapter with some care.
- **Discussion Questions.** These questions, 10 to 15 per chapter, expand the student's understanding. These questions might ask the student to consider how the analysis would change if an underlying assumption were to change, list additional factors that a manager would consider, and explain how the idea may apply to different settings.

We construct exercises and problems at three levels of difficulty.

- **Foundational Exercises.** The 15 or so exercises test students' basic understanding of chapter materials. These focused problems apply chapter concepts to the given setting.
- **Intermediate Problems.** These problems, 10 or so per chapter, typically require both quantitative and qualitative answers. These problems often require students to consider (trade off) multiple objectives.
- **Advanced Problems.** These problems require students to think creatively and to move beyond a direct application of chapter content. We have three to five challenging problems per chapter.

Consistent with the theme of providing a problem-solving framework, we organize many questions (particularly, intermediate and challenging problems) into three parts:

- **Application of chapter content.** This part asks students to apply a formula or concept discussed in the chapter.
- **Sensitivity analysis.** Intermediate and advanced level ("challenging") problems have one or more questions that ask the student to probe the effect of relaxing one of the "simplifying" assumptions. For example, we may ask how estimated cost changes as operations approach capacity limits.
- **Qualitative and strategic considerations.** The final part expands the analysis to include important but hard to quantify factors. For example, in this part, we may ask the student to discuss the quality implications of outsourcing a component.

Finally, each chapter has one to three mini-cases. These cases integrate most of the chapter's learning objectives and could serve as the basis for group (collaborative) activity or for a richer discussion of the issues presented in the chapter in a broader organizational context.

5. Flexibility in Sequencing Chapters

There are at least three ways to organize the chapters in this book in the context of a 15-week semester long course.

A. TRADITIONAL ORGANIZATION

Begin with Chapters 1–3 to introduce students to managerial accounting, cost terminology, and cost flows. Move to Chapters 14 and 15, which cover job and process costing. After covering product costing, revert to Chapter 4, which covers how to estimate costs for short-term decisions. From here on out, chapters unfold in a traditional sequence.

We anticipate that many instructors following this sequence will omit Chapter 16 on service department allocations. The instructors also might end the course with Chapter 12, which covers decentralization, performance measurement, and transfer pricing.

B. DECISION-MAKING FOCUS

We advocate this sequence. The only modification to the chapter sequence that we might make is to reduce the coverage of the chapters on strategic planning and control (Chapter 13) and to skim Chapter 16. We along with some of our colleagues have found that this approach works extremely well for undergraduates and MBA audiences.

C. STRATEGIC FOCUS

The sequencing of chapters allows instructors to deemphasize product costing and to increase the focus on decision making. Follow the chapter sequence, though you should ask students to skim Chapter 3. You can also skip Chapters 14 and 15 on job and process costing, as well as Chapter 16 on service department allocations.

Acknowledgments

Many people who reviewed earlier drafts went above and beyond the call of duty when giving us valuable feedback. We particularly note with gratitude input from Helen Adams (University of Washington), Arthur Francia (University of Houston), Laureen Maines (Indiana University), Robert Milbrath (University of Houston), Mark Penno (University of Iowa), Devika Subramanian (Rice University), and Michael Williamson (University of Texas at Austin). We also owe an intellectual debt to Bala Balachandran (Northwestern University), Joel Demski (University of Florida) and Shyam Sunder (Yale University), who shaped our thinking on the subject of management accounting. Several hundred students read and gave us comments on earlier versions of this book. We particularly thank Manasee Atre, Jacob Madden, Rebecca McCright, Kevin Klimes, and P. Vijay, for their detailed comments. Pamela Bourjaily, Christian Kuiate, Marina Ruseva, and Jean Thompson provided outstanding editorial support.

At Wiley, the staff who helped make this project a reality include our editor Jeff Howard, production editor Bill Murray, project editor Ed Brislin, media editor Allie Morris, marketing manager Julia Flohr, and assistant marketing manager Carly DeCandia. Mark Bonadeo, previously of John Wiley, was key in encouraging us to undertake and persevere with this challenging and rewarding task of textbook writing.

Reviewers

Helen Adams
University of Washington

Natalie Allen
Texas A&M University

Sheila Ammons
Austin Community College

Rowland Atiase
University of Texas at Austin

Jack Bailes
Oregon State University

Kashi Balachandran
New York University

Karen Bird
University of Michigan

Cynthia Birk
University of Iowa

Phillip Blanchard
University of Arizona

Donna Booker
University of Cincinnati

Kevin Bosner
St. John Fischer College

Bill Brewer
Sam Houston State University

Doug Clinton
Northern Illinois University

Jeffrey Cohen
Boston College

Constance Cooper
University of Cincinnati

Deb Cosgrove
University of Nebraska, Lincoln

Susan Cox
University of South Florida

Anthony Curatola
Drexel University

Alan Czyzewski
Indiana State University

Somnath Das
University of Illinois, Chicago

David Dearman
University of Arkansas, Fort Smith

Shane Dikolli
Duke University

Patricia Doherty
Boston University

Andrea Drake
University of Cincinnati

Rafik Elias
California State University, Los Angeles

Kurt Fanning
Grand Valley State University

Nicholas Fessler
Central Missouri State University

Timothy Fogarty
Case Western Reserve University

David Franz
San Francisco State University

Harlan Fuller
Illinois State University

Hubert Glover
Georgia State University

Stephen Goldberg
Grand Valley State University

Marvin Gordon
University of Illinois, Chicago

Marina Grau
Houston Community College

Ralph Greenberg
Temple University

Carrine Hall
Austin Community College

Rosalie Hallbauer
Florida International University

Russell Hardy
New Mexico State University, Carlsbad

James Hesford
Cornell University

Richard Hurley
University of Connecticut, Stamford

Robert Hurt
California State Polytechnic University, Pomona

Frank Ilett
Boise State University

Zafar Iqbal
California State Polytechnic University, SLO

Sanford Kahn
University of Cincinnati

Rajabali Kiani-Aslani
California State University, Northridge

Kip Krumwiede
Boise State University

Tom Lechner
University of Utah

Danny Litt
University of California, Los Angeles

Joan Luft
Michigan State University

Cathy Lumbattis
Southern Illinois University

Ajay Maindiratta
New York University

Sue Marcum
American University

Mark McCarthy
DePaul University

Noel McKeon
Florida Community College

Kevin McNelis
New Mexico State University

Robert Milbrath
University of Houston

Lisa Mueller
Franklin University

Ather Murtuza
Seton Hall University

Peggy O'Kelly
Northeastern University

Mohamed Onsi
Syracuse University

Joyce Ostrosky
Illinois State University

Chei Paik
George Washington University

Robert Picard
Idaho State University

Mina Pizzini
University of Texas, Dallas

Meg Pollard
American River College

Barbara Reider
Missoula Technical College

Mark Rieman
East Carolina University

Juan Rivera
University of Notre Dame

Anwar Salimi
California State Polytechnic University, Pomona

George Schmelzle
Indiana Purdue University, Ft. Wayne

Henry Schulman
Grossmont College

Ken Sinclair
Lehigh University

Talitha Smith
Auburn University

Toni Smith
University of New Hampshire

Jalal Soroosh
Loyola College

Charles Stanley
Baylor University

Dennis Stovall
Grand Valley State University

Carolyn Strand Norman
Virginia Commonwealth University

Krishnamurthy Surysekar
Florida International University

Scott Szilagyi
Fordham University

Kim Tan
California State University, Stanislaus

Greg Thibodeaux
University of Tennessee, Chattanooga

Lynda Thoman
Purdue University

Wendy Tietz
Kent State University

Kristy Towry
Emory University

Joan Van Hise
Fairfield University

Ramgopal Venkataraman
University of Minnesota

Ron Vogel
College of Eastern Utah

Charles Tony Wain
Babson College

Mary Ann Welden
Wayne State University

Tim West
University of Arkansas, Fayetteville

Andy Williams
Edmonds Community College

Michael Williamson
University of Texas at Austin

Rick Young
Ohio State University

Focus Group Participants

Michael Robinson
Baylor University

Jim Mackey
California State University, Sacramento

Fred Jacobs
Michigan State University

Joseph San Miguel
Naval Postgraduate School

Annie McGowan
Texas A&M University

Stan Davis
Wake Forest University

Tim West
University of Arkansas

Tammy Waymire
University of Arkansas

Sean Peffer
University of Kentucky

Zafar Khan
Eastern Michigan University

David Gray
North Central College

Sandra Vera-Munoz
Notre Dame University

Barbara Lamberton
University of Hartford

Valerie Milliron
California State University, Chico

Mark Vargas
University of Texas, Dallas

Gail Richardson
Bakersfield College

Supplements

Richard Merryman, *Jefferson County Community College—State University of New York*, PowerPoint and Study Guide author

Patricia Mounce, *University of Central Arkansas*, Test Bank author

Debra Cosgrove, *University of Nebraska—Lincoln*, Study Guide author

Eileen Shifflett, *James Madison University*, online quizzes

Diane Tanner, *University of North Florida*, *WileyPLUS* quizzes

Accuracy Checkers

LuAnn Bean, *Florida Institute of Technology*

Terry Elliott, *Morehead State University*

James M. Emig, *Villanova University*

Anthony Falgiani, *Western Illinois University*

Jill Misuraca, *Central Connecticut State University*

John Plouffe, *California State University—Los Angeles*

Rex Schildhouse, *San Diego Community College—Miramar*

Bernie Weinrich, *Lindenwood University*

Brief Contents

Contents

Module I:
INTRODUCTION AND FRAMEWORK

Module II:
SHORT-TERM PLANNING AND CONTROL:
MAXIMIZING CONTRIBUTION

Chapter 6
Decision Making in the Short Term   200

Chapter 7
Operating Budgets: Bridging Planning and Control   252

Chapter 8
Budgetary Control and Variance Analysis   304

Module III:
PLANNING AND CONTROL OVER
THE LONG TERM: MAXIMIZING PROFIT

Module IV:
COST ACCOUNTING SYSTEMS

MANAGERIAL
ACCOUNTING

Chapter 1

Accounting: Information for Decision Making

TOM AND LYNDA OWN AND OPERATE Hercules Health Club. Hercules maintains a top-notch reputation because of Tom and Lynda's attention to detail. The club is neat and clean, and offers the small conveniences and personalized services that many people appreciate. As a result, Hercules is a profitable business, even though it does not provide the latest in physical training equipment.

Well, as often happens in business, when the going gets good, the competition moves in. Tempted by the market potential, a national health-club chain, Apex Health & Fitness, recently opened a branch in the community. Compared to Hercules, Apex's larger facility provides a wider choice of equipment, a bigger swimming pool, and more classes in aerobics, karate, strength training, and yoga.

Tom and Lynda did not expect Apex to affect their business significantly, as many of Hercules' members have been loyal to the club for years. Imagine Tom and Lynda's surprise when they lost nearly 10 percent of their members to Apex within the first three months! Concerned by this development, they ask you to recommend options for regaining the lost membership and improving profits.

Darryl Leniuk/Getty Images

Tom and Lynda are proud owners of a popular gym. They are wondering how best to respond to emerging competition.

LEARNING OBJECTIVES

After studying this chapter, you will be able to:

1 Describe the four-step framework for making decisions.

2 Explain how decision making in organizations differs from decision making by individuals.

3 Understand how planning and control decisions relate to each other.

4 Differentiate between financial accounting and managerial accounting.

5 Discuss the role of ethics in decision making.

As you can see in the *Applying the Decision Framework* box on the opposing page, there are many possible strategies for you to consider. With all these questions and options available, how should you sort through them to determine Hercules' best course of action? You know other businesses routinely face similar decisions. How do they manage?

In this book, we provide you with a foundation in managerial accounting—a branch of accounting that helps you make business decisions. We begin in this chapter by describing a four-step framework that you could use to systematically structure and analyze any personal or business decision. Next, we explain how decision making in organizations differs from the decisions that we, as individuals, make in our daily lives. We then introduce you to two important kinds of organizational decisions— planning decisions and control decisions—and we discuss how organizations use managerial accounting information to make these decisions.

> **CHAPTER CONNECTIONS**
> *In Chapters 2–4, we apply the four-step decision framework to Hercules' problem.*

We end the chapter by examining how ethics, as well as societal and professional standards, influence decisions.

The Four-Step Framework for Decision Making

LEARNING OBJECTIVE 1

Describe the four step framework for making decisions.

We make decisions all the time. Do I have enough time for breakfast this morning before rushing off to school or work? What should I wear today? Should I major in accounting, finance, management, or marketing? Which car should I buy? Where should I live next year? When making decisions, most of us follow a process: we think about what we want out of the decision, identify available options, evaluate each one, and then select the option that best meets our goals. A **decision,** therefore, is simply choosing one option from a set of options to achieve a goal.

As such, we can describe decision making as consisting of the following four steps:

Step 1: Specify the decision problem, including the decision maker's goals.
Step 2: Identify options.
Step 3: Measure *benefits* (advantages) and *costs* (disadvantages) to determine the *value* (benefits reaped less costs incurred) of each option.
Step 4: Make the decision, choosing the option with the highest value.

This four-step process, the **Decision Framework,** applies equally to *all* decisions, whether personal or business-related. Only the context differs. As the book unfolds, you will see the general applicability of this framework. For now, let us look closer at each step.

STEP 1: SPECIFY THE DECISION PROBLEM, INCLUDING THE DECISION MAKER'S GOALS

Decisions help us accomplish goals. We all have **goals,** or objectives, that we strive to achieve. Tom and Lynda's primary goal is to restore Hercules' profits to the level earned before Apex arrived on the scene. Thus, their decisions should help them achieve this objective. Because of the intertwining of their personal lives and the club, however, Tom and Lynda's personal goals might influence their decisions. For example, reducing the membership fee carries the risk of permanently lowering income, if the lower fee does not lead to an increase in membership. An unwillingness to bear this risk may steer Tom and Lynda away from this option. Similarly, Tom and Lynda may not be willing to put in an extra 15 hours per week, even if doing so increases profits by $1,000 a month. Ultimately, Tom and Lynda's decisions also will depend on the relative importance they attach to other factors, such as money, risk, and leisure.

When determining their goals, individuals frequently differ in the factors they consider and the importance they attach to these factors. For example, one musician may wish to become a pop diva, while another may wish to play only for personal enjoyment. Some students attach primary importance to their grade point average (GPA), while others accept lower grades for greater involvement in extracurricular activities. As you might expect, these differences in goals often lead individuals to make different choices, even when confronted with the same options. Given an hour of free time, one person may prefer to watch television while another might exercise. While at the food court in the mall, one person might choose pizza and another might choose tacos.

As you can see, these examples illustrate the importance of clearly identifying goals before making decisions. Understanding the factors that influence the decision maker's goals and their relative importance is the first step in making effective decisions.

STEP 2: IDENTIFY OPTIONS

The second step is to identify options. Some decisions involve a small number of options. For example, consider a contestant's decision on the popular TV game show, *Let's Make a Deal!* In this show, one of three doors hides a valuable prize such as a car, while the other two doors conceal less desirable items. The contestant first chooses one of the three doors. Let's assume the contestant picks Door 1. At this point, the game-show host opens one of the other doors (say Door 2) to reveal a less desired prize. The contestant can now switch between the door initially chosen (Door 1) and the remaining door (Door 3). The host then opens the final door chosen to reveal the contestant's prize.

In this game, the contestant has two decisions: the initial choice and the follow-up choice. For both decisions, the contestant has a clear set of options; the first decision has three options (see Exhibit 1.1), and the second decision has two options.

In contrast, many decisions have a large number of options. Think about deciding where to go on vacation. Identifying all potential destinations is practically impossible. In such cases, we narrow the options to a manageable number in any number of ways, such as by placing a budget limit of $1,000 or by only considering areas in Washington.

Business decisions frequently have numerous options. For example, recall that some of Tom and Lynda's many options include reducing the membership fee, offering new programs such as yoga, and renovating the spa and steam rooms. For most businesses, identifying the set of options is one of the more important tasks of management. Managers frequently distinguish themselves by their ability to identify the most promising options. *Throughout the book, we help you sharpen these skills by considering many different types of business decisions, each with numerous options.*

Exhibit 1.1	*The Three Doors on* Let's Make a Deal! *Represent a Clear Set of Options for the Decision Maker*

(NBCU Photo Bank/©AP/Wide World Photos)

STEP 3: MEASURE BENEFITS (ADVANTAGES) AND COSTS (DISADVANTAGES) TO DETERMINE THE VALUE (BENEFITS REAPED LESS COSTS INCURRED) OF EACH OPTION

Every option presents a unique trade-off between benefits and costs. Suppose you seek to increase profit by increasing a product's sales, and you have identified two options to accomplish this goal: a price cut or an advertising campaign. A price cut will increase sales, but each unit sold will bring in less money. An advertising campaign also will increase sales, but it costs money to execute. Which of these two options should you choose? Naturally, you will choose the option that maximizes *value*, which in this case is the increase in profit.

The **value** of an option equals its benefits less its costs. Because value is the contribution of an option to the decision maker's goals, *we measure value relative to the status quo, which is not doing anything at all.* Even though most businesses measure value in terms of money, or profit, value need not be a monetary amount. We could measure value in terms of leisure time, convenience, or simply feeling good about ourselves. As such, the value of the same option might differ among decision makers.

Suppose you need to travel from Orlando, Florida, to Atlanta, Georgia, for the wedding of a family friend. You need to choose between flying and driving. As Exhibit 1.2 shows, these two options differ in terms of their costs and time required. Their value to your decision will rely on your goals for the trip, such as maximizing your time in Atlanta or minimizing your traveling costs.

Opportunity Cost

Whenever we make a decision and choose an option, we give something up. For example, if you decide to drive from Orlando to Atlanta for a wedding, you will lose the time saved by flying. If you fly, you will spend money that you would have saved by driving. Opportunity cost is the value of what you give up by making your decision.

In the Atlanta wedding example, you had only two choices, making it easy to measure value and opportunity lost. Now consider an example with many options. Suppose Megan, a college student, can make $50 running experiments for her biology professor this Saturday. Suppose Megan also has two other options this

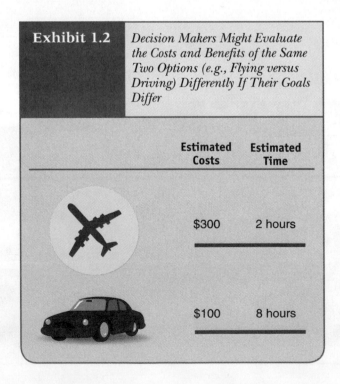

Exhibit 1.2	*Decision Makers Might Evaluate the Costs and Benefits of the Same Two Options (e.g., Flying versus Driving) Differently If Their Goals Differ*

	Estimated Costs	Estimated Time
	$300	2 hours
	$100	8 hours

Saturday—working as an usher at her school's football game and earning $75, and working at the library and making $60. Considering only money, what is her opportunity cost for running experiments—$60 or $75? It is $75. Why is this? Because $75 is the *most* she stands to lose by running experiments. The **opportunity cost** of any decision option is the value to the decision maker of the *next best* option.

Businesses typically measure value and opportunity cost in terms of money, or profit. Suppose Tom and Lynda consider offering either yoga or karate classes at Hercules. In this case, they have three options—offering a yoga class, a karate class, or neither class (the status quo of doing nothing). The value of offering the yoga class is the added profit from the yoga class relative to doing nothing. Likewise, the value of the karate class is the change in profit compared to doing nothing. If both classes are profitable, then the opportunity cost of offering the yoga class is the profit from the karate class. Similarly, the opportunity cost of offering the karate class is the profit from the yoga class.

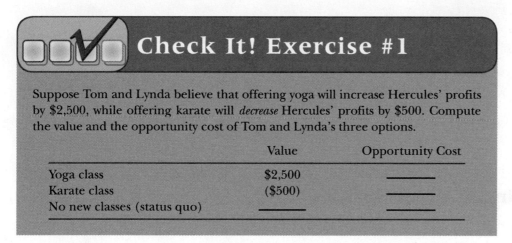

Check It! Exercise #1

Suppose Tom and Lynda believe that offering yoga will increase Hercules' profits by $2,500, while offering karate will *decrease* Hercules' profits by $500. Compute the value and the opportunity cost of Tom and Lynda's three options.

	Value	Opportunity Cost
Yoga class	$2,500	_____
Karate class	($500)	_____
No new classes (status quo)	_____	_____

Solution at end of chapter.

Effective decision makers ensure that the value of the chosen decision option exceeds its opportunity cost. This comparison makes sure that they are putting their resources to the best possible use and are maximizing their value. In essence, the concepts of value and opportunity cost emphasize that every decision involves trading off what we get with what we give up.

STEP 4: MAKE THE DECISION (CHOOSING THE OPTION WITH THE HIGHEST VALUE)

The best choice is the option with the highest value to the decision maker. This also is the only option whose value exceeds its opportunity cost. If your goal is to maximize time with family and friends, flying from Orlando to Atlanta is your best option. Similarly, if Megan's goal is to make the most money this Saturday, then working as an usher at the football game is her best option.

Throughout the book, we use these four steps to frame and describe decisions. To underscore the process, we use a box titled *Applying the Decision Framework* to

CHAPTER CONNECTIONS
In Chapter 2, we discuss the concepts associated with identifying and measuring costs and benefits to determine value and opportunity cost.

APPLYING THE DECISION FRAMEWORK

What Is the Problem?	You need to travel from Orlando to Atlanta for a wedding, where you want to spend as much time as possible with family and friends.
What Are the Options?	The two options are to drive or to fly.
What Are the Costs and Benefits?	Driving is cheaper but results in less time with family and friends. Flying costs more but requires less travel time.
Make the Decision!	After considering all of the costs and benefits, you decide to fly so that you can maximize your time in Atlanta.

show how it applies to the decision at hand. For example, you can use the framework to guide your decision regarding whether to drive or fly from Orlando to Atlanta.

Thus far, we have examined how the four-step framework applies to individual decision making. In the next section, we discuss how the framework applies to decision making in organizations.

Decision Making in Organizations

LEARNING OBJECTIVE 2

Explain how decision making in organizations differs from decision making by individuals.

The four-step decision-making framework applies equally well to *both* individual and organizational decisions. However, there are two important differences. First, unlike individuals whose goals might have several factors, organizations tend to have focused goals. For example, profit is the dominant goal of commercial organizations. As such, these organizations primarily evaluate decisions by their impact on the bottom line.

Second, because an organization is a collection of individuals, we need to think about how individual goals relate to organizational goals. Organizations don't make decisions; the people that comprise the organization do. Individual goals might differ from organizational goals, leading to actions that are not in the firm's best interests. To see this, consider a sports team. The team's goal is to win the game. However, seeking individual recognition, some players might take actions that put them in the best light even if doing so is not in the team's best interests. The lack of alignment in goals is even more of an issue when organizational goals are unclear. For an example, think back to your last team project. Some members may have wanted to work hard and receive a high grade, while others may have simply wanted to pass the class.

ORGANIZATIONAL GOALS

An **organization** is a group of individuals engaged in a collectively beneficial mission. Organizations form for many reasons. Nonprofit organizations and charities such as the Red Cross and Habitat for Humanity seek to help individuals in need and improve people's lives. Professional organizations, such as the American Bar Association, serve the public and the legal profession by promoting justice, education, and professional integrity.

A for-profit business usually specifies organizational goals according to ownership. For a family-owned venture such as Hercules, the goal is to increase family wealth, which means maximizing Hercules' profits. The goal for a publicly held business such as General Motors or IBM, collectively owned by shareholders, is to maximize **shareholder value**—that is, to maximize the returns (stream of profits or, equivalently, stream of cash flows) to shareholders investing in the company.

 **Connecting to Practice**

MISSION STATEMENTS

Corporate mission statements often specify elements of an organization's strategy for achieving its goals and its core values. Google's mission statement is to "organize the world's information and make it universally accessible and useful." Their informal corporate motto is "Don't be evil." Likewise, Microsoft's Web site says, "At Microsoft, we work to help people and businesses throughout the world realize their full potential. This is our mission. Everything we do reflects this mission and the values that make it possible."

COMMENTARY: While corporate mission statements often do not make explicit reference to maximizing profit, such statements are a means to an end. That is, a focus on pleasing customers is simply good business and leads to increased profits.

ALIGNING INDIVIDUAL GOALS WITH ORGANIZATIONAL GOALS

As we mentioned earlier, organizational goals rarely coincide with the goals of *all* individual participants. Hercules' employees care more about their own compensation, job security, and well-being than about how much money Tom and Lynda make. These employees want the gym to do well financially primarily because it ensures their continued employment, and not because of its profit potential for Tom and Lynda. Similarly, professional managers, who run large firms such as General Electric, also are employees with their own goals. While companies hire managers to act in the best interests of shareholders, these individuals wish to maximize their own compensation and happiness.

What are the implications of this divergence in goals for the four-step decision-making framework? In Step 1 of the decision process, a firm's owners would like to frame decision problems in terms of maximizing profit. However, owners do not make all of the decisions in an organization. They delegate many decisions to employees. But, as you know, employees come to the organization with their own goals. Thus, these employees will look at the *same* decision in terms of maximizing their own goals and might attach lower importance to the firm's profit. As a result, the decisions that best attain individual goals may not necessarily maximize profit, the organization's goal.

What can owners do to align individual and organizational goals? To influence employees to achieve organizational goals, firms use the following methods:

- *Policies and procedures* to define acceptable behavior. Tom and Lynda keep detailed attendance records to discourage employees from claiming payment for time not worked. Bank of America requires tellers to balance their drawers at the end of their shifts, and UPS expects its drivers to follow safe driving practices.

- *Monitoring* to enforce policies and procedures. Tom and Lynda routinely walk around the gym to make sure that their employees are doing their jobs and providing helpful and courteous service. Pilots at Delta are subject to random drug and alcohol tests at the end of every flight, and McDonald's uses a mystery shopper program to ensure quality and consistency among its restaurants.
- *Incentive schemes and performance evaluation* to motivate employees to consider organizational goals. Tom and Lynda solicit feedback from class patrons and link instructor bonuses to satisfaction ratings. Realtors at Century 21 earn commissions based on their sales, and the United States Marine Corps requires its soldiers to go through annual performance evaluations.

As these examples illustrate, firms promote goal congruence by tailoring policies and procedures, monitoring, incentives, and performance evaluation to fit their specific needs. In Chapters 8, 12, and 13 we discuss extensively the choice of specific systems to increase goal congruence.

Connecting to Practice

ENRON

Enron began operations in 1985 as a producer and seller of energy. By 2000, Enron was the seventh-largest company in the United States, employing more than 21,000 people in 40 countries. Unfortunately, Enron's success turned out to be artificial—key personnel misrepresented company profits and concealed debts from the company's records.

Enron's mission statement noted that the company prided itself on four key values: respect, integrity, communication, and excellence. Among other things, all business dealings at Enron were supposed to be "open and fair." As Enron's story unfolded in Congress and the courts, it became obvious that employees were not following the company's mission statement.

COMMENTARY: Such debacles can occur when there is a mismatch between an organization's stated goals and its actual monitoring, performance evaluation, and incentives. As some would say, "you get what you measure."

In essence, the key difference between individual and business decisions relates to Step 1 of the four-step framework—that is, organizations need to ensure that the goals of individual employees mesh with the focused goals of the organization. To accomplish their goals, then, organizations need to not only allocate resources effectively but also to motivate employees to focus on organizational goals. As we see next, these two kinds of decisions, planning and control, form part of a larger cycle.

The Planning and Control Cycle

LEARNING OBJECTIVE 3

Understand how planning and control decisions relate to each other.

Planning decisions relate to choices about acquiring and using resources to deliver products and services to customers. Planning includes deciding which products and services to offer, their prices, and the resources needed, such as materials, labor, and equipment. In a broad sense, a plan is like a blueprint that specifies the actions required to achieve a goal.

It makes little sense to plan, though, unless we intend to keep a watchful eye on how well our plans are meeting our goals. This is the purpose of **control decisions**, which relate to motivating, monitoring, and evaluating performance. As such, many control decisions involve examining *past* performance, with the purpose of improving subsequent plans. For example, at the end of last semester, you probably compared your actual GPA with what you planned to achieve. You then might have made a control decision, such as changing the amount of time you spend on extracurricular activities. Likewise, by comparing actual sales with budgeted sales, organizations can learn more about market conditions and the effectiveness of a new advertising campaign. In addition, this comparison helps management gauge the efforts of its sales force as a whole and to identify its top performers.

Planning and control are two sides of the same coin, with one following the other. Exhibit 1.3 illustrates the planning and control cycle. You can think of these four stages as the PIER cycle: **P**lan, **I**mplement, **E**valuate, and **R**evise.

The cycle begins with *Planning* which products and services to offer, what resources to acquire, how much of each resource to acquire, and where to sell products and services. The next stage involves *Implementing* these choices, which includes determining how and when to use resources, as well as setting performance standards to motivate employees to achieve the formulated plan. Note that the Implement stage has elements of both planning and control. We typically consider the use of resources to be part of planning, and motivating employees to be part of control. This overlap underscores how it is sometimes difficult to know where planning and control start and stop.

The *Evaluate* stage deals with measuring actual performance and understanding the reasons for any deviations between actual and planned results. Which deviations should we spend time investigating? Which deviations should we chalk up as normal? Answers to these questions lead to the final stage, *Revise*, where we correct, as

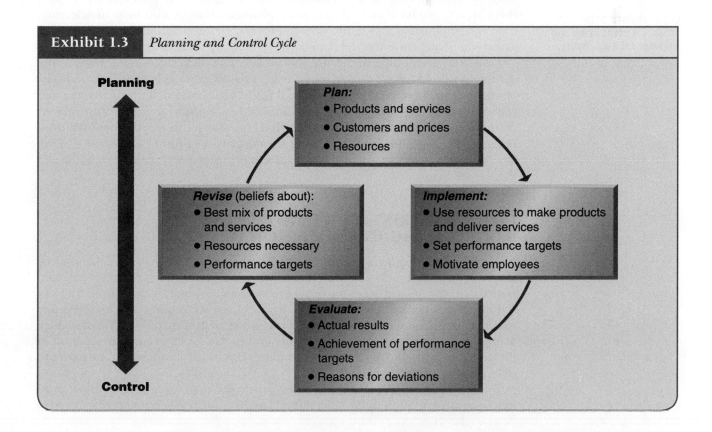

Exhibit 1.3   *Planning and Control Cycle*

Planning

Plan:
- Products and services
- Customers and prices
- Resources

Implement:
- Use resources to make products and deliver services
- Set performance targets
- Motivate employees

Evaluate:
- Actual results
- Achievement of performance targets
- Reasons for deviations

Revise (beliefs about):
- Best mix of products and services
- Resources necessary
- Performance targets

Control

necessary, beliefs about the best products and services to offer, the appropriate types and amounts of resources, the feasibility of performance targets, and the effectiveness of incentive schemes. This updated information then feeds into future planning and control decisions.

The planning and control cycle could happen within moments or it could take months. A ship's captain might bark at the crew to trim the sails and check to see if the correction is enough. Here, the entire planning and control cycle takes place in a few moments, and the captain might not consciously distinguish between planning and control. In contrast, a multimillion dollar building project, which might last years, would involve discrete steps for planning and control.

In responding to Apex, Tom and Lynda would also follow the planning and control cycle. Suppose that Tom and Lynda decide to offer yoga classes (Plan). They then need to hire appropriate instructors, get needed equipment, as well as schedule and promote the class (Implement). Tom and Lynda would then closely monitor class attendance, satisfaction ratings, and overall membership levels (Evaluate). If necessary, they would make changes, such as switching instructors or the type of yoga offered, to ensure that the program is successful and that the class is meeting their goals (Revise).

Now that you understand the kinds of decisions in organizations, let us turn to where organizations might obtain the information needed to make planning and control decisions. Not surprisingly, accounting plays an important role in this context.

Accounting and Decision Making

LEARNING OBJECTIVE 4

Differentiate between financial accounting and managerial accounting.

Courses in business address different aspects of the Decision Framework. Marketing concepts help managers understand consumers' goals and preferences, helping them to sell products more successfully. Management theories help in selecting, training, organizing, and motivating employees. Understanding finance is crucial when identifying the costs and benefits of funding operations in different ways.

How does accounting fit into the Decision Framework? Accounting plays a fundamental role in Step 3. *The primary role of accounting is to help measure the costs and benefits of decision options.* Broadly, we can think of two classes of decision makers who rely on accounting information—decision makers outside the firm who rely on financial accounting information, and decision makers inside the firm who use managerial accounting information. In Appendix A, we provide an overview of the key financial players in organizations and some professional accounting bodies in the United States.

CHARACTERISTICS OF FINANCIAL ACCOUNTING INFORMATION

Financial accounting aims to satisfy the information needs of decision makers *outside* the firm, such as shareholders, creditors, and taxing authorities. Shareholders and potential investors use accounting data to determine whether they should buy or sell shares of a company's stock. Similarly, banks use accounting data to determine whether they should lend money to a firm and at what terms. Boards of directors, acting on behalf of shareholders, use accounting data to determine the amount of dividends to pay out. The Internal Revenue Service (IRS) uses accounting data to determine the amount of taxes due.

Because the context and goals differ across the many external decision makers, their information needs also differ. Furthermore, it is not cost effective for an organization to produce individually tailored, decision-specific financial accounting information. Typically, firms satisfy the information needs of external decision makers by issuing a comprehensive set of financial statements at regular intervals (e.g., quarterly and annual reports) that relate to the firm as a whole.

Investors also have many options about where to put their money. As such, investors need to be able to compare the financial prospects of different firms using a common frame of reference. Such need for comparability of information across companies has led to standardization in the way firms prepare financial statements. In the United States, firms follow Generally Accepted Accounting Principles (GAAP) as defined by the Financial Accounting Standards Board (FASB) when preparing their financial statements. Many European and Asian firms follow standards issued by the International Accounting Standards Board. These standards reflect compromises that consider the views of the many uses for financial accounting information. For instance, the need to verify information means that the standards place greater emphasis on the reliability of the data over its relevance for any given decision.

While financial accounting information is useful for assessing an organization's overall current state and future prospects, it does not provide enough detail to address most decision needs within the firm. Managers grappling with whether to run a promotion, introduce a new product, change prices, or outsource a business process will often find financial accounting information inadequate. Instead, managers need information tailored to their specific decision problems. That is, they need managerial accounting information.

CHARACTERISTICS OF MANAGERIAL ACCOUNTING INFORMATION

Managerial accounting aims to satisfy the information needs of decision makers *inside* the firm. An organization's employees use managerial accounting data to determine, among other things, which products and services to offer, the prices of products and services, what equipment to purchase, who to hire, and how to pay them. That is, managerial accounting information is useful for both planning and control decisions.

Because organizations' policies and procedures usually prohibit sharing sensitive and detailed information with outsiders, employees have greater access to information. Moreover, they need this greater access. To make the best decisions on behalf of the organization, employees require the most relevant data, be it financial or nonfinancial, when and as needed.

To understand the differences between financial and managerial accounting, notice that Tom and Lynda will prepare financial accounting statements even though Hercules is a small, closely held organization that is not listed on any stock exchange. One use for such statements is to determine the profit for the year, so that Tom and Lynda can determine how much money they can withdraw from the business. Their bank, which has given Hercules a line of credit, also demands an audited income statement each year.

Such statements, however, are not useful for Tom and Lynda to make their decision about whether to offer yoga. This decision concerns only some costs and benefits, leaving others unchanged. Tom and Lynda cannot rely on financial reports for this decision because these reports aggregate revenues and costs. Instead, they will look to their managerial accounting system to obtain specific information for the decision at hand. In general, like all managers, Tom and Lynda will use managerial accounting information both for recurring (Are we under budget for staffing costs?) and for one-time decisions (Should we renovate the spa and steam rooms?). Exhibit 1.4 summarizes the key differences between managerial accounting and financial accounting.

Exhibit 1.4	*Financial and Managerial Accounting Information Differ on Many Dimensions*	
Characteristic	**Financial Accounting**	**Managerial Accounting**
Primary users	Persons external to the organization.	Persons internal to the organization.
Governing Principles	Generally Accepted Accounting Principles (GAAP), as established by bodies such as the Financial Accounting Standards Board (FASB) and enforced by bodies such as the U.S. Securities and Exchange Commission (SEC).	Evaluating the costs and benefits of decision options. In most situations, data are collected, reported, and analyzed as needed and do not conform to specified standards.
Unit of analysis	Usually, the entire organization, with limited disclosures about individual lines of business.	Varies, with the decision context dictating the relevant unit of analysis.
Emphasis	Information reliability, sometimes at the expense of relevance.	Information relevance valued most.
Periodicity	Fixed periodicity, with external reports usually released at the end of each quarter.	Often generated on an as-needed basis.
Types of data considered	Focus is on *past* financial data.	Collects, reports, and uses all available data, *including estimates on future performance*, whether financial or nonfinancial.

In essence, *managerial accounting information supports decisions related to the acquisition and use of organizational resources as well as decisions related to motivating, monitoring, and evaluating performance.* That is, managerial accounting supports planning and control decisions.

So far, we have discussed several aspects of decision making. We have reviewed the four-step framework of decision making, as well as how managerial accounting

Connecting to Practice

BLURRED BOUNDARIES IN MODERN ORGANIZATIONS

We have drawn a clear distinction between decision makers inside the firm and decision makers outside the firm. Modern management practices frequently blur these organizational boundaries. Today, many firms share extensive information with suppliers and customers. For example, at Bose Electronics suppliers' employees have access to Bose's production data and information systems. These persons place sales orders on behalf of Bose for the products their employers sell. Such "open-book management" is like a grocery store anticipating your food needs, stocking your pantry, and debiting your bank account for the cost.

COMMENTARY: As the example illustrates, the distinction between external and internal decision makers is becoming less sharp. Consequently, firms are broadening the scope of their managerial accounting systems.

information supports the two main types of decisions, planning and control. However, our discussion of decision making would be incomplete if we did not address the role of ethics.

Ethics and Decision Making

Ethics relates to every aspect of the Decision Framework. Consider Step 3, which involves measuring the costs and benefits of decision options. Some decision makers might approve an unethical act if it provides monetary benefits in excess of the costs. For example, a business might condone the use of child labor if it reduces manufacturing costs. And if a business makes that decision, who or what will stop it?

The issue of ethics goes beyond ensuring that decision makers do not choose an option based solely on monetary costs and benefits. In fact, as Exhibit 1.5 shows, we also could view ethics as an integral part of Steps 1 and 2, shaping decision makers' goals and influencing the set of options to consider. For example, should an organization's goal be to maximize wealth at all costs? What about its responsibility to contribute to its community? That is, we could view an organization's goal as not just one of profit maximization, but profit maximization *in an ethical manner.* Ethics could also stop decision makers from including questionable options in their choice set.

So, what stops an individual from engaging in unethical decision making? Organizations and societies play a significant role in shaping goals and motivating decision makers to act ethically. Through laws, rules, and regulations, organizations and governments specify the behaviors that cross ethical boundaries and the resulting penalties for engaging in unethical behavior.

For example, managers in the United States are subject to the Foreign Corrupt Practices Act of 1977. This act requires that firms maintain internal control systems to properly execute and record all transactions. It further prohibits managers from giving or taking bribes, even if such acts are part of the normal business practices in

LEARNING OBJECTIVE 5

Discuss the role of ethics in decision making.

Exhibit 1.5	*Ethical Considerations Influence Every Step of the Four-Step Decision Framework*
Step in Decision Framework	**How Ethical Considerations Might Influence This Step**
What Is the Problem?	Acting in an ethical manner is an important factor in the goals of most individuals and is the stated policy for numerous organizations. Thus, ethics influence how we frame decision problems.
What Are the Options?	Many decision makers will not consider unethical actions in their choice set. For instance, cadets at West Point would rather receive a failing grade than cheat on an exam.
What Are the Costs and Benefits?	Breaching ethical standards might trigger some gains but also might impose significant costs. Indeed, it is possible to view adherence to ethical standards as the outcome of a cost-benefit analysis.
Make the Decision!	Personal standards might prevent some decision makers from choosing an option that they consider unethical, even if the option satisfies prevailing legal standards.

Connecting to Practice

CHANGING THE CULTURE AT CITIGROUP

Citigroup is a world-renowned organization that operates in over 100 countries and employs over 300,000 people. Until 2003, Citigroup focused on rapid growth, acquisitions, and year-over-year gains in earnings. Perhaps because of this focus, Citigroup became embroiled in several situations that hurt its reputation. In the United States, regulators penalized the firm for blurring the line between investment bankers and analysts; in Japan, the firm lost its license for private banking; and, in the UK, the firm's bond-trading unit was chastised for dubious trading strategies. In all, the firm faced billions of dollars in fines and penalties.

COMMENTARY: Responding to these pressures, the new management of Citigroup has focused on ramping up internal controls and restoring ethics to a "center of the plate" issue. While the new focus has resulted in some high-profile turnover and some loss of earnings momentum, the approach has restored some of the firm's luster. It also might prove shrewd business: Citigroup's early settlement for transgressions related to failed firms such as Enron and WorldCom were smaller than fines levied on other banks that dragged their feet.

another country. The Sarbanes-Oxley Act of 2002 (SOX) mandates that senior executives of publicly traded companies take individual responsibility for the accuracy and completeness of financial reports. Executive and financial officers must now certify, in writing, the truthfulness of quarterly and annual reports filed with the U.S. Securities and Exchange Commission (SEC). Executives who knowingly alter, destroy, mutilate, conceal, or falsify records are subject to stiff penalties, including fines and jail time.

Individual company policies provide additional guidance regarding ethical standards. Employee handbooks usually include statements of ethical standards, as do employee rights and responsibilities documents. Some firms even impose ethical standards on their suppliers.

Finally, most professional associations expect their members to do the "right thing" even if it involves personal sacrifice. The Code of Ethics established by the Institute of Management Accountants (see Appendix B) stipulates that accountants should resign rather than participate in a questionable practice. This statement also spells out expected behaviors such as competence, confidentiality, integrity, and objectivity, and provides a road map of procedures to follow when resolving an ethical conflict. Other professional bodies, such as the American Institute of Certified Public Accountants (AICPA) and the Institute of Internal Auditors (IIA), prescribe similar standards for their members.

Laws, rules, and regulations help define expected behaviors and penalties for violations, but do we really expect that all people will voluntarily abide by these guidelines? Probably not. Thus it is that societies have a justice system, including the police and courts, to enforce the laws of the land. Organizations use monitoring mechanisms to encourage desired behavior. For instance, many firms conduct surprise audits to increase the odds of detecting unethical behavior. Coupled with severe penalties, such audits make unethical actions unattractive to employees. Similarly, the threat of expulsion and the loss of certification induce individuals to abide by the norms set forth by professional bodies.

In summary, organizations, professional bodies, and the government define ethical standards. They also expend resources to enforce the laws, rules, and regulations. Yet, in the final analysis, the main responsibility for ethical behavior rests on all of us, the individuals involved. It is up to us, whether as an accountant helping out Tom and Lynda or in some other position, to help maintain ethical standards.

In this chapter, we described a four-step framework for making decisions, distinguishing how differences in individual and organizational goals can affect business decisions. We then explained the differences between financial and managerial accounting, as well as how managerial accounting assists organizations in making planning and control decisions. Finally, we discussed the role of ethics in decision making.

Our discussion in Chapter 1 highlights that managerial accounting plays a fundamental role in Step 3 of the four-step decision-making framework. To complete this step successfully, we need to *identify* and *measure* the costs and benefits of decision options. We take up this task in Chapter 2.

RAPID REVIEW

LEARNING OBJECTIVE 1

Describe the four-step framework for making decisions.

- A decision involves choosing one option from a set of options to achieve a goal. Every decision consists of four steps: (1) specify the decision problem, including the decision maker's goals; (2) identify options; (3) measure costs and benefits to determine the value of each option; and, (4) make the decision, choosing the option with the highest value.

- We all have goals, or objectives, that we try to achieve. However, individuals differ in their goals, which lead them to make different choices even when faced with the same options.

- Business decisions frequently have numerous options. Good managers distinguish themselves in their ability to both identify good opportunities and to prune the many possible choices to the most promising few.

- The value of a decision option equals its benefits less its costs. We measure value relative to the status quo, which is not doing anything at all. The opportunity cost of any decision option is the value to the decision maker of the next best option.

- The best option has the highest value and is the only option whose value exceeds its opportunity cost.

LEARNING OBJECTIVE 2

Explain how decision making in organizations differs from decision making by individuals.

- The four-step framework for making decisions applies equally to individual and organizational decisions. The key difference between individual and business decisions relates to Step 1—that is, organizations need to ensure that the goals of individual employees mesh with the goals of the organization. Furthermore, unlike individuals whose goals might have several factors, organizations tend to have focused goals.

- An organization is a group of individuals engaged in a collectively beneficial mission. In business settings, we usually specify organizational goals in relation to ownership.

- Organizations use policies and procedures, monitoring systems, performance evaluation, and incentives to align individual goals with organizational goals.

LEARNING OBJECTIVE 3

Understand how planning and control decisions relate to each other.

- Decision making is dynamic—we make decisions, implement them, receive feedback about the quality of our decisions, and then start the process again, hoping to make better decisions the next time. That is, decisions follow a cycle of planning and control. The four stages of a planning and control cycle are Plan, Implement, Evaluate, and Revise (PIER).

- Planning decisions relate to choices about which products and services to offer, and about the resources, such as materials, labor, and equipment, necessary to make these products or deliver these services. In a broad sense, a plan is like a blueprint that specifies the actions needed to achieve an objective.

- Control decisions examine past planning decisions, with the purpose of improving future planning decisions. Control decisions also include setting performance targets and motivating employees. Control decisions naturally lead back to planning decisions.

LEARNING OBJECTIVE 4

Differentiate between financial accounting and managerial accounting.

- The primary role of accounting is to help measure the costs and benefits of decision options.

- Financial accounting information aims to satisfy the information needs of decision makers outside the firm, such as shareholders, creditors, and taxing authorities. These decision makers use financial accounting data to assess an organization's current state and future prospects. Decision makers also use financial accounting information to decide on the distribution of organizational resources.

- Generally Accepted Accounting Principles (GAAP) govern financial accounting data. This information is aggregate, issued with fixed periodicity, and focuses on verifiable (audited), monetary values.

- Managerial accounting information aims to satisfy the information needs of decision makers within the firm. These decision makers use managerial accounting information to support decisions related to the acquisition and use of organizational resources as well as decisions related to motivating, monitoring, and rewarding performance.

- Managerial accounting information relates to specific decision problems, emphasizes information relevance, is prepared on an as-needed basis, and contains both financial and nonfinancial data.

LEARNING OBJECTIVE 5

Discuss the role of ethics in decision making.

- Ethics relates to every step of the Decision Framework. One approach is to view ethics as affecting Step 3, when decision makers measure the costs and benefits of decision options. Another approach is to view ethics as affecting Steps 1 and 2, in shaping decision makers' goals and considered options. Under this approach, we could view organizations as maximizing profit but in an ethical manner.

- Societies, organizations, and professional bodies provide guidelines for expected behavior. The legal system also helps to ensure ethical behavior, by enforcing the laws of the land. Organizations use monitoring mechanisms, and professional associations use the threat of expulsion to encourage desired behavior. However, in the final analysis it is up to you, the individual, to behave in an ethical manner even if it involves personal sacrifice.

Appendix A
THE PROFESSIONAL ACCOUNTING ENVIRONMENT

In this appendix, we provide an overview of the key financial players in organizations and some of the professional accounting bodies in the United States.

Key Financial Players

Exhibit 1.6 presents a partial organization chart for a typical corporation. An **organization chart** shows the hierarchical relations among positions in an organization. This exhibit shows that a board of directors, representing shareholders, is ultimately responsible for overseeing the firm's operations. The board usually delegates

Many persons have to coordinate their efforts to run an effective and efficient organization.
(Robert Daly/Getty Images)

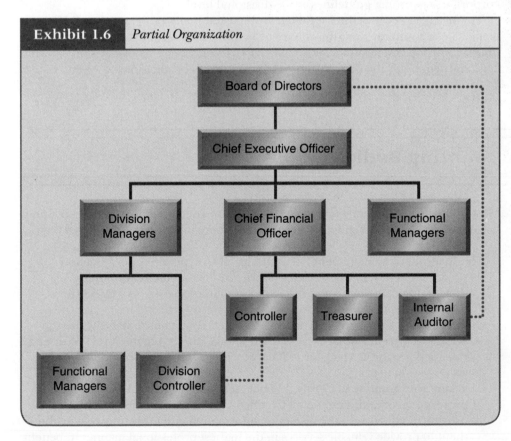

Exhibit 1.6   *Partial Organization*

most decisions to a **chief executive officer** (CEO), the highest-ranking executive in an organization. The CEO is like the captain of a ship, steering the firm's operations in the right direction.

A number of individuals assist the CEO in managing the organization. The **chief financial officer** (CFO) reports to the CEO and is responsible for all accounting and finance functions. In turn, the CFO often hires a controller to direct the accounting function and a treasurer to oversee the finance function. Many firms also have a **chief internal auditor** (CIA), who manages the internal audit function. Internal auditors frequently report directly to the audit committee of the board of directors, which helps to maintain the auditor's objectivity in presenting a full and fair picture of the firm's operations.

The **controller** manages the day-to-day accounting for the firm and oversees corporate accounting policies. The controller's staff assists in planning the firm's operations, designing and operating information systems, and fostering effective decision making. The controller is a key player in ensuring that the firm has appropriate monitoring, performance evaluation, and incentive systems in place to motivate employees to achieve organizational goals.

The **treasurer** manages the firm's cash flow and serves as the contact point for banks, bondholders, and other creditors of the firm. The treasurer ensures that the firm raises the required capital at the lowest cost and uses the capital wisely to maximize shareholder returns. The treasurer's office usually employs many finance professionals, most of whom have a strong background in accounting as well.

Other functional managers, such as the vice presidents of marketing and human resources oversee operations in key business areas. Division managers direct the day-to-day operations of product lines and markets. In turn, division managers appoint their own functional managers and a divisional controller. While divisional controllers report to division managers, they also have a "dotted line" relationship with the corporate controller. That is, the division controller must implement the corporate accounting guidelines at the divisional level.

The modern accountant is a valued and trusted member of the overall business team. The accountant gains this stature by helping division and corporate managers understand the financial and nonfinancial costs and benefits of decision options. This, in turn, helps the firm to improve the quality of its decisions.

Professional Accounting Bodies

Most countries have several professional organizations dedicated to improving the practice of accountancy. We highlight three prominent organizations in the United States.

The Institute of Management Accountants (IMA) "provides personal and professional development opportunities in management accounting, financial management, and information management." The IMA offers educational programs and supports research to further the practice of management accounting. The IMA offers certifications that designate the accounting professional as a Certified Management Accountant (CMA) or a Certified Financial Manager (CFM). For more information about the IMA, visit www.imanet.org.

The American Institute of Certified Public Accountants (AICPA) is the "national, professional organization for all Certified Public Accountants. Its mission is to provide members with the resources, information and leadership that enable them to provide valuable services in the highest professional manner to benefit the public as well as employers and clients." Among other activities, the AICPA advocates on behalf of its members before the government and standard setters. It also promotes public awareness and confidence in the integrity, objectivity, and competence of Certified Public Accountants (CPAs). For more information, visit www.aicpa.org.

The Institute of Internal Auditors (IIA) "provides dynamic leadership for the global profession of internal auditing." The IIA advocates the value of internal auditing and provides education on best practices in internal auditing. The IIA offers certification that designates a person as a Certified Internal Auditor (CIA). For more information, visit www.theiia.org.

Appendix B
THE IMA CODE OF ETHICS

We reproduce below, with permission, the code of ethics established by the Institute of Management Accountants.

ETHICAL STANDARDS

In today's modern world of business, individuals in management accounting and financial management constantly face ethical dilemmas. For example, if the accountant's immediate superior instructs the accountant to record the physical inventory at its original costs when it is obvious that the inventory has a reduced value due to obsolescence, what should the accountant do? To help make such a decision, here is a brief general discussion of ethics and the "Standards of Ethical Conduct for Members."

Ethics, in its broader sense, deals with human conduct in relation to what is morally good and bad, right and wrong. To determine whether a decision is good or bad, the decision-maker must compare his/her options with some standard of perfection. This standard of perfection is not a statement of static position but requires the decision-maker to assess the situation and the values of the parties affected by the decision. The decision-maker must then estimate the outcome of the decision and be responsible for its results. Two good questions to ask when faced with an ethical dilemma are, "Will my actions be fair and just to all parties affected?" and "Would I be pleased to have my closest friends learn of my actions?"

Individuals in management accounting and financial management have a unique set of circumstances relating to their employment. To help them assess their situation, the Institute of Management Accountants (IMA) has developed the following "Standards of Ethical Conduct for Members."

STANDARDS OF ETHICAL CONDUCT FOR MEMBERS

Members of IMA have an obligation to the public, their profession, the organizations they serve, and themselves, to maintain the highest standards of ethical conduct. In recognition of this obligation, the IMA has promulgated the following standards of ethical conduct for its members. Members shall not commit acts contrary to these standards nor shall they condone the commission of such acts by others within their organizations.

Members shall abide by the more stringent code of ethical conduct, whether that is the standards widely practiced in their country or IMA's Standards of Ethical Conduct. In no case will a member conduct herself or himself by any standard that is not at least equivalent to the standards identified for members in IMA's Standards of Ethical Conduct.

The standards of ethical conduct for IMA members are published in SMA 1C (Statement on Management Accounting).

Competence

Members have a responsibility to:

- Maintain an appropriate level of professional competence by ongoing development of their knowledge and skills.
- Perform their professional duties in accordance with relevant laws, regulations, and technical standards.
- Prepare complete and clear reports and recommendations after appropriate analyses of relevant and reliable information.

Confidentiality

Members have a responsibility to:

- Refrain from disclosing confidential information acquired in the course of their work except when authorized, unless legally obligated to do so.
- Inform subordinates as appropriate regarding the confidentiality of information acquired in the course of their work and monitor their activities to assure the maintenance of that confidentiality.
- Refrain from using or appearing to use confidential information acquired in the course of their work for unethical or illegal advantage either personally or through third parties.

Integrity

Members have a responsibility to:

- Avoid actual or apparent conflicts of interest and advise all appropriate parties of any potential conflict.
- Refrain from engaging in any activity that would prejudice their ability to carry out their duties ethically.
- Refuse any gift, favor, or hospitality that would influence or would appear to influence their actions.
- Refrain from either actively or passively subverting the attainment of the organization's legitimate and ethical objectives.
- Recognize and communicate professional limitations or other constraints that would preclude responsible judgment or successful performance of an activity.
- Communicate unfavorable as well as favorable information and professional judgments or opinions.
- Refrain from engaging in or supporting any activity that would discredit the profession.

Objectivity

Members have a responsibility to:

- Communicate information fairly and objectively.
- Disclose fully all relevant information that could reasonably be expected to influence an intended user's understanding of the reports, comments, and recommendations presented.

Resolution of Ethical Conflict

In applying the standards of ethical conduct, members may encounter problems in identifying unethical behavior or in resolving an ethical conflict. When faced with significant ethical issues, members should follow the established policies of the organization bearing on the resolution of such conflict. If these policies do not resolve the ethical conflict, such members should consider the following courses of action.

- Discuss such problems with the immediate superior except when it appears that the superior is involved, in which case the problem should be presented initially to the next higher managerial level. If a satisfactory resolution cannot be achieved when the problem is initially presented, submit the issues to the next higher managerial level. If the immediate superior is the chief executive officer, or equivalent, the acceptable reviewing authority may be a group such as the audit committee, executive committee, board of directors, board of trustees, or owners. Contact with levels above the immediate superior should be initiated only with the superior's knowledge, assuming the superior is not involved. Except where legally prescribed, communication of such problems to authorities or individuals not employed or engaged by the organization is not considered appropriate.
- Clarify relevant ethical issues by confidential discussion with an objective advisor (e.g., IMA Ethics Counseling service) to obtain a better understanding of possible courses of action. Consult your own attorney as to legal obligations and rights concerning the ethical conflict.
- If the ethical conflict still exits after exhausting all levels of internal review, there may be no other recourse on significant matters than to resign from the organization and to submit an informative memorandum to an appropriate representative of the organization. After resignation, depending on the nature of the ethical conflict, it may also be appropriate to notify other parties.

Source: **Institute of Management Accountants (www.imanet.org). Adapted with permission.**

ANSWERS TO CHECK IT! EXERCISE

Exercise #1: Value and opportunity cost of the: (a) yoga class = $2,500 and $0; (b) karate class = ($500) and $2,500; and, (c) no new classes = $0 and $2,500.

SELF-STUDY PROBLEMS

Splashin' Safari Water Park is a favorite family destination on hot summer days. From the thrilling Slidewinder to the carefree Lazy River and the family-oriented Paradise Lagoon, Splashin' Safari offers over 50 water-based fun activities for people of all ages. During the summer, Splashin' Safari draws an average of 10,000 patrons per week—40% of the park's patrons are adults and the remaining 60% are children.

The price of admission to Splashin' Safari is $15 for adults and $10 for children. Once inside the park, the average adult spends $8 on food and drinks, and the average child spends $5 on food and drinks. Management of Splashin' Safari further estimates that it costs $60,000 per week to operate the park (for staff, water, and advertising) if there are 12,500 or fewer patrons, and $65,000 per week if there are more than 12,500 patrons. The park can accommodate a maximum of 17,500 patrons a week. Finally, management estimates that for every $1.00 patrons spend on food and drinks, it costs the park $0.50 to buy the food and drinks.

Management is considering whether to offer a special for the coming week. Splashin' Safari has run two kinds of specials. The first is a "kids free" week. Under this option, each paying adult can take a child, free of charge, into the park. The special will cost nothing to advertise as management knows that word will get out quickly. Management also expects the following:

- Park attendance will increase by 6,000 patrons, to 16,000 patrons, for the coming week
- 50 percent, or 8,000, of the patrons will be adults and the remaining 50% will be children
- A paying adult will accompany each child

Management calculates that this option will lead to weekly profit of $107,000, an increase of $16,000 over the current weekly profit of $91,000.

The second option is to run additional radio advertising. Under this option, management would run the "usual" one-minute ad six more times per day on a local FM station. The extra spots will cost $16,800. Management expects attendance to increase by 1,000 patrons (to 11,000 patrons) for the week. Similar to the average week, management expects 40% of these patrons to be adults. Under this option, management calculates that weekly profit would decrease from $91,000 to $89,300.

a. *What is Splashin' Safari's decision problem, including its goals?*

As is true of most for-profit businesses, it is likely that **the goal of Splashin' Safari is to maximize profits.** In turn, **Splashin' Safari's decision problem centers on what option generates the highest profit.**

b. *What are Splashin' Safari's options for the coming week?*

Splashin' Safari's opportunity set consists of three options:

1. Maintain the status quo. That is, conduct business as usual in the coming week—do not offer the "kids free" special or run additional radio advertising.
2. Offer the "kids free" special.
3. Run additional radio advertising.

c. *What are the costs and benefits of each option? What is the value and opportunity cost of each option?*

As briefly mentioned in the text and discussed in more detail in Chapter 2, we measure costs and benefits relative to the status quo. Thus, the value of a decision option equals the change in profit relative to the profit in the status quo. Accordingly, for the status quo (option 1), there are no costs and benefits. For option 2, the benefits equal the additional admission revenues and food and drink revenues. The costs include the additional food and drink costs and park operating costs. For option 3, the benefits equal the additional admission revenues and food and drink revenues. The costs include the additional food and drink costs and advertising costs.

Using the given data, we have the following value for each option. (You can verify the specific benefits, costs, and values using the detailed problem data).

1. Status Quo: **$0** = $91,000 − $91,000 (i.e., if Splashin' Safari chooses this option, then the change in profit = $0)
2. Kids free special: **$16,000** = $107,000 − $91,000
3. Additional radio advertising: **($1,700)** = $89,300 − $91,000

The opportunity cost of an option is the value of the next best option. Thus, the opportunity cost of each option is:

1. Status Quo: **$16,000**
2. Kids free special: **$0**
3. Additional radio advertising: **$16,000**

d. *What should Splashin' Safari do this coming week?*

Splashin' Safari should choose option 2 and offer the "kids free" special this coming week. This option leads to the largest weekly profit, or $107,000, increasing Splashin' Safari's profit by $16,000. Option 2 is the only one in which value, or $16,000, exceeds opportunity cost, or $0.

GLOSSARY

Chief executive officer (CEO) The highest ranking executive in an organization. The CEO is responsible for carrying out the policies of the board of directors on a day-to-day basis.

Chief financial officer (CFO) The person in an organization who oversees all accounting and finance functions.

Chief internal auditor (CIA) The person in an organization who oversees the internal audit function.

Control decisions Decisions related to motivating, monitoring, and evaluating performance.

Controller The person in an organization who manages the day-to-day accounting and issues guidance concerning corporate accounting policies.

Decision Choosing an option from a set of options to achieve a goal.

Decision framework A four-step process that consists of specifying the decision goals, identifying available options, evaluating these options, and then selecting the option that best meets the decision maker's goals.

Financial accounting Accounting information system that aims to meet the needs of decision makers outside the organization.

Goals Objectives that decision makers try to achieve.

Managerial accounting Accounting information system that aims to meet the needs of decision makers inside an organization.

Opportunity cost The value of the next-best option.

Organization A group of individuals engaged in a collectively beneficial mission.

Organization chart A graphical representation of the hierarchical relations among positions in an organization.

Planning decisions Decisions about acquiring and using resources to deliver products and services to customers.

Shareholder value The long-run expected wealth potential of an organization to its shareholders.

Treasurer The person in an organization who manages cash flows and serves as the contact point for banks, bondholders, and other creditors.

Value The benefits less the costs of a decision option.

REVIEW QUESTIONS

1.1 LO1. What are the four steps in decision making?

1.2 LO1. Why do individuals' goals differ?

1.3 LO1. What is the value of a decision option?

1.4 LO1. What is the opportunity cost of a decision option?

1.5 LO2. What is an organization? What is the key difference between decision making in organizations and decision making by individuals?

1.6 LO2. What three methods do organizations use to motivate employees to achieve firm goals?

1.7 LO3. What are planning decisions? What are control decisions?

1.8 LO3. What are the stages of the planning and control cycle?

1.9 LO4. What is the primary role of accounting?

1.10 LO4. Who are the primary users of financial accounting information? What types of decisions do these people make?

1.11 LO4. Who are the primary users of managerial accounting information? What types of decisions do these people make?

1.12 LO4. What are the key differences between financial and managerial accounting?

1.13 LO5. How does ethics fit into the Decision Framework?

1.14 LO5. What law prohibits managers in the United States from giving or taking bribes, even if it is the customary business practice in another country?

1.15 Appendix A. Who are the key financial players in organizations? What are their roles?

1.16 Appendix B. The code of ethical conduct prescribed for members of the Institute of Management Accountants divides expected behavior into four areas. What are these four areas?

DISCUSSION QUESTIONS

1.17 LO1. You are about to graduate from college, and you have been fortunate to receive three job offers. How will you make your decision? Briefly discuss your goals and how you would rank your options.

1.18 LO1. Enlarging the number of options available can never reduce opportunity cost. Is this statement true?

1.19 LO1. You have a final exam in managerial accounting tomorrow. What is the opportunity cost of watching television tonight?

1.20 LO1. Jessica Wilde works for a leading consulting company. She wishes to leave her job and pursue a full-time MBA program. What is Jessica's opportunity cost of joining an MBA program?

1.21 LO1 (Advanced). List three sources for differences in individuals' goals. Discuss one business that relies on variations in individuals tastes for risk.

1.22 LO1 (Advanced). In the *Let's Make A Deal!* problem described in the text, the best strategy is a random initial choice followed by a switch on the second choice. Why is this the best strategy?

1.23 LO2. What do you believe are the organizational goals of a nonprofit hospital, a university, and an honor society?

1.24 LO2. Think of the class you are attending as an organization. Assume your instructor is the "owner." What are the goals of this organization? What are your individual goals in relation to this class? Do you see a divergence between your goals and your instructor's goals? How does your instructor motivate you to perform in a way that advances course goals?

1.25 LO2. Why do organizations pay commissions to salespeople? What are the advantages and disadvantages of paying sales commissions from an organization's point of view?

1.26 LO2 (Advanced). Special Forces such as the Navy SEALs and the Army Rangers represent group settings in which there is almost perfect alignment between team and individual goals, and where individuals often put team goals ahead of their personal well being. What unique features give rise to the difference between these organizations and the "typical" profit-making organization?

1.27 LO3. Referring to an experience that we are sometimes forced to endure, we often find ourselves saying things like, "That wasn't too bad." What is the implicit plan in this statement? What is the control aspect? What implications does the assessment have for subsequent plans?

1.28 LO3 (Advanced). Control can apply both to situations in which you are assessing a process ("Did I get 30 miles to the gallon?") and to situations in which you are evaluating another person's performance ("Don't slouch!"). How, if at all, does the introduction of another person change the nature of the control problem?

1.29 LO4. Examine the financial statements of a Fortune 500 company such as **ExxonMobil**, **Sears**, or **General Electric**. How useful are these data for day-to-day decision making?

1.30 LO4. Some argue that accounting systems only measure costs and not opportunity costs. Do you agree?

1.31 LO4 (Advanced). Would firms engage auditors to certify their financial statements even if they are not required to do so? (*Hint:* Think about the credibility of unaudited statements). Also discuss why reputation is an auditor's primary asset.

1.32 LO5. Suppose that you are a journalist who has obtained a video copy of a particularly violent crime. You know that a broadcast would likely cause some emotional harm to the victim's family. However, you also know that airing the tape will increase your TV station's viewership significantly. Should you air the tape, even if there are no legal restrictions against doing so?

EXERCISES

1.33 Specifying goals (LO1). Browse the Web site at http://www.microsoft.com/mscorp/mission/ to read about Microsoft's goals (corporate mission). For an additional sample of a for-profit firm's goals, browse the Web sites of **General Foods, Boeing, FedEx,** or **Unilever.** Look through these sites to identify each company's goals. Many firms list their goals in a mission statement. (Search the site using the keywords "mission statement.") Some firms label their mission statement as the vision statement; others simply include a section entitled "corporate goals."

Required:

  a. According to its Web site, what is **Microsoft's** mission? Why do you believe that Microsoft makes no explicit reference to profit maximization in its corporate mission statement?

  b. Browse the Web site http://www.metmuseum.org/visitor/faq_hist.htm and read about the **Metropolitan Museum of Art's** mission statement. For an additional sample of a not-for-profit organization's objectives, browse the Web sites of the **National Geographic Society** or **Doctors without Borders.**

1.34 Goals (LO1). Browse the Web site for Johnson & Johnson (http://www.jnj.com) and read about its credo. What conclusions do you draw about the firm's priorities? How does this square with the goal of maximizing shareholder value?

1.35 Implementing the four-step framework (LO1). Desiring to stay in shape this semester, you are debating between joining the fitness center at your university versus paying on a "per-use" basis. Joining the fitness center costs $80 for the semester, but you can use the facilities as often as you like at no additional cost. Alternatively, you can pay on a per-use basis, with each visit costing $4. You believe that you will use the fitness center once a week, or 16 times for the semester.

Required:

a. What is your goal for this decision problem?

b. What are the options available to you?

c. What is the cash outflow for the semester for each option?

d. Based on your answer to part (c), what should you do?

1.36 Calculating value, value can be negative (LO1). Toys Ahoy! has 1,000 action figures in inventory that cost $6.25 per unit to produce. Due to changing consumer preferences, the sales department is having great difficulty selling the action figures, and Toys Ahoy! must choose between two options. *Option 1*—scrap (dispose of) the action figures at a total cost of $1,000 (for transportation and landfill fees); *Option 2*—rework all of the action figures, at a total cost of $1,200 in labor and materials, and sell them to a local toy store for a total of $750.

Required:

a. What is the value of scrapping the action figures?

b. What is the value of reworking the action figures and selling them to the toy store?

c. Is the fact that Toys Ahoy! spent $6.25 to produce each action figure relevant to your value computations?

1.37 Opportunity cost (LO1). Jon Tyler is a handyman who does odd jobs such as painting, fixing leaky faucets, installing ceiling fans, and minor electrical work. Jill Safford recently contracted with Jon to paint the outside of her home, and chose a unique color that few persons would consider.

The day before he planned to paint, Jon purchased an initial batch of 20 gallons of the paint. The local hardware store, which mixed the paint to order, charged Jon $325; the store also noted its policy of "no refunds or exchanges on custom colors." Unfortunately, Jon threw his back out that evening. By the time he recovered a month later, Jill had sold her home.

Required:

a. What is Jon's opportunity cost of using the paint for a new job?

b. Suppose Jon decides to throw the paint out because no one else wants the color that Jill had picked out. As a hazardous substance, paint has to be properly disposed. The landfill will charge Jon $40 to dispose of the paint ($2 per can). In light of this new information, what is Jon's opportunity cost of using the paint for a new job?

c. Suppose Jill had paid a nonrefundable advance of $350 to Jon. How, if at all, does this information affect Jon's opportunity cost of using the paint for another job?

1.38 Implementing the four-step framework (LO1). Zap, Inc., manufactures and sells a broad-leaf herbicide that kills unwanted grasses and weeds. Via their television infomercials, Zap encourages homeowners to "take control of their yards" by purchasing one of their "ZAP" kits. Each ZAP kit includes a 32-ounce bottle of weed and grass killer concentrate and a 16-ounce bottle of poison ivy and tough brush killer concentrate. Anticipating high sales, Zap produced 50,000 ZAP kits at a cost of $7.50 per kit. Unfortunately, Zap overestimated the demand for their product. After a year of infomercials, the company had only sold 25,000 units at a price of $19.95 per unit.

The company is in a quandary about what to do with the remaining 25,000 units. Zap could sell the remaining 25,000 units to a national home-improvement store for $7.00 a unit. Alternatively, the company could sell the product via its Web site—under this option, Zap believes they could sell 60% of the remaining units if they reduced the price to $9.95. (Any remaining units would be thrown away). Finally, Zap has ruled out running additional infomercials due to the high cost of TV advertising.

Required:

a. What is Zap's decision problem, including its goals?

b. What are Zap's options with respect to the 25,000 unsold ZAP kits?

c. What is the increase in cash flow associated with each of Zap's options?

d. What should Zap do with the remaining ZAP kits?

1.39 Individual goals versus organizational goals (LO2). Consider a professional sports team such as the **Miami Heat**, the **Chicago Cubs**, or the **Colorado Avalanche**. The team comprises many individuals, each of whom is a gifted athlete and is well paid. As a multimillion dollar business, the team also has several layers of management staff in addition to the usual complement of coaches and trainers. Professional sports teams are often owned by partnerships and corporations, with a wealthy individual having controlling interest.

Required:

a. What are the goals of a team's owners? Do these goals mesh with the goals of the coaching staff and the individual players?

b. What methods do owners use to align the goals of individual players with the goals of the team?

1.40 Individual goals versus organizational goals (LO2). Many firms in the retail industry use "mystery shoppers" to evaluate the quality of their stores and employees. In addition, audit staff for fast-food restaurants such as **McDonald's** and **Burger King** use extensive checklists to evaluate the degree to which their franchisees are complying with company policies. On these unannounced audits, representatives of the company may check the freshness of the food, the average wait time for the drive through, and the cleanliness of the facilities.

Required:

Why do companies invest resources in such monitoring programs? Why is it not enough to instruct employees to follow prescribed company policies?

1.41 Planning and control cycle (LO3). Dr. Sam "Smiley" Shapiro, DDS, has just graduated from a prestigious dental school in the Western United States. He has asked for your assistance in classifying the following actions/decisions within the context of the planning and control cycle: Plan, Implement, Evaluate, and Revise.

Item #	Description
1	Whether to hire two or three dental hygienists? Dr. Shapiro has narrowed his choices to two or thee hygienists based on expected patient volume.
2	Prepare a staffing schedule so that at least one hygienist is available during all times the office is open.
3	Track the number of patients seen by each hygienist per week.
4	Reevaluate the adequacy of current staffing levels.

Required:

Classify each decision according to its stage in the planning and control cycle. Provide a brief rationale for each classification.

1.42 Planning and control (LO3). After years of working for others, Gina Matheson has decided to open her own florist shop. Over time, Gina has gained considerable experience in the nuances of selling flowers and flower arrangements in the retail market. She also has developed good contacts with flower wholesalers. She currently is contemplating the pricing of bouquets for Mother's Day. This is an important decision because, as per the Society of American Florists, sales on this day account for 15 to 20% of the annual sales of flowers in the United States. (The other critical sales day is Valentine's Day, which falls on February 14).

Required:

Identify at least one decision/action for each of the four stages of the planning and control cycle: Plan, Implement, Evaluate, and Revise.

1.43 Financial accounting and investment decisions (LO4). Suppose an individual is considering investing $50,000 in a pharmaceutical company that has been listed on a major stock exchange for several years. The pharmaceutical company currently makes six drugs and is seeking approval for selling four additional drugs.

Required:

a. How could the company's financial statements help this decision maker?

b. Other than the financial statements, what types of data would help the potential investor make a good decision? Classify these data as being financial/nonfinancial and discuss where an investor might obtain such information.

1.44 Managerial accounting (LO4). "I was trained as an engineer, I work as an engineer, and I intend to retire as an engineer. Why on earth would I want to learn accounting?" Linda Payton, a senior production engineer at a Fortune 500 firm, clearly is unhappy that her boss asked her to attend a one-week seminar on managerial accounting before taking on her new position. Linda's new duties deal with managing tools. She has overall authority for when to replace tools, whether to buy them or make them, and what quantities to purchase or produce.

Required:

The following list presents five decisions that Linda might face in her job. How can managerial accounting information help with these decisions? For each decision, list at least one information item that Linda might use and whether the item is financial or nonfinancial in nature.

1. Whether actual costs are in line with expectations?
2. Whether to make a tool in-house or buy it from a supplier?
3. How many tools to purchase for making 100,000 units of a product?
4. What is the right inventory level for a given tool?
5. Whether to make a new tool or to refurbish an existing tool?

 1.45 Ethics and decision making, travel expenses (LO5). You have spent the last two days in San Diego, California, on company business. You flew in on Wednesday morning and took the red-eye flight out on Thursday evening. During this trip, you stayed with your friend, Darren. As Darren lives in the suburbs, you rented a car and paid $80 for the rental and gas. Finally, as a courtesy, you treated Darren and his wife to dinner on Wednesday night (cost: $90). You also spent $45 toward other meals, even though you had breakfast with Darren on Thursday.

Usually, your firm puts up its employees in a downtown hotel. The average cost for San Diego is $140 per night (this is the discounted corporate rate). The firm also pays a per-diem meal allowance of $50 (no receipt required). However, if you were with clients, the firm would reimburse the actual cost for the meal (receipt required).

Required:

Prepare an expense report for your trip (excluding airfare). Assume that if you stayed at the hotel, no car would have been needed as you can walk from the hotel to your firm's office.

 1.46 Ethics and decision making, billing (LO5). Jay Kincaid is a highly sought-after tax attorney, who bills clients at $250 per hour. He has just spent 20 hours researching a unique tax shelter for one of his wealthy clients and has billed the client $5,000.

Jay just received a call from another client asking about a similar tax shelter. He realizes that he can complete the work in 5 hours or so, leveraging his earlier work. Any other similarly skilled professional would take 20 hours to do the work (and would bill $5,000). Jay is wondering about the amount to bill the second client. He knows that the two clients are good friends. There is a chance that any difference in the amount billed to the two clients would be discovered, potentially triggering the loss of one or both clients.

Required:

Discuss at least two billing options and their relative advantages. Advise Jay as to his best course of action.

PROBLEMS

1.47 Value depends on goals (LO1). You wish to work this summer to save money for college. Your goal is to maximize the amount of money you earn working. After spending a week looking for the right job, you have narrowed your prospects to two choices. Your first option is to wait tables at a local restaurant. The manager at the restaurant has guaranteed you 40 hours per week for 12 weeks. Your pay will be $4 per hour plus tips. Naturally, the amount of tips you earn depends on how busy the restaurant is and on your people skills. Not having waited tables in the past, you believe that you have a 50% chance of earning $3 per hour in tips and a 50% chance of earning $6 per hour in tips. Your second option is to work as a checkout clerk at the local supermarket for $8.25 per hour. Similar to the restaurant, the manager of the local supermarket has guaranteed you 40 hours per week for 12 weeks.

Required:

a. How much money would you earn working as a checkout clerk this summer?

b. How much money would you expect to earn waiting tables this summer?

c. Based on your calculations in parts (a) and (b), what summer job would you take? Can you see where someone else might make a different choice?

1.48 Opportunity cost, qualitative (LO1). Wynter Turner and her husband live in rural Nebraska, where Wynter has a well-paying job with the city's only major employer. Wynter and her husband purchased their home three years ago for $225,000. Because she is an avid gardener, Wynter spends much of her free time on landscaping and gardening projects around the house. Wynter estimates the cost of the improvements to her home at $40,000, which includes the imputed value of her time and the out-of-pocket cost of the trees, shrubs, flowers, and hardscape materials. The yard now looks fabulous and has been featured in the local newspaper.

Unfortunately, Wynter's employer recently decided to close the plant where she works. Wynter has been offered a comparable job in the firm's Ohio plant. Wynter has accepted the offer and put her beloved home up for sale. At Wynter's insistence, the home was listed for $275,000, even though the local real estate market has taken a big hit because of the plant closing. While numerous prospective buyers loved Wynter's yard and home, no offers were forthcoming. After a month, the realtor did manage to procure an offer but only for $200,000. The realtor also indicates that this is a "take it or leave it" offer, because the buyer is considering other properties.

Required:

a. What is the opportunity cost of accepting the $200,000 offer? (*Note:* There is not enough information to arrive at an exact number—simply discuss the factors that Wynter should consider.)

b. How would Wynter's options expand if the $200,000 offer were not a take it or leave it offer?

1.49 Appropriate compensation (LO2, LO5). In addition to a base salary that can be several hundred thousand dollars, Chief Executive Officers (CEOs) of major charities enjoy generous perquisites. Some argue that such salaries and perquisites are needed to attract and retain top-notch executive talent. Others argue that such salaries are unseemly in charitable organizations, particularly when their stated goal is to cater to the poor and the downtrodden.

Required:

a. Browse to the Web site of a charity such as the United Way (www.national.unitedway.org) and identify its goals.

b. Do you think a charity's CEO and other top executives believe in the charity's goals? If so, how can the CEO and top executives justify receiving "excessive" compensation, as is often alleged?

1.50 Value depends on goals, airline overbooking (LO1, Advanced). Airlines routinely overbook flights. For example, an airline may sell "confirmed" seats to 225 passengers even when the plane has only 210 seats. Airlines do this anticipating that some confirmed passengers will not show up because their incoming flight is late, their plans change at the last minute, or they are too sick to travel.

Of course, the airline has a problem if its expectations are wrong and more than 210 passengers with confirmed tickets show up. In this case, the airline usually solicits volunteers to be "bumped" from the flight and take the next flight to their destination. The airlines induce passengers with monetary rewards (e.g., a $200 travel certificate). It is common for the reward to increase every few minutes until such time enough people volunteer. If the flight is overbooked even after the maximum reward, then the airline takes the next step of involuntarily bumping confirmed passengers. Confidential airline policies govern who gets to fly.

Required:

a. Discuss the factors the airline considers when it decides to sell 225 confirmed seats, knowing that only 210 seats are available?

b. Why do some passengers volunteer to be "bumped" while other passengers show no interest in the airline's offers?

    c. Some passengers play a wait and see game in an overbooked situation. What is the cost of waiting until the reward reaches a "satisfactory," or high, level?

    d. What cost does the airline incur when it involuntarily bumps a passenger with a confirmed ticket? Does this cost differ across passengers? Will the airlines' ranking of passengers consider these differences, if any?

1.51 Characteristics of value (LO1). Terry Hogan is a technology buff, with a particular interest in video and audio. Terry is contemplating replacing his 55-inch regular-definition projection TV with a 55-inch high-definition projection TV (HDTV). Terry has done extensive research and has identified the specific model that he wishes to purchase. Terry purchased his "old" TV for $1,500 one year ago. The new HDTV costs $1,699 plus 6% in sales tax. Finally, Terry's neighbor has offered to purchase Terry's old TV for $600.

Required:

    a. List the costs and benefits, both quantitative and qualitative, that Terry should consider in his decision.

    b. Suppose Terry still owes $300 on his old TV set. How, if at all, does this information affect Terry's decision?

    c. Suppose a flood in Terry's basement destroys his current (i.e., "old") TV. Terry receives $600 from his insurance provider to cover the associated loss. Terry can replace the old TV with an identical model for $600. How, if at all, does this information change the value of purchasing the HDTV?

1.52 Measuring the costs and benefits of decision options, qualitative (LO1, Advanced). Barbara Maxton, the dean of a leading business school, is wrestling with a problem created by the surge in enrollment for a course entitled "Strategic Cost Management." This course currently is offered in a 20-seat classroom because the instructor uses a seminar format that relies heavily on student involvement. Projects and exams test students' critical faculties, requiring students to integrate material from several prerequisite classes. Strategic Cost Management has become a very popular course. This semester, enrollment exploded—the course hit its enrollment cap on the first day, and another 15 students have e-mailed Dean Maxton expressing their desire to take the course. Dean Maxton is considering the following three options after considering and discarding several others:

    1. Cap enrollment at 20 students. Students can always take the class the following semester or register for an alternative class. Strategic Cost Management is not required for any degree program (i.e., it is an elective course).

    2. Cancel another class with low (six students currently) enrollment to free up another 20-seat classroom. Hire an instructor for $20,000 to teach the second section. Opening a new section requires Dean Maxton to cancel an existing class because all available classrooms are fully scheduled.

    3. A class that currently is scheduled in a 45-seat classroom has only 19 enrolled students. The dean can switch the room assignments, thereby opening up the Strategic Cost Management course to more students. The current instructor for the course, however, has indicated that she cannot follow the same teaching style with 35 or more students—the format has to become more lecture-oriented. Moreover, the examinations will have more multiple-choice and fewer open-ended questions that challenge students' critical faculties.

Dean Maxton knows that most, if not all, of the students who take Strategic Cost Management carry a full course load (15 credit hours per semester). She also knows that tuition does not increase once a student enrolls for nine credit hours (e.g., a student taking 15 credit hours pays the same tuition as a student taking nine credit hours).

Required:

What costs and benefits should Dean Maxton consider in making her decision?

1.53 Implementing the four steps in decision making, qualitative (LO1). Suppose you have decided to purchase a Wintel (Windows-Intel) personal computer to assist you with your coursework. However, you have yet to decide between a laptop and a desktop. You would like to use the four-step framework to assist you in this decision.

Required:

    a. What is your decision problem, including your goals?

    b. What are your options?

c. What are the costs and benefits of each option?

d. How will you make your decision?

1.54 Implementing the four steps in decision making, qualitative (LO1, LO2). You and your best friend have just graduated from college. Before starting your jobs in the fall, the two of you wish to go on a 14-day vacation together. However, you have yet to decide where you will vacation. You and your friend would like to use the four-step decision framework to assist you in this decision.

Required:

a. What are your goals? Are both your and your friend's goals likely to be perfectly aligned?

b. What are your options?

c. What are some of the costs and benefits that you are likely to consider in evaluating your options?

d. How will you make your decision?

1.55 Implementing the four-step framework (LO1). Natalie's Knick Knacks is a boutique store that sells seasonal merchandise. For this Christmas season, Natalie paid $50,000 for an order of figurines, tree ornaments, candles, and wreaths. Natalie marks up each piece of merchandise by 100% to arrive at the selling price. Thus, if Natalie pays $20 for a figurine, she will price it at $40.

Unfortunately, sales were well below expectations, and Natalie's revenues were only $65,000 (far less than the $100,000, or $50,000 × 2, that she had hoped for). This presents a quandary for Natalie, who is contemplating what to do with the unsold merchandise. One option is for Natalie's to store the unsold merchandise for the next 10 months and attempt to sell it the next Christmas season. Natalie estimates that it would cost her $4,000 to properly pack, store, and then unpack all of the unsold merchandise. In addition, because the merchandise would be somewhat dated, Natalie believes that she will only be able to sell 30% of the remaining merchandise the following year (at the current year's retail price). Any unsold items will have negligible resale value, and Natalie plans to donate them to a local charity.

Alternatively, Natalie could hold a January after-Christmas sale. Specifically, Natalie believes that she can sell 100% of the unsold merchandise if she holds an "80% off sale," 80% of the unsold merchandise if she holds a "70% off sale," 55% of the unsold merchandise if she holds a "60% off" sale, and 40% of the unsold merchandise if she holds a "50% off" sale. (The % off is the reduction in the selling price; thus, under a 60% off sale, a figurine priced at $40 would sell for $16, or $40 − [.60 × $40]). Natalie would donate any unsold merchandise to a local charity.

Required:

a. What is Natalie's decision problem, including her goals?

b. What options does Natalie face with respect to the unsold merchandise?

c. What is the increase in cash flow associated with each of Natalie's options?

d. Based on your answer to part (c), what is the opportunity cost associated with each option?

e. What sales strategy would you recommend to Natalie?

1.56 Opportunity cost, pricing (LO2, LO3, CIMA adapted, Advanced). Wood Guardians, located in Manchester, England, manufactures a chemical used to protect fences, boardwalks, picnic tables, and other wooden structures. Manchester city officials have asked Wood Guardians for a price quote on a special job that must be completed within one week.

Completing the special job will require 100 hours of skilled labor and 50 hours of unskilled labor. Wood Guardians pays their skilled and unskilled employees £525 and £280, respectively, for 35 hours of work per week. (£ = British Pound, the official currency of the United Kingdom). Because it is the peak of the slow season, Wood Guardians anticipates having excess capacity of 75 skilled and 100 unskilled labor hours in the coming week. Wood Guardians can also hire additional skilled and unskilled labor on an hourly basis; these part-time employees are paid an hourly wage based on the wages paid to current employees.

Wood Guardians has in stock the primary raw material, chromic acid, needed to complete the city's special job. Wood Guardians purchased the chromic acid two months ago for £1,000; however, due to recent price declines the same amount of chromic acid could be purchased today for £800. Finally, Wood Guardians estimates that it would *cost* them £500 to dispose of the chromic acid (chromic acid is highly toxic, and strict regulations govern the disposal process).

Required:

a. What is Wood Guardians' opportunity cost of labor for completing the city's special job?

b. What is Wood Guardians opportunity cost of materials for completing the city's special job? Assume that Wood Guardians had planned to use the chromic acid on a job to be completed in two weeks. Thus, if Wood Guardians uses the chromic acid on the city's special job, it will need to purchase additional chromic acid.

c. Suppose Wood Guardians purchased the chromic acid for a job that recently was completed. The chromic acid currently in stock is the excess from that job, and Wood Guardians had been planning to dispose of it. Under this scenario, what is Wood Guardians' opportunity cost of materials for completing the city's special job?

d. Continue with the scenario in part (c) above. Suppose that materials and labor comprise Wood Guardians only costs for completing the city's special job. What is the minimum price that Wood Guardians should bid on this job? Do you recommend that Wood Guardians submit a higher bid? Why?

1.57 Differences in individuals' goals (LO1). Assume you have narrowed your choice of a wireless carrier down to the following three plans:

Carrier	Description of Calling Plan	Cost
A	400 anytime minutes. Unlimited nights and weekends. Nationwide calling on the carrier's network. Service is often busy and sometimes leads to dropped calls.	$39.99 per month; Two-year contract. Free phone and activation.
B	Unlimited local calling within the "calling zone" (which includes your hometown). Calls outside the zone cost $0.40 per minute. Good service and coverage.	$29.99 per month. Two-year contract. Phone and activation cost is $100.
C	500 anytime minutes within the "calling zone." Calls over the time limit and outside the zone cost $0.40 per minute. Excellent service and coverage.	$29.99 per month. No contract. Unused minutes rollover to next month. Phone and activation are free if you stay for 6 months. Otherwise, the fee is $100.

Required:

a. Discuss at least two factors that are important to you when choosing a wireless carrier.

b. What might lead one person to prefer calling plan A over calling plan B? What kind of a usage pattern would lead to a preference for calling plan C?

1.58 Monitoring in casinos (LO2). Casinos and other gambling establishments use sophisticated systems to monitor their employees. Employees, particularly dealers, are subject to stringent background checks. In addition, the entire casino is under extensive video surveillance, with security personnel monitoring the gaming operations 24 hours a day, seven days a week. (Any table with "higher than normal" losses is specially monitored). Finally, both uniformed and undercover security personnel prowl the casino looking for suspicious behavior on the part of both casino employees and patrons.

Required:

a. Why do casinos monitor their employees?

b. Identify two costs and two benefits of installing video monitors, relative to physical monitoring by stationing people on the casino floor.

c. Most casinos have *both* video monitoring and physical monitoring on the floor. In addition, they have physical controls for safeguarding chips and money. How do you explain the use of *multiple* monitoring and control measures?

1.59 Monitoring, performance measures (LO2). Felix Uribe takes pride in doing things well. Even as a child, he was neat and organized; as an adult, Felix is fastidious and pays great attention to details. Currently, Felix is considering repainting the bedrooms in his house. While he would love to do it himself, Felix's wife has been complaining about the long hours he has been putting in at work and on projects, and how little time he has for her. Felix is planning to surprise her with a romantic getaway at a bed and breakfast inn; he simply cannot seem to find a spare weekend, though.

Felix could cut the time needed for painting the bedrooms if he enlisted the help of his close friend, Oscar Monroe. With Oscar's help, Felix can get the rooms done by Friday and take the weekend off. There is one problem, however. Although high on enthusiasm, Oscar is a newcomer to painting and home maintenance. As such, his workmanship is not quite at the same level as Felix's workmanship. Another option is to contract the job out. Felix has obtained a bid for $500 from a local contractor to paint all three rooms. Felix estimates that he would spend less than $100 on paint if he did the job himself or with Oscar.

Required:

a. What are Felix's options with respect to painting the bedrooms in his house?

b. Is there a conflict between Felix's objectives and Oscar's objectives with regard to the quality of the painting job? What is the role for monitoring and control systems in this setting?

c. Is there a conflict between Felix's objectives and the contractor's objectives with regard to the quality of the painting job? What role do monitoring and control systems have in this setting?

1.60 Delegation and monitoring (LO2). The Diamond Jubilee is a floating riverboat casino that operates on the Mississippi River. The casino is open 24 hours daily and features 675 slot machines, 25 blackjack tables, 8 poker tables, 3 craps tables, and 2 roulette tables. For motivational purposes, the Diamond Jubilee links some of its general manager's compensation to the casino's profitability. Specifically, the riverboat's general manager, Sapphire Sally, receives a monthly bonus equal to 5% of the casino's pre-tax profit.

Required:

Assume that you are the managing partner in the partnership that owns the Diamond Jubilee. Given Sally's direct financial interest in maximizing casino profit, would you feel comfortable delegating all decisions to Sally and giving her complete control of the casino? In other words, does the bonus contract fully align Sally's interests with the partnership's interests?

1.61 Perquisite consumption, ethics (LO2, LO5). The movie *Holes* is based on an award-winning novel by Louis Sachar. The movie deals with troubled youths sent to a juvenile detention camp, Camp Greenlake, in central Texas. The camp's warden (played by Sigourney Weaver) has each of the boys dig a hole 5 feet wide by 5 feet deep (the shovel is the measure!) everyday to "build character." In reality, the warden has the boys dig the holes in an effort to find buried treasure.

Required:

a. To what extent is the performance measure currently in place (whether the boy has dug a 5 feet wide by 5 feet deep hole) consistent with the state's objective, which is to reform delinquent youth?

b. To what extent is the performance measure consistent with the warden's objective of finding buried treasure?

c. What could the state of Texas have done to ensure that the warden did not use the camp to further her own purposes?

1.62 Individual goals and incentives, ethics (LO2, LO5). Felipe Arrazola is a senior manager for a software consulting firm. Felipe's firm does "turnkey" software projects, with clients paying several hundred thousand to millions of dollars for project completion. The partners of Felipe's firm evaluate his performance based on the revenues he generates. Moreover, the partners expect Felipe to increase his revenues every year.

It is now near the end of the fiscal year. Felipe's current sales volume places him well ahead of last year's sales. This will be the third straight year that Felipe has increased revenues, and he is confident that one or two more years of stellar performance will vault him into the executive suite. Felipe is particularly confident in this projection, as he knows that the firm as a whole is a bit short of meeting its sales budget for the year and that he is one of the few managers who deliver steady sales growth.

One of Felipe's customers has just called to inform Felipe that he is sure to receive a major contract from her company. The contract, valued at $2 million, is almost 10% of Felipe's annual sales volume. The client wants to do the paperwork and issue the formal order after receiving the final specifications and details from Felipe.

Required:

a. Would the partners of Felipe's firm prefer that he book the $2 million contract in the current fiscal year or the next fiscal year?

b. Would Felipe prefer to book the $2 million contract in the current fiscal year or the next fiscal year?

c. Suppose Felipe decides to defer the contract until next year. Do you view this act as being unethical? Why or why not?

1.63 Aligning incentives, nonlinear schemes, ethics (LO2, LO5, Advanced). Stefan Möeller manages the European operations for a large U.S. firm. All manufacturing is done in the United States, and Stefan's primary job responsibilities entail generating sales and coordinating delivery of the goods ordered. In line with the firm's philosophy of "pay for performance," Stefan receives a base salary of €15,000 per month (€ = euro, or Europe's common currency) plus a commission, which has the following properties:

Annual Sales	Commission Rate
€0 to €10 million	0%
€10 million to €20 million	2%
Over €20 million	5%

Thus, if Stefan generated €25 million in sales for a year, his commission would be: $[(€20 \text{ million} - €10 \text{ million}) \times .02] + [(€25 \text{ million} - €20 \text{ million}) \times .05] = €450,000$.

Stefan's year-to-date sales are €16 million, and, based on market intelligence, he believes that he can increase sales by €6 million this year if he spends an additional €1 million on an intensive sales campaign. However, €4 million of the increased sales would represent customers pushing next year's sales forward to this year. This would mean that Stefan would likely only generate €12 million in sales next year rather than his normal volume of €16 million. If Stefan does not undertake the intensive sales campaign, sales are expected to be €16 million this year and next year.

Required:

a. Should Stefan undertake the intensive sales campaign? Why?

b. Assume that Stefan's parent company earns $0.40 in profit (pre-bonus) for each dollar of sales. From the parent company's standpoint, should Stefan undertake the sales campaign? Why?

c. Is there a conflict of interest between Stefan and his parent company? If yes, how might the parent company resolve this conflict?

1.64 Planning and control cycle (LO3). Vulcan Forge makes components used in automobiles and other machinery. The firm, established in 1892, has forged (!) a stellar reputation in the marketplace, allowing it to command a premium price for its products. Vulcan specializes in forging "difficult" shapes and metals. Its metallurgical department has won national and international acclaim for its innovativeness.

Vulcan's management is considering purchasing a new press to replace its existing press. With normal use, this machine will last five years and will be used to make a number of products.

Required:

a. Consider the period from the time of buying the new press until Vulcan scraps it for another press. Describe key decisions that correspond to the four stages of the planning and control cycle.

b. During the time it owns the press, Vulcan would make several decisions that relate to the machine but might only affect operations for a few days or weeks. How do these "smaller" decisions fit into the overall scheme that you describe in your answer to part (a)?

1.65 Planning and control cycle (LO4). Your friend, Drew, is a strong personality. When you explain the planning control cycle, Drew balks at the entire notion. He says, "I know precisely what I want to do. Only indecisive people look back and revise their decisions. I only look forward, never back!" Drew also says, "The belief that every decision follows a clean 4-stage cycle is absurd. Every decision worth making will have many sub-decisions. Take for example, our coach's decision about who plays varsity. By the time Coach revisits this decision at the end of your planning-control cycle, he might have changed the starters several times. In fact, Coach changes the players in the game every few minutes. Each of these actions is a decision as well. How does this fit with the overall planning-control cycle for the decision of which players to have on the varsity team?"

Required:

Comment on Drew's assertions.

1.66 Managerial accounting (LO4). Suppose Tom and Lynda are considering offering a class on yoga. They have sought your help in evaluating the profit impact of this decision.

Required:

List five items that Tom and Lynda should consider in this decision. Characterize each item as to whether it is a cost or benefit, financial or nonfinancial in nature, and if it is measured objectively or subjectively. Describe how Tom and Lynda might compute the magnitude (e.g., $ spent) of each item.

1.67 Managerial accounting (LO4). You have been tasked with evaluating whether your firm should introduce a new product, and if so at what price. If you decide to go forward, the firm wants a three-year profit projection.

Required:

List five items that you should consider for the product launch decision. Characterize each item as to whether it is a cost or benefit, financial or nonfinancial in nature, and if it is measured objectively or subjectively. Describe how you might compute the magnitude (e.g., $ spent) of each item.

MINI-CASES

1.68 Value and opportunity cost, uncertainty, qualitative (LO1). Professor Steven K. studies large-group decision making. He collects research data by asking students to perform a variety of decision tasks in carefully controlled settings. Professor K varies the decision task across group sessions in a preplanned way so that he can isolate the effect of specific factors, such as the amount of information, on students' decisions. His current research project calls for a series of six experimental sessions; each session requires exactly 32 students.

Professor K pays students to participate in his experiments. He advertises the experiments in large-enrollment classes, and interested students can sign up for one or more experimental sessions. (While students can sign up for multiple sessions, they can only actually participate in one session.) Using the sign-up sheets, Professor K randomly selects 40 students for participation in a particular experimental session. He then sends an e-mail to the selected students, notifying them of the time and location of the experiment.

Students who receive an e-mail from Professor K and who show up at the appointed time and place receive a $5 show-up fee. Usually, more than 32 students show up (it is rare, however, that all 40 students do). In this case, Professor K randomly selects the 32 who will stay. He dismisses the students not chosen, after giving them their $5 show-up fee. While it rarely occurs, Professor K must cancel the session if fewer than 32 students show up (of course, he still pays the $5 show-up fee to the students who came). Moreover, a student who shows up for the experiment has a 90% chance of participating in the experiment and a 10% chance of not participating in the experiment.

Professor K informs the students selected to stay for the experiment that they can earn an additional $0 to $40 over the next hour and that the average student will earn approximately $20. The amount earned depends on the quality of the student's decision making. The better the decision, the greater the earnings.

Required:

a. Why does Professor K pay students a $5 show-up fee?

b. What is the student's opportunity cost of showing up for the experiment?

c. Why does Professor K construct the payout scheme so that students' earnings vary in the quality of their decisions? What is the advantage of this payout scheme relative to paying each student a flat fee of $20 for taking part in the experiment?

1.69 Health-care practice, ethics (LO1, LO2, LO4, LO5). Dr. Sarah Cleveland is a pediatrician in San Bernardino, California. Dr. Cleveland became a physician to help sick children; for her, medicine is as much a calling as it is a profession. Dr. Cleveland passionately believes that everyone is entitled to quality medical care and that physicians have an ethical obligation to reach out to the underprivileged. Consequently, Dr. Cleveland currently participates in numerous health-care programs. Her practice caters to patients enrolled in governmental programs such as Medicare and Medicaid; private insurance plans such as Blue Cross and Blue Shield; Health Maintenance Organizations (HMOs) such as Cigna and Kaiser Permanente; and to patients who pay their own way.

Dr. Cleveland sees many benefits and costs from being a part of HMOs. On the one hand, she is reluctant to drop HMOs because several insurance firms and HMOs restrict their members to "approved" physicians only. She wants to be on the approved list in order to expand her availability. On the other hand, insurance firms and HMOs can be difficult paymasters. In a bid to keep costs down, they tightly monitor utilization (e.g., did a given doctor have "excessive" referrals to a specialist?). They also cap doctors' payments at predetermined levels. For example, insurance firms and HMOs pay the same amount per visit or procedure regardless of the actual time spent. Thus, a doctor who takes more time than is "allowed" with a patient is not compensated for the higher time invested.

Increasingly, Dr. Cleveland has become tired of the many restrictions placed by HMOs and insurance firms on the amount of time she can spend with a patient. Currently, Dr. Cleveland is reimbursed at the rate of $40 for an office visit. The insurance firms and HMOs arrived at this rate by allowing doctors 12 minutes per office visit and considering the prevailing income for physicians (after deducting the cost of operating a clinic). The physical time spent with a patient is lower because the 12-minute standard includes time for reviewing the file and dictating notes. Although Dr. Cleveland has reduced the amount of time she spends with each patient to 15 minutes (including review and follow-up notes), she has found herself not being able to provide the quality of care she believes is appropriate and still earn a reasonable income.

Dr. Cleveland is considering a radical experiment. One of her closest physician friends tried this experiment a year ago and has reported being much happier. The experiment is to resign from all of the insurance and HMO plans. Dr. Cleveland would then tell her patients about her operating philosophy of providing excellent care unconstrained by insurance company requirements. The flip side, however, is that patients would have to pay Dr. Cleveland's billed charge, even if the patient's insurance would only reimburse a smaller amount. The patient, in effect, would be paying out-of-pocket for the extra time that Dr. Cleveland spends relative to the average physician.

Under the new scheme, Dr. Cleveland estimates that she would spend ½ hour with each patient, on average. Each patient would be billed (and pay) $75 for the office visit (most patients insurance companies would cover $40 of the $75 fee). Dr. Cleveland's costs of an office visit are negligible because any tests are billed separately. Based on an informal survey, Dr. Cleveland believes that she will have no shortage of patients if she switches to the "patient pays billed charges" approach.

Required:

a. What are Dr. Cleveland's goals? Are there any trade-offs among these goals?

b. Compute Dr. Cleveland's annual revenues if she stays with the HMOs and insurance plans. Also compute Dr. Cleveland's annual revenues if she switches to a "patient pays billed charges" approach. In either case, assume that Dr. Cleveland works 225 days per year and averages 8 billable hours per day worked.

c. Map Dr. Cleveland's decision into the four-step framework. Thus, in addition to Dr. Cleveland's goals, what are her options, what do you perceive to be the costs and benefits of each option, and how do you believe she will make her decision?

d. Assume that Dr. Cleveland switches to the patient pays approach. She then devotes 3 hours every week to caring for indigent patients, for free. She feels that providing such care is part of her obligation to society. What is the opportunity cost of this decision (assume that Dr. Cleveland continues to work for 8 hours per day)?

e. If she cuts down the per-patient time to 25 minutes, Dr. Cleveland can see three more patients per day under the patient pays option. What is Dr. Cleveland's annual revenue if she reduces the time spent with each patient from 30 minutes to 25 minutes? What other factors should Dr. Cleveland consider?

1.70 Elements of decision making, opportunity cost, not for profit (LO1, LO2). The directors of the Community Foundation have almost finished selecting the grants they will fund this year. Three partners in the law firm of Reddy, Willing, and Able established the Community Foundation, with the aim of promoting "equal access to justice for all." The Community Foundation disperses small and large grants designed to educate people about their legal rights and encourage voter registration and participation in the legal system. The directors are down to the last $50,000 in the grants budget for this year and have narrowed the choice to the following three projects:

Project	Description	Amount Requested
A	Help with operating expenses for legal clinics for the indigent.	$50,000
B	Add self-help law books to the local library system.	$18,000
C	Fund a team of law students to travel to a country in Eastern Europe to help with setting up their court system.	$22,000

Assume that a project is either funded at the requested level or not funded at all. Also, the foundation can add any unallocated funds to its endowment. In other words, the directors need not spend the $50,000 because any remaining money will be put in "savings" to be used for future projects.

Required:

a. What are the directors' options with regard to the remaining $50,000 in grant money?

b. What is the opportunity cost of funding Project A?

c. Suppose the directors decide on projects one at a time. Their decision rule is to fund the project if its perceived value exceeds the requested amount and to deny the project otherwise. What are the costs and benefits of using such a decision rule? Assume that the directors first consider Project C, then Project B, and finally Project A.

d. Suppose the directors assess the value of Projects A, B, and C at $50,500, $17,500, and $20,000, respectively. Which projects should they fund?

1.71 Managerial accounting, organizational goals (LO4). The last 20 years have seen a dramatic change in the way that hospitals are paid for services provided. Under the cost-plus system that existed in the 1980s, insurance firms and the government (in the form of Medicare and Medicaid payments) reimbursed hospitals for actual costs plus a reasonable profit. The current Prospective Payment System (PPS), however, classifies all diseases into Diagnostic Related Groups (DRGs). The hospital obtains a flat fee for each patient in a given DRG, independent of the hospital's actual costs for treating that patient.

Required:

a. What are management's incentives under the cost-plus regime? What information does management need to execute its strategy under the cost-plus regime? Assume management's goals are the same as the hospital owners' goals.

b. What are management's incentives under the PPS regime? What information does management need to execute its strategy under the PPS regime? Again, assume management's goals are the same as the hospital owners' goals.

c. How does the change in the regime affect the change in the type of cost information provided to management?

Chapter 2
Identifying and Estimating Costs and Benefits

CONCERNED ABOUT LOSING MEMBERS to Apex, Tom and Lynda want to take steps that will increase Hercules' profit, both immediately and over the long term. They begin by asking current members for suggestions. Some members want to make the gym more "fun" by having contests and prizes. Others would like Hercules to offer more programs and services such as yoga and karate. A few believe that the gym's facilities require major renovation, especially the spa and steam rooms.

You realize that these ideas vary greatly in terms of the resources and effort required to implement them. Organizing a contest might only take a few weeks, and it would have an immediate effect on Hercules' profit. In contrast, a renovation might take months but is likely to influence Hercules' profit for many years. In fact, Tom and Lynda may want to implement both of these suggestions, not just

APPLYING THE DECISION FRAMEWORK

What Is the Problem?	Tom and Lynda want to increase Hercules' profitability, both by attracting new members and by preventing existing members from leaving Hercules for Apex.
What Are the Options?	Members have suggested many ideas, including running contests, offering new classes, and renovating the spa and steam rooms.
What Are the Costs and Benefits?	Tom and Lynda will need to identify, measure, and compare the costs and benefits of each option.
Make the Decision!	Tom and Lynda will select the option(s) that best meet(s) their goal of increasing profitability in both the short term and the long term.

one or the other. To formulate a coordinated response, they need to identify, measure, and compare the costs and benefits of each option in both the short term and the long term.

Tom and Lynda could offer classes in Yoga and/or Karate to respond to the threat posed by Apex.

LEARNING OBJECTIVES

After studying this chapter, you will be able to:

1 Understand how to identify the costs and benefits of decision options.

2 Consider how time affects the realization of costs and benefits.

3 Explain the principles for estimating costs and benefits.

4 Describe the hierarchical nature of costs and its implications for cost measurement.

As you learned in Chapter 1, the primary role of management accounting is to measure the costs and benefits of decision options. This step consists of two tasks—*identifying* the costs and benefits to measure, and then *estimating* the amount of each identified cost and benefit. In this chapter, we focus on the principles that help managers accomplish these two tasks. We begin with the principles, *controllability* and *relevance*, that determine which costs and benefits to measure. Using these principles, we offer a way for grouping business decisions by their horizon—the time span within which an organization reaps the benefits and incurs the costs of a decision. Next, we describe the two key principles for estimating costs and benefits: *variability* and *traceability*. Finally, we extend the principle of variability to develop a hierarchy of costs, which helps to increase the accuracy of estimated costs.

CHAPTER CONNECTIONS

In Chapter 3, we discuss the kinds of accounting systems that you will encounter in the workplace. Such systems provide the data for measuring costs and benefits.

Knowing What to Measure

LEARNING OBJECTIVE 1

Understand how to identify the costs and benefits of decision options.

From Chapter 1, we know that the value of a decision option equals the benefits reaped less the costs incurred. The principles of controllability and relevance help us identify these costs and benefits.

CONTROLLABILITY

By picking an option, a decision maker *chooses* to receive some benefits and incur some costs relative to doing nothing. Conversely, by not picking an option, a decision maker *chooses* to forego the associated benefits but save on the additional costs. Thus, the benefits and costs that arise from the decision maker's choice of a particular option are controllable—the decision maker *controls* the costs that will be incurred and the benefits that will be received.

Because commercial organizations seek to maximize profit, they measure the value of a decision option as the change in profit relative to current profit. Thus, the **controllable benefits** and **controllable costs** for these organizations are the *incremental* revenues and expenditures relative to current revenues and expenditures or status quo.

Consider Tom and Lynda's decision regarding whether to offer yoga. Suppose that offering yoga increases Hercules' instructor salaries from $8,400 to $10,000 per month. This incremental amount of $1,600 for instructor salaries is a controllable cost. Similarly, suppose that offering yoga increases Hercules' membership revenues from $70,000 to $75,000 per month. This incremental amount of $5,000 for membership revenues is a controllable benefit. If these were the only incremental revenues and costs associated with this option, then the value of offering yoga is $5,000 − $1,600 = $3,400 per month.

For this decision, Tom and Lynda do not care about the amounts of many other costs and revenues, such as lease payments and rental revenues. They ignore these *noncontrollable* costs and benefits because the decision to offer yoga does not change them. Focusing on controllable costs and benefits or, equivalently, the costs and benefits incremental to the status quo, allows Tom and Lynda to evaluate each decision option and choose the best one.

In some situations, it is easier for us to consider only *some* of the controllable costs and benefits when making our choice. The principle of relevance, which we discuss next, explains how we could still make the right choice by focusing on select controllable benefits and costs.

RELEVANCE

Suppose you need a new desktop computer. How would you decide which model to buy? You would probably select several brands to consider and then compare the costs and benefits (features) of each. In making this comparison, it is logical to ignore those costs and benefits that are common to the options, such as the cost of an external hard drive, even if these costs must be incurred (i.e., they are controllable). You need only focus on controllable costs and benefits that differ. In effect, you are using the principle of relevance. This principle narrows your attention to **relevant costs** and **relevant benefits**, which are the controllable costs and benefits that *differ* across decision options.

The principle of relevance helps decision makers compare options by focusing on those costs and benefits that *matter,* and ignoring items that are *common* and *irrelevant.* Such a focus simplifies the decision-making process. For example, consider Exhibit 2.1, which compares the costs and benefits of two desktop computers, both of which meet your computing needs.

You will have to pay $1,979 if you choose Brand D and $2,054 if you choose Brand H. These amounts are the controllable costs of the options. Intuitively, you ignore the benefit derived from using the computer as not relevant to your choice. Why? The reason is that you will get the same benefit from both brands. Thus, you prefer Brand D because its total controllable costs of $1,979 are $75 less than those of Brand H.

Indeed, as Exhibit 2.2 shows, we can apply the principle of relevance to simplify the problem further by focusing only on the costs that differ across the two models. We find that the $75 difference in the relevant costs is the same as the difference in controllable costs. Do you see how Exhibit 2.2 might help you to make your decision more efficiently?

Buyers focus on key differences when choosing a computer. (Hafizov Ivan/iStockphoto)

Exhibit 2.1	Choosing a Computer by Comparing Controllable Costs	
	Brand D	**Brand H**
Base configuration (3.08 GHz Intel processor, 1 GB memory, 120GB 5400RPM hard drive, 15" flat panel display, Windows Vista Basic)	$925	$875
Upgrade to 19" flat panel display	125	125
Memory upgrade	225	225
100GB External hard drive	169	169
Upgrade to Windows Vista Professional	175	175
Office 2007 Suite	185	185
3-year service agreement	175	300
Total controllable costs	$1,979	$2,054

Exhibit 2.2	Choosing a Computer by Comparing Relevant Costs	
	Brand D	**Brand H**
Base configuration	$925	$875
3-year service agreement	175	300
Total relevant costs	$1,100	$1,175

COMPARING CONTROLLABILITY AND RELEVANCE

Will applying the concept of relevance always reduce the number of costs and benefits to consider? Not necessarily. As shown in Exhibit 2.3, the answer depends on whether the status quo is an available option. If the status quo is a feasible option, then *all* controllable costs and benefits are relevant because, by definition, they differ from the status quo. Using the concept of relevance therefore does not reduce the number of costs and benefits to consider. However, if the status quo is not a feasible option, then some controllable costs and benefits might not be relevant, letting us ignore them in our analysis.

An example will help clarify this distinction. Suppose Tom and Lynda are deciding among offering yoga, karate, or not offering either class. Furthermore, suppose that the instructor charges $1,600 per month for either class. The status quo is not to offer either class, as Hercules does not currently offer yoga or karate. In this case, the item "instructor salaries" is a controllable cost because the decision could change Hercules' salary expenses compared to the status quo. It also is a relevant cost because Hercules would only incur the additional salary expense of $1,600 for some, but not all, options. Hercules incurs the additional salary expense if it offers either karate or yoga but avoids the cost if it offers neither.

In some situations, the status quo is not a viable option. Suppose that Tom and Lynda are committed to offering yoga or karate, meaning that the status quo is not an option. In this case, the $1,600 instructor salary is still a controllable cost because Hercules' salaries change by offering the new class. However, the $1,600 is not relevant for the choice of which class to offer because it is the same for Hercules' two options.

As our discussion highlights, we can use either controllability or relevance to make effective decisions. We can use the principle of controllability to identify the incremental costs and benefits relative to the status quo, calculate the value of each option, and choose the one with the highest value. Often, however, we may want to identify the best choice quickly and efficiently; in such cases, relevance is the operative principle. We identify relevant costs and benefits by asking if they differ across the feasible options. Summing relevant costs and benefits associated with each option gives us the *relative* values of the options, enabling us to make the right choice.

Check It! Exercise #1 allows you to sharpen your understanding of relevance and controllability.

Exhibit 2.3	*Controllability and Relevance Are Closely Related Concepts*

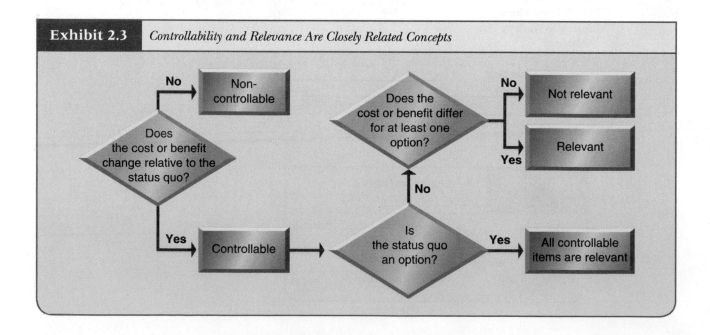

Check It! Exercise #1

After a satisfying lunch, Jason has decided to watch a movie. His choices are to watch a movie at a rundown theater close to his home or the same movie at a brand-new theater 15 miles away. Both theaters have the same ticket price. They also have the same prices for popcorn. Which of the following costs and benefits are controllable for this decision? Which of the following costs and benefits are relevant for watching the movie at the brand-new theater? Indicate your answer by marking a *Yes* or *No* in the appropriate column.

Item	Controllable?	Relevant?
(1) Amount spent for lunch today	———	———
(2) Tuition payment due next month	———	———
(3) Ticket price for movie	———	———
(4) Travel cost to the theater	———	———
(5) Utility from theater experience	———	———
(6) Amount spent for popcorn at theater	———	———

Solution at end of chapter.

Connecting to Practice

CONSUMER ELECTRONICS RECYCLING

In Europe, the Waste Electrical and Electronic Equipment (WEEE) Directive requires manufacturers to ensure that electronic products disposed of by consumers are recycled. In 2004, Hewlett-Packard (HP) and German electronics retailer Media-Markt offered customers the opportunity to return any used or unwanted IT products and receive a discount toward the purchase of any new HP product. More than 2,300 people dropped off equipment for recycling during the week-long program. In addition to these types of "trade-in" programs, HP also provides consumers the opportunity to donate working computer hardware to persons with disabilities, economically disadvantaged persons, and students.

COMMENTARY: Some decisions may unavoidably lead to *negative value* because the costs exceed the benefits for all decision options. Such decisions arise when the status quo is not a feasible option, perhaps because of legal or regulatory reasons. In the context of HP, numerous options exist for handling a product at the end of its useful life. Almost all of these options have a negative value (in terms of current profit) from the firm's perspective. Accordingly, Hewlett-Packard seeks to minimize its costs of recycling computer and printer hardware, while at the same time maintaining its reputation as a "good global citizen."

SUNK COSTS

When identifying costs and benefits, we only focus on *future* revenues and *future* costs. Why? Because the benefits and costs of an option will be realized in the future, and only if we choose the option. The cost of the exercise equipment that Tom and

Lynda installed at Hercules six months ago is a past expenditure, a **sunk cost**, which their decisions today will not affect. Sunk costs do not influence value because we cannot change the past. We define value relative to where we are today, not where we could have been or would like to be. As such, sunk costs are neither controllable nor relevant. Indeed, pharmaceutical companies such as Baxter Healthcare and Novartis often abandon failed drugs even after investing millions of dollars in research and development. These firms know not to "throw good money after bad" and when to cut their losses.

Sunk costs are never relevant because they pertain to the past. How far into the future must we look to identify controllable costs and benefits? As we discuss next, the nature of the decision influences how far we have to look and, in turn, the number of costs and benefits to consider.

Time and Controllability

LEARNING OBJECTIVE 2

Consider how time affects the realization of costs and benefits.

A decision's horizon significantly influences the controllable costs and benefits we need to consider. Suppose you, a business major, need to choose a History class to fulfill your breadth requirement. For this decision, you might consider only a few items such as the fit with your schedule and the popularity of the class. Limiting the items considered is reasonable because you will incur almost all of the costs and receive the benefits within a few months. In contrast, suppose you are thinking about whether to change your major. You will naturally consider many more factors such as how the choice will affect the set of courses taken the next semester and the change in career prospects. Intuitively, you realize that the latter decision affects costs and benefits over a longer period. Accordingly, you consider more costs and benefits relative to the number when picking a class to fulfill breadth requirements. This same intuition carries over to business decisions, leading managers to distinguish between short- and long-term decisions.

CATEGORIZING DECISIONS BASED ON TIME

As illustrated in Exhibit 2.4, a decision maker's control over costs and benefits increases as the time horizon increases. This expansion occurs because previously made commitments and obligations expire with time. For example, Hercules has considerable discretion over expenditures on routine items like towels and cleaning supplies because Tom and Lynda buy these items as needed. Salaries for instructors represent commitments over a longer period because Hercules signs six-month contracts with its instructors. If a decision calls for the immediate replacement of the Pilates instructor, the instructor's salary is noncontrollable; Hercules needs to honor the six-month contractual commitment even if Tom and Lynda replace the instructor. The cost is controllable, however, for the longer-term decision of whether to offer Pilates next year. In this case, the six-month contract will have expired.

Similarly, Hercules' lease will expire in five years. This cost is controllable for long-term decisions such as where to locate the gym, but it is not controllable for shorter-term decisions such as which classes to offer.

Whether we are addressing decisions made by Hercules or by IBM, it is important to keep the time horizon in mind. The horizon affects whether a cost or benefit is controllable for that decision.

At this point, you might ask what distinguishes short-term decisions from long-term decisions? The answer is, "The ability to change the levels of *capacity resources*

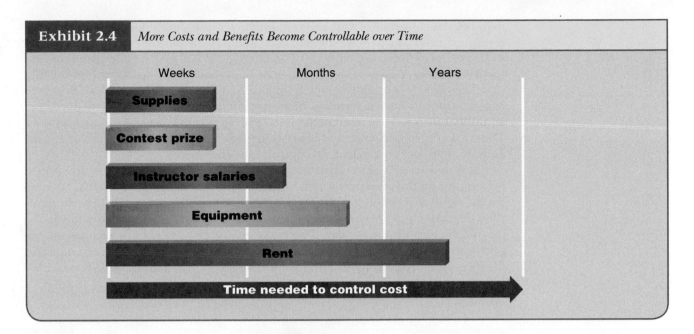

Exhibit 2.4 | *More Costs and Benefits Become Controllable over Time*

Connecting to Practice

CONTROLLABLE COSTS AND AIRLINE PRICING

Commercial airlines such as United and Northwest frequently post flight schedules months in advance of the actual flights. Such commitments trigger a set of costs, including those related to the planes needed to fly the routes and operating the facilities at serviced airports. These costs are noncontrollable once the airline finalizes its schedule.

In contrast, fares for flights change frequently, sometimes in a matter of minutes, meaning that revenues are a controllable benefit even in the short term. Airlines use computer programs to set and continuously adjust prices. They divide available seats into fare "buckets," with each bucket carrying a different fare and restrictions. Computer programs constantly adjust the number of seats available in each bucket, taking into account tickets sold, historical demand patterns, and the number of connecting passengers likely to use the route as one leg of a longer trip. It is therefore common to find that the person in the next seat has paid twice (or, worse, half) what you paid for the same flight!

COMMENTARY: Once an airline's commitment to a flight schedule expires, it could decide not to fly certain routes or service certain destinations. The cost of operating the facilities at the no-longer serviced airports is controllable for a decision that spans a longer horizon.

related to plants, equipment, and salaried staff." In the short term, these resources are fixed and noncontrollable; that is, organizations cannot substantially alter their abilities to deliver products or services in the short term. For example, United Airlines has a certain number of planes, pilots, and landing slots; it cannot decide to fly twice the number of routes next month because it simply does not have enough resources, nor can it acquire them in such a short time period.

In the long term, organizations *can* change capacity. Thus, capacity costs are controllable for long-term decisions—that is, organizations can alter their abilities to deliver products or services in the long term. For example, United can decide to expand the number of routes it flies over the next several years if it purchases additional planes, hires additional pilots, and acquires the necessary landing slots. Thus, the controllable costs and benefits for such long-term decisions include many items that are not controllable for short-term decisions.

Equivalently, we could classify decisions as relating to the short or long term depending on the time over which we experience the costs and benefits. We realize the costs and benefits of short-term decisions relatively quickly; indeed, many short-term decisions are recurring. For example, we make decisions about what to eat and what to wear every day. If we make a poor choice one day, we have the opportunity to make another choice the next day. In contrast, we make long-term decisions less frequently—it's not often that we choose a major or buy a car. We

CHAPTER CONNECTIONS

The modules in this book correspond to decisions in differing time horizons. Chapters 4–8 focus on the role of managerial accounting in short-term decisions. Sample topics include cost–volume–profit analysis, differential cost analysis, budgeting, and variance analysis. Chapters 9–13 focus on the role of managerial accounting in long-term decisions. Sample topics include activity based costing, capital budgeting, the balanced scorecard, and value chain analysis.

Connecting to Practice

VIRTUAL ORCHESTRA

An Apple computer is the newest member of the orchestra in many productions. Professional musicians are fighting a losing battle with producers who are replacing musicians with a "virtual orchestra," particularly for tours. Even though it costs upwards of $50,000 per play to install, the computer-synthesizer can cut the number of musicians needed by 50% or more. The cost savings mount up when you begin to consider the cost of transporting, housing, and feeding two dozen musicians for weeks at a time. While producers claim no appreciable difference in quality, music unions point to glitches in some shows as evidence that there is no replacing a live musician.

COMMENTARY: The decision to go with the virtual orchestra versus live musicians influences subsequent costs and commitments, such as the salaries of the musicians and the cost of moving the orchestra from one location to another. In addition, this decision may affect the quality of the musical performance.

make such decisions expecting to realize the costs and benefits over an extended period and, as such, not expecting to revisit the decision for some time. Moreover, changing our minds about our choice for a long-term decision can be difficult and costly.

Unfortunately, no unique rule enables us to classify *all* decisions per their horizon without any ambiguity. Many decisions are difficult to classify as they contain elements of both the short and the long term. That said, understanding a decision's horizon is important because time influences whether a cost or benefit is controllable. In other words, time helps us identify the costs and benefits we need to include in the decision—that is, the costs and benefits that are "on the table" and that we need to estimate.

How to Estimate Costs and Benefits

Thus far, we have focused on how to identify costs and benefits associated with decision options and which of these costs and benefits have priority in making decisions. However, knowing *what* to measure is only the first step. We now turn to the next step of *how* to estimate costs and benefits.

The core idea underlying estimation is that *costs and benefits are the result of performing activities*. When Nike engages in the activity of advertising on television, it incurs the advertising costs but also receives the benefits in terms of increased revenues. Likewise, Hercules will realize the costs and benefits of offering the yoga class by performing specific activities such as hiring a yoga instructor and scheduling classes. We therefore estimate costs and benefits by first estimating the change in activity for an option and then calculating the financial impact of this change in activity levels.

The principles of variability and traceability underlie the estimation of costs and benefits. Variability deals with *how* activities influence costs and benefits, whereas

LEARNING OBJECTIVE 3

Explain the principles for estimating costs and benefits.

 **Connecting to Practice**

ESTIMATING SOFTWARE COSTS AT INFOSYS

Infosys is a multibillion-dollar Indian company specializing in information technology and business consulting. Infosys routinely completes "turnkey" software systems for its global client base. When bidding for a new contract, the company needs to estimate the cost of project completion to ensure that it earns a reasonable profit. Common activities used to estimate software costs include lines of code, functions (e.g., complexity of inputs and outputs), and objects (e.g., number of screens displayed).

COMMENTARY: Infosys incurs numerous costs to complete any consulting project, including costs related to hardware, travel and training, networking and communications, compensation to engineers and professional staff, and central office administration. It is impractical for Infosys to estimate every cost associated with a consulting project. Instead, the company likely relies on a few activities to estimate the cost of project completion.

traceability is the degree to which we can directly relate a cost or benefit to a specific option.

VARIABILITY

Some costs change as the volume of activity changes, while other costs stay the same. **Variability** is the relation between a cost or a benefit and an activity. A **variable cost** is proportional to the volume of activity, (b) a **fixed cost** does not change as the volume of activity changes, and, (c) a **mixed cost** contains both fixed and variable components. Similar definitions apply to variable, fixed, and mixed benefits.

We can only classify a cost or benefit as variable, mixed, or fixed as it relates to a specific activity and/or a specific time horizon. For example, factory rent varies with the number of buildings leased, but it does not change with respect to weekly production levels. Likewise, we might consider Hercules' rent as fixed for short-term decisions but variable for long-term decisions.

The specific activity we choose to estimate costs and benefits depends on the item that we want to measure, the decision context, and the organization. Hercules could measure activity in terms of the number of members, Breyers could measure activity in terms of cases of ice cream sold, and Google could measure activity in search requests. Let us examine the variability of benefits and costs with regard to a common measure of activity: sales volume.

Variability of Benefits

For most businesses, sales volume (i.e., number of units sold) determines revenues. That is, as Exhibit 2.5 shows, revenues are proportional to sales volume. For example, DreamWorks's revenues increase with movie ticket sales, revenues at Dell vary with personal computer sales, and Hercules' monthly revenues reflect its current membership level.

Variability of Costs

Costs can be variable, fixed, or mixed with respect to sales volume. Variable costs for a computer assembler such as Gateway include the hard drives installed in its computers, the cartons used to pack the computers, and the hourly labor required to assemble the computers. These costs are proportional to computer sales. (Economists

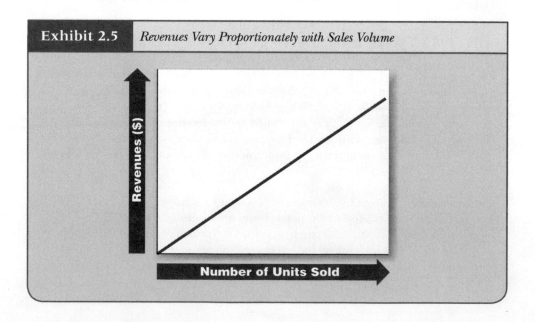

| Exhibit 2.5 | *Revenues Vary Proportionately with Sales Volume* |

often refer to variable costs as *marginal costs* because the unit variable cost is the cost of producing an additional unit.)

Gateway also incurs fixed costs, such as factory rent, salaries for technical support staff, and the cost of testing equipment. These costs are fixed as they do not change in the short term, even if sales volume changes. Mixed costs include utilities and a plant manager's compensation that has both a fixed salary component and a variable bonus component (which increases with the volume of sales beyond a certain base level). However, we can split any mixed cost into fixed and variable components. Therefore, we can represent a firm's total costs as the sum of fixed and variable costs, as Exhibit 2.6 shows. We discuss fixed and variable costs in more detail in Chapter 4.

The principle of variability means that, when estimating costs and benefits, the first step is to estimate the change in activity. For example, Tom and Lynda would estimate the increase in membership if they offered yoga. They can then apply the

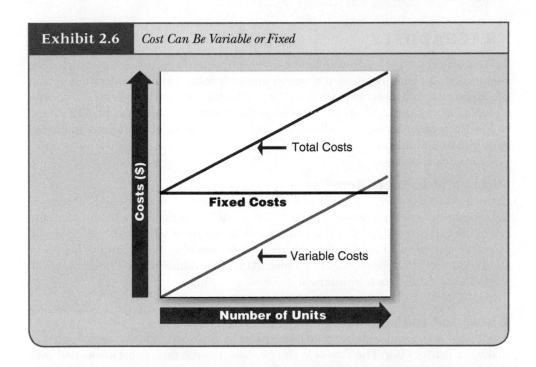

Exhibit 2.6   *Cost Can Be Variable or Fixed*

Check It! Exercise #2

The following table provides total variable costs and total fixed costs for several activity levels. Verify that the unit variable cost is the same for all activity levels, while the fixed cost per unit decreases as the volume of activity increases.

Volume of Activity	Total Variable Costs	Total Fixed Costs	Unit Variable Cost	Fixed Cost Per Unit
100 units	$1,200	$1,000	_____	_____
125 units	$1,500	$1,000	_____	_____
200 units	$2,400	$1,000	_____	_____
250 units	$3,000	$1,000	_____	_____

Solution at end of chapter.

CHAPTER CONNECTIONS

The short-term decisions that we discuss in Chapters 4–8 rely on classifying costs as being either fixed or variable, because many costs are noncontrollable (i.e., are fixed) in the short term. In Chapters 9–13, we consider long-term decisions, where most costs that we classified as fixed in the short term become controllable.

concept of variability to convert the change in membership to corresponding changes in revenues and costs. Traceability, the principle we discuss next, pertains to the confidence with which any decision maker, including Tom and Lynda, can estimate a cost or a benefit.

TRACEABILITY

Traceability is the degree to which we can directly relate a cost or revenue to a decision option. A cost or revenue that we can uniquely relate (*trace*) to a decision option is a **direct cost** or a **direct benefit**. If only a portion of the cost or revenue pertains to a particular decision option, then it is an **indirect cost** or an **indirect benefit**. Organizations frequently refer to indirect costs as *common costs* and to indirect manufacturing costs as manufacturing **overhead**.

Direct and Indirect Benefits

Assume that Frigidaire, a leading manufacturer of kitchen appliances, is determining whether to continue making a particular model of refrigerator. In this case, the company can directly identify the revenues received from sales of the refrigerator. However, the product might also provide indirect benefits. For example, buyers of the Frigidaire refrigerator might be more likely to purchase other Frigidaire appliances in the future, thereby increasing overall revenues.

Direct and Indirect Costs

Frigidaire can uniquely identify the type, quantity, and costs of raw materials used to make the refrigerator. The cost of such raw materials is a direct cost associated with the decision to make the refrigerator. However, the company may use the same machinery to produce many different refrigerators and related products. The cost of such machinery is an indirect cost.

It is important not to confuse direct and common costs with variable and fixed costs. A direct cost can be fixed or variable. The cost of a machine used only for manufacturing this refrigerator is a fixed, direct cost. The cost of raw materials is a variable, direct cost. Likewise, indirect costs also can be fixed or variable. The regular salary (e.g., not including bonuses) paid to the plant manager who oversees the production of this and other refrigerators is a fixed, indirect cost. The cost of oils and lubricants to run the machines is indirect and variable. It is variable because the amount depends on the number of refrigerators made; it is indirect because it is not possible to identify the amount of coolants used for a particular refrigerator.

We can identify direct and indirect costs in all functional areas. Direct marketing expenses include sales commissions. The expense of maintaining sales offices, however, is an indirect cost. Similarly, the royalty payment for a patent used in product development is a direct cost, while the cost of maintaining research staff is indirect.

Exhibit 2.7	Sample Costs and Benefits Classified by Controllability, Variability, and Traceability		
Item	Controllable for Decision to Offer Yoga?	Variable in Number of Members?	Traceable to Decision to Offer Yoga?
Dues from new members	Yes	Yes	Yes
Instructor salary	Yes	No	Yes
Supplies	Yes	Yes	No
Rent for gym	No	No	No

The instructor's salary is controllable and traceable to the decision to offer yoga. (Masterfile)

When evaluating whether Hercules should offer the yoga class, we must consider both the variability and the traceability of the associated costs and benefits. Exhibit 2.7 lists and labels some of the costs and benefits that Tom and Lynda will consider when deciding whether to offer yoga.

It is easier to estimate direct costs and benefits than indirect costs and benefits. Why? By definition, direct costs and benefits relate entirely to a decision option. In contrast, only a part of the indirect cost or benefit relates to the decision option. Thus, we need to determine the portion of an indirect cost or benefit attributable to the option. This allocation of costs often requires assumptions and is therefore imprecise. In the next section, we extend the principle of variability to develop a **cost hierarchy**, which can help increase the accuracy of estimated costs.

Hierarchical Cost Structure

Say you and your friends decide to travel to a concert. You might need one car for four of you, but two cars for five. As Exhibit 2.8 shows, this example illustrates a step cost. **Step costs** stay at the same level for a certain activity range (one to four people), but jump to a higher amount if the volume of activity increases beyond this range (adding a fifth person to the group). For Hercules, the cost of the yoga instructor is a step cost. Until a volume of 30 members, say, the cost is fixed. If enrollment in the yoga class exceeds 30 members, Hercules may need to schedule an additional class to ensure quality instruction, thereby increasing its costs. Sales staff at the Gap is another example of step costs because it is not possible to hire sales persons by the minute.

Step costs relate to fixed costs and variable costs in a straightforward way. A step cost behaves more like a variable cost as the step size decreases. It behaves more like a fixed cost as the step size increases. For example, consider bicycles, buses, and trains as modes of transportation. Trek bicycles have a step size of one rider, a Greyhound bus has a step size of 50 passengers or more, and an Amtrak train has a step size in the hundreds. Like a variable cost, the number of bicycles needed increases for each additional person; the number of buses required increases with about every 50 passengers, behaving like a step cost; and we only need one train over a very large range of passenger volume, a fixed cost.

In sum, when we classify all costs as fixed or variable with respect to sales volume, we are saying that *all* costs are either independent of or proportional to sales volume.

LEARNING OBJECTIVE 4

Describe the hierarchical nature of costs and its implications for cost measurement.

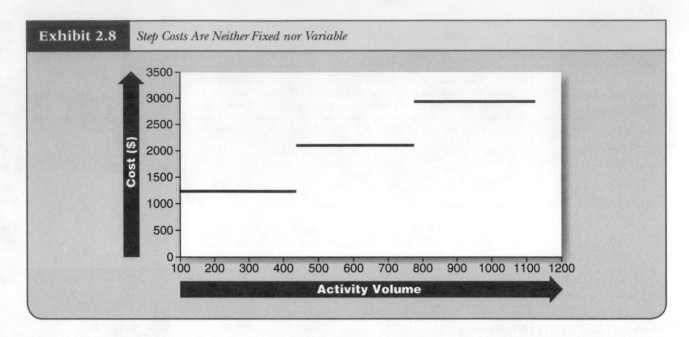

| Exhibit 2.8 | *Step Costs Are Neither Fixed nor Variable* |

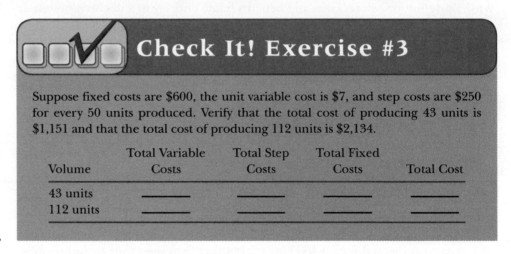

Check It! Exercise #3

Suppose fixed costs are $600, the unit variable cost is $7, and step costs are $250 for every 50 units produced. Verify that the total cost of producing 43 units is $1,151 and that the total cost of producing 112 units is $2,134.

Volume	Total Variable Costs	Total Step Costs	Total Fixed Costs	Total Cost
43 units	_____	_____	_____	_____
112 units	_____	_____	_____	_____

Solution at end of chapter.

While practical and frequently used, this assumption often results in imprecise measurements. As a result, when decision makers need finer estimates, they use the cost hierarchy. Generalizing the classification by using the cost hierarchy allows us to consider *unit-, batch-, product-, and facility-level activities,* which in turn helps us to estimate better the costs of a decision option.

Consider the cost structure for Deluxe Checks, which prints customized checkbooks (see Exhibit 2.9). For each printing job, the cost of the paper and direct labor varies proportionally with production volume. We refer to such costs, which we earlier termed variable costs, as **unit-level costs**. Unit-level costs increase or decrease in direct proportion to the number of units produced. The step size for these costs is a unit.

Each job produced, however, requires some setup and production planning. Deluxe has to prepare the printing machine for the next job by loading a new program. Setup costs include all changeover costs incurred to prepare the production process for the next product. These costs vary with the number of setups done, not with the number of units produced. That is, the setup costs are the same whether Deluxe produces 200, 500, or 1,000 checks after the setup. Because the step for such

Exhibit 2.9	*Using the Cost Hierarchy Allows Deluxe Checks to Improve the Accuracy of Cost Estimates*

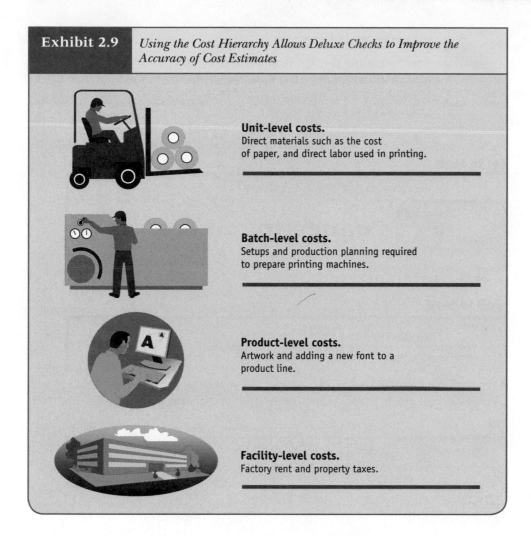

Unit-level costs.
Direct materials such as the cost
of paper, and direct labor used in printing.

Batch-level costs.
Setups and production planning required
to prepare printing machines.

Product-level costs.
Artwork and adding a new font to a
product line.

Facility-level costs.
Factory rent and property taxes.

costs depends on the number of batches produced (number of setups) instead of units, we refer to these costs as **batch-level costs**.

Each job also requires some artwork. This work does not depend on the number of batches and units. Such **product-level costs** include advertising, research and development, and the cost of specialized equipment. For example, if Deluxe adds more fonts and backgrounds for customizing checks, this increases its product-level costs, as the firm will need to reprogram its computers and update its product catalogs. These costs change only as the company changes the number of products.

Finally, costs that do not vary at the unit level, the batch level, or the product level are **facility-level costs**. Examples include the fixed costs of operating a factory, such as rent and property taxes, which firms incur to sustain their place of business. Even these costs, however, might vary in the long term; they change with the number of plants operated by Deluxe, meaning that the step size is an entire factory.

For Hercules, the cost of serving members is a unit-level (member-level) cost. This cost will proportionately rise as the club attracts new members. The yoga instructor's salary is an example of a batch-level cost that will only increase with every 30 members in the yoga class. The money spent on buying a massage table is a product-level cost because the cost relates to offering massage services. The rent paid by Tom and Lynda is a facility-level cost.

Understanding Hercules' cost structure will help you in measuring the yoga class's costs and benefits more accurately. But where do we go to get the data to measure these costs and benefits? In the next chapter, we discuss the accounting systems that provide the data for measuring costs and benefits.

CHAPTER CONNECTIONS
Understanding the cost hierarchy is important when using activity-based costing (ABC) to estimate the cost of products and services over an extended horizon. We discuss activity-based costing in Chapter 11.

Connecting to Practice

ART.COM

Art.com is an e-tailer that specializes in selling framed and unframed prints. An analysis of the firm's operations revealed the following cost structure:

Cost type	% of total cost	Examples
Unit-level costs	31%	Materials, labor, packing, and freight
Batch-level costs	7%	Purchasing, receiving, order processing
Product-level costs	49%	Web site, inventory management, marketing
Facility-level costs	13%	Administration

COMMENTARY: At Art.com, product-level costs comprise approximately half of total costs. Thus, classifying costs as purely fixed or variable could lead to poor decisions in this setting. Accordingly, management may wish to use both product- and unit-level activities when estimating costs.

APPLYING THE DECISION FRAMEWORK

What Is the Problem?	Tom and Lynda want to increase Hercules' profitability, both by attracting new members and by preventing existing members from leaving Hercules for Apex.
What Are the Options?	Members have suggested many ideas, including running different types of contests, offering more programs and services, and renovating the spa and steam rooms.
What Are the Costs and Benefits?	The costs and benefits differ greatly across individual decisions— the number of controllable costs and benefits for renovating the spa and steam rooms exceeds the number for running a contest.
Make the Decision!	Tom and Lynda classify renovating as a long-term decision and offering more classes and running contests as short-term decisions. This grouping enables Tom and Lynda to understand when the costs and benefits of each decision will materialize and, in turn, estimate the costs and benefits of each option.

SUMMARY

The primary role of management accounting is to *measure* the costs and benefits of decision options. This step consists of two tasks—*identifying* the costs and benefits to measure, and then *estimating* the amount of each identified cost and benefit.

In this chapter, we described the two principles, controllability and relevance, for identifying the costs and benefits of decision options. We established an important link between controllability and time. Based on this link, we distinguished between short- and long-term decisions. We next considered the two principles, variability and traceability, that are used to estimate costs and benefits. Finally, we broadened the principle of variability to develop a hierarchy of costs.

A firm's accounting system is the natural spot that we look to for help with identifying and estimating costs and benefits. How do firms accumulate and report costs, revenues, and profit? We take up this task in Chapter 3.

RAPID REVIEW

LEARNING OBJECTIVE 1

Understand how to identify the costs and benefits of decision options.

- A cost or benefit for a decision option is controllable if it differs from *current* expenditures and revenues. The value of a decision option equals such incremental benefits less incremental costs and is the change in profit relative to current profit.

- A cost or benefit is relevant if its amount differs across decision options. Focusing on relevant costs and benefits provides the relative value of the decision options.

LEARNING OBJECTIVE 2

Consider how time affects the realization of costs and benefits.

- A decision maker's control over costs and benefits increases with the passage of time because commitments and obligations expire with time.

- The ability to change the levels of *capacity resources* related to plant, equipment, and salaried staff distinguishes short-term decisions from long-term decisions. In the short term, these resources are fixed and noncontrollable—that is, organizations cannot substantially alter their abilities to deliver products or services. In the long term, organizations have a greater ability to do so.

LEARNING OBJECTIVE 3

Explain the principles for estimating costs and benefits.

- The core idea underlying estimation is that controllable costs and benefits are the outcomes of activities.

- Variability is the relation between a cost or a benefit and the chosen activity. A cost or benefit is (1) variable if it is proportional to the volume of activity; (2) fixed if it does not change as the volume of activity changes; and (3) mixed if it contains both fixed and variable components.

- Revenues are variable in units sold. Costs can be variable, fixed, or mixed with respect to sales volume.

- Traceability is the degree to which we can relate a cost or a benefit with a decision option. We can attribute the entire amount of a direct cost or a direct benefit to a decision option. If only a portion of the cost or revenue pertains to a particular decision option, then it is an indirect cost or an indirect benefit.

- While variability allows us to convert activity estimates to estimates of costs and benefits, traceability influences our confidence in our estimates.

LEARNING OBJECTIVE 4

Describe the hierarchical nature of costs and its implications for cost measurement.

- The cost hierarchy broadens the principle of variability, allowing us to consider multiple activities. The cost hierarchy recognizes four types of costs: (1) unit-level costs; (2) batch-level costs; (3) product-level costs, and (4) facility-level costs.

- Unit-level costs increase or decrease in proportion to the number of units produced. Unit-level costs are synonymous with variable costs.

- Batch-level costs increase or decrease in proportion to the number of batches of units made. Many refer to batch-level costs as step costs.

- Product-level costs increase or decrease in proportion to the number of products.

- Facility-level costs are required to sustain the business. They do not vary at the unit-, batch-, or product-level.

- Misclassification of costs across the cost hierarchy introduces errors in cost estimation.

ANSWERS TO CHECK IT! EXERCISES

Exercise #1: (1) Noncontrollable, not relevant; (2) Noncontrollable, not relevant; (3) Controllable, not relevant; (4) Controllable, relevant; (5) Controllable, relevant; (6) Controllable, not relevant. Notice that item (3), the ticket price, and item (6), the amount spent on popcorn, are controllable but irrelevant to Jason's decision. They are controllable because Jason has yet to pay for the movie and the popcorn. They are not relevant because Jason will pay the same amount regardless of which theater he attends.

Exercise #2: Unit variable cost = $12. Fixed cost per unit = $10, $8, $5, and $4.

Exercise #3: $600 + (43 × $7) + ($250 × 1 step) = $1,151; $600 + (112 × $7) + ($250 × 3 steps) = $2,134.

SELF-STUDY PROBLEMS

SELF-STUDY PROBLEM #1:
Controllability and Relevance

For a new product, Mega Manufacturing is deciding whether to buy 500 units of a component from an outside supplier or to make them in-house. If Mega buys the component from an outside supplier, it will pay the supplier $12 per unit. Mega will also pay $1 per unit to inspect the component and spend an additional $9 per unit in materials and labor to convert each component into a finished product. Mega will sell the finished product to consumers for $30 per unit.

Making the component in-house requires $6 worth of steel and $3 worth of a special alloy. Mega routinely purchases and uses steel in its operations, and it does not currently have any steel in inventory. The special alloy is unique to the component in question, and Mega currently has $2,000 worth in stock. If it chooses the buy option, Mega will dispose of the special alloy. Disposal costs equal salvage value, meaning that Mega's net proceeds from disposal are $0. Making the component in-house also requires that Mega hire new workers at a cost of $16 per hour—workers can make four units of the component per hour.

As under the buy option, Mega will pay $1 per unit to inspect the component and spend an additional $9 per unit in materials and labor to convert each component into a finished product. Mega will then sell the finished product to consumers for $30 per unit.

a. *What are the controllable costs and benefits associated with the buy option? What are the controllable costs and benefits associated with the make option?*

As discussed in the text, a cost or benefit is controllable if it changes relative to current expenses and revenues. Compared to current profit, the following costs and benefits change under the buy and make options:

Costs and Benefits—Buy Option

Item	Amount per unit	Total (500 units)
Revenues—Finished Units	$30	$15,000
Total Controllable Benefits		*$15,000*
Purchase Price	$12	$6,000
Inspection	$1	$500
Additional Materials and Labor	$9	$4,500
Total Controllable Costs		*$11,000*
Value (benefits − costs)		*$4,000*

Costs and Benefits—Make Option

Item	Amount per unit	Total (500 units)
Revenues—Finished Units	$30	$15,000
Total Controllable Benefits		*$15,000*
Steel	$6	$3,000
Special Alloy*	$0	$0
Labor**	$4	$2,000
Inspection	$1	$500
Additional Materials and Labor	$9	$4,500
Total Controllable Costs		*$10,000*
Value (benefits-costs)		*$5,000*

* The $2,000 of special alloy in inventory is a sunk cost, and Mega does not plan to purchase additional special alloy if it makes the component in house. Thus, the cost is non-controllable.
** $4 per unit = $16 per hour/4 units per hour.

b. *What is the value of the make option? What is the value of the buy option?*

Value = Controllable benefits − Controllable costs. Based on our calculations in part (a):
Value (buy) = $15,000 − $11,000 = $4,000
Value (make) = $15,000 − $10,000 = $5,000

Mega should choose the make option because it has the higher value.

c. *Compared to the buy option, what are the relevant costs and revenues associated with the make option?*

The revenues received from the finished product do not differ between the two options. Given this, *the relevant revenues are $0.*

In addition, three of the costs do not differ between the make and buy options: (1) the inspection cost, (2) the additional labor and materials required to convert the component to a finished product, and (3) the sunk cost of the special alloy. Accordingly, these costs are irrelevant. The three costs that differ are: (1) the steel, (2) the labor, and (3) the purchase price. Thus, we have:

Relevant Costs—Make Option

Item	Amount per Unit	Total (500 units)
Steel	$6	$3,000
Labor	$4	$2,000
Purchase Price	($12)	($6,000)
Total Relevant Costs		*($1,000)*

Using the principle of relevance, we find that Mega still prefers the make option because its cost is $1,000 less than the cost of the buy option. Notice that we subtracted the purchase price in our computations. We did so because, compared to buying, Mega *saves* $12 per unit by making the component.

Thus, the principles of relevance and controllability give us the same ranking of options. Relevance also preserves the difference in value between the two options, or $1,000. Finally, notice that compared to controllability, relevance allows us to focus our attention on fewer items.

d. *Suppose Mega did not have the alloy in stock and had to purchase it. How does this information change your analysis?*

This information means that the cost of alloys is now controllable. It also is relevant. Thus, the controllable costs of the make option would increase to $11,500, making the buy option more attractive. Likewise, the relevant cost of making versus buying is $500, again meaning that buy is the preferred option. Both analyses show that Mega gains $500 by buying the component over making it, if the firm has to purchase the alloy.

Self-Study Problem #2:
Variability, Traceability, Cost Hierarchy

Dudley Brothers offers waste management services, specializing in construction waste. The firm has two product lines: regular waste disposal and hazardous waste disposal. Because hazardous waste requires extra handling and care, Dudley Brothers has specialized equipment for handling materials such as asbestos and lead-based paint.

In a typical engagement, Dudley places one or more dumpsters at the client's construction site. These dumpsters are emptied every week. The dumpsters may be emptied sooner if the construction crew informs Dudley that the dumpster is full. Dudley then hauls the waste to the landfill, disposing of it properly. The landfill charges Dudley a fee based on the number of pounds dumped as well as the type of waste dumped (the landfill fee for hazardous waste is higher than the fee for regular waste).

The following table lists eight costs incurred by Dudley:

Cost #	Description of Cost
1	Gasoline costs for hauling waste to the landfill
2	Landfill fee for dumping regular waste
3	Landfill fee for dumping hazardous waste
4	Cost of weekly scheduled pickups
5	Annual city permit fee to handle hazardous materials
6	Cost of the truck to haul waste (Dudley's truck can haul dumpsters with either regular or hazardous waste)
7	Cost of new dumpster to handle hazardous waste
8	Salary to receptionist at the firm's office

Classify each cost as per the cost hierarchy—that is, classify each cost as being a unit-, batch-, product-, or facility-level cost. In addition, classify each cost as being direct (D) or indirect (I) with respect to Dudley's two product lines. Provide a brief rationale for each classification.

The following listing provides the cost classifications, including comments pertaining to the rationale underlying each classification:

1. Gasoline costs for hauling waste to the landfill   ***Unit level, Indirect***
    This cost depends on the volume of waste (more waste = more trips). This cost is indirect because Dudley can make multiple trips with a single tank of gas. However, one could argue that this is a batch-level cost inasmuch as regularly scheduled pickups must be made regardless of actual volume.
2. Landfill fee for dumping regular waste   ***Unit level, Direct*** (*regular waste*)
    The cost varies in the volume of waste handled and is traceable to the regular waste product line.
3. Landfill fee for dumping hazardous waste   ***Unit level, Direct*** (*hazardous waste*)
    The cost varies in the volume of waste handled and is traceable to the hazardous waste product line.
4. Cost of weekly scheduled pickups   ***Batch level, Indirect***
    The cost is incurred once a week, regardless of how full the dumpster is. Furthermore, the cost is indirect because a single customer may have both types of waste.
5. Annual city permit fee to handle hazardous materials   ***Product level, Direct*** (*hazardous*)
    This cost does not vary in the number of loads or the volume handled. Dudley incurs the cost to operate the hazardous product line.
6. Cost of the truck to haul waste   ***Facility level, Indirect***
    This is a facility-level cost because it pertains to *all* of Dudley's product lines. If Dudley were to get into another line of business that does not use the truck, then it would be a product-level cost.
7. Cost of new dumpster to handle hazardous waste   ***Product level, Direct*** (*hazardous*)
    This is a product level cost because it does not vary in the amount of waste or the number of loads. The cost is traceable to the hazardous waste product line.
8. Salary to receptionist at the firm's office   ***Facility level, Indirect***
    This cost is incurred to sustain the business, and is not traceable to either product line.

This problem shows that, in many cases, costs do not fall neatly into fixed and variable categories. The cost hierarchy helps managers structure their thinking about the underlying reason for a cost and suggests why a given cost would increase or decrease. In turn, such understanding can facilitate decision making, as misclassifications could lead to poor estimates of cost (e.g., assuming a cost is variable or fixed when, in fact, it is a batch- or product-level cost).

Nonetheless, for many decisions, organizations do classify costs as being purely fixed or purely variable, because the ease of resulting computations outweighs the errors introduced by the classification.

This problem also helps with the distinction between direct and indirect costs. It is important to remember that traceability depends on the unit of analysis. For example, while the salary of the receptionist is an indirect cost with respect to Dudley's two product lines, it is a direct cost with respect to the firm as whole.

GLOSSARY

Batch-level cost A cost that varies in proportion to the number of batches of units made (used synonymously with step cost).

Controllable cost, controllable benefit A cost or benefit that a decision maker chooses to incur, relative to doing nothing.

Cost hierarchy The classification of costs into unit-, batch-, product-, and facility-level.

Direct cost, direct benefit A cost or benefit that is uniquely related to a decision option.

Facility-level cost Cost that does not vary at the unit-, batch-, or product-level. Cost required to sustain the organization.

Fixed cost A cost that does not change as the volume of activity changes.

Indirect cost, indirect benefit A cost or benefit that is not unique to a decision option—only a portion relates to a decision option.

Mixed cost A cost that contains both fixed and variable components.

Overhead The costs of capacity resources.

Product-level cost A cost that varies in proportion to the number of products.

Relevant cost, relevant benefit A cost or benefit that differs across decision options.

Step cost A cost that increases in discrete steps as the volume of activity increases.

Sunk cost A past expenditure that cannot be changed.

Traceability The degree to which we can directly relate a cost or a revenue to a decision option.

Unit-level cost A cost that increases or decreases in direct proportion to the number of units produced (used synonymously with variable cost).

Variability The relation between a cost or a benefit and an activity.

Variable cost A cost that is proportional to the volume of activity.

REVIEW QUESTIONS

2.1 LO1. What does it mean for a cost or benefit to be controllable?

2.2 LO1. How is value related to controllable costs and benefits?

2.3 LO1. What does it mean for a cost or benefit to be relevant?

2.4 LO1. When is a controllable cost relevant? When is a controllable cost not relevant?

2.5 LO2. Why does time influence the controllability of costs and benefits?

2.6 LO2. What is the key difference between a long-term and a short-term decision?

2.7 LO2. Why is it not possible to sharply distinguish between short- and long-term decisions?

2.8 LO3. What is the central principle underlying the estimation of revenues and costs?

2.9 LO3. Are revenues usually variable, mixed, or fixed? Why?

2.10 LO3. What are variable, fixed, and mixed costs?

2.11 LO3. What is traceability?

2.12 LO3. What are direct and indirect costs?

2.13 LO4. What is a step cost?

2.14 LO4. How many kinds of costs are there in the cost hierarchy? List these kinds of costs.

DISCUSSION QUESTIONS

2.15 LO1. We know that the controllable benefits less the controllable costs of an option equals its value. Can focusing only on relevant costs and benefits ever give us value?

2.16 LO1. Many decisions often involve qualitative factors. How can you reconcile this fact with the concept of relevant costs?

2.17 LO1. Every relevant cost is controllable. However, not all controllable costs are relevant. Why are these two statements correct?

2.18 LO1. When might the magnitude of a sunk cost be relevant for a decision? How do you reconcile this answer with the maxim that a sunk cost is not relevant for decision making? (*Hint*: Consider taxes or a decision maker's reputation.)

2.19 LO2. Identify a personal decision that could affect your life for 10 years or more. Discuss how this decision sets the stage for subsequent decisions that may only span a few years or perhaps even a few months.

2.20 LO2. Consider your school. How would you classify the following decisions as per their time horizon: (a) whether to open an additional section for an existing class or to reassign rooms among classes, (b) whether to offer a new program of study, and (c) whether to remodel the cafeteria in the dormitory?

2.21 LO2. Television manufacturers such as Pioneer, Sony, Toshiba, and Mitsubishi introduce new models constantly. In your judgment, how long is the short-term horizon for such television companies? Identify two short-term decisions that these companies might make to improve their profit.

2.22 LO2. Consider the decision to purchase an automobile to commute to school and/or to work. What costs do you commit to/do not commit to when making your choice?

2.23 LO2. From your life experience, identify a decision that appeared to have a short-term horizon but had unintended long-term consequences.

2.24 LO3. If a firm drops a product line, it will lose the revenue from that product. This loss is controllable and direct with respect to the decision to keep or drop the product. Dropping a product might also affect the sales of the firm's other products. Give two examples—one in which the spillover effect increases the revenue from other products and one in which the spillover effect decreases the revenue from other products. Are these spillover effects controllable and direct to the decision to drop the product?

2.25 LO3. We can think of a cost or revenue estimate as a draw from many possible values of some distribution. Evaluate the following statement, "Variability is helpful in assessing the mean of the probability distribution while traceability speaks to the variance."

2.26 LO4. Some companies impose a minimum charge for services. For example, a caterer may charge $12 per person, with a minimum charge of $120 to host a small dinner party. What is the rationale for a minimum charge? (*Hint*: Think about the caterer's costs in terms of the cost hierarchy)

2.27 LO4. Batch- and product-level costs are not relevant for decisions that only affect the volume of production. Do you agree with this assertion? Why or why not.

2.28 LO4. Some costs, such as a dedicated field service agent, might be specific to a given customer. How does the cost hierarchy accommodate these customer level costs? Describe decisions for which grouping costs per an alternate hierarchical classification (i.e., by customer rather than by product) might be useful.

EXERCISES

2.29 Controllability and relevance (LO1). Sarah is not currently using the fitness loft, a special area of the gym that houses state-of-the-art cardio and strength training equipment. Based on a visit as a friend's guest, Sarah has decided to enroll in the loft. She is deciding between buying a pass to the fitness loft (cost: $120 per semester) and buying a pass for each use (cost: $4 per visit). She wants to work out at least three times a week, which translates to 45 times for the semester. Towel rental at the loft is $0.50 per use. Sarah pays a facilities fee of $175 per semester with her tuition; this fee entitles her to "free" use of one locker.

Required:

a. Is the facilities fee of $175 relevant or controllable for Sarah's decision?

b. Is the towel rental of $0.50 per visit controllable or relevant for this decision?

c. Is the per-use fee controllable or relevant for this decision?

2.30 Controllability and relevance (LO1). Alex has just graduated from college and has accepted a job at a different city. Rather than move his furniture, Alex decides to sell it. Alex sets his price by noting that removing the bolts that now anchor his bunk bed to the wall will leave unsightly holes. Alex estimates that the property owner will deduct $100 from his refundable deposit to cover the cost of repairs. Thus, Alex prices the furniture at $100. He considers this a "steal" because he had spent nearly $500 to buy the furniture three years ago.

Much to his surprise, he does not receive any takers. Indeed, Alex has even lost all hope of getting anyone to take the furniture for free. Tomorrow is moving day, and Alex has to turn the apartment over to the owner. Alex knows that he will need to rent a truck and pay landfill fees if he wants to put the furniture in the city's landfill. Another option is to discard the furniture on the street. Although many students junk their furniture in this fashion, Alex knows that it is illegal. He also knows that the city incurs considerable expenses to clean up after moving day.

Required:

a. Is the amount that Alex paid for the furniture ($500) controllable for his decision? Is it relevant?

b. Is the estimated cost of repairs ($100) controllable for the decision? Is it relevant?

c. List two relevant costs for Alex's decision. Why are these costs relevant?

d. When and how could the value of a decision be negative?

2.31 Controllability (LO1). Suppose that Tom and Lynda are considering reducing Hercules' membership fee by 10%.

Required:

List Tom and Lynda's two options. Next, identify two costs and benefits that are controllable for this decision.

2.32 Controllability and relevance (LO1). Sam Walters is leaving tomorrow for a three-day business trip and is trying to decide the most economical way to get to and from the airport and his home. Sam could either drive (using his own car) or take the shuttle. If Sam drives, then he estimates that it will cost $0.30 per mile driven in operating costs (e.g., for gas and oil) and $7.50 per day for parking. The one-way cost of the shuttle is $25. Sam's home is exactly 30 miles from the airport.

Required:

a. What are the controllable costs for Sam's decision?

b. What are the relevant costs and benefits for Sam's decision?

c. Are the controllable costs the same as the relevant costs for Sam's decision? If so, why? Can controllability and relevance give the same costs and benefits even when the status quo is not a feasible option?

2.33 Controllability and relevance (LO1). Akawasi Sudawa is a production manager for HAL, a firm that specializes in manufacturing high-precision aircraft components. For a new product, Akawasi is trying to decide whether his company should make a particular component internally or whether he should buy it from an outside supplier. In either case, HAL would supply all of the needed materials and connectors to ensure that the finished component meets quality standards. Akawasi expects the supplier to use 5% more in materials than HAL would for in-house manufacturing because the supplier would not have access to the same specialized machines as HAL does. However, the number of connectors used would be the same under both options. Finally, the status quo of doing nothing is not feasible—HAL will either make or buy the component.

Required:

a. Classify: (1) the cost of the materials used to make the components, (2) the cost of the connectors used to make the components, and (3) Akawasi's annual salary of $105,000 as being controllable (C) or noncontrollable (NC), and relevant (R) or not relevant (NR) for the above decision. Provide a brief rationale for each of your classifications.

b. Assume the status quo of not doing anything is a viable option. That is, HAL does not have to make or buy the component—it can choose to do neither. How does this change in the opportunity set affect your classifications in part (a)?

    c. Assume HAL currently makes the component internally. Thus, the status quo is the "make" option as this represents the existing state of affairs. How does this change affect your classifications in part (a)?

2.34 Controllability and relevance (LO1). Seeking to find gainful part-time employment, Sarah Spencer is choosing between two job offers. The first, a sales position at a department store, pays a flat salary of $8 per hour. As Sarah plans to work 80 hours per month, she expects to earn $640 per month. The second job, at a stereo store, pays a monthly salary of $400 for a 1/2 time position (20 hours per week or 80 hours per month) plus commissions. The store manager informs Sarah that, on average, 1/2 time salespeople earn commissions of $300 per month.

Both job sites are about 25 miles from Sarah's home, and Sarah estimates that, regardless of the position taken, she will incur about $125 in travel costs per month. Sarah currently shares an apartment with three friends. Her share of the rent and utilities is $250 per month.

Required:

a. Classify the following costs and benefits as to their controllability and relevance for Sarah's decision: (1) Job salaries; (2) commissions; (3) transportation costs; (4) rent and utilities.

b. Using controllable costs and benefits, estimate the value and opportunity cost of Sarah's two decision options.

c. Evaluate Sarah's decision using relevant costs and benefits.

2.35 Classifying decisions according to their time horizon (LO2). The following table lists nine decisions you are likely to make during your college career:

Decision #	Description of Decision
1	Choosing a major.
2	Choosing whether to wake up at 7:30 a.m. when your alarm goes off or hit the snooze button and wake up in another 9 minutes at 7:39 a.m.
3	Choosing whether to buy a desktop or a laptop computer.
4	Choosing whether to bring a car to campus or use university and local transportation (i.e., the "bus").
5	Choosing whether to take a required course this semester or next semester.
6	Choosing whether to have pizza or a sub-sandwich for dinner this coming Friday.
7	Choosing whether to stay at your current school or transfer to another school.
8	Choosing whether to lease a two-bedroom apartment or stay in the dormitory next year.
9	Choosing whether to buy a semester pass for the fitness center or pay on a per-use basis.

Required:

a. Classify each decision according to its horizon, short term or long term. Provide a brief rationale for each classification.

b. It is easy to find examples where a short-term decision has long-term consequences. The lecture you attended to be with a friend might spur your interest in a career path and shape the rest of your life. Given this linkage, what is the benefit from classifying decisions according to their time horizon? (*Hint:* Think about the benefits of breaking down a large assignment into manageable pieces).

2.36 Classifying decisions according to their time horizon (LO2). Saburo and Akiko Watanabe have been married for a bit less than three years and just had their first baby. They want to have another child within two or three years and look forward to "settling down" into the classic American dream of a home with a large yard, a dog, and BBQs on lazy summer afternoons.

Both Saburo and Akiko have professional degrees and well-paying jobs. Each of them earns roughly $80,000 per year, which has allowed them to save up for a down payment on a nice house. Currently, they are wondering if one of them should take some time off (for say, five to ten years) from work and devote the freed-up time to building a family. They both care deeply about instilling the right mixture of Japanese and American values in their children and are worried that without adequate parental involvement, their children may lose track of their Japanese heritage.

The following lists nine decisions that Saburo and Akiko will be facing in the near future:

Decision #	Description of Decision
1	Reconsidering the decision to give up one income (neither person has quit yet).
2	Deciding whether to buy a second car (Saburo and Akiko currently only have one car because they live in the city).
3	Deciding whether to pay this month's mortgage payment by check or electronic transfer.
4	Deciding whether to hire a housekeeper.
5	Deciding the type of dog to get.
6	Deciding whether to spend $10,000 on a 4-week tour to Japan and Southeast Asia.
7	Deciding whether to have the stay-at-home spouse look for part-time, home-based employment.
8	Deciding whether to grill steak or fish for their dinner party this coming Saturday.
9	Deciding which house to buy.

Required:

a. Classify each decision according to its time horizon, short term or long term. Provide a brief rationale for each classification.

b. As discussed in the text, many short-term decisions have longer-term implications. Given this linkage, what is the benefit from classifying decisions according to their time horizon? (*Hint:* Think about the benefits of breaking down a large assignment into manageable pieces.)

2.37 Variability and traceability (LO3). The following are some common statements that we find students making.

- A variable cost is always controllable.
- A fixed cost is always noncontrollable.
- A direct cost is always a variable cost.
- Fixed costs are always indirect.
- Virtually every cost is variable with respect to some activity.

Required:

Classify each statement as True or False, and justify your response.

2.38 Variability (LO3). Excalibur Steel incurs three types of costs (*a*, *b*, and *c*) in its manufacturing process. The following table presents total costs for each type for two different activity levels.

	Cost		
	A	*B*	*C*
5,000 units	$25,000	$28,000	$50,000
7,500 units	$37,500	$35,000	$50,000

Required:

Identify whether each cost is variable, fixed, or mixed.

2.39 Variability: choice of activity (LO3). The following table lists 10 costs commonly incurred by manufacturing firms.

Cost #	Description of Cost
1	Cost of raw materials used
2	Electricity used to operate machines
3	Cost of packing materials
4	Equipment maintenance

Cost #	Description of Cost
5	Janitorial supplies used to clean the factory
6	Cost of human resources department
7	Cost of purchasing department
8	Sales commission paid
9	Travel expenses for sales persons
10	CEO salary

Required:

a. For each cost, identify and justify the underlying activity whose volume determines the amount incurred for that cost. That is, what activity, if any, makes the cost variable?

b. Is there one activity that "stands out?" Does this help us understand why organizations often use sales or production levels to assess cost variability?

2.40 Traceability (LO3). The Greek Corporation makes two products: Kappa and Gamma. Although each product uses a different type of raw material, the firm produces both products in its Eastern plant. The products make use of the same equipment as well. Greek Corporation produces Kappa during the day shift and Gamma during the night shift.

The following list presents six costs incurred by the Greek Corporation to produce Kappa:

Cost #	Description of Cost
1	Eastern plant rent
2	Raw materials purchased to produce Kappa
3	Eastern plant utilities and water
4	Salary of the Eastern plant manager
5	Equipment maintenance
6	Salary of a production employee who works the day shift at the Eastern plant

Required:

For each cost, classify whether it is direct (D) or indirect (I) with respect to Greek's decision to produce the Kappa product. Provide a brief rationale for each classification.

2.41 Revenue variability and traceability, not for profit (LO3). The Johnson County Arts Foundation aims to promote the appreciation and practice of art in Johnson County and surrounding areas. Consistent with this mission, the foundation sponsors a number of exhibitions, conducts art classes, and promotes local artists. The foundation is considering three ways to raise money toward covering its operating expenses.

1. Issue lottery tickets ($50 each) for a "dream art vacation" for two to the "world-famous museums of London and Paris." The foundation estimates the cost of the vacation at $6,000.

2. Host a charity dinner, with each ticket costing $100. The caterer has offered the foundation a $2,000 discount of his usual price. Select donors (who are likely to give money in the future as well) would be recognized and honored during the dinner.

3. Conduct a silent auction for works by local artists. The artists and the foundation will share equally in the proceeds. The silent auction is a way for artists to gain exposure and potentially sell more of their work.

Required:

Identify the controllable benefits for each of three fund-raising options. Classify each benefit as being direct (D) or indirect (I) to the decision option. In addition, classify each revenue source as variable (V) or fixed (F).

2.42 Hierarchical cost structure: cost classifications (LO4). Creative Tiles produces tiles embossed with leaf prints and other images in silhouette. When used on a wall or a floor, these tiles add color and texture, in addition to providing a focal point for the eye.

The process for making a tile is relatively straightforward. The first step is to prepare a clay-like bisque containing aluminum silicates, sand, and other commodity inputs. Since each type of tile designed is a unique product (Creative Tiles' customers can choose from over 100 leaf prints), the tiles are formed using a custom mold and printed via a custom screen-printing process. The next step is to fire (i.e., bake) a batch of up to 1,000 tiles in an oven at temperatures that exceed 2,000° F. After cooling, the tiles are finished, packed, and palleted. Using a forklift, workers move each pallet to the storeroom.

The following table lists eight costs incurred by Creative Tiles:

Cost #	Description of Cost
1	Sand used
2	Oven rental for the year
3	Power for firing the oven
4	Molds used
5	Hourly wages to employees who mix the clay
6	CEO salary
7	Prepare leaf print for image
8	Using forklifts to move finished goods from the factory floor to the storeroom.

Required:

Classify each cost as per the cost hierarchy. (i.e., classify each cost as being a unit-, batch-, product-, or facility-level cost). Provide a brief rationale for each classification.

2.43 Hierarchical cost structure: cost classifications (LO4). Sun and Sand Hotels (S&S), an exclusive beach resort, offers all-inclusive vacations—the package price includes the room, food, and access to all facilities. However, alcoholic beverages and special services (e.g., boat tours) are extra. S&S offers many attractions such as an enclosed lagoon within which guests may pet dolphins. The resort also offers snorkeling and diving tours at a nearby coral reef. Sun and Sand is interested in calculating its cost to host a typical member. Customers usually are couples, and the average couple stays for three nights and four days.

Required:

Treating the number of couples as a unit of activity, identify a unit-, batch-, product- and facility level cost for Sun and Sand.

2.44 Step costs (LO4). Consider the following two settings. Setting 1: Westin, Inc., is estimating the cost of supervision at its many plants. The firm's policy is to have one supervisor per 15 employees. Westin's cost analyst mistakenly classified the supervision costs as a unit-level cost that varies in the number of employees.

Setting 2: Westin also employs one product engineer per product line. The cost analyst also incorrectly classified this product-level cost as a unit-level cost. He then divided the cost by the number of units Westin expects to produce to calculate a product engineering cost per unit.

Required:

a. Suppose Westin uses the analyst's estimate of the cost of supervision per employee to estimate supervision cost. Would you expect the estimate to be higher, lower, or the same as the true cost?

b. Suppose Westin uses the analyst's estimate of the product engineering cost to estimate the cost associated with the product engineer. Would you expect the estimate to be higher, lower, or the same as the true cost?

PROBLEMS

2.45 Controllability and relevance (LO1). Rams Ramachandran is considering the wisdom of reducing the number of suppliers his firm uses. Currently, Rams uses 25 suppliers to purchase goods worth $2,500,000 per year. To manage the orders and coordinate with suppliers, Rams employs one manager and two clerical staff. The manager earns $65,000 per year and each clerical staff person earns $35,000 per year. (As VP, Rams earns $175,000 annually.) Reducing the number of suppliers from 25 to 6 would allow Rams' firm to free up one of the clerical staff. While the manager would supervise fewer people, she also would interact more with each supplier; thus, her workload would not change appreciably.

Rams bargains aggressively with suppliers, and, with 25 suppliers, he was anticipating a 3% savings in purchase costs next year. With only six suppliers, however, each supplier would have greater bargaining power, eliminating Rams' ability to reduce the prices paid for goods. Finally, Rams believes that better coordination with fewer suppliers would increase service quality (e.g., a lower risk of stock outs and other problems), and he estimates the cost savings at $100,000 per year.

Required:

a. Classify the following costs as to their controllability and relevance for Rams' decision: (1) Cost of goods purchased; (2) Clerical staff salaries; (3) Manager's salary; (4) Service quality cost savings; and (5) Rams' salary.

b. Should Rams use 25 or 6 suppliers?

2.46 Controllability and relevance (LO1). Brandt Heating and Cooling is a reputed HVAC (heating, ventilation, and air-conditioning) contractor. Tim Brandt has a reputation for doing quality work and for treating the customer "right." Brandt serves both homeowners and building contractors. The following table presents Brandt's income statement for the most recent year:

Item	Amount	Detail
Revenues from homeowners	$275,000	
Revenues from contractors	525,000	
Direct costs	500,000	Materials used in jobs plus the cost of hourly labor.
Rental cost	30,000	For the office building.
Trucks and other equipment	65,000	Brandt has a fleet of trucks used by technicians to travel to job sites. This amount also includes costs for operating and maintaining trucks and other equipment.
Administrative costs	85,000	For the part-time accountant, receptionist, and supervisor.
Profit	$120,000	

Tim believes that while contractors are important from a volume perspective, homeowners are more profitable. Unlike homeowners, building contractors "know the business" and negotiate aggressively.

Required:

For each of the following three decisions, classify whether each item on Brandt's income statement is controllable and/or relevant. Explain why an item may be controllable/relevant for some decisions but not for other decisions.

1. Whether to give a $50 discount to a regular homeowner customer who complained about the technician showing up late.

2. Whether to send a technician to obtain training in high-voltage work. (This service would appeal to contractors but not homeowners.)

3. Whether to replace an aging truck with a newer model.

2.47 Controllability and relevance (LO1). Motown Manufacturing makes trumpets and other fine musical instruments. Motown currently is deciding whether to buy 100 units of a component for piccolos from an outside supplier or to make them in-house. The status quo option of doing nothing is not feasible—Motown will either buy the component or make the component.

If Motown buys the component from an outside supplier, it will pay the supplier $500 per unit. Motown will also pay $50 per unit to inspect the component and spend an additional $400 per unit in materials and labor to convert each component into a finished product. Motown sells the finished piccolos to consumers for $1,500 each.

Making the component in-house requires $200 worth of brass and $175 worth of a special African Blackwood called Mpingo. Motown routinely purchases and uses brass in its operations, and it does not currently have any brass in inventory. The special wood is unique to the component in question, and Motown currently has $10,000 worth in stock. Motown will dispose of the Mpingo wood (at a net value of zero) if the company pursues the buy option. Making the component in-house also requires labor at a cost of $25 per hour. It takes employees 10 hours to make one component.

As under the buy option, Motown will pay $50 per unit to inspect the component if it is made in-house and spend an additional $400 per unit in materials and labor to convert each component into a finished product. Motown will then sell the finished piccolos to consumers for $1,500 each.

Required:

a. What are the controllable costs and benefits associated with the buy option? What are the controllable costs and benefits associated with the make option?

b. What are the relevant costs and benefits associated with the make option? What are the relevant costs and benefits associated with the buy option?

2.48 Controllability and relevance (LO1). Exactly one year ago, Gamma Machinery purchased a lathe for $300,000. At the time of purchase, Gamma expected the lathe to generate a net cash inflow of $120,000 per year for three years. Recently, another firm located in the same industrial park went into bankruptcy. The bankrupt firm's liquidators have offered to sell their client's sophisticated lathe to Gamma for $400,000 even though their client paid $800,000 for it one year ago.

The bankrupt firm's lathe has a superior control system that would significantly improve Gamma's machining capabilities. Moreover, if Gamma replaces its current lathe, it will be able to increase its net cash inflow to $250,000 per year for each of the next two years. If Gamma purchases the lathe, the company can either retain its current lathe for miscellaneous jobs or sell it. The miscellaneous jobs will produce an additional net cash inflow of $50,000 per year for the next two years. Gamma can sell its current lathe today for $170,000. Both lathes will be worth $0 in two years.

Gamma must decide whether to purchase the bankrupt firm's lathe and, if it does, what to do with its own lathe. Gamma's goal is to maximize its net cash flow over the next two years. (As discussed in Chapter 1, the goal of maximizing profits is, in the long run, equivalent to the goal of maximizing cash flows).

Note: A lathe is a machine tool that spins a block of material, such as steel or wood, about a horizontal axis. Applying cutting tools to the block produces an object symmetric with respect to the axis of rotation. Sophisticated lathes use many tools and can shape the material along all three axes. Examples of products produced using lathes include candlesticks, table legs, and baseball bats.

Required:

a. Identify Gamma's decision options. Is the status quo a feasible option?

b. What are the controllable and relevant costs and benefits for Gamma's decision?

c. Assume that Gamma is committed to buying the new lathe. Thus, the status quo is not a feasible option. In this case, what are the controllable and relevant costs and benefits for Gamma's decision?

2.49 Controllability of revenues and decision horizons (LO1, LO2, Advanced). The Terrapin Coffeehouse currently has one downtown location. The shop offers a number of different types of coffees and espressos, brewed to the customer's order. Terrapin also offers a limited selection of cakes and pastries.

Required:

Classify each of the following decisions as to its horizon. Indicate whether the effect on revenue arises primarily from the decision's impact on the *price* of goods and services, the *quantity* of goods and services demanded, or *both*. What conclusions do you draw about the controllability of price and quantity (the components of revenue) across decision horizons?

1. How much to spend on advertising in the local newspaper. Terrapin is relatively new to the area and does not have the name recognition enjoyed by some of the other coffeehouses competing in the same market.

2. Offering a points program with 1 point for each dollar spent in the store. Customers can redeem 25 points for a beverage of their choice.

3. Increasing the variety in the types of coffees offered from four to eight. Management has noticed that about 10% of customers would not find their chosen flavor and would have to settle for their second (and occasionally third) choice.

4. Adding to product variety by offering goat milk and soymilk-based drinks.

5. Increasing the flow of customers by reconfiguring the counter layout. Currently, having as few as five customers in line can block the entrance and make the shop look full from the outside even though plenty of seating is available inside.

6. Opening a branch in a suburb renowned for housing many "single and affluent professionals."

2.50 Controllability and time (LO1). The following are three decisions that Joel Stager needs to make. Joel manages an up-market restaurant in Miami, Florida, and has considerable discretion over its operations.

Decision 1: Whether to convert the restaurant from a European to an Asian theme. This change will require substantial redecoration.

Decision 2: Which celebrity chefs to showcase? The restaurant usually invites three or four celebrity chefs during the year to take over the restaurant for a week. In consultation with the regular chef, the celebrity chef designs the menu for that fortnight, often contributing several secret recipes or helping build a theme.

Decision 3: Whether to accept a booking for a wedding reception. The reception will take over the entire restaurant for one evening. While some costs will increase (e.g., for rearranging seating), others will decrease (everyone will have the same meal).

Required:

a. Classify each of the three decisions as per their time horizon.

b. Classify the following costs and benefits as being controllable or noncontrollable with respect to the three decisions.

1. Average revenue per patron
2. Cost of meals served
3. Cost of printing restaurant menus
4. Salaries for chef and other kitchen staff
5. Building rental cost

2.51 Classifying decisions by time; cost commitment (LO2). Anne Larson graduated from Prestige U. three years ago with a degree in accounting. She currently is a rising star in a national accounting firm. Although she enjoys her job, Anne has decided to leave and pursue an MBA as a way to accelerate her career. To this end, Anne has procured admission to two top-tier MBA programs in California. Having grown up in Baltimore, Maryland, and currently stationed in Cleveland, Ohio, Anne is eager to spread her wings and explore sunny California!

The following table lists nine decisions that Anne likely will be making in the near future:

Decision #	Description of Decision
1	Reconsider the decision to get an MBA. (Anne has not yet quit her job!)
2	Decide whether to pay first-semester tuition by check or by credit card. (Each month, Anne pays off her credit card balance in full.)
3	Choose a major (accounting, finance, or marketing).
4	Choose the courses to take in the first semester.
5	Decide whether to buy new clothes (to fit the student lifestyle) or to make do with her current business clothes.
6	Decide whether to have a part-time job while in the MBA program.
7	Decide whether to spend the next few weeks brushing up on math and economics or to spend the time taking a vacation before school starts.
8	Decide whether to live in a studio apartment or to share a two-bedroom apartment.
9	Choosing which of the two MBA programs to join.

Required:

a. Classify each decision according to its time horizon (short term or long term). Provide a brief rationale for each classification.

b. Consider the following three costs associated with going to school: (1) tuition, (2) housing, and (3) books. For decisions 1 and 2 (i.e., reconsidering whether to get the MBA and deciding how to pay tuition), classify whether or not each of these three costs is controllable. What relation do you observe between the decision horizon and cost controllability?

2.52 Variability and controllability (LO1, LO3). The Malabar Company specializes in imported novelty items from Asian countries such as Thailand, Indonesia, and China. The firm, headquartered in San Jose, California, has franchised over 70 stores in upscale malls throughout the United States. Currently, Malabar's management is deciding whether to open a new store in a large mall in Chicago, Illinois.

The following table lists ten of Malabar's costs:

Cost #	Description of Cost
1	Sales commissions
2	Cost of merchandise
3	Salaries to sales staff
4	Salary to store manager
5	Display and stocking expenses
6	Advertising on national television
7	Advertising in local newspapers
8	Store cleaning and maintenance
9	Transportation of goods to stores
10	Central purchasing department

Required:

Classify each cost as being fixed (F), mixed (M), or variable (V) with respect to the sales volume in any given store. In addition, classify each cost as being controllable (C) or noncontrollable (NC) for the decision regarding whether to open the new store in Chicago. Provide a brief explanation of your answers.

2.53 Cost traceability and decision contexts (LO3). Kyle Corp. is a diversified firm with numerous plants. Each plant is devoted to producing one or two product lines. Management is considering several options concerning the plant in Grand Junction, Nebraska. This plant currently makes toy farm equipment and miniature cars.

> **Decision 1:** Whether to continue producing a deluxe version of the farm toys? The deluxe version uses the same machines as used by the regular models, but it has additional finishing and accessories.
>
> **Decision 2:** Whether to continue making farm toys? The firm will dispose of the machines used for this product line if the firm discontinues the line. Most of the machines used for making farm toys are unique to the line but some of the die-casting machines are also used to stamp out miniature cars.
>
> **Decision 3:** Whether to close the Grand Junction plant?

Required:

Classify the following costs with respect to their traceability for the three decisions listed.

1. Cost of special die used to make the deluxe version of farm toys. Each die can make enough toys to meet a year's demand.

2. Labor used to make the deluxe farm toy.

3. Cost of dedicated machines used to make farm toys.

4. Engineering support provided solely to maintain the farm toy line.

5. Advertising for farm toys.

6. Salary paid to the manager of the Grand Junction plant.

7. IT support provided by the head office to the Grand Junction plant.

2.54 Controllability and cost hierarchy (LO1, LO4). Consider the following list of costs and decisions for a retail store.

Cost items:

a. Cost of goods purchased for resale

b. Conducting orientation session for new employees.

c. Setting up seasonal display of items

d. Cost of shelving used in store.

Decisions:

1. Whether to offer a 10% price discount on specific items?
2. Whether to schedule orientation sessions on a weekly or bi-weekly basis.
3. How often to change seasonal displays.
4. Whether to change store layout to improve traffic patterns.

Required:

a. Classify each cost as per the cost hierarchy.

b. Classify the decisions as to their time horizon.

c. Prepare a table that indicates the costs controllable for the given decision. Designate the four costs by letters, a through d.

d. Based on your answers to the above parts, what inferences could you draw about the controllability of costs and the cost hierarchy?

2.55 Traceability and cost hierarchy (LO3, LO4, Advanced). "I don't understand the purpose of the cost hierarchy," complained Erika Vijh, a seasoned plant manager at a Fortune 500 firm. Erika argues that, ultimately, the units produced in her factory must cover all of the costs in the plant. Otherwise, the head office will shutter the plant. In other words, she argues that it makes sense to somehow charge each unit of the product with its "fair" share of all costs, wherever the cost appears in the cost hierarchy.

Required:

How would you respond to Erika's criticism? Your answer should include how the items in the cost hierarchy relate to the concepts of controllability and traceability, and how the relations help managers make effective decisions.

2.56 Traceability and variability (LO1, LO3, Advanced). It is difficult to distinguish between direct and indirect labor in many modern manufacturing plants. An employee might participate in a design review team, work on maintenance, and produce components, all in the same day. Moreover, these plants are organized as a "factory within a factory," meaning that each production line might be dedicated to a single product line. Thus, rather than grouping like machines together, the factory is organized around production processes for an individual product line. Each line would have its own labor, supervisors, production engineers, and so on, enabling it almost to act as a separate factory. This organization contrasts sharply with traditional systems where many product lines might share the machines.

Required:

What implication does the modern organization have for the traceability of costs? How does this change affect the controllability of costs for decisions that affect the volume of production? Decisions to add or drop products?

2.57 Traceability and variability (LO1, LO3, Advanced). Many firms outsource jobs today to countries with lower labor costs. Firms such as Apple outsource virtually all of their production. Over the last decade, U.S. firms also have outsourced business functions (e.g., telephone support, document processing) to firms in India and China.

Required:

What are the implications of outsourcing for the variability and traceability of costs? For concreteness, consider the outsourcing of (1) a product based on a piece-rate contract, and (2) a business process for a fixed-fee contract.

MINI-CASES

2.58 Traceability, variability, controllability, and relevance (LO1, LO3). You and your four closest friends all love winter sports. Accordingly, you decide to spend some time during winter break at a nearby ski resort. You have reserved a chalet that will sleep six people, and you have paid a nonrefundable deposit for three nights (the resort has informed you that, if you decide to extend your trip, you can rent the chalet for up to three more nights at the same daily rate). You are contemplating driving as a group to the resort, even though it would be a cramped ride. Finally, you decide that while each person will pay for his or her own food and drinks during the trip, you will equally share all common expenses.

Required:

a. Classify (1) the cost of gasoline for driving, (2) the cost of food and drink, and (3) the cost of the chalet rental (for the first three nights) as being direct (D) or indirect (I) with respect to both the trip as a whole and each person.

b. Classify (1) the cost of gasoline, (2) the cost of food and drinks, (3) the cost of the chalet rental for the first three nights, and (4) the cost of the chalet rental after the first three nights as being variable (V) or fixed (F). If the cost is variable, what activity determines the magnitude of the cost? How can you use these classifications to estimate the total cost of the vacation?

c. Classify the following costs as per the cost hierarchy.

  1. Cost of food and drink during the trip

  2. Cost of the chalet rental

  3. Cost of obtaining premium TV channels in chalet

  4. Cost of time spent in planning trip

d. Suppose that, instead of driving, you and your friends could take a bus to the ski resort. In this case, each person will pay his or her own bus fare. Classify the following costs as being controllable (C) or noncontrollable (NC) and relevant (R) or not relevant (NR) with respect to the friends' two transportation options (drive or take the bus) for the trip.

  1. Costs of operating the car

  2. Cost of the bus fare

  3. Cost of the chalet rental for the first three nights

  4. Cost of the chalet rental after the first three nights

2.59 Cost variability, step costs (LO3, LO4). Christine Mbai owns and operates an extremely popular Montessori school in suburban Chicago. The school has its own private pickup and drop-off facilities. The following lists 12 costs Christine incurs in running her school:

Cost #	Description of Cost
1	Rent on school building
2	Lunches and lunch supplies (lunches are catered-in)
3	Teacher salaries
4	Utilities and water
5	Bus driver salaries
6	Art supplies
7	Janitorial services
8	Brochures and pamphlets (including monthly newsletter)
9	Receptionist salary
10	Field trip to the Museum of Science and Industry
11	Repainting the hallway
12	Fuel for buses

Required:

For each cost, classify and discuss whether you believe it will be fixed (F), variable (V), mixed (M), or jump in steps (S) with respect to the number of enrolled students in the coming term (semester). In addition, discuss any arguments that support a classification other than the one you have assigned.

Chapter 3
Cost Flows and Cost Terminology

TOM AND LYNDA APPRECIATE THE help you have given them in structuring their decision problem. They now want you to help them figure out the profit they could expect to make from offering a yoga class. Naturally, you turn to Hercules' accounting system for revenue and cost data. To estimate the change in profit from offering yoga you need to understand how Hercules' accounting system works. More generally, knowing how firms track revenues and costs enables you to tailor data from the accounting system to the decision problem at hand.

APPLYING THE DECISION FRAMEWORK

What Is the Problem?
What data should you use to estimate the profit impact of offering yoga?

What Are the Options?
You naturally turn to the accounting system to obtain cost and revenue data. Your options relate to whether and how to modify Hercules' system to suit your needs.

What Are the Costs and Benefits?
Modifying the system is costly in terms of time, effort, and the expertise required. However, it can lead to benefits in terms of a more accurate profit estimate.

Make the Decision!
Your decision hinges on the benefits of obtaining a more accurate estimate versus the costs of obtaining this estimate. As the stakes increase, firms are more likely to modify their systems to facilitate internal decisions.

Andrea Wyner/Getty Images

Tom and Lynda rely on their accounting system to help them figure out the profit from offering a yoga class.

LEARNING OBJECTIVES

After studying this chapter, you will be able to:

1 Distinguish product costs from period costs.

2 Understand the flow of costs in service firms.

3 Discuss how inventories affect the flow of costs in merchandising firms.

4 Explain the cost terminology and the flow of costs in manufacturing firms.

5 Allocate overhead costs to products.

In this chapter, we discuss the kinds of accounting systems you will encounter in the workplace. Most firms design their financial records to track costs by business function, such as whether they relate to manufacturing, selling, or administration. Why? Because formal accounting systems typically are set up to help with financial reporting, and Generally Accepted Accounting Principles (GAAP) requires financial reports to group costs by business function.

We begin this chapter with a short look at how firms accumulate costs for financial reporting purposes. We then examine cost accumulation in three types of organizations: service, merchandising, and manufacturing. We discuss the similarities and differences in the flow of costs in these organizations, focusing particularly on how they accumulate costs for valuing inventory and reporting income. Because cost allocations play an integral role in this process, we end with a brief overview of the mechanics of cost allocations.

CHAPTER CONNECTIONS

An organization's accounting information system provides considerable detail regarding its activities. As you learned in Chapter 1, decision makers aggregate and analyze these detailed data for different purposes. In many cases, data in financial accounting reports are not directly useful for internal decision making because these reports aggregate costs and benefits by business function. For any given decision, GAAP statements combine controllable costs and benefits with noncontrollable costs and benefits and fixed costs with variable costs. This feature means that decision makers must modify financial data to suit their needs. In Chapter 4, we will show you how to construct accounting reports that group costs by their variability. This is a first step in modifying GAAP statements to obtain controllable costs and benefits.

Product and Period Costs

LEARNING OBJECTIVE 1

Distinguish product costs from period costs.

In Chapter 1, you learned that one important function of accounting is to provide data for the preparation of financial statements such as the income statement, balance sheet, and statement of cash flows. These statements convey information about the performance and value of a firm to its shareholders, lenders, banks, and the government. You also learned that these statements must conform to GAAP and the reporting standards put out by the Financial Accounting Standards Board.

Exhibit 3.1 displays Hercules' GAAP income statement for the most recent month. This income statement informs us that Tom and Lynda made $10,000 last month. Hercules generated revenues of $80,000 and, by adding up the two reported costs, spent $70,000. Why does Hercules report costs in two separate lines? The answer is that, to comply with GAAP, Hercules' income statement must separate *product costs* from *period costs*. Let us examine this distinction.

In the line below revenues, Hercules reports that it incurred costs of $55,000 for providing programs and services. These costs directly relate to Hercules' primary business function. They include items such as instructor salaries, depreciation of

Product costs at a gym include the cost of equipment used by members. (Michael Grecco/Getty Images)

Exhibit 3.1	*Hercules Health Club: GAAP Income Statement for the Most Recent Month*
Revenues	$80,000
Costs of providing programs and services	55,000
Gross margin	25,000
Management salaries, marketing, and administration	15,000
Profit before Taxes	$10,000

equipment, utility costs in the gymnasium, equipment maintenance, and supplies. In financial accounting terms, the costs associated with getting products and services ready for sale are **product costs**.

Product costs always appear "above the line" for **gross margin**, which is revenues less product costs. Hercules' gross margin of $25,000 equals its revenues of $80,000 less its product costs of $55,000.

In the line below gross margin, Hercules reports that it spent $15,000 on costs related to management salaries, marketing, and administration. These costs, which are not a part of the costs of providing programs and services, are period costs. **Period costs** do not directly relate to readying products or services for sale. Rather, these costs, which include office rent, advertising, customer service, and sales force compensation, relate more to the passage of time. Period costs, *which are all costs that are not product costs,* always appear "below the line" for gross margin. We subtract period costs from the gross margin to arrive at profit before taxes.

The matching principle in GAAP is the answer for why we need to separate product and period costs. GAAP requires that we match the revenues and costs associated with making and selling a product or service during the same accounting period. We flow product costs through inventory accounts to enable such matching. There is no need to match period costs, as they are not associated with making and selling a product or service. Thus, we immediately expense, or charge to the income statement, all of our period costs.

GAAP provides considerable flexibility regarding reporting formats. Many firms follow a multistep presentation of income statements and separately report product and period costs. However, it is easy to find firms that employ single-step reporting. In their detailed records, these firms also distinguish between product and period costs for costing purposes. However, their income statements may not show a line for gross margin nor do they report the costs separately. Throughout this text, we will use the two-step presentation to emphasize the distinction between product and period costs. Moreover, GAAP relies on managerial judgment in determining cost categories because most firms incur at least some costs not readily classified as product or period costs.

Although these costs exist in all organizations, their nature, the kinds of systems used to accumulate them, and the complexity of the calculations all depend on the type of organization. In the following sections, we discuss cost accumulation procedures in the three main types of organizations—service firms, merchandising firms, and manufacturing firms.

Cost Flows in Service Organizations

Consulting firms such as Accenture, hoteliers such as Marriott, and airlines such as JetBlue are service firms. What distinguishes service firms from other firms? Like all organizations, these firms use a mix of human and capital resources to perform their functions. However, unlike merchandising and manufacturing firms, the products **service firms** offer are not tangible or storable. For example, we enjoy the hotel experience when we are at Marriott, but we cannot store the experience for a later period. In essence, service firms make their facilities available to others for a fee—Accenture, Marriott, and JetBlue "rent" their consultants, rooms, and planes, respectively.

Hercules is a service firm, making its facilities available to members for a fee. Exhibit 3.2 illustrates the cost flows in Hercules and distinguishes product costs from period costs.

Now, let us turn to Tom and Lynda's yoga decision. Does Hercules' GAAP income statement in Exhibit 3.1 provide enough information to make this decision? The

LEARNING OBJECTIVE 2

Understand the flow of costs in service firms.

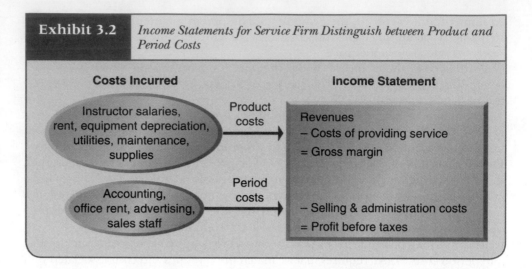

Exhibit 3.2 *Income Statements for Service Firm Distinguish between Product and Period Costs*

answer is "no." Tom and Lynda rely on their business experience, not GAAP financial statements, to estimate the number of additional members the gym could attract by offering yoga. Furthermore, GAAP statements provide limited information about opportunity costs. For example, offering yoga might prevent Hercules from offering a new karate class. Yet we cannot determine from GAAP reports the possible profit from offering karate. For such reasons, it frequently is vital to modify accounting reports and use nonfinancial data to estimate the controllable costs and benefits of a decision option.

Although the GAAP income statement separates product costs from period costs, it combines controllable costs with noncontrollable costs and fixed costs with variable costs. For example, the cost of providing services includes the depreciation on exercise equipment as well as the cost of supplies. The cost of supplies, which is variable, will increase if the yoga class attracts new members. However, the amount of equipment depreciation will not change if Hercules offers yoga. Similarly, period costs contain both controllable and noncontrollable costs. For example, offering yoga will change administrative expenses such as fees Hercules pays to banks for processing credit card transactions but not the salary paid to office staff. As such, simply dividing total product or period cost by the number of members would yield a poor estimate of the cost per member associated with offering yoga.

In Chapter 4, we learn some techniques for modifying GAAP statements to estimate the controllable costs of a decision. For now, let us expand our discussion about the flow of costs to merchandising firms. Unlike service firms, inventories play a vital role in merchandising firms because a retailer's products are both tangible and storable. The presence of inventory adds some complexity to the accounting system; we explore this issue next. Later in the chapter, we will also address the role of inventories for manufacturing firms.

Cost Flows in Merchandising Organizations

LEARNING OBJECTIVE 3

Discuss how inventories affect the flow of costs in merchandising firms.

Examples of merchandising firms include retailers such as JCPenney and Sears, grocery stores such as Kroger, and office products stores such as Office Depot and Staples. **Merchandising firms** buy goods from suppliers and resell substantially the same products to customers. Unlike service firms, merchandising firms maintain an inventory of goods that they buy and sell. They use this inventory to make

Connecting to Practice

BLURRED BOUNDARIES

It is sometimes difficult to determine whether a firm is a service, merchandising, or manufacturing firm. For example, is Kinko's a service firm? Its final product, copies, is both storable and tangible to consumers, but the firm itself does not maintain any inventories of its final product. And is Bank of America a service firm? When we cash a check, we receive money, which is both tangible and storable. On the other hand, banks provide financial advice and analysis to their customers.

COMMENTARY: As these examples illustrate, not all firms fall cleanly in the service, merchandising, and manufacturing distinctions. Some firms exhibit characteristics of each type, making them difficult to classify. However, regardless of their classification, all firms distinguish between product and period costs.

goods available in the quantities, varieties, and delivery schedules demanded by customers.

INVENTORY EQUATION

Because inventories are a necessary part of a merchandiser's business, such firms need to distinguish the cost of goods *purchased* from the cost of goods *sold*. For financial reporting purposes, firms expense the cost of items when they sell the items, not when they purchase them.

Suppose a merchandiser buys and stores some items in one month, expecting to sell them next month. The cost of this merchandise, or goods, flows through the inventory account, becoming part of **cost of goods sold** only when the firm sells the items. We capture this flow using the following inventory equation.

> Cost of beginning inventory
> + Cost of goods purchased during the period
> − Cost of ending inventory
> = Cost of goods sold (COGS) during the period

Applying this inventory equation in practice is not as simple as it appears. Retail firms often buy several batches of an item at different times and at different prices. Thus, at any given time, firms might have different "layers" of inventory of the same item. At the time of sale, it becomes necessary to determine which batch or layer the items belong to, in order to use the corresponding prices to compute the cost of sales. Firms achieve this by making inventory cost flow assumptions such as First-In-First-Out (FIFO) or Last-In-First-Out (LIFO). For simplicity, we use the FIFO method whenever we require an inventory cost flow assumption.

Check It! Exercise #1

For the month of June, you have the following data for Mega Mart, a merchandising firm: (1) cost of beginning inventory = $3,450,200; (2) cost of ending inventory = $3,745,600; (3) cost of goods purchased during June = $24,795,740. Verify that the cost of goods sold for Mega Mart for June is $24,500,340.

Solution at end of chapter.

Connecting to Practice

INVENTORIES IN SERVICE ORGANIZATIONS

NCS Pearson offers a wide range of testing and scoring services. Many states use its services to test and evaluate students and schools, particularly in connection with the federal No Child Left Behind Act. NCS often undertakes special projects for clients, with some projects lasting many years.

COMMENTARY: Some service firms, like NCS, report an inventory in their annual reports. Such an inventory consists of costs incurred on partially completed projects yet to be billed. NCS cannot expense these amounts if it has not recognized the associated revenue. The firm would expense the inventory when it bills the client per the terms of the project.

INCOME STATEMENT

Exhibit 3.3 depicts the typical flow of costs in a merchandising firm. Except for the presence of the inventory account, the cost flows in merchandising firms resemble the flows for service firms.

Exhibit 3.4 presents the most recent annual income statement for Office Gallery, a merchandizing firm that sells three standard lines of office furniture: desks, chairs, and bookshelves.

As with Hercules, the two main cost categories are the costs incurred to obtain and prepare the goods for sale (product costs) and the costs associated with sales and administration (period costs).

The major item in the first group is the cost of purchasing goods from suppliers. This item includes not only the amounts paid to suppliers but also the cost of transportation and the cost of preparing the goods for sale. Office Gallery normally does not sell all of the furniture it purchases in a given month. Thus, it adds the cost of all purchases to its inventory account. As it sells items from its inventory, Office Gallery removes the associated costs from the inventory account and expenses them in the income statement. You can see this flow of costs in a condensed manner in Exhibit 3.4's income statement.

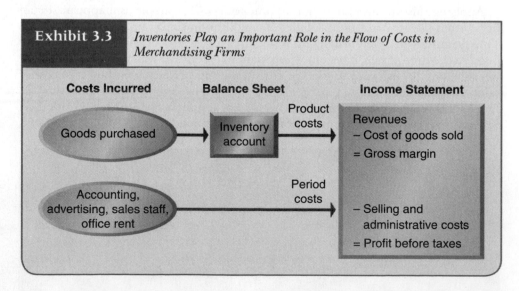

| Exhibit 3.3 | *Inventories Play an Important Role in the Flow of Costs in Merchandising Firms* |

Exhibit 3.4	Office Gallery: GAAP Income Statement

		Total
Revenues		$63,832,500
Beginning inventory	$18,245,300	
= + Cost of goods purchased	45,283,550	
− Ending inventory	18,427,500	
Cost of goods sold		$45,101,350
Gross margin		$18,731,150
Administrative costs	$5,491,840	
Sales salaries and commissions	4,750,300	
Marketing, advertising, and distribution	4,867,320	
Total S&A (period) costs		$15,109,460
Profit before taxes		$3,621,690

As with service firms, period costs appear below the line for gross margin. Office Gallery then computes profit before taxes as the gross margin less period costs. As we will see next, the cost flows are even more complex in manufacturing firms.

Cost Flows in Manufacturing Organizations

Unlike merchandising firms, **manufacturing firms** use labor and equipment to transform inputs such as raw materials and components into outputs. For instance, Sony purchases plasma screens, frames, and circuit boards from suppliers. It makes additional components itself using basic inputs. Employees at Sony then assemble these components into its award-winning televisions. Because Sony has inventories

LEARNING OBJECTIVE 4

Explain the cost terminology and the flow of costs in manufacturing firms.

 ## Connecting to Practice

MANAGING LOGISTICS

Merchandising operations range in size from your neighborhood mom-and-pop store to global behemoths such as Wal-Mart. Nevertheless, all successful merchandisers share two key traits: efficiently managed inventory and a strong focus on reducing support costs. The business discipline of "supply chain management" is concerned with helping the firm have the right product at the right place at the right time and for the right price!

COMMENTARY: Supply chains today span the globe. Seeing a Chinese-made product at your local store would not surprise you in the least. The rise of global supply chains allows merchandisers to offer increasing product variety at ever-lower prices. However, global sourcing also is a major headache because the firm now needs to manage more suppliers in foreign locales. Entire industries have sprung up to help firms deal with this problem in their quest to achieve operational excellence.

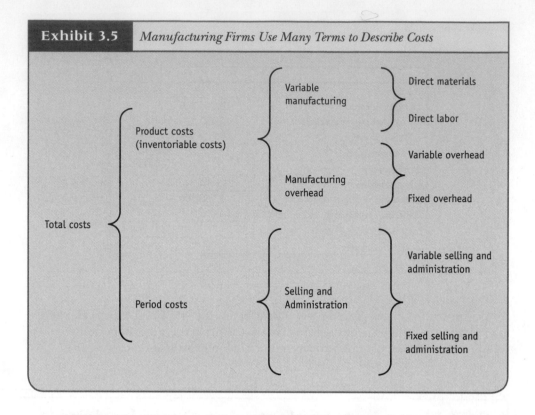

Exhibit 3.5 *Manufacturing Firms Use Many Terms to Describe Costs*

of raw materials and components, partly finished items, and finished goods, its flow of costs is more complex than that for a typical service or merchandising firm.

The many kinds of costs and variations in manufacturing production processes result in a dizzying array of cost terms. Exhibit 3.5 summarizes the most important of these terms commonly found in practice.

COST TERMINOLOGY

We've already shown that total costs are the sum of product costs and period costs. Let's first look further at product costs, which, as you know, are the costs of manufacturing the products. Typical inputs in a manufacturing firm include *materials*, such as steel, leather, canvas, and plastic, and *labor*, the physical work required to convert materials to a finished product. These items represent variable manufacturing costs as expenditures on these items vary proportionally with production volume. Moreover, because firms frequently can trace materials and labor costs directly to products, they are direct costs. As such, many refer to materials and labor costs as **direct materials** and **direct labor**, respectively.

In addition to materials and labor, manufacturers use other inputs—including factories, equipment, machines, and production support staff—to make their product. The costs of these resources represent indirect costs because many products share these resources; we cannot trace these costs directly to a specific product. We refer to the total of all these indirect manufacturing inputs as **overhead**, or sometimes as **manufacturing overhead**.

Some overhead costs, such as the costs of supplies and packaging materials, might vary with production volume. In contrast, the costs of other overhead resources, such as factory rent and equipment depreciation, are fixed. For example, automobile manufacturers such as Suzuki and Ford might classify the cost of power needed to operate an assembly line as a variable indirect cost, and the cost of a salaried production supervisor as fixed and indirect. We refer to the variable portion of these costs as **variable overhead** and the fixed portion as **fixed overhead**.

Direct materials, direct labor, and overhead (both variable and fixed) are all product costs because they are connected with getting the product ready for sale. Some firms emphasize this definition by referring to product costs as **inventoriable costs**, for these are the costs that firms attach to inventories of work in process and finished goods.

Of course, manufacturing firms also incur nonproduction related costs. Some of these costs, such as the cost of transporting goods to customers and sales commissions, are variable. Other costs, such as rentals for sales offices and salaries to marketing personnel, are fixed. Firms also incur administration costs associated with managing the organization itself. Such costs include management salaries, the cost of maintaining a legal staff, accounting and payroll costs, and other corporate level expenses. Collectively, we refer to these costs as **selling and administration costs**. From a financial reporting perspective, selling and administration costs are period costs. GAAP prohibits firms from attaching these costs to inventories. Consequently, firms expense these costs in the income statement during the period they are incurred.

Exhibit 3.6 introduces some additional terminology that firms use to refer to groups of costs. Manufacturers such as Timken refer to the sum of materials and labor costs as **prime costs** because these are the primary inputs into the manufacturing process. Likewise, firms refer to the sum of their variable and fixed overhead as **capacity costs** because these indirect costs provide the firm with the ability they need to make their products. Finally, firms such as Monsanto refer to the sum of labor and overhead as **conversion costs**; these expenditures are required to convert their raw materials to finished goods.

TYPICAL PRODUCTION PROCESS

Now that you understand the cost terminology used in manufacturing firms, let us turn to how their accounting systems accumulate and report these costs. We begin by examining the physical flow of resources in a manufacturing firm. This is a useful step because accounting flows mirror this physical flow.

Exhibit 3.7 illustrates a typical production process. When firms purchase raw materials, they add the cost to the materials inventory account. Firms accumulate labor and overhead costs incurred during a given accounting period in temporary "control" accounts, which are zeroed out at the end of each accounting period.

Exhibit 3.6 *Firms Give Names to Groups of Costs to Show Their Function*

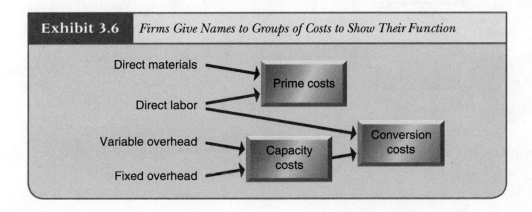

Connecting to Practice

HOW MUCH DOES THAT WII COST?

Teardown analysis includes disassembling a product to determine its components. The sum of the costs of individual components provides a good estimate the cost of direct materials, and thus the manufacturer's margin. Such analysis yields the following estimates for some popular products (data as of January 2007):

Product (firm)	Price	Teardown Cost	Items included
Wii (Nintendo)	$ 199 (wholesale)	$ 158.95	Materials only
30 GB Ipod (Apple)	$ 249 (retail)	$ 130.90	Materials only
Q phone (Motorola)	$ 199 (discounted)	$ 158.00	Materials & assembly
iPhone (Apple)	$ 499 (retail)	$ 229.85	Manufacturing cost
HD-DVD (Toshiba)	$ 499	$ 674.00	Materials only

COMMENTARY: Firms guard their cost data well because knowledge of this information helps the competition. Unlike Apple, which makes a substantive margin on its products, the estimate for Wii shows that Nintendo likely experiences a loss from the sale of the Wii. This fact is not surprising because firms that sell game systems make most of their profit from selling games and not the consoles themselves. In the same way, Verizon (which buys the Q from Motorola) likely sells the Q below cost, hoping to make money from wireless services. Likewise, by pricing the DVD player aggressively, Toshiba hopes to increase market share for its video format and ensure its long-run viability.

The product cost for a Wii includes the cost of materials, labor, and manufacturing overhead. (Reuters/Yuriko Nakao/Landov LLC)

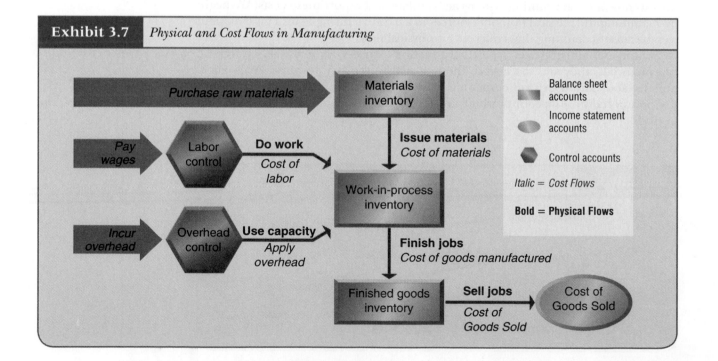

Exhibit 3.7 *Physical and Cost Flows in Manufacturing*

Connecting to Practice

MANUFACTURING PROCESSES

Firms vary greatly in their raw materials and production processes. Firms such as Alcoa convert bauxite ore into aluminum. Other manufacturers such as Caterpillar use steel, aluminum, and plastic to make components and then assemble these components into construction equipment. Construction firms such as Toll Brothers use Caterpillar's products to build new homes.

COMMENTARY: As seen above, the types of input materials used as well as the production processes and the products vary widely across manufacturers. This variety has led to a considerable range of manufacturing practices, including Just-in-Time production and lean manufacturing.

As production commences, firms assign the cost of materials, labor, and overhead from the respective inventory and control accounts to a *work-in-process* (WIP) account. The sum of materials, labor, and overhead costs added to the work-in-process account during the period are the total manufacturing costs charged to production.

Often, the production process consists of many steps, with new materials and/or labor added at each step. Each step also consumes some overhead resources. Cost assignments mirror this physical flow. At every step, we add the costs of materials, labor, and overhead consumed in that step to the WIP account to "build" the cost of the work performed on a specific product.

Once the production process is completed, firms transfer finished work physically from work-in-process inventory to *finished goods* (FG) inventory. Correspondingly, they transfer the **cost of goods manufactured** (COGM) from the work-in-process inventory account to the finished goods inventory account.

When firms sell finished goods, they physically transfer the goods to buyers. At the same time, firms remove the associated cost from the FG inventory account and transfer it to the cost of goods sold (COGS) account. Cost of goods sold appears as a deduction from revenues in the income statement, with gross margin equaling the difference between revenues and COGS.

INCOME STATEMENT

Using an example, Vulcan Forge, let us take a closer look at the cost flows for a manufacturing company.

Vulcan Forge owns and operates a plant that makes a single product: 5-ton hooks used in cranes. Vulcan buys raw materials such as steel and converts them into hooks. Following the flow in Exhibit 3.7, let us begin with raw materials. Exhibit 3.8 presents the raw materials inventory account.

The work-in-process account, shown in Exhibit 3.9, informs us that Vulcan began the year with $2 million worth of work in process. To this amount, the firm added $10 million of raw materials, as we learned from Exhibit 3.8. Vulcan also spent $8 million on labor and $16 million on manufacturing overhead during the year. We add these three amounts, which we collectively refer to as the **total manufacturing costs charged to production**, to the WIP account. As with raw materials, Vulcan applies the inventory equation to the WIP account to obtain cost of goods manufactured.

Exhibit 3.8	*Vulcan Forge: Cost of Raw Materials Used*

	Total
Beginning inventory of raw materials	$1,500,000
+ Purchases of raw materials	9,000,000
− Ending inventory of raw materials	500,000
= Cost of materials used	$10,000,000

Exhibit 3.9	*Vulcan Forge: Cost of Goods Manufactured for the Most Recent Year*

	Total
Cost of beginning work-in-process inventory	$2,000,000
+ Cost of materials used (from Exhibit 3.8)	10,000,000
+ Direct labor	8,000,000
+ Manufacturing overhead	16,000,000
− Cost of ending work-in-process inventory	1,000,000
= Cost of goods manufactured	$35,000,000

Exhibit 3.10	*Vulcan Forge: Cost of Goods Sold for the Most Recent Year*

	Total
Cost of beginning finished goods inventory	$2,000,000
+ Cost of goods manufactured (Exhibit 3.9)	35,000,000
− Cost of ending finished goods inventory	5,000,000
= Cost of goods sold	$32,000,000

Exhibit 3.11	*Vulcan Forge: Income Statement for the Most Recent Year*

	Total
Revenues	$45,000,000
Cost of goods sold	32,000,000
Gross margin	$13,000,000
Selling and administration	11,000,000
Profit before taxes	$2,000,000

As discussed earlier, the cost of goods sold represents the product costs associated with the items *sold* during the year. It is not necessarily the same as the cost of goods manufactured during the year. As shown in Exhibit 3.10, Vulcan Forge uses the inventory equation to reconcile cost of goods manufactured and cost of goods sold. As we see from this exhibit, we obtain the cost of goods sold ($32 million) by adding together the beginning finished goods inventory ($2 million) and the cost of goods manufactured ($35 million from Exhibit 3.8) and subtracting the cost of ending finished goods inventory ($5 million).

Notice that the cost of goods manufactured exceeds the cost of goods sold by $3 million. Naturally, Vulcan's finished goods inventory increases by the same amount: $2 million at the start to $5 million at the end of the period.

Finally, Exhibit 3.11, which conforms to GAAP, presents Vulcan's income statement for the most recent year of operations.

Exhibit 3.12 shows an alternate view of the flow of costs at Vulcan Forge. Recall from Exhibit 3.3 that a merchandising firm has one significant inventory

CHAPTER CONNECTIONS

Virtually every organization allocates costs. Allocating manufacturing overhead to value inventory is a prominent reason. This reason does not apply to service and merchandising firms. Even so, these firms allocate costs for a variety of planning and control decisions. We study the many roles for cost allocations in Chapter 9.

Exhibit 3.12   *Flow of Costs through Inventory Accounts in Manufacturing Firms*

Raw Materials Inventory Account

Beginning Inventory	$1,500,000	To Work in Process	$10,000,000
Purchases	9,000,000		
Ending Inventory	$ 500,000		

Cost of raw materials used

Work-in-Process Inventory Account

Beginning Inventory	$ 2,000,000	To finished goods	$35,000,000
Materials used	10,000,000		
Direct labor	8,000,000		
Overhead	16,000,000		
Ending Inventory	$ 1,000,000		

Cost of Goods Manufactured

Finished Goods Inventory Account

Beginning Inventory	$2,000,000	To income statement	$32,000,000
COGM	35,000,000		
Ending Inventory	$5,000,000		

Cost of Goods Sold

Income Statement

Cost of goods sold	$32,000,000	Revenues	$45,000,000
Selling & admin. costs	11,000,000		
		Profit	$2,000,000

Check It! Exercise #2

Suppose Mason Manufacturing provides the following data for the most recent quarter: raw material purchases of $1,200,000; labor costs of $845,000; and manufacturing overhead of $760,500. Mason also informs you that it had $240,000; $50,000; and $375,000 as its beginning inventories for raw materials, work in process, and finished goods, respectively. The corresponding ending inventory values were $320,000; $100,000; and $294,500, respectively. Verify that (1) the cost of raw material used is $1,120,000, (2) cost of goods manufactured is $2,675,500, and (3) cost of goods sold is $2,756,000.

Solution at end of chapter.

account: merchandise inventory. A manufacturing firm, however, has three inventory accounts: raw materials, work in process, and finished goods. Yet the final income statement looks the same for service, merchandising, and manufacturing firms.

Cost Allocations

Allocate overhead costs to products.

We next turn to an issue of how firms assign overhead costs, for example, when multiple products exist. In such cases, a firm will have multiple work-in-process and finished goods accounts, one for each product. We can directly assign the costs of materials and labor to each WIP and FG account because we can trace these costs to each product.

However, assigning manufacturing overhead to *individual* work-in-process accounts poses a problem. Overhead costs are indirect and, as such, are not traceable to each product. We did not face this issue with Vulcan Forge because it has one WIP account and one FG account related to its one product, 5-ton hooks. Firms with multiple products resolve this issue by *allocating* overhead costs to products on some justifiable basis. In this section, we describe the cost allocation procedures commonly used in organizations.

A **cost allocation** is a procedure that allocates, or distributes, a common cost. Suppose two families share a $60 meal. The Smith family has three persons—an adult couple and their child. The Jones family has two persons—an adult couple. How might we allocate the $60 cost of their meal? Exhibit 3.13 illustrates the allocation process we might follow.

We start by considering four elements that are in every cost allocation: cost pools, cost objects, cost drivers, and allocation volume.

- **Cost Pool**—the total costs to allocate. Our cost pool is $60, the cost of the meal.
- **Cost Objects**—the items or entities to which we allocate the costs in the cost pool. In our example, we have two cost objects: the Smith family and the Jones family.
- **Cost Driver (Allocation Basis)**—attributes that we can measure for each cost object. For example, we could use the number of persons in each family as the attribute, or the number of adults, the number of males, the number of left-handed people, and so forth. For our example, if we select the number of persons as the allocation basis, then the Smith family has three units of the cost driver, and the Jones family has two units. Suppose the restaurant had a "kids eat free" promotional special. Then we might select the number of adults as the allocation basis, in which case the Smith and the Jones families each have two units of the cost driver. While we can choose any attribute to be an allocation basis, we often choose attributes that have a *causal* relation between the attribute and the costs incurred. We distinguish such allocation basis by terming them a *cost driver*.
- **Allocation Volume (Denominator Volume)**—the sum of the cost driver amounts across all cost objects. In our example, if the number of persons is the cost driver, then the allocation or denominator volume is five persons. If the number of adults is the cost driver, then the allocation volume is four persons. Managers emphasize causal links by reserving the term *denominator volume* for allocations that employ cost drivers.

After considering these elements, the allocation procedure itself consists of two steps. The yellow boxes in Exhibit 3.13 represent these steps.

- **Determine the Allocation Rate (Overhead Rate).** Calculate the **allocation rate** by dividing the amount in the cost pool by the denominator volume. When the number of persons is the cost driver, our allocation rate is $60/5 persons = $12

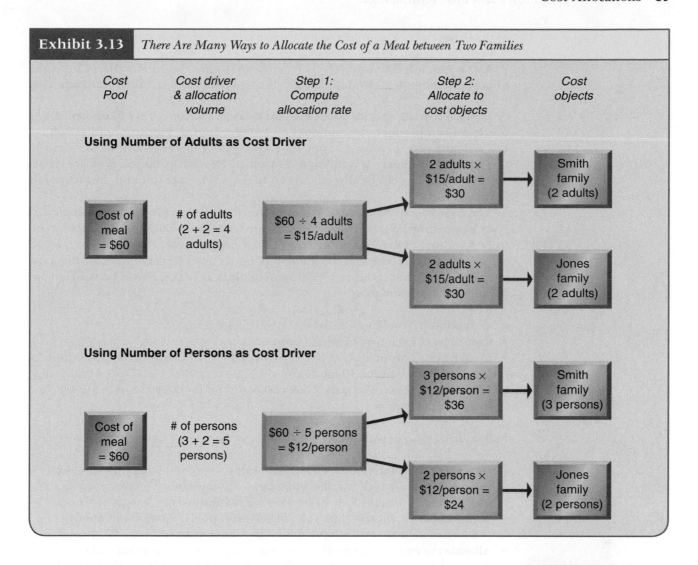

Exhibit 3.13	*There Are Many Ways to Allocate the Cost of a Meal between Two Families*

Cost Pool	Cost driver & allocation volume	Step 1: Compute allocation rate	Step 2: Allocate to cost objects	Cost objects

Using Number of Adults as Cost Driver

Cost of meal = $60

# of adults (2 + 2 = 4 adults)

$60 ÷ 4 adults = $15/adult

2 adults × $15/adult = $30 → Smith family (2 adults)

2 adults × $15/adult = $30 → Jones family (2 adults)

Using Number of Persons as Cost Driver

Cost of meal = $60

# of persons (3 + 2 = 5 persons)

$60 ÷ 5 persons = $12/person

3 persons × $12/person = $36 → Smith family (3 persons)

2 persons × $12/person = $24 → Jones family (2 persons)

per person. When the number of adults is the cost driver, our allocation rate is $60/4 adults = $15 per adult. Because overhead costs are the subject of most cost allocations, many refer to the allocation rate as the **overhead rate**.

- **Allocate the Cost.** Multiply the number of cost driver units contained in each cost object by the allocation rate. When the number of persons is the cost driver, then the Smith family pays 3 persons × $12/person = $36, whereas the Jones family pays 2 persons × $12/person = $24. However, when the number of adults is the cost driver, then both cost objects (both families) pay the same amount: 2 adults × $15 per adult = $30 per family.

We often share the cost of a meal. Such sharing is a cost allocation. (Radius Images/Masterfile)

Notice that, regardless of the cost driver we choose, the sum of the allocations equals the cost pool. When the number of persons is the cost driver, the allocations total $36 + $24 = $60. When the number of adults is the cost driver, the allocations total $30 + $30 = $60.

As you can see from the example, allocations divide the costs in the cost pool in proportion to the number of cost driver units in each cost object. When the number of persons is the cost driver, we allocate 60% of the cost to the Smith family because this family accounts for 60% of the cost driver units (persons). When the number of adults is the cost driver, each family pays $30 instead of the $36/$24 split. Therefore, we allocate 50% of the cost to each family because each family contributes 50%

of the driver units. Regardless of the chosen cost driver, *the proportion of cost allocated to a cost object equals the proportion of driver units in that cost object.*

As our example illustrates, the cost driver we choose can greatly affect the results of cost allocations. In Module III, we discuss how to select the appropriate cost driver.

How do cost allocations affect the cost flows at Vulcan Forge? Suppose Vulcan produces two products, 5-ton hooks and 10-ton hooks. Vulcan would now have two WIP and two FG accounts, one for each product. Because Vulcan can identify the amount of materials and labor consumed by each product, both materials and labor costs would be directly traced to each WIP account and, in turn, each FG account.

The issue then rests on what Vulcan would do with the $16 million in overhead costs (see Exhibit 3.9). Because these costs are common to both products, they need to be allocated to determine the cost of each product. Assume Vulcan decides to allocate these costs based on the number of hooks produced and that, for the most recent year, Vulcan produced 15,000 5-ton hooks and 10,000 10-ton hooks. First, we identify the four elements:

- **Cost pool.** $16 million, the overhead to be allocated.
- **Cost object.** Each type of hook (5-ton hook and 10-ton hook)
- **Cost driver.** The quantity of hooks produced (15,000 units of the 5-ton hook and 10,000 units of the 10-ton hook)
- **Allocation volume.** The sum of the cost driver units. 15,000 units + 10,000 units = 25,000 units

Following the two-step allocation procedure, we have:

- **Determine the allocation rate (overhead rate).** In general, regardless of the number of products or the allocation basis, *this step consists of calculating the overhead rate by dividing the total overhead cost (the cost pool) by the total of the driver units (allocation volume).* Thus $16,000,000 (cost pool)/25,000 total hooks (allocation volume) = $640 per hook (allocation rate).
- **Allocate the cost.** In general, *the overhead allocated to an individual unit or product line is the number of driver units contained in that unit or product line times the overhead*

Connecting to Practice

GUMP ACCOUNTING

The blockbuster movie, *Forrest Gump*, grossed over $657 million in the box office. It generated millions more in video sales and product tie-ins. While analysts believe that the movie generated over $350 million in net cash flows, Paramount Studio's account suggested that the movie lost $62 million. The movie *Coming to America* also suffered a similar fate. In both cases, the studio arrived at the loss after allocating the common costs it incurs to make and distribute all movies.

COMMENTARY: The studio chose cost drivers such as gross receipts to allocate common costs. Part of the rationale for such a choice might be to reduce the payout to movie stars, screenwriters, and others who receive a cut of the profit from the movie. This argument has lost bite in recent years as movie stars and directors now contract for the payout to be a percentage of the gross revenue, which is unaffected by any cost allocation.

Check It! Exercise #3

Suppose Vulcan Forge decides to allocate the $16,000,000 in overhead costs on the basis of direct labor hours. Each 5-ton hook requires 25 labor hours, and each 10-ton hook requires 42.50 labor hours. Verify that Vulcan would allocate $7,500,000 in overhead to the 5-ton hooks and $8,500,000 in overhead to the 10-ton hooks.

Solution at end of chapter.

CHAPTER CONNECTIONS

While the essential allocation process is the same, actual accounting systems must deal with numerous types of costs and products. Firms usually tailor their accounting systems to their production processes. Grouping firms by the nature of their product, we can anchor one end with firms that make one-of-a-kind products and the other end with firms that produce large volumes of standardized goods. In Chapters 14 and 15, we study job-costing and process-costing, which are the accounting systems that correspond to these two extremes.

rate per driver unit. Thus, for the cost object of 5-ton hooks, Vulcan would allocate 15,000 hooks × $640 per hook = $9,600,000 in overhead. For the 10-ton hooks, Vulcan would allocate 10,000 hooks × $640 per hook = $6,400,000 in overhead.

Therefore, in addition to the direct materials and direct labor costs traceable to each hook, the $9,600,000 and $6,400,000 in allocated overhead would flow through each product's WIP account. When the hooks are finished, these costs would flow through to the FG accounts. They will become part of the COGS when Vulcan sells the associated products.

GAAP gives firms considerable leeway regarding their choices of how to allocate manufacturing overhead to products. Commonly used allocation bases include direct labor hours, direct labor cost, machine hours, and the number of units. Usually, firms pick a *cost driver* that exhibits a cause-effect relation with the cost being allocated. As we will learn in Chapter 9, their choice arises from their desire to use the allocation both to value inventory and to estimate the long-run change in capacity costs. Thus, firms often allocate supervisory costs and materials handling costs using direct labor cost and materials cost, respectively, as the allocation basis. They expect that, over the long term, changes in labor cost will trigger or "drive" a proportional change in supervisory costs. A similar rationale holds for using materials cost as the basis for allocating the costs of handling materials.

BEWARE OF ALLOCATED COSTS WHEN MAKING DECISIONS

As we discussed earlier with Hercules, GAAP income statements combine controllable costs with noncontrollable costs and fixed costs with variable costs. As a result, it is difficult to use the summary data provided by GAAP income statements for internal decision making. Indeed, as Exhibit 3.14 illustrates, allocating overhead costs can make non-controllable fixed costs appear to be controllable and variable.

Exhibit 3.14	*GAAP Income Statement*	
	Amount per unit	**Total**
Number of units sold		30,000
Price/Revenues	$25.00	$750,000
Cost of goods sold:		
Direct materials	6.00	180,000
Direct labor	8.00	240,000
Allocated manufacturing overhead (50% is variable, 50% is fixed)	4.00	120,000
Gross margin	$7.00	$210,000
Selling and administration (30% is variable, 70% is fixed)	5.00	150,000
Profit before taxes	$2.00	$60,000

This report suggests that the firm increases its profit by $2.00 for each additional unit sold. The report also suggests that the product costs $23.00 to make and sell, meaning that a price lower than $23.00 would be unacceptable. Thus, the firm would reject a one-time offer to buy 1,000 units at $22.50, even if the firm had the capacity to accommodate this request.

While intuitively appealing, this decision would be incorrect! Why? The answer is that the report combines variable costs (direct materials, direct labor, variable overhead, variable selling and administrative) and fixed costs (fixed overhead, fixed selling, and administration). Only the revenues and variable costs would be controllable in the short term. Here, the variable cost per unit consists of $6.00 direct materials + $8.00 direct labor + $2.00 variable overhead + $1.50 variable selling and administration, or $17.50 per unit. Therefore, the offer to buy the units at $22.50 per unit actually increases profit by $5.00 per unit, and a total of $5,000 in increased profit for 1,000 units.

To facilitate decisions, many firms prepare reports that regroup costs by their variability, as shown in Exhibit 3.15. In Chapter 4, we will closely examine these statements, which we call contribution margin income statements.

WRAPPING IT UP

Now that you understand cost flows and reporting systems, what is the best course of action with regard to Hercules? Hercules is a service organization—it does not

Exhibit 3.15	*Contribution Margin Income Statement*	
	Amount per unit	**Total**
Number of units sold		30,000
Price/Revenues	$25.00	$750,000
Direct materials	6.00	180,000
Direct labor	8.00	240,000
Allocated variable overhead	2.00	60,000
Variable selling and administration	1.50	45,000
Contribution margin	$7.50	$225,000
Allocated fixed overhead	2.00	60,000
Fixed selling and administration	3.50	105,000
Profit before taxes	$2.00	$60,000

APPLYING THE DECISION FRAMEWORK

What Is the Problem?	What data should you use to estimate the profit impact of offering yoga?
What Are the Options?	You naturally turn to the accounting system to obtain cost and revenue data. Your options relate to whether to modify and how to modify Hercules' system to suit your needs.
What Are the Costs and Benefits?	Modifying the system is costly in terms of time, effort, and the expertise required. However, it can lead to benefits in terms of a more accurate profit estimate.
Make the Decision!	You decide that you can rely on expenses reported in financial statements to estimate the costs and benefits of offering yoga. However, you will first have to estimate variable and fixed costs. You also have to consider if any fixed costs would change because of the decision.

have much in the way of inventories. However, you still need to modify Hercules' accounting system to determine the variable and fixed costs, and thus the change in profit associated with offering yoga. We take up this task in Chapter 4.

SUMMARY

In this chapter, we discussed accounting systems that you are likely to encounter in the workplace. Most firms' accounting systems are set up to comply with GAAP, sharply delineating between product and period costs. We discussed how such systems accumulate costs for financial reporting purposes as well as the similarities and differences in cost flows for service, merchandising, and manufacturing firms. Finally, we illustrated how allocations play an important role in determining inventory values and cost of goods sold in manufacturing firms and how the use of summary income statement data can lead to poor decisions.

In the next module (Chapters 4−8), we examine short-term decisions. Because financial reporting requirements influence accounting systems, the data we find often are not suitable for decision making. To make effective decisions, we need information about the controllability and variability of costs and benefits. In the next chapter, we examine how to modify the data from accounting systems to suit the needs of internal decision makers.

RAPID REVIEW

LEARNING OBJECTIVE 1

Distinguish product costs from period costs.

- One of the important functions of accounting systems in organizations is to provide information for the preparation of financial statements such as the income statement, balance sheet, and statement of cash flows.
- Financial accounting systems classify costs according to business function. Costs related to the primary business function are product costs, and costs related to support functions are period costs.

- Product costs appear "above the line" in computing the gross margin. Period costs appear "below the line" after computing the gross margin.

LEARNING OBJECTIVE 2

Understand the flow of costs in service firms.

- The hallmark of a service firm is that the products it offers are neither tangible nor storable.
- Because service firms' products are neither tangible nor storable, they do not maintain inventories of their final products.

Discuss how inventories affect the flow of costs in merchandising firms.

• Merchandising firms sell substantially the same products they purchase. Most merchandising firms maintain an inventory of goods that they buy and sell; they use this inventory to display items, obtain volume discounts, and ensure product availability.

• The presence of inventory means that costs on purchases often do not equal the expense related to the cost of goods sold.

• Merchandising firms use an inventory equation to determine the cost of goods sold during the period. Cost of goods sold = the value of beginning inventory + the cost of purchases − the value of ending inventory.

• Because merchandising firms buy goods at different times and different prices, they make inventory cost flow assumptions such as FIFO or LIFO to compute the value of inventory and cost of goods sold.

• As with service firms, merchandising firms' income statements report the cost of goods sold above the line for gross margin, and all other costs below this line.

Explain the cost terminology and the flow of costs in manufacturing firms.

• Unlike merchandising firms, manufacturing firms use labor and equipment to substantially transform inputs such as raw materials and components into outputs.

• While merchandising firms have one primary inventory account, manufacturing firms have three: raw materials, work-in-process, and finished goods. Given this, and the variations in manufacturing production processes, manufacturing firms have complex cost flows and cost terminology.

• Typical inputs in a manufacturing firm include direct materials, direct labor, and overhead. Prime costs are the sum of direct materials and direct labor costs, and conversion costs are the sum of direct labor and manufacturing overhead costs.

• Product costs are the sum of all manufacturing costs. These costs flow through the firm's inventory accounts. Nonmanufacturing costs are period costs. Firms expense these costs in their income statements during the period incurred.

• Applying the inventory equation to the raw materials inventory yields the costs of materials used. This amount plus the cost of direct labor and manufacturing overhead is the input into the work-in-process (WIP) account. Adjusting the total by the beginning and ending balances in the WIP account yields the cost of goods manufactured, which is the inflow into the inventory of finished goods (FG). Once again, adjusting for beginning and ending balances in the FG account yields the cost of goods sold, the amount expensed in the income statement.

Allocate overhead costs to products.

• To allocate is to distribute, and a cost allocation is a procedure that distributes a common cost among the items giving rise to the cost. Firms need to allocate overhead costs because they are common to products. In contrast, direct materials and direct labor can be traced to products.

• There are four elements in every cost allocation:
  (1) Cost pool—the total costs to allocate
  (2) Cost objects—the items or entities to which we allocate costs
  (3) Cost driver (allocation basis)—attributes that we can measure for each cost object; they are used to distribute costs in the cost pool among cost objects
  (4) Allocation volume (denominator volume)—the sum of the cost driver amounts across all cost objects

• Cost allocation procedures consist of two steps:
  (1) Calculate the allocation rate by dividing the cost pool by the allocation volume.
  (2) Use the allocation rate to assign costs to each cost object by multiplying the cost driver units contained in a specific cost object by the allocation rate.

• Every allocation divides the costs in the cost pool in proportion to the number of cost driver units corresponding to each cost object.

• While allocations play an important role in calculating product cost for financial reporting purposes, it is important to remember that such allocations—found in GAAP income statements—mingle controllable and noncontrollable costs and variable and fixed costs.

ANSWERS TO CHECK IT! EXERCISES

Exercise #1: We have:

Cost of beginning inventory	$3,450,200
+ Cost of goods purchased	+ 24,795,740
− Cost of ending inventory	− 3,745,600
= Cost of goods sold	= $24,500,340

Exercise #2: Raw materials used = Beginning materials inventory + purchases − ending materials inventory. Thus, $1,120,000 = $240,000 + $1,200,000 − $320,000.
Beginning WIP inventory + materials used + labor cost + manufacturing overhead − ending WIP inventory = Cost of goods manufactured.
Thus, $50,000 + $1,120,000 + $845,000 + $760,500 − $100,000 = $2,675,500.
Beginning FG inventory + COGM − ending FG inventory = Cost of goods sold. Thus, $375,000 + $2,675,500 − $294,500 = $2,756,000.

Exercise #3: Allocation volume = (15,000 5-ton hooks × 25 labor hours per hook) + (10,000 10-ton hooks × 42.50 labor hours per hook) = (375,000 labor hours + 425,000 labor hours) = 800,000 labor hours.
Allocation rate = $16,000,000 in overhead costs/800,000 labor hours = $20 per labor hour.
Amount allocated to 5-ton hooks = allocation rate × cost driver units = $20 per labor hour × 375,000 labor hours = $7,500,000.
Amount allocated to 10-ton hooks = allocation rate × cost driver units = $20 per labor hour × 425,000 labor hours = $8,500,000.

SELF-STUDY PROBLEMS

SELF-STUDY PROBLEM #1:
Cost Flows in Manufacturing Firms

DigJam Industries makes dyes used to color fabrics. The following data pertain to its operations for the most recent year:

Raw materials beginning inventory	$60,000
Raw materials ending inventory	$80,000
WIP beginning inventory	$80,000
WIP ending inventory	$105,000
Finished goods beginning inventory	$300,000
Finished goods ending inventory	$250,000
Raw materials issued to production	$225,000
Manufacturing overhead	$360,000
Total manufacturing costs charged to production (= raw materials issued to production + direct labor + manufacturing overhead)	$885,000
Cost of goods available for sale (= beginning balance in finished goods + cost of goods manufactured)	$1,160,000
Revenues	$1,150,000
Selling and administrative costs	$147,000

a. *Calculate the cost of raw materials purchased during the year.*
The inventory equation for the raw materials account is:

> Ending balance = Beginning balance + Raw materials purchased − Raw materials issued to production. Thus,
> $80,000 = $60,000 + raw materials purchased − $225,000.
> Raw materials purchased = **$245,000**.

b. *Calculate the cost of direct labor charged to production.*

> Total manufacturing costs charged to production = raw materials issued to production + direct labor cost + manufacturing overhead.
> $885,000 = $225,000 + Direct labor cost + $360,000.
> Direct labor cost = $885,000 − $225,000 − $360,000 = **$300,000**.

c. *Calculate the cost of goods manufactured during the year.*
The inventory equation for the work-in-process account is:

> Ending balance = Beginning balance + Total manufacturing costs charged to production − Cost of goods manufactured.
> 105,000 = $80,000 + $885,000 − Cost of goods manufactured.
> Cost of goods manufactured = **$860,000**.
> <u>Alternatively</u>, we can calculate:
> Cost of goods manufactured = Cost of goods available for sale − Beginning balance in finished goods.
> $1,160,000 − $300,000 = **$860,000**.

d. *Calculate the cost of goods sold during the year.*

We can express cost flows through the finished goods account using the following equation:

Ending balance = Beginning balance + Cost of goods manufactured − Cost of goods sold.

$250,000 = $300,000 + $860,000 − Cost of goods sold.

Cost of goods sold = **$910,000**.

<u>Alternatively</u>, we can calculate:

Cost of goods sold = Cost of goods available for sale − Ending balance in finished goods.

$1,160,000 − $250,000 = **$910,000**.

e. *Prepare DigJam's GAAP income statement for the most recent year.*

The following table presents DigJam's GAAP income statement for the most recent year.

DigJam Industries
Income Statement for the Most Recent Year

Revenues		$1,150,000
Beginning FG inventory	$300,000	
+ Cost of goods manufactured	860,000	
− Ending FG inventory	250,000	
= Cost of goods sold		$910,000
Gross margin		$240,000
Selling & administration costs		147,000
Profit before taxes		$93,000

SELF-STUDY PROBLEM #2:

Cost Allocations, Product Cost

Precision Bearings manufactures several kinds of roller bearings. This past year, Precision spent $11,750,000 on manufacturing overhead costs and $23,500,000 for direct labor. Precision produced 5,875,000 bearings and sold 5,500,000 bearings during the year.

The following table provides the direct materials, direct labor, and selling and administrative (S&A) costs per unit for three of Precision's bearings:

	Model 6203	Model 6210	Model 30207
Direct materials	$1.00	$1.75	$3.00
Direct labor	$3.00	$4.00	$7.00
S & A	$0.50	$0.75	$1.00

a. *Assume that Precision allocates overhead costs using the number of units produced as the cost driver. What is the unit product cost (inventoriable cost) for each of the three bearings?*

Under GAAP, product cost is the sum of direct materials, direct labor, and manufacturing overhead. Product cost does not include any selling or administrative costs; these costs are treated as period expenses.

Furthermore, Precision allocates overhead costs to products using units produced as the cost driver. We now use the two steps outlined in the text for allocating costs.

Step 1: We first calculate the allocation rate by dividing the costs contained in the cost pool by the denominator volume.

$11,750,000/5,875,000 units = $2.00 per unit

Notice that we use total production to allocate costs as the $11,750,000 relates to units produced, not just units sold.

Step 2: With the allocation rate in hand, we can determine the unit product cost for each kind of bearing:

	Model 6203	Model 6210	Model 30207
Materials cost	$1.00	$1.75	$3.00
Labor cost	3.00	4.00	7.00
Allocated overhead	2.00	2.00	2.00
Product cost	**$6.00**	**$7.75**	**$12.00**

Again, we emphasize that selling and administrative costs are not included in inventoriable costs.

b. *Assume that Precision allocates overhead costs using direct labor costs as the cost driver instead of the number of units produced. What is the unit product cost (inventoriable cost) for each of the three bearings?*

This change in the cost driver will change the rate that we use to allocate overhead costs.

Step 1: Compute the allocation rate. Plugging in the numbers from the problem, $11,750,000/$23,500,000 in labor costs = $0.50 per labor $

Step 2: Allocate costs. With this rate in hand, we can determine the unit product cost for each bearing:

	Model 6203	Model 6210	Model 30207
Materials cost	$1.00	$1.75	$3.00
Labor cost	3.00	4.00	7.00
Allocated overhead	1.50	2.00	3.50[1]
Product cost	**$5.50**	**$7.75**	**$13.50**

[1] $1.50 = $3.00 labor $ × $0.50/labor $; $2.00 = $4.00 labor $ × $0.50/labor $; $3.50 = $7.00 labor $ × $0.50/labor $.

For each bearing, we compute the allocated manufacturing overhead as the labor cost of each bearing × allocation rate per labor $. Notice again that we do not use S&A costs to determine product costs.

c. *Compare your answers to parts (a) and (b), and discuss any differences in product cost.*

We find that the product cost for 6203 has decreased, the product cost for 30207 has increased, and the product cost for 6210 has not changed.

To understand the difference, notice that when Precision allocates overhead costs using units, each bearing gets an equal share of overhead. However, when Precision allocates using labor cost, allocated overhead is proportional to the bearings' labor cost.

The "average bearing" consumes $4 of labor ($23,500,000/5,875,000 bearings). *There would be no difference due to the change in the allocation basis only if each kind of bearing actually did consume $4 per bearing in labor costs.* However, this equivalence is not true. Thus, bearings with lower than average labor cost (e.g., 6203) will experience a reduction in reported cost if Precision changes its allocation basis from units to labor cost. Conversely, bearings with higher than average labor cost (e.g., 30207) experience an increase in reported costs.

Note: Although the product cost of each individual bearing changes depending on the allocation basis chosen, the total overhead costs allocated to all bearings will be $11,750,000—*regardless of the allocation basis chosen.*

d. *Do you believe product cost, as computed under GAAP, is sufficient for determining a product's profitability?*

Unfortunately, the product cost computed under GAAP is not enough for assessing a product's profitability. Why? For assessing a product's profitability, we wish to include all controllable costs and exclude all noncontrollable costs. As discussed in the text, GAAP excludes selling and administrative costs, both variable and fixed, from a product's product cost. Many of these costs, such as those related to shipping, distribution, and sales commissions are controllable at the product level. Accordingly, it is important to include such costs when assessing a product's profitability.

In addition, by allocating all fixed manufacturing costs, noncontrollable costs often are included in product cost. This could occur, for example, with items such as factory rent, which may not be controllable even over an extended horizon.

GLOSSARY

Allocation basis Same as "cost driver."

Allocation rate The cost pool divided by the allocation volume.

Allocation volume The sum of the cost driver amounts across all cost objects.

Capacity costs The sum of variable and fixed overhead costs.

Conversion costs The sum of direct labor and manufacturing overhead costs.

Cost allocation A procedure that distributes a common cost among the items giving rise to the cost.

Cost driver Attributes that we can measure for each cost object that are used to distribute the cost pool among cost objects.

Cost of goods manufactured (COGM) The cost of items finished and transferred from work in process inventory to finished goods inventory.

Cost of goods sold (COGS) The cost of products sold in a period. The cost of items transferred from finished goods inventory to the income statement.

Cost objects The items, or entities, to which costs are to be allocated.

Cost pool The total costs to be allocated.

Denominator volume Same as "allocation volume."

Direct labor Labor costs than can be traced to individual units of a product in a cost-effective manner.

Direct materials Materials costs than can be traced economically to individual units of a product.

Fixed overhead Indirect manufacturing costs that do not vary with production volume.

Gross margin Revenues less product costs.

Inventoriable costs See Product costs.

Manufacturing firm A firm that uses labor and equipment to transform inputs such as materials and components into outputs.

Manufacturing overhead The sum of all indirect manufacturing costs.

Merchandising firm A firm that resells essentially the same product it buys from suppliers.

Overhead Same as manufacturing overhead.

Overhead rate Term frequently used to refer to "allocation rate."

Period costs A financial accounting concept under GAAP. Any cost that is not a product cost. A cost related to the selling of goods and the administration of the organization.

Prime costs The sum of direct materials and direct labor costs, as these are the primary inputs into the production process.

Product costs A financial accounting concept under GAAP. Any cost associated with getting products and services ready for sale.

Selling and administration costs Nonmanufacturing costs. A term frequently used to refer to "period costs."

Service firm A firm whose product is neither tangible nor storable.

Total manufacturing costs charged to production The sum of materials, labor, and overhead added to the work-in-process account during the period.

Variable overhead Indirect manufacturing costs that vary with production volume.

REVIEW QUESTIONS

3.1 LO1. What is the difference between a product cost and a period cost?

3.2 LO1. What is the gross margin?

3.3 LO1. Why does GAAP require firms to distinguish between product and period costs?

3.4 LO2. What is the key characteristic of a service firm?

3.5 LO3. What is the key characteristic of a merchandising firm?

3.6 LO3. What is the inventory equation?

3.7 LO4. What is the key characteristic of a manufacturing firm?

3.8 LO4. Why do we frequently refer to materials and labor costs as being both direct and variable?

3.9 LO4. What is the difference between variable manufacturing overhead and fixed manufacturing overhead?

3.10 LO4. Define the terms *prime costs and conversion costs.*

3.11 LO5. What are the four elements of every cost allocation?

3.12 LO5. Describe the two-step procedure for allocating costs.

3.13 LO5. What is the relation between the proportion of cost allocated to a cost object and the proportion of driver units in the cost object?

DISCUSSION QUESTIONS

3.14 LO2. Consider a consulting firm that completes large software projects that often take two or more years to complete. What is the nature of inventory for such a firm? How should it value this inventory?

3.15 LO2. A restaurant converts inputs into substantially different outputs, a key characteristic of a manufacturing firm. Yet, most would classify a restaurant as a service firm. How would you classify a restaurant? Why?

3.16 LO2 (Advanced). Consider a firm such as U-Haul that supplies trucks that we could rent to move goods. (Ignore other aspects of U-Haul's operations.) To meet demand, which is usually seasonal and focused on a

few weeks each year, U-Haul keeps a large supply of trucks. Would you classify this firm as a service firm or as a merchandising firm? What conclusions do you draw about the distinctions between service and merchandising firms?

3.17 LO3. List three reasons why a merchandising firm holds inventory.

3.18 LO3. Should a retail firm include the cost of receiving and stocking goods when computing inventory values?

3.19 LO3 (Advanced). Many merchandising firms charge the entire amount of transportation costs to cost of goods sold. Other merchandising firms perform a year-end allocation to distribute the cost between the inventory and cost of goods sold. How might firms justify not tracing transportation costs to individual products and flowing these costs through the inventory accounts?

3.20 LO4 (Advanced). GAAP excludes most research and development costs from its definition of inventoriable costs. Why do you believe GAAP mandates such a treatment?

3.21 LO1, LO4 (Advanced). Do you expect reported income and operating cash flows for a service firm to be close in magnitude? Would your answer differ for a manufacturing firm? Why?

3.22 LO4. As you know, direct materials, direct labor, and manufacturing overhead are the three major components of manufacturing costs. Expressing each part as a percentage of the total manufacturing cost, how do you think the percentages of these costs have changed over the last 50 years?

3.23 LO4 (Advanced). Give an example of a manufacturing firm where labor is a major cost component. Give

another example in which labor is a negligible part of total manufacturing cost. How do you reconcile these observations?

3.24 LO5. Assume a firm is deciding between labor hours and machine hours as a cost driver. When would these drivers yield the same allocations?

3.25 LO5. "Depreciation is nothing but an allocation of the purchase price over different accounting periods." Do you agree with this statement? If so, identify the elements of cost allocations (cost pool, cost objects, cost driver, allocation volume) implicit in the computation of depreciation. If not, identify differences between cost allocations and depreciation.

3.26 LO1, LO5. What is the most important asset for a professional services firm? Given your answer, what is a reasonable basis for allocating the costs of this "asset" to individual projects?

3.27 LO5. Usually, we think of cost allocations as the process of splitting the cost of a shared resource among its users. When might a firm allocate *revenue*?

EXERCISES

3.28 Product versus period cost (LO1). The following are some of the costs incurred by a consulting firm.

Salary paid to consultants	Fee for attending training seminar
Salary to office administrator	Corporate office rent
Cost of general-purpose software	Travel to client site

Required:

Classify each cost as a product cost (above the line for gross margin) or a period cost (below the line for gross margin).

3.29 Cost flows in a service firm (LO2). The following data pertain to Boyd Associates, a consulting company.

Revenues	$1,600,450
Gross margin	450,000
Profit before taxes	275,400

Required:

Complete a GAAP income statement to determine (a) the firm's cost to provide service and (b) its marketing and administration costs.

3.30 Cost flows in a service firm (LO2). The following data pertain to Skogg Consulting. Skogg provides advice on structural engineering for large projects such as stadiums and bridges. Clients seek Skogg out because it has extensive contacts and can find the person who is "right" for the job. This is a nontrivial task, as often fewer than 10 persons worldwide might have the required expertise. Skogg bills clients at the rate of $350 per hour plus actual expenses for travel and board. The firm draws consultants from a roster it maintains, and it pays the consultant $300 per hour. The balance of $50 goes toward administrative support. The firm expects to accumulate 9,000 consulting hours for the year and projects a profit before taxes of $230,000.

Required:

Complete a GAAP income statement to determine (a) the firm's cost to provide service and (b) its marketing and administration costs.

3.31 Cost flows in a service firm, cost classifications (LO1, LO2). Brad Timberlake is known throughout the world for his insights on effective and efficient time management. Currently, Brad offers 35 daylong seminars each year at locations throughout North America,

Europe, and Asia. The average seminar has 125 participants, each of whom pays a $400 fee. The variable costs (folder, worksheets, copy of Brad's book, and food) amount to $75 per participant. In addition, setting up the seminar itself (the use of a hotel or convention center, hotel staff, and Brad's travel expenses) costs $20,000 per seminar. Finally, Brad pays a coordinator a salary of $50,000 per year to organize his seminars and incurs $250,000 in fixed costs annually to maintain a central office and support staff.

Required:

a. Preparing a GAAP income statement for Brad's operations, calculate Brad's gross margin and profit before taxes for the year. Remember to classify all administration costs as below the gross margin and all costs connected with offering the seminar above the gross margin.

b. Classify Brad's costs as being unit-, batch-, product-, or facility-level costs, as defined in Chapter 2.

c. How does the cost classification in part (b) correspond to the classification of costs into product and period costs in part (a)? Would this correspondence between costs per the cost hierarchy into product and period costs always hold? Provide counterexamples.

3.32 Product versus period cost (LO1, LO3). The following are some of the costs incurred by a merchandising firm.

Cost of merchandise sold
Stocking goods on shelves
Cost of display cases
Store manager's salary
Transportation in
Store rental

Required:

Classify the costs as a product cost (above the line for gross margin) or a period cost (below the line for gross margin).

3.33 Cost flows in a merchandising firm (LO3). MegaLo Mart provides the following information relating to its most recent year of operations. MegaLo Mart charges off the entire cost of transportation in to the income statement for the period.

Revenues	$14,568,800
Beginning inventory, 1/1	245,600
Ending inventory, 12/31	260,400
Purchases	10,950,325
Transportation in	102,500
Sales commissions	437,064
Store rent	1,435,000
Store utilities	134,675
Other administration	879,345

Required:

Complete a GAAP income statement to determine MegaLo Mart's profit before taxes.

3.34 Cost flow in a merchandising firm (LO3). The following is a condensed income statement for Sweets & Treats, a confectionary.

Sweets & Treats
GAAP Income Statement

Item		Amount
Revenues		$2,250,300
Beginning inventory, 1/1	$125,000	
Purchases	?	
Ending inventory, 12/31	$112,400	
Cost of goods sold		?
Gross margin		$639,055
Sales & administration		?
Profit before taxes		$203,555

Required:

Determine (a) the cost of purchases and (b) costs associated with sales and administration.

3.35 Cost categories in manufacturing firms (LO4). Consider the following expenses frequently incurred by manufacturing firms.

1. Connectors used to make a product
2. Labor to machine product components
3. Steel used to make components
4. Drill bits, saw blades, and other tools
5. Salary paid to the factory manager
6. Factory maintenance costs
7. Depreciation on materials-handling equipment
8. Holiday pay paid to assembly workers

Required:

Classify each expense as being direct materials, direct labor, variable manufacturing overhead, or fixed manufacturing overhead. Please note that, for some of the eight expenses, a portion of the cost could be in one category and another portion could be in another category.

3.36 Cost classification, product versus period cost (LO1, LO4). The following costs relate to a manufacturing organization:

Sales commissions	Sales manager salary
Distribution costs	Production supervisor
Factory rent	Corporate office expenses
Product components	Supplies used in manufacturing
Direct manufacturing labor	Plant manager salary

Required:

Classify the costs as product costs or period costs. Also classify the costs as variable or fixed with respect to the volume of production. What inferences do you draw about the correspondence between the two concepts?

3.37 Inventoriable cost (LO4, LO5). The following information pertains to the production of 120,000 units of a product.

Sales price per unit	$45
Direct materials cost	$2,400,000
Direct labor cost	720,000
Factory overhead	Allocated to each unit at 140% of labor cost
Sales commission	6% of price
Distribution costs	$960,000
Selling costs	$480,000

Required:

a. Calculate the inventoriable cost per unit of this product.

b. Do you believe that the inventoriable cost is adequate for evaluating this product's profit per unit?

3.38 Cost flows in manufacturing (LO4). Ace Welding Company's accounting records show that, for the most recent year, the raw materials inventory account had a beginning balance of $24,000. During the year, Ace purchased $82,000 of raw materials. At year-end, the raw materials inventory account had a balance of $25,000.

Required:

a. What was the cost of materials issued out to work in process during the year?

b. Suppose the work-in-process account had a beginning balance of $220,000. During the year, the total manufacturing costs charged to operations (including the cost of raw materials, direct labor, and all manufacturing overhead) amounted to $800,000. The balance of the work-in-process account at the end of the year was $180,000. What was the cost of goods completed and transferred to finished goods during the year?

c. Suppose the finished goods account had a beginning balance of $40,000 and an ending balance of $85,000. Calculate the cost of goods sold during the year.

3.39 Cost flows in manufacturing (LO4). Dan Wenman makes stainless steel containers used by medical laboratories and other institutions that handle biohazards. Dan has provided you with the following data from the most recent year of operations:

Beginning balance in materials inventory	$14,000
Beginning balance in work in process	$28,200
Beginning balance in finished goods	$8,200
Purchases of materials	$86,450
Payments for direct labor	$134,500
Factory overhead charged to products	$67,250
Ending balance in materials inventory	$13,750
Ending balance in work in process	$25,400
Ending balance in finished goods	$10,300

Required:

Determine (a) the cost of goods manufactured and (b) the cost of goods sold for the most recent year. (Notice that the data do not distinguish between variable and fixed manufacturing overhead. Rather, the problem refers to the total amount as factory overhead.)

3.40 Determining job cost (LO4). Kim and Tim Landry are painting contractors. For an upcoming job, Kim and Tim estimate that they need $250 worth of paint. In addition, they expect to spend 45 person-hours on the job. Kim and Tim pay their workers $12 per hour (including all benefits). They also expect to use several brushes, scaffolding, and other ancillary items, although it is difficult to estimate this use exactly. Finally, Kim and Tim estimate that they will spend four hours in preparing the bid; this includes driving to the customer's home to evaluate the work required and going to the store to buy paint. Kim and Tim price their time at $20 per hour. In preparing bids, Kim and Tim mark up the total cost of materials and labor (including their labor) by 40% to cover administrative overhead and profit.

Required:

a. Determine Kim and Tim's bid for this job.

b. How would the cost sheet change if Kim and Tim's explicitly allocated overhead to jobs? Assume that Tim and Kim apply overhead at the rate of 20% of materials cost and 50% of direct labor cost.

3.41 Allocation mechanics (LO5). Casey Corporation is organized into three divisions: Northwest, Midwest, and Southern. The firm has provided you with the following data, pertinent to allocating its annual corporate overhead cost of $3,200,000.

	Northwest Division	*Midwest Division*	*Southern Division*	*Total*
Head count	250	300	250	800
Revenue	$50,000,000	$60,000,000	$50,000,000	$160,000,000
Profit	$2,000,000	$1,800,000	$1,200,000	$5,000,000

Required:

a. Determine the overhead cost allocated to each division if Casey uses head count as the allocation basis. Repeat the exercise with revenue as the allocation basis and with profit as the allocation basis.

b. Compare the costs allocated to the divisions under each of the three cost drivers. Why is the allocation using head count the same as the allocation using revenue? Why is the allocation using head count different from the allocation using profit?

3.42 Forming cost pools and choosing cost drivers (LO5). Alex, Mark, John, and Jason met during freshman orientation in college. They bonded almost instantly and became very good friends. During their junior year, they found a four-bedroom house for rent in a quiet residential neighborhood near their school. Alex found the house and signed the lease, fully anticipating that the others would be glad to room with him.

As the first person in, Alex chose for himself the only bedroom with an attached bath. Drawing straws for the other three rooms, Mark got the room with the best view and John got the largest room. The friends then started to figure out how they would handle the various expenses associated with living in a house. They wanted an equitable basis for allocating the rent and utilities (electricity, water, and cable TV; each has his own cell phone). In addition, they wanted to figure out a way to allocate food expenses as they anticipated cooking at home.

Required:

a. Discuss three ways that the friends could allocate the rental cost among themselves. What are the costs and benefits of each method?

b. Would you recommend that the friends choose different allocations for the different expenses? Justify your answers by indicating the change in the circumstances that triggers the need for a change in the allocation procedure.

3.43 Service firm, GAAP income statement (LO2). Green Acres is a full-service lawn service. In addition to mowing, Green Acres provides a full array of seeding, aerating, and fertilizing services. The service has recently expanded to include pruning and related care of shrubs and trees. During the fall season, the service also rakes lawns, and does miscellaneous cleanup. Noticing that his trucks and rider mowers are idle during winter, Shawn, the owner, is contemplating whether to expand the service to include snow removal.

The following data pertain to operations for the most recent year.

Revenues from lawn mowing	$525,200
Revenue from fertilizing services	$640,000
Miscellaneous revenue	$76,450
Beginning inventory of fertilizer and supplies	$34,350
Purchases of fertilizer & supplies	$395,400
Ending inventory of fertilizer and supplies	$29,460
Depreciation of lawn mowing equipment	$45,000
Equipment repair and maintenance	$78,000
Fuel and other costs	$54,000
Crew salaries	$285,600
Office rent	$82,000
Advertising	$128,000
Accounting and payroll	$45,000
Depreciation of Shawn's personal truck	$4,000

Required:

Prepare a GAAP income statement. What detail would help increase the value of this statement?

3.44 Cost flows in merchandising (LO3). The following data pertain to Natalie's Knick Knacks, a store that specializes in seasonal decorations, curios, and other collectibles.

Beginning inventory of goods	$238,600
Purchases for the year	$879,830
Ending inventory	$178,450

Natalie typically prices items at a 100% markup. That is, if she paid $30 for an item, she would price it at $60. Of course, she does not expect to sell all items at the full markup. The following represents the pattern of sales in a typical year: 10% of her sales are at the full markup, 60% of sales are with a 25% discount off the list price, 20% at 50% off the list price, and 5% at 80% off the list price. The remainder (5%) represents unsold items, breakage, and so on.

Natalie also incurs $136,800 towards the rental of her store, supplies (e.g., bags, tissue), utilities, and so on. She incurs $64,500 toward salaries paid to her employees.

Required:

Prepare a GAAP income statement for the most recent year of operations.

3.45 Allocations in merchandising (LO3, LO5). Serene Comfort sells a wide range of mattresses, beds, and other bedroom furniture. For the most recent year, they provide the following data:

Beginning inventory	$2,450,000
Cost of purchases	23,125,000
Ending inventory	2,225,000
Transportation in	179,050

The firm informs you that it has traditionally written off the cost of transportation in to the cost of goods sold account. However, the firm has a new auditor this year. This auditor insists that the cost of transportation in, a product cost, should flow through the inventory account.

Required:

a. Determine the cost of goods sold, ignoring the cost of transportation in.

b. Allocate the cost of transportation in between ending inventory and cost of goods sold, using the account values as the allocation basis. The accountant informs you that there is no need to adjust the beginning inventory value for last year's values.

c. What arguments could you make to justify the procedure in (b) as a reasonable way to deal with the accountant's objections? How, if at all, could you justify Serene Comfort's earlier action of writing off the entire amount to COGS?

3.46 Merchandising cost flows, two product lines (LO3). The Great Plains Cooperative Society (GPC) offers a wide range of gourmet foods (including organic foods) as well as an extensive selection of wine at its only store. To deal with rising costs and recent losses, as well as a major cash shortage, the cooperative store is planning to raise prices. The board has assembled the following data:

Gross sales	$4,345,800
Cost of goods sold	3,524,600
Store staff salaries	235,320
Store rental & utilities	145,290
Other miscellaneous expenses	97,000

Digging deeper, you find the following additional data:

	Wine	*Groceries*
Beginning inventory	$284,600	$145,600
Ending inventory	395,340	128,900
Purchases	1,450,240	?
Sales	?	$2,080,000

Moreover, you find that $180,000 of the salaries are directly attributable to groceries and $230,000 to the wine department. The remainder is for persons common to both departments. The store manager informs you that it is not meaningful to separate out the area devoted for wine separately as the aisles and displays are intermingled.

Required:

Prepare a brief memo to the board as background materials for the meeting. Be sure to include an income statement and possible solutions to the loss and cash crunch.

 3.47 Allocations and cost flows (LO4, LO5). Amanda Corporation makes two kinds of hulls used to make speedboats. The regular hull is model R-750, and the deluxe model is D-800. For the year, Amanda furnishes you with the following information:

	R-750	*D-800*
Beginning inventory (WIP)	$280,000	$147,500
Raw materials used	690,000	545,000
Labor used	985,000	1,342,600
Cost of goods manufactured	2,250,000	2,346,900

You also learn that Amanda incurred $1,358,500 in manufacturing overhead expenses during the year. Amanda allocates overhead to products using raw materials cost as the allocation basis. She does not distinguish between variable and fixed overhead.

Required:

Determine the value of the ending inventory of the two products.

3.48 Overhead charges and contractor pricing (LO1, LO5). Ly Tien believes that his remodeling contractor is overcharging him for materials. Specifically, Ly can get exactly the same item, sometimes even from the same store, for 20 to 30% less than what the contractor charges. Upon further investigation, Ly finds out that most skilled workers such as electricians and tile masons earn about $15 to $20 per hour. Yet, Ly's contractor bills out labor at $30–$45 per hour.

Required:

a. What might explain the difference between the contractor's charge for materials and the price at the retail store? Would a similar rationale apply for labor costs as well?

b. Contractors typically get 30 to 40% of the jobs that they bid on. Yet, many contractors will submit a bid free of charge, even though it may take them a full day's work to assemble a bid. What are the costs and benefits of asking the potential customer to pay for the work required to assemble a bid?

3.49 Unitized costs and decision making (LO5). The following is a product cost report for component A-103. The firm has received a bid to supply all needed units for $32 per unit and must decide whether to accept the bid or continue making the product. The firm has sought your help in this decision, particularly because current capacity utilization is only 40% of available capacity. The firm will need the component for six more months; the new model of its product contains a redesigned component. The firm's accountant tells you that the decision to make or buy the component will not affect the firm's total outflow for fixed overhead costs.

Materials	$12.00 per unit	
Direct labor	9.00	
Variable overhead	4.50	50% of labor cost
Fixed overhead	9.00	100% of labor cost
Total	$34.50 per unit.	

Required:

Should the firm make or buy component A-103 for the next six months?

3.50 Allocated costs and decision making (LO5). "I was losing my shirt on field service calls. My consulting firm tells me that each call is costing me $495! I have really cut back on the number of calls, and do not dispatch a technician unless the customer has called the office at least three times. Many times, the problem seems to solve itself, saving me nearly $500!" This is Grace Daughtery's response to complaints from her salespeople that their firm is acquiring a reputation for poor after-sales service. Grace's firm sells process control systems used in manufacturing and maintains them under contract. Grace is the service manager for the Midwestern region.

Upon further inquiry, you discover that indirect costs account for a large proportion of the total costs connected with Grace's operations. Indirect costs include items such as the salaries of service technicians, facility rental, trucks, office maintenance, and the cost of storing spare parts. The consulting firm went though an extensive allocation exercise to drive these costs down to individual activities such as making a field service call.

Required:

Evaluate the wisdom of Grace's decision. In your answer, be sure to describe (1) how the consulting firm might have arrived at its estimate and (2) how, if at all, Grace should use the estimate for making effective decisions. (*Hint:* Be sure to consider the time horizon over which Grace's indirect costs would be controllable.)

3.51 Allocations and GAAP inventory valuation (LO4, LO5). Pringle and Company manufactures several kinds of canoes. This past year, Pringle spent $11,750,000 on fixed manufacturing costs, $1,762,500 on fixed selling and administrative costs, and $23,500,000 on direct labor. Pringle produced 58,750 canoes and sold 55,000 during the year.

The following table provides the direct materials and labor costs for three of Pringle's canoes:

	Model X-5	Model XV-10	Model XV-20
Materials cost	$100	$175	$300
Labor cost	$300	$400	$700

Required:

a. GAAP dictates that all manufacturing costs be included in product cost. Assume that Pringle allocates fixed costs using the number of units produced as the allocation basis. Under GAAP, what is the inventoriable cost per unit of each of the three canoes?

b. Assume that Pringle allocates fixed costs using direct labor costs as the allocation basis. Under GAAP, what is the inventoriable cost per unit of each of the three canoes?

c. Compare the answers to parts (a) and (b). Comment on any differences in inventoriable cost.

3.52 Unit costs and decisions (LO4, LO5). Sheridan Manufacturing provides the following data about its three products.

Product number	A-104	RJ-95	XL-435
Units per year	10,000	15,000	12,500
Machine hours/unit	2.5	2.6	3.25
Materials cost/unit	$5.00	$6.50	$ 9.00
Labor cost/unit	$7.50	$9.60	$12.40

You also know that the firm has $39,000 in materials-related overhead, $486,200 in labor-related overhead, and $784,687.50 in machine-related overhead costs. The firm allocated materials- and labor-related overhead as a percentage of materials and labor costs, respectively. Machine hours are the allocation basis for machine related overhead.

Required:

a. Determine the inventoriable cost per unit for each of the firm's three products.

b. The firm's managers argue that the unit inventoriable cost is the floor for prices. After all, they say, the number even excludes controllable sales and administration costs. Do you agree?

3.53 Role of cost allocations, allocation mechanics (LO5). Hank, Bill, Dale, and Boomer are friends who live in northern Maine. Being frugal, they use wood-burning stoves in their homes to provide heating during winters. The friends harvest timber from land that Boomer owns. Each friend pays Boomer for the raw timber they consume at the prevailing market rate.

Each winter, the friends rent an industrial-strength hydraulic log-splitter to cut the timber into smaller logs that would fit a wood stove. Hank typically uses up 1/2 cord (the unit of measure for logs). Bill and Dale typically consume an entire cord. Boomer, who has a large house, splits 1.5 cords. Fully utilized, the log-splitter, which costs $200 to rent for the day, could split five cords of wood per day. Hank, Bill, and Boomer split the majority of their own logs; however, the friends typically help Dale split his logs because he has a tendency to throw his back out when lifting the logs into the machine.

The friends use Bill's trailer to haul the log-splitter from the rental store and from house to house. At day's end, the friends accompany Bill to return the splitter to the rental store, after which they adjourn for some "refreshments" at a nearby bar.

Required:

a. What costs would you allocate in this setting? Should Bill be compensated for the use of his trailer? Should the friends add the cost of helping Dale to the cost pool?

b. Discuss two ways the friends could allocate the cost(s) you identified in part (a). What are the costs and benefits of each method?

 3.54 Allocation mechanics, choice of driver (Challenging, LO5). Molded luggage is one of the main product lines for the Traveler Corporation. Traveler uses large molding machines to press a specially formulated chemical compound into metal molds corresponding to different suitcase sizes and shapes. The molded product is then trimmed, lined with fabric, and fitted with accessories such as locks and hinges before being packed and shipped.

The following data pertain to setting up one of the molding machines, which costs $40,000 per year.

Product (Suitcase Type)	Number of Setups per Year	Hours per Setup	Total Number of Setup Hours for the Year
24" Two-suiter	7	14	98
26" Three-suiter	2	18	36
30" Jumbo Wheeler	1	26	26
Total	10	n/a	160

Required:

a. Suppose Traveler allocates setup costs to products by using the number of setups as the allocation basis. What is the setup cost allocated to each product?

b. Suppose Traveler allocates setup costs to products using the total number of setup hours as the allocation basis. What is the setup cost allocated to each product?

c. Why do your answers for requirements (a) and (b) differ? What condition is necessary for the two answers to coincide?

3.55 Cost flows in not-for-profit organization (LO1, Advanced). Dollars for Scholars is a national organization that provides scholarships (usually $500 to $1,000 each) to qualified high school seniors pursuing higher education. The national organization sponsors independent local charities (e.g., Greater Coralville Dollars for Scholars, Clear Lake Dollars for Scholars). Each chapter raises its own money, decides on scholarships, and otherwise manages itself. Each chapter conducts a variety of programs (e.g., Battle of the Bands, Silent Auctions) to raise money.

The following data pertain to the Clear Lake DFS group for the most recent year.

Program receipts	$25,459.93
Program costs	$14,345.55
In kind donations (for programs)	2,450.00
Cash donations (not related to programs)	14,000.00
Interest income	2,396.48
Administration expenses:	
Office expenses	2,440.00
Postage and printing	845.00
Board meetings	143.50
Scholarships handed out	$23,000.00
Beginning fund balance	$47,500.00

Required:

Prepare financial statements that might be useful to the board of the Clear Lake DFS. (*Hint:* Consider preparing statements for program-related revenues and costs, sources and uses of funds, and a balance of funds.)

MINI-CASE

3.56 Cost flows and overhead application (LO4, LO5). Baber, Inc., manufactures custom scaffolding used in construction projects. The following data pertain to its operations for the most recent year:

Raw materials beginning inventory	$23,000
Raw materials ending inventory	$42,000
WIP beginning inventory	$98,500
WIP ending inventory	$76,400
Finished goods beginning inventory	$124,350
Finished goods ending inventory	$138,750
Raw materials purchased	$190,000
Labor cost	$145,000
Selling and administration expenses	$87,600
Revenues	$694,740

You also know that Baber, Inc., uses two allocation bases to charge overhead to products. It calculates a rate of 20% of materials cost for materials-related overhead. The rate for all other manufacturing overhead is 150% of labor cost.

Required:

a. Calculate the cost of raw materials issued to WIP during the year.

b. Calculate the cost of manufacturing overhead charged to production.

c. Calculate the cost of goods manufactured during the year.

d. Calculate the cost of goods sold during the year.

e. Prepare a GAAP income statement.

f. For a particular custom truss, Baber informs you that it incurred $7,800 toward materials and $12,300 toward labor costs. What is the inventoriable cost of this truss?

g. Comment on whether the value of the units as reported in the ending inventory account is a good estimate of the products' costs for decisions such as setting pricing.

Module II

SHORT-TERM PLANNING AND CONTROL: MAXIMIZING CONTRIBUTION

In Chapter 1, you learned the Plan-Implement-Evaluate-Revise (PIER) cycle, which leads us to classify decisions as relating to *planning* or *control*. In Chapter 2, you learned that more costs and benefits become controllable as a decision's horizon increases, which leads us to classify decisions as *short term* or *long term*. Exhibit II.1 integrates these two ideas.

Like breaking down a large problem into manageable pieces, Exhibit II.1 groups business decisions to provide a systematic approach to decision making. *This exhibit provides the conceptual basis for organizing the remaining chapters in this book.* We classify decisions as short term or long term, and we discuss them in Modules 2 and 3, respectively. We cover planning decisions at the start of each module and control decisions at the end of each module.

ORGANIZATION OF MODULE II

We devote Module II (Chapters 4–8) to short-term decisions. For these decisions, organizations expect to realize most of the costs and benefits relatively quickly. Capacity costs, which arise from long-term commitments related to property, plant, equipment, and personnel, are not controllable over this horizon. These costs, which we often refer to as *fixed costs*, are therefore not relevant for short-term decisions. Accordingly, short-term decisions focus on getting

the most from available resources, as well as the efficient use of these resources.

In Chapter 3, you learned how accounting systems are designed to conform to GAAP and, as such, focus on distinguishing product costs from period costs. This focus, however, frequently is not useful for decision making because it mingles controllable costs with noncontrollable costs and fixed costs with variable costs. In Chapter 4, we show you how to modify the data from accounting systems to separate fixed costs from variable costs and controllable costs from non-controllable costs.

We devote Chapter 5 to Cost-Volume-Profit (CVP) analysis, a tool based on the linear relations among costs, volume, and profit. As you will learn, the CVP relation helps with short-term profit planning, evaluating short-term decision options, and assessing operating risk.

While the CVP relation is useful for many short-term decisions, it is not well suited for solving problems arising from temporary imbalances between the supply and demand for capacity resources. In Chapter 6, we discuss how to frame and solve such short-term decision problems. We examine several common contexts, including make-or-buy, accepting a special order, and allocating a scarce resource.

Chapter 7 examines operating budgets. Budgets incorporate planning decisions on how and where to

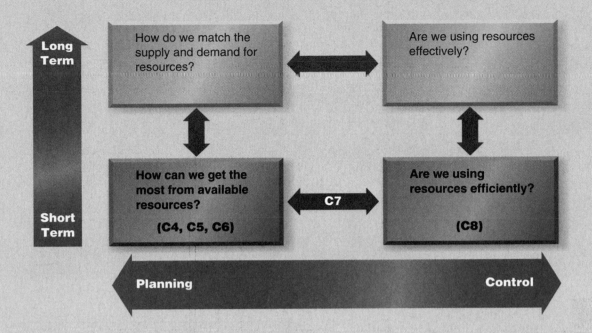

Exhibit II.1 Classifying decisions by time and planning/control provides a systematic approach to decision making.

deploy resources. Budgets also serve as the benchmark for evaluating actual results, a control decision. In this way, budgets bridge the planning and control dimensions. We underscore the tension between the planning and control roles for budgets in our discussion of both the mechanics of budgeting and the budgeting process.

The last chapter in the module, Chapter 8, focuses on short-term control decisions. We begin by introducing the concept of a variance, which is the deviation between a budgeted and actual result. We then present the mechanics of variance analysis, with a focus on using variances to reconcile budgeted and actual profit. Finally, we emphasize the link back to planning decisions by discussing how to use variances to determine possible corrective actions.

Chapter 4
Techniques for Estimating Fixed and Variable Costs

YOU NOW UNDERSTAND THAT MOST accounting systems, such as the one at Hercules, are set up to comply with Generally Accepted Accounting Principles (GAAP). Unfortunately, these systems combine controllable costs and benefits with non-controllable costs and benefits. Thus, you need to modify Hercules' system to accurately estimate the profit from offering yoga. How can you accomplish this task? More generally, how do managers modify their GAAP-based accounting systems to identify controllable costs and make effective internal decisions?

APPLYING THE DECISION FRAMEWORK

What Is the Problem?	Hercules is losing membership to the competition, Apex Health & Fitness. This erosion in membership adversely affects Tom and Lynda's goal of maximizing the profit from their health club.
What Are the Options?	(1) Offer yoga; (2) do not offer yoga.
What Are the Costs and Benefits?	We will use Hercules' accounting system to estimate the revenues and costs associated with offering yoga.
Make the Decision!	Offer yoga if it increases Hercules' profit. Otherwise, consider other options, such as karate.

Thomas Northcut/Getty Images

Tom and Lynda could use several techniques to estimate the costs and benefits from offering yoga.

LEARNING OBJECTIVES

After studying this chapter, you will be able to:

1 Prepare a contribution margin statement.

2 Use the account classification method to identify fixed and variable costs.

3 Compute fixed and variable costs using the high-low method.

4 Perform regression analysis to estimate fixed and variable costs.

5 Construct segmented contribution margin statements.

In this chapter, you will learn how to use available financial data to estimate the profit of short-term decision options, such as the decision to offer yoga. In the short-term, many costs are fixed and non-controllable. Examples include costs relating to property, plant, and equipment. In contrast, most variable costs are controllable. Accordingly, separating variable costs from fixed costs is a useful step for estimating controllable costs.

We begin this chapter by introducing the contribution margin, a concept central to short-term decisions. We then describe three techniques firms use to estimate variable and fixed costs, and therefore contribution margins, using available financial data from the systems we studied in Chapter 3. We illustrate how these techniques help firms make effective decisions. Finally, we show you how to construct segmented contribution margin statements, corresponding to individual products, customers, or geographical regions.

CHAPTER CONNECTIONS

In Chapter 5, we discuss cost-volume-profit analysis, a short-term planning tool that helps managers understand how revenues, costs, and profit vary as the volume of business varies.

Contribution Margin Statement

LEARNING OBJECTIVE 1

Prepare a contribution margin statement.

In Exhibit 4.1, we reproduce Hercules' income statement for the most recent month of operations.

Recall that Tom and Lynda use this statement for external reporting. The statement groups costs by business function. Such a functional classification is not helpful for decision making because it does not separate costs by their variability. For example, the item "costs of providing programs and services" contains variable costs such as supplies. But it also contains fixed costs such as equipment depreciation. Thus, Tom and Lynda cannot use this statement to answer questions such as "how much will costs increase if we add another 50 members?" because adding members will increase only the variable costs. The fixed costs stay the same, unless additional equipment or instructors are necessary to support the increased membership, in which case there will be a "step" increase in the fixed costs. The *contribution margin statement*, which we consider next, helps answer such questions.

ORGANIZING INFORMATION TO HELP MAKE DECISIONS

Exhibit 4.2 presents Hercules' **contribution margin statement**. This statement reorganizes the data in Exhibit 4.1, grouping costs by their variability. That is, it reports variable and fixed costs as separate line items.

The term **contribution margin** denotes *the amount that remains after subtracting variable costs from revenues*. It is the amount that *contributes* toward recovering fixed costs and earning a profit. Like revenues and variable costs, the contribution margin changes proportionately with activity volume.

The contribution margin statement is well suited to evaluate short-term decision options. As you learned in Chapter 2, an essential aspect of decision making in the short term is that the decision maker cannot change capacity. In other words, capacity costs are not controllable in the short-term. The contribution margin statement captures this aspect by separating out fixed costs, which relate to the cost of

Exhibit 4.1	*Hercules Health Club: Income Statement for the Most Recent Month*
Revenues	$80,000
Costs of providing programs and services	55,000
Gross margin	$25,000
Management salaries, marketing, and administration	15,000
Profit before taxes	$10,000

CHAPTER CONNECTIONS

Hercules reports the same profit in Exhibit 4.1 and Exhibit 4.2. This is because, as a service firm, Hercules has no inventory of finished goods. In Chapter 9, we show how inventories could cause the reported income under GAAP to differ from income reported under the contribution margin statement.

Exhibit 4.2	Hercules Health Club: Contribution Margin Statement for the Most Recent Month
Number of Members	1,000
Revenues	$80,000
Variable costs	30,000
Contribution margin	$50,000
Fixed costs	40,000
Profit before taxes	$10,000

capacity resources. Moreover, by calculating the contribution margin, the statement focuses attention on revenues and variable costs, items usually controllable in the short-term.

Now that you understand the features of a contribution margin statement, let us turn to two natural questions: *How do we use the information in Exhibit 4.2 to make good decisions? Second, how do we modify the traditional income statement in Exhibit 4.1 to prepare the statement in Exhibit 4.2?*

USING THE CONTRIBUTION MARGIN STATEMENT

Consider Tom and Lynda's problem. They hope that offering yoga will increase Hercules' membership relative to the status quo. Increasing membership will bring in more revenues, but it will increase Hercules' variable costs as well. Offering yoga also might add to fixed costs such as instructor salaries and advertising. The value of offering yoga then is the change in revenues less the change in costs.

The contribution margin statement helps us identify these components of value. Consider revenues first. Assume Tom and Lynda expect to gain 30 new members from offering yoga. From Exhibit 4.2, we know that total revenues are $80,000 and the total membership is 1,000. Thus, the monthly revenue per member is $80. Using this estimate, we calculate the expected additional revenues as 30 new members × $80 = $2,400 per month, or $28,800 per year.

Next, estimate the change in costs. The contribution margin statement separates fixed and variable costs, alerting us to differences in cost behavior. It presents total costs as the sum of (1) fixed costs and (2) the variable cost per member times the number of members. Thus, we can estimate the cost of a decision option as the sum of (1) the change in fixed costs and (2) the unit variable cost times the change in activity volume.

In most cases, we can easily identify the change in fixed costs arising from a decision. For example, Hercules needs a yoga instructor for the yoga class. The yoga instructor's annual salary of $10,000 is a fixed cost that we can trace to the

Check It! Exercise #1

Why does your estimate of the controllable fixed costs of offering yoga ignore what Tom and Lynda pay for rent? Suppose that offering yoga would permit Hercules to terminate its contract with the Pilates instructor. How would this affect the costs and benefits of offering yoga?

Solution at end of chapter.

decision to offer the yoga class. In addition, Tom and Lynda plan to spend $2,000 annually advertising the yoga program. This expenditure also increases the club's fixed costs. Combining the $10,000 in salary and the $2,000 in advertising, we can estimate the additional fixed costs connected with the yoga class at $12,000 per year.

Going back to Exhibit 4.2, we can divide the total variable costs of $30,000 by the 1,000 members to estimate the variable cost per member at $30. Multiplying this $30 variable cost per member by the 30 new members shows that variable costs would increase by $900 per month, or $10,800 annually.

Collecting annual revenues and costs, we have:

Increase in revenues	$28,800
− Increase in variable costs	10,800
− Increase in fixed costs	12,000
= Increase in profit	$6,000

We also could compute the increase in profit directly by using the contribution margin per member. Again using Exhibit 4.2, dividing the $50,000 contribution margin by the 1,000 members shows that each member contributes $50 per month toward fixed costs and profit. (We can confirm this by subtracting $30 in variable costs per member from $80 in revenue per member.) Adding 30 members would increase annual contribution by 30 members × $50 per member × 12 months = $18,000. Finally, subtracting from this amount the increase of $12,000 in fixed costs yields an increase in profit of $6,000.

ESTIMATING COST STRUCTURE

The above analysis shows how the contribution margin statement can help us make effective decisions. But, to construct such statements, we must first estimate a company's **cost structure** or, in other words, the variable and fixed portions of a company's costs.

Most firms rely on historical data to estimate their cost structure, assuming that past relations will continue into the future. As Exhibit 4.3 indicates, a systematic approach begins by examining historical data to understand the extent to which costs have varied with changes in activity levels in the past. Scatter plots, such as those illustrated in Exhibit 4.4, help in inspecting the historical data. The horizontal axis of the scatter plot represents the activity level or volume (such as membership in the Hercules example), and the vertical axis reflects the total cost. Each dot in the plot reflects the total cost incurred in a prior period for a certain activity volume.

The scatter plot in panel A of Exhibit 4.4 reflects no clear pattern. In panel B, we see that total cost appears to stay more or less the same for different activity volumes, indicating that a significant proportion of total cost is likely fixed. In contrast, panel C indicates a linear relationship between the total cost and activity volume.

Exhibit 4.3   *Methods for Using Historical Data for Estimating the Relation between Activities and Costs*

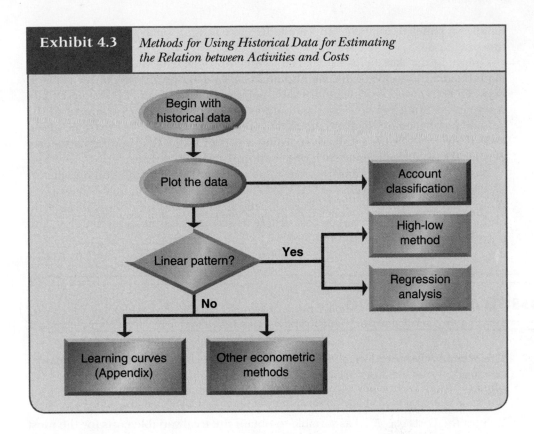

Exhibit 4.4   *Scatter Plots Reveal Relations between Costs and Activities*

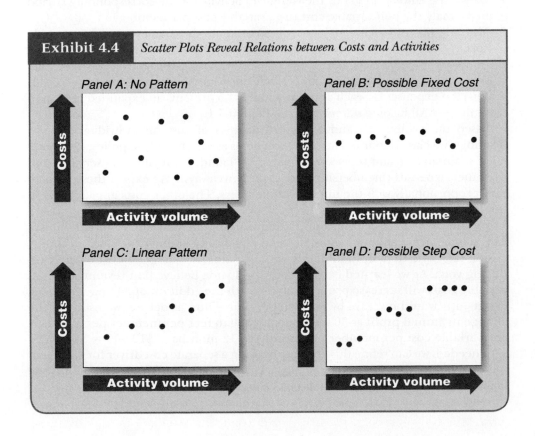

Finally, in panel D, total cost appears to be increasing in small steps as activity volume increases.

Graphing the data helps us determine the appropriate technique to use to estimate fixed and variable costs. We also obtain a visual confirmation of the relation between the chosen activity and the cost, helping us select a suitable driver. Finally, scatter plots often reveal a few data points that do not appear to conform to the general pattern emerging from other data points. Such "outliers" or extreme observations are typically the result of recording errors or unusual activities in a specific period. We usually eliminate such observations from our analyses.

Based on our scatter plot, we determine whether a linear function adequately describes our data. If the answer is yes, as is often the case, we then have to estimate the parameters of the linear equation. In the next section, we discuss three techniques that firms use to estimate cost structure: account classification, high-low, and regression analysis (see Exhibit 4.3).

Account Classification Method

LEARNING OBJECTIVE 2

Use the account classification method to identify fixed and variable costs.

The **account classification method** involves systematically categorizing a company's cost accounts as fixed or variable. We then estimate the change in variable costs as follows:

1. Sum the costs classified as variable to obtain the total variable costs for the most recent period.
2. Divide the amount in (1) by the volume of activity for the corresponding period to estimate the unit variable cost (e.g., variable cost per member).
3. Multiply (2) by the change in activity to estimate the total controllable variable cost.

We obtain the data for the account classification method from accounting records that list the expenses for each account. Exhibit 4.5 presents an expanded version of Hercules' GAAP income statement from Exhibit 4.1.

Based on Exhibit 4.5, and a detailed analysis of costs in individual account headings, we classify four of Hercules' cost items as variable: (1) supplies; (2) equipment maintenance and replacement parts; (3) laundry and janitorial services; and (4) other expenses (membership badges and giveaways). We expect these costs to vary proportionally with the number of members. The other costs appear fixed in the short term.

We can then construct the contribution margin statement shown in Exhibit 4.6. This statement is naturally a more detailed version of Exhibit 4.2.

For each line item in Exhibit 4.6, we calculate the change in cost from introducing yoga. As we learned earlier, Tom and Lynda believe that revenues and all variable costs will increase proportionately with the addition of 30 new members. Fixed costs would increase by $12,000 per year. Thus, as before, we estimate the change in annual profit as 30 members × [$80 in fees per member per month − $30 variable cost per member per month] × 12 months − $12,000 = $6,000.

If needed, we can refine this estimate by using a separate cost driver for each item rather than use the number of members as the only driver. We also could include features such as steps in costs. (In our example, we ignore these refinements for simplicity.)

Exhibit 4.5   *Hercules Health Club: Income Statement for the Most Recent Month*

Membership revenues		$80,000
Costs of providing programs and services		
Supplies (sports supplies, bath supplies)	$8,000	
Equipment maintenance and replacement parts	12,000	
Salaries for physical instructors and coaches	9,000	
Laundry and janitorial services	6,000	
Staff salaries (for member services)	5,500	
Space rental for the club	8,500	
Renting the parking space for the club	2,000	
Other expenses (membership badges and giveaways)	4,000	
Total		$55,000
Gross margin		$25,000
Management, marketing, and administration		
Management salaries	8,500	
Staff salaries (for administration)	4,500	
Marketing costs	2,000	
Total		15,000
Profit before taxes		$10,000

Exhibit 4.6   *Hercules Health Club: Contribution Margin Statement for the Most Recent Month*

Membership Revenues		$80,000
Variable Costs		
Supplies (sports supplies, bath supplies)	$8,000	
Equipment maintenance and replacement parts	12,000	
Laundry and janitorial services	6,000	
Other expenses (membership badges and giveaways)	4,000	
Total variable costs		30,000
Contribution Margin		$50,000
Fixed Costs		
Salaries for physical instructors and coaches	9,000	
Staff salaries (for member services)	5,500	
Space rental for the club	8,500	
Renting the parking space for the club	2,000	
Management salaries	8,500	
Staff salaries (for administration)	4,500	
Marketing costs	2,000	
Total fixed costs		40,000
Profit before taxes		$10,000

Connecting to Practice

GRANTS FOR RESEARCH

Many faculty members support their research with grants from governmental agencies such as the National Institutes of Health and the National Science Foundation. Private foundations also provide grants to individuals and organizations. Some, such as the Kauffman Foundation or the Sapling Foundation, specifically support socially relevant activities.

COMMENTARY: Budgetary requests for grants usually include a list of expenditures (e.g., salaries, equipment, and travel) and associated amounts. The grantor also will request periodic reports summarizing actual expenditures on these line items and the status of the funded research. Account analysis for estimating and reporting costs is appropriate in these settings. Each project is unique, and applicants do not have historical cost data they could use to estimate costs.

EVALUATION OF THE ACCOUNT CLASSIFICATION METHOD

Because account classification requires us to examine each cost account in detail, it can provide very accurate estimates. Often, this analysis requires us to plot each cost account and examine the graph to determine its behavior. While some cost items will exactly correspond to the classical definitions of a fixed or variable cost, other cost items will require considerable judgment.

The major disadvantage of the account classification method is the difficulty associated with implementing it. Consider large firms such as **General Motors** or **Microsoft.** They offer a wide range of products, use a huge number of resources in their operations, and have expansive account lists. Even with advances in computer and information technologies, the account classification task would be daunting for such companies. Moreover, there is an element of subjectivity involved in classifying costs into variable and fixed categories. Classifications frequently require considerable knowledge and experience. Incorrectly classifying a fixed cost as variable (or vice versa) could lead to substantial errors in cost estimates.

Because the account classification method is both time-consuming and subjective in nature, many firms use techniques such as the high-low method and regression analysis. Such techniques are quantitative, objective, and less time consuming to implement.

High-Low Method

LEARNING OBJECTIVE 3

Compute fixed and variable costs using the high-low method.

The **high-low method** uses two observations of *aggregate* cost data to estimate *total* fixed costs and the unit variable cost. By doing so, the high-low method avoids the need to classify individual cost items as fixed or variable, making it less demanding than the account classification method.

To understand the high-low method, let us refer back to the scatter plots in Exhibit 4.4. As we observed earlier, panel A of this exhibit reveals no clear pattern in the data as observations are all over the place. Panels B and C, though, reflect clear patterns indicating that there is an underlying "true" cost structure that relates the total cost to the activity volume. In the presence of such a definite relationship, the high-low method does a good job of identifying the fixed and variable portions of the total cost.

Exhibit 4.7 provides a graphical illustration of the high-low method. Let us assume that some "true" association exists between the total cost and the activity volume (as is the case, for example, in panel C of Exhibit 4.4). We represent this unknown true cost relation using a solid line. This line shows that fixed costs stay the same (the solid line AB) for all activity levels in the normal range of operations. The variable cost per unit (the slope of solid line AC) also remains the same. Then, for any volume of activity, total costs are:

$$Total\ costs = Fixed\ costs + (Unit\ variable\ cost \times Volume\ of\ activity).$$

Unfortunately, we do not *know* the *true* cost line; if we did, there would be no need to estimate anything! We only know actual costs and actual activities, and we must rely on these observations to *estimate* the true cost line.

In Exhibit 4.7, each observation (marked with "●") represents actual costs and actual activities for some period, such as a month. Actual activity levels vary across these periods because of demand fluctuations, causing total costs to

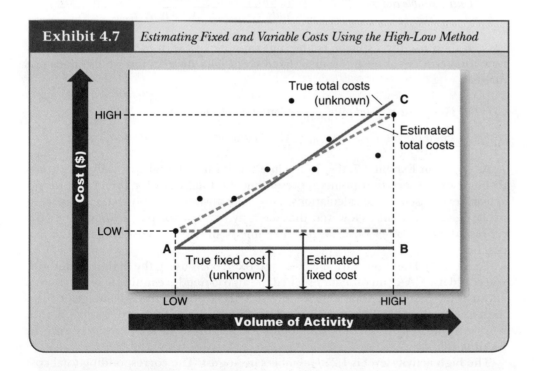

Exhibit 4.7 — *Estimating Fixed and Variable Costs Using the High-Low Method*

CHAPTER CONNECTIONS
The high-low method classifies costs as either fixed or variable. This classification is useful for short-term decisions. As a decision's horizon expands, some fixed costs become controllable. In Chapter 9, we discuss methods that firms use to estimate the change in "fixed" costs over an extended horizon.

change as well. Actual costs differ from expected costs because of changes in prices and efficiencies. The dotted line that we will construct using the information from actual costs and activities represents our estimates of fixed and variable costs.

MECHANICS OF THE HIGH-LOW METHOD

The high-low method uses two observations to estimate total fixed costs and the variable cost per unit, or *unit variable cost*. By convention, managers use the two observations pertaining to the *highest and lowest activity levels*. These values are most likely to define the normal range of operations. (As is the case in Exhibit 4.7, the observations with the highest and lowest activity levels may not be the observations with the highest and lowest costs.) We then apply the cost equation to these two points:

$$Total\ costs_{HIGH\ ACTIVITY\ LEVEL} = Fixed\ costs + (Unit\ variable\ cost \times Activity\ level_{HIGH})$$

$$Total\ costs_{LOW\ ACTIVITY\ LEVEL} = Fixed\ costs + (Unit\ variable\ cost \times Activity\ level_{LOW})$$

From these equations, we can calculate the unit variable cost as:

$$Unit\ variable\ cost = \frac{Total\ costs_{HIGH\ ACTIVITY\ LEVEL} - Total\ costs_{LOW\ ACTIVITY\ LEVEL}}{Activity\ level_{HIGH} - Activity\ level_{LOW}}$$

We can then use this estimate of the unit variable cost with *either* the HIGH or the LOW total cost equation to estimate fixed costs. The observation we use does not matter.

$$Fixed\ costs = Total\ costs_{HIGH} - (Unit\ variable\ cost \times Activity\ level_{HIGH}).$$

$$Fixed\ costs = Total\ costs_{LOW} - (Unit\ variable\ cost \times Activity\ level_{LOW}).$$

As shown in Exhibit 4.7, the dotted line for estimated total costs will always pass through the observation points representing the total costs for the high and low activity levels used in the calculations. Why? The answer is simply that the line connects these two points. However, the line may or may not pass through the "o"s representing the other observations. The line is an *estimated* cost line, not the *true* cost line.

To estimate Hercules' variable costs and fixed costs using the high-low method, you could use GAAP income statement data; all you need are multiple observations about total costs and total activity levels. This is one of the advantages of the high-low method. To help you implement this method, Tom and Lynda provide you with their GAAP income statements for the previous six months, shown in Exhibit 4.8.

The high activity level is 1,250 members in August. The corresponding total cost ($63,000 in product costs + $15,000 in period costs) is $78,000. The low activity level is 1,000 members in January, and the corresponding total cost ($55,000 in product costs + $15,000 in period costs) is $70,000. Using these two data points, we estimate the following monthly variable cost per member and fixed costs under the high-low method:

$$Monthly\ variable\ cost\ per\ member = \frac{\$78,000 - \$70,000}{1,250 - 1,000} = \$32.$$

$$Monthly\ fixed\ costs = \$78,000 - (\$32.00 \times 1,250\ members) = \$38,000.$$

Exhibit 4.8	Hercules Health Club: Income Statements for the Most Recent Six Months					
	Jan	**Dec**	**Nov**	**Oct**	**Sep**	**Aug**
Volume of Activity						
Number of members	1,000	1,075	1,100	1,150	1,200	1,250
Revenues	$80,000	$86,000	$88,000	$92,000	$96,000	$100,000
Costs of providing programs and services	55,000	58,000	58,000	59,000	61,000	63,000
Gross margin	$25,000	$28,000	$30,000	$33,000	$35,000	$37,000
Management salaries, marketing, and administration	15,000	15,000	15,000	15,000	15,000	15,000
Profit before taxes	$10,000	$13,000	$15,000	$18,000	$20,000	$22,000

Notice that we could have calculated monthly fixed costs using the low activity point, in which case our calculation would be:

Monthly fixed costs = $70,000 − ($32.00 × 1,000 members) = $38,000.

Be mindful that the fixed cost number above represents the *total* fixed costs at the current level of operations. For the decision regarding yoga, we are interested in the change in fixed costs. We focus on the change because controllability, which identifies the costs and benefits to measure, refers to the change relative to the status quo.

Recall that, for Hercules, the change in annual fixed costs for the yoga decision is $12,000. Tom and Lynda expect the yoga program to lead to a net increase of 30 members. Using the high-low method, you estimate the total change in annual variable costs as ($32 variable cost per member per month × 30 members × 12 months) = $11,520. Therefore, you estimate total costs for the year to be $12,000 + $11,520 = $23,520.

Using the high-low method, you can now project the increased annual profit if Hercules offers yoga: ($28,800 in revenues − $23,520 in costs) = $5,280. Notice that our profit estimate of $5,280 differs from our estimate under the account classification method ($6,000); we are using a different method and different data to estimate the unit variable cost.

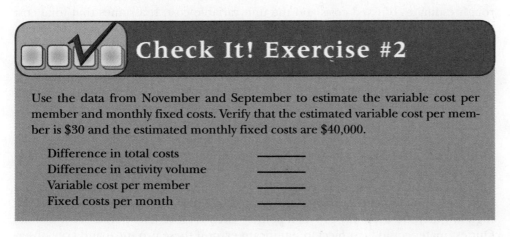

Check It! Exercise #2

Use the data from November and September to estimate the variable cost per member and monthly fixed costs. Verify that the estimated variable cost per member is $30 and the estimated monthly fixed costs are $40,000.

Difference in total costs   _____

Difference in activity volume   _____

Variable cost per member   _____

Fixed costs per month   _____

Solution at end of chapter.

Connecting to Practice

PREDICTING PROFITS AT AMAZON.COM

For the third quarter of 2002, Amazon.com reported the following numbers:

Revenues = $851.29 million
Cost of goods sold = $635.12 million, and
Profit = $216.17 million.

For the fourth quarter of 2002, Amazon.com reported:

Revenues = $1,428.68 million
Cost of goods sold = $1,093.49 million, and
Profit = $335.19 million, respectively.

Using these two points, we can estimate cost of goods sold as a function of revenues. The resulting relation is:

Cost of goods sold = −$40.67 million + (0.7938 × Revenues).

Applying this equation to actual revenues of $1,083.59 million in the first quarter of 2003 gives a cost of goods sold estimate of $819.54 million and a profit estimate of $264.05 million. These estimates are close to the numbers actually reported, $813.01 million and $270.58 million, respectively.

COMMENTARY: Using the high-low method and sales forecasts, we can predict profits at Amazon.com with reasonable accuracy. Notice, however, that our fixed cost estimate is negative. This illustrates that the estimated cost equation is only valid for the normal range of operations, which does not include zero sales!

Classifying costs as being fixed or variable can help improve decisions. (Mark Richards/ZUMA Press/©Corbis)

EVALUATING THE HIGH-LOW METHOD

The high-low method is straightforward to use. It requires only aggregate department- or company-level cost data, readily available from a company's financial and cost records. Unlike the account classification method, it does not require analysis of the data at the individual account level. We can apply the high-low method even if we know only total revenues, total costs, and activity volume.

The high-low method poses two major concerns, however. First, it yields only rough estimates of fixed costs and the unit variable cost. It assumes that total cost varies *proportionately* with the volume of activity within the normal range of operations, and that this relation *does not change from period to period.* As we discussed in Chapter 2, some costs increase in proportion to the number of batches produced (batch-level costs), or only when there is an increase in the number of products produced (product-level costs). Because the high-low method does not separate such cost items, it misidentifies batch- and product-level costs as either variable or fixed costs, reducing the accuracy of the resulting estimates. It is possible to refine the high-low method to include batch-level and product-level costs. However, such refinements are cumbersome and diminish the high-low method's simplicity and ease of use.

Second, unusual cost deviations in the HIGH and LOW observations affect the high-low estimates and could increase estimation error significantly. Recall that the high-low method uses only two data points—even if more data points are available. Our estimates could be subject to significant error if these two HIGH and LOW observations are not representative. You could reduce the error by plotting the data, using Excel or another spreadsheet program, and inspecting the plot for unusual observations. You also could guard against unusual cost deviations by generating multiple estimates of the unit variable cost using different sets of points to represent the HIGH and LOW activity levels. You could then average the estimate after discarding extreme values.

Would a more sophisticated method such as regression analysis overcome the deficiencies of the high-low method? Let us consider this question next.

Regression Analysis

Regression analysis is a statistical method for estimating fixed and variable costs. In contrast to the high-low method, which only uses two past observations to estimate fixed and variable costs, the regression method uses *all* available observations to come up with a line that best "fits" the data. (To be precise, the regression line minimizes the sum of the squared deviations between the points and the line.) Although each observation may deviate somewhat from the line, regression analysis efficiently uses the information in each observation. Consequently, this method results in the least error between the estimated and the true total cost line.

LEARNING OBJECTIVE **4**

Perform regression analysis to estimate fixed and variable costs.

Explaining the mechanics of regression analysis is beyond the scope of this book. Instead, we show you how to use Excel to fit a regression line to a given set of data. We also discuss how to interpret the results provided by Excel.

Exhibit 4.9 provides the past 12 months of membership and cost data for Hercules, starting with the most recent month. The following steps will fit a regression line to this data.

1. Open Excel. Enter the months in column A, the volume of activity (# of members) in column B, and the total costs in column C. (Use a heading, or title, for each column).
2. From the *Tools* menu, choose the *Data Analysis* option.
3. From the *Options* box, choose *Regression*.

Exhibit 4.9	Hercules Health Club: Membership and Cost Data for the Past 12 Months	
Month	**Volume of Activity (# of members)**	**Total Costs**
Jan	1,000	$70,000
Dec	1,075	73,000
Nov	1,100	73,000
Oct	1,150	74,000
Sep	1,200	76,000
Aug	1,250	78,000
July	1,240	76,250
June	1,260	77,500
May	1,235	75,500
April	1,275	76,800
March	1,300	80,500
Feb	1,280	79,000

4. You will see a dialog box, as shown in Exhibit 4.10.

    a. Enter the *y*-axis cell range (total costs) and the *x*-axis cell range (# of members) as shown.

    b. Check the *Labels* option to include the title cells in the range.

    c. Choose the *Line Fit Plots* option if you would like to see a graph of the fitted line.

    d. Click *OK*, and you should see the results (as in Exhibit 4.11) in a separate worksheet.

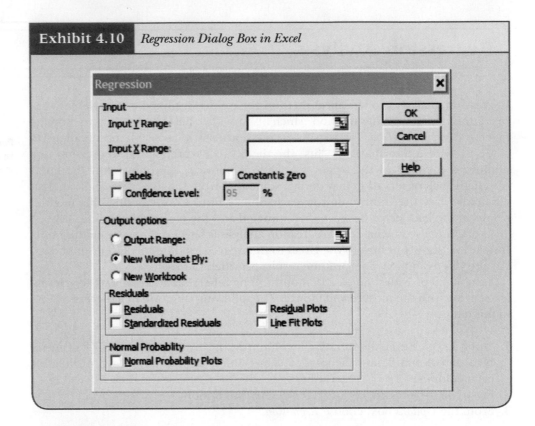

Exhibit 4.10   *Regression Dialog Box in Excel*

Exhibit 4.11   *Excel Screenshot of Regression Output*

	A	B	C	D	E
1					
2		*Regression Statistics*			
3		Multiple R	0.951128423		
4		R Square	0.904645277		
5		Adjusted R Square	0.895109805		
6		Standard Error	946.5090968		
7		Observations	12		
8					
9	ANOVA				
10		*df*	*SS*	*MS*	*F*
11	Regression	1	84993496.96	84993497	94.87158
12	Residual	10	8958794.704	895879.5	
13	Total	11	93952291.67		
14					
15		*Coefficients*	*Standard Error*	*t Stat*	*P-value*
16	Intercept	40715.87661	3611.912408	11.27266	0.01
17	Activity level (# of members)	29.30452354	3.008614941	9.740204	0.01

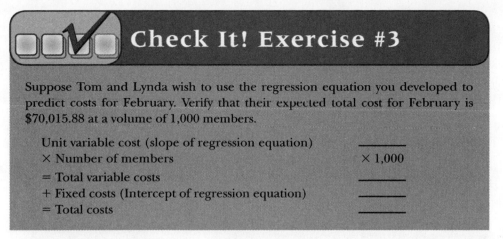

Check It! Exercise #3

Suppose Tom and Lynda wish to use the regression equation you developed to predict costs for February. Verify that their expected total cost for February is $70,015.88 at a volume of 1,000 members.

Unit variable cost (slope of regression equation)	————
× Number of members	× 1,000
= Total variable costs	————
+ Fixed costs (Intercept of regression equation)	————
= Total costs	————

Solution at end of chapter.

To interpret the results, refer to Exhibit 4.11. The first cell under the column headed *Coefficients* estimates the intercept of the line. This amount, $40,715.88, represents our estimate of Hercules' monthly fixed costs. The second cell under the column headed *Coefficients* estimates the slope of the regression line. This amount, $29.30, is our estimate of Hercules' variable cost per member per month.

Because regression is a well-defined statistical method, it provides a number of other statistics that help us evaluate the fitted line. We draw attention to the R-square for the regression and the p-value for each coefficient. The value of the R-square indicates the goodness-of-fit. The R-square will always lie between zero and one. The closer this number is to one, the better the fit. The R-Square for this regression is 0.9046, which indicates a very good fit. The p-value indicates the confidence that the coefficient estimates reliably differ from zero. Usually, we look for p-values lower than 0.05, with lower values representing tougher thresholds to meet. In other words, a p-value of less than 0.01 indicates a sufficiently high level of confidence in the estimates.

For Hercules, recall that controllable fixed costs are $12,000 and that Tom and Lynda expect the yoga program to lead to a net increase of 30 members. Using the regression analysis value of $29.30 for the unit variable cost, you estimate the annual controllable costs from offering yoga as

$$\$12,000 + (29.30 \times 30 \text{ members} \times 12 \text{ months}) = \$22,548.$$

In turn, calculating ($28,800 in revenues − $22,548 in costs), you project an increase in annual profit of $6,252 if Hercules offers yoga. Again, because we used a different method and different data, our estimate under regression analysis differs from our earlier estimates.

EVALUATION OF THE REGRESSION METHOD

A major drawback of using regression analysis is that the technique makes a number of assumptions about the data, and accounting data sometimes do not satisfy these assumptions. In these cases, users are required to correct the data or adjust the analysis. For example, one might think that expenditures on equipment maintenance are consistent throughout the year, with monthly and weekly checkups. However, firms usually schedule maintenance after periods of heavy usage. Thus, machine hours in one month might relate to maintenance expenditures in the following month. Obtaining reliable estimates also requires many observations. Overall, while we introduce you to regression analysis, we also urge caution when using it.

Connecting to Practice

STATISTICAL ANALYSIS AND CREDIT SCORING

Credit ratings influence the interest rates that consumers pay on loans. Rating agencies such as Experian provide credit scores for individuals in the United States. A poor rating could raise the interest rate on a mortgage considerably. Organizations such as Standard and Poor's provide a similar service for businesses.

COMMENTARY: Rating agencies develop and use regression models to determine the weights that aggregate these factors into a composite credit rating. In these regression models, credit rating is the dependent variable (like total costs in our cost model), and factors such as previous payment behavior, amount of outstanding debt, type of credit used (e.g., credit card versus home loan), and proportion of total available credit being used are independent variables (like the activity volume in our cost model).

CHOOSING AN APPROPRIATE METHOD

Each of the three techniques we considered for estimating fixed and variable costs has pluses and minuses. Fortunately, as shown in the accompanying summary table, all three methods show that Hercules would increase annual profit by at least $5,280 if it offers yoga. Your recommendation is clear.

Will the methods always agree? What happens if the methods lead to different choices? How should you pick the best method? Fortunately, in most instances, the three methods lead to similar results. The choice of a particular method depends on how best we can implement each of these techniques in a given setting. For example, given its ease of implementation, the high-low method may be

---

APPLYING THE DECISION FRAMEWORK

What Is the Problem?	Hercules is losing membership to the competition, Apex Health & Fitness. This erosion in membership adversely affects Tom and Lynda's goal of maximizing the profit from their health club.
What Are the Options?	(1) Offer yoga; (2) do not offer yoga.
What Are the Costs and Benefits?	It will cost Hercules $10,000 to hire a yoga instructor for the year, and Tom and Lynda plan to spend $2,000 advertising the program. Finally, Hercules expects to attract 30 new members by offering yoga. In sum, we calculated the change in profit from offering yoga as: Account classification $6,000 High-low method $5,280 Regression analysis $6,252
Make the Decision!	Based on your calculations, you expect the yoga class to increase Hercules' annual profit by at least $5,280. You recommend to Tom and Lynda that they offer the yoga class.

particularly appropriate and sufficiently accurate when the variability of costs is relatively stable over time.

We might prefer account analysis in other settings. Suppose the TB Alliance, a nonprofit organization dedicated to the development and distribution of tuberculosis drugs, is planning to open a clinic in Africa. In this case, there may not be any past data to analyze, and the high-low method and regression analysis might only be of limited use. You might find that account analysis, which helps to project the change in individual cost elements, provides the most reliable estimates. The high-low method and regression analysis might be of less use here because the underlying cost structure of the new operations might differ from the current state of affairs.

Regression analysis is particularly useful in extracting information about complex patterns in cost data. Investing in such analysis is most worthwhile for large problems that involve significant cash flows and where small errors can be extremely costly.

Keep in mind that we have focused our attention only on those costs and revenues that are quantifiable. Often, it is difficult to quantify certain costs and benefits in dollar terms. Nonprofit organizations such as the **Gates Foundation** might spend several million dollars on advertising that promotes the health benefits from vaccinations. Commercial enterprises such as **Nike** advertise to promote their image. In both cases, expected benefits are hard to express in dollar terms. The benefits of image advertising are not as measurable as those from a promotional campaign where customers must return a coupon to receive a product discount.

Similarly, organizations consider the effect on employee morale when making layoff decisions. Do the remaining employees work harder to prove they deserve to hold on to their jobs. Or does their morale drop, leading to lower productivity, increased absences, and greater job turnover? How should we include such *hard to quantify* costs or benefits? Usually, we have to rely on subjective estimates or approximations. Good managers consider tangible costs first and fold in the intangibles second, even if only on a subjective or judgmental basis. They then combine both the objective and subjective factors to pick the option that meshes best with their goals.

Remember that, for all three techniques, we assumed that revenues and variable costs are proportional to activity volume. This assumption is only valid in the **relevant range**, or the normal range of operations. In the relevant range, we expect a stable relation between activity and cost. Outside the relevant range, costs and revenues may not bear the same direct relation with activity volume, or fixed costs may change.

Consider a firm that normally produces between 1,500 and 3,000 units per month. Suppose that we estimate fixed costs at $25,000 per month and the unit variable cost at $12. Then, the estimated total monthly cost of producing and selling 2,000 units is:

Total monthly cost of producing 2,000 units = $25,000 + ($12 × 2,000) = $49,000.

Can we use this equation to predict costs for making 20,000 units a month? Using the equation, our estimate of total costs is $265,000 (= $25,000 + $12/unit × 20,000 units). However, we cannot trust this estimate. Fixed costs are likely to be much higher if the firm increases its volume of operations that significantly. Existing capacity may

Check It! Exercise #4

Verify that the total monthly cost of producing 1,600 units is $44,200 and that the total monthly cost of producing 2,750 units is $58,000.

Solution at end of chapter.

be sufficient to support only the normal range of 1,500 to 3,000 units. For 20,000 units a month, more capacity may be required, meaning that fixed costs will increase well beyond the estimate of $25,000 per month. Similarly, due to economies of scale and learning by doing, the unit variable cost may decrease if the company substantially increases output volume. In Appendix A, we discuss a more advanced technique for cost estimation in situations where learning takes place.

What does this mean for Hercules? Based on the information in Exhibit 4.9, Hercules' relevant range spans from 1,000 to 1,300 members. Tom and Lynda can be more confident when using the cost equations we estimated for a volume of 1,150 members than for a volume of 2,000 members. Outside the relevant range, both fixed and variable costs may differ significantly from our estimates.

Now that you understand how to estimate the variable and fixed portions of a company's cost structure, and how to present this information clearly and conveniently using the contribution margin format for a single product, the next step is to extend these concepts to more general settings.

Segmented Contribution Margin Statements

LEARNING OBJECTIVE 5

Construct segmented
contribution margin
statements.

Most firms offer many products and operate in multiple geographical regions. The "segmented" contribution margin statement is one way these firms modify the contribution margin statement to reflect the greater complexity of their operations.

PRODUCT-LEVEL CONTRIBUTION MARGIN

Exhibit 4.12 presents a contribution margin statement, organized by product, for Office Gallery, the merchandising firm we studied in Chapter 3. Each column in the statement begins with sales volume and revenues. For simplicity, we do not show the flow of merchandise inventory for each product. Total revenues and profit before taxes correspond to the amounts reported earlier in Exhibit 3.4. As with Hercules, for each product, the *contribution margin* equals revenues less variable costs.

For each product, we compute the **segment (product) margin** by subtracting the fixed costs traceable to that product from its contribution margin. These

Exhibit 4.12	*Office Gallery: Product-Level Contribution Margin Statement*			
	Chairs	**Desks**	**Bookshelves**	**Total**
Sales volume (in units)	45,250	32,200	52,000	
Revenues	$24,887,500	$23,345,000	$15,600,000	$63,832,500
Cost of merchandise sold	17,557,000	16,422,000	11,122,350	45,101,350
Variable transportation in	543,000	901,600	1,396,300	2,840,900
Variable selling & administrative costs	407,250	418,600	421,020	1,246,870
Contribution margin	$6,380,250	$5,602,800	$2,660,330	$14,643,380
Traceable Fixed Costs	1,950,000	1,745,000	2,857,000	6,552,000
Segment (product) margin	$4,430,250	$3,857,800	($196,670)	$8,091,380
Common Fixed Costs				4,469,690
Profit before taxes				$3,621,690

Verify that Office Gallery's contribution margin and profit would *decrease* by
$26,000 if a customer offered to buy 1,000 desks for $525 per desk.

Solution at end of chapter.

fixed costs are not relevant for decisions involving increasing or decreasing production volumes. However, these fixed product-level costs are controllable with
respect to the decision of adding or dropping a segment. For example, Office
Gallery could lower fixed costs by $2,857,000 if it decides to stop producing
bookshelves.

We compute profit before taxes by summing all segment margins and then
subtracting common fixed costs. These common fixed costs, or facility-level costs,
do not relate to any product in particular but to the entire business. They are not
controllable at the product level.

How does such detail help? Suppose that Office Gallery has a one-time offer
from a customer to purchase 1,000 chairs for $500 per chair. Even though the offer
is below the usual selling price of $550 per chair ($550 = $24,887,500 in chair
revenues/45,250 chairs sold), Office Gallery is willing to consider this offer for
strategic reasons, provided the deal does not "lose money."

Accepting the offer increases Office Gallery's revenues by 1,000 chairs × $500
per chair = $500,000. From Exhibit 4.12, we can calculate that the variable cost per
chair is $18,507,250 total variable costs/45,250 chairs = $409. Accepting the offer
increases total variable costs by 1,000 chairs × $409 per chair = $409,000. Thus,
accepting the offer increases Office Gallery's contribution margin by $500,000 −
$409,000 = $91,000. This also is the net change in profit because neither traceable
nor common fixed costs would change due to this decision.

REGION- AND CUSTOMER-LEVEL CONTRIBUTION MARGIN STATEMENTS

When constructing segmented statements, we use the term *segment* in a broad sense,
with the specific meaning dependent on the decision context. Exhibit 4.12 defines
each product as a segment. Thus, we could have used the term *product margin* instead
of segment margin. In a similar fashion, we could define a specific store, region, or
customer as a segment. The corresponding statements would yield store-level,
regional, and customer-level contribution margins and profit.

Suppose that Office Gallery sells its products throughout the United States. It
divides the country into its three primary geographical regions for organizing its
sales and distribution activities. Assume the company is considering whether to
continue its presence in a specific geographical region. For this decision, Office
Gallery would prepare a contribution margin statement that divides the firm by
geographic region, informing management of the profit by region. In this case,
each geographic region is a segment.

We could combine two or more segments into one statement. For example,
regional statements might also break out regional sales by product line. Thus, we
could identify the contribution from the sale of chairs in the Mid-Atlantic region.
In theory, there is no limit to how many segments we report. In practice, the
difficulty of determining the traceability of costs to each segment limits the detail
reported.

Connecting to Practice

SEGMENT DISCLOSURE

Johnson & Johnson reports select financial data such as sales, operating profit, and assets by its three major segments: (1) Consumer; (2) Pharmaceutical; and, (3) Medical Devices and Diagnostics. Johnson & Johnson also reports data by four geographic areas: (1) United States; (2) Europe; (3) the Western Hemisphere excluding the United States; and (4) Asia-Pacific/Africa.

COMMENTARY: We have discussed organizing information *within* the firm to facilitate effective decisions. However, firms that have significant operations in foreign countries and/or in distinct product markets *must report* investment, sales, and profit information by geographic region and/or operating segment. Regulators believe these data help an investor better value the firm's future prospects.

SUMMARY

In this chapter, we discussed how to use available financial data to estimate the profit of short-term options. Because many costs are fixed and noncontrollable in the short term, we need to separate variable costs from fixed costs. We described three techniques to accomplish this objective: the account classification method, the high-low method, and regression analysis, as well as the advantages of each method. We learned how we could use these techniques, and the resulting contribution margin statement, to make effective decisions. Finally, we learned how to construct segmented contribution margin statements for firms that have multiple products and customers or that operate in multiple geographical regions.

In Chapter 5, we build on the material in the current chapter by expressing a firm's profit as a function of price, unit variable cost, sales volume, and fixed costs. We then illustrate how to use the resulting equation for profit planning, breakeven analysis, assessment of operating risk, and short-term decision making.

RAPID REVIEW

LEARNING OBJECTIVE 1

Prepare a contribution margin statement.

- The contribution margin statement groups costs by their variability, reporting fixed costs and variable costs as separate line items. The contribution margin is the amount that remains after subtracting variable costs from revenues, contributing toward recovering fixed costs and earning a profit.

- The contribution margin statement is particularly helpful for short-term decisions because variable costs are controllable for short-term decisions, whereas fixed costs are not.

- Firms use three techniques to construct contribution margin statements: (1) account-classification, (2) high-low method, and (3) regression analysis.

LEARNING OBJECTIVE 2

Use the account classification method to identify fixed and variable costs.

- The account classification method involves systematically classifying a company's list of cost accounts into fixed and variable categories.
- The account classification method is detailed and can provide very accurate estimates if done correctly. However, it is time consuming and subjective.

LEARNING OBJECTIVE 3

Compute fixed and variable costs using the high-low method.

- The high-low method uses historical cost data to estimate total fixed and unit variable costs. The method uses two observations—the high activity level and the low activity level—to estimate the cost equation.
- The high-low method is straightforward to use. However, it assumes that the cost structure of a company does not vary over time and uses only two data points.

LEARNING OBJECTIVE 4

Perform regression analysis to estimate fixed and variable costs.

- Regression analysis is a statistical method for estimating fixed and variable costs. The regression method uses all available data to come up with a line that best fits the data.

- The major advantage of regression analysis is that it uses all available data to estimate the cost equation. It also provides a number of statistics to help evaluate the fitted equation.
- A major drawback of using regression analysis is that the technique makes a number of assumptions about the structure of the data. Accounting data may not satisfy these assumptions, requiring users to make adjustments.

LEARNING OBJECTIVE 5

Construct segmented contribution margin statements.

- Firms operating with many product lines and/or in many regions might construct a segmented contribution margin statement.
- A segmented contribution margin statement reports the following: (1) contribution margin, which equals revenues less all variable costs; (2) segment margin, which equals the contribution margin less traceable fixed costs, and (3) profit before taxes, which equals the segment margin less common fixed costs. This detail allows the firm to make decisions at the level of an individual product, segment, or the firm as a whole.

Chapter 4 Appendix
LEARNING CURVES AND COST ESTIMATION

On many repetitive projects, such as the manufacture of airplanes, ships, computers, and spacecraft, the amount of labor time required decreases with every succeeding unit. Why? As people gain experience, they can produce each unit more efficiently than the preceding one. For example, on the first unit, a worker may frequently consult a blueprint to install virtually every part. On the second unit, the worker may remember what part of the blueprint to look at in order to find out how to install a part. Eventually, the worker may simply remember where and how to install a particular part, without referring to the blueprint. Consequently, the required labor time decreases, which should also decrease labor cost.

Studies conclude that an exponential curve represents well the relation between labor time and production. Rather than going into all of the technical details, we illustrate what is termed a "doubling approach." This approach says that as the production volume doubles, the average time required decreases by a fixed percentage. For example, if it takes 500 hours to produce the first unit of production, and the product is subject to a 90% learning effect, then the average time to produce two units (a doubling of production) will be 90% of 500 hours, or 450 hours. Similarly, the average time to produce four units (another doubling of production) will be 90% of 450 hours, or 405 hours.

Notice that the calculation results in the *average* time to produce all units to date. Thus, to find the *total* time to produce the first two units, we multiply the average

Exhibit 4.13	*Example of Cost Behavior with Learning (90% Learning Effect)*	
Total Number of Units Produced	**Average Time to Produce all Units to Date***	**Total Time to Produce all Units to Date****
1	500.00	500.00
2	450.00	900.00
4	405.00	1,620.00
8	364.50	2,916.00
16	328.05	5,248.80

* The first unit takes 500 hours. Every time production doubles, we take the previous average time and multiply it by 0.90 to obtain the new average time. For example, the average time to produce 8 units = 405 × 0.90 = 364.05.

** Total number of units produced × Average time to produce all units to date.

Exhibit 4.14   *Learning by Workers Reduces Total Cost in a Predictable Way*

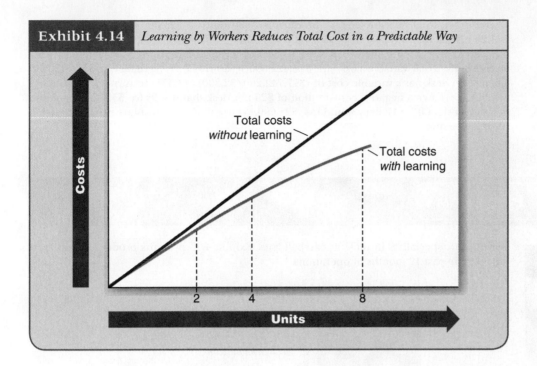

time for the two units by 2, to yield 450 hours × 2, or 900 hours. Similarly, the time to produce four units is 405 hours × 4, or 1,620 hours. Exhibit 4.13 represents costs with learning in a tabular format. Exhibit 4.14 provides the graphical intuition, showing that costs increase at a decreasing rate with learning.

If we wish to know the time to produce just the third and fourth units, we must calculate the total time to produce all four units and subtract the time to produce the first two units. In this way, we get the additional time to produce the last two units. In the example given, the last two units should require 1,620 hours − 900 hours, or 720 hours to complete.

Learning curves are an empirical phenomenon. There is little theoretical basis for figuring out why a certain learning curve exists. Organizations use prior experience to forecast learning effects and cost savings. The cost savings can be huge. For example, a handful of firms, including Intel, dominate the market for computer chips because the learning that new entrants require poses a significant entry barrier. Thus, when analyzing costs, we find it useful to ask if learning is expected and, if so, to determine its magnitude.

ANSWERS TO CHECK IT! EXERCISES

Exercise #1: Hercules' rental cost does not change by offering yoga. Hercules will incur this cost regardless of Tom and Lynda's decision. The decrease in salaries paid would be a benefit. We would include the amount as a controllable fixed cost with a negative value.

Exercise #2: Difference in total costs = $76,000 − $73,000 = $3,000; Difference in activity volume = 1,200 − 1,100 = 100 members; Variable cost per member = $3,000/1,000 = $30; Fixed costs per month = $76,000 − ($30 × 1,200) = $40,000 OR, equivalently, $73,000 − ($30 × 1,100).

Exercise #3: Unit variable cost = $29.30; Total variable costs = $29.30 × 1,000 = $29,300; Fixed costs = $40,715.88; Total costs = $29,300 + $40,715.88 = $70,015.88.

Exercise #4: Total monthly cost of producing 1,600 units = $25,000 + ($12 × 1,600) = $44,200; Total monthly cost of producing 2,750 units = $25,000 + ($12 × 2,750) = $58,000

Exercise #5: Total variable costs are $16,422,000 + $901,600 + $418,600 = $17,742,200. Thus, each desk has a variable cost of ($17,742,200/32,200) = $551. In turn, Office Gallery would experience a negative contribution of $26 per desk that it sells for $525. At a volume of 1,000 desks, Office Gallery would lose $26,000. Notice that fixed costs are not controllable for this decision.

SELF-STUDY PROBLEMS

Total costs increase with the number of bats produced. (©John Sommers II/ Reuters/©Corbis)

Gwynn, Inc. specializes in making baseball bats. Exhibit 4.15 presents production and cost data for the past 12 months of operations.

Exhibit 4.15	Gwynn, Inc.: Monthly Production & Cost Information	
Month	**Bats Produced**	**Total Costs**
January	18,500	$ 875,000
February	35,000	1,340,000
March	45,000	1,472,000
April	27,000	1,050,000
May	30,000	1,215,000
June	34,000	1,300,000
July	42,000	1,541,000
August	38,000	1,445,000
September	33,000	1,275,000
October	17,000	840,000
November	18,000	870,000
December	15,000	812,000

a. *Graph the relation between Gwynn's total costs (y-axis) and the number of baseball bats produced (x-axis). Do any particular data points strike you as being "odd?"*

The graph in Exhibit 4.16 depicts the relation between Gwynn's total costs and bats produced. Please note that this scatter plot sorts the data in Exhibit 4.15 by the number of bats produced to help us evaluate the relation between the driver (bats produced) and costs.

Two features of the data are particularly notable. First, the total cost of $1,472,000 for producing 45,000 bats in March is *lower* than the total cost of $1,541,000 for producing 42,000 bats in July. Cost has decreased even though production volume has increased! This anomaly suggests caution in using the data from March. It is possible that the firm recorded some costs incorrectly or, worse, failed to record some costs.

Second, the plot shows a somewhat marked increase in total costs when production increases from 27,000 bats in April to 30,000 bats in May (the line connecting the April and May data is steeper than any other line). This jump suggests the presence of some step costs—perhaps Gwynn needed to purchase some additional equipment or hire more salaried personnel. Detailed account analysis can help identify these specific costs.

Exhibit 4.16	*Gwynn, Inc.: Scatter Plot of Total Costs and Bats Produced*

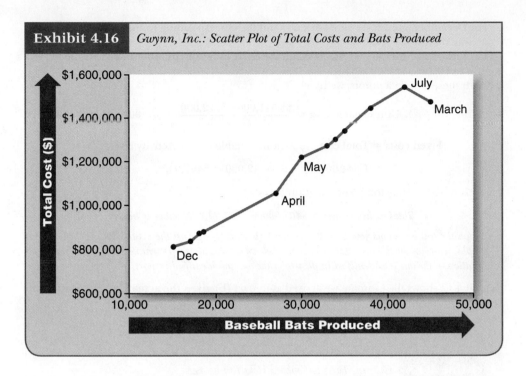

b. *Estimate Gwynn's monthly total fixed costs and variable cost per bat produced using the high-low method.*

The highest level of activity, measured in the number of bats produced, is in March (45,000 bats, total cost = $1,472,000). Recall that we identified March as being somewhat of an unusual month in part (a) and advocated caution using the data from this month. In this part, we will continue to view March as having the highest level of activity, but will address some concerns from doing so later in parts (c) and (d). The lowest level of activity is in December (15,000 bats, total cost = $812,000). Thus:

$$\text{Activity level}_{HIGH} = 45,000 \text{ bats; Activity level}_{LOW} = 15,000 \text{ bats}$$

$$\text{Total cost}_{HIGH} = \$1,472,000; \text{ Total cost}_{LOW} = \$812,000$$

The high-low estimate for the unit variable cost is:

$$\text{Unit variable cost} = \frac{\text{Total cost}_{HIGH} - \text{Total cost}_{LOW}}{\text{Activity level}_{HIGH} - \text{Activity level}_{LOW}}$$

$$= \frac{\$1,472,000 - \$812,000}{45,000 - 15,000} = \$22.00$$

$$\text{Fixed costs} = \text{Total cost}_{HIGH} - (\textit{Unit variable cost} \times \text{Activity level}_{HIGH})$$

$$= 1,472,000 - (22.00 \times 45,000) = \$482,000$$

Equivalently, we can also calculate fixed costs using Total cost$_{LOW}$ and Activity level$_{LOW}$ as

$$\text{Fixed costs} = \text{Total cost}_{LOW} - (\textit{Unit variable cost} \times \text{Activity level}_{LOW})$$

$$= \$812,000 - (22.00 \times 15,000) = \$482,000$$

The resulting monthly cost equation is:

Total monthly costs = $482,000 + ($22.00 × Number of bats)

c. *Estimate Gwynn's monthly fixed costs and variable cost per bat produced using the data from December and July.*

For December, total costs were $812,000 and the corresponding number of bats produced was 15,000.

For July, total costs were $1,541,000 and the corresponding number of bats produced was 42,000.

With these two data points, we have:

$$\text{Unit variable cost} = \frac{\$1,541,000 - \$812,000}{42,000 - 15,000} = \$27.00$$

$$\text{Fixed costs} = \text{Total cost}_{\text{JULY}} - (\text{unit variable cost} \times \text{Activity level}_{\text{JULY}})$$

$$= 1,541,000 - 27.00 \times 42,000 = \$407,000$$

The resulting monthly total cost equation is:

Total monthly costs = $407,000 + ($27.00 × Number of bats)

d. *Graph the cost equations you estimated in parts (b) and (c) against the actual data. Based on your graphs, which of the two cost equations do you believe is likely more representative of Gwynn's true cost equation— the one you identified in part(b) or the one you identified in part(c)?*

Exhibit 4.17 shows the estimate we arrived at in part (b) given the actual data for March and December.

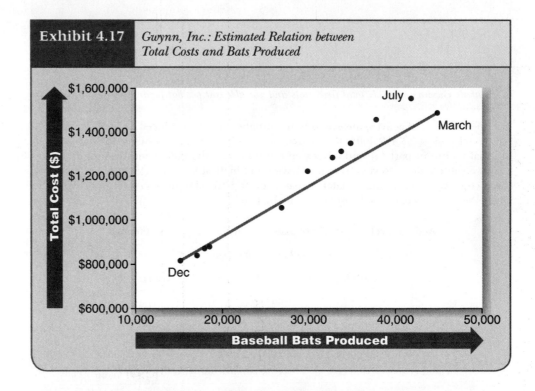

Exhibit 4.17   *Gwynn, Inc.: Estimated Relation between Total Costs and Bats Produced*

Exhibit 4.18 shows the estimate we arrived at in part (c) given the actual data for July and December.

With the exception of March, the estimate in part (c) appears to fit the data better than the estimate in part (b). That is, using the data from December and July leads to smaller differences between actual and predicted costs than using the data from December and March. (This preference occurs even though we used the month of December in both specifications.) In short, it is likely that the estimate in part (b) contains error because of the "odd" behavior of the data for March.

This scenario underscores the importance of graphing the data. Graphing the data and ensuring data reliability are crucial steps before using any technique to estimate costs. Graphing

Exhibit 4.18 *Gwynn, Inc.: Estimated Relation between Total Costs and Bats Produced*

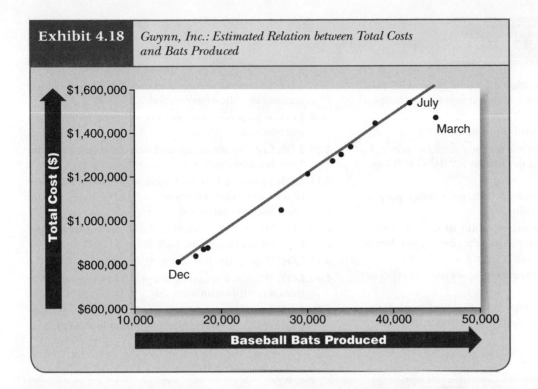

the data is an excellent way to gain intuition regarding the relation between activity levels and costs. Graphs are also useful in identifying unusual and extreme observations that should not be used in estimation.

e. *Estimate Gwynn's monthly total fixed costs and variable cost per bat produced using regression analysis. Follow the steps outlined in the chapter and use all available data.*

Following the steps outlined in the chapter, we arrive at the following cost equation using regression analysis.

Total monthly costs = $411,422 + ($25.81 × Number of bats)

This estimate is "closer" to the estimate we arrived at in part (c), further increasing our confidence that the cost equation we arrived at in part (c) better represents Gwynn's costs than the cost equation we arrived at in part (b).

GLOSSARY

Account classification method A cost estimation technique that involves systematically classifying a company's list of cost accounts into fixed and variable categories.

Contribution margin Revenues less variable costs.

Contribution margin statement An income statement that groups costs by their variability, reporting variable costs and fixed costs as separate line items.

Cost structure The proportion of total costs that are fixed and variable.

High-low method A cost estimation technique that uses two observations pertaining to the highest and lowest activity levels to estimate fixed and variable costs.

Regression analysis A statistical method that uses all available observations to estimate fixed and variable costs.

Relevant range A firm's normal range of operations. Over this range, we expect a stable relation between activity and cost.

Segment (product) margin The contribution margin of a segment (e.g., product, customer, geographical region) less traceable fixed costs.

REVIEW QUESTIONS

4.1 LO1. Why is the traditional income statement, used for financial reporting, often not helpful for decision making?

4.2 LO1. What is the contribution margin?

4.3 LO1. How does the format for the contribution margin statement differ from the format for the GAAP-based income statement?

4.4 LO1. Does the contribution margin change proportionally with activity volume?

4.5 LO1. How does the organization of data in a contribution margin statement help firms make better decisions?

4.6 LO2. What are the three techniques used to estimate costs?

4.7 LO2. What three steps are followed under the account classification method to estimate the change in variable costs?

4.8 LO2. List one advantage and one disadvantage of the account classification method.

4.9 LO3. Which two observations are used by the high-low method?

4.10 LO3. List one advantage and one disadvantage of the high-low method.

4.11 LO3. In contrast to the high-low method, how many observations does regression analysis use to estimate fixed and variable costs?

4.12 LO4. What are two statistics that help us evaluate the results from regression analysis?

4.13 LO4. What is the relevant range?

4.14 LO5. What is a segment margin? How does it differ from a contribution margin?

4.15 LO5. List three possible ways in which a company might wish to segment its contribution margin income statement.

DISCUSSION QUESTIONS

4.16 LO1. Which of the following would trigger a larger decrease in unit contribution margin: a 5% decrease in the selling price or a 5% decrease in variable costs? Why?

4.17 LO1. Why might investors prefer an income statement in the gross margin format even though managers might prefer to organize the data in the contribution margin format?

4.18 LO1. Why is the contribution margin statement more useful for making short-term decisions than it is for long-term decisions?

4.19 LO1. How can plotting the data help improve cost estimation?

4.20 LO1. Suppose you are plotting monthly data (12 observations) from last year. Why might you wish to sort the data by activity volume before plotting it? That is, why might you not use months as the *x*-axis in your graph?

4.21 LO2. Why is account classification a preferred method for estimating costs when submitting a proposal for grant funding? For example, a not-for-profit organization might apply to the Gates Foundation for a program grant.

4.22 LO2. A manager might not be as confident in her ability to estimate costs for large, one-of-a-kind projects as for smaller decisions that are of a routine nature. Yet, we might prefer account classification for large projects and mechanical methods such as the high-low method for smaller, routine decisions. Explain this seeming inconsistency.

4.23 LO3. As discussed in the chapter, the accuracy of the cost estimates derived using the high-low method depends crucially on picking the "right" observations.

How can you visually verify that the high and low data points are "representative?"

4.24 LO2, LO3. Can you identify two reasons why the high-low estimate of Hercules' variable cost per member differs from the account classification estimate?

4.25 LO3. "It is important to remove outliers in the high-low method because we only use two observations. Removing extreme observations that might not skew results is not as important when using regressions because an outlier is only one of many observations." True or False? Explain.

4.26 LO4. Going back to obtain historical data from many years is one way to increase the number of data points we use in a regression. What are the potential issues with this approach?

4.27 LO4 (Advanced). How could we include batch- and product-level activities in regression analysis? Is it appropriate to interpret the intercept as "facility-level costs?"

4.28 LO4 (Advanced). Gyms such as Hercules often offer both individual and family memberships. For example, a family membership would give access up to four individuals, but the family membership will cost less than four individual memberships. How does this feature affect the estimation methods described in this chapter? What additional assumptions, if any, do we need to implement these methods?

4.29 LO5. Does it make sense to construct a contribution margin statement by customer? Why or why not? What kinds of decisions might such a statement facilitate?

4.30 LO5. If a firm drops a product line, it will lose the revenue from that product. This loss is controllable and direct with respect to the decision to keep or drop the product. Dropping a product might also affect the sales of the firm's other products. Give two examples—one where the spillover effect increases the revenue from other products and one where the spillover effect decreases the revenue from other products. Are these spillover effects controllable and direct to the decision to drop the product?

4.31 LO5. Browse the Web site of General Electric Corporation (http://www.ge.com) or another firm of your choice. Locate the *Investor relations* section and browse the latest annual report. Can you identify the data reported by segments? (*Hint:* These data are often reported in the "notes to the financial statements," with the results being discussed in the "management discussion and analysis.")

EXERCISES

4.32 Contribution margin statement (LO1). Suppose a firm provides you with the following information for the most recent period of operations: (a) Sales = 500 units; (b) Revenues = $15,000; (c) Variable manufacturing costs = $5,000; (d) Variable selling and administrative costs = $1,000; (e) Fixed manufacturing costs = $6,000, and; (f) Fixed selling and administrative costs = $2,000.

Required:

Calculate both the unit contribution margin and contribution margin, and prepare a contribution margin statement.

4.33 Contribution margin statement (LO1). The following is the income statement from Ajax Corporation, a merchandising firm.

Ajax Corporation Income Statement for the Most Recent Year

Revenue	$1,525,000
Cost of goods sold	900,000
Transport in	24,500
Gross margin	$600,500
Administration costs	220,000
Selling costs	240,000
Profit	$140,500

You learn that $18,000 in transport in represents fixed costs, and Ajax pays its sales persons a commission of 6%. That is, a person selling $1,000 worth of items would earn a commission of $60.

Required:

Prepare an income statement in the contribution margin format.

4.34 Contribution margin statement (LO1). Jindal Manufacturing Company provides you with the following income statement.

Jindal Manufacturing Company Income Statement for the Most Recent Year

Revenue	$2,435,000
Cost of goods sold	1,246,760
Gross margin	$1,188,240
Administration costs	425,000
Selling costs	558,950
Profit	$204,290

You learn that Jindal incurred manufacturing overhead costs of $248,750 for the year and that all of this cost is fixed. Moreover, the only variable selling costs are sales commissions at 5% of revenue. Finally, all administration costs are fixed.

Required:

Prepare an income statement in the contribution margin format. For simplicity, assume that the Jindal began and ended the year with zero inventories of any kind.

4.35 Cost estimation: Account classification (LO2). Dean Previts is considering increasing the number admitted into an MBA program from 400 to 450. He anticipates that the increase will add eight sections in total. Staffing ratios have usually run about 1 staff person per 50 students.

Required:

Using account classification, estimate the increase in the following costs because of the decision to increase enrollment.

Student related variable costs	$2,500 per student per year
Faculty related costs	$150,000 per faculty member.

Each professor teaches four sections per year.

Administration costs	$60,000 per full time employee
Building maintenance	$150,000 per year

4.36 Cost estimation: Account classification (LO2). Mega Manufacturing is considering whether to increase the production of one of its products, the Mega Rototiller. The product has done better than expected, and management wishes to figure out the costs of increasing production (and sales) from 10,000 units to 12,500 units per month.

The following data pertain to the current production of 10,000 units per month.

Number of Units	10,000	Detail
Materials and components	$120,000	Traced
Direct labor	115,000	Traced
Supplies	11,500	Determined as 10% of labor cost
Oils and lubricants	4,500	At $1.50 per machine hour
Machine depreciation	67,500	At $22.50 per machine hour
Plant heating and lighting	20,000	Based on area occupied
Plant rental	12,000	Based on area occupied
Freight out	2,500	Actual cost
Sales commissions	20,000	At 4% of sales revenue
Sales office administration	25,000	Allocated based on sales $
Corporate office costs	2,400	Allocated based on head count
Total product cost	$400,400	

Required:

Determine the expected increase in costs if Mega decides to produce 12,500 units per month. This increase would last for two months, and then Mega would revert to its production level of 10,000 units per month. Be sure to consider the nature of the cost and its controllability in your answer.

4.37 Cost estimation: Account classification (LO2). MidWest University offers executive MBA programs in Singapore. The dean has charged you with estimating the cost of offering the program. You identify the following:

Item	Detail
Tuition revenue	$35,000 per participant. 40 participants expected.
Partner fee	The partner in Singapore takes 35% of revenue. In return, the partner provides all marketing, student recruitment, local logistics, and classrooms.
Instructor costs	$20,000 paid as salary to instructor. Travel reimbursed on actual cost basis, averaging $4,500 per trip. The program comprises 16 classes.
Textbooks, copies, and so on	These costs amount to $200 per student per course.
Administration costs	Between them, the dean and the associate dean make three trips costs per year (cost: $6,500 per trip). They also estimate that the work at the U.S. location accounts for 1.5 full-time equivalent (FTE) employees (average salary: $54,000). The dean estimates that she spends 5% of her time on this program and the associate dean spends 10% of his time on the program. The dean earns $350,000, and the associate dean $225,000 per year.

Required:

a. Prepare a statement that shows (a) the contribution margin, (b) the program margin, and (c) the profit margin (after including allocated costs) for the Singapore program. Identify decisions for which (a) the contribution margin would be the focus and (b) the program margin is the relevant amount.

b. A local firm in Singapore has offered to enroll three of its managers in the program but only if the program reduces the fee to $25,000 per participant. Estimate the net increase in profit if the university accepts this offer.

4.38 **Cost estimation: High-low method (LO3).** Silk Flowers & More is an on-line company that specializes in selling silk flower arrangements, offering their customers free shipping on all orders. Management currently is interested in understanding how shipping costs vary with the number of flower arrangements sold. To this end, they have provided you with the following data for the most recent five months of operations:

Month	Flower Arrangements Sold	Shipping Costs
January	5,000	$27,500
February	7,500	$33,750
March	6,000	$30,250
April	6,500	$31,000
May	7,000	$32,375

Required:

a. Use the high-low method to estimate Silk Flowers & More's monthly shipping cost equation.

b. Assume Silk Flowers & More expects to sell 5,500 flower arrangements in June. Use the cost equation you developed in part (a) to estimate Silk Flowers & More's June shipping costs.

c. Discuss why management of Silk Flowers & More would want an estimate of the cost equation for monthly shipping costs.

4.39 **Cost estimation: High-low method (LO3).** Ginsburg and Company provide you with the following data:

Month	Supervision Cost	Labor Hours	Machine Hours
January	$27,500	2,400	5,040
February	$27,500	2,560	5,300
March	$32,540	3,360	6,600
April	$30,000	2,880	6,500
May	$32,630	3,300	6,750

Required:

a. Use the high-low method to estimate Ginsburg's monthly fixed supervision cost and the cost per labor hour. (i.e., assume Ginsburg uses labor hours as its measure of activity).

b. Use the high-low method to estimate Ginsburg's monthly fixed supervision cost and the cost per machine hour (i.e., assume Ginsburg uses machine hours as its measure of activity).

c. Which of the two estimates, the answer to question (a) or question (b), is likely to be more representative of actual cost behavior?

d. Why might a manager believe that neither equation is a good way to estimate supervision costs?

4.40 **Cost estimation: High-low method, decision making (LO3, LO1).** Frame & Show is the name Megan Dee selected for her custom framing shop. Megan opened Frame & Show two years ago and has seen a steady improvement in her business. Megan's customers really seem to appreciate the extensive range of moldings and mat boards Frame & Show offers as well as Megan's artistic talents in frame design. Condensed income statements for Frame & Show's first two years of operations follow:

	Year 1	Year 2
Number of items framed	3,000	3,500
Total revenue	$318,000	$371,000
Total costs	$310,000	$332,500
Profit before taxes	$8,000	$38,500

Both the average frame price and Megan's cost structure have remained the same during Frame & Show's first two years of operations and Megan believes they are likely to remain the same in the near future.

Required:

a. Use the high-low method to estimate Frame & Show's annual cost equation (i.e., use the data from years 1 and 2 to estimate Frame & Show's annual fixed costs and variable cost per framing).

b. Megan has been asked to participate in the local "Thieves Market." If she decides to participate in the market then, in addition to the variable cost of each framing, Megan will have to pay a booth fee of $2,500 to the sponsors. Megan estimates that, above and beyond her normal business, she will also be able to sell 150 framings at the market. By how much is Frame & Show's profit expected to change if Megan participates in the Thieves Market?

4.41 Regression method for estimating the cost equation (LO4). Refer to the previous exercise, Silk Flowers & More.

Required:

a. Use the regression method to estimate Silk Flowers & More's monthly shipping cost equation.

b. Assume Silk Flowers & More expects to sell 5,500 flower arrangements in June. Use the cost equation you developed in part (a) to estimate Silk Flowers & More's June shipping costs.

4.42 Regression method for estimating the cost equation: Interpreting regression output (LO4). The GPS Company is trying to derive a cost equation that predicts its monthly materials-handling costs. GPS estimated the following two equations using regression analysis.

Equation 1:
Materials-handling costs per month = $24,543.34 + ($0.027 × value of materials handled)

R-square = 54.17%
Both coefficients have *p*-values of 0.05 or lower.

Equation 2:
Materials-handling costs per month = $12,452.56 + ($10.45 × number of material moves)
R-square = 76.34%
Both coefficients have *p*-values of 0.01 or lower.

Required:

Which of these two equations do you believe better predicts GPS's monthly materials-handling costs? Why?

 4.43 Regression method for estimating the cost equation: Interpreting regression output (LO4). O'Conner and Company provide you with the following data regarding their transportation costs.

Month	Number of Cases Shipped	Total Costs
January	1,200	$13,750
February	1,440	$15,500
March	1,680	$16,250
April	2,100	$17,000
May	2,400	$17,500
June	2,640	$18,500
July	2,880	$20,000
August	3,000	$20,313
September	2,400	$18,125
October	1,920	$16,250
November	1,500	$15,000
December	1,320	$21,250

Required:

a. Using regression analysis, estimate O'Conner's monthly fixed costs and the cost per case shipped.

b. Evaluate the goodness of fit of the regression equation.

4.44 Organizing information for decision making: Creating a product contribution margin statement (LO5). Caylor Company is a biotechnology firm that specializes in developing drugs based on monoclonal antibodies. The firm has obtained FDA approval for two drugs: RX-560 and VR-990. RX-560 is a recent approval and commands a premium price. In contrast, competition from superior formulations and from generic drugs is eroding the market for VR-990.

The firm provides you with the following information from its most recent income statement. While the income statement conforms to Generally Accepted Accounting Principles, management wishes to redo the income statement to provide better information for making product-level decisions.

Caylor Company
Income Statement for the Most Recent Year

Revenues	$17,400,000
Cost of goods sold	4,840,000
Gross margin	$12,560,000
Selling, general and administrative (SG&A) expenses	12,270,000
Profit before taxes	$290,000

You also collect the following product-specific information:

	RX-560	VR-990
Number of doses sold	180,000	2,000,000
Price per dose	$30	$6
Variable manufacturing cost per dose	$3	$1
Variable SG&A cost per dose	$4	$4
Traceable fixed manufacturing costs	$500,000	$500,000
Traceable fixed SG&A costs	$1,000,000	$1,350,000

Finally, you determine that Caylor spent a total of $2,500,000 on fixed costs common to both products (i.e., the $2,500,000 is not directly traceable to either product). Of this amount, Caylor spent $1,300,000 on manufacturing costs and the remaining $1,200,000 on SG&A costs.

Required:

a. Create a product-level contribution margin statement for Caylor Company.

b. How might Caylor use the product contribution margin statement to make better decisions?

4.45 Organizing information for decision making: Creating segmented contribution margin statements (LO5). The Omega Corporation sells two different lines of bathroom fixtures: standard and deluxe. Omega began its operations in the eastern part of the United States and recently expanded its operations to the western United States.

Omega has provided you with the following monthly sales and variable cost data by product and geographical region:

Product	Revenue per Month Eastern Region	Revenue per Month Western Region	Variable Manufacturing Costs*	Variable Selling Costs*
Standard	$1,000,000	$400,000	55%	3%
Deluxe	$1,000,000	$200,000	75%	2%

* As a percentage of sales revenue.

In addition to the above information, you find that Omega currently spends $750,000 each month on fixed costs. By geographical region, $250,000 of the $750,000 is traceable to the Eastern region and $225,000 is traceable to the Western region. The remaining $275,000 is not traceable to either region. By product, $275,000 of the $750,000 is traceable to the Standard line, whereas $225,000 is traceable to the Deluxe line. The remaining $250,000 is not traceable to either product.

Required:

a. Create a monthly contribution margin statement by geographical region (Eastern and Western) for the Omega Corporation.

b. Create a monthly contribution margin statement by product (Standard and Deluxe) for the Omega Corporation.

c. How might the contribution margin statements you created in parts (a) and (b) assist Omega's management in making better decisions?

4.46 Learning curves (Appendix). Atman Enterprises assembles satellites using customer-supplied parts and materials. A customer has asked Atman to bid on a new model of satellites and estimates purchasing eight units. Atman believes that it would take 20,000 hours to assemble the first satellite. Atman's labor cost is $25 per labor hour.

Required:

a. Determine the total number of hours required to assemble all eight satellites, assuming no learning takes place. What is the associated labor cost?

b. Repeat requirement (a) assuming that Atman expects to realize a 90% learning curve for such jobs.

c. Comparing your answers for parts (a) and (b), what conclusions do you draw about the importance of including the effects of learning when bidding for jobs?

PROBLEMS

4.47 Cost estimation: Hierarchical cost structure and account classification (LO1, LO2). When she was a child, Amy Nicholson spent a lot of time in Southeast Asia. Consequently, Amy is well versed in the local languages (she is fluent in Thai and Tagalog) and customs. Over time, Amy has parlayed her experience and expertise into a profitable business: she organizes tours to Southeast Asia for vacation travelers from North America. Not surprisingly, Amy's profit depends a great deal on the number of tours she organizes. Amy charges $4,000 per person and can accommodate a maximum of 50 persons per tour. While she seeks to fill up each tour, some tours have less than 50 persons. Amy cancels the tour if she has fewer than 35 persons. Amy estimates that each tour costs $98,000 to set up and organize. This cost is in addition to the variable cost of $1,200 she incurs for each person on the tour. Finally, Amy incurs fixed expenses of $50,000 per quarter to maintain her central office in Carmel-by-the-Sea, California.

Required:

a. Classify each of Amy's three types of costs (cost per person, per tour, and per quarter) as per the cost hierarchy.

b. Using your cost classifications from part (a), calculate Amy's total quarterly costs if (1) she has two tours with 40 persons per tour, and (2) she has five tours with 50 persons per tour.

c. Why would Amy cancel a tour if it has fewer than 35 persons?

4.48 Cost estimation: Account classification, allocations (LO2, Advanced). Shringar Industries is a leading manufacturer of cosmetic products. The following data concern one of the firm's products:

	Sales Volume	
Item	10,000 units	12,000 units
Direct materials	$2.50	$2.50
+ Direct labor	2.14	2.14
+ Departmental overhead: Direct	0.45	0.45
+ Departmental overhead: Indirect	3.10	2.58
+ Factory overhead	2.14	2.14
= Factory cost	10.33	9.81
+ Selling & administration overhead	3.62	3.43
= Total cost per unit	$13.95	$13.24

You know that Shringar allocates factory overhead based on labor cost and that the charge for selling and administration cost is 35% of factory cost. Digging deeper, you learn that direct departmental overhead comprises supplies and other consumables. The indirect overhead is traceable to the product as it represents the cost of direct supervision.

Required:

Shringar has been producing 10,000 units per month. Suppose, for the next month alone, the firm wishes to increase its level of production from 10,000 to 11,500 units per month. Determine the controllable costs the firm should use for this decision. That is, what is the cost of increasing production by 1,500 units?

4.49 Cost estimation: Account classification and hierarchical cost structure, decision making (LO1, LO2). Comfort Pillows makes "ultra-luxury" goose-down pillows encased in 500-thread count fabric. In recent years, Comfort Pillows has operated at only 60% of its available capacity. Spooked by market volatility, many persons in Comfort Pillows' target market have scaled back on ostentatious purchases. As a result, the firm currently is producing only 12,000 pillows per month rather than the 20,000 pillows it could produce. Comfort Pillows makes its pillows using labor paid on an hourly basis. While machine capacity is difficult to adjust in the short term, it is easy to adjust the amount of labor.

Seeking to make gainful use of its machine capacity, Comfort Pillows is considering an order from a high-end department store. The department store wants Comfort to make 5,000 pillows. The department store will sell the pillows under its own brand name. Comfort Pillows has asked you to analyze its accounts and prepare a price estimate. The firm plans to arrive at its selling price by adding a 25% markup to the controllable costs associated with accepting the order. The following data are available:

Item	Cost
Fabric	$2.50 per pillow
Fill	$18.00 per pillow
Industrial sewing machines	1/2 hour per pillow; the long-term lease cost is $100,000 per year; Comfort Pillows has enough sewing machines to produce 20,000 pillows per month.
Labor	1/2 hour per pillow; labor costs $12 per hour.
Plastic wrap & other packing	$0.50 per pillow
Cartoning & crating	$10.00 per 25 pillows.
Transportation	$1,500 for a truckload of 2,500 pillows
Purchasing & manufacturing support	$32,500 for 12,000 pillows per month. Comfort expects this cost to increase by $15,000 per month (to $47,500 per month) if volume increases to 15,000 or more pillows per month.
Advertising brochures	$150,000 per year
Office expenses	$300,000 per year. The current office staff can support a volume of 20,000 pillows per month.
Sales & customer support	$200,000 per year for 250 customers. The department store is not a regular customer. Comfort expects to spend a total of $1,000 in arranging logistics and incorporating the department store into its regular client list.

Required:

a. Classify each of the cost items as being controllable (C) or noncontrollable (NC) for pricing the department store's order. Next, calculate the price per pillow, assuming Comfort Pillows adds a 25% markup to the controllable costs associated with accepting the order.

b. What is the price per pillow if the department store's order is for 4,000 pillows?

4.50 Cost estimation: High-low method, relevant range (LO3). Although only open for one year, Pizzeria Paradise has established a reputation as serving excellent deep-dish pizza and recently won a "Best of City" award. Management is interested in using the data from the first year of operations to estimate the firm's cost structure. To this end, they have provided you with the following data for the first four quarters of operations:

Quarter	Number of Pizzas Sold	Total Costs
First	25,000	$115,000
Second	30,000	$150,000
Third	35,000	$175,000
Fourth	40,000	$190,000

Required:

a. Use the high-low method to estimate Pizzeria Paradise's quarterly cost equation (i.e., use the high-low method to estimate Pizzeria Paradise's quarterly fixed costs and variable cost per pizza).

b. How would you interpret the estimate of fixed costs if it were below zero?

c. Use the cost equation you developed in part (a) to predict Pizzeria Paradise's total quarterly costs for a volume of 50,000 pizzas. How confident are you in your estimate of total quarterly costs?

4.51 Cost estimation: High-low method, relevant range (LO3). Zap, Inc., manufactures and sells a broadleaf herbicide that kills unwanted grasses and weeds. Via their television commercials, Zap encourages homeowners to "take control of their yard" by purchasing one of their "ZAP" kits for $39.95. Each "ZAP" kit includes a 32-ounce bottle of weed and grass killer concentrate and a 16-ounce bottle of poison ivy and tough brush killer concentrate. A review of the firm's production and cost data for the previous four quarters revealed the following:

Quarter	ZAP Kits Sold	Total Costs
First	5,400	$187,800
Second	9,600	$268,200
Third	6,000	$192,000
Fourth	4,500	$181,500

Required:

a. Use the high-low method to estimate Zap's quarterly cost equation (i.e., use the high-low method to estimate Zap's quarterly fixed costs and variable cost per ZAP kit sold).

b. Using the four data points provided, graph Zap's total costs (*y*-axis) as a function of the number of ZAP kits sold (*x*-axis). Does any particular data point strike you as being unusual?

c. Since the data point for the second quarter appears to be "different" from the other data points, you decide to ask management whether anything unusual occurred in this quarter. Management informs you that, similar to prior years, the firm runs extra advertising in the second quarter, just before the peak summer months when weeds are most active. How does this information affect your analysis? Reestimate Zap's quarterly cost equation, ignoring the data from the second quarter. Use this new cost equation to estimate the amount Zap spent on extra advertising during the second quarter.

d. What inferences do you draw about graphing the data and ensuring data validity before estimating a firm's cost structure?

4.52 Cost estimation: Step costs, multiple cost drivers (LO2, LO3; Advanced). Carlton Stokes owns and operates a car-detailing business named "SuperShine & Detailing." For $150, Carlton's business will hand wash and wax customers' cars, vacuum the interior, and thoroughly clean the upholstery, wheels, tires, and windows. In addition, Carlton's business will pick up each customer's car in the morning and return it to the customer's workplace or home, as instructed.

Buoyed by the success of his first shop, Carlton plans to expand his business to another location. Similar to his current location, Carlton is committed to using only full-time employees at the new location. As his business expands, Carlton believes it will become increasingly important to understand his cost structure. To this end, he seeks your help in estimating his fixed costs, the variable cost of detailing a car, and the annual cost per employee. Carlton has provided you with the following data for the most recent three years of operations at his present location:

Year	Cars Detailed	No. of Employees	Total Costs
1	1,200	2	$129,000
2	1,600	2	$137,000
3	2,400	3	$183,000

Carlton believes that his cost structure has not changed over the last three years and that one employee, working diligently, can detail three cars per day. SuperShine & Detailing is open for business 300 days a year.

Required:

a. How does the cost of employees vary with the number of cars detailed? Is the cost of employees a fixed cost, a variable cost, or a step cost? Why?

b. Using the data provided, estimate Carlton's annual fixed costs, the annual cost per employee, and the variable cost per car detailed.(*Hint:* Notice that two of the three years have the same number of employees.)

4.53 Cost estimation: Contrasting high-low and account classification methods (LO2, LO3; Continuation of Comfort Pillows). As an alternative to the detailed account analysis, management at Comfort Pillows desires to use the high-low method to estimate the variable cost associated with producing a pillow. The firm plans to add 25% to the variable cost to arrive at the price charged to the department store. Management of Comfort Pillows has provided you with the total costs associated with the highest (September) and lowest (March) monthly production volumes for the most recent year of operations.

Month	Pillows Sold	Total Costs
March	10,000	$420,000
September	15,000	$560,000

Required:

a. Use the high-low method to estimate Comfort Pillows' monthly cost equation (i.e., use the high-low method to estimate Comfort Pillows' monthly fixed costs and variable cost per pillow produced).

b. Using the variable cost estimate, calculate the price per pillow that Comfort will charge the department store.

c. Explain why your answer to part (b) above differs from your answer to part(a) in the previous problem. Which of these two estimates do you believe is better/more reliable? Why?

4.54 Regression method for estimating the cost equation (LO4). Watson College includes the cost of all textbooks, lab supplies, and course packets in its tuition. Facing increasing financial pressures, Watson College is interested in predicting the costs associated with copying class notes (i.e., making course packets for students). Watson's vice president of finance has provided you with the following data regarding the total costs of printing course packets, and the corresponding class size for six representative classes:

Class Size (Students)	Total Costs of Making Course Packets for the Class
10	$175
20	$225
30	$268
40	$290
50	$345
60	$370

Required:

a. Plot the relation between the total cost of making course packets for a class (*y*-axis) and class size (*x*-axis). Does the relation between the cost of making course packets and class size appear to be linear?

b. Using Excel, fit a regression line to Watson College's course packet data. What are the fixed costs per class associated with preparing a course packet, and what is the variable cost per student?

c. Comment on the results. Does the regression line appear to "fit" the data? How might the vice president further increase the accuracy of the cost estimate?

4.55 Regression method for estimating the cost equation: Matching time periods (Advanced, **LO4).** Frank Fletch manages a plant that produces a variety of ball bearings and cylindrical roller bearings. Seeking to better understand his cost structure, Frank collected the following data regarding the number of machine hours worked and the number of maintenance hours for the past nine quarters (2.25 years) of operations:

Quarter	Machine Hours	Maintenance Hours
Q1, 2007	10,000	810
Q2, 2007	12,200	655
Q3, 2007	13,400	886

Quarter	Machine Hours	Maintenance Hours
Q4, 2007	15,300	971
Q1, 2008	12,000	1,041
Q2, 2008	13,500	700
Q3, 2008	15,000	814
Q4, 2008	18,000	966
Q1, 2009	12,250	1,203

Required:

a. Using Excel, estimate the following regression equation: *Maintenance hours = FC + (UVC × machine hours)*.

b. Why do you believe that the equation you developed in part (a) does not predict the number of maintenance hours worked in a quarter? You know that Frank usually schedules preventive maintenance during "off" times when the machines are not being fully utilized.

c. Modify the equation in part (a) so that maintenance hours are regressed on machine hours from the prior quarter. That is, estimate the following regression equation: *Maintenance hours = FC + (UVC × machine hours$_{quarter-1}$)*.

 4.56 Regression method for estimating the cost equation: Specification issues (LO4, Advanced). PermaPictures uses computer-guided lasers to etch pictures from photographs on granite. The firm's management advertises heavily because it believes that advertising and product recognition is a key factor in generating sales. The following data pertain to the previous eight quarters of operations:

Advertising Costs	Sales Revenue
$200,000	$1,235,000
$225,000	$1,369,000
$240,000	$1,403,000
$275,000	$1,408,000
$180,000	$1,132,000
$220,000	$1,212,000
$210,000	$1,260,000
$230,000	$1,345,450

Required:

a. Plot the relation between advertising costs (*y*-axis) and sales revenue (*x*-axis). Does the relation between advertising costs and sales revenue appear to be linear?

b. Using Excel, estimate the following regression equation: *Advertising Costs = Fixed costs + (UVC × Sales Revenue)*. That is, use sales revenue as the cost driver for advertising costs.

c. Using the regression equation you developed in part (b), estimate PermaPictures' advertising costs for a sales volume of $1,750,000. Comment on the validity of this estimate and, more generally, on the validity of the underlying cost equation being estimated. (*Hint:* Consider whether it is sensible to specify advertising costs as a function of sales revenue.)

4.57 Organizing information for decision making: Assessing segment contributions (LO5). Carousel Motors is an auto dealership that specializes in selling used cars. Carousel also has a small service station that it uses to (1) make minor repairs on the cars it buys and (2) provide both paid and courtesy repairs and maintenance on customers' cars. For example, Carousel often runs ads that offer "free maintenance for one year with any auto purchase," and restricts the maintenance to regularly scheduled items such as oil changes and tire rotations. The following data pertain to Carousel's most recent year of operations:

	Used Cars	Service Department	Total
Revenue	$2,500,000	$200,000	$2,700,000
Variable costs	1,200,000	200,000	1,400,000
Contribution margin	$1,300,000	$0	$1,300,000
Traceable fixed costs	750,000	250,000	1,000,000
Segment margin	$550,000	($250,000)	$300,000
Common fixed costs			200,000
Profit before taxes			$100,000

* Common fixed costs equal the salary of the owner plus the salary of the general manager.

You are puzzled by the service department's zero contribution margin since you know that the service department marks up its variable cost by 100% to arrive at the price charged to an external customer. Digging into the data, you learn that the service department only spent one-half of its time servicing external customers. The remainder of its time was spent repairing cars bought to replenish Carousel's inventory of used cars and providing courtesy (free) repairs on the used cars sold. For the service department, the above income statement only shows the revenues derived from sales to external customers, while it shows the costs associated with all of its service activities. Moreover, the used car division does not record any costs for the repairs provided by the service department.

Required:

a. Modify Carousel's contribution margin statement so that the service department's revenues and the used car's costs fully reflect the market value of the services provided by the service department to the used car department (i.e., assume that the service department charges used cars what it charges external customers). (*Hint:* Carousel's overall profit before taxes will not change.)

b. Jim Carew, the owner of Carousel Motors, believes that closing the service department will increase overall company profit. Based on your calculations in part (a), by how much will Carousel's overall profit increase or decrease if the service department is closed? (Assume that the used car department will pay an independent service station for the minor repairs on the cars it buys and for the courtesy repairs and maintenance on the used cars sold—all of this will be done at market price, or the amount you calculated in part [a].) What other factors should Jim consider before making the decision to close the service department?

c. Assume that closing the service department will reduce used car sales by 10%. How does this information affect your answer to part (b)? That is, by how much will Carousel's overall profit increase or decrease if the service department is closed and used car sales decrease by 10%? (Assume that the reduction in sales is not enough to affect used car's traceable fixed costs).

4.58 Learning curves and cost estimation (Appendix). FlyWell Avionics produces sophisticated guidance systems that are used in military satellites. FlyWell currently is bidding on a government contract to supply 32 specialized guidance systems over the next two years. FlyWell estimates that the variable cost of the first guidance system will be $1,200,000, which is comprised of $600,000 in labor costs, $400,000 in material costs, and $200,000 in variable overhead (i.e., other variable manufacturing) costs. While the materials and variable overhead costs are expected to remain constant over the 32 guidance systems, FlyWell believes that labor costs will be subject to a 90% learning curve. That is, as workers become familiar with producing the new guidance system, they are expected to become more efficient in performing their duties. Consequently, the average labor hours and, in turn, labor costs per guidance system are expected to decrease as the number of guidance systems produced increases.

On this particular government contract, management of FlyWell plans to submit a bid that equals the total variable costs of producing the 32 guidance systems plus a 50% markup (i.e., the bid = 1.50 × total variable costs).

Required:

a. What are the total variable costs FlyWell expects to incur in producing the 32 guidance systems?

b. What is the bid that FlyWell plans to submit? If it wins the contract, what is FlyWell's expected contribution margin from producing the 32 guidance systems?

c. Suppose that FlyWell obtains the contract but, due to budgetary pressures, the government is forced to scale back its order to 16 systems. Because the order size has been cut in half, the government is only willing to pay half of FlyWell's bid calculated in part (b). What is the actual contribution margin and markup that FlyWell will realize from this contract?

4.59 (Advanced) Learning curves and cost estimation (Appendix). Zeron, a medical equipment company, is expanding its product line and plans to manufacture testing equipment that calibrates magnetic resonance imaging (MRI) machines. Zeron plans to manufacture the MRI testing equipment in batches of 100 units. The firm estimates that the variable costs of producing the first batch will equal $1,000,000, which is comprised of $150,000 in materials costs, $50,000 in variable overhead costs, and $800,000 in labor costs ($800,000 = 32,000 labor hours × $25 per labor hour).

While the materials and variable overhead costs are expected to remain constant over time, Zeron believes that labor costs will be subject to a learning curve. Specifically, Zeron estimates that the second batch of 100 units will only consume 22,400 labor hours. Zeron plans to price the MRI testing equipment at the average variable cost to produce batches 17 to 32 plus a 75% markup (i.e., the unit selling price = 1.75 × average unit variable cost for units produced in batches 17 through 32).

Required:

a. What is the planned unit selling price of the MRI testing equipment? (Remember to adjust the batch cost to obtain a unit cost.)

b. What is the expected profit from the MRI testing equipment in year 1 if Zeron plans to produce 16 batches in the first year? Assume Zeron will incur fixed costs of $3 million per year to produce the MRI testing equipment.

c. What is the expected profit from the MRI testing equipment in year 2 if Zeron plans to produce batches 17–32 in the second year? Again, assume Zeron will incur fixed costs of $3 million per year to produce the MRI testing equipment.

MINI-CASES

4.60 Cost estimation: High-low method (LO3). The Yin-Yang Yogurt Shoppe serves the best chocolate-vanilla frozen yogurt in the city. While Yin-Yang's management tracks the cups of yogurt sold and total costs incurred each month, they are woefully unaware of which costs do and do not vary with the cups of yogurt sold (i.e., which costs are fixed and which costs are variable). Yin-Yang's management is hoping that you can figure out their cost structure. To this end, they have provided you with the following data for the past 12 months of operations:

Month	Cups of Yogurt Sold	Total Costs
January	1,000	$5,500
February	1,200	$6,200
March	1,400	$6,500
April	1,750	$6,800
May	2,000	$7,000
June	2,200	$7,400
July	2,400	$8,000
August	2,500	$8,125
September	2,000	$7,250
October	1,600	$6,500
November	1,250	$6,000
December	1,100	$8,500

Required:

a. Plot (i.e., graph) the relation between Yin-Yang's monthly total costs (*y*-axis) and cups of yogurt sold (*x*-axis).

b. Estimate Yin-Yang's monthly total cost equation using the data from January and February (i.e., use the data from January and February to estimate Yin-Yang's monthly fixed costs and variable cost per cup of yogurt sold).

c. Estimate Yin-Yang's monthly total cost equation using the two observations associated with the highest and lowest total monthly *cost* levels.

d. Estimate Yin-Yang's monthly total cost equation using the two observations associated with the highest and lowest total monthly *activity* levels (i.e., use the high-low method).

e. Estimate Yin-Yang's cost structure using regression analysis. Perform the analysis with and without the data for December.

f. Comment on the results. Specifically, which cost estimate do you believe is best? Why do you believe the estimate you chose leads to a better specification of Yin-Yang's monthly total costs than the other two estimates?

4.61 Cost hierarchy, cost estimation, decision making (LO1, LO2, LO3) Brad Timberlake is known throughout the world for his insights on effective and efficient time management.

Brad has authored several best-selling self-help books (also available in audio and video tape). In addition, Brad offers daylong seminars in major metropolitan areas. Brad has hired you (he does not have the time to do this himself!) to figure out if he should change the way he offers seminars.

Currently, Brad offers 35 daylong seminars each year at locations throughout North America, Europe, and Asia. The typical seminar is comprised of an initial talk followed by a break-out session in which participants complete worksheets that help them assess how they have been managing their time. After a coffee break, Brad critiques the "typical" worksheet and identifies the "time demons," as he calls time-wasting activities. The chastised participants adjourn for lunch. After lunch, Brad offers tips and solutions for better time management. Participants then go back to their break-out groups and redo their worksheets. The grand finale is a comparison of a pre- and post-time allocation sheet from a "random" participant.

Each seminar lasts the better part of a day. The average seminar has 125 participants, each of whom pays a $400 fee. The variable costs (folder, worksheets, copy of Brad's book, and food) amount to $75 per participant. In addition, setting up the seminar itself (the use of a hotel or convention center, hotel staff, and Brad's travel expenses—he always travels first class) costs $20,000 per seminar. Finally, Brad pays a coordinator a salary $50,000 per year to organize his seminars and incurs $250,000 in fixed costs annually to maintain a central office and support staff.

The following table provides summary data for Brad's seminars for the most recent four years (starting with the most recent year):

	Year 4	Year 3	Year 2	Year 1
Number of seminars	35	40	28	30
Total number of participants (number of seminars × 125)	4,375	5,000	3,500	3,750
Total revenues (number of participants × $400)	$1,750,000	$2,000,000	$1,400,000	$1,500,000
Total costs	1,328,125	1,475,000	1,122,500	1,181,250
Profit before taxes	$421,875	$525,000	$277,500	$318,750

Brad is getting tired of the endless travel and is considering offering fewer seminars. In particular, Brad wants to do no more than 20 seminars per year. To keep up with demand (and to try to keep his profit at the same level), Brad plans to increase the size of each seminar so that the average seminar has 230, rather than 125, participants. Because each participant would receive less personal attention, Brad also plans to reduce his seminar fee from $400 to $350 per person.

Required:

a. Brad wishes to use the high-low method to estimate his annual fixed costs and variable cost per seminar participant. That is, Brad wishes to represent his total annual costs as: Total costs = Fixed costs + (Variable cost per seminar participant × Total number of seminar participants). Using the data from the past four years, estimate Brad's annual fixed costs and variable cost per participant under the high-low method.

b. Using the cost equation you derived in part (a), what is Brad's estimated annual profit associated with offering 20 seminars under the proposed format (i.e., 230 participants per seminar, with each participant being charged $350)? How does this profit compare to Brad's current profit (i.e., 35 seminars under the current format)?

c. Not satisfied with your answer to part (b), Brad wants to dig a little deeper into the problem. On one of his trips, Brad learned about the cost hierarchy. (Brad excels at multitasking!) He asks you to classify each of his four types of costs (i.e., the variable cost per participant, seminar costs, coordinator's salary, and central office) as per the cost hierarchy.

d. Your classification of Brad's costs vis-à-vis the cost hierarchy leads you to reconsider your analysis in part (b). Taking a closer look at Brad's costs, you learn that the change in the seminar format would not affect the per-participant variable cost, the seminar coordinator's salary, or Brad's central office costs. However, because of the increased enrollment, the cost of hosting each seminar would increase by $5,000 (i.e., from $20,000 to $25,000 per seminar). Using your knowledge of the cost hierarchy, what will Brad's profit be if he switches to the new seminar format? That is, use the account classification method to estimate Brad's profit associated with offering 20 seminars under the proposed format.

e. Do your answers from parts (b) and (d) differ? If so, why?

4.62 Cost estimation, sunk costs, decision making (LO1, LO2, LO3). Molly's Music is an independent record store located in Seattle, Washington. Molly, a self-described "music junkie," started her business after she encountered repeated difficulties finding music that was not produced by one of the major record labels. Molly wanted a store that had just about everything in stock, from the most popular artists to the most obscure artists in all musical genres, be it rock or roots. She also wanted a store that supported local musicians by carrying their CDs.

Albeit slowly, Molly has seen her business grow over the years and, on any given day, Molly's 25,000 square-foot store has 75,000 titles in stock. Molly also has assembled an eclectic, knowledgeable staff that lives for music and can assist customers with just about any musical question or request. A review of Molly's sales, costs, revenue, and profit data for the previous 12 months revealed the following:

Month	CDs Sold	Total Costs	Revenue	Profit
January	8,500	$145,675	$144,075	($1,600)
February	8,000	$142,500	$135,600	($6,900)
March	8,800	$144,590	$149,160	$4,570
April	10,800	$162,880	$183,060	$20,180
May	7,900	$138,425	$133,905	($4,520)
June	7,000	$128,000	$118,650	($9,350)
July	9,500	$150,100	$161,025	$10,925
August	6,000	$125,000	$101,700	($23,300)
September	10,000	$151,305	$169,500	$18,195
October	9,600	$157,875	$162,720	$4,845
November	8,800	$147,500	$149,160	$1,660
December	12,000	$170,000	$203,400	$33,400
Total:	106,900	$1,763,850	$1,811,955	$48,105

While you find Molly's proceeds from her business impressive, you believe that she could do better if she reduced the average selling price per CD. Specifically, over the past several years, you (as one of Molly's employees) have heard numerous customers rave about Molly's knowledgeable and courteous staff and vast array of CD titles. However, you also have heard numerous customers say that Molly's average price of $16.95 per CD is "unreasonable." Moreover, you have witnessed individuals come into the store, ask for your advice, and then leave without making a purchase. Your supposition is that once these customers decide on the CDs they want, they actually buy their CDs from one of the local chain stores where the average price per CD is $14.95.

To be competitive with the chain stores, you believe that Molly should reduce the average selling price of a CD by $2.00 to $14.95. Based on your experience and an informal customer survey, you estimate that such a move would increase CD sales by 30%. You also believe that the increased sales volume would be well within Molly's relevant range—that is, if sales increased by 30% Molly would not have to invest in additional fixed costs related to space, equipment, or personnel.

Molly believes that your idea is "nuts" because your recommended selling price is lower than the average cost per CD. Molly calculates that she would lose $14.95 − $16.50 = ($1.55) per CD if she followed your advice. Molly arrived at the $16.50 cost per CD by dividing her total costs for the most recent year, or $1,763,850, by the total number of CDs sold during the most recent year, or 106,900.

Required:

a. Before performing any calculations, prepare a brief paragraph or two discussing the soundness of Molly's logic regarding her response to your suggested price decrease.

b. Help Molly better understand the "big picture" by plotting (i.e., graphing) the relation between her total costs and number of CDs sold (*x*-axis). Is this graph informative about Molly's cost structure?

c. Using the high-low method, estimate Molly's monthly cost equation (i.e., use the high-low method to estimate Molly's monthly fixed costs and variable cost per CD sold). Add a line representing Molly's estimated cost equation to your graph in part (b). Does your model appear to fit the data well?

d. Based on the cost model you developed in part (c), does it make sense for Molly to lower the selling price per CD to $14.95? That is, by how much do you estimate that Molly's expected yearly profit will increase or decrease if she follows your advice?

e. Molly is impressed with your business acumen and wonders whether the cost model you developed can help her with another business decision. Specifically, Molly is considering hiring another employee at a total cost of $52,150 per year in salary and benefits. Molly believes that this employee, who is an expert in international folk music, will increase monthly sales by 750 CDs. Assuming Molly decides to reduce the average price of a CD to $14.95, by how much is Molly's annual profit expected to increase or decrease if she hires this employee?

f. Molly has one final question for you. Ten years ago, she purchased 10 "Greatest Hits from the 70's" CDs (Molly was a huge fan of KC and The Sunshine Band, and they are featured on the CD's cover). Molly paid the record company $5 for each CD and priced them at $12.95 each. Molly sold six "Greatest Hits from the 70's" CDs in the first three years after acquiring them; however, Molly has not sold any of the remaining four CDs in the last seven years (the CDs have been sitting on the shelf collecting dust). Recently, one of Molly's college-age customers offered to buy the four remaining CDs for $15. (The customer thinks they will make nice gifts for his older relatives.) Molly is reluctant to accept the offer because she paid $5 for each CD. Before declining, though, she asks you for your advice. What would you recommend to Molly? Why?

4.63 Organizing information for decision making: Creating a customer contribution statement (LO5). Denzel Adams runs a carpet cleaning business in Tupelo, Mississippi. Denzel serves two major types of customers: motels and residential homes. Currently, Denzel spends three days each week cleaning the carpets and upholstery in six motels. He devotes the remaining two days of each week to cleaning the carpets and upholstery of individual residences. Denzel has asked for your help in determining whether he should drop his motel customers and focus solely on residences. Although he likes the steady business the motels provide, he does not like the price—Mina Patel, the owner of the six motels, drives a hard bargain.

You gather the following additional information about Denzel and his business:

- Denzel works 50 weeks a year. He works 10 hours a day Monday through Wednesday, the days he cleans the motels. He works an average of 6 hours a day on Thursday and Friday, the days he cleans residential homes. Denzel does not work weekends. Denzel values his work time at $15 per hour.

- Denzel receives $150 in revenue for each motel he cleans and $80 (on average) in revenue for each house he cleans. Denzel cleans two motels per day on Monday through Wednesday and three houses per day on Thursday and Friday.

- Denzel uses a higher grade cleaner for residences than motels. Denzel figures that he spends $20 in supplies per residential customer and $30 in supplies per motel. Denzel leases his van and other equipment for $7,000 per year. Of this, $1,500 worth of equipment is used only for the motel cleaning jobs.

- Denzel takes out ads in the local newspapers and yellow pages to drum up residential business. (Denzel does not incur advertising costs related to the motels since he's had the motel business for years.) He estimates this cost at $5,000 per year.

- Because he is under contract, Denzel needs to hire another company to clean the motels during the two weeks that he is on vacation (this company does not clean any residences for Denzel during these two weeks). While Denzel still receives the $150 fee per motel, he pays the other cleaning company a flat wage of $175 per motel (the other company uses its own supplies and employees to do all the work).

- Denzel works out of his home and uses his kitchen table as his office. He figures that he spends about $500 a year on supplies and $1,000 on telephone expenses. (These expenses cannot be directly traced to either motels or residences.)

Required:

a. Create an annual contribution margin statement by customer (motels and residences) for Denzel. (Be sure to include $15 per hour for Denzel's time.)

b. Based on your analysis, should Denzel drop his motel clients? Assume that if he drops the motel business, Denzel can double his residential business if he also doubles his advertising budget. (Be sure to consider the value of any savings in Denzel's time.)

Chapter 5
Cost-Volume-Profit Analysis

SIERRA PLASTICS MANUFACTURES A patented plastic, Perlast, used to make milk, fruit juice, and water containers. Sierra's chief executive officer and founder, Ben Brady, started the company because scientific tests showed that Perlast did a better job than existing plastics in preserving freshness for longer periods.

While Sierra has always been profitable, Ben believes that the company could do better. He and his staff are considering three options to increase profit for the coming year (see the the Decision Framework box at right for details).

Ben is unsure how to evaluate these options and chart the best course of action. He believes it will be difficult for Sierra to pursue more than one option initially. Thus, Ben would like to start with the option that has the maximum profit impact, then revisit the other two options later. Ben seeks your help in selecting the best option.

APPLYING THE DECISION FRAMEWORK

What Is the Problem?
How can Sierra Plastics increase its profit?

What Are the Options?
Ben and his staff have identified three promising options:

1. Decrease the price of Perlast to increase demand.
2. Purchase new inspection technology to reduce the unit variable cost of Perlast.
3. Offer different grades of Perlast to meet the specific needs of individual market segments.

What Are the Costs and Benefits?
You will perform Cost-Volume-Profit (CVP) analysis to estimate the costs and benefits of each option.

Make the Decision!
After performing CVP analysis, you will be able to recommend the best option for Sierra.

Sierra Plastics is considering several options to increase profit.

How many tickets do the Chicago Cubs need to sell for a game to break even? How much will profit increase if Starbucks sells another 1 million cups of coffee a year? When facing lower than expected demand, would reducing the selling price be more profitable for Nike than increasing advertising? Cost-Volume-Profit analysis, the focus of this chapter, is the tool we use to answer such questions.

We begin this chapter by examining the Cost-Volume-Profit (CVP) relation. We then show you how to use the CVP relation for profit planning and for evaluating the profit impact of short-term decisions. Following this, we extend the CVP relation to include multiple products. Finally, we discuss the limitations of CVP analysis.

CHAPTER CONNECTIONS

CVP analysis is useful for profit planning and for making short-term decisions that pertain to the firm as a whole. However, it can be difficult to adapt CVP analysis to decisions that deal with individual products, resources, or customers. We consider such decisions in Chapters 6.

The Cost-Volume-Profit (CVP) Relation

LEARNING OBJECTIVE 1

Understand the CVP relation.

The Cost-Volume-Profit (CVP) relation follows directly from the contribution margin statement that we studied in Chapter 4. In this statement, we calculated profit by subtracting variable costs and fixed costs from revenue. In other words:

$$\textit{Profit before taxes} = \textit{Revenues} - \textit{Variable costs} - \textit{Fixed costs}$$

Both revenues and variable costs are proportional to sales volume. Revenues equal the number of units sold multiplied by the price per unit. Likewise, variable costs equal the number of units sold multiplied by the unit variable cost. Combining these observations, we can rearrange this profit equation to highlight the Cost-Volume-Profit relation:

$$\textit{Profit before taxes} = [(\textit{Price} - \textit{Unit variable cost}) \times \textit{Sales volume in units}] - \textit{Fixed costs}$$

Notice that, over the short term, fixed costs do not change with the number of units sold.

This expression captures the essence of the CVP relation because it relates sales volume with profit and costs.

Next, we define **Unit contribution margin** = *Price* − *Unit variable cost*. Using this definition, we have:

$$\textit{Profit before taxes} = (\textit{Unit contribution margin} \times \textit{Sales volume in units}) - \textit{Fixed costs}$$
$$= \textit{Contribution margin} - \textit{Fixed costs}$$

This final expression emphasizes that *contribution margin is the appropriate measure for evaluating short-term decisions.* Why does this conclusion follow? Because fixed costs generally do not change in the short term, increasing contribution margin increases profit by an identical amount. That is, for every unit sold, profit increases by an amount equal to the unit contribution margin.

For Sierra, Ben provides you with the information in Exhibit 5.1 for the most recent year of operations.

We can construct Sierra's CVP relation using the information in Exhibit 5.1. We have price = $25, unit variable cost = $10, sales volume in units = 100,000, and fixed costs = $1,200,000. Thus, we express Sierra's profit as:

$$\textit{Profit before taxes} = [(\textit{Price} - \textit{Unit variable cost}) \times \textit{Sales volume in units}] - \textit{Fixed costs}$$
$$\textit{Profit before taxes} = [(\$25 - \$10) \times 100,000] - \$1,200,000 = \$300,000$$

Because we know the unit contribution margin is $25 − $10 = $15, we can also write:

$$\textit{Profit before taxes} = (\$15 \times 100,000) - \$1,200,000 = \$300,000$$

Exhibit 5.1	*Sierra Plastics: Key Operating Data*		
Item	**Amount**	**Item**	**Amount**
Sales of Perlast in pounds	100,000	Manufacturing capacity (in pounds)	200,000
Selling price per pound	$25		
Variable manufacturing costs		Fixed manufacturing costs	
Direct materials per pound	$3	Equipment	$150,000
Direct labor per pound	$4	Supervisory personnel	$170,000
Packaging per pound	$2	Factory rent	$290,000
Variable selling costs		Fixed selling & administration cost	
Sales commissions per pound	$1	Advertising	$40,000
		Sales staff	$250,000
		Office space rental and expenses	$300,000
Total variable costs per pound	$10	Total fixed costs	$1,200,000

Exhibit 5.2 uses the data in Exhibit 5.1 to construct a contribution margin statement for Sierra. Notice that this statement shows the same profit we calculated using the CVP relation. This equivalence underscores the fact that the CVP relation is simply a convenient way to express the contribution margin statement.

HOW FIRMS USE THE CVP RELATION

Firms frequently use the CVP relation to estimate profit at different sales volumes. At the current sales volume of 100,000 pounds, Sierra's profit is $300,000. As shown in Exhibit 5.3, you can use the CVP relation to calculate Sierra's profit before taxes at differing sales volumes.

Exhibit 5.2	*Sierra Plastics: Income Statement*	
Item	**Detail**	**Amount**
Revenues		$2,500,000
Variable costs	100,000 pounds × $25 per pound	
Manufacturing	100,000 pounds × $9 per pound	$900,000
Selling	100,000 pounds × $1 per pound	100,000
Contribution margin		$1,500,000
Fixed Costs		
Manufacturing	From Exhibit 5.1	$610,000
Selling & administration	From Exhibit 5.1	590,000
Profit before taxes		$300,000

Exhibit 5.3	*Sierra's Expected Profit before Taxes at Differing Sales Volumes*			
	Sales Volume of Perlast in Pounds			
	90,000	*100,000*	*120,000*	*140,000*
Profit before taxes = ($15 × Sales volume in pounds) − $1,200,000	$150,000	$300,000	$600,000	$900,000

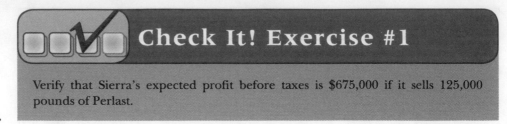

Check It! Exercise #1

Verify that Sierra's expected profit before taxes is $675,000 if it sells 125,000 pounds of Perlast.

Solution at end of chapter.

Exhibit 5.3 shows that a relatively modest increase in sales volume leads to a substantial increase in profit. For example, increasing Sierra's sales by 20%, from 100,000 pounds to 120,000 pounds, increases profit before taxes by 100%, from $300,000 to $600,000. Similarly, a modest decrease in sales volume reduces profit substantially. Decreasing quantity sold by 10%, from 100,000 pounds to 90,000 pounds, reduces profit before taxes by 50%, from $300,000 to $150,000. Such large changes in profit as the sales volume changes indicate that Sierra faces some risk in its operations. As shown in Exhibit 5.4, and as you will learn later, firms use the CVP relation for many purposes.

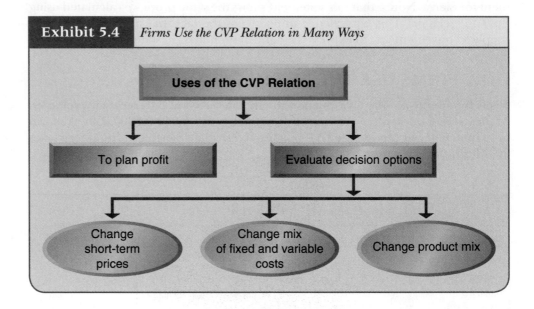

Exhibit 5.4   *Firms Use the CVP Relation in Many Ways*

The CVP Relation and Profit Planning

LEARNING OBJECTIVE 2

Use the CVP relation to plan profit.

While most organizations want to make a profit, at the very least they want to generate enough business to avoid making a loss. What volume of business must a company generate to guarantee that there will be no loss? What volume of business would yield a certain minimum profit? We refer to the use of the CVP relation to answer such questions as *profit planning*.

BREAKEVEN VOLUME

Breakeven volume is the sales volume at which profit equals zero. Exhibit 5.5 is useful in understanding the breakeven point. The line for total costs equals fixed costs

Exhibit 5.5   *The CVP Relation Shows How Fixed Costs, Variable Costs, and Price Determine Breakeven Sales Volume*

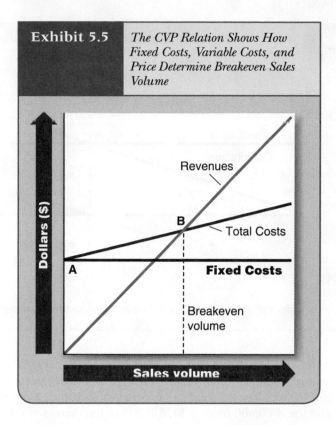

plus variable costs. Point A shows where the total costs line intercepts the *y*-axis. At this point, when there are no sales, revenues are zero and total costs equal fixed costs. As sales volume increases, total costs increase proportionally due to the variable costs associated with making and selling products.

At the breakeven volume, point B, the firm makes zero profit, meaning that revenues equal total costs. The firm is profitable if the quantity sold exceeds the breakeven volume. However, the firm incurs a loss if sales dip below this level. Exhibit 5.5 also highlights that, for a viable business, the revenues line must be steeper than the total costs line. Why is this? If the total costs line is steeper than the revenues line, the two lines will never meet—profit will always be negative. Thus, to have any chance of making a profit, a firm must have a positive unit contribution margin; that is, price must exceed the unit variable cost.

Exhibit 5.6 shows another way to look at breakeven. In this graph, we directly plot contribution margin and profit. When sales volume is zero, the firm incurs a loss equal to its fixed costs. You can see this relationship where the contribution margin line and the profit line intercept the *y*-axis. For every unit sold, both contribution margin and profit increase at the same rate, by an amount equal to the unit contribution margin. When we sell enough units to make contribution margin equal to fixed costs (point A), profit equals zero (point B). This amount of units is the breakeven volume. The greater the unit contribution margin, the steeper the profit line and the more the firm's profit increases for a given increase in sales volume.

A positive unit contribution margin by itself does not guarantee profit, however. The firm must sell enough units so that the contribution margin at least covers fixed costs. For example, how many pounds of Perlast must Sierra sell to avoid a loss? We know that Sierra's unit contribution margin equals $15 and its fixed costs are $1,200,000. Because profit equals zero at the breakeven volume, we set profit equal to $0 to calculate the breakeven volume as:

$$0 = Breakeven\ volume \times Unit\ contribution\ margin - Fixed\ costs$$

$$Breakeven\ volume = \frac{Fixed\ costs}{Unit\ contribution\ margin}$$

| Exhibit 5.6 | *We Can Use the CVP Relation to Directly Plot Contribution and Profit* |

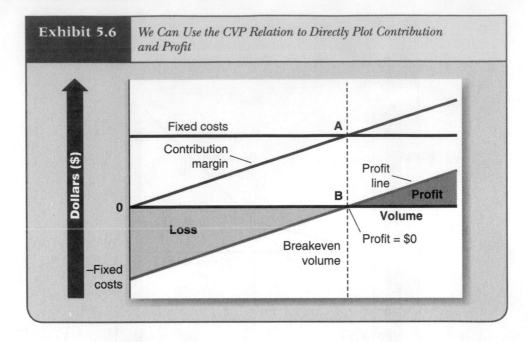

Thus, Sierra needs to sell 80,000 pounds (fixed costs of $1,200,000 divided by the unit contribution margin of $15) to break even. We can verify this answer by using the CVP relation to calculate that Sierra has zero profit at this volume: $15 in unit contribution margin × 80,000 units − $1,200,000 of fixed costs = profit of $0.

Connecting to Practice

RECYCLING

Tomra Corporation operates kiosks where consumers return aluminum cans. Located near supermarkets, these brightly lit and clean kiosks provide a convenient way for environmentally conscious consumers to recycle.

Tomra's business plan is straightforward. Each kiosk costs $36,000 a year to operate in fixed costs. The kiosk receives $0.02 in revenue for each can delivered to the scrap metal dealer, but consumes $0.01 in processing costs. Accordingly, Tomra estimates that it needs to process 3,600,000 cans per year, or 300,000 cans per month, for a kiosk to break even.

The state of California goes a step further by providing Tomra with a subsidy of $21,600 per year to cover fixed costs and $0.01 per can toward processing costs. These subsidies reduce both Tomra's fixed costs and the unit variable cost, making it easier to reach breakeven. California hopes that Tomra will then open more kiosks, making it even more convenient for consumers to recycle.

COMMENTARY: With the information provided, we express Tomra's profit for a kiosk as, *Profit before taxes* = [($0.02 − $0.01) × *Sales volume in units*] − $36,000. Thus, each kiosk needs to process $36,000/0.01 = 3,600,000 cans per year, or 3,600,000/12 = 300,000 cans per month, to break even. With the California subsidies, Tomra's profit is *Profit before taxes* = ($0.02 × *Sales volume in units*) − $14,400. In turn, we calculate the breakeven point as $14,400/0.02 = 720,000 cans per year. This substantial reduction in the breakeven volume to 60,000 cans per month makes it more attractive for Tomra to open new kiosks.

Variable costs for recyclers can be low because they often do not pay for their raw materials. (Pete Starman/Getty Images)

BREAKEVEN REVENUES

Organizations frequently prefer to express the breakeven point in terms of *revenues* rather than in terms of units. Why? Well, money is the language of business. Ultimately, managers focus on dollars and the bottom line rather than on physical units.

Breakeven revenues are the sales dollars needed to break even:

$$Breakeven\ revenues = Breakeven\ volume \times Price$$

For Sierra, we know the breakeven volume is 80,000 pounds of Perlast and the price is $25 per pound. Thus, we calculate breakeven revenues as:

$$Breakeven\ revenues = 80,000\ pounds \times \$25\ per\ pound = \$2,000,000$$

While this calculation is helpful, organizations often report only total revenue and cost data; they often do not report the unit-level data. The absence of such detail makes it difficult to determine a product's unit contribution margin or price. Thus, it may not be possible to calculate breakeven revenues as above.

Fortunately, we can compute breakeven revenues directly. To do so, it is necessary to understand the notion of a contribution margin ratio. The **contribution margin ratio** is simply the unit contribution margin divided by price. That is,

$$Contribution\ margin\ ratio = \frac{Unit\ contribution\ margin}{Price} = \frac{Price\text{-}Unit\ variable\ cost}{Price}$$

Sierra's contribution margin ratio is:

$$Contribution\ margin\ ratio = \frac{\$25 - \$10}{\$25} = \frac{\$15}{\$25} = 0.60\ or\ 60\%$$

Intuitively, the contribution margin ratio is the portion of every sales dollar that remains after covering variable costs—it is the portion that contributes toward covering fixed costs and, ultimately, to profit. For Sierra, 40% of the $25 revenue from each pound of Perlast sold goes toward covering variable costs ($10/$25 = 0.40 or 40%). The remaining 60% contributes to covering fixed costs and to profit.

We can calculate the contribution margin ratio either using unit-level data or using total revenues and variable costs. If only total revenues and variable cost information are available, we calculate the contribution margin ratio as

$$Contribution\ margin\ ratio = \frac{Contribution\ margin}{Revenues} = \frac{Revenues - Variable\ costs}{Revenues}$$

For Sierra, we refer to Exhibit 5.2 and compute the contribution margin ratio as

$$Contribution\ margin\ ratio = \frac{\$2,500,000 - \$1,000,000}{2,500,000} = 0.60$$

The contribution margin ratio represents the portion of revenues that contribute to covering fixed cost and profit. Therefore, we can express a firm's profit as

$$Profit\ before\ taxes = (Contribution\ margin\ ratio \times Revenues) - Fixed\ costs$$

In turn, we can calculate breakeven revenues by setting profit equal to zero and solving as follows:

$$0 = Breakeven\ revenues \times Contribution\ margin\ ratio - Fixed\ costs$$

$$Breakeven\ revenues = \frac{Fixed\ costs}{Contribution\ margin\ ratio}$$

Given Sierra's contribution margin ratio of 60% and fixed costs of $1,200,000, we calculate Sierra's breakeven revenues as $1,200,000/0.60 = $2,000,000. This amount is exactly what we found earlier when we multiplied the breakeven volume by the selling price.

Check It! Exercise #2

Suppose Sierra sells Perlast for $50 a pound, the unit variable cost is $30, and annual fixed costs equal $1,500,000. Verify that the breakeven volume is 75,000 pounds and that breakeven revenues are $3,750,000 under both the *unit contribution margin* and *the contribution margin ratio* approaches:

Unit contribution margin approach
_____

Profit before taxes = (Unit contribution margin × Sales volume in units) − Fixed costs.

Unit contribution margin _____

Breakeven volume _____

Breakeven revenues
(= Breakeven volume × Price) _____

Contribution margin ratio approach
_____

Profit before taxes = (Contribution margin ratio × Revenues) − Fixed costs.

Contribution margin ratio _____

Breakeven revenues _____

Breakeven volume
(= Breakeven revenue/Price) _____

Solution at end of chapter.

TARGET PROFIT

Organizations frequently specify annual, quarterly, and monthly profit goals for their product and divisional managers. These goals guide managers' actions during the period. For example, managers will want to know the level of sales required to achieve the targeted profit. Is this sales level possible at the current price? Is additional advertising necessary? Are price discounts necessary? Managers can use the CVP relation to answer such questions.

To illustrate, suppose Sierra wants to earn a profit before taxes of $450,000 in the coming year. How many pounds of Perlast must the company sell? How much revenue does it need to generate? Let us first answer these questions using the unit contribution margin. As you know,

Profit before taxes = (Unit contribution margin × Sales volume in units) − Fixed costs

Setting profit before taxes equal to $450,000, we have:

$$\$450,000 = (\$15 \times \textit{Sales volume in units}) - \$1,200,000$$

Solving, we find that Perlast needs a sales volume of 110,000 pounds to achieve a profit of $450,000. At this volume, revenues equal $2,750,000 ($25 price per pound × 110,000 pounds).

We can also use the contribution margin ratio to answer these questions.

Profit before taxes = (Contribution margin ratio × Revenues) − Fixed costs

From our earlier calculations, we know that the contribution margin ratio for Perlast is 0.60, or 60%. Therefore, setting profit before taxes equal to $450,000,

$$\$450,000 = (0.60 \times \textit{Revenues}) - \$1,200,000$$

Solving, we find that revenues of $2,750,000 are necessary to achieve a profit of $450,000, the same sales figure we obtained earlier!

CVP Analysis and Taxes

Taxes are an unavoidable part of doing business. As a result, firms usually are interested in earning a target profit *after* taxes. We can readily modify the CVP relation to include taxes:

$$Profit\ after\ taxes = Profit\ before\ taxes - (Profit\ before\ taxes \times Tax\ rate)$$
$$= Profit\ before\ taxes \times (1 - Tax\ rate)$$

Keep in mind that we can calculate profit before taxes using either the unit contribution margin approach or the contribution margin ratio approach.

Suppose Ben wishes to make $450,000 in profit *after* taxes and that Sierra faces a 40% tax rate. How many pounds of Perlast does Sierra need to sell? How much revenue must Sierra generate? Using the unit contribution margin approach, we have:

$$\$450,000 = [(\$15 \times Sales\ volume\ in\ units) - \$1,200,000] \times (1 - 0.40)$$

Solving, we find that the required sales volume is 130,000 pounds. Multiplying this volume by the price of $25 per pound translates to $3,250,000 in required revenues. These answers exceed our earlier answers of 110,000 pounds and $2,750,000 in revenues because taxes reduce the profit retained.

Let us verify these numbers using the contribution margin ratio approach:

$$\$450,000 = [(0.60 \times Revenues) - \$1,200,000] \times (1 - 0.40)$$

Solving, we find once again that revenues of $3,250,000 are required to achieve $450,000 in profit after taxes.

Exhibit 5.7 re-draws the profit graph from Exhibit 5.6 to show how taxes affect the CVP relation. Taxes reduce profit by a certain percentage beyond the breakeven point. In Exhibit 5.7, we see that, above the breakeven point, the slope of the profit line decreases by the taxes paid. Below the breakeven point, no tax is due; therefore, the CVP relation remains the same as in Exhibit 5.6.

Armed with an understanding of the CVP relation, let us now use it to evaluate Sierra's options.

Exhibit 5.7	*Income Taxes Change the Slope of the Profit Line*

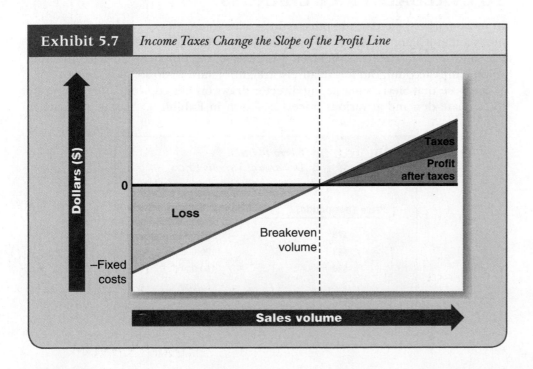

Using the CVP Relation to Make Short-Term Decisions

LEARNING OBJECTIVE 3

Make short-term decisions using CVP analysis.

In addition to planning profits, the CVP relation helps organizations make short-term decisions. As noted in the opening paragraphs of this chapter, Sierra's current profitability gives Ben some comfort, yet he desires to improve profit. Recall that he and his staff identified three options:

1. Decrease the price of Perlast to increase demand.
2. Purchase new inspection technology to reduce the unit variable cost of Perlast.
3. Offer different grades of Perlast to meet the specific needs of individual market segments.

Under the first option, decreasing the selling price per pound reduces the unit contribution margin—the change reduces price, but not the unit variable cost. Because each pound sold contributes less to profit, Sierra's overall profit will increase only if the reduction in the unit contribution margin is more than offset by the additional sales volume that price cuts typically generate.

Under the second option, the unit contribution margin will increase because Sierra expects the inspection technology to reduce the unit variable cost. Consequently, each pound of Perlast sold will contribute more to profit. However, this option also increases fixed costs. Sierra can justify the expenditure only if the increased contribution margin exceeds the increase in fixed costs.

The final option is to tailor grades of Perlast to individual market segments, allowing Sierra to increase total sales volume and use existing capacity more effectively. Producing and marketing multiple products is likely to increase Sierra's fixed costs. As with the second option, Sierra can justify expanding its product offerings only if the increased contribution margin exceeds the increase in fixed costs.

In sum, we can analyze each option in terms of the CVP relation and its effect on various elements that make up Sierra's profit. Let us first evaluate Ben's pricing decision.

USING THE CVP RELATION TO EVALUATE PRICE CHANGES

In most markets, increases in price reduce sales volume. Conversely, retail companies such as JCPenney, Mattress Firm, and Sears reduce prices in an effort to stimulate sales. Thus far, we have not taken this "inverse" relation between price and sales volume into account. But it is relatively straightforward to do so.

Suppose that Sierra's marketing director draws on her considerable experience to estimate demand at various prices, as shown in Exhibit 5.8. Using the data in

Exhibit 5.8	*Sierra Plastics: Demand at Various Prices*

Price (per pound)	Expected Sales Volume (in pounds)
$25	100,000
$23	120,000
$20	160,000
$18	184,000
$16	200,000

Exhibit 5.8 and Sierra's CVP relation, you can estimate profit at each price, quantity combination. Exhibit 5.9 shows the results of these calculations.

Notice that of the prices listed, a price of $20 yields the highest profit even though reducing the price by $5 decreases the unit contribution margin from $15 to $10. We obtain this result because the corresponding change in sales volume, from 100,000 pounds to 160,000 pounds, overcomes the negative effects of the lower unit contribution margin. The net result of this tradeoff is an increase in short-term profit before taxes of $100,000.

Exhibit 5.10, which depicts the trade-off in a graph, shows two classic relations. As shown by the demand curve, increases in price reduce demand. Second, there is an inverted U shape relation between price and profit. At low prices, increasing prices to raise contribution overcomes the effect of lost demand. But, as prices increase even more, the demand loss overcomes the effect of gaining more contribution from each unit sold.

Exhibit 5.9	Sierra Plastics: Cost-Volume-Profit Analysis to Evaluate Price Changes				

Price	Unit Variable Cost	Unit Contribution Margin	Fixed Costs	Expected Sales Volume	Profit before Taxes
$25	$10	$15	$1,200,000	100,000	$300,000
$23	$10	$13	$1,200,000	120,000	$360,000
$20	$10	$10	$1,200,000	160,000	$400,000
$18	$10	$8	$1,200,000	184,000	$272,000
$16	$10	$6	$1,200,000	200,000	$0

Exhibit 5.10	Firms Trade Off Unit Contribution with Volume When Choosing Prices

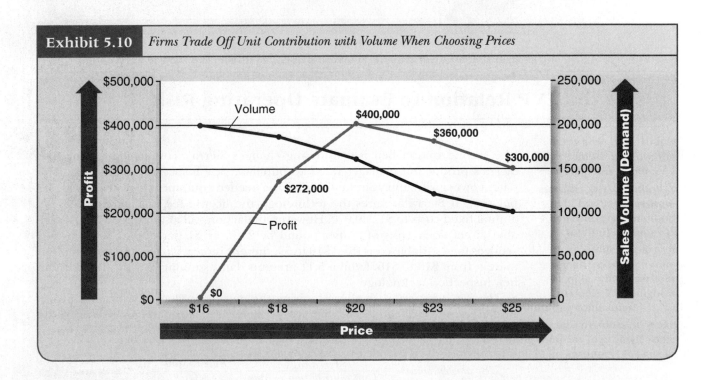

Sierra's current price is $25 per pound. Thus, lowering price to $20 increases profit. However, reducing the price too much could hurt profit. If Ben sells Perlast for $18 per pound, Sierra experiences high-capacity utilization (184,000 pounds/200,000 pounds of capacity = 92% utilization). However, even such a high volume is not sufficient to offset the effect of the lower unit contribution margin. Profit before taxes is $272,000, less than the $300,000 currently earned. This example demonstrates how CVP analysis allows firms to evaluate the trade-off between price and quantity, and their effect on profit.

A word of caution before we move on. When performing such computations, keep in mind the *short-term focus* of CVP analysis. Price reductions may pay off in the short term, but they often are not beneficial in the long term. For example, competing firms may decide to cut their prices as well. In that case, the demand estimates in Exhibit 5.8 may not hold in future periods. Ben must consider these longer-term consequences before reducing prices permanently.

CHAPTER CONNECTIONS

At the time Ben founded Sierra, he would have considered the long-term price, costs, and demand for Perlast. The outcome of this decision process resulted in Sierra installing capacity to make 200,000 pounds of Perlast annually. We consider such capital budgeting decisions in Chapter 13. However, the actual demand for a year might be higher or lower than the long-term average. If the actual demand falls short of the capacity of 200,000 pounds in a given year, Ben may have to reduce the selling price to stimulate demand. Thus, the focus of such short-term decisions is to respond to immediate demand conditions and to make the most profitable use of available capacity. The cost of the capacity itself is not controllable for these decisions.

Using the CVP Relation to Evaluate Operating Risk

The second option Ben is considering changes Sierra's cost structure. Suppose Sierra's production manager wants to purchase new inspection technology. The patent owner will supply Sierra with all of the needed equipment for a fee of $40,000 per year. If Sierra acquires the technology, the license fee will increase Sierra's annual fixed costs to $1,240,000. However, the action will also reduce Sierra's variable direct labor costs of $4 per pound by 25%, or $1 per pound. This savings reduces total variable costs from $10 to $9, thereby increasing the unit contribution margin from $15 to $16. Exhibit 5.11 presents data assuming Sierra purchases the new inspection technology.

The key question is whether acquiring the new technology will increase profit. Because we are evaluating each option separately, we perform this analysis using the original Perlast price of $25 per pound. We start by calculating Sierra's revised breakeven volume:

$$Breakeven\ volume = \frac{Fixed\ costs}{Unit\ contribution\ margin} = \frac{\$1,240,000}{\$16} = 77,500\ pounds$$

With the new inspection technology, Sierra requires only 77,500 pounds of Perlast, rather than 80,000 pounds, to break even. With an expected demand of 100,000 pounds, a higher volume contributes directly to annual profit. In addition, each pound contributes one dollar more to profit than before (i.e., $16 versus $15 per pound).

As Exhibit 5.12 shows, these factors lead to a $60,000 *increase* in Sierra's profit before taxes. Because it reduces the required volume to break even and increases profit, the new inspection technology seems like a good option. However, this option also changes Sierra's cost structure and adds to fixed costs. Firms are usually reluctant to add to fixed costs because they represent a sure outflow. In contrast, actual revenues and variable costs are uncertain because their amounts depend on the actual demand. Thus, the new technology might subject Sierra to greater risk. If the risk is "too much," Ben might even forego the additional profit from adopting the new technology.

How should we evaluate the risk arising from a firm's choice of cost structure? In this section, we discuss two common measures of *operating* risk. These two measures—margin of safety and operating leverage—originate from the CVP relation.

MARGIN OF SAFETY

The CVP relation allows firms to evaluate risk by considering the amount by which expected sales exceeds breakeven sales. We refer to this cushion, expressed in percentage terms, as the firm's **margin of safety:**

$$\text{Margin of safety} = \frac{\text{Sales in units} - \text{Breakeven volume}}{\text{Sales in units}} = \frac{\text{Revenues} - \text{Breakeven revenues}}{\text{Revenues}}$$

For Sierra, without adding in the new technology, current sales are 100,000 pounds and current revenues are $2,500,000. The breakeven volume is 80,000 pounds, and breakeven revenues are $2,000,000. Thus, we have:

$$\text{Margin of safety (current)} = \frac{100,000 - 80,000}{100,000} = \frac{\$2,500,000 - \$2,000,000}{\$2,500,000}$$
$$= 0.20 \text{ or } 20\%$$

Exhibit 5.11	Sierra Plastics: Data with New Inspection Technology		
Item	**Amount**	**Item**	**Amount**
Sales (in pounds)	100,000	Available capacity (pounds)	200,000
Selling price per pound	$25		
Variable costs per pound		**Fixed costs**	
Variable cost per pound	$10	Fixed costs (Exhibit 5.1)	$1,200,000
Decrease in variable cost	*$1*	*Increase in fixed costs*	*$40,000*
New variable cost	$9	New fixed costs	$1,240,000

Exhibit 5.12	Sierra Plastics: CVP Analysis with and without New Inspection Technology						
	Price	**Unit Variable Cost**	**Unit Contribution Margin**	**Fixed Costs**	**Breakeven Volume**	**Expected Sales**	**Profit before Taxes**
With new technology	$25	$9	$16	$1,240,000	77,500	100,000	$360,000
Without new technology (current operations)	$25	$10	$15	$1,200,000	80,000	100,000	$300,000

If Sierra maintains sales at the current level of 100,000 pounds and revenues of $2,500,000, it has a 20 percent margin of safety.

With the new technology, breakeven volume is 77,500 pounds and breakeven revenues are $1,937,500 (77,500 × $25). Thus, we have:

$$\textit{Margin of safety (new technology)} = \frac{100,000 - 77,500}{100,000} = \frac{\$2,500,000 - \$1,937,500}{\$2,500,000}$$
$$= 22.5\%$$

By reducing the breakeven point, and thereby increasing the margin of safety, the new technology lowers Sierra's operating risk at the expected level of operations.

To firm up our understanding, let us revisit the decision to reduce prices from the perspective of margin of safety. We know from Exhibit 5.9 that lowering the price of Perlast to $20 will increase profit. But is there any downside to reducing the price? What happens to Sierra's margin of safety? Because the price reduction decreases Sierra's unit contribution margin to $10, Sierra's breakeven volume increases to 120,000 pounds (fixed costs of $1,200,000/unit contribution margin of $10). Ben expects to sell 160,000 pounds of Perlast at the new price; therefore, Sierra's expected margin of safety is

$$\textit{Margin of safety} = \frac{160,000 - 120,000}{160,000} = 0.25 \text{ or } 25\%$$

Thus, decreasing price increases both expected profit *and* the margin of safety (calculated earlier at 20%). However, in the final analysis of option 1, Ben will need to weigh the comfort he gains from the larger cushion against the pressure of needing to sell an additional 40,000 pounds to break even.

In general, the higher the margin of safety, the lower the risk of a loss should actual sales fall short of expectations. There is no hard and fast rule on what is an appropriate margin of safety. It varies from industry to industry and from firm to firm. In industries with stable demand conditions, a small margin of safety might be enough to reduce the risk of losses to acceptable levels. Conversely, firms that face highly variable demand conditions might require high margins of safety.

Margin of Safety and Profit Sensitivity

We can use the margin of safety to calculate the percent change in profit that results from any given percent change in sales, as follows:

% change in profit before taxes = % change in *Sales volume* × (1/*Margin of safety*)
= % change in *Revenues* × (1/*Margin of safety*)

Using the current data (without the new technology and with the current price of $25 per pound), we know that Sierra's current sales are 100,000 pounds and its margin of safety is 20%. Then, if sales were to increase by 10% to 110,000 pounds, this equation indicates that Sierra's profit change would be

% change in profit before taxes = 0.10 × (1/0.20) = 0.50 or 50%

Check It! Exercise #3

Assume that Sierra sells Perlast for $50 a pound, the unit variable cost is $30, annual fixed costs equal $1,500,000, and current sales total 80,000 pounds. Verify that the margin of safety = 6.25% using both sales volume in units and revenues. In addition, verify that if sales were to increase by 20%, profits would increase by 320%, from $100,000 to $420,000.

Solution at end of chapter.

Sierra's profit before taxes would increase by 50% of $300,000, or $150,000. Adding this $150,000 to the original profit of $300,000 gives a revised profit before taxes of $450,000. As we saw in Exhibit 5.3, a small change in sales can have a large impact on profit. The effect is particularly large for sales volumes near the breakeven point, where margins of safety are very low.

OPERATING LEVERAGE

By their choice of technology, firms can influence the proportion of fixed and variable costs they incur. Typically, firms with higher fixed costs have lower variable costs and, hence, higher contribution margins. However, at lower volumes, higher fixed costs impose higher risk because they result in greater total costs. Moreover, the greater the fixed cost, the more sensitive is profit to changes in volume.

Exhibit 5.13 is useful for understanding this trade-off between fixed and variable costs. This exhibit shows the total cost lines for two companies that have different cost structures. Company M, represented by the solid line, is machine intensive, whereas Company L, represented by the dotted line, is labor intensive. At zero sales volume, there are no variable costs—this is the point where each line intercepts the y-axis. At this point, total costs are higher for Company M because it has higher fixed costs from its investment in machinery. As sales volume increases, total costs increase at a smaller rate for Company M because its unit variable cost is lower than that for labor-intensive Company L. For low sales volumes, Company M has higher total costs than Company L.

As volume increases, the difference in total costs narrows and vanishes at some point. This point, marked in the graph as point A, represents the *crossover* volume. At this point, the total costs for the two companies are equal. Beyond this point, the total costs for Company L exceed those of Company M. Higher volumes favor Company M because the benefits from its lower variable costs more than offset the disadvantage it faces from higher fixed costs.

Exhibit 5.13	*Alternate Cost Structures Trade Off Fixed Costs with Variable Costs*

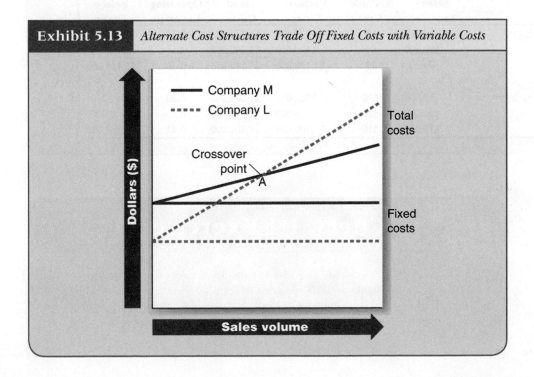

Firms use **operating leverage** as a measure of risk arising from having more fixed costs. We calculate operating leverage as follows:

$$Operating\ leverage = \frac{Fixed\ costs}{Fixed\ costs\ +\ Variable\ costs} = \frac{Fixed\ costs}{Total\ costs}$$

Let us consider how the technology changes Sierra's operating leverage. Exhibit 5.14 shows Sierra's operating leverages and profits for different sales volumes, with and without the new technology.

Exhibit 5.14 shows that while the new technology does increase operating leverage, the increase is not substantial. In general, we prefer the technology with a smaller operating leverage at lower sales volumes and technology with a larger operating leverage at higher volumes. To see this, notice that under both cost structures (with and without new technology), Sierra will report an identical profit (a loss of $600,000) at the crossover volume of 40,000 pounds. At volumes below 40,000 pounds, Sierra prefers the current technology (with the lower operating leverage) because this choice results in a *lower* loss. If he expects sales beyond this level, however, Ben will want to select the new technology as it results in a lower loss or higher profit.

In summary, at the current sales level of 100,000 pounds, the new inspection technology creates only a small difference in Sierra's operating leverage. The additional risk associated with acquiring the new technology is small. In fact, the new technology substantially improves profit for sales volumes over 40,000 pounds. Overall, it appears that Ben should seriously consider the new technology. However, before he makes that decision, he needs information about the third option, expanding Sierra's product offerings. Evaluating this alternative will require us to perform *multiproduct* CVP analysis.

Exhibit 5.14	*Sierra Plastics: Analysis of Operating Leverage with and without New Technology*

	Sales Volume	Unit Variable Cost	Variable Costs	Fixed Costs	Operating Leverage	Profit before Taxes
With new technology	30,000	$9	$270,000	$1,240,000	0.82	($760,000)
	100,000	$9	$900,000	$1,240,000	0.58	$360,000
	170,000	$9	$1,530,000	$1,240,000	0.45	$1,480,000
Without new technology	30,000	$10	$300,000	$1,200,000	0.80	($750,000)
	100,000	$10	$1,000,000	$1,200,000	0.55	$300,000
	170,000	$10	$1,700,000	$1,200,000	0.41	$1,350,000

Check It! Exercise #4

When comparing profits with and without the inspection technology, verify the crossover point of 40,000 pounds. You can determine the crossover point by solving for the sales volume at which both cost structures yield the same total cost. You can ignore revenues in your computation because it is the same for both decision alternatives.

Solution at end of chapter.

Connecting to Practice

OUTSOURCING AND OPERATING LEVERAGE

Chrysler outsources many of the components in its auto assembly lines rather than making the components in-house. In-house manufacturing requires higher fixed costs due to costly investments in plant and equipment. However, the variable costs of producing in-house are likely to be less than those from outsourcing because of economies of scale and scope.

COMMENTARY: A low operating leverage strategy allows companies such as Chrysler to offer new models, and not be limited by the capabilities of existing plant and equipment. A cost structure with less operating leverage offers companies *flexibility* because it involves fewer upfront cost commitments (i.e., fewer fixed costs). Companies confronting uncertain and fluctuating demand conditions are likely to opt for this flexibility because it allows them greater discretion in pricing and in offering product variations to stimulate sales. On the other hand, companies facing stable and predictable demand conditions might opt for high operating leverage by investing in fixed resources. Such a strategy allows them to benefit from economies of scale and scope and keep the variable costs of production down.

Outsourcing operations changes a firm's cost structure. (Mark Joseph/Getty Images)

Multiproduct CVP Analysis

In this section, we extend CVP analysis to settings in which a firm makes multiple products or many versions of the same product. Because products share resources such as the plant, equipment, and supervisors, and such costs are fixed in the short term, it does not make sense to allocate or assign these fixed costs to any particular product. Consequently, it is not advisable to perform CVP analysis on a product-by-product basis. Rather, it is necessary to perform CVP analysis by taking into consideration all products *at once* as a group. We refer to a group of products as a *portfolio* of products.

Fortunately, CVP analysis with many products is essentially the same as for a single product. Like the single-product CVP relation, the multiproduct CVP relation also stems from the contribution margin statement. However, each of a firm's many products usually has a different unit contribution margin. Therefore, we now have to consider a *segment* contribution margin statement, as in Chapter 4, where we separately computed Office Gallery's contribution margin derived from desks, chairs, and bookshelves. In addition, we total *all* of the fixed costs and represent them as one sum.

In the context of Sierra, recall that as a third option, Ben is considering offering many grades of Perlast. Specifically, in addition to selling Standard Perlast, Ben is considering producing and selling an economy version of Perlast. Because it will sell for only $15 per pound, Ben expects that Economy Perlast will expand Sierra's customer base, increase sales volume, and better utilize existing capacity. The company already has most of the equipment to produce both products, but will need some new equipment to permit the greater variation in prepping the raw materials

LEARNING OBJECTIVE 5

Perform CVP analysis with multiple products.

and in finishing operations. Sierra can lease this equipment for $75,000 per year. Exhibit 5.15 summarizes key information for this third option.

Combining Standard and Economy sales, the total sales volume of 164,000 pounds represents a significant increase over current sales. Ben estimates that for every three pounds of Standard Perlast sold, Sierra will sell five pounds of Economy Perlast. This mix underlies his estimate that he would sell 102,500 pounds (5/8 × 164,000) of Economy and 61,500 pounds (3/8 × 164,000) of Standard Perlast. Thus, while the introduction of Economy Perlast will add new customers, it also will take sales away from Standard Perlast. We refer to the relative proportion in which Sierra expects to sell the two products as the **product mix**—in this case, three pounds of Standard to five pounds of Economy. Knowledge of the product mix is crucial to performing multi-product CVP analysis.

We can now prepare Sierra's segmented contribution margin statement, as in Exhibit 5.16, to evaluate the profit from adding Economy Perlast.

We learn that even though adding Economy Perlast will *increase* overall sales, the move will *lower* Sierra's profit before taxes to $262,500 from the current level of $300,000. While Exhibit 5.16 answers Ben's question about this specific option, how, in general, do we plan profit when multiple products exist? To address this question, we need a multiproduct version of the CVP relation—we tackle this topic next.

PROFIT PLANNING WITH MULTIPLE PRODUCTS

There are two equivalent methods for performing multiproduct CVP analysis: the *weighted unit contribution margin method* and the *weighted contribution margin ratio method*. We begin with the weighted unit contribution margin method.

Weighted Unit Contribution Margin Method

In a multiproduct CVP analysis, the **weighted unit contribution margin** is simply the contribution margin per average unit. From Exhibit 5.16, we can calculate the weighted unit contribution margin as the total contribution margin of $1,537,500 divided by the total sales of 164,000 pounds, or $9.375 per pound.

Exhibit 5.15	*Sierra Plastics: Multiple-Product Data*				
	Type of Perlast				
	Economy	*Standard*	**Fixed Costs**		**Amount**
Unit (per pound) price	$15	$25	Current fixed costs		$1,200,000
Unit variable cost	9	10	**Lease—New equipment**		75,000
Unit contribution margin	$6	$15	Total fixed costs		$1,275,000
Sales volume (pounds)	102,500	61,500			

Exhibit 5.16	*Sierra Plastics: Product-Level Contribution Margin Statement*		
	Economy	**Standard**	**Total**
Sales volume (in units)	102,500	61,500	164,000
Revenues	$1,537,500	$1,537,500	$3,075,000
Variable costs	922,500	615,000	1,537,500
Contribution margin	$615,000	$922,500	$1,537,500
Common fixed costs			$1,275,000
Profit before taxes			$262,500

CHAPTER CONNECTIONS

Whether to offer more grades of Perlast is a good example of the fuzzy boundaries between decision horizons. We would consider this option as a long-term decision if it substantially *changes the firm's productive capacity and fixed costs. Such a decision to alter the firm's product portfolio allows it to target new markets and obtain new capabilities. We address these types of decisions in Chapters 9, 11, and 12. In contrast, a decision to alter the mix of current products to respond to changing demand is a short-term decision. This decision seeks the best way to use* available *capacity by changing the emphasis of products in the current portfolio. Sierra's decision lies between these two classes of decisions. Even though it leads to a small change in fixed costs and capabilities, it does not alter productive capacity.*

Connecting to Practice

DIET COKE

In 1982, the **Coca-Cola Company** introduced Diet Coke (in some regions, Diet Coke is marketed as Coca-Cola Light). Since its inception, sales of the zero-calorie beverage have steadily increased. It currently ranks as the third largest-selling soft drink in the world (Coca-Cola® & Pepsi® are the number 1 and 2 selling soft drinks, respectively). The **Coca-Cola Company** markets and sells both Coke and Diet Coke in over 150 countries worldwide.

COMMENTARY: We could analyze **Coca-Cola**'s decision to introduce Diet Coke within the context of the CVP relation. The decision to produce and sell Diet Coke increased **Coca-Cola**'s overall fixed costs but added a new product that would contribute to covering fixed costs and profit. In essence, **Coca-Cola** hoped the increased contribution margin exceeded the increase in fixed costs. In hindsight, the decision to introduce Diet Coke worked out well for **Coca-Cola**. Not all of **Coca-Cola**'s new-product decisions have been as successful, though, as evidenced by **Coca-Cola**'s decision to replace Classic Coke with "New Coke" in 1985. The decision proved to be a disaster, and the firm quickly reversed it.

We can also calculate the weighted unit contribution margin using unit-level data. In Sierra's case, Ben expects *unit sales* to consist of 5/8 or 62.50% Economy Perlast and 3/8 or 37.50% Standard Perlast. Therefore, the weighted unit contribution margin is

Weighted unit contribution margin $= (0.625 \times \$6) + (0.375 \times \$15) = \$9.375$

Because the weighted unit contribution margin is the contribution margin of an average unit, we can write Sierra's profit in terms of the total number of pounds sold as:

Profit before taxes = (Weighted unit contribution margin $\times$ Total sales volume in pounds) $-$ Fixed costs

For Sierra, we have,

$$\textit{Profit before taxes} = (\$9.375 \times \textit{Total sales volume in pounds}) - \$1,275,000$$
$$= \$9.375 \times 164,000 - \$1,275,000 = \$262,500$$

Just as we did for a single product, we can use the multiproduct CVP relation to find Sierra's breakeven volume or the volume needed for target profit. Setting profit before taxes to zero (for breakeven), we divide its fixed costs of $1,275,000 by the weighted unit contribution margin of $9.375 to get 136,000 total units. In turn, 5/8 of these units should be Economy Perlast and 3/8 of them Standard Perlast. Thus, Sierra would break even by selling 85,000 pounds of Economy and 51,000 pounds of Standard Perlast. Exhibit 5.17 summarizes our calculations:

Check It Exercise #5 asks you to verify calculations for earning a target profit of $225,000.

Weighted Contribution Margin Ratio Method

Thus far, we have defined product mix in terms of units sold. Frequently, managers find it more convenient to express product mix in terms of revenues. As with the single-product setting, managers of multiproduct firms usually work with the share of revenue from various products rather than units sold.

Comparing contribution margin ratios across products often makes more sense than comparing unit contribution margins. After all, comparing the unit contribution margin of a sports car such as a Ford Mustang with that of an entry-level vehicle such as a Ford Fusion is like comparing apples and oranges. Moreover, firms often use different units for their products. John Deere sells tractors and health insurance, and cannot express both products in the same unit. On the other hand, we can always compare contribution margin ratios because they represent the fraction of each sales dollar that goes toward covering fixed costs and profit.

As with the weighted unit contribution margin, we can compute the **weighted contribution margin ratio** either from the segment contribution margin statement or from unit-level data. From Exhibit 5.16, we know that total revenues are $3,075,000 and the total contribution margin is $1,537,500. Thus, the weighted contribution margin ratio, or the contribution ratio per average dollar, is $1,537,500/$3,075,000 = 50%.

We also could obtain this value by weighting each individual product's contribution margin ratio by its expected share of *revenues*. For Sierra, the contribution margin ratios of Economy and Standard are 0.40 ($6/$15) and 0.60 ($15/$25), respectively. Moreover, from Exhibit 5.16 we know that each product contributes 50% of total revenue.

Exhibit 5.17	*Sierra Plastics: Multiproduct CVP Analysis* *Weighted Unit Contribution Margin Method*	
Description	**Economy**	**Standard**
Expected product mix (in pounds)	5	3
Proportion of each product in the expected product mix	5/8	3/8
Selling price per pound	$15	$25
Variable cost per pound	9	10
Unit contribution margin	$6	$15
Weighted unit contribution margin	(5/8 × $6) + (3/8 × $15) = $9.375	
Fixed costs	$1,275,000	
Breakeven volume	$1,275,000/$9.375 = 136,000 total units	
Breakeven volume in individual products (= total units × proportion of each product in the mix)	136,000 × 5/8 = 85,000 lb	136,000 × 3/8 = 51,000 lb

 **Check It! Exercise #5**

Suppose the new product mix is that for every 2 pounds of Standard Perlast sold, Sierra will sell 5 pounds of Economy Perlast. Verify that if Sierra wants to earn a target profit before taxes of $225,000, it must sell 175,000 weighted units. Then verify that at this volume of sales, Sierra will sell 50,000 pounds of Standard Perlast and 125,000 pounds of Economy Perlast.

Item	Economy	Standard
Expected product mix (in pounds)	5	2
Proportion of each product in the expected Product mix		
Unit contribution margin	$6	$15
Weighted unit contribution margin		
Fixed costs	$1,275,000	
Target profit	$225,000	
Required volume in pounds of weighted units		
Required volume of individual products		

Solution at end of chapter.

Weighted contribution margin ratio = (0.50 × 0.40) × (0.50 × 0.60) = 0.50 or 50%

Using the weighted contribution margin ratio, we write profit as

Profit before taxes = (*Weighted contribution margin ratio* × *Total revenues*) − *Fixed costs*

Let us consider an example to solidify our understanding. Suppose Sierra wants to earn $315,000 after taxes in the coming year and that it faces a tax rate of 40%. How much total revenue must Sierra generate? What does this translate to in terms of sales of Economy and Standard?

For Sierra, because the weighted contribution margin ratio is 50%, we have:

Profit before taxes = (0.50 × *Total revenues*) − $1,275,000

In order to earn profit after taxes of $315,000, Sierra must earn $315,000/0.60 = $525,000 in profit before taxes. (Note that 1 − the tax rate of 40% = 60% or 0.60.) We can now solve for the total revenue required:

$525,000 = (0.50 × *Total revenues*) − $1,275,000

We find *Total revenues* = $3,600,000. Each product contributes 50% to revenue or $1,800,000 each for Economy and Standard. This level equals $1,800,000/$15 per pound = 120,000 pounds of Economy and $1,800,000/$25 per pound = 72,000 pounds of Standard.

Check It Exercise #6 allows you to develop your skills further. In this exercise, you will use the weighted contribution margin ratio approach to calculate breakeven revenues and verify that it is equivalent to the weighted unit contribution margin method.

MAKING DECISIONS USING CVP ANALYSIS

We have now completed evaluating Ben's three options using CVP analysis. The accompanying Decision Framework box summarizes our recommendation.

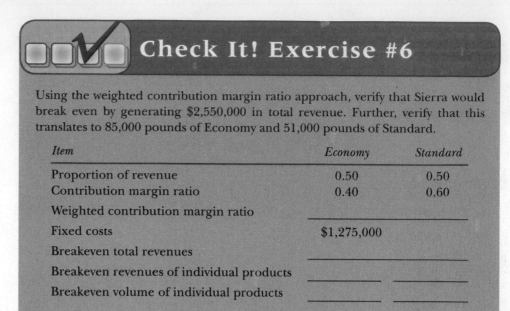

Check It! Exercise #6

Using the weighted contribution margin ratio approach, verify that Sierra would break even by generating $2,550,000 in total revenue. Further, verify that this translates to 85,000 pounds of Economy and 51,000 pounds of Standard.

Item	Economy	Standard
Proportion of revenue	0.50	0.50
Contribution margin ratio	0.40	0.60
Weighted contribution margin ratio		
Fixed costs	$1,275,000	
Breakeven total revenues		
Breakeven revenues of individual products		
Breakeven volume of individual products		

Solution at end of chapter.

For administrative reasons, Ben did not want to consider multiple options at the same time. However, it seems logical to lower the price *and* to acquire the inspection technology. The inspection technology increases operating leverage because it increases fixed costs and reduces variable costs. Thus, its profit effect is greater at higher sales volumes. Because a price reduction leads to greater volume, a price cut also increases the attractiveness of the inspection technology. As such, you might recommend that Ben include the combined choice as a fourth option.

Decisions may not reinforce each other's profit impact. For example, if Ben decides to expand Sierra's product line, he may not want to invest in the new inspection technology unless he can also use the technology for Economy Perlast. Likewise, if Ben decides to expand Sierra's product line, reducing the selling price on Standard Perlast is probably unwise. Each of these combinations adds another twist to Ben's decision.

APPLYING THE DECISION FRAMEWORK

What Is the Problem?
How can Sierra Plastics increase its profit?

What Are the Options?
Ben and his staff have identified three promising options:
1. Decrease the price of Perlast to increase demand.
2. Purchase new inspection technology to reduce the unit variable cost of Perlast.
3. Offer different grades of Perlast to meet the specific needs of individual market segments.

What Are the Costs and Benefits?
Summarizing each option's profit impact, we have:

Option	Effect on Profit before Taxes
Reduce price to $20	Increase to $400,000.
Acquire inspection technology	Increase to $360,000.
Offer more varieties of Perlast	Decrease to $262,500.

Make the Decision!
You recommend that Ben lower the price of Perlast to $20 per pound, as this appears to be the best way to boost short-term profits.

Expanding the analysis to include every possible combination of stand-alone options usually is not advisable. Combining each choice with every other choice rapidly expands the opportunity set. Good managers excel in narrowing their choices to those that complement each other and are most promising.

CVP Analysis—A Critical Evaluation

As we have seen, the CVP relation crisply captures how revenues, costs, and profit vary as the volume of business varies. It enables decision makers to assess how much volume they need to avoid a loss (break even) or to maintain a certain margin of safety. Moreover, CVP analysis is useful for numerous short-term decisions related to pricing, advertising, cost structure, and more. However, any decision tool is only as good as the assumptions needed to make it work. Consequently, we need to understand the assumptions underlying CVP analysis and the extent to which they are likely to be valid.

LEARNING OBJECTIVE 6

List the assumptions underlying CVP analysis.

1. *Revenues increase proportionally with sales volume.* CVP analysis assumes that the selling price *per unit* is constant and does not vary with sales volume. This assumption reflects general practice, as most companies tend to adopt stable pricing policies. If needed, we can use CVP analysis to examine "flexible" pricing policies such as special-order pricing problems.
2. *Variable costs increase proportionally with sales volume.* CVP analysis assumes that the *unit variable cost* is constant and does not vary with sales volume. Referring to Chapter 4, this assumption says that the firm is operating in the "relevant range." While batch- and product-level costs likely exist, most firms estimate costs via linear approximation, as we have done.
3. *Selling prices, unit variable costs, and fixed costs are known with certainty.* Managers deal with numerous sources of uncertainty all the time. Because managers cannot be sure when a machine will break down or when an employee will call in sick, they cannot be 100% sure about unit variable costs or fixed costs. Likewise, it is impossible to perfectly predict demand at a given price. Some of the end-of-chapter problems help you understand how to combine the basics of probability and expected value with CVP analysis.
4. *Single-period analysis.* The typical CVP analysis assumes that all revenues and costs occur in a single period. CVP analysis does not allow a role for inventory, which means that we might incur the costs of production this period but realize the associated sales revenue the next period. The tax assumption in CVP also assumes a single-period focus as it does not allow for complex tax provisions such as carrying losses to future periods. Finally, CVP analysis does not take into account the *time value of money*, which reflects the notion that the buying power of a dollar today is not the same as the buying power of a dollar a year from now. This assumption again underscores that CVP analysis is primarily a tool for *short-term* decision making.
5. *Product-mix assumption.* With many products, CVP analysis assumes a known and constant product mix. Companies generally base such estimates on a history of past sales data and input from the Marketing Department. Nevertheless, managers also extensively evaluate alternate product-mix assumptions to assess their confidence in estimated profit, as changes in product mix can significantly affect profit.
6. *CVP analysis does not always provide the "best" solutions to short-term decisions.* Rather, CVP analysis is a tool that helps managers improve profit by answering "what if" questions. For example, CVP analysis suggests that Sierra's profit before taxes will decrease by $37,500 if the company manufactures Economy Perlast

in addition to Standard Perlast. What CVP analysis does not do, however, is to determine the optimal product mix—in other words, whether Sierra could increase profit by producing and selling Economy and Standard Perlast in a proportion other than 3:5.

7. *Availability of capacity.* CVP analysis is not well suited for a setting in which available capacity is not sufficient to meet all demand, meaning that companies have to decide which products to cut back on. In these cases, companies turn to other methods, which we discuss in Chapter 6.

SUMMARY

In this chapter, we discussed how the Cost-Volume-Profit (CVP) relation expresses a firm's profit as a function of price, the unit variable cost, sales volume, and fixed costs. We then illustrated how to use the CVP relation for profit planning, assessing operating risk, and making short-term decisions. Finally, we extended the CVP relation to settings with many products and discussed the assumptions underlying CVP analysis.

While CVP analysis is extremely useful, it can be difficult to use the CVP relation when decisions deal with individual products, resources, or customers. We consider such settings in Chapter 6.

RAPID REVIEW

LEARNING OBJECTIVE 1

Understand the Cost-Volume-Profit (CVP) relation.

- The Cost-Volume-Profit (CVP) relation expresses profit before taxes as a function of the selling price per unit, the unit variable cost, sales volume, and fixed costs.

  Profit before taxes = [(Price − Unit variable cost) × Sales volume in units] − Fixed costs = (Unit contribution margin × Sales volume in units) − Fixed costs

- Firms perform CVP analysis for three primary purposes: (1) profit planning; (2) calculating measures that help assess operating risk; and (3) evaluating the profit impact of short-term decision alternatives.

LEARNING OBJECTIVE 2

Use the CVP relation to plan profit.

- Breakeven volume is the volume of sales needed to avoid a loss. At breakeven, profit equals zero, and the contribution margin exactly equals fixed costs. Additional volume beyond breakeven contributes directly to profit.

  Breakeven volume = Fixed costs/Unit contribution margin

- Managers calculate the breakeven point in terms of revenues using the contribution margin ratio. The contribution margin ratio is the unit contribution margin divided by the price per unit. The contribution margin ratio represents the fraction of each dollar in revenue that goes first toward covering fixed costs and then to profit.

  Breakeven revenues = Fixed costs/Contribution margin ratio

- Just as firms use the CVP relation to compute breakeven volume and breakeven revenue, they use the CVP relation to calculate the sales volume or revenues required to earn a target profit, either before or after taxes.

LEARNING OBJECTIVE 3

Make short-term decisions using CVP analysis.

- When evaluating short-term decisions, organizations use the CVP relation to estimate the effects on price, unit variable cost, sales volume, and fixed costs.

- Marketing personnel in organizations often develop schedules showing the trade-off between price and demand. The CVP relation allows managers to compute profit at the various price-quantity combinations to identify the profit-maximizing choice.

Measure risk using the CVP relation.

- Organizations need to consider the effects of uncertainty, or risk, on their decisions. The CVP relation provides two measures of operating risk.
- Margin of safety is the percentage by which current sales exceed breakeven sales.

  Margin of safety = Sales (in units or dollars) − Breakeven sales (in units or dollars)/Sales (in units or dollars)

  Percent change in profit = Percent change in sales × (1/Margin of Safety)

- Higher operating leverage implies higher risk. We measure operating leverage as

$$\text{Operating leverage} = \frac{\text{Fixed Costs}}{\text{Total Costs}}$$

Perform CVP analysis with multiple products.

- Multiproduct firms perform CVP analysis at the portfolio, or aggregate, level. Firms do so because products share resources such as plant, equipment, and supervisors, and such costs are fixed in the short term. Thus, it does not make sense to allocate or assign fixed costs to any particular product.

- Product mix, or the relative proportion in which a firm expects to sell its products, is a crucial input to multiproduct CVP analysis.
- There are two arithmetically equivalent approaches for performing multiproduct CVP analysis: (1) the weighted unit contribution margin approach; and, (2) the weighted contribution margin ratio approach.

List the assumptions underlying CVP analysis.

- Revenues increase proportionally with sales volume.
- Variable costs increase proportionally with sales volume.
- Selling prices, unit variable costs, and fixed costs are known with certainty.
- Single-period analysis—all revenues and costs occur in a single period.
- In multiproduct CVP analysis, the product mix is known and constant.
- CVP analysis does not always provide the "best" solution to short-term decisions. While useful for answering "what if" questions, CVP analysis does not necessarily provide the optimal selling price or product mix.
- Availability of capacity—CVP analysis assumes that firms do not encounter capacity constraints that force them to ration capacity.

ANSWERS TO CHECK IT! EXERCISES

Exercise #1: $675,000 = ($15 per pound × 125,000 pounds) − $1,200,000.

Exercise #2:
Unit contribution margin approach:
Unit contribution margin = $50 − $30 = $20; Breakeven volume
= $1,500,000/$20 = $75,000;
Breakeven revenues = 75,000 × $50 = $3,750,000
Contribution margin ratio approach:

Contribution margin ratio = $\frac{\$50-\$30}{\$50}$ = 0.40;

Breakeven revenues = $1,500,000/0.40 = $3,750,000;
Breakeven volume = $3,750,000/$50 = 75,000

Exercise #3:
Breakeven volume = $1,500,000/$20 = 75,000; Breakeven revenues = $1,500,000/0.40 = $3,750,000. In addition, current revenues = 80,000 × $50 = $4,000,000

Margin of safety = $\frac{80,000-75,000}{80,000}$ = $\frac{\$4,000,000-\$3,750,000}{\$4,000,000}$ = 0.0625, or 6.25%

If sales were to increase by 20%, then the percent change in profit before taxes = 0.20 × (1/0.0625) = 3.20, or 320%. Because current profit before taxes = [($20 × 80,000) − $1,500,000] = $100,000, profit would increase by $100,000 × 3.2 = $320,000. In turn, $100,000 + $320,000 = $420,000.

Exercise #4:
With the new technology, total costs = $1,240,000 + ($9 × *Sales volume in units*).
Without the new technology, total costs = $1,200,000 + ($10 × *Sales volume in units*).

Setting these two equations equal to each other, we have:

$1,240,000 + ($9 × *Sales volume in units*) = $1,200,000 + ($10 × *Sales volume in units*)

Solving, we find *Sales volume in units* = 40,000 pounds.

Exercise #5:

Weighted unit contribution margin = (5/7 × $6) + (2/7 × $15) = $60/7 = $8.5714 (rounded)

Required volume in total units = ($1,275,000 + $225,000)/$8.5714 = 175,000 pounds

Required volume of individual products: 175,000 pounds × 5/7 = 125,000 pounds of Economy, and 175,000 × 2/7 = 50,000 pounds of Standard.

Exercise #6:

Weighted contribution margin ratio = (0.50 × 0.40) + (0.50 × 0.60) = 0.50. Thus, Breakeven total revenues = $1,275,000/0.50 = $2,550,000. Breakeven revenues of individual products: $2,550,000 × 0.50 = $1,275,000 for Economy, and $2,550,000 × 0.50 = $1,275,000 for Standard.

Breakeven volume of individual products: $1,275,000/$15 = 85,000 pounds of Economy, and $1,275,000/$25 = 51,000 pounds of Standard.

SELF-STUDY PROBLEMS

SELF-STUDY PROBLEM #1:
Single-Product CVP Analysis

Silicon Cards makes a high-capacity memory card, SC-100, for use in electronic equipment. Silicon's owner, Monique Mejia, started the company because she believed that memory cards would gain widespread acceptance. Monique believed the demand for portable electronics would increase and, in turn, stimulate the demand for memory cards.

During the upcoming year, Silicon expects to sell 450,000 SC-100 cards at an average selling price of $30 per card. Silicon's unit variable cost is $18 per card, and its annual fixed costs equal $4,800,000.

a. *What is Silicon's annual profit equation?*

Using the information provided, we can write Silicon's profit equation as

Profit before taxes = [(Price − Unit variable cost) × Sales volume in units] − Fixed costs, or

Profit before taxes = [($30 − $18) × Sales volume in units] − $4,800,000

$$= (\$12 \times \textit{Sales volume in units}) - \$4,800,000$$

b. *How many cards does Silicon need to sell to breakeven? What does this translate to in revenue?*

Breaking even implies a profit of $0. Using the CVP relation from part (a) and setting profit equal to $0, we have:

$0 = ($12 × *Breakeven volume*) − $4,800,000

Solving, we find *Breakeven volume* = **400,000 cards**

We could also compute breakeven volume by dividing fixed costs by the unit contribution margin.

$$\textit{Breakeven volume} = \frac{\textit{Fixed costs}}{\textit{Unit contribution margin}} = \frac{\$4,800,000}{\$12} = \textbf{400,000 cards}$$

Next, we calculate Silicon's breakeven point in revenue by multiplying the breakeven volume by price. We have:

Breakeven revenues = Breakeven volume × Price = 400,000 × $30 = **$12,000,000**

c. *What is Silicon's contribution margin ratio? Compute Silicon's breakeven revenues using the contribution margin ratio approach.*

Using the formula in the text, Silicon's contribution margin ratio is given by

$$\textit{Contribution margin ratio} = \frac{\textit{Unit contribution margin}}{\textit{Price}} = \frac{\$12}{\$30} = 0.40, \text{ or } \textbf{40\%}$$

Computing breakeven revenues directly using the formula in the text, we find:

$$\text{Breakeven revenues} = \frac{\text{Fixed costs}}{\text{Contribution margin ratio}} = \frac{\$4,800,000}{.40} = \mathbf{\$12,000,000}$$

This is exactly what we arrived at in part (b).

d. *What is Silicon's expected margin of safety during the coming year? What would sales volume need to be if Monique desires a 20% margin of safety?*

We know from part (b) that the breakeven volume is 400,000 cards. Because Monique expects sales to be 450,000 cards, Silicon's expected margin of safety is

$$\text{Margin of safety} = \frac{450,000 - 400,000}{450,000} = \frac{50,000}{450,000} = 0.1111, \text{ or } \mathbf{11.11\%}$$

For a margin of safety of 20%, we work backward to find the necessary sales volume:

$$\frac{\text{Required sales} - 400,000}{\text{Required sales}} = 0.20, \text{ or } \text{Required sales} = \mathbf{500,000 \text{ cards}}$$

e. *How many cards would Silicon need to sell to earn an annual after-tax profit of $1,800,000? Assume Silicon pays income taxes equal to 40% of profit before taxes.*

We know that:

Profit after taxes = Profit before taxes $\times$ *(1 − Tax rate)*

Using the CVP relation we developed in part (a) and modifying it for the tax rate yield:

Profit after taxes = [($12 $\times$ *Sales volume in units*) − $4,800,000] $\times$ (1 − .40)

Setting profit after taxes equal to $1,800,000, we have:

$1,800,000 = [($12 $\times$ *Required sales volume*) − $4,800,000] $\times$ 0.60, or

Required sales volume = **650,000 cards**

Silicon needs to sell 650,000 cards to generate profit after taxes of $1,800,000.

f. *Silicon's Marketing Manager is requesting an additional $750,000 for advertising and promotion. How would Silicon's breakeven volume change if Monique agrees to this expenditure? Assume that the Marketing Manager believes that sales will increase by 100,000 cards if Silicon spends an additional $750,000 on advertising and promotion. By how much will Silicon's profit after taxes increase or decrease due to the advertising? As with part (e), assume Silicon's tax rate is 40%.*

With the additional $750,000 in advertising and promotion, Silicon's fixed costs increase from $4,800,000 to $5,550,000. To compute the new breakeven volume, we repeat part (b) with the new level of fixed costs. Doing so yields

$$\text{Breakeven volume} = \frac{\$5,550,000}{\$12} = \mathbf{462,500 \text{ cards}}$$

Alternatively, we can compute the *additional* number of cards to cover the *additional* fixed costs of $750,000. We can then add this number to the breakeven volume we calculated in part (b). Following this approach, we find that Silicon needs to sell an additional $750,000/$12 = 62,500 cards. Because 400,000 cards are required to cover the original fixed costs of $4,800,000, the new breakeven volume is 400,000 + 62,500 = 462,500 cards.

Silicon's Marketing Manager expects sales volume to increase by 100,000 cards due to increased advertising and promotion. Out of this volume, 62,500 cards are required just to cover the additional advertising and promotion expenditure of $750,000. The remaining 37,500 cards contribute directly to profit. Because the unit contribution margin on each card is $12, the *additional* profit before taxes would be 37,500 $\times$ $12 = $450,000. After taxes, Silicon would have an increase in profit of $450,000 $\times$ 0.6 = **$270,000**. Assuming the marketing manager's demand estimate is accurate, spending an additional $750,000 on advertising and promotion is justified.

SELF-STUDY PROBLEM #2:
Multiproduct CVP Analysis

Refer to Self-Study Problem #1. The owner of Silicon Cards, Monique Mejia, wishes to evaluate the possibility of using existing excess production capacity to make another product—SC45 cards.

Monique expects to sell the proposed SC-45E cards for $20 each and estimates that the unit variable cost of producing each SC-45E card will be $10. Monique also believes that there is enough excess plant and equipment capacity to accommodate the expected sales volume of 300,000 SC-45E cards. Thus, for every three SC-100 cards sold, Silicon expects to sell two SC-45E cards. (Recall from Self-Study problem #1 that Silicon expects to sell 450,000 SC-100 cards; in turn, 450,000:300,000 = 3:2.) In order to accommodate the increased sales volume, Monique will need to hire additional sales and administrative personnel, increasing annual fixed costs by $800,000.

a. *What is Silicon's annual profit equation (before taxes) if Monique decides to offer both SC-100 and SC-45E cards?*

Compared to Self-Study Problem #1, Silicon's profit will change in two ways.

First, fixed costs increase by $800,000, from $4,800,000 to $5,600,000; Silicon's profit calculation needs to reflect this change. Second, introducing the SC-45E line will mean that another product is contributing to Silicon's overall profit. Each SC-45E card has a unit contribution margin of $10 ($20 selling price − $10 unit variable cost). With these two modifications, we rewrite Silicon's profit before taxes as

Profit before taxes = ($12 × *Sales volume of SC-100 cards*)
+ ($10 × *Sales Volume of SC-45E cards*) − $5,600,000

b. *Assume Monique decides to offer both SC-100 and SC-45E cards. What is Silicon's breakeven volume in total cards and breakeven revenues for each type of card?*

Notice from the CVP relation in part (a) that multiple sales quantity combinations of SC-100 and SC-45E cards would satisfy the breakeven condition. Thus, with multiple products, we need to specify a product mix, which is the proportion (expressed in units) in which Silicon expects to sell the products. This proportion is 3:2, as Monique expects to sell three SC-100 cards for every two SC-45E cards.

This product mix allows us to calculate a weighted unit contribution margin, which is $(3/5 \times \$12) + (2/5 \times \$10) = \$11.20$.

Rewriting Silicon's profit in terms of total units, we have:

Profit before taxes = ($11.20 × *Sales volume in total units*) − $5,600,000

We are now in a position to use the breakeven equation from the text. We have:

$$\text{Breakeven volume} = \frac{\text{Fixed costs}}{\text{Weighted unit contribution margin}} = \frac{\$5,600,000}{\$11.20}$$

= 500,000 total cards

Because three out of every five cards are SC-100, the breakeven volume is 300,000 SC-100 cards and 200,000 SC-45E cards. Breakeven revenue for the SC-100 cards is 300,000 × $30 = $9,000,000, and breakeven revenue for the SC-45E cards is 200,000 × $20 = $4,000,000.

c. *Given the sales projections for the SC-45E card, does it make sense for Monique to expand her product line? What other considerations might weigh into Monique's decision to expand her product line? Assume that Silicon pays income taxes equal to 40% of profit before taxes.*

First, we rewrite Silicon's CVP profit to incorporate taxes:

Profit after taxes = [($12 × *Sales volume of SC-100 cards*)
+ ($10 × *Sales volume of SC-45E cards*) − $5,600,000] × (1 − 0.40)

According to Monique's sales projections, Silicon expects to sell 450,000 SC-100 cards and 300,000 SC-45E cards. Plugging these projections into the expression for profit, we have:

Profit after taxes = [($12 × 450,000) + ($10 × 300,000) − $5,600,000)]
× (1 − 0.40) = **$1,680,000**.

If Silicon does not introduce the SC-45E card, then it expects to sell 450,000 SC-100 cards (as in the previous year), and its profit after taxes would be $360,000 (we can verify this number using the CVP relation from part (e) of Self-Study Problem #1). Thus, the incremental profit of introducing the SC-45E cards is $1,680,000 − $360,000 = $1,320,000. It makes economic sense for Silicon to introduce the SC-45E line.

In general, introducing a new product line is a long-term decision that is subject to many strategic considerations. Monique should consider her competition's reaction, what other memory card manufacturers are likely to do, and whether introducing the SC-45E line will affect the demand for her popular SC-100 card. For example, do we really believe that demand for the SC-100 will equal 450,000 regardless of whether Silicon introduces the SC-45E line? Moreover, Silicon should not base such a decision on expectations formed for a single period. It is important to remember that CVP analysis is primarily a short-term decision aid; we should use it cautiously for decisions involving longer horizons.

d. *Compute Silicon's operating leverage with and without the SC-45E card. What can you conclude about the effect of introducing the SC-45E card on Silicon's operating leverage?*

Recall that operating leverage is the ratio of fixed costs to total costs. Also recall that the unit variable cost of SC-100 is $18 and that the unit variable cost of SC-45E is $10. Annual fixed costs equal $4,800,000 if Silicon produces only the SC-100 card and $5,600,000 if Silicon produces both the SC-100 and SC-45E cards. Thus, the operating leverage with and without the SC-45E card is

$$\text{Operating leverage (SC-100 only)} = \frac{\text{Fixed costs}}{\text{Total costs}} = \frac{\$4,800,000}{\$4,800,000 + (\$18 \times 450,000)}$$
$$= \mathbf{0.372}$$

$$\text{Operating leverage (SC-100 + SC-45E)} = \frac{\$5,600,000}{\$5,600,000 + (\$18 \times 450,000) + (300,000 \times \$10)}$$
$$= \mathbf{0.335}$$

Silicon's operating leverage is expected to decrease if Monique introduces the SC-45E card. Intuitively, the decrease occurs because introducing the SC-45E line will allow Silicon to use its existing capacity more fully and gainfully. Moreover, producing the SC-45E card will not require any additional plant or equipment—the $800,000 is for additional sales and administrative personnel. To the extent that operating leverage can be viewed as a measure of risk, we see that introducing the SC-45E line reduces Silicon's profit risk—lower operating leverage implies lower risk.

GLOSSARY

Breakeven revenues The sales volume in revenues at which profit equals zero.

Breakeven volume The sales volume in units at which profit equals zero.

Contribution margin ratio The unit contribution margin divided by the unit price. The contribution margin ratio represents the portion of each sales dollar that, after covering variable costs, goes toward covering fixed costs and, ultimately, profit.

Margin of safety The percentage by which current sales exceed breakeven sales.

Operating leverage The ratio of fixed costs to total costs (total costs = fixed costs plus variable costs).

Product mix The proportion, expressed in units, in which products are expected to be sold.

Unit contribution margin The contribution margin per unit.

Weighted unit contribution margin Unit contribution margin averaged across multiple products, with each product's unit contribution margin being weighted by the product mix (i.e., its share of total sales in units).

Weighted contribution margin ratio Contribution margin ratio averaged across multiple products, with each product's contribution margin ratio being weighted by its share of revenues (which is a function of both the product mix and prices).

REVIEW QUESTIONS

5.1 LO1. What is the CVP relation?

5.2 LO1. What does the CVP relation follow directly from?

5.3 LO2. What is breakeven volume?

5.4 LO2. What are breakeven revenues?

5.5 LO2. What is the contribution margin ratio?

5.6 LO2. How do taxes affect the CVP relation?

5.7 LO3. How can we use the CVP relation to analyze the profit effect of price changes?

5.8 LO4. What is the margin of safety?

5.9 LO4. How could we use the margin of safety to calculate the percent change in profit given a percent change in sales?

5.10 LO4. What is operating leverage?

5.11 LO5. What is a product mix?

5.12 LO5. What is a weighted unit contribution margin?

5.13 LO5. What is a weighted contribution margin ratio?

5.14 LO5. Why do managers often prefer to calculate CVP relations using the weighted contribution margin ratio approach?

5.15 LO6. What are the assumptions underlying CVP analysis?

DISCUSSION QUESTIONS

5.16 LO1. Which action has a greater effect on the unit contribution margin: (1) increasing the unit selling price by 10% or (2) reducing the unit variable cost by 10%?

5.17 LO1. In an article in the *Wall Street Journal*, you read that a firm reported a contribution margin equal to 40% of revenues and profit before taxes equal to 15% of revenues. If fixed costs were $200,000, what were the firm's revenues?

5.18 LO2. We could readily extend CVP analysis to consider cash breakeven by considering *cash* fixed costs only. That is, we exclude noncash items such as depreciation from the analysis. Which kinds of firms would value this approach?

5.19 LO2. If fixed costs increase, but the unit contribution margin stays the same, can we calculate the additional volume needed to break even by dividing the change in fixed costs by the unit contribution margin? Why or why not?

5.20 LO2. In the text, we refined the CVP relation to incorporate taxes that are proportional to pretax profit. How could we further refine the CVP relation to include multiple tax brackets, where the tax rate depends on the magnitude of the profit?

5.21 LO2 (Advanced). Could we modify the CVP relation to include step costs? What complications might arise in the context of CVP analysis with step costs?

5.22 LO3. Is the contribution margin ratio of a software firm such as Microsoft likely to be higher or lower than the contribution margin ratio of an auto maker such as Ford? What does this imply about the sensitivity of profit to sales?

5.23 LO3. What do you think of the business practice of charging customers different prices for essentially the same good? Can you list some examples where you see this practice?

5.24 LO4. How might managers use the margin of safety concept in decision making?

5.25 LO4. Why does operating leverage decrease as sales volume increases?

5.26 LO4. Why is operating leverage viewed as a measure of risk?

5.27 LO5. Consider a large multidivisional firm such as John Deere or Johnson & Johnson. Does it make sense to perform CVP analysis for such firms as a whole? More generally, how could such firms use CVP insights effectively?

5.28 LO5. The text suggests that comparing the unit contribution margin of a sports car with an entry-level vehicle is like comparing apples and oranges, but that comparing the contribution margin ratios is a fair comparison. Do you agree? Why? Can you think of an example where it may be more appropriate to compare unit contribution margins but not contribution margin ratios?

5.29 LO6. Think about each of the assumptions underlying CVP analysis. Do you believe each assumption accurately depicts reality? Can you think of a setting where each assumption is likely to be violated?

EXERCISES

5.30 CVP relation and profit planning, unit contribution margin approach (LO1, LO2). Ajay Singh plans to offer gift-wrapping services at the local mall during the month of December. Ajay will wrap each package, regardless of size, in the customer's choice of wrapping paper and bow for a price of $3. Ajay estimates that his variable costs will total $1 per package wrapped and that his fixed costs will total $600 for the month.

Required:

a. Express Ajay's profit before taxes in terms of the number of packages sold.

b. How many packages does Ajay need to wrap to break even?

c. How many packages must Ajay wrap to earn a profit of $1,400?

5.31 CVP relation and profit planning, unit contribution margin approach (LO1, LO2). From Exercise 5.30, we know that Ajay Singh's gift-wrapping service charges $3 for each package wrapped. Ajay estimates that his variable costs will total $1 per package wrapped and that his fixed costs will total $600 for the month.

Required:

a. Suppose Ajay's variable costs were to increase by 50% per package. What is Ajay's breakeven sales volume?

b. Suppose Ajay estimates that he will be able to wrap 3,000 packages in a month. Assume also that he wishes to earn $2,400 in profit for the month. What is the minimum price that Ajay must charge to reach his profit goal?

c. How much profit would Ajay earn if December revenue were $4,500 for the month?

5.32 CVP relation and profit planning, contribution margin ratio approach (LO1, LO2). Gina Matheson owns and operates a successful florist shop in Bloomington, Indiana. Gina estimates that her variable costs are $0.25 per sales dollar (i.e., variable costs represent 25% of revenue) and that her fixed costs amount to $6,000 per month.

Required:

a. How does Gina's monthly profit increase as revenue increases? (*Note:* given the absence of unit-level data, you will need to express Gina's monthly profit in terms of revenue.)

b. How much revenue does Gina need to generate each month to break even?

c. How much profit would Gina earn if her revenues were $10,000 per month?

5.33 CVP and profit planning, Hercules (LO1, LO2, LO3). Tom and Lynda own Hercules Gym. An individual membership costs $100 per month. Tom and Lynda estimate variable costs at $35 per member per month and fixed costs at $40,950 per month. They currently have 950 members.

Required:

a. How many members does Hercules need to break even?

b. Suppose Hercules pays income taxes that amount to 35% of income. How many members does Hercules need to report after tax profits of $11,375?

c. Using the contribution margin ratio, calculate the revenue required to earn an after-tax profit of $11,375.

d. What is Hercules' margin of safety?

e. What is Hercules' operating leverage?

5.34 Contribution margin, unit level costs (LO1). J&R Audio Company manufactures digital keyboards. At a volume of 15,000 units, per-unit price and cost data for the year just ended follow:

Item	Value per Unit
Selling price	$800
Variable manufacturing costs	440
Fixed manufacturing overhead	50
Gross margin	$310
Variable selling costs	40
Fixed selling and administrative costs	110
Profit margin	$160

Required

What is J&R Audio's breakeven point in units?

5.35 CVP relation and solving for unknowns, contribution margin ratio approach (LO1, LO2). Gina Matheson owns and operates a successful florist shop in Bloomington, Indiana. Gina estimates that her variable costs are $0.25 per sales dollar (i.e., variable costs represent 25% of revenue) and that her fixed costs amount to $6,000 per month.

Required:

a. How much revenue does Gina need to generate to earn a profit of $3,600 per month?

b. Suppose Gina estimates that she will be able to generate revenue of $15,000 in a month. Assume also that she wishes to earn $4,000 in profit each month. What is the maximum amount that she can spend on fixed costs?

c. Suppose Gina's variable costs were to increase by 50%. What is Gina's breakeven revenue per month?

5.36 CVP relation and profit planning, unit contribution margin approach, taxes (LO1, LO2). SpringFresh provides commercial laundry and linen services to local hospitals, hotels, and restaurants. SpringFresh charges its customers $1.50 per pound laundered, regardless of the items to be cleaned (e.g., sheet, towel, garment, tablecloth). SpringFresh's variable costs equal $0.50 per pound laundered, with fixed costs amounting to $50,000 per month. SpringFresh's income tax rate is 25%.

Required:

a. Write down the expression for SpringFresh's annual after-tax profit.

b. How much will SpringFresh pay in taxes if it processes 750,000 pounds of laundry this year? What would SpringFresh's profit after taxes be?

c. What is SpringFresh's annual breakeven volume in pounds of laundry processed?

5.37 Solving for unknowns, tax brackets, unit contribution margin approach, taxes (LO1, LO2). SpringFresh charges its customers $1.50 per pound laundered, regardless of the items to be cleaned. SpringFresh's variable costs equal $0.50 per pound laundered, with fixed costs amounting to $50,000 per month. SpringFresh's income tax rate is 25%.

Required:

What is the volume of laundry (in pounds) that must be processed if SpringFresh desires to earn $120,000 in profit after taxes for the year?

5.38 CVP relation in nonprofits, contribution margin ratio approach (LO1, LO2). The local chapter of the Rotary Foundation is planning a fundraiser. They estimate that renting the auditorium and paying for the sound system and performers and other costs would come to $15,000. They expect to charge $50 per person. Variable costs are negligible.

Required:

a. What is the required attendance for the chapter to raise $21,000 toward charity?

b. The chapter also proposes to have a cash bar at the event. They estimate that the average patron would spend $20 and that the contribution margin ratio would be 50%. How does this data change your answer to part (a)?

5.39 CVP and profit planning, contribution margin ratio approach, taxes (LO1, LO2). Arena Auto Body specializes in repairing automobiles involved in accidents. Arena has contracts with most insurance providers, enabling Arena to directly bill (and collect from) customers' insurance companies. Arena estimates that its variable costs equal 30% of billings and that fixed costs equal $14,000 per month. Furthermore, Arena pays income taxes equal to 35% of profit.

Required:

a. How does Arena's monthly after-tax profit increase as revenue increases? (*Note:* Given the absence of unit-level data, you will need to express the profit in terms of revenues, or billings.)

b. What is Arena's monthly breakeven point in billings?

c. Suppose Arena's billings for March were $50,000. What is Arena's profit before taxes? What is Arena's profit after taxes?

d. Suppose Arena wants to have profit after taxes of $7,280 per month. What is the required level of monthly billings?

5.40 CVP relation, inferring cost structure, extension to decision making (LO2, LO3). Zap, Inc., manufactures an organic insecticide that is marketed and sold via television infomercials. Each "ZAP" kit sells for $22, which includes a base price of $20 per "ZAP" kit plus $2 in shipping and handling fees. Zap's contribution margin ratio is 60%. In addition, Zap expects to break even if it sells 17,500 "ZAP" kits per month.

Required:

a. What is the unit variable cost of a "ZAP" kit?

b. What are Zap's monthly fixed costs?

c. Suppose Zap introduces an offer for "free" shipping and handling. How many additional "ZAP" kits must be sold each month to break even?

5.41 CVP relation and decision making, pricing based on a demand schedule (LO3). Greg Green is a schoolteacher who, during the summer months, operates a successful lawn-mowing business. Before advertising his services in the local newspaper, Greg needs to decide on his rate, or price per lawn. Greg is keenly aware that the lower his rate, the more business he will get and vice versa. He is determined to figure this relationship out and select the price that maximizes his summer profit. After conducting some market surveys, Greg believes that the local summer demand is as follows:

Price	Expected Demand (total # of lawns)
$32.50	300
$30.00	350
$27.50	400
$25.00	450
$22.50	500

Greg's variable costs amount to $6 per lawn mowed, and his fixed costs total $3,000 for the summer.

Required:

What price should Greg charge to maximize his profit from mowing lawns?

5.42 CVP relation and decision making, choosing a cost structure, operating leverage (LO3, LO4). Leticia Gonzalez is in charge of the concession stands division for all 100 theaters owned and operated by Midwest Cinema. Theaters range in size from single-screen (mostly in small towns) to multiplexes with 10 or more screens. Leticia wants to develop a system that will enable her to select the optimal popcorn machine for any given theater location. Leticia can rent commercial popcorn machines in small, medium, or large sizes. The fixed annual rental cost for each machine differs, as does the variable cost associated with operating and maintaining the machine. For example, the large popcorn machine costs the most to rent but requires minimal staff attention and maintenance. The following table shows the annual fixed costs and variable costs associated with operating each popcorn machine:

Size of Popcorn Machine	Annual Fixed Operating Costs	Variable Costs per Patron
Small	$6,000	$0.50
Medium	$12,000	$0.35
Large	$18,500	$0.25

Required:

a. Help Leticia determine the optimal size popcorn machine for a given theater. In other words, how many moviegoers does a theater need to have before Midwest Cinema should rent the medium and large popcorn machines?

b. Assume one of Midwest Cinema's theaters expects 65,000 moviegoers in the coming year. What is the operating leverage for each popcorn machine?

5.43 CVP relation and decision making, margin of safety, operating leverage, cash-basis break-even analysis (LO3, LO4). The Cottage Bakery sells a variety of gourmet breads, cakes, pies, and pastries. Although its wares are considerably more expensive than those available at supermarkets and other bakeries, the Cottage Bakery has a loyal clientele willing to pay a premium price for premium quality. In a typical month, the Cottage Bakery generates revenue of $150,000 and earns a profit of $7,500. The Cottage Bakery's contribution margin ratio is 40%.

Required:

a. What is the Cottage Bakery's margin of safety at its current sales level?

b. What is the Cottage Bakery's operating leverage?

c. What is the revenue required for Cottage Bakery to break even on a cash basis? Assume that 30% of the Cottage Bakery's fixed costs represent noncash items (e.g., depreciation expense on the ovens, furniture, and fixtures). All other expenses are paid in cash and all revenues are received in cash.

5.44 Multiproduct CVP analysis, unit contribution margin approach (LO5). Mountain Maples is a mail-order nursery dedicated to growing, selling, and shipping beautiful Japanese Maple trees. Located on a ridge-top in Mendocino County, northern California, Mountain Maples offers two distinctive types of Japanese Maples: Butterfly and Moonfire. The trees are sold after five growing seasons, and revenue and cost data for each tree type (for the most recent year) are as follows:

	Butterfly	Moonfire
Quantity sold	800	1,600
Selling price per tree	$200	$100
Variable cost per tree	$100	$50

Mountain Maples' fixed costs for the most recent year were $75,000.

Required:

a. How many Japanese Maples must Mountain Maples sell in a year to break even? At this sales volume, how many Butterfly and Moonfire trees are sold?

b. At the current product mix, how many Butterfly trees must Mountain Maples sell in a year to earn a profit of $50,000?

c. Assume that Mountain Maples product mix changes to 50% Butterfly and 50% Moonfire. How does this information change your answer to part (a)?

5.45 Multiproduct CVP analysis, contribution margin ratio approach (LO5). Select Auto Imports is a regional auto dealership that specializes in selling high-end imported luxury automobiles. Select Auto Imports sells both new and pre-owned (used) cars. Financial data for the most recent year of operations are as follows:

	New Cars	Used Cars	Total
Revenue	$1,500,000	$500,000	$2,000,000
Variable costs	750,000	200,000	950,000
Contribution margin	$750,000	$300,000	$1,050,000
Fixed costs			840,000
Profit before taxes			$210,000

Required:

a. Assuming the product mix remains constant, what is Select Auto Import's breakeven point in revenue? At the breakeven point, what is the revenue from new and used autos, respectively?

b. What level of revenue is required to ensure that Select Auto Imports earns a profit of $1,050,000 in the coming year? What is the revenue from new and used autos, respectively?

 5.46 Multiproduct analysis, weighted contribution margin & weighted contribution margin ratio approach, Hercules (LO5). Tom and Lynda operate Hercules Gym. The club currently has 900 individual members and 300 family memberships. The fee for individual memberships is $100 per month, and families pay $150 per month. Variable costs are $35 per month for individual and $60 per month for a family. Monthly fixed costs amount to $42,750.

Required:

a. Calculate Hercules' weighted contribution margin. Use this answer to calculate the number of individual and family memberships at breakeven volume

b. Calculate Hercules' weighted contribution margin ratio. Use this answer to calculate the total revenue to achieve breakeven.

PROBLEMS

5.47 CVP relation, profit planning, unit contribution margin approach, extensions to decision making (LO1, LO2, LO3). Garnet's Gym is a fitness and aerobic center located in Atlanta, Georgia. With over 25,000 square feet of space, Garnet's offers its customers an unparalleled fitness experience, including the finest equipment for cardiovascular training, resistance training, and free-weight training. Garnet's also features state-of-the-art aerobics, spinning, yoga, and tai chi classes taught by nationally certified instructors. Finally, when not working out, patrons can enjoy other amenities such as Garnet's tanning salon, hot tub, sauna, and juice bar.

The owners of Garnet's Gym currently are working on their operating plan for the coming year, and they have provided you with the following average membership and cost data for the previous year:

Membership fee	$500 per member
Number of members	5,000
Variable costs (supplies, etc.)	$200 per member
Fixed costs (equipment, salaries, etc.)	$1,200,000

The owners anticipate that, for the coming year, both total fixed costs and the variable cost per member will remain unchanged from the previous year.

Required:

a. Write down the expression for Garnet's annual profit.

b. How many members must Garnet's Gym have to break even?

c. Assuming the same number of members as last year, what is Garnet's expected profit for the coming year?

d. The owners of Garnet's Gym are considering reducing the membership fee by 10%. They believe that this action will increase membership to 6,500 for the coming year. What will profit be if the owners adopt this alternative? (*Note:* The membership fee for all members will be reduced by 10%.) Does this seem like a good option?

e. As an *alternative* to reducing the membership fee by 10%, the owners of Garnet's Gym could increase membership to 6,500 by adopting a special advertising campaign. What is the maximum amount that the owners should pay for the advertising campaign? (*Hint:* The amount you calculate will make the owners just indifferent between lowering the membership fee by 10% and adopting the advertising campaign.)

f. The owners of Garnet's Gym noticed that you used the unit contribution margin approach in arriving at your answers. They wonder if your answers would change if you used a contribution margin ratio approach. Briefly explain to the owners why your answers would, or would not, change.

5.48 CVP relation, profit planning, contribution margin ratio approach, extensions to decision making (LO1, LO2, LO3). You are the chief financial officer of a jewelry manufacturing and wholesaling company, Precious Stone Jewelry, Inc. (Your company's motto is "Romantic selections to suit every budget.") At this morning's executive meeting, you distributed last month's income statement—which contained the following information:

Precious Stone Jewelry
Income Statement

Revenues	$1,000,000
Variable costs	600,000
Contribution margin	$400,000
Fixed costs	260,000
Profit before taxes	$140,000
Taxes (25% of profit before taxes)	35,000
Profit after taxes	$105,000

During the meeting, the various officers of the company made the following reports:

- The marketing director indicated that, due to a competitor leaving the market, Precious Stone could raise the unit selling price on all products by 20% without affecting demand.

- The operations director indicated that, due to recent advances in technology, the company's unit variable costs could be reduced by 20%.

- The controller distributed a new tax bill, just signed into law, that will increase the company's tax rate to 30% of profit before taxes.

Required:

a. What is your company's current breakeven revenue? (For this question, ignore all of the changes announced at the meeting.)

b. Ignoring the other two changes, what effect would raising the unit selling price by 20% have on breakeven revenue?

c. Ignoring the other two changes, what effect would decreasing the unit variable cost by 20% have on the breakeven revenue?

d. Ignoring the other two changes, what effect does a change in the tax rate have on the breakeven point?

e. Suppose all of the changes announced at the meeting do take place. What will your company's profit after taxes be next month? Support your answer with a pro-forma income statement ("pro-forma" means the income statement for a time period that has not yet occurred).

5.49 CVP relation and profit planning, solving for unknowns (LO1, LO2). You read an article in your local newspaper, *The Herald Times*, about your city's expenditures on snow removal for the most recent winter. *The Herald Times* reports that there were 20 major snowfalls this past winter and that snow removal costs totaled $300,000. The article goes on to mention that the $300,000 was comprised of both fixed costs (e.g., plows, trucks, and some salaries) and variable costs per major snowfall (e.g., salt and sand). The article concludes by noting that the heavy snowfall this past winter has placed the city in somewhat of an unexpected budget bind—the city's snow removal budget for the current year was based on last year's snow removal costs of $228,000 and 12 major snowfalls.

Assume that your city's cost structure for snow removal has remained the same in recent years. That is, the fixed costs have been the same each year and the variable costs per snowfall have been the same each year. Moreover, the city does not anticipate any change in its snow removal cost structure for the coming years.

Required:

a. Fascinated by this article, you wonder if it is possible to back into your city's cost structure for snow removal costs using the two data points that the local newspaper provides. What are the city's fixed and variable costs for snow removal?

b. The *Farmers' Almanac* predicts that next year's winter will be a real "doozy" and has forecasted 26 major snowfalls for your city. Based on this forecast, how much should your city budget for in snow removal costs?

5.50 Building a CVP relation that incorporates taxes and bonus payments using a contribution margin ratio approach (LO1, LO2). The Diamond Jubilee is a floating riverboat casino that operates on the Mississippi River. The casino is open 24 hours daily and features 675 slot machines, 25 blackjack tables, 8 poker tables, 3 craps tables, and 2 roulette tables.

On average, for every $1.00 wagered at the Diamond Jubilee $0.82 goes back to the gamblers as winnings, and $0.08 covers the casino's variable costs. The remaining $0.10 goes toward covering the casino's fixed costs and contributing toward profit. The Diamond Jubilee's fixed costs amount to $27,500 per month, and the casino pays combined state and federal taxes equal to 25% of pretax profit.

For motivational purposes, the Diamond Jubilee links some of its general manager's compensation to the casino's profitability. Specifically, the riverboat's general manager, Sapphire Sally, receives a monthly bonus equal to 5% of the casino's pretax profit.

Required:

How much do Diamond Jubilee patrons have to wager in a month for the casino to earn an after-tax and after-bonus profit of $28,500? (*Note:* The bonus is deductible for tax purposes, and, thus, taxes are paid on pre-bonus profit less the bonus.)

5.51 CVP relation and profit planning, choosing a cost structure (LO1, LO2, LO3). Cecelia's Custom Cabinets specializes in making handcrafted custom cabinets for the discriminating homeowner. Over time, the owner of Cecelia's Custom Cabinets, Cecelia Tyson, has developed a strong reputation for superior craftsmanship and attention to detail—Cecelia uses only the finest hardwood materials and employs only the most expert carpenters. Currently, Cecelia and her staff do most of their work with hand tools and only sparingly use sophisticated woodworking machines.

Given the recent advances in woodworking technology, Cecelia is considering buying some state-of-the-art planing and cornicing machines. Cecelia believes that these machines will not only reduce the amount of time she and her staff spend on making cabinets but also will significantly reduce the level of scrap and wasted materials.

Under her current cost structure (i.e., without the new machines), Cecelia estimates that her fixed costs average $36,000 per month and that her contribution margin ratio is 40%. If Cecelia acquires the woodworking machines, then her fixed costs would increase to $60,000 per month; however, her contribution margin ratio would also increase to 60%.

Required:

a. What is Cecelia's monthly breakeven revenue under her current cost structure? What would Cecelia's monthly breakeven revenue be if she acquired the new machines?

b. Which cost structure would you recommend to Cecelia if her monthly revenue was $95,000? Which cost structure would you recommend to Cecelia if her monthly revenue was $150,000?

c. Calculate the sales level at which Cecelia is indifferent (that is, has the same profit) under both cost structures.

5.52 CVP relation and decision making, pricing based on a demand schedule (LO3). Innova Solutions has developed a software product that enables users to electronically prepare and file their state and federal tax returns. Innova Solutions has asked for your help in pricing this product. Preliminary market research indicates that if Innova Solutions prices its tax software at $25 per copy, then it will sell 75,000 copies in the first year. Demand would increase to 150,000 copies in the first year if the selling price were $15 per copy and to 300,000 copies in the first year if the selling price were $5 per copy.

As you know, end-users invest considerable time in learning how to use new software packages. As a result, they tend to stick with the same software year after year. Moreover, initial acceptance is extremely important; you expect that the number of copies sold in the first year will equal the number of copies sold in the second year. Thus, if Innova Solutions sells 75,000/150,000/300,000 copies in the first year, it also expects to sell 75,000/150,000/300,000 copies in the second year (as long as the price in the second year is not outrageous—in this case, $25 or less).

Innova Solutions is contemplating a strategy of setting a low introductory price in the first year followed by a more competitive price of $25 per copy in the second year. The following table summarizes Innova Solutions' pricing options in years 1 and 2 and the corresponding demand for each year:

Price (year 1)	Demand (year 1)	Price (year 2)	Demand (year 2)
$25	75,000	$25	75,000
$15	150,000	$25	150,000
$5	300,000	$25	300,000

Innova Solutions' fixed costs amount to $1,500,000 per year, and the variable costs associated with producing and distributing the software equal $1 per copy.

Required:

a. For each of the two years (and overall), calculate Innova Solutions' profit under each of three introductory pricing scenarios: $25 per copy; $15 per copy; and $5 per copy. For each of the three scenarios, the price in the second year will be $25 per copy.

b. How would your answer to part (a) change if Innova Solutions' fixed costs amounted to $200,000 per year and its variable costs associated with producing and distributing the software equaled $15 per copy?

c. What inferences can you draw about the wisdom of using low introductory prices (i.e., "low-balling") to gain market share? Does the effectiveness of this strategy change depending on the organization's cost structure?

5.53 CVP relation and margin of safety (LO4). Brenda Wong is a licensed real estate broker specializing in vacation homes and investment properties in the Sedona, Arizona area. Because of her affiliation with a large national real estate agency and her attention to detail, Brenda has been able to build a very successful business. Brenda receives a 3% commission, based on the property's selling price, for every successful transaction. (The realtor representing the other party also receives a 3% commission. Typically, the owner of the property being sold pays both commissions.) Brenda has a nice office and support staff to assist her in operating her business. Brenda's fixed costs equal $18,000 per month; her variable costs are negligible and, thus, can be ignored.

Required:

a. What is the volume of transactions (in dollars) that Brenda must successfully complete in a month to break even?

b. Assume Brenda currently averages a transaction volume of $1,000,000 per month. What is her margin of safety?

c. What is Brenda's margin of safety if she averages a transaction volume of $1,200,000 per month. What is Brenda's margin of safety if she averages a transaction volume of $1,600,000 per month?

d. What do you notice about the relation between Brenda's margin of safety and her monthly transaction volume?

5.54 CVP relation and decision making, operating leverage, margin of safety (LO3, LO4). Dan Wenman has approached your bank for a loan to start a hazardous waste management business. There are a number of biotechnology and chemical companies in Dan's community, and such companies generate a fair amount of hazardous medical, chemical, and radioactive waste. Dan wants to start a business that focuses on all aspects of the waste management process; his goal is to provide for the safe and cost-effective storage, transportation, and disposal of industrial waste.

Dan has approached your bank with two proposals. His first proposal calls for him to "go it alone." As such, Dan would be responsible for acquiring all of the necessary personnel, equipment, and facilities for waste treatment. Under this proposal, Dan expects to incur fixed costs of $1,500,000 per year. His expected contribution margin ratio is 60%.

The second proposal calls for Dan to outsource the disposal portion of his business (i.e., Dan would focus on the containment and transportation of waste). Here, Dan would enlist (and pay for) the services of a privately owned landfill, waste combustor, and incinerator (rather than buying his own landfill, waste combustor, and incinerator). The benefit of this option is that it reduces Dan's fixed costs to $675,000 per year. The cost, however, is that Dan's contribution margin ratio would decrease to 30%. Dan is confident that both options are comparable on all other dimensions, such as quality and safety.

Required:

a. Suppose Dan estimates that revenues from his business will be $2,750,000 per year. What is Dan's profit under each proposal? What is Dan's operating leverage under each proposal? What is Dan's margin of safety under each proposal? As Dan's potential lender, which proposal would you likely support?

b. Suppose Dan estimates that sales revenue from his business will be $4,500,000 per year. What is Dan's profit under each proposal? What is Dan's operating leverage under each proposal? What is Dan's margin of safety (in $) under each proposal? As Dan's potential lender, which proposal would you likely support?

5.55 **Multiproduct CVP analysis (LO5).** Campus Bagels bakes and sells authentic New York-style kettle-boiled bagels. For the most recent year, Campus Bagels sold 250,000 bagels at a selling price of $1 per bagel. During this same year, Campus Bagels incurred fixed costs of $100,000 and variable costs of $0.40 per bagel.

Management of Campus Bagels is considering extending their product line to include bagel sandwiches. Management estimates that adding bagel sandwiches would increase their total fixed costs by $25,000 per year and that the variable cost per bagel sandwich would be $1.25.

Required:

a. Ignoring the new product line, how does Campus Bagels' profit increase or decrease with number of bagels sold? Using this model, what was Campus Bagels' profit for the most recent year?

b. How would adding bagel sandwiches change Campus Bagels' profit? What information do you need before you can determine how introducing bagel sandwiches would affect Campus Bagels' overall profit? Is it reasonable to assume Campus Bagels will still sell 250,000 bagels?

c. Assume Campus Bagels believes that, in addition to selling 250,000 bagels in the coming year, it also can sell 25,000 bagel sandwiches. What price should Campus Bagels charge per bagel sandwich if it wishes to increase overall profit by $50,000?

d. Assume Campus Bagels believes that it can sell 25,000 bagel sandwiches but that this will reduce the number of bagels sold by 25,000 to 225,000 (i.e., there is a one-for-one trade-off between bagels and bagel sandwiches). What price should Campus Bagels charge per bagel sandwich if it wishes to increase overall profit by $50,000?

5.56 **Multiproduct CVP analysis and fixed cost allocations.** Jan Van Voorhis is a florist in Sedona, Arizona. Dividing his clients into two major categories, he provides the following income statement. He stresses that, for most florists (including himself), each segment accounts for 50% of total revenues.

	Retail	*Institutional*	*Total*
Revenues	$450,000	$450,000	$900,000
Variable cost	150,000	270,000	420,000
Contribution margin	300,000	180,000	480,000
Traceable fixed costs	175,000	80,000	255,000
Segment margin	125,000	100,000	225,000
Common fixed costs			200,000
Profit before taxes			$25,000

Required

a. Suppose Jan allocates common fixed costs equally between the two segments. Treating each segment as a separate business, determine the breakeven revenue for institutional revenues and for retail revenues. Does Jan's shop, as a whole, break even with these revenues?

b. Compute Jan's Weighted Contribution Margin Ratio using the product mix provided in the problem text. Determine breakeven revenues using this revenue shares.

c. Why do the answers for parts (a) and (b) differ? What key feature of Jan's business is not captured in the answer to part (a)? What do you conclude about the wisdom of allocating common costs and performing breakeven analysis separately by segment?

d. When would a firm perform breakeven analysis for a segment?

5.57 Multiproduct CVP analysis (LO5). Kim Kane sells lunches from a pushcart in a pedestrian mall near a busy office area. Over time, Kim has established a reputation for selling quality sandwiches, soups, and salads. Kim sells each sandwich for $4, each bowl of soup for $3, and each salad for $3. Customers also can purchase a bottle of water or a can of soda from Kim for $1.

For every ten customers, three customers purchase both a soup and a sandwich; three customers purchase both a soup and a salad; two customers purchase only a sandwich; one customer purchases only a bowl of soup, and one customer purchases only a salad. Six of every ten customers also purchase a bottled water or soda with their food. Kim does not offer any price discounts for purchasing multiple items; thus, a customer who purchases both a soup and a sandwich is charged $7 (i.e., $4 for the sandwich + $3 for the soup.)

Kim estimates that her variable costs are as follows: $1.25 for each sandwich; $1.00 for each bowl of soup; and $0.75 for each salad. She buys soda and water in bulk for $0.25 a can (or bottle). Finally, Kim estimates that her fixed costs (which include the cost of her time, her pushcart license, plastic and paper products, condiments, and so on) total $4,950 per month.

Required:

a. How many customers does Kim need to serve in a month to break even? What does this mean in monthly revenue? (*Hint:* Use sales per 10 customers to determine Kim's weighted contribution margin ratio.)

b. Suppose Kim decides to offer a free can of soda or bottle of water to customers who purchase a sandwich-soup-salad combo (as you know, no one currently purchases this combination). Assume that the three of every ten customers who currently purchase both a soup and a sandwich will be enticed by this offer. Also, assume that these three customers had always purchased a soda or water with their soup and sandwich. Kim's offer will have no effect on her other customer groups. How many customers does Kim need to serve in a month to break even? What does this translate to in monthly revenue?

5.58 Multiproduct CVP analysis, weighted contribution margin ratio approach (LO5). The University Bookstore sells both new and used textbooks. New textbooks are sold to students at the publisher's suggested retail price and are purchased from publishers for 75% of the suggested retail price. University Bookstore also incurs additional variable costs in selling a new textbook; variable selling costs amount to 5% of the publisher's suggested retail price.

University Bookstore sells used textbooks for 75% of the price of a new textbook. However, University Bookstore can purchase a used textbook for 25% of the suggested retail price of a new textbook. Variable selling costs (*in dollars per textbook*) are the same for both new and used textbooks. University Bookstore's annual fixed costs amount to $360,000.

Required:

a. If used books account for 40% of revenue, what is University Bookstore's breakeven revenue? (*Hint:* To calculate breakeven revenue, you will need to pick a number for the price of a new book—any number will do. Why?)

b. When students purchase a textbook for a course, they purchase either a used book or a new book, but not both. On average, would University Bookstore prefer to sell a student a new textbook or a used textbook? Why? (Assume University Bookstore has yet to purchase books for the coming semester, so the cost of textbooks is not sunk).

c. The University Bookstore has decided that, for fairness reasons, it should price used textbooks so that the contribution margin ($ contributed toward profit) per used book is the same as the current contribution margin on a new book. To accomplish this objective, what would the price of a used textbook be as a percentage of the price of a new textbook? (Recall that used textbooks currently sell for 75% of the price of a new textbook).

5.59 Multiproduct CVP analysis, how best to spend advertising dollars (LO3, LO5). The Tornado Vacuum Cleaner Company produces and sells three different types of upright vacuum cleaners: (1) the F1, (2) the F3, and (3) the F5. Each vacuum cleaner shares certain basic features such as a 15-inch cleaning width, edge groomers, headlight, and 31-foot power cord. However, the vacuums differ in the power offered (the F5 has a 12-amp motor and dual agitators), versatility (the F5 comes with five cleaning tools, whereas the F3 comes with three cleaning tools and the F1 has only one cleaning tool), and ease of use (both the F3 and the F5 are manufactured without belt drives—thus, customers do not need to purchase or install a replacement belt as they ultimately would have to for the F1).

Management of Tornado has provided you with the following data for their most recent year of operations:

	Vacuum Cleaner		
	F1	*F3*	*F5*
Selling price per unit	$150	$200	$400
Variable cost per unit	$75	$110	$240
Quantity sold	25,000	15,000	10,000

In addition, management has informed you that annual fixed costs amounted to $3,860,000.

Required:

a. What was Tornado's profit for the most recent year?

b. Assume that Tornado wants to spend $150,000 on advertising. To maximize impact, management believes it should focus all advertising dollars on one of the three vacuum cleaners. Regardless of the product chosen, Tornado estimates that sales of the targeted vacuum cleaner will increase by $600,000, whereas sales for each of the other two vacuum cleaners are expected to decrease by $60,000. Which vacuum cleaner should be the focus of the advertising campaign? By how much is profit expected to increase as a result of the advertising campaign?

c. In part (b), Tornado's management assumed that, regardless of the product chosen for the advertising campaign, the increase in sales revenue will be constant at $600,000. What assumption is management making? Likewise, management also assumed that the decline in sales revenue associated with the two vacuum cleaners not selected for the advertising campaign will be constant at $60,000. Do you believe these assumptions accurately depict reality? Why?

5.60 CVP analysis—A critical evaluation: nonlinear cost function, linear approximation, and decision making (LO3, LO6, Advanced). Jackrabbit Trails is a family camp located in Kings Canyon National Park, California. Open from mid-May to Labor Day, Jackrabbit Trails offers week-long family summer vacation packages that include lodging, three meals a day, and numerous activities such as horseback riding, waterskiing, sailing, canoeing, archery, fishing, hiking, and mountain biking. To provide families with a restful experience, Jackrabbit Trails limits the number of families to 20 per week. Moreover, the camp motto is "Follow the fun without following the herd."

Jackrabbit Trails believes that the following function captures the "true" underlying relation between the number of families at the camp in a given week and the total costs of running the camp for a week:

$$Total\ cost\ (\$) = 1,000 + 300\ (Families) - 20\ (Families)^2 + (Families)^3$$

Required:

a. Plot (graph) Jackrabbit Trails' weekly total costs as a function of the number of families for 0 to 20 families. Does the shape of this cost function look familiar to you (think back to microeconomics)? What are some of the properties of this cost function?

b. Suppose Jackrabbit Trails approximates its cost function via a linear model using the endpoints of its relevant range from 4 families to 16 families per week. Write out the linear cost model and plot it on the same graph you developed in part (a). Over what range does the linear cost function strike you as a reasonable approximation to Jackrabbit Trails' true underlying cost curve?

c. Suppose Jackrabbit Trails believes that the following equation captures the relation between the price (per family), and weekly demand (number of families) for their summer camp:

$$Price = 1{,}200 - (50 \times Families)$$

What price and quantity maximize Jackrabbit Trails' weekly profit when the total cost is nonlinear? What price and quantity maximize Jackrabbit Trails' weekly profit when the total cost is linear? What does Jackrabbit Trails sacrifice and/or gain by adopting the linear cost model?

5.61 CVP analysis—A critical evaluation: Nonlinear CVP relation, pricing (LO3, LO6, Advanced). Chul Park & Sons manufacture and sell specialized automotive testing equipment, including alternator testers, solenoid testers, and voltage regulator testers. Over the past 15 years, Chul Park & Sons has established a national reputation as a producer of accurate, reliable, and functional computerized products for testing automotive electrical and electronic components.

Chul Park & Sons, however, is only one of many companies that manufacture automotive testing equipment. Customers can choose from among numerous automotive suppliers, and, as a result, Chul Park & Sons' sales are quite sensitive to the selling price it sets for each product. Mr. Park currently is working on setting the selling price for his main product, a universal (3 in 1) tester. He believes that the following equation nicely captures the relation between the selling price and demand for his universal tester:

$$Quantity - 32{,}500 - (10 \times Price)$$

where *Quantity* represents the demand for Chul Park & Sons' universal tester and *Price* represents the unit selling price established by Mr. Park. Mr. Park also informs you that the variable cost per universal tester is $750 and that the fixed costs associated with producing and selling the universal tester equal $14,000,000 per year.

Required:

a. What is Chul Park & Sons' expression for annual profit for its universal tester? (*Hint:* Substitute the demand equation for quantity in the expression for profit in the text.)

b. Determine the price at which Chul Park & Sons maximizes profit on its universal tester. What is the profit on the universal tester at this price? (*Hint:* If you are familiar with calculus, take the first derivative of the profit model [with respect to *Price*] and set it equal to 0; otherwise, plot the profit equation, varying the price between 0 and $3,000 in increments of $100.)

MINI-CASES

5.62 Made to order caps. Jessica James is considering a business venture—selling custom-embroidered baseball caps from a pushcart kiosk at College Mall. The caps will be available in 12 different colors and one-size fits all. The caps' unique feature is that almost any name, phrase, or logo, can be stitched onto the cap while the customer waits. Thus, a customer can obtain a cap with his or her own name, monogram, special saying, or favorite logo in a wide variety of thread colors, sizes, and fonts. Based on preliminary market research and input from the franchising company, Jessica plans on selling each embroidered cap for $20.

Jessica plans to acquire the necessary technology (two industrial strength sewing machines hooked up to PCs with scanners and all of the necessary software) by obtaining a franchise from Made to Order Caps, Inc. Made to Order Caps, Inc., sells all of the necessary equipment and technology and provides the inventory of caps and other supplies. In addition, Made to Order Caps, Inc., trains prospective franchisees such as Jessica in the basics of running the business and operating the machines.

Jessica will need to buy the caps from Made to Order Caps, Inc., for $4 per cap and pay a royalty to the franchising company of $2 per cap sold. In addition, Jessica believes that each cap will use about $2.50 worth of supplies (including thread, replacement of sewing needles, machine maintenance, etc.). Finally, Made to Order Caps, Inc., requires that each franchisee invest $250 per month on leaflets and brochures to advertise the product.

Jessica discovers that College Mall would supply her with the pushcart and all of the necessary equipment for proper display. The license from the mall also allows Jessica to use several electrical outlets and two telephone outlets. College Mall will pay for Jessica's electricity consumption, but she will have to obtain two business telephone lines at a cost of $50 per line per month. College Mall is willing to license the space and equipment to Jessica on a monthly basis for $1,970 per month.

To generate maximum sales, Jessica wants to keep the pushcart open for business from 10 A.M. to 10 P.M. Monday through Friday, and from 10 A.M. to 6 P.M. on Saturday and Sunday. Jessica is willing to put in 50 hours at the kiosk, and she can obtain additional part-time help at $10 per hour (only one individual is required to operate the business). Jessica's only other significant expense is setting up to accept credit cards. Jessica anticipates that 75% of her sales will be credit card sales, and the credit card company charges Jessica a fee of 2% of the selling price.

Required:

a. Write down the expression for Jessica's monthly profit. (Assume that there are exactly four weeks per month.)

b. Calculate Jessica's monthly breakeven point in baseball caps. What does this translate to in revenue?

c. How much profit would Jessica earn in a month if she sold 1,000 caps? How many caps would Jessica have to sell to earn a target profit of $4,032 per month?

d. Jessica has been toying around with how the quantity of caps she can sell is likely to vary inversely with the selling price. Jessica is keenly aware that the lower the price per cap, the more caps she can sell and vice versa. She is determined to figure this relationship out and find the best price. After conducting extensive market surveys, Jessica believes that the local monthly demand for embroidered baseball caps is as follows:

Price per Cap	Demand
$20	300
$25	250
$28	220
$30	200
$32	180
$34	160

How does this piece of information alter Jessica's profit calculation? What price per cap should Jessica charge to maximize profit? How much profit does she earn at this price?

e. Jessica is almost done—she realizes that she forgot to include taxes as part of her decision model. Jessica believes that combined local, state, and federal taxes will be 25% of her profit before taxes. Does this piece of information affect Jessica's decision in part (d)? Does this change the profit-maximizing price? Does it change Jessica's profit?

f. What do you think of Jessica's business venture?

 5.63 Short-term decisions, multiproduct CVP, service firm (LO1–LO5). Rick's English Hut (Rick's) is a restaurant located in North Myrtle Beach, South Carolina on a saltwater marsh, surrounded by stately oak trees. Rick's appetizers and entrees run the gamut, from tasty burgers and sandwiches to authentic Mexican plates and succulent ribs. Rick's also has two bars that feature a dozen beers on tap and a wide-variety of wines and mixed drinks. With 15 televisions and seating for 250 patrons, Rick's is *the* place to enjoy good food and warm hospitality with friends while watching your favorite sports team.

For the most recent month, Rick's generated $60,000 in revenue, 55% of which came from the sale of alcoholic beverages and 45% of which came from the sale of food items. On average, alcoholic beverages sell for $4 and have a variable cost of $2; the average food item sells for $5 and has a variable cost of $4. Rick's fixed costs for the month totaled $10,950.

Rick's recent operating results present the proprietors with a dilemma. Specifically, for state licensing purposes Rick's currently is classified as a "restaurant" and, as such, has the appropriate liquor license associated with this status—Class B. With a Class B liquor license, Rick's is allowed to sell alcohol on the premises. However, alcohol sales must not exceed 50% of total revenue—otherwise Rick's would be classified as a bar, a classification that requires a Class A liquor license. Currently, Rick's pays $150 per month for its Class B liquor license; this cost is included in the fixed costs of $10,950 above.

Rick's proprietors would have to pay an additional $850 a month for a Class A liquor license. Furthermore, Rick's liquor liability insurance premiums would increase due to the increased liabilities associated with a higher proportion of alcohol sales (e.g., increased possibility of injury on the premises due to inebriation, increased chance of serving alcohol to minors, and so on). Rick's insurance provider has informed the proprietors that their insurance premiums will increase by $318 per month if the establishment is licensed as a bar rather than a restaurant.

The South Carolina State Liquor and Alcoholic Beverage Control Agency closely monitors alcohol consumption in the state and has informed Rick's that if it continues operating at the current sales mix level, Rick's will need to operate under a Class A license. The agency has informed Rick's that it will not impose any penalties on the restaurant as a result of the most recent month's operating performance. The agency has, though, informed Rick's that it needs to get its business in order starting this month.

In terms of moving forward, the proprietors of Rick's have discussed the following three options.

- *Option 1:* Change the licensing status of the establishment from restaurant to bar. This option would entail obtaining a Class A liquor license and paying the increased monthly licensing fees and insurance premiums. Rick's would plan on selling alcohol and food at their current sales-mix percentages and levels (i.e., total revenue and the proportion associated with food and alcohol would not change).

- *Option 2:* Close the restaurant one-half hour earlier each night. This option would reduce alcohol sales such that alcohol sales exactly equal the *current* level of food sales (i.e., the revenues from both products would be equal). In addition, it would reduce Rick's fixed costs by $450 per month. Finally, Rick's would continue to operate as a restaurant under its Class B license.

- *Option 3:* Offer a brunch on Saturday and Sunday mornings (no alcohol would be served at the brunch). To ensure that revenues from the brunch are sufficient to *bring up* food sales *to equal current alcohol revenue,* Rick's would need to price each brunch at $4. Unfortunately, Rick's has determined that the variable cost of offering the brunch (including labor, food, etc.) will be $4.08 per brunch and that fixed costs will increase by $105 per month. However, a benefit of offering the brunch is that Rick's could continue to operate as a restaurant under its Class B license.

Rick seeks your expertise in evaluating the efficacy of each option.

Required:

a. Calculate Rick's profit and breakeven point in revenue for the most recent month (i.e., before considering the options).

b. Calculate Rick's monthly profit and breakeven point in revenue under *option 1.*

c. Calculate Rick's monthly profit and breakeven revenue under *option 2.*

d. Calculate Rick's monthly profit and breakeven revenue under *option 3.*

e. Prepare a brief paragraph or two discussing the key insights Rick's has learned. Can you link these insights to some commonly observed business practices? Try listing some examples.

5.64 **Constructing and interpreting CVP graphs (LO1, LO2).** The Yin-Yang Yogurt Shoppe serves the best chocolate-vanilla frozen yogurt in the city. Each cup of yogurt sells for $4, with variable costs amounting to $2 per cup. Yin-Yang's fixed costs equal $3,000 per month.

Required:

a. Graph Yin-Yang Yogurt Shoppe's total costs as a function of the number of cups of yogurt sold (going from 0 to 2,500 cups of yogurt in increments of 500 cups). What does the *y*-intercept (i.e., the point where the total cost line crosses the *y*-axis) represent? What does the slope of the total cost line represent?

b. Add a plot of the Yin-Yang Yogurt Shoppe's total revenue (as a function of the number of cups of yogurt sold) to your graph from part (a). Identify the breakeven point in your graph. Identify the profit and loss areas.

c. Construct a profit graph for the Yin-Yang Yogurt Shoppe. Form a single line that depicts Yin-Yang's profit as a function of the number of cups of yogurt sold. What does the intercept of the profit line represent? What does the slope of the profit line represent? How do you interpret the point at which the profit line crosses the horizontal (i.e., *x*) axis? Identify the profit and loss areas.

d. Suppose Yin-Yang pays taxes at the rate of 40% of profit. How does this affect the profit line?

e. (*Advanced*) Assume you do not have unit-level data; in other words, assume you only know that Yin Yang's monthly fixed costs equal $3,000 and that its contribution margin ratio is 50% (you gather this information from Yin Yang's financial statements). Construct a profit graph that allows you to identify Yin Yang's breakeven point and profit and loss areas. (*Hint:* Without unit-level data, you will need to measure a variable other than units on the *x*-axis.) Ignore taxes.

5.65 CVP analysis with alternative cost structures, demand uncertainty, and risk (LO3, LO4, LO6, Advanced). Sally Sturgeon owns a company that manufactures and sells fishing rods. Sally's latest creation is the Bass-O-Matic, a graphite fishing rod designed with a trigger-stick Portuguese cork handle and Sally's revolutionary titanium guide system. Compared to other fishing rods on the market, Sally believes her Bass-O-Matic not only will reduce hand and arm fatigue but also will allow anglers to make longer and more precise casts with smoother retrieves.

Sally can make the Bass-O-Matic with one of two available technologies. The first technology is a labor-intensive technology; if Sally chooses this technology, then she will incur fixed costs of $500,000 per year and a variable cost of $50 per fishing rod. The second technology is a capital-intensive technology; if Sally chooses this technology, then she will incur fixed costs of $2,500,000 per year and a variable cost of $25 per fishing rod. Both technologies lead to identical product quality and an identical selling price of $75 per fishing rod.

Required:

a. What is Sally's breakeven point in units with the labor-intensive technology? What is Sally's breakeven point in units with the capital-intensive technology?

b. Which technology is preferred if sales are expected to be 40,000 units? Which technology is preferred if sales are expected to be 90,000 units? At what sales level would the two technologies yield identical profit?

c. On the same graph, draw a profit line for each of the two technologies (*Hint:* Measure profit on the *y*-axis and quantity in units on the *x*-axis; allow quantity to range from 0 to 100,000 units in increments of 20,000 units.) Using your graph, intuitively explain your answer to part (b) above.

d. Suppose Sally believes that there is a 50% chance that sales will equal 40,000 units and a 50% chance that sales will equal 90,000 units. What is Sally's expected profit with the labor-intensive technology? What is Sally's expected profit with the machine-intensive technology? (*Hint:* Expected profit is the average of the profit for the two demand estimates.)

e. What is the range of profit (using 40,000 and 90,000 as the lowest and highest possible demand estimates) under each technology? Which technology has the greater range in profit? Explain your answer using the profit graph you constructed earlier. What inference do you draw about the variability of profit under the two technologies? (*Hint:* Range is a statistical term for the difference between the highest and lowest values of a distribution.)

5.66 CVP relation and profit planning, taxes, ethics (LO1, LO2, Advanced). Ganesh Bidi manufactures bidis in Andhra Pradesh, India. A bidi is a blended-tobacco product that is hand-wrapped in a tendu (type of plant) leaf, then roasted in charcoal to remove moisture and provide flavor. In India, bidis often are referred to as the "poor person's cigarette."

Ganesh sells his bidis directly to wholesalers for 3.00 Indian Rupees per pack of 20 (1 Indian Rupee = approximately $0.02). Each pack of bidis costs Ganesh 0.75 Indian Rupees in materials and 0.25 Indian Rupees in labor. Ganesh's fixed costs amount to 1,075,000 Indian Rupees per month.

Required:

a. Assume Ganesh does not pay any taxes. How many packs of bidis must Ganesh sell to earn a profit of 750,000 Indian Rupees per month?

b. Assume Ganesh pays income taxes equal to 40% of profit. How many packs of bidis must Ganesh sell to earn a profit after taxes of 750,000 Indian Rupees per month?

c. In addition to income taxes equal to 40% of profit, assume Ganesh also pays a value-added tax (VAT) of 20% per pack of bidis. The Indian government assesses the 20% value-added tax based on the selling price less the cost of the materials. (A value-added tax is levied on the difference between the price of outputs and the value of materials input.) How many packs of bidis must Ganesh sell to earn a profit of 750,000 Indian Rupees per month?

d. In addition to income taxes equal to 40% of profit and a value-added tax of 20%, assume the Indian government requires Ganesh to pay an excise tax of 0.05 Indian Rupees per pack of bidis. (An excise tax is a manufacturing tax usually levied as a percentage of manufacturing cost. Sometimes, it is a fixed amount per unit of the product.) How many packs of bidis must Ganesh sell to earn a profit of 750,000 Indian Rupees per month?

e. Briefly discuss how you modified the standard CVP relation to include income, value-added, and excise taxes. What does each tax vary with? Do you think sales taxes would affect the CVP model?

Chapter 6

Decision Making in the Short Term

CULINARY CREATIONS SPECIALIZES in catering weddings, corporate outings, and dinner parties. As most of these events take place on weekends, Culinary is booked solid Friday through Sunday. Weekdays, however, are far less active than weekends, and Culinary often cannot generate enough business to keep the staff busy Monday through Thursday.

A charity organization has just called to ask whether Culinary Creations could cater its annual fundraising dinner. The charity would like to hold the dinner either on a Wednesday or on a Saturday. The charity expects 150 people to attend if the dinner is on Wednesday and 200 people if the dinner is on Saturday. Because it has a limited budget, the charity is willing to pay only $26 per attendee, regardless of the day scheduled.

Culinary Creations' owner, Monica, wants you to handle the details of the deal. While Monica is willing to reduce her normal

profit markup for charitable causes, she does not want to lose money on the event. She asks you to figure out whether Culinary should cater the event, and if so, on what day.

APPLYING THE DECISION FRAMEWORK

What Is the Problem?	Should Culinary Creations cater the charity's annual fundraising dinner?
What Are the Options?	Culinary Creations has three options:
	1. Do not cater the charity event.
	2. Cater the charity event on Wednesday.
	3. Cater the charity event on Saturday.
What Are the Costs and Benefits?	We will directly estimate the controllable costs and benefits of each option.
Make the Decision!	After estimating the controllable costs and benefits, we will be able to recommend the best option for Culinary Creations.

Culinary Cuisine is a well-regarded catering service. Its owner, Monica, is preparing a bid to cater a charity dinner.

LEARNING OBJECTIVES

After studying this chapter, you will be able to:

1 Understand the factors that trigger short-term decisions.

2 Evaluate decision options using alternate approaches.

3 Solve short-term decisions such as make versus buy and special-order pricing.

4 Determine the best use of a resource in short supply.

5 Consider the qualitative and longer-term aspects of short-term decisions.

In Chapter 5, we learned that the Cost-Volume-Profit (CVP) relation is useful for understanding how revenues, costs, and profit vary as the volume of business varies. Organizations use the CVP relation for many purposes: planning profit over the short-term, measuring operating risk, and analyzing short-term decision problems. However, many short-term decisions deal with specific products, customer orders, or departments. In these cases, it often is more convenient to estimate the costs and benefits of decision options directly.

We begin this chapter by discussing the central feature of short-term decision problems. We then discuss ways in which to evaluate such decisions. We illustrate these approaches in the context of Culinary's decision as well as other typical short-term decisions, including make versus buy and product promotion. Finally, we discuss some of the qualitative and longer-term considerations that often play a role in short-term decisions.

CHAPTER CONNECTIONS

In Chapter 7, we discuss operating budgets, which bridge the gap between short-term planning and control. One important output from budgeting is an income statement, which shows the cumulative profit effect of numerous short-term decisions.

Characteristics of Short-Term Decisions

LEARNING OBJECTIVE 1

Understand the factors that trigger short-term decisions.

Most short-term decisions *deal with temporary gaps between the demand and supply of available capacity.* These temporary gaps result because, in the short term, businesses have a fixed supply of capacity but confront changing demand.

FIXED SUPPLY OF CAPACITY

Capacity is the maximum volume of activity that a company can sustain with available resources. The Staples Center, where the Los Angeles Lakers play basketball, has the capacity to seat 18,997 persons. Commercial printing presses, such as those used at the *Chicago Sun-Times,* can produce approximately 60,000 pages per hour. A primary-care physician has the capacity to see one patient every 10 to 15 minutes.

The decision of how much capacity to put in place is a long-term decision. Organizations make capacity decisions based on the expected volume of operations over a horizon often spanning many years. They build plants, buy equipment, rent office space, and hire salaried personnel in anticipation of the demand for their products and services. Once installed, however, it is not easy to change the capacity level. It takes time, effort, and money to build a new stadium, acquire and install a commercial printing press, or hire another doctor. These actions are not easily reversible. Consequently, in the short term, businesses must do the best with the capacity that they have when dealing with fluctuations in demand.

Monica has made several long-term decisions concerning Culinary Creations. For example, she considered whether she needed one, two, or three chefs to satisfy her expected long-term demand. She purchased kitchen equipment and signed a multiyear lease for the facility. Monica entered into such long-term cost commitments to provide Culinary Creations with the capacity to supply a certain level of catering service every day of the week.

DEMAND CHANGES FREQUENTLY

Even though Culinary Creations has access to the same kitchen facilities each day of the week, most of the demand for catering service is during weekends. As a result, Culinary often does not utilize its capacity fully during weekdays. In contrast, demand exceeds supply on many weekends. Monica simply cannot accommodate *all* weekend business opportunities.

Exhibit 6.1 illustrates the unavoidable temporary imbalances between the demand and supply of organizational resources. This exhibit shows that we cannot change the supply of capacity in the short term and that demand varies. Sometimes demand exceeds available supply (i.e., there is **excess demand**), while at other times available supply exceeds demand (there is **excess capacity/excess supply**).

For example, Radio City Music Hall in New York City cannot accommodate *all* patrons wishing to see a popular new show even though the facility has 5,910 seats.

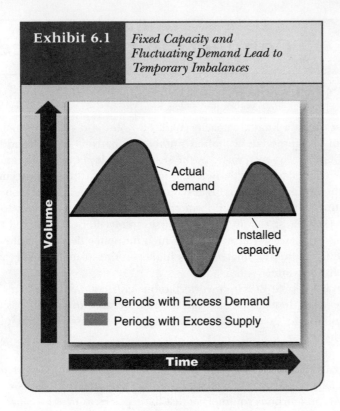

Exhibit 6.1 | *Fixed Capacity and Fluctuating Demand Lead to Temporary Imbalances*

At other times, however, it has seats to spare. From Radio City's standpoint, both situations are undesirable. The theater is foregoing profit in the first instance and has unused capacity in the second.

CLOSING THE GAP BETWEEN DEMAND AND SUPPLY

Effective managers anticipate the likelihood of such short-term gaps between supply and demand when planning for capacity. Monica knows that weekends are busier than weekdays for almost all caterers. It makes sense for her to work out an arrangement with her chefs so that they work long hours during weekends and lighter schedules during weekdays. Similarly, electric utilities such as Ameren have standby plants that they bring on-line only in times of peak demand. Most companies also manage demand by raising prices during such periods. Companies such as Apple and Hewlett-Packard, which sell PCs via retail outlets, anticipate demand spikes and buildup inventories. Firms such as Toro Corporation make snow throwers *and* lawn mowers in the same plant to deal with seasonal demand patterns for these products. Despite such adjustments, businesses can rarely match supply and demand exactly *all the time*. The core problem of having to deal with some excess capacity or some excess demand in the short term remains.

We can classify most short-term decisions into two broad categories.

- *Decisions that deal with excess supply.* Examples include reducing prices to stimulate demand, running special promotions, processing special orders, and using extra capacity to make some production inputs in-house (i.e., making parts versus purchasing them from an outside supplier).
- *Decisions that deal with excess demand.* Examples include increasing prices to take advantage of favorable demand conditions, meeting additional demand by outsourcing production, and altering the product mix to focus on the most profitable ones.

Golf greens fees vary from season to season with demand.
(Eric Risberg/©AP/Wide World Photos)

Connecting to Practice

GOLF GREENS FEES

Golf courses have a limited capacity. With 18 holes and only so much daylight, courses can accommodate a limited number of patrons daily. In addition, the demand for golf frequently varies by the season, the day of the week, and the time of day. For example, in Myrtle Beach, South Carolina, the self-proclaimed "golf capital of the world," demand is highest during the spring and fall seasons. Demand decreases during the summer and winter, when it is either too hot or too cold for many golfers. Because the number of courses in Myrtle Beach is fixed (currently, there are more than 100), greens fees, which influence demand, follow a similar pattern—rates are approximately 100% higher in the spring and fall than during the summer and winter.

In contrast, Pebble Beach, a world famous golf course located in California, experiences high demand throughout the year because the weather is California is usually suitable for golfing. As we would expect, its greens fees exhibit little variation over the year.

COMMENTARY: Similar to golf courses, hotels and airlines find it difficult to adjust available capacity. Their demand also is seasonal and varies daily. As we know, hotels and airlines routinely adjust their prices to match realized demand conditions. Airlines offer "last-minute specials" to stimulate demand and increase passenger load. Hotels in college towns charge premium rates during graduation weekend.

Recall from Chapter 2 that the opportunity cost of a decision option is the value of the next best option. The opportunity cost of *excess capacity* is zero because there is no other profitable use for it. Therefore, any use of this excess capacity that generates a positive contribution margin is worth considering. With *excess demand*, it becomes necessary to forego some profitable uses of available capacity. The opportunity cost of capacity is positive because we have to let go of some opportunity. In this case, the decision is one of which opportunities to let go.

As you go through this chapter, please keep in mind that most short-term decisions have longer-term implications. For example, a stellar catering job may not only result in a long-lasting relationship with the charity, but also lead to engagements with other charities or businesses. Because it is often difficult to measure the profit impact of these long-term effects, managers usually focus their initial analysis on the short-term costs and benefits, and then qualitatively consider any longer-term implications. We discuss these qualitative considerations in detail later in the chapter.

CONTEXTS FOR SHORT-TERM DECISION MAKING

Exhibit 6.2 illustrates some short-term decision contexts. When available capacity exceeds demand, firms take actions to boost demand. Examples include pricing special orders aggressively, favoring making versus buying components, and executing product promotions. These actions make sense because they put capacity that is otherwise idle to productive use. Conversely, when there is excess demand, firms try to allocate capacity to the most profitable use. They set a high bar for accepting special orders and look for components that they could buy from suppliers rather

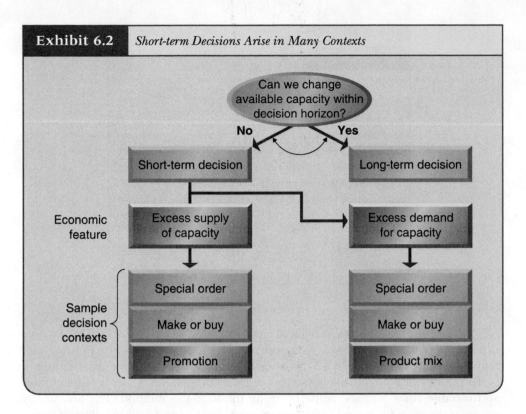

Exhibit 6.2 *Short-term Decisions Arise in Many Contexts*

than produce internally. They also try to change their product mix to focus on the most profitable products.

As Exhibit 6.2 also shows, dealing with temporary gaps between capacity and demand is the essence of short-term decisions. However, whether we deal with excess supply or with excess demand, the principles of controllability and relevance that we discussed in Chapter 2 continue to guide us in identifying costs and benefits that we must consider in making these short-term decisions. Let us see how we can put these principles to work.

Evaluating Options

The excess supply/excess demand classification is a helpful way for us to evaluate Culinary Creations' decision problem, a special order. Let's begin by checking whether Culinary has engagements on the charity's requested dates. Wednesday is open, and it is highly unlikely that Culinary will receive another catering request for that date. Currently, Saturday is also open. However, Culinary almost surely will receive another catering request for that date, at the average size of 120 persons. Thus, one decision option features excess supply, and another deals with excess demand.

To evaluate these options, let's start with Culinary's income statement, shown in Exhibit 6.3. Using this information, you calculate Culinary's average cost per person served as \$900,000/30,000 persons = \$30. Because the charity will pay only \$26 per attendee, it appears at first look that accepting this proposal will result in a loss. If you based your recommendation on this information alone, you would tell Monica to decline the engagement.

However, you realize that it is premature to make this recommendation. Exhibit 6.3 is not in the contribution margin format. You know that some of the costs in this exhibit are controllable with respect to Culinary's options, but others are not. As a result, you realize you need to refine your analysis.

LEARNING OBJECTIVE 2

Evaluate decision options using alternate approaches.

Exhibit 6.3	Culinary Creations: Income Statement for the Most Recent Year
Revenues	
Total number of people served = 30,000	$1,080,000
Expenses	
Food and supplies	$300,000
Utilities (gas, electricity, and water)	30,000
Wages for temporary (serving) staff	75,000
Transportation to and from engagements	45,000
Kitchen equipment and utensils	50,000
Salaried staff	325,000
Rent	75,000
Total expenses	$900,000
Profit before taxes	$180,000

The revenue portion is relatively straightforward. Dividing $1,080,000 in revenues by 30,000 persons served, you estimate that Culinary obtains $36 from each regular patron, compared to $26 from each person attending the charity dinner.

To figure out controllable costs, you begin as in Chapter 4 by identifying fixed and variable costs. You also settle on using the high-low method. The accountant provides you with Culinary's income statements for the past four quarters of operations, shown in Exhibit 6.4. You observe that the fourth quarter has the highest activity level, with 9,000 people served and a corresponding total cost of $243,750. The first quarter has the lowest activity level, with 6,000 people served and a corresponding total cost of $206,250. Using these two cost observations, you estimate the variable cost per person served as $12.50 and the quarterly fixed costs as $131,250.

With these estimates in hand, you can identify the value of each of Culinary's options. Of course, one option available for Culinary is to maintain the status quo by not catering the charity event at all (option 1)—thus, the value of this option is $0. As in Chapter 2, we define the value of the other options by calculating the incremental revenues and costs relative to the status quo. In the language of Chapter 2, these are the *controllable* costs and benefits of a decision option. Thus, relative to not catering the charity event (the status quo):

- If Culinary caters the charity dinner on Wednesday, it expects to serve 150 additional persons at a price of $26 per person. Incremental revenues, therefore, are $3,900. At $12.50 per person, incremental costs for 150 persons are $1,875. Subtracting the incremental costs from the incremental revenues, the value (change in profit) of catering the charity dinner on Wednesday is $2,025.

CHAPTER CONNECTIONS

In Chapter 4, we discussed three methods—account classification, high-low, and regression analysis—to estimate the unit variable cost and total fixed costs. Recall that the high-low method uses two observations—the high activity level and the low activity level—to estimate the cost equation.

Exhibit 6.4	*Culinary Creations: Income Statements for the Past Four Quarters*				

			Quarter		
	Total	*Fourth*	*Third*	*Second*	*First*
Total number of people served	30,000	9,000	7,000	8,000	6,000
Revenue	$1,080,000	$324,000	$252,000	$288,000	$216,000
Expenses					
Food and supplies	$300,000	$90,000	$70,000	$80,000	$60,000
Utilities	30,000	8,250	7,250	7,750	6,750
Wages for temporary (serving) staff	75,000	21,000	18,000	19,500	16,500
Transportation	45,000	12,000	11,000	11,500	10,500
Kitchen equipment and utensils	50,000	12,500	12,500	12,500	12,500
Salaried staff	325,000	81,250	81,250	81,250	81,250
Rent	75,000	18,750	18,750	18,750	18,750
Total expenses	$900,000	$243,750	$218,750	$231,250	$206,250
Profit before taxes	$180,000	$80,250	$33,250	$56,750	$9,750

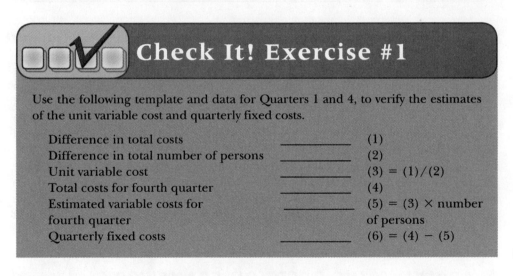

Check It! Exercise #1

Use the following template and data for Quarters 1 and 4, to verify the estimates of the unit variable cost and quarterly fixed costs.

Difference in total costs	_____	(1)
Difference in total number of persons	_____	(2)
Unit variable cost	_____	(3) = (1)/(2)
Total costs for fourth quarter	_____	(4)
Estimated variable costs for fourth quarter	_____	(5) = (3) × number of persons
Quarterly fixed costs	_____	(6) = (4) − (5)

Solution at end of chapter.

- If Culinary caters the charity dinner on Saturday, it expects to serve 200 additional persons at a price of $26 per person, generating $5,200 in revenue. However, Culinary will also lose the business of 120 regular patrons at $36 per person, or $4,320. Incremental revenues are, therefore, $5,200 − $4,320 = $880. Culinary would also incur additional variable costs of $1,000, which represents the $12.50 cost per person for the 80 *extra* meals served (200 meals it could serve at the charity dinner − 120 meals it otherwise expects to serve). Thus, the value of catering the charity dinner on Saturday is $880 − $1,000 = ($120).

Exhibit 6.5 summarizes this information. You find that catering the charity dinner on Wednesday is the best option for maximizing short-term profit. Your calculations also reveal that Culinary will realize more profit if it rejects the catering event rather than accepting it for Saturday. (Why? Because accepting the charity event for Saturday results in a *loss* of $120 relative to the status quo of not catering the charity event.)

Exhibit 6.5	Culinary Creations: Incremental Costs and Revenues Relative to not Catering the Charity Event		

		Cater on Wednesday	Cater on Saturday
Incremental revenues from catering the charity organization			
(= $26 × 150; $26 × 200)		$3,900	$5,200
Lost revenues from regular business			
(= $36 × 0; $36 × −120)		$0	($4,320)
Net incremental revenues		$3,900	$880
Incremental costs associated with catering the charity event			
(= $12.50 × 150; $12.50 × 200)		$1,875	$2,500
Cost savings from regular business			
(= $12.50× 0; $12.50× −120)		$0	($1,500)
Net incremental costs		$1,875	$1,000
Incremental contribution margin		$2,025	($120)
Less: Avoidable fixed costs		$0	$0
Value (incremental profit)		$2,025	($120)

Why is it profitable for Monica to accept the charity event for Wednesday but reject it for Saturday? The answer is that Culinary has excess capacity on Wednesday but not on Saturday. On Wednesday, Monica has no alternative use for her catering capacity. Thus, each person attending the charity dinner has a unit contribution margin of $13.50—the revenue of $26.00 per person less the unit variable cost of $12.50. Culinary will increase profit by accepting the charity event. The value from using the capacity for the dinner, $13.50 per person, exceeds its opportunity cost of $0—that is, it is better than letting the capacity be idle.

The excess demand for Saturday changes the story. Each person attending the charity dinner still contributes $13.50 in contribution margin. However, we have an alternate use for the capacity. Thus, the opportunity cost is $23.50 per person, the unit contribution margin from each regular customer ($36.00 price − $12.50 unit

APPLYING THE DECISION FRAMEWORK

What Is the Problem?	Should Culinary Creations cater the charity's annual fundraising dinner?
What Are the Options?	Culinary Creations has three options: 1. Do not cater the charity event. 2. Cater the charity event on Wednesday. 3. Cater the charity event on Saturday.
What Are the Costs and Benefits?	You summarize your estimates of the costs and benefits as follows:

Option	Value (Change in profit)
Do not cater the charity event	$0
Cater charity event on Wednesday	$2,025
Cater charity event on Saturday	($120)

Make the Decision!	You recommend that Culinary Creations cater the charity event on Wednesday, as this option leads to the highest profit.

variable cost) displaced. Even after adjusting for the contribution margin from 80 additional persons served at the charity event, it is still more profitable to serve regular customers, as our calculations in Exhibit 6.5 show.

RELEVANT COST ANALYSIS

Recall from Chapter 2 that in picking the best decision option from among a set of available decision options, we could consider *controllable* costs and benefits <u>or</u> *relevant* costs and benefits. As mentioned earlier, we identify controllable costs and benefits depending on the change relative to the status quo. We defined relevant costs and benefits as those costs and benefits that differ across options and showed that focusing on relevant costs, or performing **relevant cost analysis**, often simplifies the analysis.

Relevant cost analysis is particularly useful when maintaining the status quo is not feasible. In such cases, we choose *any* feasible option as a baseline or a "benchmark" against which to evaluate other options. Relevant cost analysis involves focusing on only those costs and revenues that differ from this benchmark option. For this reason, some refer to relevant cost analysis as the **incremental** or **differential method**.

Exercise #2 lets you practice the incremental approach. After you complete this exercise, use the profit estimates in Exhibit 6.5 to verify that Monica would gain $2,145 by catering the charity event on Wednesday rather than on Saturday.

CHAPTER CONNECTIONS
Recall from Chapter 2 that a cost or benefit is relevant if its amount differs for at least one decision option.

Check It! Exercise #2

Suppose that Culinary commits to catering the charity event—thus, the status quo is not a viable option. Show that Monica would lose $2,145 if she were to cater the event on Saturday instead of Wednesday. Use catering the event on Wednesday as the benchmark option and calculate the relevant change in demand, costs and benefits.

	Number of Persons	Amount per Person	Cater on Saturday
Additional revenue from charity event	50	_____	_____
Lost revenue from regular business	_____	$36	_____
Total relevant revenues			($3,020)
Additional variable costs from charity event	50	$12.50	_____
Variable costs saved by not serving regular customers	120	_____	_____
Total relevant costs			_____
Change in profit (relative to catering the event on Wednesday)			_____

AN ALTERNATE APPROACH

Relevant cost analysis uses the fewest calculations necessary to evaluate Culinary's options. However, when decision options involve numerous cost items, many managers find it more convenient to include some or even all noncontrollable costs or revenues in their calculations. This approach makes the calculations more mechanical because we do not have to decide whether a cost or benefit is controllable or relevant. Moreover, the amounts for each option correspond more closely with the actual cash flow under each option. In essence, depending on whether the manager considers some or all of the noncontrollable costs and benefits, this approach involves putting together a partial or complete contribution margin statement for each option.

Such a mechanical approach, if done correctly, does not alter the rankings of the options—the inclusion of noncontrollable costs affects the contribution margin of each option by an identical amount. Some call this method the **totals or gross approach** because it considers the gross revenues and costs associated with each option, rather than the incremental amounts relative to the benchmark option.

To illustrate the difference between this approach and relevant cost analysis, consider the item "Lost revenues from regular business" in Exhibit 6.5. As reported there, Culinary expects Saturday night revenues from its regular customers of $4,320 if it does not cater the charity event or caters it on Wednesday. However, it expects Saturday night revenues of $0 from its regular customers if it caters the charity event on Saturday.

Back in Exhibit 6.5, we calculated the *incremental* revenue from regular clients as $0 for the Cater on Wednesday option. That option did not affect the amount of revenue expected during the week from regular clients. However, we calculated the *incremental* revenue from regular clients as –$4,320 for the Cater on Saturday option because Culinary would lose that amount of revenue—from regular clients—if Culinary were to cater the charity event on Saturday.

In contrast, the amounts in Exhibit 6.6 represent gross amounts associated with the different options. If Culinary chooses not to cater the event at all, or decides to cater the event on Wednesday, then the revenue from regular customers will be $4,320. If Culinary chooses to cater the event on Saturday, then the revenue from regular customers will be $0. You can follow the same steps in identifying the gross amounts for the variable costs.

Notice that the *ranking* of the two catering options is the same in Exhibit 6.6 as it is in Exhibit 6.5. If you compare Culinary's anticipated profit from catering the

Exhibit 6.6	*Culinary Creations: Evaluating Decision Options with a (limited) Contribution Margin Statement*		
	Do not Cater Event	**Cater on Wednesday**	**Cater on Saturday**
Revenue from charity organization (= $26 × 0; $26 × 150; $26 × 200)	$0	$3,900	$5,200
Revenue from regular business (= $36 × 120; $36 × 120; $36 × 0)	4,320	4,320	0
Total Revenue	$4,320	$8,220	$5,200
Less: Variable costs (= $12.50 × 120; $12.50 × 270; $12.50 × 200)	$1,500	$3,375	$2,500
Contribution margin	$2,820	$4,845	$2,700
Less: Fixed costs	0	0	0
Profit before taxes	$2,820	$4,845	$2,700

event on Wednesday, or $4,845, to the anticipated profit of $2,820 for not catering the event at all, the increase in profit is $2,025 for catering the event on Wednesday. A similar comparison of the profit for catering on Saturday, or $2,700, with the $2,820 profit from not catering the event shows a loss, or $120, from catering the event on Saturday. These amounts—$2025 and ($120)—correspond exactly to our calculations in Exhibit 6.5.

COMPARING THE METHODS

As you can see, we get the same answer with all three approaches. As in Exhibit 6.5, we can choose by comparing the value of each option, identifying controllable costs and benefits as the items that change relative to the status quo. In *Check it! Exercise #2*, we ranked options by choosing a feasible option as the benchmark, and identifying relevant costs and benefits as the items that change relative to this benchmark. Finally, rather than focus on incremental items (relative to the status quo or any feasible option), in Exhibit 6.6, we considered some noncontrollable costs and benefits to construct a partial contribution margin statement. (The statement is partial because we do not consider costs and revenues for the entire week or consider fixed costs.) We can then directly compare the profit earned under the options.

In general, analysis that considers only controllable or relevant costs is more efficient when decision options differ only with respect to a few benefit and cost items. It allows us to pick the best option quickly by evaluating each relative to the status quo (as we did for Culinary Creations in Exhibit 6.5). The totals method might be preferable in decisions involving many costs and benefits. Ultimately, all the methods are equivalent, but certain decision problems lend themselves better to one approach relative to the other. You are also likely to encounter all of these approaches in your workplace.

Additional Examples of Short-Term Decisions

In this section, we present two additional examples of short-term decisions. The first looks at short-term promotions to deal with excess capacity. The second considers a make-versus-buy decision in a setting with excess demand. We encourage you to work through these examples to solidify your understanding of how to approach short-term decisions.

LEARNING OBJECTIVE 3

Solve short-term decisions such as make versus buy and special-order pricing.

EVALUATING SHORT-TERM PROMOTION DECISIONS

Superior Cereals estimated demand for its generic breakfast cereal poorly. Therefore, it currently has more boxes of "toasted honey flakes" than it could sell at the product's usual price. Superior normally sells toasted honey flakes to supermarkets for $2.00 per box and earns $0.72 in unit contribution margin.

Superior's management has come up with the following two options to address the current inventory of 50,000 boxes:

- *Emphasize Institutional Sales:* Sell 25,000 boxes of toasted honey flakes to supermarkets for $2 per box, and the remaining 25,000 boxes to institutional buyers (e.g., hospitals, schools) for $1 per box.
- *Issue a Rebate:* Print a coupon in the local newspaper, offering consumers a rebate of $0.50 for every box top of toasted honey flakes submitted to Superior.

Superior Cereals is considering the use of rebates to stimulate demand. (image100/ Age Fotostock America, Inc.)

It will cost Superior $5,000 to advertise the campaign in local newspapers and process the rebates. Superior anticipates supermarket sales of 45,000 boxes and paying out the rebate on 22,000 boxes. Superior will sell the remaining 5,000 boxes for $1 per box to institutional buyers.

Our first step is to figure out the status quo. How many boxes would Superior sell if it did nothing? We do not have this information. However, not having this information does not hinder our analysis. We can address Superior's issue using relevant cost analysis where we use either of the options as the benchmark. We also could make the decision using the totals or gross approach where we calculate gross revenues and costs.

Exhibit 6.7 presents the calculations for Superior's decision under the gross approach. *Check It! Exercise #3* asks you to make the decision using relevant cost analysis.

In Exhibit 6.7, we set the variable costs for each decision option to equal $0. Why? Because Superior has already incurred the variable costs for making the 50,000 boxes, these costs are *sunk*. Thus, we exclude them from the analysis. However, we could have included variable costs, noncontrollable for this decision, in our analysis. Including this item does not change the rank ordering of options, or the *difference* in profits between options, meaning that our decision would not change as well.

Exhibit 6.7 shows that Superior maximizes its short-term profit by issuing a rebate. This option increases profit by $4,000 over the "emphasize institutional sales" option.

MAKE-VERSUS-BUY DECISIONS

Precision Piston Rings manufactures piston rings for automobile engines. The company anticipates that it will produce 470,000 piston rings in the coming year and earn a contribution of $5 per ring. At this level of production, Precision will operate at 94% of its available capacity of 500,000 piston rings. Equivalently, because Precision produces eight rings per hour, the anticipated production will consume 58,750 of its available 62,500 machine hours.

Exhibit 6.7	*Superior Cereals: Evaluating Options Using the Gross Approach*	
	Emphasize Institutional Sales	**Issue Rebate**
Supermarket sales—full price	25,000 boxes	23,000 boxes
Supermarket sales—rebate	—	22,000 boxes
Institutional sales	25,000 boxes	5,000 boxes
Wholesale price per box	$2.00	$2.00
Price per box with rebate	—	$1.50
Institutional price per box	$1.00	$1.00
Supermarket sales—full price	$50,000	$46,000
Supermarket sales—rebate	—	33,000
Institutional sales	25,000	5,000
Total revenues	$75,000	$84,000
Variable costs	0	0
Contribution margin	$75,000	$84,000
Advertising and processing costs	0	5,000
Profit	$75,000	$79,000

Check It! Exercise #3

Verify that the incremental profit from the "issue a rebate" option relative to "emphasize institutional sales" option is $4,000.

	Incremental Boxes Relative to "Emphasize Institutional Sales"	Incremental Cost or Benefit for "Issue Rebate"
Incremental revenues		
Supermarket sales—full price	−2,000 (= 23,000 − 25,000)	_____
Supermarket sales—rebate	+22,000 (= 22,000 − 0)	_____
Institutional sales	−20,000 (= 5,000 − 25,000)	_____
Total incremental revenues		_____
Less: incremental variable costs		_____
Incremental contribution margin		_____
Less: incremental fixed costs		$5,000
Incremental profit		_____

Solution at end of chapter.

Patrick O'Toole, the owner of Precision Piston Rings, notes that Precision has unused capacity of 3,750 machine hours (62,500 − 58,750). Thus, he wonders if he could increase profit by using this capacity to make the jigs and fixtures he needs and not buy them from a supplier. Currently, Precision pays an outside supplier $162,500 for 25 jigs, or $6,500 per jig. (Jigs and fixtures, which wear out on a regular basis, hold the ring in place during machining operations.)

Making the jigs in-house will cost $25,000 per year in additional fixed costs (for new tools and equipment), $4,000 per jig in materials and labor costs, and consume 200 hours of machine time per jig. Because of design and quality considerations, Patrick believes that he should either make *all* of the jigs or buy all of the jigs (i.e., he is not interested in making some jigs and buying the rest).

We can therefore summarize Patrick's two options as follows:

- *Buy jigs*: Continue to buy the 25 jigs from an outside vendor at a price of $6,500 per jig.
- *Make jigs*: Make the jigs in house using 200 machine hours per jig, spending $25,000 per year in fixed costs for tools and $4,000 per jig for materials and labor.

Buying 25 jigs at $6,500 per jig costs $162,500. At first look, making 25 jigs at $4,000 each plus $25,000 in fixed costs will total $125,000. Thus, you might conclude that Patrick should make the jigs, as doing so saves $37,500.

This conclusion is incorrect, however. When you calculate incremental revenues and costs, you see that Precision's annual profit will *decrease* by $12,500 if it makes the jigs in-house, as Exhibit 6.8 shows.

Why is our initial calculation of a savings of $37,500 incorrect? Precision's plant is operating near capacity. Therefore, it cannot make all of the jigs *and* all of the rings using its current facilities. Making all of the jigs requires that Patrick cut back on the number of rings, as he will have to divert some machine hours from making piston rings. This excess demand means that capacity has a positive opportunity cost. For Precision, this cost is the loss in contribution margin of $50,000 (10,000 rings × $5 per ring) that Precision could have otherwise generated. Consequently, it is *relatively* more profitable for Precision to use the capacity for its primary product, piston rings, and purchase the needed jigs from its supplier. Relative to making jigs, profit in this case would improve by $12,500 ($50,000 − $37,500).

Exhibit 6.8	*Precision Piston Rings: Evaluating Options Using the Incremental Approach*

	Detail	Buy (status quo)	Make
Jigs per year		25	25
Machine hours needed to make jigs	200 hours/jig × 25 jigs	—	5,000
Machine hours available	62,500 − 58,750 hours	3,750	3,750
Machine hours diverted from making rings	5,000 − 3,750 hours	0	1,250
Piston rings that could be made with diverted machine hours	8 rings/hour × 1,250 hours	0	10,000
			Increment Due to Make
Saved payments to outside vendor	$6,500/jig × 25 jigs		$162,500
Materials and labor costs to make jigs	$4,000/jig × 25 jigs		(100,000)
Tools and equipment	Given		(25,000)
Apparent savings from Make			$37,500
Lost contribution from using machine hours to produce jigs in house	10,000 rings × $5/ring		($50,000)
Incremental profit (value)			($12,500)

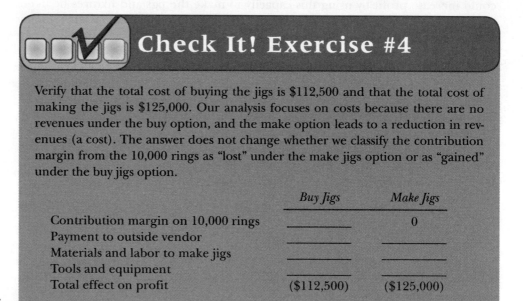

Check It! Exercise #4

Verify that the total cost of buying the jigs is $112,500 and that the total cost of making the jigs is $125,000. Our analysis focuses on costs because there are no revenues under the buy option, and the make option leads to a reduction in revenues (a cost). The answer does not change whether we classify the contribution margin from the 10,000 rings as "lost" under the make jigs option or as "gained" under the buy jigs option.

	Buy Jigs	Make Jigs
Contribution margin on 10,000 rings	_____	0
Payment to outside vendor	_____	_____
Materials and labor to make jigs	_____	_____
Tools and equipment	_____	_____
Total effect on profit	($112,500)	($125,000)

Solution at end of chapter.

Determining the Best Use of a Scarce Resource

LEARNING OBJECTIVE 4

Determine the best use of a resource in short supply.

So far in this chapter, we have evaluated short-term decisions that have a *limited* number of options. We identify all of the options and then evaluate them either by performing incremental analysis or by constructing a (partial) contribution margin statement for each option, then comparing the contribution margins.

In some cases, however, the number of available options can be very large. Consider a company that is deciding how best to use 1,000 hours of machine time to make its

Connecting to Practice

PRICE-GOUGING WHEN DEMAND IS HIGH

The Federal Energy Regulatory Commission's report on the 2001 power crisis in California provides an example of price gouging and its consequences. The report alleges that a firm prolonged an outage at a power plant to take advantage of higher prices the state was paying at the height of the crisis. That is, the firm reduced capacity in a period with peak demand, driving up prices for the capacity that stayed on line. The report estimates that the firm earned more than $10 million extra in energy sales from its other plants. The investigation ended when the firm agreed to refund the state $8 million, without any admission of guilt.

COMMENTARY: Price gouging occurs when a firm exploits temporary excess demand to raise prices to unreasonable levels. Such excess demand frequently stems from natural disasters such as floods and hurricanes.

Source: FERC report, CNN, November 17, 2002; *Atlanta Business Journal,* March 3, 2003; WSWS.org, September 28, 2002.

three products. The problem is that 1,000 machine hours are not enough to meet the demand of *all* three products.

How should the company decide how much of each product to produce? When demand is high and a resource is in short supply, we should rank products by the contribution margin *per unit of the resource* and not by the contribution margin *per unit of the product.* This is a general rule for solving problems with excess demand. The logic is that, for a resource in short supply, the opportunity cost of the resource is positive (as we saw in the Precision Piston Rings example). Consequently, we put the resource to its *best* possible use. This means ensuring that the contribution margin per unit of the resource from this use exceeds that foregone by putting it to the next best use.

To illustrate this rule, let's consider an example—Aero Toys, which manufactures and sells toy airplanes. Aero, owned and operated by Amelia Hart, has a factory in Boston, Massachusetts, and manufactures three different kinds of toy planes: FighterJet, JumboJet, and SuperJet. The demand for Aero's planes is highest during the months of October and November, when retailers want a large stock available for holiday shopping. Expecting this trend to continue, Amelia wonders about how best to utilize her available capacity. What combination of toy planes should she produce? Exhibit 6.9 presents key operating data.

As Exhibit 6.9 shows, Aero has 9,000 production hours available for November. At a production rate of 50 per hour, Aero could produce a maximum of 450,000 units of FighterJet if it uses all of its production capacity to make this product. At a rate of 25 units per hour for JumboJet and 15 units per hour for SuperJet, Aero could produce a maximum of 225,000 units of JumboJet and 135,000 units of Super-Jet, respectively. Thus, Aero could meet the *individual* demand for any one of the product comfortably.

Unfortunately, meeting the demand for *all* the jets is impossible. Producing 200,000 FighterJets at 50 units per hour would require 4,000 hours. Similarly, producing 100,000 JumboJets at 25 units per hour and 60,000 SuperJet at 15 units per hour would require 4,000 hours for each line. Thus, producing all the Jets at full demand requires 12,000 total production hours. Amelia does not have that much

Exhibit 6.9	*Aero Toys: Key Operating Data*		
	FighterJet	**JumboJet**	**SuperJet**
Demand (in units) for November	200,000	100,000	60,000
Unit price	$40	$60	$80
Unit variable cost	$25	$35	$40
Unit contribution margin	$15	$25	$40
Production rate (units per hour)	50	25	15
Available production hours in November			9,000
Total monthly fixed costs			$4,000,000

capacity at her disposal. She has only 9,000 hours, not 12,000 hours. The question then is how many of each plane should Amelia produce to maximize the profit for November?

To answer this question, Amelia carefully studies the profitability of each toy plane. Looking again at Exhibit 6.9, Amelia notices that the high-priced SuperJet has the highest unit contribution margin ($40), followed by the JumboJet ($25), and the FighterJet ($15). Based on this information, Amelia decides to give the highest priority to the SuperJet and meet its demand. If any unused capacity remains, she will consider the JumboJet and, finally, the FighterJet.

If Amelia implements this decision rule, meeting all of the SuperJet's demand of 60,000 units will require 4,000 production hours. Of the 5,000 production hours that remain, Amelia will use 4,000 to meet all of the demand for the JumboJet. The company will then have 1,000 production hours available for FighterJet, which will allow Amelia to produce only 50,000 units. Although uncomfortable with losing a sizeable portion of the demand for FighterJet, Amelia believes that she will be doing the best she can with the available capacity.

Let us calculate Amelia's expected profit from this decision. The contribution margin from making and selling 60,000 units of SuperJet, 100,000 units of JumboJet, and 50,000 units of FighterJet is (60,000 × $40) + (100,000 × $25) + (50,000 × $15) = $5,650,000. Subtracting the $4,000,000 in fixed costs, we therefore estimate Amelia's profit before taxes as $1,650,000. Amelia is pleased with this profit estimate.

After a couple of sleepless nights, Amelia realizes how she can do even better. From an Executive MBA program she had attended some time ago, Amelia recalls the general rule that we described earlier: To maximize profit when capacity is in short supply, *maximize the contribution margin per unit of capacity.* Amelia quickly revises her analysis of each jet's profitability. Exhibit 6.10 presents her findings.

Notice from panel A of Exhibit 6.10 that for the FighterJet, a production hour yields a contribution margin of $750, which equals 50 units produced times the $15 unit contribution margin. Similarly, a production hour devoted to making JumboJet yields a contribution margin of $625, and a production hour devoted to making SuperJet yields a contribution margin of $600. Thus, giving top priority to FighterJet makes the most sense. JumboJet is the next ranked product, with SuperJet taking up any residual capacity.

Panel B of Exhibit 6.10 shows the time allocation under Amelia's revised ranking of the products. Aero will use 4,000 hours each (or 8,000 production hours in total) to meet all of the demand for FighterJet and JumboJet, yielding a combined contribution margin of $5,500,000. With the remaining 1,000 hours, Aero will produce and sell 15,000 units of SuperJet, earning an additional contribution margin of $600,000. This product combination yields a total profit before taxes of $2,100,000. This amount is $450,000 greater than the $1,650,000 profit before taxes from her previous choice.

Exhibit 6.10	Aero Toys: Most Profitable Production Schedule for November

Panel A: Determine Contribution Per Unit of Scarce Resource

	FighterJet	JumboJet	SuperJet
Demand (in units) for November	200,000	100,000	60,000
Unit price	$40	$60	$80
Unit variable cost	$25	$35	$40
Unit contribution margin	$15	$25	$40
Production rate (units per hour)	50	25	15
Contribution margin per production hour	$750	$625	$600
(= unit contribution margin × production rate)			
Product rank for scheduling production	1	2	3

Panel B: Allocation of Time Among Products

Product	Time Available (hours)	Production Rate (units /hr)	Units Made	Time Used (hours)	Unit Contribution Margin	Total Contribution
FighterJet	9,000	50	200,000	4,000	$15	$3,000,000
JumboJet	5,000	25	100,000	4,000	$25	2,500,000
SuperJet	1,000	15	15,000	1,000	$40	600,000
Total contribution						$6,100,000
− Fixed cost						4,000,000
= Profit						$2,100,000

Check It! Exercise #5

Assume the production rates of FighterJet, JumboJet, and SuperJet are 50, 25, and 20 units per hour, respectively (all other information is the same). Verify that the most profitable schedule calls for production of 200,000 units of FighterJet, 50,000 units of JumboJet, and 60,000 units of SuperJet. Also verify that Aero's profit before taxes will be $2,650,000 at these production levels.

	FighterJet	JumboJet	SuperJet
Maximum demand (units)	200,000	100,000	60,000
Unit contribution margin	$15	$25	$40
Production rate (units per hour)	50	25	20
Contribution margin per production hour	_____	_____	_____
Rank for scheduling production	_____	_____	_____

Product	Time Available	Production Rate	Units Made	Time Used	Contribution Margin
_____	_____	_____	_____	_____	_____
_____	_____	_____	_____	_____	_____
_____	_____	_____	_____	_____	_____

Total contribution margin _____
Total monthly fixed costs _____
Profit before taxes _____

In the Aero example, we considered a case in which there is only one resource whose supply is limited. Often, organizations face this situation with multiple resources at the same time. Managers must therefore consider the constraints posed by all of the resources. Multiple-resource cases are similar to the one-resource case presented above. However, dealing with them requires applying the advanced methods of *linear and integer programming,* topics discussed in upper-level classes in operations management.

We have examined four contexts for short-term decisions: special order, product promotion, make or buy, and product mix. In Appendices A and B, we examine two more contexts: "sell now or process further" decisions and "product add/drop" decisions. As you will notice there, the key issue in these settings is dealing with some significant costs that are not controllable and thus not relevant for the decision at hand.

Connecting to Practice

THEORY OF CONSTRAINTS

Aero Toys' solution relates to a core message of the Theory of Constraints (TOC). Eli Goldratt, who established the Goldratt Institute, popularized this approach to problem solving that deals with excess demand by identifying and obtaining the maximum value from the factors that constrain profitability. A key prescription is to maximize the value of the amount of production (throughput) processed in the constraining resource. TOC looks to maximize *throughput margin,* defined as unit price less materials cost, by focusing on those products that yield the largest throughput margin per capacity unit of the constraining resource.

COMMENTARY: In her solution, Amelia maximizes the contribution margin per unit of the scarce resource because she defines *all* variable costs (materials, labor, variable overhead, and variable selling expenses) as controllable with respect to her product-mix decision. Her solution would coincide with the TOC prescription if she defines only materials costs as controllable. The specifics of the individual situation and the decision horizon determine whether a given cost or benefit is controllable. The solution methodology is the same after classifying costs and benefits per their controllability.

Qualitative Considerations

LEARNING OBJECTIVE 5

Consider qualitative and longer-term aspects of short-term decisions.

In the previous sections, we focused on how managers could improve short-term profit when faced with a temporary gap between supply and demand. We illustrated how the concepts of controllability and relevance guide the proper choice from a set of options. In these analyses, however, we ignored the potential longer-term implications of these short-term actions. Because these long-term effects could vary across decision options, they might be relevant. Why then does our approach make sense? Why are we ignoring potentially *relevant* long-term costs and benefits?

The short answer is that we want to keep the decision problem as simple as possible. Such simplification frequently is the first step for many managers. Quantifying the longer-term implications of short-term actions is difficult. In many cases, qualitative assessments are the only ones possible, and large estimation errors accompany such assessments. As a result, many managers follow a "peel the onion" approach. They first estimate the short-term effects and then expand the range of considered factors.

Quantitative analysis of different decision options is extremely important, yet it constitutes just one input into decision making. Effective managers articulate and consider the longer-term implications of short-term decisions, even if only on a qualitative basis. It is important for managers to do so because of potential trade-offs between short-term and long-term interests. An option may cost the company in the short term but may be the most beneficial one from a long-term perspective. Looking out for long-term profit by not turning away loyal clients and preserving reputation in the marketplace might sway the manager from the option that maximizes short-term profit.

Almost every business example that we have discussed in this and the previous chapters offers us the opportunity to appreciate such a trade-off. Let us begin with the vignette in Chapters 1 through 4, Hercules Health Club. Self-sustaining classes such as yoga have long-term value because they preserve some *flexibility* with respect to future choices. If Tom and Lynda offer the yoga class and it turns out not to be attractive, they could cancel it and reconsider lowering the membership fee. Suppose they lower the membership fee now and it proves insufficient to stem defections to Apex. They may then find it hard to raise fees to the original levels and try out the yoga class as an alternate strategy. Indeed, the differential ease in lowering versus raising prices is why firms offer discounts rather than reduce the list price. It is much easier to cancel the discount program! Managers often use the term *real options* to denote the flexibility associated with different options and use advanced mathematical techniques to value the real options.

The case of Precision Piston Rings is also instructive. The quality of piston rings is extremely important to the functioning of an automobile engine. The market for piston rings is very competitive because many suppliers vie for business from the major automobile companies. It may be in Precision's best interest to make its own jigs and fixtures and other needed machine tools *in-house* because the quality of those items determines the quality of the piston rings. The improved quality may result in Precision being better off in the end, even if the short-term costs of in-house production are higher. Of course, this decision is much easier if in-house production also lowers short-term costs.

In the case of Culinary Creations, short-term interests and long-term interests are aligned closely. In the short term, it is profitable for Culinary Creations to accept the charity engagement's Wednesday offer. This action is probably in Culinary Creations' long-term best interests as well. It may lead to future business with the charity organization, build community goodwill, and secure future business with individuals who are attending the charity event.

Conceptually, many long-term implications arise because people outside the firm, such as customers, suppliers, and competitors, respond to the firm's decisions and actions. Precision's higher quality might generate more business from its customers. Similarly, catering the charity dinner may build community goodwill for Culinary Creations. Successful managers' choices account for how such external parties are likely to respond to the various options.

As Exhibit 6.11 illustrates, financial considerations might be the meat, but qualitative and long-term considerations provide essential ingredients that can help determine which short-term option to implement. In the case of Superior Cereals, the manager in charge of a national brand is probably well aware that local store brand manufacturers will mimic any new product introduction. They will account for this behavior when scheduling the promotion and advertising campaigns. In

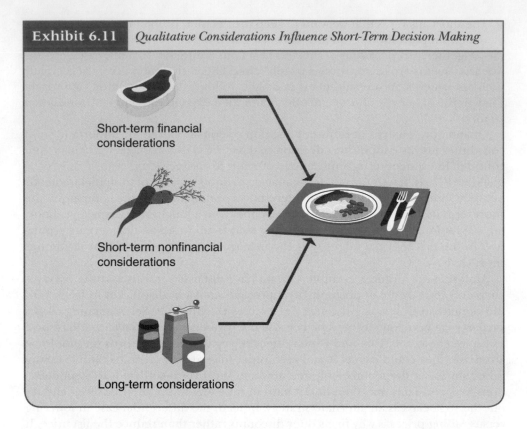

Exhibit 6.11 *Qualitative Considerations Influence Short-Term Decision Making*

Short-term financial considerations

Short-term nonfinancial considerations

Long-term considerations

turn, Superior's management will consider such intentions on the part of national brand manufacturers when taking appropriate actions. Game Theory, a branch of economics, deals with the formal study of such strategic behavior of decision makers. You may encounter this topic in your economics courses.

SUMMARY

In this chapter, we discussed the nature of short-term decisions and developed an excess supply/excess demand "lens" with which to view such problems. We then discussed and illustrated how businesses could evaluate options for closing the gap between the supply and demand of available capacity. Our examples, which span service (Culinary Catering), manufacturing (Precision Piston Rings), and merchandising (Superior Cereal), underscore the universal applicability of these ideas. Finally, we discussed some of the qualitative and longer-term issues that invariably play a role in short-term decision making.

In the next chapter, we bridge the gap between short-term planning and control. Our primary focus is on budgeting, a subject of importance to all organizations.

RAPID REVIEW

LEARNING OBJECTIVE 1

Understand the factors that trigger short-term decisions.

• Managers choose capacity levels to match long-term expected demand and supply. However, demand realizations rarely match expectations, creating an imbalance between the supply of and the demand for capacity.

• Short-term decisions are responses to a mismatch between supply (capacity) and demand. During demand downturns, capacity utilization goes down. During demand upturns, there is a shortage of available capacity. Short-term decisions attempt to close these gaps between the supply of and demand for capacity resources.

• During demand downturns, managers may reduce prices to stimulate demand or accept special orders to increase capacity utilization. Such actions are profitable because the opportunity cost of temporarily idle capacity is zero.

- During demand upturns, managers may increase prices to reduce demand or outsource work. These actions may be profitable because excess demand results in capacity having positive opportunity cost.

LEARNING OBJECTIVE 2

Evaluate decision options using alternate approaches.

- We could formulate short-run decisions by focusing on controllable costs or by using relevant costs.

- In either of these incremental approaches, we express the benefits and costs of the various options *relative to* one of the options. If the status quo is a viable option, we usually pick the status quo as the benchmark and focus on controllability. If the status quo is not a feasible option, then we could still apply the incremental approach by choosing any option as the basis for evaluating the remaining options. It is usually efficient to perform a relevant cost analysis by focusing only on relevant costs and benefits.

- We also could consider *all* costs and benefits associated with each regardless of whether some costs are controllable or relevant. Doing so does not change the rankings of options.

LEARNING OBJECTIVE 3

Solve short-term decisions such as make versus buy and special-order pricing.

- Superior Cereals examines the viability of short-term promotions to deal with excess supply. Superior confronted the decision of how to sell 50,000 boxes of cereal it already produced—a situation akin to a manufacturing firm that has to deal with excess capacity because of lean demand.

- Precision Piston Rings considers a make-versus-buy decision in a setting with excess demand. Precision faced excess demand on its machining capacity because it could not make all of the jigs *and* all of the rings using its current facilities. The excess demand led to a positive opportunity cost for capacity, and we found that it was more profitable for Precision to buy the jigs and devote its attention to its primary product, piston rings.

LEARNING OBJECTIVE 4

Determine the best use of a resource in short supply.

- With a limited number of options, it is possible to list them all and pick the best one. In some cases, the number of available options can be very large. In such cases, it is not feasible to list all of the options and calculate their values.

- The general rule for solving such problems when excess demand exists is: When demand is high and a resource is in short supply, rank products by the contribution margin per unit of the resource and not by the contribution margin per unit of the product.

LEARNING OBJECTIVE 5

Consider the qualitative and longer-term aspects of short-term decisions.

- Many short-term decisions have longer-term implications. These implications arise because people outside the firm, such as customers, suppliers, and competitors, respond to the firm's decisions and actions.

- Quantifying the longer-term implications of short-term actions is difficult. Frequently, only qualitative assessments are possible.

- Effective managers do consider the qualitative implications of short-term decisions. While it is possible that short-term and long-term goals coincide, the best action from a short-term perspective does not always guarantee long-term profitability.

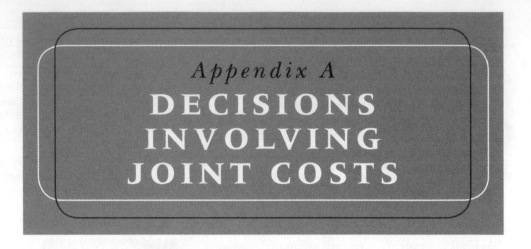

Appendix A

DECISIONS INVOLVING JOINT COSTS

Heritage Farms processes raw milk to make cream and liquid milk. It processes the cream further to make butter. Heritage sells both the butter and milk to supermarkets. As with Heritage, in many companies across many industries, a single process often yields many outputs. Firms such as BHP Billiton process ore to extract copper and other metals such as zinc and lead from the *same* ore. Likewise, when firms such as Amoco refine crude oil, they obtain a number of products including aviation fuel, kerosene, oil-based resins, and automobile fuel. The unique aspect of such processes is that we cannot modify them to yield just one product or the other. The nature of the process means that we will obtain many outputs from a single input. Such processes are joint processes, and their outputs are **joint products**.

As shown in Exhibit 6.12, every week, Heritage converts 20,000 gallons of raw milk into 18,000 gallons of processed milk and 6,750 pounds of cream. It pays $18,000 to dairy farmers. It incurs an additional $5,000 to separate the cream. At some point in the process, Heritage can separately identify milk and cream. This step in the production process is the **split-off point**. Costs incurred before the split-off point are **joint costs** that we cannot trace to individual products. Heritage's joint costs are, therefore, $23,000 per week.

Usually, firms process individual products further beyond the split-off point. Heritage incurs additional costs of $8,000 to pasteurize and package milk for retail sale, and $3,000 to process and package 6,750 pounds of cream into 6,500 pounds of butter. Unlike joint costs, we can trace these costs, which are incurred after the split-off point, to individual products, thereby eliminating any need for allocations.

Heritage sells each gallon of milk for $1.50 and each pound of butter for $2.00.

In general, there are two broad classes of decisions in settings with joint products.

Exhibit 6.12	*Heritage Farms: Cost Flows in Milk Processing Unit*

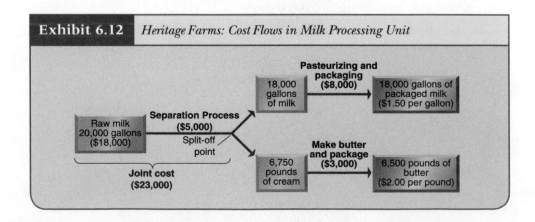

- Determine whether the entire process is profitable. This is a long-term decision.
- Determine whether we should sell any particular joint product at the split-off point, or if we should incur additional costs to process it further into a different product. Such "sell now or process further" decisions are usually short term in nature, for the decision will change based on prevailing prices.

Let us examine whether it is profitable for Heritage Farms to operate the entire process. Exhibit 6.13 provides a statement of income per week. The format for this income statement is the same as that for Office Gallery, the example we used in Chapter 4 to illustrate segmented income statements.

Notice that in calculating income, there is no need to allocate joint costs to individual products. As long as the total contribution margin from the joint products exceeds the total joint cost, the process is profitable.

Suppose Heritage Farms has the option of selling milk in bulk at the split-off point for $1.20 per gallon and cream at the split-off point for $1.40 per pound. Should Heritage process the bulk milk further, pasteurizing and packaging the milk for retail sale? Should it convert cream into butter for retail sale? Or should Heritage sell either the milk or the cream (or both) at the split-off point?

Exhibit 6.14 presents the calculations for these decisions. As we know from Exhibit 6.13, the contribution margin from processing 18,000 gallons of liquid milk further is $19,000. By selling the 18,000 gallons immediately at the split-off point as bulk milk for $1.20 per gallon, the company can generate $21,600, and there are no additional processing costs. Heritage makes $2,600 more by selling the milk in bulk. Similar calculations show that it is more profitable for Heritage Farms to convert cream into butter instead of selling the cream directly at the split-off point.

Each decision turns on whether the increase in revenue from additional processing exceeds the cost of additional processing. *We do not consider the joint cost of $23,000, nor how it might be allocated between the two products, in these sell now or process further decisions.* The reason is that the joint cost is not relevant for product-related decisions *beyond* the split-off point. Heritage has no choice but to incur the joint cost regardless of its decisions regarding selling now or processing further. For these decisions, the joint cost is sunk.

Exhibit 6.13	Heritage Farms: Product-Level Contribution Margin Statement		
	Milk	**Butter**	**Total**
Sales volume (in units)	18,000 gal	6,500 lb	
Revenues	$27,000	$13,000	$40,000
Traceable processing costs	8,000	3,000	11,000
Segment (product) margin	$19,000	$10,000	$29,000
Joint costs			23,000
Profit before taxes			$6,000

Exhibit 6.14	Heritage Farms: Should We Sell Now or Process Further?	
	Milk	**Butter**
Sales volume (in units)	18,000 gal	6,500 lb
Process further		
Revenue	$27,000	$13,000
Traceable processing costs	8,000	3,000
Segment (product) margin	$19,000	$10,000
Sell at split-off point		
Revenue (for raw milk/cream)	$21,600*	$9,450**
Traceable processing costs	0	0
Segment (product) margin	$21,600	$9,450
Decision	Sell as bulk milk at split-off point	Process further into butter

*18,000 gallons of milk × $1.20 per gallon
**6,750 lb of cream × $1.40 per lb

Appendix B
ADDING/ DROPPING PRODUCT LINES

The Toys section of Fair Value stores has been losing money for several months now because a specialty store like Toys R Us has opened in the neighborhood. How should Fair Value evaluate whether it is profitable to close the section and reallocate the resources to, say, a bookstore?

Let us begin by considering whether the decision pertains to the short term or to the long term. The answer is ambiguous because managers might be interested in considering both the short- and long-term effects on profitability. We defer a detailed discussion of how to estimate the long-term impact to Chapter 9. Here, we present a method for evaluating the decision's short-term impact. Fortunately, the basic approach to decision making still remains the same as discussed in Chapter 2. We only consider costs and benefits controllable over the short term.

Exhibit 6.15 provides a section-level income statement for Fair Value. This income statement reflects the firm's policy of allocating its fixed costs to its various sections based on square feet of space usage. As we can tell, the Toys section appears to be unprofitable.

However, we should not rely on income statements such as that in Exhibit 6.15 to evaluate the effect on short-term profit. Why? Because they allocate common costs to product lines or sections, such statements mingle controllable and noncontrollable costs.

If Fair Value closes the Toys line, it will lose the contribution of $1,225,000 − $722,500 − $172,500 = $330,000. It also will save the $95,000 of fixed costs traceable to the Toys division. However, the statement also suggests that Fair Value will not incur the $281,250 in allocated fixed costs allocated to the Toys line if it discontinues the line. Such a reduction is not likely, at least in the short term. While the common fixed costs might decrease, the decline may not be $281,250. A detailed account analysis of the accounting records indicates that the common fixed costs

Exhibit 6.15	*Fair Value Stores: Section-Level Income Statement*		
	Toys	**Other Departments**	**Total**
Square feet	12,000	52,000	64,000
Revenues	$1,225,000	$11,375,000	$12,600,000
Cost of merchandise	722,500	6,212,500	6,935,000
Variable salaries to sales staff	172,500	509,500	682,000
Traceable fixed costs	95,000	277,800	372,800
Allocated fixed costs	281,250	937,500	1,218,750
Profit before taxes	($46,250)	$3,437,700	$3,391,450

Exhibit 6.16	Fair Value Stores: Department-Level Contribution Margin Statement		
	Toys	**Other Departments**	**Total**
Square feet	12,000	52,000	64,000
Revenues	$1,225,000	$11,375,000	$12,600,000
Cost of merchandise	722,500	6,212,500	6,935,000
Variable salaries to sales staff	172,500	509,500	682,000
Segment contribution	$330,000	$4,653,000	4,983,000
Traceable fixed costs	95,000	277,800	372,800
Segment Profit	235,000	4,375,200	4,610,200
Fixed costs avoided if toys line is closed	85,500		85,500
Unavoidable fixed costs			1,133,250
Profit before taxes			$3,391,450

would decline only by $85,500 if Fair Value discontinues the Toys line. (Some refer to such costs as **avoidable fixed costs**.) However, Fair Value will continue to incur other costs such as the lease payment for the building. Such costs are not avoidable or controllable over the short term. Thus, they are not relevant for evaluating the profit effect from closing the line.

The segmented income statement we discussed in Chapter 3 offers a convenient way to evaluate short-term profit effects. Exhibit 6.16 presents the same data as in Exhibit 6.15, but in the familiar segmented contribution margin format.

The Toys section is generating a positive margin of $149,500 even after deducting the avoidable fixed costs. Therefore, unless the manager can rent the space for more than $149,500 annually, it is not advisable to close down the Toys section.

ANSWERS TO CHECK IT! EXERCISES

Exercise #1: (1) $243,750 − $206,250 = $37,500; (2) 9,000 − 6,000 = 3,000 persons; (3) $37,500/3,000 = $12.50; (4) $243,750; (5) $12.50 × 9,000 = $112,500; (6) $243,750 − $112,500 = $131,250.

Exercise #2: (1) Additional revenue from charity is 50 × $26 = $1,300; (2) lost revenue is −120 × $36 = ($4,320); (3) Additional variable costs for charity are $625; (4) variable costs saved from not serving regular customers are $1,500; (4) The total relevant cost is ($875) − that is, it costs less in total variable costs if we cater on Saturday because Culinary serves 70 fewer customers; (5) Relevant profit = ($3,020) − ($875) = ($2,145).

Exercise #3: Incremental profit from issuing a rebate:
  Incremental revenue from supermarket sales − full price = $2 × −2,000 = − $4,000
  Incremental revenue from supermarket sales − rebate = $1.50 × 22,000 = $33,000
  Institutional sales = $1 × −20,000 = − $20,000
  Less
  Incremental variable costs = $0
  Incremental fixed costs = $5,000
  Incremental profit = $4,000

Exercise #4: Total cost of buying: Contribution of $5 × 10,000 rings − Payment to outside vendor of $162,500 less contribution margin from being able to make the additional 10,000 rings ($5 × 10,000) = ($112,500); Total cost of making = $125,000 = $4,000 × 25 jigs + $25,000.

Exercise #5: Contribution margin per production hour = $750, $625, and $800, respectively for FighterJet, JumboJet, and SuperJet. Starting with SuperJet (with the highest contribution margin per production hour): Produce 60,000 units (full demand). Requires 60,000 units/20 units per hour = 3,000 hours. Contribution = 60,000 units × $40 per unit = $2,400,000. Remaining hours = 9,000 − 3,000 = 6,000 hours. FighterJet has the next highest contribution margin per production hour. Produce 200,000 units (full demand). Requires 200,000 units/ 50 units per hour = 4,000 hours. Contribution = 200,000 units × $15 per unit = $3,000,000. Remaining hours = 6,000 − 4,000 = 2,000. With 2,000 remaining hours, Aero can produce 2,000 hours × 25 units per hour = 50,000 units of JumboJet. Contribution = 50,000 units × $25 per unit = $1,250,000. Total contribution margin = $2,400,000 + $3,000,000 + $1,250,000 = $6,650,000. Fixed costs = $4,000,000. Profit before taxes = $6,650,000 − $4,000,000 = $2,650,000.

SELF-STUDY PROBLEMS

SELF-STUDY PROBLEM #1:
Allocation of a Scarce Resource

Suppose you are taking an examination that contains three types of questions: (1) multiple choice, (2) short answer, and (3) essay. Your instructor informs you that the exam will contain 14 multiple-choice questions worth 2 points each (28 points total), 8 short-answer questions worth 4 points each (32 points total), and 4 essay questions worth 10 points each (40 points total). Thus, the maximum score on the exam is 100 points.

You believe that you can correctly answer 90% of the multiple-choice questions you attempt, receive 80% of the possible points on each short-answer question you attempt, and receive 70% of the possible points on each essay question you attempt. In addition, you need 4 minutes to answer each multiple-choice question, 5 minutes to answer each short answer question, and 10 minutes to answer each essay question. The exam is scheduled to last only two hours—sadly, your instructor has vastly different ideas about the amount of time students need to answer these questions.

To maximize your expected score, which type of question should you answer first? Which type of question should you answer last? What is your expected score?

In this problem, time is in short supply. Thus, maximizing total points requires you to maximize the points earned per available minute. Exhibit 6.17 summarizes the analysis:

Exhibit 6.17	*Expected Points per Minute of Exam Time*		
	Multiple Choice	**Short Answer**	**Essay**
Maximum points per question	2	4	10
Probability correct	0.90	0.80	0.70
Expected points if question attempted	1.8	3.2	7
Time per question in minutes	4	5	10
Expected points per minute	0.45	0.64	0.70

To maximize the expected score on the exam, you should attempt the essay questions first, followed by the short-answer questions and finish with the multiple-choice questions. Such a strategy leads to the following expected score:

Exhibit 6.18   *Expected Exam Score*

	Allocated Time (min.)	Expected Points	Time Left (min.)
Start of exam			120
Allocated to essay questions	40	28.00*	80
Allocated to short-answer questions	40	25.60**	40
Allocated to multiple-choice questions	40	18.00***	0
Expected Total Score		71.60	

*There are four essay questions worth 10 points each. Each question takes 10 minutes to answer, and, on average, you receive 70% of the possible points. Thus, you will take $4 \times 10 = 40$ minutes to answer these questions and receive $4 \times 10 \times .7 = 28.00$ points (i.e., 40 minutes $\times$ 0.70 points per minute = 28 points).

**There are 8 short-answer questions worth 4 points each. Each question takes 5 minutes to answer and, on average, you receive 80% of the possible points. Thus, you will take $5 \times 8 = 40$ minutes to answer these questions and receive $4 \times 8 \times .8 = 25.60$ points (i.e., 40 minutes $\times$ 0.64 points per minute = 25.6 points).

***There are 14 multiple-choice questions worth 2 points each. Each question takes 4 minutes to answer, and, on average, you will receive 90% of the possible points. With only 40 minutes remaining, however, you can answer only 10 multiple-choice questions. Thus, you spend the remaining 40 minutes on multiple-choice questions and receive $2 \times 10 \times .9 = 18.00$ points (i.e., 40 minutes $\times$ 0.45 points per minute = 18 points).

This problem shows that even though you have a greater probability of being correct on the multiple-choice questions, they should be attempted last because they take too much time. Essentially, you will only get an average of 0.45 points per minute spent on the multiple-choice questions, whereas you can get an average of 0.70 points per minute spent on the essay questions. As you can see, the principles of short-term decision making can be applied to aspects of our daily life.

SELF-STUDY PROBLEM #2:
Excess Supply Using Alternate Approaches

Refer to the Superior Cereals problem in the text. Suppose Superior's managers have identified the following option, in addition to the "emphasize institutional sales" and "issue a rebate" options.

- Store Display: Offer supermarkets a sum of $17,500 for a prominent store display. Superior anticipates that this option would result in selling 40,000 boxes of toasted honey flakes at $2 per box. Institutional buyers would snap up the remaining 10,000 boxes at $1 per box.

  a. *Determine the best option for Superior Cereals.*
  Exhibit 6.19 presents the costs and benefits associated with each of Superior's three decision options. As in the text, we consider total costs and revenues associated with each option because we do not have information on the status quo.
      The option with the highest value is the issue a rebate option. While the store display option generates the highest contribution margin of the three options, the increase in fixed costs swamps the increase in contribution margin. Thus, the issue a rebate option remains the best option for Superior Cereals.

  b. *Using relevant cost analysis, determine the best option for Superior Cereals.*
  Exhibit 6.20 recasts the information for Superior's three decision options using relevant cost analysis and evaluates the issue rebate and store display options relative to the emphasize institutional sales option.
      Notice that the relevant cost analysis does not require any information about the status quo. Our analysis confirms that the issue a rebate option is the most attractive because it offers the *largest (positive) incremental profit.*

Exhibit 6.19   *Superior Cereals: Evaluating Available Options*

	Detail	Emphasize Institutional Sales	Issue Rebate	Store Display
Supermarket sales— full price		25,000 boxes	23,000 boxes	40,000 boxes
Supermarket sales—rebate		—	22,000 boxes	—
Institutional sales		25,000 boxes	5,000 boxes	10,000 boxes
Wholesale price per box		$2.00	$2.00	$2.00
Price per box with rebate		—	$1.50	—
Institutional price per box		$1.00	$1.00	$1.00
Supermarket sales— full price	25,000 × $2; 23,000 × $2; 40,000 × $2	$50,000	$46,000	$80,000
Supermarket sales—rebate	22,000 × $1.50	—	33,000	—
Institutional sales	25,000 × $1; 5,000 × $1; 10,000 × $1	25,000	5,000	10,000
Revenues		$75,000	$84,000	$90,000
Variable costs		0	0	0
Contribution margin		$75,000	$84,000	$90,000
Advertising & processing costs		—	5,000	—
Display space rental		—	—	17,500
Profit		$75,000	$79,000	$72,500

Exhibit 6.20   *Superior Cereals: Relevant Cost Analysis*

	Emphasize Institutional Sales	Increment Due to	
		Issue Rebate	Store Display
Incremental revenue			
Supermarket sales − full price (= $2 × −2,000; $2 × 15,000)	—	−$4,000	$30,000
Supermarket sales − rebate (= $1.50 × 22,000; $1.50 × 0)	—	33,000	0
Institutional sales (= $1 × −20,000; $1 × −15,000)	—	−20,000	−15,000
Total incremental revenue	—	$9,000	$15,000
Incremental variable costs	—	0	0
Incremental contribution margin	—	$9,000	$15,000
Incremental fixed costs (= $5,000; $17,500)	—	5,000	17,500
Incremental profit	$0	$4,000	−$2,500

GLOSSARY

Avoidable fixed costs Costs that need not be incurred if an option is not chosen. Same as controllable fixed costs.

Capacity The maximum volume of activity that a company can sustain with available resources.

Excess capacity/Excess supply A condition that obtains when available capacity exceeds realized demand.

Excess demand A condition that obtains when realized demand exceeds available capacity.

Incremental (differential) approach An approach for framing and solving decisions that involves expressing the benefits and costs of the various decision options *relative* to one of the options.

Joint cost A cost that is common to two or more products. Costs of a joint process.

Joint product Products that are produced in a joint process. It is not possible to produce one joint product without producing the others as well.

Relevant cost analysis See Incremental (differential) approach.

Split-off point Step in a joint process after which we can identify and process the joint products separately.

Totals (gross) approach An approach that includes non-controllable costs and benefits to construct a contribution margin statement for each decision option.

REVIEW QUESTIONS

6.1 LO1. What do short-term decisions deal with in most business environments?

6.2 LO1. What does the term "capacity" mean?

6.3 LO1. Why is the decision of how much capacity to put in place a long-term decision?

6.4 LO1. What are the two broad classifications of short-term decisions? List two examples of each.

6.5 LO2. Briefly describe the incremental or differential method approach to making short-term decisions.

6.6 LO2. Briefly describe the totals or the gross approach to making short-term decisions.

6.7 LO2. Which approach, incremental or totals, requires more computations? Why?

6.8 LO2. When might the gross approach be preferable to the incremental approach for making short-term decisions?

6.9 LO3. Are sales promotion decisions typically responses to an excess supply situation or an excess demand situation?

6.10 LO3. What is a make-or-buy decision?

6.11 LO4. When does it make sense to compute the contribution margin per unit of a particular resource in making short-term decisions?

6.12 LO4. What is the general rule for allocating a scarce resource to making multiple products?

6.13 LO5. How might managers deal with the possible long-term implications that may arise from short-run decisions?

DISCUSSION QUESTIONS

6.14 LO1. The definition of "short-term" depends on the business context. What would General Motors consider as short-term? Is this period longer than what a bakery would consider as short-term? Why?

6.15 LO1. Automobile dealers frequently advertise sales because their lots are "overflowing." The ads suggest a shortage of storage capacity but the price-cutting action indicates a demand shortfall. How can you reconcile these seemingly contradictory inferences? (*Hint:* Think about defining capacity in terms of vehicles sold per day.)

6.16 LO1, LO5. After a heavy snowfall, hardware stores often experience a run on snow shovels and other snow removal equipment. However, they rarely raise prices even though there is a temporary spike in demand. What considerations, legal and otherwise, do you think govern their actions? (*Hint:* Do an Internet search on the phrase "price gouging" for some provocative articles.)

6.17 LO1. Identify the one resource whose daily supply is fixed for each person. How could we improve the effectiveness with which we consume this resource?

6.18 LO2. Some people argue that the gross method is also, at some level, "incremental." Evaluate this argument. (*Hint:* Think about how the gross method treats Superior Cereal's other costs and revenues.)

6.19 LO3, LO5. When faced with a sudden spurt in demand, why does it sometimes make sense for a company to increase prices? For example, why do airlines raise fares during peak travel periods? Why might it not be a good idea for consulting companies?

6.20 LO3. In periods of excess capacity, does it make sense for a manufacturing company to produce some products to stock (i.e., build up inventory) for sale in future periods of high demand? Give two examples of industries where this might be a good idea. Give two examples where it might be a bad idea.

6.21 LO3. How does holding inventory help reduce the expected gap between available capacity and uncertain demand?

6.22 LO3 (Advanced). Inventory is one mechanism that a firm could use to protect itself from the impact of fluctuating demand. What are other long-term strategies a company could adopt to insulate itself against uncertain demand?

6.23 LO4. Often, the capacity of the most expensive machine defines a plant's capacity. That is, firms will deliberately install excess capacity in "cheap" resources. Why might this practice be optimal?

6.24 LO4 (Advanced). The general allocation procedure in the text assumes few constraints on how we could use resources. Why might this general rule not hold when individual uses require a *minimum* amount of the resource? (For example, if we are allocating space, each use might need a minimum of 10 units of space.) How might we modify our approach to incorporate lumpy uses of capacity?

6.25 LO4. How does the notion of maximizing the contribution per unit of the scarce resource apply when some products have *minimum* production quantities?

6.26 LO5. Outsourcing is the practice of having an external party take over some business and/or manufacturing processes. How does outsourcing change a firm's cost structure and, therefore, its ability to be nimble in responding to competition? What are some long-term costs and benefits of outsourcing?

6.27 LO5. We often dip our toes in the water to check the temperature before jumping in. How might this analogy pertain to a firm introducing a new product? How does test marketing provide greater flexibility to the firm relative to a national launch?

6.28 LO5. Suppose that buying a component is estimated to save $50,000 annually over making it in-house. However, outsourcing the component means that 20 long-term employees would be laid off, adversely affecting employee morale. How might a manager trade off these two factors?

EXERCISES

6.29 Framing and solving short-term decisions using controllable cost and gross approaches (LO1, LO2). Ajay Singh offers gift-wrapping services at the local mall. Ajay wraps each package, regardless of size, in the customer's choice of wrapping paper and bow for a price of $3. Ajay's variable costs total $1 per package wrapped, and his fixed costs amount to $600 per month.

Due to the anticipated increase in demand over the holiday season, Ajay is considering hiring a helper, at a cost of $8.50 per hour, to help him wrap packages. With the helper, Ajay estimates that he can wrap 110 packages in a 10-hour day. Without the helper, Ajay estimates that he can wrap 60 packages in a 10-hour day. Ajay plans on operating his business for thirty 10-hour days during the holiday season.

Required:

a. Does Ajay's decision deal with excess supply or excess demand?

b. Using the gross approach, determine whether Ajay should hire the helper.

c. Using controllable cost analysis, determine whether Ajay should hire the helper.

d. Assume Ajay's fixed costs were $1,000 rather than $600. Would this affect Ajay's decision to hire a helper?

6.30 Special-order pricing using the controllable cost analysis (LO2, CIMA Adapted). Magic Maids is one of England's largest commercial office cleaning services. The company has set a price of £120 for cleaning the "standard" business office. (£ = British Pound, the official currency of the United Kingdom). Magic Maids derived this price as follows:

Cleaning materials	£12.50[1]
Labor (3 hours @ £15 per hour)	45.00[2]
Variable overhead	7.50[3]
Fixed overhead (3 hours @ £5 per hour)	15.00[4]
Total cost	80.00
Profit markup (50%)	40.00
Price	£120.00

[1] Magic Maids provides all of the cleaning supplies.

[2] All Magic Maids employees receive a fixed salary. Magic Maids computes the "hourly" rate of £15 per hour by dividing the total salary by the total number of hours available.

[3] Variable overhead consists of costs such as scrub brushes and vacuum bags that depend on the number of offices cleaned.

[4] Magic Maids arrived at this estimate by dividing its total fixed overhead of £150,000 (which is comprised mainly of office rent and administrative salaries) by the total number of available labor hours, or 30,000.

A local conglomerate based in London approached Magic Maids about the possibility of cleaning 150 standard business offices next week. The conglomerate needs the work done on a rush basis due to an unexpected visit by a dignitary. Magic Maids has all of the requisite supplies in stock. It believes that it could complete 60% of the job during normal business hours. To complete the remaining 40%, however, some employees will have to work overtime; these employees receive £22.50 per hour, or 1.5 times the hourly rate, for their overtime hours.

Required:

a. Does Magic Maids' decision deal with excess supply or excess demand?

b. What is the incremental cost associated with cleaning the 150 offices?

c. How might Magic Maids use the incremental cost number you calculated in part b for decision making?

6.31 Special-order pricing, time-based pricing (LO1, LO2, LO3). Erin and Kyle Kouri operate a highly regarded Bed & Breakfast inn located in the historic district of Montpelier, Vermont. The inn has six rooms—each room has its own theme and rents for $180 per day. While the rooms are usually occupied on weekends (Friday, Saturday, and Sunday), it is rare for more than two rooms to be occupied during the week.

This past week, Erin received a telephone call from a customer who wishes to rent four rooms from Monday afternoon through Thursday morning (three nights). The customer and her three friends are planning a vacation and picked Montpelier for its recreational and cultural activities. However, the customer indicated that $180 a day was beyond their budget. She suggested a flat sum of $200 per person for the entire stay. She also requested that each person be accommodated in a separate room.

Erin and Kyle are not quite sure what to do. If they do not accept the customer's offer, then the rooms will remain empty. In addition, Erin and Kyle figure that it only costs them $10 per day to clean a room and change the linens. On the other hand, Erin and Kyle are concerned about renting the rooms for less than 50% of the standard rate.

Required:

a. Does Erin and Kyle's decision deal with excess supply or excess demand?

b. What should Erin and Kyle do?

6.32 Make versus buy (LO1, LO2, LO3). Jen Ahrens is a part-time artist who produces exquisite Japanese calligraphy prints on rice paper. Jen typically makes 50 prints per month and sells most of the prints for $75 each. Jen estimates that the variable cost of the paper and supplies amount to $8 per print and that her monthly fixed costs (the studio and utilities) amount to $250. (Jen's fixed costs are low because she works in a small room in her home.) Finally, Jen has each print framed and pays a local framing shop $25 per print for this service.

Due to a slowing economy, Jen's sales have slumped. Jen has only sold 30 prints in each of the past three months, and she believes that the demand for her prints will remain at 30 a month for the foreseeable future. Accordingly, Jen has reduced her production to 30 prints per month. Jen ruled out lowering her price because it will take her below the "price point" for her target audience, and she worries that reducing the price would lead customers to believe that her work is of low quality. Rather, Jen seeks your advice regarding doing her own framing. Jen believes that it would only cost her $10 per print to frame her own work and that she could do as good a job as the framing shop.

Required:

a. Does Jen's decision deal with excess supply or excess demand?

b. What is the cost of Jen doing her own framing versus having it done by a framing shop?

c. Assume that Jen will only be able to produce 15 prints a month if she does her own framing. How does this information affect your answer to part (b)? For simplicity, assume that Jen either frames all or none of her prints.

6.33 Product promotion, excess capacity (LO2). Tom and Lynda, owners of Hercules, are considering whether to offer valet parking as an optional feature of membership. They estimate that offering the service would increase monthly costs by $2,500 for salaries paid to attendants, increase in insurance rates, and so on. They also estimate that 400 members would use the service if it were priced at $5 per month. At this price, the club would also attract 20 new members. The number using the service would be 300 and the number of new members would be 10 if valet parking were priced at $10 per month. You estimate membership fees at $100 per month and variable costs at $35 per month.

Required:

a. At what price, if at all, should Tom and Lynda offer valet parking as an optional feature of the membership? Justify with supporting calculations.

b. What other factors might Tom and Lynda consider in their decision?

6.34 Excess capacity & excess demand (LO1, LO2). Marjorie Myers, a nurse, has approached Tom and Lynda, owners of Hercules, with an intriguing proposal. Marjorie wishes to offer specialized classes to small groups of expectant mothers. She believes that the exercise room at Hercules is perfect for her service, guarantees that she will not use any other part of the gym, will bring her own supplies, and promises not to interfere with the gym's operation in any way.

Required:

a. Marjorie is willing to pay $600 per month for use of the room, three days per week. She is willing to hold the class between 1 and 3 P.M. on weekdays. During this time, the gym is usually deserted and no classes are scheduled. Should Tom and Lynda accept Marjorie's offer?

b. Assume the same facts as in part (a) except that Marjorie wishes to hold one of her classes from 6 to 7 P.M. for three weekdays. She will increase payment from $600 to $700 per month. (She will schedule the other class from 1 to 2 P.M.) This schedule will disrupt the current schedule and make some of Hercules' current classes less convenient. Tom and Lynda anticipate losing eight members as a consequence. You know that monthly membership is $100 and monthly variable costs are $35 per member. Should Tom and Lynda accept Marjorie's offer? Assume that Marjorie will not accept a deal that does not include the requested evening time slot.

c. Suppose Marjorie is willing to accept the terms in part (a) or in part (b). Using the situation in part (a) as the base, calculate the *incremental* profit from scheduling evening classes.

6.35 Working with unit-level data, pricing (LO2). The Déjà Vu Card Company offers greeting cards for every occasion at unmatched prices. The following information comes from Déjà Vu's accounting records for December of the most recent year:

Greeting cards sold	100,000 cards
Selling price	$1.00 per card
Fixed costs:	
Manufacturing	$0.30 per card
Marketing & administrative	$0.21 per card
Variable costs:	
Manufacturing	$0.15 per card
Marketing & administrative	$0.08 per card

Required:

Déjà Vu has an extra stock of 5,000 holiday greeting cards. The company is considering two options: (1) holding a 50% off sale and (2) holding an 80% off sale. Déjà Vu expects to sell 1,500 cards if it holds a 50% off sale and 4,000 cards if it holds an 80% off sale. The remaining cards would be discarded. Which option should Déjà Vu pursue?

6.36 Effect of cost structure on decision making, gross approach (LO2). You and your four closest childhood friends ("The Fab Five," as you like to call yourselves) all attend the same university. Collectively, you are trying to determine the best way to organize transportation to and from your home town over the winter break; you have come up with two options:

1. *Drive.* While it will be cramped, your car can accommodate all five people. Operating your car will cost $0.30 per mile driven (in oil, gas, expected wear and tear of car, etc.), but this cost will be split five ways. In addition, because the 800-mile, one-way trip home will take more than 12 hours, you expect that each person will spend $20 on food and refreshments each way (i.e., the $20 cost will be incurred twice—on the trip home and on the return trip).

2. *Fly.* One of your friends, Amy, has found a cheap, round-trip, Internet-only fare for $169 per person. You can use the mass-transit system for transportation to and from the airport—this will cost $6 per person each way. Your parents will pick you up and drop you off at the other end. Finally, because the airline schedule calls for the trip to last 4 hours and 19 minutes (this estimate does not include travel time to and from the airport), you expect that each person will spend $5 on refreshments each way.

Required:

a. What is the per-person, round-trip cost for each option? Which option is cheaper?

b. Suppose it was just you and one friend (the "Terrific Two") rather than you and four friends. How does this information change your answer to part (a) above? That is, what is the per-person, round-trip cost for each option? Which option is cheaper?

c. What other factors would you consider in deciding whether to drive or to fly?

d. Is this a problem of excess demand or excess supply?

6.37 Joint cost allocation (Appendix A). Myers Quarry produces coarse gravel and sand in an 8:2 ratio. Joint costs for a month (volume = 9,000 tons of rocks input) amount to $225,000. Values at the split-off point are $30 per ton for gravel and $40 per ton for sand.

Required:

a. Allocate joint costs to the two products using the relative sales value at split off as the allocation basis.

b. Suppose Myers can run the sand through a sieve to remove small rocks and make fine sand used to fill sandboxes. The process will, however, reduce the yield of sand from 1,800 tons to 900 tons. This superior grade of sand ("sandbox" quality) retails for $160 per ton. However, Myers will incur $18,000 to process the sand into "sandbox" quality. Should Myers sell the coarse sand as is or process it further into sandbox quality sand?

6.38 Calculating incremental costs and revenues, special promotion (LO2, LO3). Mihir Patel is in charge of a multiplex operated by Majestic Cinema. In an attempt to boost profit, Mihir is considering a two-for-one promotion. Under this scheme, any customer attending a matinee show can exchange their ticket stub for a free pass at the end of the matinee. The pass is valid for the next seven days on any matinee show in any of the screens in the multiplex. Mihir believes the scheme is a winner because just about every matinee has empty seats, and the cost of showing a movie (e.g., projection, utilities) will not change if a matinee attracts a few more patrons.

Mihir estimates that running the promotion will increase overall weekly attendance at matinee shows from 2,000 to 2,500 persons. However, Mihir expects that running the promotion actually will decrease matinee ticket sales from 2,000 to 1,800 (in other words, Mihir expects 700 people to take advantage of the promotion and actually use their free pass). Mihir does not expect the promotion to affect attendance and sales on nonmatinee shows. The average matinee ticket sells for $3.95. Mihir believes that the lost matinee ticket revenue would be offset by increased sales at the concession stand. Moreover, Mihir figures that roughly half of his customers patronize the concession stand. The average moviegoer who visits the concession stand spends a total of $6 on drinks, popcorn, and candy. Variable costs in the concession stand amount to 15% of concession revenue, and weekly fixed costs for the concession stand equal $2,000.

Required:

Calculating controllable costs and benefits, determine the value of the promotion.

6.39 Product interdependencies, incentive conflict (LO3, Appendix B). Greg Gordon manages the 10,000-square-foot multilevel laser tag arena at LazerLite. This arena combines cutting-edge computer technology with action-oriented team play; in a futuristic environment with boggling mazes, fantastic fog swirls, and adrenaline-pumping music, players attempt to score points by "tagging" opponents and targets with a laser phaser. LazerLite charges its customers $7.50 to play a 10-minute game of laser tag. The fixed costs associated with operating the laser tag arena amount to $2,500 per week, with variable costs equaling $3.00 per person per game. On average, 1,400 persons visit LazerLite per week, each playing one game of laser tag.

LazerLite also offers its customers a fully stocked video arcade. When not playing laser tag, customers can enjoy some of the hottest video games and coolest simulator rides. Approximately 75% of all customers who play laser tag each week patronize the video arcade. Once inside the arcade, customers spend approximately $6 on video games and rides. The variable costs of running the video arcade equal 10% of video arcade revenue, while the fixed costs of running the video arcade total $2,000 per week.

The owners of LazerLite are considering running an after-school special Monday through Thursday from 3:30 P.M. to 5:30 P.M. The after-school special will reduce the price of a laser tag game from $7.50 per person to $5.00 per person (thus, there will be a $2.50 savings per game of laser tag during this time). Management expects that 500 people, each playing one game of laser tag, will take advantage of the special each week. However, management also expects that, because of the special, weekly demand for laser tag games at the normal price of $7.50 per game will decrease by 300 (thus, the special will attract a net of 200 additional people). The incremental fixed costs associated with running the after-school special are expected to equal $150 per week (for advertising).

Required:

a. From Greg's perspective, is the after-school special desirable? Assume that as the manager of the laser tag arena, Greg receives an annual bonus tied to the profitability of the laser tag arena.

b. From the perspective of LazerLite, is the after-school special desirable?

6.40 Discontinuing a product line, incremental approach, qualitative considerations (LO2, LO3, LO5, Appendix B). Gerry's Guitar Shack is the "happening" place in Wichita, Kansas. Gerry has 400 square feet of usable retail space on the first (ground) floor and an additional 200 square feet upstairs. The first floor is stocked with guitars, amps, music books, and other related items. Currently, the second floor is comprised of six 6-foot by 4-foot sound-proof cubicles and 80 square feet of common space. The cubicles are used by local musicians to give lessons.

Gerry figures that he generates $5,000 of revenue per year per square foot from the ground floor. His typical markup is such that he makes $0.25 in contribution margin per dollar of revenue. Gerry also figures that each of his four salespersons costs him $50,000 annually, with additional fixed costs (rent, etc.) amounting to $100,000 a year.

The upstairs music cubicles also generate some revenue. Each ½ hour rental generates a $5 fee to the Guitar Shack. Gerry estimates that each cubicle is used 40 times a week during the 50 weeks a year the store is open. There are negligible variable costs associated with the cubicles, and traceable maintenance and other fixed expenses amount to $7,500 per year. (These costs are included in the $100,000 amount above.)

Gerry is getting somewhat tired of the music lessons. He believes that he spends too much time scheduling the rooms and dealing with conflicts and changes. Many of the musicians who give lessons also invariably spend time chatting with Gerry and the salespersons, and Gerry believes that such chatting does not help productivity. Given all of these factors, Gerry is considering remodeling the upstairs portion of his store to remove the cubicles and convert it to retail space. He figures that he can get 150 square feet of usable retail space, bringing the shop total to 550 square feet. Similar to the downstairs space, Gerry believes the remodeled upstairs would generate $5,000 in revenue per year per square foot. The added sales volume, however, would also trigger the need for two more salespersons. Finally, Gerry estimates that the traceable maintenance and other expenses for the remodeled upstairs space would amount to $10,000 per year.

Required:

a. Using controllable cost analysis, compute the expected change in Gerry's annual profit associated with converting the upstairs to retail space.

b. What additional considerations do you believe Gerry needs to consider in this decision. For example, do you believe Gerry will be able to generate the same revenue per square foot in the expanded facility?

6.41 Excess demand, manufacturing, qualitative considerations (LO3, LO4, LO5). Justin Brass specializes in marine pumps. Justin's monthly contribution and profit are $125,000 and $50,000 at its current monthly volume of 2,500 pumps. At this volume, Justin's firm fully uses its available capacity of 10,000 labor hours.

Justin's management has been trying to branch out into making valves. A buyer has contacted Justin for an order of 500 valves. Each valve will consume 3 labor hours and yield a contribution of $30 per unit.

Required:

a. By how much will Justin's monthly profit change if the valve order is accepted?

b. Determine the price per valve at which Justin's monthly profit is the same whether it accepts or rejects the valve order.

c. Discuss two qualitative considerations that might affect Justin's decision.

6.42 Optimal allocation of scarce resource (LO4). SuperSound Stereos sells high-end stereo equipment to specialty audio and video shops. SuperSound serves three different types of customers: small, medium, and large. Customers are placed into these categories based on the average revenue generated per visit—"small" customers yield average revenue of less than $20,000 per visit, "medium" customers yield an average revenue of $20,000 to $40,000 per visit, and "large" customers yield an average revenue of over $40,000 per visit. Data for a typical sales territory are provided below:

	Customer Category		
	Small	Medium	Large
Number of customers in the territory	50	25	10
Average sales revenue per visit	$15,000	$30,000	$45,000
Average time to visit a customer	1.0 hour	2.0 hours	5.0 hours

Salespersons can realistically spend 125 hours per month visiting customers and generating orders. Salespersons' remaining time is spent in the head office filling out paperwork, learning about the company's products, and attending sales meetings. With only 125 hours available per month to visit customers and generate sales revenue, salespersons unfortunately cannot visit all of the potential customers in their territory.

Required:

a. Traditionally, SuperSound's salespersons have given top priority to large customers because these customers generate the most revenue per visit. Calculate monthly revenue in a typical sales territory if, in a given month, a salesperson first visits all the large customers, then visits all the medium customers and, finally, squeezes in as many small customer visits as possible.

b. Trey Foster is SuperSound's top salesperson. In contrast to conventional wisdom, Trey focuses first on the small and medium customers and, if time permits, the large customers. He tells anyone who will listen that large customers are not worth the bother—"You can win a game with singles" is the mantra that Trey preaches. Calculate monthly revenue using Trey's sales strategy. How do you explain Trey's success?

6.43 Qualitative Aspects of short-term decisions (LO3, LO5). After spending five years working for a prestigious consulting firm, Christine Kuhl enrolled in a top MBA program. Christine believes that obtaining an MBA is necessary to achieve her goal of becoming a partner in a major consulting firm. Christine is paying for her MBA (i.e., tuition, books, and living costs) with $25,000 in savings and a $45,000 loan. The MBA program requires four full trimesters of coursework; each trimester spans four months, including time for breaks. Most students complete the MBA program in 16 months.

Halfway into her third trimester, Christine's ex-employer called and offered her an attractive two-month assignment that perfectly meshes with her interests and expertise. Because this is a rush job, her previous employer is willing to pay Christine $50,000 to complete the two-month assignment. Unfortunately, accepting the assignment would require Christine to drop her current classes and retake them the following trimester. Since the tuition and fees are nonrefundable, Christine will spend $8,000 to re-register for these classes. In addition, her graduation will be delayed by four months (one trimester). Realistically, Christine estimates that she will earn a starting annual salary of

$120,000 immediately upon graduating. Her current and future living expenses amount to $2,000 per month.

Required:

a. Based on the information provided, what is the net monetary benefit associated with accepting the assignment?

b. In your opinion, is the net monetary benefit large enough for Christine to accept the assignment? If not, what qualitative considerations are likely to guide Christine's decision?

6.44 Qualitative aspects of short-term decisions (LO3, LO5). "I paid three C-notes for each ticket—I don't want to miss the game!" This was Charlie's reaction upon being informed by his assistant that a major client had unexpectedly arrived in town and wanted to have dinner with Charlie. The client was in town briefly and had a full schedule. Dinner was the only available time that the client could meet with Charlie.

Charles Watson III is the scion of a publishing family. As vice president of marketing, Charlie has propelled his company to the forefront of e-publishing. This particular client controls major magazines, and Charlie is in the thick of negotiating an important contract with her company. However, Charlie also is a die-hard Knick's fan and had worked his contacts to obtain the two center-court playoff tickets he referred to in his outburst.

Note: A "C-note" or just "C" is slang for $100, as the Roman numeral system uses the letter "C" to denote a hundred. The Knicks, based in New York, are part of the National Basketball Association and a high-powered team with a loyal following.

Required:

a. Does Charlie's decision deal with excess supply or excess demand?

b. Is the price paid for the two Knicks tickets ($600) relevant to Charlie's decision?

b. What are the qualitative factors that are likely to guide Charlie's decision?

PROBLEMS

6.45 Product-line Decisions, gross approach (LO2, Appendix B). Pete's Pets is an independent pet store located in Hoboken, New Jersey. Pete collects and reports operating data by "product line," with all revenues and costs being placed into one of three summary categories: (1) dogs, (2) cats, (3) birds & fish. For the most recent year of operations, Pete reported the following results:

	Dogs	Cats	Birds & Fish	Total
Revenue	$218,000	$142,500	$92,500	$453,000
Variable costs	87,200	42,750	46,250	176,200
Contribution margin	$130,800	$99,750	$46,250	$276,800
Traceable fixed costs	31,500	22,600	27,500	81,600
Common fixed costs*	35,000	35,000	35,000	105,000
Profit	$64,300	$42,150	($16,250)	$90,200

Common fixed costs relate to rent. Since dogs, cats, and birds and fish each use one-third of the available space, Pete allocates these costs equally among the three pet-related

While pleased with his overall profit and the profit on dogs and cats, Pete is concerned about the loss on birds and fish. He is thinking about discontinuing the birds and fish product line, and using the space to expand his offering of dogs and cats and their related supplies. Pete believes this option would increase both dog and cat revenue by 12%; however, it would also increase dog-related traceable fixed costs by $12,500 and cat-related traceable fixed costs by $8,000.

Required:

a. Using the gross approach, evaluate whether Pete should discontinue the birds and fish product line.

b. For decision-making purposes, do you believe Pete needs more detailed information than is currently provided in his financial statements? Why?

6.46 Incentives and sales promotions, relevant cost analysis, qualitative considerations (LO2, LO5, CMA Adapted). The Fangorn Forest Furniture Company makes outdoor furniture from aged wood. Fangorn's two primary product lines are chairs and tables. Pippin Took, founder and owner of the Fangorn Forest Furniture Company, is somewhat dismayed that sales of tables are not going as well as planned. Data for the most recent quarter (three months) of operations are as follows:

	Chairs	Tables	Total
Quantity sold	8,000	1,500	
Revenue	$800,000	$375,000	$1,175,000
Direct materials	288,000	140,625	428,625
Direct labor	192,000	46,875	238,875
Contribution margin	$320,000	$187,500	$507,500
Traceable fixed costs	125,000	100,000	225,000
Common fixed costs*	75,000	75,000	150,000
Profit	$120,000	$12,500	$132,500

These costs relate to space, equipment, and personnel used by both the chairs and tables product lines (e.g., costs of running the factory, administrative costs, Pippin's salary). Because these costs are common to both product lines, Pippin has allocated an equal amount to each product line.

Pippin was certain that the lagging sales on tables were due to a lack of effort on the part of his sales force (Pippin believes that his sales force is pushing the lower-priced chairs rather than the higher-priced tables). To spur sales of tables, Pippin is considering rewarding the salesperson who sells the most tables in each quarter with an all-expense paid vacation for two to Hawaii.

Required:

a. Suppose the Hawaii vacation will cost Pippin $6,000. How many additional tables need to be sold each quarter to justify running the sales contest?

b. Pippin believes that offering the trip to Hawaii will increase table sales by 288 units per quarter. By how much is quarterly profit on the tables product line expected to increase?

c. Pippin's close friend, Merry Brandybuck, mentions to Pippin that since the contest only rewards sales of tables, chair sales actually may decrease. What do you think—is this possible? By how much would sales on chairs have to decrease before it is no longer profitable for Pippin to offer the trip to Hawaii (as in part [b], assume the trip is expected to increase quarterly table sales by 288 units)?

d. In addition to the consideration in part (c), what other factors should Pippin consider before running the sales contest?

6.47 Excess supply, controllable cost analysis, pricing (LO1, LO2, LO3). The Cottage Bakery sells a variety of gourmet breads, cakes, pies, and pastries. Although its wares are considerably more expensive than those available at supermarkets and other bakeries, the Cottage Bakery has a loyal clientele willing to pay a premium price for premium quality.

The Cottage Bakery sells a variety of fresh-baked muffins daily for $1.50 each. The variable cost of making each muffin is $0.90. Invariably, approximately 20 muffins are left over at day's end, and Cottage currently donates these muffins to the local homeless shelter. Joe Smart, a bright young man on Cottage's counter-staff, suggests selling the unsold muffins the next day, labeling them as "day-old" and selling them at a 50% discount. Joe believes that sales of "day-old" muffins would average 15 per day and would not affect the sales of regular muffins.

Management of Cottage Bakery likes Joe's proposal, but they were considering using the remaining counter space to sell fresh raspberry-filled croissants for $2.00 each. The variable cost of making each croissant is $1.20, and management expects sales to average 20 croissants per day without affecting the sales of other (e.g., chocolate) croissants. In addition, management estimates that, on average, 2 raspberry-filled croissants would be left over at day's end (i.e., Cottage plans to produce 22 croissants per day). Any leftover croissants would be donated to the local homeless shelter as there would not be any space to sell "day-old" croissants. Moreover, if Cottage sells fresh raspberry-filled croissants, it will not have any space to sell "day-old" muffins.

Required:

a. List all of the options in Cottage Bakery's opportunity set with respect to the remaining counter space. What is the status quo? Is it a viable option?

b. Compared to the status quo, what is the incremental daily profit associated with Cottage Bakery's other options?

c. What should Cottage Bakery do with the remaining counter space?

6.48 **Joint cost allocation (Appendix A).** Chemco employs a joint process (cost: $100,000) that produces two chemicals, JAV-100 and YAZ-200. At the current volumes, the value of these products at the split-off point is $80,000 and $40,000, respectively. Chemco has the option of spending $25,000 to further process YAZ-200 into YAZ-400, with a sales value of $80,000.

Required:

a. Suppose Chemco does not process YAZ-200 further. Allocate joint costs to the two products using the revenue from the product as the allocation basis. Calculate the profit earned from each product, taking the allocated costs into account. (Round all numbers to the nearest dollar.)

b. Repeat the exercise in part (a) except assume that Chemco does process YAZ-200 into YAZ-400.

c. Focusing on the product level profit calculated in parts (a) and (b), should Chemco process YAZ-200 into YAZ-400? Why is this comparison suspect?

6.49 **Special-order, unitized data, relevant cost analysis (LO2, LO3, CMA Adapted).** Award Plus manufactures medals and trophies for winners of athletic competitions and other contests. Award Plus's manufacturing plant has the capacity to produce 10,000 medals per month. Currently, Award Plus is operating at 75% of available capacity, producing 7,500 medals per month. Pertinent data for this level of operations follows:

Medals produced and sold	7,500
Selling price	$175 per medal
Fixed costs:*	
Manufacturing	$46 per medal
Marketing & administrative	$34 per medal
Variable costs:	
Direct materials	$50 per medal
Direct labor	$40 per medal
Profit	$5 per medal

*Award Plus calculates fixed costs per medal by dividing the annual fixed cost by the number of medals it expects to produce during the year.

Recently, Award Plus received an inquiry from a national Little League baseball organization about the possibility of producing 1,800 medals next month. The Little League organization plans to give the medals to the winners of the upcoming state tournaments. Since there are 50 states, 3 age brackets, and approximately 12 players per team, the organization needs 1,800 medals (i.e., $1,800 = 50 \times 3 \times 12$). The Little League organization, however, indicates that they are somewhat strapped for cash and can only pay $100 for each medal.

Required:

a. Using the following table, indicate whether each item is relevant or not relevant for computing the incremental profit on the special order. Assume that Award Plus's relevant range of operations is between 5,000 and 10,000 medals.

Item	Relevant? (Y or N)	Reason
Regular selling price ($175)		
Special order price ($100)		
Direct materials cost		
Direct labor cost		
Fixed manufacturing cost		
Fixed marketing & administrative cost		

b. By how much will Award Plus's profit increase or decrease if it accepts the special order?

c. Assume that Award Plus's manufacturing plant has the capacity to produce only 9,000 medals per month rather than 10,000 medals per month. This means that if Award Plus accepts the special order, it will have to forego sales of 300 medals to its regular customers (i.e., the special order cannot be partially fulfilled). How does this information affect your answer to part (b)? That is, by how much will Award Plus' profit increase or decrease if it accepts the special order when plant capacity is only 9,000 medals?

6.50 Sales promotion, controllable costs (LO2, LO3). Hōgyoku Tamukeyama owns and operates a successful dry cleaning business in Bangor, Maine. Summary financial data for a typical month of operations are as follows:

Revenue	$30,000
Variable costs (40% of revenue)	12,000
Contribution margin	$18,000
Fixed costs	10,000
Profit	$8,000

Because it is the end of winter, Hōgyoku is considering running a special promotion on parkas, comforters, and other winter items. During the month-long promotion Hōgyoku plans to reduce the charge for cleaning each of these bulky winter items from $9 to $6. Hōgyoku plans to spend $1,000 advertising the promotion in various print media, and she expects the promotion to increase the coming month's sales by 1,500 winter items. Hōgyoku's average monthly revenue on winter items during a typical month amounts to $4,500.

Required:

By how much will Hōgyoku's profit increase or decrease in the coming month if she runs the promotion?

6.51 Eliminating a product line, gross approach (LO2, LO3, Appendix B). SpringFresh provides commercial laundry and dry cleaning services to local hospitals, hotels, and restaurants. Management believes that the dry cleaning business is a "loser," even though dry cleaning operations yield a high contribution margin. Moreover, based on summary financial data from the most recent year of operations (presented here) management is seriously considering getting out of the dry cleaning business.

	Laundry	Dry Cleaning	Total
Revenue	$3,000,000	$1,000,000	$4,000,000
Variable costs	1,000,000	200,000	1,200,000
Contribution margin	$2,000,000	$800,000	$2,800,000
Traceable fixed costs	1,000,000	500,000	1,500,000
Common fixed costs*	500,000	500,000	1,000,000
Profit	$500,000	($200,000)	$300,000

* These costs relate to the sales force, reception, and delivery trucks that are common to both lines of business. Management has arbitrarily allocated an equal amount to each line.

Required:

a. Assume that common fixed costs would decrease by $200,000 if the dry cleaning business were closed. By how much will SpringFresh's profit increase or decrease if it closes the dry cleaning operations?

b. Suppose that closing the dry cleaning business would increase overall laundry revenue by 10%. Specifically, while some customers would be lost because they value one-stop cleaning convenience, the sales force will be better able to focus its efforts because there will be only one product line. How does this information affect your answer to part (a)? That is, by how much will SpringFresh's profit increase or decrease if it closes the dry cleaning operations?

6.52 Excess supply, structuring promotions (LO1, LO3). GoGo Juice is a combination gas station and convenience store that is located at a busy intersection in a major metropolitan area. Recently, a national chain opened a similar store two blocks away, and, as a result, GoGo Juice's profits have decreased. In an effort to boost profit, GoGo Juice is considering running a special promotion. Under the special promotion, customers would receive $0.01 in free merchandise for every $0.20 spent on gasoline. For example, a customer purchasing $12.60 in gasoline would receive ($12.60/$0.20) × .01 = $0.63

in free merchandise (the customer could use the $0.63 toward the purchase of a soda, candy bar, etc.).

Management of GoGo Juice believes that the special promotion will increase gasoline sales by 8% from their current levels. In addition, management believes that overall merchandise sales will increase by 12% from their current levels. Most of the increase in merchandise sales will result from persons redeeming their free merchandise money; indeed, management expects that everyone will use their free merchandise money. However, merchandise sales also are expected to increase because, in the process of using their free merchandise money, people will spend more. For example, a person receiving $0.63 in free merchandise may decide to purchase a $0.75 candy bar (thus, the individual will have to pay GoGo Juice $0.12 for the candy bar). Without the free merchandise money, this same person might not have purchased the candy bar (i.e., he or she may only have purchased gasoline).

The following table provides data regarding current monthly sales and variable costs for both gasoline and merchandise:

	Gasoline	Merchandise
Sales revenue	$150,000	$75,000
Variable costs	$0.75 for every $1.00 in sales	$0.50 for every $1.00 in sales

GoGo Juice also incurs fixed costs of $60,000 per month.

Required:

a. Does GoGo Juice's decision deal with excess supply or excess demand?

b. By how much is GoGo Juice's monthly profit expected to change if it runs the special promotion?

c. Assume that GoGo Juice is considering altering the special promotion in the following way: Rather than give $0.01 in free merchandise for every $0.20 spent on gasoline, management would give customers $0.50 in free merchandise for every $10.00 spent on gasoline. Under this scheme, a customer spending $8.00 on gasoline would not receive any free merchandise, whereas a customer spending $18.00 on gasoline would receive $0.50 in free merchandise. Discuss what you perceive to be the costs and benefits of altering the special promotion in this fashion.

6.53 Working with unit-level data, dropping a product line, gross approach (LO2, LO3, Appendix B). Timmy N. runs a small shop that manufactures and sells battery testers and solenoid testers for quick, easy use around the home. The following information related to these two products has been gathered from Timmy's accounting records for the most recent year:

	Battery Tester	Solenoid Tester
Sales in units	20,000	10,000
Unit selling price	$35	$20
Total unit cost	$28	$22

Furthermore, the total unit cost of each product is calculated as follows:

	Battery Tester	Solenoid Tester
Fixed costs:		
Manufacturing	$10 per unit	$10 per unit
Marketing & administrative	$4 per unit	$4 per unit
Variable costs:		
Manufacturing	$12 per unit	$6 per unit
Marketing & administrative	$2 per unit	$2 per unit
Total	$28 per unit	$22 per unit

Both fixed manufacturing and fixed marketing and administrative costs are assigned to products based on the number of units sold. That is, Timmy's accountant takes the total fixed costs incurred and divides them by the total number of units sold to arrive at a fixed cost per unit. Moreover, Timmy expects to incur $420,000 in total fixed costs each year regardless of production volume. Because Timmy's shop produced 30,000 total units in the most recent year, each product was assigned $420,000/30,000 = $14 per unit in fixed costs.

Required:

a. What was Timmy's overall profit for the most recent year? What was Timmy's reported profit for each product?

b. What was Timmy's total contribution margin for the most recent year? What was Timmy's contribution margin on each product?

c. Since the unit cost of the solenoid tester exceeds the unit price, Timmy believes that his business would be more profitable if he stopped producing solenoid testers. Is this true? By how much will Timmy's profit increase or decrease if he stops producing and selling solenoid testers?

d. Based on your answers to parts (a) through (c), what inferences do you draw about the value of expressing fixed costs as the amount allocated per unit rather than the total of the expenditure?

6.54 Special-order, qualitative considerations (LO3, LO5). Randy Quench manages the Science Station in Lansing, Michigan. One of the station's key attractions is a big-screen IMAX theater. As stated in the IMAX Web site, "The IMAX experience is the world's most powerful and involving film experience. With breathtaking images up to eight stories high and wrap-around 12,000-watt digital sound, IMAX technology takes you to places only imagined." The IMAX Theater has been very popular and has increased attendance and interest in the Science Station.

The average IMAX show at the Science Station attracts 125 patrons (50 children and 75 adults) at a ticket price of $7.95 for children under 12 and $9.95 for adults. Randy estimates that the variable costs per IMAX show are $250. In addition, fixed costs of $600 are allocated to each show, a number that is computed by dividing the annual estimate of the total fixed costs (associated with running the IMAX Theater) by the annual estimate of the number of IMAX shows.

The local middle school has approached Randy about scheduling an extra show for its eighth graders. One hundred students and five teachers are expected to attend the special screening on the International Space Station, a feature that is currently showing. The school has asked Randy for a price quote. The special screening will take place in the mid-morning hours when the IMAX is not traditionally open.

Required:

a. Based on the data provided, what is the minimum amount that Randy should charge the school so that the Science Station does not incur a loss on the special screening?

b. What other financial factors, though not listed in the problem, could be relevant to Randy's price quote?

c. Are there any nonfinancial factors you believe Randy should consider?

6.55 Health care, relevant cost analysis, ethics (LO2, LO3, LO5). Quincy Heil is the chief financial officer for General Hospital, located in Port Chester, New York. General Hospital currently is experiencing some financial difficulties because of the pricing pressures created by Health Maintenance Organizations (HMOs) and Medicare. Quincy believes that aggressive cost management is the only way to improve the hospital's financial performance as there is little room for increasing prices or patient volume.

Based on a detailed cost study, Quincy estimates that the per-patient variable cost per hospital-day equals $125. (This cost excludes the cost of any tests, medications, procedures, and other professional services.) Quincy wants the hospital to reduce the average patient length of stay (LOS) from 1.8 days to 1.5 days. Given the current annual volume of 10,000 patients, this would save the hospital 3,000 patient days. In addition, hospital revenue would not be affected because payments are based on the episode (i.e., reason for visit) and are not directly linked to length of stay.

When presented with this plan, the hospital's chief of staff concurred with the cost savings but pointed out that any pressures to reduce LOS would inevitably lead to some patients being discharged earlier than is optimal from a medical perspective. Early discharge increases the risk of patients not fully recovering and experiencing added complications and discomfort. In short, the chief of staff estimates that reducing the LOS from 1.8 days to 1.5 days will increase the readmission rate (admissions within 30 days of discharge) from 2% to 4%. Based on the current annual patient volume of 10,000 patients, this amounts to about 200 additional patients per year.

In his response to the chief of staff, Quincy pointed out that readmissions typically qualified as a new episode and triggered a new payment from the insurance company or Medicare. Moreover, Quincy indicated that, on average, insurance companies and Medicare pay the hospital $500 per readmission, whereas the hospital's total incremental costs associated with increasing the readmission rate to 4% were likely to amount to $50,000. The chief of staff, clearly disconcerted by Quincy's analysis, has decided to raise the issue with you, the hospital's chief executive officer.

Required:

As General Hospital's chief executive officer, the decision to reduce length of stay is ultimately your call. What would you do? By how much is hospital profit expected to increase if you decide to reduce length of stay? What other factors are important in this decision?

6.56 Offering a product via the internet (LO3, LO5). TaxPlan Solutions, a software firm, has developed a software product that enables users to electronically prepare and file their state and federal tax returns. TaxPlan traditionally has sold a stand-alone version that users install on their personal computers. This year, the firm's marketing director wants to offer a stripped-down version of the product via the Internet, in addition to offering the stand-alone version. The modified Internet version will allow users to prepare and file their tax returns using the World Wide Web. The product, which meets the needs of 75% of tax-filers, will be offered to all for free. Moreover, the marketing director feels that the Web-based product will allow TaxPlan to market itself as a company that seeks to help the "person on the street" and, hopefully, also lead to some financial benefits. TaxPlan has provided you with the following information:

- TaxPlan already has spent $500,000 in developing the Web-based tax-filing product. If TaxPlan decides to offer the product, then it expects to spend $420,000 each year (including this year) maintaining the servers, providing technical support, and so on.

- The marketing director believes that the free tax-filing offer will induce users to sample the convenience of electronically managing their personal finances. She believes that many users will like the process and, consequently, end up purchasing TaxPlan's software for managing personal finances. The personal finance software retails for $25. TaxPlan incurs variable costs of $1 per unit to produce, package, and distribute their personal finance software package. TaxPlan also incurs $1 million in fixed costs each year to maintain and market the personal finance software package.

- The marketing director believes that the Web-based tax-filing service will allow TaxPlan to collect names and contact information to be used for marketing purposes. She estimates that 80% of the 250,000 people expected to use the free software *will not* opt out of the mailing list. (The opt-out box is buried deep in the program and takes much effort to find.) Currently, TaxPlan buys names and contact information from bulk-mailers and other sources and pays $0.09 per usable name. Thus, the Web-based tax-filing product will allow TaxPlan to avoid paying for this service.

Required:

a. How many personal-finance software packages does TaxPlan Solutions need to sell to ensure that it covers at least the incremental costs associated with offering the Web-based tax-filing software? (Also, express this number as a proportion of the number of people expected to use the free Web-based tax-filing product.)

b. List two other factors that TaxPlan should consider in its decision regarding whether to introduce the free Web-based tax-filing product.

c. TaxPlan's chief financial officer wants to lobby the Internal Revenue Service (IRS) for a grant of $300,000 to develop and market the free Web-based tax-filing product. Do you believe the federal government has a financial interest in whether TaxPlan offers such a product? Why or why not?

6.57 Equipment replacement, sunk costs, reputation effects (LO3, LO5). The Diamond Jubilee is a floating riverboat casino that operates on the Mississippi River. The casino is open 24 hours daily and offers a "full house" of gaming, including numerous slot and video poker machines and a variety of table games such as blackjack, Caribbean stud, craps, and roulette. On average, the Diamond Jubilee earns $0.10 in contribution margin for every $1.00 wagered. The remaining $0.90 goes to the gamblers as winnings and to cover the casino's variable costs.

Lucy "Lucky" Johnson is in charge of the Diamond Jubilee's slot machines, which includes both mechanical and video machines. Based on Lucy's recommendation, casino management recently replaced, at a total cost of $1,250,000, their 250 video poker machines. The 250 machines just acquired are expected to last two years. At the end of their two-year life, the machines would have zero salvage value—their sale price would be exactly offset by the cost of dismantling the machines, packing, and shipping.

Unfortunately, days after the new machines arrived, Lucy learned from her industry contact of an even better video poker machine. Compared to the machines recently purchased, these machines have sound that is more vivid, more stunning visual effects, and other attention grabbers. Moreover, Lucy believes that the total wagered in one video poker machine would increase by $30,000 a year if the casino had purchased 250 of these machines rather than the 250 machines actually purchased.

The better video poker machines, however, cost $5,500 each. Similar to the machines recently purchased, these machines also last for two years and have zero salvage value at the end of their two-year life. In addition, the operating costs of the better machine and those recently purchased are identical. Finally, like new cars, once they are driven off the lot, video poker machines depreciate substantially after they are put in use. For the Diamond Jubilee, this means that each recently acquired video poker machine would only net $1,000 if it were sold today.

Required:

a. By how much will the Diamond Jubilee's profit increase or decrease over the next two years if it purchases the new video poker machines and sells the recently acquired video poker machines? Ignore tax effects and the time value of money in your analysis.

b. A key part of Lucy's job is to keep track of trends in the gaming industry and the new products coming into the market. Suppose that only Lucy knows about the better video poker machines. The Diamond Jubilee's other managers would learn of the better machine's availability only in a year or so. Would Lucy recommend replacing the recently purchased video poker machines with the better machines?

c. Would your answer to requirements (a) and (b) change if the Diamond Jubilee had paid $2,500, rather than $5,000, for each of the recently acquired video poker machines?

6.58 Equipment replacement, sunk costs, Taxes, continuation of the previous problem (LO3, Advanced). Suppose the Diamond Jubilee pays combined state and federal taxes equal to 25% of profit. Since the casino is highly profitable, this means that any increase in casino revenues will be taxed at the rate of 25%. It also means that depreciation on the machines is deductible for tax purposes. Finally, it means that the casino can write off the loss if it sells the recently acquired video poker machines. That is, the loss on the recently acquired video poker machines produces a benefit to the Diamond Jubilee because it shields income from being taxed.

Required:

a. If taxes are ignored, does the $1,250,000 cost of the recently acquired video poker machines affect the decision to purchase the better video poker machines?

b. With taxes, how does the $1,250,000 cost of the recently acquired video poker machines affect the Diamond Jubilee's taxes if the old machines are retained? How does the $1,250,000 cost of the recently acquired machines affect the Diamond Jubilee's taxes if the old machines are sold and the new machines are purchased? In both cases, assume the Diamond Jubilee depreciates all of their gaming equipment using straight-line depreciation and zero assumed salvage value. Ignore the time value for money in your computations.

c. Considering tax effects, by how much will the Diamond Jubilee's profit increase or decrease over the next two years if it purchases the new video poker machines and sells the recently acquired video poker machines?

d. What do you conclude about the relevance of sunk costs?

6.59 Equipment replacement decision, depreciation (LO3, Advanced). Gina Matheson owns and operates a successful florist shop in Bloomington, Indiana. Two years ago, Gina purchased a refrigerated display case for $20,000, expecting to use it for 10 years. Unfortunately, Gina's assistant recently (and accidentally) left the case's door open during the night and the motor burned out. The local repair shop has informed Gina that it will cost $4,500 in parts and labor to fix the refrigerated display case (the case needs a new motor and wiring). On the upside, if the existing case is repaired then it will last another 10 years.

Rather than repair the existing display case, Gina is considering purchasing a new refrigerated display case. A new display case would cost Gina $21,000 and last 10 years. In addition, the new case has better insulation than the existing case, and Gina believes that purchasing the new case will save her $100 per month in utility bills.

Ignore the time value of money in all of the subsequent questions. Also, ignore income taxes except where instructed otherwise.

Required:

a. Should Gina repair the existing case or purchase the new case? In addition to the facts above, assume that the existing case has a book value of $16,000 but, given its current condition, cannot be sold (i.e., the existing case has a current sales value of $0).

b. Assume the existing display case has a book value of $10,000 rather than $16,000. Would this information affect your answer to part (a)?

c. Assume the existing case has a book value of $16,000 and can be sold in its current condition for $5,000 (rather than $0 as assumed in part [a]). Would this information affect your answer to part (a)?

d. (**Advanced**). Assume that the existing case has a book value of $16,000 and can be sold for $5,000. In addition, assume that Gina pays income taxes equal to 30% of profit. Finally, Gina depreciates all of her assets using straight-line depreciation and zero assumed salvage value. In light of this information, should Gina repair the existing case or purchase the new case?

e. What other factors should Gina likely consider in her decision regarding whether to repair or replace her existing refrigerator display case?

6.60 Special-order, capacity costs (LO2, LO3). Bob Wright is a skilled machinist who has identified a need for specialized, custom-made containers that store and move biological materials. This market is particularly active in Bob's community because of the human genome research at the local university and the numerous biotechnology firms that operate in the area.

Recently, one of Bob's long-time customers, a professor at the local university, asked Bob for a 25% discount in the coming year. The professor has requested the discount because one of her major federal grants was canceled and it will be at least another year before she can find replacement funding. She expects to place about $50,000 worth of orders (at the pre-discount price) in the coming year, after which she expects to pay full price. Absent a discount, she will not have the funds to place the order.

Bob knows that for each $100 in sales, he spends $45 on variable cost items for materials, labor, and so on. He figures that his remaining expenses are fixed at $175,000 per year. Bob expects sales for the coming year (without the professor's order) to equal $675,000 or 90% of capacity. Bob measures capacity in pre-discounted revenues—that is, as revenue at normal prices.

Required:

a. By how much will Bob's profit increase or decrease if he gives the 25% discount to the professor?

b. Assume that at $675,000 in sales Bob will be operating at 96% of capacity rather than 90% of capacity. Also, assume that the professor's order cannot be partially fulfilled—it must be taken in full or rejected entirely. How does this piece of information change your answer to part (a)? That is, by how much will Bob's profit increase or decrease if he gives the 25% discount to the professor?

c. Continue with part (b), except that at $675,000 in sales Bob will be operating at 100% of capacity rather than 90% of capacity. How does this piece of information change your answer to part (a)? That is, by how much will Bob's profit increase or decrease if he gives the 25% discount to the professor?

6.61 Excess supply, qualitative aspects of short-term decisions (LO3, LO5). Edmund Heil, Jr., CPA, has his own accounting firm in Golden, Colorado. Edmund caters primarily to small businesses and, over the last 15 years, has built a loyal list of clients. Edmund offers his clients a full range of audit, tax, and business advisory services, typically charging his clients $100 per hour plus out-of-pocket expenses. (The client pays for any direct costs related to Edmund's travel, filing tax returns, and so on.) Moreover, almost all of Edmund's costs are fixed and relate to his office operating expenses such as rent, support staff, and his own compensation.

It is now mid-August, a traditionally slow period; the busy tax and audit season is nearly five months away. Edmund normally uses this time for rest, relaxation, and recreation. Indeed, Edmund is an avid mountain and rock climber, which partly motivated his move to Colorado.

On August 15, a long-time but relatively small-volume customer approached Edmund with an interesting project. However, the client's business is in the doldrums, and the client wants Edmund to give them a 50% "loyalty" discount. Edmund is trying to decide whether he should accept the project.

Required:

What are the quantitative and qualitative factors Edmund should consider in deciding whether to accept the long-time client's project? Assume that the job would take 20 hours and that the client would cancel the job before paying full price.

6.62 Product-Mix Decision with a scarce resource (LO4, Loosely adapted from HBS case 198-085, LeHigh Steel). Sylvester's Steel Works is a mini mill that recycles shredded scrap steel into usable products such as alloy (e.g., communication equipment), coils (e.g., appliances), steel bars (e.g., reinforcing concrete), and wire (e.g., cable connectors). Sylvester's starts with a basic feed stock of shredded scrap steel and then melts and purifies the steel via its high-powered electric furnace. The molten metal is next transferred for processing in Sylvester's Cold Rolling Mill (CRM), which is the bottleneck machine in Sylvester's manufacturing process.

Management of Sylvester's has provided you with the following data regarding the company's four primary product lines, and the amount of time (in minutes) a pound of each product requires in the Cold Rolling Mill (CRM).

	Alloy	Coils	Steel Bars	Wire
Contribution margin per pound	$1.40	$0.45	$0.98	$0.75
Minutes per pound in CRM	0.10	0.03	0.35	0.30

Sylvester's fixed costs amount to $2,400,000 per year.

Required:

a. Suppose the Cold Rolling Mill can be operated for 24,000 minutes per month. What product(s) should Sylvester produce in the coming month? If management follows your production advice, how much profit will Sylvester earn next month?

b. Do you believe the solution you arrived at in part (a) is feasible? What additional data would you require before deciding which product Sylvester's Steel Works should emphasize?

6.63 Allocating a scarce resource (LO4, Advanced). "Crash" Johnson manages the 1,500-square-foot video arcade and game center at a popular mall. Seeking to renovate and upgrade the arcade, Crash recently removed some old games, freeing up 300 square feet of space. Crash has narrowed his options for new games to the following:

- Install video games that simulate high-adrenaline activities such as driving a motorcycle and skiing. Each of these machines would consume 50 square feet of space and generate revenues of $20 per fully occupied hour. Based on the expected 40% occupancy rate, each installed machine would generate maintenance costs of $100 per week. Crash believes that, at a maximum, he could install up to five such machines.

- Install a dance game. This game allows one or two players to "dance" on pads to match the moves displayed on the screen. Because good players attract considerable numbers of bystanders, Crash budgets 75 square feet per game. While most arcades have at least one such game, Crash does not wish to have more than two games. (He does not currently have the game available.) The dance game generates $40 in revenue per occupied hour. With estimated usage at 30%, Crash projects maintenance expenses of $300 per week per machine.

- Install simple games (e.g., "Whack-a-Mole") aimed at pre-teens and children. These games occupy 10 square feet each and require virtually no maintenance (for all practical purposes, assume it is $0 per week). To maintain balance in his arcade, Crash believes that he could install a maximum of six simple games. Finally, while the simple games generate $15 in revenue per hour occupied, the occupancy rate hovers around 10%.

Crash believes that he could deploy any combination of these three options and still maintain the overall balance of games in his video arcade.

Required:

a. Determine the contribution margin per week per square foot devoted to each kind of game. Based solely on the ranking of the games as per their profitability, allocate the 300 feet in available space to maximize Crash's expected profit per week. What is Crash's expected profit with this allocation? Assume that the arcade is open for 100 hours per week.

b. Explain why your solution in part (a) may not fully use all available capacity.

c. Suggest an alternative configuration that might help Crash improve his expected profit per week.

d. (Advanced) What do you conclude about the validity of the rule "allocate scare capacity among uses to maximize the contribution margin per unit of the scarce resource?"

6.64 Optimal allocation of a scarce resource, expected value (LO4, Advanced). Vidya Patel operates a newspaper stand in Grand Central Station, New York. As you might imagine, space is at a tremendous premium, and Vidya uses every inch of her 300 cubic feet (think in three dimensions—length, width, and height) of available space to stock a wide selection of newspapers, magazines, and snack-food items.

Vidya estimates that her contribution margin ratios on newspapers, magazines, and snack-food items are 10%, 25%, and 20%, respectively. In addition, for equivalent sales in dollars, newspapers take up 5 times as much space as magazines and 10 times as much space as snacks. However, since newspapers are the primary draw for Vidya's customers, she believes that at least 50% of her available space, or 150 cubic feet, must be devoted to newspapers. Finally, Vidya believes that 10% of her available space is enough to stock all of the popular snack-food items (i.e., she could devote less than 10% of her space to snack-food items, but devoting more than 10% would be wasteful as it would not generate additional snack-food sales).

Required:

a. What is Vidya's optimal allocation of space to newspapers, magazines, and snack-food items?

b. Suppose that Vidya allocates space according to your recommendation in part (a). For Vidya to recover her fixed costs of $2,700 per month, how much total sales revenue must she generate per cubic foot each month?

6.65 Excess supply of capacity, pricing special services (LO1, LO2). "Cadillac" Cody operates a shuttle-bus service between the Miami, Florida International Airport and the Florida Keys. A popular vacation getaway, the Florida Keys are a string of islands located off the southern tip of Florida. The Keys offer year-round warm weather, white sandy beaches, and sunny skies. Vacationers can spend the day in a variety of water sports such as surfing, snorkeling, sailing, and scuba diving. Numerous charter boats also offer would-be anglers the opportunity to experience deep-sea fishing and snare game fish such as marlin, mahi-mahi, swordfish, and snapper.

Partly out of a desire to keep the Keys pristine, Miami is the closest large airport. The Miami International Airport is roughly 80 miles away from Key Largo, one of the nearest islands, and a bit less than 200 miles away from Key West, the southernmost island. Most individuals and families visiting the Keys rent a car at the Miami airport and drive to their final destination. Most large groups (e.g., church groups, corporate outings, senior groups), however, prefer to take a shuttle bus due to the substantial cost savings and because they generally do not need transportation after reaching their final destination (i.e., their activities are preplanned and include transportation). Cody's business is aimed at these groups; for a fixed fee Cody will meet a group at the airport and transport them to their hotel, campsite, or charter boat. Cody is, of course, delighted to offer return transportation as well.

Cody owns a mini-bus that can seat up to 24 people. His air-conditioned bus comes with many conveniences like two video monitors and DVD players. Having lived in the area his entire life, Cody also has a wealth of information about area attractions, local celebrities, surfing, and fishing. All in all, both Cody and his customers have a blast. Cody has built a sterling reputation and has a core group of loyal clients that use his services exclusively whenever they visit the Keys. This core group also serves a valuable role in directing other groups toward Cadillac Cody.

Cody offers two primary products: A one-way trip between Miami and Key Largo (the Upper Keys), and a one-way trip between Miami and Key West (the Lower Keys). Under Cody's straightforward pricing scheme, groups are charged $300 for a one-way trip to the Upper Keys and $500 for a one-way trip to the Lower Keys. (Cody does not offer any discounts for booking round-trip travel. Also, the price is the same regardless of the direction of travel.) This fee entitles a group to exclusive use of Cody's mini-bus (i.e., Cody only transports one group at a time). Gratuities also are a part of Cody's business, and, without exception, clients give Cody a 15% tip (as suggested in the brochure). Rightfully, Cody views gratuities as personal income rather than business income.

A one-way trip to the Upper Keys takes about two hours of Cody's time (this includes 80 miles of driving plus time for passenger loading and drop offs). As a result, Cody believes that at best he can squeeze in two round-trips (four one-way trips) to the Upper Keys in a day. A one-way trip to the Lower Keys takes about 3 hours and 45 minutes of Cody's time (this includes 200 miles of driving plus time for passenger loading and drop-offs), and, as a result, Cody believes that only one round trip (two one-way trips) to the Lower Keys per day is feasible.

Cody's work schedule is somewhat erratic. During the peak tourist season, which lasts roughly from October 1 through March 31 (6 months), it is common for Cody to go two or three weeks without a break. Off-peak, however, it is equally common for Cody to work a three-day week. Analysis of Cody's travel log from the prior year showed that Cody made 400 paid one-way trips to the Upper Keys and 200 paid one-way trips to the Lower Keys (sometimes, Cody will only have a paid trip on the drive to or from the Keys; one-way trips where the bus is empty are called "deadhead" trips). Of these 400 and 200 one-way trips, 275 and 140, respectively, were during the peak season. Moreover, of the 100,000 miles Cody drove last year (this number includes trip mileage and business-related errands), Cody estimates that 62,500 miles were driven during the peak season and 37,500 miles were driven during the off-peak season.

The following table details Cadillac Cody's business income statement for the most recent year:

Item	Amount
Revenue[1]	$220,000
Cost of bus (net of salvage value)[2]	($60,000)
Office operating expenses[3]	($45,000)
Fuel & oil costs[4]	($30,000)
Bus-related insurance & maintenance costs[5]	($25,000)
Brochures & advertising costs[6]	($5,000)
Business income	$55,000

[1] $220,000 = (400 one-way trips to the Upper Keys × $300) + (200 one-way trips to the Lower Keys × $500).

[2] Cody purchases a new bus each year. A new bus, with all of the amenities Cody desires, costs approximately $85,000. At the end of the year, Cody sells the bus for approximately $25,000.

[3] Cody has a small office at the airport and a part-time administrative assistant to help with running the business (e.g., to help with scheduling and paperwork).

[4] Cody spends approximately $0.30 in gas and oil per mile: $30,000 = (62,500 + 37,500) × $0.30.

[5] Insurance costs are fixed, but maintenance costs vary with miles driven. Cody estimates that maintenance costs amount to $0.15 per mile: $25,000 = $10,000 + (62,500 + 37,500) × $0.15.

[6] Cody has a local advertising company put together a nice color brochure each year.

In addition to his business income, Cody earned $220,000 × 0.15 = $33,000 in tips last year. Thus, Cody's overall (business plus personal) income in the most recent year was $55,000 + $33,000 = $88,000.

Required:

a. Two groups recently contacted Cody about employing his services. Unfortunately, both groups will be arriving at the Miami airport this coming Tuesday, and one group wants to book a one-way trip to the Upper Keys while the other group wants to book a one-way trip to the Lower Keys. Cody already has scheduled a trip to the Upper Keys for the morning, so he will only be able to take one of the two groups. (*Note*: if he takes the group wishing to go to the Lower Keys, this will make for a long day.) On this particular Tuesday Cody will not be able to book a group for either return trip (i.e., his bus will be empty on the drive back). Which group should Cody book, and by how much will Cody's overall (business + personal) income increase by booking this group?

b. Assume that if Cody books the group traveling to the Upper Keys, then he will be able to book another group for the return trip to the Miami airport. Unfortunately, Cody will not be able to book another group for the return trip if he goes to the Lower Keys. How does this piece of information affect your answer to part (a)? In other words, which group should Cody book, and by how much will his overall (business + personal) income increase by booking this group?

c. Cody and his wife are planning an upcoming vacation (their first vacation in years). They would like to take a week (7 days) off and are considering taking their vacation in either the first week in March (during Cody's peak business season) or during the second week in July (during Cody's off-peak business season). How much business and personal income would Cody expect to sacrifice if he and his wife schedule their trip for March? How much business and personal income would Cody expect to sacrifice if he and his wife schedule their trip for July? (*Hint*: Prepare a contribution margin statement segmented by trips made during the peak season and trips made during the off-peak season; consider both business and tip income).

d. One of Cody's friends mentions to him that hotels and airlines seem to offer discounts during their off-peak seasons (to spur additional demand). This friend suggests that Cody follow a similar strategy. Since most of Cody's costs are fixed, the friend believes that Cody could clean up with such a strategy. Specifically, Cody's friend believes that Cody would increase his off-peak volume by 60% if he cut his fares by 25% during the off-peak season. By how much would Cody's overall income increase if the friend's numbers are accurate (assume Cody's mileage during the off-peak season will increase by 40%, and not 60%, because he will have fewer deadhead trips). Next, evaluate the friend's advice—in particular, why might such a strategy work well for higher-priced items like airfare and hotels but not work as well for lower-priced items like a shuttle bus?

6.66 Excess demand, LO1, LO2. Hannah Turnbull manages Elegant Suites, a hotel in a small town 10 miles inland from Florida's beautiful gulf coast. Elegant Suites has a capacity of 320 suites and offers a small, but well managed, conference center. Since opening, Elegant Suites has established a good reputation among small and medium-sized business clients as a nice place to hold annual meetings and retreats.

Hannah currently is in a quandary regarding hotel bookings for the last weekend in February. One of Elegant's long-standing clients, Piedmont Publishing, recently called Hannah about the possibility of holding its annual three-day sales conference at the end of February. Piedmont wants to reserve 75 rooms each day (= 225 total room days). Per its usual arrangement, Piedmont would pay $120 per day per room and $5,000 per day for use of the convention center. Because this is a bulk booking, the room rate is lower than the normal rate of $150 per day. Like all clients, however, the Piedmont attendees would spend additional money at the hotel. Hannah expects this miscellaneous expenditure to be $25 per person per day.

Shortly after receiving the call from Piedmont, Hannah received a call from Capelli Fashion Designers. Capelli, a prospective first-time client, wants to hold its annual three-day fashion event at Elegant Suites at the end of February. Capelli would book 225 suites per day (for a total of 675 room days) and is willing to pay $120 per suite per day. Also, Capelli would be willing to pay the normal daily rate of $5,000 for use of the convention center, although it wants Hannah to construct a runway at a cost of $3,000. Hannah was ecstatic to receive the Capelli call until she realized that the dates Capelli wants coincide with Piedmont's annual sales meeting.

Trying to figure a way out, Hannah calls both Capelli and Piedmont to see if either party would be willing to move its event to different dates. However, both Capelli and Piedmont are committed to holding their respective events at the end of February. Next, Hannah looks at her reservations chart to see if she can hold both events. She realizes that 60 suites already are committed to other individual clients during that time. Hannah believes strongly that she must honor these reservations.

Hannah provides you with the following summary financial data for a typical month of operations.

Summary Financial Data for a Typical Month of Operations

Number of occupied suite-days	6,000
Average Suite rate	$130
Revenues:	
Suites	$780,000
Convention Center	75,000
Food, telephone, movies, and other incidentals	150,000
Total Revenues	$1,005,000
Variable costs:	
Food, laundry, supplies, telephone, and movies	$180,000
Labor (kitchen help, cleaning staff)	210,000
Contribution margin	**$615,000**
Fixed costs:	
Labor (hotel management)	$125,000
Building and Grounds	350,000
Profit before taxes	**$140,000**

Hannah also informs you that if she stays with Piedmont, she is likely to sell another 57 suites to individual parties for each of the three days at the standard rate of $150 per suite. If she accepts Capelli, she will be able to sell the remaining 35 suites to individual parties for each of the three days at the standard rate of $150 per suite. However, as booking Capelli would cause an abnormally high occupancy rate (100%), Hannah anticipates the need to pay her hourly staff an overtime premium of 50% for the three-day period (i.e., the average hourly wage will be the base wage $\times$ 1.50).

Required:

a. Identify Hannah's decision options.

b. Identify Hanna's best option.

c. Suppose 75 and 225 suites per day is the number of suites that Piedmont and Capelli wish to block for their conventions. However, the actual demand might be less than this estimate. While Piedmont is sure to occupy at least 60 suites, Capelli estimates that total demand might range from 150 to 225 suites. Because actual demand would not be known till late, Hannah would not be able to fill unused suites with paying guests. How might this information affect Hannah's decision?

d. Considering long-term implications, what should Hannah do?

6.67 Excess demand, real estate (LO1, LO3). Brenda Stowers is a licensed real estate agent in the Sedona, Arizona area. Because of her affiliation with a large national real estate agency and her attention to detail, Brenda has been able to build a very successful business. In the United States, people selling their home hire an agent who "lists" the home. The agent representing the potential buyers "shows" the home. If a sale occurs, the seller pays a commission to both the agent listing the house (i.e., their own agent) *and* the agent representing the buyers. Each agent typically receives a commission equal to 3% of the home's selling price. On occasion, the listing agent is also the agent for the buyer. In this case, the listing agent receives both commissions; that is, as the agent for both the buyer and the seller, the agent receives a total commission of 6%.

On behalf of an owner, Brenda currently has listed a home with an asking price of $250,000. Brenda believes that if she holds an open house this coming Sunday, the home will attract many visitors. (An open house is a designated period, say 2–4 P.M., when the house is open to visitors. Anybody can walk into the house and look around without a prior appointment). Since this is a new listing, Brenda believes that there is a 10% chance one of the visitors to the open house actually will purchase the house. The prep for the open house plus the time it takes to host the open house will consume an entire day. In addition, variable costs related to signs and ads in the local newspaper will cost Brenda $250. Finally, almost all buyers who look at open houses are likely to be under contract with another realtor, implying that Brenda expects to receive a 3% commission if the home sells.

Alternatively, Brenda could spend this coming Sunday showing homes to some of her clients who are looking to buy a house. Brenda estimates that, on any given day that she devotes to showing homes, there is a 4% chance that she will sell a house that is not her listing (thereby receiving a 3% commission), and a 1% chance that she will sell a house that is her listing (thereby receiving a 6% commission). The average asking price of the houses Brenda shows is $220,000. Brenda's variable costs of showing homes are negligible and, thus, can be ignored. Finally, on average, houses (including open houses) sell for 95% of the asking price.

Required:

a. Does Brenda's decision deal with excess supply or excess demand?

b. What is Brenda's expected profit from holding the open house this coming Sunday?

c. What is Brenda's expected profit from showing homes (to some of her clients who are looking to buy a house) this coming Sunday?

d. What should Brenda do this coming Sunday?

e. As you might suspect, the chances of selling a home during an open house decline after the first open house. Assume Brenda's first open house does not lead to a sale. What would the chances of a sale during the second open house need to be so that Brenda prefers holding a second open house rather than showing homes to potential buyers (assume everything but the chance of sale remains the same)?

6.68 Outsourcing, qualitative considerations (LO3, LO5). Jackrabbit Trails is a family camp located in Kings Canyon National Park, California. Open from mid-May to Labor Day, Jackrabbit Trails offers week-long family summer vacation packages that include lodging, three meals a day, and numerous activities such as horseback riding, waterskiing, sailing, canoeing, archery, fishing, hiking, and mountain biking. To provide families with a restful experience, Jackrabbit Trails limits the number of families to 20 per week. Moreover, the camp motto is "Follow the fun without following the herd."

Jackrabbit Trails is planning on adding another activity to their repertoire—whitewater rafting. Management currently is trying to decide whether to offer patrons this service via a local company, Tributary Tours, or to provide the service "in house." If Jackrabbit Trails provides its own whitewater rafting tours, then management estimates that annual fixed costs will increase by $40,000 and that they will earn $0.60 on each dollar of whitewater rafting tour revenue (i.e., for every dollar of whitewater rafting revenue, there would be $0.40 in variable costs and $0.60 in contribution margin). On the other hand, if Jackrabbit Trails routes patrons to Tributary Tours for their whitewater rafting experience, annual fixed costs will not increase and Tributary Tours will pay Jackrabbit Trails $0.20 for each dollar of whitewater rafting tour revenue (that is, for tours booked through Jackrabbit trails). Management of Jackrabbit Trails expects gross whitewater rafting revenues to be the same under either scenario.

Required:

a. Suppose Jackrabbit Trails expects whitewater rafting revenue to be $75,000 per year. Should management outsource the whitewater rafting tours or operate them internally? Would your decision change if revenues were expected to be $125,000 per year?

b. What is the whitewater rafting revenue at which Jackrabbit Trails is indifferent (i.e., has the same profit) between its two choices?

c. What other factors should Jackrabbit Trails consider in making its decision?

6.69 Excess demand, qualitative considerations, ethics (LO1, LO5). Robin Spurlock is the director of the Mossbank Museum of Science and Natural History in Des Moines, Iowa. The museum is housed in an architecturally renowned facility. The five-story atrium provides a magnificent place to hold gala receptions and other events. Robin currently is in a quandary and seeks your advice.

A local children's charity has talked with Robin about using the atrium for the first Saturday of October. (They have not gotten around to signing a contract yet.) The conversation occurred almost a year ago because the charity wanted to get the best rate. Robin was delighted to help out, particularly because October typically is a slow month for the museum. She only charged the charity $500 to rent the atrium rather than the normal rate of $2,000 per day, even though the event would have no catering or other direct monetary benefits to the museum. The children's charity plans to use the atrium for the grand finale of a well-advertised art contest they are holding to raise money. The 100 finalists in the art contest would have their paintings showcased in the atrium, and numerous prizes would be awarded. Robin knows that the contest has spurred a great deal of interest among grade school children, including her own daughter, Emma.

It is now the middle of September, and one of the museum's corporate donors has contacted Robin about renting the atrium for the first Saturday in October. The corporate donor wishes to use the facility to hold a black tie event welcoming their new president and chief executive officer. The firm is willing to pay the full $2,000 rental fee. In addition, Robin knows that the museum will get 10% of the catering contract in return for use of the museum's kitchen and other facilities. The catering contract is likely to be around $15,000.

After Robin apprised the corporate donor of the conflict, she received a call from one of the corporation's directors. In a cordial conversation, the director implored Robin to consider fitting the event in because other dates and locations would not work as well. The director also took the opportunity to gently remind Robin of his corporation's past support for the museum and the board's desire to "do it right" for the reception. He also hinted that the museum might get a nice "surprise" during the event.

Robin would like to both honor her commitment to the children's charity and be responsive to the corporate donor. However, she knows that it is not physically feasible to hold both events the same day.

Required:

What quantitative and qualitative factors should Robin consider in her decision? Which factors do you believe are most important to Robin's decision?

Chapter 7
Operating Budgets: Bridging Planning and Control

AMARILLO TOYS IS A MEDIUM-SIZED company earning revenues of $29 million during the most recent year. Since its inception, Amarillo Toys has manufactured and marketed the same two products: BuildIT and BuildIT-PLUS building block sets. The BuildIT set is affordable but somewhat plain. While the BuildIT-PLUS set is more attractive and has more features, it also is more expensive.

During the first few years of operations, Amanda Barsky, Amarillo's founder, personally managed all aspects of the business. However, as the company grew, the volume of work overwhelmed her. Currently, Amarillo has two separate product divisions, one for BuildIT and one for BuildIT-PLUS, each with its own product manager. Within each division, individual managers oversee the marketing, production, and purchasing functions. Amanda allows her managers considerable latitude in decision making because she believes this is the best way to run a company of Amarillo's size.

APPLYING THE DECISION FRAMEWORK

What Is the Problem?	Over the coming year, what actions should Amarillo take to maximize profit?
What Are the Options?	Amarillo could follow many paths. We can view each path, and the accompanying set of decisions by Amarillo's employees, as a decision option.
What Are the Costs and Benefits?	Each set of possible decisions imposes different requirements on Amarillo's employees and resources. We can evaluate the profit effect of these decisions using budgeting.
Make the Decision!	By providing a detailed financial model, a budget allows us to consider the costs and benefits of various options and choose the best one.

Amanda attributes much of Amarillo's success to careful planning. She emphasizes the budgeting process and involves all of her key employees in drafting budgets. Once the budgets are set, she holds everybody accountable for achieving them.

Amanda Barsky of Amarillo Toys relies on detailed budgets to guide her operations.

LEARNING OBJECTIVES

After studying this chapter, you will be able to:

1 Understand the roles budgets serve in organizations.

2 Link individual budgets together to form an organization-wide plan.

3 Construct a cash budget and understand cash management.

4 Describe factors that affect the budgeting process.

As you learned in Chapters 5 and 6, organizations make short-term decisions to maximize the value derived from available capacity resources. These decisions affect activities throughout the firm. For example, offering a price discount increases sales and influences operations in the production, scheduling, and purchasing departments. Budgeting is a vehicle that many firms use to consolidate and coordinate such decisions. Budgets allow organizations to examine the collective impact of localized decisions by showing their overall effect on firm resources and profit.

We begin this chapter by discussing the three primary roles of budgets—*planning, coordination,* and *control*. We next turn our attention to the process of preparing a budget. We describe the components of a typical budget and illustrate them in the context of Amarillo Toys, underscoring the planning and coordination roles. As you will learn, the use of budget targets as benchmarks for performance, or the control role for budgets, also

CHAPTER CONNECTIONS

In Chapter 8, we focus on the control role for budgets by performing variance analysis, a technique used to determine the causes for deviations between budgeted and actual results.

affects the budgeting process. Accordingly, we consider how organization structure, management style, and reliance on past performance influence budgeting.

What Is a Budget?

A **budget** is a plan for using limited resources. Budgets specify the goals we hope to achieve in a specific period, and how we plan to achieve these goals. With unlimited resources, we can satisfy all of our wants. However, people and organizations have *limited* time and money. Hence, our plans must trade off among competing priorities when using available resources.

Because a budget reflects decisions on how to use scarce resources, it is the outcome of a decision process. Indeed, many of the benefits from budgeting arise because preparing budgets forces managers to examine various ways in which to get the most from organizational resources.

WHY DO FIRMS USE BUDGETS?

Organizations use budgets for three primary purposes:

- *Planning*: Budgets promote a culture of organization-wide planning by compelling managers to choose the best course of action from available options.
- *Coordination*: Budgets serve as a means by which different units of the organization communicate with each other and synchronize their actions.
- *Control (performance evaluation and feedback)*: Budgets provide a frame of reference, or a benchmark, for providing feedback and for evaluating actual performance.

Let us examine each of these purposes, paying particular attention to how each role bridges different aspects of an organization's operations.

Planning

Most companies prepare budgets for different horizons—from daily and weekly budgets to budgets that span several years. Multiyear budgets are strategic plans that specify the direction in which a company desires to head. For example, Dell has long-term budgets specified in terms of growth, profit, and market share. Such long-term plans set the stage for **operating budgets**, which bridge short-term decisions and long-term plans. Like a step on a path, operating budgets help companies reach their long-term goals. Dell's operating budgets would specify expected revenues, production costs, purchasing patterns, and marketing activities for the coming year. In this way, operating budgets reflect the outcomes of numerous short-term decisions designed to achieve long-term goals. **Financial budgets** quantify the outcomes of operating budgets in summary financial statements.

Connecting to Practice

STRATEGIC PLANS

Strategic planning focuses outside the organization, scanning the environment for threats and opportunities. Threats can come from competing technologies—for example, the failure to anticipate the move to digital cameras cost Kodak dearly, as the trend substantially reduced the market for film, Kodak's main product. On the other hand, innovation and changing demographics can generate opportunities. For example, eBay's success as an on-line auction house stems from the widespread use of the Internet and consumers becoming more comfortable with using computers to make on-line purchases.

COMMENTARY: Operational budgets have an inward focus. Companies develop these budgets within the confines of their strategic plans. For example, once Amazon decides to enter foreign markets, it needs to change its operating strategy to fit. Examples include opening warehouses in foreign countries and establishing Web sites in foreign languages.

Kodak's strategic plans must incorporate the growth of digital photography. (Paul Sakuma/©AP/Wide World Photos)

A **master budget** for a period is a plan that presents the expected revenues, costs, and profit corresponding to the expected sale volume as of the beginning of that period. As shown in Exhibit 7.1, it consists of a comprehensive set of operating and financial budgets. The master budget involves all facets of operations and links organizational activities. For example, Dell's master budget would specify sales targets for individual products, production cost targets, promotional expenses, and warranty costs.

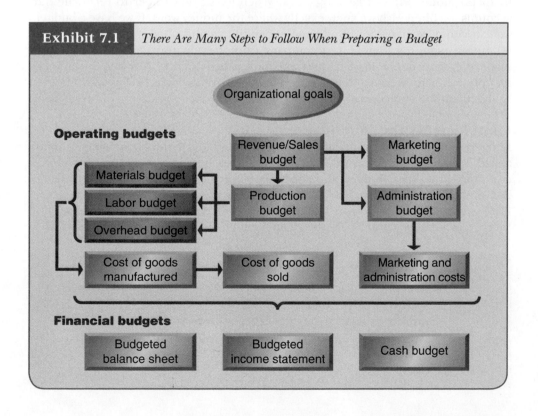

Exhibit 7.1 *There Are Many Steps to Follow When Preparing a Budget*

Study Exhibit 7.1 carefully as it provides the overall structure that links the many steps in budgeting. The exhibit uses a separate color for a group of related steps. When we discuss individual steps, we will use these colors again so that you can place those steps within the overall context.

Coordination

As a company grows, it is difficult for one person to manage all aspects of the business. When Amarillo was still a small company, Amanda could oversee all operations, including purchasing, production, sales, and marketing. To cope with the growing demands, however, she hired a marketing manager, a production manager, and a purchasing supervisor to oversee these functions for each of her two product lines. Thus, Amanda moved from a **centralized decision-making** environment in which she was making all the decisions to a **decentralized decision-making** environment in which she *delegated* decision making to individuals with relevant expertise and knowledge.

In decentralized companies, departments must *communicate* and *coordinate* with each other to ensure that everyone is working toward the same corporate goals. If the Marketing Department can sell only 1,000 units of a product in a given quarter because of weak demand, there is no sense in the Production Department making 2,000 units just because it can. Budgets are a good way of communicating the plan targets to everyone in the organization.

Budgets also enable various departments to coordinate their activities in a way that benefits the company as a whole. They highlight linkages among departments and force each department to consider how its actions influence the actions of other departments. In this way, budgets help department managers make the best decisions from the company's standpoint. As you see in Exhibit 7.1, the master budget links several component budgets. Because of these linkages, preparing a budget is a joint effort that requires participation from all concerned. Many firms use cross-functional teams that include employees from several departments to prepare the budget.

Control (Performance Evaluation and Feedback)

Budgets provide a basis or a *benchmark* for evaluating actual performance. Many of us spend money without keeping track. When we sit down later to reconcile our accounts, we often wish we knew exactly where the money went. If we have a budget, we can compare actual and budgeted expenditures and obtain valuable feedback for future planning. Similarly, a company cannot evaluate whether its managers made the right decisions if it does not have a benchmark. Nor can a company identify problem areas so that it can take corrective actions. In this way, budgets bridge planning and control decisions.

Complements and Conflicts

Budgets have both a planning and a control role. Budgets force managers to think ahead and find the best way to use scarce resources, linking the organization's long- and short-term plans. Budgets also effectively communicate corporate objectives and link multiple departments, leading to a coherent plan for the entire organization. Finally, the planned targets in budgets become the benchmark for actual results, thereby facilitating control. As shown in Exhibit 7.2, the control role leads to a

CHAPTER CONNECTIONS

In Chapter 8, we discuss the role of budgets in variance analysis, which is a tool for performance evaluation and control. Profit variance analysis reconciles the income projected in the master budget with actual income and identifies the key reasons for any discrepancies.

Exhibit 7.2	*Operating Budgets Link Long- and Short-term Plans and Are Part of the PIER Cycles*

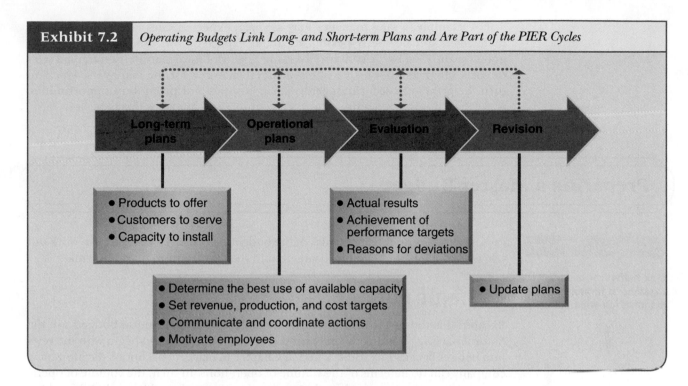

reexamination of the assumptions made during the planning process. Notice that this cycle mirrors the planning and control cycle that we discussed in Chapter 1.

The dual planning and control roles for budgets can create conflicts in the budgeting process, however. Firms want to use the best available information when making planning decisions. In decentralized operations, employees at lower levels in the organization often have the most up-to-date and relevant information about local operating conditions. Thus, firms ask employees for this information when making the budget. But these employees may not be forthright in sharing their information.

 **Connecting to Practice**

ARE BUDGETS GOOD FOR BUSINESS?

A survey of 212 top executives from a range of manufacturing and service firms shows that 66% of executives believe that their firms derive good to excellent value from it. Moreover, respondents indicate overwhelmingly that they could not manage without budgets. These data confirm the widespread use of budgets as a critical part of a firm's planning and control systems.

COMMENTARY: The survey also indicates room for improvement. Budgets take an average of 10.3 weeks to complete. Moreover, nearly 30% of surveyed managers agreed that budgets are "too time consuming," "slow to detect problems," and "not reliable for performance measurement."

Source: T. Libby and R. Lindsay, "Beyond Budgeting or Better Budgeting," *Strategic Finance*, August 2007, 47–51.

For example, a sales manager may *downplay* expected sales, while a production manager might be overly pessimistic about expected costs. Such actions are not good for the firm because they reduce the quality of information used to plan sales or costs. However, they lead to more achievable targets for the managers, which, in turn, help them in securing performance bonuses and promotion opportunities. A well-functioning budgeting process recognizes and manages this behavior.

Preparing a Master Budget

LEARNING OBJECTIVE 2

Link individual budgets together to form an organization-wide plan.

Let us now dig into the mechanics of the budgeting process. Our goal is to work our way toward a budgeted income statement in the contribution margin format.

REVENUE BUDGET

Because it is the first line item on the income statement, revenue budgets are the natural starting point for the master budget. Organizations also begin with the revenue budget because, as you learned in Chapter 6, market conditions dictate what a company can do in terms of the volume of operations. In turn, the volume of operations drives many costs, such as those related to materials and labor. Exhibit 7.1A is the relevant portion of the overall budgeting process illustrated in Exhibit 7.1 emphasizing the importance of preparing the revenue budget before preparing the production budget.

Exhibit 7.3 presents Amarillo's revenue budget by product for each quarter of the coming year. Sales projections are in lots of 100 units, and the expected price for each lot of BuildIT and BuildIT-PLUS is $2,900 and $4,800, respectively.

Firms spend considerable time and effort in preparing a revenue budget, as its accuracy is crucial in putting together a good master budget. Marketing departments typically update historical sales trends utilizing their knowledge of the market, customer surveys, the company's products and pricing decisions, and competitors' products and prices. Many firms also use consultants to gather information about product markets and forecasted demand.

PRODUCTION BUDGET

After the revenue budget, the logical next step is to prepare the production budget. The production budget combines the demand information provided by the revenue budget and the company's inventory policy regarding finished goods to determine production levels in the coming period. Exhibit 7.4 presents Amarillo's production budget by quarter for the coming year. In this exhibit, we compute each quarter's budgeted production using the inventory equation that we studied in Chapter 3.

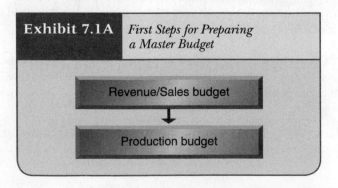

Exhibit 7.1A *First Steps for Preparing a Master Budget*

Revenue/Sales budget

↓

Production budget

Exhibit 7.3	Amarillo Toys: Revenue Budget

	Quarter				
	Quarter 1	Quarter 2	Quarter 3	Quarter 4	Total
BuildIT					
Sales in lots	1,500	1,500	2,000	3,000	8,000
Price per lot	$2,900	$2,900	$2,900	$2,900	$2,900
Revenue	$4,350,000	$4,350,000	$5,800,000	$8,700,000	$23,200,000
BuildIT-PLUS					
Sales in lots	400	400	500	700	2,000
Price per lot	$4,800	$4,800	$4,800	$4,800	$4,800
Revenue	$1,920,000	$1,920,000	$2,400,000	$3,360,000	$9,600,000
Total revenue	$6,270,000	$6,270,000	$8,200,000	$12,060,000	$32,800,000

Connecting to Practice

USING INTERNAL MARKETS FOR FORECASTING

Hewlett-Packard (HP) is among the firms using a novel technique, internal markets, for developing forecasts. These markets, restricted to HP marketing and sales personnel, allow employees to trade "futures" contracts for sales of a particular product. For example, for a given product, HP might set up contracts for sales less than 10,000 units, from 10,001 to 15,000 units, from 15,001 to 20,000 units, or over 25,000 units. People who believed sales would be 10,001 to 15,000 units could post a price to buy a contract with that characteristic. They could also sell the other contracts (e.g., for the contract stipulating sales would be under 10,000 units) to other employees with different beliefs. Only the persons holding the "right" contract, as defined by actual sales, would receive a reward. Over time, as employees bought and sold their futures contracts, the summary market price varied according to the collective opinions of everyone participating in the market. It turned out that this market's predictions beat every other prediction!

COMMENTARY: Firms use many techniques to gather information about demand and forecast sales. Companies go to great lengths to obtain these estimates because of the importance of getting an accurate revenue budget.

It is difficult to forecast sales for products such as toys because buyer tastes often vary unpredictably. (©Dylan Ellis/Corbis)

As shown in Exhibit 7.4, Amarillo expects to end the current year with 75 lots of BuildIT and 15 lots of BuildIT-PLUS in inventory. These quantities become the beginning inventory for the forthcoming year. At the end of each quarter, Amarillo targets to have finished goods inventory equal to 10% of the following quarter's sales volume. Thus, Amarillo desires to have 200 lots of BuildIT in inventory at the end of the second quarter, or 10% of the 2,000 lots it expects to sell in the third quarter. Based on tentative sales projections five quarters out, Amarillo plans to end the year with 90 lots of BuildIT and 20 lots of BuildIT-PLUS in stock.

Exhibit 7.4	Amarillo Toys: Production Budget

	Quarter				
	Quarter 1	*Quarter 2*	*Quarter 3*	*Quarter 4*	*Total*
BuildIT					
Sales in lots	1,500	1,500	2,000	3,000	
+ Desired ending inventory	150	200	300	90	
= Total requirements	1,650	1,700	2,300	3,090	
- Beginning inventory	75	150	200	300	
= Lots to be produced	**1,575**	**1,550**	**2,100**	**2,790**	**8,015**
BuildIT-PLUS					
Sales	400	400	500	700	
+ Desired ending inventory	40			20	
= Total requirements	440	*See Check It!*		720	
- Beginning inventory	15	*Exercise #1*		70	
= Lots to be produced	**425**	**410**	**520**	**650**	**2,005**

✓ Check It! Exercise #1

Complete the missing cells in Exhibit 7.4 for BuildIT-PLUS for Quarters 2 and 3. Verify that Amarillo expects to produce 410 and 520 lots of BuildIT-PLUS in Quarters 2 and 3, respectively.

	Quarter 2	Quarter 3	
Sales in lots	400	500	From Exhibit 7.3
+ Desired ending inventory	_____	_____	10% of next quarter's sales
= Total requirements	_____	_____	
− Beginning inventory	_____	_____	Ending inventory of prior quarter
= Lots to be produced	410	520	

Solution at end of chapter.

Preparing the production budgets requires Amarillo's marketing managers and production managers to coordinate and address some important questions. For example, is there enough production capacity to meet projected sales? If not, should the company add more capacity, temporarily or permanently? Is it more profitable to reduce the volume of one of the products and sell less? In addition, the managers need to decide on inventory levels for each product, trading off the costs of carrying too much inventory with the costs of having too little inventory. The production managers need to coordinate how best to schedule the two products on shared machinery and equipment, and the resources necessary to ensure efficient production.

DIRECT MATERIALS USAGE BUDGET

Once we formulate a production budget, we know the output targets. As the relevant portion of Exhibit 7 excerpted in Exhibit 7.1B shows, we use these output targets to derive the budgets for materials, labor, and overhead. In turn, these *usage* budgets enable us to estimate variable and fixed manufacturing costs.

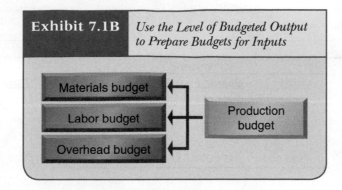

Exhibit 7.1B *Use the Level of Budgeted Output to Prepare Budgets for Inputs*

We begin with the direct materials usage budget. Amarillo's two products consume four types of direct materials—standard-grade plastic for BuildIT, special-grade plastic for BuildIT-PLUS, dyes for color, and boxes for packaging. Amarillo uses the same dyes for BuildIT and BuildIT-PLUS. One lot of direct materials denotes the amount of materials necessary to produce a lot of each product.

Amarillo's production manager and purchasing supervisor estimate that at the start of the coming year, the company will have the following direct materials in beginning inventory:

- 65 lots of standard-grade plastic at $600 per lot
- 30 lots of special-grade plastic at $1,000 per lot
- 125 lots of dyes at $500 per lot
- 75 lots of BuildIT boxes at $400 per lot
- 25 lots of BuildIT-PLUS boxes at $400 per lot

The purchasing supervisor believes that direct materials prices will remain the same for all materials. With this information, Exhibit 7.5 presents Amarillo's direct materials usage budget.

For simplicity, we prepare Amarillo's budgets assuming that prices will not change. What happens if we do expect prices to change? Then, the firm will expect to have different layers of inventory of the same material but at different prices. We have to make some assumptions, such as FIFO or LIFO, regarding cost flows to determine the cost of materials used. The appendix to this chapter describes how Amarillo can deal with such situations in its budgets.

The purchasing and production managers coordinate closely to prepare the materials usage budget because it requires both price and quantity estimates. Most companies estimate direct material quantities based on internal standards for the

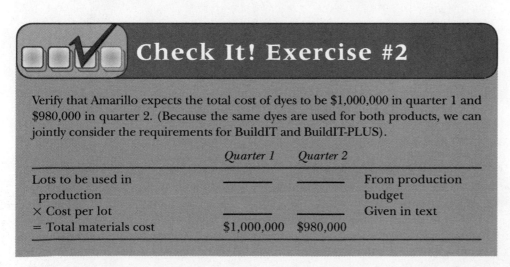

Check It! Exercise #2

Verify that Amarillo expects the total cost of dyes to be $1,000,000 in quarter 1 and $980,000 in quarter 2. (Because the same dyes are used for both products, we can jointly consider the requirements for BuildIT and BuildIT-PLUS).

	Quarter 1	Quarter 2	
Lots to be used in production	_____	_____	From production budget
× Cost per lot	_____	_____	Given in text
= Total materials cost	$1,000,000	$980,000	

Solution at end of chapter.

Exhibit 7.5   *Amarillo Toys: Direct Materials Usage Budget*

	Quarter				
	Quarter 1	*Quarter 2*	*Quarter 3*	*Quarter 4*	*Total*
Plastic: Standard Grade					
Lots to be used in production					
(from Exhibit 7.4)	1,575	1,550	2,100	2,790	
Cost per lot	$600	$600	$600	$600	
Total Materials cost	$945,000	$930,000	$1,260,000	$1,674,000	$4,809,000
Plastic: Special Grade					
Lots to be used in production					
(from Exhibit 7.4)	425	410	520	650	
Cost per lot	$1,000	$1,000	$1,000	$1,000	
Total Materials cost	$425,000	$410,000	$520,000	$650,000	$2,005,000
Dyes					
		See Check It! Exercise #2			
Total Materials Cost	$1,000,000	$980,000	$1,310,000	$1,720,000	$5,010,000
Packing Boxes					
BuildIT					
Lots to be used in production	1,575	1,550	2,100	2,790	
Cost per lot	$400	$400	$400	$400	
Packing cost for BuildIT	$630,000	$620,000	$840,000	$1,116,000	
BuildIT-PLUS					
Lots to be used in production	425	410	520	650	
Cost per lot	$400	$400	$400	$400	
Packing cost for BuildIT-PLUS	$170,000	$164,000	$208,000	$260,000	
Total Packing Cost	$800,000	$784,000	$1,048,000	$1,376,000	$4,008,000
Cost of all direct materials to be used					**$15,832,000**

materials needed to make one unit of output. Direct material prices are more difficult to estimate. Their accuracy depends on the experience and knowledge that purchasing has about conditions in the marketplace for materials.

DIRECT LABOR BUDGET

Similar to the direct materials usage budget, the direct labor budget follows from the production budget. Labor standards at Amarillo indicate that BuildIT requires 8 labor hours per lot and BuildIT-PLUS requires 12 labor hours per lot. On average, labor costs $15 per hour. Exhibit 7.6 presents Amarillo's direct labor budget for the coming year.

Often, the labor budget is more detailed than what we see in Exhibit 7.6. Depending on a company's production technology, different grades of labor may be necessary for jobs requiring different skills and expertise. For example, Amarillo may require special skills for plastic molding and extrusion operations. In such settings, we would separately identify each type of labor.

Like the direct materials usage budget, the labor budget helps Amarillo plan working capital needs. Most organizations maintain a Human Resources Department to manage labor relations. Besides hiring and firing decisions, the human resource

Exhibit 7.6	Amarillo Toys: Direct Labor Budget

	Quarter				
	Quarter 1	Quarter 2	Quarter 3	Quarter 4	Total
BuildIT					
Lots to be produced	1,575	1,550	2,100	2,790	
Labor hours per lot	8	8	8	8	
Labor cost per hour	$15	$15	$15	$15	
Direct labor cost	$189,000	$186,000	$252,000	$334,800	$961,800
BuildIT-PLUS		*See Check It! Exercise #3*			
Direct labor cost	$76,500	$73,800	$93,600	$117,000	$360,900
Total labor cost	**$265,500**	**$259,800**	**$345,600**	**$451,800**	**$1,322,700**

Check It! Exercise #3

Verify the BuildIT-PLUS direct labor cost numbers in Exhibit 7.6.

	Quarter 1	Quarter 2	Quarter 3	Quarter 4
Lots to be produced	_____	_____	_____	_____
× Labor hours per lot	_____	_____	_____	_____
× Labor cost per hour	_____	_____	_____	_____
= Direct labor cost	_____	_____	_____	_____

Solution at end of chapter.

function is responsible for the cost of labor in much the same way the purchasing function is responsible for getting the best price for raw materials. Thus, preparing the labor budget requires close coordination between the Production Department, which determines labor requirements for production, and the Human Resource Department, which has information about labor costs and helps ensure the availability of labor.

MANUFACTURING OVERHEAD COST BUDGET

Having identified materials and labor needs, our next task is to prepare the manufacturing overhead cost budget. Manufacturing overhead consists of both variable and fixed costs. Variable items include the supplies used by employees, oils used in the machining process, and the plastic film used to wrap cartons. While it is possible for Amarillo to estimate each item in its variable overhead separately, it usually is more efficient to estimate total expenditures on variable overhead as a proportion of manufacturing activity.

In keeping with industry practice, Amarillo uses direct labor cost as its measure of manufacturing activity. In recent years, the variable manufacturing overhead rate has remained steady at $0.50 per direct labor dollar. Because Amarillo expects this rate to hold in the coming year, we multiply the budgeted direct labor cost from Exhibit 7.6 by the variable overhead rate of $0.50. This leads us to the budgeted variable manufacturing overhead in the top half of Exhibit 7.7.

Exhibit 7.7	*Amarillo Toys: Manufacturing Overhead Cost Budget*

	Quarter				
	Quarter 1	*Quarter 2*	*Quarter 3*	*Quarter 4*	*Total*
Variable manufacturing overhead					
Budgeted direct labor cost (from Exhibit 7.6)	$265,500	$259,800	$345,600	$451,800	
Variable overhead rate per DL$	$0.50	$0.50	$0.50	$0.50	
Total variable overhead	**$132,750**	**$129,900**	**$172,800**	**$225,900**	**$661,350**
Fixed manufacturing overhead					
Cash expenses	$950,000	$950,000	$950,000	$950,000	$3,800,000
Annual equipment depreciation					1,450,000
Total fixed overhead					**$5,250,000**
Total Overhead Costs					**$5,911,350**

In addition to variable overhead, Amarillo also expects to incur costs related to machines, salaried employees, warehousing, and other capacity resources. These costs make up fixed manufacturing overhead, which is usually a large fraction of total costs. Firms usually carefully estimate the expected costs for each category of fixed overhead. They then add these costs up to estimate the total amount.

Amanda expects fixed overhead to equal $5,250,000 in the coming year. As shown in the bottom half of Exhibit 7.7, fixed overhead contains cash expenses related to salaries, rent, and property taxes as well as noncash expenses related to equipment depreciation.

VARIABLE COST OF GOODS MANUFACTURED BUDGET

Now that we have the budgets for materials, labor and overhead, we are now in a position to calculate the total variable manufacturing cost of the units Amarillo expects to produce during the coming year (Exhibit 7.1C reproduces the relevant portion of Exhibit 7.1). Exhibit 7.8 presents this computation. To keep the exhibit simple, we present only the annual budget and do not present the details on a quarter-by-quarter basis.

Exhibit 7.1C	*Consolidate Costs of Inputs to Determine Costs of Goods Manufactured and Sold*

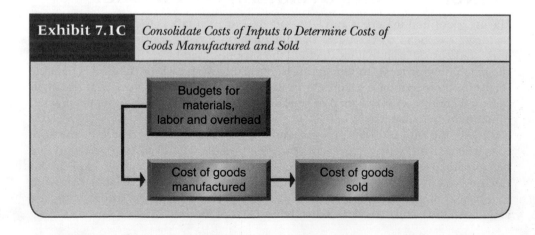

Exhibit 7.8	Amarillo Toys: Variable Cost of Goods Manufactured Budget

	From Exhibit	BuildIT	BuildIT-PLUS	Total
Plastic: Standard-grade	7.5	$4,809,000		$4,809,000
Plastic: Special-grade	7.5		$2,005,000	2,005,000
Dyes	7.5	4,007,500	1,002,500	5,010,000
Packaging materials	7.5	3,206,000	802,000	4,008,000
Direct manufacturing labor	7.6	961,800	360,900	1,322,700
Variable manufacturing overhead	7.7	480,900	180,450	661,350
Variable cost of goods manufactured		**$13,465,200**	**$4,350,850**	**$17,816,050**

The variable cost of goods manufactured is the sum of several cost items: materials, labor, and variable overhead. We obtain the cost of materials used from the direct materials usage budget in Exhibit 7.5. Notice that Exhibit 7.8 separates the total cost of the dyes and packing boxes from Exhibit 7.5 into portions attributable to the two product lines. We obtain labor costs from the labor budget in Exhibit 7.6. We also break out the variable manufacturing overhead costs by product. For example, the $480,900 in variable manufacturing overhead for BuildIT is the product of the $961,800 in BuildIT direct labor costs from Exhibit 7.6 multiplied by the variable overhead rate of $0.50 per direct labor dollar.

VARIABLE COST OF GOODS SOLD BUDGET

Our next step is to estimate the variable cost of goods sold, which takes us even closer to Amarillo's budgeted income statement. To calculate cost of goods sold, we apply the inventory equation to finished goods. We calculate:

Cost of goods sold = Cost of beginning finished goods inventory + cost of goods manufactured − cost of ending finished goods inventory

We start by obtaining the cost of beginning finished goods inventory.

Beginning Finished Goods Inventory

As you know from the production budget (Exhibit 7.4), Amarillo expects to have 75 lots of BuildIT and 15 lots of BuildIT-PLUS on hand at the beginning of the year. What is the cost of each lot, and what is the total cost of this inventory that we expect to have at the end of last year? Exhibit 7.9 provides this information. In this exhibit, the cost of each lot includes the cost of materials, labor, and variable overhead. These estimates take into account the costs incurred the prior year as this year's beginning inventory would have been produced last year.

Exhibit 7.9	Amarillo Toys: Beginning Finished Goods Inventory

	BuildIT	BuildIT-PLUS
Variable cost per lot	$1,680	$2,170
Number of Lots	75	15
Total variable cost	**$126,000**	**$32,550**

Ending Finished Goods Inventory

Exhibit 7.4 shows us that Amarillo expects to have 90 lots of BuildIT and 20 lots of BuildIT-PLUS on hand at the end of the year. What is the cost per lot, and what is the total cost of this inventory? Exhibit 7.10 provides the detailed calculations.

Notice that the cost per lot is the same at the start and at the end of the year. This is because Amarillo is not forecasting any change in the prices of materials, labor, or variable overhead. If Amarillo did expect prices to change, as shown in the Appendix, the cost per lot would change over time. Consequently, Amarillo would use a cost flow assumption such as FIFO to calculate the cost of goods sold.

Variable Cost of Goods Sold

Now that we have the cost of beginning finished goods inventory, the cost of goods manufactured, and the cost of ending finished goods inventory, we can calculate Amarillo's cost of goods sold. Exhibit 7.11 shows our calculations for the year (without the quarterly detail).

Marketing and Administrative Costs Budget

We next turn our attention to the budget for marketing and administrative expenses. These inputs usually relate to the volume of *sales* activity, meaning that they link to the revenue budget (Exhibit 7.1D). As we see in Exhibit 7.12, some of Amarillo's marketing and administrative expenses, such as sales commissions and shipping, are variable because they change proportionally with sales. As noted in the top half

---

Exhibit 7.10 | *Amarillo Toys: Ending Finished Goods Inventory*

	BuildIT	BuildIT-PLUS
Variable cost per lot		
Plastic	$600	$1,000
Dyes	500	500
Packing boxes	400	400
Direct labor	120	180
Variable manufacturing overhead	60	90
Total	$1,680	$2,170
Number of Lots	90	20
Total variable cost	**$151,200**	**$43,400**

Exhibit 7.11 | *Amarillo Toys: Variable Cost of Goods Sold Budget*

	Exhibit Reference	BuildIT	BuildIT-PLUS	Total
Beginning finished goods inventory	7.9	$126,000	$32,550	$158,550
+ Cost of goods manufactured	7.8	13,465,200	4,350,850	$17,816,050
= Cost of goods available for sale		$13,591,200	$4,383,400	$17,974,600
- Ending finished goods inventory	7.10	151,200	43,400	194,600
= Variable Cost of goods sold		$13,440,000	$4,340,000	$17,780,000

of Exhibit 7.12, Amarillo estimates that the variable portion is $185 for each lot of BuildIT sold and $225 for each lot of BuildIT-PLUS sold.

As is evident from Exhibit 7.12, other marketing and administrative expenses, such as administrative salaries and office space, are fixed. Similar to fixed manufacturing overhead, these costs contain both cash and noncash items.

Exhibit 7.12 also shows that Amanda plans to invest $1 million toward research and development (fixed R&D expenses). Such expenses are discretionary and do

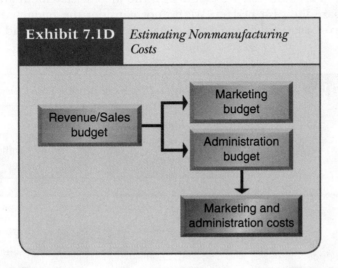

Exhibit 7.1D   *Estimating Nonmanufacturing Costs*

Exhibit 7.12   *Amarillo Toys: Marketing and Administrative Costs Budget*

	Quarter				
	Quarter 1	*Quarter 2*	*Quarter 3*	*Quarter 4*	*Total*
Variable marketing and administrative costs					
BuildIT					
Sales in lots	1,500	1,500	2,000	3,000	
Variable cost per lot	$185	$185	$185	$185	
Variable costs	$277,500	$277,500	$370,000	$555,000	$1,480,000
BuildIT-PLUS					
Sales in lots	400	400	500	700	
Variable cost per lot	$225	$225	$225	$225	
Variable costs	$90,000	$90,000	$112,500	$157,500	$450,000
Total variable marketing and administrative costs	$367,500	$367,500	$482,500	$712,500	$1,930,000
Fixed marketing and administrative costs					
Cash expenses	$1,120,000	$1,120,000	$1,120,000	$1,120,000	$4,480,000
Fixed R&D expenses	250,000	250,000	250,000	250,000	1,000,000
Annual depreciation					$1,020,000
Total fixed costs					$6,500,000
Total marketing and administrative costs					$8,430,000

not contribute to current period sales, and they are best viewed as investments in the company's future. Firms have to invest today to have a solid product line tomorrow.

BUDGETED INCOME STATEMENT

We are finally in a position to project Amarillo's financial statements: the balance sheet, the income statement, and the cash budget (Exhibit 7.1E presents the relevant portion of Exhibit 7.1). We first discuss the income statement and then show how to prepare the cash budget. We do not consider the budgeted (sometimes called the pro-forma) balance sheet in detail, as that topic is beyond the scope of this book.

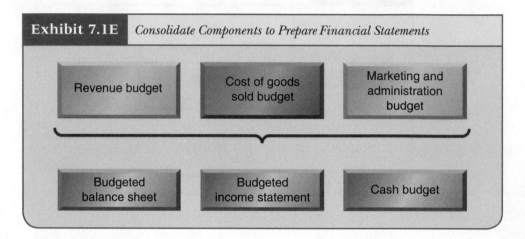

Exhibit 7.1E | *Consolidate Components to Prepare Financial Statements*

Exhibit 7.13 presents our calculations for the income statement.

Exhibit 7.13 | *Amarillo Toys: Budgeted Income Statement*

	Exhibit Reference	BuildIT	BuildIT-PLUS	Total
Budgeted sales in lots	7.3	**8,000**	**2,000**	
Revenue	7.3	$23,200,000	$9,600,000	$32,800,000
Variable costs				
Manufacturing	7.11	13,440,000	4,340,000	$17,780,000
Marketing & Administration	7.12	1,480,000	450,000	1,930,000
Contribution Margin		$8,280,000	$4,810,000	$13,090,000
Fixed costs				
Manufacturing	7.7			$5,250,000
Marketing & Administration	7.12			6,500,000
Profit before Taxes				$1,340,000
Taxes (at 35% of pre-tax profit)				469,000
Profit after Taxes				$871,000

Consistent with other contribution margin statements, Exhibit 7.13 begins with revenue. We first subtract all variable costs to arrive at each product's contribution margin. Next, we subtract fixed costs to arrive at profit before taxes. We then subtract estimated income taxes to arrive at profit after taxes. Amanda's focus is on profit after taxes because this is the amount available for paying out dividends or for reinvesting in the business.

Connecting to Practice

TAX PLANNING AND BUDGETING

Suppose you are planning to sell some appreciated stock next year. When calculating your cash flow, you budget for the receipt from the sale of stock *and* the taxes that you will pay on the realized gain. To reduce taxes owed, you might consider deferring some deductible donations from this year to the next, or paying two years worth of property taxes next year.

COMMENTARY: Prudent tax planning includes taking actions to time expenses to coincide with recognition of income so that the taxpayer can reduce income taxed at higher rates. Multinational firms such as Roche, Baxter, and Caterpillar routinely engage in such tax planning. Because these actions influence the accounting recognition of revenues and expenses, as well as the timing of cash payments, these firms often review their tax plans when preparing their budgets.

Exhibit 7.13 indicates substantial contribution margins for both BuildIT and BuildIT-PLUS. The budgeted contribution margins provide a sound basis for evaluating the performance of Amarillo's two product managers in the coming year. Firms often prepare similar statements for each quarter or month to facilitate timely monitoring of results.

ITERATIVE NATURE OF THE BUDGETING PROCESS

Exhibits 7.3 to 7.13 present an orderly manner of arriving at Amarillo's budgeted income statement for the coming year. These exhibits help us understand the flow of numbers and the linkages among various functions of an organization.

Actual budgeting processes are quite iterative. Most companies rework their budgets numerous times. The sales staff, the marketing manager, and Amanda would go through several iterations before agreeing to the revenue budget. Even with intense scrutiny of individual steps, firms often end up reworking entire budgets. For instance, the first budget iteration may have produced an estimated profit of $700,000. Amanda and other senior managers would evaluate this estimate in light of the firm's overall goals and plans. If the estimate falls short of their goals, they would ask the budget team to reexamine all plan assumptions to find areas where Amarillo could reduce costs or enhance revenue.

They might also reexamine the budget to see if they have made the correct assumptions. Perhaps the price of special-grade plastic will increase from $1,000 to $1,050 in the second quarter. Measures to improve efficiency may have reduced the variable manufacturing overhead rate from 50 to 45%. The sales analysts may believe that the company's reputation is leading to a shift by some consumers so that sales of the basic kit are expected to fall by 10%, but sales of the plus kit are expected to increase by 20%. (We address the price change assumptions in the Appendix.)

In general, a careful review of operating assumptions and estimates adds value to the budgeting process. A well-prepared budget allows the firm to make the best possible decisions and extract the maximum value from its available resources.

In addition to the overall budgets we prepared for Amarillo, companies prepare numerous other budgets for subunits. Each division, department, or even project may also have its own revenue and/or cost budget. Even individual employees may have detailed budgets for their time, sales quotas, or expenditures related to travel. In the next section, we examine another important budget in organizations, the cash budget.

APPLYING THE DECISION FRAMEWORK

What Is the Problem? Over the coming year, what actions should Amarillo take to maximize profit?

What Are the Options? Amarillo could follow many paths. We view each path, and the accompanying set of decisions by Amarillo's employees, as a decision option.

What Are the Costs and Benefits? Each set of possible decisions imposes different requirements on Amarillo's employees and resources. We can evaluate the profit effect of these decisions using budgeting.

Make the Decision! *Amanda is satisfied that the budgets in Exhibits 7.3 through 7.13 represent the best possible use of Amarillo's resources in the coming year.*

Cash Budget

The cash budget is important for managing a firm's working capital. The **cash budget** allows companies to determine whether they will have enough money on hand to sustain projected operations. Companies can manage cash shortfalls by accelerating revenues, deferring payments, altering the timing of special cash inflows, or borrowing. Effective working capital management can save companies money in terms of interest payments on costly short-term loans.

As shown toward the bottom of Exhibit 7.14, the cash budget has three major components: inflows from operations, outflows from operations, and special items. Each of these relate to a specific part of the budgets we prepared to arrive at the income statement. As the exhibit also shows, we have to adjust revenues and costs to determine the cash inflow or outflow.

Exhibit 7.14 *Steps for Preparing a Cash Budget*

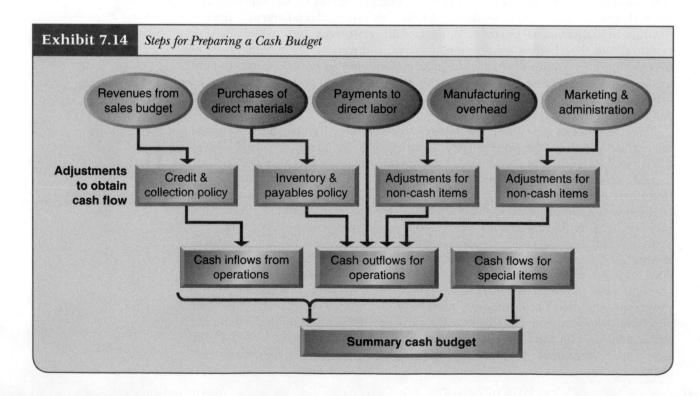

CASH INFLOWS FROM OPERATIONS

Proceeds from sales are the primary cash inflows from operations. However, in order to compute the expected inflow of cash, we need to adjust revenue by the firm's credit policy. Most businesses offer credit terms to customers. Therefore, they receive cash only a few days, weeks, or months after the sale occurs. At Amarillo, experience indicates that 60% of revenue is collected in the quarter the sales occurred, 35% is collected in the quarter following the sales, and 5% in the quarter thereafter.

Exhibit 7.15 builds on the revenue budget in Exhibit 7.3 to provide Amarillo's estimated cash inflows from operations for the coming year. During the first quarter, Amarillo collects 60% of first-quarter sales, or 0.60 × $6,270,000 = $3,762,000 (see Exhibit 7.3). In addition, Amarillo collects 35% of fourth-quarter sales from the previous year and 5% of third-quarter sales from the previous year. (Collectively, these two amounts total $2,625,000.)

We compute the cash collections for the other quarters in an identical fashion. In the fourth quarter, Amarillo expects to collect 60% of fourth-quarter sales, or 0.60 × $12,060,000 = $7,236,000. Amarillo also collects $2,870,000 from third-quarter sales (0.35 × $8,200,000) and $313,500 from second-quarter sales (0.05 × $6,270,000).

Exhibit 7.15 indicates that Amarillo expects to collect all of its revenues. Firms, however, often have to deal with uncollectible credit sales because some customers default on their payments. How would uncollectible sales affect our computations? We would show collections as being less than 100% of revenues, with the reduction being

Exhibit 7.15 *Amarillo Toys: Budgeted Cash Inflows from Operations*

[EXBTCH]	Quarter 1	Quarter 2	Quarter 3	Quarter 4	Total
[EXTB]Last year's sales	$2,625,000	$350,000			$2,975,000
Quarter 1 sales	3,762,000	2,194,500	$313,500		6,270,000
Quarter 2 sales		3,762,000	2,194,500	$313,500	6,270,000
Quarter 3 sales			4,920,000	2,870,000	7,790,000
Quarter 4 sales				7,236,000	7,236,000
Total cash collected	$6,387,000	$6,306,500	$7,428,000	$10,419,500	$30,541,000

Check It! Exercise #4

Verify Amarillo's budgeted cash inflows from operations for the third quarter. Use Exhibit 7.3 to obtain the revenue data.

Quarter of Sales	Revenues	% Collected in Q3	Amount Collected
1	_____	_____	$313,500
2	_____	_____	2,194,500
3	_____	_____	4,920,000
Total	_____	_____	$7,428,000

Solution at end of chapter.

the percent of uncollectible sales. From an accounting recordkeeping perspective, we also need to adjust the balance of accounts receivable and reported income to reflect the uncollectible debt.

CASH OUTFLOWS FROM OPERATIONS

There are four types of cash outflows from operations: purchases of direct materials, payments for labor, expenditures on manufacturing overhead, and outflows for marketing and administration costs.

Purchases of Direct Materials

Just as Amarillo extends credit to its customers, the company expects credit from its suppliers. Amarillo pays 40 percent of its accounts payable in the quarter purchases are made and 60 percent in the following quarter. To calculate Amarillo's cash payment for purchases, we first need to calculate the expected direct materials purchases in the coming year.

We prepare the direct materials purchases budgets based on Amarillo's direct material usage and inventory policy. As in the case of finished goods inventory, Amarillo targets 10 percent of the next period's production usage as the desired ending inventory for direct materials in any given period. Based on Amarillo's production budget in Exhibit 7.4 and the amounts of beginning inventory for each material reported in the text, we prepare Exhibit 7.16.

| Exhibit 7.16 | *Amarillo Toys: Direct Materials Purchase Budget* |

	Quarter				
	Quarter 1	*Quarter 2*	*Quarter 3*	*Quarter 4*	*Total*
Standard-grade plastic					
Lots used in production (Exhibit 7.4)	1,575	1,550	2,100	2,790	
+ Desired ending inventory	155	210	279	100	
= Total requirements	1,730	1,760	2,379	2,890	
- Beginning inventory	65	155	210	279	
= Lots to be purchased	1,665	1,605	2,169	2,611	8,050
Purchase price per lot	$600	$600	$600	$600	
Purchases	$999,000	$963,000	$1,301,400	$1,566,600	$4,830,000
Special-grade plastic					
Lots used in production (Exhibit 7.4)	425	410	520	650	
+ Desired ending inventory	41	52	65	25	
= Total requirements	466	462	585	675	
- Beginning inventory	30	41	52	65	
= Lots to be purchased	436	421	533	610	2,000
Purchase price per lot	$1,000	$1,000	$1,000	$1,000	
Purchases	$436,000	$421,000	$533,000	$610,000	$2,000,000
Dyes	*See Check It! Exercise #5 Below*				
Purchases	$1,035,500	$1,013,000	$1,351,000	$1,610,500	$5,010,000
Packing boxes (Detailed calculations not shown)					
Purchases	$838,400	$810,400	$1,080,800	$1,288,400	$4,018,000
Total Purchases	$3,308,900	$3,207,400	$4,266,200	$5,075,500	$15,858,000

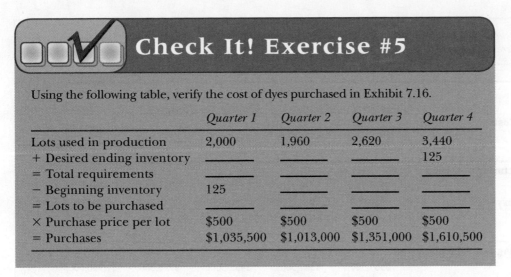

Check It! Exercise #5

Using the following table, verify the cost of dyes purchased in Exhibit 7.16.

	Quarter 1	Quarter 2	Quarter 3	Quarter 4
Lots used in production	2,000	1,960	2,620	3,440
+ Desired ending inventory	_____	_____	_____	125
= Total requirements	_____	_____	_____	_____
− Beginning inventory	125	_____	_____	_____
= Lots to be purchased	_____	_____	_____	_____
× Purchase price per lot	$500	$500	$500	$500
= Purchases	$1,035,500	$1,013,000	$1,351,000	$1,610,500

Solution at end of chapter.

With the information in Exhibit 7.16 and Amarillo's payment policy, we can plan the cash outflow for materials purchases during the coming year. Exhibit 7.17 presents the details.

As an example, Amarillo's cash outflows for purchases in the third quarter total $3,630,920, which is the sum of payments for second-quarter purchases ($3,207,400 × 0.60 = $1,924,440) and payments for third-quarter purchases ($4,266,200 × 0.40 = $1,706,480).

Labor Costs

Panel A of Exhibit 7.18 projects Amarillo's cash outflows for direct labor costs. We obtain this information directly from Exhibit 7.6, Amarillo's direct labor budget. Notice that the cash outflow for labor depends on production volume and not on sales volume. Production employees expect payment when they render service, which occurs when they make the product.

Manufacturing Overhead

Panel B of Exhibit 7.18 projects cash outflows for manufacturing overhead costs. Referring to Exhibit 7.7 (the manufacturing overhead cost budget), we see that the expense from depreciating equipment, $1,450,000, is a substantial part of the fixed manufacturing overhead cost of $5,250,000. We exclude this noncash item when estimating the cash outflows associated with manufacturing overhead.

Exhibit 7.17 *Amarillo Toys: Cash Outflow for Purchases*

	Quarter				
	Quarter 1	Quarter 2	Quarter 3	Quarter 4	Total
Last year's purchases	$2,130,000				$2,130,000
Quarter 1 purchases	1,323,560	$1,985,340			3,308,900
Quarter 2 purchases		1,282,960	$1,924,440		3,207,400
Quarter 3 purchases			1,706,480	$2,559,720	4,266,200
Quarter 4 purchases				2,030,200	2,030,200
Total cash outflow	**$3,453,560**	**$3,268,300**	**$3,630,920**	**$4,589,920**	**$14,942,700**

Exhibit 7.18	*Amarillo Toys: Cash Outflows for Labor, Manufacturing Overhead, & Marketing and Administrative Expenses*

	Quarter				
	Quarter 1	*Quarter 2*	*Quarter 3*	*Quarter 4*	*Total*
Panel A: Labor Costs					
Total	$265,500	$259,800	$345,600	$451,800	$1,322,700
Panel B: Manufacturing overhead					
Variable costs	$132,750	$129,900	$172,800	$225,900	$661,350
Fixed costs (cash only)	950,000	950,000	950,000	950,000	3,800,000
Total	$1,082,750	$1,079,900	$1,122,800	$1,175,000	$4,461,350
Panel C: Marketing and Administrative					
Variable costs	$367,500	$367,500	$482,500	$712,500	$1,930,000
Fixed costs (cash only)	1,120,000	1,120,000	1,120,000	1,120,000	4,480,000
Fixed research	250,000	250,000	250,000	250,000	1,000,000
Total	$1,737,500	$1,737,500	$1,852,500	$2,082,500	$7,410,000

CHAPTER CONNECTIONS

Cash outflows for depreciable items such as machinery take place in lump sums, when the firm purchases the equipment. Firms capitalize this cost and depreciate it over the asset's useful life. The cash inflows associated with purchasing equipment (e.g., increases in revenue or reductions in operating costs) accrue over several years, meaning that we need to consider the time value of money in our decision process. In Chapter 12, we discuss how to make these longer-term capital budgeting decisions.

Nonmanufacturing Costs

Panel C of Exhibit 7.18 projects the cash outflow for Amarillo's marketing and administrative costs. Again, we adjust this expense for noncash-related items to forecast the cash outflows. Subtracting the $1,020,000 of depreciation from the fixed cost of $6,500,000 estimated in Exhibit 7.12 means that the associated annual cash outflow for fixed costs is $5,480,000.

NET CASH FLOW FROM OPERATIONS

We are now in a position to estimate Amarillo's net cash flow from operations, as shown in Exhibit 7.19. This exhibit combines the summary information from Exhibit 7.15, Exhibit 7.17, and the three panels in Exhibit 7.18.

Exhibit 7.19 indicates some potential problems. Amarillo has a negative net cash flow from operations in the first and second quarters. Barring a reserve of cash at the beginning of the year or inflows from special items, Amarillo will need to find ways to make up for this expected shortfall.

PULLING IT ALL TOGETHER

We next consider the cash flow for special items and then consolidate all of the information into one overall cash budget.

Exhibit 7.19	Amarillo Toys: Net Cash Flow from Operations

	Quarter			
	Quarter 1	*Quarter 2*	*Quarter 3*	*Quarter 4*
Collections from revenue	$6,387,000	$6,306,500	$7,428,000	10,419,500
- Purchases	3,453,560	3,268,300	3,630,920	4,589,920
- Labor expenses	265,500	259,800	345,600	451,800
- Manufacturing overhead	1,082,750	1,079,900	1,122,800	1,175,900
- Marketing & administrative	1,737,500	1,737,500	1,852,500	2,082,500
Net operating cash flow	($152,310)	($39,000)	$476,180	$2,119,380

Special Items

Thus far, our analysis of Amarillo's cash budget has considered inflows and outflows from operations. This analysis is consistent with the focus of preparing an income statement for the budget period. Firms, however, experience cash inflows and outflows for other reasons.

Purchasing a machine that will last for several years leads to a cash outflow. However, such an outflow would not be included in cash flows from operations. Neither would the payment of dividends or making a scheduled payment on a loan. Special items also can result in cash inflows, as would occur from the sale of a machine, the sale of stock in the capital market, or a loan.

Amarillo does not anticipate any unusual cash inflows in the coming year. However, Amanda informs you that Amarillo expects to pay a dividend of $225,000 during the first quarter. She also notes that replacement of machines and other capacity resources will result in cash expenditures of $50,000, $175,000, $150,000, and $195,000 in quarters 1 through 4, respectively.

Recall that Amarillo's total estimated tax is $469,000. The IRS requires that firms make estimated tax payments each quarter. Accordingly, Amanda wants to budget for estimated income tax payments of $118,000 each quarter.

Financing Needs

Exhibit 7.20 presents Amarillo's cash budget for the coming year.

Exhibit 7.20	Amarillo Toys: Summary Cash Budget

	Quarter			
	Quarter 1	*Quarter 2*	*Quarter 3*	*Quarter 4*
Beginning balance	$750,000	$204,690	($127,310)	$80,870
± Net operating cash flow	(152,310)	(39,000)	476,180	2,119,380
± Special items	(275,000)	(175,000)	(150,000)	(195,000)
- Estimated taxes	(118,000)	(118,000)	(118,000)	(118,000)
Ending balance before financing	$204,690	($127,310)	$80,870	$1,887,250

Amanda projects that she will open the coming year with cash of $750,000 because of receipts from fourth-quarter holiday sales for the current year. However, the cash needed in quarter 1 of the coming year will severely deplete this balance. Amarillo has a negative cash flow from operations, as operating outflows exceed collections by $152,310. The payment of dividends of $225,000, the capital expenditures of $50,000 and estimated taxes further increase the outflow by $393,000 to yield a total outflow of $545,310. The ending cash balance is only $204,690.

The cash picture worsens in quarter 2. The beginning cash balance of $204,690 is not enough to overcome the small deficit in operating flows, $39,000, and the other outflows of $293,000. She projects a negative balance of $127,310 at the end of quarter 2. Therefore, Amanda will need to arrange short-term financing. However, the picture for the entire year is positive. Cash inflows exceed cash outflows in quarters 3 and 4, allowing Amarillo to build a comfortable cash balance by the end of the year.

A summary cash budget such as the one in Exhibit 7.20 is invaluable in helping firms anticipate financing needs. Amarillo might wish to arrange now for a line of credit of perhaps $200,000 so that it can tide over its cash shortfall in quarter 2. Alternatively, the firm can explore whether it can accelerate collections or defer purchases. In particular, it seems wise to defer the dividend payment to the fourth quarter, when ample cash is available. As shown in *Check It! Exercise #6*, this change would be enough to remove the need for any loans.

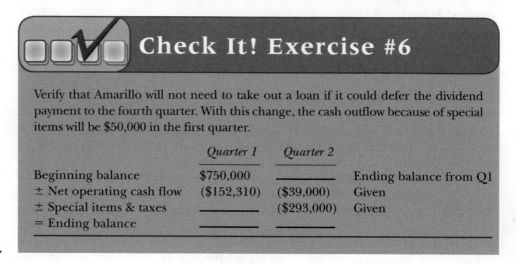

Check It! Exercise #6

Verify that Amarillo will not need to take out a loan if it could defer the dividend payment to the fourth quarter. With this change, the cash outflow because of special items will be $50,000 in the first quarter.

	Quarter 1	Quarter 2	
Beginning balance	$750,000	_____	Ending balance from Q1
± Net operating cash flow	($152,310)	($39,000)	Given
± Special items & taxes	_____	($293,000)	Given
= Ending balance	_____	_____	

Solution at end of chapter.

Like most firms, Amarillo would have a target level for its "inventory" of cash. Suppose Amanda's target level for Amarillo is $100,000. The cash budget in Exhibit 7.20 alerts Amanda that she will have considerable excess cash at the end of the next year. She might, therefore, begin to make plans for investing the excess (over that required to sustain operations) into expanding the business, investing it elsewhere, or returning the capital to shareholders as dividends.

Thus far, we have focused on the somewhat mechanical linkages among individual budgets. However, budgeting is more than an accounting exercise. As we discuss next, managing the process of preparing and administrating budgets is a challenging task.

Factors Influencing the Budgeting Process

LEARNING OBJECTIVE 4

Describe factors that affect the budgeting process.

The quality of the information obtained for budgeting, as well as the way in which budgets are developed and used in organizations, depends on several factors, including organizational structure and management style. We discuss these factors next.

ORGANIZATIONAL STRUCTURE

Firms delegate decisions to individuals likely to have the best information pertinent to that decision. For example, firms typically entrust their marketing personnel with decisions related to developing and maintaining the customer base, advertising, and improving market share. Such delegation of decision rights is sensible because marketing personnel have the best knowledge about market trends and demand conditions. In this way, delegation can help the organization make better and faster decisions.

We use the term **responsibility accounting** when referring to concepts surrounding decentralization—each organizational subunit is a **responsibility center**. Over the years, three common forms of responsibility centers have evolved, each based on the type of decision rights delegated.

1. **Cost centers:** Organizational units that have control over the costs incurred in offering products or services. A production plant is a classic example.
2. **Profit centers:** Organizational units that have control over both revenue and costs. A region or a product line is an example.
3. **Investment centers:** Organizational units that have control over revenues, costs, and long-term investment decisions. Stand-alone divisions are usually evaluated as investment centers.

Exhibit 7.21 presents the organization chart for Amarillo Toys. Referring to this chart, Amanda treats each product division as a profit center and holds each product manager accountable for the profit generated by his or her division. She treats the Production departments within the product divisions as cost centers, responsible for the cost side of the equation. The several sections within each product department are cost centers as well. Amanda uses the organizational structure effectively to co-locate knowledge and decision making.

Decentralization of decision-making authority comes at a cost, however. As you learned earlier, differences between the firm's goals and employees' goals mean that employees may not always take actions that are in the firm's best interests. For example, marketing personnel may use company resources for expensive dinners and fancy hotel accommodations. This conflict leads to the need for performance evaluation and incentives schemes to help align interests.

Exhibit 7.21	*Amarillo's Simplified Organization Chart*

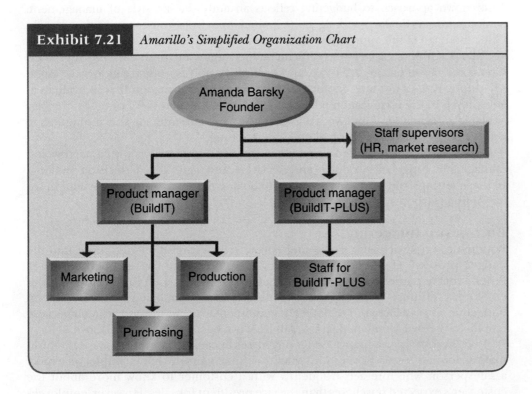

CHAPTER CONNECTIONS

In Chapter 1, we discussed the lack of congruence between organizational and individual goals. This incongruence means that individuals have to be motivated, through incentive schemes and performance evaluation systems, not to use company resources in order to advance their own goals at the expense of organizational goals.

What does all of this mean for budgeting? It means that Amanda will use Amarillo's budgets to motivate, evaluate, and reward her employees. Under responsibility accounting, Amanda will hold managers accountable for the revenue and cost items that they control—the production manager of BuildIT would be held accountable for differences between the actual and budgeted costs of producing BuildIT, but not BuildIT-PLUS. Similarly, product managers would be held accountable for differences between the actual and budgeted profit for their specific products. An organization's structure also dictates who is responsible for preparing certain budgets and the extent of communication and coordination necessary to consolidate the budgets. For example, to obtain the overall revenue budget, Amanda would need to consolidate the individual revenue budgets prepared by the marketing managers of BuildIT and BuildIT-plus.

MANAGEMENT STYLES

In addition to organizational structure, management styles also vary across organizations. Some managers are authoritarian while others, like Amanda, prefer to build consensus. The quality of the information obtained, the cost of budgeting, and the commitment to budgets frequently depend on management style. Two widely used characterizations are **top-down budgeting** and **bottom-up budgeting**.

Top-down Budgeting

A top-down approach to budgeting reflects an authoritarian style of management. Senior managers finalize the budget with limited input from lower organizational levels. One advantage of this approach is that it is not time consuming. A top-down approach also allows senior managers to set difficult budget targets and push the company in new directions. However, the top-down approach does not use organization-wide input. Therefore, it does not take advantage of the superior information that individuals at lower levels in the organization possess, meaning that budgets may not reflect the best available information. Employees also may lack the commitment and motivation to achieve budget goals that they had no input in setting.

Top-down budgeting is most suitable in smaller organizations with a narrow and manageable range of products and services, and centralized decision making. In these settings, top managers are likely to possess detailed enough information for budgeting purposes.

Bottom-up Budgeting

Bottom-up, or participative, budgeting encourages organization-wide input into the budget process. The usefulness of budgeting relies on having good forecasts. Proponents of participative budgeting argue that it makes sense to take advantage of employees' intimate knowledge of operations when formulating plans. Bottom-up budgeting also can increase employees' commitment to achieving budget goals because employees helped set the budgets—goals have not been imposed from above.

A drawback of participative budgeting arises because employees have *better* information about operating conditions than their managers do. For example, we expect a salesperson who interacts frequently with a customer to know more about the customer's expected purchases than the vice president for sales. However, employees have incentives to be strategic when revealing the information that only they know. Why would employees do this when they know that not revealing their information would lead to inaccurate data for planning? Employees do so because a lower performance benchmark is easier to beat. For example, cost-center managers have incentives to overstate costs, or pad the budget, making it easier to beat the budget and creating the appearance of a better than expected performance.

Recognizing these incentives, organizations using participative budgets go through several iterations to obtain as good a forecast as possible. This means that participative budgeting can become a very time-consuming and effort-intensive process, especially in large decentralized organizations.

 **Connecting to Practice**

PARTICIPATIVE BUDGETING IN PORTO ALEGRE

The city of Porto Alegre dramatically changed its budgeting practices in 1998. Instead of bureaucrats developing budgets behind closed doors and obtaining approval in a city council meeting, the city chose to involve the population in the budgeting process. Every March, the public receives preliminary budget documents. Extensive public discussions ensue for 10 months before the city approves the final budget in December.

COMMENTARY: For many municipalities, the budgeting process focuses on "saving money" rather than on what expenditures best serve the community. In contrast, the budgeting process in Porto Alegre begins by asking what services the community wants, with a focus on identifying overall city priorities. While the participative budgeting process is time consuming and expensive, benefits can accrue when everyone has a say in the process.

Source: Based on "The Participative Budget in Porto Alegre: Insights from a Study Visit of a Canadian Councillor," *The Innovation Journal*, updated April 15, 2004.

Our descriptions of top-down and participative budgeting represent two ends of the spectrum. Most firms implement a combination of the two methods where some aspects of the budget are top-down and other aspects are bottom-up. Reconciling the different plan assumptions and targets among the different parts often requires many meetings, reexamination of assumptions, and prioritizing needs. However, these time-consuming steps often pave the way for getting the maximum benefit from the budgeting process.

Budget Goals

The top-down or bottom-up nature of the budgeting process also affects the nature of the plan targets. Top-down budgets often lead to goals that are difficult to achieve. While hard goals may motivate employees to deliver their best, employees may simply give up if they perceive the targets to be unattainable. Bottom-up processes, on the other hand, can generate loose or easy targets because employees have a natural incentive to ensure that the targets used to evaluate their performance are easily achievable. Such loose targets are not likely to motivate employees to do their best.

Popular wisdom characterizes the best targets as "tight but attainable," or targets that employees can achieve if they put their best foot forward. While we cannot provide a precise definition of "tight but attainable," surveys and experimental data suggest that roughly 80% of all employees will meet a tight but attainable target if they deliver their best efforts.

PAST PERFORMANCE AND THE BUDGETING PROCESS

Past performance and past trends can be useful in budgeting because they help future projections. Indeed, many organizations use the budget for the previous year or period as the starting point in the budgeting process. These organizations evaluate the previous year's actual performance relative to the budget and desired changes in performance targets. They then use this information to update budgetary items.

This incremental approach to budgeting is pragmatic. It focuses peoples' attention on making *changes* to the previous year's budget based on actual performance and new information. Incremental changes are easier to justify and communicate; it is human nature to compare performance across people and periods.

While it often makes sense to use prior performance as the starting point for developing budgets, there are at least two concerns with this approach. First, the incremental approach can foster a business-as-usual mentality, and lead organizations to miss the "forest for the trees." It may blind decision makers to the need for drastic changes in business by making them focus narrowly on small changes from the status quo. Second, an incremental approach can lead to *ratcheting*. Organizations have a natural tendency to ratchet up performance expectations, but are less likely to ratchet down. Managers are more likely to approve cost reductions than cost increases and to set higher sales targets than lower sales targets. Anticipating this behavior, a subordinate might deliberately tailor effort levels to meet or just beat the current year's budget. This incentive arises because exceeding today's target substantially might lead to a much higher target for the next year.

SUMMARY

In this chapter, we discussed budgeting, a means for showing the collective impact of decisions on organizational resources and profit. We first articulated the three primary roles—planning, coordination, and control—that budgets serve in organizations. Next, we illustrated the detailed mechanics associated with preparing the master budget and the cash budget. Finally, we discussed how organizational structure, management style, and past performance influence the budgeting process.

Having focused primarily on the planning and coordination roles of budgets in this chapter, we turn our attention to the control role of budgets in the next chapter. Our focus in Chapter 8 is profit variance analysis, a technique used to determine the causes for deviations between budgeted and actual results.

RAPID REVIEW

LEARNING OBJECTIVE 1

Understand the roles budgets serve in organizations.

- A budget is a plan for using limited resources. Budgets serve three major roles: (1) planning, (2) coordination, and (3) control (performance evaluation and feedback).

- Operating budgets reflect the outcomes of numerous short-term decisions designed to achieve long-term goals. Financial budgets quantify the outcomes of operating budgets in summary financial statements.

- As a company grows, it usually transitions from centralized to decentralized decision making. Under decentralization,

departments need to communicate and coordinate among themselves to ensure that all are working toward the same corporate goals. Budgets are a good way of communicating organization-wide plan targets and highlighting the linkages among organizational subunits.

- Budgets provide a benchmark for evaluating actual performance. Without such a benchmark, it is difficult to assess whether employees made the right decisions or to identify problem areas so that the firm can take corrective actions.

- The three roles for budgets complement each other, but also can lead to conflicts during the budgeting process. The central tension in the budgeting process stems from the interplay between the planning and control roles.

Link individual budgets together to form an organization-wide plan.

- The master budget comprises several components. The revenue budget is the starting point and anchors the rest of the budgets. The firm's policy on finished goods helps translate the sales forecast in the revenue budget into the production budget. In turn, organizations use the production budget to estimate materials, labor, and overhead budgets. Firms then consolidate these budgets to obtain the costs of goods manufactured and sold.

- Sales and marketing personnel develop budgets for selling, distribution, and administrative expenses.

- Budgeted financial statements, such as the income statement, consolidate all of the component budgets in the master budget.

- The usual budgeting process is iterative, with planners reworking estimates numerous times throughout the budgeting process. Such intense examination of operating assumptions and estimates adds value to the budgeting process. By scrutinizing all estimates, a well-prepared budget allows the firm to make the best possible decisions and extract the maximum value from its resources.

Construct a cash budget and understand cash management.

- The cash budget helps firms manage their working capital. The cash budget allows companies to assess whether they will have enough money on hand to sustain projected operations. Constructing a cash budget is important because credit sales, on-account purchases, and other accrual accounting practices mean that the flow of cash will not correspond exactly to the flow of revenues and expenses.

- The cash budget comprises three major components: inflows from operations, outflows from operations, and special items.

- Proceeds from sales are the primary cash inflows from operations. Just about every business offers credit terms to its customers—with credit sales, cash comes in *after* the sale occurs. Accordingly, firms need to adjust revenue by their credit policies to compute the expected inflow of cash.

- There are four general types of cash outflows from operations: purchase of materials, payments for labor, payments for manufacturing overhead, and payments for nonmanufacturing costs. Firms forecast cash outflows for materials by examining the purchase budget and adjusting for their payment policy, for labor from the production budget, and for overhead expenses from the individual overhead budgets.

- Cash inflows and outflows due to special items arise from capital budgeting and financing decisions.

Describe factors that affect the budgeting process.

- The budgeting process depends on numerous factors such as organizational structure, management style, and the perceived role budgets play in organizations.

- We use the term *responsibility accounting* when referring to concepts surrounding decentralization and the attendant performance evaluation. Over the years, three common types of responsibility centers have evolved: (1) cost centers, (2) profit centers, and (3) investment centers.

- Most firms use a combination of top-down and bottom-up (or participative) approaches to budgeting. The top-down approach is suitable for small firms with managers intimately involved in day-to-day operations. The participative approach seeks input from all participants, thereby encouraging information transfer and buy-in to budget targets. However, the control role for budgets means that the participative process also encourages employees to set easy targets by understating revenue estimates or padding costs. Regardless of the process, the objective is to set tight but attainable targets to best motivate employees.

- Incremental budgets generate forecasts by adjusting past performance but could lock in current practices.

Appendix
BUDGETING AND COST FLOW ASSUMPTIONS

For simplicity, the chapter illustrates Amarillo's budget under the assumption that prices of input materials do not change during the budgeting period or relative to last year. If this assumption is not true, as is often the case, Amarillo needs to employ a cost flow assumption such as FIFO or LIFO to value the cost of materials used. This change will ripple through to the cost of goods manufactured and cost of goods sold budgets. It also will affect the cash budget.

In the text, we assumed the cost of special-grade plastic to be $1,000 per lot for the entire period. Suppose instead that Amarillo forecasts prices to be $1,050 for quarters 2 and 3 and $1,100 for quarter 4.

Exhibit 7.22 shows how this change would affect the direct materials usage budget (see Exhibit 7.5 for a benchmark comparison). As you see, we now have to distinguish between lots of special-grade plastic because we have inventory layers with differing prices. Notice that the total cost of materials used has increased from $2,005,000 (in Exhibit 7.5) to $2,111,200.

This change in the cost of special-grade plastic in turns affects the variable cost of goods manufactured, as shown in Exhibit 7.23. Notice how the increase affects the cost per lot of BuildIT-PLUS produced. Rather than staying at $2,170 per lot for the entire period, the cost per lot changes gradually from $2,170 to $2,265. In turn, this cost affects the value of inventory of BuildIT-PLUS.

Exhibit 7.24 then shows how the change affects the cost of goods sold for BuildIT-PLUS. For ease of reference, the top of this exhibit shows the physical flow of lots

Exhibit 7.22	*Amarillo Toys: Direct Materials Usage Budget (special-grade plastic only)*

	Quarter				
	Quarter 1	*Quarter 2*	*Quarter 3*	*Quarter 4*	*Total*
Lots to be used in production	425	410	520	650	
(from Exhibit 7.4)					
Lots from beginning inventory	30	41	52	65	
Lots to be used from purchases	395	369	468	585	
Cost per lot of beginning inventory	$1,000	$1,000	$1,050	$1,050	
Cost of materials from inventory	$30,000	$41,000	$54,600	$68,250	
Cost per lot of purchases	$1,000	$1,050	$1,050	$1,100	
Cost of materials purchased	$395,000	$387,450	$491,400	$643,500	
Total Cost	$425,000	$428,450	$546,000	$711,750	$2,111,200

Exhibit 7.23   *Amarillo Toys: Variable Costs of Goods Manufactured (BuildIT-PLUS only)*

	Quarter 1	Quarter 2	Quarter 3	Quarter 4	Total
Lots produced	425	410	520	650	
Plastic: Special-grade	$425,000	$428,450	$546,000	$711,750	$2,111,200
Dyes	212,500	205,000	260,000	325,000	1,002,500
Packaging materials	170,000	164,000	208,000	260,000	802,000
Direct manufacturing labor	76,500	73,800	93,600	117,000	360,900
Variable manufacturing overhead	38,250	36,900	46,800	58,500	180,450
Variable cost of goods manufactured	$922,250	$908,150	$1,154,400	$1,472,250	$4,457,050
Cost per lot of BuildIT-PLUS in ending inventory (= total variable cost of goods manufactured / lots produced)	*$2,170*	*$2,215*	*$2,220*	*$2,265*	

Exhibit 7.24   *Amarillo Toys: Variable Costs of Goods Sold (BuildIT-PLUS only)*

	Quarter 1	Quarter 2	Quarter 3	Quarter 4	Year
Lots in beginning inventory	15	40	50	70	15
+ Lots manufactured	425	410	520	650	2005
- lots in ending inventory	40	50	70	20	20
= Lots sold	400	400	500	700	2000
Value of beginning inventory	$32,550	$86,800	$110,750	$155,400	$32,550
+ Variable cost of goods manufactured	922,250	908,150	1,154,400	1,472,250	4,457,050
- Value of ending inventory	86,800	110,750	155,400	45,300	45,300
= Variable Cost of goods sold	$868,000	$884,200	$1,109,750	$1,582,350	$4,444,300

for BuildIT-PLUS. The value of the beginning inventory is, of course, the value of the ending inventory from the prior quarter (recall that he amount was $2,170 per lot at the end of the prior year). We can then use the data in Exhibit 7.22 to calculate the variable cost of goods sold. Again, notice that the variable cost of goods sold for the year has increased from $4,340,000 in Exhibit 7.11 to $4,444,300.

The above exhibits show how changing prices affect the amounts in the accounting records. Of course, changing prices would also affect the cash budget. Rising prices for inputs such as materials, labor, and overhead mean that we will owe more to our suppliers and employees, increasing the outflow of cash. On the other hand, holding volumes constant, higher prices for Amarillo's products would increase the inflow of cash.

As you can see, a seemingly small change in a budget assumption affects calculations in many subsequent steps. Firms deal with such issues by using linked spreadsheets to prepare their budgets. This approach allows them to change one value and have the effect ripple through the rest of the budget. The approach also helps firms analyze more "what if" scenarios for alternate assumptions about demand, efficiencies, and prices.

CHAPTER CONNECTIONS

Suppose prices were constant for the entire period. Then, we can express the budgeted income statement in the form of a multiproduct CVP equation that we studied in Chapter 5. In particular, the unit contribution margins for BuildIT and BuildIT-PLUS are $1,035 and $2,405, respectively, and total fixed costs are $11,750,000. Thus, we can express the income statement in Exhibit 7.13 as

$$\text{Profit before taxes} = \$1,035 \times BuildIT + \$2,405 \times BuildIT\text{-}PLUS - \$11,750,000$$

This representation is not possible with changing prices because different layers of inventory of the same product would have different contribution margins. While CVP is an aggregate and easy-to-use model, budgeting is a detailed exercise that can account for the complexities of business operations.

ANSWERS TO CHECK IT! EXERCISES

Exercise #1: For quarter 2, desired ending inventory = 500 × 0.10 = 50, and beginning inventory = 40 (the ending inventory from quarter 1); thus, 400 + 50 − 40 = 410. For quarter 3, desired ending inventory = 700 × 0.10 = 70, and beginning inventory = 50 (the ending inventory from quarter 2); thus, 500 + 70 − 50 = 520.

Exercise #2: For quarter 1, the lots to be used in production = 1,575 BuildIT + 425 BuildIT-PLUS = 2,000, and the cost per lot = $500; thus, 2,000 lots × $500 per lot = $1,000,000. For quarter 2, the lots to be used in production = 1,550 BuildIT + 410 BuildIT-PLUS = 1,960, and the cost per lot = $500; thus, 1,960 lots × $500 per lot = $980,000.

Exercise #3: For quarter 1, 425 lots to be produced (see Exhibit 7.4) × 12 labor hours per lot × $15 per labor hour = $76,500. For quarter 2, 410 lots × 12 labor hours per lot × $15 per labor hour = $73,800. For quarter 3, 520 lots × 12 labor hours per lot × $15 per labor hour = $93,600; for quarter 4, 650 lots × 12 labor hours per lot × $15 per labor hour = $117,000.

Exercise #4: $6,270,000 × 0.05 = $313,500; $6,270,000 × 0.35 = $2,194,500; $8,200,000 × 0.60 = $4,920,000.

Exercise #5: For quarter 1, desired ending inventory = 1,960 × 0.10 = 196, and beginning inventory = 125 (from text); thus, [(2,000 + 196 − 125) × $500] = $1,035,500. For quarter 2, [(1,960 + 262 − 196) × $500] = $1,013,000. For quarter 3, [(2,620 + 344 − 262) × $500] = $1,351,000. For quarter 4, [(3,440 + 125 − 344) × $500] = $1,610,500.

Exercise #6: For quarter 1, ending balance = $750,000 − $152,310 − ($50,000+$118,000) = $429,690. For quarter 2, ending balance = $429,690 − $39,000 − (175,000+$118,000) = $97,690.

SELF-STUDY PROBLEM

Jack's, a popular discount store, is formulating its budget for the second quarter of the coming year. Revenue estimates are $1,495,000 for April, $1,430,000 for May, and $1,560,000 for June. While markups on individual items vary, Jack's management estimates that the average selling price exceeds the average purchase cost by 25%. In terms of inventory, Jack's targets to have merchandise on hand equal to 30% of the following month's cost of goods sold.

In addition to the cost of goods purchased, Jack's budgets 80 hours of labor, at a cost of $10 per hour, for every $10,000 of revenue. Like many stores, Jack's tends to adjust the number of checkout clerks, stocking personnel, and other labor based on actual sales, which influences the volume of work needed. Jack's supervisory staff costs $24,500 per month, and rent and utilities amount to $38,000 per month. All other expenses, including $12,000 for depreciation on storage racks, equal $74,000 per month.

a. *Construct Jack's purchases budget for May.*

$100 in purchases generates $125 in sales ($100 × 1.25 = $125). Thus, $100 of revenue requires purchases of $100/1.25 = $80.

Per Jack's inventory policy, the ending inventory for May equals 30% of the cost of goods sold in June. Further, the beginning inventory for May equals 30% of the cost of goods sold in May. (Jack's will use May revenue to generate the ending inventory for April, which, in turn, becomes the beginning inventory for May.) With this information, we use the inventory equation to compute Jack's budgeted purchases for May.

Cost of goods sold in May $1,430,000/1.25	$1,144,000
+ Desired ending inventory ($1,560,000/1.25) × 0.30	374,400
− Beginning inventory ($1,430,000/1.25) × 0.30	343,200
= **Goods to be purchased**	$1,175,200

b. *Construct Jack's direct labor budget for May.*

Jack's direct labor budget follows directly from its revenue budget. Jack's budgets 80 hours of labor per $10,000 of revenue and plans to pay $10 per labor hour. Given the revenue information for May, we have:

Labor hours required ($1,430,000/10,000) × 80	11,440
Labor cost per hour	$10
Direct labor cost (11,440 × $10)	$114,400

c. *Construct Jack's budgeted income statement for May.*

Exhibit 7.25 provides the required statement.

Exhibit 7.25	*Jack's: Budgeted Income Statement for May*

	Detail	Amount
Revenue	Given	$1,430,000
Variable costs		
Cost of goods sold	Revenue/1.25	1,144,000
Hourly labor	See part [b]	114,400
Contribution Margin		$171,600
Fixed costs		
Supervisory salaries	Given	$24,500
Rent and utilities	Given	38,000
Other expenses	Given	74,000
Profit before Taxes		$35,100

Jack's appears to be in good financial condition. Its profit before taxes is $35,100, or 2.45% of revenue. The markup on purchases appears to be in line with industry averages.

Not surprisingly, employees are the single largest operating expense other than cost of goods sold. "Other expenses" amount to $74,000, and no detail is provided. Jack's might benefit from a thorough examination of the costs in this classification and determine if they yield commensurate benefits.

d. *Construct Jack's cash budget for May. Assume that Jack's collects 90% of its revenue in the month of sale and the remainder in the following month. Jack's pays for 70% of its purchases in the month of purchase and the remainder in the following month. Jack's also expects to buy and pay for some new display units, costing $24,000, in May. Finally, Jacks expects to begin May with a cash balance of $25,000.*

Exhibit 7.26 provides Jack's cash budget for May.

Exhibit 7.26   *Jack's: Cash Budget for May*

	Amount	Amount	Detail
Beginning balance		$25,000	
+ Cash inflows from operations			
Collections – April Sales	149,500		10% of April sales
Collections – May sales	1,287,000	1,436,500	90% of May sales
– Cash outflows from operations			
Purchases – April	-354,120		30% of April purchases*
Purchases – May	-822,640		70% of May purchases
Hourly labor	-114,400		See part [b]
Supervisory salaries	-24,500		Given
Rent and utilities	-38,000		Given
Other expenses	-62,000	-1,415,660	$74,000 – $12,000 in
+/- Special items			
Display units		-24,000	For display units
Ending balance		**$21,840**	

* April purchases = $1,196,000 cost of goods sold in April + $343,200 desired ending inventory – $358,800 beginning inventory = $1,180,400.

We compute cash inflow from operations by adjusting the revenue estimates for the pattern of collections. Likewise, we calculate the cash flow from purchasing by applying the payment policies to the monthly purchases. We estimate all other expenses directly, with the only adjustment for depreciation, which is a noncash expense.

Our calculations reveal that Jack's expects to end May with a cash balance of $21,840. If management of Jack's believes that this is a sufficient beginning balance for June, then the company does not need to undertake any borrowing activities. If, however, the company has a policy of maintaining a minimum balance of, say, $25,000, then Jack's will have to find some short-term financing.

GLOSSARY

Bottom-up budgeting A process by which lower-level employees actively participate in setting budgets.

Budget A plan for using limited resources.

Cash budget A budget that focuses on the inflow and outflow of cash.

Centralized decision making An organizational setting where a few top managers make all the decisions.

Cost center Organizational unit that has control over and is accountable for costs incurred in offering products or services.

Decentralized decision making An organizational setting where decision-making authority is dispersed throughout the firm.

Financial budgets Budgets quantifying the outcomes of operating budgets in summary financial statements.

Investment center Organizational unit that has control over and is accountable for revenues, costs, and long-term investment decisions.

Master budget Comprehensive set of operating and financial budgets.

Operating budgets Budgets reflecting the collective expression of numerous short-term decisions that conform to the direction set by long-term plans.

Profit center Organizational unit that has control over and is accountable for both revenues and costs.

Responsibility accounting Set of concepts pertaining to decision rights and performance evaluation in decentralized organizations.

Responsibility center An organizational subunit.

Top-down budgeting A process by which top management sets the budgets.

REVIEW QUESTIONS

7.1 LO1. What is a budget?

7.2 LO1. What are the three reasons firms use budgets?

7.3 LO1. What are: (a) an operating budget, (b) a financial budget?

7.4 LO2. What is the natural starting point for the budgeting process? Why?

7.5 LO2. What budget typically is prepared immediately after the revenue budget?

7.6 LO2. What budgets follow from the production budget?

7.7 LO2. What equation do firms use to calculate the cost of goods sold budget?

7.8 LO3. Why is the cash budget important?

7.9 LO3. What are the three main components of the cash budget?

7.10 LO3. Why is a firm's credit policy important for translating the revenue budget into the budgeted inflows of cash?

7.11 LO3. What are the four types of cash outflows from operations?

7.12 LO3. What are some special items that might affect a firm's cash budget?

7.13 LO4. What is a responsibility center? What are the three types of responsibility centers?

7.14 LO4. What is the difference between top-down budgeting and bottom-up budgeting?

7.15 LO4. What are the advantages of using last year's data as the starting point for this year's budget?

DISCUSSION QUESTIONS

7.16 LO1. The owner of a small clothing store says, "I run a small operation. I know my employees well. They are very loyal to me. I also know my business well. I know what to do to generate revenues and how to control costs. I don't need formal budgets." Do you agree with this statement? Why or why not?

7.17 LO1. "In large organizations, formal budgets are perhaps the only effective means for organization-wide communication." Comment on this statement.

7.18 LO1. Actual events rarely unfold exactly as expected, particularly in complex scenarios. Thus, budget assumptions are likely to be proven wrong as actual events unfold. What then is the value of a budget?

7.19 LO1. Firms use budgets as a benchmark for performance evaluation, especially in large organizations. Since close supervision may not be possible in such organizations, is this role of budgets simply a substitute for close supervision? Comment.

7.20 LO2. "Budgets are only as good as the forecasts upon which they are based." In some industries, it is very difficult to forecast demand accurately, while in other industries demand conditions are relatively stable. Discuss the role of budgeting in these two settings.

7.21 LO2. Sales forecasts and overhead estimates are the two activities that consume the most time during the budgeting process. Discuss why this is the case.

7.22 LO2. "Sales and production budgets are the same in firms that follow a just-in-time inventory policy." Is this assertion correct? Comment on whether the materials usage budget would be the same as the materials purchase budget for JIT firms.

7.23 LO2. The text portrays the budgeting process as a linear progression from one budget to another. In practice, budgets are rarely linear and are much more recursive. What are the costs and benefits of going through several iterations before finalizing a budget?

7.24 LO3. What are the similarities and differences between the cash budget as described in the text and the cash flow statement that we find in firms' financial reports?

7.25 LO1, LO2, LO3. Do you believe that budgets lead organizations to place too much emphasis on financial performance and not enough emphasis on the qualitative and nonfinancial aspects of performance? Why or why not?

7.26 LO4. Some experts argue that budgets have to be "loose" and "flexible" for companies that are in their growth phase. Other experts believe that good planning and control through well-formulated budgets can never hurt. Which line of reasoning do you agree with? Are these two arguments necessarily inconsistent?

7.27 LO4. Participative, or bottom-up, budgeting is a time-consuming process in large organizations. Yet, it is perhaps most beneficial to these companies. Discuss the advantages and disadvantages of participative budgeting in large organizations.

7.28 LO4. When would a top-down budgeting be preferable to bottom-up or participative budgeting?

7.29 LO4 (Advanced). Investigate line-item budgeting. Why is line-item budgeting more prevalent in government and nonprofit organizations than it is in commercial companies? Explain.

7.30 LO4. (Advanced) A criticism of budget lapsing is that it forces decision makers to find ways to spend the money allocated to them in the budget, even when there is no real need. Do you agree with this criticism? Can you think of situations where budget lapsing would actually be beneficial to an organization?

EXERCISES

7.31 Revenue budget (LO2). Premium Windows makes one type of standard windows for residential buildings. Premium desires to end March with 2,500 windows in stock. Premium's inventory on March 1 is 1,750 windows, and its budgeted production for the month is 8,000 windows. Each window sells for $60.

Required:

Prepare Premium's revenue budget for March.

7.32 Revenue budget, price-sales trade-off (LO2). Premium Windows makes one type of standard windows for residential buildings. Premium believes that if it prices each window at $60, then it will sell 2,500 windows in January and that sales will increase by 100 units a month through August. Sales would then decrease at the rate of 150 units per month through December. However, if Premium prices each window at $57, then sales for January would be 2,600 units. Sales would increase at the rate of 125 per units per month through August and then decrease at the rate of 150 units per month through December.

Required:

a. Which price should Premium choose, $57 or $60, to maximize its revenues for the year?

b. What other factors should Premium consider before making its pricing decision?

7.33 Revenue and production budgets (LO2). The following table presents select information for three of Premium Windows' monthly budgets for the coming year.

Number of Windows	April	September	December
Desired ending inventory	1,800	2,000	?
Beginning inventory	1,200	?	2,200
Budgeted sales	10,000	15,000	20,000
Budgeted production	?	14,000	21,000

Required:

Fill in the missing information, computing the value of each "?."

7.34 Revenue and production budgets, inventory policy (LO2). The following table presents select information for three of Premium Windows' monthly budgets for the coming year. Premium's inventory policy is to have ending inventory equal to 15% of next month's sales.

Number of Windows	February	March	April
Desired ending inventory	?		3,000
Beginning inventory	1,500	?	?
Budgeted sales	10,000	15,000	20,000
Budgeted production	?	?	?

Required:

Fill in the missing information, computing the value of each "?."

7.35 Revenue budget, income statement, Hercules (LO2). Tom and Lynda own Hercules Health Club. They provide the following information regarding expected membership. You also know that the monthly fee for an individual membership is $100 and the fee for a family membership is $160. Variable costs are $35 and $60, respectively, for the individual and family membership. Fixed costs amount to $40,000 per month.

Month	Individual Memberships	Family Memberships
August	700	300
September	690	300
October	680	295
November	675	290

Required:

a. Prepare a revenue budget and an income statement for August-November.

b. Tom and Lynda are concerned about the downward trend in memberships. They propose to run an advertising campaign that costs $10,000. If they run the ads in September, they expect to obtain 10 more individual members and 5 additional family memberships every month. Revise the budget in part (a) for this action.

c. Should Tom and Lynda run the ad campaign? Be specific about what assumptions, if any, you may need before you can make such a recommendation.

7.36 Purchases and overhead, Hercules (LO2). Tom and Lynda own Hercules Health Club. They provide the following information regarding their expected inventories of supplies and other materials.

Month	Individual Memberships (number)	Family Memberships (number)	Beginning Inventory $
August	700	300	$5,000
September	690	300	$5,000
October	680	295	$4,500
November	675	290	$4,500

Tom and Lynda also inform you that each individual member consumes $10 worth of supplies ($22 per family) each month.

Required:

Calculate the amount of supplies purchased each month for August through October.

7.37 Cash budget, Hercules (LO3). Tom and Lynda own Hercules Health Club. They provide the following information regarding their expected inventories of supplies and other materials.

Month	Individual Memberships (number)	Family Memberships (number)	Purchases ($)
August	700	300	$13,600
September	690	300	$13,000
October	680	295	$13,500

Tom and Lynda also inform you that the monthly individual membership fee is $100 and the family fee is $160. Hercules offers a 10% discount if a member pays the entire year's fee in a lump sum. About 180 individuals and 60 families take this offer. The number up for renewal is spread evenly through the year.

Hercules pays for 60% of its purchases during the month of the purchase, and the remainder the next month. Other variable costs (paid in cash) amount to $25 per month for individuals and $45 per month for families. Hercules also incurs $41,000 (including $12,500 in depreciation) toward fixed costs each month. Finally, Tom and Lynda inform you that they have to pay $20,000 toward the purchase of new equipment in September, and take out $15,000 each month as their profit. (They do not draw a salary.)

Hercules began August with a cash balance of $6,000.

Required:

Prepare a cash budget for September.

7.38 Production budget, budget revision (LO2). At the beginning of the year, Gantz Company budgeted to have an inventory of 22,000 units at the end of April. Budgeted production for April was 120,000 units, and budgeted inventory at the beginning of April was

15,000 units. A few days before the end of March, the company's marketing executive cut the sales forecast for both April and May by 10 percent. In addition to affecting April and May sales, this revision means that the targeted ending inventory for April needs to be revised down by 10 percent. Naturally, April's production budget will also be affected. However, Gantz still expects to begin April with 15,000 units because it's too late in the month to alter March production.

Required:

Calculate Gantz's revised production budget for April.

 7.39 Revenue and production budgets, multiple products (LO2). Bosworth Boxes makes cardboard boxes in three sizes—small, medium, and large. Betty Bosworth currently is working on the monthly budgets for March and April and provides you with the following information:

	Box Type		
	Small	*Medium*	*Large*
Budgeted sales for March	10,000	25,000	15,000
Budgeted sales for April	15,000	30,000	20,000
Budgeted sales for May	20,000	40,000	25,000
Budgeted price per unit	$2.75	$3.75	$5.00

Desired ending inventory for each type of box = 20% of the following month's sales.

Required:

Prepare Bosworth Boxes' revenue and production budgets for March and April.

 7.40 Direct materials usage and purchase budgets (LO2, LO3, Appendix). Bosworth Boxes makes cardboard boxes. For March and April, Bosworth expects to produce 12,000 and 15,800 boxes, respectively.

The main material input for Bosworth's boxes is cardboard. To make one box, Bosworth budgets to use 12 linear feet of 2-foot-wide cardboard at a cost of $0.75 per linear foot. Further, while Bosworth expects to begin March with 50,000 linear feet of 2-foot-wide cardboard, its direct materials inventory policy is to have 40 percent of the next month's total material needs in ending inventory.

Required:

a. Prepare Bosworth's cardboard purchases budget for March.

b. Prepare Bosworth's cardboard usage budget for March. Assume that Bosworth's beginning inventory of cardboard is also valued at $0.75 per linear foot and that Bosworth uses the First-In-First-Out (FIFO) inventory method.

c. (Appendix) Suppose Bosworth values its beginning inventory of cardboard at $0.70 per linear foot, but still expects to pay $0.75 per linear foot for March purchases. Assuming Bosworth uses a FIFO cost flow assumption, what is Bosworth's cardboard usage budget for March?

7.41 Cash inflows from operations, sales (LO3). Bruce Jaffee is a wholesaler of spices, importing them from countries such as Thailand, India, and Sri Lanka. Bruce repackages the spices and sells them to organic food stores and gourmet groceries. Bruce sells most of his products on credit; he estimates that he collects 30% of his revenues in the month of sale, 40% in the following month, 25% two months after the sale, and the remaining 5% the month thereafter.

Bruce provides you with the following budgeted revenue information for the coming five months:

	Month				
	August	*September*	*October*	*November*	*December*
Revenues	$120,000	$135,000	$140,000	$135,000	$150,000

Required:

Compute Bruce's budgeted cash inflows for November and December.

7.42 Cash outflows from operations, purchases (LO3). Bruce Jaffee, the wholesaler of spices from the previous exercise, purchases most of his products on credit; he estimates that he pays 60% of his accounts payable in the month of purchase, 30% in the month following purchase, and 10% in the month thereafter.

Bruce provides you with the following information about his expected purchases for the next five months:

	Month				
	August	*September*	*October*	*November*	*December*
Purchases	$90,000	$95,000	$120,000	$110,000	$120,000

Required:

Compute Bruce's budgeted cash outflows for October, November, and December.

7.43 Summary cash Budget, borrowing/lending (LO3). The following cash budget for the fourth quarter of the current year has some missing information. The company has a policy of starting each month with a minimum cash balance of $9,500. Any necessary short-term borrowing is done using the firm's line of credit, which is $40,000. The firm prefers to pay off its loans as quickly as possible, without violating its minimum cash policy.

Cash Budget—Fourth Quarter			
	October	*November*	*December*
Beginning cash balance	$9,500	$9,500	$9,500
Cash receipts	14,100	?	?
Total cash available	?	27,400	27,900
Cash disbursements			
Payments for materials	4,400	?	4,100
Payments for direct labor	8,450	7,250	?
Payments for overhead	?	5,920	5,720
Total payments	18,300	16,800	17,030
Balance prior to financing	?	?	?
Minimum cash balance	9,500	9,500	9,500
Financing			
Borrowing/repayment	?	?	?
Ending cash balance with loans & repayments	?	?	?

Required:

Fill in the missing information, computing the value of each "?." Assume the firm began October with no loans.

7.44 Cash budget (LO3). Gilbert Ortega operates a small boutique in Scottsdale, Arizona that sells Kachina dolls. Gilbert expects to generate revenues of $40,000, $50,000, and $60,000 during October, November, and December, respectively. Gilbert's cost of goods sold average 60 percent of revenues, and his budgeted marketing and administrative costs are $4,000, $6,000, and $5,000 for October, November, and December, respectively.

Gilbert expects to receive 70% of his revenues in cash during the month of sale and 30% in the following month. Gilbert receives his dolls on consignment, with the purchase price being due at the time of sale. Thus, Gilbert's cash outflow for goods sold equals his cost of goods sold. Finally, Gilbert pays for all marketing and administrative expenses in cash as they are incurred.

Required:

Prepare Gilbert's cash budget for November and December. Assume that Gilbert expects to have $16,000 in cash on November 1.

7.45 Cash receipts and disbursements, integration with the balance sheet (LO4, Advanced). Kris VanKemp is a wholesaler of flowers, shipping them throughout the Pacific Northwest. Kris expects her April 1 balances in accounts receivable and accounts payable to be $25,000 and $6,000, respectively.

Kris also informs you that she expects sales of $50,000, $40,000, and $46,000 during the months of March, April, and May, respectively. Kris collects 50% of her sales in cash during the month of sale and the remaining 50% in the following month.

Kris purchases all of her flowers from local growers. She pays for 80% of her purchases in the same month and the remaining 20% in the following month. Kris expects her purchases to be $30,000, $32,000, and $40,000 for March, April, and May, respectively.

Required:

a. Compute Kris's expected balance for accounts receivable as of May 31.

b. Compute Kris's expected balance for accounts payable as of May 31.

7.46 Budget discretion, ethics (LO4). Wilma Turner, the budget manager at Norton Company, is working on the budget for the forthcoming year. In discussions with Scott Ford, the marketing manager, Wilma discovers that Scott's projections are 15 to 20% below what he truly believes is feasible. "We always give ourselves some breathing room," Scott says, "As you know, Roy (the company's founder) is fanatical about making budget and is not shy about showing his feelings in the bonus check. Plus, everyone around here builds a little cushion; you should too, in your department's budget."

Wilma finds Scott's assessment accurate. When she pushes, Jake Lewis, the production manager, admits to inflating costs by 5% or more. He sees his actions as a valid hedge against unpredictable price swings and efficiency losses. Moreover, he uses the extra allowance for needed repairs and other ancillary costs. "Roy would never spend a dime on something that does not go into the product," Jake says, "but I need to keep the plant going and this is a way of getting some discretionary funds."

Required:

What should Wilma do?

7.47 Budget rigidity (LO4). "Our biggest customer had a fire in their plant, torpedoing all of our sales projections. We will be lucky if we can come in at 80% of budget. Yet, Carrie refuses to adjust the budget, destroying my bonus and the sales morale. I pleaded with Carrie to give a little but she flat out refused and even threatened to replace me!" This outburst, from Jim Benjamin, neatly summarizes the current dispute at Simon and Company. Carrie Simon, the founder's granddaughter, has been managing the business for over 15 years. Her hard-nosed approaches to budget targets and aggressive tactics have earned her the nickname "Cutthroat Carrie."

When you approach Carrie, she readily admits that the current targets are now unrealistic. Yet she says that making one revision will start the firm down a slippery slope where there is no accountability for estimates.

Required:

Evaluate the costs and benefits of revising budget targets.

PROBLEMS

7.48 Production budget and capacity (LO2). BlueSteel makes premium quality filing cabinets. The firm has one factory with a production capacity of 10,000 cabinets per month.

BlueSteel provides you with the following budgeted sales information in units by quarter. Furthermore, the firm expects to realize the same level of sales for each of the three months within each quarter.

	Quarter 1	*Quarter 2*	*Quarter 3*	*Quarter 4*
Sales for quarter	24,000	28,500	33,000	27,000
Sales per month	8,000	9,500	11,000	9,000

Required:

a. On an annual basis, does BlueSteel have enough production capacity to meet its sales forecast?

b. Assume that BlueSteel begins the first quarter with zero inventory. Formulate a production budget consistent with its sales forecast.

c. The firm's CEO is contemplating going to a "no inventory" policy because she is convinced that inventory just ties up valuable capital. Comment on the effect of this strategy on BlueSteel's ability to meet next year's anticipated sales.

d. What conclusions do you draw about the relation between capacity and inventory?

7.49 Cash budget, bad debts, credit sales (LO3). Mina Pizzini owns Mina's Miniatures, a store that deals in "life's little things." Items sold range from Bonsai trees to miniature paintings to doll furniture. Mina believes that 30% of any month's sales are for cash, with the remaining

70% being on credit. Of the credit sales, Mini collects 40% during the month after the sale, and 50% in two months. After much effort, Mini recovers a further 8% of credit sales three months after the sale occurs. She writes off 2% of credit sales as uncollectible.

Mina provides you with the following information regarding budgeted sales for the next six months:

			Month			
	July	August	September	October	November	December
Sales	$85,000	$95,000	$125,000	$164,000	$175,000	$190,000

Required:

Determine Mina's expected cash collections, by month, for October through December.

7.50 Cash budget, prepaid purchases (LO3). Ashwini Gupta owns a retail store that sells hand-made leather goods from around the world. Unfortunately, overseas suppliers are less than trusting when dealing with small clients, as it is common for people not to pay their bills. Thus, most suppliers require a letter of credit before they ship any items. Ashwini deals with a local bank for such letters of credit. The bank will put a hold on Ashwini's account for the amount guaranteed. The actual payment, however, will take place only after the supplier produces evidence of having shipped the items.

Ashwini expects to receive $150,000 worth of items in May, $185,000 worth of items in June, and $210,000 worth of items in July. Ashwini usually commits to a letter of credit a month before she receives the items.

Required:

What should Ashwini budget as "cash outflow for purchases" for April, May, and June?

7.51 Cash budget and income statement (LO2, LO3). Gary Siegel recently opened a steel warehouse. Gary buys his steel only after he receives a firm order from a customer; thus, Gary only buys what he sells in a particular month. Nevertheless, Gary projects that he will experience some cash flow problems toward the end of the year. While Gary is confident about the fundamentals of his business, he is wondering if he is perhaps too generous with his credit terms to customers.

Gary informs you that he currently collects 30% of revenues in the month after sale and the remaining 70% two months following the sale. Gary pays for 50% of his purchases in the month of purchase and 50% in the following month. His monthly fixed costs amount to $95,000, including $10,000 in noncash expenses. Finally, Gary marks up his products by 25% over the purchase price.

Gary provides the following information regarding projected sales for the next five months.

August	September	October	November	December
$468,750	$468,750	$475,000	$525,000	$562,500

Required:

a. Construct Gary's budgeted contribution margin income statement for October, November, and December.

b. Construct Gary's cash budget for October, November, and December. Assume that, because of a special payment to be made at the end of the third quarter, Gary plans to begin October with $5,000 in cash on hand.

c. Explain why Gary is facing a cash flow problem even though his business is profitable. Identify two things that Gary could do to alleviate the anticipated cash crunch.

7.52 Cost of goods manufactured and cost of goods sold budgets (LO2). Kincaid Casting Works provides you with the following information from the company's monthly budgets for May and June:

	May	June
Beginning work-in-process inventory	$180,000	?
Ending work-in-process inventory	?	?
Direct materials usage	$250,000	$280,000
Direct labor	$265,500	$345,000
Variable overhead	$125,000	$145,000
Variable cost of goods manufactured	$545,000	$574,000
Beginning finished good inventory	$220,000	?
Ending finished goods inventory	?	$225,000
Variable cost of goods sold	$615,000	?

Required:

Fill in the missing information, computing the value of each "?."

7.53 Budgeted income statement (LO2). Naomi Soderstrom sells over-boots for use in wintry conditions. Naomi's products, worn over shoes, provide traction on ice and packed snow, helping prevent falls. Naomi's income for her most recent year of operations is as follows:

Revenues (120,000 units × $20)		$2,400,000
Variable costs		
Direct materials	$480,000	
Direct labor	720,000	
Selling and administration	120,000	$1,320,000
Contribution margin		$1,080,000
Fixed costs		
Manufacturing	$540,000	
Marketing and sales	120,000	
General administration	228,000	888,000
Profit before taxes		$192,000

Naomi believes that while the cost of direct materials and direct labor varies with the number of units, the cost of variable selling and administration expenses are proportional to revenues.

Not satisfied with her current profit and 8 percent return on sales ($192,000/ $2,400,000), Naomi wants to improve profits in the coming year. She is considering changing her selling price. If Naomi increases her selling price to $22 per unit, then she expects sales to stay at 120,000 units in the coming year. However, if she reduces her selling price to $19 per unit, then she expects sales to increase to 175,000 units.

Regardless of her pricing strategy, Naomi expects next year's costs to be as follows:

- Direct material costs to increase by 10 percent.
- Direct labor costs to increase by 5 percent.
- Variable selling and administration costs to stay the same as a fraction of each sales dollar.
- Total fixed costs to stay the same at $888,000.

Required:

Prepare a budgeted income statement for each of Naomi's two pricing choices. What price should Naomi choose?

7.54 Top-down versus bottom-up budgeting (LO4). "Nobody in my firm is held to targets they don't accept. But, once they sign off, I expect them to deliver." These statements summarize Tim West's budgeting philosophy. Tim, who owns and operates a medium-sized firm that makes road sealant, is a no-nonsense person with little formal education beyond high school. He attributes his financial success to hard work, risk-taking, and his ability to get the best from his employees.

"Sure, we have a participative budget!" says Melanie Leichty, Tim's plant manager. In a wry tone, she adds, "Including Tim, we have 10 in our management team. In this team, we all get one vote. However, as owner, Tim gets 11 votes! And, of course, we rely on a majority vote when making decisions!"

Digging deeper into the budgeting process for sales, you discover the following steps:

- Each of the five salespersons prepares a customer-by-customer listing of sales for the past three years. Based on this information and their knowledge about customer needs, they project an overall sales goal for each customer, by month.
- The sales manager aggregates all of this information and modifies it a bit. In particular, the sales manager looks at differences in sales growth and corrects low projections to be in line with the average. He, of course, discusses this correction with the concerned salesperson. The usual tactic is to hold up the other forecasts and attribute lack of sales growth to lower talent.
- The sales manager then meets with Tim. By this time, Tim has backed out of his sales expectations for next year based on his desired profit. He discusses the overall target with the sales manager. The usual result is a 3 to 7% increase in projected sales, which the sales manager evenly allocates among the five salespersons.

- Of course, Tim insists that the sales manager discuss and negotiate any change with the sales force. Drawing on his experience as a successful salesperson who has never missed a target, Tim believes that the adjustment is to correct for padding by the sales manager. He just believes that with suitable logic and persuasion, he could set high but achievable targets for his sales team.

Required:

Comment on the participative nature of the sales budgeting process at Tim's firm. What kinds of positive and negative behaviors do such processes encourage?

7.55 **Flexible budgeting, subjective nature of the budgeting Process (LO2, LO4, Advanced).** Essex Fuel Pumps sells its product directly to auto manufacturers as well as in the replacement market. The owner and CEO of the company, Claire Balderson, believes in keeping tight control over operations through careful planning. Over time, Claire and her accountants have followed a practice of starting the annual budgeting process around December 15 of every year for the following calendar year. They first come up with an initial draft of the budget based on marketing forecasts and actual results from the prior three years. Formulating this initial draft is a four-step process.

- The marketing manager projects the demand in units. The projected selling price per unit is the average price over the last three years.
- The accountant classifies all expenses into fixed and variable categories. The accountant makes this classification by examining the cost per unit for manufacturing expenses and the cost per sales dollar for selling, general, and administrative expenses. If the cost per unit or sales dollar remains relatively stable as activity volume changes, then the expense is classified as variable. However, if the cost per unit or sales dollar decreases substantially as activity volume increases, then the expense is classified as fixed.
- For each expense classified as fixed, the accountant uses the average expense over the last three years as the estimate for the initial budget.
- For expenses classified as variable, the accountant calculates the average amount per unit (for manufacturing expenses) or the average amount per sales dollar (for selling, general, and administrative expenses) for each year and then averages these amounts over the three years. The accountant then uses these estimates to project variable costs for the coming year.

It is now time to initiate the 2009 budget. Essex's operating results for the last three years were as follows (even though the 2008 year has not ended yet, only two weeks remain and therefore the operating results for the year are available):

	2006	2007	2008
Sales in units	80,000	110,000	95,000
Revenues	$4,480,000	$6,160,000	$5,320,000
Direct materials	$816,000	$1,111,000	$950,000
Direct labor	1,140,000	1,595,000	1,401,250
Plant maintenance	720,000	742,500	736,500
Plant depreciation	420,000	440,000	427,500
Indirect labor	163,200	227,700	193,800
Engineering design	220,000	230,000	240,000
Utilities	81,600	113,300	95,950
Plant administration	325,000	312,500	310,000
Marketing administration	180,000	185,000	190,000
Sales force commissions	134,400	184,800	159,600
Plant supervision	275,000	280,000	300,000

The marketing manager is very optimistic about 2009, and projects the demand for 2009 to be 150,000 fuel pumps. Obviously pleased, Claire sets about the task of preparing the annual budget for the coming year.

Required:

a. Classify each of Essex's expenses as being a (1) variable manufacturing cost; (2) variable selling cost; (3) fixed manufacturing cost; or (4) fixed selling cost.

b. Prepare estimates for revenues and each cost category for 2009. Using these estimates, prepare Essex's budgeted income statement for 2009.

	2006	2007	2008
Units	80,000	110,000	95,000
Revenues	$4,480,000	$6,160,000	$5,320,000
Unit price	*$56.00*	*$56.00*	*$56.00*
Direct materials	$816,000	$1,111,000	$950,000
Direct labor	1,140,000	1,595,000	1,401,250
Indirect labor	163,200	227,700	193,800
Utilities	81,600	113,300	95,950
Total	$1,956,245	$3,047,000	$2,641,000
Cost per unit	*$27.51*	*$27.70*	*$27.80*
Sales force commissions	$134,400	$184,800	$159,600
Cost per sales $	*$0.03*	*$0.03*	*$0.03*
Plant maintenance	$720,000	$742,500	$736,500
Plant depreciation	420,000	440,000	427,500
Engineering design	220,000	230,000	240,000
Plant administration	325,000	312,500	310,000
Marketing administration	180,000	185,000	190,000
Plant supervision	275,000	280,000	300,000
Total fixed costs	*$2,140,000*	*$2,190,000*	*$2,204,000*

c. Evaluate the assumptions underlying the budget in light of the unusually optimistic demand projection by the marketing manager.

7.56 Budget coordination, continuation of the previous problem (LO2, LO4). Refer to the information in the previous problem for Essex Fuel Pumps. Pleased with the initial budget, the CEO of Essex Fuel Pumps, Claire Balderson, distributes the document to the production, planning, and purchasing managers to seek their inputs and to help them gear up for the coming year. Both the production and planning managers were concerned. "Look, Claire, our maximum capacity is 120,000 pumps, and we can perhaps stretch it to make 125,000 pumps. There is no way we can make 150,000 pumps without additional investment. We need to increase our capacity by at least 25,000 pumps to be able to make the budget. This means that we have to buy some equipment and invest in human resources. For your convenience, I am giving you an estimate of what it would cost to increase capacity. But, before you decide to expand capacity, we need to make sure that we are not responding to a temporary surge in demand. What would we do with this additional capacity if the demand were to recede to normal levels the following year?" Pierre Grosjean, the planning manager, wanted to know. The following table summarizes the additional capacity costs that would need to be incurred to increase Essex's capacity to 150,000 fuel pumps.

Increase in plant maintenance	$225,000
Increase in plant depreciation	$125,000
Increase in plant administration	$100,000
Increase in marketing administration	$40,000
Increase in plant supervision	$75,000

Required:

a. Assume that demand is likely to continue at the level of 150,000 pumps over the next several years and that unit variable costs stay the same as estimated in the previous problem. Prepare a revised budgeted income statement for 2009 after incorporating the additional fixed cost estimates.

b. What would budgeted income be if Claire decides not to incur the additional capacity costs but, rather, decides to produce the maximum number of fuel pumps (i.e., 125,000 fuel pumps) with existing capacity?

c. Is it more profitable for Essex to increase capacity to 150,000 units or decrease production to 125,000 units?

7.57 Merchandise company—budgeted income statement (LO2). Matt Domby is the owner of Domby's Boot Store. Matt currently is formulating his budget for the coming year and provides you with the following information about expected quarterly sales.

	Quarter			
	1	*2*	*3*	*4*
Sales	$406,000	$529,250	$420,500	$594,500

Matt believes revenues will be highest in Quarters 2 and 4 because of his semiannual "*20% off everything*" sale held during May and November. Indeed, Matt estimates that half of Quarter 2 and Quarter 4 sales will be at the sale prices. However, Matt informs you that the sales estimates in the table above are gross amounts; that is, they represent expected revenues *before any discounts*.

Matt notes that 80% of his sales are paid with credit cards and that he pays a 2% transaction fee to the credit card company. (*Note:* Credit card fees are based on net sales—that is, on what the customers actually pay.) Matt's normal prices include a 45% markup on his cost, and he spends $35,000 on fixed costs per month.

Required:

Prepare a quarter-by-quarter income statement for Domby's Boot Store. (Round all numbers to the nearest dollar.)

7.58 Service industry, budgeted income statement (LO2). Media Mogul owns the cable TV franchise for Spudcity, Idaho. Dan Trevino, the manager in charge of the Spudcity franchise, is responsible for all operational decisions, including preparing the monthly budget.

Dan provides you with the following information regarding the activities of the Spudcity franchise.

Subscription Fees	$20 per month for basic service, $50 per month for "extended basic," and $10 per month for each premium channel. Customers receive a 20% discount on each premium channel if ordering more than one.	50,000 total subscribers—5% receive basic service and the remainder have extended basic. 15,000 premium channel subscriptions—4,000 are at discount.
Internet Fees	$45 per month. $3 per month for modem rental.	26,000 subscribers—20,000 have a rented modem. Bundling cable and Internet generates a $5 discount to the customer. 500 of the 26,000 subscribers have Internet only.
Content and Franchise Fees	Fees paid by Media Mogul to content providers.	$1,400,000 per month. Each premium channel hooked up is an additional $6 per month.
	Spudcity also taxes Media Mogul for using the public right of way. (This amount is in excess of the public, educational, and government channels provided for free to all subscribers.)	Spudcity also levies taxes at 10% of net revenues (i.e., revenues after all discounts are given).
Internet Connection Fees	Variable costs include the costs for leasing high-speed lines and anticipated repairs. Fixed costs include those related to equipment and depreciation.	$35 per line per month. Fixed costs amount to $85,000 per month.

Operating Costs	Fixed costs include the rent, trucks, and salaries to office personnel.	$450,000 per month.
	Variable costs comprise installations, repairs, and maintenance. Dan estimates 250 installations and 600 repair calls per month. He also estimates that he will perform 35 line maintenance actions.	Variable cost is $60 per installation, $35 per repair, and $75 per line maintenance.

Required:

a. Prepare Dan's budgeted monthly income statement.

b. Comment on the similarities and differences, if any, between Media Mogul's budget and the budget for a manufacturing firm.

7.59 Not-for-profit, program budgets, qualitative (LO4, Challenging). Lori Koenig is the executive director of the Mid-Atlantic Region of I-Care, a not-for-profit group that facilitates corneal transplants and healthy vision. The group is best known for collecting corneas from the recently deceased, storing them safely, and moving them to the hospitals with patients who need corneas.

I-Care operates three separate, but related, programs. The first harvests eyes from cadavers and transports them for transplantation. The second is an educational outreach program aimed at young children. This program conducts free eye tests and stresses the importance of proper eye care. The third program targets senior citizens, testing for age-related degenerative eye diseases.

Each program is funded by grants from individuals, charities, and the government. Indeed, fund raising is one of I-Care's more important activities. There are little, if any, direct revenues from any of its three programs.

Required:

Discuss the budgeting and reporting requirements for I-Care and how they might differ from those in a for-profit organization.

 7.60 Budgeted income statement, comprehensive (LO2). Peterson Pipes prepares detailed budgets for all four quarters of the year. The following information pertains to Peterson's budget for 2009:

	Revenues	Direct Labor	Materials Purchases	Beginning Materials Inventory	Beginning Finished Goods Inventory
First quarter	$795,200	$240,000	$235,000	$400,000	$380,000
Second quarter	834,200	244,500	211,200	420,000	390,400
Third quarter	864,450	238,500	222,300	415,000	385,600
Fourth quarter	856,250	248,600	207,500	425,000	391,250
First quarter, 2010				410,000	396,500

Peterson expects fixed manufacturing overhead to be $150,000, $172,250, $169,250, and $174,300 for quarters 1 through 4 of 2009, respectively. Also, Peterson expects fixed selling and administrative costs to be $80,000, $95,000, $106,000, and $100,000 for quarters 1 through 4, respectively. Peterson does not incur any expenditure related to variable overhead or any variable selling and administrative costs. Finally, Peterson plans to begin and end each quarter with zero work in process inventory.

Required:

Prepare a budgeted contribution margin income statement for Peterson Pipes for each quarter of 2009.

 7.61 Cash budgeting, comprehensive (LO3). Refer to the data in the previous problem for Peterson Pipes. Peterson expects its first-quarter opening balances in cash, accounts receivable, and accounts payable to be $75,000, $125,000, and $126,500, respectively. The following additional information also is relevant for preparing Peterson's cash budgets:

- Peterson expects to earn the same amount of revenues for each of the three months within a quarter. Experience indicates that Peterson collects 60 percent of its sales in the month of sale and 40 percent in the following month.

- Peterson expects to make the same amount of materials purchases for each of the three months within a quarter. Peterson pays for 50 percent of its materials purchases in the month of purchase and the remaining 50 percent in the month following purchase.

- Each quarter's fixed manufacturing overhead includes $15,000 of noncash expenses. The remaining overhead expenses occur uniformly throughout the three months of each quarter and are disbursed immediately in cash.

- Fixed selling and administrative expenses occur uniformly throughout the three months of each quarter, and are disbursed immediately in cash.

Required:

Prepare Peterson's cash budget for each quarter of the coming year.

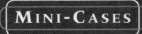

7.62 Budgeting, comprehensive (LO3). Manasee Atre is an award-winning innovator who makes educational toys for preschool children. Manasee's company, which she whimsically named Pumpkin Patch, makes plastic pieces that can be assembled to create imaginative animal and human models. The standard set consists of several types of "head gear," "noses," "eyes," "ears," "arms and legs," as well as "foot wear." The deluxe set adds to the number of options under each category.

For the second half of 2008, estimated sales in units for each set are as follows:

Month	Standard	Deluxe
July	10,000	3,500
August	11,400	4,000
September	12,000	4,500
October	15,600	5,000
November	18,000	5,500
December	22,000	6,000
January 2009	18,000	4,200

Manasee provides you with the following additional information:

Sales price: The actual sales for May and the forecasted sales for June were $150,000 and $155,000, respectively, for the standard set. The relevant numbers for the deluxe set are $70,000 (May sales) and $65,000 (June sales).

Manasee prices the standard set at $17 per unit and the deluxe set at $26 per unit.

Inventory policy for finished goods: Manasee's policy for finished goods inventory is to stock 25% of the forecasted demand for the next month. As of June 30, Manasee expects to have 2,500 units of the standard set and 875 units of deluxe set in stock. These inventories were valued at $12.00 and $17.00 per unit, respectively. Pumpkin Patch uses the FIFO (First-In-First-Out) method to value its inventories.

The company's long-term plans call for it to have 4,000 units of the standard set and 1,000 units of the deluxe set on January 31, 2009.

Production requirements: The standard set consumes 1 pound of plastic per unit, whereas the deluxe set consumes 1.50 pounds of plastic per unit. Plastic costs $3.00 per pound. The cost of all other materials is $1.00 per unit for the standard set and $1.25 per unit for the deluxe set.

The standard set requires 0.50 direct labor hours per unit, and the deluxe set requires 0.75 labor hours per unit. Labor costs $16 per hour.

Fixed manufacturing overhead is expected to be $48,000 per month. Of this amount, $22,000 represents depreciation and other noncash expenses. Pumpkin Patch does not have any variable manufacturing overhead.

Inventory policy—raw materials: With regard to the plastic used to produce each set, Manasee likes to have an ending materials inventory to meet all of the material needs for the next month's anticipated production.

Pumpkin Patch expects to have 13,000 pounds of plastic in inventory as of June 30, 2008. (*Note:* The beginning inventory does not follow the stated stocking policy exactly.)

Manasee's long-term plans call for her to have 10,000 pounds of plastic in inventory as of January 31, 2009.

Payables policy: Pumpkin Patch pays for half of its material purchases in the month of purchase and the remainder the following month.

Accounts payable for materials and other items were expected to be $19,500 on June 30, 2008.

All other materials are purchased on a cash basis during the month when they are used.

Collection policy: For both the standard and deluxe set, 40 percent of any month's sales are for cash. Ten percent of the credit sales are collected in the month of sale, 70% are collected the following month, and 18% are collected in the second month after the sale. The remaining 2% of receivables are deemed uncollectible. Pumpkin Patch writes off bad debts to the income statement during the month the debt is deemed uncollectible (i.e., two months after the sale occurs). The firm makes no accruals for estimated bad debts in the month of sale.

Sales and administration costs: Monthly nonmanufacturing expenses consist of the following:

Salaries and wages	$3,000
Commissions	6% of sales revenue
Rent	$7,000
Other expenses	4% of sales revenue
Depreciation	$1,500 (for office equipment)

Except depreciation, all nonmanufacturing expenses are paid in cash when incurred.

Cash and financing: Pumpkin Patch maintains a minimum cash balance of $15,000. Borrowing can make up any anticipated shortfalls. Ignore interest on the loan in your calculations. For simplicity, assume that the bank will only lend (and accept repayments) in $1,000 increments. (Minimize the amount borrowed, however.)

Cash on hand on June 30 is expected to be $16,000.

Special items for cash budget: Pumpkin Patch needs to make a payment of $15,000 during July for equipment previously purchased on credit. The firm also has scheduled a dividend payment of $20,000 in September.

Required:

a. Prepare Pumpkin Patch's contribution margin income statement for each of the last six months of 2008.

b. Prepare Pumpkin Patch's cash budget for each of the last six months of 2008.

c. Write a brief report summarizing Pumpkin Patch's budget for the second half of 2008.

7.63 Budgeting, sales force compensation (LO4). Bartlett Drugs makes generic prescription drugs. It relies on its sales personnel to market and sell its products widely to pharmacies, doctors, and hospitals. While Bartlett has always been profitable, revenues have been stagnant over the last five years. In contrast, other generic drug companies recorded significant revenue growth over the same period.

After careful investigation, Bartlett's CEO, Mary Stone, concludes that an important reason for the lack of revenue growth is the way the incentive system is set up for the company's sales personnel, coupled with the role sales personnel play in the annual budgeting process. Currently, an average salesperson receives a fixed annual salary of

$40,000, and a bonus of $20,000 for meeting or exceeding an annual sales target of $400,000. A look at the records was enough for Mary to realize that hardly any member of the sales team exceeded the target of $400,000 by much (the maximum recorded sales was only $426,000), and many of them were just about meeting this target. The sales target itself was set every year in consultation with the sales team, and the target had not moved up in the last five years to reflect any growth.

It was clear to Mary that the sales team was "low-balling" the target to be able to comfortably meet it and qualify for the bonus. They also seemed to stop once they met the target. Yet, Mary realized that the sales personnel were in the best position to assess market trends and to help set realistic targets for the company's planning process. After consulting with experts on sales force compensation, Mary has come up with four options:

- Remove the bonus for meeting the target and increase the annual salary to $60,000.
- Set the target at a level that is 10 percent higher than what the sales team recommends. Implement a sales commission system whereby a salesperson earns 5 percent of the amount by which actual sales exceed 90% of the target.
- Set the target based on industry growth and keep the existing bonus system.
- Implement a tournament scheme wherein sales personnel are ranked into five performance-based groups, and vary the bonus across groups.

Required:

Discuss the relative merits and drawbacks of each scheme from the company's point of view. Which scheme is likely to put the company on a path of sales growth?

7.64 Forecast Revisions, Not-for-profit, ethics (LO4). Eshe works for a not-for-profit group that recycles computers and other equipment to communities in rural Africa. The group collects two- to three-year-old PCs and peripheral equipment from businesses, refurbishes the PCs, ships them to Africa, and distributes them for a nominal fee (which is often waived). Even though businesses donate the computers and equipment, Eshe's group needs cash for operating expenses. It therefore seeks grants from foundations such as the Gates Foundation and the Rockefeller Foundation that support charitable endeavors. Eshe's dilemma concerns one such grant that could fund a substantial portion of next year's operations.

Eshe's problem is that the volume of computers distributed has stabilized and has even begun a slight downturn. Businesses began to keep their machines for longer periods, and the rapid change in technology has made obsolescence a major issue. Eshe had prepared the grant application with the best available data and her best estimate of the volume next year (down 5% from current volumes). The application also shows a similar downtrend for the near future.

Eshe's supervisor, the charity's CEO, is convinced that the grant application would be denied if the group projects a declining activity level. Without adequate funds, he will have to scale back dramatically. He further notes that restarting the initiative two to three years later is like starting over because the government and other contacts in Africa would have atrophied. He thinks that the downturn is temporary and that volume would pick up over the next two to three years. He accordingly asks Eshe to revise her estimates and show a 5% *increase* in volume for next year. He argues that even the best estimate is "gazing into a crystal ball" and that a 5% increase *might* occur, even though it is not a high probability event.

Required:

What should Eshe do?

7.65 Budgeting and performance evaluation (LO4). Florida Cruises operates a fleet of glass bottom boats that give tours of the coral reefs off Key West, Florida. Since its inception, the firm has fetched its owner a healthy return on investment. One reason the company does so well is that the owner believes in keeping tight control over operations. Every December, the owner and the manager evaluate the prior year's operations and carefully plan next year's operations. At the end of these discussions, they project income for the coming year. The manager and other operating staff receive a large bonus if actual income exceeds budgeted income.

This incentive scheme appeared to work well in the past. The manager and the staff worked hard to reap bonuses at the end of each year. However, the performance for the most recent year did not quite measure up to expectations, as the following data indicate:

Florida Cruises		
Income Statement for Year Ending December 31		
	Budgeted	*Actual*
Revenues	$2,800,000	$2,050,000
Less		
Variable costs		
Direct materials (fuel, supplies)	480,000	520,000
Direct labor	1,100,000	950,000
Variable overhead	175,000	148,000
Fixed costs		
Operating overhead (boats, pier, salaries)	320,000	420,000
Marketing and administration	380,000	325,000
Profit before taxes	**$345,000**	**($313,000)**

Naturally, the manager and staff did not receive a bonus. However, the manager was upset with this turn of events. "We all worked extra hard this year. It was a tough year. The fuel prices more than doubled. We lost three months' worth of revenues because of hurricanes—people were fleeing the Florida Keys. How can we expect tourists to come in and see coral reefs at a time like that? We should not be punished for what is not under our control," he complained.

To make his point, the manager provided the following additional information to the owner:

• The loss in revenues is mostly attributable to two devastating hurricanes. While hurricanes are common in Key West, the past year set a record in terms of the number and severity of hurricanes that passed over the Keys.
• The increase in direct material costs is attributable to a sharp increase in fuel prices (the price run-up was not anticipated at the time of budgeting).
• About $140,000 of fixed operations overhead was attributable to the expenses that were incurred to protect the boats from the hurricanes and to fix some unavoidable damage to the pier and sheds.

The manager claimed that if the budget were revised to account for these factors, the actual performance would appear much more reasonable given the circumstances.

Required:

Should a bonus be awarded to the manager and operating staff?

Chapter 8

Budgetary Control and Variance Analysis

CINDY'S CAKES MAKES AND SELLS specialty cakes to supermarkets and convenience stores. For the month of March, Cindy budgeted to sell 3,500 cakes and earn a profit of $9,275. During March, actual sales were 3,800 cakes, but profit was only $5,481. These results puzzle Cindy. She wonders, "How is it possible to sell more cakes than budgeted but earn less profit?" She seeks your assistance in figuring out what happened.

APPLYING THE DECISION FRAMEWORK

What Is the Problem?	Cindy's actual profit in March is lower than her budgeted profit. This shortfall occurred even though sales volume exceeded expectations.
What Are the Options?	Cindy's actual profit might differ from her budgeted profit for a number of reasons, including a lower than expected selling price, baker inefficiencies, higher input prices, material waste, and oven failure.
What Are the Costs and the Benefits?	We will perform variance analysis to isolate the profit impact of individual input and output factors. Once Cindy understands the causes for the lower profit, she can evaluate specific corrective actions.
Make the Decision!	After looking at individual variances, we will be able to suggest which option Cindy should follow.

Peter Dazeley/Getty Images

Cindy's Cakes is a thriving bakery.

LEARNING OBJECTIVES

After studying this chapter, you will be able to:

1 Understand how companies use budgets for control.

2 Perform variance analysis.

3 Interpret variances to determine possible corrective actions.

4 Explain how nonfinancial measures complement variance analysis.

As we know, it is not enough just to make plans. We need to check periodically to see whether everything is going according to plan and whether any corrective actions are necessary. For example, we might review a day's activities. Did we accomplish what we set out to do? Do we need to change our schedule for the next day? Similarly, large organizations compare actual revenues, costs, and profits with budgeted amounts to determine whether they need to make changes to their products, marketing policies, production processes, or purchasing procedures.

In this chapter, we focus on short-term measures of control. We begin by discussing the role of budgets in the control process. We then present the mechanics of **variance analysis**, a technique firms use to determine *why* actual revenues, costs, and profit differ from their budgeted amounts. Variance analysis helps organizations determine whether their people and processes are performing as expected. It also helps organizations motivate their employees and improve *future* planning decisions. Finally, we discuss how organizations can use nonfinancial measures, in addition to variance analysis, to help control operations.

CHAPTER CONNECTIONS
While variance analysis is a tool for short-term control, trends in variances could signal underlying issues with longer-term plans regarding products, customers, and processes. We consider such control decisions in Chapters 12 and 13.

Budgets As the Basis for Control

LEARNING OBJECTIVE 1

Understand how companies use budgets for control.

As you learned in Chapter 7, a good plan is the foundation for effective control. Without a well-conceived plan against which to compare actual performance, it is difficult to determine how we are doing or what we could do to improve. For most organizations, including Cindy's Cakes, a budget is the benchmark for evaluating actual performance.

The starting point for Cindy's monthly budget is projected sales. Based on her experience, Cindy expects to sell 3,500 cakes at a price of $20.95 per cake during March. This sales target shapes the rest of Cindy's monthly budget.

Cindy makes the following assumptions to estimate costs.

- *Raw Materials Quantities:* Exhibit 8.1 presents the materials required by Cindy's recipe. Cindy uses the recipe and expected sales to calculate how much of each raw material to purchase each month. Because she uses only fresh ingredients, Cindy's Cakes does not inventory materials. Thus, Cindy's usage budget corresponds exactly to her purchases budget.
- *Raw Materials Prices:* Cindy expects the purchase price of each ingredient (shown in Exhibit 8.1) to hold steady for the upcoming month.
- *Labor Requirements:* Cindy estimates that bakers take an average of 30 minutes per cake.
- *Wage Rate:* Cindy budgets to pay each baker $20 per hour.

Cindy's bakers follow her special recipes. (©Helen King/Corbis)

Exhibit 8.1	*Cindy's Recipe for a Specialty Cake*		
Item	**Quantity**	**Price**	**Cost per Cake**
Butter	1.5 cups (3/4 pound)	$2.40/pound	$1.80
Granulated sugar	3 cups (1 pound)	$0.80/pound	0.80
Eggs	5 large	$0.12/egg	0.60
All-purpose flour	3 cups (3/4 pound)	$0.40/pound	0.30
Extracts & other items	Various	Various	0.25
		Total	**$3.75**

Exhibit 8.2	Cindy's Cakes: Master Budget		
			Amount
Revenue	3,500 cakes × $20.95 per cake		$73,325
Variable costs			
Raw materials	3,500 cakes × $3.75 per cake	$13,125	
Direct labor	3,500 cakes × 0.50 hours/cake × $20/hour	35,000	
Variable overhead	3,500 cakes × 0.50 hours/cake × $1.10/hour	1,925	
Total variable costs			$50,050
Contribution margin			$23,275
Fixed costs			
Rent		$2,500	
Equipment costs		10,000	
Transportation		1,500	
Total fixed costs			$14,000
Profit before taxes			$9,275

- *Variable Overhead:* Variable overhead includes utilities and baking supplies. Cindy expects variable overhead to amount to $1.10 per baker hour (or $1.10 × 0.50 baker hours per cake = $0.55 per cake).
- *Fixed Costs:* Cindy expects to pay $14,000 in fixed costs each month. This amount includes rent, the salaries of Cindy's marketing associate, office manager, and janitorial staff, as well as the cost of the vans used to deliver the cakes to the various stores.

Based on this information, Cindy prepared her **master budget** for March. Recall from Chapter 7 that a master budget for a period is a plan that presents the expected revenues, costs, and profit corresponding to the expected sales volume as of the beginning of that period. As we see in Cindy's master budget for March in Exhibit 8.2, she expected to sell 3,500 cakes and earn $9,275 in profit. As you already know, this did not happen. In the next section, we begin to figure out why.

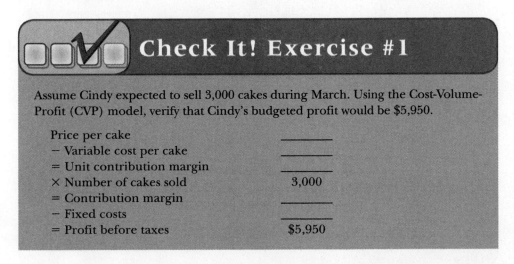

Check It! Exercise #1

Assume Cindy expected to sell 3,000 cakes during March. Using the Cost-Volume-Profit (CVP) model, verify that Cindy's budgeted profit would be $5,950.

Price per cake	_____
− Variable cost per cake	_____
= Unit contribution margin	_____
× Number of cakes sold	3,000
= Contribution margin	_____
− Fixed costs	_____
= Profit before taxes	$5,950

Solution at end of chapter.

How to Calculate Variances

LEARNING OBJECTIVE 2

Perform variance analysis.

A **variance** is the difference between an actual result and a budgeted amount. We classify a variance as favorable or unfavorable based on their effect on *current* profit. As Exhibit 8.3 shows, a **favorable (F) variance** means that performance exceeded expectations—actual revenue exceeded budgeted revenue or actual cost was less than budgeted cost. An **unfavorable (U) variance** means that performance fell short of expectations—actual revenue was less than budgeted revenue or actual cost exceeded budgeted cost.

We denote favorable variances with positive numbers and unfavorable variances with negative numbers. Thus, we calculate sales, contribution margin, and profit variances as the actual result less the budgeted amount (e.g., actual profit − budgeted profit). In contrast, because costs represent outflows, we calculate cost variances as the budgeted amount less the actual result (e.g., budgeted labor cost − actual labor cost). For instance, if budgeted labor costs exceed actual labor cost, the variance is favorable and positive.

How do Cindy's actual results compare with her budget? Cindy tracks revenues and expenses on an ongoing basis and prepares monthly financial statements. During the first few days of April, Cindy prepared the income statement shown in Exhibit 8.4, summarizing her actual results for March.

Using the data in Exhibits 8.2 and 8.4, you can prepare Exhibit 8.5, which shows the variance for each revenue and expense on Cindy's income statement. We mark all favorable variances with an "F" and all unfavorable variances with a "U."

Looking at Exhibit 8.5, we see that Cindy sold 300 more cakes and realized $2,485 more in revenue than budgeted during March. However, Cindy's variable costs were $5,779 higher than budgeted, and her fixed costs were $500 over budget. Thus, Cindy's actual profit was $5,481 or $3,794 *lower* than budgeted. That is, Cindy's **total profit variance** = $5,481 − $9,275 = ($3,794), or $3,794 U.

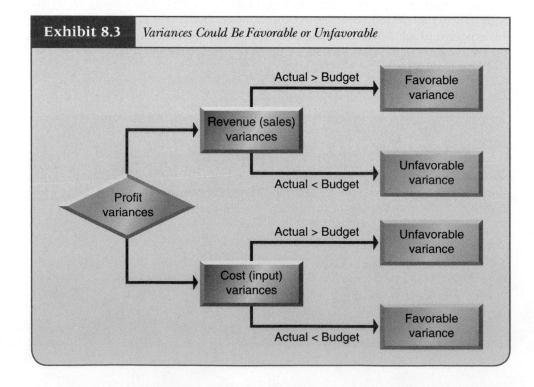

Exhibit 8.3   *Variances Could Be Favorable or Unfavorable*

Exhibit 8.4	Cindy's Cakes: Actual Results for March	
		Amount
Number of cakes sold		3,800
Revenue		$75,810
Variable costs		
Raw materials	$14,567	
Direct labor	39,000	
Variable overhead	2,262	
Total variable costs		$55,829
Contribution margin		$19,981
Fixed costs		
Rent	$2,500	
Equipment costs	10,500	
Transportation	1,500	
Total fixed costs		$14,500
Profit before taxes		$5,481

Exhibit 8.5	Cindy's Cakes: Actual versus Budgeted Results for March			
	Master Budget	**Actual Results**	**Variance**	
Number of cakes sold	3,500	3,800	300	F
Revenue	$73,325	$75,810	$2,485	F
Variable costs				
Raw materials	$13,125	$14,567	($1,442)	U
Direct labor	35,000	39,000	(4,000)	U
Variable overhead	1,925	2,262	(337)	U
Contribution margin	$23,275	$19,981	($3,294)	U
Fixed costs				
Rent	$2,500	$2,500	$0	
Equipment costs	10,000	10,500	(500)	U
Transportation	1,500	1,500	0	
Profit before taxes	$9,275	$5,481	($3,794)	U

$$Total\ Profit\ Variance = Actual\ Profit - Master\ Budget\ Profit$$

Cindy would like to get her business back on track. To do so, however, she needs to know *what* caused the total profit variance. Exhibit 8.5 reveals two basic sources:

- Actual sales exceeded budgeted sales. Because each cake has a positive unit contribution margin, Cindy should have *exceeded* her profit target.
- Actual costs exceeded budgeted costs. The increase in costs has more than offset the positive effect on profit from the increase in sales.

The two sources of variances are related. Part of the $4,000 increase in labor costs is probably due to an increase in sales volume. Because Cindy made 300 more cakes than budgeted, we should expect the labor cost to increase as well. However, the increase in the labor cost may also have resulted from bakers taking more time than budgeted to make each cake. Furthermore, the actual wage rate may have exceeded the budgeted rate. Unfortunately, Exhibit 8.5 does not provide us with enough detail to determine exactly what happened. We need a systematic approach for breaking down the total profit variance to pinpoint these causes.

BREAKING DOWN THE TOTAL PROFIT VARIANCE

As Exhibit 8.6 shows, in a series of steps, we can break down the total profit variance into several components. Each component informs us about how a certain aspect of operations, such as a change in sales volume or a change in the selling price, affects profit.

As the first step, we use a *flexible budget* to decompose the total profit variance into two major components: the sales volume variance and the flexible budget variance.

Exhibit 8.6	*We Can Decompose Variances into Smaller Pieces*

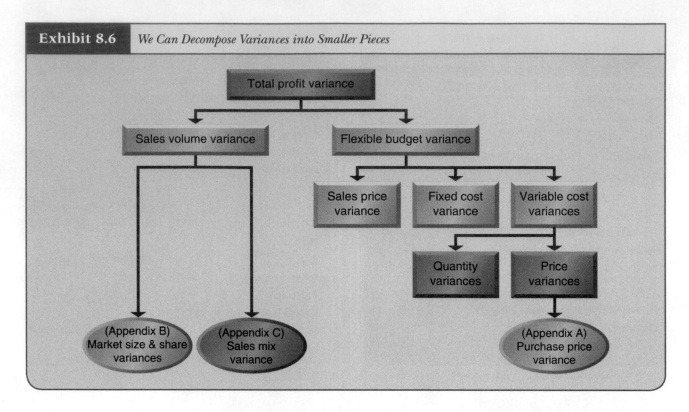

Exhibit 8.6A	*Overview of Variance Analysis*

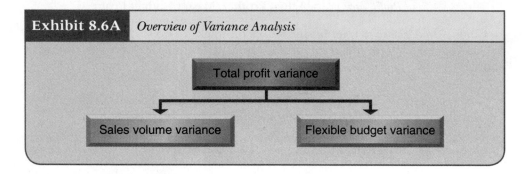

FLEXIBLE BUDGET

Let us begin by breaking down the total profit variance into the sales volume variance and the flexible budget variance. (Exhibit 8.6A reproduces the relevant portion of Exhibit 8.6 to help you place this step in context.) Using the assumptions in the master budget, companies can develop a CVP relation that projects the profit for any sales level. We refer to this exercise as *flexing* the master budget. Flexing the master budget changes total budgeted revenues and total budgeted costs to correspond to any sales level. In this exercise, be sure to notice that only variable costs change; fixed costs are the same for all sales volumes.

As shown in *Check It! Exercise #2*, we can construct a budget for any sales volume. In variance analysis, we are particularly interested in *the budget at the actual level of sales*, or the **flexible budget**. For Cindy's Cakes, because the actual sales turned out to be 3,800 cakes, the flexible budget is the budget corresponding to 3,800 cakes.

Why are we interested in the flexible budget? The answer is that *any profit difference between the master and flexible budgets is due solely to the difference between budgeted and actual sales.* That is, sales quantity is the only item that differs between the master budget and the flexible budget. Otherwise, both budgets assume the same sales and input prices, as well the same input usage per unit of output. Exhibit 8.7 compares

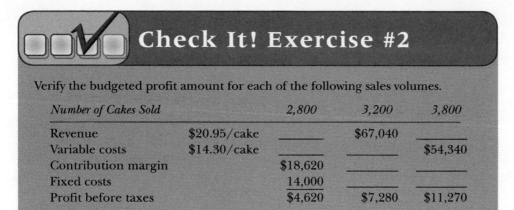

Check It! Exercise #2

Verify the budgeted profit amount for each of the following sales volumes.

Number of Cakes Sold		2,800	3,200	3,800
Revenue	$20.95/cake	_____	$67,040	_____
Variable costs	$14.30/cake	_____		$54,340
Contribution margin		$18,620	_____	_____
Fixed costs		14,000	_____	_____
Profit before taxes		$4,620	$7,280	$11,270

Solution at end of chapter.

Connecting to Practice

FLEXIBLE BUDGETS AND SNOW REMOVAL COSTS

In early 2003, three major storms wreaked havoc with the snow removal budget for the City of Oneonta in New York. At the beginning of March, the city was already over budget even though 10 months remained in the year.

COMMENTARY: Cities and counties develop their budgets for snow removal costs based on data about the amount and frequency of snowfall in previous years. For example, a budget may anticipate six snowfalls with an average of 3 inches of precipitation per snowfall. To judge the efficiency of the snow removal services, however, the city must account for any unanticipated snowfall—a primary driver of removing snow from streets. It is the flexible budget that allows the city to consider snowfall in excess of, or less than, master budget predictions.

Exhibit 8.7	Cindy's Cakes: Sales Volume and Flexible Budget Variances				
	Master Budget	Sales Volume Variance	Flexible Budget	Flexible Budget Variance	Actual Results
Number of cakes	3,500		3,800		3,800
Revenue	$73,325	$6,285	$79,610	($3,800)	$75,810
Variable costs					
Raw materials	$13,125	($1,125)	$14,250	($317)	$14,567
Direct labor	35,000	(3,000)	38,000	(1,000)	39,000
Variable overhead	1,925	(165)	2,090	(172)	2,262
Contribution margin	$23,275	$1,995F	$25,270	($5,289)U	$19,981
Fixed costs					
Rent	$2,500	$0	$2,500	$0	$2,500
Equipment costs	10,000	0	10,000	(500)	10,500
Transportation	1,500	0	1,500	0	1,500
Profit before taxes	$9,275	$1,995F	$11,270	($5,789)U	$5,481

Cindy's master budget (Exhibit 8.2), flexible budget, and actual results (Exhibit 8.4). Let us consider the variances resulting from these comparisons.

Sales Volume Variance

Because the flexible and master budgets only differ in sales volume, we refer to the difference in profit between the two budgets as the **sales volume variance**, and we compute it by subtracting master budget profit from flexible budget profit.

Cindy's sales volume variance for March = $11,270 − $9,725 = $1,995 F. This difference in profit also equals the difference in contribution margins ($25,270 − $23,275 = $1,995) because the master and flexible budgets have the same fixed costs. We also note that, because they make identical assumptions about sales price and variable costs, the *budgeted unit contribution margin* is the same for both the master and the flexible budgets. Therefore, changing the volume of sales proportionately changes profit by the budgeted unit contribution margin, as follows:

$$\text{Sales Volume Variance} = \text{Flexible Budget Profit} - \text{Master Budget Profit}$$
$$= (\text{Actual Sales Quantity} - \text{Budgeted Sales Quantity})$$
$$\times \text{Budgeted Unit Contribution Margin}$$

It is important to note that the *individual* revenue and cost components of the sales volume variance are neither favorable nor unfavorable. The variances for each line item simply represent changes in revenue and costs that are strictly proportional to the change in sales volume. Cindy should expect these variances given the volume increase of 300 cakes. Thus, the net profit effect, which also equals the difference in contribution margins, is all we should interpret.

In Appendix B, we discuss how firms can split the sales volume variance into two pieces—a market size variance and a market share variance—to gain additional insight regarding the reasons underlying a sales volume variance.

Flexible Budget Variance

The difference in profit between the actual results and the flexible budget is the **flexible budget variance.**

$$\text{Flexible Budget Variance} = \text{Actual Profit} - \text{Flexible Budget Profit}$$

Exhibit 8.7 shows that Cindy's flexible budget variance was $5,481 − $11,270 = ($5,789), or $5,789 U. Our next task is to look at the components of this variance.

Before we move to the component variances, let us first look at the sales volume variance and the flexible budget variance graphically. Exhibit 8.8 shows how variances isolate the effect of one factor while controlling for other factors. Point A marks the budgeted profit given the budgeted volume of activity (this amount comes from the master budget). For Cindy's specialty cakes, this point would be $9,275 in profit for 3,500 cakes. Once we know the actual volume of activity, we use the flexible budget to calculate what the expected profit is—the budgeted profit given the

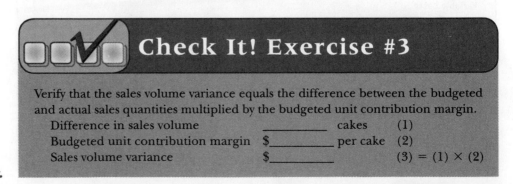

Check It! Exercise #3

Verify that the sales volume variance equals the difference between the budgeted and actual sales quantities multiplied by the budgeted unit contribution margin.

Difference in sales volume	_____ cakes	(1)
Budgeted unit contribution margin	$_____ per cake	(2)
Sales volume variance	$_____	(3) = (1) × (2)

Solution at end of chapter.

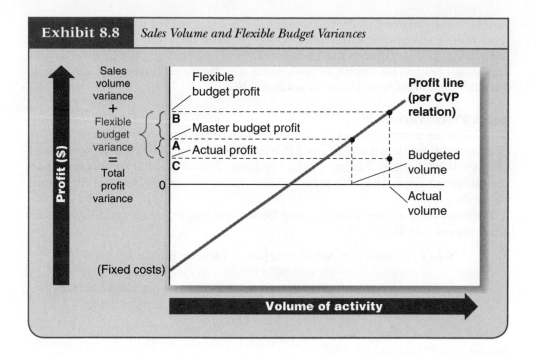

Exhibit 8.8   *Sales Volume and Flexible Budget Variances*

actual volume. In Exhibit 8.8, that relationship is marked by point B. When Cindy sells 3,800 cakes instead of 3,500, she expects her profit to be $11,270. We then look at the actual results, showing both the actual volume of activity and the actual profit. This relationship is marked by point C. As per the CVP relation, Cindy might expect her profit to be $11,270 for 3,800 cakes, but her profit turns out to be $5,481 instead.

On the graph, the difference between points A and C on the *y*-axis, the profit or loss in dollars, is the total profit variance. This variance is the difference between the master budget and the actual results and is made up of two components. The first, the difference between points A and B, between the master budget and the flexible budget, is the sales volume variance. The second, the difference between points B and C, between the flexible budget and the actual results, is the flexible budget variance.

COMPONENTS OF THE FLEXIBLE BUDGET VARIANCE

In the next step of variance analysis (see Exhibit 8.6B), we split the flexible budget variance into three components: the sales price variance, fixed cost variances, and

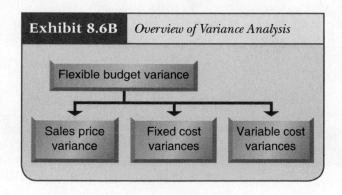

Exhibit 8.6B   *Overview of Variance Analysis*

variable cost variances. Exhibit 8.9 summarizes information from Exhibit 8.7 to show these variances for Cindy's Cakes. We calculate these individual variances by comparing the lines for revenue and each kind of cost between the flexible budget and actual results. Be careful to notice that we classify an increase in revenue as favorable but an increase in cost as unfavorable.

Sales Price Variance

Recall that the flexible budget provides the expected revenue for the actual number of cakes sold. Yet, actual revenue of $75,810 differed from the expected revenue of $79,610. Why? Because the actual price Cindy was able to get per cake was *lower* than the budgeted price. The sales price variance captures the effect of this difference on profit.

We compute the **sales price variance** between actual revenues and flexible budget revenues, as follows:

$$
\begin{aligned}
\textit{Sales Price Variance} &= \text{Actual Revenue} - \text{Flexible Budget Revenue} \\
&= (\text{Actual Sales Price} \times \text{Actual Sales Quantity}) \\
&\quad - (\text{Budgeted Sales Price} \times \text{Actual Sales Quantity}) \\
&= (\text{Actual Sales Price} - \text{Budgeted Sales Price}) \\
&\quad \times \text{Actual Sales Quantity}
\end{aligned}
$$

Fixed Cost Variance

Next, let's consider fixed costs. We refer to any difference between budgeted and actual fixed costs as a **spending variance**.

$$
\textit{Fixed Cost Spending Variance} = \text{Budgeted Fixed Costs} - \text{Actual Fixed Costs}
$$

Exhibit 8.9	Components of the Flexible Budget Variance	
Item		**Amount**
Sales price (revenue) variance		($3,800) U
Raw materials variance	($317) U	
Direct labor variance	(1,000) U	
Variable overhead variance	(172) U	
Total variable cost variances		(1,489) U
Fixed cost variance		(500) U
Flexible budget variance		**($5,789) U**

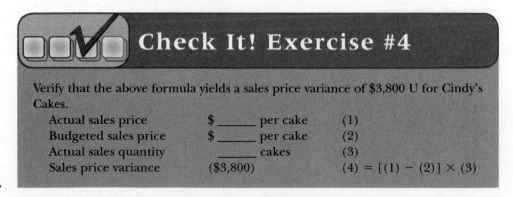

Check It! Exercise #4

Verify that the above formula yields a sales price variance of $3,800 U for Cindy's Cakes.

Actual sales price	$ _____ per cake	(1)
Budgeted sales price	$ _____ per cake	(2)
Actual sales quantity	_____ cakes	(3)
Sales price variance	($3,800)	(4) = [(1) − (2)] × (3)

Solution at end of chapter.

Recall from Chapter 5 that the CVP relation assumes that fixed costs should be the same for all sales levels within the relevant range. However, even in the short term a firm's actual expenditure on fixed costs could differ from the budgeted amount. Such differences could arise because of unforeseen changes in expenses related to rent, equipment, salaried employees, utilities, property taxes, and insurance.

Cindy had budgeted $14,000 for fixed costs, but actual fixed costs amounted to $14,500. Thus, Cindy realized a fixed cost spending variance of $500 U for March.

Variable Cost Variances

Finally, let's consider each of Cindy's variable cost variances. As shown in Exhibit 8.9, Cindy realized a total variance of $317 U for raw materials, $1,000 U for direct labor, and $172 U for variable overhead. These variances are the differences between the budgeted costs (from the flexible budget) and the actual costs. Cindy should not attribute these variances to the increased sales volume. Why? The reason is that the costs in the flexible budget—the benchmark for this variance—are already adjusted for the actual volume of operations.

The next step is to break down each variable cost variances into two components: a price variance and a quantity variance.

INPUT QUANTITY AND PRICE VARIANCES

Cindy's final step is to calculate input quantity and price variances corresponding to variable costs (see Exhibit 8.6C). A variable cost variance equals the amount in the flexible budget less the actual cost. Let us examine how we arrive at these two amounts. To calculate the flexible budget cost, we multiply the budgeted input per unit of sales by the actual sales quantity. The product is the *flexible budget quantity* of the input. We then multiply this quantity by the budgeted cost per unit of the input to find the flexible budget cost.

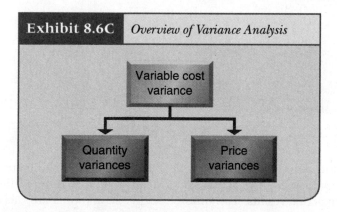

Exhibit 8.6C | *Overview of Variance Analysis*

Cindy's budget calls for 0.75 pound of butter per cake. The actual sales quantity for March is 3,800 cakes. Thus, the *flexible budget quantity* for butter is 0.75 lb per cake × 3,800 cakes = 2,850 lb of butter. We also know that Cindy budgeted to pay $2.40 per pound of butter. Therefore, the *flexible budget cost* for butter is $2.40 per pound × 2,850 lb = $6,840. This is Cindy's expected cost for butter at a volume of 3,800 cakes.

Exhibit 8.10 provides similar calculations for each input. The actual total cost of any input is the actual cost per unit of the input times the actual quantity of the input used. Exhibit 8.11 shows the actual costs and quantities of Cindy's inputs for March. For example, the actual price of butter during March was $2.40 per pound, and Cindy used 2,775 pounds of butter during the month. Thus, the total actual cost of butter during the month was $2.40 per pound × 2,775 pounds = $6,660.

Exhibit 8.10	*Flexible Budget Costs for Cindy's Variable Inputs*			
	Quantity Budgeted for One Cake	**Flexible Budget Input Quantity (3,800 cakes)**	**Budgeted Cost per Unit of Input**	**Flexible Budget Cost**
Raw materials				
Butter	0.75 pound	2,850 pounds	$2.40/pound	$6,840
Granulated sugar	1 pound	3,800 pounds	$0.80/pound	3,040
Eggs	5 eggs	19,000 eggs	$0.12/egg	2,280
All-purpose flour	0.75 pound	2,850 pounds	$0.40/pound	1,140
Other	$0.25	3,800 cakes	$0.25/cake	950
Direct labor	0.50 hours	1,900 hours	$20/hour	38,000
Variable overhead	0.50 hours	1,900 hours	$1.10/hour	2,090
Total variable costs				**$54,340**

Exhibit 8.11	*Actual Costs for Cindy's Variable Inputs*		
	Actual Cost per Unit of Input	**Actual Input Quantity (for 3,800 cakes)**	**Actual Total Cost**
Raw materials			
Butter	$2.40/pound	2,775 pounds	$6,660
Granulated sugar	$0.75/pound	3,820 pounds	2,865
Eggs	$0.14/egg	18,600 eggs	2,604
All-purpose flour	$0.50/pound	2,900 pounds	1,450
Other	$0.26 per cake	3,800 cakes	988
Direct labor	$20/hour	1,950 hours	39,000
Variable overhead	$1.16 per hour	1,950 hours	2,262
Total variable costs			**$55,829**

Cindy carefully tracks the actual amounts of ingredients used. (Angie Norwood Browne/ Getty Images)

In sum, the amounts in the flexible budget represent budgeted prices and budgeted quantities for the actual sales. Meanwhile, actual quantities and actual prices dictate actual results. The differences in the amounts are the variances for variable costs. This variance can relate to either input quantity or input price.

To separate these two effects, we introduce an "as if" budget. This budget represents the results with actual input quantities but with prices in the master budget. Exhibit 8.12 shows this "as if" budget for each of Cindy's inputs for March.

With this budget in hand, we compute the price and quantity variances for each input, as shown in Exhibit 8.13. Comparing line items in the flexible budget to the "as if" budget isolates a change in *input quantity*. Comparing the "as if" budget to the actual results isolates a change in *input price*.

For each of the line items, the **input price variance** is the difference between the "as if" budget and actual results. Comparing the column headings in Exhibit 8.13, notice that an input price variance arises only if the actual price of an input differs from its budgeted price. If the actual input price is greater than the budgeted input price, then the variance will be unfavorable; if it is less than the budgeted input price, the variance will be favorable.

Exhibit 8.12	Variable Costs under "As If" Budget		
	Actual Input Quantity (from Exhibit 8.11)	Budgeted Cost per Unit of Input (Exhibit 8.10)	Cost in "As If" Budget
Butter	2,775 pounds	$2.40/pound	$6,660
Granulated sugar	3,820 pounds	$0.80/pound	3,056
Eggs	18,600 eggs	$0.12/egg	2,232
All-purpose flour	2,900 pounds	$0.40/pound	1,160
Other	3,800 cakes	$0.25/cake	950
Direct labor	1,950 hours	$20/hour	39,000
Variable overhead	1,950 hours	$1.10/hour	2,145
Total variable costs			$55,203

Exhibit 8.13	Cindy's Cakes: Input Price and Quantity Variances							
	Flexible Budget (Flexible budget input quantity × Budgeted input price)	Input Quantity Variance		"As If" Budget (Actual input quantity × Budgeted input price)	Input Price Variance		Actual Results (Actual input quantity × Actual input price)	
Butter	$6,840	$180	F	$6,660	$0		$6,660	
Granulated sugar	3,040	(16)	U	3,056	191	F	2,865	
Eggs	2,280	48	F	2,232	(372)	U	2,604	
All-purpose flour	1,140	(20)	U	1,160	(290)	U	1,450	
Other	950	0		950	(38)	U	988	
Total (raw material)	$14,250	$192	F	$14,058	($509)	U	$14,567	
Direct labor	$38,000	($1,000)	U	$39,000	$0		$39,000	
Variable overhead	$2,090	($55)	U	$2,145	($117)	U	$2,262	
Total variable costs	$54,340	($863)	U	$55,203	($626)	U	$55,829	

The **input quantity variance** is the difference between the amounts in the flexible budget and the "as if" budget. These two numbers will only differ if the budgeted quantity is different from the actual quantity. If the actual quantity is greater than the flexible budget quantity, then the variance is unfavorable. If it is less than the flexible budget quantity, then the variance is favorable. Many also refer to the input quantity variance as the *input efficiency variance* because it captures the efficiency of input resource use.

Referring to Exhibit 8.13, we observe that Cindy has an unfavorable **materials price variance** for eggs, flour, and other ingredients. That is, for these inputs, she paid a higher price than budgeted. However, she has a favorable *price* variance for sugar. We also note that, with the exception of butter and eggs, all of the **materials efficiency variances** are unfavorable.

The direct labor price variance, also known as the direct **labor rate variance**, is zero because the actual labor rate of $20 per hour turned out to be the same as the budgeted labor rate. As in the case of materials, many refer to the labor quantity variance as the **labor efficiency variance** because it reflects the efficiency of the labor input. In Exhibit 8.13, this variance is $1,000 U.

The variable overhead price and quantity variances are $117 U and $55 U, respectively.

The box that follows provides a summary of variance calculations associated with variable costs.

Flexible Budget Quantity = Actual sales quantity
$\qquad\qquad\qquad$ × Quantity of input budgeted for 1 unit of sales)

Flexible Budget Cost = Flexible budget quantity × Budgeted cost per unit of input

Actual Input Cost = Actual input quantity × Actual cost per unit of input

Input Price Variance = (Budgeted price per unit of input
$\qquad\qquad\qquad$ − Actual price per unit of input) × Actual input quantity.

Input Quantity Variance = (Flexible budget quantity of input
$\qquad\qquad\qquad$ − Actual quantity of input) × Budgeted price per
$\qquad\qquad\qquad\qquad$ unit of input

Now that we have completed calculating all of the necessary variances, our next step in the control process is to use the variances to evaluate the different organizational functions.

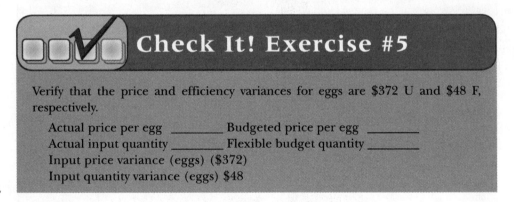

Check It! Exercise #5

Verify that the price and efficiency variances for eggs are $372 U and $48 F, respectively.

Actual price per egg _____ Budgeted price per egg _____
Actual input quantity _____ Flexible budget quantity _____
Input price variance (eggs) ($372)
Input quantity variance (eggs) $48

Solution at end of chapter.

CHAPTER CONNECTIONS

Recall from Chapter 7 that inventory cost flow assumptions, such as FIFO, could lead to different budgeted prices for individual units of the same input resource. For example, we may budget to use 100 units of materials from inventory at $3.00 per unit and to purchase an additional 100 units of materials at $3.25 per unit. In variance analysis, we typically use a single estimate for the budgeted input price. In general, we use the most recent price (in our example, $3.25). Consequently, the computed price variance would include the profit effect due to anticipated price changes.

Interpreting and Using Variances

Companies generally prepare a **budget reconciliation report** that provides management with a summary that bridges actual and expected performance. This report helps pinpoint which areas to investigate in order to take appropriate corrective actions. It also highlights areas of exceptional performance so that the organization as a whole can learn from success stories.

LEARNING OBJECTIVE 3

Interpret variances to determine possible corrective actions.

Exhibit 8.14 presents the budget reconciliation report for Cindy's Cakes for March. We start with the master budget profit, *add* each profit-increasing variance (i.e., favorable revenue and cost variances, and *subtract* each profit-decreasing variance (i.e., unfavorable revenue and cost variances) to arrive at actual profit. Thus, we first add the favorable sales volume variance, and then we add or subtract the flexible budget variances.

We are now ready to interpret the variances in the budget reconciliation report. Variances could arise for three main reasons.

- Variances could arise during the normal course of operations. For example, a machine might unexpectedly break down or several employees might call in sick.
- Variances could arise because of a more permanent change in the firm's operating environment. For example, a competitor introduces a new product or a supplier raises prices.
- Variances could arise because budgets or standards are either too tight or too loose.

Exhibit 8.14	Cindy's Cakes: Budget Reconciliation Report		
Master Budget			
Profit			$9,275
Sales volume variance	$1,995	F	$1,995
Flexible budget variances			
Sales price variance	($3,800)	U	(3,800)
Materials variances			
Price variances (total)	($509)	U	
Efficiency variances (total)	192	F	
Total	($317)	U	(317)
Labor variances			
Price variance	$0		
Efficiency variance	(1,000)	U	
Total	($1,000)	U	(1,000)
Variable overhead			
Price variance	($117)	U	
Efficiency variance	(55)	U	
Total	($172)	U	(172)
Fixed cost spending variance	($500)	U	(500)
Actual profit			$5,481

GENERAL RULES FOR ANALYZING VARIANCES

There are three general rules to follow in a variance investigation:

- Investigate all significant variances, whether favorable or unfavorable.
- Examine trends.
- Consider the total picture.

Let's see how these rules help us get the most out of variance analysis.

Investigate All Large Variances

Small variances probably indicate random factors at work. It is possible that Cindy's sales volume variance occurred because of an unexpected increase in demand. If so, and the increase were purely temporary, Cindy needs no further action. Similarly, it is possible that the cost variances occurred because of fluctuating input prices. This might be especially true for Cindy's Cakes; as we know from our own grocery shopping experiences, prices change frequently. Again, this would not be cause for alarm. (In Appendix A, we discuss the *purchase price variance*, which is a slight variation on the materials price variance.)

In contrast, large variances could signal a permanent change in the operating environment. For instance, Cindy might have reduced the price per cake because she felt that sales would have fallen short of the budgeted 3,500 cakes otherwise. If true, the ensuing sales price and sales volume variances suggest a change in the

Connecting to Practice

OPEN BRIEFINGS FROM AUSTRALIA

Seeking to improve disclosure, the Australian Stock Exchange (ASX) periodically posts "Open Briefings" by CEOs of firms listed in the ASX. The following is an excerpt from one such briefing.

Interviewer: Domestic Liquefied Petroleum Gas (LPG) sales volumes for Kleenheat Gas were below budget, and LPG input prices were up from last year. Therefore, can you explain why earnings were above budget and whether there's more outperformance to come from Kleenheat?

CEO: Kleenheat has had a particularly good year because its profits are significantly up at a time when its raw material input price has risen. This is the first time that the negative correlation between LPG prices and Kleenheat profits has been broken. Usually if LPG prices rise then we expect to see Kleenheat profits fall. The main reason for the good performance is that David Robb has instituted better management practices across the business. We've restructured the organization, improved the contractual pricing arrangements and achieved quite significant cost savings. Although we've made the majority of cost savings, we hope Kleenheat will continue its improved performance in the coming years.

COMMENTARY: The previous excerpt highlights management's focus on understanding the reasons for variances and using these reasons as the basis for corrective actions.

Source: www1.wesfarmers.com.au/uploads/pdfs/WES03-079.pdf

price/demand relationship. Because this change likely has long-term implications, it is important to understand its cause. Is it new competition, a price reduction from existing competition, or a change in customer tastes? Cindy must explore each possibility and initiate suitable corrective action.

Trends in Variances

Trends in variances often point to inherent problems. Suppose Cindy repeatedly finds her labor efficiency variances to be unfavorable, even though the variance for any one period is not particularly large. Such a trend, especially if the amount of the variance is increasing over time, might indicate a developing problem in the manufacturing process. Cindy would be prudent to investigate and fix the problem before it becomes a significant issue.

Trends in variances also could arise because of biases that influence the setting of standards. In most organizations, the forecasting process begins with the marketing/sales function. As you learned in Chapter 7, marketing personnel are in the best position to predict future demand trends because of their intimate knowledge of the market. However, marketing personnel have an incentive to deliberately underestimate demand to give themselves a better chance of exceeding targets. Similarly, production personnel might overstate costs to give themselves additional leeway in operations. All of these factors increase the likelihood of favorable variances. Finding mostly favorable variances over time might therefore suggest that the underlying plans contain significant slack.

CHAPTER CONNECTIONS

In Chapter 7, you learned that employees have incentives to build slack into budgets by inflating costs or by low-balling sales. By lowering the standard for expected performance, such slack increases the chances of obtaining a favorable variance.

Linking Variances—The Big Picture

We often get so caught up in the specific calculations and analysis of each variance that we forget to look at the big picture. It is important to step back and see how the variances are connected to each other. For instance, Cindy must consider whether the increase in demand was due to a reduction in the sales price, which, as we know, generates an unfavorable sales price variance. That is, unfavorable sales price variances could lead to favorable sales volume variances. Cindy needs to consider how changing the price would affect the sales quantity at the time of planning, as illustrated in Exhibit 8.15.

Many other linkages occur among variances. For example, the purchasing department typically acquires the raw materials needed for production. An excessive focus on generating favorable input price variances provides the purchasing manager with a natural incentive to look for "good" deals by sacrificing quality, purchasing in bulk quantities, or agreeing to flexible delivery schedules. Such practices could lead to unfavorable variances elsewhere in the organization. Cheaper ingredients lead to a favorable price variance, but they also may lead to unfavorable quantity variances because of poor quality. Similarly, agreeing to delivery schedules that suit the supplier may save money. However, such a deal may also prevent materials from being available on a timely basis, leading to excessive idle time.

Finally, revenue and cost variances sometimes have the same underlying cause. It is possible that the unexpected increase in sales volume contributed to the unfavorable

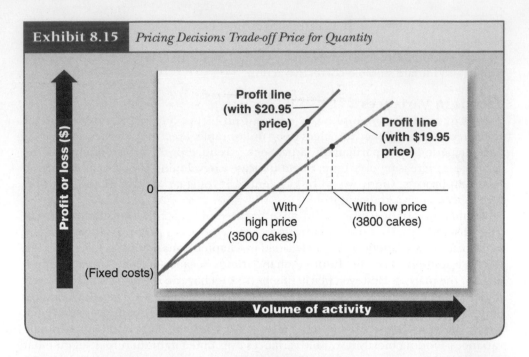

Exhibit 8.15 *Pricing Decisions Trade-off Price for Quantity*

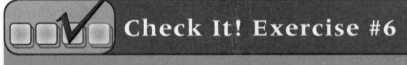

Check It! Exercise #6

Assume that at the time of planning, Cindy knew that she could sell 3,800 cakes in March if she dropped the price to $19.95. Verify that Cindy's budgeted profit would have been $7,470 at this price-volume combination. Further verify that the sum of the sales price and sales volume variances captures this drop in profit.

Solution at end of chapter.

labor efficiency variance. For example, Cindy might have hired some temporary help who were not as skilled as her regular bakers, leading to the unfavorable labor efficiency variance. Cindy has to draw on other information about her operations to discern such links.

MAKING CONTROL DECISIONS IN RESPONSE TO VARIANCES

We have come to the end of the evaluation step. Analyzing individual variances for a specific period is just a starting point. Firms should use all of the variances to investigate the validity of underlying budget assumptions and targets. They then need to collect additional information to choose among alternate explanations. Only then should companies decide on suitable corrective actions.

After contacting numerous suppliers, Cindy concludes that the price of eggs is likely to stay at the higher level for the next few months. She therefore decides to revise her budgets to reflect the increase. Specifically, Cindy will reduce her estimate of the unit contribution margin by $0.10 because the price of eggs increased $0.02 per egg and each cake requires five eggs. If she plans to sell 3,500 cakes, this adjustment would reduce expected monthly profit by $350.

With regard to the unfavorable labor efficiency variance, Cindy discovers that one of the ovens malfunctioned. The oven failed to work efficiently for several days and then cost $500 for repairs. Cindy believes that this explains both the unfavorable labor efficiency variance and the unexpected increase in fixed costs. Thus, Cindy decides not to revise her labor standards or fixed costs in the coming month.

Finally, Cindy decides to hold her marketing and salespeople answerable to *any* volume variance—*positive or negative.* She believes this will reduce the incentive to "low-ball" demand forecasts. Cindy further decides to institute a new policy regarding price changes—she must personally approve all price changes.

While we have used a single-product firm to highlight the concepts and mechanics underlying variance analysis, most companies usually offer a range of products to meet diverse customer needs. How does variance analysis change for such multiproduct companies? The answer is, "Not much." We calculate and interpret all of the cost variances in a multiproduct firm exactly as we would for a single-product firm. However, when analyzing the revenue variances from multiproduct firms, we need to consider one additional aspect—sales mix. In Appendix C, we illustrate the computation of sales mix variances for multiproduct firms. As you will learn there, the multiproduct variance analysis uses the same ideas, weighted unit contribution margin and weighted contribution margin ratio, which you learned when performing multiproduct CVP analysis in Chapter 5.

Nonfinancial Controls

Thus far, we have focused on a specific control process—variance analysis—that helps ensure that an organization's people and processes are performing as expected. Variance analysis is an extremely useful tool for control and, indeed, organizations routinely perform this analysis. Yet, it has some limitations. These limitations apply whenever controls are based on financial data from a firm's accounting system.

LEARNING OBJECTIVE **4**

Explain how non-financial measures complement variance analysis.

APPLYING THE DECISION FRAMEWORK

What Is the Problem?	Cindy's actual profit in March is lower than her budgeted profit. This shortfall occurred even though sales volume exceeded expectations.
What Are the Options?	Cindy's actual profit might differ from her budgeted profit for a number of reasons, including a lower than expected selling price, baker inefficiencies, higher input prices, material waste, and oven failure.
What Are the Costs and the Benefits?	Our analysis of Cindy's profit variances indicates that her actual profit was lower than her budgeted profit primarily because of a large, unfavorable sales price variance, an unfavorable labor efficiency variance, and an unfavorable fixed cost spending variance. We also found minor deviations in the materials prices and efficiencies.
Make the Decision!	After looking at the individual variances, Cindy decides to chalk up the fixed cost spending variance and the labor efficiency variance to an unexpected oven failure. Given the magnitude of the sales price and sales volume variances, Cindy decides to personally approve all price changes and change the incentives of her sales and marketing personnel. Finally, Cindy decides to revise her forthcoming budgets to reflect the changes in raw materials prices.

The primary limitations of variance analysis pertain to *timeliness* and *specificity*. Because they rely on accounting data, firms compute variances on a weekly or monthly basis. Numerous business functions require quicker feedback, however. If a key machine breaks down, we need to take corrective action immediately, and not at the end of the week or month when a variance report reveals a large, unfavorable variance. Similarly, if a customer is unhappy, we must correct the problem immediately, and not wait until an unfavorable sales volume variance reveals that the customer is no longer purchasing goods or services.

Financial measures also are aggregate. It is difficult for Cindy to evaluate the performance of each of her ovens using financial data. Specific nonfinancial measures, such as a temperature gauge on each oven, are of greater use. The lack of timeliness and specificity in financial variances force organizations to use other, primarily nonfinancial controls to ensure that they are meeting organizational objectives.

NONFINANCIAL MEASURES AND PROCESS CONTROL

Nonfinancial measures can provide immediate and specific feedback to employees about the status of the environment and the outcomes of their decisions. To perform their jobs well, pilots need to know, among other things, the plane's speed, altitude, fuel status, and direction. For these reasons, the airline cockpit is a maze of instruments, providing the pilot with numerous nonfinancial measures regarding every aspect of the flight. If any of these measures deviates from the flight plan, the pilot has to take immediate corrective action or risk catastrophe.

In a like fashion, employees need feedback regardless of their level in the organization's hierarchy. A line operator at United States Steel needs to continuously monitor steam pressure. A purchasing manager at Macy's needs to know which goods are in stock and which are not. Maytag's CEO needs information on attributes such as customer satisfaction, the rate of innovation, and product quality to ensure that the firm is executing its strategy. We all need feedback, or control, information to perform our jobs effectively.

As you can see from these examples, the nature of the information required by a manager differs depending on the type of job and the type of organization. Some controls, such as those required by operating personnel at lower hierarchical levels, need to give immediate, or "real-time" feedback. Cindy's bakers need real-time information about oven temperatures, not after the fact. Many firms use *process control charts* and statistical control methods to help employees track performance on a real-time basis. These methods indicate, on a continuous basis, whether the processes, such as a machine, are functioning within defined limits and can immediately highlight any deviations. Because these measures focus on one aspect (a single machine, for instance), the corrective action is often obvious. Employees on site, such as the machine operator, would take corrective steps.

Exhibit 8.16 shows a representative process control chart. This chart has a graph representing the expected value as well as lines representing lower and upper control limits. Observations within the control limits are likely due to random fluctuations. However, observations outside these limits indicate a significant change and trigger an investigation. Even within the control limits, trends in observations could signal an impending problem. As with financial variances, when a process is performing as planned, we expect to see random fluctuations around the expected value (the mean) of the performance measure and within the control limits.

Supervisors and managers, who are higher up in the hierarchy, may only need information on a daily or weekly basis. A manager at a local Wal-Mart may total sales each day or each shift but not each hour. A sales manager at Hoover may track the number of client contacts made per salesperson each week. The longer time for

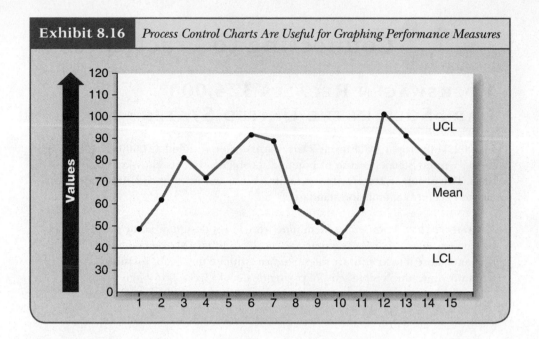

Exhibit 8.16 | *Process Control Charts Are Useful for Graphing Performance Measures*

the feedback measures is appropriate because the decisions taken by the employees receiving the feedback spans a longer time horizon.

Top management often tracks metrics such as quality and customer satisfaction. These measures, called *critical success factors*, are vital to achieving the firm's strategy. By tracking these measures over time, top management can determine whether the firm is executing its strategy effectively. Firms often collect and report these measures only once a month or quarter because the measures represent the outcomes of longer-term decisions.

In all cases, there is an expected or budgeted value for each measure. We then compute the actual value and compare it with the budgeted value. Next, we diagnose the deviations and take corrective actions. Thus, in a broad sense, we can compute a variance for each nonfinancial measure as:

$$\textit{Nonfinancial Measure Variance} = \text{Actual Value} - \text{Budgeted Amount}$$

 **Connecting to Practice**

PROCESS CONTROL CHARTS

Dr. Boggs et al. report how they use process control charts to monitor patients with asthma and adjust their medication. This application shows the value of these charts to both clinicians and managed care organizations.

COMMENTARY: Numerous companies use process control charts that allow employees to track performance on a real-time basis. For example, to ensure uniform, high quality, Mattel uses process control charts in the manufacture of their popular "Barbie" dolls and "Hot Wheels" cars.

Source: P. B. Boggs et al. "Control Charts to Guide Medication Decision Making in Asthma Care," *Drug Benefit Trends* 11(8), 1999:42–52.

Connecting to Practice

VOLKSWAGEN RECALLS 324,000 CARS SOLD IN THE UNITED STATES

In 2002, Volkswagen AG, Europe's largest carmaker, recalled 324,000 vehicles sold in the United States because of potential problems with its emission control systems. The problems stemmed from faulty oxygen sensors that caused certain vehicles to exceed U.S. emission standards.

COMMENTARY: Poor quality stemming from faulty design or faulty processes can be very expensive. For Volkswagen, the recall could tarnish the company's reputation and cause it to lose future sales. Studies estimate that such "invisible" costs can be many times the "visible" cost of paying dealers to fix the problem.

NONFINANCIAL MEASURES AND ALIGNING GOALS

In addition to helping firms identify problems with their processes, nonfinancial measures also help align goals. This dual role for nonfinancial measures is similar to that for financial measures. For example, we could use the sales volume variance both to validate demand assumptions and to evaluate the sales manager. In a like manner, firms use nonfinancial measures not only to provide ongoing feedback to employees but also to evaluate them. A sales manager might use the number of calls per salesperson per month to assess the overall productivity. She might use the same metric to identify individual salespersons operating above and below expectations. In turn, a regional manager can compare the metric across branches or sales offices to identify high-performing sales managers.

In general, financial controls are more useful for evaluating managers at higher levels in an organizational hierarchy, whereas nonfinancial controls are more useful for monitoring and evaluating employees at lower levels, engaged in day-to-day operations. Problems that are not fixed in a timely manner when and where they arise will give rise to unfavorable financial variances at the end of the week or the month, and it becomes a manager's responsibility to take corrective actions next time around.

SUMMARY

In this chapter, we discussed how organizations use short-term control measures to follow up on planning decisions and to motivate employees. We described variance analysis, a technique used to determine why actual profit differs from budgeted profit. We explained the mechanics of variance analysis and how variances help verify whether an organization's people and processes are performing as expected. Finally, we discussed how nonfinancial measures complement financial variances in controlling operations.

In the next module (Chapters 9–14), we examine issues that arise when measuring costs and benefits for long-term planning and control decisions.

RAPID REVIEW

Understand how companies use budgets for control.

- As plans determine the benchmark of evaluating actual performance, a good plan is the foundation for effective control. Without a well-conceived benchmark, or budget, it is difficult to evaluate how we are doing or what we can do to improve.

- A master budget is the quintessential example of a plan. A master budget specifies the expected sales and profit during the plan period, and the organizational resources to be used to achieve this profit level. To prepare a master budget, an organization must form expectations about sales prices, sales quantities, input efficiencies, and input costs.

Perform variance analysis.

- A variance is the difference between an actual result and a budgeted amount. A favorable variance means that actual revenue exceeded budgeted revenue or actual cost was less than budgeted cost. An unfavorable variance means that actual revenue was less than budgeted revenue or actual cost exceeded budgeted cost.

- We denote favorable variances with positive numbers and unfavorable variances with negative numbers. Thus, we calculate revenue, contribution margin, and profit variances as actual results less budgeted amounts. In contrast, because costs represent outflows, we calculate cost variances as budgeted amounts less actual results.

- The total profit variance is the difference between actual profit and master budget profit. To split the total profit variance into its two component variances, the sales volume variance and the flexible budget variance, we need to prepare the flexible budget. A flexible budget is the budget corresponding to the actual level of sales achieved.

- The sales volume variance is the difference between flexible budget profit and master budget profit. Whenever actual sales differs from budgeted sales, we have a sales volume variance.

- The flexible budget variance is the difference between actual profit and flexible budget profit. The flexible budget variance is comprised of the sales price variance, the variable cost variances, and the fixed cost spending variance.

- The sales price variance is the difference between actual revenue and flexible budget revenue. A sales price variance arises whenever the actual selling price differs from the budgeted selling price.

- We refer to any variance in fixed costs as a spending variance. The fixed cost spending variance equals the difference between budgeted fixed costs and actual fixed costs.

- An input price variance is the difference between the budgeted price per unit of the input and the actual price per unit of the input, multiplied by the total actual quantity of the input. An input price variance arises whenever the actual price of an input, such as materials, labor, or variable overhead, differs from its budgeted price assumed in planning.

- An input quantity variance is the difference between the flexible budget quantity of the input and the actual quantity of the input, multiplied by the budgeted price per unit of the input. An input quantity variance arises when the actual quantity of materials, labor, or variable overhead consumed differs from the budgeted quantity that should have been consumed given the actual sales level.

Interpret variances to determine possible corrective actions.

- To explain the difference between actual and budgeted results for any given period, organizations prepare a budget reconciliation report.

- Variances serve as important diagnostic controls in organizations. When using variances, it is important to: (a) investigate all significant variances, whether they are favorable or unfavorable; (b) examine trends; and, (c) consider the total picture, as actions that lead to a favorable variance in one aspect of operations can result in offsetting unfavorable variances elsewhere.

Explain how nonfinancial measures complement variance analysis.

- Relative to financial measures, nonfinancial measures often are *more timely* and *more specific*. Consequently, firms supplement variance analysis with nonfinancial performance measures. The specific measures depend on the nature of the job and the organization.

- Nonfinancial measures provide the feedback necessary for employees to discharge their responsibilities effectively. The frequency of nonfinancial reports tends to decrease as we move up the organizational hierarchy. Employees at lower levels may need real-time controls and process control charts. In contrast, it may be enough for top management to track key success factors such as quality and customer satisfaction on a monthly or quarterly basis.

- As with variances, firms use nonfinancial measures to achieve both process control and align goals. In both instances, firms follow the same steps as with financial measures—they establish a benchmark or budget, measure actual performance, compare it with the budget, diagnose deviations, and take corrective actions.

Appendix A

PURCHASE PRICE VARIANCE

In the text, we calculated the materials price variance using the actual quantity of materials used in operations. However, the actual quantity of materials used in operations could differ from the actual quantity of materials *purchased*. An organization might purchase less material than it plans to use when it has excess raw materials, and more materials than it plans to use when it wishes to increase its inventory. Many organizations compute the materials price variance using the actual quantity of materials purchased rather than the actual quantity of materials used. That is, they calculate a **purchase price variance** as

$$Purchase\ Price\ Variance = (Budgeted\ input\ price - Actual\ input\ price) \\ \times Actual\ quantity\ purchased$$

For Cindy's Cakes, assume the office manager actually purchased 4,200 pounds of sugar. The purchase price variance is therefore:

$$Purchase\ price\ variance = (\$0.35 - \$0.32) \times 4{,}200 = \$126,\ or\ \$126\ F$$

Because Cindy's Cakes actually used 3,820 pounds of sugar in March, the remaining 380 pounds would go into inventory.

Which variance, the materials price or purchase price, should we use? Some argue that by holding the manager responsible for the quantity purchased, the purchase price variance provides a better measure for evaluating the purchasing function. Others argue that the purchase price variance amplifies the manager's incentive to buy in bulk to get price discounts, leading to undesirable inventory buildups. In practice, the difference between the purchase price variance and the materials price variance is often negligible. We focus on the materials price variance as it helps reconcile actual profit with master budget profit.

Appendix B
MARKET SIZE AND MARKET SHARE VARIANCES

A favorable or unfavorable sales volume variance could arise due to a change in (1) the market as a whole or (2) the firm's share of the market. Distinguishing between these factors is important because they can lead to different corrective actions. If an unfavorable sales volume variance is due to a shrinking of the overall market size, then the firm may wish to focus its efforts on other products. Alternatively, if an unfavorable sales volume variance is due to lower market share, then the firm may wish to increase advertising.

Suppose Cindy had budgeted sales of 3,500 cakes in March based on capturing a 20% share of the market, estimated at 17,500 cakes. The actual sales volume of 3,800 cakes in March represented a 19% share of the market of 20,000 cakes. Finally, recall that Cindy's budgeted contribution margin per cake was $6.65.

As in the text, we can calculate Cindy's sales volume variance as:

Sales Volume Variance
= (Actual Sales Quantity − Budgeted Sales Quantity) × BUCM
= (3,800 cakes − 3,500 cakes) × $6.65/cake = $1,995, or $1,995 F

We can express the actual sales quantity as actual market size times actual share (3,500 = 0.20 × 17,500), and the budgeted sales as the product of budgeted market size and share (3,800 = 0.19 × 20,000).

We can therefore express sales volume variance as

Sales Volume Variance = [(Actual Market Size × Actual Market Share)
   − (Budgeted Market Size × Budgeted Market Share)]
   × BUCM

This computation shows that both market size and market share affect the sales volume variance. With suitable algebraic manipulations, we disentangle the effects of market size and market share by rewriting the sales volume variance as follows:

Market Share Variance = Actual Market Size × (Actual Market Share
   − Budgeted Market Share)
   × Budgeted Unit Contribution Margin.

Market Size Variance = (Actual Market Size − Budgeted Market Size)
   × Budgeted Market Share
   × Budgeted Unit Contribution Margin

Note that the **market share variance** holds market size constant while examining variations between budgeted and actual market share. The **market size variance** holds market share constant while examining variations between actual and budgeted market size.

For Cindy's Cakes, we have:

Market Share Variance = $20,000 \times (.19 - .20) \times \$6.65 = (\$1,330)$, or $\$1,330$ U

Market Size Variance = $(20,000 - 17,500) \times .20 \times \$6.65 = \$3,325$, or $\$3,325$ F

Sales Volume Variance = $\$1,995$ F = $\$3,325 - \$1,330$

This decomposition shows that the increase in Cindy's sales volume was due to an increase in the size of the overall market for specialty cakes. Even though Cindy reduced her price per cake, her market share dropped. This pattern of results may give Cindy some cause for concern because it signals changing consumer preferences for Cindy's cakes. If the pattern continues, Cindy will need to think about further price decreases, increased advertising, or perhaps even changing her recipe. If, however, the market size variance were unfavorable, Cindy might need to think about changing the type of cake she sells; such a variance would signal that consumer preferences are changing from specialty cakes to some other cake or dessert item.

Finally, we emphasize that while splitting the sales volume variance into market size and market share variances could be informative, it requires data regarding both the size of the overall market and the firm's share of the market. Such data might be available via trade organizations and industry associations. If not, managers must subjectively evaluate the causes for the variances.

Appendix C

SALES VARIANCES IN A MULTIPRODUCT FIRM

When analyzing the variances of multiproduct firms, we need to consider two additional variances—the sales mix variance and the sales quantity variance. The two variances together add up to the sales volume variance. Recall that we define the sales volume variance as

$$Sales\ Volume\ Variance = \text{Flexible budget profit} - \text{Master budget profit}$$
$$= \text{Flexible budget } CM - \text{Master budget } CM$$
$$= (Actual\ sale - Budgeted\ sales) \times BUCM$$

where $BUCM$ = budgeted unit contribution margin.

In Chapter 5, we defined the sales mix as the proportion, expressed in units, in which a company expects to sell products. We used the notion of a sales mix to incorporate multiple products into CVP analysis. In one approach, we used the budgeted sales mix to compute a weighted unit contribution margin ($WUCM$). In terms of calculating the sales volume variance for a multiproduct firm, the question is: how do we calculate the $WUCM$ for the master budget and the flexible budget?

For the master budget, we calculate the $WUCM$ using the budgeted sales mix and the budgeted unit contribution margin for each product. For the flexible budget, we retain all budget assumptions except for sales volume. Therefore, for the flexible budget, we calculate the $WUCM$ using the actual sales mix and the budgeted unit contribution margin. With these clarifications, we have:

$$Sales\ Volume\ Variance = (\text{Actual Total Sales} \times WUCM_{\text{flexible budget}})$$
$$- (\text{Budgeted Total Sales} \times WUCM_{\text{master budget}})$$

In the single-product case, the $WUCM$ in the master and flexible budgets is identical because we have only one product.

The above expression shows that the sales volume variance in a multiproduct firm could arise because of changes in the total units sold and changes in the weighted unit contribution margin for the units sold. With some algebraic manipulation, we can split the sales volume variance for a multiproduct firm into a sales mix variance and a sales quantity variance:

$$Sales\ Mix\ Variance = \text{Actual Total Sales}$$
$$\times (\text{WUCM}_{\text{flexible budget}} - \text{WUCM}_{\text{master budget}})$$
$$Sales\ Quantity\ Variance = (\text{Actual Total Sales} - \text{Budgeted Total Sales})$$
$$\times \text{WUCM}_{\text{master budget}}$$

The **sales mix variance** captures the profit effect of changes in the sales mix from the budgeted level. The **sales quantity variance** tells us the effect of the aggregate change in sales quantity, holding the sales mix at the budgeted level. You might find it convenient to think of the sales quantity variance as the mix-adjusted sales volume variance.

An Example

Suppose Pacific Telephones manufactures two different types of cordless telephones, the PT1000 and the PT2000. The PT1000 is a basic telephone, with a handset and a base station. The PT2000 model contains all the features of the PT1000 plus a built-in digital answering machine. Exhibit 8.17 presents Pacific Telephones' budgeted and actual results for the most recent quarter.

Exhibit 8.17 *Pacific Telephones: Budgeted and Actual Results for the most Recent Quarter*

Budgeted Results

Product	Sales Price per Unit	Unit Variable Cost	Sales in Units	UCM
PT1000	$29.95	$8.50	150,000	$21.45
PT2000	$59.95	$24.00	50,000	$35.95
Total			200,000	

Actual Results

Product	Sales Price per Unit	Unit Variable Cost	Sales in Units	UCM
PT1000	$29.00	$8.45	154,000	$20.55
PT2000	$60.50	$24.25	47,000	$36.25
Total			201,000	

Exhibit 8.18 *Pacific Telephones: Sales Volume and Flexible Budget Variances*

	Master Budget	Sales Volume Variance	Flexible Budget	Flexible Budget Variance	Actual
Units (PT1000)	150,000	4,000	154,000		154,000
Units (PT2000)	50,000	(3,000)	47,000		47,000
Total units	200,000	1,000	201,000		201,000
Revenue (PT1000)	$4,492,500	$119,800	$4,612,300	($146,300) U	$4,466,000
Revenue (PT2000)	2,997,500	(179,850)	2,817,650	25,850 F	2,843,500
Total revenue	$7,490,000	($60,050)	$7,429,950	($120,450) U	$7,309,500
Variable cost (PT1000)	$1,275,000	($34,000)	$1,309,000	$7,700 F	$1,301,300
Variable cost (PT2000)	1,200,000	72,000	1,128,000	(11,750) U	1,139,750
Total variable costs	$2,475,000	$38,000	$2,437,000	($4,050) U	$2,441,050
Contribution margin	$5,015,000	($22,050) U	$4,992,950	($124,500) U	$4,868,450

Exhibit 8.18 presents the sales volume and flexible budget variances for Pacific Telephones. Relative to the one-product example (Cindy's Cakes), note that the only difference is the separate revenue and cost line for each product. Otherwise, we calculate the total sales volume variance of $22,050 U and the flexible budget variance of $124,500 U in the same way.

Interpreting the sales volume variance for Pacific Telephones is difficult. In particular, the sales volume variance is unfavorable, even though actual total sales exceeded budgeted sales by 1,000 units. The added sales should have increased, rather than decreased, profit. We cannot point to costs as an explanation because we assume the same cost structure for both the master and the flexible budgets. (Recall that we construct the flexible budget with the same plan assumptions as the master budget, except for sales volume.) What could account for the odd result?

The answer is that while, relative to budget, Pacific Telephones sold more of the PT1000, the firm sold less of the PT2000. Furthermore, the PT1000 has a lower unit contribution margin relative to the PT2000. Thus, while overall sales volume increased by 1,000 units, this increase came from selling 4,000 more units of the less profitable PT1000 and 3,000 fewer units of the more profitable PT2000. Pacific Telephones replaced higher profit units with lower profit units! Its sales mix, which affects the contribution received, changed adversely.

Our observations underscore the importance of splitting the sales volume variance for a multiproduct firm into a sales mix variance and a sales quantity variance. Exhibit 8.19 shows this analysis for Pacific Telephones. We find that the sales mix variance is $47,125 U and that the sales quantity variance is $25,075 F. The negative profit effect of the change in sales mix more than offsets the positive profit effect due to selling more units.

In terms of moving forward, Pacific Telephones may wish to investigate whether reducing the price on the PT1000 and increasing the price on the PT2000 led to the unfavorable sales mix variance. (Exhibit 8.21, presented in Self-Study Problems, reveals that the sales price variance is $146,300 U for the PT1000 and the sales price variance is $25,850 F for the PT2000.) Moreover, the slight increase in the overall volume of sales was not enough to counter the unfavorable sales mix variance and the net unfavorable sales price variance. Pacific Telephones might wish to reconsider its product mix and product pricing strategy. Finally, if required, we can apply the techniques from Appendix B to decompose the sales quantity variance into a market size and a market share variance.

Exhibit 8.19	Pacific Telephones: Sales Mix and Sales Quantity Variances	
	Master Budget	**Flexible Budget**
Total sales	200,000	201,000
Percent sales from PT1000	75.00%	76.62%
Percent sales from PT2000	25.00%	23.38%
Unit contribution margin PT1000	$21.45	$21.45
Unit contribution margin PT2000	$35.95	$35.95
Weighted unit contribution margin	$25.08	$24.84
Sales mix variance[1]	$47,125 **U**	
Sales quantity variance[2]	$25,075 **F**	
Total (sales volume variance)	$22,050 **U**	

[1] = actual total sales × (*WUCM* in flexible budget − *WUCM* in master budget).

[2] = (actual total sales − budgeted total sales) × *WUCM* in master budget.

ANSWERS TO CHECK IT! EXERCISES

Exercise #1: Price per cake = $20.95; unit variable cost = $3.75 in materials + $10.00 in labor ($10.00 = $20 per hour $\times$ 0.50 hours per cake) + $0.55 in variable overhead = $14.30; unit contribution margin = $20.95 − $14.30 = $6.65; contribution margin = 3,000 $\times$ $6.65 = $19,950; fixed costs = $14,000; profit before taxes = $19,950 − $14,000 = $5,950.

Exercise #2: For 2,800 cakes, revenue = $58,660, and variable costs = $40,040; For 3,200 cakes, variable costs = $45,760, contribution margin = $21,280, and fixed costs = $14,000; For 3,800 cakes, revenue = $79,610, contribution margin = $25,270, and profit = $11,270.

Exercise #3: (1) 3,800 cakes − 3,500 cakes = 300 cakes; (2) $6.65; (3) $1,995 = 300 $\times$ $6.65.

Exercise #4: (1) $75,810 actual revenue ÷ 3,800 cakes actually sold = $19.95 per cake; (2) $20.95; (3) 3,800; (4) ($19.95 − $20.95) $\times$ 3,800 = $3,800 U.

Exercise #5: Actual input price = $0.14; Budgeted input price = $0.12; Actual input quantity = 18,600; Flexible budget quantity = 19,000 = 5 eggs per cake $\times$ 3,800 cakes; Input price variance = $372 U = ($0.12 − $0.14) $\times$ 18,600; Input quantity variance = $48 F = (19,000 − 18,600) $\times$ $0.12.

Exercise #6: At a sales price of $19.95, the unit contribution margin = $19.95 − $14.30 = $5.65; budgeted fixed costs = $14,000; thus, budgeted profit = 3,800 $\times$ $5.65 − $14,000 = $7,470. The sales volume and sales price variances capture the effect of this error in planning. The sales volume variance = $1,995 F and the sales price variance = $3,800 U; the net effect is $3,800 − $1,995 = $1,805 U, which corresponds to the difference in budgeted profit. That is, $1,805 U = $7,470 in budgeted profit at the $19.95 price and 3,800 cakes combination − $9,275 in budgeted profit at the $20.95 and 3,500 cakes combination.

SELF-STUDY PROBLEMS

SELF-STUDY PROBLEM #1:
Splitting the Total Profit Variance into Sales Volume and Flexible Budget Variances

Serene Brakes manufactures brake pads for motorcycles. For the month of June, Serene budgeted to manufacture and sell 8,000 sets of brake pads (a set includes pads for the front and rear wheels) at a price of $32 per set. Serene's management estimated the unit variable cost at $20 per set and budgeted fixed costs of $54,000 for the month. During June, Serene actually sold 7,200 sets of brake pads, earning $259,200 in revenue. In addition, Serene's actual total variable and fixed costs amounted to $160,000 and $50,000, respectively.

a. *Compute Serene's total profit variance for June.*

As discussed in the text, the total profit variance = Actual profit − Master budget profit. Given the information in the problem, we have Exhibit 8.20:

Exhibit 8.20	Serene Brakes: Total Profit Variance		
	Master Budget[1]	**Total Profit Variance**	**Actual Results**
Sets of brake pads	8,000		7,200
Revenue	$256,000		$259,200
Variable costs	160,000		160,000
Contribution margin	$96,000		$99,200
Fixed costs	54,000		50,000
Profit before taxes	$42,000	$7,200 F	$49,200
[1]Master budget revenue = 8,000 $\times$ $32; Variable costs = 8,000 $\times$ $20.			

The master budget profit is $42,000, while actual profit is $49,200. Thus, Serene's total profit variance = $7,200 F = $49,200 − $42,000.

b. *Split Serene's total profit variance for June into a sales volume variance and a flexible budget variance.*

To split Serene's total profit variance into a sales volume variance and a flexible budget variance, we need to create Serene's flexible budget for June. This requires us to redo Serene's master budget for the actual sales volume of 7,200 sets of brake pads.

As discussed in the text, the sales volume variance is the difference between flexible budget profit and master budget profit. The flexible budget variance is the difference between actual profit and flexible budget profit.

Exhibit 8.21 provides the required analysis. Serene's sales volume variance for June was $9,600 U, and its flexible budget variance for June was $16,800 F.

Exhibit 8.21	*Serene Brakes: Sales Volume Variance and Flexible Budget Variance*				
	Master Budget	**Sales Volume Variance**	**Flexible Budget**	**Flexible Budget Variance**	**Actual Results**
Sets of brake pads	8,000		7,200		7,200
Revenue	$256,000		$230,400	$28,800 **F**	$259,200
Variable costs	160,000		144,000	(16,000) **U**	160,000
Contribution margin	$ 96,000	($9,600) **U**	$86,400	$12,800	$99,200
Fixed costs	54,000		54,000	4,000 **F**	50,000
Profit before taxes	$42,000	($9,600) **U**	$32,400	$16,800 **F**	$49,200

The sales volume variance + the flexible budget variance = the total profit variance for Serene, $9,600 U + $16,800 F = $7,200 F

c. *Break out Serene's flexible budget variance into a sales price variance, the variable cost variance, and a fixed cost spending variance.*

Exhibit 8.18, presented earlier, provides the necessary data for performing the required computations. In particular, we have:

Sales price variance = Actual revenue − Flexible budget revenue.
= $259,200 − $230,400 = $28,800 F.

Variable cost variance = Flexible budget variable costs − Actual variable costs.
= $144,000 − $160,000 = ($16,000) U

Fixed cost variance = Budgeted fixed costs − actual fixed costs
= $54,000 − $50,000 = $4,000 F

The sum of these variances yields the flexible budget variance of $16,800 F.

SELF-STUDY PROBLEM #2:
Variable Cost Variances

Classic Woodworks manufactures wood doors for residential homes. The company has established the following materials and labor budgets for making one door:

Materials: 24 square feet of wood at $15 per square foot.
Labor: 6 hours of labor at $25 per hour.

Classic Woodworks budgets to manufacture 1,200 doors each month.

For the most recent month, the actual materials and labor costs incurred in making 1,225 doors were as follows:

Materials: 29,500 square feet of wood purchased and used at a total cost of $413,000.
Labor: 8,250 hours at a total cost of $214,500.

a. *Calculate the materials and labor price and quantity variances for the most recent month.*

Direct Materials

With the information provided in the problem, we have:

Flexible budget materials quantity = 24 square feet of wood per door × 1,225 doors
= 29,400 square feet of wood

Budgeted price per square foot of wood = $15

Actual materials quantity = 29,500 square feet of wood

Actual material price = Actual price per square foot of wood

$$= \frac{\$413,000}{29,500} = \$14 \text{ per square foot}$$

Following the text,

Flexible budget cost = Flexible budget quantity × Budgeted input price
= 29,400 sq feet × $15 = $441,000

"As if" budget cost = Actual input quantity × Budgeted input price
= 29,500 × $15 = $442,500

Actual cost = Actual input quantity × Actual input price
= 29,500 × $14 = $413,000

Direct Labor

Flexible budget labor hours = 6 hours per door × 1,225 doors = 7,350

Budgeted labor rate = $25 per hour

Actual labor hours = 8,250

Actual labor rate = $214,500/8,250 hours = $26 per hour

Therefore,

Flexible budget cost = Flexible budget quantity × Budgeted input price
= 7,350 × $25 = $183,750

"As if" budget cost = Actual input quantity × Budgeted input price
= 8,250 × $25 = $206,250

Actual cost = Actual input quantity × Actual input price
= 8,250 × $26 = $214,500

Arranging this information as in Exhibit 8.13 of the text, we have:

	Flexible Budget	Input Quantity Variance	"As if" Budget with Actual Efficiency	Input Price Variance	Actual Results
Materials	$441,000	($1,500) **U**	$442,500	$29,500 **F**	$413,000
Direct labor	$183,750	($22,500) **U**	$206,250	($8,250) **U**	$214,500

The materials quantity variance is $441,000 − $442,500 = $1,500 U and the materials price variance is $442,500 − $413,000 = $29,500 F.

The direct labor quantity or efficiency variance is $183,750 − $206,250 = $22,500 U and the labor price or rate variance is $206,250 − $214,500 = $8,250 U.

Alternatively, we can use the expressions for variances in Exhibit 8.14. That is,

Input price variance = (Budgeted price per unit of input − Actual price per unit of input)
× Actual input quantity.

Input quantity variance = (Flexible budget quantity of input − Actual quantity of input)
× Budgeted price per unit of input.

For direct materials:

Materials price variance = ($15 − $14) × 29,500 = 29,500 F
Materials quantity variance = (29,400 − 29,500) × $15 = $1,500 U

For direct labor:

Direct labor price or rate variance = ($25 − $26) × 8,250 = $8,250 U
Direct labor quantity or efficiency variance = (7,350 − 8,250) × $15 = $22,500 U

b. *What factor(s) might explain this pattern of materials and labor variances?*

One explanation for this pattern of results is that Classic Woodworks purchased lower quality wood for a lower price. The lower price leads to a favorable materials price variance. Poor materials quality also could lead to unfavorable materials and labor quantity variances because of more waste in making the doors and carpenters taking more time to fabricate the doors.

A second explanation relates to labor scheduling. The unfavorable labor quantity variance could be the result of scheduling more people than necessary for a particular shift. The unfavorable labor price variance may be the result of scheduling higher paid employees (e.g., more experienced carpenters) than was budgeted.

GLOSSARY

Budget reconciliation report A report that uses variances to reconcile the difference between master budget profit and actual profit.

Favorable variance A difference between an actual result and a budgeted amount that leads to an *increase* in profit.

Flexible budget A budget made for the actual level of sales, retaining all other plan assumptions in the master budget.

Flexible budget variance The difference between actual profit and flexible budget profit.

Input price variance Profit effect associated with the difference between the budgeted and actual price of an input.

Input quantity variance Profit effect associated with the difference between the budgeted and actual input quantity used.

Labor efficiency variance See Input quantity variance

Labor rate variance See Input price variance

Market share variance (Appendix B) The profit effect due to differences between the actual and budgeted share of the market for a product.

Market size variance (Appendix B) Profit effect due to differences between the actual and budgeted size of the market for a product.

Master budget The budget as prepared at the start of the accounting period.

Materials efficiency variance See Input quantity variance

Materials price variance See Input price variance

Purchase price variance (Appendix A) The difference between the budgeted and actual price of materials multiplied by the actual quantity of materials *purchased*.

Sales mix variance (Appendix C) Used in multiproduct firms, it captures the effect of changes in the sales mix from the budgeted level.

Sales price variance The difference between actual revenues and flexible budget revenues.

Sales quantity variance (Appendix C) Used in multiproduct firms, it captures the effect of an aggregate change in sales quantity, holding the sales mix at the budgeted level.

Sales volume variance The difference in profit between the flexible budget and the master budget.

Spending variance The difference between budgeted fixed costs and actual fixed costs.

Total profit variance The difference between actual profit and master budget profit.

Unfavorable variance A difference between an actual result and a budgeted amount that leads to a *decrease* in profit.

Variance The difference between an actual result and a budgeted amount.

Variance analysis Technique for determining why actual revenues, costs, and profit differ from their budgeted amounts.

REVIEW QUESTIONS

8.1 LO1. For many organizations, what is the benchmark for evaluating actual performance?

8.2 LO1. What is a master budget?

8.3 LO2. What is a variance?

8.4 LO2. What does it mean when a variance is favorable? What does it mean when a variance is unfavorable?

8.5 LO2. What is the total profit variance?

8.6 LO2. What two subsidiary variances make up the total profit variance?

8.7 LO2. What is a flexible budget?

8.8 LO2. What is the sales volume variance?

8.9 LO2. What is the flexible budget variance? What three subsidiary variances make up the flexible budget variance?

8.10 LO2. What is the sales price variance?

8.11 LO2. What is the fixed cost spending variance?

8.12 LO2. Each variable cost variance can be decomposed into two variances. What are these variances?

8.13 LO2. What is an input price variance?

8.14 LO2. What is an input quantity variance?

8.15 LO3. What is the function of a budget-reconciliation report?

8.16 LO3. What are the three primary reasons variances occur?

8.17 LO3. What are the three main rules to follow when conducting a variance investigation?

8.18 LO4. What are the two primary reasons organizations use nonfinancial measures in addition to financial measures for control purposes?

DISCUSSION QUESTIONS

8.19 LO1. Each of us regularly uses budgets and benchmarks to evaluate how we are doing or what we could do to improve. Can you list three examples from everyday life?

8.20 LO1. Some argue that making the master budget hard to achieve or "tight" can help eliminate waste and make organizations more efficient. Others argue that master budgets should be "loose" because they provide room for discretion in decision making. What do you think?

8.21 LO2. Can you list some examples of variances that you calculate in everyday life? Think about getting a test back or analyzing other people's actions (e.g., we often say things like "I can't believe they did that!"). Do you think "variances" influence the behavior of animals such as family pets? What does this say about the widespread use of variance analysis?

8.22 LO2. When will the sales volume variance be unfavorable? When will the sales price variance be unfavorable? Is it possible to have an unfavorable sales volume variance and an unfavorable sales price variance?

8.23 LO2. If the sales volume variance is favorable, does this imply that for inputs such as materials and labor, the actual quantity of the input used will be greater than the flexible budget quantity of the input? Why or why not?

8.24 LO2, LO3. When will the materials price variance be unfavorable? Does an unfavorable materials price variance necessarily indicate a control problem? Explain why or why not.

8.25 LO2, LO3. When will the materials quantity variance be unfavorable? Might an unfavorable materials

quantity variance be related to other variances, such as the materials price variance and the labor quantity variance? Explain why or why not.

8.26 LO3. Many firms (particularly firms using a Just-in-Time inventory philosophy) enter into long-term contracts with a few suppliers. Do you believe this has implications for the materials price variance? Just-in-Time firms also encourage workers to stop production rather than produce a defective unit. Could this policy have implications for the labor quantity variance?

8.27 LO3. Why might a favorable sales volume variance lead to an unfavorable fixed cost spending variance? How does your answer reconcile with the fixed cost/variable cost classification of costs?

8.28 LO4. Statistical control charts establish upper and lower control limits. Observations falling outside these limits or a sequence of observations above or below the expected value, even if within the control limits, trigger an investigation. How does this practice conform to our description of how firms use profit variance analysis?

8.29 LO4. If nonfinancial measures are both more timely and more specific than financial measures, why do firms use financial measures at all? (*Hint:* Consider whether a manager should implement a decision that increases one nonfinancial measure but decreases another nonfinancial measure. For example, decreasing the mean time per call handled increases the efficiency of customer support staff but potentially decreases service quality and customer satisfaction.)

EXERCISES

 8.30 Calculating and interpreting sales variances (LO1, LO2, LO3). Midwestern University, never a football powerhouse, has only won a total of 12 football games in the past four years. Because of this, and the University's heavy emphasis on basketball, football attendance currently averages only 50% of the stadium's capacity of 52,180 seats.

At the beginning of the year, Midwestern University's associate athletic director prepared the following master budget for football.

	Football Master Budget
Sales (seats per game)	26,000
Number of home games	6
Average ticket price (per seat, per game)	$25
Variable cost (per seat, per game)	$5
Fixed costs (for the season)	$2,000,000

During the summer, the athletic director wondered if there might be a way to put more "bodies in the stadium." To boost attendance, the athletic director decided to reduce the average ticket price by $6 per seat. Indeed, as shown in the actual results in the accompanying table, the athletic director's decision increased average home attendance by 15,000 per game.

	Football Actual Results
Sales (seats per game)	41,000
Number of home games	6
Average ticket price (per seat, per game)	$19
Variable cost (per seat, per game)	$5
Fixed costs (for the season)	$2,000,000

Everyone in the Athletic Department was excited by these numbers.

Required:

a. What was Midwestern University's total profit variance for football?

b. Calculate Midwestern University's football sales volume variance and football sales price variance.

c. Comment on Midwestern University's football performance for the most recent year.

8.31 Calculating and interpreting sales variances (LO1, LO2, LO3). Select Auto Imports is a regional auto dealership that specializes in selling high-end imported luxury automobiles. Master budget data and actual results for the most recent month of operations are as follows:

	Master Budget	Actual Results
Sales (# of cars)	60	70
Sales price per car	$50,000	$45,000
Variable cost per car	$40,000	$40,000
Fixed costs	$350,000	$350,000

Required:

a. What is Select Auto Imports' total profit variance for the most recent month?

b. Calculate Select Auto Imports' sales volume variance and sales price variance for the month.

c. What factor(s) might explain the sales volume and sales price variances you calculated in part (b)?

8.32 Calculating and interpreting sales variances (LO1, LO2, LO3). Garnet's Gym is a fitness and aerobic center located in Atlanta, Georgia. The following table reports Garnet's master budget and actual results for the most recent year:

	Master Budget	Actual Results
Membership fee (per member)	$500	$550
Number of members	5,000	4,000
Variable cost (per member)	$200	$200
Fixed costs	$1,200,000	$1,200,000

With regard to the discrepancies between the budgeted and actual membership fee and the budgeted and actual number of members, the owners of Garnet's Gym inform you that in early January they decided to raise the membership fee from $500 to $550. The owners believed that such an action would only reduce membership by 500 rather than 1,000, as actually occurred.

Required:

a. What was Garnet's total profit variance for the most recent year?

b. Calculate Garnet's sales volume variance and sales price variance for the most recent year. Did raising the membership fee turn out to be a good idea?

c. Would raising the membership fee have been a good idea if membership decreased by 500 (as predicted) rather than 1,000?

8.33 Calculating sales and flexible budget variances (LO1, LO2). For the month of April, Tom and Lynda had forecasted gym membership at 950 members. Tom and Lynda expect to collect $100 as the monthly fee from each member and to spend $35 in variable costs per member per month. Tom and Lynda budget $42,000 toward fixed costs.

They are careful to note that the $100 per month fee is an average. The nominal fee is $115 per month. The $100 is the fee they expect to receive per member after discounts for length of membership, percent off coupons, and other adjustments.

Actual results for April show membership at 975 members, revenues at $98,100, fixed costs at $43,000, and profit at $20,975.

Required:

Calculate the (1) sales volume variance, (2) sales price variance, (3) variable cost variance, and (4) fixed cost variance. Be sure to mark each variance as being favorable (F) or unfavorable (U).

8.34 Calculating materials and labor price and quantity variances (LO2). The Glass Vessel Company has established the following budget for producing one of its hand-blown vases:

Materials (silica)	2 pounds @ 1.25 per pound
Labor	1.5 hours @ $15.00 per hour

In March of the most recent year, Glass Vessel produced 300 vases using 650 pounds of materials. Glass Vessel purchased the 650 pounds of materials for $845. Labor costs for March were $7,200 for 480 hours worked.

Required:

a. What were Glass Vessel's materials price and materials quantity variances for March?

b. What were Glass Vessel's labor price and labor quantity variances for March?

8.35 Purchase price variance (Appendix A, continuation of the previous problem). Suppose Glass Vessel purchased 700 pounds of materials during March at a total cost of $910. Recall that the firm actually used 650 pounds to make the 300 vases during March and that it budgets to pay $1.25 per pound of materials.

Required:

a. What was Glass Vessel's purchase price variance for March?

b. Why might Glass Vessel be interested in computing a materials price variance with the amount of materials purchased rather than the amount of materials used?

8.36 Calculating and interpreting materials price and quantity variances (LO2, LO3). Big Bob's Burgers is justifiably famous for its whopping 1-pound hamburger made with fresh ground beef and cooked to order. Together with a side of "all you can eat" country style French fries, one of Big Bob's hamburgers makes for a very satisfying meal. On an average day, Big Bob serves 200 1-pound hamburgers. Big Bob budgets to use 225 pounds of ground beef to make 200 1-pound hamburgers because some hamburgers invariably are overcooked or dropped on the floor (and therefore must be discarded). Finally, Big Bob budgets to pay $3 per pound of ground beef.

For the most recent week (Big Bob's is open 7 days a week), Big Bob served 1,200 1-pound hamburgers using 1,250 pounds of ground beef. In addition, Big Bob paid his supplier $3.20 per pound of ground beef for the 1,250 pounds he used during the week.

Required:

a. What were Big Bob's ground beef price and quantity variances for the most recent week?

b. What factor(s) could explain Big Bob's ground beef variances?

 8.37 Materials price and quantity variances (LO2, LO3). Tom and Lynda own Hercules Health Club. For the month of April, they had forecasted gym membership at 972 members. Tom and Lynda expect to go through 1 towel (cost $3 per towel) per four members each month at this volume. Actual results for April show that Hercules had 969 members. Hercules bought (and used) 270 new towels for April at a cost of $837.

Required:

For April, calculate the efficiency and prices variance for towels.

8.38 Calculating and interpreting labor price and quantity variances (LO2, LO3). QuickyLube specializes in the routine maintenance of automobiles, including changing a car's oil and other vital fluids as well as checking tire pressure and lights, replacing wiper blades, and the functioning of all filters. Management of QuickyLube budgets to service 275 automobiles a week and has adopted the following labor standard for their technicians: ½ hour per car serviced at a wage rate of $12.50 per hour.

During the past week, QuickyLube actually serviced 210 automobiles. In addition, QuickyLube paid their technicians $1,470 for 140 hours worked.

Required:

a. What were QuickyLube's labor price and quantity variances for the most recent week?

b. What factor(s) could explain QuickyLube's labor variances?

8.39 Calculating materials price and quantity variances (LO2). Homer's D'ohnuts makes tasty chocolate-glazed doughnuts. The main ingredient in doughnuts is flour, and, for the most recent month, Homer budgeted to purchase and use 625 pounds of flour at $0.25 per pound. Budgeted output was 2,500 chocolate-glazed doughnuts (i.e., Homer budgets to make four doughnuts per pound of flour). Homer actually purchased and used 720 pounds of flour at $0.22 per pound; actual output for the month was 3,240 chocolate-glazed doughnuts.

Required:

What were Homer's flour price and quantity variances for the most recent month?

8.40 Solving for unknowns (LO2). GripRite manufactures high-grade golf grips. Variance data for the polymer material used in the grips for the most recent month of operations follows:

Materials price variance	$3,150 U
Materials quantity variance	$4,500 F
Flexible budget quantity	18,000 pounds
Budgeted price	$1.50 per pound

Required:

How much of the polymer material (in pounds) did GripeRite actually use in production during the most recent month? What was the actual price per pound of the polymer material?

8.41 Nonfinancial boundary controls, tailoring performance measures to the job setting (LO4). Guardian Services is a firm that provides security services to apartment buildings and offices. Smartly dressed in dark blue uniforms, Guardian's security officers are placed in visible locations (typically in the building's foyer) and serve to increase safety and deter theft and other crimes. In many buildings, Guardian's officers monitor the feed from video cameras that are strategically located throughout the building. These cameras often are hooked up to a personal computer (PC) at the security station; the officer can then use the PC to adjust the camera angle and zoom in on any suspicious activity. All feeds also are captured on videotape, which is archived for a minimum of seven days.

Required:

a. As you might imagine, overcoming boredom is a big challenge in the security officer's job. Usually, little activity of interest occurs, and it is not uncommon for officers to doze off when on duty. How might Guardian Services mitigate this problem? In other words, what kinds of controls might Guardian Services put in place to ensure that its security officers are awake and alert?

b. Would you use different types of controls to evaluate the activities of police officers who are cruising the streets in their patrol cars? What kinds of controls might you put in place to ensure that police officers are doing their job?

c. Why do the control mechanisms differ in the two job settings described above?

8.42 Choosing performance measures for loan (LO4). Dan Bergstrom has approached your bank for a loan to start a hazardous waste management business. There are a number of biotechnology and chemical companies in Dan's community, and such companies generate a fair amount of hazardous medical, chemical, and radioactive waste. Dan wants to start a business that focuses on all aspects of the waste management process; his goal is to provide for the safe and cost-effective storage, transportation, and disposal of industrial waste. Dan has approached your bank for a loan of $7 million. Under his business plan, Dan would be responsible for recruiting all of the necessary personnel, and acquiring the needed equipment and facilities for waste treatment. Dan expects to incur fixed costs of $1.5 million per year, and his expected contribution margin ratio is 60%. Dan also expects to contribute $2.5 million of equity (from himself, his family, and friends) toward setting up the business.

Required:

a. Assume that Dan's business proposal is sound and that your bank has decided to lend Dan $7 million to start his business. What two performance measures would you like to monitor on a regular basis to ensure that your bank's money (principal + interest) is recouped?

b. Rather than asking for a $7 million business loan, assume Dan has asked for a $200,000 home mortgage. What type of performance measures would you use in this scenario?

c. Why do the performance measures differ between scenarios (a) and (b)?

8.43 Choosing financial and nonfinancial performance measures (LO4). Assume that you are a franchisee of a fast-food chain, "Pita Palace," that serves made-to-order pitas. The menu, prices, and decor are dictated by the national office; further, you are required to purchase all of your supplies through a specified distributor. Your primary responsibility is to ensure adequate staffing and to exercise quality control. Naturally, as the franchisee, you also are keenly interested in your store's profitability.

Required:

a. As the franchisee, list two financial measures and two nonfinancial measures that you would monitor on a short-term (e.g., weekly) basis.

b. Why do think it is important to use both financial and nonfinancial measures?

8.44 Use of Nonfinancial measures for employee evaluation (LO4). Darjeeling Tea is famous the world over for its complex and delicate flavors. The basic input for Darjeeling's teas, tea leaves from tea shrubs, are hand-picked by workers on tea estates. Tea pickers are paid based on both the quantity and quality of tea leaves that they pick (mature leaves have less value than young leaves). There is very little in the form of other controls; pickers can start and stop whenever they want. Moreover, some pickers bring their children with them to work and make frequent stops to feed or change their babies.

Required:

How would you characterize the performance measures used for tea pickers—are they financial or nonfinancial? Why doesn't Darjeeling tea specify start and stop times and/or output quotas?

 8.45 Market size and share variances (Appendix B). For April, Tom and Lynda have budgeted to obtain a 15% share in their target market. They estimate the actual size of the market at 6,075 memberships. Their budgeted contribution margin per member is $65, and the actual contribution was $62. Moreover, their budgeted sales volume is 950 members and the actual sales volume was 975 members.

Required:

Calculate the market size and market share variances.

 8.46 Sales volume and mix variances (Appendix C). Tom and Lynda own Hercules Health Club. For the month of April, they had forecasted gym membership at 700 individual members and 300 family memberships. Individual members pay $100 per month and families pay $150 per month. Variable costs are $35 and $60 per month, respectively.

Actual results for April show membership at 750 individual and 250 family members.

Required:

a. Determine Hercules' sales volume variance.

b. Decompose the sales volume variance into a sales mix variance and a sales quantity variance.

c. Why did Hercules' contribution decrease even though the total memberships were the same?

 8.47 Sales variances in a multiproduct firm (Appendix C). The Tornado Vacuum Cleaner Company produces and sells three different types of upright vacuum cleaners: (1) the F1, (2) the F3, and (3) the F5. Each vacuum cleaner shares certain basic features such as a 15-inch cleaning width, edge groomers, headlight, and 31-foot power cord. However, the vacuums differ in the power offered (the F5 has a 12-amp motor and dual agitators), versatility (the F5 comes with five cleaning tools, whereas the F3 comes with three cleaning tools and the F1 has only one cleaning tool), and ease of use (both the F3 and the F5 are manufactured without belt drives—thus, customers do not need to purchase or install a replacement belt as they ultimately would have to for the F1).

Management of Tornado has provided you with the following data regarding their budget for their most recent year:

	Vacuum Cleaner		
	F1	*F3*	*F5*
Selling price per unit	$150	$200	$400
Variable cost per unit	$75	$110	$240
Quantity sold	25,000	15,000	10,000

In addition, management budgets annual fixed costs of $3,860,000.
Actual results for the most recent year were as follows:

| | Vacuum Cleaner | | | |
	F1	F3	F5	Total
Quantity sold	30,000	10,000	10,000	50,000
Revenue	$4,500,000	$2,000,000	$4,000,000	$10,500,000
Variable costs	2,250,000	1,100,000	2,400,000	5,750,000
Contribution margin	$2,250,000	$900,000	$1,600,000	$4,750,000
Fixed costs				3,860,000
Profit				$890,000

Required:

a. Determine Tornado's sales volume variance and flexible budget variance for the most recent year.

b. Decompose Tornado's sales volume variance into a sales mix variance and a sales quantity variance.

c. Why did Tornado's profit decrease even though the total number of units sold, the unit sales prices, the unit variable costs, and fixed costs were all exactly in line with expectations?

PROBLEMS

8.48 Calculating and interpreting sales volume and flexible budget variances (LO1, LO2, LO3). Space Toys manufactures a popular toy rocket ship. The company's master budget and actual operating results for the most recent quarter (three months) of operations are as follows:

	Master Budget	Actual Results
Rocket ship sales	15,000 units	12,000 units
Revenue	$375,000	$300,000
Variable costs	75,000	54,000
Contribution margin	$300,000	$246,000
Fixed costs	150,000	141,000
Profit	$150,000	$105,000

The owner of Space Toys is alarmed that actual revenue decreased by 20% and, more importantly, that actual profit decreased by 30% compared to the master budget. Because of these numbers, the owner is convinced that both the marketing director, who is responsible for sales, and the production manager, who is responsible for controlling costs, did not do a good job last quarter.

Required:

a. What was Space Toys' flexible budget for the most recent quarter of operations?

b. What were Space Toys' sales volume and sales price variances for the most recent quarter?

c. What were Space Toys' variable cost and fixed cost variances for the most recent quarter?

d. In light of your answers to parts (b) and (c), who do you believe is to blame for Space Toys' poor profit performance last quarter?

8.49 Market size and market share variances (Appendix B, continuation of the previous problem). Suppose that Space Toys' quarterly budgeted sales in units were based on an estimated 10% market share. Actual market size, based on research data, was 100,000 rocket ships for the most recent quarter.

Required:

Compute Space Toys' market size and market share variances. Do these variances cast the marketing manager's performance in a different light?

8.50 Calculating the sales volume and flexible budget variances, budget reconciliation report (LO1, LO2, LO3). During the holiday season, Ajay Singh offers gift-wrapping services at the local mall. Ajay budgets to wrap 1,250 packages per month for $3 per package. Ajay estimates that his variable costs (supplies) will equal $1 per package wrapped and that his fixed costs (rent and utilities) will equal $600 per month.

For the month of December, Ajay actually wrapped 1,500 packages, receiving $4,500 in revenue. However, Ajay spent $1,600 on supplies (he had to make an emergency purchase of bows at retail price). In addition, Ajay paid $700 to the mall's management for rent and utilities. (This past December was unseasonably cold, and Ajay is charged a percentage of the mall's actual utility bill.)

Required:

a. What was Ajay's master budget profit and actual profit for December?

b. By how much did Ajay's profit increase or decrease in December due to changes in sales volume (i.e., what was the sales volume variance)?

c. What was Ajay's variable cost variance and fixed cost spending variance for the month of December? Is there enough information to decompose Ajay's variable cost variance into price and quantity components?

d. Prepare a budget reconciliation report for Ajay for the month of December.

8.51 Calculating and interpreting materials and labor price and quantity variances (LO1, LO2, LO3). Pizzeria Paradise has established the following dough and labor standards for making one 14" pizza:

Dough   ½ pound at $2 per pound

Labor   ¼ hour at $8 per hour

For the most recent month (June), the actual dough and labor costs incurred in making 12,000 pizzas were as follows:

Dough   6,800 pounds purchased and used $1.90 per pound
Labor   3,200 hours at a total cost of $26,400

Required:

a. What are the dough price and quantity variances for June?

b. What are the labor price and quantity variances for June?

c. What factors might explain the dough and labor variances you calculated in parts (a) and (b)?

8.52 Labor variances in a bank (LO1, LO2, LO3). Alvin Jefferson is the manager of the Storm Lakes branch of a small credit union located in Birch Run, Michigan. One of Alvin's duties is to monitor the cost of tellers. Scheduling tellers is complicated because transaction volume (i.e., deposits, withdrawals, inquiries) tends to vary significantly by the day of the week and the time of day. There also are activity surges prior to long weekends and holidays. Alvin's challenge is to staff enough tellers so that the lines are manageable and customers do not get upset, but not so manageable that tellers are idle. Moreover, Alvin's budget is for each teller to process 20 transactions per hour. Alvin's credit union only uses part-time employees as tellers and budgets to pay them $12.50 per hour.

This past November, the tellers at Alvin's branch worked a total of 1,520 hours, received $19,000 in wages, and processed 32,000 transactions. Because of the impending holiday season, the volume of transactions in November was significantly higher than the average monthly volume of 24,000 transactions.

Required:

a. What is the planned (master budget) cost of tellers in an average month when transactions are expected to equal 24,000? What is the planned (flexible budget) cost of tellers for this past November when transactions equaled 32,000?

b. What is the difference between the master budget teller costs for an average month and the actual teller costs for November? Do you believe it is appropriate to evaluate Alvin's performance for the month of November using this variance? Why or why not?

c. Calculate the teller price and teller quantity variances. Based on these variances, does it appear that Alvin did a good job managing teller costs for the month of November?

8.53 Multiple labor variances in a CPA firm (LO1, LO2, LO3). Shari Greenshade, CPA, has her own accounting firm in Sioux Falls, South Dakota. Shari recently and successfully bid on a job for a local retailer. This particular client wanted Shari to streamline the store's inventory and book-keeping systems, and to educate his staff about how to maintain the books using a PC and software such as Quickbooks®. Shari bid $9,000 for the job. She arrived at this bid in the following way. First, Shari budgeted a total of 150 hours for the job, 50 hours of her own time, and 100 hours of her assistant's time. Next, Shari budgeted her cost at $50 per hour and her assistant's cost at $20 per hour. Finally, Shari added a 100% markup to her total budgeted labor cost to arrive at her bid; in other words, [($50 × 50 hours) + ($20 per hour × 100 hours)] × 2 = $9,000.

Shari recently completed the job, and the storeowner could not have been more pleased with the quality and reliability of the service provided. To help her in future bids, Shari wanted to calculate her profit from this job. While Shari received the $9,000 in full from the storeowner, she calculated that she actually spent 70 hours on the assignment, whereas her assistant spent 65 hours on the assignment (Shari underestimated her hours and overestimated her assistant's hours). The actual cost per hour for both Shari's and her assistant's time, however, equaled the budgeted cost $50 and $20, respectively.

Required:

a. What were Shari's master budget profit and actual profit from this job?

b. Compute the price and quantity variances for both Shari's labor and the labor of her assistant.

c. Compute the total labor quantity variance. Does this explain the difference between Shari's actual profit and master budget profit? Do you believe it makes more sense for Shari to compute the labor quantity variance for each type of labor or in total?

8.54 Solving for unknowns (LO2). The FeelGood Company manufactures vitamins. Feel-Good has prepared the following budget for producing one bottle of Vitamin C; each bottle contains 100 tablets, and each tablet contains 500 mg. of Vitamin C.

Materials	52,500 mg. @ $0.0001 per mg.
Labor	6 minutes @ $12.00 per hour

For the most recent month, FeelGood produced 2,500 bottles of Vitamin C and reported the following variance data:

Materials price variance	$3,000 F
Materials quantity variance	$1,875 U
Labor price variance	$188 F
Labor quantity variance	$180 U

Required:

a. What was the actual quantity of materials (in mg) used during the most recent month?

b. What was the actual price paid for materials (per mg) during the most recent month?

c. What was the actual quantity of labor (in hours) used during the most recent month?

d. What was the actual price paid (per hour) for labor during the most recent month?

8.55 Working backwards (LO2, Advanced). The following data pertain to the most recent quarter of operations for CoolCo, a manufacturer of styrofoam coolers:

Actual profit	$100,000
Fixed cost spending variance	$2,000 U
Materials quantity variance	$2,500 F
Total profit variance	$5,000 F
Labor price variance	$500 U
Sales price variance	$4,000 U
Materials price variance	$1,500 U
Variable cost variance	$4,000 F

Required:

a. What was CoolCo's master budget profit?

b. What was CoolCo's sales volume variance?

c. What was CoolCo's flexible budget profit?

d. What was CoolCo's labor quantity variance?

8.56 Variance analysis with contribution margin ratios, budget reconciliation report (LO2, Advanced). Gina Matheson owns and operates a successful florist shop in Bloomington, Indiana. Gina estimates that her variable costs amount to $0.25 per sales dollar (i.e., variable costs represent 25% of revenue) and that her fixed costs amount to $6,000 per month. Gina budgets for $16,000 in revenue per month.

This past May, Gina's actual revenue was $21,000. Gina attributes part of the increase to seasonal holidays (Mother's Day, Memorial Day) and part of it to higher prices. She figures that, taking advantage of a surge in demand, she was able to increase her prices by 5% this past month. Gina's actual total costs for May were $12,100, which included $6,300 in fixed costs.

Required:

a. What was Gina's master budget profit and actual profit for May? What was Gina's total profit variance for May?

b. Decompose Gina's total profit variance for May into four numbers: (1) the sales volume variance, (2) the sales price variance, (3) the variable cost variance, and (4) the fixed cost spending variance.

8.57 Market size and market share variances, analysis with contribution margin ratios (Appendix B, Continuation of the previous problem, Advanced). Assume Gina's budget of $16,000 in monthly revenue is based on an estimated 2% market share. Actual market size for the month, based on industry data, was $1,250,000 in revenue.

Required:

Compute Gina's market size variance and market share variance for the most recent month.

8.58 Calculating and interpreting materials and labor flexible budget variances (LO2, LO3). SpringFresh provides commercial laundry and linen services to local hospitals, hotels, and restaurants. SpringFresh charges its customers $1.50 per pound laundered, regardless of the items to-be cleaned (e.g., sheet, towel, garment, tablecloth).

SpringFresh budgets to launder 70,000 pounds each month and, for each pound laundered, budgets to spend $0.10 on materials and $0.40 cents on labor. For the most recent month, SpringFresh actually laundered 60,000 pounds and spent $4,000 on materials and $20,000 on labor.

Required:

a. Calculate the materials and labor flexible budget variances for the most recent month.

b. In the absence of any other information, does it appear that SpringFresh's management has done a good job controlling costs in the most recent month?

c. Assume that in recent months, SpringFresh has received numerous complaints about the quality of their services. Specifically, several customers have complained that their laundry is "not as clean as it used to be" and, even worse, that some of their items have come back stained due to bleeding. Does this information cast the favorable variances and management's performance in a different light?

8.59 Profit reconciliation (LO1, LO2, LO3). Famous Footwear is a store that specializes in shoes targeted to people who lead an "active life." The Chicago mega-store has a special area called the "Locker Room" that is dedicated to shoes for various sports and activities like jogging, tennis, and basketball. Budgeted profit for the Locker Room is computed using an average cost of $44 per pair of shoes and an average selling price of $80 per pair of shoes.

The manager of the Locker Room has considerable discretion in setting prices and in staffing the area. Typically, the Locker Room is staffed for 700 hours per month at a budgeted wage rate of $5 per hour. In addition to this base wage, sales staff receives a commission equal to 5% of revenues. Normally, the staffing level would not be expected to change in response to "small" (defined as ±10%) changes in budgeted shoe sales. For October, the Locker Room had budgeted sales of 4,000 pairs of shoes and 700 staffing hours.

Actual results for October were as follows:

Pairs of shoes sold	4,250
Revenue	$323,000
Cost of shoes	170,000
Labor − commissions	16,150
Labor − base wages	3,000 (the actual base wage was $5 per hour)
Profit	$133,850

Required:

a. What was the Locker Room's master budget profit and flexible budget profit for October? What was the Locker Room's total profit variance for October?

b. Decompose the Locker Room's total profit variance into four numbers: (1) the sales volume variance, (2) the sales price variance, (3) the flexible budget shoe cost variance, and (4) the flexible budget labor cost variance.

c. Prepare a budget reconciliation report for the Locker Room for October. Comment on the results—in particular, what factor(s) do you believe may cause the pattern of variances?

8.60 Labor performance measures, use of boundary, and other controls (LO3, LO4). Factory workers who work on an assembly line often have to punch in and out of work using a time clock. In addition, there are penalties for being tardy as well as detailed policies regarding both the number and duration of breaks. Thus, for many factory workers, firms exercise strict control over the amount of time spent at the workstation.

At the other extreme, faculty at universities enjoy considerable flexibility regarding the amount of time they spend on campus. Other than the time when a class is scheduled to meet, faculty can come and go as they please. Thus, there is very little control over the time faculty spends at their workstation.

Many office workers lie between these two extremes. Office workers often exercise some freedom under flextime policies and adjust their arrival and departure times to suit their personal schedules. Under a typical policy, staff are expected to arrive between 7 and 10 A.M. and leave between 3 and 6 P.M., subject to putting in at least 40 hours per week.

Required:

a. Why do you believe there are differences in the time controls used for assembly-line workers, office workers, and faculty?

b. More generally, the performance measures used for factory workers tend to be input based, whereas the performance measures used for faculty tend to be output based. Why do you believe this is the case?

8.61 Balancing the use of financial and nonfinancial measures (LO4). The Yin-Yang Yogurt Shoppe serves the best chocolate-vanilla frozen yogurt in the city. Yin-Yang's business plan was made under the assumption that each cup of yogurt will have a unit contribution margin of $2, monthly fixed costs will equal $3,000, and monthly revenue will equal $12,000.

Because frozen yogurt frequently is purchased on impulse, Yin-Yang's management is acutely aware of the impact of quality and the store's ambience on sales. Staff, who are mostly college students hired on a part-time basis, are constantly reminded about the need to follow food-safety procedures, to maintain a clean workplace, and to create a friendly atmosphere.

Required:

a. As the owner of the Yin-Yang Yogurt Shoppe, list two performance measures that you would monitor on a *daily* basis. Briefly explain why you selected each measure.

b. As the owner of the Yin-Yang Yogurt Shoppe, list two performance measures that you would monitor on a *monthly* basis. Briefly explain why you selected each measure.

c. Do the daily measures tend to be more nonfinancial or financial in nature? What about the monthly measures? Briefly discuss any patterns you observe.

8.62 The use of nonfinancial labor performance measures (LO4). Seeking to manage customer service costs, many U.S. firms locate their call centers for handing customer-service inquiries overseas. The cities of Bangalore and Hyderabad in India are centers for much of this action. Employees at these locations are trained in American English usage, accents, and slang, and watch U.S. television shows (on company time!) to be current with social trends and norms. Using Western names (e.g., Alice for Anjali, Sarah for Sharmila, and Sam for Shankar) and pop-up screens based on the customer's zip code to learn about "local" weather conditions, these employees become indistinguishable in the customer's perception from a person located in mainland United States.

Required:

a. Suppose that you are the supervisor of such a call center. What kinds of nonfinancial measures and controls might you use to ensure that employees are optimally utilized and that costs are managed to their lowest level?

b. Suppose one measure you adopt is the amount of time spent per call. What are the costs and benefits of using this measure?

c. Why do many companies also permit the supervisor to monitor (on a random basis and invisible to both the customer and the call center employee) calls received by the call center? (U.S. laws require that the firm disclose such monitoring practices to the customer.)

8.63 Purchase price variance (Appendix A). The Armstrong Company manufactures bicycle frames. Armstrong budgets to use 5 pounds of a carbon-composite material to produce one frame. Armstrong budgets to pay $40 per pound of the carbon-composite material.

In December of the most recent year, Armstrong manufactured 225 bicycle frames using 1,125 pounds of the carbon-composite material. To obtain a quantity discount, however, Armstrong's purchasing manager actually acquired 1,500 pounds of the carbon-composite material during December at a total cost of $56,250.

Required:

a. What is Armstrong's material price variance for December? What is Armstrong's purchase price variance for December?

b. Which variance, the materials price variance or the purchase price variance, would you recommend that Armstrong use?

8.64 Purchase price variance (Appendix A, Advanced). Rush and Company values all of its inventories at standard cost. This feature also means that Rush values at standard cost all materials issued out from inventory into production.

Rush began the month of August with 4,000 kilograms (kg) of chromic acid in stock and valued this inventory at $8,000. During August, the following transactions occurred:

Date	Transaction	Units	Cost
August 10	Purchase	1,000 kg	$2,150
August 15	Issued out	2,000 kg	?
August 22	Purchase	800 kg	$1,632
August 29	Issued out	1,000 kg	?

Required:

a. What is the value of Rush's ending inventory and the cost of chromic acid issued out for August?

b. What is Rush's purchase price variance for August?

c. Fill in the following table to illustrate the relations between the purchase price, the purchase price variance, and inventory values.

Item	Kgs.	Value
Beginning inventory		
+ Purchases		
− Issued out		
+/− Purchase price variance		
= Ending inventory		

8.65 Sales variances in a multiproduct firm (Appendix C). Mountain Maples is a mail-order nursery dedicated to growing, selling, and shipping beautiful Japanese Maple trees. Located on a ridge-top in Mendocino County, Northern California, Mountain Maples offers two distinctive types of Japanese Maples: Butterfly and Moonfire. The trees are sold after five growing seasons. Budgeted revenue and cost data for each tree type for the most recent year follow:

	Butterfly	*Moonfire*
Quantity sold	800	1,600
Selling price per tree	$200	$100
Variable cost per tree	$100	$50

Mountain Maples' budgeted annual fixed costs are $75,000.
Actual results for the most recent year were as follows:

	Butterfly	Moonfire	Total
Quantity sold	700	1,700	
Revenue	$147,000	$178,500	$325,500
Variable costs	84,000	93,500	177,500
Contribution margin	$63,000	$85,000	148,000
Fixed costs			76,000
Profit			$72,000

Required:

a. Calculate Mountain Maples' total profit variance for the most recent year.

b. Decompose Mountain Maples' total profit variance into a sales volume variance and a flexible budget variance.

c. Decompose the flexible budget variance into a sales price variance, a variable cost variance, and fixed cost variance.

d. Compute the sales mix variance and the sales quantity variance, and show that they sum to the sales volume variance.

e. Using a budget reconciliation report, discuss the overall performance for Mountain Maples for the most recent year.

8.66 Sales variances in a Multiproduct firm, weighted contribution margin ratio approach (Appendix C, Advanced). Tom Carroll operates a bike shop in Omaha, Nebraska. Tom budgets to earn $100,000 in revenue each month; he also expects 40% of this revenue to be from deluxe bikes and the remainder to be from standard bikes. Tom budgets for a contribution margin ratio of 40% on the deluxe bike and 30% on the standard bike. After accounting for $27,000 in fixed costs per month, Tom budgets to earn $7,000 in monthly profit.

For the most recent month, Tom earned $120,000 in revenue. However, deluxe bikes only accounted for 30% of total revenue. Actual selling prices, contribution margin ratios, and fixed costs, were all as budgeted.

Required:

a. Calculate Tom's total profit variance for the month.

b. Decompose Tom's total profit variance into a sales volume variance and a flexible budget variance.

c. Compute the sales mix variance and the sales quantity variance, and show that they sum to the sales volume variance.

d. Discuss the overall performance for Tom's bike shop for the most recent month.

MINI-CASES

8.67 Calculating and interpreting variances (LO1, LO2, LO3). Scotty Grace's goal has always been to design the finest putters for the best golfers in the world. For years, Scotty toiled in isolation, crafting putters using a table-top mill in his mother-in-law's garage. All of that changed in 1994, however, when a famous professional golfer used one of Scotty's creations to win the PGA Championship. Scotty's putters became an "overnight success," and Scotty received several thousand orders in the next two weeks for the putter that the PGA professional had used.

Scotty's latest invention is the Amazing Grace, a triangular-shaped mallet-style putter that has the highest moment of inertia of any putter ever made. The putter, which is milled from high-tech aircraft aluminum, has a substantial amount of mass located several inches behind the putter face, giving it a deep center of gravity. This deep center of gravity makes the Amazing Grace very stable and forgiving, which, in turn, should help the golfer make more putts!

At the beginning of the year, Scotty's management team developed the following master budget for the Amazing Grace (the master budget was based on last year's actual results):

Master Budget		
(Amazing Grace Putter)		
Sales (# of putters)		5,000
Sales price per putter		$280
Material costs (per putter):		
Aluminum & weights (for putter head)	1,000 grams per putter @ $0.06 per gram	$60
Shaft (steel)	1 per putter @ $8.00	$8
Grip	1 per putter @ $10.00	$10
Labor costs (per putter)	3 hours @ $20/hr.	$60
Fixed costs (for the year)		$250,000

Upon seeing these figures, Scotty wondered if there was a way to increase his company's profit from the Amazing Grace putter. Scotty had two ideas. The first was to reduce the selling price to $245. He believed that the $35 reduction in the selling price would substantially increase putter sales.

Scotty's second idea was to rent a new milling machine for the coming year. The rental would cost Scotty $50,000 for the year, but he hoped that the machine would reduce both the materials waste and the labor time associated with making each putter. Moreover, since each finished putter head weighed only 350 grams, Scotty wanted to find a way to reduce the 650 grams (1,000 − 350) of high-tech aircraft aluminum and other materials (tungsten) that were wasted in the production process. He also reasoned that reducing material waste would reduce the labor time needed to fabricate each putter.

Scotty implemented both of his ideas, and at the end of the year, the actual results were as follows:

Actual Results		
(Amazing Grace Putter)		
Sales (# of putters)		5,600
Sales price (per putter)		$245
Material costs (per putter):		
Aluminum & weights (for putter head)	700 grams per putter @ $0.06 per gram	$42
Shaft (steel)	1 per putter @ $8.00	$8
Grip	1 per putter @ $12.00	$12
Labor costs (per putter)	2.5 hours @ $20/hr.	$50
Fixed costs (for the year)		$300,000

Required:

a. What was the master budget profit for Scotty's Amazing Grace putter for the most recent year?

b. What was Scotty's actual profit from his Amazing Grace putter for the most recent year?

c. Prepare Scotty's flexible budget for his Amazing Grace putter for the most recent year.

d. Did reducing the selling price turn out to be a good idea? Which variances help you assess the quality of this decision? By how much did Scotty's profit increase or decrease as a result of lowering the selling price?

e. Did renting the new milling machine turn out to be a good idea? Which variances help you assess the quality of this decision? By how much did Scotty's profit increase or decrease as a result of renting the new milling machine?

f. Prepare a brief paragraph or two discussing why Scotty should care about the variances you calculated and how they might be used to improve Scotty's decision making.

8.68 Calculating and interpreting variances (LO1, LO2, LO3). Kim and Tim Landry started College Painters in 1988 when they were seniors in college. Fully bonded and insured, College Painters specializes in faux finishes using techniques such as sponging, washing, marbleizing, and ragging. While Kim and Tim used to do all of the painting themselves, they now manage the business, employing a mix of college students and other individuals who have some experience and interest in decorative painting. Kim and Tim also provide extensive training in faux finishing techniques to all of their employees and routinely visit worksites to ensure that jobs meet their quality standards.

Kim and Tim budget for 25,000 square feet of business a month. The average job is 500 square feet, and, for such a job, Kim and Tim expect to incur the following costs:

Materials (paint)	1.6 gallons @ $25.00 per gallon
Materials (supplies)	$10.00
Labor (includes surface preparation and applying the paint and the faux finish)	16 hours @$15.00 per hour

To arrive at a selling price, Kim and Tim mark up the budgeted paint cost by 50% and the budgeted labor cost by 100% and add the budgeted cost of supplies. Thus, the starting point for constructing a bid is $550 = (1.50 × 1.6 × $25) + (2.00 × 16 × $15) + $10. Of course, Kim and Tim adjust this starting price to reflect prevailing market conditions and so on. For instance, they will charge more for a rush job, or they will give a discount if the customer is unhappy with the final product. Finally, Kim and Tim budget to pay a total of $2,000 per month in fixed costs related to office rent, utilities, advertising, and the company car.

For August of the most recent year, College Painters earned $25,333 in revenue for several different jobs totaling 24,000 square feet. College Painters used 72 gallons of paint and 765 hours of labor during August. The 765 hours of labor cost Kim and Tim $11,475, which includes the 32 hours it took to clean up the mess in a customer's home because an employee accidentally tipped over a full can of paint.

According to the bill from the hardware store, Tim and Kim spent $2,160 on paint and $480 on painting supplies during August. The bill for paint was higher than normal because Kim and Tim decided to try a newer, more expensive paint in the hope that it would lead to improved paint and labor efficiencies (Tim and Kim did not expect this decision to affect the amount of supplies used). Finally, Kim and Tim spent $2,250 for the month on fixed costs.

Required:

a. What was College Painters' master budget profit and actual profit for August? What was College Painters' total profit variance?

b. Prepare a budget reconciliation report for College Painters for August. Your report should include all of the variances that make up the total profit variance. For this part, do not consider the costs of the accident separately.

c. Considering each variance, determine Kim and Tim's costs related to the accident involving the spilled can of paint. Separate the costs relating to the accident into out-of-pocket and opportunity costs. Revise your budget reconciliation report to highlight the cost of the accident.

d. Did switching paint increase College Painters' profit in August? Which variances help you in assessing the quality of this decision?

e. Prepare a brief memo evaluating College Painters' performance in August vis-à-vis their budgeted performance.

Module III

PLANNING AND CONTROL OVER THE LONG TERM: MAXIMIZING PROFIT

We devote Module III (Chapters 9–13) to long-term decisions. In the long term, costs associated with property, equipment, and salaried personnel ("capacity resources"), which are fixed in the short term, become controllable and relevant. Accordingly, long-term decisions focus on matching the supply and demand of these capacity resources and making the most effective use of capacity resources.

It is often difficult, however, to estimate the controllable capacity costs related to equipment, space, and personnel. This difficulty arises because products and customers share capacity resources; that is, such costs are not directly traceable to individual products and customers. In the language of Chapter 2, capacity costs are indirect costs. As a practical solution, firms use cost allocations to approximate the long-term change in capacity costs.

Chapter 9 provides an integrated discussion of the various demands for cost allocations within an organization. We first examine how and why firms make frequent use of cost allocations for long-term decisions. We then present and discuss other reasons for allocations: reporting income to external parties such as shareholders and the IRS, justifying cost-based reimbursements, and influencing behavior within the organization.

In Chapter 10, we take a close look at the use of allocations for decision making. We focus particularly on activity-based costing (ABC), and illustrate how ABC can lead to better decisions by refining estimates of controllable capacity costs. We also discuss how ABC systems facilitate activity-based management, enabling firms to optimize their products, customers, and resources.

Despite their widespread use, allocations have two limitations: (1) They do not consider the time value of money; and (2) they do not consider the lumpy nature of capacity resources. These limitations are of particular concern when the firm is considering a large expenditure on a long-lived resource. For such expenditures, organizations routinely engage in capital budgeting, which is the focus of Chapter 11.

Chapter 12 examines long-term control decisions. In the long term, the goal is to measure whether we are putting organizational resources to their best or most effective use. A key step in doing so is to ensure that a firm's performance-evaluation and reward system fits with its organizational structure. Accordingly, we first describe the common forms of decentralization and the different types of responsibility centers found in organizations. Following this discussion, we consider the principles governing performance measurement and then apply them to each type of responsibility center.

We focus on *strategic* planning and control in Chapter 13, the final chapter in this module. Strategy is a commitment to pursue a particular approach to business—it defines how a firm *positions* its products

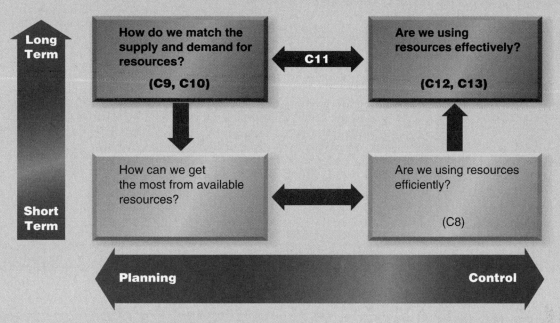

Exhibit III.1 Classifying Decisions by Time and Planning/Control

and services and *distinguishes* itself from its competitors to maximize returns. Organizations that successfully implement their strategies know their value chain and link their performance measures to critical success factors. Accordingly, we discuss how management accounting helps a firm identify and configure its value chain. Finally, we discuss the balanced scorecard, a measurement system that provides a framework for motivating and monitoring strategic initiatives and outcomes.

Chapter 9

Cost Allocations: Theory and Applications

THE EZ-REST MATTRESS COMPANY sells two types of mattresses, Standard and Deluxe, to university dormitories and hospitals. While both mattresses are the same size, the Deluxe mattress has extra padding and is of higher quality. Demand is high for both mattresses, allowing EZ-Rest to operate at full capacity.

However, Craig Edwards, the chief executive officer (CEO) of EZ-Rest, is not satisfied with the firm's performance. Currently, EZ-Rest sells 18,000 Standard mattresses and 12,000 Deluxe mattresses, for 30,000 total units every year. Craig wonders whether EZ-Rest could make more money by selling more of the Deluxe mattresses. His plan is to keep total sales volume the same, but to sell 20,000 Deluxe mattresses and 10,000 Standard mattresses. Craig believes that the company can achieve this goal within the next three years. Before he makes the necessary changes to the company's operations, Craig asks you to evaluate the merits of this decision.

APPLYING THE DECISION FRAMEWORK

What Is the Problem?	Even though EZ-Rest currently operates at capacity, CEO Craig Edwards wants the company to increase its profit.
What Are the Options?	We will examine two options: (1) Change the product mix to emphasize Deluxe mattresses; (2) Stay with the current product mix.
What Are the Costs and Benefits?	We will use cost allocations to estimate the change in EZ-Rest's profit due to this long-term decision.
Make the Decision!	After estimating the profit associated with EZ-Rest's two options, we will be able to recommend the best option to Craig.

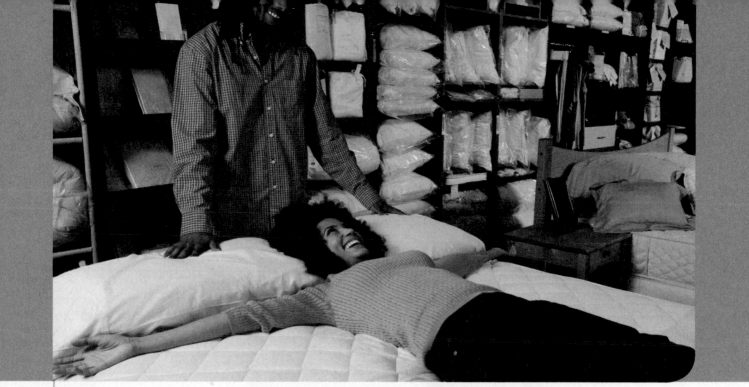

EZ-Rest is trying to figure the best mix of the two models of mattresses it makes.

LEARNING OBJECTIVES

After studying this chapter, you will be able to:

1 Understand how to use cost allocations to make long-term decisions.

2 Explain how cost allocations affect income under absorption costing relative to variable costing.

3 Describe the role of incentives in the choice of allocation procedures.

In Chapters 4–8, we examined short-term decisions for which the costs associated with capacity resources, such as property, plant, and equipment, were not controllable. Accordingly, our goal was to make the best use of *available* capacity resources by maximizing contribution margin. In this chapter, we shift our attention to longer-term decisions. The key feature distinguishing these decisions is the controllability of capacity costs, or the ability to *change* capacity levels.

We begin this chapter by discussing why firms frequently allocate capacity costs for long-term decisions. We then review the mechanics of cost allocations and allocate EZ-Rest's capacity costs to its two products. Such allocations are a practical and often used method for estimating long-term costs of decision options. Finally, we describe other reasons why firms allocate capacity costs.

CHAPTER CONNECTIONS

In Chapter 10, we focus on activity-based costing, a technique that refines the cost allocation procedures to make allocated costs more suitable for making effective decisions.

Long-Term Decisions and Cost Allocations

LEARNING OBJECTIVE 1

Understand how to use cost allocations to make long-term decisions.

In the previous module, we frequently used contribution margin income statements to address short-term decision problems. Exhibit 9.1 presents EZ-Rest's contribution margin income statement and accompanying unit-level data for the most recent year of operations.

Exhibit 9.1 *EZ-Rest Mattress Company: Income Statement for the Most Recent Year*

	Mattress Type		
	Standard	**Deluxe**	**Total**
Sales volume (in units)	18,000	12,000	30,000
Revenue	$11,700,000	$10,500,000	$22,200,000
Variable costs			
Direct materials	$5,310,000	$4,200,000	$9,510,000
Direct labor	1,350,000	1,800,000	3,150,000
Marketing and sales	432,000	864,000	1,296,000
Contribution margin	$4,608,000	$3,636,000	$8,244,000
Fixed costs			
Manufacturing			$5,040,000
Marketing and sales			1,560,000
Administration			960,000
Profit before taxes			$684,000
Unit-level data	**Standard**	**Deluxe**	
Selling price	$650	$875	
Direct materials	295	350	
Direct labor	75	150	
Variable marketing & sales	24	72	
Unit contribution margin	$256	$303	

EZ-Rest's Deluxe mattress is more comfortable but is also more costly to make than the Standard mattress. (Gregory Kramer/Getty Images)

Craig's proposal is to change the product mix to 10,000 Standard and 20,000 Deluxe mattresses. Using the data in Exhibit 9.1, we estimate the profit from Craig's proposal as:

Contribution margin from Standard mattresses	10,000 × $256/unit	$2,560,000
Contribution margin from Deluxe mattresses	20,000 × $303/unit	$6,060,000
Total contribution margin		$8,620,000
Fixed costs		($7,560,000)
Profit		$1,060,000

This profit is up substantially from the current profit of $684,000. Craig's proposal appears to be a good one, right? Not necessarily!

EZ-Rest's decision to change its product mix over the next three years is not a short-term decision. Shifting emphasis from Standard to Deluxe mattresses would take time and require a replanning of existing capacity resources. EZ-Rest may have to replace equipment, reorganize the factory, and change personnel. These changes would likely alter both the nature and magnitude of EZ-Rest's "fixed" capacity costs.

To evaluate Craig's proposal properly, we need to estimate the change in capacity costs. Treating them as fixed, as we would for a short-term decision, is not appropriate.

EZ-Rest's long-term decision relates to changing the product mix. Other examples of long-term decisions include adding or dropping products and services, expanding or scaling down operations, and changing target markets. These decisions usually involve altering the level and mix of capacity resources in place. Dropping a product or scaling down operations could idle some existing equipment and machinery. Meanwhile, adding a new product or expanding operations frequently requires additional space, equipment, and staff. Commitments and contractual obligations expire with the passage of time. When excess supply exists in the long term, firms can dispose of unneeded capacity. Similarly, when excess demand exists, firms can acquire extra capacity.

Because capacity costs are controllable over the long term, we need to consider them in our decision-making process. This feature changes our focus from maximizing contribution margin to maximizing profit margin. As we learned in Chapter 4, contribution margin equals revenues less variable costs. **Profit margin** equals contribution margin less allocated capacity costs and, thus, takes into account the change in capacity costs. *While contribution margin is the appropriate measure of value for short-term decisions, profit margin is the appropriate measure for long-term decisions.*

How can we systematically estimate the cost of capacity resources? We discuss two general approaches: direct estimation and cost allocation.

DIRECT ESTIMATION

Direct estimation of capacity costs involves systematically examining each cost account to evaluate whether (and how much) a decision would change a capacity cost. For example, Ram Gupta, EZ-Rest's chief operations officer, estimates that

Connecting to Practice

GENERAL MOTORS SHEDDING JOBS

In November 2005, General Motors announced plans to cut as many as 30,000 jobs, indicating that it would close operations in nine North American factories. Chairman and Chief Executive Officer Rick Wagoner said the move should help General Motors save as much as $7 billion by the end of 2006.

COMMENTARY: Downsizing staff reduces General Motors' capacity for producing automobiles. A firm might decide to downsize to match capacity with revised beliefs about the demand for the firm's products. Downsizing imposes both explicit and implicit costs. Explicit costs are in the form of paying severance to employees and meeting various contractual obligations. Implicit costs arise because of the cost to the surrounding community from loss of employment and loss of morale among retained employees.

Source: Wall Street Journal, November 22, 2005, p. A3.

Downsizing assembly line capacity is a major decision for an automobile company because it imposes significant costs on the firm, its employees, and the surrounding community. (Al Goldis/©AP/Wide World Photos)

shifting the product mix would increase costs for supervisory staff by $325,000, tools by $206,000 and equipment by $359,000. The sum of these costs, $890,000, would then be the controllable capacity costs for this decision.

With this estimate, Craig's proposal does not appear to be wise. We estimate the profit from Craig's proposal as:

Contribution margin from		
Standard mattresses	10,000 × $256/unit	$2,560,000
Contribution margin from		
Deluxe mattresses	20,000 × $303/unit	$6,060,000
Total contribution margin		$8,620,000
Current fixed costs		($7,560,000)
Increase in fixed costs		($890,000)
Profit		$170,000

In many ways, direct estimation is like the account classification method that you learned in Chapter 4. It involves identifying, on an account-by-account basis, which capacity costs would change, and by how much, for each decision option. Direct estimation of changes in capacity costs can be difficult and time-consuming. Moreover, its accuracy depends on the expertise and incentives of the person making the estimates. For these reasons, firms frequently use cost allocations, a simpler but potentially less-accurate approach to estimate controllable capacity costs.

CHAPTER CONNECTIONS

In Chapter 4, we discussed the account classification method. This method allows firms to directly estimate the costs associated with an option by analyzing each cost item separately. While the account classification method can lead to accurate estimates, it is tedious and time consuming, and is subject to the biases and incentives of the decision maker.

COST ALLOCATIONS

Recall from Chapter 3 that to allocate is to distribute a common cost or benefit among two or more entities. For EZ-Rest, capacity costs (such as the costs of plant and machinery) are the common costs incurred to make the two product lines.

Suppose we decide to allocate EZ-Rest's fixed capacity costs to its two product lines using direct labor dollars (DL$) as the allocation basis. Referring back to Exhibit 9.1, the cost pool is the total fixed costs of $7,560,000, made up of $5,040,000 for manufacturing, $1,560,000 for marketing and sales, and $960,000 for administration. The cost objects are the two product lines (Standard and Deluxe mattresses). The cost driver is direct labor dollars, and the total number of direct labor dollars ($3,150,000) is the denominator volume. With this information, we can perform the two-step cost-allocation procedure for EZ-Rest:

1. Calculate the **allocation rate** by dividing the costs in the cost pool by the denominator volume:

$$\text{Allocation rate} = \frac{\$7,560,000}{\$3,150,000 \text{ DL\$}} = \$2.40 \text{ per DL\$}$$

Connecting to Practice

PRODUCT COSTING AT NISSAN

In his study of Nissan Motor Company, Professor Robin Cooper reports that Nissan uses product costs, which include allocated costs, for four primary purposes: (1) For assessing long-term profitability; (2) for selecting the product mix, (3) for identifying nonprofitable variants of models, and (4) for maintaining cost control.

COMMENTARY: The first three uses are classic long-term decisions that we study in this chapter and Chapter 10. We discuss the fourth use in Chapter 12. Nissan also uses an extensive costing system to determine the profitability of products yet to enter production. We discuss such target costing systems in Chapter 13.

Businesses often refer to this rate as the **overhead rate** because capacity costs are also termed **overhead costs**. Some firms refer to this rate as the **burden** because they charge, or burden, each product with this amount.

2. For each product, multiply the cost driver units by the allocation rate:

Standard = $1,350,000 DL$ × $2.40 per DL$ − $3,240,000
Deluxe = $1,800,000 DL$ × $2.40 per DL$ = $4,320,000

In this way, the allocation divides the total fixed costs of $7,560,000 between the two product lines. As you can verify in *Check It! Exercise #1*, the proportion of fixed costs allocated to each mattress line is identical to the proportion of direct labor dollars (the cost driver) in each product line (cost object).

Dividing $3,240,000 by 18,000 Standard mattresses, we determine the allocated cost as $180 per Standard mattress. Similarly, dividing $4,320,000 by 12,000 mattresses gives us an allocated cost of $360 per Deluxe mattress. Alternatively, we could obtain the allocated cost per unit by multiplying the unit labor cost of each type of mattress by the overhead allocation rate of $2.40 per every labor dollar:

Standard mattress = $75 DL$ × $2.40 per DL$ = $180 per mattress
Deluxe mattresses = $150 DL$ × $2.40 per DL$ = $360 per mattress

Check It! Exercise #1

When allocating EZ-Rest's fixed costs of $7,560,000 to mattresses, using direct labor dollars as the allocation basis, verify that the percentage of the cost allocated to each mattress line equals the percentage of direct labor dollars.

	Standard	Deluxe	Total
Direct labor dollars (DL$)	_____	_____	$3,150,000
Percentage of DL$	_____	_____	100%
Amount allocated	_____	_____	$7,560,000
Percent of cost allocated	_____	_____	100%

Solution at end of chapter.

Notice that with labor cost as the allocation base, the allocated cost per unit for Deluxe mattresses ($360 per mattress) is twice the amount allocated to each unit of the Standard mattress ($180 per mattress).

How do allocations help long-term decisions? Allocations break up capacity costs into pieces attributable to individual products. We then use the product-level estimates to compute expected costs for a new volume of operations or a revised product mix. That is, allocations estimate long-run capacity costs as proportional to the volume of the underlying cost driver. Exhibit 9.2 presents the product-level income statement for EZ-Rest for the projected product mix using the above allocations.

Our new estimate of capacity costs for Standard mattresses multiplies 10,000 units × $75 DL$ per unit × $2.40 allocation per DL$ = $1,800,000. For Deluxe mattresses, the capacity cost estimate is 20,000 units × $150 DL$ per unit × $2.40 allocation per DL$ = $7,200,000. The revised estimate represents a large increase in capacity costs. EZ-Rest's profit actually would decrease from a profit of $684,000 in Exhibit 9.1 to a loss of $380,000—a profit margin decrease of $1,064,000—if Craig changes the product mix.

It is important to understand that the accuracy of our estimates depend crucially on the specific allocation procedure used. *Check It! Exercise #2* emphasizes this observation. This exercise asks you to verify that EZ-Rest's estimated capacity costs would *not* change from its current amount of $7,560,000 if we use sales volume in units as the allocation basis. Why is there no change? The answer is that the change in capacity cost is proportional to the change in the total units of the cost driver. In this exercise, the total number of units sold (the cost driver for this allocation) does not change

Exhibit 9.2	*EZ-Rest Mattress Company: Projected Profit with Modified Product Mix Using Allocations*		
	Mattress Type		
	Standard	**Deluxe**	**Total**
Sales volume (in units)	10,000	20,000	30,000
Revenue	$6,500,000	$17,500,000	$24,000,000
Direct materials	2,950,000	7,000,000	9,950,000
Direct labor	750,000	3,000,000	3,750,000
Variable marketing and sales	240,000	1,440,000	1,680,000
Contribution margin	$2,560,000	$6,060,000	$ 8,620,000
Allocated fixed costs	1,800,000	7,200,000	9,000,000
Profit margin	$760,000	($1,140,000)	($380,000)

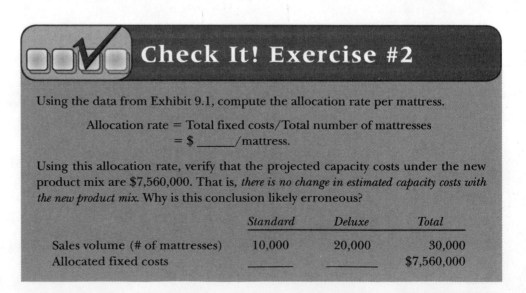

Check It! Exercise #2

Using the data from Exhibit 9.1, compute the allocation rate per mattress.

Allocation rate = Total fixed costs/Total number of mattresses
= $ _____/mattress.

Using this allocation rate, verify that the projected capacity costs under the new product mix are $7,560,000. That is, *there is no change in estimated capacity costs with the new product mix.* Why is this conclusion likely erroneous?

	Standard	Deluxe	Total
Sales volume (# of mattresses)	10,000	20,000	30,000
Allocated fixed costs	_____	_____	$7,560,000

between the current and proposed product mix. Thus, the total cost will remain the same. (In our calculations above, the cost driver was labor dollars, not units sold.)

REFINING THE ALLOCATION

When we use allocated costs to make decisions, the quality of our decision depends on how well the allocation estimates the capacity cost associated with the various options. Constructing the right allocation procedure is a critical step in obtaining the best estimate of controllable capacity costs. A procedure that is too simple might give inaccurate estimates because it does not capture how different products consume capacity resources. On the other hand, highly sophisticated procedures may be difficult to implement because of the many measurements that may be required. The decision context, ease of collecting and analyzing data, and magnitude of the decision all play a role in determining how detailed an allocation procedure to use.

Let us consider two ways to improve the accuracy of allocation procedures.

Using Multiple-Cost Pools and Cost Drivers

Sarah Andrews, the marketing director at EZ-Rest, points out a potential issue in the allocation procedure we used earlier. Sarah agrees that the capacity costs associated with manufacturing the mattresses are likely to vary in proportion to the direct labor cost of each mattress. After all, greater labor cost means more manufacturing time, which means greater use of the factory's capacity. Thus, she supports the use of direct labor costs to estimate the change in manufacturing overhead costs. However, she sees no connection between direct labor cost and the effort needed to market and sell the mattresses. In her experience, it takes the same amount of time to sell either a Deluxe or a Standard mattress. Moreover, the time taken for general administration, processing, and delivering the order is independent of the kind of mattress ordered. Sarah believes that sales volume is better suited for assigning the fixed marketing and administrative costs to the two product lines.

Sarah's observation highlights that a firm's total capacity cost is the sum of the costs of many resources. Products generally consume different capacity resources in different proportions. A driver that is appropriate for some resources may not be appropriate for other resources. How should we deal with this problem?

The solution is to use multiple-cost pools. For each resource or class of similar resources, we could use a separate cost pool. We then allocate the costs in this pool using an allocation basis that best captures the consumption of the associated resources. For example, when estimating the cost of operating a checking account, Citicorp might use separate cost pools for the costs of operating the ATM network and of processing checks. It could then allocate these costs to individual accounts using the number of ATM transactions and the number of checks as the allocation bases, respectively.

In the case of EZ-Rest, let us break the total fixed costs into two separate pools. The first pool contains manufacturing capacity costs and the second, marketing costs. Using the data from Exhibit 9.1, we classify $5,040,000 of the total fixed costs of $7,560,000 as manufacturing costs and the remaining $2,520,000 as marketing and administration costs. Next, we use direct labor dollars for allocating manufacturing costs, and units sold for allocating marketing and administrative costs.

As Exhibit 9.3 shows, after repeating the two cost allocation steps for each cost pool separately, we have $3,672,000 allocated to the Standard mattresses and $3,888,000 allocated to the Deluxe mattresses. Panels A and B in Exhibit 9.4 show the computations for the one- and two-pool systems, respectively.

If using two cost pools is better than using one pool, how about using three cost pools? For instance, why not separately allocate the cost of machines, currently included with manufacturing costs, using machine hours as a third driver? In this case, we would use three cost pools—machining costs, manufacturing costs other than machining costs, and marketing costs—to assess the profit impact of the change in product mix. Such a refinement could make sense if the pattern of machine usage differs from how products use labor.

Exhibit 9.3 *EZ-Rest Mattress Company: Allocation with Two Cost Pools*

	Mattress Type		
	Standard	Deluxe	Total
Pool 1: Manufacturing costs			
Step 1			
Total fixed manufacturing costs			$5,040,000
Total direct labor $	$1,350,000	$1,800,000	$3,150,000
Rate per direct labor $			$1.60
Step 2			
Allocate costs to product lines			
(= DL $ × rate per DL $)	$2,160,000	$2,880,000	$5,040,000
Pool 2: Marketing and administrative costs			
Step 1			
Total fixed marketing and administration costs			$2,520,000
Total units	18,000	12,000	30,000
Rate per unit			$84.00
Step 2			
Allocate costs to product lines			
(= # of units × rate per unit)	$1,512,000	$1,008,000	$2,520,000
Total allocated cost	$3,672,000	$3,888,000	$7,560,000
Allocated cost per unit			
(= total allocated cost / total units)	$204	$324	

Exhibit 9.4 *Refining Cost Estimation by Using Two- versus One-pool Systems*

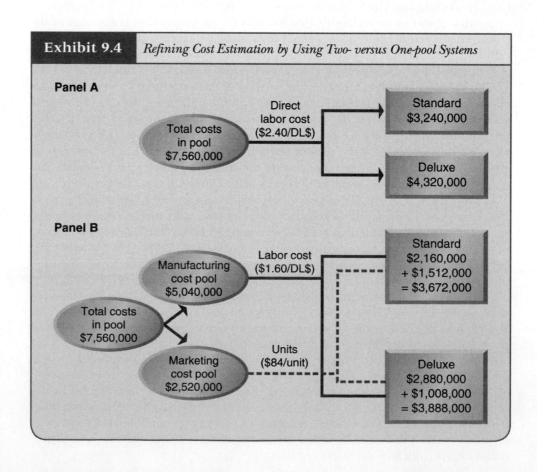

CHAPTER CONNECTIONS
*Activity-based costing, the topic of Chapter 10, is a refined
methodology for estimating allocated costs used to make decisions.*

In principle, we could divide the total fixed costs of $7,560,000 into as many
pools as needed. There is no hard and fast rule that determines how many different
cost pools to use. Some firms use only a few cost pools, while other firms such as Siemens use several hundred pools. Firms that use a single rate are often characterized
as using a **plantwide rate**, whereas firms that develop many rates, usually one per
department, are labeled as employing **departmental rates**.

Excluding Some Capacity Costs

The second refinement to EZ-Rest's system concerns which costs to allocate. Both
the one- and two-pool systems assume that EZ-Rest's entire capacity costs of
$7,560,000 are controllable. This assumption may be inaccurate in some contexts.
After all, some of these costs, such as factory rent and other facility-level costs, could
be noncontrollable for the product-mix decision. That is, regardless of the product
mix, these costs stay the same. Ideally, we should exclude such noncontrollable costs
from the allocation process. We have not done so in the case of EZ-Rest for simplicity; we will revisit this issue in detail in Chapter 10.

PULLING IT ALL TOGETHER

You are now ready to estimate EZ-Rest's income for the proposed product mix
using the allocated costs from the two-pool system. Exhibit 9.5 presents the
income statement for the proposed product mix. It shows that the estimated
capacity costs total $8,520,000, representing an increase of $960,000 from the
current level of $7,560,000. With this increase, you project the profit with the
new mix at $100,000, which is significantly lower than EZ-Rest's current profit
of $684,000. You recommend that Craig consider other avenues for increasing
EZ-Rest's profitability.

Exhibit 9.5	*EZ-Rest Mattress Company: Income Statement—Proposed Product Mix and Allocated Costs from Two-Pool System*			
		Mattress Type		
	Detail	*Standard*	*Deluxe*	*Total*
Sales volume (in units)		10,000	20,000	30,000
Revenue	10,000 × $650;			
	20,000 × $875	$6,500,000	$17,500,000	$24,000,000
Variable costs	10,000 × $394;			
	20,000 × $572	3,940,000	11,440,000	15,380,000
Contribution margin		$2,560,000	$6,060,000	$8,620,000
Estimated fixed costs	10,000 × $75 × $1.60;			
(manufacturing)	20,000 ×$150 × $1.60	1,200,000	4,800,000	6,000,000
Estimated fixed costs	10,000 × $84;			
(Marketing)	20,000 × $84	840,000	1,680,000	2,520,000
Profit before taxes		**$520,000**	**($420,000)**	**$100,000**

APPLYING THE DECISION FRAMEWORK

What Is the Problem?
Even though EZ-Rest currently operates at capacity, CEO Craig Edwards wants the company to increase its profit.

What Are the Options?
We examined two options: (1) Change the product mix to emphasize Deluxe mattresses, (2) Stay with the current product mix.

What Are the Costs and Benefits?
Using the single-pool cost allocation system, we estimate profit will decrease to ($380,000) if EZ-Rest changes its product mix. Using the two-pool cost allocation system, we estimate profit will decrease to $100,000 if EZ-Rest changes its product mix.

Make the Decision!
Because we estimate that changing the product mix to emphasize Deluxe mattresses will actually decrease profit, we recommend that Craig explore alternative ways to increase his company's profitability.

Exhibit 9.6	*Organizations Allocate Capacity Costs for Many Reasons*

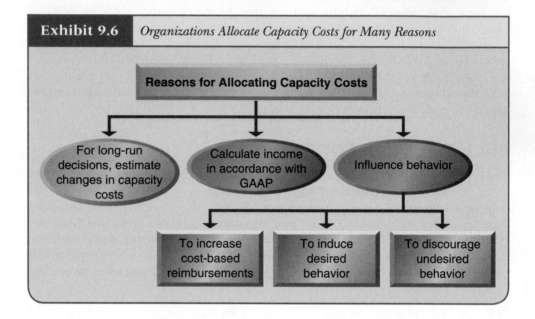

As shown in Exhibit 9.6, helping with decisions is just one of the many reasons firms allocate costs. We now turn our attention to three other common applications of cost allocations: (1) Reporting income to external parties such as shareholders and the IRS; (2) justifying costs, including cost-based reimbursements; and (3) influencing behavior.

Cost Allocations for Reporting Income

LEARNING OBJECTIVE 2

Explain how cost allocations affect income under absorption costing relative to variable costing.

Recall from Chapter 3 that firms must prepare income statements and balance sheets in accordance with the Generally Accepted Accounting Principles (GAAP). GAAP requires firms to use **absorption costing**, which separates product costs from period costs, for external reporting purposes.

Under absorption costing, the value of a unit of a product includes all product costs. Thus, the value includes direct manufacturing costs such as materials and direct labor, as well as indirect manufacturing costs, such as machine depreciation and factory rent. Because indirect manufacturing costs are not traceable to individual products, companies must allocate them to prepare income statements for

CHAPTER CONNECTIONS

As you learned in Chapter 3, product costs are the expenditures required to make a product ready for sale. Examples include the costs of direct materials, direct labor, as well as a variable and fixed manufacturing overhead. Period costs include all selling and administration expenses.

external reporting under GAAP. (You also might wish to review the discussion in Chapter 3 concerning the flow of costs in manufacturing firms, and Exhibits 3.7 and 3.12 in particular.) Thus, EZ-Rest calculates $295 (materials) + $75 (labor) + $120 (manufacturing overhead at $1.60 per labor $) = $490 as the inventoriable value for each Standard mattress. The corresponding number is $350 + $150 + $240 = $740 for each Deluxe mattress. Notice that we do not include variable or fixed selling and administration costs when calculating these values.

To understand how absorption costing affects reported income, assume that EZ-Rest continued to *make* 18,000 Standard and 12,000 Deluxe mattresses as in Exhibit 9.1, but *sold* only 17,000 Standard and 11,600 Deluxe mattresses. That is, the firm put 1,000 Standard and 400 Deluxe mattresses into its inventory of finished goods. How does this change affect reported income from $684,000 in Exhibit 9.1?

Let us begin by calculating what the change in income would be under the now familiar contribution margin format. Exhibit 9.7 presents these calculations. Because this format groups variable costs and fixed costs separately, many also refer to the method as either **direct costing** or **variable costing**. As we expect, the reduction in sales volume reduces income from $684,000 in Exhibit 9.1 to $306,800. This reduction is as predicted by the CVP equation (see *Check it! Exercise #3*). Notice that

Exhibit 9.7	*EZ-Rest Mattress Company: Variable Costing Income Statement*		
	Mattress Type		
	Standard	*Deluxe*	*Total*
Production volume (in units)	18,000	12,000	30,000
Sales volume (in units)	17,000	11,600	28,600
Revenue	$11,050,000	$10,150,000	$21,200,000
Variable costs			
Direct materials ($295 × 17,000; $350 × 11,600)	$5,015,000	$4,060,000	$9,075,000
Direct labor ($75 × 17,000; $150 × 11,600)	1,275,000	1,740,000	$3,015,000
Marketing and sales ($24 × 17,000; $72 × 11,600)	408,000	835,200	$1,243,200
Contribution margin	$4,352,000	$3,514,800	$7,866,800
Fixed costs			
Manufacturing overhead			$5,040,000
Marketing and sales			1,560,000
Administration			960,000
Profit before taxes			$306,800
Unit-level data for inventory value	*Standard*	*Deluxe*	
Direct materials	295	350	
Direct labor	75	150	
Inventoriable cost per unit	$370	$500	
× # of units in inventory	1,000	400	
Value of inventory (total)	$370,000	$200,000	$570,000

 Check It! Exercise #3

Verify that the decline in income from $684,000 in Exhibit 9.1 to $306,800 in Exhibit 9.7, a reduction of $377,200, is as predicted by the CVP equation for EZ-Rest.

First, write down the CVP equation for EZ-Rest:

Profit before taxes = UCM of _____ × # of Standard mattresses
+ UCM of _____ × # of Deluxe mattresses
− fixed costs of _____.

Next, use the equation to calculate the reduction in profit if sales decline by 1,000 units of Standard and 400 units of the Deluxe mattress.

Solution at end of chapter.

Exhibit 9.8	EZ-Rest Mattress Company: Absorption Costing Income Statement		

| | Mattress Type | | |
	Standard	Deluxe	Total
Production volume (in units)	18,000	12,000	30,000
Sales volume (in units)	17,000	11,600	28,600
Revenue	$11,050,000	$10,150,000	$21,200,000
Product costs			
Direct materials ($295 × 17,000; $350 × 11,600)	$5,015,000	$4,060,000	$9,075,000
Direct labor ($75 × 17,000; $150 × 11,600)	1,275,000	1,740,000	3,015,000
Manufacturing overhead ($120 × 17,000; $240 × 11,600)	2,040,000	2,784,000	4,824,000
Gross margin	$2,720,000	$1,566,000	$4,286,000
Period costs			
Variable marketing and sales ($24 × 17,000; $72 × 11,600)	$408,000	$835,200	1,243,200
Fixed marketing and sales			1,560,000
Administration			960,000
Profit before taxes			$522,800
Unit-level data for inventory values	Standard	Deluxe	
Direct materials	295	350	
Direct labor	75	150	
Allocated overhead	120	240	
Inventoriable cost per unit	$490	$740	
× # of units in inventory	1,000 units	400 units	
Value of inventory (total)	$490,000	$296,000	$786,000

the amount of manufacturing overhead cost expensed in the income statement is still $5,040,000—it is unaffected by the change in the number of units sold.

Exhibit 9.8 presents the absorption costing income statement with the revised assumption about units sold. Again, as we expect, reported income declines relative to $684,000, the income when EZ-Rest sold all the units that it made. In this statement, consistent with GAAP, we use the product cost of $490 and $740 per Standard and Deluxe mattress to calculate the cost of goods sold and inventory values.

Notice that the drop in income is much smaller in Exhibit 9.8 than in Exhibit 9.7. Why is this? The answer is that we allocate fixed manufacturing costs to individual products under absorption costing so that we can comply with GAAP and account for overhead as a product cost. Intuitively, absorption costing "burdens" each unit with some fixed manufacturing overhead as it moves through the production process. This allocation results in fixed manufacturing overhead "traveling" with the units.

At the end of an accounting period, in addition to the units we sell, we may have added units to the finished goods account. The cost of goods sold account will include the fixed manufacturing costs of units sold. Similarly, the finished goods inventory account will contain the fixed manufacturing costs of units produced but not sold. Focusing only on the fixed manufacturing costs, we see in Exhibit 9.8 that the cost of goods sold contains $4,824,000 of the $5,040,000 of fixed manufacturing overhead, and the finished goods inventory contains the remainder. In contrast, the contribution margin statement (i.e., variable costing statement) summarized in Exhibit 9.7 expenses all $5,040,000 of manufacturing overhead. This difference of $216,000 in overhead costs contained in the inventory is also the difference in the income reported under the two methods.

Exhibit 9.9 represents the cost flows pictorially. Panel A shows the underlying physical flow of units: EZ-Rest made 18,000 Standard and 12,000 Deluxe mattresses and sold 17,000 and 11,600 units, respectively. As shown in the leftmost circles of panels B and C, EZ-Rest also spent $5,040,000 in fixed manufacturing costs. Panel B shows that, under variable costing, we expense the entire amount to the income statement. However, as shown in panel C, under absorption costing, we first allocate the amount to individual

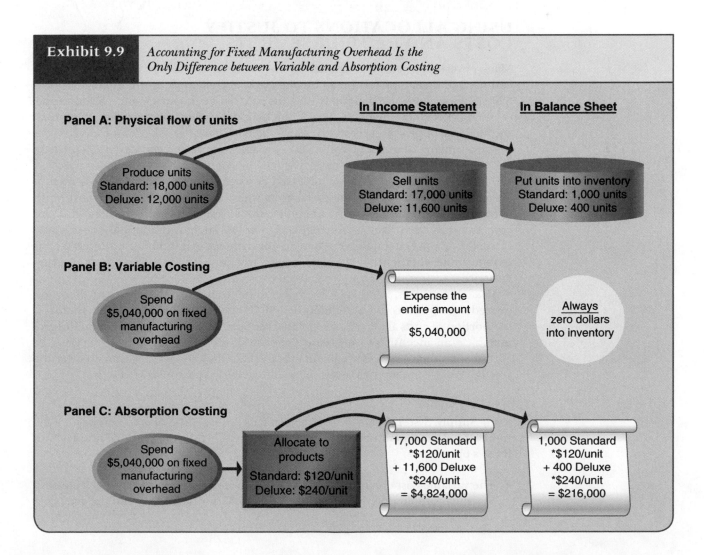

Exhibit 9.9   *Accounting for Fixed Manufacturing Overhead Is the Only Difference between Variable and Absorption Costing*

In Income Statement   **In Balance Sheet**

Panel A: Physical flow of units

Produce units
Standard: 18,000 units
Deluxe: 12,000 units

Sell units
Standard: 17,000 units
Deluxe: 11,600 units

Put units into inventory
Standard: 1,000 units
Deluxe: 400 units

Panel B: Variable Costing

Spend $5,040,000 on fixed manufacturing overhead

Expense the entire amount
$5,040,000

Always zero dollars into inventory

Panel C: Absorption Costing

Spend $5,040,000 on fixed manufacturing overhead

Allocate to products
Standard: $120/unit
Deluxe: $240/unit

17,000 Standard
*$120/unit
+ 11,600 Deluxe
*$240/unit
= $4,824,000

1,000 Standard
*$120/unit
+ 400 Deluxe
*$240/unit
= $216,000

units. This means that the overhead associated with units sold appears in the income statement, and the overhead for the units put into inventory appears in the balance sheet. When EZ-Rests adds units to inventory, this accounting for overhead leads to greater reported income, relative to the income reported under variable costing.

The Appendix to this chapter provides an in-depth comparison of variable and absorption costing. For now, it is enough that you know firms must allocate manufacturing overhead to products when valuing inventories. Such allocations result in the overhead cost flowing through the inventory account. Consequently, when inventory levels change, the amount recognized in the income statement for overhead may not correspond to the amount spent. How the firm allocates overhead determines the portion recognized in the income statement and, therefore, reported income.

Incentives and Cost Allocations

LEARNING OBJECTIVE 3

Describe the role of incentives in the choice of allocation procedures.

As you have learned thus far, the amount of cost allocated to a particular cost object depends on what costs we allocate, how we group them into cost pools, and which drivers we choose. Companies often choose allocation procedures in a way that allows them to achieve certain goals. In this section, we provide some examples of how companies use allocations in contract negotiations and as a means of influencing workplace behavior.

USING ALLOCATIONS TO JUSTIFY COSTS AND REIMBURSEMENTS

Many government entities, such as the Department of Defense (DoD), contract to compensate their suppliers on a cost-plus basis. For example, if the supplier's cost is $200 and the agreed-on markup is 10%, the supplier's reimbursement is $220. Suppliers such as Rockwell Collins often prefer such contracts when there is uncertainty about the final cost or project success, as it allows them to share the risk of cost overruns with the government. Absent such contracts, companies may be reluctant to accept the risky and expensive projects such as developing the next generation of combat aircraft.

Many organizations also use allocated costs to justify prices. Hospitals such as Massachusetts General use allocated costs when negotiating rates with insurance companies and other payers. A communications company like Qwest uses allocated costs to justify the prices set for regulated services such as residential phone rates. Managers in the Federal Reserve Bank, a government institution, use allocated costs to determine whether they should continue to offer services such as check clearing and wire transfers that large commercial banks also offer.

In such instances, firms have incentives to be strategic in the choice of allocation procedures. Qwest could potentially benefit by choosing a procedure that increases the portion of costs allocated to regulated services. Managers at the Federal Reserve may have an incentive to decrease the cost allocated to competitive services, to "prove" that their services are profitable and that they should continue to offer the service. We use a numerical example to illustrate this incentive next.

An Example
Ryan Supply Systems sells ready-to-eat meals to both the armed forces and the public (e.g., campers and hunters). We have the following information about Ryan's operations:

- The variable cost of a meal supplied to the armed forces is $4. The variable cost of a meal supplied to the public is $5, due to better packaging and the greater variety of meals available.

Connecting to Practice

DETECTING COST SHIFTING

A recent study of defense contractors shows that the contractors enjoyed higher than normal profits during 1984–1989, which was a period of unusually low competition. The authors examine the hypothesis that these firms were able to generate abnormal profits because they exploited their bargaining power to shift more costs to cost-plus contracts with the defense department.

COMMENTARY: The study looked for evidence of cost shifting by comparing the profits reported by three segments—commercial, defense, and mixed—for a sample of defense contractors. Surprisingly, despite extensive analysis of the firms' financial data, it did not find any evidence that the higher profitability resulted from the alleged cost-shifting behavior. Thus, while cost shifting is a much talked about phenomenon, it might be hard to detect and prove.

Source: Vendrzyk, V., and A. McGowan. "The relation between cost shifting and segment profitability in the defense contracting industry." *The Accounting Review* 2002 77(4): 949–969.

- Annual fixed costs equal $8 million.
- Sales to each the military and the public equal 2 million meals per year. Because of the greater variety of meal packages sold to the public, Ryan estimates that the 2 million meals sold to the public consume 60% of the plant's capacity of 100,000 machine hours; the 2 million meals sold to the military consume the remaining 40%.
- The price of a meal sold to the public is $8; the price to the military allows for a 20% markup on cost.

Because Ryan's reimbursement from the armed forces depends on cost, it must decide how to allocate the fixed costs of $8 million between the military and the public. The military contract allows Ryan to use either the number of meals or machine hours to allocate fixed costs. Which basis should Ryan use to maximize its profit?

Allocations Using Units
Using meals as the allocation basis, we find:

- The allocated fixed cost per meal is $2 (= $8,000,000 fixed costs/4,000,000 meals) for both the armed forces and the public.
- The total cost per meal is $6 for the military contract ($6 = $4 variable cost per meal + the allocated fixed cost of $2 per meal).
- Adding the markup of 20% to this cost, the military pays $7.20 per meal (= $6 × 1.2).

Allocations Using Machine Hours
If Ryan were to choose machine hours as the basis for allocation:

- The allocation rate is $80 per machine hour (= $8,000,000 fixed costs/100,000 machine hours).
- Ryan uses 40% of its 100,000 hours of machine capacity, or 40,000 machine hours, to produce meals for the military. Multiplying this amount by the allocation rate of $80 per machine hour, Ryan allocates $3,200,000 of the fixed costs to the military contract, for an allocated cost of $1.60 per meal (= $3,200,000/2,000,000).

- The total cost per meal is $5.60 for the military contract ($5.60 = $4 variable cost per meal + $1.60 of allocated fixed cost).
- Adding the markup of 20% to this cost, the military price is $6.72 (= $5.60 × 1.2).

Exhibit 9.10 provides a condensed income statement under the two allocation methods. We find that Ryan increases its profit by $960,000 merely by changing the basis for its allocation. Using meals instead of machine hours as the allocation basis increases the amount allocated to the military sector from $3.2 million to $4 million, an increase of $800,000. The additional reimbursement combines this $800,000 and the 20% markup of $160,000, for a total increase of $960,000 in profit. The change in the allocation basis does not affect other costs and revenues. Choosing units as the allocation basis merely shifts a greater portion of the fixed costs to the military contract, and increases the associated revenue.

Buyers like government agencies understand firms' incentives to engage in this cost-shifting behavior. As a result, government contracts typically specify how the supplier should determine the allocated cost. These agencies also conduct audits to ensure compliance. Nevertheless, because of the unavoidable ambiguity in allocating common costs, the contracting parties must strike a delicate balance. The contract must devise procedures that allow suppliers to recoup a fair share of their costs while controlling their incentive to manage cost estimates to their advantage.

Check It! Exercise #4

Suppose that the meals sold to the public consume 55% of the plant's capacity of 100,000 machine hours. Verify that Ryan would still prefer to allocate costs based on meals.

Solution at end of chapter.

Connecting to Practice

TAXES AND NOT-FOR-PROFIT ORGANIZATIONS

Under U.S. tax laws, not-for-profit organizations owe income taxes on the profit they make from activities not related to their charitable mission. For example, a university must pay taxes on income it receives from renting out the stadium for a rock concert. But revenue from tuition is not taxable because it relates to the university's educational mission. We usually find many shared costs among the activities that generate related and unrelated business income. The not-for-profit must therefore allocate costs to determine taxable income.

COMMENTARY: Research finds that more than half of the surveyed not-for-profits that reported positive revenue from unrelated businesses also reported taxable income of exactly zero! That is, their costs *exactly* equaled their revenue. It appears that many not-for-profit organizations allocate costs strategically to minimize their taxable income.

Exhibit 9.10	*Ryan Supply Systems: Condensed Income Statements*			
	Unit Data (Public/Military)	**Public**	**Military**	**Total**
Sales volume (in units)		2,000,000	2,000,000	
Panel A: Using Units as the Allocation Basis				
Revenue	$8.00 / $7.20	$16,000,000	$14,400,000	$30,400,000
Variable costs	$5.00 / $4.00	10,000,000	8,000,000	18,000,000
Allocated fixed costs	$2.00 / $2.00	4,000,000	4,000,000	8,000,000
Gross Margin		$2,000,000	$2,400,000	$4,400,000
Panel B: Using Machine Hours as the Allocation Basis				
Revenue	$8.00 / $6.72	$16,000,000	$13,440,000	$29,440,000
Variable costs	$5.00 / $4.00	10,000,000	8,000,000	18,000,000
Allocated fixed costs	60% / 40%	4,800,000	3,200,000	8,000,000
Gross margin		$1,200,000	$ 2,240,000	$3,440,000

USING COST ALLOCATIONS TO INFLUENCE BEHAVIOR

Well-designed cost allocation procedures can influence the mix of resources that an organization uses. In particular, cost allocations may dissuade the use of one resource in favor of another resource. Recall that allocated cost equals the number of driver units used multiplied by the cost per driver unit. Therefore, the cost allocated to the manager is proportional to the number of driver units consumed by the manager. By changing the quantity of driver units consumed, managers can change the costs allocated to their units. From a manager's perspective, the allocated cost *behaves* like a variable cost.

Why do managers care about the costs allocated to their individual departments or divisions? After all, the total cost is the same and fixed for the company as a whole. The allocation merely changes the distribution of this fixed cost among units. It might seem that the firm or its managers should not care about how the firm allocates this cost. However, managers' performance evaluations frequently depend on their unit's performance more than overall firm performance. The cost allocated to a division is an integral part of that division's reported profit and performance. Reducing the number of driver units consumed benefits managers by lowering the cost allocated to their units, even though the change may have no effect on the firm as a whole.

Cost allocations therefore provide subtle, yet effective, means to achieve change. It is often difficult for organizations to implement change; people generally resist change. Of course, one way to force people to change is by leaving them with no other option. However, such autocratic approaches usually create resentment and motivational problems. Instead, using carefully chosen allocation methods can induce desired behavior and dissuade undesired behavior. We next look at two examples to show how firms can accomplish this.

Allocations to Induce Desired Behavior

Consider a company that has five divisions, each of which manufactures a different product line. A year ago, the company invested in sophisticated equipment and technology to automate production processes. The company believed that the technology would help improve quality and productivity in every division. Moreover, this technology would help divisions reduce their reliance on direct labor by automating production processes. Surprisingly, the divisions appeared to continue existing practices, adopting the new technology at a slower-than-expected pace.

Faced with the task of motivating its workforce to use the new technology, corporate headquarters reexamines its employee incentives. Employees receive a straight salary and a bonus based on divisional profit. Divisional profit includes an allocation for corporate administrative and overhead costs. Although the allocation results in a substantial charge to each division's profit, the head office does provide numerous support services to the divisions. Currently, the firm allocates administrative costs equally among the five divisions.

As a motivation to use the new technology, the chief financial officer (CFO) suggests changing this allocation procedure and using direct labor hours as the basis for allocating corporate overhead. Thus, the company would allocate the most corporate overhead to the division that uses the most direct labor hours in its production process. That division's profit would accordingly decrease, thereby reducing employee bonuses. The result is a natural incentive for the workforce in the division to opt for new technology and automation to lower the amount of direct labor used. As Exhibit 9.11 shows, the quantity demanded of any resource (vertical axis) decreases as its price (horizontal axis) increases. Allocating overhead costs in proportion to the usage of a resource effectively increases its price, and, therefore, the quantity demanded goes down.

In this example, allocating corporate overhead based on direct labor is arbitrary. Direct labor use may have little to do with corporate overhead costs. However, even arbitrary allocations, if well designed, can serve the purpose of encouraging desired organizational behavior.

Allocations to Induce Efficient Use

By discouraging wasteful use, cost allocations also can induce efficient utilization of resources shared by multiple users. Suppose the Department of Accounting at Prestige University recently hired Brad Gates, a talented computer service specialist, to help with the computing needs of its faculty and staff. The department offered Brad a three-year contract at an annual salary of $60,000.

At the start, Brad seemed to provide a welcome solution to the department's mounting computer hardware and software woes. However, after only a few months, Melanie Brooks, the department chair, began to hear complaints regarding Brad's tardiness and inability to cope. After investigating the issue, Melanie notes that Brad,

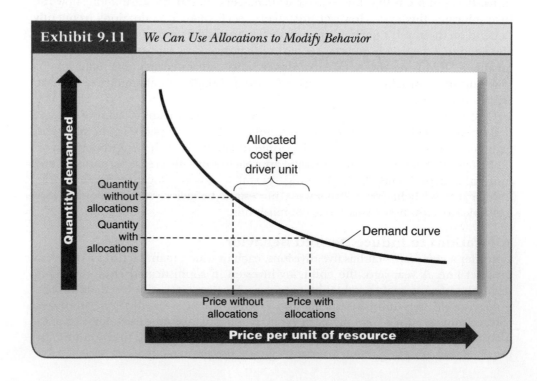

| Exhibit 9.11 | *We Can Use Allocations to Modify Behavior* |

in fact, is competent and puts in long hours. However, Brad spends much of his time attending to minor jobs that faculty and staff could easily handle themselves.

Melanie concludes that the faculty and the staff are using Brad's services inefficiently because they view Brad's time as a "free good." As there is no charge for Brad's time, everyone asks for Brad's help, even for minor problems. Being an astute accountant, Melanie decides to charge the faculty and staff an hourly rate for using Brad's services. Assuming 250 working days in a year, and eight working hours in a day, Melanie comes up with an hourly rate of $30 per hour ($60,000/(250 days $\times$ 8 hours per day)). Any time a faculty member uses Brad's services, she decides to charge the faculty person's spending account at the rate of $30 per hour.

As Melanie expected, the faculty initially react to this decision with some disapproval. Soon, however, everybody seems happy with Brad's performance. The faculty only brings to Brad's attention those problems that need his expertise. Thus, everybody uses Brad's services more efficiently.

What happened? Given the three-year contract, Brad's salary is a fixed and noncontrollable cost. Thus, the $30 per hour rate at which the department allocates this cost is arbitrary. However, this rate creates an opportunity cost for faculty requesting Brad's help. It forces faculty members to evaluate whether it is worth paying for Brad's services at $30 per hour, or whether they should resolve the problem themselves. Because the allocated cost serves as the price for using Brad's services, Melanie can further increase efficiency. That is, she can increase or decrease the demand for Brad's time by changing the hourly rate.

Many universities use such cost allocation procedures to cut unnecessary and wasteful use of expensive resources. Firms such as British Petroleum and Principal Financial Group use similar procedures with respect to administrative, maintenance, IT, and other support services. The use of cost allocations for this purpose serves as a simple and effective way to influence employees' use of resources, especially the expensive ones.

CONTROLLABILITY AND ALTERNATE DEMANDS FOR COST ALLOCATIONS

Thus far, we have described three different demands for cost allocations: estimating long-run capacity costs, determining reported income, and influencing behavior. Let us now consider how these uses differ in terms of the costs to allocate and choice of drivers.

Connecting to Practice

COST ALLOCATIONS IN JAPAN

After an extensive study of Japanese firms such as Nissan, Komatsu, and Citizen Watch, Professor Robin Cooper concluded that the product costing systems of these firms follow traditional practices. They also have cost control as their primary focus. That is, they use large cost pools and use drivers such as labor dollars and machine hours.

COMMENTARY: The primary goal of these costing systems is to support cost control during the production process. Firms engage in this practice to motivate their managers to reduce labor content to the maximum extent feasible. These firms do not use this allocation when determining prices, an economic decision. The firms use detailed target costing systems for this purpose. We discuss target costing in Chapter 13.

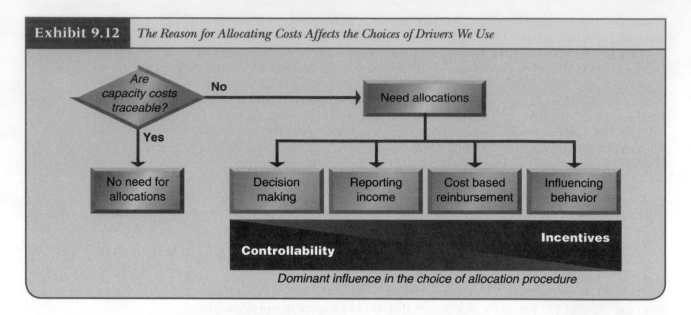

Exhibit 9.12 *The Reason for Allocating Costs Affects the Choices of Drivers We Use*

At the start of this chapter, our goal was to determine the profit impact of changing EZ-Rest's product mix. For this decision, the need for cost allocations arose from two fundamental principles: (1) *controllability* of capacity costs over the long term resulted in EZ-Rest measuring these costs for appropriate decision making; (2) the lack of *traceability* of capacity costs to individual products led to a demand for allocations.

Controllability is the criterion that determines what costs to measure. In the context of a long-term decision (such as the product-mix choice), the cost of a decision option may include direct and allocated costs across all functional areas including manufacturing, marketing, and administration. Indeed, surveys indicate that numerous companies, including John Deere, Siemens, and Lehigh Steel, allocate capacity costs to estimate product profitability for making product-mix decisions. These firms employ a many-pool system with multiple drivers to estimate how costs would change as the volume of the underlying activities changes.

When allocating costs to value inventory, traceability is the underlying reason why firms allocate rather than directly measure capacity costs. Controllability is less important. In particular, GAAP mandates that we allocate manufacturing overhead to products, even if they are not controllable. Furthermore, firms do not allocate selling and distribution costs to units in inventory even though these costs may be controllable. Firms also tend to employ simple one-pool systems when allocating costs for valuing inventory.

As Exhibit 9.12 shows, the link to controllability is even weaker when using allocations to determine reimbursements or to influence behavior. In these cases, the focus is on what behavior we wish to encourage or deter—controllability is less of an issue.

We must always keep the specific context in mind when seeking to understand, design, and use cost allocation systems. Ideally, firms need to use separate systems for each purpose. Unfortunately, multiple systems increase the potential to confuse users, most firms use one cost allocation for all purposes. Managers therefore must modify available data often to make it suitable for the specific purpose at hand.

SUMMARY

In this chapter, we discussed the how and the why of cost allocations. We learned that organizations use cost allocations for several purposes, including decision making, reporting income to external parties, justifying reimbursements, and influencing behavior. We studied each of these uses as well as the mechanics underlying allocations. While controllability is the driving force behind the use of allocations for decision making, incentives drive the choice of allocation procedures for the other three uses.

In Chapter 10, we examine in detail the use of cost allocations as decision aids. Our primary focus is activity-based costing (ABC), a technique to help improve our estimates of product profitability. In Chapters 14 and 15, we consider further the external reporting role of allocations, examining job and process costing systems, respectively.

RAPID REVIEW

LEARNING OBJECTIVE 1

Understand how to use cost allocations to make long-term decisions.

- The key feature distinguishing long-term decisions from short-term decisions is the ability to change the level of capacity supplied and, thus, capacity costs. In the long term, we can sell excess capacity or acquire additional capacity. Accordingly, we need to consider the cost of capacity resources when evaluating long-term decisions.

- There are two general approaches to estimating the change in capacity costs: (1) direct estimation and (2) allocations. While potentially accurate, direct estimation is difficult and time-consuming. In addition, its accuracy depends on the expertise and incentives of the person making the estimates. For these reasons, organizations make frequent use of cost allocations. An allocation distributes a common cost or benefit among two or more cost objects (e.g., products, departments).

LEARNING OBJECTIVE 2

Explain how cost allocations affect income under absorption costing relative to variable costing.

- Under variable costing, sales, the unit contribution margin, and fixed costs determine reported income. We do not need to use cost allocations to arrive at net income or inventory values when constructing the contribution margin statement.

- Cost allocations play an important role in determining income reported under Generally Accepted Accounting Principles (GAAP). GAAP specifies that a cost of a unit in inventory should include the direct manufacturing costs of materials and labor as well as the indirect manufacturing costs such as machine depreciation and factory rent. Because these costs are indirect, firms use cost allocations to value inventory and, in turn, determine cost of goods sold and net income. The matching principle, a fundamental precept of GAAP, underlies this use of cost allocations.

- A common criticism of absorption costing is that it provides incentives to produce more than what is necessary to satisfy demand. This incentive arises because a firm can report higher income merely by increasing production.

- Increases or decreases in inventory levels will cause income under variable costing to differ from income under absorption costing. We reconcile this difference as:

Income reported under variable costing
+ Fixed manufacturing costs in ending inventory
− Fixed manufacturing costs in beginning inventory
= Income reported under absorption costing

LEARNING OBJECTIVE 3

Describe the role of incentives in the choice of allocation procedures.

- Numerous organizations use allocated costs to justify prices. In such instances, firms can be strategic by choosing a procedure that increases the portion of costs allocated to the goods and services priced on a cost-plus basis. By merely changing the basis for cost allocation, organizations can sometimes increase their profitability.

- Cost allocations are a way to penalize and, therefore, dissuade the use of one resource in favor of another resource. For example, cost allocations based on labor may encourage managers to automate production processes. In addition, cost allocations can induce the efficient use of resources shared by multiple users by discouraging wasteful use.

- While controllability is central when allocating costs for decision making, it is subordinate to incentives when allocating costs for other uses, such as valuing inventory, justifying costs, and influencing behavior.

Appendix
VARIABLE AND ABSORPTION COSTING

In this appendix, we use an example to provide an in-depth comparison of variable and absorption costing. Consider Bath Technologies, a firm that makes enamel-coated steel bathtubs. Exhibit 9.13 presents Bath's variable costing income statement for the most recent quarter of operations.

We begin by noting that variable costing conforms to the CVP relation you learned in Chapter 5. Thus, we could express Bath's monthly profit before taxes as:

$$\text{Monthly profit before taxes} = (\text{Sales in units} \times \$416) - \$3,725,000$$

Exhibit 9.13 also shows that Bath accumulated inventory of 200 bathtubs in August; the firm produced 10,000 tubs but only sold 9,800. Bath values this inventory at the variable manufacturing cost of $270 per unit ($120 in direct materials + $150 in direct labor). Variable selling costs are not included in ending inventory values because Bath would not have incurred selling expenses for the unsold units in its inventory.

In essence, sales, the unit contribution margin, and fixed costs determine income reported under variable costing. Whether Bath accumulates inventories (as in

Exhibit 9.13	*Bath Technologies: Variable Costing Income Statement*			
	Per unit	**July**	**August**	**September**
Sales volume (in units)		10,000	9,800	10,200
Production volume (in units)		10,000	10,000	10,000
Revenue	$700	$7,000,000	$6,860,000	$7,140,000
Variable costs				
Direct materials	$120	1,200,000	1,176,000	1,224,000
Direct labor	$150	1,500,000	1,470,000	1,530,000
Marketing and sales	$14	140,000	137,200	142,800
Contribution margin	$416	$4,160,000	$4,076,800	$4,243,200
Fixed costs				
Manufacturing		2,550,000	2,550,000	2,550,000
Marketing and administration		1,175,000	1,175,000	1,175,000
Profit before taxes		$435,000	$351,800	$518,200
Inventory:				
Units in ending inventory		0	200	0
Value per unit	$270		$270	$270
Value of ending inventory		$0	$54,000	$0

Check It! Exercise #5

Using Bath's monthly CVP equation, verify its income before taxes for the months of July, August, and September as reported in Exhibit 9.13.

Solution at end of chapter.

August) or depletes inventories (as in September) does not affect reported income. We also note that Bath does not use any cost allocations to arrive at monthly income or inventory values when constructing the variable costing income statement. However, as mentioned in the chapter, this approach is not acceptable under GAAP for external reporting purposes.

Absorption Costing

Absorption costing separates costs that are required to ready goods for sale (product costs) from all other costs (period costs). Exhibit 9.14 recasts Bath's data using the absorption costing approach. Some refer to this format as **full costing** because accounting convention terms a product's inventoriable cost as its full cost.

To comply with GAAP, Bath allocates fixed manufacturing costs to units *produced*. That is, Bath divides its monthly fixed costs ($2,550,000) by its monthly production (10,000 units) to arrive at a fixed manufacturing rate of $255 per unit. Bath adds this allocated cost to variable manufacturing costs ($270), thereby valuing each tub at $525. Thus, Bath computes its COGS as the number of tubs sold × $525. Likewise, it values the inventory of 200 tubs in August at $105,000 (200 tubs × $525 per tub).

Exhibit 9.14	Bath Technologies: Absorption Costing Income Statement and Inventory Values			
	Revenue/ Cost per unit	July	August	September
Sales volume (in units)		10,000	9,800	10,200
Production volume (in units)		10,000	10,000	10,000
Revenue	$700	$7,000,000	$6,860,000	$7,140,000
Cost of goods sold				
Direct materials	$120	1,200,000	1,176,000	1,224,000
Direct labor	$150	1,500,000	1,470,000	1,530,000
Allocated fixed manufacturing costs	$255	2,550,000	2,499,000	2,601,000
Total cost of goods sold	$525	5,250,000	5,145,000	5,355,000
Gross margin	$175	$1,750,000	$1,715,000	$1,785,000
Period costs				
Variable marketing and sales	$14	140,000	137,200	142,800
Fixed marketing and sales		1,175,000	1,175,000	1,175,000
Profit before taxes		$435,000	$402,800	$467,200
Inventory:				
Units in ending inventory		0	200	0
Inventoriable cost per unit		$525	$525	$525
Value of ending inventory		$0	$105,000	$0

Recall that because manufacturing overhead "travels" with the units, the cost of goods sold account will include the fixed manufacturing costs of units sold. The finished goods inventory account will contain the fixed manufacturing costs of units produced but not sold. Thus, focusing only on the fixed manufacturing costs, we see that the cost of goods sold contains $2,499,000 of the $2,550,000 of fixed manufacturing overhead, and the finished goods inventory contains the remainder of $51,000.

ABSORPTION COSTING AND THE MATCHING PRINCIPLE

The matching principle, a fundamental tenet of GAAP, requires firms to recognize costs in the same period in which the associated revenue occurs. GAAP specifies that fixed manufacturing costs are part of the cost of producing a unit and requires that companies record the product cost as an expense only in the period in which they make the sale and recognize the associated revenue. Absorption costing accomplishes this goal by allocating fixed manufacturing costs to units in inventory. When the sale eventually takes place, fixed manufacturing costs are included in cost of goods sold for that accounting period.

INCENTIVES TO OVERPRODUCE UNDER ABSORPTION COSTING

A common criticism of absorption costing is that it provides incentives to produce more than what is necessary to satisfy demand. This incentive arises because a firm can report a higher income merely by increasing production. To illustrate, assume that Bath increases production from 10,000 to 15,000 tubs during July, but sales remain at 10,000 units. In this case, the new allocation rate is $170 per unit ($2,550,000/15,000 units). Why? The additional production decreases the overhead rate from $255 per unit ($2,550,000/10,000 units) to $170 per unit. Because this change in allocation rate does not change either revenue or variable costs, the gross margin per unit increases by $85 per unit, from $175 per unit to $260 per unit. As a result, income increases by 10,000 units × $85 per unit = $850,000, to $1,285,000.

This increase is illusory. The firm now has 5,000 units in inventory, whereas previously it had none. Inventory contains $850,000 (5,000 units × $170 per unit) of July's fixed overhead costs. This "hiding" of the overhead cost in inventory is the source for the additional "profit" in July. This cost will become part of cost of goods sold in some future period, when Bath sells these 5,000 units.

Why might managers seek to boost current income in this manner? Managers may be overly optimistic about the future. They might view the inventory buildup as a way to use currently available capacity to meet future demand. Managers also might want to increase reported income if they receive bonuses based on the income that they report.

Reconciling Variable and Absorption Costing Income

Over the lifetime of the firm, both variable and absorption costing will lead to the same total income, as the firm begins and ends with zero inventories. However, within a shorter period, any increase or decrease in inventory levels will cause the two incomes to differ. We can reconcile this difference as follows:

> Income reported under variable costing
> + Fixed manufacturing costs in ending inventory
> − Fixed manufacturing costs in beginning inventory
> = Income reported under absorption costing

Check It! Exercise #6

Complete the following table to reconcile the income numbers reported under variable costing and absorption costing. Recall that the fixed manufacturing cost per unit − $255

	July	August	September
Units in beginning inventory	0	___	___
Units in ending inventory	___	___	0
Income reported under variable costing	$435,000	$351,800	$518,200
+ Fixed manufacturing costs in ending inventory	___	___	___
− Fixed manufacturing costs in beginning inventory	___	___	___
= Income reported under absorption costing	$435,000	$402,800	$467,200

Solution at end of chapter.

In our example, Bath reports income of $435,000 for July under both variable and absorption costing because production equaled sales and the firm had zero units in beginning inventory. There was no change in inventory levels. Therefore, income reported under absorption costing equaled income reported under variable costing.

Referring to Exhibits 9.13 and 9.14 for the month of August, we find that income under absorption costing is $51,000 higher than income under variable costing ($402,800 − $351,800). Note that this difference in income corresponds to the difference in ending inventory values—ending inventory under absorption costing is $105,000, whereas it is only $54,000 under variable costing. The $51,000 represents the fixed manufacturing costs in ending inventory under absorption costing (200 unsold bathtubs × $255 fixed manufacturing cost per bathtub).

In September, income reported under absorption costing is $51,000 *less* than income reported under variable costing because Bath *sold* its inventory of 200 tubs. Accordingly, the income statement for September includes the costs attached to these units. Under variable costing, these costs include direct materials and direct labor. Under absorption costing, however, the cost also includes the $51,000 in fixed manufacturing costs allocated to the ending inventory of 200 units in August. These costs become a part of the COGS for September when Bath sells the units it inventoried in August. Thus, September income decreases by the same $51,000.

ANSWERS TO CHECK IT! EXERCISES

Exercise #1: Direct labor dollars (DL$) = $1,350,000 and $1,800,000; Percentage of DL$ = 42.86% and 57.14%; Amount allocated = $3,240,000 and $4,320,000; Percent of cost allocated = 42.86% and 57.14%.

Exercise #2: Allocation rate = $7,560,000/30,000 = $252 per mattress; Allocated fixed costs = $2,520,000 ($252 × 10,000) and $5,040,000 ($252 × 20,000). The total does not change because we have 30,000 units both under the current and projected mix. Furthermore, when we choose units as the allocation basis, the fixed overhead estimate is proportional to total units. This estimate is likely to be erroneous because manufacturing capacity costs are not likely to be related to units sold—that is, Standard and Deluxe mattresses consume varying amounts of resources. As discussed in the text, the Deluxe mattresses use much more labor time, which, in turn, leads to greater use of the factory's capacity.

Exercise #3: Unit contribution margin is $256 per Standard mattress and is $303 per Deluxe mattress. We can calculate these values as $4,352,000/17,000 Standard mattresses and $3,514,800/11,600 Deluxe mattress. Thus, the contribution lost because of the lower sales volume (relative to the volume in Exhibit 9.1) is (1,000 Standard $\times$ $256) + (400 Deluxe $\times$ $303 per mattress) = $377,200.

Exercise #4: The allocation rate is $80 per machine hour. Thus, $4,400,000 would be allocated to public meals (= 0.55 $\times$ $8,000,000), and $3,600,000 would be allocated to the military contract (= 0.45 $\times$ $8,000,000). The gross margin for public meals is therefore $1,600,000 (= $16,000,000 − $10,000,000 − $4,400,000). The gross margin for the military is $2,320,000 (= [$8,000,000 + $3,600,000] $\times$ 0.20). The total gross margin = $1,600,000 + $2,320,000 = $3,920,000, which is still lower than the $4,400,000 total gross margin using meals as the allocation basis.

Exercise #5: July: (10,000 $\times$ $416) − $3,725,000 = $435,000; August: (9,800 $\times$ $416) − $3,725,000 = $351,800; September: (10,200 $\times$ $416) − $3,725,000 = $518,200.

Exercise #6: July: 0, $0, $0, 435,000 + $0 − $0 = $435,000; August: 0, 200, $351,800 + $51,000 − $0 = $402,800; September: 200, 0, $518,200 + $0 − $51,000 = $467,200.

SELF-STUDY PROBLEMS

Susan Brown, a talented engineer, holds the patent on a device that helps cap oil wells. Susan runs a small firm that makes and sells this product, which we refer to as the "cap." Susan has provided you with the following data regarding her operations:

Sales volume	1,500 units per month
Selling price	$350 per unit
Direct materials costs	$120 per unit
Labor hours consumed	3 hours per unit
Variable marketing and selling costs	$25 per unit

Susan pays her labor $20 per hour. She also incurs fixed manufacturing costs of $135,000 per month and fixed marketing and administrative costs of $30,000 per month. Finally, Susan currently is operating at full capacity, which she defines in terms of labor hours.

a. *One of Susan's customers approaches her to make a new component. This component has materials cost of $200 per unit and would consume 2 hours of labor per unit. In addition, it would cost Susan $10 per unit in variable marketing and selling costs. The customer needs 450 units urgently and knows that Susan's factory has the needed equipment. The customer's regular supplier had a fire in its factory and cannot supply the units this month. For this short-term decision, what is the minimum price that Susan should charge per unit for this new component so that her monthly profit does not decrease?*

In this situation, Susan faces a short-term decision with excess demand (as we studied in Chapter 6). The decision is short term because it pertains to a one-time special order. The situation is one of excess demand as Susan currently is operating at full capacity and the special order would put her over the top. Because Susan cannot expand her capacity in the short term, contribution margin is the relevant concept.

In the following table, we compute the incremental costs for this decision.

Item	Detail	Cost
Direct materials cost for new component	450 units × $200 per unit	$90,000
Direct labor cost for new component	450 units × 2 hours per unit × $20 per hour	$18,000
Variable marketing and sales costs for new component	450 units × $10 per unit	$4,500
Lost contribution margin from selling 300 fewer caps	300 caps × $145 per cap*	$43,500
Total incremental costs		$156,000

* Unit contribution margin for current caps = $350 − $120 − (3 labor hours × $20 per hour) − $25 = $145. Because the new component would consume 900 labor hours (= 450 units × 2 hours per unit), Susan would have to give up production of 300 caps (= 900 hours/3 hours per cap).

Our analysis reveals that the minimum price for the new component is $156,000 for the order of 450 components, or $156,000/450 = $346.67 per component.

b. *Suppose Susan's customer has approached her with the intention of switching suppliers rather than filling a temporary need. The customer would give Susan time to acquire the additional capacity resources required to handle the increase in monthly production volume. Thus, rather than having to sacrifice regular business, Susan can acquire the needed capacity to handle both her regular business and the additional business. Susan believes that her fixed manufacturing costs relate to direct labor cost, while her fixed marketing and administration costs relate to sales volume in units. For this long-term decision, what is the minimum price that Susan could charge per unit for the new component without decreasing her profit?*

Susan now faces a long-term decision as she is contemplating a long-lasting change to her product line. Thus, we can no longer use contribution margin to determine all controllable costs and benefits, which now include the opportunity cost of capacity. The problem indicates that labor cost is the appropriate driver for fixed manufacturing costs, and sales volume in units is the appropriate driver for fixed marketing and administration costs. Using the data from current operations, we have:

Item	Fixed Manufacturing Costs	Fixed Marketing Costs
Amount in cost pool	$135,000	$30,000
Cost driver	Labor cost	Units sold
Denominator volume	$90,000*	1,500 units
Allocation rate	$1.50 per labor $ (= $135,000/$90,000)	$20 per unit (=$30,000/1,500 units)

* $90,000 = 1,500 units × 3 labor hours per unit × $20 per labor hour

Using this data, we could project the increase in fixed manufacturing and fixed marketing and administration costs required if Susan produces the new component. Including the variable costs, we calculate the controllable cost of producing the new component as:

Item	Detail	Cost
Direct materials cost	Given	$200
Direct labor cost	2 hours per unit × $20 per hour	40
Variable marketing cost	Given	10
Allocated fixed manufacturing costs	$40 labor per unit × $1.50 per labor $	60
Allocated fixed marketing costs	$20 per unit	20
Total controllable costs per unit		$330

Thus, over the long-term, Susan's minimum price for the new component is $330 per unit. Notice that this price is lower than the price we computed in part (a). Rather than having to ration capacity as she did in the short term, Susan has the option of acquiring additional capacity in the long term. This ability to adjust capacity expands Susan's options and, in this example, reduces the price per unit for the new component.

c. *(Appendix) For parts (c), (d), and (e), ignore data pertaining to the new component. Assume that for the most recent month, Susan produced 1,500 caps but only sold 1,350 caps. Determine her monthly income and the value of her ending inventory as reported under variable costing. Assume Susan had zero units in beginning inventory.*

The following table provides Susan's monthly income and the value of her ending inventory under variable costing. This statement is in the contribution margin format as it groups fixed and variable costs.

Sales volume (in units)		1,350
Production volume (in units)		1,500
Revenue	$350 per unit	$472,500
Variable costs		
Direct materials	$120 per unit	$162,000
Direct labor	$60 per unit	81,000
Marketing and sales	$25 per unit	33,750
Contribution margin		$195,750
Fixed costs		
Manufacturing		135,000
Marketing and administration		30,000
Profit before taxes		$30,750
Inventory:		
Units in ending inventory		150
Value per unit	$120 dm + $60 dl	$180
Value of ending inventory		$27,000

d. *(Appendix) As in part (c), assume that for the most recent month Susan produced 1,500 caps but only sold 1,350 caps. Determine her monthly income and the value of her ending inventory if she prepared financial statements in accordance with Generally Accepted Accounting Principles (GAAP) as under absorption costing. To comply with GAAP, Susan allocates fixed manufacturing costs to units produced. Assume that Susan uses units produced to allocate manufacturing overhead to products and that Susan had zero units in beginning inventory.*

Under absorption costing, the method specified by GAAP, Susan needs to allocate fixed manufacturing costs to units produced. These costs then "travel" with the units via the inventory account to cost of goods sold. Susan incurs fixed manufacturing costs of $135,000 per month. Her allocation rate is therefore $90 per unit = $135,000/1,500 units. In turn, Susan's inventoriable cost per unit is $270 = $120 for materials + $60 for labor + $90 for allocated manufacturing overhead.

With this information, the following table provides the income reported under absorption costing. This statement is in the gross margin format as it groups manufacturing costs and non-manufacturing costs.

Sales volume (in units)		1,350
Production volume (in units)		1,500
Revenue	$350 per unit	$472,500
Cost of goods sold		
Direct materials	$120 per unit	$162,000
Direct labor	$60 per unit	$81,000
Allocated fixed costs	$90 per unit	$121,500
Gross margin		$108,000
Period costs		
Variable marketing and sales	$25 per unit	$33,750
Fixed marketing and administration		$30,000
Profit before taxes		$44,250
Inventory:		
Units in ending inventory		150
Value per unit	$120 + $60 + $90	$270
Value of ending inventory		$40,500

e. *(Appendix) Reconcile the incomes reported under variable costing and absorption costing. Explain your logic.*

The income reported under the two methods differs owing to the differing treatment of fixed manufacturing costs. Under variable costing, we expense all of the fixed manufacturing costs in the income statement. Under absorption costing, we allocate this cost to units produced. We expense the cost only when we sell the units. Thus, any discrepancy between the number of units produced and sold would lead to some fixed manufacturing cost being added to or taken out of the inventory accounts. This amount also appears as a difference in the incomes reported under the methods.

Using the formula from the text, we have:

Income reported under variable costing	from part (c)	$30,750
+ Fixed manufacturing costs in ending inventory	(1,500 − 1,350) units × $90 per unit	$13,500
− Fixed manufacturing costs in beginning inventory	given	$0
= Income reported under absorption costing	from part (d)	$44,250

Notice that the difference in incomes reported under the variable and absorption costing methods corresponds to the differences in ending inventory values (i.e., $40,500 − $27,000 = $13,500).

GLOSSARY

Absorption costing A method whereby a product's inventoriable cost includes direct manufacturing costs, such as materials and direct labor, as well as indirect manufacturing costs such as machine depreciation and factory. Generally Accepted Accounting Principles (GAAP) requires absorption costing.

Allocation rate Equals the costs in the cost pool divided by the allocation (denominator) volume.

Burden Term frequently used to refer to "allocation rate."

Departmental rates The use of many rates, usually one per department, for allocating capacity (overhead) costs to products.

Direct costing Term frequently used to refer to "variable costing."

Full costing Term frequently used to refer to "absorption costing."

Overhead costs Term frequently used to refer to "capacity costs."

Overhead rate Term frequently used to refer to "allocation rate."

Plantwide rate The use of one rate for the entire company when allocating capacity costs (overhead) to products.

Profit margin Contribution margin less allocated capacity costs.

Variable costing A method that separates variable costs from fixed costs. Under this method, the cost of a unit of product in inventory includes only variable manufacturing costs, such as direct materials, direct labor, and variable manufacturing overhead.

REVIEW QUESTIONS

9.1 LO1. What is the appropriate measure of value for long-term decisions?

9.2 LO1. What is the difference between a contribution margin and a profit margin?

9.3 LO1. What are the two approaches for estimating the controllable cost of capacity resources over the long term?

9.4 LO1. Describe the direct estimation method for estimating controllable capacity costs. List one advantage and one disadvantage of this approach.

9.5 LO1. In addition to decision making, what are the other common uses of cost allocations?

9.6 LO2. Which of the two methods, variable costing or absorption costing, is allowed under GAAP?

9.7 LO2. What costs does the value of a unit of product include under absorption costing?

9.8 LO2. Under variable costing, how does sales volume affect the amount of fixed manufacturing overhead expensed in the income statement?

9.9 LO2. Under absorption costing, how does sales volume affect the amount of fixed manufacturing overhead expensed in the income statement?

9.10 LO2. When will income reported under variable costing be the same as income reported under absorption costing?

9.11 LO3. Why might the Department of Defense pay some of its suppliers on a cost-plus basis?

9.12 LO3. Why might a firm be strategic in the choice of allocation procedures to determine reimbursable costs?

9.13 LO3. How could a firm induce desirable behavior or dissuade undesirable behavior by changing its cost allocation procedures?

9.14 LO3. What are the two main influences that guide the choice of a cost allocation procedure?

9.15 Appendix. What is the formula for reconciling income reported under variable costing with income reported under absorption costing?

DISCUSSION QUESTIONS

9.16 LO1. Many firms dedicate separate production facilities to each of their product lines. What are some of the advantages and disadvantages of this approach from the perspective of allocating costs for decision making?

9.17 LO1. Suppose a firm currently makes three products using the same capacity resources and that one of the products has a negative profit margin. Identify two reasons why the firm may wish to continue making the unprofitable product.

9.18 LO1. We define "long term" as the time needed to change capacity resources. What do you think constitutes the "long term" for the following industries: (a) Automobiles, (b) Toys, (c) Computers, and (d) Construction Equipment?

9.19 LO1 (Advanced). When using allocated costs for decision making, we assume that capacity costs will change in proportion to changes in the cost driver. How can a company validate this assumption when it chooses cost drivers? (*Hint:* Consider the techniques we used in Chapter 4 to determine the link between activity volume and variable costs.)

9.20 LO2 (Advanced). Do you believe GAAP should allow variable costing for external reporting? Why or why not?

9.21 LO2. GAAP usually excludes research and development costs from its definition of inventoriable costs. Why do you believe GAAP mandates such a treatment?

9.22 LO2. "Depreciation is nothing but an allocation of the purchase price over different accounting periods." Do you agree with this statement? If so, identify the elements of cost allocations (cost pool, cost objects, cost driver, denominator volume) implicit in the computation of depreciation. If not, identify differences between cost allocations and depreciation.

9.23 LO2. Assume a firm's overall inventory has increased during the period. Is it possible for income under variable costing to exceed income under absorption costing? (*Hint:* think about multiproduct firms or changing prices and inventory layers).

9.24 LO3. Cost uncertainty creates more opportunities to exaggerate costs. Yet, cost reimbursement is more prevalent in situations with high cost uncertainty. How might we reconcile these contradictory tensions?

9.25 LO3. The IRS exempts qualified charities from income taxes, provided the income relates to their charitable activities. The provision exists because many charities conduct activities deemed unrelated to their core charitable mission. For example, a museum may earn income on its cafeteria sales or by renting out its lobby for a corporate reception. Such unrelated business income is taxable. Determining the portion of income that is taxable often involves extensive cost allocations. How might a charity be strategic in its choice of allocation methods? (*Hint:* An academic study found that nearly 30% of sampled charities reported *exactly* $0 as their unrelated business income.)

9.26 LO3. Suppose a firm produces two products, both of which are sold in competitive markets. Are there any incentives to be strategic when allocating costs between these two products?

9.27 LO3. Firms that allocate costs based on head count motivate their managers to reduce the number of employees. What kind of dysfunctional and profit-destroying (from the firm's perspective) behavior might such allocations engender?

9.28 LO3. Suppose a firm allocates costs to its individual product lines using labor cost as the allocation basis. Further assume that each product line's manager is evaluated based on the line's reported profit. How might this allocation affect a manager's short-term decision to make or buy individual components?

9.29 LO3. Even when a decision is short term, the use of allocated costs in managerial performance evaluation implicitly makes the manager behave as if the decision were a long-term decision. Do you agree with this statement?

9.30 LO3. Governments often use tax policy to induce desired behavior (e.g., allow mortgage interest to be deducted) or to dissuade undesired behavior (e.g., "sin taxes" on cigarettes). Can you give two additional examples of how tax policy influences behavior? Discuss the similarities and differences between the use of tax policies and cost allocations to modify behavior.

EXERCISES

9.31 Contractor pricing, qualitative (LO1). Service providers such as plumbers and electricians often charge $60 per hour even in rural areas where a factory job that pays perhaps $20–$25 per hour would be considered a "good job." Furthermore, factory workers often have training that equals that of most plumbers and electricians.

Required:

Explain the seeming discrepancy in the prices for labor services. Please note that many plumbers and electricians operate small businesses.

9.32 Increase in volume of business and cost projections (LO1). David Sharma sells masks, textiles, and other goods imported from Africa. David usually marks up his purchases by 300% (that is, if he pays $10 for an item, he lists it at $40). His annual sales range from $1,400,000 to $1,700,000, with sales for the current year expected to be $1,500,000. He also incurs fixed costs related to the rental for his store, travel, and other items. Such fixed costs generally amount to $900,000 per year.

Required:

a. Suppose David anticipates sales of $1,700,000 next year. Calculate his expected profit for the current year and for next year, assuming that he does not change his pricing strategy. Use the contribution margin format.

b. Suppose David anticipates sales of $2,800,000 next year because he expects African art to come into "fashion." Calculate expected profit. The new level of fixed costs is $1,600,000.

c. Why is it reasonable to think of fixed costs as being controllable when computing the answer for part (b) but not for part (a)? How might David reasonably estimate the "fixed" costs if he expects sales of $2,800,000 next year?

9.33 Increase in volume of business and cost projections (LO1). Acme Manufacturing Company has approached Hercules Health club with a plan to provide discounted memberships to its employees. In particular, Acme will start a match program (i.e., Acme will pay a part of the club fees charged to its employees) to motivate its employees to join the fitness club. In return, Acme wants Hercules to give a 25% discount—that is, the fee to Acme employees would be $60 per person instead of the normal charge of $80 per person per month.

You learn that Hercules currently has 1,000 members and incurs variable costs of $35 per member per month and fixed costs of $40,000 per month. Tom and Lynda tell you that the club can accommodate the 200 members that would be added if they accepted Acme's proposal. However, they also tell you that more than 200 additional members would strain the club's capacity.

Required:

a. What is the additional contribution margin if Hercules were to accept Acme's proposal?

b. Is the answer in part (a) the correct way to evaluate Acme's proposal?

c. How might allocations help Tom and Lynda improve their decision making? Justify with suitable supporting calculations.

9.34 Absorption costing, income, and inventory effects of alternative allocation bases (LO2). Charlie Stumpf manufactures and sells high-quality, handmade wooden toys. Charlie began the current year with zero inventories. During the year, Charlie produced toys that consumed $24,000 in materials and $30,000 in labor. At year-end, Charlie estimated that his inventory comprised toys that had $5,000 of materials content and $7,500 of labor content. Based on his actual fixed manufacturing overhead costs, Charlie added overhead to products at the rate of 100% of labor cost.

Required:

a. What is the value of Charlie's ending inventory under absorption costing?

b. Repeat requirement (a) assuming that Charlie allocates overhead to products using material cost, rather than labor cost, as the allocation basis.

c. Which of the two allocation bases, labor cost or materials cost, will cause Charlie to report higher income for the year? Why?

9.35 Allocations under absorption costing, GAAP inventory valuation (LO2). Precision Bearings manufactures several kinds of roller bearings. This past year, Precision spent $11,750,000 on fixed manufacturing costs, $1,762,500 on fixed selling and administrative costs, and $23,500,000 for direct labor. Precision produced 5,875,000 bearings and sold 5,500,000 bearings during the year.

The following table provides the direct materials and labor costs for three of Precision's bearings:

	Model 6203	Model 6210	Model 30207
Materials cost	$1.00	$1.75	$3.00
Labor cost	$3.00	$4.00	$7.00

Required:

a. Assume that Precision allocates fixed costs using the number of units produced as the allocation basis. Under absorption costing, what is the inventoriable cost per unit of each of the three bearings?

b. Assume that Precision allocates fixed costs using direct labor costs as the allocation basis. Under absorption costing, what is the inventoriable cost per unit of each of the three bearings?

c. Compare the answers to parts (a) and (b). Comment on any differences in inventoriable cost.

 9.36 Variable costing versus absorption costing, Income Reconciliation (LO2). Horizon Manufacturing provides you with the following information for the most recent month of operations:

Units in beginning inventory	0
Units produced	2,000
Units sold	1,600
Selling price	$50 per unit
Fixed manufacturing costs	$24,000
Fixed selling and administrative costs	$10,000
Variable manufacturing costs	$16 per unit
Variable selling and administrative costs	$6 per unit

Required:

a. What is Horizon's reported income and cost of ending inventory under variable costing?

b. What is Horizon's reported income and cost of ending inventory under absorption costing? Assume Horizon allocates cost using units produced.

c. Reconcile the difference between Horizon's income under variable costing and absorption costing.

 9.37 Variable costing versus absorption costing (LO2). Creative makes tiles in batches of 1,000 tiles each, the standard "unit" in the industry. Each batch consumes $70 in materials and $140 in labor costs. Manufacturing overhead amounts to $1,500,000 and is allocated equally among the batches produced during the year. Creative had no inventories at the beginning of the most recent year. During the most recent year, Creative made 15,000 batches. The firm sold 13,500 batches for an average price of $450 each. Creative incurred variable marketing costs of $50 per batch and fixed marketing costs of $625,000 for the year.

Required:

a. Prepare a contribution margin statement for Creative Tiles for the most recent year. In addition, compute the value of the Creative Tiles' ending inventory under variable costing.

b. Prepare a gross margin statement for Creative Tiles for the most recent year. Also compute the value of the Creative Tiles' ending inventory under absorption costing.

c. Reconcile the income reported under variable costing and absorption costing. Briefly explain the reason for the difference.

9.38 Allocations for taxes (LO3). Located in Madras, India, Shah Company manufactures and sells leather garments in India and in Europe. For the most recent year of operations, Shah sold 20,000 garments each in Europe and India. Each garment sold in India consumes 4 hours of labor, while each garment sold in Europe consumes 7 hours of labor. Shah currently allocates fixed manufacturing overhead costs, which amount to $660,000 per year, using the number of garments produced for the allocation basis.

Shah's income-tax rate in Europe is 40% and 30% in India. Assume that each jurisdiction (Europe, India) taxes only income reported in that jurisdiction.

Required:

Compute the net savings in taxes paid if Shah were to allocate overhead costs using labor hours rather than garments as the allocation basis.

9.39 Change in product mix (LO1). Bradshaw Industries makes two varieties—Standard and Deluxe—of its one product. The following data are available:

	Standard	Deluxe
Number of units	250,000	50,000
Labor hours per unit	2	4
Price per unit	$14	$18
Variable costs	$8	$9
Contribution margin	$6	$9

You also know that Bradshaw incurs common fixed costs of $1,400,000.

Suppose Bradshaw is considering changing its product mix to sell equal amounts of its Standard and Deluxe products. Total sales would remain at 300,000 units. This change would be implemented over the next two to three years.

Required:

a. Why should Bradshaw consider the common fixed costs as being controllable for this decision?

b. Allocating common fixed costs as per the number of units, calculate Bradshaw's expected profit with the new product mix.

c. Repeat part (b) except use the number of direct labor hours to allocate costs to the two products.

d. Which of the two estimates, in part (b) or part (c), do you feel is a superior estimate of profit with the new mix? Why?

9.40 Allocations under absorption costing, GAAP inventory valuation, two departments (LO2). The Boston Box Company has two departments, fabrication and assembly. Boston uses machine hours to allocate overhead costs in the fabrication department and labor hours to allocate overhead costs in the assembly department. Pertinent data for each department follows:

Item	Fabrication	Assembly
Overhead costs	$66,000	$39,000
Labor hours	4,000	6,000
Machine hours	12,000	6,500

Required:

a. One of Boston Box's products has direct materials costs of $50 per unit and direct labor costs of $42 per unit. This product uses one machine hour in the fabrication department and two labor hours in the assembly department. Finally, the product incurs $6 in variable selling costs and $5 in allocated fixed marketing costs per unit. Determine the inventoriable cost of this product under absorption costing.

b. Briefly discuss whether the inventoriable cost, as computed under absorption costing, is the appropriate cost estimate to use when determining a product's long-term profitability.

9.41 Allocations and inventory valuation, incentives (LO2, LO3). Atsuko Ito makes custom skates that sell for $750 a pair. Atsuko began the most recent year with zero inventory. She produced 3,500 pairs of skates during the year and sold 3,300 of them. Atsuko figures that the skates in inventory at year end have materials worth $50,000 and labor of $62,500. Atsuko also informs you that she spent $700,000 on materials, $1,050,000 on labor, $525,000 on manufacturing overhead, and $250,000 on selling and administrative costs during the year.

Required:

a. Using labor dollars to allocate manufacturing overhead costs, determine the value of Atsuko's ending inventory under GAAP.

b. Using the ending inventory value derived in requirement (a), determine Atsuko's reported income for the year.

c. Suppose it is near the end of the fiscal year. Because of the lead-time required, Atsuko has received all of the orders relating to the current year. Revenues from any new orders would be booked in the financial statements for the following year. Discuss one way in which Atsuko could temporarily boost her current year's reported income.

9.42 Inventory valuation, variable overhead, multiple cost pools (LO2). Xenon Corporation makes a number of industrial products. Xenon estimates annual factory overhead at $1,500,000, materials cost at $600,000, and labor cost at $1,000,000. In addition, Xenon considers one-third of its overhead to be variable, as these costs pertain to items such as supplies, oils, and lubricants. Xenon uses direct labor cost to allocate manufacturing overhead to products. One of Xenon's products, a pump, requires $12 in materials and $30 in labor. Each pump sells for $90.

Required:

a. Determine the contribution margin per pump. Assume that pumps do not incur any variable selling and administrative costs.

b. Determine the gross margin per pump.

c. Suppose Xenon analyzes its fixed overhead and determines that $240,000 relates to materials and the remainder relates to labor-related expenses. Xenon allocates materials-related fixed overhead using materials cost as the allocation basis and labor-related fixed overhead using labor cost as the allocation basis. As before, Xenon allocates variable overhead using labor cost as the allocation basis. Determine the gross margin per pump.

d. Why is the gross margin in (c) higher than the gross margin in (b)?

9.43 Allocation for reimbursement, arbitrary nature of some allocations (LO3). Shibin expects to receive his Ph.D. soon from a highly-regarded program. Seeking to hire him for their faculty, the accounting group at State University in New York City invited Shibin to interview. After finalizing dates, Shibin purchased a round-trip airline ticket for $400. Just after he purchased the ticket, Shibin received a call from Prestige University, a private university, also in New York City. The accounting faculty at Prestige had heard that Shibin was coming to State University and wanted to interview him for a position at Prestige as well. They were willing to conduct their interview the day after the interview at State. Shibin, of course, was ecstatic with the chance to interview at two well-regarded institutions.

Shibin called his travel agent to change his ticket. The travel agent informed Shibin that while the price would stay the same, as per airline rules, the change in plans would trigger a penalty of $100.

Required:

How should Shibin allocate the total cost of the airfare (i.e., $500) between the two schools? What is the purpose of this allocation? What factors should he consider as he chooses among alternate splits? (Assume that the split will have no effect on the probability of his getting an offer from either school.)

9.44 Cost allocations and reimbursement (LO3). Pamela Bourjaily is a consultant. Two of Pam's current projects have considerable overlap, meaning that the same background research benefits both projects. The first project, from Apollo Corporation, pays cost plus 50%. The second project, from Troy Brothers, pays cost plus 30%. Apollo is a long-time customer while Troy is a future prospect, which is part of the reason for the price break.

Pam estimates that she has spent $6,000 on travel, books, and databases for work that is common to both projects. She also provides the following additional data.

	Apollo	Troy
Budgeted hours	40	40
Pam's sales for the year to the client	$100,000	$25,000
Client's annual sales	$50 million	$200 million

Required:

a. Calculate the cost allocated to the two clients using budgeted hours as the allocation basis. Repeat the exercise using Pam's sales to the clients as the allocation basis and the clients' annual sales as the allocation basis.

b. Advise Pam on the appropriate choice of an allocation basis.

PROBLEMS

9.45 Short vs. long-term considerations in pricing (LO1, qualitative). "My boss simply doesn't get it. We are operating at 60% of capacity, and this situation is not likely to improve for at least six months. I just convinced a regular client to double her order. But, I had to cut the price below cost to get the order. Even with the price cut, we are making a good contribution. Therefore, this is a good deal. But the VP has nixed the deal insisting that all orders must cover full costs, including allocated fixed costs." This is Brian Baxter's rant, after learning that his latest deal has fallen through.

Brian is a star salesman for an equipment manufacturing company that is subject to a six-year business cycle. That is, the firm usually experiences three years of high demand followed by three years of low demand. The firm is currently on the down cycle. An upswing is expected in 6 to 12-months.

Required:

a. How could Brian justify taking an order that generates positive contribution margin but a negative profit margin?

b. What arguments could the VP for sales advance to justify her decision to nix the sale?

9.46 Direct estimation vs. allocated costs (LO1). Catlow Corporation is trying to estimate the costs associated with increased volume of operations. The firm currently has a capacity for 10,000 machine hours, spread over five machines. That is, each machine provides 2,000 hours of capacity. It is not feasible to buy machines with smaller capacity (e.g., to buy a machine with 480 hours or capacity, or rent a machine on a half-time basis).

Currently, the firm makes two products, Alpha and Beta. Alpha, with a volume of 2,900 units, takes two machine hours per unit. Beta, with a volume of 1,400 units, consumes three machine hours per unit. Each machine hour costs has a variable overhead rate of $20 per machine hour (for power, oils, lubricants and other consumable items), and $30 as an allocation for fixed costs (e.g., machine depreciation).

Catlow is considering expanding the volume of its operations to produce 3,400 units of Alpha and 2,000 units of Beta.

Required:

a. Using the cost per machine hour to estimate capacity costs, calculate the total cost of machining time for the two products.

b. How could you refine the estimate in part (a) above? What conclusions do you draw about the relative costs and benefits of direct estimation of capacity costs versus using allocated costs to estimate them?

9.47 Change in product mix (LO1). Sunder Corp. makes two main products in its factory in Birmingham, Alabama. Because of intense competition for standardized products, particularly from overseas firms, Sunder is considering switching its emphasis to custom-made products.

The following data are available:

Item	Standard Products	Custom Products
Average price per unit	$130 per unit	$175 per unit
Contribution margin ratio	50%	60%
Profit margin per unit	$25	$65
Machine hours per unit	2	4
Number of units	75,000	25,000

Required:

a. Calculate the variable cost and the allocated fixed cost per unit of the standard and the custom product. Comment on the validity of the implied allocation mechanism.

b. Calculate the profit margin for the two products, assuming that Sunder allocates costs to products using machine hours as the allocation basis.

c. Sunder believes that, with suitable marketing, it can change its product mix to be 50,000 units each of the Standard and Custom products. Using fixed costs allocated on the number of units to project the change in capacity costs, estimate Sunder's profit with the proposed product mix.

d. Repeat part (c) except allocate capacity costs using machine hours.

 9.48 Change in customer segments (LO1). N&N Sanitation offers waste management services for residential and commercial clients. The following select operating data are available:

	Residential	Commercial	Total
Number of customers	500	100	600
Number of pickups per week	500	500	1,000
Revenue	$800,000	$1,200,000	$2,000,000
Variable costs	$140,000	$240,000	$380,000
Traceable fixed costs	$150,000	$225,000	$375,000
Common fixed costs	NA	NA	$1,100,000

Believing its commercial customers to be more profitable, N&N is thinking of moving its business more toward the business segment. Management would like to see a mix of 200 residential and 300 commercial clients in three years' time.

Required:

a. Estimate the change in profit arising from the change in product mix. For now, assume that traceable and fixed common costs do not change from current levels.

b. Suppose N&N believes that, in the long run, fixed costs would change in proportion to sales revenue. Calculate the expected profit with the new customer mix. Allocate common fixed costs in proportion to the revenue from the two segments when performing this exercise.

c. Repeat the exercise in part (b), except allocate common fixed costs to segments and in proportion to the number of pickups from each segment. That is, assume that pickups are the cost driver for traceable and common fixed costs.

d. Which of the three estimates, for parts (a) through (c), is likely to be a good estimate of N&N's profits three years hence if it changes its customer mix as indicated?

9.49 Product introduction decisions, qualitative (LO1). "I spend half my time trying to figure out these accounting reports," said Paul Hribar in total frustration. He was trying to figure out whether to introduce a new product and was referring to the latest "Product Cost Estimate" he had received from accounting. He thinks the report is wrong. He argues that "No one will be hired or fired in accounting if I add or do not add this product. But I am being charged for the accounting department's costs and am expected to recover it in the product price. How can this make sense?"

Product Cost Sheet (Estimate)	Model Number: KX –245/R2	
Number of units		50,000
Estimated unit price		$80.00
Materials cost	$13.00	
Labor cost (1 hour @ $22/labor hour)	$22.00	
Variable factory overhead (@$7 per machine hour)	$10.50	
Materials handling (10% of materials cost)	$1.30	
Other factory costs (150% of labor cost)	$33.00	
Total factory cost		$79.80
Gross margin		$0.20
Variable selling costs	$6.45	
Fixed selling costs (5% of price)	$4.00	
Total selling costs		10.45
Net profit		($10.25)

Required:

Explain why the product cost report contains allocations for manufacturing and SG&A overhead.

9.50 Direct estimation vs. using allocated costs (LO1). The following data pertain to the budgeted overhead for Waymire, Inc., which makes wires and coils.

Item	Amount
Materials handling and inventory	$2,400,000
Supervision	460,000
Payroll	640,000
Factory administration	1,600,000
Machine depreciation	3,450,000
Machine operations	1,410,000
Sales offices	840,000
Travel and other customer development	1,200,000
Selling administration	1,500,000
Total capacity costs	$13,500,000

Waymire, Inc., has asked for your help in estimating capacity costs if it implements an ambitious plan to rationalize its product portfolio. The change would also increase the amount of automation in the plant. If implemented, the change would dramatically alter Waymire's activity profile. Waymire provides you with the following additional information concerning activity levels before and after the change in product portfolio.

Item	Current Amount (prior to change)	Expected Amount (after the change)
Materials cost	$48,000,000	$52,000,000
Labor hours	135,000 hours	121,500
Machine hours	81,000 hours	132,300
Revenue	$162,000,000	$175,000,000

Required:

a. Waymire currently uses labor hours to allocate all capacity costs (including SGA costs) to products. Using the allocation rate per unit of this driver, estimate the capacity cost after the change in operations.

b. Repeat the exercise with machine hours and revenue as the sole drivers.

c. Could you construct a better estimate using a combination of these four drivers to model the change in activity levels?

d. How does the refinement in part (c) bring the analysis closer to direct estimation of capacity costs? Comment on the relative merits and demerits of direct estimation and using allocations to estimate capacity costs.

9.51 Choice of cost drivers, behavior modification (LO1, LO3). "I simply don't understand this! I went from a winner to a loser in one month because some bozo in accounting changed his spreadsheet," griped LuAnne Leffler, a sales representative for DisplayCo, a firm that sells display stands to stores.

LuAnne and other sales representatives call on prospective clients to update them regarding new products and prices, to assess customer needs, and to take orders. LuAnne was the top salesperson last year, generating $5 million of DisplayCo's total annual revenue of $60 million. Much of LuAnne's success stemmed from her close relationship with a major client that generated $3 million in annual revenue. LuAnne likes this client a great deal even though the client's average order was smaller than DisplayCos's overall average revenue per order of $8,000.

DisplayCo compensates its sales representatives based on their "margin," computed as sales revenue *less* manufacturing and marketing costs. Under the current system, total manufacturing and marketing costs are allocated on the basis of revenue. For the most recent year, total manufacturing costs equaled 80% of revenue and total marketing costs amounted to 13.50% of revenue.

Recently, DisplayCo's accountant decided to allocate marketing costs by the number of sales orders rather than revenue. The accountant based the marketing allocation rate on last year's total marketing costs and sales orders. Manufacturing costs continue to be allocated at 80% of revenue. LuAnne's reaction is to the new allocation procedure. Under the new system, she has slipped to second place for the most recent month, even though Betty Barnett, the first-place salesperson, recorded monthly sales of only $350,000 from 35 orders when LuAnne had raked in $400,000 from 60 orders.

Required:

a. For the most recent month, compute both LuAnne's and Betty's margin under the allocation system in place before the accountant revised the basis for allocating marketing costs.

b. Compute both LuAnne's and Betty's margin for the most recent month under the accountant's revised allocation system.

c. Which system, the old system or the accountant's revised version, do you believe better captures the profit from a customer? How can you further improve the allocation of marketing costs to customers when assessing the margin generated by individual salespersons?

d. How could a manager use information regarding the margin generated by each sales representative to motivate and reward her sales force?

9.52 Choice of drivers, qualitative (LO1, LO3). Governments and other regulators often finance roads via tolls and other fees paid by motorists. One can view the charge to a motorist as an allocation for the cost of building and maintaining the toll way. Some examples include the New Jersey Turnpike and the "Coastal Highway," a controlled access, high-speed road link between major cities in Tamil Nadu in India.

Required:

Evaluate the costs and benefits of the following four pricing schemes.

1. A flat charge per vehicle, charged when the vehicle enters the toll way.

2. A flat charge per category of vehicle. That is, there is a different charge for a car, a small truck, and an 18-wheeler.

3. A graduated charge based on the vehicle's actual weight, paid when the vehicle enters the toll way.

4. A graduated charge based on vehicle weight and distance traveled on the road. This fee requires a tollbooth at both the entrances to and the exits from the toll way.

9.53 Allocation mechanics, choice of allocation basis, qualitative (LO1, LO3). Municipalities often allocate the cost of new infrastructure such as sewer lines to property owners who benefit from the improvements. Such improvements often take place when a city expands its services to newly annexed areas. The choice of an allocation basis is often contentious as the cost is significant (often in the thousands of dollars per house) and the benefit is hard to quantify.

Required:

a. Evaluate the following three possibilities as to their suitability for allocating the cost of improving the sewer lines to property owners.

  1. Equally across all homeowners.

  2. Based on linear feet of road front for the property.

  3. Based on property value.

b. Discuss how, if at all, your relative ranking of the allocation bases would change if the improvement were to install sidewalks instead of laying a sewer line.

9.54 Different allocations for different purposes (LO1, LO3, Advanced). Maggie Chen, the owner of the Yin Yang Yogurt Shop, is very pleased with how her business has grown over the past two years. She now has five branches in various suburbs in addition to her flagship store. Maggie has asked for your suggestions regarding the wisdom of allocating the following central office costs to the branches. Each branch has its own store manager and staff.

  Payroll Processing. The firm administers payroll from its main office. However, each branch manager handles the hiring and firing of employees (mostly hourly workers). The number of people on the payroll drives the expense for payroll processing and, of course, the payroll itself. In addition, there is one-time paperwork every time a new employee is hired or an existing employee is let go.

  Advertising. The firm runs ads in the local newspaper, as well as radio spots on the morning talk shows. Maggie believes that sales would drop 15%, across the board, if she were to discontinue the advertising.

  Purchasing and Inventory Handling. All purchasing is done centrally. The firm replenishes branch inventory from a central warehouse each morning. The amount delivered depends on the branch manager's estimate of demand. Branch managers differ in their ability to forecast demand. Some branches have a greater tendency to run out of a flavor and ask for an additional delivery in the afternoon.

Required:

Help Maggie decide if she should allocate any of the listed cost items to branches. Distinguish between using the allocation for the purpose of managerial performance evaluation and using the allocation for the purpose of evaluating branch profitability.

9.55 Cost allocations in real estate, qualitative (LO1, LO3, Advanced). The Great Lakes Company specializes in real estate. Great Lakes purchases large tracts of land in a city's outlying areas. The company improves the land by putting in roads, sewer systems, and so on, and then subdivides the improved property into parcels sold to individual homeowners and homebuilders. To make the property more attractive, Great Lakes always designates some land as green-space (i.e., parks and other recreational areas). It also reserves land for an elementary school, a community center, and other "public-use" property. Finally, Great Lakes reserves about 5% of the property for retail use (i.e., for neighborhood stores). From start to finish, a typical deal consumes anywhere from three to seven years.

In a recent transaction, Great Lakes spent $1.6 million to buy 160 acres of property near a fast-growing city. It then spent an additional $1.4 million to develop the property. In line with its usual practice, the firm reserved 20 acres for green space, 4 acres for an elementary school, 3 acres for a church, and 3 acres for a community center. In addition, roads and out-lots (i.e., unusable parcels) consumed 5 acres. Thus, the firm could sell 125 acres to homeowners, to homebuilders, and as retail space.

Required:

a. Discuss two reasons why Great Lakes may wish to allocate its costs to individual parcels of land.

b. List at least two bases Great Lakes could use to allocate its costs to the individual parcels of land.

c. Considering the differences among buyers (school district, church, home builder, retailer), list at least three criteria that Great Lakes would employ to choose the allocation basis. Explain.

9.56 Variable costing versus absorption costing, income reconciliation (LO2, Advanced). For April, Quick Test Enterprises prepared, in accordance with Generally Accepted Accounting Principles (GAAP), the following income statement using absorption costing.

Quick Test Enterprises		
Gross Margin Statement—April		
Sales volume (in units)	1,500	
	Total	*Per Unit*
Revenue	$150,000	$100
Cost of goods sold	105,000	70
Gross margin	$45,000	$30
Selling, general, and administrative (SG&A) expenses	18,000	12
Profit before taxes	$27,000	$18

Quick Test uses a FIFO (i.e., First-In-First-Out) inventory cost flow assumption to compute cost of goods sold and the value of ending inventory. At the *beginning* of April (i.e., at the end of March), Quick test had 750 units in inventory with a total cost of $45,000. Of the $45,000, $11,250 represents allocated fixed manufacturing overhead costs.

Quick Test produced 1,250 units during April. The variable manufacturing cost per unit produced during April was $50. In addition, fixed selling, general, and administrative expenses for April were $12,000.

Required:

a. Compute the value of Quick Test's inventory at the end of April under variable costing.

b. How much did Quick Test actually spend on fixed manufacturing overhead costs during April?

c. Prepare Quick Test's variable costing income statement for April.

d. Reconcile the difference between Quick Test's April income under variable costing and April income under absorption costing.

9.57 Control role for allocations, (LO3, qualitative). Southeast University's Business College created the Horn Technology Center to centralize all of the computing services within the college. The center coordinates computer purchases for faculty, staff, classrooms, and the computer labs. The center also selects software and administers it. In addition to word processing and spreadsheet programs, the center's staff maintains large and complex research databases. They design, build, and maintain the college's extensive website. Finally, the Center provides help on special projects such as developing a Web-based questionnaire or database.

Because it considers itself part of the college, the center does not charge any of its "internal customers" for work done. The Center's budget comes from the college and comprises staff salaries and equipment such as servers. (The Center bills out, at cost, any computing equipment purchased for a specific user.)

The Center's director recently approached the dean for approval to charge faculty and departments a flat rate of $50 per hour for any work on special projects. She argued that the Center is handling too many requests for special projects. The dean is puzzled because, a few years ago, the director herself had proposed the idea of special projects as a way to fill in the unevenness in the Center's workload. It was widely understood that these projects would be completed when time became available. Thus, the projects were using a temporarily idle resource, with no increase in the college's overall cash outflow.

When he put these arguments to the Center's director, she argued that the volume of special projects had increased by an order of magnitude over the years, as faculty and staff gained expertise in using the World Wide Web. She also mentioned that it was personally embarrassing to miss promised delivery dates several times in a row. She believed that the charge is a compromise between charging faculty for the full rate (outside consultants may charge up to $100 per hour) and giving them a value-added service for "free."

Required:

Evaluate the arguments for and against allocating the Center's cost to faculty and departments. Assume that the Center's overall expenditure will not change whether or not they continue to do the special projects. (The charge of $50 per hour merely moves money from one account to another and does not alter the total outflow for the college.)

9.58 Allocations for eliciting demand, qualitative (LO1, LO3, Advanced). Matt Mouw is in charge of providing computing and other information technology services to his firm. Matt's firm has four distinct product lines, each operated as a stand-alone business. Profit is the primary criterion for evaluating product-line managers, and the entire firm has a competitive culture that takes pride in meeting tight targets. Support department managers, such as Matt, are expected to allocate their costs to their internal customers and break even.

Matt has identified a new software product that would help all four product lines improve their data storage, analysis, and reporting. The product would bring considerable standardization to Matt's department as well and allow him to provide more effective and efficient customer service. The product will cost $750,000 plus a license fee for each user. The managers of product lines A and B, the two largest products, have expressed considerable interest in installing the system. The existing software package has become obsolete, and the divisions see the new software as increasing their competitive edge. The manager of product line C indicates that a number of other initiatives are underway. She will be able to indicate interest, or lack thereof, only after a period of six months or so. The manager of product line D wants to wait for another year because his division is too small to take a gamble. He wants to see how things go with the "big boys" before committing the human and other resources needed to roll out the new system.

Required:

a. What is the purpose of allocating the cost of the new software product to the users? In particular, should the firm allocate the acquisition cost to the four product lines?

b. Assume that the firm has decided to allocate the software cost. List two different ways the firm could allocate the software cost to the product divisions. What are the costs and benefits of each method?

c. Suppose that the software cost was allocated to Divisions A and B alone because they are the only immediate users. Six months later, Division C wants to implement the software as well. The division manager for C argues that the acquisition cost is now sunk, meaning that none of it should be allocated to her division. Evaluate the merits of this argument.

9.59 Alternate allocation basis, homeowner's association (LO1, LO3). The City of Pleasantville created The Peninsula as a model subdivision. In contrast to traditional subdivisions, The Peninsula mingled condominiums, town homes, and single-family homes. The City designed the project so that many key amenities (a bank, the post office, shops, and so on) are within an easy walk from any residence. The development is located in a river's oxbow and almost constitutes a stand-alone entity. Indeed, the City believed this feature to be critical in developing a sense of neighborhood and in creating a vibrant, self-sufficient community. With all of these features, the City realized high demand for the properties, and within a few years, The Peninsula was fully occupied.

The current dilemma concerns the homeowner's association. Until The Peninsula became sustainable, the City used monies from a federal grant to maintain many of the amenities such as the pond, parks, hiking trails, shelters, and landscaping. A homeowner's association was formed to discharge these duties. The association learns that the City spent $150,000 last year on these amenities. Thus, the homeowner's association needs to find a way to raise $150,000 from the homeowners and the retail establishments.

Required:

Evaluate the following methods of raising the $150,000. Identify at least one positive feature and one negative feature associated with each allocation basis.

1. Value of property.
2. Head count, based on the number of persons living at each residence.
3. Equal division, counting each residence and store as one unit.
4. Fee-based, as far as practicable, with the remainder being allocated.

9.60 Allocations and reimbursement, ethics (LO3). Because he is a senior executive, Jean-Pierre's firm allows him to travel business class, particularly for international travel. The firm wants its executives to be well rested and ready for business when they reach their destination. Jean-Pierre seeks your advice regarding the appropriate amount to allocate toward reimbursable expenses.

  a. Jean-Pierre recently took a trip for which the business class airfare is $5,000. The airline offered a deal whereby Jean-Pierre could obtain a second business class ticket for the price of a coach ticket, which is $1,800. Jean-Pierre used the offer to have his wife travel with him.

  b. Consider the setting in (a) above. Assume the airline offers a "companions fly free" program, which Jean-Pierre frequently uses to take his wife with him. However, the program requires companions to have the same travel itinerary. Jean-Pierre's wife wanted to spend an extra day at the foreign locale. Consequently, Jean-Pierre stayed a day longer than he would have stayed if he had traveled alone. The hotel costs $450 per night, and Jean-Pierre can (and usually does) charge his firm up to $200 per day for meals.

  c. Consider the setting in (a) above. Assume the airline is willing to swap one business class ticket for two tickets in coach class. Jean-Pierre and his wife took advantage of the offer. Jean-Pierre extended his stay by another day, and enjoyed a wonderful weekend getaway.

  Required:

  Discuss the appropriate course of action for each of the three settings.

9.61 Allocations and behavior modification (LO3). Allocations influence behavior because they serve as a "tax" on the cost driver. Thus, users are induced to decrease the quantity of driver units consumed. The following depict situations in which allocated costs can potentially affect behavior.

  1. You are a division manager, and a large part of your bonus derives from your division's reported profit. Your firm allocates corporate office expenses to divisions based on the number of employees in each division.

  2. You are part of a team designing a new circuit board. Your firm allocates materials-handling costs to products using the number of components used as the driver.

  3. You are part of a team designing a new circuit board. Your firm allocates materials-handling costs to products using the number of unique components (i.e., the number of components used by this product alone) as the driver.

  4. You are a product manager. Your firm allocates all manufacturing overhead to products using materials cost as the driver.

  5. You are a product manager. Your firm allocates all manufacturing overhead to products using labor costs as the cost driver.

  Required:

  a. For each of the preceding situations, describe the kinds of actions you might take to reduce the amount of overhead allocated to you. Do these actions necessarily increase the firm's overall profitability?

  b. What might be the firm's logic in using the specified drivers in each instance. That is, what do you perceive to be the costs and benefits of each allocation mechanism?

9.62 Cost allocations and behavior (LO3). "I can't believe what just happened back there," Julie exclaimed to her friend, Becky, as they were returning to their apartment after a dinner at an upscale restaurant to celebrate their passing the bar exam. Julie, Becky, and four other friends had gone through law school together, studied together for the bar exam, and were all excited at clearing the final hurdle before they could practice law. The meal was excellent, the conversation upbeat and scintillating, and the wine flowed freely.

  Julie's complaint related to her share of the cost. When the final check (which made Julie gulp in shock) arrived, someone proposed an equal split. The proposal was quickly seconded. Although some looked uncomfortable, no one objected. The bill was settled and the friends dispersed.

  Julie felt that the scheme was unfair. She had consumed only soda and the cost for the liquor represented at least half of the total bill. However, she felt awkward about complaining and spoiling an otherwise excellent evening. She expressed her discomfort only when she and Becky were returning to their apartment.

Becky sympathized with Julie. As a vegetarian, Becky could not consume many of the appetizers and had to settle for an inexpensive pasta while the others splurged on lobster and other expensive delicacies. The two friends felt that they wound up paying for the other four friends' meals.

Required:

a. What is the objective of allocating the cost of the bill among the six friends? What considerations come into play when choosing an allocation mechanism?

b. In addition to equally splitting the cost among all diners, list at least two other methods that the friends could have used to allocate the cost among themselves. What are the costs and benefits of each method?

c. Assume that none of the friends were teetotalers and none were vegetarian. Suppose the friends had agreed, at the start of the meal, to split the cost equally. Would you expect the total bill to differ if the friends had agreed, at the start, to track individual orders for drinks and entrees? Why or why not?

9.63 Allocations for estimating capacity costs (LO1). Color Graphics (CG) specializes in printing glossy magazines. CG currently has orders for four magazines, with each magazine being issued on its own cycle. With the four magazines, CG's capacity is 100% utilized from Thursday through Sunday, every week. The press run 14 hours for each of these days, and CG's management believes that it is counterproductive to run the machines any longer than 14 hours (i.e., two shifts) in a day. However, CG has considerable excess capacity from Mondays through Wednesdays.

CG prices at an average rate of $0.07 per page. Variable costs amount to $0.02 per page. CG groups its fixed costs into two main pools—Machinery and Support staff. The four-color printing machines cost $4 million two years ago, and are expected to last another two years at the current rate of usage. Currently, CG uses each machine for approximately 3,000 hours per year, meaning that an average machine has a useful life of 12,000 hours, printing 20,000 pages per hour. Support staff and other indirect costs amount to an additional $2 million per year.

a. CG's marketing manager wants to bid for a catalog. The job will consume 20 hours and contain 400,000 pages. The customer has some flexibility regarding delivery dates, meaning that CG could print the job during weekdays. This is a one-time job as the store's regular printer had an unexpected machine malfunction. What is the minimum price that CG can charge for this job, without lowering their profit?

b. Suppose CG enters the catalog market. The marketing manager argues that the catalogs are merely using up extra capacity. Even including machining costs, she argues that any price over $0.0325 a page is "pure profit." She wants to move aggressively and price the product at $0.06 a page, which is substantially below the current price of $0.07 a page. Evaluate the merits of this argument, being sure to show how the marketing manager might have arrived at her estimate.

c. The firm's accountant argues that the catalogs are consuming capacity and must be charged for it. He expects machine usage to increase from 3,000 hours to 4,000 hours per year if the firm pursues the catalog business. In addition, while existing personnel can handle some of the work associated with printing catalogs, more people need to be hired, increasing the cost of support staff by $250,000. He believes that CG should take the **total** support staff cost and allocate it to both magazines and catalogs using machine hours as the allocation basis. Calculate the cost per page for the catalogs per the accountant's proposal. Determine the price per page, if the firm adds a 10% markup and rounds to the nearest 1/100 of a penny. Evaluate the merits of the accountant's argument.

d. The marketing manager sees some logic in the accountant's argument, although she is not happy with the implied cost for printing catalogs. However, she also sees a positive aspect. She wants to reduce the price per page for printing magazines because now the cost to print magazines has decreased. She wants to use the lower cost to justify a price concession that would relieve her of some the intense price pressure in the market place. Evaluate the merits of this argument.

 9.64 Variable versus absorption costing (LO2). "I don't understand how I can go from a profit to a loss when I sell more units." This comment aptly sums Emily Johnson's frustration with her accounting statements. Emily owns and operates a small firm that sells prefabricated sheds used for storing lawn equipment. Her business is seasonal, exhibiting wide swings in sales and production.

Emily's one product sells for $1,000 per unit. Variable manufacturing costs are $200 per unit, with fixed manufacturing costs amounting to $750,000 per month. Emily's monthly marketing costs are given by the equation $100,000 + ($25 × units sold). Each month, Emily allocates costs to units based on actual expenses and production.

Emily began March and ended April with zero inventories. She sold 1,000 units in March and 1,250 units in April. Emily produced 1,500 units in March.

Required:

a. Prepare Emily's income statement for March and April under absorption costing. In addition, determine the cost of Emily's March ending inventory under absorption costing.

b. Prepare Emily's income statements for both March and April under variable costing.

c. Reconcile the difference between variable costing net income and absorption costing net income.

d. Comment on the reconciliation, and indicate why Emily's total profit over the two months is the same under both methods. Also indicate why Emily's absorption costing income decreases from March to April even though she sold more units in April than in March?

 9.65 Allocations and reimbursements, ethics (LO3). Sue Malloy works as a project manager for C3 Systems, a firm that designs sophisticated circuit boards. The firm's boards are used in communications satellites and other civilian uses. C3's circuit boards also form the guts of cryptography equipment used by governmental security agencies.

Sue's primary responsibility is to work on a board that potentially could open up a new civilian market for C3 systems. The firm developed the technology used in this board primarily for an application in the armed forces. Deep into the development, Sue realized the complementary civilian application. Sue is wondering how best to allocate the cost of her time as well as that of key research personnel between the government project and the civilian application. She knows that the government contract would reimburse C3 for its development expenses at cost plus a 10% markup. Both the government and C3 systems had agreed that development costs could amount to $8 to $10 million. Clearly, there is no explicit recovery of development expense in the civilian application.

Sue and her team have spent $7 million to date, and anticipate spending another $3 million if they develop both the civilian and the military application. They will spend only an extra $2 million on development if the firm abandons the civilian application.

Once the product goes into production, the civilian product will have $18 million of materials cost and $12 million of labor cost. The military product will have $15 million each of materials and labor cost, for a total of $30 million. The common manufacturing overhead, for both of the products, will be $6 million. This overhead comprises $2 million in materials-related overhead and $4 million in labor-related overhead. Sue expects the civilian application to produce revenues of $40 million. The firm will negotiate a fixed price contract with the government. These fixed prices are set such that the firm obtains a 10% markup on expected product cost.

Required:

a. List two different allocations Sue could use to allocate the development cost between the military and the civilian applications. What are the comparative merits of the two schemes that you suggest?

b. Consider the cost of manufacturing the two products. What is the overhead cost that would be allocated to the military line if (1) all overhead is allocated to products based on labor cost, (2) all overhead is allocated to products based on materials cost, and (3) if materials-related overhead is allocated based on materials cost and labor-related overhead is allocated based on labor cost? Which of the three mechanisms do you recommend? Why?

c. Suppose Sue decides to allocate $8.5 million of development cost (= $7 million spent already plus half of the next $3 million to be spent) to the government contract. Do you believe this choice conforms to the norms for ethical behavior?

9.66 Cost Allocations and induced behavior, ethics (LO3). Bjorn and Karl work as product managers for a medium-sized manufacturing firm in Cologne, Germany. Both are evaluated on their respective product's reported profit and are given considerable autonomy in terms of production methods, distribution, and pricing.

Their firm has adopted a strategy of automating the production process as much as possible. Yet, as it has done for many years, the firm continues to allocate all overhead to individual products based on the number of labor hours consumed by each product.

During drinks one evening, Bjorn and Karl started talking shop. Bjorn complained that the allocation mechanism penalizes his product line because of its high labor content. Karl laughed and said, "There is an easy way to fix that problem! Start buying more components from suppliers instead of making them yourself."

Required:

a. Evaluate the merits of the firm's choice to continue allocating overhead based on labor hours, although the strategy is to foster automation. What is the impact on the accuracy of reported product cost? What countervailing benefits, if any, does the allocation mechanism provide?

b. How does Karl's recommended strategy reduce the amount of overhead allocated to Bjorn's product line?

c. Suppose Bjorn follows Karl's advice. Will the firm's overall expenditure on overhead costs increase, decrease, or stay about the same? What about the firm's total costs, which includes the cost of materials and labor?

d. Does Karl's recommended course of action fall within the norms for ethical behavior? Why or why not?

Chapter 10
Activity-Based Costing and Management

DAVID MASON OWNS AND OPERATES Mason Kitchen Cabinets (MKC) in High Point, North Carolina. Each of MKC's three product lines targets a distinct market segment: (1) the *Silver* line is low-priced and functional; (2) the *Gold* line is a mid-market product with a touch of elegance; and (3) the *Platinum* line offers the finest design features and highest quality. Within each product line, individual models offer different door paneling styles, woods or veneers, and colors.

David is particularly proud of the Platinum line because it is a testament to his company's workmanship. The market, too, appears to perceive the value of this line, as evidenced by the recent growth in Platinum sales. Despite all the success, MKC's profit has decreased over the last few years. Puzzled, David asks you to take a closer look at the profitability of each of MKC's products.

APPLYING THE DECISION FRAMEWORK

What Is the Problem?	MKC's profit has shown a decreasing trend in recent years.
What Are the Options?	There are numerous options, including changing the product mix and contracting or expanding capacity levels.
What Are the Costs and Benefits?	We need to gather information regarding the long-term profitability of each product line. We will use cost allocations and, in particular, activity-based costing, to estimate the costs of the resources used by each product.
Make the Decision!	Once we know the costs of the resources used by each product and each product's profitability, we will be able to suggest where David should focus his efforts.

Mason Kitchen Cabinets is famous for its workmanship. Although the sales of its Platinum line has been increasing, profits have not kept pace.

In Chapter 9, we examined how cost allocations facilitate long-term decisions by estimating each product's share of capacity costs. In this chapter, we take a closer look at the use of cost allocations for long-term decisions. We discuss how activity-based costing (ABC) could improve these estimates and thus provide a better picture of long-term product profitability.

We begin this chapter by reviewing the concept of a profit margin, which is important in making long-term decisions. We then describe the steps associated with designing product-costing systems and develop an activity-based costing (ABC) system for MKC. We conclude by illustrating how to use the data from ABC systems for product planning, customer profitability analysis, and targeting process improvements.

CHAPTER CONNECTIONS

In Chapter 11, we examine capital budgeting, a technique used for long-term resource planning. We discuss how to include the time value of money when evaluating long-term projects and how to best allocate capital among competing projects.

Elements of Activity-Based Costing (ABC) Systems

LEARNING OBJECTIVE 1

Understand the elements of an activity-based costing (ABC) system.

Exhibit 10.1 presents MKC's income statement for the most recent year of operations. MKC prepares this gross margin statement after allocating fixed manufacturing costs to products in proportion to their actual labor cost. Consistent with GAAP, MKC expenses all sales, marketing, and administrative costs in the period incurred.

Based on the data similar to that in Exhibit 10.1, David expanded the Platinum line and scaled down the Silver line several years back. Unfortunately, MKC's profit has decreased in the years following this decision. David knows something is not right.

As you learned in Chapter 9, David's problem might exist because he uses gross margin as a measure of product profitability. This metric is designed for financial reporting. It is not suited for decision making because it often excludes controllable costs and includes noncontrollable costs. Contribution margin, too, is not appropriate for this decision because it ignores changes in capacity costs. **Profit margin**, which equals a product's contribution margin less the cost of capacity resources needed to support its production, is the appropriate measure for evaluating long-term profitability.

Exhibit 10.1	*Mason Kitchen Cabinets: Gross Margin Income Statement for the Most Recent Year*

	Silver	Gold	Platinum	Total
	Cabinet Type			
	Silver	*Gold*	*Platinum*	*Total*
Sales volume (in linear feet)	225,925	135,960	112,370	474,255
Revenue	$10,618,475	$8,837,400	$9,888,560	$29,344,435
Cost of Goods Sold				
Direct materials	$5,196,275	$4,894,560	$5,618,500	$15,709,335
Direct labor	1,807,400	1,359,600	1,573,180	4,740,180
Allocated fixed manufacturing costs	1,717,030	1,291,620	1,494,521	4,503,171
Gross Margin	**$1,897,770**	**$1,291,620**	**$1,202,359**	**$4,391,749**
Period Costs				
Variable selling costs	316,295	203,940	191,029	$711,264
Fixed sales and marketing				1,750,000
Fixed general administration				850,000
Profit before Taxes				**$1,080,485**
Amount per Linear Foot	*Silver*	*Gold*	*Platinum*	
Selling price	$47.00	$65.00	$88.00	
Unit Contribution Margin	$14.60	$17.50	$22.30	
Unit Gross Margin	$8.40	$9.50	$10.70	

Firms use cost allocations as a practical way to *estimate* the cost of capacity resources that they assign to each product when measuring the profit margin. Exhibit 10.2 shows four key steps in designing a product costing system:

1. Determine how to form cost pools
2. Identify which cost pools to allocate
3. Identify the cost driver to use for allocating each cost pool
4. Determine the appropriate denominator volume of each cost driver to calculate allocations rates

Steps 1, 3, and 4 correspond to defining elements that are common to all cost allocations: cost pools, cost drivers, and the denominator volume. We saw these

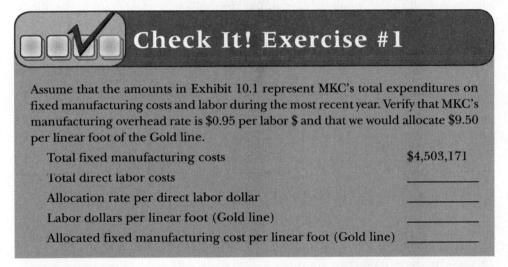

Check It! Exercise #1

Assume that the amounts in Exhibit 10.1 represent MKC's total expenditures on fixed manufacturing costs and labor during the most recent year. Verify that MKC's manufacturing overhead rate is $0.95 per labor $ and that we would allocate $9.50 per linear foot of the Gold line.

Total fixed manufacturing costs	$4,503,171
Total direct labor costs	_____
Allocation rate per direct labor dollar	_____
Labor dollars per linear foot (Gold line)	_____
Allocated fixed manufacturing cost per linear foot (Gold line)	_____

Solution at end of chapter.

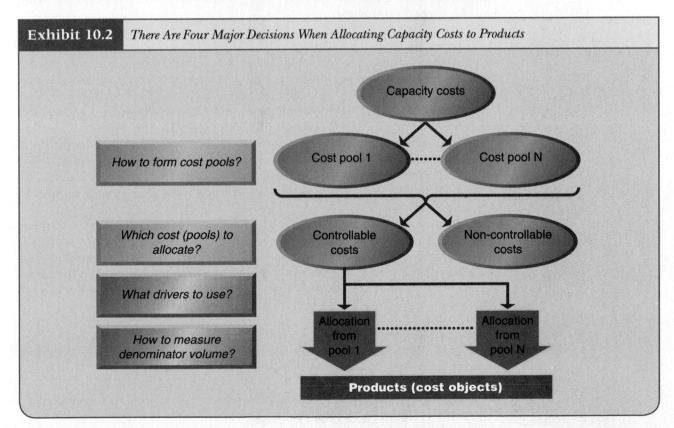

Exhibit 10.2   *There Are Four Major Decisions When Allocating Capacity Costs to Products*

CHAPTER CONNECTIONS

In Chapter 3, we learned that every cost allocation has four elements: cost pools, cost objects, cost driver, and denominator volume. Products are the cost objects in every product costing system. Activity-based costing provides finer cost estimates because it carefully considers choices regarding the other three elements.

elements in Chapter 3 when we first discussed cost allocation procedures in organizations. Step 2 (which pools to allocate) corresponds to a refinement in the allocation process from Chapter 3. This refinement is to separate the costs of capacity resources into controllable and noncontrollable costs to properly evaluate the impact of various long-term decisions on profitability.

Activity-based costing (ABC) is an approach to determining product costs. This method assigns the controllable costs of capacity resources more reliably than traditional systems do. As you will see, traditional and activity-based product costing systems differ from each other in each of the four steps involved in a developing a product costing system. We will describe the activity-based system as we lead you through these four steps.

STEP 1: FORMING COST POOLS

The first step in designing a product costing system is to group capacity costs into cost pools. Recall from Chapter 3 that a cost pool is a collection of the costs of similar resources. We could form cost pools by functions (as we did with EZ-Rest in Chapter 9), departments, or any other logical basis. ABC systems use *activities* as the basis for forming cost pools.

Activities as Building Blocks

Activity-based costing views an organization as a set of coordinated business processes. A **business process** converts organizational inputs into a measurable output. Examples of business processes in a manufacturing firm include purchase order processing, inventory management, production scheduling, production operations, quality control, and sales order processing. In turn, each business process is a collection of **activities**. Purchase order processing includes the activities of soliciting bids from potential vendors, preparing purchase orders, ensuring proper execution of purchase orders, and paying vendors on time. Exhibit 10.3 shows the activities in UPS's main business process—moving a package from a shipper to a receiver.

Each product (a package in the case of UPS) requires one or more business processes. The cost of a product equals the sum of the costs of the resources it consumes in each of these business processes. That is, in ABC, we form cost pools by the activities that make up a business process. At a fundamental level, *activity-based costing systems capture the notion that products require activities and activities consume resources.*

Activity Hierarchy

We classify organizational activities into one of four categories. These categories correspond to the cost hierarchy that we discussed in Chapter 2.

- **Unit-level activities** are proportional to production volume. Examples include assembly, inspection, and machining. The more units a firm produces, the

Exhibit 10.3	*Shipping a Package Triggers Many Activities and Business Processes*

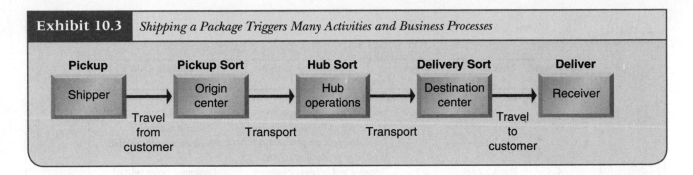

greater the machining, assembly, and inspection times. MKC has two kinds of unit-level activities. The first concerns the work of production employees, and the second relates to the operation of equipment.

For a company such as Citibank, unit-level activities include ATM and teller transactions, as these activities increase in proportion to the number of customers.

- **Batch-level activities** pertain to a group of units. When starting production, a firm performs activities such as setting up a machine and first-part inspections. These activities enable the firm to produce many units of the same product in a single run. MKC makes its cabinets in batches. It must schedule each batch, purchase appropriate material, and set up machines. Similarly, for each customer order, it must issue a pick list that specifies the items in the order, pack ordered materials, invoice the customer, and collect payment. These batch-level activities relate to executing production orders and customer orders that may pertain to many units.

For Citibank, opening a bank account is a one-time activity that allows the customer to execute many ATM and teller transactions.

- **Product- or customer-level activities** relate to a specific product or a specific customer. Examples include product-specific advertising and the work of product managers and product engineers. At MKC, each product line has dedicated tools, jigs, and fixtures. In addition, each product line has dedicated supervisory staff. The lines also occupy differing amounts of warehouse space. Moreover, MKC expends considerable effort to promote its three product lines, with the Platinum line accounting for the lion's share. Thus, MKC has three product-level activities: production support, marketing support, and warehousing.

For Citibank, maintaining the ATM computer network is a product-level activity. Such activities do not relate to production volume or batches. Rather, these activities relate to introducing a product, maintaining it, or enhancing its features.

- **Facility-level activities** sustain the business. Examples include the activities performed by security personnel, building and grounds maintenance, and general administration staff. These activities are not specific to any particular unit, batch, or product, but pertain to the business as a whole. MKC's facility-level costs relate to the long-term lease on factory and office space, including office and general administration.

ABC systems require forming cost pools by activities. Therefore, we obtain four kinds of cost pools, corresponding to the four categories of activities in the cost hierarchy. There could be many pools for each category of activity. For MKC, we form eight cost pools corresponding to eight activities, as listed in Exhibit 10.4.

For a company such as Citibank, unit-level activities include ATM and teller transactions, as these activities increase in proportion to the number of customers. (©Justin Lane/epa/©Corbis)

Exhibit 10.4	*Mason Kitchen Cabinets: Forming Cost Pools*

Cost Pool Number	Cost Hierarchy Category	Underlying Activity	Name for Cost Pool
1	Unit Level	Assembly of products (includes intricate carpentry)	Labor related
2	Unit Level	Machining of product components	Machine related
3	Batch Level	Issue and process production orders (including production scheduling)	Production order related
4	Batch Level	Receive and process customer orders (including invoice)	Customer order related
5	Product Level	Provide production support (includes design updates)	Production support
6	Product Level	Provide marketing support (includes trade shows)	Marketing support
7	Product Level	Warehouse products	Warehousing
8	Facility Level	General Administration	General administration

Connecting to Practice

COST HIERARCHY

Lord Corporation is a worldwide diversified, technology-based company. Lord's original cost system allocated materials-handling costs to products as a percent markup on the part cost. Analysis showed a greater association between inspections (a batch-level activity) and handling costs than between part costs and handling costs.

COMMENTARY: Attempts to manage materials-handling costs under Lord's original system would focus on managing part cost. However, ABC analysis shows that the true driver is the need for inspections, with moving materials to and from inspection consuming the majority of overhead costs. Management, therefore, shifted its emphasis to improving the certified vendor program, which eliminates the need for inspections altogether. This simplification of the business process allows Lord Corporation to eliminate the associated costs.

Determine the Costs in Each Cost Pool

We look to the firm's accounting records to determine the costs in each pool. Usually, firms organize accounts by the kind of expense (e.g., salary, equipment, supplies, and rent) rather than the activity supported by the expense. This means that a single account, such as salaries for marketing personnel, might contain costs related to many activities, such as providing support for production, customer order processing, warehousing, and general administration. With an ABC system, we need to analyze each account to determine the activities facilitated by the expenditure.

Exhibit 10.5 presents the results of such analysis for MKC. We allocate the total capacity costs of $7,103,171 (made up of fixed manufacturing costs, fixed sales and marketing costs, and fixed general administration costs from Exhibit 10.1) among the eight cost pools identified. Some of these costs, such as the cost of machine depreciation, relate uniquely to one-cost pool: machine-related activities. Other costs relate to multiple-cost pools. For instance, the supervisory staff spends a portion of their time supervising direct labor and a portion providing general production support such as scheduling. Therefore, we split the cost of the supervisory staff between two cost pools—the labor-related cost pool and the production support cost pool—in proportion to time. Many refer to this allocation of costs from accounts to cost pools as Stage 1 allocations.

STEP 2: DECIDING WHICH COSTS TO ALLOCATE

An accurate estimate of a product's profit margin includes all capacity costs that would change by the decision to make (or eliminate) the product. It excludes all other capacity costs that would remain unaltered. By focusing on controllable costs, activity-based systems differ from the traditional approach, which allocates all manufacturing costs and expenses all selling costs, regardless of their controllability.

In the context of MKC, we have to classify the costs in each of the eight cost pools as controllable for the product planning decision. Discussions with key personnel at

Exhibit 10.5 *Mason Kitchen Cabinets: Analyze Each Account to Allocate Its Costs Among Cost Pools*

	Expense						
Cost Pool	*Supervisory staff*	*Supplies, tools, jigs, and fixtures*	*Machine depreciation*	*Other fixed manufacturing costs*	*Sales, marketing, and customer support*	*General administration*	**Total**
1. Labor related	$458,171			$729,329		$237,500	$1,425,000
2. Machine related		$229,329	$1,720,671				1,950,000
3. Production order related				600,000			$600,000
4. Customer order related				150,000	$600,000		$750,000
5. Production support	395,000	220,671					$615,671
6. Marketing Support					525,000	150,000	$675,000
7. Warehousing					225,000		$225,000
8. General administration					400,000	462,500	$862,500
Total	$853,171	$450,000	$1,720,671	$1,479,329	$1,750,000	$850,000	$7,103,171

Check It! Exercise #2

Suppose a salesperson, earning $60,000 per year, informs you that she spends 70% of her time calling on customers and providing marketing support, 20% coordinating customer orders with the factory, and 10% on general administrative work. Allocate this person's salary expense among the eight cost pools identified in Exhibit 10.5. Verify that five of the eight pools would have zero cost allocated to them.

Solution at end of chapter.

MKC lead us to conclude that the costs in Pools 1–7 are controllable for product level decisions, whereas the costs in the general administration pool are not. The costs in Pool 8 include expenses, such as the salaries of administrative personnel that are only controllable at the business level.

STEP 3: IDENTIFYING COST DRIVERS

Our next task is to identify an appropriate cost driver/allocation basis for each pool. Exhibit 10.6 lists our choice for each of MKC's eight cost pools.

An appropriate cost driver is one that has the strongest causal relation with the costs in the cost pool. Thus, we use labor costs to allocate costs from the first pool, labor-related capacity costs. In the long term, a change in the driver volume should trigger a proportionate change in the costs contained in the pool. We also want the driver to be easily measured, readily understood, and believable. Techniques such as regression analysis, discussed in Chapter 4, help identify the most appropriate cost driver.

Moving on to the product-level cost pools, we can trace some costs to product lines directly. For MKC, the costs in the production-support cost pool include

Exhibit 10.6	*Mason Kitchen Cabinets: Designing an ABC System — Identifying a Cost Driver for Each Cost Pool*

Cost Pool	Cost Driver
1. Labor related	Labor cost
2. Machine related	Machine hours
3. Production order related	Number of production orders
4. Customer order related	Number of customer orders
5. Production support	Traced to each product line
6. Marketing support	Subjective estimate
7. Warehousing	% area occupied
8. General administration	(Not allocated)

Connecting to Practice

CLUB MEMBERSHIP PERKS

Like most car rental firms, National Car Company has a loyalty program, the Emerald Club. Members can rent cars in an expedited process because National's computer system has most of the required data for the club member. Why does National incur product-specific costs to set up and maintain the club?

COMMENTARY: The benefits occur both as increased revenue and decreased costs. The speedier processing might spur consumers to choose National over competing firms. In addition, every time a customer rents a car directly from the Emerald Club, National saves a little on the cost of processing that rental transaction.

items such as dedicated supervisory staff, and product-specific tools, jigs, and fixtures. We directly trace, rather than allocate, these costs to the product lines.

In contrast, the marketing support cost pool contains costs related to marketing and sales staff. These personnel serve all products, requiring the allocation of the associated costs. As is the case for MKC, this allocation often is subjective because marketing and sales staff do not keep detailed time sheets. We allocate warehousing using the number of square feet as the driver.

STEP 4: MEASURING DENOMINATOR VOLUME

Unlike traditional systems, ABC systems frequently use practical capacity as the denominator volume when calculating allocation rates. In traditional systems, we compute allocation rates by dividing the costs in a cost pool by the actual (or budgeted) volume in any given period. This procedure spreads all capacity costs over *actual* (or *budgeted*) volume—regardless of whether we use, or expect to use, available capacity fully. Thus, during periods when production volume is low and there is idle capacity, we spread capacity costs over a smaller production volume, driving up allocation rates. Products will seem *costlier* than normal in periods of low demand simply because of the way we allocate capacity costs.

ABC systems use **practical capacity**, an estimate of the maximum possible activity level, as the basis to allocate capacity costs. The advantage of a practical capacity-based allocation rate is that it does not change across periods. If a product consumes the same amount of resources, the cost allocated to it will also stay the same. In other words, this method assigns capacity costs to products strictly in proportion to use.

Unallocated activity cost is the difference between allocated activity costs and actual *spending* on capacity resources. It represents the cost of *unused capacity*. For example, suppose the direct labor cost is $250,000 in a given month, but only

---

Check It! Exercise #3

MKC's selling and administration costs include $225,000 toward warehousing. The warehouse has a capacity of 100,000 square feet. Currently, the Silver, Gold, and Platinum lines occupy 45,000, 20,000, and 15,000 square feet of space, respectively. Verify that (1) there is zero unused capacity if we use actual capacity as the denominator volume, and that (2) the cost of unused capacity is $45,000 if we use practical capacity to allocate costs.

	Actual Capacity	*Practical Capacity*
Cost to be allocated	_____	_____
Number of driver units	80,000 sq. feet	100,000 sq. feet
Allocation rate ($/sq. foot)	_____	_____
Cost allocated to Silver line	_____	_____
Cost allocated to Gold line	_____	_____
Cost allocated to Platinum line	_____	_____
Total allocated cost	_____	_____
Unallocated cost (cost of unused capacity)	_____	_____

Solution at end of chapter.

$225,000 is allocated to activities performed. Then the difference, $25,000, is the cost of underutilizing direct labor during that month; that is, it is the cost of unused labor capacity.

Highlighting the cost of unused capacity is valuable for managing costs. If a portion of the cost remains unallocated period after period, the company may as well cut back on wasteful spending by eliminating the unused capacity. From a decision-making perspective, identifying and isolating the cost of unused capacity is the primary reason for using practical capacity as the denominator volume. In the Appendix, we discuss accounting for the cost of unused capacity in detail.

Having made choices concerning each of the four elements of a product costing system, we are now in a position to compute the cost of each of MKC's product lines and examine how data from an ABC system can help in decision making.

Connecting to Practice

ACTIVITY-BASED COSTING IN PRACTICE

AIRCO, located in Arkansas, makes industrial air-conditioner units in the 5- to 20-ton range. Each air conditioner has over 200 parts, some made in-house and others purchased from suppliers. To understand the profitability of its products better, AIRCO installed an ABC system, forming eight activity cost pools. Sample pools include materials handling, product changeover, and customer service.

COMMENTARY: Following implementation of ABC, AIRCO discovered that the 5-, 6-, and 12.5-tons units were unprofitable at their current selling prices, while the popular 7.5- and 15-tons units were quite profitable. More importantly, AIRCO personnel were motivated to streamline their materials-handling processes by reducing raw material and parts transport distances within the factory layout. Improved production scheduling also helped to reduce product changeovers.

Source: Industrial Engineer, 2004.

Decision Usefulness of ABC Systems

LEARNING OBJECTIVE 2

Comprehend the decision usefulness of ABC systems.

By grouping capacity costs into carefully designed cost pools, ABC systems allow us to estimate the cost of capacity resources consumed by each product accurately. We can then use these estimates to project the controllable capacity costs associated with a decision option such as a new product mix. Let us begin by computing the cost of MKCs product lines.

COMPUTING PRODUCT COSTS

Because ABC is an allocation, it consists of the two steps involved in any allocation: (1) Compute the allocation rate, and (2) multiply the rate by the number of cost driver units in a cost object. We perform these steps for each cost pool. We then sum the costs across cost pools to determine product cost. Many refer to this allocation of costs from cost pools to products as Stage 2 allocations.

To obtain the activity rate for each cost pool, we divide the total cost in each pool by the practical capacity of its associated driver. Exhibit 10.7 presents these computations.

For the second step, we measure the number of cost driver units consumed by each product. Exhibit 10.8 provides this information for each of MKC's three product lines. For example, the Gold line consumes 40,788 machine hours. Therefore, we allocate 40,788 machine hours × $13 per machine hour = $530,244 to this product line from the machine-related cost pool. In total, we allocate $1,432,124 in capacity costs to the Gold line.

Note that we do not allocate $101,946 of the machine-related costs to any of the three product lines. The expenditure of $1,950,000 on machine-related costs provides MKC with 150,000 machine hours of capacity. However, current production only utilizes 142,158 machine hours, leaving 7,842 hours of unused capacity. The unallocated cost represents the cost of unused capacity (7,842 machine hours × $13 per machine hour = $101,946). The owner of MKC, David Mason, might wish to investigate why there is this much unused capacity.

Exhibit 10.7 *Mason Kitchen Cabinets: Compute the Cost Rate for Each Pool*

Cost Pool	Cost Driver	Total Cost in Pool	Practical Capacity	Activity Rate
1. Labor related	Labor cost	$1,425,000	$4,750,000	$0.30 per labor $
2. Machine related	Machine hours	$1,950,000	150,000 machine hours	$13.00 per machine hour
3. Production order related	Number of production orders	$600,000	1,000 orders	$600.00 per production order
4. Customer order related	Number of customer orders	$750,000	1,500 orders	$500.00 per customer order
5. Production support	Traced to each product line	$615,671	n/a	n/a
6. Marketing support	Subjective estimate	$675,000	100%	$6,750 per percent of support
7. Warehousing	% area occupied	$225,000	100%	$2,250 per percent area occupied
8. General administration	Not applicable	$862,500	n/a	n/a
Total cost		**$7,103,171**		

Exhibit 10.8 *Mason Kitchen Cabinets: Assign Costs to Products*

	Cost Pool								Total
	1. Labor related	2. Machine related	3. Production order related	4. Customer order related	5. Production support	6. Marketing support	7. Warehousing	8. General administration	
Activity driver (Exhibit 10.6)	Labor cost	Machine hours	Production orders	Customer order	N/A	N/A	% area	N/A	
Activity Rate: (Exhibit 10.7)	$0.30 per labor $	$13 per machine hour	$600 per production order	$500 per customer order	Traced	$6,750 per percent of support	$2,250 per % of area occupied	N/A	
Driver units consumed by (data collected at product level):									
Silver line	$1,807,400	45,185	200	300	n/a	30%	45%		
Gold line	$1,359,600	40,788	100	200	n/a	20%	20%		
Platinum line	$1,573,180	56,185	600	700	n/a	50%	15%		
Cost allocated to: (= driver units consumed × rate per driver unit)									
Silver line	$542,220	$587,405	$120,000	$150,000	$184,500	$202,500	$101,250		$1,887,875
Gold line	$407,880	$530,244	$60,000	$100,000	$154,000	$135,000	$45,000		$1,432,124
Platinum line	$471,954	$730,405	$360,000	$350,000	$277,171	$337,500	$33,750		$2,560,780
Unallocated	$2,946	$101,946	$60,000	$150,000	$0	$0	$45,000	$862,500	$1,222,392
Total cost allocated	$1,425,000	$1,950,000	$600,000	$750,000	$615,671	$675,000	$225,000	$862,500	$7,103,171

Now that we have completed our ABC system for MKC, we are ready to report ABC data.

REPORTING ACTIVITY-BASED COSTING DATA

Exhibit 10.9 presents a profitability report for the Silver line after using activity-based costing to determine product cost. Pay particular attention to two important points.

First, the report captures the complexity in the production process. If MKC produces the Silver line in smaller batches, we expect product cost to increase. The ABC product cost report would reflect this expected increase because the number of production orders would increase. In contrast, the original gross margin report in Exhibit 10.1 would not reflect this cost increase because it uses only a unit-level driver, direct labor costs. Indeed, reporting unit cost, obtained by dividing the total cost by linear feet to obtain a cost per linear foot, could mislead managers into thinking that cost varies in proportion to production volume. By breaking out the detailed activities and grouping them per the cost hierarchy, the ABC report alerts managers to the complexities of the production process.

Check It! Exercise #4

Verify that MKC should allocate $100,000 customer order related costs to the Gold line.

Cost in customer order cost pool	$750,000
Denominator volume	_____ customer orders
Rate per customer order	_____
# of Customer orders for Gold line	_____
Customer order cost allocated to Gold line	_____

Solution at end of chapter.

Exhibit 10.9	*Mason Kitchen Cabinets: Product Profitability Report for Silver Line*

Category	Detail	Description of driver	Driver volume	Activity Rate Per driver unit		Cost
	(Exhibit 10.5)	(Exhibit 10.6)	(Exhibit 10.8)	(Exhibit 10.7)		
Sales volume						225,925
Revenue		Linear feet	225,925 feet	$47.00		$10,618,475
Variable costs						
	Direct materials	Linear feet	225,925 feet	$23.00	$5,196,275	
	Direct labor	Linear feet	225,925 feet	$8.00	$1,807,400	
	Variable selling expenses	Linear feet	225,925 feet	$1.40	$316,295	$7,319,970
Contribution margin						$3,298,505
Unit-level costs	Labor related	Labor cost	$1,807,400 labor $	$0.30	$542,220	
	Machine related	Machine hours	45,185 machine hours	$13.00	$587,405	$1,129,625
Batch-level costs	Production support	Production orders	200 production orders	$600.00	$120,000	
	Customer support	Customer orders	300 customer orders	$500.00	$150,000	$270,000
Product-level costs	Production support	Traced	n/a	Traced	$184,500	
	Marketing support	Estimated %	30% of support	$6,750,000	$202,500	
	Warehousing	% area	45% of area	$2,250,000	$101,250	$488,250
Facility-level costs	General administration	Unallocated	n/a	n/a		
Profit margin						$1,410,630

Second, the ABC report uses batch-, product-, and facility-level drivers. Neverthe-less, unit-level costs still account for a substantial part of capacity costs. Consider the total firm level data shown in Exhibit 10.7. By adding labor-related costs and machine-related costs, we find that unit-level costs equal $3,375,000, which is 47.5% of the total overhead of $7.1 million. Thus, the volume of operations is still an important driver of the capacity resources consumed by the product.

Exhibit 10.10 provides a product-profitability statement for MKC, using ABC to evaluate each product line's profit margin. Notice that MKC's profit before taxes under the ABC method remains the same as in Exhibit 10.1. This equivalence shows that ABC is just another cost allocation system. Changing the method for allocating costs does not change total cost. Aggregate net income will stay the same.

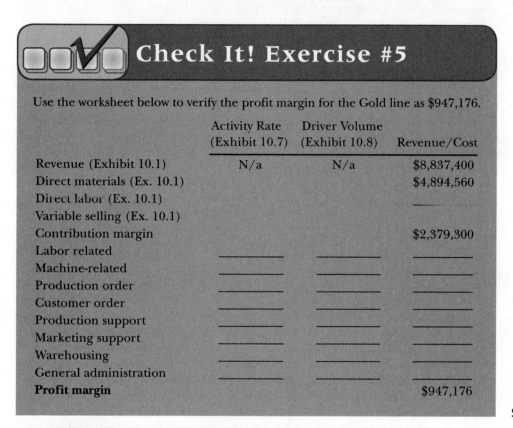

Check It! Exercise #5

Use the worksheet below to verify the profit margin for the Gold line as $947,176.

	Activity Rate (Exhibit 10.7)	Driver Volume (Exhibit 10.8)	Revenue/Cost
Revenue (Exhibit 10.1)	N/a	N/a	$8,837,400
Direct materials (Ex. 10.1)			$4,894,560
Direct labor (Ex. 10.1)			——
Variable selling (Ex. 10.1)			
Contribution margin			$2,379,300
Labor related			
Machine-related			
Production order			
Customer order			
Production support			
Marketing support			
Warehousing			
General administration			
Profit margin			$947,176

Solution at end of chapter.

Exhibit 10.10	Mason Kitchen Cabinets: Product Profitability Statement

	Cabinet Type			
	Silver	Gold	Platinum	Total
Sales volume (in linear feet)	225,925	135,960	112,370	474,255
Revenue	$10,618,475	$8,837,400	$9,888,560	$29,344,435
Variable costs	7,319,970	6,458,100	7,382,709	$21,160,779
Contribution margin	$3,298,505	$2,379,300	$2,505,851	$8,183,656
Unit level costs	1,129,625	938,124	1,202,359	3,270,108
Batch-level costs	270,000	160,000	710,000	1,140,000
Product-level costs	488,250	334,000	648,421	1,470,671
Product Profit Margin	$1,410,630	$947,176	($54,929)	$2,302,877
Facility level costs				862,500
Unallocated costs				359,892
Profit before Taxes				$1,080,485

However, changing the allocation method affects the reported profit margins for each of the product lines. As we see in Exhibit 10.11, ABC dramatically alters the ranking of products per their profitability. Contrary to David's belief, the Platinum line incurs a loss on a fully allocated basis! There are logical reasons for this reversal in profitability. The Silver line is popular among high-volume low-cost homebuilders. Order sizes typically are large, and the production lot sizes are large as well. On the other hand, the Platinum line is popular among custom builders. While MKC receives numerous orders for this line, the order sizes are usually small. The ABC report factors in the cost of processing the additional orders, which leads to lower profitability for the Platinum line.

Why does the gross margin report in Exhibit 10.1 not reflect these features? The answer is that we allocate more than a proportionate share of capacity costs to high-volume products when we use volume-based drivers such as direct labor hours. Because total overhead is the same, volume-based allocations generally underreport costs for low-volume products. Managers refer to this phenomenon as the high-volume product **cross subsidizing** the low-volume product.

Finally, notice that the product profit margins reported in Exhibit 10.10 do not include $862,500 of facility-level costs or $359,892 of the cost of unused capacity. We did not allocate the $862,500 among the three product lines because this cost is not controllable at the product level. Furthermore, changing the product mix is unlikely to affect the magnitude of this cost. The cost is relevant, however, when evaluating firm profitability. For example, the facility-level cost is controllable for the decision to keep MKC going or to shut it down. The remaining $359,892 represents the cost of unused capacity in various cost pools (see last line in Exhibit 10.8). This amount includes, for example, the 20% of unused warehouse space.

DECISIONS AT MKC

David sees the logic and merit in the design of the ABC system. He agrees that ABC data provide a more realistic estimate of the capacity resources consumed by the products, relative to the absorption costing system MKC currently uses. Based on the ABC data, he identifies several paths for MKC to increase profitability.

- *Deemphasize the Platinum line:* This move will allow David to use the freed-up resources to produce more of the Silver or Gold lines. However, David believes that the Platinum line contributes significantly to the company's reputation as a quality kitchen cabinetmaker. Reputation is hard to quantify but should not be ignored. Cost information should not be the *only* basis for making product-related decisions. Strategically, MKC might prefer to maintain a limited production of the Platinum line.

Exhibit 10.11	*Mason Kitchen Cabinets: Comparing Product Margins Using Contribution Margin, Gross Margin, and ABC*

	Cabinet Type		
System	*Silver*	*Gold*	*Platinum*
Contribution Margin	$3,298,505	$2,379,300	$2,505,851
Gross Margin (traditional method)	$1,897,770	$1,291,620	$1,202,359
ABC system	$1,410,630	$947,176	($54,929)
Margin per linear foot			
Contribution Margin	$14.60	$17.50	$22.30
Gross Margin (traditional method)	$8.40	$9.50	$10.70
ABC system (rounded to nearest cent)	$6.24	$6.97	($0.49)

- *Increase the price of the Platinum line* : This may be a viable option for David if he still wants to emphasize the Platinum line. It is possible that the customer segment for the Platinum line is not price-sensitive. Customers should be willing to pay the price at which MKC can profitably sell this line. David may have underpriced this line based on inaccurate cost information from the old cost system.
- *Manage costs* : A third option is to find ways to improve production efficiencies within the organization and cut costs. As it turns out, the ABC system provides valuable information to manage costs effectively. We discuss this process, activity-based management, later in this chapter.

These options are not mutually exclusive. David should also consider pursuing a combination of these avenues.

APPLYING THE DECISION FRAMEWORK

What Is the Problem?	MKC's profits have shown a decreasing trend in recent years.
What Are the Options?	There are numerous options, including changing the product mix and contracting or expanding capacity levels.
What Are the Costs and Benefits?	The ABC product costing system shows the Silver line to be more profitable than believed, while the Platinum line is less profitable.
Make the Decision!	David decides to change the emphasis among and the prices of his three lines. This strategy could include a number of decisions such as increasing the price for the Platinum line, focusing only on some market segments, and rearranging production processes to reduce cost.

 # Connecting to Practice

ABC AT UPS

Deregulation of interstate commerce freight provided the impetus for detailed ABC implementation at UPS, the world's largest package distribution company. UPS transports more than 3.1 billion parcels and documents annually. With over 500 aircraft, 157,000 vehicles, and 1,700 facilities providing service in over 200 countries, UPS has made a worldwide commitment to serving the needs of the global marketplace. Prior to deregulation, UPS based its prices on weight and distance alone. The revised system considers numerous factors such as location of pickup/drop-off, the nature of delivery, and the number of packages shipped in determining the price charged to a customer.

COMMENTARY: Many events can spur ABC implementations, including fluctuating profit margins and the adoption of new technologies. Moreover, external change such as deregulation or the emergence of new competition can also trigger a reexamination of the firm's business processes and costing systems.

UPS makes extensive use of detailed cost data when setting prices. (REUTERS/ John Sommers II/Landov LLC)

IMPLEMENTING ACTIVITY-BASED COSTING

Of course, there is no free lunch! ABC provides a firm with improved data for planning and control. The firm gains by basing its decisions on better data. However, implementing a full-fledged activity-based costing system is often a costly, time-consuming, and tedious exercise. ABC advocates the use of multiple-cost pools and cost drivers to capture more accurately the consumption of resources by cost objects. Therefore, it also requires more detailed information systems. Thus, there is a substantive cost associated with designing, implementing, and maintaining an ABC system. Indeed, a survey by the Institute of Management Accountants shows that only 54% of responding firms in the United States use activity-based costing.

Activity-Based Management

LEARNING OBJECTIVE 3

Explain the importance of activity-based management (ABM) in planning products, customers, and resources.

In this section, we discuss how to use the information from ABC systems to *improve* profitability by managing products, customers, and resources. We refer to this use of activity-based costing information as **activity-based management**, or simply ABM.

PRODUCT PLANNING

As we have learned in this chapter so far, ABC provides useful information for **product planning** by providing accurate estimates of profit margins. Like MKC, firms routinely rebalance their product portfolios to remain competitive as new market trends emerge and as technologies change. For example, two decades ago only a few automobile manufacturers marketed sports utility vehicles (SUVs). Now, virtually all auto manufacturers, including BMW, Mercedes, and Porsche, offer SUVs. Some industries, such as consumer electronics, have dynamic market conditions. Firms in those industries must rebalance their product portfolios more frequently. Companies such as Fisher continuously update their audio and CD product lines. In industries characterized by stable market conditions, such as energy and staple foods, product portfolio rebalancing occurs less frequently.

In the case of MKC, the Platinum line has a *positive contribution margin*. Yet we found that it has a *negative profit margin*. As we learned in Chapters 5 and 6, a product with a positive contribution margin may help improve short-term profits. Over an extended horizon, however, a firm cannot survive unless its products have positive profit margins. Absent strategic considerations, MKC should either raise the price on the Platinum line or consider dropping the product from its portfolio.

Decisions about product pricing and quantity determine the revenue received from products. Typically, we conceive of an inverse relation between price and quantity—the lower the price, the higher the quantity demanded and vice versa. While reducing the price of a product decreases its profit margin, a firm may be able to make up for the lost margin by selling more of the product. Nevertheless, in the long-term, the ABC cost provides a floor for setting the price. If the firm is not able to generate a unit price above this cost, dropping the product from its portfolio may be the best option.

CUSTOMER PLANNING

As we have seen, ABC systems help greatly in accurately evaluating the profitability of various products. However, we have assumed thus far that selling a product generates the same amount of profit regardless of *who* buys it, which is often not the case. Some customers are more demanding, requiring more of an organization's time and resources. Selling to these customers at the same price would yield lower profits.

Firms perform **customer planning** to examine the profitability of individual customers and market segments, and take appropriate actions to improve profitability. For example, MKC supplies kitchen cabinets to high-end custom homebuilders as well as retail home improvement stores. Knowing the profitability of each of these two market segments is clearly important for MKC in making decisions such as which segment to focus on, how to price their cabinets in the two segments, and how to allocate its resources. As Exhibit 10.12 shows, we can use an ABC system to measure the profitability or profit potential of an individual customer or a market segment. Instead of the product, we simply use the customer or the market segment as the cost object or the unit of analysis. That is, we allocate controllable capacity costs to various customers, rather than products, in proportion to their relative use to the capacity resources.

Customer-focused analysis is important because sales and administration costs associated with acquiring, servicing, and retaining customers often account for a significant portion of total costs, as they do for firms in the financial services industry like Citibank and FirstUSA. For many businesses, a few large customers account for a significant portion of total revenue. For example, Motorola is a major customer for Air Products & Chemicals. WalMart is often the major customer for many of its suppliers. It is good business practice for firms to measure customer costs and monitor the profitability of major customers. They may then effectively manage these relationships to improve profitability.

Customer costs include the unit-, batch-, product-, and facility-level capacity costs consumed by specific customers. Unit-level costs are proportional to customers' order volume and include items such as packaging and freight. Batch-level costs relate to customers' frequency of ordering or order sizes. Product-level costs may include the costs associated with tailoring a product to customers' desires. Facility-level costs may

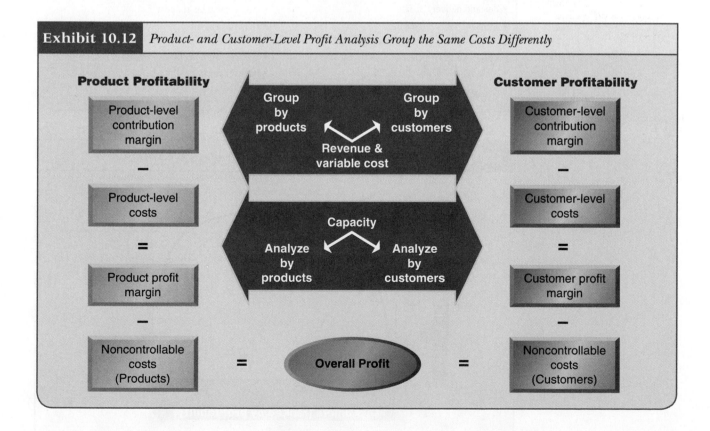

Exhibit 10.12   *Product- and Customer-Level Profit Analysis Group the Same Costs Differently*

include warehousing of customers' products. Exhibit 10.13 presents typical profiles of customers with high and low costs that emerge from analyzing information provided by ABC systems.

Most businesses have a mix of high- and low-profit customers. The graph in Exhibit 10.14, known as a **whale curve**, represents most firms' experience in customer profitability. The *x*-axis of this graph arranges customers in decreasing order of profitability, with the most profitable customer being the first from the origin. The *y*-axis is the cumulative profit. As we can see from this graph, the top 20% of the customers account for more than 220% of the company's overall profit! How can this happen? Because the remaining customers are unprofitable for the company, they actually bring profit *down* by 120%.

Why don't firms simply get rid of unprofitable customers and increase profit? In general, it is poor business practice to turn away customers. In some sense, serving unprofitable customers is an unavoidable cost of doing business. However, firms should know which customers contribute to profit and which do not. Effective management then works with "undesirable" customers to convert them into "desirable" ones.

Exhibit 10.13 *Characteristics of Low- and High-Profit Customers*

Low-Profit Customers	**High-Profit Customers**
• Small order sizes	• Large order sizes
• Unpredictable ordering pattern, hard to plan for	• Predictable ordering patterns, easy to plan for
• Frequent order change requests	• Minimal order change requests
• Demand immediate deliveries	• Planned deliveries
• Need to carry inventory to satisfy customer demands	• Minimal inventory requirements
• Require more customization	• Require minimal customization
• Demand delivery at site	• Less pre-sales support
• Frequent sales force contact	• Less after sales support
• Demand immediate and frequent after sales service	• Easy to deal with, has well organized purchase procedures
• Rigid requirements	• Flexible relationship
• Not paying on time	• Pays on time

Exhibit 10.14 *A Plot of Customer Profitability Produces a Whale Curve*

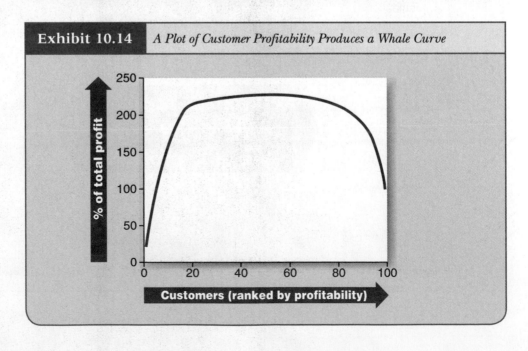

Connecting to Practice

CUSTOMER PROFITABILITY AT A CREDIT UNION

The following (disguised) data are from a credit union. All data are in percentages.

Household Group (most to least profitable)	Profit	Deposits	Loans
Tier 1 (7.9%)	146.9%	16.1%	55.3%
Tier 2 (14.6)	36.6	12.9	18.4
Tier 3 (16.5)	8.4	7.8	6.9
Tier 4 (40.4)	−18.2	11.2	6.2
Tier 5 (20.6)	−73.8	52.0	13.2

COMMENTARY: The data clearly show that a few households contribute to the bulk of the Credit Union's profit. The top 39% of households are profitable, while the bottom 61% are not profitable. Furthermore, loans appear to be a primary driver of profitability. Notice, however, that the credit union needs the Tier 5 households to obtain the capital that it lends! Thus, just as we consider product portfolios, we also need to consider customer portfolios to take account of the relations among different customer segments.

RESOURCE PLANNING

By estimating product costs based on resource usage, an ABC system enables us to determine the capacity levels required by a proposed product portfolio. When a firm contemplates a change in the product portfolio, it can use ABC to determine how much additional capacity is needed or how much can be freed up. With such **resource planning** information, the firm can evaluate how its profits will change under various product planning options.

Firms plan their capacity levels to match demand conditions over the long term. Once machines are purchased, factories are built, and other commitments are made, it is difficult to make quick changes. There is no sense in installing more capacity than required, or investing in insufficient capacity.

Activity-based costing helps resource planning in a number of ways. First, it pinpoints activities and business processes that are costly. Firms can then target these specific areas for improving efficiencies. Second, it isolates the cost of excess capacity from the productive use of capacity, so that firms can find profitable ways of dealing with the excess capacity.

Improving Business Process/Activity Performance

In a competitive environment, it is important for firms to perform various activities efficiently to ensure that they stay in business for a long time. Firms must therefore constantly look out for ways to improve their operations. But we must first know where to look. This is not an easy task; organizations have many business processes and a multitude of activities. It is both difficult and inefficient to go through every activity systematically and then analyze it in detail. How then does a firm decide which activities to target for improvement?

There is no simple answer to this question. Frequently, firms will emphasize costly activities or business processes. Improving efficiencies with respect to these activities can make a significant difference in the firm's cost structure. To identify costly activities and processes, firms can use their ABC system. For example, by using ABC, MKC has found that it currently spends a total of $1,350,000 on order-related activities. Each production order currently costs $600, and each customer order currently costs $500. These are two processes that MKC may target for improving efficiencies, leading to lower costs.

Once a process is selected, the following steps describe how we can go about improving its efficiency:

- ***Develop a process map for each activity/process chosen.*** Understand *how* it works. Each element in the process performs a function and consumes resources.
- ***Identify value- and non-value-adding activities.*** Non-value-adding activities cost money but do not provide commensurate benefits. Firms can identify non-value-adding activities by asking, "If we eliminate this activity, would the customer notice?" An activity such as issuing the production order clearly adds value. However, entering the customer's order in multiple data systems adds no value from the perspective of the customer. Eliminating non-value-adding activities improves costs and efficiencies—by eliminating the need for MKC's various personnel to enter the customer's order, it may be possible to reduce the activity rate from $500 to, say, $400.
- ***Seek ways to improve value-adding activities.*** One way of reducing the cost of customer inquiries is to set up an informative Web site with all the necessary details and provide on-line access to a database of frequently asked questions and responses. Although developing and maintaining this Web site has its own costs, the site may well be a cheaper alternative.

Firms also may focus on activities that appear inefficient compared to industry best practices. Many companies "benchmark" their activities and business processes against the best industry practice or a market rival in order to identify areas of improvement. Usually, benchmarking exercises involve consulting with industry experts. Firms compare the ABC cost of performing these activities and businesses processes with these benchmarks. They can then determine the competitiveness of their operations and assess the extent to which they need to improve to become competitive. In this way, activity-based management is a valuable tool for companies in achieving their business goals.

 **Connecting to Practice**

RESOURCE PLANNING IN HOSPITALS

The *Des Moines Register* reports that patients had to wait for up to 23 days to schedule a CAT scan at "University Hospital," a real hospital that chose to remain anonymous. After studying the process, the hospital had the patients drink the "contrast material" needed for the scan when they first arrived rather than after completing the preparatory work.

COMMENTARY: How can this seemingly small change in the process improve the waiting time?

It eliminated the need for a staging room, allowing for better coordination of high-cost screening equipment, which require technicians' and nurses' time. Patients now wait no more than a day to schedule a scan, the hospital does 12 more scans each day, and the patient time in the office has dropped 38 minutes.

Source: *Des Moines Register,* October 31, 2004.

SUMMARY

In this chapter, we discussed activity-based costing (ABC) systems. We showed that ABC systems could improve estimates of controllable capacity costs and assessments of product profitability. ABC accomplishes this by refining three elements of the allocation procedure: cost pools, cost drivers, and the choice of denominator volume. We also examined how to use the information from activity-based costing (ABC) systems for activity-based management (ABM). ABM helps firms improve their profitability by focusing on the elements of long-term profit: products, customers, and resources.

Because it is an allocation, ABC suppresses issues concerning the time value of money and the lumpy nature of capacity resources. Thus, when decisions involve significant outlays, organizations often supplement analyses using allocated costs with capital budgeting techniques. We study capital budgeting in Chapter 11.

RAPID REVIEW

LEARNING OBJECTIVE 1

Understand the elements of an activity-based costing (ABC) system.

- Profit margin, rather than gross margin or contribution margin, is the appropriate metric for long-term decisions. The profit margin is contribution margin less the controllable cost of capacity resources.

- ABC refines three elements of the allocation procedure: cost pools, cost drivers, and the choice of denominator volume. The fourth element, cost objects, is the same for all product costing systems.

- The first step in designing an ABC system is to group capacity costs into cost pools. Activities are the building blocks of ABC systems and are used to form cost pools. ABC considers four categories of activities:
  1. *Unit-level activities* are proportional to production volume.
  2. *Batch-level activities* pertain to a group of units.
  3. *Product- or customer-level activities* relate to a specific product or customer.
  4. *Facility-level activities* are required to sustain the business.

- After forming cost pools and deciding on which costs to allocate, we identify appropriate cost drivers for each pool. We look for drivers that have the strongest causal relation with the cost in the cost pool.

- In choosing denominator volume, ABC systems attempt to isolate the productive use of capacity from excess or idle capacity. To accomplish this objective, ABC allocates costs in strict proportion to usage. Thus, ABC uses practical capacity rather than actual capacity to compute activity rates. This feature allows us to calculate the cost of unused capacity.

LEARNING OBJECTIVE 2

Comprehend the decision usefulness of ABC systems.

- Because an ABC system is a series of allocations, we compute product cost by performing the two steps involved in any allocation: (1) compute the allocation rate and (2) multiply the rate by the number of cost driver units in a cost object.

- We obtain the activity rate for each cost pool by dividing the total cost in each pool by the practical capacity of its associated driver.

- For the second step, we measure the number of cost driver units consumed by each product.

- ABC systems highlight product profitability. We can use ABC product cost reports to make product emphasis, pricing, and cost management decisions.

- Because ABC requires extensive information systems, implementing a full-fledged ABC system can be a costly, time-consuming, and tedious exercise in most organizations.

LEARNING OBJECTIVE 3

Explain the importance of activity-based management (ABM) in planning products, customers, and resources.

- Activity-based management involves the use of ABC information for product, customer, and resource planning.

- Product planning involves making appropriate add/drop decisions. It also involves ensuring that in the long run product prices are set so that they deliver positive profit margins.

- Customer planning involves identifying profitable and unprofitable customers, and taking actions to improve customer profitability.

- Resource planning involves improving the efficiency of resource usage by first identifying value-adding and non-value-adding activities and business processes. It then focuses on putting organizational resources to more profitable use.

Appendix
ACCOUNTING FOR THE COST OF UNUSED CAPACITY

Because ABC uses practical capacity to calculate allocation rates, it helps isolate the cost of unused capacity. How should firms deal with the cost of unused capacity?

The correct way to deal with the cost depends on the reason for the idle capacity. It is possible that the unused capacity has no gainful purpose whatsoever. In this case, the firm should avoid the cost by ridding itself of the excess capacity. However, it also is possible that the unused capacity is attributable to a temporary lull in demand, such as when demand is seasonal, as is the case for a utility company like MidAmerican Energy. In such instances, firms cannot dispose of this capacity because it will need the capacity in times when demand peaks. Accordingly, we attribute the cost of having to carry excess capacity during lean months to the production in peak months.

Another reason for carrying excess capacity is that it serves a strategic role. For instance, analysts speculate that Monsanto built a large glyphosate plant in Camacari, Brazil, partly to deter entry from competitors. In this case, we attribute the cost of unused capacity to management strategy. Other reasons for unused capacity include planning for growth or uncertain demand from a large customer.

By isolating the cost of unused capacity, ABC helps management investigate the underlying reason and charge the cost to its cause (e.g., the customer or product deriving the related benefit). If no one gets any benefit, we should dispose of the capacity or redeploy it into value-adding projects.

Excess Capacity and the Downward Demand Spiral

Identifying unused capacity is particularly important when firms engage in cost-based pricing. Firms experience unused capacity in periods with low demand. Allocation rates based on actual capacity increase in such periods because fixed costs do not decrease proportionally with activity volume. Naturally, the *reported* costs of all products increase. If the firm responds to the higher reported cost by raising prices, it risks setting off a dangerous trend. Higher prices would lower demand even more, raising allocation rates yet again. Use of practical capacity to calculate allocation rates guards against this phenomenon by isolating the cost of unused capacity rather than including it in the allocation rate and, in turn, reported product costs.

GAAP and the Cost of Unused Capacity

At present, GAAP does not recognize the use of practical capacity for computing allocation rates. Under GAAP, the cost of unused capacity would appear as underapplied overhead. At year end, we must reallocate this cost to products or, if the amount is small, write it off to cost of goods sold. This approach effectively ensures that reported product costs correspond to the costs computed using actual activity as the denominator volume. The Financial Accounting Standards Board, which oversees GAAP, is reviewing this issue.

CHAPTER CONNECTIONS

We discuss the concepts of under- and overapplied overhead in Chapter 14, where we discuss the details of cost accumulation and reporting systems in different production settings.

ANSWERS TO CHECK IT! EXERCISES

Exercise #1: Total direct labor costs = $4,740,180; Allocation rate per direct labor dollar = $4,503,171/$4,740,180 = $0.95 per labor $; Labor cost per linear foot = $10 (= $1,359,600/135,960); Allocated fixed manufacturing cost per linear foot (Gold line) = $10.00 direct labor per linear foot × $0.95/labor $ = $9.50.

Exercise #2: Marketing support = 0.70 × $60,000 = $42,000; Customer order related = 0.20 × $60,000 = $12,000; General administration = 0.10 × $60,000 = $6,000. All other cost pools would have zero cost allocated to them.

Exercise #3: *Actual capacity:* Cost to be allocated = $225,000; Allocation rate = $225,000/80,000 = $2.8125 per square foot; Cost allocated to Silver line = 45,000 square feet × $2.8125/square foot = $126,562.50; Cost allocated to Gold line; $56,250; Cost allocated to Platinum line; $42,187.50; Total allocated cost = $225,000; Unallocated cost = $0. *Practical Capacity:* Cost to be allocated = $225,000; Allocation rate = $225,000/100,000 = $2.25 per square foot. Cost allocated to Silver line = 45,000 square feet × $2.25/square foot = $101,250; Cost allocated to Gold line; $45,000; Cost allocated to Platinum line; $33,750; Total allocated cost = $180,000; Unallocated cost = $45,000 (= $225,000 − $180,000).

Exercise #4: Denominator volume = 1,500 orders; Rate per customer order = $750,000/1,500 of practical capacity = $500 per order; the Gold line has 200 customer orders; Cost allocated to the gold line = 200 orders × $500/order = $100,000.

Exercise #5: Revenue = $8,837,400; direct materials = $4,894,560; direct labor = $1,359,600; supplies and utilities = $203,940; unit-level labor related = $407,880; unit-level machine related = $530,244; batch-level production support = $60,000; batch-level customer support = $100,000; product-level production support = $154,000; product-level marketing support = $135,000; product-level warehousing = $45,000; facility-level general administration = $0; profit margin = $947,176.

SELF-STUDY PROBLEM #1:
Profit Margins and Activity-Based Costing

Ritchie Simmons sells two versions, Deluxe and Premium, of his firm's only product, the GoGoJuicer. The GoGoJuicer uses patented technology to extract the last drop of juice from most fruits. The Premium version can handle larger fruit and has more options relative to the Deluxe version. The following table provides the financial results for the most recent year of operations. Labor costs $16 per hour, and each product requires one hour of labor. Ritchie currently allocates all fixed manufacturing costs to products, using labor hours as the allocation basis. He also allocates all fixed selling and administrative expenses, using revenue as the allocation basis.

	Deluxe	Premium	Total
Units	90,000	10,000	100,000
Revenue	$6,300,000	$900,000	$7,200,000
Materials	1,080,000	250,000	1,330,000
Labor	1,440,000	160,000	1,600,000
Contribution margin	$3,780,000	$490,000	$4,270,000
Allocated fixed manufacturing costs	3,420,000	380,000	3,800,000
Allocated fixed selling and administrative expenses	251,563	35,937	287,500
Profit margin	$108,437	$74,063	$182,500
Unit profit margin	$1.2048	$7.4063	

a. *Although the unit profit margin of the Deluxe Juicer is rather low, Ritchie believes that it is important to keep this model in the product mix. However, Ritchie believes that he can tailor his promotion and sales strategies to improve the sales mix to a 6:4 ratio from the current 9:1 ratio of Deluxe to Premium juicers, with total volume staying the same at 100,000 units. Using the current fixed manufacturing costs activity rate and the current fixed selling and administrative costs activity rate, compute Ritchie's expected profit if sales change to 60,000 Deluxe Juicers and 40,000 Premium Juicers.*

The current fixed manufacturing costs activity rate = $3,800,000/100,000 labor hours = $38 per labor hour. (Because each product requires 1 hour of labor, the total labor hours equals the total number of units produced). The current fixed selling and administrative expenses activity rate = $287,500/$7,200,000 = $0.03993 per $1 of revenue. Finally, we calculate the unit prices, materials, and labor costs by dividing revenue, materials costs, and labor costs by the number of units. For example, the materials cost per unit of a Premium juicer = $250,000/10,000 units = $25 per unit.

The following table provides the income statement for the new product mix:

	Deluxe	Premium	Total
Units	60,000	40,000	100,000[1]
Revenue	$4,200,000	$3,600,000	$7,800,000[2]
Materials	720,000	1,000,000	1,720,000[3]
Labor	960,000	640,000	1,600,000[4]
Contribution margin	$2,520,000	$1,960,000	$4,480,000
Allocated fixed manufacturing costs	2,280,000	1,520,000	3,800,000[5]
Allocated fixed selling and administrative expenses	167,706	143,748	311,454[6]
Profit margin	$72,294	$296,252	$368,546

[1] 100,000 units sold in a 6:4 ratio
[2] (60,000 Deluxe × $70 per unit) + (40,000 Premium × $90 per unit)
[3] (60,000 Deluxe × $12 per unit) + (40,000 Premium × $25 per unit)
[4] (60,000 Deluxe × $16 per unit) + (40,000 Premium × $16 per unit)
[5] (60,000 Deluxe × 1 hour × $38 per hour) + (40,000 Premium × 1 hour/unit × $38 per hour)
[6] ($4,200,000 × $0.03993) + ($3,600,000 × $0.03993)

Notice that we also could have used the unit profit margins to calculate expected profit under the proposed product mix. Specifically, $368,546 \approx (60,000 \times \$1.2048) + (40,000 \times \$7.4063)$. (*Note*: The total profit numbers do not agree by $6 due to rounding of the selling and administrative costs in the summary table.)

b. *Ritchie is pleased to discover that, as per the existing cost estimates, the new sales mix is expected to more than double his profit. When Ritchie shares his insight with his staff, they express some reservations. His production manager, Debra, indicates that $1.1 million of the $3.8 million in fixed manufacturing costs (approximately 30%) pertains to batch-related activities such as scheduling production runs. Because the Premium Juicer is run in smaller batches (250 per batch rather than 500 per batch for the Deluxe model), she conjectures that fixed manufacturing costs are unlikely to stay at $3.8 million if the sales mix changes as proposed. Likewise, Brett, the marketing manager, indicates that while it takes 10 sales visits to sell 1,000 units of the Deluxe Juicer, it takes 25 visits to sell 1,000 Premium Juicers.*

Reverting to the original problem data, determine the cost per batch if $1.1 million of fixed manufacturing costs relate to batch-level activities. In addition, determine the cost per sales visit if all selling and administrative costs are allocated using sales visits, rather than revenue, as the cost driver. Finally, determine the activity rate per labor hour for the remaining fixed manufacturing costs of $2.7 million.

We now have three cost pools instead of two. We have split the fixed manufacturing costs into two pools: batch costs (allocated by the number of batches) and other manufacturing costs (allocated by labor hours). We also have changed the cost driver for selling costs from revenue to the number of sales visits. We have:

Total number of batches: (90,000 deluxe units/500 units per batch)
+ (10,000 premium units/250 units per batch) = 220 batches

Total number of sales visits: [(90,000 deluxe units/1,000) × 10]
+ [(10,000 premium units/1,000) × 25] = 1,150 visits

Using these estimates of activity volumes, we have:

Rate per batch = $1,100,000/220 = $5,000 per batch
Rate per labor hour = $2,700,000/100,000 labor hours = $27 per labor hour
Rate per sales visit = $287,500/1,150 visits = $250 per visit

c. *Using the original product mix (i.e., 90,000 Deluxe Juicers and 10,000 Premium Juicers), determine Ritchie's expected profit using the three cost pools and cost drivers you derived in part (b). Compare your profit estimate with Ritchie's current profit of $182,500.*

The following table provides the income statement for the old product mix with the new cost pools and cost drivers:

Units	Deluxe	Premium	Total
	90,000	10,000	100,000[1]
Revenue	$6,300,000	$900,000	$7,200,000[2]
Materials	1,080,000	250,000	1,330,000[3]
Labor	1,440,000	160,000	1,600,000[4]
Unit-related fixed manufacturing costs	2,430,000	270,000	2,700,000[5]
Batch-related fixed manufacturing costs	900,000	200,000	1,100,000[6]
Fixed selling and administrative expenses	225,000	62,500	287,500[7]
Profit margin	$225,000	($42,500)	$182,500

[1] 100,000 units sold in the original 9:1 ratio
[2] (90,000 Deluxe × $70 per unit) + (10,000 Premium × $90 per unit)
[3] (90,000 Deluxe × $12 per unit) + (10,000 Premium × $25 per unit)
[4] (90,000 Deluxe × $16 per unit) + (10,000 Premium × $16 per unit)
[5] (90,000 Deluxe × 1 hour × $27 per hour) + (10,000 Premium × 1 hour × $27 per hour)
[6] [(90,000 Deluxe/500 units per batch) + (10,000 Premium/250 units per batch)] × $5,000 per batch
[7] [900 visits for Deluxe + 250 visits for Premium] × $250 per sales visit

Although we changed the number of cost pools and the drivers used, our profit estimate equals Ritchie's original profit. The reason is that the changes in the allocation system merely redistributes the costs between the two products.

Notice, however, that the change in our allocation system dramatically alters the profit attributable to each of the two product lines. The revised data indicate that the Deluxe model is highly profitable while the Premium model loses money.

d. *Using the proposed product mix (i.e., 60,000 Deluxe and 40,000 Premium Juicers), determine Ritchie's expected profit using the three cost pools and cost drivers you derived in part (a). How does this profit estimate compare to the profit you computed in part (a)?*

The following table provides the income statement for the new product mix with the new cost pools and cost drivers.

	Deluxe	*Premium*	*Total*
Units	*60,000*	*40,000*	*100,000*[1]
Revenue	$4,200,000	$3,600,000	$7,800,000[2]
Materials	720,000	1,000,000	1,720,000[3]
Labor	960,000	640,000	1,600,000[4]
Unit-related fixed manufacturing costs	1,620,000	1,080,000	2,700,000[5]
Batch-related fixed manufacturing costs	600,000	800,000	1,400,000[6]
Fixed selling and administrative expenses	150,000	250,000	400,000[7]
Profit margin	$150,000	$(170,000)	$(20,000)

[1] 100,000 units sold in the proposed 6:4 ratio
[2] (60,000 Deluxe × $70 per unit) + (40,000 Premium × $90 per unit)
[3] (60,000 Deluxe × $12 per unit) + (40,000 Premium × $25 per unit)
[4] (60,000 Deluxe × $16 per unit) + (40,000 Premium × $16 per unit)
[5] (60,000 Deluxe × 1 hour × $27 per hour) + (40,000 Premium × 1 hour/unit × $27 per hour)
[6] [(60,000 Deluxe/500 units per batch) + (40,000 Premium/250 units per batch)] × $5,000 per batch
[7] [600 visits for deluxe + 1,000 visits for Premium] × $250 per sales visit

Our revised profit estimate clearly shows that it is unwise to change the product mix to favor the premium model.

The old method for estimating capacity costs used unit-level drivers only. Thus, most of the capacity costs are allocated to the Deluxe line because it accounts for most of the labor costs and units. Consequently, when Ritchie projects future capacity costs, his estimates do not change much. After all, the total volume in terms of labor hours and in terms of units has not changed. However, the detailed activity analysis information provided by Debra and Brett indicate a significant increase in the activities needed to support the new product mix. This increase in activity volume will naturally trigger an increase in capacity costs. By partitioning the capacity costs into smaller pools and using cost drivers that capture the underlying activities, the revised cost system provides a better estimate of the capacity costs needed to support the new product mix.

SELF-STUDY PROBLEM #2:
Customer Profitability Analysis

Four clients account for all of Hogan Medical Supplies' business. Two of Hogan's clients are small pharmaceutical stores, and the remaining two clients are large discount stores with attached pharmacies. Hogan prices its products at 25% above variable cost, although all four customers demand and receive a sizable discount off the list price.

The following data are available for the most recent quarter of operations. In addition to this information, management of Hogan informs you that they can trace $18,000 of general administration costs to small pharmaceutical stores and $43,000 of general administration costs to the large discount stores.

Item	Small Stand-alone Pharmaceuticals		Large Pharmaceuticals Attached to Discount Stores		Activity Rate
	Dolan	Ryan	MegaMart	BiLo Stores	
Number of orders	20	45	30	15	$150
Order size	$8,000	$4,000	$85,000	$80,000	n/a
Average discount	5%	10%	18%	12%	n/a
Regular deliveries	20	45	30	15	$75
Expedited deliveries	10	0	10	0	$250

a. *Prepare a customer-profitability report that shows the profit from each customer and each customer channel, stand-alone pharmaceuticals, and large pharmaceuticals attached to discount stores.*

The table below provides the required information for each of Hogan's customers as well as each customer channel, stand-alone pharmaceuticals, and large pharmaceuticals attached to discount stores.

Hogan Medical Supplies: Customer Profitability Report

	Dolan	Ryan	Channel Total	Mega Mart	BiLo	Channel Total
Revenue at list price[1]	$160,000	$180,000	$340,000	$2,550,000	$1,200,000	$3,750,000
Discount[2]	8,000	18,000	26,000	459,000	144,000	603,000
Net revenue	$152,000	162,000	$314,000	$2,091,000	$1,056,000	$3,147,000
Variable costs[3]	128,000	144,000	272,000	2,040,000	960,000	3,000,000
Contribution margin	$24,000	$18,000	$42,000	$51,000	$96,000	$147,000
Order processing[4]	3,000	6,750	9,750	4,500	2,250	6,750
Regular deliveries[5]	1,500	3,375	4,875	2,250	1,125	3,375
Expedited deliveries[6]	2,500	0	2,500	2,500	0	2,500
Customer profit	$17,000	$7,875	$24,875	$41,750	$92,625	$134,375
Channel costs			18,000			43,000
Channel profit			$6,875			$91,375

[1] = Number of orders × order size.
[2] = Revenue at list price × average discount.
[3] = Revenue at list price × 0.80 because list price = VC × 125% or VC = list price/1.25.
[4] = Number of orders × $150 per order.
[5] = Number of regular deliveries × $75 per delivery.
[6] = Number of expedited deliveries × $250 per delivery.

b. *Based on your analysis, recommend how Hogan could improve its profit.*

Hogan is barely breaking even with small pharmaceuticals. Dolan is much more profitable than Ryan because Ryan receives a higher discount. Moreover, although sales volumes are similar, Ryan places more orders. These costs outweigh the favorable aspect of Ryan not demanding expedited deliveries. Hogan could coordinate with Ryan to increase order size and also try to negotiate a smaller discount. Likewise, it might try to work with Dolan to reduce the number of expedited deliveries even if the action increases order frequency.

Hogan makes substantial profit from the large pharmaceuticals. BiLo is more than twice as profitable as MegaMart with half the sales volume. The primary reason is the aggressive pricing for MegaMart. BiLo also is a very desirable customer as its orders are for large quantities and the company requires little extra attention. Hogan could possibly increase profit by cultivating BiLo further. Hogan may have no choice but to deal with MegaMart as a less profitable customer, because MegaMart accounts more than 50% of Hogan's sales.

GLOSSARY

Activity The basic element of any business process.

Activity-based costing (ABC) An allocation methodology used to estimate the controllable cost of capacity resources.

Activity-based management (ABM) Using information from ABC systems to improve profitability by managing products, customers, and resources.

Batch-level activities Activities that pertain to a group of units.

Business process Converts a set of organizational inputs into a measurable output.

Cross-subsidization Some cost allocation systems allocate systematically lower amounts to some products and higher amounts to allocate other products. In such instances, products receiving higher allocations are said to cross-subsidize products receiving lower allocations.

Customer planning The set of decisions to assess the profitability of individual customers and customer segments, including the actions taken to improve their profitability.

Facility-level activities Activities that are required to sustain the business.

Practical capacity A realistic estimate of the maximum possible activity level.

Product-/customer-level activities Activities that relate to a specific product or a specific customer.

Product planning The set of decisions about which products to offer and their prices.

Profit margin Contribution margin less the controllable cost of capacity resources.

Resource planning Decisions that pertain to improving the efficiency and effectiveness of organizational processes.

Unit-level activities Activities that are proportional to production volume.

Whale curve A curve that plots customer profitability, after ranking customers in order of their profitability. Has the appearance of a "whale."

REVIEW QUESTIONS

10.1 LO1. What is the definition of unit profit margin?

10.2 LO1. What are the four key steps in designing a product costing system?

10.3 LO1. What is a business process? How are activities and business processes related?

10.4 LO1. What is the basis that ABC systems use to form cost pools?

10.5 LO1. What is the primary criterion that we should use when choosing a driver to allocate costs from an activity pool to products?

10.6 LO2. What is practical capacity? How does it differ from budgeted capacity? How does it differ from actual capacity?

10.7 LO2. Why does allocating costs using an ABC system not change the total reported income for the organization as a whole?

10.8 LO2. What is cross-subsidization?

10.9 LO2. List three ways in which a company can improve profitability using ABC data.

10.10 LO3. What are the two key customer-planning decisions that companies face?

10.11 LO3. What are the differences between product-level profit analysis and customer-level profit analysis?

10.12 LO3. List five characteristics of customers that are "high cost-to-serve" customers. List five characteristics of customers that are "low cost-to-serve" customers.

10.13 LO3. What is a whale curve?

10.14 LO3. What is the key objective of resource-planning decisions?

10.15 LO3. What is a non-value-adding activity?

DISCUSSION QUESTIONS

10.16 LO1. Some might argue that the costs of developing a product are sunk at the time the product goes into production. Thus, these costs are not controllable for any decisions. Should we allocate these costs to products to determine their profit margin?

10.17 LO1. Suppose we are choosing between two drivers to allocate the costs in the "perform setup" cost pool: the number of setups or the number of setup hours. When will the choice not matter

(i.e., will result in the same amount costs being allocated to the various products from this pool?) What factors do we need to consider when making this choice?

10.18 LO2. What are some of the problems that we are likely to encounter in measuring practical capacity? For concreteness, consider measuring the practical capacity of a purchasing department that has five persons, and whose primary activity is issuing purchase orders.

10.19 LO2. Surveys show that over 40% of all firms do not employ ABC systems. What might be the underlying reasons for this finding?

10.20 LO2. Suppose your firm is currently employing a traditional volume-based product costing system. Further, suppose that you begin to improve this system by incrementally modifying one cost pool at a time by refining its drivers and so on. Would such actions always increase the accuracy of reported product costs? Justify your response.

10.21 LO2 (Advanced). Organizations have employed ABC systems with multiple objectives corresponding to the four reasons for allocating costs (see Chapter 9). Consider an ABC system whose primary objective is to facilitate decision making versus another whose objective is to induce desired behavior. How, if at all, would the difference in objectives manifest itself in choices regarding the number of cost pools and activity drivers?

10.22 LO3. Is the activity "inspect incoming materials for requisite quality" a value-adding activity? Justify.

10.23 LO3. Consider the retail operations for a bank. For these operations, how should the bank define its customer? Should each individual be the customer? Alternatively, should each household be the unit of analysis?

10.24 LO3. Cell phone companies, credit card issuers, and cable companies are prominent examples of firms that spend large amounts to acquire customers. How do these firms justify these investments? How could we modify the traditional customer profitability report to assess a customer's lifetime value?

10.25 LO3. Suppose a firm increased the efficiency of all of its processes. The firm needs fewer resources to produce the same volume and mix of goods and services. However, the firm does not cut spending on the resources freed up as a result. What is the effect of these actions on the firm's reported profit? What is the key additional step required to translate efficiency improvements into profit gains?

10.26 LO3. Describe a process that you undertake each day (e.g., pack for school in the morning). Further, describe how you could improve the process with virtually no investment of capital (e.g., pack the bag the prior night). Finally, describe how the change improves the process (e.g., avoids searching for items).

10.27 LO3. Iguana Insurance allows its customers to pay their premiums in full, in four quarterly payments, or as twelve monthly payments. Iguana adds a surcharge of $3 per payment if the customers choose a mode other than annual payment. It offers a rebate of $1 per payment if the customers set up an automatic withdrawal plan with their bank. How might Iguana justify these surcharges and discounts?

10.28 LO3 (Advanced). Because of the way a firm is organized, different managers (representing different regions or products) might negotiate with the same customer. Moreover, the customer's profit profile may not be the same across regions and/or products. The customer might even be a marginal or loss-making customer for some regions/product lines. Discuss the costs and benefits of alternate incentive schemes that a firm could employ to motivate its managers to consider a customer's entire relationship with the firm when negotiating with the customer.

10.29 Customer actions and resource planning, qualitative (LO3). Airlines have sought to reduce long lines by introducing self-service kiosks and on-line services for passenger check in. What might be the reasoning that underlies the introduction of such initiatives?

EXERCISES

10.30 Computing cost of activity (LO2). The University Credit Union (UCU) has engaged your services to determine the cost of its various activities. The following data are available for a representative branch.

	Process Deposits	Process Checks	Balance Inquiries	Other Activities	Total Cost
Tellers	30%	40%	10%	20%	$150,000
Assistant manager	10%	10%	5%	75%	75,000
Managers	2%	3%	5%	90%	90,000

The average branch processes 600,000 deposits and 1,250,000 check transactions each year.

Required:

Compute the cost per deposit and the cost to process a check.

10.31 Volume based and ABC allocations, manufacturing (LO2). The Acme Corporation manufactures a number of different kinds of sprinklers in three broad product lines. The following table provides relevant information about the product lines.

	Hand-Held	Lawn Sprinklers	Estate Sprinklers
Units	1,000,000	2,000,000	40,000
Price per unit	$9.00	$8.50	$15.00
Variable costs	2.00	4.00	4.50
Labor hours /unit	2.2 hours	1.9 hours	2.1 hours
Batch size	10,000 units	5,000 units	1,000 units

Currently, Acme incurs total overhead of $12,776,400 per year and allocates it to individual products using labor hours as the allocation basis.

Required:

a. Determine product profitability under the current method for allocating overhead costs.

b. Based on your answers to part (a), Acme's CEO wishes to expand the sales of estate sprinklers and deemphasize lawn sprinklers. However, because the firm's operating personnel seem cool to this idea, the CEO asks you to refine the product cost estimates and shore up her case. You find that $7,300,800 of the overhead is labor related, with the remainder relating to the number of batches run. How does this new information affect your estimates of product profitability?

10.32 Alternate allocation basis, manufacturing (LO2). Alex Rodriguez is a product manager. Historically, his product has been a mainstay for the firm, with per-unit usage of material and labor staying at the same levels. However, the firm's accounting systems show that over the past five years, this product has become more expensive to make, even after adjusting for changes in the prices of materials and labor. This period is also the time over which the firm aggressively expanded into new product lines and markets.

Alex provides you with the following data:

Number of units made   200,000
Labor hours per unit   24 minutes/unit
Overhead per unit $8.40

Alex also informs you that, under the current scheme, 70% of the firm's total overhead is allocated to his product.

Required:

a. Compute the firm's total overhead cost and the overhead rate.

b. Suppose 50% of the overhead relates to labor, meaning that it is appropriate to use labor hours as the cost driver for this pool. An additional 30% relates to batch-level cost; Alex's product consumes 45% of all batch-level activities. Of the product level costs (15% of total), only $100,000 is traceable to Alex's product and the remainder is traceable to other products. The remaining 5% represents facility-level overhead costs. Determine the overhead cost per unit for Alex's product, incorporating this additional information.

10.33 Volume and batch level Allocations, services (LO2). Marcotte and Company organizes seminars and other events for companies and professional associations. Until recently, the firm organized only large events (average of 750 persons each) and had a volume of 20 seminars per year. The past year, the firm increased its scope to include small seminars of 100 persons each as well. While this action increased total expenses to $309,000 per year, Milt Marcotte, the firm's owner and CEO, believes the action to be profit enhancing. As evidence, he points to the rapid growth of the small seminars (100 persons per seminar, 50 seminars in a year), without cutting into the number of large seminars.

Required:

a. When he only offered large seminars, Milt determined the price to charge the conference organizers by computing a cost per participant and adding a 40% markup. He continued this scheme even after he included small seminars to the product line. Under this scheme, determine the price per the average large seminar and the average small seminar.

b. One of the seminars Milt organized concerned activity-based costing. Milt caught fragments of the talk and wonders if the lessons apply to him. As a preliminary cut, he figures that costs per participant (doing mailings, preparing nametags, etc.)

cost $225,000 per year. The remainder of $84,000 per year relates to coordinating with the hotel and caterers, organizing AV equipment, hanging banners, and so on. Using activity-based costing, determine the price per large seminar and the average small seminar.

10.34 Product planning (LO2). The following table provides the ABC report for product KJ-29.

Item	Detail	Cost per Unit/Batch	Total Cost for 6,000 Units
Unit-level expenses			
Material	Traced	$0.52	
Material-related overhead	10% of materials cost	0.05	
Direct labor		4.40	
Direct labor-related overhead	120% of direct labor cost	5.28	
Machine-related overhead	($16.50/Machine. hr)	2.12	
Total per unit		12.37	$74,220
Batch-level expenses (12 batches)			
Setup	$35 per hour	$350.00	
Production order	$145 per order	145.00	
Material moves	$23.50/move	188.00	
Total per batch		683.00	8,196
Product-level expenses			945
Facility-level expenses	$0.01 per $ of unit level costs		742
Total cost			$84,103
Cost per unit			$14.017

The firm currently sells 6,000 units of KJ-29 for $16 per unit.

Required:

The firm is considering lowering the price of KJ-29 to $15.25 per unit. Because this action will increase sales by 25%, the firm is also considering increasing the batch size to 750 units. Compute expected profit if the firm implements both actions.

10.35 Activity rate, stages 1 and 2 (LO2). Yousef Ibrahim manages a plastics plant. He has provided you with the following data.

Tools, jigs and fixtures	650,000	Traceable to individual products
Machine operators	240,000	Salaried employees
Oils, coolants and lubricants	67,500	Required to operate machines
Factory power	125,000	30% is used for general heating and lighting
Machine depreciation	$1,200,000	Although the average machine lasts many years, Yousef spends considerable amounts to replace worn-out machines each year.
Factory lease	144,000	60% occupied by various machines. The plant is in year 3 of a 10-year lease.
Total costs	$2,436,500	

Yousef believes that the factory has a practical capacity of 25,000 machine hours. He wants to determine the full cost of a machine hour to use in determining his product mix over the next two to three years.

Required:

Forming a cost pool that contains all machine related costs in the above accounts, compute the overhead rate per machine hour.

10.36 Volume and ABC allocations (LO2). A world-famous photographer of wild animals and nature, Sonja Rego sells framed prints of select photographs over the Internet. Regardless of the picture bought, she offers buyers a choice in framing: a plain black frame or a fancy frame with a certificate of authenticity.

Based on initial cost estimates, Sonja believes the Deluxe frames to be more profitable than the Standard frames. However, her profits have slipped every quarter even as the proportion of Deluxe frames sold has increased. She has asked for your help in figuring out what she might be doing wrong. She provides the following data:

	Deluxe	Standard
Units/year	1,000	5,000
Price per unit	$350	$210
Materials	100	65
Labor	75	50

She further informs us that her total overhead is $390,000 per year.

Required:

a. Calculate the profit per unit for the Deluxe and Standard prints, if Sonja allocates overhead using labor hours as the allocation basis.

b. You find that only $156,000 of Sonja's cost relates directly to labor. Of the remainder, $136,500 corresponds to batch-level activities and $58,500 to product-level activities. She runs separate batches (50 prints for Deluxe, 250 for Standard) for Deluxe and Standard pictures. The product-level costs, she believes, are equally attributable to both product lines. The remaining facility-level costs relate to the rent on her studio, hosting the Web site, and other such business-sustaining actions. Prepare an income statement for Sonja, clearly highlighting the allocation from each cost pool.

c. Based on the answers to parts (a) and (b), what insights could you offer to Sonja?

10.37 Product interdependency in product planning (LO3). The QwikFill Corporation recently hired David Oxley to figure out ways to improve profit. David notes that, like virtually all gas stations, QwikFill's stations also had an air pump that customers could use to fill air in their tires. As per David's detailed cost report, an air pump's fully allocated cost is around $1,200 per year. Variable costs are negligible.

David offers two solutions. One is to eliminate the pump and save $1,200 each year. The second is to charge a quarter (25 cents) for each minute of operation. Currently, about 20 customers use the pump each day in any given gas station. The average customer takes about 3 minutes to check and inflate all tires.

Required:

a. At the current volume of operations, identify the increase in profit if David's first proposal were to be implemented at all 243 of QwikFill's stations. What is the profit with the second proposal?

b. Do you recommend following either of David's proposals? Why or why not?

10.38 Resource planning (LO3). Carolyn Evans manages the lunchroom at West High, a large (approximately 1,600 students) school in Scottsdale, Arizona. The current cash payment system requires four cashiers (paid $8 per hour), employed for about 6 hours a day. The lunchroom operates approximately 250 days a year.

Carolyn is considering an electronic system, where a student could just swipe an ID card for payment. This system would cost $15,000 to set up and $2,000 per year to operate. Carolyn believes that she could manage with two cashiers if she were to implement the system.

Required:

a. Ignoring the time value of money, estimate the five-year cost savings from implementing the system.

b. What other qualitative costs and benefits should Carolyn consider in her decision? Comment on how such process reconfigurations help improve the effectiveness of organizational resources.

10.39 Activity cost pools, financial services, qualitative (LO2). A checking account is a primary product for many banks. The typical account permits teller and ATM transactions, in addition to allowing the owner to write checks. Furthermore, while banks still mail paper statements each month (increasingly only upon request), most banks encourage account holders to check balances and perform other transactions electronically.

Required:

a. Prepare a list of activities that might help determine the cost of a checking account for the average customer. Classify each activity as a unit-level, batch- or process-level activity.

b. How might a bank use the information from the activity map to tailor multiple versions of its checking accounts?

c. Should the bank allocate the cost of advertising its checking accounts (a product-level activity) to individual accounts, when assessing its profitability?

10.40 Symptoms of failing systems. Qualitative (LO2, advanced). David Chang, a student, mows lawns part-time. He determined that the *average* lawn mowing charge in his neighborhood is $30 per lawn, and he set his price to match. Soon, he had enough demand to fill his self-imposed quota of 12 lawns. As and when existing customers decided to mow their own lawns or hired another lawn mowing service, David would seek new engagements. Over time, David notices that he is spending more and more time mowing lawns. Whereas he was devoting 15 hours a week when he started, he finds himself putting in more than 20 hours during recent times. This trend puzzles him as he is still mowing only 12 lawns per week and the average rate in the neighborhood is still $30 per lawn.

Required:

Help David understand the root causes for the increase in the time required to mow 12 lawns.

10.41 Product pricing, qualitative (LO3). United Parcel Services (UPS) is a multibillion dollar corporation that offers numerous options for shipping documents and parcels. Until the mid-1980s, UPS priced deliveries based solely on weight and on distance. During this era, UPS used trucks to move most goods, and it focused on delivering small parcels to businesses. However, after deregulation of interstate freight and the emergence of competition such as FedEx, UPS's pricing for the same service now considers many factors such as the time of pickup/delivery, place of pickup/delivery, size of package, and customer ID in addition to weight and distance.

Required:

a. Why might these factors be relevant for pricing parcel delivery in this now intensely competitive business?

b. How might ABC help UPS with its attempt to discern the costs of various types of services and to fine-tune its pricing strategy?

PROBLEMS

10.42 Volume based and ABC allocations, distribution (LO2). Jim Vermeer is a flower wholesaler. Jim prices his product (as is the industry custom) at 12 cents over the price he pays to the exporter. Current volume is 50,000 stems per day. Jim is happy with this state of affairs as it costs him only 10 cents per stem in overhead charges (i.e., his overhead cost is $150,000 per month or $5,000 per day).

Jim's daughter recently joined the business. Exploiting her artistic talents, JoAnne expanded the product line to include bouquets. The average bouquet contains 24 stems and yields a contribution of 15 cents per stem.

Jim is delighted at this chance to increase his profit per stem. Indeed, he is considering expanding the bouquet business from 10 to 30% of his overall volume. However, his enthusiasm is somewhat tempered because his profit has dropped to only $750 a day, even though total daily volume is steady at 50,000 stems. He knows that there is more work in assembling a bouquet but has no reason to doubt the cost system that has worked well for many years.

Required:

a. Compute Jim's overhead using the new product mix, profit, and contribution margins.

b. How could expanding into a product line with higher contribution margin erode the firm's profit margin?

c. What features of the new business line might account for the surge in overhead?

10.43 ABC allocations, service (LO2). Vanessa Xu is the general manager for "The Grand" Hotel in Hong Kong. Vanessa is pondering about how to respond to a request from a major client regarding long-stay rates. A long stay would be a single visit of a week or more.

Vanessa has assembled the following data to help with her decision.

Regular room rate	HK$1,800 per day	At current rates USD1 = HK$7.8.
Variable cost	HK$150 per day	Cleaning, supplies, water, utilities
Room maintenance	HK$300 every three days	The hotel changes sheets every three days as a matter of course. However, the hotel will change sheets everyday if asked. Most people do not request new sheets every day. Of course, the hotel changes sheets when a guest departs.
Check in and Check out	HK$150 per guest; HK$250 for long-stay guests	Includes cost of welcome basket (cost: HK$150) for long-stay guests
Concierge service	HK$100 per day for first 3 days. HK$50 per day afterwards.	Usage declines as guests become more independent and less reliant on the hotel's services
Guest spending on meals, etc.	HK$450 per day	The hotel's variable cost is 40% of billed amounts
Guest spending on miscellaneous services	HK$400 per short-term guest; HK$2,500 for long-stay guests.	The hotel's variable cost is 40% of billed amount.

Required:

a. Compute the total cost of a long stay (9 days average) and a short stay (2 days) guest.

b. What advice do you give Vanessa Xu re the price discount to offer the client for long-stay guests?

10.44 Volume based and ABC allocations, batch size and pricing (LO2). Anna works for a firm that makes a machine that makes single shots of coffee, teas, and espresso-based drinks using a proprietary "pod" technology. The average pack of pods (with 12–16 pods) sells for $8.99 and has a unit contribution margin of $4.00. The typical order is for four packs. While some orders are for four packs of the same drink, the average order contains two separate kinds of drinks (e.g., 3 packs of coffee and 1 of tea). Currently, the customer pays a shipping fee of $2.99 per order, regardless of the number of packs in the order. The firm projects sales of 4 million packs this year.

Anna is considering free shipping for orders for six or more packs. She believes that because it would increase average order size, the promotion would decrease the total number of orders to 60% of the current volume. However, only half of all orders would qualify for free shipping. Finally, the larger order size would also increase the kinds of drinks per order to three (from the current two kinds per order).

Anna notes that whenever an order comes in, the firm has to pick and put the requisite packs into a carton (for shipping), at a cost of $0.10 per pack. Moreover, each kind of drink in the order adds $0.50 to the cost of processing an order. Finally, the firm incurs costs of $6.00 per order to pack and ship the order. (For simplicity, assume that packing and shipping costs are the same regardless of order size.)

Required:

Evaluate the merits of Anna's idea.

10.45 Computing cost of activity, stage 1 (LO2). Sheila Baldwin is a manager for Bath Technologies, a firm that makes designer bathtubs and bath fixtures. You collect the following data from interviewing Sheila.

• There are nine people in her department, including Sheila. Five of the staff members are paid $60,000 each, the two assistant managers are paid $90,000 each, Sheila earns $120,000, and her administrative assistant earns $35,000. Sheila's department is responsible for inventory management, production planning, and purchasing.

• Two staff members work exclusively on inventory management and one staff member each is devoted to production planning and purchasing. The fifth staff person splits her time equally on inventory management, production planning, and purchasing activities. One assistant manager is responsible for production planning, and the other for purchasing.

- Sheila spends about 30% of her time overseeing the managers and staff. She also spends 10% of her time attending meetings with senior managers and coordinating with other departments. She spends the remaining time on inventory management.

- The administrative assistant spends 75% of his time working for Sheila, and the remainder for the two assistant managers.

- Accounting records indicate that Sheila's department spent $75,000 last year on supplies, travel, and other items. Accounting tells you that it is difficult to break out the expense by person as it would require some manual sorting of travel records and such. Sheila believes that each activity consumes supplies equally.

Required:

Allocate the cost of Sheila's department among the activities performed.

10.46 Computing activity cost, stages 1 and 2 (LO2). Lim Chee Wah is conducting a study of order processing costs for his company, a wholesaler of Chinese handicrafts. He has identified that every new customer order triggers the following actions.

- Sales representatives generate customer orders and enter them into the system. The firm estimates that each of its six salespersons earns $65,000 annually. Total order volume in a typical year is 5,000 orders. Sales representatives spend 80% of their time in these activities.

- The shipping department assembles the various products contained in the order, and then packs and ships the order. The shipping department employs two people full time and occupies 12,000 square feet of warehouse space. These two persons are paid $40,000 each; warehouse rental and upkeep is $48,000 for the year. The employees believe that 70% of their time is devoted to assembling, packing, and shipping an order. They estimate the time needed to enter the order into the system and such at 20%. These employees are also responsible for the general upkeep of the warehouse (10% of time).

- The Accounting Department issues an invoice, once per month, for each customer who has placed an order or has an outstanding balance. This invoice lists all of the orders placed that month. Most customers place multiple orders each month. The accounting manager estimates her department's budget at $140,000 and believes that invoicing and collections occupy 30% of her department's time. She believes that 40% of her department's effort is spent on coordinating purchases, 10% is spent on payroll, and 20% on general accounting and special projects.

Required:

Collecting all costs related to order processing in one pool and using expected activity levels as the denominator volume, compute the cost to process a customer order. Be sure to justify your choice if you exclude any of the costs listed above from the order-processing cost pool.

10.47 Customer planning (LO3). Aqua Distribution buys bottled water at $12 per case and sells it to retail clients at $14.40 per case. Data pertaining to four customers are as follows:

	Quinn	Ralph	Sutliffe	Thorne
Cases sold	8,750	60,800	31,800	3,900
Actual price	$14.16	$13.20	$13.92	$12.96
Number of orders	25	30	25	30
Customer visits	3	6	2	3
Deliveries	30	60	40	20
Miles/delivery	4	3	8	40
Expedited deliveries	0	0	0	1

The firm estimates the following rates:

Number of orders	$100 per order (number of cases in a order varies)
Customer visits	$80 per visit
Delivery	$2 per delivery mile traveled
Product handling	$0.50 per case sold
Expedited deliveries	$300 per incident

Required:

Evaluate customer profitability and suggest remedial actions if necessary.

10.48 Customer planning (LO3). Sylvester Steel manufactures specialty steel in various forms (ingots, wires, rounds, and so on). In essence, the firm melts scrap steel, adds trace elements (e.g., magnesium), and processes the resulting alloy. The firm has provided you with data regarding the following three customers.

	Customer A	Customer B	Customer C
Annual sales volume	$1.3 million	$1.2 million	$850,000
Average contribution margin ratio (based on last year's mix)	25%	30%	22%
Number of orders	8	4	6
Number of shipments	12	4	12
Number of order changes	3	0	5
Days outstanding for receivables (average)[1]	8	29	38
Requests for new products	0	0	2

[1] Sylvester offers 1% cash discount if the invoice is paid within 10 days of invoicing date. (All invoices are transmitted electronically.)

[1] Sylvester offers 1% cash discount if the invoice is paid within 10 days of invoicing date. (All invoices are transmitted electronically.)

Sylvester's management gives the following results from a detailed study of its cost structure.

Transaction	Revenue/Cost
Number of orders	$300 per order
Number of shipments	$500 per shipment
Number of order changes	$2,500 per change
Cost of capital	15%
Requests for new products	$10,000 to develop a new product

Required:

a. Compute the profitability of the three representative customers.

b. What actions do you recommend that Sylvester initiate to improve the profitability of these representative customers?

 10.49 Customer planning ((LO2, LO3). The University Credit Union has provided you with data regarding representative clients from three broad market segments.

	Student	Homeowners	Retirees
Checking account balance	$250	$1,100	$800
Teller transactions per month	0.5	1	2
ATM transactions per month	8	4	0.5
Number of checks	0	4	7
Number of telephone enquiries	0	2	1
Number of bills via Bill Pay	0	20	0
Number of overdrafts	0.25	0.1	0
Average savings balance	$5	$100	$5,000
Credit card balance	$450	0	$0
Safe deposit box (% of customers)	2%	90%	80%
Auto loan (% of customers)	20%	0%	5%
Electronic statement (% of customers)	90%	40%	2%
Monthly household income	<$1,000	$5,500	$3,000
Household net worth	<$55,000	$75,000	$45,000

The UCU informs you that it earns 6% per year on deposits and pays out 4% for savings accounts. Checking accounts do not earn interest, unless the balance is over $1,000, in which case they earn 3%. The bank also has conducted a detailed ABC study that reveals the following:

Transaction	Revenue/Cost
Teller transactions per month	$2
ATM transactions	$0.25
Number of checks	$0.03 per check
Number of telephone enquiries	$0.50
Number of overdrafts	Bank charges $10, but incurs little cost
Credit card balance	Earn interest at 24% per annum
Safe deposit box	Average box loses $10 per year. This is seen as an "essential service."
Bill Pay	$0.02 per bill paid by bank,
Auto loan	Average loan balance is $5,000, and annual profit margin is 10% of balance.
Cost per statement	$1.50

Required:

a. Compute the monthly profitability of the three representative accounts.

b. What actions do you recommend that UCU initiate to improve its profitability?

10.50 Process simplification (LO3). Moin Ahmed is a process engineer at Xyon Technologies, which manufactures power supply systems. Moin notices that one of the steps involved requires 4.2 hours of setup per batch. The firm currently estimates setup costs to be $65 per hour.

Moin believes that the firm should acquire quick-change dies that could be preloaded when the current job is still running. These dies, specific to each product, cost $5,000 each and would last two years. With the dies, setup times would be reduced to 5 minutes per changeover. Moin argues that acquiring the dies makes sense from a strategic perspective. The dies would allow the company to reduce batch size from 750 units per batch to a much smaller number. This reduction would reduce inventories, thereby adding to the company's flexibility in matching demand with supply. He also thinks that the change would improve product quality because it might be easier to detect errors in a smaller batch.

Required:

a. Compute the cost savings from acquiring the quick-change die for a product with an annual volume of 6,000 units and for a product with an annual volume of 7,500 units.

b. Considering the qualitative benefits, what do you recommend?

10.51 Resource planning, classifying activities (LO3). Spring Distribution has expanded its operations into a number of different soft drinks. It has classified its warehousing activities into the following steps (the steps are scrambled and not in the sequence performed):

	Activity	Hours
A.	Products physically stored	1,400
B.	Location of product to ship identified	700
C.	Inventory records updated for supply	200
D.	Vehicle unloaded (for supplies)	1,300
E.	Products checked for damage	500
F.	Return damaged product to supplier	300
G.	Products compared to purchase order	400
H.	Incorrect products sent back to supplier	300
I.	Products labeled and packaged per customer order	400
J.	Orders placed on loading dock for shipment	30
K.	Vehicle loaded for shipment to customer	1,400
L.	Invoice and notification prepared	400
M.	Products retrieved from storage	1,500
N.	Inventory records updated for shipment	500

Required:

a. Suppose Spring Fresh staffs its warehouse with a five-person team. Average annual salary is $32,000, based on 2,000 hours per person. Compute the cost of unused capacity.

b. Suggest actions that might help Spring Distribution manage its warehousing costs. You might wish to begin rearranging the steps into a logical flow and then rating each activity on a 1- to 5-point scale with 5 being the highly valued and 1 as non-value-adding. Generate an estimate of possible cost savings.

10.52 Effective resource usage (LO3). The following data pertain to usage at the computer lab for a business school.

Activity	Percent of Users Accessing Application during Session	Percent of Time that the Application Is "Active"	Average Time Application Is Used
E-mail	90%	30%	5 minutes
Printing	60%	10%	10 minutes
Web browsing	70%	20%	20 minutes
Course management	40	5%	5 minutes
Word, Excel, …	35%	25%	45 minutes
Course specific (e.g., simulation game)	10%	5%	35 minutes
Other	5%	5%	20 minutes

* Total of percent used exceeds 100% because many users access more than one application during a session. The percent time is the time when the application is "active" during the session.

The director of the computer lab wonders if this current usage pattern is the best use of the state-of–the-art machines in the computer lab. She notes that students often stand in line for 15 minutes or more to check email for 5 minutes or to use course management software (e.g., blackboard or WebCT) to print the notes and other handouts (again, a 5-minute job). Finally, the director notes that machines that are several years old can easily accommodate these tasks. While the director has 20 to 30 of these old machines in storage, the computer lab does not have space to deploy them.

Required:

Offer three suggestions that might help improve the usage of the computer lab. Please identify salient costs and benefits for each option.

10.53 Product pricing (LO2, LO3). Insight Research uses focus groups and other techniques to test consumer reaction to new products. The CEO, Manasee Agrawal, is puzzled as to why her profits are so much lower than expected even though her total volume is per projections.

She informs you that she charges client companies $50 per participant. As anticipated, she billed $4 million this year for 80,000 participants. She is proud that she has increased the number of distinct products tested from 10 last year to 18 this year. However, she thinks that she might have taken on too many jobs that did not involve national testing (400–600 groups per product) but rather involved regional tests only (150–300 groups per product). Each group typically has 10 to 20 consumers.

Manasee also informs you that her primary costs are payments to participants ($30 per participant). She also incurs setup costs of about $300 per group session. Setting up a national test incurs up-front costs of $15,000. A regional test costs $10,000.

Required:

a. Suppose Manasee expected to handle eight national products and seven regional products this year for a total of 4,500 groups and 80,000 participants. Estimate her total profit for this mix of groups and jobs.

b. Suppose the actual data show that Manasee had 6 national and 12 regional jobs for this year. The average national job only had 500 groups, and the average regional job had 250 groups. Compute Manasee's profit with the realized product mix.

c. Comment on the discrepancy between her projected and actual profit.

10.54 Cost estimation for changing product mix, Not-for-profit (LO2). Manuela Gomez is the director of a nongovernment organization (NGO) that operates eye clinics in developing nations. The NGO contracts with leading eye surgeons in Europe and the United States (usually, physicians donate their services) to set up clinics for diagnosing and treating diseases such as macular degeneration. Manuela's problem concerns clinic location: whether to operate fewer large clinics in a central town or many smaller clinics in outlying areas.

Manuela informs you that it costs $5,000 to set up a clinic in a major town. Equipped like a mini-hospital, such a clinic facilitates advanced treatments. This clinic usually is in place for two weeks and can treat 1,000 patients during this period. About 50 of these cases require advanced treatment. The clinics attract many people from nearby areas. However, it is also true that some patients have to travel many miles (some came from as far as 200 miles away), enduring difficult traffic conditions. Most patients consume supplies worth $3; however, each patient with an advanced condition consumes supplies worth $250.

The alternative is to use the time to set up three smaller clinics (three to four days each) in outlying areas. Each of the smaller clinics costs $2,500 to set up. Travel adds another $1,500 or so to the costs per clinic. The smaller clinics cannot deal with advanced cases but can reach people who otherwise could not get treatment. Usually, each small clinic handles about 250 patients, although the physicians have to turn away patients with advanced conditions. Variable costs for each patient amounted to $3.

For this year, Manuela's NGO offered three large trips and seven small trips.

Required:

a. The sponsoring agency has requested that Manuela's NGO become more cost efficient in delivering its services. Recent media articles about excessive spending by NGO and lack of controls prompted a clamp-down on costs. Calculate the current year's cost per patient.

b. Help Manuela prepare a budget for the forthcoming year. She expects to offer six trips with small clinics and four trips with large clinics during the year. Use the cost per patient to estimate total costs for the year. Do you trust this estimate?

c. What justifications would you offer to the funding agency for why it should fund the higher cost per patient?

10.55 ABC implementation, choices in system design (LO2). Bill Huang is one of six salespersons who worked for GT Corporation, a firm specializing in industrial gears. GT has recently implemented activity-based costing at its factory and is in the process of expanding the application to include its sales force. In particular, GT is interested in estimating the cost to serve each customer. To this end, GT accumulates the cost of the sales staff as follows:

Salaries and benefits	$330,000
Travel	32,000
Office supplies	12,400
Total	$374,400

GT believes that all other sales-related expenses, such as the rent for the sales building, are not controllable in the medium term and are not directly related to the number of sales orders. GT wishes to allocate the total cost of each sales person to its customers based on the number of sales calls made. The sales team made 1,440 calls for the last year.

Bill believes that this method is flawed. He says that while larger customers may have fewer sales calls, each sales call lasts a long time. It is not unusual for the salesman to spend the entire day with the larger customer. It also is common for the salesman to visit two or three smaller customers in a day. Most of Bill's customers are smaller customers. If these customers are deemed unprofitable, Bill will have less leeway in dealing with them. In addition, Bill believes that the firm should distinguish among local and long-distance customers. All of Bill's customers are within easy driving distance, and Bill believes that their "cost to serve" should not include any allocation for travel expenses.

Required:

a. Compute the cost per order, as the firm currently calculates it.

b. Evaluate the merits of Bill's arguments.

10.56 Practical capacity, classroom (Appendix). Barry Butler is the dean of the Engineering School at State University. Barry's data indicate that the Bio-Mechanical Engineering Department offers six elective classes using two faculty. (The standard load is three sections per academic year per faculty person.) The department offers these classes in 35-seat classrooms, as smaller classrooms do not contain the required equipment. The department, however, has only 20 students; all of them take all six elective classes. No other students take these specialized elective classes. Estimating the cost of a faculty person at $125,000 per year and capacity utilization at 58% (= 20 students/35 seats), Barry estimates the cost of the unused capacity at $105,000. (Barry multiplies $125,000 per faculty person $\times$ 2 faculty persons $\times$ $(1 - 0.58)$ = cost of unused capacity). He informs the department chair that she must decrease this waste of valuable resources or risk being closed down.

Required:

Focusing just on elective classes, is Barry correct in asserting that the Bio Mechanical Department is not fully utilizing its capacity? What is the capacity resource in this setting, and what is the right measure of capacity utilization?

10.57 Effect of loss of product (Appendix). Innova Machines (Pvt) Limited, located in Chennai, India, supplies automotive components to two-wheeler (scooters, motorcycles, mopeds, and such) manufacturers. A dozen major customers located within India account for most of its sales. The largest customer accounted for 20% of the sales, and the smallest accounted for about 6% of the sales volume. As elsewhere in the world, the market for automotive components is extremely competitive, and price is the key determinant of which supplier gets the order.

For 2006, management estimated materials cost at Rs. 80,000,000 (Rs. denotes Rupees—Rupee is the Indian currency), labor at Rs. 120,000,000, and manufacturing overhead at Rs. 75,000,000. The (industry) standard of 15% markup on manufacturing cost yielded total revenue of Rs. 316,250,000. The firm made a modest profit after accounting for selling and administration expenses.

One of Innova's smaller customers (accounting for 8% of sales) went bankrupt and closed at the end of 2006. Innova's management tried hard to replace the business but was unsuccessful, and budgeted manufacturing overhead at Rs. 72 million for 2007. They then computed prices based using the standard markup.

Despite heroic efforts from its sales force, the firm lost another customer in 2007— a customer who accounted for 15% of 2006 sales. Despite another saving of Rs. 7 million in budgeted overhead costs for 2008, it appeared that the firm had succumbed to nimbler competitors making the product at lower cost.

Required:

Help management figure out what is going on. (*Hint:* Compute the overhead rate per labor Rupee over time, assuming that labor cost will decline proportionately as demand declines).

10.58 Allocations in new product setting, choice of denominator (Appendix, Advanced). Vijay Srirangan, a successful entrepreneur, set up Indipan Industries to manufacture and sell convenience gadgets such as rice cookers, steamers, and tabletop grills to the burgeoning middle class in India. He believed strongly that, with the rise of two-career couples, the demand for these products would skyrocket. He wanted in on the ground floor!

Vijay teamed up with a well-known Japanese firm to set up his plant with the capacity to produce 50,000 rice cookers per month. However, because the product was new to most consumers in the target market, current production is only 20,000 cookers per month.

Vijay's total materials cost is Indian Rs. 6 million, and labor cost is Rs.9 million. Overhead amounts to an additional Rs.18 million per month. Vijay seeks his accountant's help in pricing the cooker. The accountant divides the total cost of Rs. 33 million per month into the expected production volume of 20,000 cookers, and determines the cost per cooker to be Rs. 1,650. With a nominal markup of 10%, the accountant recommends pricing the product at Rs. 1,850 per cooker.

Vijay is not happy with this estimate. He believes that he can sell fewer than 7,500 cookers a month if he prices them at Rs. 1,850 each. He had used a price of Rs. 1,400 per cooker when projecting demand at 20,000 cookers a month. He believes that eventually, the consumer will value convenience, and demand will rise to 50,000 cookers per month, as long as the price is less than Rs. 1,500 per cooker.

Required:

a. Do you believe that the accountant's cost estimate accurately reflects the cost to produce each cooker? Why or why not?

b. Vijay's marketing manager argues that the accountant's cost estimate is high only because the factory is operating under capacity. She argues that, with full production of 50,000 cookers, the cost per cooker is only Rs. 1,110 (= Rs 300 for materials +

Rs. 450 for labor + Rs. 360 for overhead). A 10% markup then leads to a price of about Rs. 1,250 per cooker. Evaluate the merits of this argument.

c. Suppose that Vijay follows his marketing manager's recommendation and allocates only Rs. 360 (= Rs. 18 million/50,000 cookers) to each cooker. How should Vijay deal with the cost of unused capacity of 30,000 cookers?

MINI-CASES

10.59 ABC Allocations & pricing (LO3). Carolyn McKinsey is in charge of the copy center at Midwest University's Business College. Carolyn seeks your help in figuring out how she should price the course packets that she prepares for many of the courses offered in the college. Her internal customers for course packets are the academic departments. The school charges each student a fixed fee for textbooks and notes, with each student getting the appropriate books and notes during the first class.

After investigating her costs and analyzing her operations, you determine that her major activities comprise the following:

Obtain copyrights for articles	This step applies to some articles only. The copy center must repeat this step each semester, even if the same article is used. Carolyn handled this step and estimated that a small course pack (5 or fewer articles) took about an hour to complete. Every additional article would consume about 10 minutes. The average fee is $2 per article.
Make a master copy	This step is done once per course pack. Faculty members usually change the pack slightly each semester, meaning that a new master must be made. Her assistant took ½ hour per course pack for this step.
Set up machine	Load the appropriate type of cover, printing, and binding options. The staff person handled this chore and consumed ½ hour per order. This step was taken each time the job was run, regardless of the number of copies made.
Print and bind the copies	The number of copies made depends on the order from the department. Each course pack contains a different number of pages. Traditionally, the academic departments underestimate the number of copies needed. When enrollment is finalized, they ask for a rush job to make up the shortfall. Student assistants ran the copy machine. Carolyn insisted that a student stand by the machine in case of paper jams and such. The last thing she desires is for the machine to break down at the start of a semester.
Deliver to classroom	The number of deliveries depends on the number of sections. One delivery per 30 course packs is a good rule of thumb. The student assistants did the delivery, averaging about ½ hour for each delivery.

Carolyn's primary costs comprised the following.

Copy paper	$0.02 per sheet.
Other supplies (binders, clips, and so on)	$2,500 per semester
Copy machine supplies	$0.01 per copy made (cost of toner etc)
Copy machine capacity	The manufacturer advertises the machine cost (including maintenance) as only $0.01 per copy and is the lowest in the industry. The manufacturer arrived at this number by dividing the total machine cost (including machine supplies) by the total number of copies over its lifetime. The machine could print 60 copies per minute. An average course pack contained 240 pages. Some course packs, though, were only 30 pages, and others were "monsters" that ran to 500+ pages.
Personnel	$35,000 for Carolyn, $27,500 for her one assistant. Student employees are paid $8 per hour. Carolyn and her assistant worked 2,000 hours each year. The university does not charge the Center for the space and power used, for the furniture, and so on.

Required:

a. Help Carolyn develop the price for a course pack that contains 12 articles (7 copyrighted) and that contains 240 copies (120 sheets of paper with double-sided printing). The instructor estimates the demand at 30 students. (*Note*: It is much easier to work with total costs than cost per pack.)

b. The day before classes began, the instructor for the class discovered that actual enrollment is 40 students. Thus, Carolyn has to run an extra 10 copies. What is the cost of the resources consumed by the additional run?

c. The head of the Management and Organizations Department (a department that has many classes with large course packs) believes that the pricing scheme should only include the cost of papers and other consumables. He argues that the cost of the machine, Carolyn's salary, and other such expenses are fixed costs and therefore are not relevant for the pricing decision. He further argues that this is a short-term decision because each course pack is valid only for one semester. Evaluate the merits of this argument.

 10.60 Volume based allocations, inventory values, rationing scarce resource, & ABC (LO1, LO2 and LO3). Mark Ahren is an award-winning potter whose primary products are custom-designed cups and mugs in unique shapes. Mark estimates that the variable costs (clay bisque, pigments, glaze, and so on) are $3.50 per mug. He estimates 75% of this cost relates to materials, and the other 25% to labor and variable overhead. The average mug weighs a pound and sells for $13.

Mark also incurs costs for operating his office ($50,750 per year), travel to fairs, and so on ($26,250), and, most important, for firing his custom-built, high-temperature oven ($77,000).

For the past couple of years, Mark has expanded his product line to include larger items such as water pitchers and vases. Pitchers weigh in at 2 pounds per unit, have a variable cost of $6 per unit, and retail for $20. Corresponding data for vases are 3 pounds, $8 per unit, and $24 per unit. Mark believes that materials constitute 75% of the variable cost for these items as well. For the coming year, he estimates producing 29,000 mugs and 3,000 units each of the larger items, or 35,000 pieces in total.

Mark emphasizes the importance of having a high-quality reliable oven in his line of work. Indeed, he tells you that the oven capacity essentially controls what he could do in terms of product volume. In particular, he claims that he could easily hire more labor to mix the clay and do other miscellaneous tasks. While it might take several months, he also believes that he could also expand his sales and administrative capacity by hiring appropriate staff. However, replacing the oven will take close to two years. In addition to the substantial investment, Mark has to coordinate with the manufacturer so that the oven meets Mark's exacting specifications. Mark notes that he started with a smallest possible oven, with a capacity of 25,000 pounds. Each replacement oven has been larger, although he thinks he might have reached the limit for a single oven.

Finally, because of the time required to set up, load, and unload the oven, Mark could fire the oven only 200 times (or about 40,000 pounds) per year. He could produce 250 mugs, 50 vases, or 100 pitchers per firing. Mark is careful to note that the actual number of firings in any given year might be a bit higher or lower. Moreover, he observes that the time required for a firing depends on the weight of the products fired. Because most firings have a combination of mugs, vases, and pitchers, the actual time per firing of the oven varies quite a bit.

Required:

a. Suppose Mark allocates all overhead to products using the number of units as the allocation basis. Determine the unit contribution and unit profit margin for each of Mark's three product lines. What is the implication for which products to emphasize and which to deemphasize?

b. Repeat requirement (a) assuming that Mark allocates all overhead using the number of pounds as the allocation basis. What is the implication for which products to emphasize and which to deemphasize?

c. Continue with pounds as the allocation basis. For each product, what value could Mark attach to a unit in inventory? Recall that Mark would employ this unit for computing reported income, meaning that the allocation choices must conform with GAAP.

d. Is there a clear choice for the basis (pounds versus units) that Mark should choose for valuing inventory? for assessing product profitability? Justify your answer.

e. Mark also learns about activity-based costing. Again, he understands the logic of this method. He therefore wants to compute product profitability using the expected number of firings (200) to allocate oven-related costs and the number of units to allocate selling costs. He wants to allocate all other costs at the rate of $0.10 per revenue dollar. Perform this computation and rank order products as per their ABC profit margin.

f. Compute Mark's total income using ABC to allocate costs. Why do you expect this income to be the same (subject to rounding) as the income computed when you use the number of units to allocate costs?

g. Under what conditions would you expect the ABC income you computed for part (g) to differ from the income reported under GAAP?

h. By now, Mark is thoroughly confused as to which of his three products is the most profitable, and deserves more emphasis in his product mix. Please be sure to outline the implicit assumptions and requirements for each of the methods (the two volume-based allocations, inventory value, and ABC).

10.61 Refining Cost Drivers. LO1-LO3. Tom and Lynda are considering several actions in response to another gym opening nearby. Tom believes that Hercules should focus on actions that target family memberships, as he believes family memberships to be more profitable than individual memberships. He therefore wishes to add more classes and other activities of greater interest to families. Lynda is less sure because she thinks that families also use the gym more intensively. She thinks that individuals might cost less (even if their apparent usage is more) because they tend to focus on using easy to maintain and long-lasting exercise equipment (e.g., dumbbells) rather than costly items such as the pool. They provide the following data regarding uses and costs.

	Individuals	Family
Number of memberships	500	200
Persons per membership (average)	1	2
# of visits per month per person	8	2
Minutes on exercise equipment per month	120	30
# of class sessions attended per person	3	12
Minutes on cardio machines per month per person	120	120
# of visits to pool per person	0.2	0.5
% of members paying with credit card	0.5	0.8
Membership fee per month	$100	$160

Variable costs

Supplies—towels, etc.	22,500
Supplies—for classes	2,500
Water (50% relates to pool and 50% relates to showers)	3,000
Credit card fees	1,012

Fixed costs

Estimated wear and tear on cardio equipment	1,500
Estimated wear and tear on weights and related equipment	900
Instructor salaries and other class-related costs	12,000
Pool maintenance	1,200
Utilities (electric and gas)	2,500
Staff salaries (front desk, office)	13,500
Rental and maintenance for building	5,000
Other admin expenses	3,500
Total costs	$69,112

Required:

a. Calculate profit per individual and family membership. Allocate all costs (fixed and variable) using the number of visits as the allocation basis.

b. Calculate profit per individual and family membership. Develop suitable drivers for each of the costs except for the items deemed to be facility-level costs.

c. Based on your answers to the above parts, what advice do you offer Tom and Lynda?

d. Would you classify the analysis in part (b) as activity-based costing?

 10.62 LO1, LO2, LO3. ABC model of product costs. Zeus Optical is a specialist manufacturer of optical instruments. Zeus has recently expanded its core product market of binoculars into making eyepieces for microscopes/telescopes, and screw-on lenses for digital SLR cameras. The firm believes that it makes little money selling binoculars, and that these new markets have great profit potential.

Somewhat to Zeus's surprise, it finds it tough to make money with eyepieces. As of now, the firm is selling the product at a negative profit margin. Yet, Zeus faces intense price pressure in this segment and thinks that it might have to lower prices by 5% or more to stay competitive. The market for binoculars has been stable for several years, and Zeus expects the trends to continue for the near future. Zeus is most excited about entering the market for screw-on lenses for digital SLR cameras. Although current volumes are small (relatively), Zeus believes that there is substantial market potential for this product. Leveraging its excellent reputation for optics and lenses, Zeus believes that it could reach and sustain three times the current volume of this product. This strategy also makes sense financially as this product is the most profitable of the three lines, per the firm's accounting records.

The following table provides key information about the product lines. (*Note:* All data have been disguised for confidentiality. However, relations among data items have been preserved.)

	Eyepieces	Binoculars	Camera Lens
Sales volume (units)	16,000	20,000	3,000
Price	**$53.00**	**$78.00**	**$160.00**
Unit variable cost	30.00	45.00	118.00
Unit contribution margin	$23.00	$33.00	$42.00
Unit profit margin	($2.50)	$0.70	$6.30
Labor hours/unit	1.5	1.9	2.1

Currently, the firm incurs $1,161,100 in overhead costs annually. It allocates this overhead among product lines using the number of labor hours used by each product line. Zeus's management realizes that moving to camera lenses is a major shift in their product and market focus. Moreover, they know that factory personnel have complained about the increased coordination required for producing lenses. Thus, management wants you to conduct a detailed study of product costs.

You collect the following data.

	Eyepieces	Binoculars	Camera Lens
Sales volume (units)	16,000	20,000	3,000
batch size	3,200	1,000	200
# of batches	5	20	15
# of receiving transactions	20	35	50
# of products	1	1	1
Components	2	6	20

Analyzing the overhead, you discover the following:

Item	Amount
Labor related	$341,500
Machine related	273,200
Production order	88,000
First part inspection	100,000
Inventory management	110,000
Receiving and shipping	46,250
Parts administration	90,000
General administration	112,150
Total	$1,161,100

You are wondering how best to allocate these costs into cost pools. You settle on forming five pools.

- Volume-related costs, allocated to products using labor hours.
- Cost related to executing a production order (this would include first part inspections), allocated using the number of batches.
- Costs related to inventory, receiving, and shipping. These costs would be allocated using the number of transactions per product line (= components × number of transactions).
- Costs related to parts administration, which will be equally shared by all product lines.
- Facility-level costs. You decide not to allocate these costs to individual product lines, reasoning that these costs are not controllable at the product level.

Required:

a. Verify the profit margin data reported in the problem text, using the current allocation system.

b. Compute the amounts in the five cost pools and the rate per driver unit for each cost pool.

c. Using the driver rates you computed in part (b), determine the product cost for each product line. That is, compute the profit margin for each product line using activity-based costing.

d. Based on the ABC profit margins, what actions would you recommend for Zeus's management.

e. How could you further improve the accuracy of reported product costs, using the ABC system? Be sure to indicate the additional data, if any, which you might need to implement your suggestions.

Chapter 11

Managing Long-Lived Resources: Capital Budgeting

As THE CHIEF ADMINISTRATOR OF
St. Vincent's Hospital, Dr. Maria Rodriguez is facing increasing pressure to acquire magnetic resonance imaging (MRI) equipment. St. Vincent's patients now get the needed tests done at a nearby hospital. However, Dr. Rodriguez knows that St. Vincent's patients often must endure long waits for their appointments. She is concerned that these delays could tarnish St. Vincent's reputation and erode its customer base. Preliminary inquiries indicate that setting up an MRI facility, which has an estimated life of 10 years, will require an outlay of $1.5 million.

Before committing to such a large expenditure, Dr. Rodriguez needs to know whether St. Vincent's would recoup the $1.5 million through future benefits. She also needs to ensure that purchasing the MRI equipment is the best use of St. Vincent's limited capital.

APPLYING THE DECISION FRAMEWORK

What Is the Problem?
Dr. Rodriguez of St. Vincent's Hospital wonders whether it is worthwhile to acquire magnetic resonance imaging (MRI) equipment.

What Are the Options?
The options are to acquire MRI equipment or to continue with the current arrangement of patients getting the tests done at a nearby hospital.

What Are the Costs and Benefits?
The new MRI equipment will require a large up-front expenditure. In addition, the hospital will incur both variable and fixed operating costs. However, St. Vincent's will increase its revenue. Additional considerations include more timely diagnosis and treatment, and increased customer satisfaction, as well as the potential increase in exposure to a malpractice suit.

Make the Decision!
Using the tools for capital budgeting, we will estimate the financial impact of acquiring the MRI equipment. Based on our analysis, along with an understanding of the nonfinancial factors, we will be able to recommend a course of action for Dr. Rodriguez.

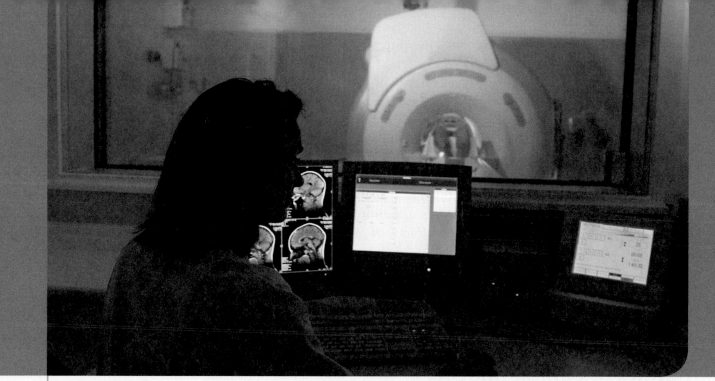

Dr. Rodriguez of St. Vincent's is considering whether to invest in MRI equipment.

LEARNING OBJECTIVES

After studying this chapter, you will be able to:

1 Understand the reasons for capital budgeting.

2 List the components of a project's cash flows.

3 Apply discounted cash flow techniques.

4 Compare various methods for evaluating projects.

5 Explain the role of taxes and the depreciation tax shield in project evaluation.

6 Describe issues in allocating scarce capital among projects.

In Chapters 9–10, we examined a number of long-term decisions involving the acquisition and disposal of capacity resources. In our discussions, however, we did not consider that money has a time value: a dollar today is worth more than a dollar tomorrow. We also did not consider that capacity resources are "lumpy." That is, capacity resources come in discrete sizes—we cannot buy part of a car or an MRI machine. These considerations are especially important in the acquisition of long-lived resources. In this chapter, we discuss capital budgeting, a tool that explicitly incorporates the time value of money and the lumpy nature of resources in decisions involving significant long-term investments.

We begin this chapter by examining why organizations use capital budgets to evaluate expenditures on long-lived, or capacity, resources and list the features of capital budgets. We then illustrate techniques such as net present value (NPV) and internal rate of return (IRR) analyses that firms use to evaluate projects. Next, we consider how taxes affect project value and address some qualitative issues that often do not enter into financial cost-benefit calculations. Finally, we discuss how a firm might allocate scarce capital among competing projects.

CHAPTER CONNECTIONS

Firms usually review their capital budgets at the same time they construct their operating budgets, the topic of Chapter 7. Such a linkage exists because the firm's cash budget needs to account for the outflows due to expenditures on capacity resources.

Roles of Capital Budgets

When firms open new stores, they evaluate cash inflows and outflows over a long time horizon. (Paul Sakuma/©AP/Wide World Photos)

LEARNING OBJECTIVE 1

Understand the reasons for capital budgeting.

Just like St. Vincent's Hospital, organizations routinely face decisions involving significant outlays. Machines and equipment depreciate with use and need replacement. As markets grow, expenditures on new plants and machinery become necessary to exploit new opportunities. Every time Starbucks opens a new coffee shop, Chipotle opens a new restaurant, or Foley's opens a new department store, these firms incur substantial expenditures related to buying the necessary land, constructing a building or leasing store space, furnishing the store, purchasing equipment, and hiring staff. To judge whether such investments are worthwhile, we need to estimate the benefits and costs over many years. We also must decide whether a proposed investment is the best use of available funds, or whether we can put these funds to a more profitable use. **Capital budgeting** refers to the set of tools companies use to evaluate such large expenditures.

Before describing the mechanics of capital budgeting, let us first place capital budgeting in the context of earlier topics that we studied, including cost allocations and budgeting.

CAPITAL BUDGETING AND COST ALLOCATIONS

In Chapters 9 and 10, we learned that cost allocations help us estimate the cost of capacity resources for long-term decisions related to people, products, customers, and resources. Despite the widespread use of allocations for decision making, they suffer from two drawbacks that are particularly important when evaluating long-lived resources. They do not account for either the time value of money or the lumpy nature of capacity resources.

The **time value of money** arises because a dollar today is worth more than a dollar tomorrow. To see why, suppose you invest a dollar today in a Certificate of Deposit (CD) that promises an annual return of 10%. When the certificate matures in a year, you will have $1.10. Thus, your dollar today is worth $1.10 a year from now. Conversely, $1.10 a year from now is only worth $1 now.

Intuitively, money is a productive asset. Its opportunity cost is the time value of money. Unlike cost allocations, capital budgeting explicitly considers this time value by **discounting** future cash inflows and outflows to their current or

present value. It allows us to express *all* future cash flows—cash flows occurring at *different* future points in time—in terms of their respective present values. This way, we can put these different cash flows on an equal footing and compare them.

It is easy to match supply and demand for some resources. We can buy raw materials and acquire electricity on an as needed basis. The amounts we purchase during a month or year closely match the amounts we need. However, it is difficult to match the supply and demand for capacity resources over a period of months or even years. The difficulty arises because many capacity resources are "**lumpy**." We cannot purchase half of a television set. St. Vincent's cannot buy three-fourths of an MRI machine. At some point, if you want to produce one more unit of a good, you need to purchase another piece of equipment and not just enough to make one more unit.

Cost allocations ignore the lumpy nature of capacity resources and estimate costs as if we can match supply and demand continuously and smoothly. However, capital budgeting techniques do not. These techniques consider the timing and magnitude of *all* of the cash inflows and outflows associated with resource acquisition, use, and disposal. Thus, particularly when evaluating large outflows, firms supplement their cost allocation estimates with capital budgeting techniques.

CAPITAL BUDGETS AND BUDGETING

Most companies prepare budgets for different time horizons—from short-term operating budgets to long-term strategic plans. Strategic plans span many years and flesh out how the firm's overall mission and core competencies will influence operations. These plans specify *how* the company intends to achieve its long-term objectives, and dictate *what* resources the firm needs to execute its plans. St. Vincent's strategic plans call for it to be the "preferred hospital in its market by providing personalized care for patients and their families." The MRI equipment would help St. Vincent's meet this goal.

Operating budgets, which we examined in Chapter 7, are short-term plans that aim for the maximum possible contribution from available capacity resources. As we know, short-term decisions treat capacity levels as fixed and capacity costs as noncontrollable. Once St. Vincent's acquires the MRI equipment, its capacity is fixed for decisions involving its utilization. The hospital will periodically review its own demand for MRI in order to decide whether to grant other hospitals access to it.

A capital budget links strategic and operating budgets. It helps determine *how much of each capacity resource an organization should acquire* and how it should invest its capital in specific assets such as plant, equipment, building, and technology. Whether to spend $1.5 million on MRI is a typical capital budgeting decision.

Like most firms, St. Vincent's performs capital budgeting in two steps. First, it identifies and evaluates individual investment proposals. Second, it prioritizes the proposals and decides which ones to execute. Just as operating budgets allocate the firm's productive capacity among products, capital budgets allocate scarce capital among available investment opportunities. Let us first consider how to evaluate an individual project.

CHAPTER CONNECTIONS
We discuss strategic planning and control in Chapter 13.

Connecting to Practice

CAPITAL BUDGETING AT STANFORD UNIVERSITY MEDICAL SCHOOL

The School of Medicine (SOM) at Stanford University indicates that its "annual Capital Planning and Budgeting process occurs in four phases, progressing from more general and long-term plans to more specific annual budgets." These process phases are the University Capital Plan, SOM long-range forecast, SOM capital plan, and the SOM annual capital budget. Each of the phases lasts several months, with the phases executed sequentially, as the results of one phase provide the needed inputs into the next phase. The overall process is also iterative because the results of later evaluations cause the SOM to revisit earlier decisions.

COMMENTARY: The SOM constructs its plans and budgets to be in tune with the university's plan. Similarly, divisions in firms such as General Motors and Johnson & Johnson construct their own plans, which are subject to corporate approval. Such layering of the capital budgeting process is common in large decentralized organizations.

Source: Medfacilities.stanford.edu/facilities/downloads/SoM_capital_plan_process.pdf (3/15/05)

Elements of Project Cash Flows

LEARNING OBJECTIVE 2

List the components of a project's cash flow.

Exhibit 11.1 highlights the four important elements of a capital-expenditure decision about a single project:

1. *Initial Outlay.* What are the costs associated with acquiring the resource and getting it ready for use?

Exhibit 11.1	*There Are Four Important Elements of a Project's Cash Flow*

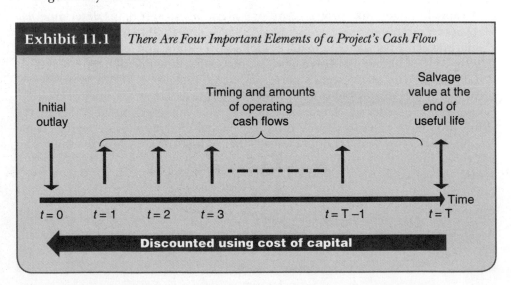

2. *Estimated Life and Salvage Value.* How long do we expect to keep the resource? At the end of this period, are there any costs associated with disposing of the resource? Can we sell the resource to someone else when we are done with it?

3. *Timing and Amounts of Operating Cash Flows.* What are the expected operating expenses every year? What are the expected revenues or cost savings?

4. *Cost of Capital.* What is the opportunity cost of capital required for the proposed investment?

Let us examine each of these elements in more detail.

INITIAL OUTLAY

The **initial outlay** includes all costs incurred to ready the asset for its intended use. These costs include the purchase price, shipping and delivery costs, taxes, and any installation and training charges. For St. Vincent's, the initial investment of $1,500,000 includes all of these costs.

Just as we might sell our old car when buying a new car, firms often replace their old assets with new assets. The proceeds received from the sale of old assets would be deducted from the initial investment in arriving at cash outflow at time $t = 0$. In the case of St. Vincent's, this inflow is not applicable because it does not currently have its own MRI equipment.

ESTIMATED LIFE AND SALVAGE VALUE

Assets lose their productivity with use. They also become obsolete as new, more efficient technologies emerge. The MRI equipment considered by Dr. Rodriguez

 **Connecting to Practice**

LEASING CAPITAL ASSETS

IBM offers a sales-leaseback arrangement to its customers. As stated on the firm's Web site, with a sales-leaseback arrangement, "you actually sell your equipment—and transfer your title of ownership—to IBM Global Financing for the fair market value of the assets. Then you lease the equipment back at regular, low monthly payments over a flexible payment period. The cash or credit you receive can be used to acquire upgrades or new equipment, can be applied to your monthly payments, or used as you see fit. At the end of the lease term, you can choose to extend the lease, or simply transfer possession of the equipment to IBM Global Financing so you can replace it with the latest IT solutions. IBM Global Financing will even manage the disposal of your assets in accordance with EPA guidelines and U.S. federal, state, and local laws."

COMMENTARY: The large initial outflow of capital prevents many firms from investing and upgrading capital equipment. Buying firms may also be reluctant to employ traditional methods such as a bank loan to borrow the money needed. As a liability on their balance sheet, the loan might adversely affect the firm's debt-to-equity ratio. Sellers of capital assets have devised several methods to finance the purchase, but without the implicit loan showing up in the buyer's book. IBM's offer is one such example.

represents cutting-edge technology and will last 10 years with little fear of obsolescence.

Using a reasonable and realistic estimate of life expectancy is important. Too low of an estimate understates the profitability of the investment and could result in the firm rejecting profitable opportunities. Too high of an estimate overstates the profitability of the investment and could lead to a wasteful use of scarce capital.

Firms also must consider an asset's salvage value when evaluating an investment. The **salvage value** is the residual value from disposing of the asset at the end of its useful life. While salvage value is often positive because it is a cash inflow from selling the asset, it could also be negative to mark a cash outflow. For example, to satisfy regulatory requirements, mining firms often incur significant expenses to restore the land to productive use after they stop extracting ore.

TIMING AND AMOUNTS OF OPERATING CASH FLOWS

Operating cash inflows increase directly through increased revenues. They also may increase indirectly through decreased outflows due to cost savings. When evaluating cash flows, a reduction in outflow is equivalent to an increase in inflow. Operating cash outflows typically include increases in variable costs that are proportional to the increase in revenue, increases in annual fixed costs related to hiring additional personnel, and costs associated with periodic repairs and maintenance.

Exhibit 11.2 presents the estimated cash inflows and outflows over the 10-year horizon for the MRI equipment. Dr. Rodriquez expects the following controllable cash inflows and outflows.

Exhibit 11.2	*St. Vincent's Hospital: Expected Cash Inflows and Outflows from the MRI Project*			
	Year 0	**Cash Flow for Each of Years 1–3**	**Cash Flow for Each of Years 4–5**	**Cash Flow for Each of Years 6–10**
Initial outlay	($1,500,000)			
Internal use (# of images)		2,400	2,400	2,400
Outside sales (# of images)		960	1,200	1,600
Cash inflows				
Internal use		$480,000	$480,000	$480,000
Outside sales		192,000	240,000	320,000
Total inflow		$672,000	$720,000	$800,000
Cash outflows				
Variable operating costs		(168,000)	(180,000)	(200,000)
Fixed operating costs		(150,000)	(150,000)	(150,000)
Maintenance expenses		(20,000)	(20,000)	(20,000)
Total cash outflow		(338,000)	(350,000)	(370,000)
Net cash outflows/inflows	($1,500,000)	$334,000	$370,000	$430,000

- *Cash Inflow—Internal Use:* The MRI equipment has a practical capacity of 4,000 images per year. St. Vincent's expects to receive an average of $200 per image for 2,400 images. Dr. Rodriguez expects the internal demand to remain constant, yielding annual revenue of $480,000 (2,400 images per year × $200 per image).

- *Cash Inflow— External Sales:* Dr. Rodriguez expects to earn additional revenue by renting out the MRI equipment's spare capacity of 1,600 images. St. Vincent's will directly bill the patient's insurance company for the MRI, again at an average rate of $200 per image. In years 1–3, Dr. Rodriguez expects outside sales of 960 images, for a revenue of $192,000 (960 images × $200 per image). She estimates outside use of 1,200 images per year in years 4 and 5 (revenue of $240,000 per year) and 1,600 images for each of years 6–10 (revenue of $320,000 per year).
- *Cash Outflow—Initial Investment.* To get the MRI equipment up and running requires a one-time outlay of $1,500,000.
- *Cash Outflow—Variable Operating Costs:* Variable operating costs are $50 per image. Thus, in years 1–3, annual variable costs amount to $168,000 ((2,400 + 960) images × $50 per image). By similar calculation, annual variable costs amount are $180,000 per year for years 3–5 and $200,000 per year for years 6–10.
- *Cash Outflow—Fixed Operating Costs.* Dr. Rodriguez expects to incur fixed operating costs of $150,000 per year for technician and staff salaries and use of the hospital space. She estimates maintenance expenses of $20,000 per year. Thus, the MRI machine would increase the hospitals' total fixed costs by $170,000 per year. We note that Dr. Rodriguez might rely on cost allocations, as might be obtained from an ABC system, to calculate the estimated increase in St. Vincent's fixed costs.
- *Cash Inflow/Outflow—Salvage Value.* The equipment has no salvage value at the end of 10 years. The costs of dismantling and selling the equipment will offset the expected sale price.

Exhibit 11.3 depicts these cash flows pictorially.

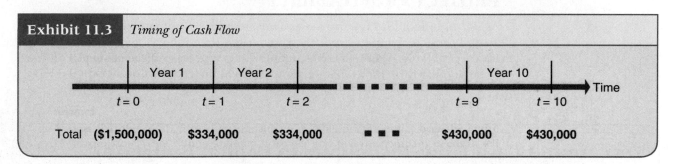

| **Exhibit 11.3** | *Timing of Cash Flow* |

	Year 1	Year 2		Year 10	
	t = 0	t = 1	t = 2		t = 9	t = 10
Total	($1,500,000)	$334,000	$334,000	■ ■ ■	$430,000	$430,000

It is important to note that Exhibits 11.2 and 11.3 focus on before-tax *cash flows* and not accounting expenses. In particular, the accounting depreciation of the MRI equipment is not relevant for cash flow computations. While depreciation is an expense, it does not involve a cash outflow. We return to depreciation later in the chapter when we consider after-tax cash flows because the amount of depreciation affects taxes paid, a cash outflow.

COST OF CAPITAL

The **cost of capital** is the opportunity cost for money. We measure the cost of capital as the rate of return that providers of capital (such as shareholders, lenders, and banks) expect from their investments. We use this rate of return as the **discount rate** to calculate the *present* value of *future* cash inflows and outflows.

Estimating the cost of capital is difficult because the return expected by capital providers varies with the risks they face and other investment opportunities they have. A lender will demand a higher rate of return for a riskier project, much as a bank charges a higher interest rate for a person with poor credit. Other factors such as inflation and the state of the economy also influence the discount rate for an investment. For St. Vincent's, the treasurer informs Dr. Rodriguez that the hospital

Exhibit 11.4	*There Are Many Ways to Evaluate Project Profitability*

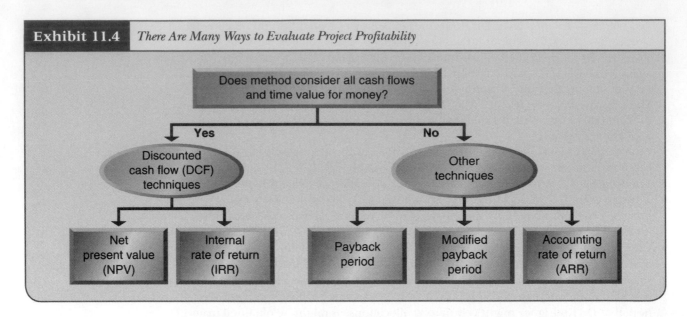

uses a rate of 12% to discount cash flows. That is, the hospital needs to earn at least a 12% return before it is willing to commit to an investment.

METHODS FOR EVALUATING PROJECT PROFITABILITY

As shown in Exhibit 11.4, firms use many methods to evaluate project profitability. Two of these techniques explicitly consider the time value of money and discount future cash flows. Although conceptually weaker, the other three methods continue to be popular for reasons that we discuss later in the chapter.

Discounted Cash Flow Techniques in Capital Budgeting

LEARNING OBJECTIVE 3

Apply discounted cash flow techniques.

Cash outflows and inflows associated with capital investments are spread over many years. Therefore, most firms use discounted cash flow (DCF) techniques to state future cash flows in terms of their respective present values. These techniques make all cash inflows and outflows comparable. The two main DCF techniques are net present value (NPV) and internal rate of return (IRR).

In Appendix A, we explain the mechanics of computing both the present and future values of cash flows. Before proceeding to the next section, we encourage you to complete *Check It! Exercise #1* to ensure that you are comfortable with present and future value calculations.

NET PRESENT VALUE

The **net present value (NPV)** of an investment is the total present value of *all* of its cash flows. We can compute this value by using the present value tables. Spreadsheet programs and most calculators calculate NPV by using the present value formula. *An investment is desirable if its NPV is positive.*

The initial investment amount shown in Exhibit 11.1 is already at its present value, that is, in current dollar terms. It requires no discount. However, $1 today

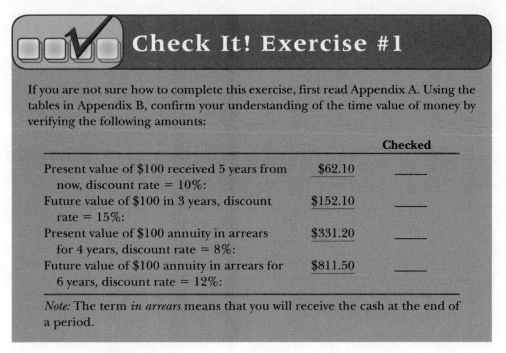

Check It! Exercise #1

If you are not sure how to complete this exercise, first read Appendix A. Using the tables in Appendix B, confirm your understanding of the time value of money by verifying the following amounts:

		Checked
Present value of $100 received 5 years from now, discount rate = 10%:	$62.10	_____
Future value of $100 in 3 years, discount rate = 15%:	$152.10	_____
Present value of $100 annuity in arrears for 4 years, discount rate = 8%:	$331.20	_____
Future value of $100 annuity in arrears for 6 years, discount rate = 12%:	$811.50	_____

Note: The term *in arrears* means that you will receive the cash at the end of a period.

Solution at end of chapter.

would have grown to $(1 + r)$ dollars in one period, if our discount rate is r. Conversely, if we receive NCF dollars at the start of period 1, then the present value of this cash flow is $NCF_1/(1 + r)$. As you go further out in time, the **discount factor** (also known as the *present value factor*), the amount by which we need to multiply the future cash flow to obtain the present value, decreases. The present value of the cash flow in some future period t is $NCF_t/(1 + r)^t$; the discount factor for this cash flow is $1/(1 + r)^t$. Adding together all of the present values provides the NPV.

Exhibit 11.5 shows that NPV declines as the discount rate increases. A higher discount rate leads to a more conservative estimate of an investment's NPV. Accordingly, firms often use larger discount rates to evaluate riskier projects.

Exhibit 11.5	*Higher Discount Rates Lower the NPV of a Cash Flow*

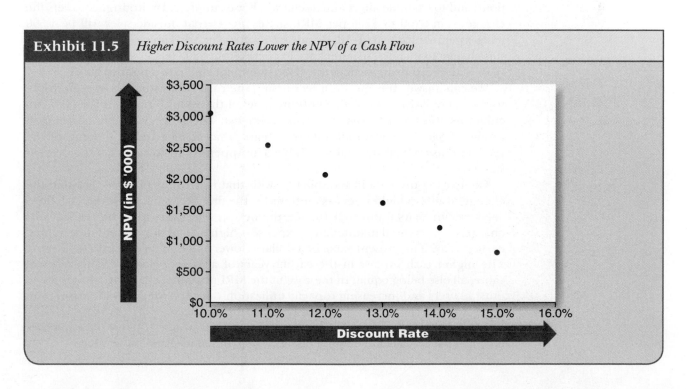

Exhibit 11.6	St. Vincent's Hospital: Present Value of the MRI Project		

Initial Investment = $1,500,000, Life 10 years, Cost of Capital 12%

Year	Net Cash Flow	Present Value Factor	Present Value
Initial investment	($1,500,000)	1.000	($1,500,000)
Year 1	$334,000	0.893	298,262
Year 2	334,000	0.797	266,198
Year 3	334,000	0.712	237,808
Year 4	370,000	0.636	235,320
Year 5	370,000	0.567	209,790
Year 6	430,000	0.507	218,010
Year 7	430,000	0.452	194,360
Year 8	430,000	0.404	173,720
Year 9	430,000	0.361	155,230
Year 10	430,000	0.322	138,460
Net present value (NPV)			**$627,158**

Recall that Dr. Rodriguez uses a discount rate of 12% to evaluate St. Vincent's investment in the MRI machine. The calculations in Exhibit 11.6 discount the cash flows from Exhibit 11.2 using Table 1 in Appendix B. Our analysis shows a positive NPV, indicating that investing in the MRI equipment is profitable.

Sensitivity Analysis

Like the Cost-Volume-Profit model of Chapter 5, the NPV method allows the user to perform "what if" sensitivity analysis with respect to various estimates and assumptions, and to examine alternative scenarios. For example, if Dr. Rodriguez lowers the charge from $200 to $190 per MRI, she estimates that outside sales will be 1,600 images per year for Years 1–10. (Inside sales will stay at 2,400 images.) She also expects this change to increase maintenance expenses from $20,000 per year to $25,000 per year. With these changes, does the MRI equipment still have a positive NPV?

We can answer this question by revising the cash flow estimates as seen in the top panel of Exhibit 11.7. The bottom panel of this exhibit presents the NPV calculations. *The net cash flows are the same every year.* Therefore, we treat the net cash inflow of $385,000 as an annuity in arrears (that is, received at the end of the year) and use the annuity tables (Table 3 in Appendix B) to calculate the present value.

Comparing the data in Exhibit 11.7 with that in Exhibit 11.6, we find that the change results in higher net cash inflows for the first five years. However, cash flows are lower in Years 6 through 10. Yet, the net present value with the revised MRI charge and increased maintenance expense is higher than the amount determined earlier. Why? The present value of a dollar is lower as we go farther into the future. The higher cash inflows in the earlier years of a project yield a higher present value, all else being equal. In the case of the MRI machine, charging a lower fee to outside users and increasing capacity utilization is a good idea as it increases overall profit.

In a similar vein, we could examine the sensitivity of our NPV estimate to other changes, such as a change in the discount rate, initial investment, or usage.

Exhibit 11.7	St. Vincent's Hospital: MRI Project—Sensitivity Analysis			
	Year 0	Years 1–3	Years 4–5	Years 6–10
Initial outlay	($1,500,000)			
Internal use (# of images)		2,400	2,400	2,400
Outside sales (# of images)		1,600	1,600	1,600
Cash inflows				
Internal use		$456,000	$456,000	$456,000
Outside sales		$304,000	$304,000	$304,000
Cash outflows				
Variable operating costs		(200,000)	(200,000)	(200,000)
Fixed operating costs		(150,000)	(150,000)	(150,000)
Maintenance expenses		(25,000)	(25,000)	(25,000)
Net cash flows		$385,000	$385,000	$385,000
Present value of annuity in arrears of $425,000 million per year for 10 years @12%		$385,000 × 5.650		$2,175,250
Less: Initial investment				(1,500,000)
Net present value (NPV)				$675,250

* Notice that the PV of an annuity in arrears is the sum of the present values of the cash flows for individual years, which data we used in Exhibit 11.6. That is, 5.650 = 0.893 + 0.797 + ... + 0.322.

Assumptions in NPV Analysis

In performing the NPV calculations illustrated above, we made some assumptions that affect our calculations.

1. The initial cash outflow takes place at the *beginning of the period*. Referring to Exhibit 11.3, time 0 designates the time of the initial investment, which is now. This assumption is the reason for not discounting the initial outlay.
2. Subsequent cash inflows and outflows occur at the *end of the relevant period*. That is, the net cash flow in year 1 occurs as a lump sum at the end of year 1, which is time $t = 1$, or a year from time $t = 0$. We used this assumption to calculate the value of the annuity in Exhibit 11.7.

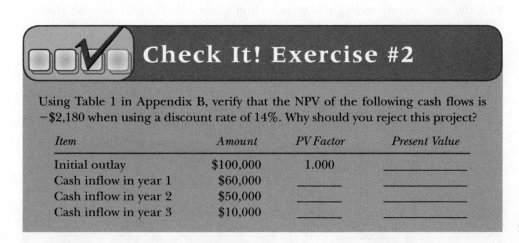

Check It! Exercise #2

Using Table 1 in Appendix B, verify that the NPV of the following cash flows is −$2,180 when using a discount rate of 14%. Why should you reject this project?

Item	Amount	PV Factor	Present Value
Initial outlay	$100,000	1.000	_____
Cash inflow in year 1	$60,000	_____	_____
Cash inflow in year 2	$50,000	_____	_____
Cash inflow in year 3	$10,000	_____	_____

Solution at end of chapter.

3. NPV calculations assume that firms reinvest future cash inflows in projects that yield a return that equals the cost of capital.

Are these assumptions reasonable? While the third assumption is acceptable, the first two assumptions may seem unrealistic. After all, firms likely receive revenue and incur costs throughout the year, not just at the beginning and end of accounting periods. Advanced accounting and finance textbooks discuss techniques that account for a continuous flow of costs and benefits during a period. Here, our purpose is to introduce you to the important concept of net present value and the need to discount future cash flows. Thus, we will continue to make these assumptions.

INTERNAL RATE OF RETURN

The **internal rate of return (IRR)** is the discount rate at which a project has zero NPV. *A project is profitable if its IRR exceeds its opportunity cost of capital.* For example, the MRI machine would be a profitable investment if its IRR exceeds 12%, the cost of capital for St. Vincent's.

Unequal Cash Flows

As is typical of most projects, St. Vincent's project has unequal cash flows over time (see Exhibit 11.2). The variance in cash flows occurs because Dr. Rodriguez projects an increasing demand for the MRI machine over time. Manually computing the IRR for a project with unequal operating cash flows spread over many years used to be difficult because the process involves a lot of trial and error. Fortunately, electronic spreadsheet programs greatly simplify this task.

Using the IRR formula in Excel, Dr. Rodriguez finds that the IRR for the MRI project is approximately 20.9%, which is considerably higher than the cost of capital of 12%. Thus, the IRR method confirms the profitability of the MRI machine.

IRR with Equal Cash Flows

The internal rate of return is easier to compute when the net cash flow is the same every year. Consider a project involving an initial investment of $50,000 and yearly net cash inflow of $15,000 for the next five years. Because the cash inflow is an annuity, we can calculate its present value using the annuity factor in Table 3. We can then calculate the annuity factor that results in a net present value of zero. In other words, we calculate

$$\$15{,}000 \times \text{Annuity Factor} = \$50{,}000, \text{ or Annuity Factor} = 3.3333$$

Referring to the present value of an annuity table (Table 3 in Appendix B), we find the row corresponding to five years and locate the column with an amount closest to this factor. For this example, the factor lies between 15 and 16%. Using Excel, we verify that the IRR = 15.24%.

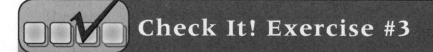 **Check It! Exercise #3**

Using the formula for IRR in Excel, verify that the IRR of the cash flows in *Check It! Exercise #2* is 12.40%. You also can determine that the IRR is between 12 and 13% by verifying that the NPV is positive with a discount rate of 12% and negative with a discount rate of 13%. Use Table 1 in Appendix B to help with these calculations.

Solution at end of chapter.

Assumptions in IRR Analysis

Like the NPV method, the IRR method assumes that the initial cash outflow takes place at the beginning of the period, and that subsequent cash flows occur as a lump sum at the end of the respective periods. The IRR method assumes that firms reinvest future cash inflows in projects that yield a return equaling the project's IRR. That is, if the current project has an IRR of 22%, the IRR method assumes that the firm invests future cash in projects that yield an IRR of 22%.

COMPARING NPV AND IRR

Many people prefer the NPV method to the IRR method because NPV is simpler to compute and provides a unique value for each project. In contrast, it turns out that the IRR method could result in multiple values of IRR for the same projects. In such instances, qualitative judgment is needed to select the right IRR.

Another key difference between the methods is their assumption about reinvestment of subsequent cash flows. The IRR method assumes that the firm has other investment opportunities that will yield the same rate of return as the project under consideration. Particularly for projects with a high IRR, this assumption is frequently not a realistic one because *highly profitable* reinvestment opportunities may not always be available. In contrast, the NPV method assumes that a firm reinvests interim project cash flows at its cost of capital.

Finally, NPV ranks projects based on the *magnitude* of the net present value, while IRR ranks projects based on the *rate* of return. Thus, NPV tends to favor larger projects with higher absolute *profit* while IRR tends to favor smaller projects that have greater *profitability*.

Collectively, these differences between NPV and IRR often result in these techniques ranking a set of available investment proposals differently, which could be a problem when firms have limited capital available—they cannot choose *all* positive NPV projects or *all* projects whose IRR exceeds the cost of capital. In such instances, firms need to rank available projects so that they can choose the combination of projects that maximizes overall profitability. Unfortunately, the NPV and IRR techniques may not agree on what that right combination might be.

Other Evaluation Criteria for Capital Budgeting

Although firms generally use NPV and IRR to evaluate investments, they also use other methods. In this section, we discuss three other methods that firms use to evaluate expenditures on long-lived resources: payback, modified payback, and accounting rate of return.

LEARNING OBJECTIVE 4

Compare various methods for evaluating projects.

PAYBACK METHOD

Under the payback method, we compute how long it takes to recoup the initial investment using *undiscounted* cash flows. We refer to this length of time as the **payback period**. Consider a project that requires an initial investment of $60,000 and that generates a net cash inflow of $24,000 a year for the next four years. The payback period for this project is two and one-half years ($60,000/$24,000 per year = 2.50 years).

What is the payback period for St. Vincent's MRI project? Because the net cash flows differ every year, determining the payback period is more involved. In this case, Dr. Rodriguez calculates the payback period by adding the net cash flows over time. As the calculations in Exhibit 11.8 indicate, accumulated net

Exhibit 11.8	St. Vincent's Hospital: Payback Period for the MRI Project		
Year	**Net Cash Flow (Exhibit 11.2)**	**Cumulative Cash Inflows (Undiscounted)**	
Initial investment	($1,500,000)		
Year 1	$334,000	$334,000	
Year 2	334,000	$668,000	
Year 3	334,000	$1,002,000	
Year 4	370,000	$1,372,000	
Year 5	370,000	$1,742,000	> $1,500,000
Year 6	430,000	$2,172,000	
Year 7	430,000	$2,602,000	
Year 8	430,000	$3,032,000	
Year 9	430,000	$3,462,000	
Year 10	430,000	$3,892,000	

Check It! Exercise #4

Suppose that a machine costs $310,000 and that annual cash inflows are $60,000 in years 1–3 and $50,000 in years 4–7. Verify that the payback period is 5.60 years.

Solution at end of chapter.

cash flows exceed the initial cash outlay of $1,500,000 somewhere between years 4 and 5. Assuming cash inflows occur uniformly throughout the year, we calculate the payback period as: 4 years + ($1,500,000 initial investment − $1,372,000 cumulative cash inflows through year 4)/$370,000 cash inflow in year 5 = 4.35 years.

The greatest advantage of the payback method is that the payback period is easy to compute and to understand. We do not need to determine the opportunity cost of capital, which can be difficult to measure. The payback method also focuses on a project's downside risk. Managers may prefer a project with a shorter payback period because it reduces the risk of losing the initial investment.

To use the payback method to accept or reject a project, a firm needs a criterion or a payback cutoff. Is a payback period of five years acceptable or is it too long? What is the minimum acceptable payback period? While prior experience with similar projects can help in this respect, it is still arbitrary.

As you know, the payback method ignores the time value of money and thus overvalues the future cash inflows it considers. Accordingly, the payback method *understates* the length of time actually required to recoup initial investment. Moreover, it ignores all cash flows that occur after the payback period, and thus favors projects that yield more cash inflows in earlier years relative to projects that take longer to bear fruit. Exhibit 11.9 provides an example in which two projects, A and B, require the same initial outlay but generate different cash flow patterns over four years of life. Project A has a shorter payback period, but Project B has a higher NPV (based on a cost of capital of 8%). Many firms use the modified payback method to address this concern.

Exhibit 11.9	Comparison of Payback Method and NPV	
Year	**Project A**	**Project B**
Initial investment	($50,000)	($50,000)
Year 1 cash flows	30,000	10,000
Year 2 cash flows	20,000	15,000
Year 3 cash flows	10,000	20,000
Year 4 cash flows	10,000	40,000
Net present value ($r = 8\%$)	$10,213	$17,397
Payback period	2 years	3.125 years

MODIFIED PAYBACK

The **modified payback method** computes the payback period using *discounted* cash flows, meaning that the method accounts for the time value of money. Under this method, we accumulate the present value of future cash flows over time and compare the cumulative value with the initial cash outlay. The year in which the accumulated present value of future cash flows exceeds the initial cash outflow determines the modified payback period.

As shown in Exhibit 11.10, the present value of future cash flows for the MRI project exceeds the initial outlay of $1,500,000 sometime in year 7. We calculate the payback period as 6 years + ($1,659,748 − $1,500,000)/$194,360 = 6.82 years. Under the traditional payback method, we calculated the payback period to be 4.35 years (Exhibit 11.8). Thus, the payback period increases by 2.47 years when we account for the time value of money. This disparity confirms our earlier observation that the traditional payback method understates the true length of time required to recoup the initial investment.

The modified payback method is an improvement over the simple payback method because it takes into account the time value of money. Still, it does not consider *all* future cash flows from a project as the NPV method does. In particular, it

Exhibit 11.10	St. Vincent's Hospital: Modified Payback Method			
Initial Investment = $1,500,000, Life 10 years, Cost of Capital 12%				
Year	**Net Cash Flow (Exhibit 11.2)**	**Present Value Factor**	**Present Value**	**Cumulative Present Value**
Year 1	$334,000	0.893	$298,262	$298,262
Year 2	334,000	0.797	266,198	564,460
Year 3	334,000	0.712	237,808	802,268
Year 4	370,000	0.636	235,320	1,037,588
Year 5	370,000	0.567	209,790	1,247,378
Year 6	430,000	0.507	218,010	1,465,388
Year 7	430,000	0.452	194,360	**1,659,748**
Year 8	430,000	0.404	173,720	1,833,468
Year 9	430,000	0.361	155,230	1,988,698
Year 10	430,000	0.322	138,460	2,127,158

ignores cash flows that occur after the payback period. Consequently, the payback and the modified payback methods generally are less preferable to NPV or IRR when evaluating projects, even though these methods are easier to use and understand.

ACCOUNTING RATE OF RETURN

Some firms compute an **accounting rate of return (ARR)** to evaluate long-lived resources. We compute ARR as follows:

$$ARR = \frac{\text{Average annual income from the project}}{\text{Average annual investment}}$$

We compute accounting income by subtracting annual depreciation expense from annual net cash flows. St. Vincent's plans to depreciate the MRI equipment using the straight-line method and assuming zero salvage value.

- First, we decrease the book value of the MRI equipment by the depreciation amount.
- Next, we calculate the average investment balance for each year as the average of the beginning and ending book values.
- The final step is to compute ARR as the ratio of the average income to the average investment over the life span of the investment.

As shown in Exhibit 11.11, the MRI project has an expected ARR of 31.89%.

Exhibit 11.11	St. Vincent's Hospital: Accounting Rate of Return

Initial Investment = $1,500,000, Life 10 years, Cost of Capital 12%

Year	Opening Book Value	Net Cash Flow (Exhibit 11.2)	Depreciation	Accounting Income	Ending Book Value	Average Book Value
Year 1	$1,500,000	$334,000	$150,000	$184,000	$1,350,000	$1,425,000
Year 2	1,350,000	334,000	150,000	184,000	1,200,000	1,275,000
Year 3	1,200,000	334,000	150,000	184,000	1,050,000	1,125,000
Year 4	1,050,000	370,000	150,000	220,000	900,000	975,000
Year 5	900,000	370,000	150,000	220,000	750,000	825,000
Year 6	750,000	430,000	150,000	280,000	600,000	675,000
Year 7	600,000	430,000	150,000	280,000	450,000	525,000
Year 8	450,000	430,000	150,000	280,000	300,000	375,000
Year 9	300,000	430,000	150,000	280,000	150,000	225,000
Year 10	150,000	430,000	150,000	280,000	0	75,000
		Average		239,200		$750,000

Accounting Rate of Return (ARR) = $239,200/$750,000 = 31.9%

Like the payback methods, ARR is relatively straightforward to compute. However, like the traditional payback method, it ignores the time value of money. Thus, we caution against the exclusive use of these methods for project acceptance decisions.

POPULARITY OF DISCOUNTED CASH FLOW TECHNIQUES

Exhibit 11.12 provides a comparison of the various methods for evaluating projects. As you can tell, the discounted cash flow (DCF) techniques are the conceptually

Exhibit 11.12	Comparison of Methods for Evaluating Project Proposals

Feature of Method	Net Present Value	Internal Rate of Return	Payback	Modified Payback	Accounting Rate of Return
Considers time value of money	Yes	Yes	No	Yes	No
Considers all cash flows	Yes	Yes	No	No	Yes
Return earned on invested cash inflows	Cost of capital	IRR	Not applicable	Not applicable	Not applicable
Ease of computations	Moderate	Moderate to difficult	Easy	Easy to moderate	Easy to moderate
Greater focus on avoiding losses than on making profit	No	No	Yes	Yes	No
Integrates well with accounting performance measures	No	No	No	No	Yes

Exhibit 11.13	Capital Budgeting Techniques—Usage Patterns

	Often or Always	Sometimes	Rarely or Never
NPV	85.1%	10.9%	4.0%
IRR	76.7	15.4	7.9
Payback	52.6	21.9	25.5
Modified payback	37.6	19.1	43.3
ARR	14.7	18.6	66.7

Source: P. A. Ryan and G. P. Ryan, "Capital Budgeting Practices of the Fortune 1000: How Have Things Changed?" *Journal of Business and Management* 8 (4), 2002.

correct way to evaluate projects, although they are computationally intensive. Perhaps because of growing comfort with spreadsheet programs, over the years, the popularity of DCF techniques has grown. Most major corporations use these techniques, particularly for large outlays. Nevertheless, as the survey data in Exhibit 11.13 indicate, even some Fortune 1000 firms still use the payback method to complement NPV and other DCF techniques, perhaps because of their simplicity.

Taxes and Capital Budgeting

Regardless of the method they use to evaluate projects, firms need to consider one very important factor: taxes. Taxes affect both the amount and timing of cash flows. A firm pays taxes on accounting income, not on cash flows. Therefore, it needs to compute accounting income to determine taxes.

Operating cash inflows and outflows influence accounting income significantly. However, net cash flows do not typically equal accounting income. A major reason is depreciation, which is an accounting expense but does not involve any cash outflow.

LEARNING OBJECTIVE 5

Explain the role of taxes and the depreciation tax shield on capital budgets.

Tax laws allow corporations to deduct depreciation when calculating taxable income. Thus, depreciation offers a *tax shield* that reduces the cash outflow associated with tax payments. Let us explore this idea further.

DEPRECIATION TAX SHIELD

We compute the depreciation tax shield as

Depreciation tax shield in a year = Tax rate × Depreciation deduction in that year

Consider the cash flow data presented in Exhibit 11.2 for the MRI project. Assume that St. Vincent's follows a straight-line depreciation method for tax purposes. Also, assume that the applicable tax rate is 30% and that St. Vincent's is a for-profit hospital. Given an initial investment of $1,500,000 and a useful life of 10 years, the annual depreciation is $150,000.

Exhibit 11.14 presents cash flow calculations for the first year of the MRI project with and without the depreciation tax effect. In the first column, the cash inflow for year 1 is $334,000. This amount triggers a 30% tax payment of $100,200, which reduces the after-tax cash flow to $233,800.

The second column shows the effect of depreciation. Subtracting the allowable depreciation deduction reduces taxable income from $334,000 to $184,000. Taxes paid also decrease, from $100,200 to $55,200. The net after-tax cash flow is then $278,800. We add back depreciation to after-tax income when we calculate this after-tax cash flow. We do this because depreciation is a noncash expense, but we deducted it earlier to compute taxable income. Notice too that the depreciation tax shield of $45,000 equals the tax rate of 30% times the depreciation amount of $150,000.

After revising the cash flows to reflect taxes and the depreciation shield, we can then apply the NPV or IRR techniques to evaluate the project. For example, incorporating taxes and depreciation into St. Vincent's MRI decision, we find that the NPV = $243,306 and the IRR = 15.6%. Thus, the MRI project is still profitable even after considering tax effects and using the two most popular DCF techniques.

Exhibit 11.14	*St. Vincent's Hospital: Illustration of Depreciation Tax Shield*	
Initial Investment = $1,500,000, Life 10 years, Cost of Capital 12%		
	Without Depreciation	**With Depreciation**
Year 1 cash flows of the MRI project (Exhibit 11.2)		
Cash inflows		
Internal use	$480,000	$480,000
Outside sales	192,000	192,000
Cash outflows		
Variable operating costs	(168,000)	(168,000)
Fixed operating costs	(150,000)	(150,000)
Maintenance expenses	(20,000)	(20,000)
Depreciation deduction	0	(150,000)
Taxable income	$334,000	$184,000
Tax payments (30%)	(100,200)	(55,200)
Add back depreciation	0	150,000
Net cash flows	$233,800	$278,800
Difference (Depreciation tax shield = $150,000 × 0.30)		$45,000

Check It! Exercise #5

Refer back to Exhibit 11.2. Verify that when considering taxes and depreciation, the net cash flows from the MRI equipment are $304,000 in year 5 and $346,000 in year 10.

Solution at end of chapter.

Connecting to Practice

MODIFIED ACCELERATED COST RECOVERY SYSTEM (MACRS)

In addition to the straight-line depreciation method, U.S. tax laws also allow depreciation deductions as stipulated by the Modified Accelerated Cost Recovery System (MACRS). The total undiscounted amount of depreciation is the same under both methods. However, MACRS allows firms to take higher depreciation charges earlier in the asset's life. In turn, because a dollar saved in tax payments today is worth more than a dollar saved tomorrow, firms generally prefer MACRS.

COMMENTARY: Tax policies can spur investment by allowing firms to realize tax benefits earlier in an asset's useful life. Such benefits often include an investment tax credit that allows the organization to write off some portion (usually 10%) of the initial outlay in the first year and accelerated depreciation schedules such as MACRS.

SALVAGE VALUE AND TAXES

Recall that salvage value is the value of an asset at the end of its useful life. Even though an asset may have lost its productive use, a company may be able to sell some parts of the asset in the replacement market. This sale price constitutes a cash inflow at the end of the asset's useful life. If a company can estimate the salvage value of an asset when acquiring it, it should include it in present value calculations. Ignoring the salvage value will *understate* the net present value of the asset.

How do taxes affect salvage value? Accounting depreciation usually does not equal the economic decline in value. Therefore, the value of an asset in the firm's books frequently differs from its economic or market value. When a firm disposes of an asset, it might realize a gain or loss due to the sale, a taxable amount. The tax code provides alternate rates for different kinds of income (e.g., earned income, dividend income, income from capital gains). For simplicity, we assume that the same tax rate applies for all kinds of income.

At the end of 10 years, St. Vincent's will have recognized 10 years of depreciation expense at $150,000 a year, or $1,500,000 in total. As net book value is the purchase cost less accumulated depreciation, the machine will have zero book value. Assume that Dr. Rodriguez believes St. Vincent's can sell the MRI equipment for $100,000 at the end of 10 years. While St. Vincent's will receive the $100,000 in cash, the entire amount is taxable. After subtracting $30,000 in taxes, St. Vincent's after-tax cash flow from disposition will be $70,000. In turn, that $70,000 has a present value of $22,540.

Similarly, a loss reduces the amount of taxes paid. For example, suppose that the hospital sells the MRI machine at the end of 9 years, foregoing the revenues and costs for year 10. At this time, the MRI equipment will have a book value of $150,000. If St. Vincent's then sells the machine for $130,000, the hospital's after-tax cash flow will be $130,000 plus the tax savings of $6,000 (= $20,000 loss × 0.30 tax rate) on the loss from sale. That is, the loss of $20,000 *reduces* the taxes owed on *other* income.

Allocating Capital Among Projects

LEARNING OBJECTIVE 6

Describe issues in allocating scarce capital among projects.

Thus far, we have examined how to evaluate any given project, discussing how firms project future cash flows, and how to use discounted cash flow techniques to gauge the project's worth. Ideally, firms should fund any investment whose NPV is positive or whose IRR exceeds the cost of capital. However, firms have limited access to the capital, managerial talent, and other organizational resources needed to undertake new projects. They cannot undertake all positive NPV projects. Many companies use a subjectively determined internal hurdle rate instead of the cost of capital as the benchmark for project acceptance decisions. The **hurdle rate** is the minimum expected rate of return of the management from any project. Thus, any project that has an IRR greater than the hurdle rate (which means that the project will have a positive NPV when discounted at the hurdle rate) would be acceptable.

We also find that firms may not always allocate capital to their highest-ranking projects. They may make such a seemingly bad decision to take advantage of synergies *across* projects. That is, the value of a portfolio of projects may exceed the sum of the NPVs of the individual projects in the portfolio. Moreover, some projects may align better with the firm's overall strategy than other projects. While some firms use sophisticated techniques to quantify these synergies and strategic fits, others qualitatively consider these factors in choosing which projects to fund.

Connecting to Practice

EQUIPMENT REPLACEMENT AT U.S. NAVY

In its proposal to replace three old cranes with a 151-ton dock crane, the Portsmouth Naval Ship Yard stresses the safety aspects, reduced environmental impact, and consistency with the Navy's overall strategic plans. The proposal also highlights the cost savings accruing from installing the new crane.

COMMENTARY: Capital expenditures commit organizational resources for many years. It is therefore vital that such expenditures reinforce the organization's overall missions and goals. As a result, strategic and qualitative considerations play a key role in equipment replacement decisions. Many organizations require that proposals for capital expenditures have a direct tie-in or justification based on the organization's strategic plans.

Source: U.S. Department of Navy, Justification Management System, 164.224.25.30 /fy04. nsf/($reload)/ 85256CAE007091FC8 5256BC80046665C/$FILE/Shipyards_Fund9b_ FY0405PB.pdf on March 11, 2005

NONFINANCIAL COSTS AND BENEFITS

Estimating future cash inflows and outflows, and identifying the appropriate discount rate for present value calculations is not enough. Companies also need to determine the future nonfinancial costs and benefits from a capital expenditure. This is not an easy task. In the case of St. Vincent's MRI project, how would it quantify the benefits from more timely diagnoses and better patient service?

Ignoring future benefits because they are hard to quantify can lead to lost opportunities. Using judgment to arrive at reasonable estimates, and performing sensitivity analyses to determine how changes in these estimates would impact investment decisions, could go a long way in helping managers make the right decisions.

Fit with Overall Strategy

Firms must consider how proposed projects affect the firm's ability to compete in the evolving marketplace. By virtue of their longevity, capital investments entail substantial risk, as it is hard to predict many years into the future. Some firms demand high rates of return to compensate for the risk from taking on such projects. Thus, they may use a high hurdle rate to discount future cash flows. Such practices lead to conservative investments. Such conservatism may come with a high price tag, as it erodes the firm's ability to compete.

Indeed, many experts cite unduly high discount rates as a primary reason why U.S. companies lost their technological advantage to Japanese firms in the 1970s, especially in the implementation of Just-in-Time and flexible manufacturing systems. Because they considered such investments risky, U.S. manufacturers such as Ford and Chrysler invested less than their Japanese counterparts did. However, these investments gave a significant competitive advantage to Japanese firms such as Toyota and Honda, allowing them to make substantial inroads into and become the dominant vendors in the U.S. automobile market.

Considering strategic impact is particularly important. The status quo may not be a viable option. As Exhibit 11.15 illustrates, an investment may be unattractive

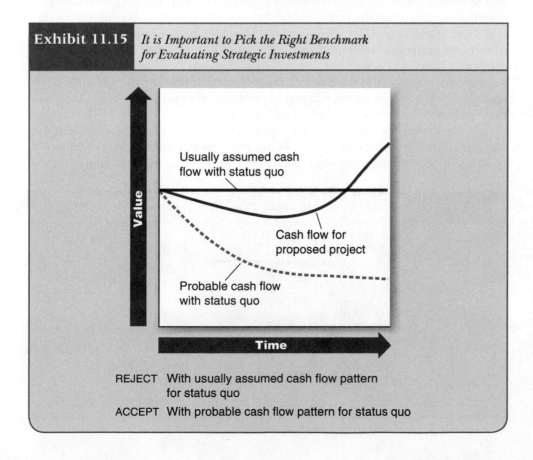

| Exhibit 11.15 | *It is Important to Pick the Right Benchmark for Evaluating Strategic Investments* |

REJECT   With usually assumed cash flow pattern for status quo

ACCEPT   With probable cash flow pattern for status quo

relative to the status quo, which implicitly asserts that the existing state of affairs will continue. However, this may not be a realistic assumption. Market forces may dictate that the status quo itself is not viable. Therefore, no action would significantly erode expected cash flows. The new investment may well be justified when compared to a revised benchmark that considers market forces on competitive position and expected cash flows.

FLEXIBILITY AND REAL OPTIONS

Flexibility is the ability to defer, abandon, expand, or contract an investment. Investments differ greatly in the flexibility they afford. Nike gains considerable manufacturing flexibility because it outsources all production. If the firm owned a plant to make its sneakers, it would not be as nimble in responding to market changes. Likewise, many firms begin projects on a small scale or on a pilot basis to gather information. Favorable outcomes lead to expansion, while failures are abandoned. Consumer firms such as Procter and Gamble and Lever Brothers routinely test new products in select markets before committing to a national launch. Amazon's substantial investment to develop its customer base, brand name, and information infrastructure for its core book business added substantial value by giving the firm the ability to extend its operations into a variety of new businesses. As seen in these examples and in Exhibit 11.16, increasing a firm's future flexibility is a key element of value, particularly for projects with considerable uncertainty in their estimated cash flows.

Many firms subjectively incorporate flexibility into project evaluation and capital allocation decisions. In recent years, both academics and practitioners have developed sophisticated mathematical models to place a quantitative value on flexibility. This branch of study, known as **real options analysis**, complements standard techniques such as NPV and IRR. It allows companies to blend strategic intuition with analytic rigor.

As a member of the hospital's executive board, Dr. Rodriguez is acutely aware that the hospital faces many demands for its limited capital. The surgeons have petitioned to upgrade the operating room, the hospital's roof is overdue for repairs, and there is a strong effort to expand the hospital's prize-winning geriatric ward. After considering these competing investments, Dr. Rodriguez still ranks the MRI project as her first choice. She believes that the new machine will substantively decrease patient turnaround time for procedures that require an MRI. The board also believes that the machine will add to the hospital's excellence in geriatric care because many diagnoses for age-related illness make use of the MRI machine. Finally, Dr. Rodriguez thinks that the downside risk is small. She is confident that she can sell the excess capacity in MRI machines to other hospitals and clinics if, contrary to current expectations, demand from St. Vincent's own patients drops.

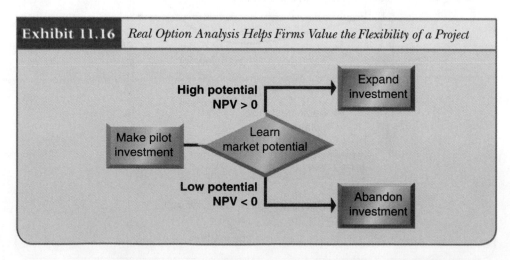

Exhibit 11.16   *Real Option Analysis Helps Firms Value the Flexibility of a Project*

 ## Connecting to Practice

OPTIONS AND PHARMACEUTICAL RESEARCH

Joint ventures and shared research arrangements are common in the high-risk biotechnology and drug development industry. For example, several years ago Merck paid Biogen $15 million up front, plus up to $130 million in milestone payments, to help it develop and bring an asthma drug to market. During the development process, Biogen faced expanded tests, a changing asthma drug market, and the risk of abandonment for safety reasons. Meanwhile, Merck could have abandoned the contract at any time without cause.

COMMENTARY: We can view this transaction as Merck purchasing a stream of options, including the option to market the drug or to abandon the product. A CSFB study, using real options analysis, revealed that the deal was worth more than the $145 million of up-front and milestone payments, making it a profitable venture for Merck. From Biogen's perspective, the venture gave it a ready stream of cash at a time of need and allowed it to partner with a pharmaceutical giant.

Source: Adopted from *Get Real: Using Real Options in Security Analysis,* Research Report by CSFB, June 1999, Merck press release, Biogen press release.

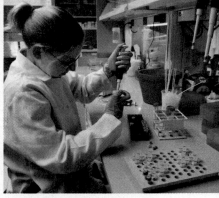

Drug development often contains exit and escalation clauses to react to future contingencies. (Emile Wamsteker/Bloomberg News/Landov LLC)

APPLYING THE DECISION FRAMEWORK

What Is the Problem?	Dr. Rodriguez of St. Vincent's Hospital wonders whether it is worthwhile to acquire magnetic resonance imaging (MRI) equipment.
What Are the Options?	The options are to buy the MRI equipment or to continue with the current arrangement of patients getting the tests done at a nearby hospital.
What Are the Costs and the Benefits?	The MRI equipment has a substantially positive NPV, and the IRR exceeds the hospital's cost of capital. Considerable nonfinancial benefits also appear to exist. However, the investment will tie up capital for many years and reduce the hospital's flexibility in terms of future investments.
Make the Decision!	Dr. Rodriguez confidently recommends that St. Vincent's proceed with its plans to acquire the MRI machine.

SUMMARY

In this chapter, we studied how firms evaluate expenditures on long-lived resources using the tools of capital budgeting. We discussed many capital budgeting techniques that firms use in decision making, including net present value, internal rate of return, payback period, and accounting rate of return analyses. Finally, we discussed the role of taxes in capital budgeting and the need to consider qualitative considerations, such as the strategic fit of a project and the flexibility afforded in project execution.

In the next chapter, we consider how firms track the results associated with expenditures on long-lived resources. Just as variance analysis helps firms evaluate the outcome of short-term plans and budgets, measures such as the return on investment (ROI) and residual income (RI) help firms evaluate the outcomes of their capital budgeting decisions.

RAPID REVIEW

Understand the reasons for capital budgeting.

- Capital budgeting is the collective term for the mechanisms and tools used to evaluate expenditures on long-lived resources.

- Capital budgeting complements the use of cost allocations for decision making by considering the time value of money and the "lumpy" nature of capacity resources.

- Capital budgets provide the link between strategic and operating budgets by determining how much capacity to acquire.

List the components of a project's cash flow.

- A project's cash flow has four elements: (1) the initial outlay; (2) the useful life and salvage value; (3) the timing and amounts of operating cash flows; and (4) the cost of capital.

- The initial outlay includes all costs incurred to ready the asset for its intended use. Using a reasonable and realistic estimate of life expectancy is important as the estimate significantly influences the profitability of the investment. The salvage value is the residual value from selling the asset at the end of its useful life. Operating cash inflows come in the form of revenue increases or cost reductions. Operating cash outflows typically include increases in variable costs and increases in controllable fixed costs. The cost of capital is the opportunity cost of foregone monetary returns. The cost of capital is higher for riskier projects and can be difficult to estimate.

Apply discounted cash flow techniques.

- The time value of money (a dollar today is worth more than a dollar tomorrow) is an important consideration when evaluating capital expenditures. By discounting future cash flows, we place all cash inflows and outflows on an equal footing.

- The net present value (NPV) of a project is the sum of all discounted future cash flows less the initial outlay. A profitable project has a positive NPV, and an unprofitable project has a negative NPV. NPV analysis also allows users to perform "what if" analysis with respect to assumptions regarding the timing and magnitude of cash flows and the cost of capital.

- The internal rate of return (IRR) is the discount rate at which a project has zero NPV. A profitable project has an IRR that exceeds the firm's cost of capital.

- NPV computations assume that firms reinvest all cash inflows at the cost of capital used in the discounting process. IRR computations assume that firms reinvest all cash inflows at the IRR. Because of their differing assumptions about reinvestment, NPV and IRR could rank projects differently.

Compare various methods for evaluating projects.

- The payback period is the number of periods required to recoup the initial outlay in undiscounted dollars. The modified payback adjusts for the time value for money. The accounting rate of return computes profit over average book value to determine project profitability.

- Though widely used, the payback method suffers from several disadvantages, including ignoring cash flows after the payback period and ignoring the time value of money. However, it does play a role in measuring downside risk. Surveys show that DCF techniques are the dominant method for evaluating capital investments.

Explain the role of taxes and the depreciation tax shield in project evaluation.

- Though not a cash flow, depreciation expense is tax deductible. The reduction in taxes payable due to depreciation is the depreciation tax shield.

- Salvage value is the proceeds received from disposing of the asset. The gain or loss due to the sale, which is the salvage value less the book value, is taxable and therefore affects cash flows.

Describe issues in allocating scarce capital among projects.

- Most organizations have capital constraints that limit the number of projects they can execute. Organizations therefore look at portfolios of projects, as well as nonfinancial considerations when choosing among projects.

- It is difficult to estimate cash flows due to intangible benefits such as reputation. However, ignoring these nonfinancial costs and benefits, such as the fit with overall strategy, can distort a project's value.

- Much like a financial option, the real option stemming from the flexibility in expanding, contracting, modifying, or abandoning a project has value. Firms use sophisticated mathematical models to estimate the value of these real options, which can be substantial in many instances.

Appendix A
PRESENT AND FUTURE VALUE CALCULATIONS

We illustrate present and future value computations using a series of four examples. These computations require the use of the present and future value tables in Appendix B.

Example 1: Future Value of an Investment

Sam Williams recently inherited $20,000 from a distant aunt. He invests the money in a stock fund that promises an expected annual return of 8% for a period of 10 years. Sam reinvests any interim proceeds in the same fund.

How will Sam's money grow in the fund? How much will Sam expect to get back at the end of 10 years? In other words, what is the future value of $20,000 at the end of 10 years if the annual rate of return is 8%?

Suppose Sam invests $20,000 at the beginning of year 1. At the end of year 1, Sam expects to have $20,000 plus the annual return of $1,600 ($20,000 × 0.08). That is, Sam expects to have $21,600.

$$\text{Future value at the end of year } 1 = 20{,}000 \times (1 + 0.08) = \$21{,}600$$

How much will Sam have at the end of year 2? Sam will have invested $21,600 at the end of year 1. This amount will grow by 8% during year 2. Thus, he will have $23,328 at the end of year 2. We could also compute the future value at the end of year 2 as

$$
\begin{aligned}
\text{Future value at the end of year } 2 &= 21{,}600 \times (1 + 0.08) \\
&= [20{,}000 \times (1 + 0.08)] \times (1 + 0.08) \\
&= 20{,}000 \times (1 + 0.08)^2 = \$23{,}328
\end{aligned}
$$

Proceeding along these lines, the future value at the end of 10 years is

$$\text{Future value at the end of year } 10 = 20{,}000 \times (1 + 0.08)^{10} = \$43{,}178.50$$

In general, the future value of a principal amount P at the end of n periods given a rate of return of $r\%$ per period is

$$FV(P, r, n) = P \times (1 + r)^n$$

where $(1 + r)^n$ is the future value factor.

We can compute future values by using the built-in formula in spreadsheet programs. Alternatively, we could look up the future value factor for $1 from a table (such as Table 2 in Appendix B). The rows of this table correspond to the rate of return per period (e.g., quarter, year), and columns correspond to the number of periods. Using the table, a rate of return of 8% and a horizon of 10 years corresponds to a factor of 2.159. Thus, we compute the future value at $43,180 = $20,000 × 2.159 (the $1.50 difference in answers is due to rounding).

Example 2: Present Value of a Future Financial Need

Suppose Sam wishes to add some of his own money to the $20,000 he inherited, so that when he retires 16 years from now, he will have access to a sum of $100,000. As before, he expects to earn 8% from his investments. How much should Sam add to the inheritance?

In this case, because we know what the future value should be at the end of 16 years, we need to calculate its present value. That is, we wish to calculate the principal amount P in the formula for future value:

$$FV(P, r, n) = P \times (1 + r)^n \Leftrightarrow P = FV(P, r, n) \left(\frac{1}{(1 + r)^n} \right)$$

The factor $1/(1 + r)^n$ is the present value factor. Applying the formula, we have

$$\$100,000 = P \times (1.08)^{16} \text{ or } P = \$29,189.04$$

OR, $P = \$100,000 \times 1/(1.08)^{16} = \$100,000 \times 0.2918904 = \$29,189.04$

Because he already has $20,000 from the inheritance, Sam needs to invest $9,189.04 ($29,189.04 − $20,000) more to reach his target.

We can compute the required factor by either using the formula above or by referring to the discount factor from Table 1 in Appendix B. Using the table, a rate of return of 8% and a horizon of 16 years corresponds to a factor of 0.292. Thus, we compute the present value as $100,000 × 0.292 = $29,200 (the difference in answers is due to rounding). In either case, we compute the present value by discounting the future value at 8%, hence the term *discount rate* for the 8% rate of return expected from the investment.

Example 3: Present Value of an Annuity in Arrears

Sam is planning for the college education expenses of his daughter, Samantha, who will finish high school in a year's time. Sam estimates that college tuition is $10,000 per year. This amount is due at the start of each year for the next four years. Sam would like to set aside enough money now to cover these expenses. He decides to invest sufficient money in a low-risk mutual fund, which yields a return of 6%.

How much should Sam invest now? Notice that Sam needs the first installment one year from now, the second two years from now, the third three years from now, and the final one four years from now. One way to compute the answer is therefore to compute the present value of $10,000 a year from now, two years from now and so on, and add the present values. This approach, however, can get tedious if we consider cash flows that span more than a few years.

Another approach takes advantage of the fact that the cash flow is the same amount for each year. Such a cash flow is termed an **annuity**. We modify the present value formula slightly to compute the present value of an annuity in arrears (i.e., payment at the end of a period).

$$\text{Present Value of an Annuity Factor} = \frac{1 - (1 + r)^{-n}}{r}$$

Using the formula, we get the annuity factor for four years (n) and 6% (r) as 3.465, which means that Sam needs to invest $10,000 × 3.465 = $34,650 to satisfy his anticipated cash needs. Alternatively, we can use Table 3 in Appendix B, the present value of an annuity table, to get the annuity factor of 3.465 corresponding to four years and 6% discount rate. With this factor, we calculate the required present value as $10,000 × 3.465 = $34,650. Sam needs to invest $34,650 now to achieve his goal of having $10,000 available at the start of each year for the next four years.

Example 4: Future Value of an Annuity in Arrears

Sam believes that he can save $7,500 at the end of each year. How much money will Sam have in 10 years if he invests his savings in a fund that returns 10% per year?

For each year's contribution, we calculate its future value for the remaining years in the 10-year horizon. Thus, for the first contribution, we calculate the future value at the end of the remaining 9 years [$FV(0.10,9,0,7500) = \$17,684.61$]. The amount grows for 9 years only as Sam invests the first installment at the end of year 1. For the second year, we calculate the future value at the end of the remaining 8 years [$FV(0.10,8,0,7500) = \$16,076.92$], and so on. Notice that the last installment will have an FV factor of 1. We can then sum the future values to determine that Sam will have $119,542.50.

Alternatively, we can use Table 4 in Appendix B to find the Future Value of an Annuity in Arrears Factor. Using this table, a rate of return of 10% and a horizon of 10 years corresponds to a factor of 15.937. Therefore, the future value of annuity of $7,500 over 10 years at a rate of return of 10% is ($7,500 × 15.937) = $119,527.50 (the difference is due to rounding).

Appendix B
PRESENT AND FUTURE VALUE TABLES

Table 1: Present Value of \$1; $\frac{1}{(1 + r)^n}$

Rate of return	Number of Periods 1	2	3	4	5	6	7	8	9	10	12	14	16	20	25
6%	0.943	0.890	0.840	0.792	0.747	0.705	0.665	0.627	0.592	0.558	0.497	0.442	0.394	0.312	0.233
7%	0.935	0.873	0.816	0.763	0.713	0.666	0.623	0.582	0.544	0.508	0.444	0.388	0.339	0.258	0.184
8%	0.926	0.857	0.794	0.735	0.681	0.630	0.583	0.540	0.500	0.463	0.397	0.340	0.292	0.215	0.146
9%	0.917	0.842	0.772	0.708	0.650	0.596	0.547	0.502	0.460	0.422	0.356	0.299	0.252	0.178	0.116
10%	0.909	0.826	0.751	0.683	0.621	0.564	0.513	0.467	0.424	0.386	0.319	0.263	0.218	0.149	0.092
11%	0.901	0.812	0.731	0.659	0.593	0.535	0.482	0.434	0.391	0.352	0.286	0.232	0.188	0.124	0.074
12%	0.893	0.797	0.712	0.636	0.567	0.507	0.452	0.404	0.361	0.322	0.257	0.205	0.163	0.104	0.059
13%	0.885	0.783	0.693	0.613	0.543	0.480	0.425	0.376	0.333	0.295	0.231	0.181	0.141	0.087	0.047
14%	0.877	0.769	0.675	0.592	0.519	0.456	0.400	0.351	0.308	0.270	0.208	0.160	0.123	0.073	0.038
15%	0.870	0.756	0.658	0.572	0.497	0.432	0.376	0.327	0.284	0.247	0.187	0.141	0.107	0.061	0.030
16%	0.862	0.743	0.641	0.552	0.476	0.410	0.354	0.305	0.263	0.227	0.168	0.125	0.093	0.051	0.024
18%	0.847	0.718	0.609	0.516	0.437	0.370	0.314	0.266	0.225	0.191	0.137	0.099	0.071	0.037	0.016
20%	0.833	0.694	0.579	0.482	0.402	0.335	0.279	0.233	0.194	0.162	0.112	0.078	0.054	0.026	0.010
22%	0.820	0.672	0.551	0.451	0.370	0.303	0.249	0.204	0.167	0.137	0.092	0.062	0.042	0.019	0.007
24%	0.806	0.650	0.524	0.423	0.341	0.275	0.222	0.179	0.144	0.116	0.076	0.049	0.032	0.014	0.005

Table 2: Future Value of \$1; $(1 + r)^n$

Rate of return	Number of Periods 1	2	3	4	5	6	7	8	9	10	12	14	16	20	25
6%	1.060	1.124	1.191	1.262	1.338	1.419	1.504	1.594	1.689	1.791	2.012	2.261	2.540	3.207	4.292
7%	1.070	1.145	1.225	1.311	1.403	1.501	1.606	1.718	1.838	1.967	2.252	2.579	2.952	3.870	5.427
8%	1.080	1.166	1.260	1.360	1.469	1.587	1.714	1.851	1.999	2.159	2.518	2.937	3.426	4.661	6.848
9%	1.090	1.188	1.295	1.412	1.539	1.677	1.828	1.993	2.172	2.367	2.813	3.342	3.970	5.604	8.623
10%	1.100	1.210	1.331	1.464	1.611	1.772	1.949	2.144	2.358	2.594	3.138	3.797	4.595	6.727	10.835
11%	1.110	1.232	1.368	1.518	1.685	1.870	2.076	2.305	2.558	2.839	3.498	4.310	5.311	8.062	13.585
12%	1.120	1.254	1.405	1.574	1.762	1.974	2.211	2.476	2.773	3.106	3.896	4.887	6.130	9.646	17.000
13%	1.130	1.277	1.443	1.630	1.842	2.082	2.353	2.658	3.004	3.395	4.335	5.535	7.067	11.523	21.231
14%	1.140	1.300	1.482	1.689	1.925	2.195	2.502	2.853	3.252	3.707	4.818	6.261	8.137	13.743	26.462
15%	1.150	1.323	1.521	1.749	2.011	2.313	2.660	3.059	3.518	4.046	5.350	7.076	9.358	16.367	32.919
16%	1.160	1.346	1.561	1.811	2.100	2.436	2.826	3.278	3.803	4.411	5.936	7.988	10.748	19.461	40.874
18%	1.180	1.392	1.643	1.939	2.288	2.700	3.185	3.759	4.435	5.234	7.288	10.147	14.129	27.393	62.669
20%	1.200	1.440	1.728	2.074	2.488	2.986	3.583	4.300	5.160	6.192	8.916	12.839	18.488	38.338	95.396
22%	1.220	1.488	1.816	2.215	2.703	3.297	4.023	4.908	5.987	7.305	10.872	16.182	24.086	53.358	144.210
24%	1.240	1.538	1.907	2.364	2.932	3.635	4.508	5.590	6.931	8.594	13.215	20.319	31.243	73.864	216.542

Table 3: Present Value of an Annuity of $1 in Arrears; $\dfrac{1 - (1 + r)^{-n}}{r}$

	Number of Periods														
	1	2	3	4	5	6	7	8	9	10	12	14	16	20	25
6%	0.943	1.833	2.673	3.465	4.212	4.917	5.582	6.210	6.802	7.360	8.384	9.295	10.106	11.470	12.783
7%	0.935	1.808	2.624	3.387	4.100	4.767	5.389	5.971	6.515	7.024	7.943	8.745	9.447	10.594	11.654
8%	0.926	1.783	2.577	3.312	3.993	4.623	5.206	5.747	6.247	6.710	7.536	8.244	8.851	9.818	10.675
9%	0.917	1.759	2.531	3.240	3.890	4.486	5.033	5.535	5.995	6.418	7.161	7.786	8.313	9.129	9.823
10%	0.909	1.736	2.487	3.170	3.791	4.355	4.868	5.335	5.759	6.145	6.814	7.367	7.824	8.514	9.077
11%	0.901	1.713	2.444	3.102	3.696	4.231	4.712	5.146	5.537	5.889	6.492	6.982	7.379	7.963	8.422
12%	0.893	1.690	2.402	3.037	3.605	4.111	4.564	4.968	5.328	5.650	6.194	6.628	6.974	7.469	7.843
13%	0.885	1.668	2.361	2.974	3.517	3.998	4.423	4.799	5.132	5.426	5.918	6.302	6.604	7.025	7.330
14%	0.877	1.647	2.322	2.914	3.433	3.889	4.288	4.639	4.946	5.216	5.660	6.002	6.265	6.623	6.873
15%	0.870	1.626	2.283	2.855	3.352	3.784	4.160	4.487	4.772	5.019	5.421	5.724	5.954	6.259	6.464
16%	0.862	1.605	2.246	2.798	3.274	3.685	4.039	4.344	4.607	4.833	5.197	5.468	5.668	5.929	6.097
18%	0.847	1.566	2.174	2.690	3.127	3.498	3.812	4.078	4.303	4.494	4.793	5.008	5.162	5.353	5.467
20%	0.833	1.528	2.106	2.589	2.991	3.326	3.605	3.837	4.031	4.192	4.439	4.611	4.730	4.870	4.948
22%	0.820	1.492	2.042	2.494	2.864	3.167	3.416	3.619	3.786	3.923	4.127	4.265	4.357	4.460	4.514
24%	0.806	1.457	1.981	2.404	2.745	3.020	3.242	3.421	3.566	3.682	3.851	3.962	4.033	4.110	4.147

Rate of return (row axis label)

Table 4: Future Value of an Annuity of $1 in Arrears; $\dfrac{(1 + r)^n - 1}{r}$

	Number of Periods													
	2	3	4	5	6	7	8	9	10	12	14	16	20	25
6%	2.060	3.184	4.375	5.637	6.975	8.394	9.897	11.491	13.181	16.870	21.015	25.673	36.786	54.865
7%	2.070	3.215	4.440	5.751	7.153	8.654	10.260	11.978	13.816	17.888	22.550	27.888	40.995	63.249
8%	2.080	3.246	4.506	5.867	7.336	8.923	10.637	12.488	14.487	18.977	24.215	30.324	45.762	73.106
9%	2.090	3.278	4.573	5.985	7.523	9.200	11.028	13.021	15.193	20.141	26.019	33.003	51.160	84.701
10%	2.100	3.310	4.641	6.105	7.716	9.487	11.436	13.579	15.937	21.384	27.975	35.950	57.275	98.347
11%	2.110	3.342	4.710	6.228	7.913	9.783	11.859	14.164	16.722	22.713	30.095	39.190	64.203	114.413
12%	2.120	3.374	4.779	6.353	8.115	10.089	12.300	14.776	17.549	24.133	32.393	42.753	72.052	133.334
13%	2.130	3.407	4.850	6.480	8.323	10.405	12.757	15.416	18.420	25.650	34.883	46.672	80.947	155.620
14%	2.140	3.440	4.921	6.610	8.536	10.730	13.233	16.085	19.337	27.271	37.581	50.980	91.025	181.871
15%	2.150	3.473	4.993	6.742	8.754	11.067	13.727	16.786	20.304	29.002	40.505	55.717	102.444	212.793
16%	2.160	3.506	5.066	6.877	8.977	11.414	14.240	17.519	21.321	30.850	43.672	60.925	115.380	249.214
18%	2.180	3.572	5.215	7.154	9.442	12.142	15.327	19.086	23.521	34.931	50.818	72.939	146.628	342.603
20%	2.200	3.640	5.368	7.442	9.930	12.916	16.499	20.799	25.959	39.581	59.196	87.442	186.688	471.981
22%	2.220	3.708	5.524	7.740	10.442	13.740	17.762	22.670	28.657	44.874	69.010	104.935	237.989	650.955
24%	2.240	3.778	5.684	8.048	10.980	14.615	19.123	24.712	31.643	50.895	80.496	126.011	303.601	898.092

Rate of return (row axis label)

ANSWERS TO CHECK IT! EXERCISES

Exercise #1: $62.10 = $100 × 0.621; $152.10 = $100 × 1.521; $331.20 = $100 × 3.312; $811.52 = $100 × 8.115.

Exercise #2: The PV factors are 1.000, 0.877, 0.769, and 0.675, yielding present values of −$100,000, $52,620, $38,450, and $6,750 for years 0–3. Thus, the NPV = $6,750 + $38,450 + $52,620 − $100,000 = −$2,180. We reject the project because it has a negative NPV.

Exercise #3: In Excel, enter cash flows in cells A1 to A4 (starting with the −$100,000 for the initial outlay in A1). In cell A5, type "=IRR(A1:A4)" and Excel will reveal that the IRR = 12.40%. Using the same approach as in *Check it! Exercise #2*, we can calculate NPV(12%) = $550; NPV(13%) = −$820, and confirm the validity of our estimate. Finally, we reject the project because its IRR is lower than the cost of capital (14%).

Exercise #4: Cumulative cash inflows through year 5 = $60,000 year 1 + $60,000 year 2 + $60,000 year 3 + $50,000 year 4 + $50,000 year 5 = $280,000. Payback period of 5.6 = 5 years + ($310,000 initial investment − $280,000 cumulative cash inflows through year 5)/$50,000 cash flow in year 6.

Exercise #5: $304,000 in year 5 = $370,000 net cash inflow from Exhibit 11.2 − [($370,000 − $150,000 depreciation expense) × 0.30 in taxes due]. *Alternatively,* $370,000 − $150,000 = $220,000 in taxable income; $220,000 × 0.30 = $66,000 in taxes. Thus, $304,000 = $220,000 in income − $66,000 in taxes + $150,000 in depreciation in expense. $346,000 in year 10 = $430,000 net cash inflow from Exhibit 11.2 − [($430,000 − $150,000 depreciation expense) × 0.30 in taxes due].

SELF-STUDY PROBLEM

The Clinging Vine Café is considering the purchase of a new dishwashing machine. This machine will cost $60,000 now. When sold as scrap at the end of three years, it will fetch $3,000. Alternatively, the café can continue hiring college students on a part-time basis to wash dishes, at an annual payroll cost of $22,000. While the dishwasher will increase outflows for power and water, manual washing leads to greater breakage. Considering all of these costs, the dishwasher would save $2,000 annually in operating costs. If the Café purchases the new dishwashing machine, it will depreciate the washer over three years using straight-line depreciation.

In each of the following three cases, use the net present value method to determine whether The Clinging Vine Café should purchase the dishwashing machine. Treat each case independently.

a. *Ivy, the owner of the Clinging Vine Café, claims that she puts all of her money in her mattress and never goes near banks. This would mean that to Ivy, the opportunity cost of capital is just a less lumpy mattress. Ignore taxes for now.*

From the perspective of buying the dishwasher, we have:

Initial outlay	($60,000)
Salvage value	$3,000
Savings—student wages for three years ($22,000 × 3)	$66,000
Savings—Broken dishes for three years ($2,000 × 3)	$6,000
NPV (with 0% as cost of capital)	$15,000

Thus, The Clinging Vine saves $15,000 by purchasing the new dishwashing machine.

b. *Ivy meets an investment banker and expands her horizons. She now estimates that her cost of capital is 10%. Again, ignore taxes.*

First, let's draw a time line from the perspective of buying the dishwasher.

	Year 0	Year 1	Year 2	Year 3
Sell machine				$3,000
Student wages		$22,000	$22,000	$22,000
Broken dishes		$2,000	$2,000	$2,000
Buy machine	($60,000)			
Total flow	($60,000)	$24,000	$24,000	$27,000

Next, we obtain the discount factors from Table 1 in Appendix B. We calculate the NPV by applying these factors to the raw cash flows each year.

Year	Cash Flow	PV Factor (10%)	NPV
0	($60,000)	1	($60,000)
1	$24,000	.909	$21,816
2	$24,000	.826	$19,824
3	$27,000	.751	$20,277
		NPV	$1,917

Thus, we still find that the café should purchase the dishwashing machine.

c. *Redo the analysis for part(b) assuming a tax rate of 40%.*

In addition to discounting, we also have to consider tax effects. Let's again create a time line from the perspective of buying the dishwasher; for illustration purposes we consider *all individual* cash flows. We place cash inflows above the line and cash outflows below the line.

	Year 0	Year 1	Year 2	Year 3
Sell machine				$3,000
Depreciation tax shield = $20,000 depreciation expense × 0.40 tax rate		$8,000	$8,000	$8,000
Student wages		$22,000	$22,000	$22,000
Broken dishes		$2,000	$2,000	$2,000
Buy machine	($60,000)			
Tax savings lost − student wages		($8,800)	($8,800)	($8,800)
Tax savings lost − broken dishes		(800)	(800)	(800)
Tax on gain from sale = ($3,000 in proceeds − $0 salvage value) × 0.40 tax rate				(1,200)
Total cash flow	−$60,000	$22,400	$22,400	$24,200

Tax savings lost − student wages = (student wages × tax rate)
Tax savings lost − broken dishes = (cost broken dishes × tax rate)

Our next step is to discount the cash flows:

Year	Cash Flow	PV Factor (10%)	NPV
0	($60,000)	1	($60,000.00)
1	$22,400	.909	$20,361.60
2	$22,400	.826	$18,502.40
3	$24,200	.751	$18,174.20
		NPV	($2,961.80)

We find that the NPV is negative; thus, the café should keep the students! This problem illustrates the importance of considering both the time value of money and tax effects when making decisions regarding long-lived resources. Moreover, our answers differ in both direction and magnitude depending on whether we incorporate the opportunity cost of capital and taxes.

Alternate Approach

We underscore the link between capital budgeting and decision making by evaluating the two options separately. If Ivy keeps the students, she would spend $24,000 (= $22,000 + $2,000) annually. Because this expenditure is deductible when computing taxable income, the expense reduces taxes paid by 40% × $24,000 = $9,600, leading to a net cash outflow of $14,400 per year. Using the annuity factor for three years (Table 3 in the Appendix), Ivy computes a discounted cash flow of ($14,400 × 2.487) = $35,812.50, where $14,400 = $24,000 − $9,600.

If Ivy buys the dishwasher, she incurs an immediate cash flow of $60,000. She get a depreciation tax shield of $8,000 (= 40% × $60,000/3) for each of three years. Finally, she gets sale proceeds of $3,000 but pays taxes of $1,200 (= 40% × $3,000) on the gain from the sale. The discounted value of these flows is $38,760.20 (use the PV factors from Table 1 in Appendix B). Keeping the students has a lower cost and saves her $2,947.70 per year. (The difference of $14.40 is due to rounding in the PV factor calculations.)

GLOSSARY

Accounting rate of return (ARR) The average annual income from a project divided by the average annual investment in the project.

Annuity A stream of cash flow with the property that the cash flows per period.

Capital budgeting The collective term for the mechanisms and tools used to evaluate expenditures on long-lived resources.

Cost of capital The opportunity cost of money in the form of returns from alternate investments.

Discounting The practice of expressing a future cash flow in terms of its present value.

Discount factor The amount by which a future cash flow is multiplied to obtain its present value.

Discount rate The rate of return employed to compute the present value of future cash flows.

Hurdle rate Minimum required rate of return chosen by management. Often exceeds the cost of capital.

Initial outlay All costs connected with purchasing an asset and getting it ready for its intended use.

Internal rate of return (IRR) The discount rate at which a project's net present value is zero.

Lumpy resource Resources for which it is difficult to match the demand for capacity with the supply.

Modified payback method/period The length of time it takes to recoup the initial investment using discounted cash flows.

Net present value (NPV) The present value of all of the cash flows associated with a resource.

Payback method/period The length of time it takes to recoup the initial investment using undiscounted cash flows.

Present value The value today of a future cash flow.

Real option analysis A collection of mathematical techniques for valuing the flexibility associated with a project.

Salvage value The final one-time costs or benefits associated with disposing of a resource.

Time value of money Phrase used to denote that a dollar today is worth more than a dollar tomorrow.

REVIEW QUESTIONS

11.1 LO1. What is capital budgeting?

11.2 LO1. What does the notion "time value of money" mean? Why is it important for project evaluation?

11.3 LO1. "Capacity resources are lumpy in nature." What does the term *lumpy* mean in this statement? Why is it relevant in the context of capital budgeting?

11.4 LO1. What is the difference between a capital budget and an operating budget?

11.5 LO2. What are the four important elements of a capital expenditure decision?

11.6 LO3. Define the term *net present value.* Describe how you would calculate the NPV for a project proposal.

11.7 LO3. Define the term *internal rate of return* or IRR. Describe how you would calculate the IRR for a project proposal.

11.8 LO3. List three assumptions underlying the NPV method.

11.9 LO4. List two key advantages of the payback method.

11.10 LO4. What is the difference between the payback and modified payback methods?

11.11 LO4. Define the accounting rate of return.

11.12 LO5. Why are taxes important in capital budgeting?

11.13 LO5. What is a depreciation tax shield? Is this tax shield a cash inflow or a cash outflow?

11.14 LO6. What is a hurdle rate?

11.15 LO6. Why do many firms begin projects on a small scale before making considerable investments?

DISCUSSION QUESTIONS

11.16 LO1, LO2. In Chapters 9 and 10, we used cost allocations to estimate the cost of capacity resources, and to measure the long-term profitability of investing in resources and products. In what ways does this approach differ from capital budgeting principles discussed in this chapter?

11.17 LO1, LO2. "I don't do any capital budgeting for buying my machines. They typically last for more than 10 years. If I have to do capital budgeting, I need to estimate my future cash inflows and outflows for the next 10 years, which is very difficult to do. I don't have time for all that. I know that my company is making money now, and if I need to buy a new machine and replace an existing machine, I just do it." How would you respond to this argument?

11.18 LO2, LO5. What are the tax implications of selling an asset when it still has some economic value? Consider, in particular, the issue when we use an accelerated depreciation schedule for calculating taxable income.

11.19 LO3. List and discuss two advantages of the net present value method relative to the internal rate of return method.

11.20 LO3. The net present value method assumes that future cash inflows are reinvested at the cost of capital. The internal rate of return method assumes that the reinvestment takes place at the internal rate of return. Which is a better assumption and why?

11.21 LO3. What are some of the considerations that go into the choice of discount rate under the net present value method?

11.22 LO2, LO3, LO4. "I don't see any reason to do this net present value stuff. The payback method works well for me. It tells me how many years it takes to recoup the initial money I put in. As long as my payback period is as good as anybody else's in the industry, I am okay." How would you respond to this argument?

11.23 LO3. Discounted cash flow techniques allow us to evaluate a long-term investment by taking future financial benefits into account. However, there could be many nonfinancial costs and benefits as well. Many experts are of the view that when it comes to these non-financial aspects, "it is better to be approximately right than precisely wrong." Do you agree? Explain.

11.24 LO4. Even though the payback method ignores time value of money, many firms continue to use it when evaluating projects. Why might this practice be in the *manager's* best interest?

11.25 LO4. List and discuss two advantages and two disadvantages of the accounting rate of return method.

11.26 LO3. Under the internal rate of return method, how would you decide which projects to accept and which projects to reject? Explain.

11.27 LO3, LO6. Is it always advisable to accept projects with the highest (positive) NPVs? IRRs? Why or why not?

11.28 LO5 (Advanced). Research the term *Modified Accelerated Cost Recovery System* (MACRS) and explain its relevance to project evaluation.

11.29 L05. Often, firms will employ different schedules for computing the depreciation expense for computing accounting and taxable income. Which schedule is relevant from a project evaluation perspective?

11.30 LO6. In the context of investing in advanced manufacturing technologies, why is the current state of affairs an inappropriate baseline for evaluating project benefits?

EXERCISES

11.31 Present value calculations (LO3). Refer to the data in the following table:

Setting	Initial Outlay	Life (years)	Discount Rate (compounded annually)	Future Value (at the end of life)
1	$225,000	5	10%	?
2	?	10	12%	$400,000
3	$157,950	8	?	$450,000
4	$150,000	?	12%	$371,400

Required:
Treating each row of the table independently, compute the missing information. Use the present value/future value tables at the end of the book.

11.32 Annuity calculation (LO3). Kim Barth decides to start a small restaurant near a busy shopping mall. She applies for a loan of $150,000, to be repaid in five annual installments, with each installment due at the end of each of the next five years. The bank charges an interest rate of 10%, compounded annually.

Required:

Compute the annual installment amount. Use the annuity tables at the end of the book.

11.33 Mortgage loan (LO3). Diana and Jason just bought a house for $484,000, inclusive of title insurance and closing costs. They plan to make a down payment of $84,000. They were able to secure a 30-year fixed mortgage loan at an annual percentage rate of 6%, compounded *monthly* from a mortgage lending company.

Required:

a. Using Excel, calculate the monthly payment that Diana and Jason have to make to the mortgage lending company. Because interest is compounded monthly, remember to convert the annual rate into a monthly rate, and convert the number of periods in the mortgage loan from years to months.

b. What would be the outstanding loan balance at the end of five years (*Hint:* Use the annuity as calculated in part (a) above, and consider only the remaining monthly installment payments)?

11.34 Future value calculation (LO3). Haidan and Ying Li just had a baby girl, Julie. They want to make sure that they will have enough money to send Julie to college. They estimate that, 18 years from now, college will cost $35,000 per year for four years. Assume that these cash flows occur at the start of years 18–21. Further, Haidan and Ying believe that they could earn 8% a year on their investments.

Required:

a. How much money should they invest right now (as a lump sum) to have the required amount on hand at the start of year 18? That is, what is the present value of the future payments?

b. Haidan and Ying do not have the necessary cash to make a lump-sum investment today for Julie's college costs. Rather, they plan to save systematically for the next 18 years. How much should they save each year to cover the expected cost? Notice that there will be 18 investments, starting now at the start of year 1 and ending at the start of year 18.

11.35 Depreciation tax shield (LO2, LO5). Quality Metal Works, Inc., is considering a proposal to buy a new furnace for $2,500,000 (all costs included). The furnace will have a useful life of 10 years, with no expected salvage value at the end of its life. The firm requires a rate of return of 8% on all its investments. For convenience, assume that cash flows occur at the end of each year. Assume straight-line depreciation for tax purposes. The applicable tax rate is 30%.

Required:

a. Ignore the depreciation tax shield. What are the minimum annual cash inflows that this furnace must generate for the company to justify the investment?

b. How much is the annual depreciation tax shield? What is the present value of the depreciation tax shield?

c. If you take into account the depreciation tax shield, will the minimum annual cash inflows from operations (pretax) needed to justify this investment increase or decrease? By how much?

11.36 Gain/loss on asset sale, taxes (LO5): Pringle Plastics recently sold a forklift for $12,500. The firm, which pays taxes on income at the rate of 45%, had purchased the forklift for $50,000. The firm's books show accumulated depreciation of $38,700.

Required:

What is the after-tax cash flow due to the sale of the forklift?

11.37 Net present value, depreciation tax shield (LO2, LO3, LO5). The owner of Polyplast, Inc., Joshua Ronen, is trying to decide what to do with a capital of $500,000 at his disposal. Ronen is considering two options: invest the money in shares of another company or expand the capacity of his plastics plant by buying a new injection molding machine. With the first option, he expects to earn a return of 12% over the next 10 years. With the second option, he expects to make annual net cash inflow of $108,000. The tax rate is 30%, and the machine will not have any salvage value at the end of its useful life of 10 years.

Required:

What should Ronen do? (Assume straight-line depreciation for tax purposes.)

11.38 Internal rate of return (LO2, LO3, LO5). Refer to the data in Exercise 11.37. The company has been using the internal rate of return approach to evaluate its long-term investments in the past, and its policy has been to invest in only those projects with internal rates return in excess of 14%.

Required:

a. What is the internal rate of return from investing in the injection molding machine? As per company policy, will it accept or reject this option?

b. Assume that the only other option is the one described in Exercise 11.37—invest the money in the shares of another company. Will Ronen's company be making the right choice if it adheres to its policy of requiring an internal rate of return in excess of 14%? What is the right "hurdle" rate to use for this decision?

11.39 Payback, ARR (LO1, LO2, LO4). Refer to the data in Exercise 11.37.

Required:

a. What is the payback period corresponding to investing in the injection molding machine?

b. What is the modified payback period corresponding to investing in the injection molding machine?

c. What is the accounting rate of return corresponding to investing in the injection molding machine?

11.40 Payback and ARR (LO4). Rego and Associates plans to invest $1,200,000 in modernizing their call centers. They expect productivity to increase and generate 8,000 more billable hours annually. The current bill rate is $50 per hour. The effect of the investment on productivity will last for over five years, although the effects become harder to predict for beyond five years. The company uses a discount factor of 10% on its capital projects.

Required:

a. What is the payback period on this project?

b. What is the modified payback period on this project?

c. What is the project's accounting rate of return? Ignore taxes.

11.41 Payback and ARR (LO4). Gleason and Company is planning to invest $5 million in a new, stand-alone project. Before depreciation, it expects this project to yield a positive cash flow of $1.4 million each year for five years. The firm expects to depreciate the investment on a straight-line basis over five years and with zero salvage value. The applicable discount rate is 12% and the tax rate is 30%.

Required:

a. What is the payback period on this project?

b. What is the modified payback period on this project?

c. What is the project's accounting rate of return?

11.42 Net present value and IRR, equal cash flows (LO3, LO4, LO5). To stave off a sudden increase in competition in the cookware industry, Rahul Sheth of Delight Cookware, Inc., is considering several cost-saving proposals to remain profitable. One such proposal promises an expected cost saving of $275,000 annually over the next five years. The required rate of return on the investment is 8%. Ignore tax effects.

Required:

a. What is the maximum amount that Rahul will be willing to invest in the project?

b. Assuming that Rahul invests the amount you calculate in a. above, what is the payback period on the project?

c. What is the project's internal rate of return?

11.43 Net present value and IRR, equal cash flows (LO3, LO4, LO5). Acme Industries is considering several ideas for expanding its scope of operations. It is planning to open an office in California to tap the Western market. Such an office would require an initial investment of $3.4 million and annual cash operating expenses of $750,000. The office, however, would generate a contribution of $1.6 million per year before considering operating expenses. Acme expects to depreciate (using a straight-line basis) the assets over an eight-year period. At the end of eight years, Acme expects to sell the California office for $400,000. Acme pays taxes at the rate of 30% of income and uses a discount rate of 10% on its capital projects.

Required:

a. Calculate the net present value (NPV) and the internal rate of return (IRR) for the California office. Based on these criteria, should Acme open the office in California?

b. What would be the payback period for this project?

11.44 NPV, IRR, Unequal cash flows (LO3). The following table presents the initial cash outlay and cash flow projections for a new line of digital cameras that DigiCam, Inc., is evaluating.

Initial cash outlay	$2,350,000
Net pretax cash inflows—year 1	$1,000,000
Net pretax cash inflows—year 2	$1,200,000
Net pretax cash inflows—year 3	$1,300,000
Salvage value (at the end of year 3)	$250,000

The company uses a discount rate of 10% for evaluating such projects. The corporate tax rate is 30%. Assume straight-line depreciation for tax.

Required:

a. What is the net present value of the project?

b. Using Excel, calculate the internal rate of return (IRR) for this project.

11.45 NPV, IRR, alternate methods, unequal cash flows (LO3, LO4, LO5). The following table presents the initial cash outlay and cash flow projections for a new store that TopSports, Inc., is planning to open in Boston, Massachusetts

Initial cash outlay	$6,750,000
Net cash inflows—year 1	$2,250,000
Net cash inflows—year 2	$2,250,000
Net cash inflows—year 3	$1,000,000
Net cash inflows—year 4	$700,000
Net cash inflows—year 5	$250,000
Salvage value (at the end of year 5)	$750,000

The company uses a discount rate of 8% for such project evaluations. The corporate tax rate is 30%. Assume straight-line depreciation for tax purposes.

Required:

a. What is the net present value of the project?

b. What is the payback period for the project?

c. What is the modified payback period for the project?

PROBLEMS

11.46 Equipment replacement, totals approach (LO2, LO3, LO5). Copy Center, Inc., offers a variety of document and computer services to the business community in midtown Cleveland. It is considering replacing one of its copiers. The old copier has a book value of $5,000 but can be sold for $12,000. The new copier being considered will cost $90,000 and offers a number of attractive features. The expected life is three years with no expected salvage value at the end of its life. The company expects that the new copier will generate $40,000, $35,000, and $25,000 in after-tax cash flows, respectively, in the first, second, and the third year of operations. The firm's manager, however, tells you that this estimate does not include the depreciation tax shield.

On the other hand, the old copier is in a relatively good condition and can last three more years with careful maintenance. Demand, though, is expected to be lower because the old copier lacks the features of the new copier. Taking these factors into account, the company projects that the old copier will generate $10,000, $8,000, and $5,000 in after tax cash flows over the next three years. Again, this estimate excludes any tax shield arising from depreciating the copier. At the end of three years, this old copier will have no salvage value.

Copy Center uses a cost of capital of 12% for discounting purposes. Copy Center depreciates its copiers on a straight-line basis over a period of three years. The corporate tax rate is 25%, and *all* taxes are paid at the end of each year. If Copy Center decided to retain the old copier, it will depreciate the remaining $5,000 book value over the next three years.

Required:

a. Compute the net present value of the new copier, assuming that the company goes ahead with the replacement decision.

b. Compute the internal rate of return from investment in the new copier (round off to the nearest percentage), assuming that the company goes ahead with the replacement decision.

c. What is the net present value from keeping the old copier?

d. Under the net present value method, which is the better option? What assumption does this method make with respect to the money that is freed up if the company were to retain the old copier? Does this assumption seem reasonable?

e. Discuss some of the qualitative/nonfinancial factors that may be relevant to this decision.

11.47 Net present value (LO3, LO5). The owner of WS Industries, Jayant Krishnan, is considering the purchase of an advanced milling machine. This machine costs $2,500,000 to purchase. Installing the machine, calibrating it and training operators will cost another $500,000. Jayant expects the machine to reduce materials costs by 20% and labor time by 40%. He expects the machine to have a useful life of five years, with zero salvage value.

Currently, Jayant makes 200,000 units of the product annually. For each unit, he incurs $8 in materials cost and $12 in labor costs. WS Industries' cost of capital is 14% and it pays income taxes at the rate of 35%. Assume straight-line depreciation for tax purposes.

Required:

What is the NPV for the project?

11.48 Net present value and IRR, growing cash flows (LO2, LO3, LO5). Thompson and Company plans to invest $8 million in a new product line. It expects the product to sell for $20 per unit. Variable costs are $8 per unit, and annual fixed operating costs (excluding depreciation) are $750,000. The firm expects sales to begin at 200,000 units and grow by 10% a year for four years, leveling off thereafter. Sales will decrease by 25% a year starting in year 8. Thompson expects to close the plant and discontinue the product line at the end of year 10, realizing zero salvage value. The required rate of return on the investment is 12%, and the company uses straight-line depreciation for tax purposes. The corporate tax rate is 30%.

Required:

a. Calculate the annual net after-tax cash flows for each of the 10 years of the proposed product line.

b. What is the net present value of the project?

c. What is the IRR for this project? (Use Excel to calculate the IRR.)

11.49 Ranking projects (NPV vs. IRR) (LO1, LO2, LO3, LO5). Consider the two alternate investment proposals presented in the following table:

	Proposal 1	Proposal 2
Initial outlay	$1,500,000	$1,000,000
Useful life	10 years	10 years
Salvage value at the end of useful life	0	0
Annual revenues	800,000	800,000
Total variable costs	350,000	475,000
Annual fixed costs (excluding depreciation)	100,000	100,000
Required rate of return	12%	12%
Corporate tax rate	30%	30%

Proposal 1 requires higher up-front investment than Proposal 2 but helps in keeping the annual variable costs at a lower level than Proposal 2. If Proposal 2 is chosen, assume that the capital of $500,000 (i.e., the difference between the initial outlays of the two proposals) can be invested elsewhere at the cost of capital.

Required:

a. Rank the alternatives using the NPV method.

b. Rank the alternatives using the IRR method.

c. Some argue that the NPV does not control for project size. In other words, larger projects tend to have higher NPV, everything else remaining the same. Is this argument applicable in this problem? Explain.

d. What is the annual operating leverage under each proposal? (Refer to Chapter 5 for a definition and description of operating leverage.) Discuss the relative operating leverages of the two proposals in light of their rankings using the NPV and IRR methods in (a) and (b) above.

11.50 Ranking projects (Payback and adjusted payback) (LO1, LO2, LO3, LO5, Advanced). Refer to the data regarding two alternate investment proposals in the previous problem.

Required:

a. Rank the alternatives using the payback period method.

b. Rank the alternatives using the modified payback period method.

The modified payback period method identifies when the present value future cash flows covers initial investment.

c. Rank the alternatives using the accounting rate of return method.

d. Compare and contrast the rankings using payback period, adjusted payback period, accounting rate of return, NPP, and IRR methods.

 11.51 Equipment Replacement (LO3, LO4, LO6). Tom and Lynda are contemplating the purchase of some cardio machines (e.g., treadmills, elliptical trainers, and stair master). They project that the purchase of gym quality machines would cost $25,000. Operating expenses such as power and maintenance would be $1,200 per year. Tom and Lynda project that the machines would last three years. While current clients would appreciate access to newer equipment, no new members would be added if Tom and Lynda replaced the machine. Each member generates $65 in contribution per month.

Required:

a. Calculate the net present value (NPV) of the purchase at 15%. Assume that the cash outflow takes place now, that all cash inflows take place at the end of the year, and that the machines have zero salvage value at the end of three years. Ignore taxes in your analysis.

b. Suppose Tom and Lynda tell you that not replacing the machines would lead to the loss of 15 members this year, 20 more the next, and 25 the year following. Redo the analysis in part (a).

c. What inference do you draw about the role of the status quo option in NPV analysis?

11.52 Make vs. buy (LO1, LO2, LO3, LO5, Advanced). Simco Blenders makes different kinds of electrical blenders, mixers, and grinders for various kitchen needs. These products are powered by small electric motors. Presently, Simco buys these motors from an outside vendor. However, Simco is considering setting up a facility to make these motors in house. The following table presents financial information for both of these options.

Option 1: Making motors in house

Initial outlay	$1,500,000
Useful life	10 years
Salvage value at the end of useful life	0
Unit variable cost	$16
Annual fixed costs (excluding depreciation)	$200,000
Required rate of return	12%
Corporate tax rate	30%
Annual demand for motors	250,000
After-sales customer support cost (per unit)	$1

Option 2: Buying motors from vendor

Unit price	$18
After-sales customer support cost (per unit)	$2

Required:

What should Simco Blenders do?

11.53 Long-term pricing and capital budgeting (LO1, LO2, LO3, LO5, Advanced). Precision Medicals makes medical instruments. It wishes to introduce a new line of electronic blood pressure gauges for use in hospitals and homes. The company will set up a new division solely for this purpose, and the division manager will be fully responsible for all aspects of the business. After much research, the chief financial officer of the company put together the following table to evaluate this proposal.

Initial outlay	$22,250,000
Maximum production capacity	100,000 units
Useful life	15 years
Salvage value at the end of useful life	zero
Unit variable cost	$85
Annual fixed costs (excluding depreciation)	$400,000
Required rate of return	12%
Corporate tax rate	25%
Expected annual sales	80,000 units

Required:

Assume that the company wishes to maintain a stable pricing policy over the entire 15-year horizon. What is the minimum price per unit that the company needs to sell this product in order for this investment to be justifiable in the long run?

11.54 NPV versus payback (LO3, LO4). The following table presents financial information regarding two alternative proposals.

	Proposal 1	Proposal 2
Initial cash outlay	$8,750,000	$8,750,000
Net cash inflows—year 1	$3,750,000	750,000
Net cash inflows—year 2	$4,250,000	1,000,000
Net cash inflows—year 3	$2,000,000	3,250,000
Net cash inflows—year 4	$700,000	3,875,000
Net cash inflows—year 5	$250,000	4,250,000

The salvage value is expected to be zero for both proposals at the end of five years. The company uses a discount rate of 10% for such project evaluations. Ignore income taxes.

Required:

a. Rank the two projects using the net present value method. Which project is preferable?

b. Rank the two projects using payback periods. Which project is preferable?

c. What conclusions can you draw about using the payback period method for project selection?

11.55 NPV versus Payback (LO1, LO2, LO3, LO4, LO6). The following table presents financial information regarding two alternative projects.

	Project 1	Project 2
Initial cash outlay	$6,750,000	$6,750,000
Net cash inflows—year 1	2,000,000	2,500,000
Net cash inflows—year 2	2,000,000	2,500,000
Net cash inflows—year 3	2,000,000	2,500,000
Net cash inflows—year 4	1,400,000	800,000
Net cash inflows—year 5	1,400,000	800,000

The salvage value is expected to be zero for both projects at the end of five years. The company uses a discount rate of 10% for such project evaluations. Ignore income taxes.

Required:

a. Rank the two projects using the net present value method. Which project is preferable?

b. Rank the two projects using payback periods. Which project is preferable?

c. Rank the two projects using *modified* payback periods. Which project is preferable?

MINI-CASES

11.56 Asset replacement, an incremental approach (LO1, LO2, LO3, LO4). STC & Tweety, LLP, own and operate a canary breeding farm. For the most recent year, STC & Tweety generated revenues of $250,000, incurred cash operating costs of $120,000, and had an after-tax net income of $77,000.

STC & Tweety are considering replacing their canary breeding barn. The current ("old") breeding barn has a book value of $60,000 and could be sold today for $45,000. Alternatively, the current barn could be used for the next three years, after which if could be sold for $3,000.

If STC & Tweety decide to keep using the old barn then they anticipate spending $10,000 to fix (repair) the barn at the end of the first year. These costs are considered a routine maintenance expense and will not increase the barn's book value.

A new canary barn would cost $180,000, but it would save STC & Tweety $70,000 in before-tax operating costs for each of the next three years. In addition, after the third year STC & Tweety could sell the new barn to a local farmer for $5,000.

STC & Tweety depreciate all of their assets using straight-line depreciation and zero assumed salvage value. Their required rate of return (cost of capital) is 10%, and their tax rate is 30%.

Assume all operating cash flows occur at year end.

Required:

a. Define the status quo.

b. Define the alternative.

c. What is the incremental *initial* after-tax cash outflow associated with the alternative you have defined? Be sure to include all relevant cash flows.

d. What is the alternative's incremental after-tax cash inflow for the end of year 2?

e. Draw a time line that shows all of the incremental cash flows associated with the alternative you have defined.

f. Should STC & Tweety, LLP invest in the new barn?

 11.57 New product introduction (LO3, LO4, LO5). ComCo makes wireless routers and other network communication products. Since its inception in the early 1990s, ComCo has successfully implemented a strategy of investing heavily in product development and introducing a new model with more enhanced features every three to four years. Every time a new model of a product is introduced, the old model is slowly phased out by first cutting prices on the old model to push as much of the inventory out as possible, and then abandoning the model.

In January, 2008 ComCo introduced the next generation of wireless broadband routers, C200H, and quickly abandoned the previous model. The following table presents the initial outlays and cash flow estimates for the next four years for C200H, based on which the CEO of ComSys, Martha Kline, gave a green light to introducing the product.

Initial cash outlay	$9,000,000
Net cash inflows—year 1	$5,000,000
Net cash inflows—year 2	$6,500,000
Net cash inflows—year 3	$4,000,000
Net cash inflows—year 4	$1,000,000
Salvage value (at the end of year 5)	0

The company expects 14% rate of return on all its projects. The corporate tax rate is 30%. In August, 2008, Lara Garcia, one of the product development engineers, burst into Martha's office all excited. Her product development team had just successfully tested a new and much improved router. This was truly an innovative product. It did not take long for Martha to realize that she had a jewel in her hand. Her senior associates agreed. The new product, C300G, had the potential of propelling the company leaps and bounds ahead of the competition.

Soon, however, an unsettling calm set in as the management team tried to get a handle on the decision they were facing. They came up with a list of issues to take into account and address:

- The new router, C300G, could be introduced as early as January 2009. However, it would require a separate production facility from the existing facility used for making C200H.

- Introduction of C300G in January 2009 would mean that the existing router, which was beginning to do well in the market, would lose some of its market because most customers would prefer C300G over C200H.

- It was only a matter of time before other competitors came up with a technology comparable to C300G. The team estimated that they had about a year's head start on this new technology. So, while delaying the introduction of C300G to the following year could help sell the existing product (C200H) and recoup some of the investment in that product, it could cost the company some market share in C300G (the company would lose the timing advantage).

Members of the management team were split in their opinions on what was the right course of action, and decided to prepare a report providing a financial comparison of two options:

1. Introduce C300G on January 1, 2009, and phase out C200H over the next three years.
2. Introduce C300G on January 1, 2010, and phase out C200H over the next two years.

Under both options, the company will continue to produce as much of C200H as it can sell over the remaining years. The management team performed a careful analysis and presented a report to Martha with their recommendations. The following two tables present the financial estimates corresponding to the two options:

Option 1 (introduce C300G in Jan 2009)	C300G	C200H
Cash outlay to introduce C300G	$15,000,000	
Net cash inflows—2009	$10,000,000	$2,200,000
Net cash inflows—2010	$6,000,000	$850,000
Net cash inflows—2011	$4,000,000	$250,000
Net cash inflows—2012	$2,000,000	—
Salvage value (at the end of 2012)	0	

Option 2 (introduce C300G in 1/2010)	C300G	C200H
Net cash inflows—2009	—	$6,500,000
Cash outlay to introduce C300G at the end of 2009	$15,000,000	—
Net cash inflows—2010	$6,000,000	$500,000
Net cash inflows—2011	$4,500,000	$150,000
Net cash inflows—2012	$2,000,000	—
Net cash inflows—2013	$1,000,000	
Salvage value (at the end of 2013)	0	

Required:

a. What should Martha do? Assume that all equipment is depreciated over four years, using the straight-line method.

b. What are some of the qualitative considerations that Martha and her management team should take into account?

Chapter 12

Performance Evaluation in Decentralized Organizations

AFTER MANAGING A COPY CENTER FOR several years, Aaron Knight began his own business, Knight Copy & PC Center (KCPC). Located in midtown Manhattan, Aaron began KCPC with an initial investment of $1.5 million and a staff of five. A loyal clientele quickly developed because of the personalized, high-quality service that KCPC provides. Within a few years, Aaron opened several branches in Manhattan and surrounding areas.

Aaron soon found it difficult to manage the day-to-day operations in all of KCPC's branches from his main office. As a result, he hired managers for each store, and three regional managers. However, Aaron is worried that the firm is losing momentum because his managers do not bring the same level of commitment and drive to the business as he does. Aaron seeks our help both in evaluating his branch and regional offices, and in motivating better performance from his managers.

APPLYING THE DECISION FRAMEWORK

What Is the Problem?
Aaron is worried about the performance of KCPC's branch offices and the commitment of its managers.

What Are the Options?
Aaron has numerous options for defining each manager's role, and for putting in a performance measurement and evaluation system to motivate, monitor, and reward managers.

What Are the Costs and Benefits?
We will examine the costs and benefits of delegating decision making (decentralizing) as well as the costs and benefits of using various performance measures and incentives.

Make the Decision!
After looking at the various issues associated with performance measurement and evaluation systems in decentralized organizations, Aaron can select the best portfolio of control measures.

Aaron Knight of Knight's Copy & PC center is trying to figure out how to motivate, monitor, and reward his employees.

LEARNING OBJECTIVES

After studying this chapter, you will be able to:

1 Explain the costs and benefits of decentralization.

2 Apply the principles of performance measurement.

3 Rate the performance of cost and profit centers.

4 Evaluate the performance of investment centers.

5 Describe transfer pricing.

In Chapters 9 through 11, you learned how to make planning decisions to support operations over the long run. As we learned in Chapter 1, however, it is not enough just to make plans. Periodically, firms need to evaluate whether everything is going as planned and whether everyone in the organization is on the same page. In this chapter, we discuss how organizations use monitoring, incentives, and performance evaluation systems for these purposes.

We begin this chapter by describing **decentralization**, the practice of delegating decisions to lower-level managers. We then examine some common forms of decentralization and illustrate how effective performance evaluation is vital in decentralized organizations. Following this, we discuss the principles of performance measurement and apply them to decentralized organizations. Finally, we discuss transfer pricing, an important issue that arises when multiple divisions within an organization engage in business transactions with each other.

CHAPTER CONNECTIONS
Our discussion in this chapter complements the material presented in Chapter 8, which focused on profit variances and short-term measures of operating efficiency. Specifically, we consider how organizations can design performance measures to ensure that its employees are motivated to generate favorable outcomes.

Decentralization of Decision Making

LEARNING OBJECTIVE 1

Explain the costs and benefits of decentralization.

Most organizations grapple with the issue Aaron faces. As firms grow, both the number and type of decisions they must make increase rapidly. We cannot expect any one individual to have all of the relevant expertise and knowledge required to make decisions related to production, marketing, finance, and human resources management. Like Aaron, organizations have no choice but to decentralize by giving lower-level managers the authority to make *specified* decisions.

Consider Hewlett-Packard (HP), a leading manufacturer of personal computers and printers. These two product lines account for a significant portion of HP's business operations. However, one manager cannot manage all aspects of *both* product lines. Therefore, HP has organized the personal computer and the printer divisions as two semi-independent organizations run by division managers. The division managers, in turn, assemble their own teams and delegate authority further.

Exhibit 12.1 shows KCPC's organizational structure. The three regional managers make decisions concerning pricing, promotion, office management, and

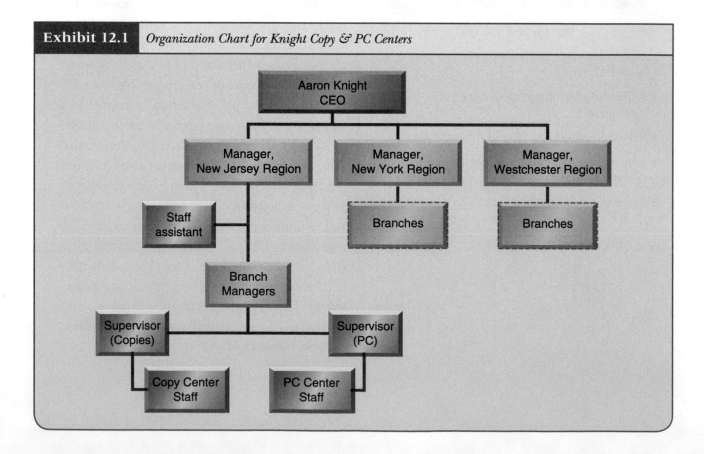

Exhibit 12.1 *Organization Chart for Knight Copy & PC Centers*

coordination of the KCPC locations within their region. The branch managers are in charge of a specific store and rely on supervisors to oversee the copy centers and PC operations. Each region also has administrative staff.

BENEFITS AND COSTS OF DECENTRALIZATION

Organizations vary considerably in the extent to which they decentralize. This variation occurs because decisions about whether and how much to decentralize affect numerous costs and benefits. Moreover, the magnitude of these costs and benefits depends on individual circumstances. Exhibit 12.2 summarizes the costs and benefits.

Let us further examine each of these benefits and costs relative to centralized decision making:

Benefits

1. *Permits timely decisions with the best available information.* Employees at lower levels in an organization typically have access to more detailed and timely information than those at higher levels. It is costly and often impractical for lower-level managers to communicate all of the relevant information to top management. For example, a shop floor supervisor can take timelier actions to deal with a machine breakdown or a quality problem than an operations manager could. It therefore makes sense to give local managers the authority to deal with decisions that rely on local knowledge.

2. *Tailors managerial skills and specializations to job requirements.* As organizations grow, managing each aspect of business becomes more challenging. Marketing one product in a local market is much easier than marketing many products nationwide. Both the expertise and experience required to manage each business function increase in the firm's size and complexity. Delegating decision making to individuals with appropriate functional experience enhances decision quality.

3. *Empowers employees and increases job satisfaction.* Decentralizing authority empowers employees at the lower levels. Empowerment is a powerful motivational tool because it gives employees a sense of ownership and often results in increased job satisfaction.

4. *Trains future managers.* A well-managed organization develops and maintains a pool of managerial talent. Ensuring smooth succession is important for the survival of any company. Decentralization prepares employees at the lower level for higher-level positions as they move up the organizational hierarchy.

Costs

1. *Leads to decisions that emphasize local goals over global goals.* Lower-level managers may not understand the "big picture." As a result, they might make decisions

Exhibit 12.2	*Costs and Benefits of Decentralization*

Benefits	Costs
• Permits timely decisions	• Might lead to an emphasis on local versus global goals
• Tailors managerial skills and specializations to job requirements	• Requires costly coordination of decisions
• Empowers employees and increases job satisfaction	• Leads to improper decisions because of divergence between individual and organizational goals
• Trains future managers	

without considering the impact on other organizational units. For example, a purchasing manager might sacrifice quality for price without considering that the quality of incoming materials adversely affects production efficiencies and customer satisfaction.

2. *Requires costly coordination of decisions.* Effective decision making in decentralized organizations requires careful coordination of the decisions by managers at various levels. Having proper internal information systems such as networked computers and other formal coordination mechanisms such as weekly meetings is important to ensure that all managers work toward the same organizational goals. The costs of coordination increase with an organization's size and complexity.

3. *Triggers improper decisions because of the divergence between individual and organizational goals.* As we learned in Chapter 1, divergence of individual goals from organizational goals means that managers might pursue their own objectives instead of acting in the organization's best interests. Decentralization worsens this problem by giving control over organizational resources to lower-level managers who are far-removed from the top management/owners of the firm.

A major part of top management's responsibility is to figure out how to maximize the benefits and minimize the costs associated with decentralization. We can increase benefits by carefully identifying the decisions under each manager's purview, matching the scope of decisions with the manager's skills and knowledge. We can also help lower-level managers understand the firm's strategy, values, and goals.

It is not possible to completely eliminate the costs of delegating decisions. Accordingly, as we discussed in Chapter 1, organizations use monitoring, performance evaluation, and incentive schemes to manage these costs. Because planning and control go hand-in-hand, the choice of which measures to use depends on the extent of decentralization and the coordination systems in place. Overall, decisions concerning how much to decentralize, the performance measures to use, and the incentive systems to employ are among the most complex decisions in organizations.

RESPONSIBILITY CENTERS

Building on our discussion in Chapter 7 and as shown in Exhibit 12.3, let us consider in detail the three common forms of **responsibility centers** listed below. Each of these organizational subunits corresponds to the nature of decisions made by the managers of the subunit.

- Cost centers
- Profit centers
- Investment centers

Let us now review the decision rights delegated to each type of responsibility center. In this review, we focus on the first issue of how to pick performance measures for each kind of responsibility center. We address the second issue, transfer pricing, later in the chapter.

Cost Centers

Cost center managers exercise control over costs, but not revenues and investments. Their charge is to *minimize the cost of producing a specified level of output or the cost of delivering a specified level of service.* The objective of cost center managers is to improve the *efficiency* of operations by finding ways to cut costs and minimize waste. Examples

Exhibit 12.3 | *There Are Several Kinds of Responsibility Centers*

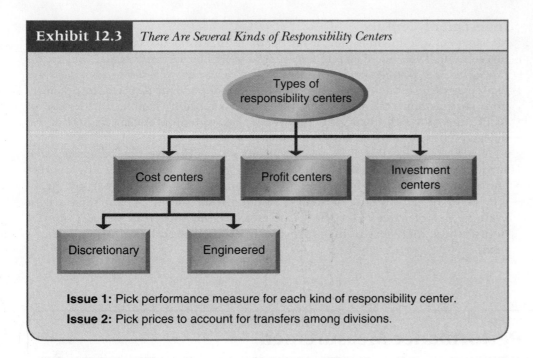

Types of
responsibility centers

Cost centers   Profit centers   Investment centers

Discretionary   Engineered

Issue 1: Pick performance measure for each kind of responsibility center.

Issue 2: Pick prices to account for transfers among divisions.

of cost centers include departments such as plant maintenance, data processing, human resources, production, and general administration. We could also consider departments such as machining and assembly, both of which are involved in making product, as cost centers. In KCPC, copy operations and PC operations in each location are cost centers.

Profit Centers

Profit center managers focus on profit. Their goal is to *both minimize costs and to maximize revenues*. KCPC's operations in each of the three regions are profit centers. Other examples include individual product lines in firms such as Procter and Gamble and retail stores of firms such as Sears.

Connecting to Practice

ORGANIZATION STRUCTURE AT JOHN DEERE

John Deere, a FORTUNE 500 firm, operates worldwide in many product markets. John Deere has several manufacturing divisions organized along product lines. These divisions focus on producing agricultural equipment, commercial and consumer equipment, power systems, and construction and forestry equipment. In addition, John Deere also operates a health maintenance organization, as well as John Deere Credit.

COMMENTARY: John Deere could instead have organized itself along geographic lines. However, its focus on excellence in manufacturing probably influenced management to enter into a product-oriented organization. The credit division supports the other divisions by providing financing to farmers and others. The health division began as a service to employees.

Large firms such as Deere & Co. have complex organization structures. (David R. Frazier/ Danita Delimont Agency/Digital Railroad, Inc.)

Investment Centers

Managers of investment centers make decisions that influence costs, revenues, and investments. Their mandate is to *maximize the returns from invested capital, or to put the capital invested by owners and shareholders of their organizations to the most profitable use.* Examples of investment centers include large independent divisions in organizations such as Sony, Siemens, Microsoft, and Procter and Gamble. In the case of KCPC, the only individual with control over investments is Aaron, as he has not delegated this authority to any of his managers.

As shown in Exhibit 12.3, organizations need effective performance measurement systems to evaluate the decisions of various responsibility centers and to set appropriate incentives for their managers. Indeed, Aaron's problem at KCPC is the lack of such a system. *What* should Aaron measure to evaluate performance? *How* should he measure the chosen items? *How* should he use these measures in incentive contracts? Let us address these questions next.

Principles of Performance Measurement

LEARNING OBJECTIVE 2

Apply the principles of performance measurement.

A **controllable performance measure** reflects the consequences of the actions taken by the decision maker. Intuition suggests that we hold decision makers accountable only for costs and benefits that they can control—that is, costs and benefits that change because of their actions. Thus, we should hold a production manager accountable for production delays but not for the overall volume of production. *Marketing* managers have the authority to change prices and offer promotions that affect actual sales, which determine the required production. *Production* managers, therefore, have little control over the volume of production. It is not reasonable to hold them accountable for someone else's decisions or random market conditions. Likewise, the manager of a restaurant in a beach resort can do little to avoid losses due to a hurricane.

While intuitive, the controllability principle is not always the right approach for choosing performance measures. Instead, we should rely on the **informativeness principle**. A performance measure is *informative* if it provides information about a manager's effort, even if the manager does not have control over it.

Most controllable measures are informative. Students control their performance on a quiz, and their score is informative about their grasp of the subject matter. However, an informative measure is not necessarily controllable. Consider the practice of grading on a curve, in which a student's grade also reflects overall class performance. What does this relative grading accomplish? Well, it controls for the level of difficulty of the exam. In an exam where the top score is 70 out of 100, a score of 69 is a high mark. An individual student has little control over how the rest of the class performs. Yet, the overall class performance is useful information in evaluating each individual student's performance because it tells us how hard the exam is.

This example extends readily to business settings. If a firm incurs losses when other firms in the industry are highly profitable, we may attribute those losses to poor managerial performance. However, if other firms in the industry are doing even worse, then the firm's management may actually be doing a terrific job of dealing with adverse business conditions. Thus, evaluating a firm relative to other firms in the industry, or **relative performance evaluation**, is useful, even though the firm's managers may have little control over how other firms do.

Connecting to Practice

MUTUAL FUNDS AND RELATIVE PERFORMANCE EVALUATION

Several publications such as *Business Week* and the *Wall Street Journal,* as well as ratings firms such as Morningstar, evaluate the managers of mutual funds. Inevitably, these services rank a manager's performance relative to a comparison group. The *Wall Street Journal* ranks mutual funds into quintiles, or fifths. Only the top funds receive the coveted 5-star rating from Morningstar.

COMMENTARY: Investors in mutual funds pay managers for delivering *market-beating* returns, as investors can obtain the market return with little effort. Thus, the return in the appropriate sector (domestic, international) is the natural benchmark for performance evaluation, even though the mutual fund manager exerts no influence over market returns.

CHARACTERISTICS OF EFFECTIVE PERFORMANCE MEASURES

An ideal performance measure:

- *Aligns employee and organizational goals.*
- *Yields maximum information about the decisions or actions of the individual or organizational unit.*
- *Is easy to measure.*
- *Is easy to understand and communicate.*

A single performance measure rarely possesses *all* of these characteristics. Rewarding employees based on customer satisfaction can help align organizational and employee goals. The measure motivates employees to pay attention to customers, and happy customers are the sources of future profit. But, customer satisfaction is subjective and difficult to measure. Some school districts rely heavily on objective test scores to evaluate the performance of their employees (such as grade school teachers). These scores might divert employees' attention from building other important skills such as creative thinking, which are hard to measure. To make effective trade-offs among the attributes, organizations often use a combination of performance measures. Let us apply these principles to KCPC and select performance measures for its cost and profit centers.

Evaluating Cost and Profit Centers

Cost center managers serve two roles in organizations: achieving cost targets for a given level of output in the short term, and making continuous efficiency improvements to cut costs in the long term.

In the short term, organizations typically use budget variances to measure cost center performance. Recall from Chapter 7 that operating budgets specify the resources needed to achieve a targeted level of output or service for the plan period.

LEARNING OBJECTIVE 3

Rate the performance of cost and profit centers.

The budget makes assumptions about materials usage and prices to determine the expected quantities of raw materials and their costs. In Chapter 8, we examined the role of flexible budgets. We analyzed flexible budget variances to evaluate performance during a budget period. For example, we can employ usage variances to evaluate the Production Department and raw material price variances to evaluate the purchasing function.

Ever since Aaron began KCPC, he has followed a practice of making detailed budgets for each branch. These budgets specify expected sales volume by product and the costs of providing the requisite service. At the end of each week, Aaron performs a variance analysis, by branch, to highlight problem areas and institute immediate corrective action.

Long-term Measures

To achieve long-term reductions in cost, organizations use performance measures arising from techniques such as benchmarking and kaizen.

- **Benchmarking** is a process that involves comparing the effectiveness and efficiency of various activities and business processes in a firm against the best practices in the industry. Such best practices are not controllable by the decision maker but still are useful performance measures. For example, a firm may hold a manager accountable for achieving greater reductions in cycle time than attained by immediate competitors.
- **Kaizen** is a philosophy of continuous improvement. This initiative encourages and rewards employees who constantly seek and suggest improvements to activities and business processes. One way to implement continuous improvement is to hold managers accountable for achieving *permanent* cost reductions.

Within KCPC, Aaron has tried to instill a spirit of continuous improvement. He routinely benchmarks the costs in one branch versus the others. If a branch consistently turns in a poor performance, Aaron steps in to help the manager find ways to reduce costs. Each month, Aaron also recognizes the employee with the "best cost saving idea for the month," and implements the idea in all branches. On an inflation-adjusted basis, his goal is to obtain a 5% reduction in overall costs each year.

Discretionary Cost Centers

The above discussion focuses on evaluating cost centers for which there is a clear relation between inputs and outputs. Such centers are termed **engineered cost centers**. However, many managers oversee **discretionary cost centers** where measuring output can be difficult. For example, members of the corporate legal staff guide and counsel management, but their output is intangible as it pertains to the quality of corporate decisions. Because there is no obvious relation between inputs and outputs in discretionary cost centers, the concerned managers' evaluation is primarily subjective. Often, the manager is required to operate within a fixed budget set at top management's discretion. The manager also is responsible for meeting qualitative targets, such as promptness in responding to inquiries or anticipating and heading off problems.

Being relatively small, KCPC does not have many discretionary cost centers. Aaron has outsourced most services such as accounting, advertising, IT support, and legal. Periodically, he evaluates the efficiency and effectiveness of the purchased services by obtaining competing price quotes and querying his managers about their satisfaction with the level of service.

PERFORMANCE EVALUATION IN PROFIT CENTERS

The goal of a profit center manager is to maximize profit, either by increasing revenues or decreasing costs, or both. Like KCPC, most large organizations treat geographically dispersed locations (or segments) as profit centers. Many corporations such as Microsoft also form divisions along product lines. Some organizations such as Citigroup and Wipro form complex matrix structures, where they measure profit both by region and by product.

Firms often use *profit before taxes* to evaluate profit centers, computed as:

$$\text{Profit before Taxes} = \text{Revenue} - \text{variable costs} - \text{traceable fixed costs}$$
$$= \text{Contribution margin} - \text{traceable fixed costs}$$

Exhibit 12.4 presents a contribution margin statement for KCPC. Aaron evaluates the three regions as profit centers. For the most recent year, the operating profits for these three locations are $1,277,000, $721,832, and $751,408, respectively.

Just as budgets provide a natural benchmark for evaluating cost center performance, they also provide a natural benchmark for profit centers. Firms use the master budget as the benchmark because a profit center manager has decision rights over both outputs and inputs.

Firms often compare actual profit with past profit and with industry profit. Retail stores such as Target routinely track growth in same-store sales. Using past performance is of particular importance in organizations following a growth-oriented strategy. Likewise, using industry performance as the benchmark allows the firm to control for industry conditions that are outside its control.

Aaron uses past performance to analyze the three profit centers of KCPC. Exhibit 12.5 provides the analysis for Westchester. Note that Westchester's actual revenue is 13.9% short of budget and is almost 5% lower than prior year actual. Despite this revenue shortfall, variable costs have increased relative to last year, both in absolute terms and relative to revenue. Naturally, the contribution margin is substantially lower. As discussed earlier, Aaron could use profit variance analysis to disentangle

---

Exhibit 12.4 | *Knight Copy & PC Center: Divisional Income Statements*

	New York	Westchester	New Jersey	Total
Revenue	$5,850,000	$4,520,400	$4,880,000	$15,250,400
Variable costs	(2,223,000)	(1,898,568)	(1,978,592)	(6,100,160)
Contribution margin	$3,627,000	$2,621,832	$2,901,408	$9,150,240
Traceable fixed costs	(2,350,000)	(1,900,000)	(2,150,000)	(6,400,000)
Division profit before taxes (Segment margin)	$1,277,000	$721,832	$751,408	$2,750,240
Common (corporate) fixed costs				($750,000)
Profit before taxes				$2,000,240

Exhibit 12.5 | *Knight Copy & PC Center: Profit Variance Report (Westchester)*

		Benchmark		Variance from	
	Actual	Budget	Last year	Budget	Last year
Revenue	$4,520,400	$5,250,000	$4,752,540	13.90% U	4.88% U
Variable costs	1,898,568	1,942,500	1,805,965	2.26% F	5.13% U
Contribution margin	$2,621,832	$3,307,500	$2,946,575	20.73% U	11.02% U
Fixed costs	1,900,000	2,000,000	1,875,415	5.00% F	1.31% U
Segment margin	$ 721,832	$1,307,500	$1,071,160	44.79% U	32.61% U

CHAPTER CONNECTIONS
We revisit the issue of motivating long-term action in Chapter 13, where we discuss the Balanced Scorecard (BSC), a technique for picking performance measures that match the organization's strategy. The Balanced Scorecard emphasizes the use of both lead and lag performance measures.

the effects of these various factors on the profit shortfall and to isolate controllable deviations from those that are not controllable.

Increasingly, firms measure profit center managers' ability to meet long-term goals in addition to delivering the operating profit budgeted for the current period. Revenue-oriented measures include customer satisfaction and market share. Cost-oriented measures might focus on employee turnover or the number of process improvements. Measuring performance using these *lead* indicators ensures that profit center managers do not sacrifice future profit for current profit.

Having discussed performance measurement in cost and profit centers, let us now consider the choice of performance measures for evaluating investment centers and their managers.

Performance Measurement in Investment Centers

LEARNING OBJECTIVE 4

Evaluate the performance of investment centers.

Managers of investment centers enjoy considerable autonomy in decentralized organizations. Firms often view investment centers as a stand-alone business. Divisions of General Motors, such as Cadillac, Pontiac, and Saturn, are investment centers. These divisions even compete with each other in the market for automobiles. Other firms, such as Johnson & Johnson, also consist of many independent divisions. In such companies, the head office typically sets business priorities, provides strategic direction, allocates investment funds, and monitors the performance of its divisions.

An organization evaluates an investment center on how well it utilizes the funds made available to it. Three popular measures of investment center performance are *return on investment (ROI), residual income (RI), and economic value added (EVA)*. Firms use these measures to evaluate whether the investment center manager is meeting or exceeding performance expectations, and to allocate available funds to divisions in the most profitable manner.

RETURN ON INVESTMENT

Return on investment (ROI) is a measure of the profit generated per dollar of investment, calculated as

$$ROI = \frac{Profit}{Investment}$$

An investment center's profit results from its operations. Just as with profit centers, the profit we compute includes all revenue and expense items directly related to the center's operations. Normally, we exclude *interest and taxes* from the calculation because investment center managers usually do not influence financing or tax-related decisions. However, if a division controls short-term working capital financing, such as short-term bank loans, then we would include the cost of such short-term financing. We would include taxes only if the division's choices significantly influence the corporate tax burden.

Assets that contribute to the operations of the division include fixed assets such as plant and equipment, and current assets such as cash, inventories, and accounts receivable. We do not include assets such as marketable securities and land; the corporate office usually manages these items. Most firms use the average operating assets as a measure of invested capital. This measure equals the average of the beginning and ending value of operating assets for the period (i.e., year of evaluation).

An important issue in measuring divisional investment is how to incorporate depreciable fixed assets such as plant and equipment. Three options exist:

1. *Net book value:* Net book value is the original acquisition cost of plant and equipment less accumulated depreciation. This method is consistent with the computation of operating profit (as we include depreciation of plant and equipment in computing profit). However, the asset's age becomes a factor. As the asset becomes older, the accumulated depreciation increases and the net book value decreases. Consequently, ROI often is higher for older assets. As a result, managers may have less of an incentive to undertake timely asset replacement decisions. Net book value is, by far, the measure most commonly used to compute ROI.

2. *Gross book value:* Gross book value is the original acquisition cost. As this measure does not include depreciation charges, the asset's age is less of a factor. However, because gross book value fails to measure the change in the value of the investment with the passage of time, it fails to represent the "true" investment of the company at the time of the evaluation.

3. *Replacement or current value of the asset:* This measure of investment is more likely to represent the true value of the asset. However, identifying the replacement costs, or current value, of various assets can be difficult and tedious.

Aaron computes ROI using net book value. As Exhibit 12.6 shows, the ROI for Manhattan is 16%, compared to less than 8% for Westchester and New Jersey. We obtain the divisional profit numbers from Exhibit 12.4.

Exhibit 12.6	Knight Copy & PC Center: Return on Investment Calculations			
	Manhattan	**Westchester**	**New Jersey**	**Total**
Divisional profit	$1,277,000	$721,832	$751,408	$2,750,240
Original acquisition cost of assets	$10,000,000	$10,000,000	$10,000,000	$30,000,000
Accumulated depreciation (average)	$3,000,000	$1,500,000	$1,500,000	$6,000,000
Net book value (average)	$7,000,000	$8,500,000	$8,500,000	$24,000,000
Other operating investments (average)	1,200,000	1,500,000	1,500,000	4,200,000
Average Investment	$8,200,000	$10,000,000	$10,000,000	$28,200,000
ROI (Net book value method)				
Divisional profit	$1,277,000	$721,832	$751,408	$2,750,240
Divisional investment	$8,200,000	$10,000,000	$10,000,000	$28,200,000
ROI	16%	7%	8%	10%

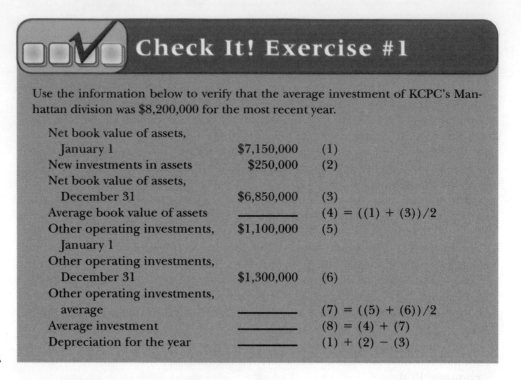

Check It! Exercise #1

Use the information below to verify that the average investment of KCPC's Manhattan division was $8,200,000 for the most recent year.

Net book value of assets, January 1	$7,150,000	(1)
New investments in assets	$250,000	(2)
Net book value of assets, December 31	$6,850,000	(3)
Average book value of assets	_____	(4) = ((1) + (3))/2
Other operating investments, January 1	$1,100,000	(5)
Other operating investments, December 31	$1,300,000	(6)
Other operating investments, average	_____	(7) = ((5) + (6))/2
Average investment	_____	(8) = (4) + (7)
Depreciation for the year	_____	(1) + (2) − (3)

Solution at end of chapter.

Advantages and Disadvantages of ROI

Surveys show that over 90% of firms use some version of ROI in their performance measurement systems. This is because ROI is an effective summary measure of business profitability. We could evaluate investments by comparing their ROIs with those of similar investments in the past, as well as the experiences of other firms in the industry. Many organizations also use ROI because it controls for size by expressing the return per investment dollar. Consequently, it is easy to compare the performance of investment centers of different size. Finally, as we show next, we can decompose ROI into smaller pieces, allowing managers to see how individual actions map into overall profitability.

The major criticism against ROI is that it fosters underinvestment. By focusing on current income and investment, ROI ignores future period considerations, making it less suitable for evaluating long-term performance. Managers would find actions that generate immediate income more desirable than actions that generate income in some future period, even though the latter actions may be more beneficial from the company's standpoint.

For example, consider a firm whose opportunity cost of capital is 15%. Suppose a division in this firm is currently generating an ROI of 22%. Finally, assume that this division has a new investment opportunity that promises an ROI of 20%. This investment opportunity is attractive for the firm because it promises an ROI greater than 15%. Yet, the manager of the division might decline this investment. Why? Because the division's ROI is greater than the investment's ROI, adopting it will lower the division's ROI and potentially reduce the manager's compensation. In practice, firms reduce the negative impact of ROI by carefully defining their measurement of ROI. Using a suitable benchmark such as budgeted ROI can help reduce the effect of measurement problems.

For KCPC, the three divisions are profit centers, not investment centers. The managers of these divisions are not concerned with ROI because it is not the basis for evaluating their performance. However, from Aaron's viewpoint, ROI is useful in evaluating how his investments in the three locations are performing. Notice that Aaron could decentralize further by treating the three locations as investment centers. However, further decentralization might not be appropriate for this relatively small, geographically focused, single-business firm.

Connecting to Practice

ROI AND INFORMATION TECHNOLOGY

A recent survey of technology executives by *InformationWeek* magazine reports that fully 80% of organizations aim to improve their return on information technology (IT) expenses. Such focus occurs because IT spending is increasing by 10% or more a year. Moreover, the industry research firm Gartner reports that $500 billion of the $2.7 trillion spent on IT in 2001 did not meet objectives.

COMMENTARY: Evaluating the ROI of a support service, such as IT, is difficult. Nevertheless, firms need to quantify the total benefits from IT and to use financial return as a key criterion when making decisions regarding spending on IT. A study by Unisys Corporation shows surprising consistency in whether firms get stellar, mediocre, or negative ROI on their IT expenses. The study also shows that successful firms spend a great deal of effort in picking the right metrics and in building a culture of getting the most out of IT expenses.

Source: Martha Heller, "The ROI of IT," *CIO magazine*, December 27, 2000.

Decomposing Return on Investment

The **DuPont model**, so named for the firm that pioneered this kind of analysis, is a method for decomposing ROI into smaller pieces.

$$\text{ROI} = \frac{\text{Profit}}{\text{Investment}} = \frac{\text{Profit}}{\text{Sales}} \times \frac{\text{Sales}}{\text{Investment}} = \text{Profit Margin} \times \text{Asset Turnover}$$

In turn, we can express profit margin as

$$\text{Profit Margin} = \frac{\text{Profit}}{\text{Sales}} = \frac{\text{Sales-Operating expenses}}{\text{Sales}} = 1 - \frac{\text{Operating expenses}}{\text{Sales}}$$

Profit margin increases if operating expenses per sales dollar decreases. In other words, if a division can generate the same amount of sales with less operating expenses or more sales with the same operating expenses, its profit margin will increase. Therefore, managers can increase profitability by *cost control* or by making operations more *efficient*.

Asset turnover (sales/investment) is a measure of *the revenue-generating ability* of operating assets. A company wants a higher turnover. It indicates that for a given level of investment in operating assets, the company is able to generate a higher level of revenues. Asset turnover increases by increasing revenue with the same level of assets or by decreasing the level of investment required for the same level of revenue.

Exhibit 12.7 shows the DuPont analysis for the three divisions of KCPC.

Exhibit 12.7	*Knight Copy & PC Center: DuPont Analysis*						
Divisions	Revenue	Operating Expenses	Operating Profit	Profit Margin	Divisional Investment	Asset Turnover	ROI
New York	$5,850,000	$4,573,000	$1,277,000	22%	$8,200,000	0.71	16%
Westchester	$4,520,400	$3,798,568	$721,832	16%	$10,000,000	0.45	7%
New Jersey	$4,880,000	$4,128,592	$751,408	15%	$10,000,000	0.49	8%

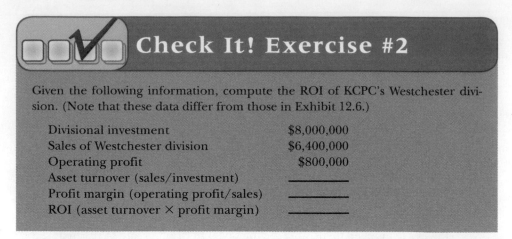

Check It! Exercise #2

Given the following information, compute the ROI of KCPC's Westchester division. (Note that these data differ from those in Exhibit 12.6.)

Divisional investment	$8,000,000
Sales of Westchester division	$6,400,000
Operating profit	$800,000
Asset turnover (sales/investment)	_____
Profit margin (operating profit/sales)	_____
ROI (asset turnover × profit margin)	_____

Solution at end of chapter.

How could Aaron improve KCPC's ROI? Assume the Westchester division can decrease its variable operating expenses from $0.42 per sales dollar to $0.40 per sales dollar. The level of revenue, fixed costs, and investment in place would remain the same. In this case, asset turnover will not change—it will remain at 0.45. However, the profit margin would increase from the current level of 16% to 18% as calculated in the following:

$$[\$4,520,400 - (\$4,520,400 \times \$0.40) - \$1,900,000]/\$4,520,400 = 18\%$$

Thus, ROI will increase from 7% to (18% × 0.45) = 8%. We could also compute the effect on asset turnover, profit margin, and ROI for other changes that Aaron might implement, such as selling off or acquiring assets. Exhibit 12.8 illustrates these effects.

RESIDUAL INCOME

Because of the limitations of ROI discussed in the preceding sections, some firms use **residual income (RI)**. Residual income is the amount an investment generates above and beyond the required rate of return on operating assets, or the residual after subtracting the expected return.

$$\text{Residual income (RI)} = \text{Profit} - (\text{Required Return} * \text{Investment})$$

Exhibit 12.8 *There Are Many Ways to Manage ROI*

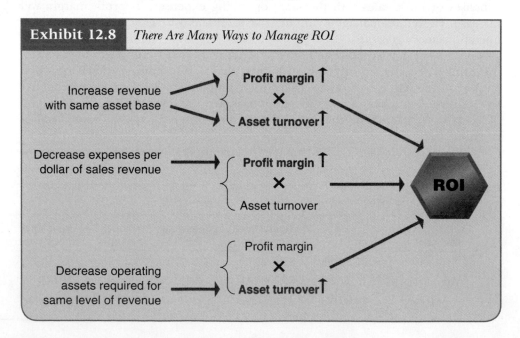

Exhibit 12.9	*Knight Copy & PC Center: Residual Income Analysis (Required Rate of Return = 10%)*

Division	Revenue	Operating Expenses	Operating Profit	Divisional Investment	RI
Manhattan	$5,850,000	$4,512,500	$1,337,500	$8,200,000	$517,500
Westchester	$4,520,400	$3,798,568	$721,832	$10,000,000	−$278,168
New Jersey	$4,880,000	$4,128,592	$751,408	$10,000,000	−$248,592

Exhibit 12.10	*Project Evaluation with ROI and RI*

Current	Investment	Profit
Current operations	$100,000	$22,000
Proposed project	$40,000	$8,000
Analysis from corporate viewpoint		
ROI of new project	$8,000/$40,000	20%
Cost of capital		15%
Decision		ACCEPT
Analysis with Return on Investment (Divisional viewpoint)		
Current ROI	$22,000/$100,000	22%
ROI with proposed project	$30,000/$140,000	21.42%
Decision		REJECT!
Analysis with Residual Income (Divisional viewpoint)		
Current ROI	$22,000 − (0.15 × $100,000)	$7,000
ROI with proposed project	$30,000 − (0.15 × $140,000)	$9,000
Decision		ACCEPT

Exhibit 12.9 calculates the residual income of KCPC's three divisions using 10% as the minimum required rate of return. Only the Manhattan division generates positive residual income, while the other two divisions have negative residual income.

Residual income represents the additional profit or value generated by an investment after meeting the required rate of return. It does not lead to underinvestment because any project with positive NPV has positive residual income, making it attractive to the manager. Exhibit 12.10 provides a numerical example of this advantage of RI as a performance measure.

Despite its conceptual advantage, RI has two key limitations that have reduced its use within modern corporations. First, the magnitude of RI depends on the size of the investment. For example, when two divisions have identical profitability (ROI), then the larger of the two would report a higher RI. Consequently, when ranking potential investment proposals, ROI and RI can yield conflicting rankings. Second, RI rankings depend crucially on the chosen rate of return. It is easy to construct examples in which the rankings of divisions using RI changes if we change the required rate of return. Exercises 12.40 and 12.41 allow you to verify these concepts.

ECONOMIC VALUE ADDED

In recent years, a modified calculation of the residual income has gained popularity among organizations. **Economic value added (EVA)** is a measure developed and popularized by a consulting firm, Stern Stewart & Company. Although similar to

CHAPTER CONNECTIONS

Estimating the risk-adjusted WACC for individual divisions is a difficult exercise. As we detail in Chapter 13, the firm is the unit of analysis for raising capital, but the division is the unit of analysis for allocating capital. Additional complications arise in international settings because divisions may operate in different tax jurisdictions.

residual income, EVA reflects the belief that managers are responsible for covering both the operating *and* capital costs of a business, including taxes. We calculate EVA as

$$EVA = NOPAT - [WACC \times (Invested\ Capital - Current\ Liabilities)]$$

where NOPAT is the net operating profit after taxes and WACC is the weighted average cost of capital.

While the formula for calculating EVA appears simple, the actual calculations are quite involved. Calculating NOPAT requires a number of adjustments to the income reported in financial statements. In essence, these adjustments "undo" the impact of many accounting rules used to prepare the financial statements. EVA computations also specify how to measure the weighted average cost of capital and the investment base.

One example of adjustments to NOPAT relates to research and development expenditures. Generally Accepted Accounting Principles (GAAP) require that research and development costs be expensed for financial reporting purposes. However, EVA computations treat these expenses in much the same way as investments in long-lived assets such as property, plant, and equipment. The proponents of EVA argue that expensing research and development costs reduces NOPAT, which will adversely affect EVA. As a result, managers will be reluctant to undertake

Connecting to Practice

EVA AND THE CHEMICAL INDUSTRY

From 1997 to 1999, Dow Chemical's sales declined 5.4%, earnings before interest and taxes (EBIT) were down 23.5%, and earnings per share (EPS) fell from $7.70 to $5.93. While each of these measures signaled a downturn and poor financial performance, what happened to the *value* of the company?

COMMENTARY: Commenting on 1999 financial results, William Stavropoulos, former president and CEO of Dow Chemical Company, says, "In what may well have been the bottom of the industry pricing cycle, our company surpassed a key financial milestone we set five years ago, earning a return well above our cost of capital—something we had never done in a trough year." That is, Dow created positive EVA in each of those years. Not surprisingly, the firm's market *value* increased by over 17% during this period.

Source: EVA and the Chemical Industry: How Do Companies Rank? John Ballow, Henri Perrson, and Fred Knechtel, *Chemical Market Reporter*, 7, Vol. 260, Issue 9, September 3, 2001.

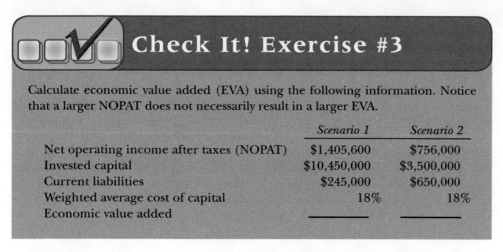

Check It! Exercise #3

Calculate economic value added (EVA) using the following information. Notice that a larger NOPAT does not necessarily result in a larger EVA.

	Scenario 1	Scenario 2
Net operating income after taxes (NOPAT)	$1,405,600	$756,000
Invested capital	$10,450,000	$3,500,000
Current liabilities	$245,000	$650,000
Weighted average cost of capital	18%	18%
Economic value added	_____	_____

Solution at end of chapter.

valuable R&D activities. Capitalizing research and development costs, and expensing them gradually over time, better reflects the fact that R&D provides benefits for many years.

We illustrate EVA calculations using a numerical example in the self-study problem at the end of the chapter.

MEASURING LONG-TERM PERFORMANCE

While useful for measuring investment center performance, it is important to recognize that ROI, EVA, and RI all focus on the short term. These measures consider current period profit and current investment. Moreover, these are lag measures, reflecting the outcomes of past decisions.

Recognizing these limitations, many firms complement ROI, RI, and EVA with other measures that have a longer-term focus, such as market share, customer satisfaction, or growth in new product sales. These measures provide information on the

APPLYING THE DECISION FRAMEWORK

What Is the Problem?
Aaron is worried about the performance of KCPC's branch offices and the commitment of its managers.

What Are the Options?
Aaron has numerous options for clearly defining each manager's role and for putting in a performance measurement and evaluation system that monitors each manager's actions.

What Are the Costs and Benefits?
Performance measures and incentive schemes help Aaron reduce the agency loss due to decentralization. However, devising, computing, and analyzing a portfolio of measures is costly in terms of managerial time. Moreover, these measures imperfectly align employee goals with KCPC's goals, meaning that there would still be some agency loss.

Make the Decision!
At the aggregate level, Aaron plans to compute the ROI and EVA for each branch to help with investment decisions. Budgets, supplemented with variance analysis, form the basis for branch manager evaluation. Aaron plans to use relative performance evaluation to determine cost targets. Aaron also decides to share the DuPont analysis with his managers and to set specific targets for improving profitability. Finally, Aaron decides to implement some nonfinancial measures to provide incentives to maximize long-term profitability.

expected long-term outcomes of current period actions. Thus, using ROI, RI, or EVA in conjunction with long-term performance measures can help in setting the right incentives for management. We discuss these long-term performance measures, such as the balanced scorecard, in Chapter 13.

So where does all this information leave Aaron? At the overall company level, Aaron decides to add EVA to ROI as a measure of divisional performance. For individual branches, he decides to pay increased attention to setting budget targets and using variances to identify any budget deviations. He also sets up nonfinancial measures such as sales targets for product lines, average wait times, and the number of new corporate accounts for continued growth. Using the fact that all branches employ similar technology, Aaron decides to use the average cost realized by the top quartile of branches for cost benchmarks. Finally, he decides to set up incentive schemes that better align the interests of his managers with KCPC.

Transfer Pricing

LEARNING OBJECTIVE 5

Describe transfer pricing.

We next turn our attention to another important issue in decentralized organizations, noted in Exhibit 12.3. The multiple divisions found within many organizations often deal with each other in the normal course of business. In such instances, the divisions divert a portion of their resources from external business to serve internal needs. Consequently, performance measurement at the divisional level will not be complete without incorporating the costs and benefits of these internal transactions.

We commonly see *intra-company*, or internal, business transactions in which an organization transfers goods or services among its divisions or segments. For example, John Deere's tractor assembly division uses parts supplied by the firm's components division. Similarly, Georgia Pacific's forest products division supplies the paper used by the company's paper division. Companies usually cite increased efficiency or a synergy in operations as the reasons for such integration.

When intra-company transfers occur, no legally recognized sale takes place because the divisions are part of the same company. Usually, no cash changes hands as well. Nevertheless, firms still recognize the economic effects of the transaction by using a **transfer price** to record a "sale" by the selling division and a "purchase" by the buying division.

DEMAND FOR TRANSFER PRICES

From the perspective of determining corporate *pretax* income, a transfer price does not serve any useful purpose. After all, the price increases the revenue of the selling division and the costs of the buying division by the same amount. These entries cancel each other out when the firm consolidates divisional operations to determine corporate profit. Exhibit 12.11 underscores this observation. It provides an example of the flow of revenue and costs in a typical transfer-pricing setting. In this example, the firm includes the transfer, valued at $1,640,000, as revenue for the selling division and as a cost for the buying division. This offset means that the transfer does not affect the consolidated total in any way.

Why, then, do we need a transfer price? The demand for a transfer price does not stem from decisions based on corporate profit. Instead it comes from decisions that are based on the profit reported by individual divisions. Not attaching a value to the internal transfer of goods and services increases the buying division's profit because the buying division does not pay anything for the goods and services

Exhibit 12.11	Accounting for Internal Transfers		
	Selling Division	**Buying Division**	**Total (after eliminating intra firm transfers)**
Revenue—External	$3,000,000	$2,450,000	$5,450,000
Revenue—Internal	**1,640,000**	0	
Total Sales	$4,640,000	$2,450,000	$5,450,000
Variable costs	1,700,000	450,000	2,150,000
Purchases—Internal	0	**1,640,000**	
Contribution margin	$2,940,000	360,000	$3,300,000
Segment fixed costs	1,500,000	200,000	1,700,000
Segment margin	$1,440,000	$160,000	$1,600,000
Corporate fixed costs			1,278,000
Profit before taxes			$322,000

received. However, it decreases the selling division's profit because the selling division does not receive any consideration. In contrast, a well-set transfer price allows firms to measure the true profit earned by divisions. This measure can then be used for decisions about resource allocation and performance evaluation. In addition, divisional managers have a keen interest in the transfer price because their individual compensation often depends on the profit reported by their division.

Tax authorities are also concerned about transfer prices. To see why, consider a firm whose divisions transfer goods and services among themselves but who operate in different tax jurisdictions. Transfer prices determine the income reported by each division and, thus, the taxes paid to different jurisdictions. Naturally, firms seek to set prices that will reduce the overall corporate tax burden. Recognizing these incentives, government agencies such as the Internal Revenue Service devote considerable effort to formulating and enforcing policies that ensure firms recognize and pay taxes on appropriate income in their country or jurisdiction.

CONFLICT IN SETTING TRANSFER PRICES

Setting effective transfer prices is difficult because the buying and selling divisions often do not agree on what constitutes a fair price. A transfer price determines what portion of the assessed value of the interdivisional transaction each division gets to keep. A low transfer price benefits the buying division, but the selling division suffers. A high transfer price has the opposite effect. A natural conflict arises because both of the divisions are profit centers. Therefore, they are interested in maximizing their respective divisional profits.

Why can't top management solve the problem by combining the divisions as a way of preserving cooperation? This solution frequently is not feasible because of strategic and economic considerations. For example, Georgia Pacific might wish to evaluate its forest products division separately from the paper division because their business models differ—that is, Georgia Pacific's top management has decided to decentralize the two divisions.

Furthermore, top management cannot step in and solve transfer-pricing disputes among its subordinates. Such a strategy might not work well for at least two reasons. First, the head office may not have the knowledge required to determine the best transfer price, which depends on the opportunity costs for each division. Second, such intervention undermines the benefits of decentralization and delegated decisions. If a division consistently makes bad decisions, the results will eventually reduce its profit and rate of return. The divisional manager then becomes accountable. A firm should respect the manager's right to make the wrong call. Even if the profit may suffer as a result in the short term, preserving divisional autonomy is likely to lead to greater profitability in the long term. Although the temptation to intervene might be strong at times, head office managers should exercise caution and judgment before stepping in to mediate a transfer-pricing dispute.

PRACTICE PATTERNS

Most companies issue guidelines for setting transfer prices. However, they usually give some autonomy to the division managers to negotiate the final terms. Some common approaches include:

1. Cost-based transfer prices (including variable and full cost)
2. Market-based transfer prices
3. Negotiated transfer prices

Variable cost-based transfer pricing is most appropriate for a short-term problem in which the selling division has excess capacity. In this context, the rule makes sense because the opportunity cost of idle capacity is zero. When the selling division has enough demand, the opportunity cost of its capacity is not zero, and its manager often will not agree to a variable cost-based transfer price unless there is a sufficiently high markup. Full cost-based pricing is more justifiable with full capacity utilization because full cost includes allocated capacity cost.

In general, there is no guarantee that cost-based transfer prices will lead to the right quantity of transfers taking place. In other words, there is no guarantee

Connecting to Practice

TRANSFER PRICING AND ACTIVITY-BASED COSTING (ABC)

Teva Pharmaceutical Industries Ltd. of Israel rejected the negotiated transfer price approach because senior executives believed that this approach would lead to endless, nonproductive arguments. Instead, the company uses activity-based costing to set its transfer prices. The firm charges marketing divisions for unit-level costs based on the actual quantities of each product they acquire. In addition, they are charged batch-level costs based on the actual number of batches their orders require. Finally, the marketing division is charged a lump-sum amount for product- and facility-level costs.

COMMENTARY: Essentially, Teva sets its transfer prices based on carefully computed costs. This system sends the marketing managers the correct signals about how much it really costs the company to produce each product. With this information, the marketing managers are better equipped to make pricing and other decisions regarding the products.

Source: Robert S. Kaplan, Dan Weiss, and Eyal Desheh, "Transfer Pricing with ABC," *Management Accounting*, May 1997, pp. 20–28.

that the actions of divisional managers will always be in the best interests of the company as a whole. Such suboptimization is one of the unavoidable costs of decentralization.

Market-based transfer prices are in theory the most sound because the market price provides the best measure of the opportunity cost of interdivisional transfer. Setting the transfer price at the competitive market price always results in both divisions voluntarily making the right decisions from the perspective of the company as a whole. In some settings, it is difficult to identify a market price because there is no ready market for the transferred goods or services. In these cases, we cannot use market-based transfer prices. Firms commonly encounter such settings, particularly when they transfer goods or services not readily available in the marketplace.

Allowing the divisions to negotiate the transfer price is appealing. It gives them considerable autonomy, which is the essence of decentralization. As long as divisional managers behave rationally and negotiate a transfer anywhere in the acceptable range of transfer prices, effective decisions will result. However, negotiations could often be time-consuming and difficult because of the conflicting interests of the divisional managers. Even well-intentioned managers may find themselves in lengthy negotiations, with personality issues clouding the discussion.

Surveys show that firms prefer to use market-based transfer prices whenever available. Such prices account for 30 to 50% of all transfer prices. Cost-based transfer prices account for 25 to 50% of transfers, with full-cost-based pricing being the most popular. Negotiated transfer prices account for the balance. In the Appendix, we illustrate how to compute economically optimal transfer prices.

INTERNATIONAL TRANSFER PRICING

Globalization brings another significant dimension to the transfer-pricing problem. Multi-national corporations (MNCs) sell goods and services in multiple markets. They locate their divisions and subsidiaries all over the world to compete effectively in these markets. Additional considerations arise in setting transfer prices for MNCs, including:

1. Transfer pricing allows MNCs to *shift* income across borders. It is in the MNC's best interest to set a transfer price that minimizes the total taxes paid by taking into account differences in income tax rules across nations, and custom duties and tariffs imposed on imports by countries. For example, MNCs can benefit by transferring income from high-tax countries to low-tax countries.
2. An MNC entering a new foreign market may want to enable its subsidiary in that country to compete effectively by charging a low transfer price. This low price in turn allows the subsidiary to charge lower prices for its products.
3. Many countries impose restrictions on foreign currency exchange. Moreover, there are inherent risks involved in foreign exchange transactions. MNCs manage these considerations by carefully adjusting transfer prices on interdivisional transfers across borders.

These considerations can outweigh the internal performance evaluation considerations for MNCs when it comes to setting transfer prices.

Of course, tax authorities in almost every country have legislation governing transfer-pricing practices. These laws are designed to prevent opportunistic transfer pricing by MNCs. While international transfer pricing provides many tax-planning opportunities, firms must take care to comply with all of the legal and ethical standards surrounding their operations.

SUMMARY

In this chapter, we examined the demand for decentralization. We discussed the costs and benefits associated with decentralized decision making, common forms of decentralization, and the need to implement performance evaluation systems and incentive schemes in decentralized environments. We focused particularly on the principles of performance measurement and on how to tailor performance measures to the specific form of decentralization. Finally, we discussed how to set up transfer prices that motivate divisions to work together to generate economic surplus, even if they compete against each other to share the surplus.

Throughout this chapter, we emphasized the short-term nature of many performance measures such as variance analysis and ROI. These measures focus on current-period performance, meaning that they provide little information about future-period performance. In the next chapter, we discuss how organizations expand the scope of their analysis beyond organizational boundaries. We also look at how they use lead measures of future financial performance, such as the balanced scorecard.

RAPID REVIEW

LEARNING OBJECTIVE 1

Explain the costs and benefits of decentralization.

- Decentralization is the delegation of the authority to make decisions throughout the organization. The benefits of decentralization are (1) bringing the best information to make timely decisions; (2) tailoring managerial skills and specializations to job requirements; (3) empowerment and job satisfaction; and (4) training of future managers. The costs of decentralization include (1) emphasizing local goals at the expense of global goals; (2) the need for costly coordination; and (3) the need for performance evaluation and incentive systems.

- Common forms of decentralization include cost, profit, and investment centers, with the labels reflecting the decision rights assigned to the managers of these units.

LEARNING OBJECTIVE 2

Apply the principles of performance measurement.

- Controllability is the idea that we hold managers accountable only for items in their control. Informativeness is the notion that any metric that provides information about a manager's effort and/or skill could be a useful performance measure. Informativeness leads to practices such as relative performance evaluation, which uses an uncontrollable benchmark to filter out common "noise" in the performance measure.

- Ideally, the best performance measures (1) reflect the decision rights assigned to the individual/organizational unit; (2) align employee and organizational goals;

(3) yield the maximum information about the decisions or actions of the individual/organizational subunit; (4) have low measurement error; and (5) are easy to understand and communicate. Firms generally use a portfolio of measures because no one measure possesses all these desired properties.

LEARNING OBJECTIVE 3

Rate the performance of cost and profit centers.

- Firms usually employ budget variances to measure cost center performance in the short term. To ensure that longer-term goals are being pursued, firms frequently use benchmarking and kaizen.

- Firms use divisional profit before taxes to measure the performance of profit centers. Divisional profit before taxes equals revenue less variable costs less traceable fixed costs.

LEARNING OBJECTIVE 4

Evaluate the performance of investment centers.

- There are three popular measures—ROI, RI, and EVA—for measuring investment center performance.

- Return on investment (ROI) equals a division's operating income divided by its investment. ROI is the most popular measure of investment center performance. It allows for a ready comparison of investment centers of different size. The major criticism of ROI is that it leads to underinvestment because managers have an incentive to reject profitable projects that exceed the firm's cost of capital but are lower than current ROI.

- Residual income (RI) equals the income that a division generates beyond the required rate of return. Unlike ROI, RI does not lead to underinvestment. However, RI does suffer from two limitations: it does not control for the size of the investment, and rankings using RI depend crucially on the chosen required rate of return.

- Economic value added (EVA) is similar in concept to RI and, as such, shares some of the same advantages and disadvantages. EVA specifies how to adjust accounting income to better capture "economic income" and how to compute the weighted average cost of capital.

LEARNING OBJECTIVE 5

Describe transfer pricing.

- Transfer prices account for the economic value of intrafirm transfers of goods and services. Nevertheless, firms still recognize the economic effects of the transaction by using a transfer price to record a "sale" by the selling division and a "purchase" by the buying division.

- Transfer prices do not affect corporate pre-tax profit. The demand for transfer pricing arises from decisions that employ divisional income. Such decisions include resource allocation and performance evaluation. Firms could also use transfer prices for tax planning when divisions are located in different tax jurisdictions.

- The conflict between the demand for decentralization that treats the divisions as stand-alone entities, and the desire to exploit synergies that treats divisions as part of a whole, is the central issue in setting effective transfer prices.

- Firms employ transfer prices that might be cost-based, market-based, or negotiated. Each method has advantages and disadvantages, although market-based prices are generally preferred when available.

- Corporations could use transfer prices strategically to reduce their tax burden. Although we expect firms to act in an ethical and equitable manner, tax authorities have a number of rules and regulations that govern international transfer pricing.

Appendix
ECONOMICALLY OPTIMAL TRANSFER PRICES

In this appendix, we dig deeper into the costs and benefits of alternate transfer pricing rules by examining the transfer-pricing issue from each division's perspective. Doing so allows us to determine the range of transfer prices that would be acceptable to both divisions *and* would lead them to act in a way that benefits the firm as a whole. Such behavior is economically optimal.

Consider the selling division—it wants to get the maximum amount for its goods and services. Its profit from internal transfer is the transfer price less the cost of the transfer. Moreover, the division would prefer to transfer only if the profit from the transfer exceeds its opportunity cost, which is the profit from alternate uses for its resources. Thus, the *minimum* price that the selling division wants from the transfer is the cost of the transfer plus the opportunity cost of the transfer. Otherwise, the selling division is better off by rejecting the offer and using its resources more profitably. Accordingly, the minimum transfer price the selling division will voluntarily agree to is

$$TP_{MIN} = \textit{Variable cost of transfer} + \textit{Selling division's opportunity cost of transfer}$$

The buying division wants to pay the least amount for the goods and services received. If the selling division is not competitive with outside suppliers, then the buying division is better off buying elsewhere. Thus, the maximum amount the buying division is willing to pay is its opportunity cost:

$$TP_{MAX} = \textit{Buying division's opportunity cost of transfer}$$

As long as the maximum price the buying division is willing to pay, TP_{MAX}, is higher than the minimum price the selling division is willing to accept, TP_{MIN}, both divisions will agree to the internal transfer at any price, say TP, between TP_{MAX} and TP_{MIN}. More importantly, such a transfer will benefit the firm as a whole. Why? The reason is that internal supply (by the selling division) is cheaper for the firm than having the buying division procure from outside.

On the other hand, if the maximum price the buying division is willing to pay, TP_{MAX}, is less than the minimum price the selling division is willing to accept, TP_{MIN}, both divisions will never agree to the internal transfer. In fact, the firm as a whole is better off if the transfer does not take place. With the transfer, the firm is giving up more in the selling division than it gains in the buying division. Thus, finding the economically optimal transfer price is an exercise in determining opportunity costs for both divisions. Let us consider an example to illustrate these points.

Transfer-Pricing Example

Consider an electronics firm that has two divisions: chip and phone. As Exhibit 12.12 shows, the chip division produces two kinds of integrated circuit chips: GPS and Mobile Phone. The GPS chip, sold on the open market, has a demand of 40,000 units at its current price of $30 per chip. The chip division currently sells 60,000 units of the mobile phone chip to the phone division. The chip division can make 100,000 GPS chips, or 100,000 mobile phone chips, or any combination thereof.

Exhibit 12.13 provides pertinent information for the two divisions. Note that the chip division's fixed costs are not relevant with respect to the decision concerning the transfer price.

We analyze three different scenarios. The scenarios, summarized in Exhibit 12.14, differ in terms of the market demand for GPS chips and the potential for savings costs from internal transfers.

SCENARIO 1

Suppose there is a competitive market for the mobile phone chips and the market price is $30 per chip. Then, there is no gain from internal transfer because the divisions can get the same value elsewhere. If it does not make a transfer, the chip

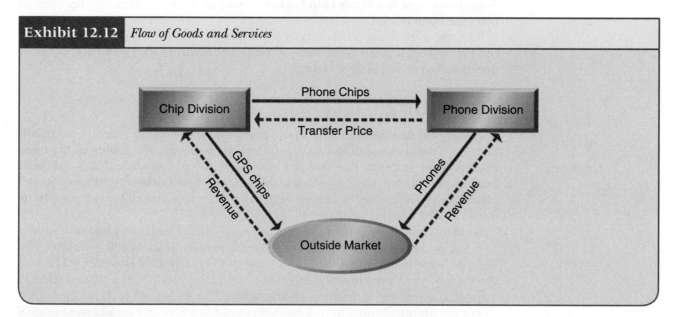

Exhibit 12.12   *Flow of Goods and Services*

Exhibit 12.13   *Transfer Pricing Example*

	Chip Division		
	Mobile Phone Chip	*GPS Chip*	**Phone Division**
Price	?	$40 per chip	$100 per phone
Variable cost	$12 per chip	$15 per chip	$22 per phone*
Demand	60,000 chips	40,000 chips	60,000 phones
Capacity	100,000 chips in total		60,000 phones
Fixed costs	$750,000 in total		$540,000

* Does not include the cost of the chip; each phone uses one chip.

Exhibit 12.14	*Scenarios Analyzed*		
	Scenario 1	**Scenario 2**	**Scenario 3**
Market demand			
GPS chip	40,000	40,000	***100,000***
Phone chip	60,000	60,000	60,000
Total demand	100,000	100,000	160,000
Available capacity	100,000	100,000	100,000
Surplus/Shortfall	0	0	(60,000)
Cost savings from internal transfer of phone chip			
Chip division	None	*$1 per chip*	*$1 per chip*
Phone division	None	*$2 per chip*	*$2 per chip*

division can sell its phone chips in the open market and make a contribution margin of $18 per chip (= $30 − $12). The chip division would lose this external sale if it transfers internally, meaning that its opportunity cost for a transfer is $18 per chip. The selling division's minimum price is therefore $30 per chip (variable cost per chip $12 + opportunity cost per chip $18).

Similarly, the buying division would not pay more than $30 per phone chip. Its opportunity cost is $30 per chip because it can procure the item for this amount from the open market.

The transfer-pricing problem is trivial because $TP_{MAX} = TP_{MIN} = \$30$. Moreover, the firm's overall profit is the same whether the divisions deal with each other or decide to buy or sell in the market.

SCENARIO 2

Now, suppose that the chip division can save $1 per phone chip by selling internally because it avoids some of the distribution costs associated with selling in the open market. That is, its variable cost per chip would be $11 instead of $12. Likewise, because the phone division is better able to coordinate deliveries, it saves $2 per phone in variable costs by buying internally. That is, its variable cost per phone would be $20 instead of $22 per phone.

As before, for every chip transferred internally, the chip division loses a contribution margin of $18 per chip from not selling it outside (price of $30 − variable cost of $12). Because the chip division's variable cost for an internal transfer is $11 now, the chip division's minimum acceptable price (TP_{MIN}) is $29, the sum of the $11 variable cost and the $18 contribution margin.

For the phone division, buying *externally* costs $30 per chip, plus $22 of additional variable costs, for a total of $52. Because the phone division incurs only $20 of variable cost with an *internal* chip, it can pay up to $32 for the *internal* transfer. Beyond

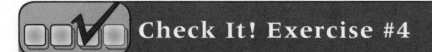

Check It! Exercise #4

Suppose the chip division's variable costs increase by $0.50 to $12.50 per phone chip if it transfers the chips internally. Assume the phone division's variable costs still decrease by $2 to $20 relative to buying externally. Verify that the range of acceptable transfer prices is $30.50 to $32.00.

Solution at end of chapter.

this price, its total cost from internal transfer would be higher than $52. Buying the chip from outside then becomes attractive. At this price of $TP_{MAX} = \$32$, the phone division is indifferent between buying internally or externally.

Thus, any price between $29 and $32 per phone chip is acceptable to both divisions. This arrangement benefits the firm as well. For each chip transferred internally, the firm saves a total $3 in variable selling and delivery costs.

SCENARIO 3

Suppose the demand for the GPS chip is 100,000 units rather than 40,000 units, at a unit price of $40 per GPS chip. As in Scenario 2, there is a $3 total savings in variable costs per chip if an internal transfer occurs.

With a demand of 100,000 units for the GPS chip at a price of $40 per chip, it makes sense for the chip division to use all of its capacity to make and sell the GPS chip exclusively. At this price, the contribution margin for the GPS chip is $25. This amount is higher than the contribution margin of $18 for the mobile phone chip. If the chip division uses up capacity to transfer a phone chip, it loses the opportunity to earn a contribution margin of $25 by making and selling a GPS chip. When we combine variable costs of $11 per chip to make the phone chip with the $25 contribution margin, we see that the chip division's minimum acceptable transfer price (TP_{MIN}) is $36 per chip.

Although the chip division's situation has changed, the phone division's situation has not. The maximum transfer price it is willing to pay (i.e., TP_{MAX}) remains at $32. Thus, the two divisions cannot agree on a price, and the transfer will not take place. The chip division will not sell for less than $36 per chip; the phone division will not purchase for more than $32 per chip. It is easy to verify that the firm loses as a whole if it forces a transfer at a price of $34 per phone chip. Thus, even though transferring the chip internally generates some cost savings, the firm gains more when it uses the capacity to make GPS chips.

Exhibit 12.15 summarizes the analyses for the three scenarios.

Exhibit 12.15	Opportunity Cost Analysis		
	Scenario 1	Scenario 2	Scenario 3
Chip Division			
Variable cost of phone chip	$12	$12	$12
Lost contribution from external sales	18	18	$25*
Cost savings realized from transfer	0	($1)	($1)
Minimum acceptable price	$30	$29	$36
Phone Division			
Market price for external purchase	$30	$30	$30
Cost savings realized from transfer	0	2	2
Maximum acceptable price for transfer	$30	$32	$32
Profit effect for overall firm			
Will divisions agree on transfer price?	Yes	Yes	No
Is transfer profitable for overall firm?	No effect	Yes	No

* The chip division loses the chance to sell one GPS chip for each phone chip transferred internally.

ANSWERS TO CHECK IT! EXERCISES

Exercise 1: Average book value of assets = ($7,150,000 + $6,850,000)/2 = $7,000,000; Other operating investments, average = ($1,100,000 + $1,300,000)/2 = $1,200,000; Average investment = $7,000,000 + $1,200,000 = $8,200,000. Depreciation for the year = $7,150,000 + $250,000 − $6,850,000 = $550,000.

Exercise 2: Asset turnover = $6,400,000/$8,000,000 = 0.80; Profit margin = $800,000/ $6,400,000 = .125 or 12.5%; ROI = profit margin × asset turnover = 0.80 × .125 = 10%.

Exercise 3: In Scenario 1, EVA = $1,405,600 − [0.18 × ($10,450,000 − $245,000)] = ($431,300). In Scenario 2, EVA = $756,000 − [0.18 × ($3,500,000 − $650,000)] = $243,000.

Exercise 4 (appendix): For the chip division, the contribution margin from an external sale = $18.00 per chip and the controllable cost = $12.50 per chip. Thus, TP_{MIN} = $12.50 + $18.00 = $30.50 per chip. For the phone division, TP_{MAX} is still $32 = $52 total variable cost of buying externally − $20 variable phone cost of buying internally. Thus, the range of acceptable transfer prices is $30.50 to $32.00. If the transfer price is set anywhere in this range, the company as a whole saves $1.50 for every chip that is internally transferred.

SELF-STUDY PROBLEMS

General Robots is an international conglomerate, operating multiple businesses in multiple countries. The data in Exhibit 12.16 pertain to three of General Robots' divisions for the most recent year of operations.

a. *Calculate each division's return on investment, using both gross book value and net book value to measure investment. In addition, compute each division's residual income and EVA. For both RI and EVA, use the required rate of return to compute the capital charge, and the net book value of assets to measure investment.*

We know that:

Return on investment = Divisional income/Divisional investment

Residual income = Divisional income
     − (Required rate of return × Divisional investment)

Economic value added = Net operating income after taxes
     − [WACC × (Investment − Current liabilities)]

Using these formulas and the information provided, we have Exhibit 12.17.

Exhibit 12.16 *Select Divisional Data for General Robots*

	Division A	Division B	Division C
Division income before taxes	$1,150,000	$2,241,000	$1,520,000
Gross book value of assets	$11,500,000	$12,450,000	$7,600,000
Accumulated depreciation	$4,312,500	$1,245,000	$1,520,000
Net book value of assets	$7,187,500	$11,205,000	$6,080,000
Current liabilities	$245,000	$325,000	$150,000
Tax rate in relevant country	30%	30%	25%
Required rate of return	14%	12%	16%

Exhibit 12.17	Performance Data for Select Divisions of General Robots		

	Division A	Division B	Division C
Return on investment			
Gross book value[1]	10.00%	18.00%	20.00%
Net book value[2]	16.00%	20.00%	25.00%
Residual income[3]	$143,750	$896,400	$547,200
EVA[4]	($166,950)	$263,100	$191,200

[1] Division A: $1,150,000/$11,500,000 = 10%; Division B: $2,241,000/$12,450,000 = 18% Division C: $1,520,000/$7,600,000 = 20%

[2] Division A: $1,150,000/$7,187,500 = 16%; Division B: $2,241,000/$11,205,000 = 20% Division C: $1,520,000/$6,080,000 = 25%

[3] Division A: $1,150,000 − 0.14 × $7,187,500 = $143,750; Division B: $2,241,000 − 0.12 × $11,205,000 = $896,400; Division C: $1,520,000 − 0.16 × $6,080,000 = $547,200

[4] Division A: $1,150,000 × (1 − 0.30) − 0.14 × ($7,187,500 − $245,000) = ($166,950); Division B: $2,241,000 × (1 − 0.30) − 0.12 × ($11,205,000 − $325,000) = $263,100; Division C: $1,520,000 × (1 − 0.25) − 0.16 × ($6,080,000 − $150,000) = $191,200

b. *Comment on the results, paying particular attention to variations in the performance measures across divisions.*

We find that Division C has the highest ROI when we measure investment using either gross or net book value. The disparity across divisions narrows somewhat with net book value. Division A appears to have the oldest assets as its ROI increases the most when we use net book value, rather than gross book value, to measure investment.

All three divisions generate positive residual income, with Division B leading the way. The differing required rates of return probably relate to risk—compared to Division C, Division B probably is in a stable, relatively risk-free business. Moreover, Division B's RI exceeds that of Division C both because it has a lower required rate of return and because Division B is larger in size.

The EVA for Division A is negative. This is because the divisions' after-tax rate of return of [16% × (1 − 0.3)] = 11.12% is lower than the required return on 16%. Adjusting for non-interest bearing current liabilities boosts EVA but not enough to overcome the lower return. Division B continues to outperform Division C in terms of EVA, even though Division B is disadvantaged in its tax environment.

This problem illustrates that the rank ordering of divisions depends on the metrics that we use to evaluate performance and, though not illustrated in the problem, the specific measures that we use for each metric (e.g., our rank ordering of ROI could change depending on whether we use gross or net book value). This example underscores the importance of selecting the right performance measures and benchmarks.

GLOSSARY

Benchmarking Systematic evaluation of various activities and business processes relative to the best practices.

Controllable performance measure A performance measure that reflects only the consequences of the actions taken by the decision maker.

Decentralization The practice of delegating authority to lower-level managers.

Discretionary cost center A cost center for which there is no clear relation between inputs and outputs.

DuPont model A method for decomposing ROI into two component parts: profit margin and asset turnover.

Economic value added (EVA) A performance measure similar to residual income. The difference is that EVA has specific guidelines on how to compute income, investment, and the weighted average cost of capital.

Engineered cost centers Cost centers for which there is a clear relation between inputs and outputs.

Informativeness principle The notion that any metric that provides information about a manager's effort or skill could be a useful performance measure.

Kaizen Philosophy of continuous improvement.

Relative performance evaluation The practice of measuring a manager's or a division's performance against other managers or divisions.

Residual income (RI) The income that a division generates over and above the required rate of return on investment.

Responsibility center An organizational subunit with specified decision rights. There are three common forms of responsibility centers: cost centers, profit centers, and investment centers.

Return on investment (ROI) A measure of profit generated per dollar of investment—equals divisional operating income divided by divisional investment.

Transfer price A notional price paid for an internal transfer of goods or services.

REVIEW QUESTIONS

12.1 LO1. Why do firms decentralize?

12.2 LO1. List two benefits and two costs associated with decentralization.

12.3 LO2. What are the three common forms of responsibility centers we find in organizations?

12.4 LO2. What are the responsibilities of a cost center manager?

12.5 LO2. What are the responsibilities of a profit center manager?

12.6 LO2. What are the responsibilities of an investment center manager?

12.7 LO2. What are the two key principles of performance measurement?

12.8 LO2. List three characteristics of an effective performance measure.

12.9 LO3. How are cost center managers commonly evaluated?

12.10 LO3. What does the term *kaizen* mean?

12.11 LO3. How are profit center managers commonly evaluated?

12.12 LO4. Define ROI. List two advantages and two disadvantages of using ROI as a measure to evaluate investment centers.

12.13 LO4. Define residual income. What is the difference between economic value added (EVA) and residual income?

12.14 LO5. Why is transfer pricing necessary in organizations with multiple divisions?

12.15 LO5. What are the three common approaches to transfer pricing? List one advantage and one disadvantage associated with each of these three approaches.

DISCUSSION QUESTIONS

12.16 LO1. Organizational experts say that decentralization "co-locates knowledge and decision rights." What does this statement mean? Is decentralization always beneficial? What are the costs associated with delegating decision making to lower levels of an organization?

12.17 LO1. Consider the various tasks that need to be accomplished within a household (e.g., take out garbage, cook, clean, mow lawn). Can you think of how a family might decentralize the execution of these tasks? Do we need motivating, monitoring, and evaluation measures as well?

12.18 LO1. Some argue that decentralization results in maximizing profit division by division. It may not lead to profit maximization at the overall firm level. Do you agree? Why or why not?

12.19 LO1. Both the U.S. Army and the University of Wisconsin are large complex entities with numerous employees. Comment on the differences to which these organizations are decentralized, as well

as variations in the monitoring and performance evaluation systems.

12.20 LO2. In choosing a performance measure, many argue that *controllability* is the operative principle in that a manager should be able to influence the metric. Some argue for *informativeness*, which says that any metric that provides insight into the manager's performance (whether controllable or not) is a good measure. Discuss, providing an example of an informative measure that is not controllable.

12.21 LO2. "Why not simply evaluate the performance of all divisional managers based on the entire firm's profit? That way, we do not have to worry about divisional managers not acting in the firm's best interests." Is this a reasonable argument? Why or why not?

12.22 LO3. Discuss the role for variance analysis (see Chapter 8) in evaluating cost center/profit center managers.

12.23 LO4. When evaluating investment centers, what are some of the disadvantages of using net book value to measure investment?

12.24 LO4. Two divisions with exactly the same return on investment (ROI) can have different residual incomes (RI). Why?

12.25 LO4. Some argue that both ROI and RI motivate managers to focus on short-term performance, since both the measures are calculated using operating performance (i.e., operating income). Yet, ROI is widely used as a performance measure. Provide a brief discussion.

12.26 LO5. Explain why capacity utilization in a supplying division is such an important consideration when choosing a transfer pricing policy.

12.27 LO5. A firm often obtains services from subsidiaries in which the firm's key officers may hold minority ownership. What incentive conflicts do such arrangements pose?

12.28 LO5. Discuss some problems that arise when pricing the transfer of intellectual property.

12.29 LO5 (Advanced). In many situations, it is difficult to determine the market price for a supplying division (because there is no ready market for the intermediate product). Discuss the options available for transfer pricing in such settings.

12.30 LO5 (Advanced). Is it advisable for the head office to interfere in transfer-pricing disputes among its divisions? Why or why not?

EXERCISES

12.31 Responsibility accounting (LO1, LO2). Karl Krader oversees a staff of over 200 persons and a budget of close to a million dollars per year. He is responsible for the upkeep of all buildings and equipment at a large university. However, any reconstruction project is budgeted and administered separately. Karl's responsibilities include selection and evaluation of personnel, negotiating with suppliers, choosing the kinds of landscaping, and so on. Karl's services, however, are not priced out to the user departments or to individual units within the university.

Required:

a. Should Karl be evaluated as a profit center or a cost center?

b. How should the university evaluate Karl's performance?

12.32 Responsibility accounting (LO1, LO2). Jose's Cantina is a chain of 20 fast-food restaurants. Gordon Martinez started the firm 10 years ago to provide affordable, fast, good quality Mexican cuisine. He locates branches near college campuses and areas with large populations of young adults. To oversee daily operations, he has hired managers for each branch and city. However, Gordon keeps a tight rein on operations. He personally approves all capital expenditures, menu changes, and so on. Branches get deliveries each day and offer a fixed menu of items at firm prices.

Required:

a. Classify the branches as being profit or cost centers. Justify.

b. Based on your answer to (a) above, briefly describe how you will evaluate the performance of each branch.

12.33 Responsibility accounting (LO1). Cynthia O'Brien has identified the following five major functional areas:

- *Marketing:* Identify and develop customers, bring in the revenues, keep track of competitive landscape, and forecast demand conditions so that the division can budget and plan effectively.

- *Production:* Meet production targets by making the most efficient use of factory resources available.

- *Planning and coordination:* Coordinate all divisional functions so that everybody is on the same page. It is responsible for budgeting and ensuring implementation of budgets.

- *Maintenance:* Ensure proper functioning of plant and equipment and provide technical support to the production function.

- *Purchasing:* Oversee procurement of various input materials and inventory management. This department also develops new vendors and evaluates outsourcing options.

Required:

Classify each of the five functions as a cost center or profit center. If classified as a cost center, discuss whether it is a discretionary cost center. Briefly describe how you will evaluate the performance of each function.

12.34 Discretionary cost centers (LO1). James Lowell heads the Strategic Planning Group for a major conglomerate. He and his staff of five are charged with helping top management formulate and implement strategy. They act as internal consultants when identifying target acquisitions or evaluating new product lines, regional expansions, and such.

Required:

What kind of a responsibility center is the Strategic Planning Group? How could we evaluate its performance?

12.35 Performance evaluation, profit center (LO3). Lori White is the chief executive of a division of Visions, Inc. Lori's division makes high-quality frames that sell for premium prices. For the most recent budget year, her division expected to sell 80,000 frames and receive $9.6 million. Actual sales and revenues were 100,000 frames and $11 million, respectively. Lori delegates all marketing and sales related decisions (including pricing) to her marketing manager.

Required:

a. Should Lori be pleased with the revenue performance?

b. Suppose instead that the actual sales were 70,000 frames for revenues of $9,100,000. Should Lori be upset with the revenue performance? List some of the issues that Lori should look into when analyzing this performance.

12.36 Cost center (LO3). The Production Department of Advent Cordless Phones is a cost center. The following table provides budgeted and actual cost information for the most recent year.

	Budget	Actual
Production volume (units)	175,000	200,000
Total variable costs	$7,875,000	$9,450,000
Total fixed costs	1,200,000	$1,350,000

Required:

Evaluate the performance of the Production Department.

12.37 Cost center (LO2). The following table provides budgeted and actual cost information for Advent Cordless Phones:

	Budget	Actual
Production volume (units)	200,000	150,000
Total variable costs	$9,200,000	$6,875,000
Total fixed costs	1,300,000	$1,350,000

Required:

a. Evaluate the performance of the Production Department during the budget year.

b. An investigation reveals a breakdown of a crucial piece of equipment during the year that restricted output considerably. It was determined that $75,000 of the fixed costs and $120,000 of the variable costs were attributable to this problem. How will your answer to part (a) change in light of this new information?

12.38 Profit center, qualitative (LO3). "In my current position, I have met my profit target for 8 quarters in a row. I am 110% confident that I can meet similar stretch goals for you, if given the opportunity." This was Greg Sierra's boast when he interviewed to be a profit center head at a large corporation. Greg had a history of turning in very good results for two to three years, and then switching jobs. As evidence of his exemplary (modestly stated, of course) managerial talent, Greg always likes to point out that his units' performance unfailingly went down after he quit.

Required:

a. What might be an alternate reason for the lower performance after Greg leaves a profit center he supervises?

b. What kinds of performance measures could you add to profit goals to ensure that Greg also pays appropriate attention to long-term goals?

12.39 Investment center performance (LO4). Refer to the data in the following table:

	Operating Income	Investment	ROI	Required Rate of Return	RI
1	$225,000	$1,800,000	?	14%	?
2	?	$2,500,000	10%	8%	?
3	$500,000	?	10%	?	$125,000
4	$150,000	$1,200,000	?	?	($18,000)

Required:

Treating each row of the table independently, compute the missing information.

12.40 Residual income and changing rates (LO4). The following data pertain to two divisions, A and B, of a large corporation:

	Division A	Division B
Profit	$3,750,000	$1,100,000
Investment	$31,250,000	$5,500,000

Required:

a. Determine the higher ranked division using residual income (with cost of capital or the required rate of return at 10%) as the criterion.

b. Repeat part (a), but using 14% as the cost of capital.

c. How do you explain the conflicting results in parts (a) and (b)?

12.41 ROI, Residual income and division size (LO4). The following data pertain to two divisions, Western and Eastern, of a large corporation. This corporation was established on the East Coast of the United States. It has recently expanded to the West Coast to take advantage of the greater profit potential in the growing western states.

	Eastern	Western
Profit	$ 3,000,000	$ 780,000
Investment	$24,000,000	$3,900,000

Required:

a. Determine the higher ranked division using residual income (with cost of capital at 10%) as the criterion.

b. Repeat the exercise in part (a), but using ROI as the criterion.

c. How do you explain the conflicting results in parts (a) and (b)?

12.42 Transfer pricing (LO5). Able Electronics makes some of its products in Thailand and sells them in the United States. Able informs you that this year, it plans to transfer 250,000 units of a product (Variable cost = $10 per unit and associated fixed costs are $1,500,000 per year) from Thailand to the United States. The product sells for $25 per unit in the United States.

Required:

a. Suppose the transfer price were set at full cost. Considering this product alone, compute the profit reported in Thailand, in the United States, and for Able as a whole.

b. Suppose the transfer occurs at a price of $20 per unit. Considering this product alone, compute the profit reported in Thailand, the United States, and for Able as a whole.

c. What inferences do you draw about the role of transfer prices in determining the pretax profit for the corporation as whole? Will your conclusion generally hold if we consider after-tax profit?

12.43 Transfer pricing (LO5). Rajdeep Scooters is organized as multiple divisions. All divisions are profit centers. The Engine Division manufactures two-stroke engines used by the assembly division. The market price of the engine is Rs. 18,000. (Rs. stands for rupees, the currency in India.) The division's cost sheet contains the following information about an engine's cost:

Item	Cost
Direct materials	Rs. 6,000
Direct labor	3,000
Variable overhead	1,000
Fixed overhead	2,000

Required:

a. What would be the transfer price if the company uses a policy of setting the transfer price at variable cost plus a 20% markup?

b. What would be the transfer price if the company uses a policy of setting the transfer price at full cost plus 10% markup?

c. Comment on whether either of the above two estimates would be a "fair" transfer price.

12.44 Transfer pricing and capacity utilization (LO5). Division A manufactures screens used in high-definition TVs. It sells its one product, a standard screen, for a price of $210 per screen. Variable costs are $90 per screen, and allocated fixed costs amount to $95 per screen. Division B has asked Division A to supply 5,000 custom-made screens. These custom screens have a variable cost of $105 per unit. Division A believes that its standard screen and the custom screen for Division B consume the same amount of capacity to make. It now has the capacity to make 20,000 screens annually.

Required:

For each of the following scenarios, what is the minimum price *per custom screen* that Division A can set for this transfer and maintain its profit at the current level?

a. Division A is currently making 12,000 standard screens.

b. Division A is operating at capacity.

c. Division A is making and selling 16,000 standard screens currently. Division B wants to buy all 5,000 screens from Division A or none at all.

PROBLEMS

12.45 Responsibility accounting (LO1, LO2, LO3). Chemco International is a large firm that has operations in numerous countries and many product lines. However, the underlying manufacturing processes in the various factories have many factors in common. Accordingly, Chemco has assembled a team of 25 chemical engineers and process specialists. Any division could call on this team for help with improving their process. The team would then charge the division a predetermined amount. Chemco expects the central research facility to recover its costs but not make a profit.

Required:

a. Should Chemco evaluate the central research group as a cost or profit center? What benefits and problems do you see with this choice?

b. What would be a good way to evaluate the performance of the central research group?

12.46 Responsibility accounting, interdependent units (LO2, LO3). AlarmTek, Inc., makes and sells high-end home security systems. It has two divisions—a production division and a marketing division. The company treats the production division as a cost center and the marketing division as a revenue center. It evaluates the production division by comparing the actual cost performance to a flexible budget. Similarly, it evaluates the marketing division by comparing actual revenues less marketing and customer care costs to the corresponding budget. The following presents budgeted and actual performance for a recent year.

	Budget	*Actual*
Production volume (units)	40,000	45,000
Revenues	$8,000,000	$8,550,000
Variable production costs	$4,000,000	$4,050,000
Total fixed production costs	800,000	$780,000
Variable marketing and customer care costs	400,000	640,000
Fixed marketing and customer care costs	250,000	450,000
Profit before taxes	$2,550,000	2,630,000

Required:

a. The production manager was very happy with his performance, but the marketing manager was fuming! Explain why by evaluating their performances.

b. The marketing manager complained severely to the head office:

> I helped sell more units, but the quality was bad! Look at my marketing costs! I did not spend any more in sales calls and promotions compared to last year. The only reason my costs are so high is because my department had to offer more after-sales service to handle a lot of customer complaints! I even lost out on revenues. I think my esteemed colleague on the production side is cutting corners to come under the cost budget. I think you have to change the way you evaluate performance.

> Do you think the marketing manager might have a legitimate case? Explain.

c. How would you improve the performance measurement and evaluation system to avoid such conflicts in the future?

12.47 Responsibility accounting, non-traditional setting (LO1, LO2, LO3). Dr. Dan Jagesia is a world-renowned surgeon who works for a university hospital. Dan receives a handsome salary from the university. In addition, he writes grant proposals and receives funds from federal and private agencies to support his research. Dan received grants totaling $2.5 million last year alone, and his total funding averages $4 million per year. In line with standard practice, the university adds, and the funding agencies pay, a 57% surcharge as overhead recovery. (This recovery is to cover administrative support, lab space, library, etc.) Dan also generates considerable revenue to the university via his clinical service (i.e., operating on patients). Dan often complains that he works for "free" as the patient revenue more than covers his salary.

Required:

How should the university evaluate Dan's performance? Is he (and his lab) a profit center or a cost center?

12.48 Performance evaluation (ROI, RI, EVA) (LO4): Superior Leather Products, Inc., has two divisions, Travel Bags Division and Leather Accessories Division. The following table presents their performance for the most recent year.

	Travel Bags	Leather Accessories
Total assets	$4,000,000	$6,000,000
Current liabilities	175,000	800,000
Operating income (before taxes)	600,000	1,200,000

Required:

a. Calculate the return on investment (ROI) for each division. Use operating income as the measure of income and use the total assets as the measure of investment.

b. Calculate the residual income for each division. Assume the required rate of return on investment is 12%.

c. Superior Leather has outstanding long-term debt with a market value of $3 million and an interest rate of 8%. Its equity capital has a market value of $7 million. The cost of equity is 12%. The income tax rate is 30%. Calculate the economic value added for each division. Recall that WACC = (1-tax rate) × % financed from debt × cost of debt + % financed from equity × cost of equity

d. Which of the three measures would you recommend? Why?

12.49 ROI, RI and EVA (LO3, LO4). The following data pertain to Hercules Health Club's operations for the most recent year.

Operating income	$125,000
Gross book value of assets	$950,000
Net book value of assets	$350,000
Liabilities	$72,000
Corporate tax rate	28%
Value of debt outstanding	$50,000
Cost of debt	12%
Estimated cost of equity	15%

Required:

a. Calculate the ROI for Hercules. Use operating income and net book value of assets as the measures for income and investment respectively.

b. Compute the residual income for Hercules, using 14% as the required rate of return.

c. Compute the economic value added (EVA) for Hercules, making sure to separately show the calculation for weighted average cost of capital.

d. What factors might explain the unusually high ROI for Hercules?

e. Suppose Tom and Lynda identify a project that has a 20% ROI. Will they choose to invest in the project? Will your answer differ if, instead of being a family-owned business, Hercules was a branch in a network of gyms? What factors are central to your argument?

12.50 Incentives and actions, cost centers (LO2, LO3). Mansoor Ali is in charge of maintenance. He is evaluated based on a flexible budget based on the number of machine hours operated. Mansoor gets a sizable bonus if his actual costs come in below budget.

In recent months, complaints against the slow pace of maintenance work reached an all-time high. The sales manager complains that she lost a major sale because of production delays, caused by slow turnaround on machine repairs. The production manager says that he does his best to squeeze the most out of every machine because any time a machine requires maintenance it seems to take forever to get it back up into production. Mansoor's response is that it takes time to do a good job. He says that if he fixed the machine in two days rather then three, the machine would be back in the shop in two instead of six months. "If I do something, I do it right," says Mansoor.

Required:

a. Discuss how, if at all, Mansoor's performance evaluation and compensation plans bear on the current situation.

b. How could you modify the systems to induce a higher level of cooperation among the managers of the various functional units?

12.51 Upper unit performance (LO2). Consider the following two settings:

Setting 1: Firm A operates a set of branch offices. Branch offices usually can fulfill customers' needs themselves. However, occasionally, they lack a specialist in the area or may not have the needed programs. In such cases, they refer the customer to other branches (or get the specialist to visit for a day). The other branch is willing to spare the specialist because many customers transact with many branches (e.g., a corporation with many divisions interacting with the many branches of a bank).

Setting 2: Firm B operates a set of branch offices. These offices are self-contained, and there is little interaction across branches. Customers tend to be branch specific.

Required:

Comment on why firm A's incentive plan for branch managers might include both local and global (e.g., regional) measures of performance. Why is such a feature of less importance in firm B?

 12.52 Performance evaluation & ROI (LO4, Advanced). MoviePlex, Inc., has giant movie theatre complexes in Houston, Atlanta, and Seattle. Each location is run independently, with the head office located in Atlanta. The three complexes are similar in size, with 12 screens each. The Seattle location is only a year old, the Atlanta location 3 years old, and the Houston location is 6 years old. The head office uses ROI to evaluate financial performance. The following table presents their performance for a recent year.

	Revenues	Variable Costs	Fixed Costs (incl. depreciation)	Invested Capital (net book value)	Annual Depreciation
Houston	$8,500,000	$2,800,000	$2,400,000	$18,000,000	$1,200,000
Atlanta	8,300,000	2,600,000	2,200,000	21,000,000	1,300,000
Seattle	8,650,000	2,250,000	2,500,000	27,000,000	1,400,000

MoviePlex, Inc., uses 10% as the required rate of return. It also depreciates its assets based on straight-line depreciation (assume that the amount for depreciation has stayed the same for the past six years).

Required:

a. Prepare a table with the three locations as rows. The four columns contain ROI and RI, each calculated using net book value and gross book value.

b. Discuss the effect of the measure and the choice of how to value investments on the ranking of the three locations.

12.53 ROI, RI, Profit projection using high-low method (Chapter 4) (LO4). Reiman Industries, a merchandising firm, provides the following information regarding one of its divisions.

	Year 2007	Year 2008
Sales	$2,400,000	$2,700,000
Cost of goods sold	1,800,000	2,010,000
Gross margin	600,000	690,000
Selling expenses	480,000	510,000
Profit before tax	120,000	180,000
Average assets	$2,100,000	$2,225,000

The firm requires a 10% rate of return from its divisions.

Required:

Suppose sales for 2009 are expected to be $3,000,000, and the average asset base was projected at $2,275,000. Calculate the firm's return on investment and residual income for 2009.

12.54 Transfer pricing and taxes (LO5). Catlow Corporation makes testing equipment used in hospitals. Usually, this equipment is made to order. However, this year, a client backed out of the deal, forfeiting a $50,000 penalty on an order worth $750,000. The U.S. division therefore has an unsold machine on which it has spent $625,000. It approached its European and Asian division heads as to whether they want the machine.

The European division says that it could pay up to $700,000 for the machine as it expects to sell the machine for $750,000. The Asian division is willing to pay $675,000 only, even though it expects to sell the machine for $775,000.

You know that the average tax rate is 45% in Europe, 20% in Asia, and 35% in the United States.

Required:

a. From the perspective of Catlow Corporation, where should the machine be sold? What is the profit-maximizing transfer price? Assume that Catlow can justify any transfer price from $625,000 to $750,000 to all involved tax authorities.

b. From the perspective of the U.S. division, which offer (from Europe or Asia) is more attractive? Why?

c. What are the benefits and costs of the corporate office stepping in to enforce the transfer as determined in part (a) rather than the transfer desired by the U.S. division in part (b)?

12.55 Transfer pricing and ethics (LO5). The machinery building factory (MBF) of Packages, Ltd., makes machines used in packaging product. These machines are sold by Packages' regional office as a complete solution: that is, the regional office will sell not only the containers but also the equipment required to fill product. MBF transfers its machines to the regional packaging units at variable cost plus 50% toward recovery of overhead. Corporate management strongly believes that a full-cost-based price would create needless complications in terms of overhead allocations. Moreover, the 50% rate makes sure that the MBF keeps a tight lid on overhead costs.

Despite heroic efforts, the MBF's management cannot contain overhead to be 50% or less of variable costs. The actual ratio for the most recent year was 0.53, and management knows that another sub par year would jeopardize their jobs. The division manager of the MBF approaches you, the division controller, to explore possible actions. She believes that the current system for classifying costs into fixed and variable is broken. She offers some suggestions that would reclassify some costs from the "fixed' to the "variable" category. She argues that this classification is just a semantic issue as ALL costs are variable in the long term.

Required:

What should you do? Be sure to consider the IMA's ethical guidelines (see Appendix to Chapter 1) in your answer.

12.56 Transfer pricing, cost pools, and ethics (LO5, Advanced). The machinery-building factory (MBF) of Packages, Ltd., makes machines that are used in packaging products such as toothpaste. These machines are sold by Packages' regional office as a complete solution: that is, the regional office will not only sell the containers but also the equipment required to fill the product. MBF transfers its machines to the regional packaging units at full cost (i.e., materials plus labor plus allocated overhead).

MBF recently branched out to sell foil printing machines in the open market. This expansion required it to purchase new computer-controlled lathes and milling machines. These machines require minimal labor input once they are set up. (The current manual lathes and milling machines could not provide the required quality. These machines have a man–machine ratio of 1, meaning that each machine hour requires one labor hour.)

During the past year, the market for foil printing machines has experienced some unanticipated shrinkage, imposing considerable price pressure on the existing suppliers (including MBF). The division is in danger of not meeting its profit goals for the third quarter in a row.

MBF's division manager comes to you, the division's controller, with a novel solution to her problem. She wishes you to modify the division's cost accounting system to a single pool system and use labor hours as the sole allocation basis.

Required:

a. How does the manager's proposal help solve her problem? Notice that the proposal neither brings in additional revenue nor reduces costs. (Assume that the change itself would be costless to implement.)

b. What should you do? Be sure to consider the IMA's ethical guidelines (see Appendix to Chapter 1) in your answer.

 12.57 Transfer price and income measurement (LO5). The following table presents the performance of two divisions—Division A and Division B—of a company. Division A supplies an intermediate product to Division B. Although there is an outside market for Division A's product, it does not sell its product to the outside market.

	Division A	Division B
Revenues		$12,500,000
Direct material costs	$2,500,000	$1,800,000*
Direct labor	$2,000,000	$1,500,000
Variable overhead	$500,000	$375,000
Fixed overhead	$1,600,000	$1,200,000
Total	$6,600,000	$4,875,000

* Does not include the cost of transfer from Division A.

Required:

a. Assume that the transfer price is 110% of Division A's full cost. Prepare an income statement for each division.

b. Assume that the transfer price is 120% of Division A's variable cost. Prepare an income statement for each division.

c. Assume that the transfer price is the market price. If Division A could sell its entire output in the intermediate market, it would realize revenues of $8,000,000. Prepare an income statement for each division.

d. What conclusions do you draw from comparing your answers? Under what conditions would you recommend the transfer-pricing schemes in requirements in parts (a), (b), and (c) above?

12.58 Transfer pricing (LO5, Appendix). Quest Computers, Inc., makes microprocessor chips and personal computers. Its Microprocessor Division makes the chips and supplies them to the Personal Computer Division. The Personal Computer buys all the other necessary parts from outside vendors and assembles personal computers for home and business use. There is also a ready outside market for microprocessor chips made by the Microprocessor Division. The following cost and market data pertains to the two divisions:

Average estimated selling price for the personal computer	$1,000
Market price for the microprocessor chip (per unit)	$250
Variable costs in Personal Computer Division (excluding chip)	$820
Variable costs for making the chip	$100

The two divisions are profit centers. While Quest Computers, Inc., would not like its Microprocessor division to sell the advanced microprocessor chip to other computer manufacturers in the outside market, it nevertheless allows its divisional managers complete latitude in decision making.

The manager of the Microprocessor Division prefers to charge the Personal Computer Division the market price for transferring the chips. The manager of the Personal Computer Division makes the following calculations

Selling price—final product		$1,000
Transferred-in costs (market)	$250	
Variable costs for completion	820	1,070
Contribution (loss) on product		$(70)

Required:

a. From the point of view of Quest Computers, should transfers be made to the Personal Computer Division if there is no excess capacity in the Microprocessor Division? Is the market price the correct transfer price?

b. Assume that the Microprocessor Division has the capacity to make 50,000 chips, and it can sell only 37,500 chips to the outside market at a price of $250 (assume for various reasons, the division is not willing to reduce this price). From the point of view of Quest Computers, should the remaining 12,500 chips be transferred to the Personal Computer Division?

c. Suppose the Microprocessor Division can sell all 50,000 chips if it reduces the market price to $225. From the point of view of Quest Computers, should transfers be made to the Personal Computer Division? If yes, is market price the correct transfer price?

12.59 ROI Computations (LO4). Tom and Lynda have approached you for clarification regarding how to compute return on investment. They inform you that their operating profit is $125,000 per year. Their accountant's statement contained a calculation of ROI based on $900,000, the net book value of their investment in Hercules. However, Tom feels that net book value is a poor measure of their return. He argues that it will take at least $1,250,000 to replace their machines and that estimate is better for figuring out what they have vested in the business. Lynda argues that even that estimate is too low. She says that they can sell the gym for about $1.7 million, mostly because the land has appreciated a great deal in their neighborhood.

Required:

Calculate the ROI for Hercules using the three estimates for investment. Which measure do you support? If different measures are useful for differing decisions, identify a context for each of the three values of ROI.

12.60 Economic value added (LO4). Refer to the following table:

	Net Operating Profit after Taxes (NOPAT)	Invested Capital	Current Liabilities	Cost of Debt Capital (k_D)	Cost of Equity Capital (k_E)	Proportion of Debt in Total Capital (d)	WACC	EVA
1	$200,000	$1,600,000	$150,000	8%	12%	0.75	?	?
2	$200,000	$1,600,000	$150,000	8%	12%	0.5	?	?
3	$200,000	$1,600,000	$350,000	8%	12%	0.5	9%	?

The weighted average cost of capital is given by WACC = $(1 - t) \times d \times k_D + (1 - d) \times k_E$, where t is the tax rate. Assume a tax rate of 25 percent.

Required:

Treating each row of the table independently, compute the missing information. What inferences can you draw by comparing your answers across rows (note that each row changes one or two items relative to the row above it)?

MINI-CASES

12.61 Project appraisal and selection, ROI (LO4). Kitchen Appliances, Inc., is a multidivision company with each major product line managed by a separate division. Divisional managers have complete autonomy with respect to operating and investment decisions. The company evaluates its division managers on ROI, calculated as operating income before taxes divided by net book value of assets (averaged over the year). The firm pays particular attention to year-over-year growth in ROI as well as budget-actual comparison of the measure.

Wendy Miller is the manager of the dishwasher division. Wendy expects that the operating income for the current year will be $2,400,000 before taxes. Given a net asset base of $6,800,000, the division's ROI would be a healthy 35%, well above the average return from other divisions. This performance has been fairly representative of the way things have been going for Wendy. She expects a similar performance next year as well and is looking forward to her promotion into the C-suite (the corporate office).

Toward the end of the current year, an investment opportunity arises for Wendy—the possibility of introducing a new dishwasher model with improved features. The following table presents some salient financial information that Wendy's managers put together for her evaluation:

Incremental cash outlay for additional equipment	$1,500,000
Useful life	10 years
Salvage value at the end of useful life	0
Annual revenues	800,000
Annual variable costs	300,000
Annual fixed costs (excluding depreciation)	100,000
Required rate of return (company stipulated)	12%
Corporate tax rate	30%

The company uses a straight-line depreciation method for accounting and tax purposes.

Required:

a. Does the investment opportunity have a positive net present value? From the company's viewpoint, should the project be accepted?

b. Will Wendy accept the project? Make a recommendation after calculating her ROI with and without the investment. Assume that investment occurs at the start of the year.

c. Assume that the company evaluates its divisional managers based on residual income, using a 12% required rate of return. What is the dishwasher division's expected residual income for the current year (without the proposed investment)? With the proposed project?

d. Comment on why ROI and RI might lead to differing incentives regarding project investments.

12.62 Decentralization and Performance Evaluation (LO1, LO2, LO3, LO4). Anne Green leveraged her love of plants and gardens into a highly acclaimed garden shop. Over the past 20 years, the business expanded rapidly and now operates in 14 states.

Anne firmly believes in giving people a free hand but exercising careful control as well. She likens managing people to growing gardens. "Once you give them the necessary tools for success and have helped through the initial growth, it is best to step aside to let them grow and thrive. But you must be prepared to pinch and prune for the best long-term results." Thus, while seen as a place that values autonomy, Annie's Gardens also has a reputation for strongly linking compensation to performance. The following describes some key aspects of the firm.

• *Strategy:* Annie believes that a small outfit like hers cannot compete in the mass market. She therefore wishes to focus on hard to find and exotic plants, as well as plants that are perceived as "more healthy and better cared for" than a customer might find at a general store. She thinks that there is a viable market (comprising middle- to upper-income households) that will pay premium prices for unique and vibrant plants that will distinguish their homes. She also feels that providing good advice (and some hand holding) is the first step when selling plants. She has accordingly expanded into garden design and renovation. However, she thinks that Annie's should play the role of a designer and supplier and hire out the actual work of making the garden.

- *Structure:* Annie's Gardens is organized into three regions—Midwest, Mid-Atlantic, and North East—each with about 20 to 30 branches. Each store has a manager and an assistant manager, who make most decisions. Many stores have one to two additional permanent employees. Stores also hire people for the season and pay them by the hour.

- *Sales:* While the central office suggests pricing for most categories of items (e.g., small shrubs for $39.99, medium for $59.99), managers are allowed to change prices to reflect local market conditions. Store managers can also design and execute targeted promotions. There is little in the form of national or regional-level advertising.

- *Purchasing:* Virtually all purchasing is centralized. Annie's negotiates prices with major growers and suppliers (e.g., for seed, fertilizer, and so on). She then circulates a list of all available plants and supplies to her stores, highlighting items that she believes have the greatest margins and are likely to "do well" this year. However, store managers and their purchasing associates (who often become managers themselves) determine what to buy and the quantities to stock. Returns, particularly of plants, are expensive to process and strongly discouraged. In practice, stores discount prices heavily to move seasonal and perishable merchandise.

- *Personnel:* The manager also is responsible for virtually all hiring, pay scales, and other decisions regarding personnel. Pay rates are negotiated locally. There is some movement of managers across stores, although it is unusual for a manager to be moved involuntarily.

- *Operations:* While the central office provides guidelines, individual store managers control store hours. They also are responsible for upkeep (e.g., making sure that the plants are watered appropriately), display, and so on. Periodic, unannounced visits (about once a month at least, with more to "problem" stores) ensure that the store meets "corporate quality standards." These standards are not spelled out but represent an informal understanding about the level of cleanliness, responsiveness to customer enquiries, and so on.

- *Investments:* Anne is very careful about this aspect. Any capital improvement over $1,000 must be personally approved by her. She is somewhat vague about her approval criteria, although her impressions about the store's prospects and its manager seem to matter a lot. After getting her MBA, she has begun to demand financial measures when managers submit investment proposals.

- *Store manager compensation:* Managers receive a base pay plus a cash bonus. The bonus formula considers the budgeted and actual return on investment (ROI) for the store. ROI is calculated as income over investment, with income defined as operating income (i.e., before taxes and finance charges). Investment includes all assets (land, buildings, equipment, and inventory are the prominent items) valued at net book value, averaged over the start and end of the year.

The bonus is based on a sliding scale. The manager earns no bonus if the actual ROI is less than 90% of budgeted ROI. At this cutoff, the manager gets an adjustment factor of 0.9 × bonus pool rate for the year × base salary. The adjustment factor increases linearly to be 1.00 when actual ROI equals budgeted ROI, and it tops out at 1.2. The bonus pool is decided at the regional level, based on both corporate and regional performance, and the bonus pool rate is calculated as the ($ in the bonus pool/total salary for bonus-eligible employees). In many cases, the bonus is nearly 50% of the manager's annual compensation.

The Situation at the Columbus Store:

Don Moser has been the manager of the Columbus store for all five years of its existence. The grapevine says that Don is likely to become region chief, when the incumbent retires in two to three years. Six months into this year, Don is projecting an ROI of 28% based on income of $92,400 and assets of $330,000 (averaged as $340,000 and $320,000 for the opening and closing values). His target ROI for the year is 25%.

The Proposal:

His second-in-command and probable successor, Deborah, has approached Don with an intriguing idea. She wants to spend $20,000 to make a specialty greenhouse that will allow the store to stock a greater variety of exotics as well as reduce the "shrinkage" (e.g., dead plants) due to adverse weather conditions. She estimates (and Don agrees) that the greenhouse would increase sales by about $17,500 during the first year but that sales would increase by 12% each year after that. Sales for the remainder of the current year would be $8,500. The greenhouse would cost $2,500 annually to operate and would last five full years (not counting the current year) without the need for substantial renovation.

Annie's usual contribution margin ratio is 50%. The firm would depreciate the greenhouse over five years and use straight-line depreciation. The current year (and the last year) will have half the normal depreciation. The required rate of return (pretax) is 20%.

Required:

a. What is Anne's implicit classification of stores (as cost/profit or investment centers). Do you agree with this classification?

b. Deborah calculates that the greenhouse has an NPV of $7,434 before considering taxes, and that its payback period is just under three years. However, Don does not seem eager to forward the proposal to Anne for her approval. What might be a source of his reluctance? (*Note:* You might wish to verify these estimates. For simplicity, assume that all cash flow, including those for the current year, take place at the end of the year. Also calculate the NPV as at the end of the current year. Verification is not needed to answer the question.)

c. Critically evaluate the choice of ROI as a performance metric and the way in which Annie's Gardens computes the measure. In particular, should Annie include or exclude some items when computing income or investment? Should she value them differently? What are the costs and benefits of using alternate measures such as residual income in place of ROI?

d. Discuss the structure of the compensation plan. What might be reasons for starting the bonus at levels below the target? for a cap on the payout ratio? for computing the bonus pool at the regional level?

12.63 Transfer Pricing (LO4, LO5, Appendix)

Brenda: Seth, I am trying to help you here. But there is no way that I can pay you $230 per unit. I have competitive bids from other vendors for about $170, and that difference means $1,200,000 in my bottom line. Because you helped me design the part, I am willing to split the difference and offer $200. This will help you ramp up your utilization and spread your fixed costs over a larger base. After all, we play for the same team, but there is a limit to the hit I can take.

Seth: I can do without help like that! I have been screaming at my sales guys to get full cost plus 15%, which is what I quoted you. I drew this line in the sand six months ago, and slowly but steadily it is paying off. I will be undercutting my own instructions if I give you the part for what you are asking. At $200, I barely break even and only if I eat the $240,000 I spent in designing the part and making mock-ups. Already, morale is low because we did not make bonus last year. Pricing at cost is a sure way for not making it this year as well.

Seth and Brenda are division managers for a large manufacturing firm that makes many different kinds of appliances. The firm operates on a decentralized basis, and division managers have considerable autonomy in pricing and sourcing. They also are held accountable for meeting divisional goals, usually set at stretch levels. Bonus compensation heavily weights divisional performance, although a portion (e.g., stock options) depends on corporate performance.

The highlighted dispute centers on an innovative part that Seth's components division had designed in collaboration with Brenda's refrigerator division. While there was no payment for the design, the intent was that Seth's outfit would be the front-runner in the bidding. However, Seth's bid of $230 per unit (for 20,000 parts annually) was substantially above other bids. The conversation excerpted above summarizes the heated exchange between the two managers.

Brenda is annoyed because she thinks she is doing Seth a favor and that he is looking a gift horse in the mouth. She knows that his division is operating at about 70% of capacity only and that his sales force is scrambling to find orders. This component would substantially increase Seth's utilization. Brenda also has a desire to keep the relationship alive because Seth's engineers have proved adept at solving thorny technical issues and his quality is decidedly better than that provided by his competitors.

Seth is upset too. He knows that Brenda would have paid for the design anywhere else. Moreover, he thinks that she saves a bundle with higher component quality. He points out that 15% is the average long-run rate of return for his segment of the industry. For his coup d'etat, he whips out an accounting statement that shows the component's variable manufacturing cost at $125 and allocated manufacturing overhead at $75 per part. He even ignored selling expenses (usually 10% of selling price) when arriving at the bid! He is planning to appeal to their joint boss to force Brenda to buy the part at $230.

Required:

a. Relative to buying for an outside supplier at $170 pr unit, calculate the change in the profit reported by Seth's division and the firm as a whole if Brenda buys the component from Seth for $170 per unit. Repeat at prices of $200 and $230 per unit. Ignore any savings in Brenda's plant due to higher quality.

b. What advice would you provide the corporate VP, who has Brenda and Seth as her direct reports? When formulating your recommendation, please be sure to consider Seth and Brenda's motivations for their respective stance.

Chapter 13

Strategic Planning and Control

AVINASH "AVI" RAM HAS AN impressive reputation for starting up retail banking operations for emerging private-sector banks in India and for globally reputed banks in the Middle East. During his career, Avi developed a large network of business contacts all over the world. He always had an acute business sense and was attracted to the mushrooming Business Process Outsourcing (BPO) industry. He felt that he had the necessary expertise and the contacts to be successful in that area. Therefore, he began toying with the idea of launching his own BPO, ClientSys. Deciding now or never, he gave up his lucrative job to embark on this exhilarating but risky journey.

APPLYING THE DECISION FRAMEWORK

What Is the Problem?
Avinash must decide the mission and the strategy of the proposed BPO, ClientSys, and design appropriate planning and control systems. He must also ensure that all organizational actions and decisions are consistent with the chosen strategy.

What Are the Options?
Strategic planning options concern the range of services (technical, voice, and/or back-office services) and target clientele (financial services versus all segments). Once Avi finalizes his strategy, he will have to design complementary control systems. Each combination of performance measures is a decision alternative for communicating strategy and monitoring its success.

What Are the Costs and the Benefits?
Because of the decision's horizon, virtually all costs and benefits are controllable. The basis for the business model is the availability of qualified and relatively inexpensive human resources in India relative to developed countries. From the control standpoint, the options vary greatly with respect to how well they communicate ClientSys's strategy to employees, and how well they align employees' goals with the firm's objectives.

Make the Decision!
We will recommend a suitable strategy, and the associated planning and control systems.

Getty Images

ClientSys, a BPO, has to pick a business strategy and long-term performance measures.

LEARNING OBJECTIVES

After studying this chapter, you will be able to:

1 Explain the role management accounting plays in guiding strategy.

2 Understand the value chain for a business.

3 Appreciate product life-cycle analysis and target costing.

4 Discuss the need for multiple measures of organizational performance.

5 Describe a balanced scorecard.

In this chapter, we consider the decision problems facing entrepreneurs such as Avi as well as managers of established firms. Perhaps the most important task for top management is to develop the organization's **strategy**. This decision charts the firm's course over the long term. The chosen strategy must allow management to create and sustain a business model that will yield sufficient returns to the suppliers of capital. In addition, the planning and control systems of the firm should support the chosen strategy. In this chapter, we discuss the role of management accounting in formulating and implementing strategy.

We begin this chapter by introducing the term *strategy*. We then describe the role management accounting plays in supporting an organization's strategy, and in identifying and configuring its value chain. We discuss two techniques, **life-cycle analysis** and **target costing**, that help a firm to incorporate a long-term view when making such strategic planning decisions. As we learned in

CHAPTER CONNECTIONS
By considering long-term planning and control decisions, this chapter brings us full circle back to Chapter 1.

Chapter 1, however, we need to follow such planning decisions with controls. We consider how to monitor the implementation of strategy. We discuss the need for multiple performance measures in organizations, and introduce the notion of critical success factors (CSFs). Finally, we describe the balanced scorecard, a widely used strategic performance measurement system that provides a framework for selecting and reporting performance measures tied to an organization's CSFs.

Formulating a Strategy

LEARNING OBJECTIVE 1

Explain the role of management accounting in guiding strategy.

To build and preserve a significant market share in any competitive market, a firm must offer a **value proposition**, the key source of customer value, to its target market. The value proposition offered by Sam's Club is to supply name-brand items at unbeatable prices. The value proposition for Saks Fifth Avenue is to sell the latest fashion apparel at premium prices in a highly personalized environment. A firm's **strategy** is the approach for creating and sustaining its value proposition. Thus, strategy defines how a firm positions its products within the target market and *distinguishes* itself from its competitors to maximize its return on investment.

DETERMINANTS OF BUSINESS STRATEGY

At least three considerations influence the formulation of a successful business strategy:

- Core competencies and capabilities
- Competitive landscape
- Sustainability

Core Competencies and Capabilities

Core competency is a term used to refer to the skill set and expertise that characterizes a firm and its employees, and advantages the firm relative to its competitors. Lucent Technologies' core competency is its R&D capabilities, while Nike relies on design expertise. Wal-Mart has the expertise and the capability in supply chains to stock its retail network with goods from around the world. Core competencies guide the value propositions of a firm. A successful business strategy builds organizational capabilities around the core competencies of its founders, key employees, or the processes it has developed over time. A strategy not anchored firmly in core competencies is destined to fail.

Avi and his business partners are clear about the competencies of ClientSys. The partners have immense experience in financial services. In addition to a vast network of contacts, they bring a wealth of knowledge on back-office business processes, research, and analysis, as well as an intimate understanding of customer needs. This experience and knowledge gives them an edge when offering BPO services to firms in the financial sector.

 **Connecting to Practice**

HP AND COMPAQ

In the early 2000s, HP merged with Compaq to gain an edge over Dell in the low-end PC market. Coupled with HP's presence in high-end computers, this move attempted to dominate the entire range of the computing equipment market, all at once.

COMMENTARY: The merger increased HP's dependence on the high-volume, razor-thin margin PC business, where it did not possess strategic advantages. The following data highlight the outcome.

	2000 Market Share	*2004 Market Share*
Compaq	13.1%	
HP	7.8%	
Combined Compaq-HP	20.9%	15.8%
Dell	11.5%	17.9%
IBM	7.4%	5.9%

However, the problem might have been implementation. After HP went through some management transitions, the firm did very well. In the late 2000's, HP was poised to become the leader in PC sales. Thus, success requires both innovative strategy *and* effective implementation.

Source: www.osnews.com, *Posted by special contributor Rahul Gaitonde on 02/24/2005.*

Competitive Landscape

When formulating a business model, it is crucial to have a good understanding of the competitive landscape. According to experts, firms should consider the five competitive forces listed in Exhibit 13.1.

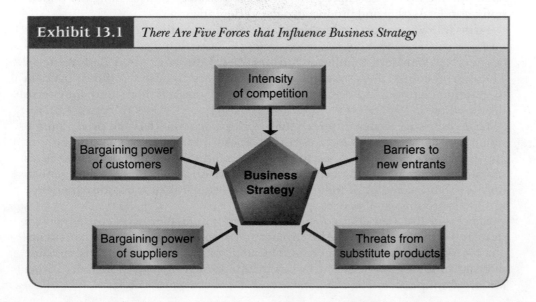

Exhibit 13.1 | *There Are Five Forces that Influence Business Strategy*

- *Industry competitors:* Who are the major competitors? What are their core competencies and capabilities? How much market share do they command? What is their cost structure? Do the firms have high or low operating leverage?
- *New entrants:* Does the chosen business segment offer enough potential to new entrants? Are there barriers to entry? What is the level of threat posed by potential new entrants?
- *Substitute products:* Is there a threat from substitute products? How well do these substitute products perform relative to the company's products? Do they offer a significant price advantage? Functional advantage?
- *Supplier power:* Will the company have to rely excessively on a few key suppliers? How important is the company's business to its suppliers? Will the company have some negotiating power with its suppliers?
- *Customer power:* How dispersed or concentrated is the target market? Is the market comprised of a few large customers? How much flexibility does a company have in dealing with its customers?

The Indian business world has numerous BPO-type operations, both large and small. Reputation and contacts count for a lot in attracting and retaining clients. Operating a successful business requires both extensive financial and human capital. The task of attracting and retaining a capable workforce is a key entry barrier in this high-turnover industry. While few substitutes exist currently, BPO operations in other low-cost countries could be a threat in a few years. However, it is difficult and expensive for clients to switch BPOs because of costs associated with training the staff in the new BPO, integrating computer systems, and so on.

Sustainability

New and existing competitors will emulate the business strategies of successful firms. A *sustainable strategy* is difficult to imitate by competitors because of the unique resource capabilities and market power it brings. It is difficult for Sears to replicate Wal-Mart's entire strategy or for United Airlines to be more like Southwest Airlines.

Avi believes that ClientSys will wow clients with its service and capabilities. This reputation for excellence and reliability at low cost will be the firm's sustainable competitive edge.

TYPES OF BUSINESS STRATEGY

As shown in Exhibit 13.2, experts classify business strategy choices along two dimensions: cost leadership and product or value differentiation.

Firms following a **cost leadership** strategy find innovative ways to improve their business processes and cut costs. Examples of firms with a cost leadership strategy include Wal-Mart, Southwest Airlines, Dell Computers, and Best Western. These firms couple their strategy with market power to raise significant barriers to potential entrants, thereby preserving their market share and long-term profitability.

Firms following a **value differentiation** strategy focus on R&D and product innovation activities. Examples include Hewlett-Packard for printers, Gucci in fashion apparel, and Disney resort hotels in the holiday and vacation industry. These firms stay ahead of competition by being quicker to develop and market the next generation of products, and by providing their target customer base a unique experience with their products and services.

Successful firms excel at combining value differentiation with cost advantage strategies. The rise of Japanese electronics and automobile firms in the late twentieth century is attributable largely to their ability to achieve cost leadership while offering products that excelled in quality and design. Examples include Toyota Motors, Olympus cameras, and Sony's consumer electronic division.

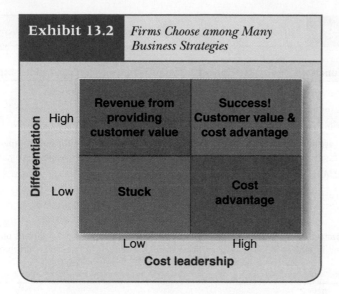

Exhibit 13.2 *Firms Choose among Many Business Strategies*

		Low Cost leadership	High Cost leadership
Differentiation	High	Revenue from providing customer value	Success! Customer value & cost advantage
	Low	Stuck	Cost advantage

For ClientSys, Avi and his partners know that the BPO industry owes its existence and rapid growth to the cost advantages it brings to its clients. Competition in this industry is primarily on the cost dimension, especially in areas such as voice services, and customer and technical support. However, clients are increasingly concerned about the quality, reliability, and range of services offered.

Because of his background, Avi identifies banking, brokerage, home mortgages, and insurance processing as the different business segments he could pursue. However, given capital and human resource constraints, he chooses to focus initially on the banking sector and expand into others as opportunities arise. Avi believes that ClientSys's core competencies should allow it to adopt a two-pronged strategy: First would be a differentiation strategy in high-value-added products in "research analytics" (investment research, valuation analysis, stock recommendations, forecasting) and investment consulting support. Second would be cost leadership strategy for routine BPO services in banking. Avi believes that these potential clients will be willing to pay a higher price for high-quality and personalized services. Even at these higher prices, Avi is confident that the clients will be also able to realize significant cost advantages relative to procuring these services within the United States. For other BPO services such as routine banking services, ClientSys would compete on cost.

MANAGEMENT ACCOUNTING AND BUSINESS STRATEGY

The cost leadership and differentiation strategies place differing demands on how a firm goes about selecting its target markets, acquiring resource capabilities, and setting up the structure of the organization. Firms following the strategy of cost leadership exploit economies of scale, institute tight cost controls, and in general adopt a firm-wide policy of cost minimization. With a differentiation strategy, innovation is more important than cost control. Naturally, as shown in Exhibit 13.3, the focus of management accounting differs across firms following these different strategies.

The price that the market is willing to pay for innovative products depends on the perceived value relative to other competing products. Thus, product costs do not play as critical a role in pricing as the market's perception of the value differentiation. To foster such innovation and to make differentiation a sustainable strategy, budgets must provide enough discretion for managers and employees to try out new ideas. Overemphasis on the use of budgets to evaluate actual performance

Exhibit 13.3	*Differences in Management Accounting Functions Across Strategies*	
Management Accounting Functions	**Product Differentiation**	**Cost Leadership**
Role of costs in pricing	Not critical	Critical
Role of budgets for planning	More discretion in budgets	Less discretion in budgets
Role of budgets in control	Loose cost control	Tight cost control
Activity-based costing for product and capacity planning	Not critical	Critical. Full capacity utilization to achieve economies of scale
Customer profitability analysis	Not critical	Critical to control costs to serve customers
Benchmarking costs against competition	Not critical	Critical to be the most efficient producer
Divisional performance evaluation and incentives	More emphasis on profit maximization through revenue generation	More emphasis on profit maximization through cost control

may prove counterproductive. Employees will be worried more about controlling costs and staying within the budget than about seeking and testing new ideas. Overall, the emphasis in cost measurement is not so much measuring the cost of each product precisely as it is on ensuring the overall profitability of the entire product portfolio.

In contrast, firms that follow the cost leadership strategy target price-sensitive market segments by offering products at as low a price as possible. Cost leadership is a high-volume, low-margin strategy. It is especially effective in established, mature markets, with little that differentiates competing products. Cost planning and control systems play a crucial role in the success of a cost leadership strategy. Knowing the cost of a product is important in ensuring that it is profitable to make and sell the product at the prevailing market price. Flexible budgets play an important role in identifying and eliminating operational inefficiencies. Inefficiencies and wastage can cost the firm its competitive edge in the price-sensitive segment.

ClientSys plans to follow a two-pronged strategy to leverage its capabilities fully. In particular, Avi decides to organize ClientSys into two units. One will focus on the "value-adding" investment and analytic services, and the other will focus on back-office BPO operations. Management controls will be looser in the first unit relative to the second. Moreover, the first unit will have a greater emphasis on output-based performance measures and a greater reliance on incentive compensation.

Avi's next task is to configure ClientSys to execute this strategy. Performing value chain analysis is useful in this task because it helps managers determine which activities to retain within the boundaries of a firm and which activities to outsource.

CHAPTER CONNECTIONS

In Chapter 8, we highlighted the role of flexible budgeting in evaluating operational efficiencies. The flexible budget variance is useful in evaluating operational performance because it provides the right benchmark against which to compare the actual performance. The flexible budget indicates what the revenues and the costs should be for the actual output level. Deviations from this budget are indicative of potential control problems with respect to the operations.

The Value Chain

In Chapter 10, we introduced the notion that an organization is a collection of activities that convert input resources such as material, labor, and machine time into products or services. We discussed the classification of activities into value-adding and non-value-adding activities to facilitate cost management. A **value chain** is a set of logically sequenced, value-adding activities that convert input resources into products or services in a manner consistent with the chosen business strategy.

LEARNING OBJECTIVE 2

Understand the value chain for a business.

BUILDING A VALUE CHAIN

Building a proper value chain ("configuring the value chain") is a crucial step in successfully implementing business strategy. An activity that adds value under one business strategy can diminish value under another strategy. Firms develop a sustainable competitive edge by carefully identifying strategy relevant activities and performing them in a manner that differentiates them from their rivals.

Whole Foods, with over 150 stores in the United States and United Kingdom, markets itself as the "World's Leading Natural and Organic Foods Supermarket." Its business strategy is to offer the highest quality, least processed, most flavorful, and naturally preserved foods with an unrelenting emphasis on customer satisfaction and employee team spirit. This strategy provides the most value to its target customers, who are health and environment conscious and are not price sensitive.

Compared to other full-service groceries such as Kroger and Safeway, Whole Foods focuses narrowly on grocery items and does not offer convenience services such as pharmacy and banking. Whole Foods seeks out suppliers from all over the world, often from small, uniquely dedicated food artisans. Activities at the store aim to provide customers a friendly and happy experience. We find customers tasting various types of food and having a sampling of gourmet coffee as they make their purchases. Thus, all aspects of the firm's operations reinforce its strategy, leading to continued growth and financial success.

Whole Food's business strategy is to offer the highest quality, least processed, most flavorful, and naturally preserved foods with an unrelenting emphasis on customer satisfaction and employee team spirit. (Elise Amendola/©AP/Wide World Photos)

 **Connecting to Practice**

PROCUREMENT AT WHOLE FOODS

The company's Web site describes its procurement activities thus:

- We feature foods that are free from artificial preservatives, colors, flavors, sweeteners, and hydrogenated fats.
- We are passionate about great tasting food and the pleasure of sharing it with each other.
- We are committed to foods that are fresh, wholesome, and safe to eat.
- We seek out and promote organically grown foods.
- We provide food and nutritional products that support health and well-being.

COMMENTARY: Each of these objectives enhances and underscores the firm's commitment to delivering natural, wholesome and unprocessed foods.

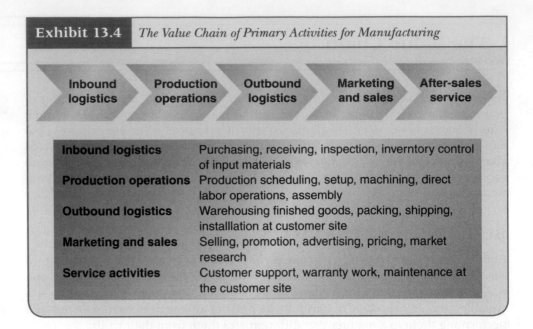

Exhibit 13.4	*The Value Chain of Primary Activities for Manufacturing*

Inbound logistics → Production operations → Outbound logistics → Marketing and sales → After-sales service

Inbound logistics	Purchasing, receiving, inspection, inverntory control of input materials
Production operations	Production scheduling, setup, machining, direct labor operations, assembly
Outbound logistics	Warehousing finished goods, packing, shipping, installlation at customer site
Marketing and sales	Selling, promotion, advertising, pricing, market research
Service activities	Customer support, warranty work, maintenance at the customer site

Extending the Value Chain Beyond the firm

As shown in Exhibit 13.4, we can classify an organization's activities into five generic categories based on the logical sequence in which these activities take place in organizations.

This classification helps us identify the specific areas in which a firm has core competencies and capabilities to gain and maintain a strategic competitive edge. It may be best for a firm to outsource or form strategic alliances with outside suppliers to perform those value activities in which it does not have a unique advantage. Dell uses mostly "off-the-shelf" parts in its assembly of personal computers because it does not have an advantage over Seagate or Western Digital in making hard drives or over Intel in making processors. Dell's advantage lies in its direct and Web-based assemble-to-order marketing, sales, and customer support network (i.e., in the marketing and sales category in Exhibit 13.4), as well as in efficient operations.

In sum, the value chain often extends beyond the boundaries of a firm. Whole Foods is part of the industry value chain that begins in small agricultural, dairy, and animal farms, continues with meat, dairy, and food processing plants before reaching the retail shelves of Whole Foods.

Exhibit 13.5 presents the industry value chain of ClientSys. ClientSys expects to enter into long-term arrangements with specialized small financial analysis firms to offer niche investment analysis. ClientSys also expects to enter into strategic partnerships with some large low-cost rival BPO firms to offer routine customer support and back-office functions to its clients.

MANAGEMENT ACCOUNTING AND THE VALUE CHAIN

Exhibit 13.6 shows how management accounting information can help configure value chains for value differentiation and cost leadership strategies. The activity-based approach to configuring the value chain is useful for both value differentiation and cost leadership strategies. However, these strategies differ in the emphasis they place on *what* each activity should achieve and how it ought to contribute to the strategy.

Under a value differentiation strategy, we evaluate activities based on how they enhance the success of a business strategy. Activities such as product research and

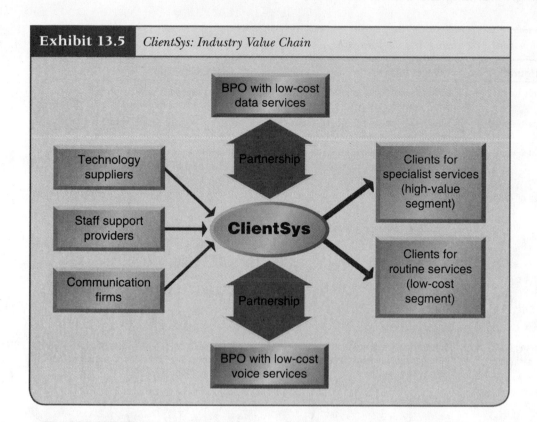

Exhibit 13.5   *ClientSys: Industry Value Chain*

Connecting to Practice

MOVING UP THE VALUE CHAIN

After years of operating computer coding and call centers, India's largest software firms, Wipro, Infosys, and Tata Consultancy Services, want more. These firms are now pursuing lucrative contracts for computer services and technology solutions outside India and have emerged as direct competitors to Accenture and IBM. The Indian firms' goal is to add to their margins by providing value-added services, leveraging the insights they have gained from operating business processes for U.S. firms.

COMMENTARY: The shift in strategy has far-reaching implications. The new approach leverages intellectual capital and expertise rather than the availability of low-skilled, low-cost labor. For the strategy to succeed, the firms will need to reconfigure their operations to measure and reward the new drivers of success.

development, and generation of new ideas, assume greater importance over systematic cost reduction initiatives.

In contrast, the cost leadership strategy sustains the competitive edge by constantly seeking ways to reduce costs throughout the value chain. Companies following this strategy intensively scrutinize costs, starting with the product design and development stage to the last operation. Over time, systems and procedures have evolved in management accounting to bring a pervasive cost focus in such organizations. These include life-cycle and target costing, functional analysis and value engineering, and kaizen costing.

Exhibit 13.6	*Management Accounting and the Value Chain*	

Steps in Value Chain Configuration	Product Differentiation	Cost Leadership
Step 1 List all activities and prepare the activity map	Lacks the cost focus to justify a full-fledged activity-based costing system	Strategy supports development of full-fledged activity-based costing system
Define scope and depth of activity-based costing.	Extends activity-based costing approach beyond the boundaries of the firm	Extends activity-based costing approach beyond the boundaries of the firm
Step 2 Identify performance linkages across activities	Focus is on contribution to value differentiation goal, after accounting for all linkages.	Identifies cost of an activity to the entire value chain by taking all linkages into account
Criteria for measuring the value of each activity		
Step 3 Engineering activities	Focus is on enhancing benefits from activity.	Focus is on cost reduction. Significant role for
Focus on engineering efforts		• Cost driver analysis
		• Scale economies
		• Benchmarking
		• Target costing
		• Kaizen
Step 4 Determine activity sourcing	Outsource any activity that does not help differentiate. Suppliers have competitive cost advantage.	Make decision based on who has the greater cost advantage, considering costs throughout the value chain.
Configure the "internal" value chain versus the "supply" chain		

CHAPTER CONNECTIONS

In Chapter 12, we discussed "Kaizen" or "continuous improvement." Popularized by Japanese companies, Kaizen costing takes an organization on a path of efficiency improvements over time.

Strategic Cost Planning

LEARNING OBJECTIVE 3

Appreciate product life cycle analysis and target costing.

As we have seen, a successful strategy requires a firm to marshal its core competencies and capabilities to develop, make, and sell the right set of products or services in a sustained manner. In this section, we discuss two techniques—life-cycle analysis and target costing—that help a firm adopt a long-term view when making long-term product planning decisions.

LIFE-CYCLE ANALYSIS

Most products have finite lives. The life cycle of a product depends on the nature of the product, the nature of the industry, the level of competition in the industry, and the rate at which technology is changing in the industry. Thus, life cycles exhibit considerable variability. A new automobile design has a life cycle of six years or so, while the life cycle of a computer chip is less than two years. Product life cycle is an important element of a business strategy because it determines the rate at which companies have to develop and introduce new products to compete effectively.

Exhibit 13.7 illustrates the five stages in a product life cycle: development, introduction, growth, maturity, and decline. As shown in Exhibit 13.8, these stages differ from each other in the types of activities performed on the product, cash outflows involved, revenues generated, and decisions involved. Consequently, the stages differ in terms of the information they need from management accounting. Let us see how.

Development

In this stage, we expect no sales revenue from products. Instead, we expect significant expenditures in product research and development activities, test runs to assess feasibility and production costs, and test marketing to evaluate market acceptance and potential. If product development is successful, we undertake necessary investments in plant, equipment, and other resources necessary to make and market the product.

Exhibit 13.7	*There Are Five Stages in a Product's Life Cycle*

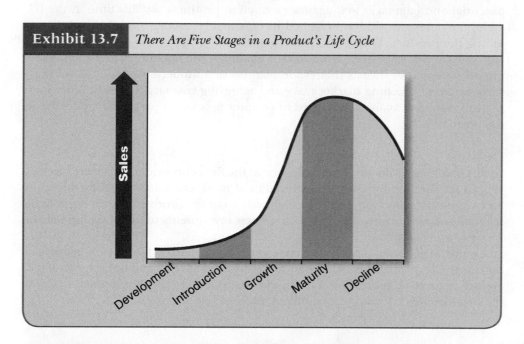

Exhibit 13.8	*Stages in Product Life Cycle and Profitability*		
Life-cycle Stages	**Key Activities**	**Management Actions**	**Profitability**
Development	Product research and development	Finalize product attributes	No profit
	Test production runs	Finalize target market	Net cash outflow
	Test marketing	Finalize operations	
	Capacity planning and investment	Finalize price point	
Introduction and growth	Marketing and distribution	Expand scale	Revenue growth
	Promotion	Increase market reach	Low profits
	Improve production efficiencies	Increase capacity utilization	
Maturity	Production, distribution, and marketing operations at maximum achievable capacity	Competitive pricing	Maximum revenue generation
		Ensure maximal efficiencies	Minimum cost of operations
		Identify and implement cost reduction initiatives	Maximum profit generation
Decline	Tap out the market	Aggressive pricing	Declining revenues and profit
	Clear inventories	Divesting in capacity and reducing scale of operations	

Introduction and Growth

In this stage, revenues begin to pick up. Attractive promotions and price discounts help penetrate the market and gain visibility. Variable costs of production costs are typically higher, especially if making the new product involves new operations and procedures. Consequently, profitability is typically low at the introduction stage. It begins to pick up in the growth stage as the scale of marketing and production goes up. The overall business strategy dictates the relative emphasis on volume versus margin. A cost leadership strategy places more weight on increasing volume relative to generating higher margins. A differentiation strategy focuses on generating and maintaining high margins for long periods.

Maturity

A product reaches the maturity stage when it has reached its targeted market potential and compares well against competing products. By this time in the life cycle, the company will have reached its maximal efficiency levels in making and selling the product. This is the "profit-generating" stage of the product life cycle. Decisions at this stage are geared toward obtaining the maximum profit and warding off competitive threats that erode margins or volume. Likewise, control measures focus on retaining market share and achieving cost targets. Techniques such as profit variance analysis, discussed in Chapter 8, become particularly effective at this stage.

Decline

In this final stage, sales and profits decline as the firm cuts prices and clears inventories, in preparation for the next generation of products. Thus, planning decisions focus more on extracting the remaining value from the product, sacrificing volume for margins. Cost control is tight, with no new investments to maintain capacity or increase efficiency.

As indicated above, product **life-cycle analysis** emphasizes that the objective is to maximize the profitability of a product over its *entire life cycle* and not stage-by-stage. We next turn to target costing, a technique that is used in the development stage of the product life cycle and that complements life-cycle analysis.

TARGET COSTING

In many industries, a large fraction of total product life-cycle costs become committed at the development stage itself, even though the firm may have spent only 15 to 20 percent of these costs by that time (Exhibit 13.9). Design decisions influence the ease with which we make the product and therefore the costs associated with the manufacturing process. Decisions about product features and functionality determine the potential revenue by defining the scope of the target market. Because of these future implications, decisions made at the design and development stage are critical. Lack of careful cost planning at this stage could result in a product failing even before it enters the introduction phase of its life cycle. Target costing, pioneered by some Japanese firms in the late 1970s, is now a common approach for cost planning at an early stage in the product life cycle.

What Is Target Costing?

Target costing is a structured approach to cost planning and management. Traditional approaches to product development first determine the cost for making a product with specified functionality and quality. We then add a desired markup to determine the price for this product. In contrast, the premise for target costing is that the firm is a price taker and that there is intense competition to acquire, retain, and grow customers. Today's customer is sophisticated and has access to information about competing products. Thus, the customer understands the value derived from

Exhibit 13.9	*Decisions made Early in the Lifecycle Exert a Large Influence on Actual Costs*

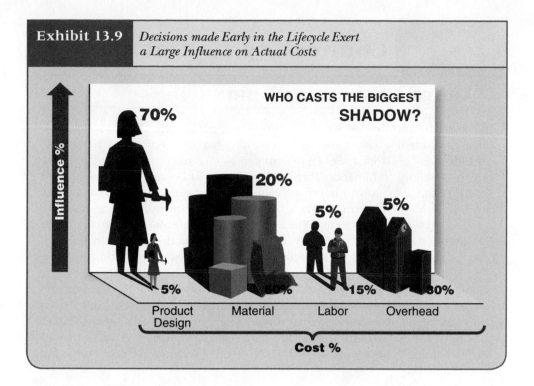

any purchase. Consequently, target costing determines cost by working backward from the customer's value.

A key innovation is to determine the allowable cost at which we must produce a proposed product with specified functionality in order to achieve a target profit margin at a given price point.

$$\text{Allowable cost} = \text{Price Point} - \text{Target Profit Margin.}$$

The **allowable cost** is often lower than the estimate of **current cost**, which is the cost estimate for making the product under current conditions. The challenge in target costing is to find a way to meet the allowable cost. The **cost gap** is the difference between the current cost and the allowable cost. The pressure to close the cost gap forces a company to consider a variety of options to ensure that the target profit margin becomes achievable before even proceeding to the introduction stage of the life cycle. Thus, target costing helps establish cost standards for various activities and business processes, standards that the company must reach in order to achieve the allowable product cost. In this way, target costing brings a cost focus at the planning stage that is crucial to ensuring that the business strategy is successful. In the Appendix we describe the specific steps involved in a typical target costing implementation.

Where Is Target Costing Effective?

The benefits of target costing depend on market characteristics. Target costing is most beneficial in industries where the intensity of competition limits firms' abilities to obtain substantial and sustainable price premiums for innovations. Nikon and Canon extensively employ target costing, although their premium products offer the latest innovations. Target costing is less useful for firms whose innovation and product differentiation allows them to command premium prices for a sustained period.

Target costing is particularly effective for products with well-defined and discrete features because it helps make proper trade-offs among price, quality, and functionality with respect to each product feature. Target costing is less effective in firms that deal with commodity-type products because there is little scope for differentiating products by their features.

Connecting to Practice

TARGET COSTING AT BOEING

Boeing is the world's leading producer of commercial aircraft. This firm, like other firms that employ target costing successfully, has cross-functional teams that include members from design engineering, manufacturing engineering, purchasing, production, and finance. Target costing teams at Boeing use a "toolbox" of management initiatives to improve productivity and reduce costs. The toolbox includes value engineering/value analysis, design for manufacturing assembly, kaizen, and lean manufacturing. The target costing system also listens to the "voice of the customer," but with a difference: the firm costs out the innovation and critically examines if the customer is willing to pay for the design innovation.

COMMENTARY: The use of cross-functional teams ensures that the team considers all of the costs and benefits associated with design and cost-planning decisions, as some of the consequences may be felt later in the value chain. Target costing is particularly effective for firms that make products with many feature combinations. Examples include automobile firms, electronics firms, and camera manufacturers.

Source: Dan Swenson et al., "Best Practices in Target Costing," *Management Accounting Quarterly (Winter 2003)*, p. 13.

Implementing Strategy

LEARNING OBJECTIVE 4

Discuss the need for multiple performance measures.

As we noted at the outset of this chapter, successful implementation requires that everyone in the organization clearly understand the chosen strategy. In addition, the organization must implement suitable monitoring and control systems.

Experts in organizational theory have discovered that a focus on financial results is not enough to help an organization implement its strategy successfully. The organization must also identify and focus some of its attention on key critical success factors (CSFs). Accordingly, we begin this section with an analysis of the need for multiple measures.

In Chapter 12, we considered ROI, RI, and EVA, which are alternate measures of an organization's financial performance. Avi periodically computes the ROI for ClientSys. He also uses the DuPont model to analyze how he could improve the firm's profitability. Yet, ROI by itself is not enough to communicate strategy. The primary reason is that ROI is a **lagging measure** that reflects *past* performance. (The same limitation is true of RI and EVA.) Lagging performance measures contain limited information about an organization's potential for *future* performance. Organizations also require **leading measures** such as customer satisfaction and product return rates, which are the drivers of *future* performance.

Because of the many factors involved in operating a business, experts in business liken managing a firm to piloting an aircraft. As shown in Exhibit 13.10, a skilled pilot simultaneously monitors many different gauges and meters to make sure that the aircraft is heading to its destination at the right direction, speed, and altitude. The pilot must also take into account weather, traffic in the air corridor,

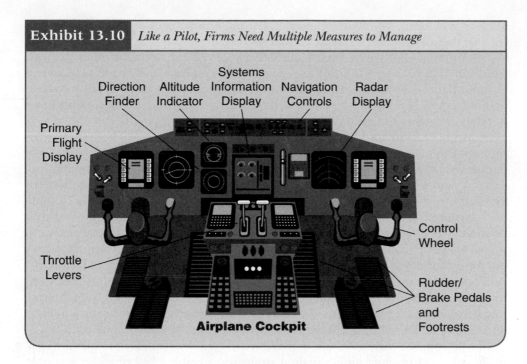

Exhibit 13.10   *Like a Pilot, Firms Need Multiple Measures to Manage*

and congestion at the destination airport. Likewise, good managers do not rely on a single measure. They know that a company will underperform in some dimensions and meet expectations in others. Therefore, they consider a combination of measures to develop a coherent picture of the organization's current health and prospects.

The need for lagging and leading indicators motivates firms to employ both financial and **nonfinancial measures** to track organizational performance. **Financial measures** suffer from the following deficiencies:

- Financial measures often reflect the aggregate performance of the entire company or division.
- Financial measures do not provide information needed in a timely manner to take immediate and on-the-spot corrective actions.
- Financial measures do not provide specific information about potential areas of concern.

Because of these reasons, organizations routinely supplement measures such as ROI with other measures of operational and strategic performance. This is the case even though many of these measures might be nonfinancial in nature and subjectively assessed. The key concern is picking those additional measures that help us measure an organization's current state of affairs and potential for future success. The concept of a critical success factor that we discuss next is central to this choice.

CRITICAL SUCCESS FACTORS

Critical success factors (CSF), also known as key performance indicators (KPIs), are performance measures that must "go right" for an organization to implement its strategy successfully and achieve its mission. Outcomes on the CSFs are the pulse of the organization's survival. On-time arrival is a CSF for commercial airlines such as United and Continental because a poor showing on this front is a recipe for failure in this competitive industry. The ability to guarantee delivery of mail by a stipulated time is a CSF for FedEx and UPS. Wireless communications companies such as

Verizon Wireless or T-Mobile compete on coverage and quality of calls—minimizing the number of dropped calls is crucial to success.

Operational CSFs are short-term metrics. These CSFs focus on the efficiency with which an organization is utilizing its resources. Operational CSFs could be financial or nonfinancial in nature. Financial metrics include cost per unit and purchase price variance. Nonfinancial metrics include average outgoing product quality level, percent defective, and yield rate.

Strategic CSFs are long-term, *firm-specific* measures. Strategic CSFs help companies monitor the success of their unique corporate and business strategies. A high-volume discount retailer like Target depends on geographical penetration and customer traffic to sustain profitability. Accordingly, measures such as sales turnover of different items are more important than assessing customer satisfaction. In contrast, a high-end retailer such as Neiman Marcus cares less about stock turnover and more about providing a delightful shopping experience for customers willing to pay premium prices. Likewise, minimizing cost per passenger mile and the time an aircraft spends on the ground for maintenance and changeovers are critical success factors for AirTran and other no-frill airlines. Though important, these factors are not paramount for an international airline such as Lufthansa because when selecting international carriers, passengers pay more attention to factors such as routes flown, schedule, and amenities. Exhibit 13.11 presents a set of CSFs for a Web-based E-tailer.

Recall from our earlier discussion that the two generic business strategies are cost-leadership and product differentiation strategies. Exhibit 13.12 provides a sample list of CSFs for each of these strategies.

Properties of a CSF

Choosing the CSFs to monitor is perhaps the most important step in the successful implementation of a strategy. A good CSF is:

- *Simple and easy to understand.* Everybody in the company must have a clear idea of what the CSF entails. On-time arrival and dropped call rate are terms that need no elaboration in the context of the airline and telecommunications industries.

Exhibit 13.11	*Critical Success Factors in E-tailing*	
CSF	**Sample Implications**	**Possible Measures**
Tell the full story	Answer every possible question a potential customer might have about the product	Number of calls to help lines
	Provide customer with as complete an experience as possible	Number of calls to help lines
Keep it simple	Help consumers narrow down their options	Percent using menu choices in Web site
	Manage a few products really well	Number of products
Full disclosure	Be upfront	Number of billing complaints
	No hidden charges in the transaction	Number of canceled transactions
Monitor consumer behavior	Learn from the consumer's Web browsing patterns	Number of page views
	Look for commonalities and design the Web experience for maximum convenience	Time spent in Web site
Inventory turnover	Stock high-demand items	Average inventory turns for SKU

Source: Martin Lindstrom, *E-Tailing's Critical Success Factors* (http://www.clickz.com/experts/brand/brand/article.php/841931)

Connecting to Practice

SHEEP FARMING

Traditional measures of success in sheep farming include lambing rate and death loss. However, these measures do not survive a hard look at their true contribution to profitability. Studies show the following to have greater impact: (1) having a low unit cost of production, (2) having enough size to be efficient, (3) adding value to the base production of the flock by feeding lambs to weights heavier than traditional weaning weights, and (4) using a mathematical measurement of flock size to the length of the lambing season.

COMMENTARY: The traditional measures relate to outcomes. The critical success factors identified by the analysis relate to the drivers of profitability. For instance, the additional cost of fattening lambs beyond their traditional weaning weight is worthwhile because it generates additional revenue. The fourth measure allows a sheep farmer to match flock size to the environment, optimizing the level of care provided.

Source: Dan Nudell, Harlan Hughes, and Tim Faller. "Critical Success Factors for Profitable Sheep Production." http://www.ag.ndsu.nodak.edu/hettinge/sheepday/critical.htm

A sheep farmer also has to monitor several critical success factors to ensure long-term financial viability. (Masterfile)

Exhibit 13.12	*Critical Success Factors and Business Strategy*
Product Differentiation	**Cost Leadership**
Operational CSFs	
Product features	Product quality
New product ideas	Cost control
	Operational efficiencies
Strategy CSFs	
Time to market new products	Market share
Product Positioning / brand image	Cost advantage
Market share	Customer value

- *Readily quantifiable.* CSFs vary in their ease of measurement. Some, such as orders delivered on time, are easy to measure. Others, such as customer satisfaction, may be equally simple and easy to understand but are harder to quantify.
- *Easy to monitor.* Performance evaluation requires measurement of CSF at regular time intervals. Ease of measurement is therefore an important consideration.
- *Linked to strategy.* A CSF must bear direct link to the strategy implemented. It does not make sense for a direct marketer such as Amazon to focus on measures such as the number of successful sales calls. As most of Dell's sales are Web-based, the number of Web hits that result in sales is more appropriate.

There is no hard and fast rule on how many CSFs to employ. The number of CSFs depends on the size of the organization, the nature of the industry, and a host of

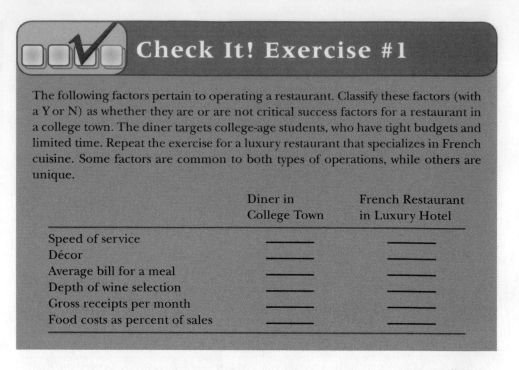

Check It! Exercise #1

The following factors pertain to operating a restaurant. Classify these factors (with a Y or N) as whether they are or are not critical success factors for a restaurant in a college town. The diner targets college-age students, who have tight budgets and limited time. Repeat the exercise for a luxury restaurant that specializes in French cuisine. Some factors are common to both types of operations, while others are unique.

	Diner in College Town	French Restaurant in Luxury Hotel
Speed of service	————	————
Décor	————	————
Average bill for a meal	————	————
Depth of wine selection	————	————
Gross receipts per month	————	————
Food costs as percent of sales	————	————

Solution at end of chapter.

other factors. However, a good performance measurement system usually has just a few key metrics. Systems that track a multitude of CSFs can provide more detailed and precise performance information. However, they often cause confusion and frustration. In contrast, a system that monitors a few carefully chosen CSFs goes a long way toward achieving a successful implementation of a strategy.

Once we choose CSFs, it is important to set targets and monitor progress (see Exhibit 13.13). In general, there is no set method or rule to determine the expected level of performance for each CSF. The top management has considerable discretion in setting these expectations as a company embarks on the implementation of a new strategy. As with budget targets (Chapter 7), we recommend setting realistic but challenging targets.

Application to ClientSys

Avi and his managers brainstorm to determine the list of CSFs for ClientSys. He is amazed by the number his team identifies. The marketing manager identifies the number of customers, market share, and the penetration into new geographic

Exhibit 13.13	*Performance Report*		
Critical Success Factor	**Target**	**Actual**	**Direction**
On-time delivery	95%	92%	▼
Product failure within 30 days of sale	0.2%	0.5%	▼
Reduction in operating costs	3%	4%	▲
Defect rate (parts per thousand)	22	15	▲
Employee turnover	15%	22%	▼
New product development (number of patents)	3	1	▼

markets and industries. The CFO identifies shareholder returns and job-by-job profit margins as key metrics, arguing that everything else is subordinate to creating shareholder value. All managers agree that monitoring employee satisfaction is important. The head of the consulting group argues for a share of revenues brought in by the back-office operations and by consulting, as well as the quality and the extent of employee training. Each of the other managers adds one or two more measures, and offers a compelling rationale for why the metric is a critical indicator of ClientSys' current and future prospects.

Somewhat to Avi's surprise, although the suggested CSFs make sense when considered in isolation, many of the CSFs appear to contradict each other. The marketing manager's desire to obtain new clients to increase the number of customers and to enter new markets is not entirely consistent with the CFO's focus on large jobs and profit margins. Investing in employee training increases the available skill set but potentially increases the chance of turnover by making employees more marketable.

Searching for a way to narrow down his choices of CSFs, Avi comes across the balanced scorecard. Let us see how this can help.

Monitoring Strategy Implementation

The **balanced scorecard** is a performance measurement system that includes a systematic approach for linking strategy to planning and control. Over the past two decades, a well-accepted structure has emerged with respect to the format and the components of a balanced scorecard. This structure allows an organization to choose among numerous CSFs representing organizational performance. Equally important, the balanced scorecard allows management to organize the measures in a way that communicates the firm's strategy, and allows all employees to see how their decisions affect other dimensions of organizational performance.

The balanced scorecard includes performance measurement along a number of different dimensions (Exhibit 13.14):

- Financial and nonfinancial measures of performance
- Short-term and long-term objectives
- Past outcome and forward looking measures of performance
- "Hard" objective and "short" subjective measures of performance
- External and internal measures of performance

LEARNING OBJECTIVE 5

Describe a balanced scorecard.

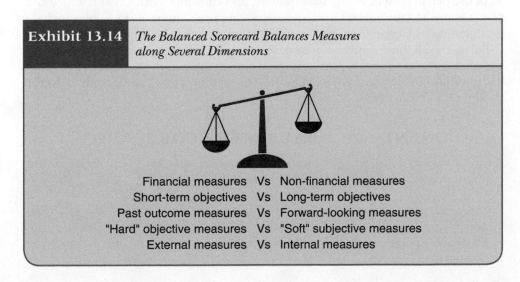

Exhibit 13.14	*The Balanced Scorecard Balances Measures along Several Dimensions*

Financial measures	Vs	Non-financial measures
Short-term objectives	Vs	Long-term objectives
Past outcome measures	Vs	Forward-looking measures
"Hard" objective measures	Vs	"Soft" subjective measures
External measures	Vs	Internal measures

Connecting to Practice

SUCCESS STORIES WITH THE BALANCED SCORECARD

The Balanced Scorecard Collaborative (www.bscol.com) is an organization that brings together materials and experts that can help organizations throughout the world build and implement the balanced scorecard to drive strategic change. Their "hall of fame" describes successful implementations in many kinds of organizations: small and large, manufacturing and service; and public and private sectors. Examples include Canon, Hilton Hotels, Duke Children's Hospital, the City of Brisbane and Fulton County Schools.

COMMENTARY: Throughout the site, we notice the tight link between an organization's strategy and its scorecard. The site takes the next step by showing how outcomes on the scorecard can help refine strategy and help a firm become a *strategy-focused organization*. This next step completes the long-term planning and control cycle.

While financial measures are still important indicators of performance, nonfinancial measures reflect drivers of future value. Firms can increase future profitability by managing these drivers well, such as finding ways in which to improve cycle times and reducing defect rates. A company needs to use both short-term and long-term critical success factors for successful implementation of a strategy. Overreliance on short-term measures can compromise long-term interests. Similarly, measures of past outcomes can be helpful in evaluating performance (e.g., the current year's profit) and control decisions, but forward-looking measures, such as customer satisfaction, are also important for planning decisions.

Some measures are "hard" in that they are quantifiable and verifiable. Examples include financial measures such as profits and asset turnover. However, "soft" qualitative measures, such as measures of customer satisfaction and effectiveness of quality improvement and employee training programs, can also be extremely valuable. Finally, some performance measures relate to constituencies outside of the traditional boundaries of the firm. For example, return on equity is a measure that captures the perspective of equity stakeholders, and customer satisfaction is a measure that pertains to customers. Other measures are purely internal. Examples include production yield, cycle time, and on-time delivery.

Balancing all these dimensions to design an effective corporate scorecard system is challenging. It requires a clear strategic vision on the part of the senior executives. It also requires free and frank communication and organizationwide buy in to the chosen set of measures.

COMPONENTS OF A BALANCED SCORECARD

A typical balanced scorecard suggests that managers look at their firms from four different perspectives, as illustrated in Exhibit 13.15.

1. **Financial perspective:** How does the company look from a shareholders' perspective?
2. **Customer perspective:** How does the company look from a customer perspective?

Exhibit 13.15 *Balanced Scorecards Often Group Measures into Four Main Perspectives*

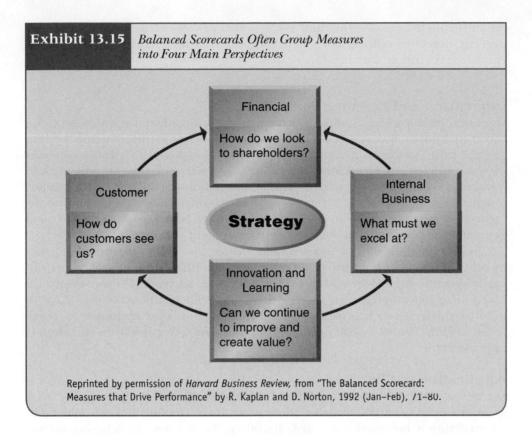

Reprinted by permission of *Harvard Business Review,* from "The Balanced Scorecard: Measures that Drive Performance" by R. Kaplan and D. Norton, 1992 (Jan–Feb), 71–80.

3. **Internal business perspective:** What are the areas in which the company must excel?

4. **Innovation and learning perspective:** What must we do to continue to improve?

Let us consider each perspective in turn.

Financial Perspective

Financial measures reflect the bottom-line impact of a company's strategy and the success with which the company is implementing the strategy. There is no sense in achieving customer satisfaction and improving business processes if these actions do not translate into financial returns for the company's owners. Typical financial measures are return on equity, sales growth, and return on net assets.

Customer Perspective

As competition has grown over the years in most product markets, firms have no choice but to become customer-focused. The balanced scorecard therefore includes factors that reflect customer perceptions. Direct measures of customer perceptions include customer satisfaction or the number of customer complaints. We can also utilize indirect measures such as market share and retention rates. For ClientSys, possible measures include the number of repeat jobs from customers and the growth in new markets.

Internal Business Perspective

As we learned in Chapter 10 in the context of activity-based costing, we could view any organization as a collection of business processes that convert inputs into outputs. Activity-based management tells us that an internal business process could add value only if it contributes to customer satisfaction, either directly or indirectly. A well-functioning organization manages both the effectiveness and the efficiency of its internal business processes. Examples of process measures include processing and cycle times, process efficiencies, yield, and percent defective output. For ClientSys, potential internal measures include employee retention, average days of delay in delivering projects, cost per transaction, and so on.

Innovation and Learning Perspective

Organizational learning is important for survival in a competitive world. So is the ability to innovate with respect to products and processes. Firms following the low-cost-producer strategy constantly seek process innovations to reduce costs and increase efficiencies. Firms following the product differentiation strategy seek to stay ahead of competition through product innovations. Some critical success factors for such firms might be the speed with which organizations learn and implement new processes, time-to-market new products, time to develop the next generation of products, and the number of new patents.

ClientSys is following a two-pronged strategy: it will compete for clients by offering low-cost back-office services but also differentiate itself by providing additional high-value-added research analytic services. These two prongs place differing emphasis on internal processes. Thus, ClientSys may have to monitor measures such as the number of training hours per employee, percent revenue from consulting services, and percent cost reduction from continuous improvement.

Application to ClientSys

Let us now consider how to implement the balanced scorecard, using ClientSys as an example. ClientSys has a well-defined strategy, the first and crucial step in constructing a balanced scorecard. Its initial focus is on the banking sector, with the eventual goal of expanding into home mortgages and insurance sectors. ClientSys aims to follow a two-pronged approach to satisfy the client. First, the firm would offer a low-cost substitute for the client's back-office operations. Second, it would differentiate itself from other BPOs by leveraging the client-specific knowledge gained to offer research analytics and other consulting services.

In a series of long and intense meetings, Avi and team identify critical success factors under each of the four perspectives of the balanced scorecard. Exhibit 13.16 presents the balanced scorecard that Avi put together for ClientSys.

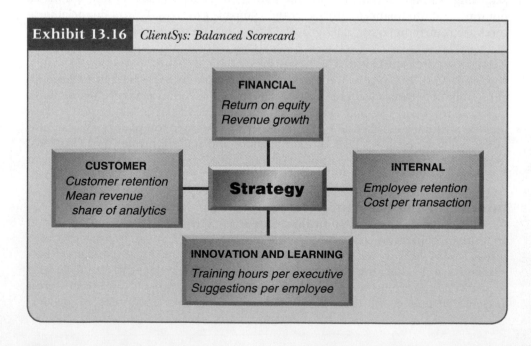

Exhibit 13.16 *ClientSys: Balanced Scorecard*

FINANCIAL
Return on equity
Revenue growth

CUSTOMER
Customer retention
Mean revenue
  share of analytics

Strategy

INTERNAL
Employee retention
Cost per transaction

INNOVATION AND LEARNING
Training hours per executive
Suggestions per employee

APPLYING THE DECISION FRAMEWORK

What Is the Problem?

Avi must decide the mission and the strategy of the proposed BPO, ClientSys, and design appropriate planning and control systems. He must also ensure that all organizational actions and decisions are consistent with the chosen strategy.

What Are the Options?

Strategic planning options concern the range of services (offer technical, voice, and/or back-office services) and target clientele (financial services versus all segments). Once Avi finalizes his strategy, he will have to design complementary control systems. Each combination of performance measures is a decision alternative for communicating strategy and monitoring its success.

What Are the Costs and the Benefits?

Because of the decision's horizon, virtually all costs and benefits are controllable. The basis for the business model is the availability of qualified and relatively inexpensive human resources in India relative to developed countries. From the control standpoint, the options vary greatly with respect to how well they communicate ClientSys's strategy to employees, and how well they align employee's goals with the firm's objectives.

Make the Decision!

Avi decides to focus on the banking sector with a two-pronged strategy of offering differentiated products for high-end analytics and cost-advantages for routine voice and data processing. Accordingly, he organizes the firm into two divisions, as these strategies require differing control systems. He outsources much of the low-cost services to specialist BPOs. He also hires suitable suppliers to obtain technical and human resources support.

To ensure successful implementation of his strategy, Avi identifies a set of critical success factors and designs a balanced scorecard.

SUMMARY

In this chapter, we discussed strategic planning and control decisions. We emphasized how strategy charts a firm's operations over the long term and the importance of aligning management planning and control systems with strategy. We then explored value chain analysis, which considers how our decisions affect costs incurred and the value derived by our suppliers and customers. Finally, we examined life cycle analysis and target costing, which underscore the importance of considering long-term costs and benefits. These techniques focus on decisions at the product design and development stage as these decisions commit us to future actions. As we learned in Chapter 2, it is important that we complement planning decisions with appropriate control mechanisms. The balanced scorecard has emerged as a popular technique for monitoring the success of strategic decisions.

RAPID REVIEW

LEARNING OBJECTIVE 1

Explain the role management accounting plays in guiding strategy.

- A strategy is an approach to compete in a product market. The strategy must identify and deliver the firm's value proposition, the core reason why customers choose the firm over others. Three considerations—core competency, competitive landscape, and sustainability—influence a firm's business strategy and its value proposition. The core competency is the skill set and expertise that characterize the firm and is at the root of its competitive advantage. Experts describe the competitive landscape in terms of current competitors, supplier power, customer power, barriers to entry, and threats from substitute products. A final consideration is the ease with which competitors, new or old, can mimic the chosen strategy.

- The two main types of business strategy are cost leadership and value differentiation. Cost leadership emphasizes advantages gained through lowering the cost of operations, while differentiation creates value by meeting previously unmet customer wants and needs.
- Management planning and control systems complement the chosen business strategy. Identifying, estimating, and managing costs are important parts of systems in organizations following the cost leadership strategy. We find looser controls and more emphasis on output-based measures in firms that follow a differentiation strategy. The focus is more on increasing profit by increasing revenue than by reducing cost.

LEARNING OBJECTIVE 2

Understand the value chain for a business.

- A value chain is a logical sequence of activities required for implementing strategy.
- Outsourcing strategy-relevant activities means that the value chain could extend beyond the firm. The entire value chain can span many firms and industries if we consider the entire process from extracting raw materials to disposition by the ultimate end-user. In this case, decisions in one part of the value chain affect costs and benefits realized in other parts. Thus, organizations can increase profit by coordinating with each other and maximizing the profit over the entire value chain.

LEARNING OBJECTIVE 3

Appreciate product life-cycle analysis and target costing.

- The useful life of a product depends on the nature of the product, industry, level of competition, and rate of innovation. Regardless, we divide a product's life cycle into five discrete stages—design and development, introduction, growth, maturity, and decline.
- The relative emphasis on revenue growth versus cost control differs systematically across the five stages in the life cycle. Consequently, different planning and control systems are appropriate at the different stages.
- Target costing is a methodology used to ensure careful attention to cost planning during the design and development stage, when all costs are controllable. We need such emphasis because decisions made during this stage commit the firm to future actions and costs. Usually, firms employ cross-functional teams to ensure that decisions at this stage consider the costs and benefits at all points in the firm's value chain.

- Target costing is particularly effective in highly competitive markets, where products have short life cycles and we can describe products in terms of features. Because target costing considers the value of each feature, some refer to it as feature-based costing.

LEARNING OBJECTIVE 4

Discuss the need for multiple measures of organizational performance.

- Critical success factors are performance measures that must "go right" for an organization to implement its strategy successfully and achieve its mission. They measure the pulse crucial to an organization's survival.
- Critical success factors must be simple and easy to understand, must be quantifiable and easy to monitor, and must bear a direct link to the strategy. Few CSFs possess all of these properties.
- The number of CSFs to track depends on the type of corporate and business strategy, the size of the organization, the nature of the industry, and a host of other factors. However, a good performance measurement system usually has a few carefully chosen measures.
- For each CSF it is necessary to specify the desired acceptable level of performance. Just as flexible budgets provide a benchmark to evaluate short-term performance, we need to stipulate a benchmark for each CSF. We also need to tie performance measures to incentives to reduce the agency conflict.

LEARNING OBJECTIVE 5

Describe a balanced scorecard.

- The usual financial measures are lagging measures of performance as they report on past actions. Many criticize financial measures as being too aggregate, not timely, and unable to provide specific enough information. Therefore, organizations also monitor leading indicators of performance, which are the drivers of future profitability.
- The balanced scorecard is a method for selecting performance measures that reflect the firm's strategy and for communicating it throughout the organization. The balanced scorecard classifies critical success factors into four organizational perspectives: customer perspective, internal business perspective, learning and growth perspective, and financial perspective.
- The balanced scorecard stresses the importance of linking long-term performance measures to the firm's strategy and of tying in the various measures in the four perspectives.

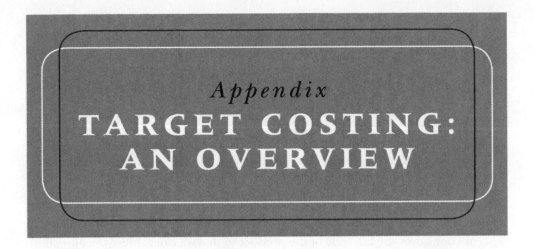

Appendix

TARGET COSTING: AN OVERVIEW

Specific implementations of target costing vary across companies and industries. However, most target costing systems share the following common steps (Exhibit 13.17):

Step 1: *Conduct market research to identify the features of proposed product.* This step involves deciding the attributes or features that the product should have, comparing it with competitive product offerings, and ensuring that the product has been positioned to appeal to the target market, in line with the firm's overall business strategy. This positioning helps set the appropriate price point at the introduction and over the product's expected life. In turn, this sequence of prices and their associated volumes determines the expected revenue from the proposed product.

Step 2: *Compute the allowable cost of the product.* We obtain the allowable cost by subtracting the targeted profit margin from the expected price point. We base the target profit on input from top management concerning

Exhibit 13.17   *An Overview of Target Costing*

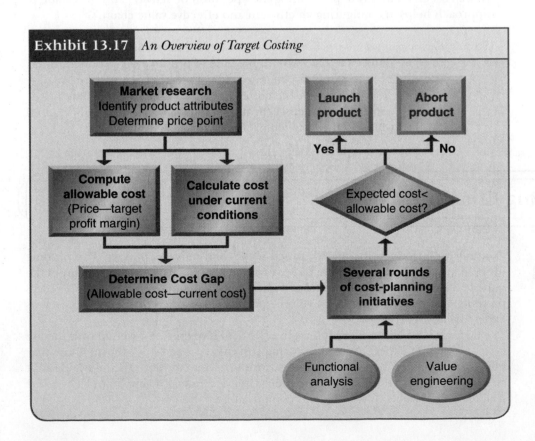

corporate goals for the product line. The allowable cost is the upper bound on the average cost of making the product over its life cycle.

Step 3: *Estimate the current cost of making the product.* Activity-based costing is useful for estimating the expected cost of making the product. It builds the overall cost from the costs of various activities to be performed. In addition, costs of other products that share some of the same features and components as the proposed product are useful in estimating the cost of the proposed product.

Step 4: *Compare the expected product cost with the allowable cost.* If the expected product cost is lower, then the target profit margin is achievable. It then makes sense to launch the product. If the expected product cost is higher than the allowable cost, then the company has the following alternatives:

- *Identify cost reduction goals at various operations/activities:* Is it possible to achieve cost reductions over the life cycle of the product so that we can achieve the allowable cost? These cost reduction goals have to be realistic. Failure to achieve these goals subsequent to product introduction can result in lower margins than targeted.
- *Perform functional analysis:* Is it possible to combine or eliminate some product functions (and thereby reduce costs) without losing much from the customer's perspective? Functional analysis involves assessing the value that the target market attaches to each function or feature of the product, and stressing only those functions that are valued the most. For example, power windows and door locks are attractive features in automobiles, yet these features may not be worth the cost for customers looking for low-priced reliable cars.
- *Provide value engineering:* Value engineering is an organized effort directed at achieving essential product functions at the lowest life-cycle cost consistent with required performance, quality, reliability, and safety. Typically, cross-functional teams consisting of individuals from design, production, and marketing divisions evaluate every operation and activity necessitated by the product design. They also assess value added to the product. They then determine whether there is a more cost-efficient way of performing the operation or activity. This systematic approach helps in configuring an efficient and effective value chain.

Step 5: *Review product launch.* Suppose, after careful evaluation of all alternatives, we determine that it is not possible to produce the product under the allowable cost. In this case, the best course of action may be to redefine the product and the target market and seek an alternate price point. We must repeat steps 1 through 4 to ensure that the reconfigured product will yield the targeted profit margin.

Target Costing Illustrated

Consider Cell Devices, Inc. (CDI), which makes and sells cell phones. The product life cycle of a cell phone is around three years. Each model typically offers many of the same features as the current model and introduces some new features. Exhibit 13.18 presents CDI's estimates of sales volume and the unit price of the model over its expected life cycle.

CDI targets an average profit margin of 15% of its expected revenue over the life cycle. It does not expect its manufacturing cost to vary materially over the three-year life. Applying the target costing model, we therefore compute the allowable unit cost of CDI323 as $150.77 (ignoring time value of money for simplicity). The *Check It!* Exercise #2 allows us to verify this computation.

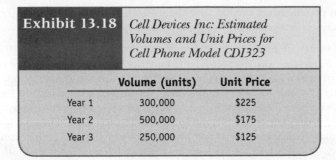

Exhibit 13.18	Cell Devices Inc: Estimated Volumes and Unit Prices for Cell Phone Model CDI323	
	Volume (units)	**Unit Price**
Year 1	300,000	$225
Year 2	500,000	$175
Year 3	250,000	$125

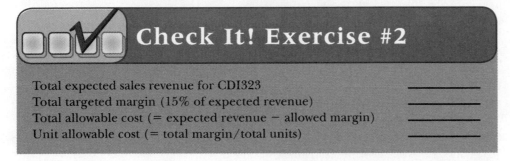

Check It! Exercise #2

Total expected sales revenue for CDI323   _____

Total targeted margin (15% of expected revenue)   _____

Total allowable cost (= expected revenue − allowed margin)   _____

Unit allowable cost (= total margin/total units)   _____

Solution at end of chapter.

Interestingly, in the final year, the unit price of $125 is less than the unit cost $150.77. That is, it appears that CDI expects to sell this model at a loss in the final year of the product life cycle. However, as we learned in Chapter 5, CDI should continue to make and sell CDI323 as long as the contribution margin is positive in the third year of the product life cycle (or, equivalently, the variable cost making CDI323 is less than $125 per unit). In addition, from a strategic perspective, it is not generally advisable to discontinue a product in the middle of a cycle if the next model is not ready for launching. Such an action may result in losing market share and market presence.

ANSWERS TO CHECK IT! EXERCISES

Check It! Exercise #1: For diner, Speed of service, Y, Room Décor, N, Average bill for a meal, Y, Depth of wine selection, N, Gross receipts per month, Y, Food costs as percent of sales, Y.

For French restaurant, Speed of service, N, Room Décor, Y, Average bill for a meal, Y, Depth of wine selection, Y, Gross receipts per month, Y, Food costs as percent of sales, Y.

Check It! Exercise #2 (appendix): Total revenue is $186,250,000, and the target profit is $0.15 \times \$186,250,000 = \$27,937,500$. Dividing the allowable cost of $158,312,500 by the total volume of 1,050,000 units gives the target cost of $150.77 per unit.

SELF-STUDY PROBLEMS

SELF-STUDY PROBLEM #1:

Orange Corporation, which makes and sells personal computers and servers, has two divisions—hardware and software. The software division's product earns universal acclaim for its elegance, functionality, and quality, particularly among graphic artists and designers. However, the software division has historically recorded a low rate of return. The hardware division, on the other hand, enjoys fat margins on its products, even though consumers often complain about the price of its products. This discrepancy is surprising because the firm usually sells its products in a bundle, and the software is optimized for the firm's hardware. In fact, the software does not work well with other hardware.

a. *What might explain the persistent discrepancy in returns between the two divisions?*

We might understand the discrepancy by looking to the bundled nature of the product. Consumers buy the hardware to gain access to the software. Thus, it appears difficult to separate the revenues of the two divisions. For strategic reasons, the firm might have priced software at low levels. For instance, many computer firms give away updates to software, even if the update consumed millions of dollars to create. Thus, we would argue that the profit discrepancy is artificial and does not reflect the underlying profitability of the two divisions.

b. *Characterize the firm's business strategy as one of cost leadership or value differentiation. Justify your choice.*

We would probably classify the firm as following a strategy of value differentiation. The innovative software is the source of value. Moreover, the firm appears to be operating in a niche market for graphic design, which values functionality and ease of use. The firm does not appear to be following a cost leadership strategy, as consumers perceive the hardware product as overpriced.

c. *List at least two strategy-relevant activities the firm might wish to conduct itself and two activities that the firm might wish to outsource.*

The firm would prefer to retain control over those activities that confer it with a competitive advantage. Product design appears crucial to the firm's success, particularly for software and for the integration of software and hardware. Marketing, particularly creating and maintaining brand equity, appears to be a second vital activity. The firm has to stay in close contact with the customer to continue to deliver cutting-edge products.

Manufacturing does not appear to be a core strength. We could argue that Orange might actually reap some cost benefits by outsourcing manufacturing to specialists. Of course, Orange will want to maintain tight control over quality. A second activity is distribution, which again appears to be a candidate best performed by specialists.

d. *As part of its corporate strategy, management is considering expanding its product line to large-format plasma and LCD TV screens. The firm has expertise with consumer electronics and has an extensive Web- and telephone-based sales and service network. Comment on the wisdom of this strategy in terms of leveraging the firm's core competency and the sustainability of the strategy.*

The strategy does not appear to be wise. The expansion does not leverage the firm's core competency in innovative software. Content providers for TVs do not coordinate with manufacturers. Moreover, competitors could mimic key features (e.g., picture in picture) easily. The distribution channel does not lend itself to the selling of expensive TVs as most consumers prefer to physically see and experiment with the TV before purchasing one. Finally, as a mature product, the market for TVs is price sensitive. Firms that enjoy cost advantages dominate this market, and Orange has little expertise in this domain.

SELF-STUDY PROBLEM #2:

"Cascades" is an exclusive inn located in scenic Sedona, Arizona, that promises to cocoon its guests from the hustle and bustle of everyday life. Its guiding principle is "all modern conveniences wrapped in old-world charm." Each of the inn's 15 villas has a separate theme, and guests often ask for a specific villa when they make reservations. Because it is located within a 250-acre estate, the inn offers its guests a wide variety of outdoor activities such as horseback riding, hiking, and so on. Guests could also while away the day lounging in the pool and availing themselves of the inn's world-famous spa. The dining room, which only has three tables for the public, is justifiably proud of its 4-star rating.

a. *Describe a reasonable strategy that is consistent with the inn's location, clientele, and reputation.*

Clearly, the inn is following a differentiation strategy that caters to wealthy clients. The inn differentiates itself via the premium services it offers. The strategy is to offer a retreat where the rich and powerful could unwind. In return for catering to the guest's every need, the inn no doubt charges a premium price. Doing otherwise is inconsistent with the general strategic thrust.

This strategy has several implications. All services must be available on tap, as the typical guest is probably not used to waiting. Service quality must be first class, with the finest in equipment and accessories. Delighting the customer is key and no request is out of line.

Trained staff must anticipate every need, while affording maximum privacy and maintaining the greatest discretion about what they may see and hear. From an information perspective, the inn must maintain a detailed database on all clients so that it can individualize each client's experience.

b. *Identify at least five critical success factors for the inn.*

Critical success factors include (this list is not exhaustive):

- Occupancy rates
- Brand image
- Maintaining service reputation (for restaurant and spa) and exceeding customer expectations
- Maintaining physical facilities in top condition
- Employee training and retention

c. *Develop a balanced scorecard for Cascades. It is enough to have two measures in each of the four perspectives.*

The following is a possible scorecard for Cascades.

Financial Perspective	Economic Value Added
	Revenue per villa
Customer Perspective	% repeat customers
	Number of customer complaints
Internal Business	Service rating for spa
	Mobil guide rank for restaurant
	Staff hours per guest
	% cost spent for maintenance
Innovation and Learning	Employee retention
	Number of new services offered

GLOSSARY

Allowable cost The cost target we must meet to achieve profit targets.

Balanced scorecard (BSC) A tool for systematically choosing performance measures linked with the firm's overall strategy.

Core competency Skill set and expertise that characterize a firm and its employees.

Cost gap The difference between the current cost and the allowable cost.

Cost leadership A strategy of competing on the basis of cost advantages.

Critical success factors (CSF) Things that must "go right" for the organization to be successful.

Current cost The cost of new product as per current configurations and production technologies.

Customer perspective One of the four perspectives in the balanced scorecard. This perspective ensures that the organization considers the customer's viewpoint.

Financial measures Metrics that rely on data recorded in a firm's accounting system.

Financial perspective One of the four perspectives in the balanced scorecard. This perspective ensures that the organization meets its ultimate goals.

Innovation and learning perspective One of the four perspectives in the balanced scorecard. This perspective ensures that the organization does not stagnate and has mechanisms that allow it to grow and stay competitive.

Internal business perspective One of the four perspectives in the balanced scorecard. This perspective ensures that the organization's processes are aligned with its customer and financial goals.

Lagging measures Measures that reflect past performance.

Leading measures Measures that capture the drivers of future performance.

Life-cycle analysis A technique that partitions a product's life into discrete stages and thereby guides efforts toward pricing and cost control.

Nonfinancial measures Measures that employ data not in the firm's accounting system.

Strategy Approach for creating and sustaining its value proposition.

Target costing A technique for cost planning during product design and development.

Value chain Set of logically sequenced activities that together execute the chosen business strategy.

Value differentiation A strategy of competing on the basis of providing customer value through innovation and service.

Value proposition The key source of customer value provided by an organization.

REVIEW QUESTIONS

13.1 LO1. What are the two types of business strategy?

13.2 LO1. What are the five forces that affect the competitive landscape?

13.3 LO1. What is a value proposition?

13.4 LO1. Traditional management accounting plays a more critical role in firms that follow a cost leadership strategy than in firms that seek to differentiate their products and services. True or False?

13.5 LO2. What is a value chain?

13.6 LO2. List the four steps in configuring a value chain.

13.7 LO3. What is life-cycle analysis?

13.8 LO3. What are the five stages in a product's life cycle?

13.9 LO3. What is target costing?

13.10 LO4. Why do organizations use both leading and lagging indicators of performance?

13.11 LO4. What are the three deficiencies of financial measures?

13.12 LO4. How does the problem of managing companies resemble the problem a pilot faces when flying a jetliner?

13.13 LO5. What is a critical success factor (CSF)? What are two kinds of CSFs? What are four properties of a well-defined CSF?

13.14 LO5. What is the balanced scorecard? What are the four components of a usual balanced scorecard?

13.15 LO3. What is the "balance" in the balanced scorecard?

DISCUSSION QUESTIONS

13.16 LO1. What is the value proposition offered by a top-tier business school such as the Wharton School, University of Pennsylvania, or London School of Business?

13.17 LO1. Consider two Internet portals, Google and AOL. What are their core competencies? How could they be different even though they compete in the same market?

13.18 LO2. Articles in the U.S. business press explore the recent trend to offshore product design and development. This trend is accelerating even among firms such as Contexant that rely on innovation for survival. What are the costs and benefits for this strategy of moving a key part of the firm's value chain to a site far removed from its corporate headquarters?

13.19 LO2. Suppose a firm is not legally liable for how its product is disposed. Should it consider disposal costs in its cost analyses? For example, consider a manufacturer of lithium ion batteries such as watches or cathode-ray-tube monitors, such as many computer monitors.

13.20 LO3. Products such as digital cameras sell at increasingly lower price points (e.g., $249, $199, and so on) as firms introduce newer models. How should we account for this feature in life-cycle analysis?

13.21 LO3. Why is target costing not necessarily useful for a firm such as Tyson Foods, which processes poultry and other animal products? Do these factors imply that cost control is not a key focus in Tyson Foods?

13.22 LO3. Suppose an intensive target costing exercise concludes that a product could not meet its allowable cost. However, the firm's strategic group argues that the product is vital for retaining the firm's presence in an important market segment. Should the firm abandon the product or develop it?

13.23 LO4. Consider a professional sports team such as the New York Yankees. What are its leading measures of performance? What implications does it have for evaluating the performance of a newly hired coach?

13.24 LO4. "Take care of the pennies, and the pounds will take care of themselves" is a popular saying. In business, this could mean that if we manage each individual process to work effectively and efficiently, the business as a whole will prosper. Is this assertion correct?

13.25 LO4. ROI, RI, and change in share prices are all summary measures of a firm's performance. Likewise, rankings issued by magazines such as *Business Week* and newspapers such as the *Wall Street Journal* and *Financial Times* are summary measures of performance of a business school. What are some deficiencies with these measures?

13.26 LO4. How could profit variance analysis (discussed in Chapter 8) help a firm monitor its operational CSFs?

13.27 LO5. What might the components of a balanced scorecard be for a municipality? for a not-for-profit hospital?

13.28 LO5 (Advanced). How should we combine the multiple measures in a balanced score-card into determining a division's overall performance?

13.29 Value proposition in same industry (LO1). Firms in the same industry offering the same end-product may offer different value propositions. For instance, consumers can obtain an airline ticket directly from the airline, a travel agent, or a travel Web site. Similarly, we can obtain clothing from a department store such as Macy's, a clothing-only store such as Aeropostale, or a designer firm such as Gucci.

Required:

a. Compare and contrast the value propositions offered by a travel site such as Expe-dia or Travelocity with that offered by a travel agent.

b. How does this insight translate to other services such as stock trading?

13.30 Sustaining competitive advantage (LO2). A firm can obtain its competitive advantage in many ways. Innovation by founders (e.g., instant photographs by Polaroid) is an obvious avenue. Location or government patronage is another.

Required:

a. List at least three other sources that a firm could use for developing a core competency.

b. For each of the three avenues, suggest actions that the firm must undertake to sus-tain its competitive advantage.

c. Describe how variations in required actions might translate into variations in the firms' management planning and control systems.

13.31 Five force analysis and monopoly (LO2). The text describes five forces (barriers to entry, customer power, supplier power, alternate sources, and intensity of competi-tion) that affect a firm's competitive landscape.

Required:

a. Describe the five forces in the context of an electric utility.

b. Use this analysis to argue why electric (and other) utilities are often subject to gov-ernment regulations.

13.32 Inferring strategy (LO2). The following are the income statements of two firms in the same industry.

	Firm A	Firm B
Revenues	$500,000	$1,000,000
Variable costs	225,000	600,000
Contribution margin	$275,000	$400,000
Fixed costs	175,000	300,000
Profit before taxes	$100,000	$100,000

Required:

a. Compute the contribution margin ratio, profit margin ratio, and sales per $ in fixed cost for the two firms.

b. Based on your answers to part (a), identify the strategy (cost leadership versus dif-ferentiation) followed by the two firms. Justify your classification. The intent of the question is fine, but the wording is moving from student to academic, followed by "conjecture" in your solution.

13.33 Target costing (LO3). True to its name, Imaging Technologies produces testing equip-ment used by forges to test their products. Imaging is considering a new X-ray machine that substantially enhances the functionality of the product it would replace. Imaging believes that it might be able to sell 4,500 units of the new product at an average price of $5,000 per unit. Management specifies a target profit margin of 5% return on sales.

Required:

a. Compute the product's allowable cost.

b. Suppose the product's current cost is $4,900 per unit. What is the cost gap (i.e., or the cost reduction that must be accomplished during the target costing process)?

13.34 Target costing, allowable costs (LO3). Fisher Industries, which makes pumps, is planning for a new product. Current sales projections call for 300,000 units at a sales price of $210 per pump. Management wants to earn a profit margin (measured as return on sales) of 5% on such products.

The following is the product's current cost structure.

Item	Unit Cost
Materials and components	$80
Direct labor	75
Manufacturing overhead (fixed)	40
SG&A costs	15
Total	$210

Required:

a. Compute the product's allowable cost and the cost reduction needed relative to current cost.

b. Suppose we find that we could get a 5% reduction in variable manufacturing costs and a 10% reduction in SG&A costs. Further reductions are thought to be infeasible. What actions do you recommend?

13.35 Life-cycle analysis, uncertainty (LO3). The following information pertains to a recent Bluetooth cordless headset produced by Optronix, Inc. This device uses Bluetooth technology to allow for hands-free operation of a cell phone. Increased awareness of the dangers of using a cell phone when driving has led to new regulations pertaining to cell phone use. Optronix expects the market for its products to increase rapidly because of these regulations.

Like most electronic products, the model has a short life cycle of about a year. The firm also expects to cut product price at least twice during the year and have a "clearance" sale at year-end.

Price	$89	$69	$49	$29
Volume	450,000	400,000	500,000	200,000

Required:

a. Compute the product's lifetime revenue.

b. Optronix knows that the demand is uncertain and that the data in the problem are just its best estimates. How can Optronix deal with this uncertainty when planning prices?

13.36 Life-cycle analysis (LO3). Imaging Technologies makes testing equipment used by forges and other manufacturers working with metal castings. The following data pertain to one of its recent products:

Design	$1,650,000
Preproduction tooling	$250,000
Manufacturing costs	$250 per unit
Selling and administration	$125,000 per year + $200 per unit
Warranty expenses	10 replacement parts per 50 units at $20 per part
	2 visits per 1,000 units (cost $1,000 per visit)

Required:

a. Suppose Imaging expects to sell 40,000 of these units over the product's life cycle of three years. Compute the product's life-cycle cost.

b. Suppose Imaging could boost sales by 25% to 50,000 units if it implements a price reduction of $60 per unit or 10% of the original price. Should Imaging choose the lower price? Justify with supporting calculations.

13.37 Multiple measures and sports (LO4). The U.S. Professional Golf Association tracks a number of statistics on its player-members. It is easy to find key statistics such as driving distance, putts per hole, greens in regulation, and fairways made. All of these measures capture differing dimensions of the game.

Golf courses exhibit considerable diversity in their design. Some have long holes but have relatively friendly greens. Other, shorter courses are more difficult, rewarding accuracy over distance.

Required:

a. Are the standard statistics leading measures of performance? Why or why not?

b. It is often the case that the best golfer (in terms of prize money or tournaments won) is not the top-ranked in any of the "standard" measures. How do you explain this discrepancy? What implications does this have for the emphasis a firm might place on differing aspects of its operations?

c. Professional oddsmakers use information to match up the characteristics of courses and golfers to determine the odds of a given golfer winning a particular tournament. What are the similarities, if any, between this practice and the fit of performance measures with a firm's critical success factors (CSFs)?

13.38 Variance analysis and CSFs (LO4). Island Spices manufactures and distributes high-quality spices to gourmet food shops and top-quality restaurants. The firm buys its spices from various regions throughout the world. The spices are cleaned, processed, and packaged at the firm's ultraclean factory before being shipped to customers. The following variances pertain to the last month of operations.

Sales volume variance	$15,000 Favorable
Sales price variance	12,000 Unfavorable
Purchase price variance	8,000 Favorable
Labor efficiency variance	7,000 Favorable
Fixed cost spending variance	1,000 Favorable

Required:

a. Identify the critical success factors for Island Spices.

b. Suppose all of the above variances arose as a consequence of deliberate managerial actions such as cutting price to increase volume. Evaluate the fit of these actions with the overall corporate strategy and critical success factors.

13.39 Multiple measures (LO4). Cost, Quality, and Time—these are the three dimensions stressed by the JHE Company in its performance evaluation of employees. Roberto Suarez, a production manager at JHE, however, thinks that JHE's management is ignorant of "facts on the ground." He says that he can deliver on *any one* of the three dimensions with ease. Low cost, or high quality or quick turnaround is no problem. Being a good manager, he can even deliver on two of the three measures. He could produce high-quality items in a cost-effective fashion if there were no demand to deliver everything today. He could also deliver quick turnaround and high quality, but the rush nature of the job would cost a pretty penny. He believes that management is shooting for the moon when it asks employees to deliver on all three dimensions.

Required:

Evaluate the reasonableness of management demanding progress on all three dimensions.

13.40 Balanced scorecard, customer metrics (LO5). Many organizations implementing the balanced scorecard have a set of measures that capture the customer or "external" perspective. Sample measures in this category include customer satisfaction and market share.

Consider Tony's Pizza and the Gallery, two restaurants with differing strategies and clientele. Tony's serves college students and prides itself on offering cheap pizza at your doorstep in 20 minutes or less. The Gallery is an up-market restaurant where the average check is over $100 per person. Both restaurants have implemented the balanced scorecard to assess and monitor their performance.

Required:

a. Considering only the customer perspective, what kinds of measures might Tony's include in its scorecard? What measures would the Gallery include?

b. Why do these two scorecards have so little in common, even though both businesses are for-profit restaurants?

13.41 Balanced scorecard, internal metrics (LO5). Culinary Creations caters weddings, office parties, and the like. Monica, the owner of Culinary Creations, offers delectable dishes and impeccable service. Her firm has gained a reputation for offering unique themed dinners and parties. Consequently, there is no shortage of demand. If a customer wants to customize a party beyond the regular "themes," the customer must reserve a date several months in advance so that Monica can plan for all contingencies and deliver perfection. Culinary charges a premium price for its unique services.

Required:

a. Describe three internal processes that Culinary must execute well to deliver on its value proposition. Justify your choices.

b. What might be the appropriate performance measures for these critical processes?

13.42 Balanced scorecard, link to incentives (LO5). Robinson's, Inc., has employed a balanced scorecard for several months now. The firm distributes high fashion accessories to boutiques and high-end department stores. At these stores, fashion-conscious, trendy customers buy these items. These customers are often not very price sensitive and are driven more by what is "in." Thus, having the right item in place is key, as the hot item last month could be in the bargain rack this month. Results for the first quarter after the full rollout are as follows:

	Budget	Actual
ROA	18.5%	17%
Customer satisfaction scores	85%	90%
Average discount per sales $	5%	8.2%
Sales from new SKU's	20%	12%
Price index relative to peers	105	94

Required:

Write a short memo evaluating Robinson's performance for the prior quarter.

13.43 Balanced scorecard, not-for-profit (LO5). Consider a not-for-profit organization such as the Lions Eye Bank, which is often affiliated with the Lions Club, a well-known business networking group that also supports a host of social services. These eye banks procure corneal tissue from eyes. Surgeons use corneal tissue to restore vision to persons who have injured or diseased corneas. Eye banks also provide corneal tissue for research and education.

Donations are the primary sources of funds for operations. Many eye banks also have endowments on which they can draw. The eye banks coordinate with local hospitals both to procure corneal tissue and to identify patients who might benefit from transplants. As in the United States, laws in many countries prohibit traffic in human organs, meaning that all tissue is donated.

Required:

A for-profit organization might use the standard scorecard categories (financial, customer, internal, and learning) to group performance measures. However, these categories might not relate well to the unique operations of an eye bank. Identify three to five categories for grouping performance measures applicable to an eye bank such as the Lions Eye Bank.

PROBLEMS

13.44 Value chain analysis, discount stores (LO1, LO2). Tim Thompson operates a highly regarded hardware store. Tim's store is the place to go if you need to get detailed advice on what kind of tools to get for the project at hand, as well as help in tracking down hard-to-find spare parts. Tim enjoys interacting with his customers and often remembers past projects that he has helped his customers complete. Thus, Tim has a loyal clientele even though his prices are usually 10% higher than those found at MegaLo Mart.

Tim's staff is also very interested in home building and maintenance. To retain them, Tim pays them an average of $15 per hour. He reckons that each of four sales persons generates an average of $20,000 in sales per month. In contrast, the average salesperson in MegaLo Mart, the discount hardware store down the street, generates only $12,000 in sales. However, the average salesperson in MegaLo Mart has less than two years experience in the retail industry and considerably less in hardware. Consequently, these salespersons earn only $8 per hour.

MegaLo Mart earns a Contribution Margin Ratio of 28% on its sales. The margin is lower even though its variable costs are only 90% of the variable costs incurred by stores such as those by Tim. (MegaLo Mart uses its volume to bargain aggressively with its suppliers.)

Required:

a. Describe Tim's strategy and value proposition. Contrast with the same items for MegaLo Mart.

b. Are Tim's expenditures on resources consistent with his strategy and value proposition?

c. How would the management control systems for store employees differ between Tim's shop and MegaLo Mart? Would you attribute the differences primarily to size or to differences in strategic thrust?

13.45 Target costing (LO3). Orange, Inc., sells portable music players and other electronic products. The firm is contemplating introducing the fifth generation of its award-winning player. The firm's engineers have reduced the size of the product by a third, even as they have increased memory capacity and video resolution. The current dispute centers on a particular custom-designed component. This component was designed at a cost of about $750,000. The head of the design group observes that developing a supplier and so on for this new component will cost an additional $100,000. Moreover, the component costs $8 per piece. All of the required functionality could be delivered by slightly modifying an existing component, used in the current fourth-generation player, with a well-established supplier. Development costs for modifying the old component are likely to be around $18,000 and unit costs at $5 per piece. However, the older component would reduce battery life by 5% relative to the new component.

Currently, Orange projects selling between 1 and 2 million units of the product over its life cycle. The exact sales volume depends greatly on whether the product generates enough buzz to become a "must have" accessory for fashionable teens and young adults. The product's average selling price is $249 per unit. Moreover, Orange usually has a 50% contribution margin ratio and a 20% profit margin on similar products.

Required:

a. For the decision of whether to launch the product with the new or old component, compute the incremental cost of using the custom-designed component over the new component.

b. What is your recommendation? Justify with appropriate supporting calculations.

13.46 Life-cycle costing (LO3). Connections, Inc., has developed an integrated cable modem and a wireless router. The product also has VOIP (phone jacks to provide telephone over the Internet) and HDMI outlets (which provide video services over the Internet). This product cost $50 million to develop; it has undergone extensive testing and is ready for production.

Currently, the firm is deciding on plant capacity, which could cost either $140 or $160 million. The additional outlay would allow the plant to increase capacity from 2 million to 3 million units.

Expected sales are 2 million units (over the product's life cycle) if priced at $199 per unit and 3 million units if priced at $174 per unit. The firm expects to have a CMR of 40% at a unit price of $199. Variable selling costs are 10% of selling price.

Required:

Advise Connections, Inc., regarding the optimal plant capacity to install. The product's life cycle is two years. The plant would have a salvage value of $25 million ($30 million if the larger capacity is chosen) at the end of two years. Ignore the time value of money and taxes in your computations.

13.47 Multiple measures and CSFs (LO4). *Quality Rules!* This is the slogan at Mason Motors, a company that supplies engine components to major automotive firms. Mason's management uses this slogan to communicate the message that quality is a critical success factor for the firm's survival. In particular, automotive firms, which account for virtually all of Mason's sales, will pay only for good items. These automotive firms also impose substantial penalties if component quality falls below prespecified levels.

Because of Just-in-Time practices, the automotive firms take an even dimmer view of missed shipments. Finally, Mason's engineers are expected to attend "quality school" to learn and implement quality control procedures, as well as participate in "cost engineering" the next generation of components.

Mason is struggling with how best to measure the intangible item, quality. Brainstorming generates numerous measures from the functional areas:

Production:	Percent reworked, scrap rates
Sales:	Average outgoing quality rate, percent on time delivery
Accounting:	Penalty payments for month
Operations:	Cycle time from receipt of order to delivery

Management is confused because each of the suggested measures seems to measure quality. Yet, management knows that if they measure all items, no single item will be most important, and it will be difficult to drive change throughout the organization. They have requested your help in sorting out how to translate a vaguely defined success factor. "Quality," into a measure that they could use to motivate, direct, and evaluate employees.

Required:

Advise management as to their best choice. Please be sure to argue regarding the costs and benefits of using separate measures for each department, as well as employing multiple measures to measure the differing dimensions of quality.

13.48 CSFs and choice of measures (LO4). Oliva Corporation is a small company that manufactures high-end stereo equipment. Oliva sells its products primarily via specialty audio-video stores. The discerning buyers of the firm's products have strong opinions about the relative merits of different brands, which means that they are not very price sensitive. The firm seeks your advice regarding how best to measure its progress on marketing and related issues. Last year's volume was just below 50,000 units; for this year, the firm projects 60,000 units and hopes to reach 100,000 units in three years.

The firm's founders strongly believe that quality is paramount. They argue that customer satisfaction with product quality (ignoring price and other issues) is key for such purchases. Thus, they wish to measure the number of 5-star reviews or customer satisfaction scores (on quality) as the measure of choice. Their nephew, who recently took over as CEO, concedes the quality point. However, pointing to the firm's plans to expand its customer base, he also wishes to measure the visibility of the firm's brands among target segments. "You can't buy what you don't know, even if it has the best quality," is his logic. Oliva's marketing manager (also a recent hire) agrees with visibility and suggests that Oliva measure market penetration, measured as the number of new stores carrying the firm's products.

Required:

a. What is Oliva's critical success factor that pertains to its interactions with its customer base?

b. Suppose Oliva wants to construct a balanced scorecard. What measures could it include in the category for capturing external perceptions? What kinds of actions would each measure encourage? Are these actions consistent with the firm's strategy?

13.49 Multiple measures (LO4). Many instructors give their students exams, pop quizzes, announced tests, and homework. Advanced and graduate classes also rely on projects and group assignments to evaluate student performance.

Required:

a. Do you believe that the instructor's goals might vary across different kinds of classes? Justify, with examples.

b. Consider an undergraduate prebusiness class on management accounting. Suppose this class has an enrollment of 500 students and is taught in two large lectures, supplemented by help sessions in smaller groups (recitation sections). What are the likely objectives of this class? What evaluation mechanisms might be appropriate for this class?

c. A favorite instructor assigns 10% of the points for attendance, 20% of the points for short multiple-choice quizzes on the assigned reading for the day, and the remainder across three examinations. How do these measures complement each other in accomplishing course objectives?

d. Continue with question c. Which of the measures are lead indicators, and which are lag indicators of the students' likely mastery of the subject material?

13.50 Core strengths and managerial actions (LO1, LO4). Techno U. is world-famous for the incredible quality of its faculty and the extreme rigor of its academic programs. Many of its graduates have gone on to become top scientists, engineers, and physicians. Almost every year, one of its graduates wins the Nobel Prize.

In recent years, however, the university has come under intense public scrutiny and criticism. First, its faculty members are among the highest paid in their respective fields, even though most of them only teach a few classes, each of which may only contain a dozen students. Second, the school admits less than 5% of applying students, basing its decision on an intense scrutiny of the applicant's profile. It is common for the university to deny admissions to persons with perfect scores on standardized tests and who are valedictorians of their class because they did not demonstrate enough excellence in other academic endeavors. Finally, the school uses its considerable endowment funds to provide scholarships to anyone who qualifies for admission but cannot afford the steep tuition. This last feature results in Techno U. receiving a large number of international applications, and many scholarships being awarded to foreign students. The U.S. press has lambasted Techno U.'s administration for taking "U.S. charity dollars" to fund the education of "foreigners."

Required:

a. What are the critical success factors for Techno University?

b. Suppose Techno U.'s administrators seek to appease the public by opening an extension college. This college will cost substantially less but also ease up on the rigor of the curriculum. How does this change affect the core strength/reputation of Techno U.?

13.51 Performance measurement, qualitative (LO4). "You can never win by doing the right thing," is George Hamada's reaction when he received a summary of his unit's performance evaluation. George, who oversees a cost center, has a staff of 40, including 32 specially trained individuals or professionals. His complaint arose because George had taken two earlier corporate initiatives to heart. The first initiative was to increase diversity; George therefore emphasized recruiting and retaining persons from underrepresented populations. He was quite successful even though he had to match outside offers for three such employees. The second initiative was to increase training for the workforce. George accordingly increased the number of professional conferences his staff could attend. He allowed each person in his department two days off to attend a seminar relevant for their job. He also allowed two of his professional staff to take advanced classes offered by specialists.

These initiatives, however, caused George to exceed his unit's cost budget. That single fact seemed to be the dominant reason for his so-so review. Indeed, the review did not even mention the increase in diversity among his staff.

Required:

a. How might George react to future "soft" initiatives that his firm might launch? Is such behavior in the firm's long-term best interests?

b. How might the firm suitably measure and reward performance on multiple dimensions? In your answer, be sure to address the claim that ultimately, all initiatives must lead to higher profit, so it is enough to measure financials alone.

13.52 Complete BSC, bank (LO1, LO2, LO4, LO5). The University Credit Union operates in a small university town in the Midwestern United States. The town, with a population of 125,000 persons, has recently been rated a top-10 place to retire because of the extent of the cultural, education, and medical resources available. Students and retirees are two of the largest segments of the town's population (20% each).

The UCU focuses on personalized service to differentiate itself. It is also heavily involved in community activities, and it expects employees to be active in civic causes. The UCU offers slightly below-market interest rates on deposits, but charges competitive rates on loans. The bank offers a full range of banking services such as safe deposit boxes and credit cards. The bank has excellent relations with local realtors and other service providers, and as a result, the bank processes the largest number of mortgages for first-time home buyers. Not surprisingly, it offers a limited range of "exotic" products such as foreign exchange conversions and letters of credit.

In recent years, UCU has encountered increasing competition. Initially, its competition consisted primarily of other local banks that also emphasized a personalized service. However, with deregulation, large national banks such as Wells Fargo and Citibank have also established branches in the community. In addition, the growth of the Internet has increased consumers' awareness of their choice set for banking services, mortgages, and so on.

Required:

Construct a balanced scorecard for UCU. Begin by identifying the critical success factors for UCU. Then, identify three to four measures for each CSF. Finally, organize select measures into logical groups that reflect UCU's strategy.

 13.53 Balanced scorecard (LO5, Advanced). Ian Thompson is the parts inventory manager for Chesapeake Airlines. In this capacity, Ian decides what engine parts to stock at various airports around the country. Ian is also responsible for coordinating with other airlines to locate a part if one is not available off the shelf.

Chesapeake is a discount carrier that competes by offering low-cost flights between underserved airports and wringing the maximum efficiency out of its assets. The airline buys only used aircraft and relies on its engineering staff to keep the plane up in the air as much as possible. Internal documents stress that a plane on the ground makes no money for the airline. On-time arrival and cost relative to other carriers are two of the key criteria the firm monitors on an almost daily basis. All bonus payments to managers depend on these measures.

Ian believes that the current system is fair to staff who operate the plane, handle baggage, or otherwise influence on-time arrival. "I can influence costs by managing inventory but making my bonus depend on on-time arrival is downright silly," he argues. Instead, he suggests that local measures such as cost per maintenance hour or the ratio of actual to standard time for the *scheduled* maintenance performed reflect his performance better. "After all, these items are within my control, and I can show you how my department is containing cost. My numbers on this front are the best in the game," he says. Probing, you discover that he is upset that his costs often spiral out of control when there is an unscheduled request for repair, requiring parts to be flown in from other airports or be bought from other airlines at premium prices.

Required:

Comment on the validity of Ian's assertion.

 13.54 Personal scorecard (LO5, Advanced). It is often instructive to construct a personal scorecard to measure your own growth and evolution. For instance, you could construct a triad of attributes that measure your personal competencies, your potential for adding value to others such as your family, employers and community, and your personal life goals. You could include items such as talent, education, and health in the first category. Items in the second group might include work ethic, ability to change, and so on. The final grouping could include work-life balance, making a difference in the world, and so on.

Required:

a. Construct a personal scorecard. Identify at least three key items in each category. Be sure to describe how you would measure these items.

b. Identify links among the items and argue how improving items in the first two categories could lead to superior measures on the third group of items.

13.55 Links among BSC categories (LO5). Sean Bobek, the head of Human Resources at a major retailer, is wondering how much he should be spending on employee training. Sean believes that there is room to improve employee skills, but he is having a hard time convincing management to spend hard cash on this intangible item. At current levels, employee skill scores have remained steady at 86 points on a 100-point scale.

Sean believes that increasing the spending by $200 per employee per year would increase employee skills by an average of 1 point on the firm's rating scale. Once skill levels reach 90, spending an additional $200 per employee per year only contributes to a ½ point increase in skill levels.

Sean knows that skilled employees have a dramatic effect on customer satisfaction. Each point increase in skill level leads to a 2-point increase in customer satisfaction, up to a score of 94 points (on a 100-point scale) and a 1-point increase thereafter. The latest survey shows a customer satisfaction score of 92%.

Satisfied customers in turn lead to greater sales. Sean estimates a 0.5% increase in firmwide sales for each percentage increase in customer satisfaction. The increase is 0.75% after scores of 95% in customer satisfaction. Currently, each employee generates $100,000 in gross sales, with an average contribution margin ratio of 35%.

Required:

How much should Sean spend on employee training?

13.56 **Links among balanced scorecard items (LO5).** That customer satisfaction leads to better financial performance is almost an article of faith among proponents of the balanced scorecard. More satisfied customers, they argue, are likely to give you a greater share of their business, which in turn translates to better financial returns.

Convinced by this intuitive logic, Kozy Kitchens invested heavily in improving its customer service functions. This online-only firm totally redesigned its Web interface to make it customer friendly. The firm hired staff to operate customer help lines 24/7. A "no questions asked" returns policy was instituted, and customers were guaranteed a price match on any item in stock.

Fred Larson, the president and CEO of Kozy Kitchens, was initially delighted to see his efforts pay off in the form of higher customer satisfaction scores. However, he has become increasingly impatient to see corresponding financial results.

	2006				2007			
	Q1	Q2	Q3	Q4	Q1	Q2	Q3	Q4
Satisfaction Index	85	88	90	92	92	94	95	95
ROA	8.5%	8.6%	9.0%	8.6%	8.4%	8.2%	8.2%	8.3%

Required:

a. Comment on why Kozy Kitchens might never experience a significant increase in ROA following an increase in customer satisfaction scores.

b. Does the seeming lack of a relation between customer satisfaction and financial performance imply that Kozy Kitchens should stop investing in providing a superior customer experience?

13.57 **Linking BSC to compensation (LO5).** Joan's Fabrics has employed a balanced scorecard for several months now. Results for the first quarter after the full rollout are as below:

	Budget	Actual
ROA	18.5%	22%
Customer satisfaction scores	85%	90%
Average discount per sales $	5%	4.5%
Sales from new SKUs	20%	26%

The firm computes the incentive payout for managers based on a formula.

- Begin by computing a score for each category. With the target scored as 100, you earn points in proportion to your actual score. Scores are truncated at 120% for each category. Thus, you get the same points whether you exceed the target by 20% or a higher amount. All percent computations are rounded to two decimal points (e.g., 90.32%). The percent discount category is reverse coded, meaning that a low discount is better than a high discount from Robinson's perspective.

- We combine scores across categories by weighting financials at 40%, customer satisfaction at 30%, and the remaining two categories at 15% each.

- The base bonus is set companywide. For this year, the base bonus is 30% of the annual salary. The bonus payable to an individual is the base bonus rate times your factor score. Thus, if you scored 120% on all four categories, your weighted factor score would be 1.2 and you would receive a bonus payout of 30 × 1.2 = 36% of your annual salary.

- No bonus, however, is payable if the score on any category is less than 90%.

Required:

Compute the bonus payable to a division manager reporting the scorecard data in the problem.

13.58 **Insider trading, leading indicators (LO5, Advanced).** Securities regulations identify the "Officers" of a firm. These persons include the Chairman, the board of directors, the treasurer, and other key executives. These officers are also termed "insiders." When they trade in the shares of their own firm, these insiders have to disclose the trades to the Securities and Exchange Commission.

Market participants keenly watch reports of insider trading. The strategy for some mutual funds is actually predicated on the belief that insider trading is a leading indicator of the stock's future performance.

Required:

a. Why might market participants reasonably believe that insider trade is a leading indicator of a firm's future performance?

b. Why do many governments issue detailed regulations concerning insider trading?

c. Insider trading is legal and unregulated in many countries. Given this fact, argue whether regulations increase or decrease the value of inside trades as a leading indicator of firm performance. More generally, what are the costs and benefits of lifting all restrictions on insider trading?

13.59 Leading indicators (LO4, Advanced). Considerable research has been done on the relation between a firm's earning stream and the market price for its stock. However, earnings explain just a small fraction of the variation in market prices, suggesting that market participants look to a variety of other measures when valuing a firm.

Required:

List five items that market participants might consider when valuing a security. Would you consider these as lead indicators of performance?

MINI-CASES

13.60 Balanced scorecard, boarding school (LO1-LO5). The Rishi Vilas School (RVS) is a residential school located in Ooty, a mountain resort in southern India. Established in 1930, the school has grown over time, and it now occupies 125 verdant acres in the rolling foothills of the Nilgiri mountain range.

Currently, the school's governing board has capped enrollment at 450 students, spread somewhat evenly among standards 7 through 12 (i.e., about 75 students would be admitted each year.) Admission decisions rely on students' academic credentials and the potential for future leadership (as judged by essays, personal interviews, athletic skills, and current accomplishments). While children of alumni receive a distinct preference, RVS tries to maintain a student body balanced along the dimensions of gender, religious affiliation, and region. Competition for admission is fierce, partly because the school uses its considerable endowment to support economically disadvantaged students. A vast majority of the students, however, pay the full tuition and board, even though some parents initially gasp upon hearing the amount.

RVS's goals are simple: Train the leaders of tomorrow in a secular and humanist environment. Thus, the school stresses the development of moral character and values as much as academic rigor. The curriculum introduces students to leaders and thoughts from various regions and religions. One would not be surprised to find students arguing about Plato's *Republic*, factors that led to the rise of communism in China, or the influence of regulator DNA on behavioral traits. Not surprisingly, the school counts numerous parliamentarians, leading scientists, top government bureaucrats, and industry titans among its alumni. The school board is particularly proud of the many alumnae who have gone on to become social entrepreneurs. In the past two years alone, the school's alumnae established three separate nongovernment organizations (NGOs) that focus on micro lending and setting up Internet kiosks in rural communities.

The focus on social awareness, humanism, and secularism does not detract from the school's academic mission. The school is among the few Asian schools that award the International Baccalaureate (IB) diploma. The curriculum is so rigorous that each year, RVS sends a few students to Ivy League schools in the United States and top-tier programs in Europe. Most of the students wind up in premier Indian institutions such as the IITs and other premier colleges.

As is the case in most boarding schools, RVS's students form lifelong friendships and develop strong ties to the school. Each student is assigned to one of four "houses" upon arrival. Housemates almost become brothers and sisters by the time a student graduates in six years. Not surprisingly, alumni networks are strong. A "Rishi" (as the alumni refer to themselves) would think nothing of receiving numerous offers for help and dinner invitations after posting her need for housing in a new location on the alumni bulletin board. Many alumni stay connected with the school throughout their lives, and it is common to find third- and fourth-generation students in the school.

Required:

a. While things have been going well, the school's headmaster is wondering whether the school is coasting on past glory and whether the school also is laying the foundations for an equally distinguished future. The headmaster therefore asks you to put together a list of linked items that would increase the probability of desired outcomes. Simply put, the headmaster would like you to clearly identify the school's outcomes (i.e., the fruits of its strategy), the processes for executing the strategy, and the resources needed to sustain the processes.

b. The headmaster also requests that you develop appropriate performance measures to measure the supply of adequate resources, the effectiveness and efficiency of the processes, and the outcomes. You can construct a scorecard along the traditional four dimensions or make up dimensions that seem more relevant to RVS.

13.61 E-Commerce, distribution, balanced scorecard (LO1-LO5). Super Steel Service Center (Triple S-C as it is known in the industry) is a "virtual" entity that operates in the steel distribution industry.

Traditionally, steel purchasers fall into one of two groups. Very large customers such as auto and appliance manufacturers fall in the first category. These customers purchase steel from mills and have it delivered to processors for cutting to specification. They might also buy direct from one or more of the approximately 3,500 steel processors or from wholesalers (normally called service centers). In all three instances, the cut steel is delivered to the customer, often on a Just-in-Time basis. The second group comprises smaller volume firms such as metal stampers and fabricators. Firms that make equipment, agricultural tools, heating, and air conditioning units also fall into the second group. These small to midsized companies, which purchase steel both as contract customers and spot buyers, but in relatively small quantities, also tend to have extensive needs for special alloy steels and odd-sizes. For the past decade, the variety of the steel demanded has steadily trended up, while the average lot size has trended down. These trends, which partly reflect increased customization and the growth of the Just-in-Time philosophy, are expected to continue, if not accelerate.

Triple S-C's founder, Remus Illies, worked at a major steel manufacturer (and was considered a rising star until he quit). Remus realized that the bulk of the distribution industry revolved around coordinating action. Managing information flow is key. Remus therefore set up Triple S-C, which does not own any warehouses or processing facilities. Instead, Triple S-C is a coordinator that buys the steel, has it processed, and has it delivered to the customer. In the process, Triple S-C might deal with as many as six separate entities. Triple S-C maintains an extensive list of firms in the steel supply chain. It also has negotiated prices and terms with many long-standing partners.

Because of its "virtual" nature and ability to put a deal together on the spot, Triple S-C provides its customers with unparalleled flexibility in terms of options for ordering, processing, and delivery. While Triple S-C accepts orders by phone or fax, it encourages customers to order via electronic data interchange (EDI) or through the Web. Slowly but surely, Triple S-C has convinced its customers about the ease of ordering via the Web and the security of the transaction. Once logged in, customers can configure products online and immediately receive multiple quotes with different volume and service parameters. Order status is continually updated and accessible to customers online. Upon execution, Triple S-C automatically debits the customer's bank account per agreed terms.

Triple S-C's advantage comes from leveraging technology to combine the orders of multiple customers to generate the volumes needed for discounts. The technology also allows Triple S-C to coordinate more effectively with processors to reduce scrap and waste. The firm also seeks to continually expand its list of processors to increase the flexibility it offers end customers. In this fashion, Triple S-C tries to build its ability to combine orders from two different customers into one processing order, which reduces the time and waste involved in loading a multi-ton coil. The firm also uses its extensive database to identify trends, which enable it to lock in both supplies of alloy steel and processing time at favorable rates. Remus's long-term goals are to deal in value-added products such as alloy steels rather than commoditized products such as carbon steel.

Currently, Triple S-C operates out of a single office in Pittsburgh, Pennsylvania, and employs just under 40 persons. Its primary market area is states east of the Mississippi River, although Remus is already thinking of westward expansion. Not surprisingly, Triple S-C's primary target market comprises small to medium-sized firms that lack the volume needed to deal with the steel mills directly and that need specialized processing.

Required:

a. Identify the critical success factors for Triple S-C. These CSFs must reflect the key processes that Triple S-C must execute well to deliver on its value proposition.

b. Construct a balanced scorecard for Triple S-C. Be sure to articulate the linkages among the metrics in the different categories.

13.62 Balanced scorecard, service firm (LO1–LO5). As you know, Hercules is a family-owned gym that is somewhat of a neighborhood tradition. It has a core of loyal followers even though it does not offer the latest physical training equipment or a bewildering array of classes. Tom and Lynda, the owners, pride themselves for providing a personal touch and offer many small conveniences that might be hard to obtain in a larger gym. An illustrative example is a particularly finicky guest, who is pathologically afraid of using a towel used by someone else. While such a guest has no choice but to bring his own towels at a large gym, Tom and Lynda stock a few towels to be used by this guest only. Tom and Lynda take care of most of the daily operations, along with a small permanent staff, and a rotating staff (mostly college-age students recruited from the local community college).

Required:

a. Identify at least three critical success factors for Hercules.

b. Construct a balanced scorecard for Hercules. Your scorecard must contain at least two measures for each of the four "traditional" perspectives (financial, customer, internal processes, learning and growth).

Module IV

COST ACCOUNTING SYSTEMS

In Chapter 3, we studied the general flow of costs in service, merchandising, and manufacturing firms. In this module, we delve further into firms' cost accumulation and reporting systems, providing an overview of *cost accounting* systems. We note two points.

- The primary purpose of these systems is to determine the value of inventories and cost of goods sold. The firm's financial accounting statements use these values to determine profit reported to external parties. Consequently, these systems comply with Generally Accepted Accounting Principles (GAAP).
- The focus on inventory valuation means that decision making is not a central consideration. Thus, unlike prior chapters, we do not couch our discussion in a decision context.

An organization's production environment determines its cost accounting system. Production environments range from settings where the firm makes a few products to order (e.g., luxury yachts) to settings where the firm makes millions of units of the same product (e.g., soft drinks). In Chapter 14, we first discuss the range of production environments that you might encounter in practice. We next discuss the costing systems associated with several kinds of production environments. After this introduction, we focus the remainder of the chapter on the mechanics of job costing systems, which are suitable for organizations that make distinct products in low volumes.

In Chapter 15, we study process costing, which is suitable for firms that mass-produce similar goods. We develop a five-step report for determining inventory values, and we discuss how these firms use average costs to value individual units rather than separately track the cost of each unit. Finally, we expand the discussion to standard costing, which uses predetermined rates to value materials and labor, in addition to overhead.

In Chapter 16, we consider two refinements that apply to costing systems. The first refinement relates to service department allocations, which are necessary when some cost pools consume the output of other cost pools. The second refinement is the use of multiple rates to allocate costs from a single pool, a refinement that builds on our discussion of the cost hierarchy in Chapter 2. We discuss how both refinements can improve the decision usefulness of cost accounting systems.

Chapter 14
Job Costing

MAGNA GOLF MAKES A VARIETY OF GOLF BAGS. MAGNA'S BAGS differ in terms of size, materials, and amount of labor required. Magna makes its bags in batches of 500 to 5,000 units. Like most manufacturing firms, Magna maintains several kinds of inventories: raw materials such as leather and vinyl, components such as zippers and stands, supplies such as cutting tools and leather polish, work-in-process of partly finished bags, and completely finished bags. Magna has asked for your help in determining the values of these inventories.

Getty Images

Magna Golf, which makes a variety of golf bags, is wondering how best to value its raw materials, work-in-process, and finished goods inventories.

LEARNING OBJECTIVES

After studying this chapter, you will be able to:

1 Describe the different kinds of production environments.

2 Explain the flow of costs in a job shop.

3 Apply overhead to jobs using predetermined rates.

4 Perform end-of-period adjustments for disposing of under- or overapplied overhead.

In Chapter 3, we discussed the basic flow of costs in service, merchandising, and manufacturing firms. In that chapter, as well as in Chapter 9, we discussed how Generally Accepted Accounting Principles (GAAP) require firms to distinguish product costs from period costs. This distinction affects inventory values and cost of goods sold, thereby affecting the amount of profit a firm reports. Accordingly, firms have extensive internal accounting systems to help value cost of goods sold and inventories. Many refer to such systems as **cost accounting** systems to emphasize the link to GAAP income statements. In contrast, we use the term *management accounting* to refer to internal systems that help managers make effective decisions.

Chapters 14–16 focus on the details of cost accounting systems. As such, we follow the rules imposed by GAAP when valuing inventories and cost of goods sold. In particular, recall that we only consider *product costs*, the costs required

CHAPTER CONNECTIONS
In Chapter 15, we consider cost accumulation and reporting in process-costing environments. Job shops and process shops anchor the two ends of our classification of production environments.

for getting a product ready for sale, when valuing inventories. We expense all *period costs*, the costs connected with selling and administration, during the period we incur the costs. Because this distinction ignores controllability, the resulting data may not be suitable for making decisions. Thus, we do not use the four-step decision framework as we have done in previous chapters.

The characteristics of a firm's production process determine the features of its cost accounting system. Therefore, we begin this chapter by discussing the different types of production environments. Following this, we focus on job shops, a commonly found production setting. We also describe the mechanics of their costing systems, usually called *normal costing*. As you will learn, a key feature of such systems is the use of a predetermined rate to allocate overhead to products.

Types of Production Environments

LEARNING OBJECTIVE 1

Describe the different kinds of production environments.

Every process converts inputs to outputs. Typical inputs in manufacturing include materials, labor, and equipment. Companies differ, though, in the types of products they produce from these inputs as well as in the variety of products they produce. Some firms such as PepsiCo, which bottles soft drinks, produce many units of the same product for a long period. Other firms such as Caterpillar, which makes earthmoving and construction equipment, produce small batches of many different products. Yet others, such as a home remodeling firm, never repeat a job. Exhibit 14.1 summarizes these differences.

Exhibit 14.1 *There are Many Kinds of Production Environments*

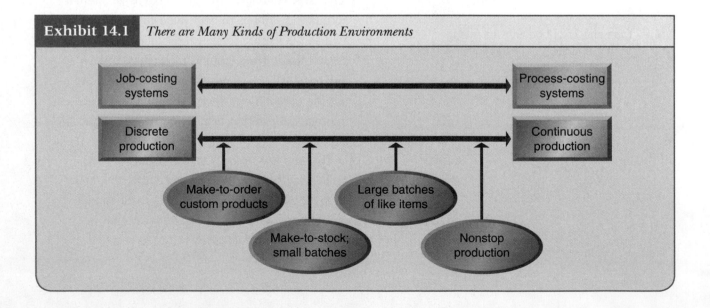

The leftmost circle in Exhibit 14.1 represents settings that involve discrete production of customized products. **Rockwell Collins**, which makes electronic equipment used in aircraft, is a good example. The nature of the product means that orders are customized and are for small quantities. Other examples include law firms and remodeling contractors. In these settings, each unit or "job" is unique. Firms with such production environments find it convenient and necessary to accumulate and analyze costs separately for each job. Naturally, we call such cost systems *job-costing systems*, and the environment a **job shop**.

The rightmost circle in Exhibit 14.1 considers environments with continuous production. **Alcoa** makes aluminum almost continuously in its smelters. **Kellogg Company** makes cereal continuously in its plants. Steel mills, paper companies, and bottlers of soft drinks offer other examples of such production environments. For such firms, it does not make sense to distinguish among the costs of virtually identical units—an average cost per unit is enough. Thus, such firms find it more convenient to accumulate and analyze costs by each process than by each job. Naturally, we call such costing systems *process-costing systems* and the environment a **process shop**.

Most production systems exhibit some characteristics of job shops and some characteristics of process shops. A garment manufacturer such as the **Gap** might have several batches of shirts, with each batch going through many processes common to all shirts, but also having some processes unique to a particular kind of shirt. Accordingly, the cost accounting system is a hybrid of job- and process-costing systems. Many refer to such systems as **operations costing**.

The middle two circles in Exhibit 14.1 represent hybrid environments. The circle for "make-to-stock" production represents firms, such as **Magna** and **SKF Bearings**, which make distinct products in small batches. Because the batch size is small, *batches or lots of a product move as a whole through the production process*. That is, a firm completes all units of a batch before moving on to the next step. For instance, Magna makes golf bags in batches of 500 to 5,000 units. For a given batch, it does not proceed to the next step before completing the prior production step for *all* units in the batch. Thus, we can think of each batch as a distinct job, with unique requirements. The costing systems in these firms resemble job costing.

The remaining circle in Exhibit 14.1 represents firms that make their products in large batches. The large batch size means that the entire batch will *not* move through the production process one-step at a time. For a firm such as **Procter and Gamble**, consider a production run to make a batch of shampoo. It is quite likely that the

Garment manufacturers such as the Gap need cost accounting systems that are a hybrid of job- and process-costing systems.
(Eric Risberg/©AP/Wide World Photos)

 **Connecting to Practice**

JOB COSTING IN LAW FIRMS

With over 650 lawyers advising a multitude of clients on virtually all aspects of corporate law, a large firm such as Arnold & Porter in Washington, D.C., is a complex job-shop environment. A job could be a specific client on a retainer or a specific case. In addition to staff time (lawyers, paralegals), each job consumes both direct (filing fees, copying, express mail) and indirect (administrative support) resources.

COMMENTARY: For effective planning and control, Arnold & Porter's managing partners will want to track budgeted and actual costs by job, by individual lawyers, by type of practice, and by industry. Not surprisingly, law firms often use specialized software such as OmegaLegal to meet their informational needs. A time log, kept by all persons in the firm, is the central element of such systems.

firm has sold some of the units to stores such CVS Pharmacy. In addition, P&G also might have some units that are finished but are unsold (waiting to be shipped), some that are still in process (e.g., need to be bottled), and finally some that it still needs to begin work on. Thus, P&G would need to allocate the costs of a batch among the bottles at different stages in the production process. This costing system is an example of process costing.

TRACEABILITY OF COSTS

Job shops and process shops differ considerably in the extent to which we can trace costs to individual units and jobs. A pure job shop makes custom products. Each unit is a separate job and is unique. It is therefore possible to trace the costs of the direct materials and direct labor to each job. However, we still need to allocate the costs of overhead and capacity resources to individual jobs. For example, a supervisor might oversee the construction of several custom homes. We need allocations to divide her cost among the homes she supervises.

In process shops, it is not possible to trace costs to individual units. Rather, we can trace the costs, even for direct materials and direct labor, only at the process or departmental level. However, this lack of traceability is not a cause for concern because, as a process shop, the firm makes the same product in large volumes. From both a valuation and a control perspective, it is enough if we can determine the cost of an average unit. Process-costing systems accomplish this task by accumulating all costs (including the cost of direct materials and direct labor) by departments or processes. We then allocate these costs to the units that have gone through the production process in that department in order to calculate the cost per average unit.

The production environments in most firms exhibit characteristics of both job and process shops. For example, each batch at SKF Bearing might have several hundred units of the bearing made. Although we can trace materials and labor costs to the specific batch (job costing), we cannot trace the cost to individual bearings. Thus, we allocate (as in process costing) the cost equally among the units that comprise the job.

Now that you understand the different types of production environments and the differences in traceability of costs, let us examine the details of job-costing systems.

Job-Costing Systems

LEARNING OBJECTIVE 2

Explain the flow of costs in a job shop.

Let us begin by recalling the general flow of costs through the inventory accounts, as illustrated in Exhibit 14.2. The cost of materials purchased increases the value of materials inventory. When a firm issues materials to the shopfloor, it removes the associated cost from the materials inventory account and adds it to the work-in-process (WIP) account. It then adds to the WIP account any labor and overhead costs for work done on the job. When it has performed all the needed work, the firm moves the units into finished goods inventory. At this time, the firm removes the associated costs from the WIP account and puts them into the finished goods (FG) account, calling the amount transferred cost of goods manufactured (COGM). Finally, when the firm sells the goods, it removes the cost from the FG inventory account and adds it to the cost of goods sold (COGS) account. That is, the firm systematically applies the inventory equation to each of materials, WIP, and finished goods inventory accounts.

Exhibit 14.5 *Magna Golf: Cost Flows in December**

Item	Amount	Item	Amount
Inventory values for December		Cost flows during December	
Opening materials inventory	$35,500	Purchase of materials	$161,750
Opening WIP inventory	94,000	Materials used	162,550
Opening FG inventory	270,100	Labor cost (direct and indirect)	82,120
		Variable overhead (nonlabor)	17,867
Ending materials inventory	?	Fixed overhead (nonlabor)	70,582
Ending WIP inventory	?		
Ending FG inventory	?	Cost of goods manufactured	?
		Cost of goods sold	?
Control accounts		Cumulative amounts as of 12/1	
Variable overhead (12/1)	$29,170	Cost of goods sold	$4,245,000
Fixed overhead (12/1)	(22,925)		

* Details of inventory balances and other items not shown.

December with some finished goods inventory: 2,300 units of model XL-100, 500 units of model XL-300 and 800 units of model FL-150. Sales records for December indicate that Magna sold 2,200 XL-100 bags, 1,400 XL-300 bags, 350 TL-50 bags, and 750 FL-150 bags.

Regarding costs, as shown in Exhibit 14.5, Magna began with $35,500 in its materials inventory, $94,000 in WIP and $270,100 in its finished goods inventory account. (The exhibit does not provide details about the individual jobs and products that comprise these inventories. We introduce the detail later as needed.) During the month, Magna bought $161,750 of materials and used up $162,550 worth. It spent $82,120 on labor, and incurred $17,867 on variable and $70,582 on fixed overhead costs. The bottom panels of the exhibit show that COGS to date is $4,245,000. These panels also show two "control" accounts relating to overhead, which we detail later in this chapter.

Magna now has to determine the values of ending work-in-process and finished goods inventory. This determination in turn will help the firm compute its cost of goods manufactured and cost of goods sold for December. This exercise is similar to the cost flow concepts you learned in Chapter 3 except that we track the costs separately for each job rather than for the company as a whole.

Analyzing Materials

Exhibit 14.6 provides details of Magna Golf's opening materials inventories as of December 1. Magna has three types of materials—components, raw materials, and supplies.

During December, Magna purchased $161,750 of materials on account: $65,750 for components, $78,000 for raw materials, and $18,000 for supplies. Consequently, the materials inventory accounts increase in value by $161,750. The offsetting entry

Exhibit 14.6 *Magna Golf: Materials Inventory as of December 1*

	Type of Material			
	Components	Raw Materials	Supplies	Total
Value	$15,000	$12,000	$8,500	$35,500

is to cash or to accounts payable, depending on the terms of purchase. Magna bases this accounting entry on source documents such as the purchase order, which establishes the unit prices for the purchased items, and material receipts.

Every time a job needs materials, Magna's production staff issues a requisition to the storeroom. The storeroom keeps track of the materials issued to specific jobs. Using an appropriate inventory cost flow assumption such as FIFO (First-In-First-Out), Magna can determine the cost of materials issued to the shopfloor. As these items physically move from the storeroom to the shopfloor, Magna transfers the associated cost from the raw materials inventory account to the individual job sheets that comprise the work-in-process account.

Referring to Exhibit 14.7, jobs in progress during December consumed $66,599 worth of components and $80,351 in raw materials. Notice that each job sheet lists details such as the specific product number and batch size.

Exhibit 14.7 also shows that Magna consumed $15,600 of supplies during December. While Magna can trace components and raw materials to individual jobs, it cannot trace supplies (e.g., oils, lubricants, cleaning materials) to specific jobs. However, it believes that the usage of these resources will be proportional to production volume. Accordingly, Magna accumulates such indirect costs in a *variable overhead control account* to facilitate their allocation to individual jobs. A **control account** is a convenient way to accumulate and allocate overhead costs, rather than dealing separately with each overhead item. For each accounting period, a control account begins and ends with a zero balance. (Exhibit 14.5 shows a non-zero balance in the control account because we usually zero out the control account only at the end of the year, and not each month.)

Exhibit 14.8 consolidates all this information with the opening balances and purchases to determine the ending balances in the materials inventory accounts. (The final column shows the aggregate inventory equation for the firm, as illustrated in Chapter 3.)

Exhibit 14.7	*Magna Golf: Material Requisitions for December*					
	Job Number (WIP account)				**Total to Work in Process**	**Variable Overhead Control**
	3000-5	**4032-7**	**5006-4**	**4045-6**		
Product	XL-100	XL-300	TL-50	FL-150		
Units	2,500	1,750	600	1,400		
Components	$20,674	$31,500	$12,000	$2,425	$66,599	
Raw materials	$28,026	$37,000	$12,500	$2,825	$80,351	
Supplies						$15,600
Total					$146,950	$15,600

Exhibit 14.8	*Magna Golf: Materials Inventory*			
	Type of Material			
	Components	*Raw Materials*	*Supplies*	*Total*
Opening balance (12/1)	$15,000	$12,000	$8,500	$35,500
+ Purchases	65,750	78,000	18,000	161,750
− Issued out (from Exhibit 14.7)	66,599	80,351	15,600	162,550
= Ending balance (12/31)	$14,151	$9,649	$10,900	$34,700

Analyzing Labor Costs

Some workers' efforts, such as those related to assembly or machining, are proportional to activity volume (e.g., number of units). Such labor costs are variable. If we can also trace the work to individual jobs, then the cost is a direct labor cost.

The work done by other employees, such as those involved in maintenance and materials handling, might also vary with activity volume. However, unlike the cost of direct labor, we cannot trace this work to individual jobs in a cost-effective fashion. As a result, the cost is an indirect labor cost. As with indirect materials, firms include such costs in variable manufacturing overhead and allocate them to individual jobs.

Finally, firms have employees such as the plant manager whose work may not be proportional to activity volume, at least in the short term. A firm classifies payments to such employees as part of its **fixed manufacturing overhead** and allocates the cost to individual jobs.

From Exhibit 14.5, we know that Magna spent a total of $82,120 on direct and indirect labor. The detail provided in Exhibit 14.9 shows that Magna spent $69,620 on direct labor. It can trace the cost of direct labor to each job, and the accounting system adds the cost of the labor used to the job cost. In a double-entry bookkeeping system, the offsetting entry is to wages and salaries payable, or cash. Exhibit 14.9 also shows that Magna spent $6,500 on indirect labor and $6,000 on salaried labor for supervision. Magna adds these costs to the variable and fixed overhead control accounts, respectively.

Exhibit 14.9	*Magna Golf: Detail of Labor Costs for December*						
	Job Number (WIP Account)				**Total to WIP Account**	**Variable Overhead Control**	**Fixed Overhead Control**
	3000-5	**4032-7**	**5006-4**	**4045-6**			
Product	XL-100	XL-300	TL-50	FL-150			
Units	2,500	1,750	600	1,400			
Direct labor	$20,520	$27,400	$15,400	$6,300	$69,620		
Indirect labor						$6,500	
Supervision							$6,000
Total					$69,620	$6,500	$6,000

 # Connecting to Practice

DIRECT AND INDIRECT LABOR

The proportion of costs represented by materials, labor, and overhead vary widely across industries. On average, materials and components are approximately 50% of each cost dollar, with labor and overhead accounting equally for the remainder. Over time, the proportion of labor costs has been decreasing while the proportion of overhead costs has been increasing.

COMMENTARY: The declining importance of direct labor costs is partly due to modern business practices that blur the distinction between direct and indirect labor. The decline in the cost of direct labor is particularly acute in the electronics industry. Some firms such as Hewlett-Packard now pool labor costs with overhead costs because it is no longer cost effective to track the items separately.

Analyzing Manufacturing Overhead

Firms accumulate indirect costs in overhead control accounts and then remove the costs from these accounts by allocating them to products. Magna has two overhead control accounts, one for variable overhead and one for fixed overhead. It allocates both variable and fixed overhead costs to products using direct labor costs as the allocation basis. Exhibit 14.10 illustrates the cost flows in and out of the overhead control account.

Referring to Exhibit 14.5, Magna spent $88,449 (=$17,867 + 70,582) on nonlabor-related overhead costs (both variable and fixed) during December. Exhibit 14.11 provides the detail for this total. Notice that the variable overhead cost pool includes $15,600 for supplies (from Exhibit 14.7). To this amount, we add $6,500 for indirect labor (from Exhibit 14.9). The fixed overhead cost pool includes the $6,000 for supervision (from Exhibit 14.9).

How should Magna deal with the overhead cost? As we discussed in Chapter 3, one option is to compute an actual overhead rate by dividing the actual overhead cost by the actual direct labor cost. For Magna, we find an actual variable overhead rate of ($24,367/$69,620) = $0.35 per direct labor dollar, and an actual fixed overhead rate of ($76,582/$69,620) = $1.10 per direct labor dollar. Magna could then combine these rates and distribute the total overhead cost to individual jobs at the

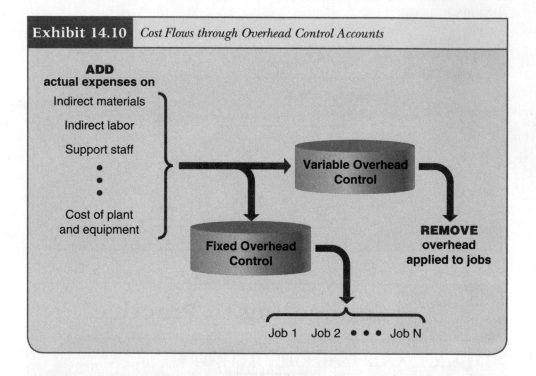

Exhibit 14.10	*Cost Flows through Overhead Control Accounts*

Exhibit 14.11	*Magna Golf: Overhead Control Accounts*

Variable Overhead Costs		**Fixed Overhead Costs**	
Supplies (Exhibit 14.7)	15,600	Depreciation	24,500
Tools and jigs	2,267	Plant administration	26,975
Total (nonlabor related)	$17,867	Materials handling	11,050
		Rent & utilities	8,057
		Total (nonlabor related)	$70,582
Indirect labor (Exhibit 14.9)	$6,500	Supervision (Exhibit 14.9)	$6,000
Total	$24,367	Total	$76,582

rate of $1.45 for each direct labor dollar. However, few firms wait until the end of the accounting period to compute actual overhead rates. Instead, most firms use predetermined rates for applying overhead to jobs.

Predetermined Overhead Rates

A firm's actual overhead cost and actual activity volume likely change from month to month. These unavoidable fluctuations occur in the normal course of business. Because of these fluctuations, overhead rates will fluctuate, as will the amounts allocated to jobs and products. Consequently, keeping track of changing product costs becomes tedious and time-consuming.

Firms avoid this problem by using **predetermined overhead rates**. Firms compute a predetermined overhead rate using *expected* overhead costs and *expected* activity levels at the start of a plan period, usually a year, as follows:

$$\text{Predetermined overhead rate} = \frac{\text{Expected overhead costs for the period}}{\text{Expected activity level}}$$

During the year, firms apply overhead to products using this predetermined rate and actual activity levels. This procedure dampens the effect of fluctuations in allocated costs, allowing firms to use a stable rate when *estimating* inventory values, cost of goods sold, and income for some future period. Because of their widespread use, we call job-costing systems that use predetermined overhead rates to apply overhead as **normal costing** systems.

In Magna's case, assume that the company budgeted to spend $850,000 on direct labor during the year. Magna would get this estimate from the annual production budget. Suppose Magna also estimates annual variable overhead at $255,000 and annual fixed overhead at $1,020,000. Then, Magna's predetermined overhead rates are as follows:

$$\text{Predetermined variable overhead rate} = \frac{\$255,000}{\$850,000} = \$0.30 \text{ per direct labor dollar}$$

$$\text{Predetermined fixed overhead rate} = \frac{\$1,020,000}{\$850,000} = \$1.20 \text{ per direct labor dollar}$$

Exhibit 14.12 shows the allocation of manufacturing overhead to Magna's individual jobs using the predetermined rates. Accountants use the term **applied overhead** for this allocation to underscore the use of the predetermined overhead rate in the procedure. You can determine the allocated amount (the *applied overhead*) by multiplying the predetermined rate and the actual labor cost incurred for the four jobs. That is, Magna applies overhead to jobs whenever it charges labor costs to the jobs. In total, Magna allocates (or applies) $20,886 of variable overhead and $83,544 of fixed overhead. The firm adds this amount to the cost of each job in the WIP account and removes it from the relevant overhead control account.

Exhibit 14.12	*Magna Golf: Applied Manufacturing Overhead Costs using Predetermined Rates*				
	Job Number (WIP Account)				
	3000-5	**4032-7**	**5006-4**	**4045-6**	**Total**
Direct labor (from Exhibit 14.9)	$20,520	$27,400	$15,400	$6,300	$69,620
Variable overhead (@ 30% of direct labor cost)	6,156	8,220	4,620	1,890	$20,886
Fixed overhead (@ 120% of direct labor cost)	24,624	32,880	18,480	7,560	$83,544
Total overhead costs applied	$30,780	$41,100	$23,100	$9,450	$104,430

CHAPTER CONNECTIONS

In Chapter 7, we emphasized that the revenue budget is the starting point for most operating budgets. Firms adjust sales volume by the finished goods inventory policy to determine the production budget. They obtain the estimated labor cost by combining the production budget with plan assumptions regarding the labor time and labor cost for each product. Similarly, they can use production volume to construct an overhead cost budget.

DETERMINING COST OF GOODS MANUFACTURED

We are now in a position to compute the cost of goods manufactured during December. From Chapter 3, recall that COGM is the outflow from the work-in-process account. Thus, you can use the inventory equation to determine COGM.

Exhibit 14.13 shows the December 1 balance in Magna's WIP account. The balance of $94,000 is the sum of the cost of Job 3000-5 for 2,500 XL-100 bags and the cost of Job 4032-7 for 1,750 XL-300 bags.

During December, Magna added $66,599 worth of components, $80,351 for raw materials, and $69,620 for direct labor costs. Magna also allocated $20,886 and $83,544 for variable and fixed manufacturing overhead costs, respectively. Exhibit 14.14 summarizes the above information in a job-cost sheet.

Exhibit 14.13	*Magna Golf: Work-in-Process Inventory as of December 1*		
	Job Number		
	3000-5	*4032-7*	*Total*
Product	XL-100	XL-300	
Units in batch	2,500	1,750	
Value	$70,000	$24,000	$94,000

Exhibit 14.14	*Magna Golf: Job-Cost Sheet*				
	Job Number (WIP Account)				**Total in WIP Account**
	3000-5	*4032-7*	*5006-4*	*4045-6*	
Product	XL-100	XL-300	TL-50	FL-150	
Number of units	2,500	1,750	600	1,400	
Opening balance (Exhibit 14.13)	$70,000	$24,000	$0	$0	$94,000
+ Components (Exhibit 14.7)	20,674	31,500	12,000	2,425	66,599
+ Raw materials (Exhibit 14.7)	28,026	37,000	12,500	2,825	80,351
+ Direct labor (Exhibit 14.9)	20,520	27,400	15,400	6,300	69,620
+ Variable overhead (Exhibit 14.12)	6,156	8,220	4,620	1,890	20,886
+ Fixed overhead (Exhibit 14.12)	24,624	32,880	18,480	7,560	83,544
Total cost of job	$170,000	$161,000	$63,000	$21,000	$415,000
Cost per unit completed	$68	$92	$105	n.a.	

From the units data in Exhibit 14.4, you know that Job 4045-6, for 1,400 units of the ladies' bag FL-150, is the only unfinished job as of December 31. The other three jobs are complete. Therefore, Magna transfers those units to finished goods inventory. Accordingly, as Exhibit 14.15 shows, the firm transfers the associated costs from the WIP account to finished goods inventory. Note that the ending balance of $21,000 is also the value of Job 4045-6, the only unfinished job as of December 31. Again, you can see that the last column in this exhibit shows the aggregate inventory equation you learned in Chapter 3.

DETERMINING COST OF GOODS SOLD

Our next task is to compute the cost of goods sold (COGS). You know that COGM is the inflow into the finished goods inventory account and that COGS is the outflow from this account. Thus, you could use the inventory equation. However, as is the case for WIP, we have to apply the equation to individual products and then sum up to obtain the aggregate flow.

Let us begin with the opening balance. From the firm's records, we know that Magna had $270,100 worth of finished goods inventory on December 1. Exhibit 14.16 provides the details that comprise this total.

From Exhibit 14.15, the inflow (i.e., the COGM) into the finished goods inventory is $394,000.

Let us now compute the COGS, the outflow from this account. From Exhibit 14.4, you know that Magna sold 2,200 XL-100 bags, 1,400 XL-300 bags, 750 FL-150 bags, and 350 TL-50 bags. Consider the XL-300 bags. From Exhibit 14.16, you know that, as of December 1, Magna had 500 of these bags in stock, valued at $90 per bag. From Exhibit 14.14, you also know that Magna completed an additional 1,750 bags during December at a cost of $161,000 or $92 per bag. Thus, Magna has two layers

Exhibit 14.15 *Magna Golf: Flow of Costs in WIP Account*

Opening balance (12/1)		$94,000
+ Costs added during December		
Total materials (Exhibit 14.7)	$146,950	
Labor (Exhibit 14.9)	69,620	
Applied variable overhead (Exhibit 14.12)	20,886	
Applied fixed overhead (Exhibit 14.12)	83,544	
Total of costs added to WIP		321,000
= Total costs in WIP account (Exhibit 14.14)	$415,000	
− Cost of goods manufactured (COGM) transferred to FG inventory		
Job 3000-5 (Exhibit 14.14)	$170,000	
Job 4032-7 (Exhibit 14.14)	161,000	
Job 5006-4 (Exhibit 14.14)	63,000	
Total COGM in December		($394,000)
= Ending balance on 12/31 (Job 4045-6)		$21,000

Exhibit 14.16 *Magna Golf: Finished Goods Inventory as of December 1*

	Product			
	XL-100	XL-300	FL-150	Total
Units	2,300	500	800	
Cost per unit	$69	$90	$83	
Value	$158,700	$45,000	$66,400	$270,100

Exhibit 14.17	*Magna Golf: Cost of Goods Sold for December*				
	Product				
	XL-100	**XL-300**	**TL-50**	**FL-150**	**Total**
Units in opening inventory	2,300	500	0	800	
Cost per unit	$69	$90		$83	
Units made in December	2,500	1,750	600	—	
Cost per unit	$68	$92	$105	—	
Total units sold	2,200	1,400	350	750	
Sold from opening inventory	2,200	500	0	750	
Sold from current production	0	900	350	0	
Costs					
Units from opening inventory	$151,800	$45,000	$0	$62,250	$259,050
Current production	0	82,800	36,750	0	$119,550
Cost of goods sold (COGS)	$151,800	$127,800	$36,750	$62,250	$378,600

of inventory for the XL-300 bag: 500 units at $90 per bag and 1,750 units at $92 per bag. Magna needs to make an inventory cost flow assumption to determine the cost of goods sold.

Magna uses a FIFO inventory flow assumption. For the XL-300 bag, this practice means that Magna computes cost of goods sold as if it sells the 500 units in stock first before selling the units produced in December. Thus, the firm values 500 of the 1,400 units sold at $90 per unit, and the remaining 900 units at $92 each. Exhibit 14.17 presents the computations for all four products.

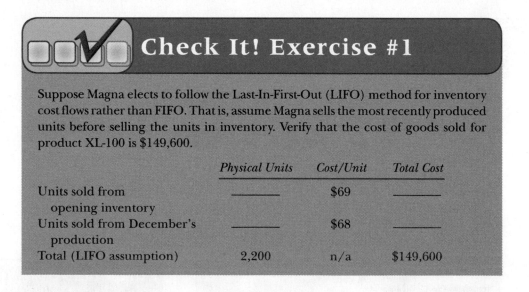

Check It! Exercise #1

Suppose Magna elects to follow the Last-In-First-Out (LIFO) method for inventory cost flows rather than FIFO. That is, assume Magna sells the most recently produced units before selling the units in inventory. Verify that the cost of goods sold for product XL-100 is $149,600.

	Physical Units	*Cost/Unit*	*Total Cost*
Units sold from opening inventory	_____	$69	_____
Units sold from December's production	_____	$68	_____
Total (LIFO assumption)	2,200	n/a	$149,600

Solution at end of chapter.

With this data in hand, we can now complete the inventory equation for the finished goods account, as shown in Exhibit 14.18. For clarity, this exhibit also shows the inventory equation in units and in dollars for each of the firm's products.

You have now completed the physical flow of materials from raw materials to the finished product delivered to the customer, and the cost flow from raw materials inventory all the way to cost of goods sold. Only some end-of-period adjustments remain.

| Exhibit 14.18 | Magna Golf: Cost Flows in Finished Goods Inventory Account for December |

	Product				
	XL-100	XL-300	TL-50	FL-150	Total
Units					
Opening inventory	2,300	500	0	800	
+ Produced in December	2,500	1,750	600	0	
− Sold in December	(2,200)	(1,400)	(350)	(750)	
= Ending inventory	2,600	850	250	50	
Costs					
Opening value (Exhibit 14.16)	$158,700	$45,000	0	$66,400	$270,100
+ Cost of goods manufactured (Exhibit 14.14)	170,000	161,000	63,000	0	394,000
− Cost of goods sold (Exhibit 14.17)	(151,800)	(127,800)	(36,750)	(62,250)	(378,600)
= Ending value	$176,900	$78,200	$26,250	$4,150	$285,500

End-of-Period Adjustments for Overhead

LEARNING OBJECTIVE 4

Perform end-of-period adjustments for disposing of under- or overapplied overhead.

During December, Magna actually incurred $24,367 in variable overhead (Exhibit 14.11), but as reported in Exhibit 14.12, Magna allocated (or applied) only $20,886. For December, this leaves an unallocated balance of $3,481 in the variable overhead control account. Similarly, Magna actually incurred $76,582 of fixed overhead costs but applied $83,544. Thus, for December, the amount applied to jobs exceeds the amount incurred by $6,962 in the fixed overhead control account.

Any unallocated balance in the overhead control account represents **underapplied overhead**—the amount applied to jobs is smaller than the amount actually spent on overhead. For December, Magna has underallocated variable overhead costs by the $3,481 remaining in the control account. When the amount applied to jobs exceeds the amount spent on overhead, we have **overapplied overhead**. This is the case for Magna's fixed overhead for December, when the applied amount exceeded the actual costs incurred by $6,962.

In general, we compute the under- or overapplied overhead as:

> Actual overhead expense for the period
> less: Applied (i.e., allocated) overhead for the period
> = Under- or overapplied overhead for the period

The use of predetermined overhead rates results in under- or overapplied overhead because these rates differ from the actual overhead rates. In the case of Magna, the predetermined variable overhead rate of $0.30 is $0.05 less than the actual rate of $0.35 for each dollar. Magna spent $69,620 on labor. This discrepancy translates to an underapplied overhead of ($69,620 × $0.05) = $3,481.

CALCULATING THE AMOUNT IN THE CONTROL ACCOUNTS

How often should Magna dispose off the under or overapplied overhead and zero out the control accounts? One option is to do the adjustment at the end of each month. However, a monthly adjustment defeats the purpose of using predetermined

Check It! Exercise #2

Verify that Magna overapplied $6,962 in fixed overhead during December.

Actual labor cost	_____	(1)
Actual fixed overhead costs	_____	(2)
Actual fixed overhead rate for the month	_____	(3) = (2)/(1)
Predetermined overhead rate	$1.20 per labor $	
Applied overhead cost	_____	(4) = (1) × $1.20
Under-/overapplied overhead	_____	(5) = (2) − (4)
Error in rate	_____	(6) = $1.20 − (3)
Error in rate × actual labor cost	_____	(7) = (1) × (6)

The numbers in (5) and (7) should be the same.

Solution at end of chapter.

rates (calculated annually) to smooth out fluctuations in overhead rates. Thus, firms usually accumulate the under- or overapplied overhead in a control account until the end of the year. At year-end, they dispose of the total amount.

Let us begin by computing the total amount in the control account. As in December, Magna would have experienced under- or overapplied overhead for the previous 11 months in its fiscal year. From Exhibit 14.5, we know that Magna had $29,170 over-applied in its variable overhead control and $22,925 underapplied in its fixed overhead control. Since Magna under-applied overhead by $3,481 in December, the net effect for the full year is $25,689, overapplied. Similarly, the net effect for the full year with respect to the fixed overhead account is $15,963, underapplied. Exhibit 14.19 summarizes this information.

GAAP permits three avenues for zeroing out the overhead control account: (1) correct the rates at year-end, (2) charge the underapplied or overapplied overhead to COGS, or (3) prorate the underapplied or overapplied overhead among the inventory accounts and COGS.

CORRECT RATES AT YEAR-END

The first choice is to correct the rate for the entire year, using actual overhead costs and actual activity volumes at the end of the year. Using the actual overhead costs and activity levels, a firm can calculate the actual overhead rates at year-end and, in turn, retrospectively revalue all of the individual jobs processed during the year. This revaluation will change the values for the WIP and FG inventories, as well as cost of goods sold. Moreover, because the firm uses actual overhead costs and actual activity volumes to compute the rates, it will allocate all overhead to products. This retroactive adjustment to product costs eliminates any under- or overapplied overhead. Modern computer-based accounting systems allow firms to accomplish this task relatively easily.

WRITE OFF TO COST OF GOODS SOLD

The second choice is to charge the under- or overapplied overhead to cost of goods sold. Writing off underapplied overhead increases cost of goods sold, thereby decreasing reported income. Why? This effect occurs because the underapplication of overhead results in a lower-than-actual production cost and cost of goods sold. Correcting the error therefore increases the amount of COGS. Similarly, over-applied overhead decreases cost of goods sold and increases income. GAAP allows firms to write off under- or overapplied overhead to cost of goods sold as long as the amount is not "material" or large.

Exhibit 14.19	Magna Golf: Under- and Overapplied Overhead for the Year	
	Variable Overhead Control	Fixed Overhead Control
Opening balance as of 12/1 (Exhibit 14.5)	$29,170	($22,925)
(Under)/overapplied overhead	(3,481)	6,962
= Ending balance as of 12/31	$25,689	($15,963)

Exhibit 14.20	Magna Golf: Adjustments to COGS Account
Unadjusted cost of goods sold (Jan–Nov)	$4,245,000
Cost of goods sold (Dec.—see Exhibit 14.18)	378,600
Total unadjusted cost of goods sold	$4,623,600
− Overapplied variable overhead for the year	25,689
+ Underapplied fixed overhead for the year	15,963
= Adjusted cost of goods sold	$4,613,874

Exhibit 14.20 shows the adjustment to the cost of goods sold account. We know from Exhibit 14.5 that Magna had a total cost of goods sold of $4,245,000 for January to November. Magna sold goods with a cost of $378,600 (see Exhibit 14.18) during December. Thus, Magna's total unadjusted COGS is $4,623,600 as of December 31. After adjusting for under- and overapplied overhead, Magna's adjusted COGS is $4,613,874.

Connecting to Practice

CONTRACTING WITH THE DoD

The Department of Defense (DoD) uses a Defense Working Capital Fund (DWCF) to compensate contractors who perform maintenance of Army depots and Army facilities. Section G in Chapter 7 of Volume 11 B of the DoD Financial Management Regulation approves the "write off to COGS" approach for dealing with under- or overapplied overhead.

COMMENTARY: The DoD issues these regulations so that it may determine the costs it should refund to a contractor. In particular, when beginning a contract, the contractor and the DoD estimate costs based on a predetermined rate. The adjustment ensures that the contractor is reimbursed for actual costs. In addition to conforming to GAAP, the DoD regulation conforms to the U.S. Standard General Ledger (USSGL) administered by the Department of the Treasury.

Check It! Exercise #3

Suppose that at year-end, Magna had underapplied variable overhead of $18,450 and overapplied fixed overhead of $12,800. Circle whether to add or subtract the numbers from unadjusted COGS. Do the arithmetic to compute Magna's adjusted COGS.

	Item	Amount	Detail
	Unadjusted COGS on 12/31	_____	From Exhibit 14.20
Add/Subtract	Underapplied variable overhead	18,450	Given
Add/Subtract	Overapplied fixed overhead	12,800	Given
=	Adjusted COGS on 12/31	_____	

Solution at end of chapter.

PRORATE AMONG INVENTORY ACCOUNTS AND COGS

The third method is to prorate (a synonym for "allocate") the under- or overapplied overhead to WIP inventory, FG inventory, and COGS *in proportion to their unadjusted ending balances*. Exhibit 14.21 provides the computations using this method for December for Magna.

COMPARING THE METHODS

Writing off under- or overapplied overhead to cost of goods sold is the easiest method, but the least accurate. To see why, recall that underapplied overhead results when the predetermined rate is smaller than the actual rate. This discrepancy results in the undervaluation of *all* jobs, whether they are in the WIP inventory, FG inventory, or sold (i.e., their costs are part of cost of goods sold). By writing off the entire underallocated amount to COGS, the "errors" in the WIP and FG inventory accounts remain unadjusted. Similar concerns apply for overapplied overhead.

Prorating (or allocating) the under- or overapplied overhead among work-in-process, finished goods, and cost of goods sold accounts partially corrects this discrepancy. It proportionately increases the value of the jobs in all three accounts. However, we usually base the allocation on the ending balances in each account, rather than the overhead contained in each account. Therefore, errors can still occur. However, because the value of the COGS tends to be much larger than the values in the inventory accounts, the COGS still receives the largest allocation. Correcting the rates at year-end is the only method that does not lead to inaccurate WIP, FG, and COGS balances.

Ultimately, the choice of which method to use depends on the magnitude of the under- or overapplied overhead. If this amount is small, it is more justifiable to write it off to cost of goods sold. It is more reasonable to follow the prorating approach or correct the rates for larger amounts.

Exhibit 14.21	*Magna Golf: Prorating (Under)/Overapplied Overhead*		
	WIP Inventory	**FG Inventory**	**COGS**
Unadjusted balance as of 12/31	$21,000.00	$285,500.00	$4,623,600.00
% of total	0.43%	5.79%	93.78%
Unadjusted balance as of 12/31	$21,000.00	$285,500.00	$4,623,600.00
− Overapplied variable overhead for the year	109.42	1,487.58	24,092.00
+ Underapplied fixed overhead for the year	67.99	924.37	14,970.63
= Adjusted values	$20,958.57	$284,936.79	$4,614,478.63

SUMMARY

In this chapter, we examined the different types of production environments and their associated costing systems. Following this, we learned that job-costing systems are suitable in settings with customized products and in settings where units, batches, or lots of a product move as a whole through the production process. We also learned that firms use predetermined overhead rates to smooth out cost fluctuations caused by the use of actual overhead rates. However, the use of predetermined rates gives rise to under- or overapplied overhead. We discussed three different methods to dispose of this amount.

In Chapter 15, we focus our attention on process-costing systems. Such systems are suitable for environments where the production process is continuous.

RAPID REVIEW

LEARNING OBJECTIVE 1

Describe the different kinds of production environments.

- Production environments range from making individual units of customized products to making millions of units of the same product. The features of a particular production process determine the extent to which we can, and need to, trace costs directly to individual units of a product and the extent to which allocations are necessary.

- In general, when units, batches, or lots of a product move as a whole through the production process, we consider the system to be job costing. In these settings, all units of a batch are completed before moving on to the next step. When different parts of a batch could be at different parts of the production process (e.g., some units are in Step 3 while other units are still in Step 1), we generally consider the system to be process costing.

LEARNING OBJECTIVE 2

Explain the flow of costs in a job shop.

- Job-shop environments allow for considerable traceability of materials and labor to individual jobs. Some job-shop environments even allow us to trace many capacity costs. Invariably, however, at least some overhead costs need to be allocated to jobs.

- We add material costs to a job when we issue materials from the storeroom to the shopfloor. We add labor when work is done. We apply overhead in proportion to the chosen activity volume. When the job is finished, we move the cost from the WIP account to the FG inventory account. Similarly, we move the cost from the FG inventory account to the COGS account when we sell the job. At the end of a period, the value of the WIP inventory is the sum of the costs of all jobs still in process, and the value of the FG inventory is the sum of all finished but unsold jobs.

LEARNING OBJECTIVE 3

Apply overhead to jobs using predetermined rates.

- Most job-costing systems use a predetermined rate to allocate overhead. Firms compute the predetermined overhead rate at the start of the year, as part of their operating budgets. Such systems are termed normal costing systems.

- Using predetermined overhead rates allows us to smooth out the inevitable fluctuations in product costs that would arise from using actual overhead rates.

LEARNING OBJECTIVE 4

Perform end-of-period adjustments for disposing of under- or overapplied overhead.

- Under- or overapplied overhead results when the predetermined rate differs from the actual rate. We underapply overhead when the predetermined rate is lower than the actual overhead rate. The reverse holds true for overapplied overhead.

- There are three methods for disposing of under- or overapplied overhead. In all three methods, underapplied overhead increases cost of goods sold and decreases income. Overapplied overhead has the opposite effect.

ANSWERS TO CHECK IT! EXERCISES

Exercise #1: Under LIFO, all 2,200 units would be sold from December's production. Thus, $2,200 \times \$68 = \$149,600$.

Exercise #2: Actual labor cost = $69,620; Actual fixed overhead costs = $76,582; Actual fixed overhead rate = $1.10/labor $; Applied overhead cost = $83,544; Overapplied overhead = $6,962; Predetermined rate is $0.10 higher than the actual rate; Error in rate $\times$ actual labor cost = $6,962.

Exercise #3: The unadjusted COGS is $4,623,600. Add underapplied overhead and subtract overapplied overhead to determine the adjusted COGS as $4,629,250.

Gordon Maderis makes and sells mouthpieces for saxophones to professional musicians at prices ranging from $300 to $1,500 per mouthpiece. Gordon began operations this year, with no inventories of any kind. During the year, Gordon purchased $194,750 worth of raw materials (wood, brass, etc.) and incurred $337,900 in labor costs. Gordon also spent $284,200 on manufacturing overhead expenses and $28,500 on selling costs.

Gordon manufactures mouthpieces in small batches of 25 to 50 pieces each. He uses a costing system in which he traces the cost of materials and labor to individual jobs and allocates overhead to jobs using a predetermined rate of 80% of actual labor cost. Recall that we termed such a system "normal costing."

a. *Job A43-05, for 30 brass mouthpieces, has materials cost of $1,375 and labor costs of $2,640. Determine the inventoriable cost of job A43-05.*

The inventoriable cost of a job is the sum of the cost of materials, the labor used by that job, and the overhead allocated to that job. We have:

Materials cost	$1,375	
Labor cost	2,640	
Allocated overhead	2,112	80% of $2,640
Total	$6,127	

b. *Gordon provides the following details at year-end, prior to disposition of any under- or overapplied overhead. Determine the amount for each cell marked with a "?."*

	Raw Materials	Work in Process	Finished Goods	Cost of Goods Sold	Total
Materials	$8,950	$11,905	$20,795	$153,100	$194,750
Labor	?	?	$32,560	$289,900	$337,900
Allocated overhead	?	?	?	231,920	?

The value of the raw materials inventory is just the cost of the materials—the labor cost and allocated overhead are $0.

Next, using the fact that there is zero labor for raw materials, we can fill in the labor cost for the WIP account by considering the row for labor costs.

Finally, we know that allocated overhead is 80% of labor cost. Thus, we can calculate the amount of overhead in the work-in-process (WIP) and finished goods (FG) inventory accounts at 80% of labor cost in the respective accounts.

	Raw Materials	Work in Process	Finished Goods	Cost of Goods Sold	Total
Materials	$8,950	$11,905	$20,795	$153,100	$194,750
Labor	0	15,440	32,560	289,900	337,900
Allocated overhead	0	12,352	26,048	231,920	270,320
Total	$8,950	$39,697	$79,403	$674,920	$802,970

c. *Calculate the under- or overapplied overhead for the year.*

Under- or overapplied overhead is the difference between the overhead allocated to production for the period and the actual overhead expense for the period. From part (b) we know the amount of overhead allocated for the period. The problem data provides the amount for actual overhead. We have:

Allocated overhead	$337,900 × 0.80	$270,320
Actual overhead	Given	284,200
Underapplied overhead		$13,880

Overhead is underapplied because the amount of overhead allocated to production is smaller than Gordon's actual expenditure. Notice that the actual cost does not include selling expenses, as GAAP does not include these costs when computing the value of inventories.

d. *Determine the COGS if Gordon disposes of the under- or overapplied overhead by (1) charging it to COGS, or (2) prorating it among the inventory accounts in proportion to their ending balances (round computations to the nearest dollar).*

As indicated in the chapter, GAAP permits both of the above methods for disposing of the under- or overapplied overhead. With either method, the adjustment will increase values as Gordon has underapplied overhead, meaning that the predetermined rate is lower than the actual rate.

Under the "write off to COGS" approach, we have:

Unadjusted COGS	$674,920
+ Underapplied overhead	13,880
= Adjusted COGS	$688,800

Under the "prorate to inventory accounts" approach, we allocate the under- or overapplied overhead to the accounts in proportion to their *unadjusted* ending balances.

	Work in Process	Finished Goods	Cost of Goods Sold	Total
Total unadjusted cost	$39,697	$79,403	$674,920	$794,020
Percent of total cost	5%	10%	85%	100%
Prorated amount	694	1,388	11,798	13,880
Adjusted cost	$40,391	$80,791	$686,718	$807,900

Note: Under either approach, the three accounts (WIP, FG, and COGS) contain the *total overhead cost* of $284,200 incurred during the period. Under the "write off to COGS" approach, overhead costs are $12,352, $26,048, and $245,800 (= $231,920 + $13,880). Under the "prorate to inventory accounts" approach, the amounts are $13,046 (= $12,352 + $694), $27,436 (= $26,048 + $1,388), and $243,718 (= $231,920 + $11,798). This equivalence underscores that the allocation process simply distributes the actual overhead costs among products and, thus, inventories.

GLOSSARY

Applied overhead The amount of overhead allocated to products using a predetermined overhead rate.

Control account A temporary holding account for accumulating costs such as direct labor and overhead. We zero out a control account at the end of an accounting period.

Cost accounting Accounting systems for calculating the values of ending inventories and the cost of goods sold.

Fixed manufacturing overhead Indirect manufacturing costs that do not vary with production volume.

Job shop Setting that involves discrete production of unique products.

Normal costing A product-costing system that uses predetermined overhead rates to apply overhead to products.

Operations costing A combination of job costing and process costing.

Overapplied overhead The difference between actual overhead and applied overhead. Arises when actual overhead is smaller than applied overhead.

Predetermined overhead rate Overhead rate computed using expected overhead costs and expected activity volumes at the start of a plan period, typically a year.

Process shop Setting that involves continuous production of homogeneous products.

Underapplied overhead The difference between actual overhead and applied overhead. Arises when actual overhead is larger than applied overhead.

REVIEW QUESTIONS

14.1 LO1. What are the two major kinds of production environments?

14.2 LO1. What is a job-costing system? Give two examples of a job-costing system.

14.3 LO1. What is a process-costing system? Give two examples of a process-costing system.

14.4 LO2. In a job-costing system, what costs are traced to products? What costs are allocated to products?

14.5 LO2. Define the terms work in process (WIP) inventory, cost of goods manufactured (COGM), and cost of goods sold (COGS).

14.6 LO3. What is a predetermined overhead rate?

14.7 LO3. Why do firms use predetermined overhead rates?

14.8 LO3. What is a normal costing system?

14.9 LO4. What do the terms *underapplied overhead* and *overapplied overhead* mean?

14.10 LO4. If a firm has underapplied overhead at year-end, its actual overhead rate is lower than its pre-determined rate. True or False? Justify your answer.

14.11 LO4. What are the three methods firms can use to deal with underapplied or overapplied overhead at the end of an accounting period?

14.12 LO4. Suppose a firm has underapplied overhead at year-end. Also assume the firm writes off this underapplied overhead to COGS. Would the adjustment increase or decrease COGS? What is the effect on net income?

14.13 LO4. Describe the proration method.

14.14 LO4. Suppose a firm has underapplied overhead at year-end. If the firm decides to use the proration approach, what accounts will be affected?

14.15 LO4. Suppose a firm has underapplied overhead at year-end. Will the income be higher or lower under the proration method relative to writing off this amount to cost of goods sold?

DISCUSSION QUESTIONS

14.16 LO1. "Variations in the traceability of costs is the key distinction between job- and process-costing systems." Comment.

14.17 LO1. "Costing systems in hospitals are like job-costing systems in many respects." Do you agree with this statement? Why or why not?

14.18 LO1. Describe service firms that are likely to have a job costing-like system; a process costing-like system.

14.19 LO1. The only difference between job- and process-costing systems relates to the size of the average batch for a product. True or False? Justify your response.

14.20 LO3. How does the use of predetermined overhead rates help with performance evaluation and cost control?

14.21 LO4. Suppose your firm disposes of under- or over-applied overhead by writing it off to cost of goods sold. How could you increase the chances of obtaining an income-increasing adjustment at year-end?

14.22 LO3, LO4. Suppose a firm, with a normal costing system, uses the number of units produced to allocate overhead to products. Use a numerical example to prove that under- or overapplied overhead equals the error in calculating the predetermined rate times the actual production in units.

14.23 LO4. Suppose you dispose of underapplied and overapplied overhead by writing it off to cost of goods sold. Would income differ compared to a setting where you use actual overhead rates to allocate indirect costs?

14.24 LO3. Suppose you dispose of underapplied and overapplied overhead by writing it off to cost of goods sold. Would income differ compared to a setting where you prorate under- and overapplied overhead among work-in-process inventory, finished goods inventory, and cost of goods sold?

14.25 LO4. Consider the following claim: "Whether firms underapply or overapply overhead is not relevant for decision making. Consequently, how they dispose of this amount is also not relevant for decision making." Do you agree? Why or why not?

EXERCISES

14.26 Basic job costing (LO2). Tubbs and Company manufactures custom motorcycles. Tubbs uses a job-cost system and provides the following information related to the work-in-process account for the month of January:

January 1 balance	$22,500
Direct material used	25,000
Direct labor incurred	24,000
Manufacturing overhead applied	36,000

Tubbs applies manufacturing overhead based on direct labor cost. Job No. 232 was the only job still in process at the end of January. As of January 31, this job, which was started in January, contains direct materials of $4,250 and direct labor of $2,500.

Required: Determine the cost of goods manufactured during January.

14.27 Predetermined overhead rates (LO3). Bayou Machinery Works budgets to spend a total of $1,200,000 on manufacturing overhead during the coming year. Of this amount, Bayou expects fixed overhead to be $500,000. Bayou applies overhead to jobs based on machine hours and expects to generate business for 10,000 machine hours in the coming year.

Required:

a. Calculate Bayou's predetermined variable, fixed, and total overhead rates for the coming year.

b. One of the jobs accepted for the coming year requires $5,000 in materials, $8,000 in direct labor, and 40 machine hours. Bayou charges its customers a 25% markup on product cost (also known as inventoriable cost). What price will Bayou charge the customer for this job?

14.28 Predetermined rates (LO3). VBK, Inc., applies overhead costs to its products using direct labor costs as its cost driver. For the most recent year, its budgeted overhead costs were $525,000, and its budgeted direct labor costs were $150,000.

During the year, VBK actually paid $140,000 for direct labor, and actual overhead costs were $530,000.

Required: Determine the firm's over- or underapplied overhead.

14.29 Predetermined rates and cost flows (LO2, LO3). Ace Company has the following (unadjusted) amounts in its accounts as of December 31:

Cost of goods sold	$100,000
Finished goods inventory	$75,000
Raw materials inventory	$50,000
Work-in-process inventory	$25,000

The company prorates over- or underapplied overhead.

Required: What will the adjusted balance in work-in-process inventory be if overhead has been overapplied by $10,000?

14.30 Basics of under- and overapplied overhead (LO3, LO4). Von Maur and Company uses a predetermined overhead rate of $5 per machine hour. A review of the company's accounting records shows that it budgeted $25,000 for overhead, and that actual overhead was $26,000. The firm also underapplied manufacturing overhead by $6,000.

Required: What were Von Maur's budgeted and actual machine hours?

14.31 Predetermined rates and cost flows (LO2, LO3). Guymon Company reported a cost of goods manufactured of $313,000. Supplemental information shows raw materials purchases of $60,000, raw materials used in production of $90,000, direct labor of $107,000, and manufacturing overhead of $113,000. You also know that the company's ending work in process was 40% of its beginning work in process (WIP).

Required: Determine the value of the firm's ending WIP.

14.32 Predetermined rates and cost flows (LO2, LO3). Osborne Products uses a predetermined overhead rate of $50 per labor hour. A review of the company's accounting records revealed actual overhead for the period of $500,000 and overapplied manufacturing overhead of $50,000.

Required: What were Osborne's actual labor hours?

14.33 Predetermined overhead rates, working backwards (LO3). Wilkinson, Inc. provides the following inventory balances and manufacturing cost data for the month of January:

Inventories	January 1	January 31		Month of January
Raw materials	$30,000	$40,000	Cost of goods sold	$530,000
Work in process	10,000	20,000	Applied manufacturing	
Finished goods	65,000	50,000	overhead	150,000
			Materials purchased	200,000
			Actual manufacturing	
			overhead	144,000

Any over- or underapplied overhead is closed to cost of goods sold at the end of the calendar year.

Required: How much direct labor cost did Wilkinson incur in January?

14.34 Disposal of underapplied overhead (LO4). Worthington Company employs a job-order costing system. Before disposition of the underapplied or overapplied overhead, selected year-end balances from Worthington's accounting records were:

Cost of goods sold	$720,000
Raw material inventory	36,000
Work-in-process inventory	54,000
Finished goods inventory	90,000

Required:

If the adjusted ending balance (after proration of underapplied or overapplied overhead) of cost of goods sold is $757,500, what is the underapplied or overapplied overhead for the period?

14.35 Predetermined overhead rates (LO3, LO4). Ortega Company uses a job-order costing system. During a year, the firm applied $280,000 of manufacturing overhead in total. At the end of the year, actual manufacturing overhead was determined to be $260,000. The following data pertain to ending account balances.

Cost of goods sold	$200,000
Finished goods inventory	$150,000
Raw materials inventory	$100,000
Work-in-process inventory	$50,000

Required:

a. Assume that Ortega closes underapplied or overapplied overhead into cost of goods sold. What is the final (i.e., adjusted) balance in cost of goods sold?

b. Calculate adjusted COGS if Ortega prorates over- or underapplied overhead.

14.36 Basic job costing (LO2, LO3). Greer Corporation, which uses a job-costing system, had two jobs in process at the start of the quarter: job no. J5-59 (beginning value: $95,000) and job no. X9-60 (beginning value: $39,500). It had a zero balance in its finished goods inventory account. The firm provides the following information:

- The predetermined overhead rate is $36 per machine hour.
- The company worked on three jobs during the first quarter. Relevant data about costs incurred during the quarter are as follows:

Job No.	Direct Material	Direct Labor	Machine Hours
J5-59	$18,000	$45,000	900
X9-60	—	20,000	200
T10-61	37,000	35,000	1,200

- Greer completed jobs J5-59 and X9-60, and sold Job J5-59.

Required:

a. Determine the cost of the job(s) still in production at the end of the first quarter.

b. Determine the value of ending finished goods inventory.

14.37 Under/overapplied overhead (LO4). Sultan and Company makes rugs, selling them to furniture and carpet stores. During the most recent year, actual fixed and variable overhead were $245,000 and $603,250, respectively. Sultan applies overhead based on the number of rugs made at the rate of $87 per rug ($25 fixed and $62 variable). Sultan made 9,750 rugs during the most recent year.

Required:

a. What was the total amount of overhead applied during the most recent year?

b. Was total overhead underapplied or overapplied? By how much were variable overhead and fixed overhead underapplied or overapplied?

14.38 Application and disposal of overhead (LO4). REPCO performs warranty repair work for name-brand kitchen appliances. REPCO bills appliance manufacturers on a cost-plus basis. It has a job-costing system that computes the cost of each order by adding the direct costs of materials and labor and then applying overhead using direct labor hours as the allocation basis.

REPCO uses flexible budgeting to forecast annual overhead. At the beginning of the year, the company projected the annual overhead budget to be $7,200,000 of fixed costs plus $80 per labor hour in variable costs. The firm treats labor costs as variable overhead because its workers do both direct and indirect work. The budgeted annual direct labor hours for the year were 100,000. During the year, REPCO actually spent $18,000,000 on overhead and labor; actual labor hours were 120,000.

Required:

a. Calculate REPCO's predetermined total overhead rate.

b. Calculate the amount of overapplied or underapplied overhead for the year.

c. REPCO's policy is to write off the amount of overapplied or underapplied overhead to cost of goods sold. By how much will REPCO's income increase or decrease for the year as a result of this policy?

14.39 Basic job costing (LO2, LO3, LO4). Fran's Custom Motors uses a job-order costing system. The firm had two jobs in process at the start of the April: job no. 401 (cost : $211,250) and job no. 402 (cost: $53,400). The following information is available:

- The company applies manufacturing overhead based on machine hours. Budgeted overhead was $275,000 and budgeted machine hours were 20,000 hours.

- There was no beginning balance in the finished goods account.

- The company worked on four jobs during the month. The following data pertain to the associated costs.

Job No.	Direct Materials	Direct Labor	Machine Hours
401	$33,000	$15,200	2,500
402	$42,500	$27,300	6,800
403	$46,000	$24,750	6,500
404	$132,750	$72,500	12,000

- Manufacturing overhead during April included charges for depreciation ($50,000), indirect labor ($53,000), indirect materials used ($26,250), and other factory costs ($168,000).

- Fran's completed job no. 401 and job no. 402 during the period. Job no. 402 was sold, producing a profit of $24,000 for the firm.

Required:

a. Determine the company's predetermined overhead application rate.

b. Calculate the ending balance for the finished goods account.

c. Calculate under- or overapplied overhead.

14.40 Overhead application (LO3, LO4). Lone Star Glassworks applies factory overhead at the rate of $8 per direct labor hour. The company has provided you with the following information for the most recent year of operations:

Direct labor hours	50,000
Direct labor	$620,000
Indirect labor	$160,000
Sales commissions	$50,000
Depreciation on manufacturing equipment	$75,000
Direct materials	$375,000
Factory fuel	$60,000
Cost of goods sold	$820,000
Factory rent	$120,000

Required:

a. Calculate the total factory overhead applied during the year.

b. Compute the amount of underapplied or overapplied overhead for the year.

14.41 Overhead application (LO3). Chopra Company, which makes golf carts and lawn tractors, uses departmental rates to allocate overhead costs. It uses direct materials costs as the basis for allocating overhead in Department A. Machine hours are the driver for Department B. Information related to product costs for last year was as follows:

	Golf Carts	Lawn Tractors
Annual production and Sales	4,000 units	2,000 units
Direct material (per unit)	$6,000	$6,000
Direct labor cost (per unit):		
Dept. A	$ 500	$1,000
Dept. B	$1,000	$750
Machine hours (per unit):		
Dept. A	10	40
Dept. B	40	20

In addition, you know that the firm budgets manufacturing overhead in department A at $9,000,000 and in department B at $3,000,000.

Required:

a. What is the overhead rate for the two departments?

b. What is the inventoriable value per lawn tractor?

14.42 Change in overhead rates over time (LO3). Serene Brakes manufactures brake pads and other automotive components. The firm's CEO is very pleased that aggressive cost cutting appears to be paying off as the firm's cost per unit has decreased from last year to this year. She provides the following data in support of her claim:

	Previous Year	Current Year
Fixed overhead	$500,000	$500,000
Variable overhead	$600,000	$750,000
Budgeted machine hours	10,000	12,500
Actual machine hours per unit	0.25	0.25
Materials + Direct labor cost per unit	$45.00	$45.00

Required:

a. Determine Serene's predetermined total overhead rate for the previous and current years. Assume Serene uses a normal costing system and applies overhead based on machine hours.

b. Determine the cost per unit for the previous year and the current year.

c. Explain why the reported cost per unit has decreased from the previous year to the current year. Would you accept the CEO's claim that costs have been reduced?

14.43 Overhead disposition, effect on income (LO4). Malcolm Manufacturing has two pools for applying overhead to products. The first pool contains labor-related overhead costs and is charged out at $0.80 per labor dollar. The second pool contains machine-related overhead costs and is charged out at $22 per machine hour.

During the year, Malcolm spent $1,800,000 on 92,000 hours of labor and used 84,000 machine hours. Actual labor-related overhead was $1,445,400 and actual machine-related overhead was $1,816,550. Prior to any adjustments for under- or overapplied overhead, Malcolm's income is $445,280.

Required:

a. Compute Malcolm's net income if the firm writes off all under- or overapplied overhead to cost of goods sold.

b. Suppose Malcolm chooses to prorate the under- or overapplied overhead to work in process, finished goods, and cost of goods sold in proportion to their ending balances. Would Malcolm's reported income be higher or lower than the answer you computed in part (a)?

PROBLEMS

14.44 Comparing methods for disposing of under/overapplied overhead (LO4). Skoll Technologies has the following year-end balances in its three inventory accounts and cost of goods sold. Skoll also informs you that actual overhead for the year was $692,415. Net income, prior to any adjustment for under- or overapplied overhead, is $122,342 for the year.

	Raw Materials	Work in Process	Finished Goods	Cost of Goods Sold
Unadjusted year-end value	$75,535.00	$143,516.50	$215,274.75	$1,076,373.75
Amount of applied overhead included in account balance	—	61,183.35	95,174.10	523,457.55

Required:

a. What is Skoll's under- or overapplied overhead for the year?

b. Suppose Skoll writes off under- or overapplied overhead directly to cost of goods sold. After the write-off, what would be Skoll's net income for the year?

c. Suppose Skoll prorates under- or overapplied overhead among the accounts that contain overhead using their unadjusted year-end balances. After proration, what would be Skoll's net income for the year?

d. Suppose Skoll prorates the under- or overapplied overhead among the accounts that contain overhead using the amount of overhead applied to each account. After this procedure, what would be Skoll's net income for the year?

e. Briefly discuss why your answers to parts (b)–(d) differ.

14.45 Application and disposition of overhead (LO3, LO4). Design Homes builds custom homes. The firm uses a job-order costing system and applies manufacturing overhead based on direct-labor hours from master artisans. Estimated manufacturing overhead for the year is $1,728,000. The firm employs 24 master artisans, who constitute the direct-labor force. Each of these employees is expected to work 2,000 hours during the year. The direct-labor rate is $50 per hour.

There was no beginning balance in the finished goods account. The company worked on three homes during the first quarter. Beginning balances, direct materials used, and direct-labor hours spent were as follows:

Job No.	Beginning Balance	Direct Materials	Artisan Labor Hours
101	$200,000	$160,000	1,000
102	0	195,000	6,500
103	0	138,000	3,000

Manufacturing overhead during the first quarter comprised of:

Depreciation	$187,500
Indirect labor	50,000
Indirect materials	30,000
Other construction costs	108,500

Design completed job no. 101 and job no. 102 during the period. Job no. 101 was sold, producing a profit of $68,000 for the firm.

Required:

a. Determine the company's predetermined overhead application rate.

b. Calculate the unadjusted balance for the cost of goods sold accounts.

c. Calculate the adjusted COGS for the period after closing any under- or overapplied overhead to the COGS account.

14.46 Cost flows and overhead application (LO2, LO3). Hawkeye Corporation provides you with the following estimates of overhead costs for the upcoming year:

Department	Budgeted Overhead	Labor Hours	Machine Hours
Materials handling	$1,500,000	150,000	100,000
Assembly	$2,500,000	50,000	100,000
Total	$4,000,000	200,000	200,000

The company just received a job order with the following information:

Department	Labor Hours Required	Machine Hours Required
Materials handling	100	400
Assembly	150	600

The job will require $5,000 of direct material. The company pays $16 per direct labor hour.

Required:

a. Calculate the estimated inventoriable cost for the job. Allocate all overhead based on a single rate based on machine hours.

b. Repeat part A, except use departmental rates to allocate overhead costs. Use labor hours as the cost driver for the Materials Handling Department and machine hours as its cost driver in the Assembly Department.

14.47 Cost flows and overhead application (LO2, LO3, LO4). DigJam Industries specializes in custom printing jobs. The following data pertains to its operations for the most recent year:

Raw materials beginning inventory	$60,000
Raw materials ending inventory	$80,000
WIP beginning inventory	$80,000
WIP ending inventory	$105,000
Finished goods beginning inventory	$300,000
Finished goods ending inventory	$320,000
Raw materials issued to production	$225,000
Total manufacturing costs charged to production (= raw materials issued to production + direct labor + applied overhead at the rate of 120% of direct labor)	$885,000
Cost of goods available for sale (= beginning balance in finished goods + cost of goods manufactured)	$1,160,000
Actual overhead incurred	$400,000

DigJam writes off any under- or overapplied overhead directly to cost of goods sold.

Required:

a. Calculate the cost of raw materials purchased during the year.

b. Calculate the cost of direct labor charged to production.

c. Calculate the cost of goods manufactured during the year.

d. Calculate the amount of underapplied or overapplied overhead.

e. Calculate the cost of goods sold during the year (including the write-off).

14.48 Overhead application, changing unit cost (LO3, Advanced). Barton Bicycles manufactures two different bicycles in its factory located in Bryan, Texas: the Cavalier and the Classic. The following information pertains to planned production for the most recent year.

	Models	
	Cavalier	*Classic*
Projected production (units)	4,800	3,200
Unit costs		
Direct materials	$20.00	$30.00
Direct labor ($12/hour)	24.00	36.00
Manufacturing overhead	48.00	72.00
Unit cost	$92.00	$138.00

Barton assigns overhead to products based on direct labor dollars, with the overhead rate being established at the beginning of the year using a flexible budget. The variable manufacturing overhead rate in the flexible budget is projected to be 40% of direct labor dollars.

Required:

a. What estimate of fixed manufacturing overhead was used in setting the overhead rate at the beginning of the year?

b. Barton's management is considering changing the allocation basis from direct labor cost to assembly hours. Each unit of the Classic takes 2.4 hours to assemble, and each unit of the Cavalier takes 0.80 hour to assemble. Calculate the overhead application rate, and compute the unit costs of Classic and Cavalier.

14.49 Overhead application and disposition (LO3, LO4). The following information is taken from the records of Cabot Cove Company. At the end of the year, Cabot Cove had only three jobs in process. Selected figures for these three jobs are:

	Job 126	*Job 130*	*Job 137*
Direct materials	$10,000	$8,000	$38,000
Direct labor	$25,000	$15,000	$40,000
Machine hours	200	100	500
Direct labor hours	80	50	200

Cabot Cove applies overhead using a budgeted rate based on direct labor dollars; the overhead application rate is calculated at the beginning of the year. Budgeted and actual figures for the most recent year were:

Budgeted total overhead	$600,000
Budgeted direct labor cost	$750,000
Actual direct labor cost	$900,000
Actual total overhead	$640,000
Finished goods inventory (at the end of the year)	$300,000
Cost of goods sold	$500,000

There were no inventories at the beginning of the year.

Required:

a. By how much was total overhead underapplied or overapplied?

b. What is the ending balance in the work-in-process account (without taking under- or overapplied overhead amounts into account)?

c. Cabot Cove prorates underapplied or overapplied overhead to work in process, finished goods, and cost of goods sold. Compute the balances in these accounts after disposing of underapplied or overapplied overhead.

d. What would be the difference in income had the company chosen to write off the entire underapplied or overapplied overhead directly to cost of goods sold?

14.50 Two overhead rates (LO2, LO3, LO4). McMaster Fabrication has two manufacturing departments: machine operations and assembly. McMaster projected the following numbers for the most recent year.

	Machine Operations	Assembly
Machine hours	7,500	1,500
Direct labor hours	10,000	20,000
Factory overhead	$600,000	$300,000

McMaster applies machine operations overhead based on machine hours and assembly overhead based on direct labor hours. The following information reflects the actual results for the most recent year.

	Machine Operations	Assembly
Machine hours	12,000	1,700
Direct labor hours	11,000	22,000
Factory overhead	$650,000	$275,000

At the end of the year, the balance in the finished goods account was $150,000, and cost of goods sold (before any adjustments for over- or underapplied overhead) was $750,000. Finally, there was only one job in process at the end of the year—Job #C252. Its job sheet revealed the following cost numbers: direct materials = $2,000; direct labor = $6,000; direct labor hours in assembly = 250; machine hours in machine operations = 40.

Required:

a. Compute the overhead rate for each of McMaster's production departments.

b. Compute the under- or overapplied overhead for each department.

c. McMaster prorates any underapplied or overapplied overhead among the work-in-process, finished goods, and cost of goods sold accounts. Compute the ending balance in each of these accounts after proration. By how much will the net income before taxes rise or fall for the year?

14.51 Cost flows, overhead application with two overhead rates (LO2, LO3, LO4). Premier Spectacles makes frames for eyeglasses. It has two main departments: Production and Assembly. The following data pertains to its operations for the most recent year.

Inventories, January 1

Direct materials (10 types)	$50,000
WIP (in assembly)	25,000
Finished goods	20,000

The manufacturing overhead budget for the most recent year was:

	Production	Assembly
Indirect labor	$100,000	$50,000
Supplies	25,000	15,000
Utilities	20,000	25,000
Repairs	75,000	25,000
Supervision	50,000	75,000
Factory rent	15,000	15,000
Depreciation on equipment	50,000	30,000
Insurance, property taxes, etc.	15,000	15,000

Manufacturing overhead is applied using budgeted rates on the basis of machine hours for Production and on the basis of direct labor cost for Assembly. Budgeted machine hours for the Production Department were 25,000; budgeted direct labor cost for Assembly was $500,000.

The following is a summary of the actual events for the year:

	Production	Assembly	Total
Direct materials purchased			$400,000
Direct materials used	$150,000	225,000	375,000
Direct labor costs incurred	200,000	550,000	750,000
Factory overhead incurred	360,000	225,000	585,000
Factory overhead applied	322,000	?	?
Sales	—	—	3,250,000
Cost of goods sold			1,650,000

The ending work in process (all in Assembly) was $22,000, and the ending finished goods inventory was $95,000.

Required:

a. Compute the budgeted overhead rates.

b. Compute the machine hours actually used in the Production Department.

c. Compute the amount of factory overhead applied in the Assembly Department.

d. Compute the gross margin after disposing of under- or overapplied overhead. Premier's policy is to write off the amount of under- or overapplied overhead direct to cost of goods sold.

14.52 Application and disposition of overhead using normal volume (LO3, LO4, Advanced). Hansen and Company's annual overhead budget equals $7,200,000 of fixed costs plus $80 per labor hour in variable costs. For the most recent year, budgeted direct labor hours were 100,000. Actual total overhead was $16,000,000 and actual direct labor hours were 110,000 during the year.

Jeremey Meyer, the CEO of Hansen and Company, believes that using the "long-term" *normal* volume of direct labor hours as the allocation base is more appropriate than using *budgeted* direct labor hours as the allocation base when computing overhead rates. Accordingly, Jeremy asks his accountant to re-compute the overhead rate using normal volume. After much deliberation and consultation with factory personnel, the accountant decides that the long-term normal volume of direct labor hours is 150,000.

Required:

a. Calculate Hansen's total annual overhead rate using normal volume.

b. Calculate the amount of overapplied or underapplied overhead for the most recent year, if Hansen used the overhead rate you derived in part (a).

c. Hansen's policy is to write off the amount of overapplied or underapplied overhead to cost of goods sold. Will Hansen's income for the year rise or fall as a result of this policy?

d. Repeat parts (a) through (c) assuming that Hansen uses the budgeted volume of direct labor hours to compute the total overhead rate.

e. What are the relative merits of using normal volume, as opposed to budgeted volume, when computing predetermined overhead rates?

14.53 Job costing and variances (LO2, LO3, Advanced; Requires Chapter 8). Jason Yao operates a successful machining shop. Jason recently submitted the following bid for a job:

Direct materials		$7,000
Labor	500 hours @ $15/hour	7,500
Fixed overhead	100% of labor cost	7,500
Total cost		$22,000
Profit at 10%		2,200
Bid		$24,200

Jason's customer negotiated the bid down to $24,000. After completing the job, Jason calculated that he spent $7,200 on materials and incurred 550 labor hours at a cost of $8,000. Jason therefore believes that he made a profit of $24,000 − $7,200 materials cost − $8,000 labor cost − $8,000 overhead cost = $800 on the job.

Required:

a. Do you agree with Jason's assessment regarding the amount of profit he made from the job?

b. Perform a variance analysis that shows the various reasons as to why actual profit differed from budgeted profit.

c. Why does the variance analysis for part (b) include a flexible budget?

14.54 Cost flows and overhead application (LO2, LO3). Tornado Company manufactures two types of vacuum cleaners—Ultimate and Deluxe. Using a plantwide manufacturing overhead rate, the firm's controller calculated the following cost estimates:

	Ultimate	*Deluxe*
Direct material	$85.00	$60.00
Direct labor (1.5 hours at $25.00 per hour)	37.50	37.50
Manufacturing overhead*	$57.00	$57.00
Total	$179.50	$154.50

* The predetermined overhead rate is $38.00 per direct-labor hour.

The following information about manufacturing overhead is available:

	Machining Department	*Assembly Department*
Budgeted variable overhead	$1 per direct-labor hour	$5 per direct-labor hour
Budgeted fixed overhead	$400,000	$630,000
Budgeted direct labor hours	10,000 hours	20,000 hours
Direct labor:		
Ultimate	0.8 hour	0.7 hour
Deluxe	0.6 hour	0.9 hour

a. Show how the company's predetermined overhead rate was determined.

b. Calculate overhead rates if the company were to use departmental predetermined overhead rates with direct labor hours as the cost driver for each department.

c. Compute the product cost for a unit of each model.

14.55 Plant versus departmental rates (LO3). Venkat and Company manufactures rotators for automobile engines: R1 and R2. Based on a plantwide overhead rate, the cost estimates for two of the firm's models for the current year are as follows:

	R1	*R2*
Direct material	$200	$300
Direct labor	$160	$160
Manufacturing overhead	$225	$225
Total	$585	$685

Each rotator model requires 12 hours of direct labor. R1 requires 9 hours in department A and 3 hours in department B. R2 requires 5 hours in department A and 7 hours in department B. The overhead costs budgeted in these two production departments are as follows:

	Department A	*Department B*
Variable cost	$20 per direct labor hour	$6 per direct labor hour
Fixed cost	$115,000	$230,000

The firm's management expects to operate at a level of 30,000 direct-labor hours in each Production Department during the current year.

Required:

a. Verify the firm's overhead rate of $18.75 per hour.

b. Suppose the company were to use departmental predetermined overhead rates with direct labor hours (DLH) as the cost driver for each department.

c. Compute the product cost of one unit of model R1 and R2.

14.56 Single versus multiple overhead rates (LO3, LO4). National Testing Systems administers standardized tests like the SAT and the GMAT. The firm bids on various jobs (e.g., state contracts) using a simple formula. Based on the estimated number of tests, National assesses the number of labor hours needed to complete the job. National then adds overhead, allocated based on labor hours, to arrive at its total cost of completing the job.

Over the past two years, National's new CEO has been aggressively pushing other "value-added" services such as longitudinal tracking of test scores and conversion of paper tests to electronic tests. National also bid on these jobs based on the number of labor hours needed. While National won almost every bid for these new services, the firm's profit has been steadily decreasing over this same time period.

The following data are available for the past three years of operations (For simplicity, we group jobs into "regular" and "new" jobs, corresponding to the traditional and new businesses):

	Year 1	Year 2	Year 3
Fixed overhead	$20.5 million	$22.0 million	$25 million
Labor hours (regular jobs)	205,000	190,000	180,000
Labor hours (new jobs)	0	15,000	35,000

You know that the overhead cost structure for the regular jobs has remained stable over this time. National has a long history with these kinds of jobs, and knows how to manage their costs. Virtually all of the increase in fixed overhead is attributable to the "new" jobs that the CEO favors.

Required:

a. Using the above data to support your argument, comment on why National appears to be less competitive on regular jobs (notice the decline in the number of hours devoted to regular jobs) but is winning "virtually all bids" on new jobs?

b. How might National change its costing system to more accurately reflect the relative amounts of capacity resources consumed by the two kinds of jobs?

14.57 Overhead application using budgeted and "normal" volumes (LO3, LO4, Advanced). Ricardo Windows specializes in making custom windows for high-end homes. Although the demand for custom windows fluctuates from year to year, the owner, Javier Ricardo, believes that it is in his company's long-term interest to maintain a stable workforce and a certain capacity level. At the end of the most recent year, the company's accountant prepared the following overhead projections for the next two years. Ricardo Windows applies overhead to jobs using a predetermined overhead rate based on direct labor dollars.

	Year 1	Year 2
Fixed overhead	$1,000,000	$1,000,000
Variable overhead per DL$	$0.40	$0.40
Budgeted direct labor cost	$800,000	$1,200,000
"Normal" volume (direct labor cost)	$1,000,000	$1,000,000

Required:

a. Compute the total overhead rate for each of the next two years using budgeted direct labor cost.

b. Compute the total overhead rate for each of the next two years using "normal" labor cost.

c. Project the amount of underapplied or overapplied overhead in each of the next two years using the overhead rates based on budgeted direct labor cost.

d. Project the amount of underapplied or overapplied overhead in each of the next two years using the overhead rates based on normal direct labor cost.

e. Provide a brief discussion of your answers to parts (c) and (d). Comment on the differences between using budgeted and normal volumes to calculate overhead application rates.

MINI-CASES

14.58 Predetermined overhead rates, overhead application, and disposition of under-/ overapplied overhead, comprehensive (LO1, LO2, LO3, LO4). Superior Auto Body & Paint Shop uses a normal costing system. Superior calculates a predetermined overhead rate at the beginning of every year and uses this rate to apply overhead to all of its jobs. For the previous year, Superior's overhead rate was $2 per labor dollar. Superior's budgeted labor costs for the previous year were $250,000, and budgeted fixed overhead was $375,000.

Required:

a. Calculate the total budgeted overhead for the previous year.

b. What was the budgeted variable overhead for the previous year?

c. Calculate the budgeted variable overhead rate for the previous year.

d. Suppose actual total overhead for the previous year was $630,000, actual direct labor cost was $300,000, and actual fixed overhead was $475,000. Calculate the total overhead applied in the previous year.

e. Calculate the amount by which total overhead was under- or overapplied.

f. Calculate the amount by which the fixed overhead was under- or overapplied.

g. Calculate the amount by which variable overhead was under- or overapplied.

h. At the end of the previous year, the following two jobs were the only jobs still in process:

	Job 125	Job 178
Direct materials	$16,000	$18,000
Direct labor	$20,000	$13,000

Calculate the balance in the work-in-process account at the end of the previous year.

i. Suppose Superior decides to write off the entire amount of under- or overapplied overhead to cost of goods sold. What would be the adjusted balance in the cost of goods sold account? Assume unadjusted cost of goods sold is $800,000.

j. At the end of the previous year, the value of Superior's finished goods inventory was $200,000. Assume Superior prorates any under- or overapplied overhead to work-in-process, finished goods, and cost of goods sold based on the balances in these accounts. Compute the adjusted ending balances for work in process, finished goods, and cost of goods sold.

k. By how much will Superior's income (before taxes) differ between the write-off (part i) and proration (part j) approaches?

14.59 Predetermined overhead rates, overhead application, and disposition of under-/overapplied overhead, comprehensive (LO1, LO2, LO3, LO4). Divine Bath Works is a leader in the bath fixtures industry, rising to prominence with the introduction of over-the-counter sinks. The following data pertain to September, the last month of Divine's fiscal year.

Type of Inventory	Balance as of September 1
Raw materials and supplies	$28,100
Work in process	$124,320
Finished goods	$245,000

The WIP inventory on 9/1 comprised one job, Job X, for 700 units of Model OO, an oval, over-the-counter sink. The finished goods inventory on 9/1 comprised the following:

Model Number (description)	Quantity	Cost per Unit	Value
OO (Oval, over-the counter)	100	$320.00	$32,000
RI (Round, in-the-counter)	400	$197.25	$78,900
OI (Oval, in-the-counter)	450	$298.00	$134,100
Total			$245,000

Divine uses a normal costing system, combined with the FIFO inventory flow assumption, to value its inventories. That is, Divine traces actual materials and labor costs to individual jobs. It allocates overhead using a predetermined rate computed at the start of the year. Divine allocates all overhead using labor dollars as the allocation basis.

Divine prepared the following annual overhead cost budget at the start of the year.

Cost Item	Budgeted Amount
Supplies	$290,000
Indirect labor	422,340
Supervision	228,520
Depreciation	425,800
Utilities	136,740
Factory rent	185,000
Total	$1,688,400

Divine also informs you that it had budgeted for 80,400 labor hours at the start of the year. As of September 1, the company had incurred 75,315 actual labor hours and spent $1,569,450 in overhead costs.

During September, Divine purchased $112,340 of raw materials and $26,430 of supplies. The following table shows the consumption of raw materials during September.

		Detail of Issues to WIP		
Job number	X	K	L	B
Model	OO	OI	RO	RI
Description	Oval, OTC	Oval, in sink	Round, OTC	Round, in sink
Units	700	500	200	700
Raw materials	$22,000	$58,000	$24,000	$11,450

Divine consumed $22,000 of supplies during September.

Divine incurred the following labor expenses during September:

Item	Job	Hours	Amount
Indirect labor			$32,000
Direct labor	X	1,920	$34,560
	K	2,430	$43,740
	L	1,678	$29,365
	B	845	$15,210

The following comprises actual overhead expenses (other than supplies and indirect labor) during the month.

Cost Item	Actual Amount (for September)
Supervision	$18,400
Depreciation	$32,650
Utilities	$8,900
Factory rent	$15,400

Finally, Divine completed all jobs except Job B during September. It also sold the following items during the month.

Model	OO	RI	OI	RO
Units Sold	750	200	400	150

Required:

Compute the following amounts:

a. The ending balance in raw materials and supplies inventory.

b. The predetermined overhead rate per labor hour.

c. The ending balance in WIP inventory.

d. The ending balance in finished goods inventory.

e. Cost of goods manufactured.

f. Cost of goods sold (prior to the adjustment for under or overapplied overhead).

g. The amount of under- or overapplied overhead.

14.60 Predetermined overhead rates, changes over time (LO2, LO3, LO4, Advanced). Vanessa Noel, owner and manager of Noel Draperies and Window Treatments, has been receiving some complaints from her loyal clientele of interior decorators and home décor consultants. For example, one of her loyal customers, Phoebe, wanted to know why she was being charged a much higher price for an order that was almost identical to an order she placed last year. Phoebe felt that the price hike was simply not justified.

Although Vanessa, when responding to Phoebe's complaint, blamed the price hike on the rising price of materials, she herself was a bit perplexed and decided to look into the matter. Vanessa asked her accountant to prepare a report for her summarizing cost and pricing data for the last three years. The accountant presented this information in the following table:

	Year 1	Year 2	Year 3
Budgeted results			
Revenue	$2,400,000	$2,700,000	$2,000,000
Direct materials	360,000	405,000	320,000
Direct labor	720,000	810,000	650,000
Variable factory overhead	144,000	162,000	130,000
Fixed factory overhead	400,000	400,000	400,000
Variable SG&A expenses	240,000	300,000	220,000
Fixed SG&A expenses	200,000	180,000	200,000
Actual results			
Revenue	$2,320,000	$2,800,000	
Direct materials	380,000	430,000	
Direct labor	725,000	900,000	
Variable factory overhead	140,000	160,000	
Fixed factory overhead	425,000	440,000	
Variable SG&A expenses	260,000	300,000	
Fixed SG&A expenses	180,000	200,000	

Vanessa believes that the last few years have been fairly representative of business volume in general. Moreover, Vanessa believes the *average* of the direct labor cost for years 1 and 2 is a fair estimate of her "normal" volume of business.

Vanessa next turns her attention to how she prices incoming jobs. When her company receives an order, Vanessa estimates the direct labor and material costs for the job, and then she applies an overhead amount to the job. Each year, the firm computes a budgeted overhead rate per dollar of direct labor. The company then prepares the order quote by adding direct material costs, direct labor costs, and applied overhead, and a 50% markup on the total cost.

Vanessa retrieves information corresponding to Phoebe's order in year 2, and compares it with the price quote the company prepared for Phoebe for her most recent order in year 3. Vanessa is not an accountant, but she is a good manager and can understand why Phoebe complained.

Required:

a. Compute the total overhead application rates for years 1, 2, and 3.

b. Compute the overapplied or underapplied overhead for year 1 and year 2.

c. The following information pertains to Phoebe's order in year 2, and her current order for year 3, which is identical to the year 2 order in terms of the draperies and the window treatments.

	Year 2	Year 3
Direct materials	$15,000	$15,500
Direct labor	$30,000	$32,000

Compute the price charged for the year 2 order and the price quoted for the year 3 order.

d. Do you agree with Phoebe that the price being quoted for her year 3 order is too high?

e. What should Vanessa do? Can you suggest an alternative way for Vanessa to develop her price quotes? Explain.

Chapter 15
Process Costing

CHEN ELECTRONICS IS ONE AMONG HUNDREDS OF ELECTRONICS firms in the Guangdong Province, People's Republic of China. Shibin Chen, the founder and CEO of Chen Electronics, has an extensive network of contacts in the United States. His firm specializes in assembling Digital Photo Display (DPD) devices. Usually, Shibin receives orders for several hundred thousand units at a time. Although shipments take place weekly, each order takes several months to complete. Shibin asks for your help in determining the cost of the units completed each month, as well as the cost of the units in process.

Chen Electronics, which assembles Digital Photo Display (DPD) devices, receives orders for several hundred thousand units at a time. Although shipments take place weekly, each order takes several months to complete. Shibin Chen wants to determine the cost of the units completed each month, as well as the cost of the units in process.

LEARNING OBJECTIVES

After studying this chapter, you will be able to:

1 Explain the mechanics of process costing.

2 Apply process costing to settings with many cost pools and beginning inventory.

3 Perform process costing using standard costs.

Chen Electronics' problem is typical of firms that produce similar units in large quantities. Like Chen Electronics, firms in the processed food, beverage, chemical, paper, pharmaceuticals, and plastics industries also mass produce relatively identical products. Examples of such companies include Tyson Foods, Heinz, Pfizer, and oil refinery units of energy giants like Exxon Mobil and BP. Firms that mass produce similar products use **process costing** to determine both the values of the inventories reported on their balance sheets and the cost of goods sold reported on their income statements.

CHAPTER CONNECTIONS
In Chapter 3, we distinguished between direct and indirect costs, noting that we could trace direct costs but needed to allocate indirect costs. Process-costing systems blur this distinction. In process-costing systems, we allocate materials and labor costs, usually termed direct costs, between the WIP and finished goods inventory accounts.

Mechanics of Process Costing

LEARNING OBJECTIVE 1

Explain the mechanics of process costing.

In Chapter 14, we outlined features of job- and process-costing systems. We learned that job costing is suitable for firms that produce customized products in small amounts. In contrast, process-costing systems are suitable for environments that involve mass production of like products. The difference in the environments results in the following key difference between job- and process-costing systems.

In settings with large batches, different units of the same batch might be at different stages of completion. However, because we still track costs for the entire batch, we need to distribute the cost of making the batch to those units that are still in process (work-in-process or WIP inventory) and to the units that have been completed during the period (cost of goods manufactured). Such *allocations* are central to process costing. We do not need them in a job-costing environment. There, a job either is in process or is completed. Thus, all the cost stays in the WIP account until the job is complete. When the job is done, we transfer the units to the FG inventory and the entire cost to the finished goods account.

How should we allocate the costs of a batch between completed and in-process units? The number of physical units in the WIP and the COGM accounts is an obvious candidate for the allocation of the costs of a batch. Let us see how. Suppose Chen began May with zero units in work-in-process inventory. During the month, Chen started production of 180,000 DPDs and completed 155,000 DPDs by May 31. Thus, 25,000 DPDs were still in process at month's end. Chen also incurred total manufacturing costs of $6,880,000 during May. Of this amount, $4,320,000 was for materials, with labor and overhead accounting for the remaining $2,560,000. Then, distributing costs proportionately, we allocate (25,000/180,000) × $6,880,000 or $955,555.56 to the WIP account and (155,000/180,000) × $6,880,000 = $5,924,444.44 to cost of goods manufactured.

Notice that such an allocation calculates, in effect, the average cost per unit of the product. We can calculate the cost as $6,880,000/180,000 units = $38.22 per unit (rounded). Because Chen produces large volumes, it is not possible to trace costs to individual units of the product. Instead, we recognize that all units are identical and employ allocations to determine the average cost per unit.

An allocation that computes costs based on the number of physical units is not quite accurate though. Why? The answer is that such an allocation attaches the same value to a unit whether the unit is in process or is complete. However, the in-process units still need more work to complete, which will involve more costs.

Process-costing systems use the concept of **equivalent units** to correct this deficiency. In particular, these systems convert *in-process* units to *equivalent* completed units. For example, suppose Chen estimates that the 25,000 units still in process are only 20% complete. Multiplying 25,000 units by 20%, Chen has the equivalent of 5,000 completed units in WIP inventory, or simply, 5,000 equivalent units.

Consumer electronics items such as the iPhone are produced in large quantities.
(Sean Gallup/Getty Images)

Meanwhile, the 155,000 units in COGM are complete in all respects, and thus contribute 155,000 (= 155,000 × 100%) equivalent units. Adding these 155,000 equivalent units with the 5,000 equivalent units from WIP inventory, we see that Chen has worked on 160,000 equivalent units during May. Here, we are implicitly assuming that cost is proportional to the work done.

Using the estimate of total equivalent units as our denominator volume, we now execute our two-step allocation process:

- Compute the allocation rate using total equivalent units as the denominator volume:

$$\frac{\$6,880,000}{(5,000 + 155,000) \text{ equivalent units}} = \$43.00 \text{ per equivalent unit}$$

- Allocate to WIP and COGM at the rate of $43 per equivalent unit:

    5,000 equivalent units × $43/equivalent unit = $215,000 to WIP, and
    155,000 equivalent units × $43/equivalent unit = $6,665,000 to COGM

Exhibit 15.1 summarizes these computations for Chen in a **process-costing report** using the following five-step procedure. The first three steps correspond to collecting the data for performing the allocation, and the last two steps are the allocation procedure itself.

1. *Track the physical flow.* Determine how many physical units are at each stage of the process. Specifically, determine how many units are still in process at the end of the period and how many units were finished during the period. Determine the percentage completion for the units still in process. (Completed units are 100% done.)
2. *Compute equivalent units.* For the units still in process, multiply the physical units by the percentage completion to obtain equivalent units. Add this amount to the units completed to obtain total equivalent units for the period.

Exhibit 15.1	Chen Electronics: Process Costing Report	
	Total	**Detail**
Step 1: Track Physical Flow		
Beginning inventory on May 1	0	
Started during May	180,000	
Total physical units to account for	180,000	
		Step 2: Compute Equivalent Units
Units completed during May	155,000	155,000 = 155,000 × 100%
Units in process on May 31	25,000	5,000 = 25,000 × 20%
Total physical units accounted for	180,000	160,000 equivalent units
Step 3: Collect Costs to Allocate		
Costs incurred during May	$6,880,000	$4,320,000 + $2,560,000
Total costs to account for	$6,880,000	
Step 4: Calculate the Rate per Equivalent Unit		
Cost per equivalent unit	$43/eq. unit	$6,880,000/160,000 eq. units
Step 5: Allocate Costs		
Units completed during May (**COGM**)	$6,665,000	$43 × 155,000 eq. units
Units in process on May 31 (**EWIP**)	215,000	$43 × 5,000 eq. units
Total costs accounted for	$6,880,000	

3. *Collect costs to allocate.* Determine the total costs in the cost pool. For Chen, this equals the total manufacturing costs of $6,880,000 incurred during May.
4. *Calculate the rate per equivalent unit.* Divide the costs in the pool by the total equivalent units.
5. *Allocate costs.* Multiply the rate by the number of equivalent units in WIP and COGM to determine the proportion of total costs allocated to each of these accounts.

In Exhibit 15.1, we assume that Chen collects all manufacturing costs related to materials, labor, and overhead into a single pool. However, most process-costing systems use multiple cost pools, which we consider next.

Process Costing with Many Cost Pools and Beginning Inventory

LEARNING OBJECTIVE 2

Apply process costing to settings with many cost pools and beginning inventory.

Chen could refine its process-costing system to incorporate several additional considerations. We discuss two important refinements: using many cost pools rather than a single cost pool, and allowing for beginning inventory.

PROCESS COSTING WITH MANY COST POOLS

Processes often require inputs at different stages. For example, many plastic manufacturing applications need a form of resin or polymer at the start of the process. At later stages, they mix in additives such as antimicrobials and bio-stabilizers to enhance the properties of the plastic. In such instances, a batch may be "complete" in all respects with regard to some inputs, and only partially complete with regard to other inputs. Accordingly, it becomes necessary to track these inputs separately in a process-costing system. Otherwise, the calculation of equivalent units will be incorrect.

When Chen starts production of a DPD, it issues all of the required materials, such as the case, screen, and circuit boards, in one basket. This basket then moves through several stations for DPD assembly. Consider units that are only 20% complete. Chen would have issued all of the materials required for these units even though the firm has completed only 20% of the assembly task for these units.

Our revised understanding of Chen's production process highlights a problem with the allocation in Exhibit 15.1. There, we allocated costs as if each in-process unit had consumed 20% of the materials, 20% of the labor, and 20% of the overhead resources. This allocation is appropriate for the **conversion costs** (labor plus overhead costs) as Chen has completed only 20% of the assembly work. However, it is incorrect for the cost of materials because Chen has already issued *all* of the needed materials. We should charge the in-process units with 100% of the material costs.

To address this problem, we compute *separate* rates for materials costs and conversion costs. As Exhibit 15.2 shows, our revised computation of equivalent units of materials accounts for the fact that in-process units are 100% complete with respect to the cost of materials. However, we still use the 20% completion rate for labor and overhead to compute the equivalent units for these costs.

Notice that, compared to Exhibit 15.1, the value of WIP inventory increases by $465,000, while the value of COGM decreases by a like amount, representing a significant change from our earlier estimates. This change occurs because our revised computation fully accounts for the materials costs in the units that are still in process.

Exhibit 15.2	Chen Electronics: Process-Costing Report with Two Cost Pools		

	Total	Detail for each Cost Pool	
		Materials	Conversion
Step 1: Track Physical Flow			
Beginning inventory on May 1	0		
Started during May	180,000		
Total	180,000		
		Step 2: Compute Equivalent Units[1]	
Units completed during May	155,000	155,000	155,000
Units in process on May 31	25,000	25,000	5,000
Total	180,000	180,000	160,000
Step 3: Collect Costs to Allocate			
Costs incurred during May	$6,880,000	$4,320,000	$2,560,000
Total costs to account for	$6,880,000	$4,320,000	$2,560,000
Step 4: Calculate the Rate per Equivalent Unit			
Cost per equivalent unit[2]		$24/eq. unit of materials	$16/eq. unit of conversion
Step 5: Allocate Costs			
Units completed during May[3] (**COGM**)	$6,200,000	$3,720,000	$2,480,000
Units in process on May 31[4] (**EWIP**)	680,000	600,000	80,000
Total costs accounted for	$6,880,000	$4,320,000	$2,560,000

[1] Materials: 155,000 × 100% + 25,000 × 100%; Conversion: 155,000 × 100% + 25,000 × 20%.
[2] Materials: $4,320,000/180,000 eq. units = $24/eq. unit of materials;
   Conversion: $2,560,000/160,000 eq. units = $16/eq. unit of conversion.
[3] Materials: 155,000 eq. units × $24/eq. unit; Conversion: 155,000 eq. units × $16/eq. unit.
[4] Materials: 25,000 eq. units × $24/eq. unit; Conversion: 5,000 eq. units × $16/eq. unit.

We can further refine Chen's process-costing system to accommodate more than two cost pools. In this case, we would calculate a separate equivalent unit basis for each cost pool. As we discuss below, process-costing systems often have several cost pools for the different types of materials and labor used during the production process.

Materials Issued at Different Points

Firms often use separate cost pools for different materials, as their consumption patterns could differ. Suppose Chen's materials cost of $4,320,000 includes $4,041,000 for the cost of the materials that make up the DPD and $279,000 for the carton, bubble wrap, and pamphlet. Although Chen issues the materials needed to make the DPD at the start of the process, it uses packing materials only at the end of the process—after it has fully assembled the DPD but before the unit is transferred to the finished goods inventory.

The above change in the physical production process changes the consumption of materials by the in-process units. The in-process units have consumed all of the materials going into the DPD but none of the packing materials. Thus, Chen needs to use three cost pools—for DPD materials, for conversion, and for packing materials—to capture the consumption of the three types of resources appropriately. *Check It! Exercise #1* allows you to verify that Chen would have zero equivalent units of packing materials for the in-process units, as these units are 0% complete with respect to this resource.

Check It! Exercise #1

Using three cost pools, one for DPD materials, one for conversion costs, and one for packing materials, verify that the value of Chen's WIP inventory as of May 31 equals $641,250 and that Chen's COGM for May equals $6,238,750.

	Total	Detail for Each Cost Pool		
		DPD Materials	**Conversion**	**Packing**
Step 1: Track Physical Flow				
Beginning inventory on May 1	0			
Started during May	180,000			
Total units to account for	180,000			
		Step 2: Compute Equivalent Units		
Units completed during May	155,000	155,000	155,000	_____
Units in process on May 31	25,000	25,000	5,000	_____
Total units accounted for	180,000	180,000	160,000	155,000
Step 3: Collect Costs to Allocate				
Costs incurred during May	$6,880,000	$4,041,000	$2,560,000	$279,000
Total costs to account for	$6,880,000	$4,041,000	$2,560,000	$279,000
Step 4: Calculate the Rate per Equivalent Unit				
Cost per equivalent unit		_____	$16/eq. unit of conversion	_____
Step 5: Allocate Costs				
Units completed during May (COGM)	$6,238,750	_____	$2,480,000	$279,000
Units in process on May 31 (EWIP)	$641,250	_____	80,000	0
Total costs accounted for	$6,880,000	$4,041,000	$2,560,000	$279,000

Solution at end of chapter.

CONSIDERING BEGINNING INVENTORY

The presence of beginning inventory can complicate a process-costing system because the units in inventory produced in a prior period might have different costs than units produced during the current period. Most process-costing systems avoid this complication by using **weighted average process costs**. *These systems do not distinguish between the costs from the prior period and costs incurred during the current period.* Keep in mind that beginning inventory for this period is the ending inventory from the prior period. The value of this inventory would be determined by costs incurred in the prior period(s). We also incur costs this period for the work done currently. Under the weighted average method, we ignore *when* costs are actually incurred. We simply add the costs from beginning inventory and the costs incurred during the period to determine the total cost in the pool. We then follow the remaining process costing steps as before.

As you determined in *Check It! Exercise #1*, Chen will begin the month of June with an inventory of 25,000 physical units that have a value of $641,250. (Notice that we considered the month of May in Exhibits 15.1 and 15.2. Of course, the ending inventory for May becomes the beginning inventory for June). Suppose that Chen starts 175,000 additional units in June. It also incurs DPD materials costs of $4,038,750, conversion

Exhibit 15.3	*Chen Electronics: Process Costing Report for June (Beginning Inventory)*			
	Total	**Detail for each cost pool**		
		DPD Materials	**Conversion**	**Packing**
Step 1: Track Physical Flow				
Beginning inventory on June 1	25,000			
Started during June	175,000			
Total physical units to account for	200,000			
		Step 2: Compute Equivalent Units[1]		
Units completed during June	185,000	185,000	185,000	185,000
Units in process on June 30	15,000	15,000	9,000	0
Total physical units accounted for	200,000	200,000	194,000	185,000
Step 3: Collect Costs to Allocate				
Costs from beginning inventory	$641,250	$561,250	$80,000	$0
Costs incurred during June	7,192,500	4,038,750	2,830,000	323,750
Total costs to account for	$7,833,750	$4,600,000	$2,910,000	$323,750
Step 4: Calculate the Rate per Equivalent Unit				
Cost per equivalent unit[2]		$23/eq. unit of DPD materials	$15/eq. unit of conversion	$1.75/eq. unit of packing
Step 5: Allocate Costs				
Units completed during June[3] **(COGM)**	$7,353,750	$4,255,000	$2,775,000	$323,750
Units in process on June 30[4] **(EWIP)**	480,000	345,000	135,000	0
Total costs accounted for	$7,833,750	$4,600,000	$2,910,000	$323,750

[1] DPD Materials: 185,000 × 100% + 15,000 × 100%; Conversion: 185,000 × 100% + 15,000 × 60%; Packing: 185,000 × 100% + 15,000 × 0%.
[2] Materials: $4,600,000/200,000 eq. units = $23/eq. unit; Conversion: $2,910,000/194,000 eq. units = $15/eq. unit; packing: $323,750/185,000 = $1.75 per equivalent unit
[3] Materials: 185,000 eq. units × $23/eq. unit; Conversion: 185,000 eq. units × $15/eq. unit; Packing: 185,000 eq. units × $1.75/eq. unit.
[4] Materials: 15,000 eq. units × $23/eq. unit; Conversion: 9,000 eq. units × $15/eq. unit.

costs of $2,830,000, and packing costs of $323,750 during the month. On June 30, Chen has 15,000 DPDs still in process. These units are 60% complete with respect to conversion costs. Given Chen's production process, these units are 100% complete with respect to all materials that go into the DPD and 0% complete with respect to packing costs. Exhibit 15.3 illustrates Chen's process-costing report for June.

Focusing on DPD materials, Chen has to account for a total cost of $4,600,000. The firm needs to allocate this amount over 200,000 equivalent units. We then calculate a rate of $23 per equivalent unit of DPD materials, leading to an allocation of $4,255,000 to COGM and the remaining $345,000 to ending WIP. Note that we add the cost of materials in beginning inventory ($561,250) to the cost of materials incurred during June ($4,088,750) before arriving at a weighted average rate of $23 per equivalent unit of materials. We perform similar calculations for the other cost pools and then use these weighted average rates to value COGM and ending WIP.

Note that during May and June, Chen produced the same DPD in large quantities. Its production technologies and other processes were substantially the same. Yet, dividing total costs by total completed units, Chen values each unit completed in May at $40.25 ($6,238,750/155,000 units) but each unit completed in June at $39.75 ($7,353,750/185,000 units). This difference arises because Chen uses the *actual costs* each month to calculate the costs per equivalent unit. Such fluctuations are unavoidable because of minor variations in actual costs from month to month. In the next section, we discuss how firms can reduce the effect of these fluctuations in their accounting records.

Standard Process Costing

Recall from Chapter 14 that job-costing systems smooth fluctuations in product costs by using a predetermined rate to apply overhead to products. In a job-cost environment, firms compute a predetermined rate for overhead costs alone, as these are the only costs that the firm allocates. In process costing, however, a firm must also allocate the cost of materials and conversion. Therefore, it might use predetermined rates for these cost categories as well.

Predetermined rates for materials and labor come from a company's engineering standards that determine quantities and from expectations regarding materials prices and wage rates. Because the predetermined rates in process costing come from company standards, we refer to these rates as standard rates and to the system as a **standard costing** system.

Firms use standard process costing for two primary reasons. First, record keeping is easier because the method attaches the same value to each completed unit, without regard to the period in which the unit was made. Second, the standard cost of work done provides a natural benchmark for actual costs. Such a benchmark helps firms determine variances from expectations.

However, it takes considerable resources and effort to compute standard costs. It makes sense to employ standard costing only in those production environments where a firm makes similar or identical units in large quantities. Standard costing has less appeal in a job shop environment because each job is unique and would require a fresh set of standards.

CHAPTER CONNECTIONS
In Chapter 7, we used predetermined rates for materials and labor to come up with materials and labor budgets.

To apply a standard process-costing system, we use the standards for materials, labor, and overhead to value COGM and ending WIP. For example, Exhibit 15.4 shows the computations for Chen Electronics for May, assuming standard rates of $22.25, $15.75, and $1.85 per equivalent unit of DPD materials, conversion, and packing, respectively.

Looking at the last three lines of Exhibit 15.4, note that Chen allocated $6,811,750, while it actually incurred costs of $6,880,000 during the month. That is, Chen has underallocated total costs by $68,250. For each cost pool, Chen will accumulate such under- or overapplied amounts for the year. At the end of the year, Chen will dispose of the cumulative under- or overapplied amounts using one of the techniques that we discussed in Chapter 14.

Exhibit 15.4	*Chen Electronics: Standard Process Costing*			
	Total	**Detail for each Cost Pool**		
		DPD Materials	**Conversion**	**Packing**
Step 1: Track Physical Flow				
Beginning inventory on May 1	0			
Started during May	180,000			
Total	180,000			
		Step 2: Compute Equivalent Units		
Units completed during May	155,000	155,000	155,000	155,000
Units in process on May 31	25,000	25,000	5,000	0
Total physical units accounted for	180,000	180,000	160,000	155,000
Step 3: Collect Costs to Allocate	*Using predetermined rates—go to Step 4*			
Step 4: Calculate the Rate per Equivalent Unit				
Predetermined standard rate per equivalent unit		$22.25/eq. unit of DPD materials	$15.75/eq. unit of conversion	$1.85/eq. unit of packaging
Step 5: Allocate Costs				
Units completed during May[1] **(COGM)**	$6,176,750	$3,448,750	$2,441,250	$286,750
Units in process on May 31[2] (EWIP)	635,000	556,250	78,750	0
Total costs allocated	6,811,750	$4,005,000	$2,520,000	$286,750
Total costs allocated (from above)	$6,811,750	$4,005,000	$2,520,000	$286,750
Actual costs incurred in May[3]	6,880,000	4,041,000	2,560,000	279,000
Favorable (unfavorable) variance	($68,250)	($36,000)	($40,000)	$7,750

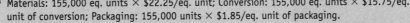

[1] Materials: 155,000 eq. units × $22.25/eq. unit; Conversion: 155,000 eq. units × $15.75/eq. unit of conversion; Packaging: 155,000 units × $1.85/eq. unit of packaging.

[2] Materials: 25,000 eq. units × $22.25/eq. unit; Conversion: 5,000 eq. units × $15.75/eq. unit of conversion; Packaging: 0 equivalent units.

[3] From *Check It! Exercise #1*.

CHAPTER CONNECTIONS

In Chapter 8, we discussed variance analysis, calculating cost variances as the difference between budgeted and actual results. Thus, favorable and unfavorable variances correspond to over- and underapplied amounts in the cost pool.

Check It! Exercise #2 extends Chen's standard process-costing system to June. Note that we use the standard costs for the work done in June as the benchmark for June's actual costs.

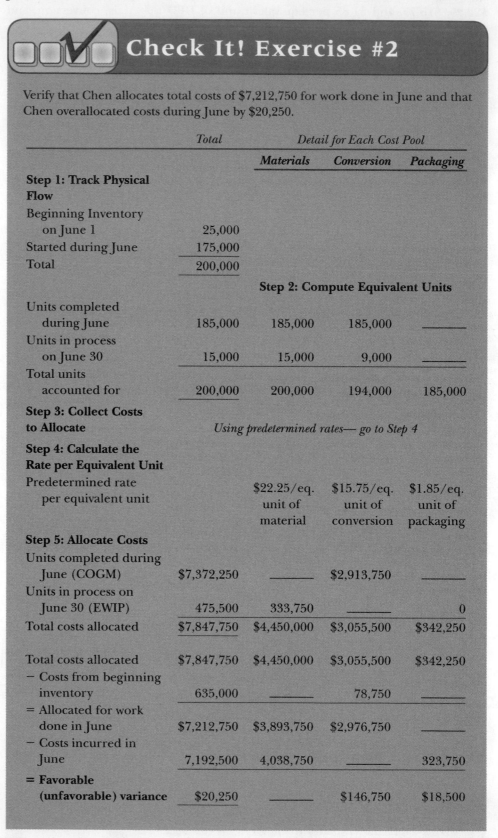

Check It! Exercise #2

Verify that Chen allocates total costs of $7,212,750 for work done in June and that Chen overallocated costs during June by $20,250.

	Total	Detail for Each Cost Pool		
		Materials	Conversion	Packaging
Step 1: Track Physical Flow				
Beginning Inventory on June 1	25,000			
Started during June	175,000			
Total	200,000			
		Step 2: Compute Equivalent Units		
Units completed during June	185,000	185,000	185,000	_____
Units in process on June 30	15,000	15,000	9,000	_____
Total units accounted for	200,000	200,000	194,000	185,000
Step 3: Collect Costs to Allocate	*Using predetermined rates— go to Step 4*			
Step 4: Calculate the Rate per Equivalent Unit				
Predetermined rate per equivalent unit		$22.25/eq. unit of material	$15.75/eq. unit of conversion	$1.85/eq. unit of packaging
Step 5: Allocate Costs				
Units completed during June (COGM)	$7,372,250	_____	$2,913,750	_____
Units in process on June 30 (EWIP)	475,500	333,750	_____	0
Total costs allocated	$7,847,750	$4,450,000	$3,055,500	$342,250
Total costs allocated	$7,847,750	$4,450,000	$3,055,500	$342,250
− Costs from beginning inventory	635,000	_____	78,750	_____
= Allocated for work done in June	$7,212,750	$3,893,750	$2,976,750	_____
− Costs incurred in June	7,192,500	4,038,750	_____	323,750
= Favorable (unfavorable) variance	$20,250	_____	$146,750	$18,500

Solution at end of chapter.

Connecting to Practice

BREAKFAST CEREALS AND PROCESS COSTING

The manufacturing process for breakfast cereals such as General Mills' *Wheaties*, marketed with the slogan, "the breakfast of champions," provides a classic setting for process costing. The production process combines raw materials such as wheat, sugar, salt, and preservatives in a continuously running mill. Almost all of the labor is indirect in this highly automated, high-volume production process. To stay competitive, General Mills likely tracks closely the costs of input materials, such as wheat and its conversion costs, as well as machine utilization. The firm also closely monitors packaging costs, a significant percentage of total costs.

COMMENTARY: General Mills may run a particular *Wheaties* box design for several weeks at a time (the firm frequently changes the packaging to highlight new champions). However, because it uses a standard costing system, the only change involves a change in the cost of the box. Standard costs and conversion rates also provide a natural benchmark for measuring operating efficiencies on a daily basis.

The manufacturing process for breakfast cereals such as General Mills' Wheaties, marketed with the slogan, "the breakfast of champions," provides a classic setting for process costing. (AP Photo/General Mills/©AP/ Wide World Photos)

SUMMARY

In this chapter, we studied process costing, a cost accumulation and reporting system found in firms that mass produce similar products over extended periods. We used the concept of equivalent units to deal with units belonging to the same batch being at different stages of completion. We then valued these equivalent units using average costs. Finally, we considered several common extensions of process-costing systems, including the use of many cost pools, the existence of beginning inventories, and the use of standard costs.

RAPID REVIEW

LEARNING OBJECTIVE 1

Explain the mechanics of process costing.

- Process-costing systems are suitable for environments that involve mass production of products. With continuous production or in settings with large batches, only part of a batch typically is completed during an accounting period. This means that we need to allocate costs between ending WIP and COGM.
- Process-costing systems use equivalent units to convert in-process units to equivalent completed units. We use equivalent units as the basis to allocate costs between ending WIP and COGM. We use percent completion to convert physical units into equivalent completed units.
- Process-costing reports use five steps: (1) track the physical flow, (2) compute equivalent units, (3) collect costs to allocate, (4) calculate the rate per equivalent unit, and (5) allocate costs.

LEARNING OBJECTIVE 2

Apply process costing to settings with many cost pools and beginning inventory.

- If we track materials and conversion costs in separate cost pools, then we should perform a separate computation of equivalent units for each pool. The computation for each pool reflects the percent of work completed for the resources whose costs are in the pool.
- If the firm begins a period with beginning inventory, it needs to make an inventory cost flow assumption. Most firms use the weighted average method for process costing. This method does not distinguish between the costs from beginning inventory and the costs incurred during the period.

LEARNING OBJECTIVE 3

Perform process costing using standard costs.

- Firms can streamline their process-costing systems by using standard rates to value the cost of materials, labor, and overhead in COGM and ending WIP inventory.

- The process of using standard rates gives rise to a variance (i.e., an under- or overapplied amount) in each cost pool. At year end, the firm needs to dispose of this balance using one of the options we discussed in Chapter 14.

ANSWERS TO CHECK IT! EXERCISES

Exercise #1: Equivalent packing units for units completed during May = 155,000 because these units are finished; equivalent packing units for units in process on May 31 = 0 because these units are yet to reach the packing stage; Cost per equivalent unit: $4,041,000/180,000 eq. units of material = $22.45 per equivalent unit of materials, and $279,000/155,000 eq. units of packing = $1.80 per eq. unit of packing. Materials cost of units completed during May, 155,000 eq. units × $22.45 per eq. unit of material = $3,479,750; Materials cost of units in process on May 31, 25,000 eq. units × $22.45 per eq. unit of material = $561,250.

Exercise #2: Equivalent packing for units completed during June = 185,000 because these units are finished; equivalent packing units for units in process on June 30 = 0 as these units are yet to reach the packing step; Materials cost of units completed in June = 185,000 units × $22.25 per eq. unit of materials = $4,116,250; packing cost of units completed in June is 185,000 units × $1.85 per eq. unit of packing = $342,250; conversion cost of work in process on June 30 is 9,000 units × $15.75 per eq. unit of conversion = $141,750.

Materials cost in beginning inventory = 25,000 eq. units × $22.25 per eq. unit of material = $556,250 (*Note:* the same standard costing rate would have been in force for May); Packing costs in beginning inventory = $0, as these units were still in process. Packing costs allocated for work done in June = $342,250. Labor cost incurred during June = $2,830,000; Materials variance in June = $145,000 U.

SELF-STUDY PROBLEMS

Kumar and Sons manufacture leather goods such as handbags and belts. In the process used for making belts, treated and dyed leather strips are first cut to their desired lengths. In the next step, the edges are folded over so that the belts can be stitched and trimmed. The belt buckle is added at the very end of the process, after the belts have been waxed and polished. Conversion costs are incurred uniformly throughout the process.

Kumar began the month of September with 500 36-inch two-tone belts in process valued at $1,100 (= $800 in materials + $300 in conversion costs). During September, Kumar started an additional 15,500 36-inch two-tone belts, completing 14,000 units during the month. Kumar also incurred $63,640 in manufacturing costs during September—$28,800 for materials (leather), $24,340 for conversion costs, and $10,500 for the buckles. Kumar estimates that the ending WIP inventory is 70% complete with respect to conversion costs.

Prepare a process costing report for Kumar and Sons for September.

Exhibit 15.5 provides the required report. Kumar values the 14,000 belts manufactured during September at $58,800, or $4.20 per belt. The ending work-in-process inventory of 2,000 belts is valued at $5,940, comprising $3,700 for the cost of the leather strips and $2,240 for conversion costs.

Exhibit 15.5	*Kumar and Sons: Process-Costing Report for September*				
		Total	**Detail for Each Cost Pool**		
			Leather Strips	*Conversion*	*Buckles*
Step 1: Track Physical Flow					
Beginning inventory on September 1		500			
Started during September		15,500			
Total physical units to account for		16,000			

| Exhibit 15.5 | Kumar and Sons: Process-Costing Report for September (continued) |

	Total	Detail for Each Cost Pool		
		Leather Strips	Conversion	Buckles
		Step 2: Compute Equivalent Units[2]		
Units completed during September	14,000	14,000	14,000	14,000
Units in process on September 30[1]	2,000	2,000	1,400	0
Total physical units accounted for	16,000	16,000	15,400	14,000
Step 3: Collect Costs to Allocate				
Costs from beginning inventory	$1,100	$800	$300	$0
Costs incurred during September	63,640	28,800	24,340	10,500
Total costs to account for	$64,740	$29,600	$24,640	$10,500
Step 4: Calculate the Rate per Equivalent Unit				
Cost per equivalent unit[3]		$1.85/eq. unit of strips	$1.60/eq. unit of conversion	$0.75/eq. unit of buckles
Step 5: Value Inventories				
Units completed during September[4] (COGM)	$58,800	$25,900	$22,400	$10,500
Units in process on September 30[5] (EWIP)	5,940	3,700	2,240	0
Total costs accounted for	$64,740	$29,600	$24,640	$10,500

[1] Ending inventory = Total units − completed units = 16,000 belts − 14,000 belts.
[2] Leather Strips: 14,000 × 100% + 2,000 × 100%; Conversion 14,000 × 100% + 2,000 × 70%; Buckles 14,000 × 100% + 2,000 × 0%.
[3] Leather Strips: $29,600/16,000 eq. units = $1.85/eq. unit; Conversion: $24,640/15,400 eq. units = $1.60/eq. unit; Buckles: $10,500/14,000 = $0.75 per equivalent unit.
[4] Leather Strips: 14,000 eq. units × $1.85/eq. unit; Conversion: 14,000 eq. units × $1.60/eq. unit; Buckles 14,000 eq. units × $0.75/eq. unit.
[5] Leather strips: 2,000 eq. units × $1.85/eq. unit; Conversion: 1,400 eq. units × $1.60/eq. unit.

GLOSSARY

Conversion costs The cost of resources, usually labor and overhead, required to convert input materials into finished goods.

Equivalent units The amount of output stated in terms of completed units. For example, 100 units in WIP that are 50% complete represent 50 equivalent units.

Process costing A costing method used by firms that mass produce similar products.

Process-costing report A format that shows the physical flow of materials, computations of equivalent units, and the allocation of total costs to WIP and COGM.

Standard costing A product-costing system that uses predetermined rates to value the materials, labor, and overhead costs.

Weighted average process costing A process-costing system that does not distinguish between the costs from beginning inventory and the costs incurred during the period.

REVIEW QUESTIONS

15.1 LO1. What production environments are most suitable for process costing?

15.2 LO1. What is the key difference between process costing and job costing?

15.3 LO1. What is an equivalent unit?

15.4 LO1. Why is the concept of an equivalent unit important in process costing?

15.5 LO1. Why is the concept of equivalent units not relevant for job costing?

15.6 LO1. What are the five steps in a process-costing report?

15.7 LO2. Why do many process-costing systems use multiple cost pools?

15.8 LO2. Suppose a factory accumulates costs in five separate cost pools. Would the equivalent units be different for each of these cost pools?

15.9 LO2. Consider the cost of materials. Why is the percentage completion for units that are finished during the period always 100%?

15.10 LO2. Consider the cost of materials added at the end of the process. Why is the percentage completion for units that are still in process always zero?

15.11 LO2. Why do most process-costing systems need to rely on an inventory cost flow assumption?

15.12 LO2. How does the weighted average process-costing system treat the costs of items in beginning inventory?

15.13 LO3. What is the key distinction between standard process costing and process costing using actual rates?

15.14 LO3. What are the two primary reasons firms use standard process costing?

15.15 LO3. How could you use standard process costing to obtain information that helps improve the efficiency of the process?

DISCUSSION QUESTIONS

15.16 LO1. Why is process costing suitable for a soft drink company but not well suited for a firm that makes luxury yachts?

15.17 LO1. What is the role for process costing in a Just-in-Time (JIT) production environment, where work-in-process inventories are negligible? For example, at any given point in time a JIT plant might only have 2 hours worth of production in process.

15.18 LO1. Why do we need process costing in industries that produce large batches of goods but not in firms that make their products in small batches?

15.19 LO1 (Advanced). Can you describe a revenue recognition setting in financial accounting that employs the concept of equivalent work? (*Hint:* Think of revenue recognition for large projects lasting several years.)

15.20 LO1. Process-costing systems involve steps where we *allocate* costs such as materials and labor that are directly traceable to a batch. Why do we need steps that allocate direct costs?

15.21 LO1. When calculating equivalent units, we assume that cost is proportional to work done. Why does this assumption make sense?

15.22 LO1. Who in the factory would be best equipped to provide estimates of the percent completion for work in process?

15.23 LO1 (Advanced). Suppose your production manager tells you that one-half the WIP is 20% complete in terms of conversion, and that the remainder is 70% complete. How would you modify the process-costing report to include this information?

15.24 LO2. The chapter illustrates how the process-costing template could be modified to include many kinds of materials, added at different points in the produc-

tion process. How could you modify process costing to include multiple overhead rates? Comment on the usefulness of such a modification for decision making.

15.25 LO2. How could we implement process costing in a plant that has a sequential production process? For example, assume a plant has two separate departments—parts are fabricated in department 1 and assembled in department 2.

15.26 LO2. Consider a multidepartment (or multistation) production environment in which not all products go though all processes. Why would we use process costing on a station-by-station basis in this setting? Does this setting reflect a blend of both job- and process-costing systems?

15.27 LO2. When you have beginning work-in-process inventory, why is the weighted average method preferred in practice over the First-In-First-Out (FIFO) and Last-In-First-Out (LIFO) methods?

15.28 LO2. In process costing, the volume of production for a period is likely to be much greater than the volume in inventory at any given point in time. This feature means that the value of inventory is a small fraction of the value of output. How does this feature help firms justify the use of the weighted average method for process costing?

15.29 LO3. How does standard process costing relate to variance analysis? Is variance analysis likely to be more or less informative in a process-costing setting relative to a job-costing setting?

15.30 LO3 (Advanced). How could you modify standard process costing so that individual batches generally follow the same process, but some batches have some unique steps (e.g., extra finishing)?

EXERCISES

15.31 Mechanics of process costing, steps 1 and 2 (LO1). Orange Computers began June with zero units of its portable music player in work-in-process inventory. During June, Orange started 250,000 units into production, completing 175,000 units by month's end. Production personnel estimate that the 75,000 units still in process on June 30 are 100% complete with respect to materials and 40% complete with respect to conversion costs.

Required: Complete steps 1 and 2 of Orange's process-costing report for June.

15.32 Mechanics of process costing, steps 1–4 (LO1). Refer to Problem 15.31. You learn that Orange spent $18,750,000 on materials costs and $7,790,000 on conversion costs during June.

Required: Complete steps 3 and 4 of Orange's process-costing report for June.

15.33 Mechanics of process costing, steps 1–4 (LO1). Refer to Problem 15.32.

Required: Complete steps 1–5 of Orange's process-costing report for June. What is Orange's cost of goods manufactured (COGM) for June and the cost of its work-in-process inventory (EWIP) on June 30?

15.34 Process-costing report, no beginning inventory, single-cost pool (LO1). The Cruise Salad Company began March with zero cases of its Thousand Island dressing in work-in-process inventory. During March, Cruise started 125,000 cases into production. On March 31, Cruise had 25,000 cases still in process, which production personnel estimated to be 30% complete.

Cruise accumulates all of its manufacturing costs in a single pool. During March, Cruise spent a total of $3,225,000 on manufacturing costs for its Thousand Island dressing.

Required:

a. Compute the number of cases finished during March.

b. Compute the number of equivalent units for cases finished during March and for cases still in process at the end of March.

c. Compute the total costs to account for.

d. Determine the cost per equivalent case.

e. Determine the cost of the cases finished during March and the cost of the cases still in process at the end of March. (The total of these two amounts should equal your answer for part (c) above.)

15.35 Process-costing report, no beginning inventory, two cost pools (LO1, LO2). Mahaska Chemicals makes a patented fertilizer in its Naperville, Illinois plant. The production process begins by mixing all of the required materials. In a series of steps, the mixed slurry is converted to a finished fertilizer that is bagged and sold. Mahaska incurs conversion costs uniformly throughout the process.

Mahaska shut its plant down for major maintenance during November and began December with zero pounds of fertilizer in beginning inventory. Mahaska started 645,000 pounds of material into production in early December and had 95,000 pounds still in process on December 31. Mahaska estimates the ending work-in-process (EWIP) inventory to be 20% complete with respect to conversion costs. (Because all materials are added at the start of the process, ending WIP is 100% complete with respect to materials.) Finally, Mahaska spent $1,935,000 on materials and $1,024,200 on conversion costs during December.

Required:

a. Compute the quantity of fertilizer completed during December.

b. Compute the number of equivalent units for pounds finished during December and for pounds still in process at the end of December. Be sure to perform the exercise separately for materials and for conversion costs.

c. Compute the total costs to account for.

d. Determine the cost per equivalent pound for materials and for conversion costs.

e. Determine the cost of the fertilizer finished during December and the cost of the WIP inventory on December 31.

15.36 Working backwards (LO1): Kang Industries provides the following partially complete process-cost report.

Item	Equivalent Units of Material	Equivalent Units of Conversion	Value
Ending WIP inventory	10,000	7,000	?
Cost of goods completed & transferred out	90,000	90,000	$270,000

The cost of goods completed and transferred out contains $162,000 toward the cost of materials and $108,000 toward conversion cost.

Required: Determine the value of Kang's ending WIP inventory.

15.37 Working backwards (LO1): Baiman and Company informs you that it completed 110,000 units during November, valued at $550,000. Its cost per equivalent unit of conversion is $2.00. Finally, you learn that Baiman has 20,000 units in ending WIP, 50% complete with respect to conversion. Baiman adds all materials at the start of the process.

Required: Determine the value of Baiman's ending WIP inventory.

15.38 Standard process costing (LO3). Igloo Electronics makes cell phones under contract to a *Chaebol*, which is the Korean term for a conglomerate. Igloo began work on a new contract in January. During January, Igloo started 150,000 units into production, completing and shipping 145,000 phones by the end of the month. Igloo estimates the remaining 5,000 units to be 30% complete with respect to conversion costs.

Igloo is primarily an assembler because the *Chaebol* supplies the casing, screens, circuit boards, and other needed materials. Thus, Igloo accumulates all costs into a single-cost pool—conversion costs. Igloo actually spent $2,270,750 on conversion costs during January.

Igloo uses standard process costing to value its inventories. Specifically, it values each equivalent unit of work (for conversion) at $15.

Required: Compute Igloo's conversion cost variance for January.

 15.39 Process-costing report, no beginning inventory, two cost pools (LO1, LO2). Rhino Car Wax makes its best-selling car wax in Mobile, Alabama. The production process begins by mixing all of the required materials. In a series of steps, the mix is then converted to a finished car wax paste. Rhino incurs conversion costs uniformly throughout the process.

Rhino began March with zero cases of car wax in beginning inventory. On March 1, Rhino started enough material for 74,500 cases of finished wax. By the end of March, Rhino had completed work on 63,250 cases, and assessed ending WIP inventory to be 60% complete with respect to conversion costs. Finally, Rhino spent $782,250 on materials and $1,697,500 on conversion costs during March.

Required:

Prepare a process-cost report to compute the cost of the cases of car wax finished during March and the cost of the cases still in process as of March 31.

15.40 Standard process costing, no beginning inventory (LO3). Refer to the information for Rhino Car Wax in the previous exercise. Rather than using actual costs, assume that Rhino uses standard process costing to value its inventories. Rhino values each equivalent unit of materials at $10 and each equivalent unit of conversion costs at $25.

Required:

a. Prepare Rhino's standard process-costing report for March. What is the cost of the cases of car wax finished during March and the cost of the cases still in process on March 31?

b. Compute Rhino's materials variance and conversion cost variance for March.

15.41 Process-costing report, no beginning inventory, three cost pools (LO1, LO2). Demski Technologies specializes in making surgical instruments. The firm closely collaborates with a German company that provides all of the needed technical expertise. The production process begins with a block of specially formulated, surgical-quality stainless steel. The instrument is formed after a number of operations to shape and trim the metal. The final step in the operation is to test each instrument for manufacturing and other defects.

Demski began July with zero instruments in process. During July, Demski began work on 4,000 instruments, completing 3,500 by month's end. Demski estimates that the units still in process as of July 31 are 30% complete with respect to conversion costs. Finally, Demski spent $600,000 on materials costs, $1,095,000 on conversion costs, and $612,500 on testing costs during July.

Required: Prepare Demski's process-costing report for July.

15.42 Process-costing report, no beginning inventory, materials added at different points (LO1, LO2). The Jogirushi Company makes a line of premium rice cookers, specially designed for the Japanese market. In February, Jogirushi launched a new model that is exclusively made in its Osaka factory.

The production process for the new model begins by forming sheet metal, the primary material, into the appropriate shape. The heating element and other electrical items are added when the unit is 40% complete. As the last step in the production process, the unit is packed in an attractive box. Jogirushi incurs conversion costs uniformly throughout the process.

During February, Jogirushi began production on 23,500 units, completing 21,200 units by month's end. Jogirushi estimates these in-process units to be 50% complete with respect to conversion costs.

During February, Jogirushi spent ¥10,575,000 on sheet metal, ¥58,750,000 on the heating element and other electrical items, ¥33,525,000 on conversion costs, and ¥12,720,000 on packing costs. (Note: ¥ is the symbol for the Yen, the Japanese unit of currency).

Required:

a. Compute the equivalent units for sheet metal, the heating element and other electrical items, conversion costs, and packing materials for Jogirushi for February.

b. Using your answer to part (a), prepare Jogirushi's process-costing report for February.

15.43 Process-costing report, working backwards (LO1, LO2). Yum Yum makes jams and other preserves from seasonal fruits and berries. The production process begins with the berries and sugar. After processing, Yum Yum packs the finished jams into glass containers prior to shipping them.

Yum Yum began June with zero cases of jam in work-in-process inventory. During June, Yum Yum started into production enough berries for 20,000 cases of jam. However, only 18,000 cases were completed during the month, with the remaining in-process cases being 80% complete at month's end. Yum Yum incurs conversion costs uniformly throughout the process.

Yum Yum estimates that the cost of the berries and sugar for the *finished cases* (i.e., COGM) equals $2,160,000. The cost of packing cases amounts to $450,000. Yum Yum further estimates that *ending WIP inventory* contains $36,000 in conversion costs.

Required:

Compute the total amount that Yum Yum spent on berries and sugar, conversion costs, and packing costs during June.

PROBLEMS

15.44 Process-costing report, beginning inventory, single-cost pool (LO1, LO2). The Cruise Salad Company began April with 25,000 cases of its Thousand Island dressing in work-in-process inventory. This inventory was valued at $225,000. During April, Cruise started 125,000 cases into production. On April 30, Cruise had 15,000 cases still in process, which production personnel estimate to be 50% complete.

Cruise accumulates all of its manufacturing costs in a single pool. During April, Cruise spent a total of $3,978,750 on manufacturing costs for its Thousand Island dressing.

Required:

a. Compute the number of cases finished during April.

b. Compute the number of equivalent units for cases finished during April and for cases still in process at the end of April.

c. Compute the total costs to account for.

d. Determine the cost per equivalent case.

e. Determine the cost of the cases finished during April and the cost of cases still in process at the end of April.

15.45 Process-costing report, beginning inventory, two cost pools (LO1, LO2). Orange Computers began July with 75,000 units of its portable music player in work-in-process inventory. These units were 100% complete with respect to materials and 40% complete with respect to conversion costs. Orange valued this inventory at $6,765,000, comprising $5,625,000 in materials costs and $1,140,000 in conversion costs.

During July, Orange started another 150,000 units to production and completed a total of 200,000 units by month's end. Production personnel estimate that the 25,000 units still in process on July 31 are 100% complete with respect to materials and 50% complete with respect to conversion costs. Finally, Orange spent $11,475,000 on materials costs and $7,147,500 on conversion costs during July.

Required: Complete Orange's process-costing report for July. What is Orange's cost of goods manufactured (COGM) for July and the cost of its work-in-process inventory (WIP) on July 31?

15.46 Process-costing report, beginning inventory, two cost pools (LO1, LO2). Damon and Company uses the weighted-average method of process costing. On January 1, the units in work-in-process (WIP) inventory were 100% complete with respect to materials and 60% complete with respect to conversion. Materials costs in beginning WIP were $330,000, and conversion costs were $432,000. Damon provides the following additional information:

- The 100,000 units in ending work-in-process (EWIP) inventory on December 31 were 100% complete with respect to materials and 80% complete with respect to conversion.
- 990,000 units started in production. Costs added during the year were $2,970,000 for materials and $1,728,000 for conversion.
- During the year, 1,000,000 units were completed and transferred to finished goods. There was no finished goods inventory on January 1. 800,000 units were sold.

Required:

a. How many units were there in beginning work-in-process (WIP) inventory on January 1?

b. Calculate the total equivalent units with respect to conversion.

c. Compute the cost per equivalent unit for materials.

d. What is the cost of the December 31, 20 × 1 work-in-process inventory?

15.47 Process-costing report, beginning inventory, two cost pools (LO1, LO2). Chang's Office Furniture manufactures office furniture by using an assembly-line process. All direct materials are introduced at the start of the process, and conversion cost is incurred evenly throughout manufacturing. An examination of the company's work-in-process account for August revealed the following selected information:

August 1 balances:	900 units, 30% complete
Value of beginning inventory	$133,800*
Production started in August	2,700 units
Direct materials used during August	$270,000
August conversion cost	$154,200
Production completed	2,100 units

* Supplementary records disclosed direct material cost of $90,000 and conversion cost of $43,800.

Conversations with manufacturing personnel revealed that the ending work in process was 80% complete.

Required:

a. Determine the number of units in the August 31 work-in-process inventory.

b. Calculate the total equivalent units with respect to conversion.

c. Calculate the cost per equivalent unit with respect to conversion in August.

d. Determine the cost of the August 31 work-in-process inventory.

 15.48 Process-costing report, beginning inventory, two cost pools (LO1, LO2). Ace Chemical Company manufactures and sells a cleaning solution. All direct materials are added at the beginning of the manufacturing process. A review of the inventory cost records disclosed the following information about the month of August:

	Units	Materials	Labor	Overhead
WIP August 1 (72% complete with respect to conversion)	?	$1,260,000	$170,000	$510,000
Units started into production during August	2,200,000			
Costs incurred during August		$3,900,000	$5,500,000	$16,500,000

During the month of August, 1,800,000 units were completed and transferred to finished goods inventory. There were 600,000 units, 60% complete with respect to conversion, in the work-in-process account on August 31.

Required:

a. How many units were in the work-in-process account on August 1?

b. Calculate the total equivalent units with respect to conversion for the month of August.

c. Determine the cost of goods manufactured for the month of August.

15.49 Process-costing report, beginning inventory, two cost pools (LO1, LO2). Guess Company manufactures a variety of natural fabrics for the clothing industry.

The following cost data are available for the month of January.

Items	Materials	Conversion
Cost of WIP on 1/1/ XX	$ 95,000	$112,000
Costs incurred during January	$ 85,000	$200,000

There were 80,000 units in process on January 1 (100% complete as to direct material and 60% complete as to conversion). The firms started 100,000 units into production in January. During January, 120,000 units were completed and transferred to finished goods. There was no finished goods inventory on January 1. We also know that 110,000 units were sold during January.

The units in ending work-in-process (EWIP) inventory on January 31 were 100% complete with respect to materials and 60% complete with respect to conversion.

Required:

a. How many units were there in ending work-in-process (WIP) inventory on January 31?

b. Calculate the total equivalent units with respect to conversion.

c. Compute the cost per equivalent unit for materials.

d. What is the cost of goods *sold* during January?

e. Suppose Guess also had beginning finished goods of 5,000 units with a unit cost of $2.90. Furthermore, Guess uses FIFO to value finished goods inventories. What is the cost of goods *sold* during January?

15.50 Process-costing report, beginning inventory, two cost pools (LO1, LO2). Tom & Jerry Corporation processes and packages ice cream. The following data are available. Conversion activity occurs uniformly throughout the production process.

Work in process, June 1—15,000 units:	
Direct material: 100% complete, cost of	$16,250
conversion: 90% complete, cost of	$85,000
Units completed during June and transferred out to finished-goods inventory	190,300
Work in process, June 30—45,200 units:	
Direct material: 100% complete	
Conversion: 75% complete	
Costs incurred during June:	
Direct material	$165,085
Conversion costs:	
Direct labor	$76,300
Applied manufacturing overhead	$235,534
Total conversion costs	$311,834

Required:

a. How many units were started during June?

b. Calculate the cost per equivalent unit with respect to conversion for the month of June.

c. Determine the cost of the June 30 work-in-process inventory. Clearly identify and label your final answer.

15.51 Process-costing report, beginning inventory, two cost pools (LO1, LO2). Mahaska Chemicals makes a patented fertilizer in its Naperville, Illinois plant. The production process begins by mixing all of the required materials. In a series of steps, the mixed slurry is converted to a finished fertilizer that is bagged and sold. Mahaska incurs conversion costs uniformly throughout the process.

Mahaska began January with 95,000 pounds of fertilizer in process, valued at $319,200. This value equals $285,000 for materials plus $34,200 for conversion costs. Mahaska started an additional 600,000 pounds into production in early January and had a total of 55,000 pounds still in process on January 31. The ending WIP inventory was estimated to be 25% complete with respect to conversion costs. Finally, Mahaska spent $1,869,500 on materials and $1,077,175 on conversion costs during January.

Required:

a. Compute the quantity of fertilizer completed during January.

b. Compute the number of equivalent units for pounds finished during January and for pounds still in process at the end of January. Be sure to perform the exercise separately for materials and for conversion costs.

    c. Compute the total costs that must be accounted for.

    d. Determine the cost per equivalent pound for materials and for conversion costs.

    e. Determine the cost of the fertilizer finished during January and the cost of the WIP inventory on January 31.

15.52 Process-costing report, beginning inventory, two cost pools (LO1, LO2). Rhino Car Wax makes its best-selling car wax in Mobile, Alabama. The production process begins by mixing all of the required materials. In a series of steps, the mix is then converted to a finished car wax paste. Rhino incurs conversion costs uniformly throughout the process.

Rhino began April with 11,250 cases of car wax in beginning work-in-process inventory. These cases were valued at $281,812.50, with $118,125 being the cost of materials and the remainder being conversion costs. Rhino estimated its April beginning WIP inventory to be 100% complete with respect to materials and 60% complete with respect to conversion costs.

On April 1, Rhino started enough material for 80,000 cases of the finished wax. By the end of April, Rhino had completed work on a total of 85,000 cases and assessed ending WIP inventory to be 70% complete with respect to conversion costs. Finally, Rhino spent $830,875 on materials and $2,008,125 on conversion costs during April.

Required:

Prepare Rhino's process-costing report for April. What is Rhino's COGM for April and the cost of its ending WIP inventory on April 30?

15.53 Standard process costing, beginning inventory (LO1, LO2, LO3). Refer to the information for Rhino Car Wax in the previous problem. Rather than using actual costs, assume that Rhino uses standard process costing to value its inventories. Rhino values each equivalent unit of materials at $10 and each equivalent unit of conversion costs at $25.

Required:

    a. Prepare Rhino's process-costing report for April. What is the cost of cases of car wax finished during April and the cost of the cases still in process on April 30?

    b. Compute Rhino's materials variance and conversion cost variance for April. (*Note:* Be sure to compute the standard cost of the *work done in April* as the basis for comparing actual costs incurred in April).

15.54 Process-costing report, beginning inventory, three cost pools (LO1, LO2). Demski Technologies specializes in making surgical instruments. The firm closely collaborates with a German company that provides all of the needed technical expertise. The production process begins with a block of specially formulated, surgical-quality stainless steel. The instrument is formed after a number of operations to shape and trim the metal. The final step in the operation is to test each instrument for manufacturing and other defects.

Demski began August with 500 instruments in work-in-process inventory. The 500 instruments were valued at $120,000, comprising $75,000 in materials plus $45,000 in conversion costs. During August, Demski started another 4,500 instruments into production, completing a total of 4,600 instruments by month's end. Demski estimates that the units still in process on August 31 are 40% complete with respect to conversion costs. Finally, Demski spent $685,000 on materials costs, $1,335,400 on conversion costs, and $828,000 on testing costs during August.

Required: Prepare Demski's process-costing report for August.

15.55 Process-costing report, beginning inventory, materials added at different points (LO1, LO2). The Jogirushi Company makes a line of premium rice cookers, specially designed for the Japanese market. In February, Jogirushi launched a new model that is exclusively made in its Osaka factory.

The production process for the new model begins by forming sheet metal, the primary material, into the appropriate shape. The heating element and other electrical items are added when the unit is 40% complete. As the last step in the production process, the unit is packed in an attractive box. Jogirushi incurs conversion costs uniformly throughout the process.

Jogirushi began May with an inventory of 2,300 units, which were 50% complete with respect to conversion costs. These units were valued at ¥8,360,000 (= ¥1,035,000 for sheet metal, ¥5,600,000 for the heating element and other electrical items, and ¥1,725,000 for conversion costs). During May, Jogirushi began production on an additional 25,000 units. At the end of May, Jogirushi had 2,200 units still in process, estimated to be 30% complete with respect to conversion.

During May, Jogirushi spent ¥11,523,000 on sheet metal, ¥55,895,000 on the heating element and other electrical items, ¥39,491,000 on conversion costs, and ¥15,311,000 on packing costs. (*Note:* ¥ is the symbol for the Yen, the Japanese unit of currency.)

Required:

a. Compute the equivalent units for sheet metal, the heating element and other electrical items, conversion costs, and packing materials for Jogirushi for May.

b. Using your answer to part (a), prepare Jogirushi's process-costing report for May.

15.56 Standard process costing, beginning inventory (LO3). Igloo Electronics makes cell phones under contract to a *Chaebol.* Continuing work on an existing contact, Igloo began February with 5,000 units in process that were 30% complete. During February, Igloo started an additional 145,000 units into production, completing and shipping a total of 148,000 phones by the end of the month. Igloo estimates the remaining 2,000 units to be 20% complete with respect to conversion costs.

Igloo is primarily an assembler, for the contractor supplies the casing, screens, circuit boards, and other needed materials. Thus, Igloo accumulates all costs into a single-cost pool—conversion costs. Igloo actually spent $2,245,000 on conversion costs during February.

Igloo uses standard process costing to value its inventories. Specifically, it values each equivalent unit of work (for conversion) at $15.

Required:

Compute Igloo's conversion cost variance for February. (*Note:* Be sure to compare the actual cost for February with the standard cost of the work done in February.)

MINI-CASES

15.57 Multiple materials, ending work in process at differing stages of completion, standard process costing (LO1, LO2, LO3). The Shalimar Paint Company makes a variety of latex- and oil-based paints for interior and exterior use. The process for making paint is virtually the same regardless of the color. Because it takes considerable time and effort to switch colors, however, the firm uses a sophisticated model to schedule colors, usually going from lighter to darker shades. Further, Shalimar produces a large quantity of each color, counting each color as a batch. Consequently, Shalimar uses a process-costing system to value its inventories.

The production process begins by mixing all of the needed materials. After a series of steps, the paint is filled in gallon-sized cans when the conversion process is 95% complete. Shalimar incurs conversion costs uniformly throughout the process.

On April 1, Shalimar had 45,000 gallons of lilac paint in work-in-process inventory. Shalimar valued this inventory at $280,350, comprising $198,000 for materials and $82,350 for conversion costs. Moreover, Shalimar estimates that its beginning WIP inventory on April 1 is 60% complete with respect to conversion costs.

During April, Shalimar started an additional 145,000 gallons of lilac paint into production. On April 30, Shalimar had only 5,000 gallons of lilac paint still in process. Of this amount, 4,000 gallons were 50% complete with respect to conversion costs, while the remaining 1,000 gallons were 98% complete with respect to conversion costs.

Shalimar spent $657,000 on materials, $481,590 on conversion costs, and $139,500 on cans during April.

Required:

a. Prepare Shalimar's process-costing report for April. What is Shalimar's cost of goods manufactured for lilac paint for April? What is the cost of Shalimar's April 30 work-in-process inventory of lilac paint?

b. Assume Shalimar uses standard process costing to value its inventories, valuing each equivalent unit for materials, conversion costs, and cans at standard costs of $4.40, $2.95, and $0.78, respectively. Compute Shalimar's materials variance, conversion cost variance, and can variance for April. (*Note:* Be sure to compare the actual costs with the standard cost for the work done in April.)

Chapter 16

Support Activity and Dual-Rate Allocations

SILVERMAN & ABBAS CONSULTING (SAC) SPECIALIZES IN designing multistory office complexes. At any given point in time, SAC works on dozens of contracts. Each contract uses activities such as structural engineering, electrical engineering, and plumbing. In addition to these *line activities*, SAC also has *support activities* such as human resources (HR), information technology (IT), purchasing, and administration.

SAC needs to track the costs for each contract for the purposes of billing and cost control. The firm has no difficulty in assigning the cost of line activities to individual contracts. Each person executing a line activity keeps a time sheet to record the time spent on the various contracts, and SAC traces the cost of materials used. However, SAC finds it difficult to deal with the cost of the support activities. For instance, only some of the purchasing activity relates directly to contracts. The purchasing activity also supports other line (plumbing) and support (IT) activities. In turn, the IT activity services both plumbing (line) and purchasing (support).

Ultimately, SAC knows that all of the activities benefit the contracts, meaning that all of the costs must be allocated to contracts. SAC seeks your help in disentangling the flow of costs to better estimate the cost of each contract.

Silverman & Abbas Consulting, which specializes in designing multistory office complexes, has support activities *such as human resources (HR), information technology (IT), purchasing, and administration. The company wants to know how to allocate the cost of the support activities to individual building contracts.*

LEARNING OBJECTIVES

After studying this chapter, you will be able to:

1 Distinguish between line activities and support activities.

2 Explain three methods used to allocate the costs of support activities to products.

3 Discuss the need for dual-rate allocations.

As we learned in Chapters 9 and 10, both traditional and activity-based costing systems have two stages of allocation. In the first stage, we group costs into cost pools that correspond to individual departments or activities. In the second stage, we allocate all costs from each cost pool directly to products. In this chapter, we consider settings in which we cannot justify allocating all costs directly to products because of interactions among the cost pools. These complex settings, of which SAC is an example, are quite common in practice.

We begin by distinguishing between line activities and support activities. We highlight the need for maintaining separate cost pools for these two different types of activities. We then discuss the flow of costs through these cost pools to the final product, and the complexities that arise because of *reciprocity of consumption* among support activities. We present three methods that firms commonly use in these situations, and discuss their relative merits and weaknesses. Finally, we discuss how dual-rate allocations can further aid decision making when allocating costs.

CHAPTER CONNECTIONS
The refinements we consider in this chapter are an extension of the product-costing systems we studied in Chapters 8 and 9.

Line and Support Activities

LEARNING OBJECTIVE 1

Distinguish between line activities and support activities.

A **line activity** directly relates to producing services or products. (The associated departments are often called line departments.) Structural and electrical engineering are line activities at SAC. Costs incurred in these departments are almost *fully* traceable to contracts undertaken. In manufacturing, the activities of production departments such as machining, assembly, and shipping are line activities. In merchandising, the sales force and store management execute line activities. A **support activity** is not directly related to making or selling a product or service but is needed to run the business. All firms need someone to handle payroll even if payroll processing does not directly relate to the firm's products or services.

For simplicity, we only considered line activities in our discussions in Chapters 9 and 10. Exhibit 16.1 shows such a two-stage allocation system, with four cost pools for four distinct activities. Recall that in the first stage of the allocation process in such systems, we group into cost pools all of the costs that we wish to allocate. These cost pools may correspond to departments in a traditional system or activities in an ABC system. In the second stage, we identify appropriate cost drivers for each pool, determine the denominator volume, and calculate the allocation rate. Using this rate, we allocate costs to individual products or jobs. We represent this second-stage allocation by the arrows linking cost pools and cost objects.

The flow of costs shown in Exhibit 16.1 implicitly assumes that products or contracts account for the *entire* activity volume corresponding to *all* cost pools. In practice, this assumption is only valid for cost pools that correspond to line activities.

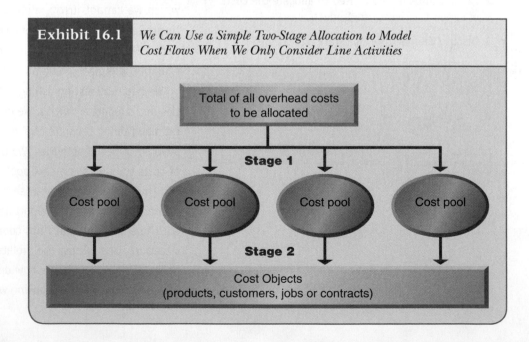

Exhibit 16.1 *We Can Use a Simple Two-Stage Allocation to Model Cost Flows When We Only Consider Line Activities*

Cost flows for support activities do not follow this simple pattern because the final cost objects (products, customers, jobs, or contracts) do not account for all of the support provided. Consider purchasing. In SAC, the Purchasing Department acquires the direct materials required for individual contracts. This department is also responsible for acquiring the supplies required by other line departments such as structural engineering *and* the supplies required by support departments such as HR, IT, and administration. In such instances, it is inappropriate to allocate all costs incurred by the Purchasing Department directly to the contracts. Some of the costs should surely be allocated directly to contracts. But some should be allocated to line departments and others to other support departments. That is, some of the costs of purchasing, itself a support activity, must flow through other line and support activities before being allocated to contracts.

When modeling this cost flow, **reciprocity in consumption** among support activities (departments) complicates cost allocation procedures. To see why, consider a second support activity. Like purchasing, HR supports both line activities such as plumbing, and support activities such as purchasing. As with purchasing, we need to allocate HR costs in proportion to use. But doing so creates a circularity. The cost of purchasing (some of which we must allocate to HR) includes an allocation from HR (which includes some costs from purchasing).

Exhibit 16.2 shows the consumption of activities and flow of costs when there is reciprocity in consumption. In this exhibit, we represent the flows among cost pools by the dotted lines. We label the support activity pools as SA1 and SA2, and the line activity pools LA1 and LA2. Notice that the costs in the pool for support activity 1 (SA1) benefit the final cost objects such as products, the activity in SA2, and the activities in the two line departments (LA1 and LA2). Likewise, costs in the pool for support activity 2 (SA2) benefit products, the support activity in SA1, and the two line activities (LA1 and LA2). However, costs in the pools for line activities are all allocated to the cost objects.

Accounting for reciprocity among support activities is important for two reasons. First, it increases the accuracy of cost estimates. SAC can therefore make more effective decisions. Second, allocating the cost of support departments helps line managers become aware of the costs of the services they consume. In decentralized firms, different managers likely oversee the activities connected with the different cost

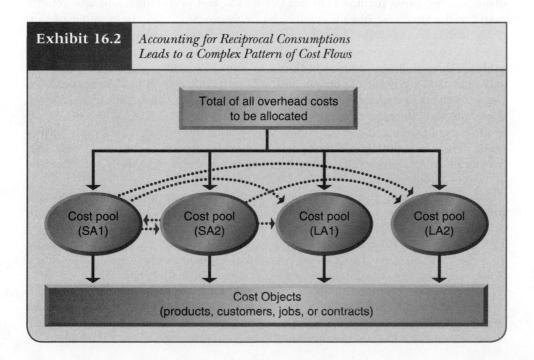

Exhibit 16.2 *Accounting for Reciprocal Consumptions Leads to a Complex Pattern of Cost Flows*

Total of all overhead costs to be allocated

Cost pool (SA1) Cost pool (SA2) Cost pool (LA1) Cost pool (LA2)

Cost Objects
(products, customers, jobs, or contracts)

CHAPTER CONNECTIONS

Understanding the costs of support departments is similar to the transfer-pricing problem we studied in Chapter 12. The key difference is that we view most support departments as cost centers, meaning that there is no demand for a markup over cost. Consistent with tradition, we employ the term transfer price *only for transfers among profit or investment centers, in which case the manager of the selling division demands a profit markup.*

pools. Cost allocation rates serve as the implicit "price" for the services line managers obtain from other support departments. Pricing such internal services correctly is critical because too high a price can lead managers to economize too much on a support resource and too low a price can lead to wasteful consumption.

Methods for Allocating Support Activity Costs

Explain three methods used to allocate the costs of support activities to products.

Firms can use one of three methods to allocate support activity costs to the other cost pools and to final cost objects: the direct method, the step-down method, and the reciprocal method. We illustrate these three methods in the context of SAC. The individual allocations in each of the three methods follow the general framework we developed in Chapter 9. Key differences relate to the sequence in which we allocate costs and the extent to which the method accounts for the reciprocity in consumption.

Let us begin by collecting some data. Consider the pattern of cost flows at SAC, restricting attention to only two pools for support activities (purchasing and administration), two pools for line activities (structural and plumbing), and one generic pool for the final cost objects (contracts). Suppose SAC uses the number of purchase orders as the cost driver for allocating purchasing costs. SAC knows that it issues 1,050 purchase orders each year, including 50 for supplies used by purchasing itself. Of the remainder, administration consumes 150 orders, plumbing 255 orders, and structural accounts 425 orders, with 170 orders directly traceable to contracts. Using this data, a useful first step for *all three methods* is to convert these activity volumes into the percentages of activities consumed.

One complication that arises is how to deal with the orders used by purchasing itself. When computing percentages for allocating costs, we ignore such **self-consumption** of a support function. Ignoring self-consumption does not affect the accuracy of allocations.

For SAC, ignoring the self-consumption of 50 orders reduces the denominator volume for purchase orders to 1,000 orders. We then calculate the consumption percentages as $150/1,000 = 15\%$, $255/1,000 = 25.5\%$, $425/1,000 = 42.5\%$ and $170/1,000 = 17\%$ for administration, structural, plumbing, and contracts. Exhibit 16.3 presents the data, in terms of percentage consumption, for other activities. (Later, we show the computations using cost drivers and allocation rates.)

Exhibit 16.3 informs us that the Structural Department consumes 28% of the services offered by administration. Recall that this means that, if SAC uses head count as the driver for allocating administration costs, the Structural Engineering Department accounts for 28% of the number of people serviced by administration.

Exhibit 16.3	Silverman & Abbas Consulting: Consumption Patterns for Activities				
	Cost Pools for Support Activities		Cost Pools for Line Activities		Final Cost Objects
	Administration	Purchasing	Structural	Plumbing	Contracts
Costs in pools	$650,000	$250,000	$1,015,000	$1,258,750	
Consumption pattern					
From Administration		30.00%	28.00%	28.00%	14.00%
From Purchasing	15.00%		25.50%	42.50%	17.00%
From Structural					100.00%
From Plumbing					100.00%

Exhibit 16.3 also indicates that there is reciprocity in consumption. The purchasing function consumes 30% of services offered by administration, while administration consumes 15% of the services offered by purchasing. Both support pools also provide services to the two line production departments: structural and plumbing. Finally, contracts directly account for some of the output from both support pools and for all of the output from the two line pools.

DIRECT METHOD

The **direct method** simplifies the allocation problem depicted in Exhibit 16.2 by ignoring reciprocity in consumption. Thus, the method assumes that the costs from support activities flow either directly to cost objects (products, jobs, contracts) or to the pools for line activities. We do not allocate costs from one support activity to another support activity. Exhibit 16.4 illustrates cost flows under the direct method.

Exhibit 16.5 presents the computations for SAC using the direct method. The first step is to re-compute the consumption percentages for the cost pools for support activities, ignoring reciprocal consumption. Consider administration costs. Purchasing, a support activity, consumes 30% of the services offered by administration.

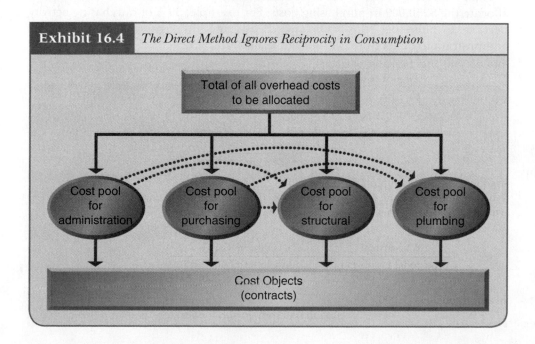

Exhibit 16.4   The Direct Method Ignores Reciprocity in Consumption

Exhibit 16.5	Silverman & Abbas Consulting: Direct Method				
	Cost Pools for Support Activities		Cost Pools for Line Activities		Final Cost Objects
	Administration	*Purchasing*	*Structural*	*Plumbing*	*Products/Jobs*
Consumption Pattern for Activities					
From Administration			40.00%	40.00%	20.00%
From Purchasing			30.00%	50.00%	20.00%
From Structural					100.00%
From Plumbing					100.00%
Cost Allocation					
Initial cost in pool	$650,000	$250,000	$1,015,000	$1,258,750	$348,750
From Administration	($650,000)		260,000	260,000	130,000
From Purchasing		($250,000)	75,000	125,000	50,000
Total costs in pools	$0	$0	$1,350,000	$1,643,750	$528,750

However, the direct method ignores this consumption and only considers the remaining 70% of the consumption when allocating administration costs. Thus, we recalculate the (revised) consumption percentages as 28%/70% = 40% for both structural and plumbing, and 14%/70% = 20% for the portion directly allocated to products. *Check It! Exercise #1* allows you to verify the computations for the purchasing cost pool.

The last four rows of Exhibit 16.5 contain the allocations. The first row shows the costs in the different cost pools. The next row allocates the cost from the administration cost pool ("from administration") to the other cost pools and jobs. As we calculated, the structural activity consumes 40% of the output from administration. Thus, we allocate $650,000 × 0.40 = $260,000 from the administration pool to the pool for structural engineering. Similarly, we allocate 40% of the cost of administration to the cost pool for plumbing. Finally, because we can link 20% of the administration consumption directly to contracts, we allocate $130,000 of administration costs to individual contracts.

After allocating the $650,000 in administration costs, we follow the same steps to allocate the $250,000 in purchasing costs. For example, 50% of purchasing activity pertains to plumbing (this is the revised estimate after ignoring the orders for administration). Therefore, we allocate $250,000 × 0.50 = $125,000 to plumbing.

Check It! Exercise #1

Verify that under the direct method, the Structural and Plumbing departments would be allocated 30% and 50%, respectively, of the purchasing activity cost.

	Admin	*Structural*	*Plumbing*	*Jobs*	*Total*
Original consumption pattern	15.00%	25.50%	42.50%	17.00%	100.00%
Eliminate support activities	0	25.50%	_____	17.00%	85.00%
Revised percentages	0	_____	_____	20.00%	100.00%
		=	=	= 0.17/0.85	

The last row shows that when all the costs for support activities have been allocated, $1,350,000 have been allocated to structural costs, $1,643,750 to plumbing costs, and $528,750 directly to contracts. This completes the allocation of support costs to line activities. We can then allocate costs from line activities to jobs as we learned in Chapters 9 and 10.

Performing the Allocation Using Rates

For simplicity in presentation, Exhibit 16.5 uses the percentage of the service consumed to calculate the amounts allocated to each cost pool. Firms often also use overhead rates for these allocations. Let us see how.

Under the direct method, we ignore any consumption by other support departments. We know that administration consumes 150 of the 1,000 purchase orders. Ignoring this consumption reduces the denominator volume for purchase orders from 1,000 orders to 850 orders. (This step achieves the same purpose as recalculating consumption percentages.) The cost in the purchasing pool is $250,000. We therefore calculate a rate of $250,000/850 orders = $294.12 (rounded) per purchase order. Using this rate, we allocate 255 orders × $294.12 per order = $75,000 to structural, 425 orders × $294.12 per order = $125,000 to plumbing, and 170 orders × $294.12 per order = $50,000 directly to contracts. These numbers, of course, are the same as the amounts we calculated in Exhibit 16.5 (see row "from Purchasing").

Why might a firm use overhead rates, a harder method to visualize, rather than percentages to perform these allocations? Firms do so to communicate the cost of support activities to managers of line activities. The allocation informs the managers of structural and plumbing that each purchase order they request increases the firm's long-run cost by $294.12. This cost information might induce them to be more careful in the use of purchase orders.

For simplicity in presenting calculations, we illustrate the step-down and reciprocal methods using percentage allocations only.

STEP-DOWN METHOD

The **step-down method** improves on the direct method by considering the reciprocity in consumption partially. We begin by rank-ordering support activity cost pools according to some criterion. Frequently, organizations use the size of the cost pool as the criterion. However, we could use other criteria such as the proportion of consumption by other support activities. SAC has chosen to allocate administration costs (with $650,000 of costs) before allocating the cost connected with the purchasing activity ($250,000).

We allocate the costs in the highest-ranked support activity pool to all other cost pools, including the *lower*-ranked support activity pools. For SAC, we would allocate the costs in the administration pool to purchasing, as well as to structural, plumbing, and directly to jobs. This allocation differs from the direct method, because under the direct method we would allocate zero costs from one support

CHAPTER CONNECTIONS

The two-step process is the detailed method for allocating costs. However, as you learned in Chapter 3, the percent of the cost allocated to a cost object equals the percent of driver units in that cost object. Thus, rather than use the two-step process for allocations, in Exhibit 16.5, we directly used the percentage data to calculate the amounts allocated.

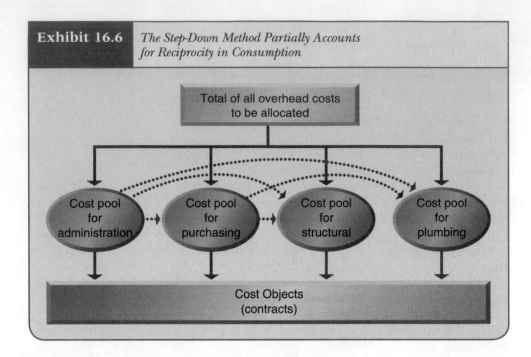

Exhibit 16.6 *The Step-Down Method Partially Accounts for Reciprocity in Consumption*

activity pool to another support activity pool (i.e., no costs flow from administration to purchasing).

As Exhibit 16.6 indicates, under the step-down method, we first allocate administration costs to the lower-ranked support activity (purchasing), to the two line activities, and to contracts. In this case, Exhibit 16.3 provides the data we use for this allocation of administration costs: 30% will go to purchasing, 28% to structural, 28% to plumbing, and 14% directly to contracts.

Next, we allocate the costs for the purchasing activity. Realize that these costs now comprise the costs originally traced as well as the costs allocated from the administration pool. Thus we allocate $ $250,000 + $195,000 = $445,000 in costs from purchasing. Where should we allocate these costs? If there were other lower-ranked support activity pools, we would allocate the purchasing costs to those pools, as well as to the line activity pools, and directly to contracts. However, we would not allocate any purchasing costs *back* to the higher-ranked administration pool. In this way, at each step, we deal with one less cost pool for support activities. We repeat the steps for the remaining cost pools until we exhaust all of the cost pools for support activities. At that point, we complete the allocation process the way we described in Chapter 9 and used to complete the direct method.

Notice that the step-down method sequentially allocates the costs of support activities. Naturally, some refer to this method as the **sequential method**.

Exhibit 16.7 provides the computations for the step-down method for SAC. Notice that the consumption pattern for administration includes the consumption of this service by purchasing, a lower-ranked support activity. However, in the row for purchasing, we re-compute the percentages for purchasing because we ignore the Administration Department's consumption of the purchasing activity. This recalculation is the same that we saw using the direct method.

As for the costs, we first allocate the $650,000 of costs contained in the cost pool to administration. Of this cost, we allocate 30%, or $195,000, to the cost pool for purchasing, increasing the costs for the purchasing activity from $250,000 to $445,000. We then allocate 28% of $650,000 to the Structural Department, 28% to plumbing and the remaining 14% directly to contracts.

We next allocate $445,000 of costs from the purchasing cost pool. Of this amount, 30% goes to structural, 50% to plumbing, and the remainder directly to contracts.

Exhibit 16.7	Silverman & Abbas Consulting: Step-Down Method				
	Cost Pools for Support Activities		**Cost Pools for Line Activities**		**Final Cost Objects**
	Administration	**Purchasing**	**Structural**	**Plumbing**	**Products/Jobs**
Consumption Pattern					
From Administration		30.00%	28.00%	28.00%	14.00%
From Purchasing			30.00%	50.00%	20.00%
From Structural					100.00%
From Plumbing					100.00%
Cost Allocation					
Initial cost in pool	$650,000	$250,000	$1,015,000	$1,258,750	$348,750
From Administration	($650,000)	195,000	182,000	182,000	91,000
From Purchasing		($445,000)	133,500	222,500	89,000
Total costs in pools	$0	$0	$1,330,500	$1,663,250	$528,750

Changing the Order of Allocations

A key step in performing a step-down allocation is to rank the support cost pools according to some criterion. However, there is no absolute criterion. The choice is often strategic because managerial incentives frequently play a role. Changing the order of allocation could change the amount of costs allocated to the cost pools and contracts. As we know from Chapter 12, managers of cost centers strive to minimize the costs of achieving a planned level of output (as specified in budgets). They would prefer a criterion that results in less support costs being allocated to cost pools under their control. Managers of profit centers act to maximize profit. They, too, would prefer a ranking scheme that would yield less allocation than more. In large organizations with multiple responsibility centers, different managers are likely to prefer different ranking criteria. It is rare that any one criterion will satisfy all managers. Moreover, the choice of a particular criterion can influence consumption patterns. Managers of cost pools receiving higher allocations of a support resource will tend to use less of the resource and vice versa.

Given these considerations, most organizations that use the step-down method follow an intuitive and a consistent criterion over time. They do not depend on consensus for their choice. The size of the support department (measured in costs) and head count are some of the commonly used ranking criteria.

In the foregoing example, we allocated the cost pool for administration activities before the purchasing cost pool. *Check It! Exercise #2* allows you to verify how the amounts allocated to the cost pools for the line activities change if SAC allocates the purchasing activity cost pool before allocating the costs for administration.

RECIPROCAL METHOD

The **reciprocal method** is conceptually the most appealing method because it takes into account *all* of the reciprocity in consumption (as depicted in Exhibit 16.2). It is convenient to represent the reciprocal method in two steps. First, we write the reciprocal relation as a system of simultaneous equations. That is, letting A and P stand for the cost of the administration and purchasing activity respectively, we have:

$$A = \$650,000 + 0.15 \times P$$
$$P = \$250,000 + 0.30 \times A$$

Check It! Exercise #2

	Support Activities		Line Activities		Cost Objects
	Adminis- tration	Purchasing	Structural	Plumbing	Products/ Jobs
Original consumption pattern					
From Administration	0%	30.00%	28.00%	28.00%	14.00%
From Purchasing	15.00%	0%	25.50%	42.50%	17.00%
From Structural					100.00%
From Plumbing					100.00%
Revised consumption pattern					
From Purchasing	15.00%	0	25.50%	42.50%	17.00%
From Administration	0	0	40.00%	_____	_____
			(= 28%/70%)		
Initial cost in pool	$650,000	$250,000	$1,015,000	$1,258,750	$348,750
From Purchasing	_____	(250,000)	63,750	_____	_____
From Administration	(687,500)	0	_____	275,000	_____
Remainder in pool	$0	$0	$_____	$_____	$_____

Solution at end of chapter.

Connecting to Practice

UTILITIES AND COST ALLOCATIONS

EPCOR is a major power and water utility in Alberta, Canada. EPCOR operates in regulated and unregulated markets. For its regulated business, EPCOR applies to the Alberta Utilities Commission for approval of revisions to its general tariffs (prices). In order to justify changes to its tariffs, EPCOR provides a detailed cost justification as part of its general tariff applications.

COMMENTARY: The Alberta Utilities Commission (formerly the Alberta Energy and Utilities Board) recognizes the incentive of rate-regulated companies to overestimate applicable costs to support tariff revisions. Accordingly, the commission requires detailed cost justification for any cost forecasts (estimates). Such estimates often include complex cost allocations including numerous interdepartmental/interunit allocations. EPCOR utilizes the services of accounting firms such as KPMG to certify its methods.

Utility companies rely on elaborate cost allocations to justify their rates to regulators. (Genesee 3—co-owned by EPCOR Utilities Inc. and TransAlta Corporation—is Canada's cleanest coal-fired power generator. The facility is situated in Alberta, where the electricity industry is deregulated and power generation is a commercial venture.)
(Courtesy of EPCOR)

The first equation yields the total cost to be allocated, A, from the administration cost pool. It consists of $650,000 directly traced to administration plus the cost of 15% of the services of the purchasing function that the Administration Department utilizes. Similarly, the second equation yields the total cost to be allocated, P, from the purchasing cost pool. It consists of $250,000 directly traced to purchasing plus the cost of 30% of the services of the administration function that the Purchasing Department utilizes. Thus, the two equations, taken together, fully consider the reciprocal relation between administration and purchasing.

We solve this system of equations by substituting the second equation into the first equation:

$$A = \$650,000 + 0.15 \times (\$250,000 + 0.30 \times A)$$

We simplify to obtain:

$$0.955\ A = \$687,500, \text{ or } A = \$719,895 \text{ (rounded)}$$

We substitute this value into the second equation and calculate:

$$P = \$250,000 + 0.30 \times \$719,895 = \$465,968 \text{ (rounded)}$$

In the second step, we use these values for A and P as the costs in the administration and purchasing activity cost pools, and we allocate using the utilization percentages from Exhibit 16.3. For example, from the adjusted administration pool of $719,895, we allocate 30% or $215,968 to purchasing, 28% or $201,571 to both structural and plumbing, and 14% or $100,785 to contracts. Exhibit 16.8 shows these computations.

While the reciprocal method is conceptually the most appealing method for allocating support costs, it is also the most complex. However, spreadsheet programs such as Excel greatly help in performing the numerous calculations involved. They also help us in readily extending the approach to more than two support pools. Nevertheless, many firms continue to employ the direct and step-down methods, which are computationally easier but yield only approximate answers.

INTEGRATION WITH PREDETERMINED OVERHEAD RATES

From an implementation perspective, an organization performs support activity (support department) allocations at the same time it computes predetermined overhead rates, a topic we studied in Chapter 14. Suppose that SAC decides to use the reciprocal method. In this case, referring to Exhibit 16.8, we allocate $719,895 and $465,968, respectively, from the administration and purchasing cost pools. Furthermore, assume SAC allocates administration costs based on head count and there are 292 persons employed at SAC (excluding administration personnel). Dividing $719,895 by 292, SAC would charge the other departments $2,465 per person for administration costs.

Check it! Exercise #3 allows you to verify the charge for each purchasing order. From the perspective of the managers of line activities (structural, plumbing), the allocations are an "overhead" charge based on their individual head count and the number of purchase orders they issue.

Exhibit 16.8	Silverman & Abbas Consulting: Reciprocal Method				
	Cost Pools for Support Activities		Cost Pools for Line Activities		Final Cost Objects
	Administration	Purchasing	Structural	Plumbing	Products/Jobs
Consumption pattern for activities					
From Administration		30.00%	28.00%	28.00%	14.00%
From Purchasing	15.00%		25.50%	42.50%	17.00%
From Structural					100.00%
From Plumbing					100.00%
Initial cost in pool	$650,000	$250,000	$1,015,000	$1,258,750	$348,750
From Administration	(719,895)	215,968	201,571	201,571	100,785
From Purchasing	69,895	(465,968)	118,822	198,036	79,215
Remaining costs in pool	$0	$0	$1,335,393	$1,658,357	$528,750

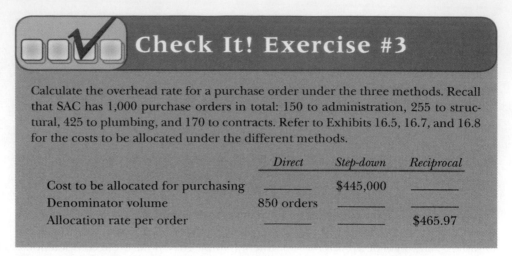

Check It! Exercise #3

Calculate the overhead rate for a purchase order under the three methods. Recall that SAC has 1,000 purchase orders in total: 150 to administration, 255 to structural, 425 to plumbing, and 170 to contracts. Refer to Exhibits 16.5, 16.7, and 16.8 for the costs to be allocated under the different methods.

	Direct	Step-down	Reciprocal
Cost to be allocated for purchasing	_____	$445,000	_____
Denominator volume	850 orders	_____	_____
Allocation rate per order	_____	_____	$465.97

Solution at end of chapter.

Check It! Exercise #3 emphasizes the effect of considering the reciprocity in consumption. Under the direct method, which ignores reciprocal consumption, SAC estimates that each order costs $294.12. The rate per order (an estimate of the long-run cost effect) jumps to $465.97 when we fully consider the interaction using the reciprocal method.

Just as we calculated the overhead rates for the support departments, we can calculate them for the line departments as well. Referring back to Exhibit 16.8, we find that the Structural Department has $1,335,393 of costs in its cost pool, after the allocations from the support activities. Suppose the Structural Department expects to bill out 12,000 hours. Its hourly cost then is $111.28.

Dual-Rate Allocations

LEARNING OBJECTIVE 3

Discuss the need for dual-rate allocations.

Printing facilities have a mixture of fixed and variable costs; their costs are best allocated using dual rates. (Tim Fan/iStockphoto)

In the previous section, we discussed three methods to incorporate the cost impact of the reciprocal relations among a firm's various line and support activities. Notice that all the three methods employ a single cost driver to allocate costs. In essence, we are assuming that all the costs in each cost pool exhibit the same level of controllability over time.

This assumption is likely not valid. Some of the costs in the cost pool for purchasing, such as the cost of traveling to meet with suppliers, are controllable in the short term. Other costs, such as the salaries paid to personnel, may only be controllable over a longer horizon. Managers of departments that use the purchasing department must understand this variation in costs. When making decisions that place demands on the purchasing function, these managers should consider only costs that are controllable over the relevant time horizon for the decision.

Consider the Printing Department at SAC. This department operates specialized equipment for printing large drawings and blueprints required during the process of planning a building. All of the line departments—structural, plumbing, and so on—use these prints, though with varying intensity. Let the number of prints be the allocation basis, and assume that the rate, using the reciprocal method, is $125 per print.

Now, consider the problem from the perspective of the Plumbing Department's manager. Her department is charged $125 for every print she orders, meaning that she will order a new print only when she believes the benefits exceed $125. From her perspective, the cost of ordering prints is:

$$\text{Total cost of prints} = \$125 \times \text{actual number of prints}$$

Decisions made with this view of costs, however, could find the Plumbing Department underutilizing the Printing Department. Not all of the costs included in the $125 rate per print are controllable in the short term. Suppose that $50 of the $125 represents variable costs, which are controllable in the short term, while the remaining $75 is a charge for the long-term costs of acquiring and maintaining the printing machines. From SAC's perspective, as long as additional capacity is available in the printing machines, the manager of the Plumbing Department ought to order a print if the benefits exceed $50 and not $125.

How can SAC communicate differences in the controllability of the underlying costs to the manager of the Plumbing Department? One answer is to use many rates. For example, we could employ two cost pools—one for long-term or fixed costs, and one for short-term variable costs—to allocate the costs from printing. Of course, we then need to compute two rates to perform the allocation and determine the charge to plumbing. Splitting the rate into two then helps inform the plumbing manager about the different levels of controllability of these costs. Naturally, we refer to the allocation as a **dual-rate** or **two-factor** allocation. (In theory, we could use many rates, with each rate corresponding to a level in the cost hierarchy. In practice, firms employ two rates only.)

Choice of Allocation Basis

When discussing ABC systems in Chapter 10, we argued that the driver we use to allocate costs should bear an economic relation with the cost we allocate. The same logic applies in the context of dual-rate allocations. Consider the cost pool for variable costs. These costs change with the volume of activity or with the number of prints made. Consequently, it is appropriate to allocate the costs in the variable cost pool using the number of prints as the driver.

Next, consider the cost pool for fixed costs. Fixed costs are the results of capacity decisions that span a longer horizon. Consequently, we need to tie the allocation to the factors that influence the long-term decision about capacity levels. The firm would have decided on capacity levels based on demand projections from the user departments. Accordingly, these long-term projections or expected demand are the appropriate basis for allocating fixed capacity costs.

In the context of SAC, assume that the Structural Engineering Department expects to use 1,500 prints during an average year, although it only used 1,300 prints during the current year. Then, the allocation to this department contains two amounts. The first amount is a lump-sum charge of $112,500, obtained by multiplying the expected 1,500 prints × $75 per print. This amount is for the fixed costs incurred by the Printing Department, where $75 per print is a charge for the long-term costs of acquiring and maintaining the printing machines. This amount is a lump-sum charge because both the long-term usage and the rate are *fixed* amounts, and do not change from year to year.

The second part is an allocation of $65,000 for the variable costs. Here we multiply the actual number of prints (1,300) by the variable rate of $50 per print. The Printing Department's variable costs are proportional to the actual number of prints made. Summing up, the following equation represents the structural engineering manager's costs for printing:

Total allocated to structural engineering department from printing
= $112,500 + ($50 × actual number of prints)

Such an allocation procedure communicates the differing controllability of costs in the Printing Department. The lump-sum charge is a committed cost that is the outcome of a long-term decision, and the variable portion is the outcome of shorter-term decisions.

In this chapter, we examined two refinements to the allocation systems that we considered in Chapters 9 and 10. The first refinement is to recognize the reciprocity in consumption among support activities. We discussed three methods that firms could use to model this consumption pattern: the direct method, the step-down method, and the reciprocal method. Second, we discussed the likelihood that a single driver (or equivalently, a single rate) is not enough to fully capture the controllability of costs contained in a cost pool. Accordingly, it may be more appropriate for firms to employ long-term expected demand to allocate fixed capacity costs and to use actual demand to allocate short-term variable costs.

RAPID REVIEW

LEARNING OBJECTIVE 1

Distinguish between line activities and support activities.

- In the two-stage allocation systems we studied in Chapters 8 and 9, we first group costs into cost pools that correspond to individual departments or activities. In the second stage, we allocate *all* costs from any given cost pool directly to products.

- In the standard two-stage allocation system, we implicitly assume that products account for the *entire* activity volume corresponding to all cost pools. While this assumption is reasonable for line activities, it does not accurately depict support activities. When a firm has support activities, we need to account for the interactions that exist among cost pools.

LEARNING OBJECTIVE 2

Explain three methods used to allocate the costs of support activities to products.

- The three methods used to account for reciprocity in consumption are the direct method, the step-down method, and the reciprocal method.

- The direct method is computationally easy, but it ignores all interactions among support departments.

- The step-down method partially accounts for the reciprocity in consumption among support activities. The first step is to rank-order support departments as per some criterion, such as size. We then allocate the cost of support activities in sequence, eliminating one support activity with each allocation, eventually allocating all costs to line activities and to products.

- The reciprocal method is conceptually the most accurate method because it fully accounts for the reciprocity in consumption. We first model the allocation as a system of equations to obtain the fully loaded cost in each support activity. We then allocate this fully loaded cost to all other support and line activities.

LEARNING OBJECTIVE 3

Discuss the need for dual-rate allocations.

- Because a cost pool accumulates costs from multiple sources, the costs in a pool often exhibit differing levels of controllability. Users of a support activity should be aware of this variation when they make decisions about their consumption levels.

- A single rate is not enough to capture the differences in controllability across different cost pools. From a user's perspective, a single rate implies that all costs are variable in the short term. We can partially address this problem by grouping costs within a cost pool into smaller pools, corresponding to the controllability of the underlying costs.

- We usually employ two subpools: one for long-term capacity costs and one for short-term variable costs. We allocate long-term costs using expected or long-term demand as the driver. This allocation is a lump-sum allocation because long-term demand is constant within an accounting period. We allocate short-term costs using the actual volume of service. We term this allocation procedure the dual-rate or the two-factor method to reflect its usage of two separate drivers.

ANSWERS TO CHECK IT! EXERCISES

Exercise #1: After eliminating consumption by administration, plumbing consumes 42.5%/85.0% = 50% of the purchasing activity and the Structural Department consumes 25.5%/85.0% = 30% of the purchasing activity. Direct consumption by contracts accounts for the remainder of 20%.

Exercise #2: There is no need to revise the pattern for purchasing as we allocate costs to all units that consume this activity. The revised consumption pattern from administration = (28%/70%) = 40% for plumbing and (14%/70%) = 20% for contracts.

Costs allocated from purchasing are (0.15 × $250,000) = $37,500 to administration, $106,250 (= $250,000 × 0.425) to plumbing, and $42,500 (= $250,000 × 0.17) directly to contracts. The total cost in administration is now $37,500 + $650,000 = $687,500.

From administration, we therefore allocate 0.4 × $687,500 = $275,000 each to structural and plumbing, and (0.20 × $687,500) = $137,500 directly to contracts. The final totals are $1,353,750 for structural, $1,640,000 for plumbing, and $528,750 for contracts.

Exercise #3: Under the direct method, total cost is $250,000 (Exhibit 16.5) and the denominator volume is 850 orders (1,050 − 50 for self-consumption − 150 for administration). Thus, the rate per order is $294.12 (rounded). For the step-down method, the cost in the pool is $445,000 (Exhibit 16.7). Because we only allocate these costs to structural, plumbing, and contracts, the denominator volume is 255 + 425 +170 = 850 orders. Thus, the rate is $523.53 per order (rounded). The denominator volume for the reciprocal method is 1,000 orders (we include the 150 orders from administration as we allocate costs back to administration). The rate is $465,968/1,000 orders = $465.97 per order.

SELF-STUDY PROBLEMS

Popov and Company make tappets, used in engines, in a small manufacturing firm in Moscow, Russia. The firm's owner, Vladimir Popov, provides you with the data shown in Exhibit 16.9.

Vladimir has requested your help in allocating the costs of the power and the maintenance activities to the line activities, machining and assembly.

a. *Perform the required allocation using the direct method.*

Under the direct method, we ignore the consumption of support activities by other support activities. Thus, as shown in the top part of Exhibit 16.10, we first re-compute the consumption percentages for the support activities. For instance, consider the row "From Power." Eliminating the 20% consumed by maintenance (see Exhibit 16.9), we obtain the consumption percentage for machining as 40%/(40% + 40%) = 50%. We follow a similar procedure to obtain the other consumption percentages.

Exhibit 16.9	*Popov & Company: Consumption Pattern for Activities*			
	Cost Pools for Support Activities		Cost Pools for Line Activities	
	Power	*Maintenance*	*Machining*	*Assembly*
Costs in pools	$288,000	$261,000	$100,000	$160,000
Consumption pattern for activities				
From Power		20.00%	40.00%	40.00%
From Maintenance	25.00%		50.00%	25.00%

Exhibit 16.10 *Popov & Company: Direct Method*

	Cost Pools for Support Activities		Cost Pools for Line Activities	
	Power	Maintenance	Machining	Assembly
Consumption pattern (re-computed)				
From Power			50.00%	50.00%
From Maintenance			66.67%	33.33%
Cost allocation				
Cost in pool after stage 1	$288,000	$261,000	$100,000	$160,000
From Power	(288,000)		144,000	144,000
From Maintenance		(261,000)	174,000	87,000
Total after allocations	$0	$0	$418,000	$391,000

Next, we use these percentages to allocate costs from the support activities to the line activities. Thus, referring to the allocation for power, we allocate 0.5 × $288,000 = $144,000 to machining and an equal amount to assembly.

b. *Perform the required allocation using the step-down method. Allocate the cost of power before allocating the cost of maintenance.*

We are given the ranking of the support activities for the allocation. (Size could be the criterion used here.) Thus, we allocate costs from the Power Department to the maintenance activity, but not vice versa.

First, let us recompute the allocation percentages shown in Exhibit 16.11. There is no need to revise the allocation percentages for power because we allocate the costs to all other support and line activities. However, we ignore consumption by the Power Department when allocating maintenance (a lower ranked department). Thus, we recompute the percentages as 50/75 = 66.67% and 25/75 = 33.33%.

The next two lines show the actual allocation. From power, we allocate 0.20 × $288,000 = $57,600 to maintenance and 0.40 × $288,000 = $115,200 each to machining and assembly. The row "From Power" shows that we allocate 66.67% of the cost to machining and 33.33% to assembly.

c. *Suppose the Maintenance Department allocates its costs using maintenance hours. Further, Popov expects to consume 21,240 maintenance hours (which includes 5,310 hours by power). Compute the cost rates per maintenance hour under the step-down method.*

Referring back to Exhibit 16.11, we know that the maintenance cost pool has $318,600 of costs. Next, under the step-down method we exclude the consumption by power as this method does not consider this link. Thus, the appropriate denominator volume is 21,240 − 5,310 = 15,930 hours. Accordingly, we have:

Rate per maintenance hour = $318,600/15,930 hours = $20 per maintenance hour

Exhibit 16.11 *Popov & Company: Step-Down Method*

	Cost Pools for Support Activities		Cost Pools for Line Activities	
	Power	Maintenance	Machining	Assembly
Consumption pattern (re-computed)				
From Power		20.00%	40.00%	40.00%
From Maintenance			66.67%	33.33%
Cost allocation				
Cost in pool after stage 1	$288,000	$261,000	$100,000	$160,000
From Power	(288,000)	57,600	115,200	115,200
From Maintenance		(318,600)	212,400	106,200
Total after allocations	$0	$0	$427,600	$381,400

d. *Perform the required allocation using the reciprocal method.*

The first step in the reciprocal method is to represent the consumption patterns as a system of equations. Representing power and maintenance by P and M, respectively, we have:

$$P = \$288,000 + (0.25 \times M)$$
$$M = \$261,000 + (0.20 \times P)$$

Plug in the second equation into the first equation to get:

$$P = \$288,000 + 0.25 \times (\$261,000 + 0.20 \times P)$$

Simplifying, we get:

$$P - 0.05\,P = \$288,000 + 65,250, \text{ or } P = \$371,842 \text{ (rounded)}$$

Plugging in the value into the second equation, we calculate M = \$335,368 (rounded).

Using these estimates, Exhibit 16.12 shows the required allocations. Notice that we allocate costs from the Power Department to the maintenance activity and vice versa.

e. *Suppose the Machining Department allocates its costs using machining hours. Further, suppose that Popov expects to consume 20,000 machine hours. Compute the cost rates per machining hour under the step-down and reciprocal methods. Comment on why the rates differ.*

Referring back to Exhibit 16.11, we know that the machining cost pool has \$427,600 of costs under the step-down method. Accordingly, we have:

Rate per machine hour (step-down)

= \$427,600/20,000 hours = \$21.38 per machine hour

Likewise, referring back to Exhibit 16.12, we obtain the cost for machining as \$416,421 under the reciprocal method. We therefore obtain:

Rate per machine hour (reciprocal)

= \$416,421/20,000 hours = \$20.82 per machine hour

The two rates differ because the methods differ in the extent to which they account for reciprocity of consumption. Unlike the step-down method, the reciprocal method fully considers the relations and is therefore more accurate.

Exhibit 16.12	*Popov & Company: Reciprocal Method*			
	Cost Pools for Support Activities		**Cost Pools for Line Activities**	
	Power	*Maintenance*	*Machining*	*Assembly*
Consumption pattern				
From Power		20.00%	40.00%	40.00%
From Maintenance	25.00%		50.00%	25.00%
Cost allocation				
Cost in pool after stage 1	\$288,000	\$261,000	\$100,000	\$160,000
From Power	(371,842)	74,368	148,737	148,737
From Maintenance	83,842	(335,368)	167,684	83,842
Total after allocations	\$0	\$0	\$416,421	\$392,579

GLOSSARY

Direct method An allocation procedure that ignores the relationship among support activities and focuses instead on the relationship between support and line activities.

Dual-rate allocations A procedure that employs two separate drivers to allocate fixed and variable costs in a cost pool.

Line activity An activity that is directly related to making and selling the firm's products and services.

Reciprocal method An allocation procedure that fully accounts for the relationship among support activities.

Reciprocity in consumption A consumption pattern in which two departments provide services to each other.

Self-consumption A support department consuming its own output.

Sequential allocation See Step-down method.

Step-down method An allocation procedure that partially accounts for the relationship among support activities.

Support activity An activity that is not a line activity. These activities help the firm execute the line activity.

Two-factor allocation See Dual-rate allocation.

REVIEW QUESTIONS

16.1 LO1. What is the distinction between a line activity and a support activity? Give two examples of each.

16.2 LO1. What complicates the allocation of support activity costs?

16.3 LO2. What are the three methods for allocating the costs of support activities?

16.4 LO2. Name one important difference between the step-down method and the direct method?

16.5 LO2. Does changing the order in which we allocate the costs of support activities matter under the step-down method? Does it matter for the direct or reciprocal methods?

16.6 LO2. How do we account for the self-consumption of resources (e.g., the power consumed by the Power Generation Department, or the Payroll Department processing checks for the employees in human resources) when we perform a step-down allocation?

16.7 LO2. Name one important difference between the reciprocal method and the step-down method.

16.8 LO3. Describe the dual-rate allocation method.

16.9 LO3. In a dual-rate allocation, what is the allocation basis for allocating capacity costs? for operating costs?

16.10 LO3. What is the advantage of using budgeted instead of actual costs when determining the overhead rates to employ for allocating the costs of support activities?

DISCUSSION QUESTIONS

16.11 LO1. What is the implicit time horizon that we assume when we allocate support activity costs to other cost objects such as products and other activities?

16.12 LO2. We rank support departments when using the step-down method. Alternate ranking criteria include department size, number of other departments serviced, and arbitrary ranking. Which method will usually produce the smallest errors, relative to the answers obtained from the conceptually accurate reciprocal method?

16.13 LO3. Why do we prefer to use predetermined rates to charge out support department costs to other departments?

16.14 LO1 (Advanced). What is the key difference between an allocation from a support department and a transfer price? Does this distinction matter for pricing the service? For evaluating responsibility center managers?

16.15 LO3 (Advanced). Suppose a support activity allocated all of its costs based on actual usage of its services and use of actual rates. In this scenario, how does the activity volume in one department affect the costs allocated to other activities? Why is such dependence undesirable?

16.16 LO3. Would the issue in the above question become moot if we employed predetermined overhead rates? Why does the answer depend on whether the decline in volume was predictable?

16.17 LO3. How does the use of practical capacity (see Chapter 10) further alleviate the issue identified in Question 16.15?

16.18 LO3. Under the dual-rate system, expected long-term demand is the allocation basis for allocating the capacity costs of support activities. What incentives does this provide to managers of line activities?

16.19 LO3. How could we accommodate the use of batch- and product-level costs in a dual-rate allocation system?

16.20 LO3. Would a dual-rate allocation make sense for allocating facility level costs? Why or why not?

EXERCISES

16.21 Direct method (LO2). The City of Pleasantville has two departments—Parks and Recreation (P&R) and Facility Maintenance (FM)—that provide services to its citizens. The P&R Department offers many programs in art, culture, and athletics, while the FM Department maintains all of the streets, buildings, and other public facilities. Behind the scenes, Pleasantville has two departments that support the activities of the P&R and FM departments. The Human Resources Department processes payroll and oversees all hiring, development, and training. The General Administration Department provides overall coordination and managerial support.

The following table provides data regarding the consumption of services by the various activity pools/departments, as well as the amount of costs traced to each activity pool.

		Human Resources	General Administration	Parks and Recreation	Facilities Maintenance
Traced costs		$100,000	$60,000	$360,000	$450,000

Service consumption pattern					
			Services consumed by		
		nan Resou	General Administration	Parks and Recreation	Facilities Maintenance
Services provided by	Human Resources		40%	30%	30%
	General Administration	20%		60%	20%

Required:

Allocate the costs of the two support departments to the line departments, using the direct method. Compute the total costs in the cost pool for the P&R and FM departments.

16.22 Step-down method (LO2). Consider the data in Exercise 16.21

Required:

a. Compute the total costs in the cost pool for the P&R and FM departments, using the step-down method to allocate the costs of the two support departments to the line departments. Allocate the costs of Human Resources before allocating the costs for General Administration.

b. Repeat requirement (a), but allocate the costs of General Administration before allocating the costs for Human Resources.

c. Comment on why you obtain different results for requirements (a) and (b).

16.23 Reciprocal method (LO2). Consider the data in Exercise 16.21.

Required:

a. Compute the total costs in the cost pool for the P&R and FM departments, using the reciprocal method to allocate the costs of the two support departments to the line departments.

b. Comment on which of the answers from Exercises 16.21, 16.22, and 16.23 provides the most accurate estimate of the cost of the support services consumed by the P&R and FM departments.

16.24 Allocations and decision making (LO2). Refer to Exercise 16.21. You have allocated the costs from the Human Resources and General Administration departments to the P&R and FM departments. Suppose you have determined that the cost pool for the P&R Department contains $473,200 in costs and the pool for the FM Department contains $506,800 in costs after these allocations. (These numbers may or may not be the answers to the requirement for Exercise 16.21.)

Required:

a. The P&R Department offered a total of 18,200 hours of instruction. What is the City's total cost per instruction hour provided by the P&R department?

b. How might the City use this information in its decision making?

16.25 Role for interactions (LO2). Sriram Motor Works manufactures scooters and other two-wheelers for sale in Asia. The firm has divided its operations into two main factories: one in Pune, India, and the other in Malaysia. The firm is contemplating the best way to allocate the support costs in the head office to the two divisions. The following data are available.

	Human Resources	General Administration	Indian Division	Malaysian Division
Traced costs	$760,000	$1,460,000	n/a	n/a
Service consumption pattern		Services consumed by		
	Human Resources	General Administration	Indian Division	Malaysian Division
Services provided by	Human Resources			40%	60%
	General Administration			50%	50%

Required:

a. Determine the costs allocated to the Indian and the Malaysian divisions using the direct method.

b. Repeat the requirement using the step-down method.

c. Why do your answers not depend on the method you use?

16.26 Direct method (LO2). T³ Technology Services provides consulting services to government and corporate clients. Because of security concerns, the firm has a separate staff servicing the two kinds of clients. However, one information systems group services the two groups of consultants. Likewise, a single administrative department provides all needed secretarial and administrative support.

T³ wishes to base its billing rates on the cost per hour of consulting provided by its staff. Assume that each person in the Government and Corporate consulting group provides 1,500 hours of billable support per year. The following table provides relevant data.

	IS	AS	Government	Corporate
Traced costs	$500,000	$300,000	$2,400,000	$3,240,000
Service consumption pattern		Services consumed by		
	IS	AS	Government	Corporate
Services provided by IS (hours)		4,000 hours	2,000 hours	4,000 hours
AS (Persons)	5		20	25

T³ Technologies allocates the costs of the IS Department using the hours of support provided and the AS Department costs by the head count in the user departments.

Required:

Determine the costs per hour of consulting provided by the Government and Corporate groups after using the direct method to allocate support department costs to the Government and Corporate groups.

16.27 Step-down method (LO2). Refer to Exercise 16.26. Suppose that Government regulations require T³ Technologies to use the step-down method to allocate the costs of support departments and activities to line departments. However, these regulations do not dictate the order in which to allocate the cost of support activities. The Government would then reimburse T³ Technologies at 115% of allowable cost, assuming 1,500 billable hours per person. The corporate clients, of course, do not care about T³ Technology's cost. They would simply refuse to hire T³ Technology's services if it charged more than the market rate of $100 per billable hour.

Required:

Advise T³ Technology's management on how it could refine its allocation procedures to maximize its reported profit.

16.28 Reciprocal method (LO2). Refer to Exercise 16.26. Suppose that government regulations require T³ Technologies to use the reciprocal method to allocate the costs of support departments and activities to line departments.

Required:

a. Determine the cost per hour billed to the Government.

b. Comment on whether T³ Technologies could boost reported profit by changing the order in which it allocates the costs of support departments to line departments.

16.29 Reciprocal method (LO2). Consider the following data pertaining to two support and two line departments.

		S1	S2	P1	P2
Traced costs		$16,000	$25,000		
Services	S1 (in hours)		200	400	400 hours
provided by	S2 (in persons)	10		30	60 persons

Required: Use the reciprocal method to determine the costs allocated to P1 and P2.

16.30 Dual-rate method (LO3). Suppose a firm's secretarial pool incurs $40,000 in fixed costs plus $15 in variable costs for each hour of service. This amount of fixed costs allows the pool to accommodate an average volume of 5,000 hours of support per month.

The following data pertain to usage patterns (in hours used) for the three departments that are the only users of the secretarial pool.

	Average Planned Usage (hours)	Actual Usage (in hours)		
		April	May	June
Department 1	2,000	2,000	2,000	2,000
Department 2	2,000	1,500	2,500	2,000
Department 3	1,000	700	700	800
Total	5,000	4,200	5,200	4,800

Actual secretarial costs for April, May, and June amounted to $110,000, $123,000, and $112,000, respectively.

Required:

a. Determine the cost allocated to each of the three departments if the firm used a single rate, based on actual costs and usage, to allocate secretarial costs to the user departments.

b. Repeat the allocation assuming that the firm uses a single rate to allocate costs but it employs costs (as determined by a flexible budget that we discussed in Chapter 8) to compute the rates.

c. Repeat the allocation assuming that the firm employs separate rates for allocating fixed and variable costs. Assume that long-run usage is the denominator volume for allocating fixed costs.

d. Which of these mechanisms would you recommend? Why?

PROBLEMS

16.31 Support department allocations (LO2). Montclair, Inc., has three support departments: Cafeteria, Janitorial, and Administration. It also has two line departments: Machining and Assembly. The following data pertain to operations for the most recent year.

		Cafeteria	Janitorial	Administration	Machining	Assembly
Traced costs		$100,000	$60,000	$360,000	$450,000	$560,000
				Services provided to		
		Cafeteria	Janitorial	Administration	Machining	Assembly
Services	Cafeteria		20%	20%	30%	30%
provided	Janitorial	25%		10%	35%	30%
	Administration	20%	10%		20%	50%

Required:

a. Allocate the costs traced to the support activities (departments) to the line activities (departments), using the direct method.

b. Allocate the costs traced to the support activities (departments) to the line activities (departments), using the step-down method. Rank support departments by size to determine the order of allocation.

c. Continue with your answer to part (b) above. Suppose the Machining Department expects to incur 10,000 machine hours for the month and the Assembly Department expects to incur 25,000 labor hours. Determine the overhead rate per machine hour in the Machining Department and per labor hour in the Assembly Department.

 16.32 Support department allocations (LO2). Pickoff and Dropoff Co. run a limousine firm. The firm has both luxury limousines rented by time and a shuttle bus support to the airport. Two separate managers, evaluated as profit centers, oversee each service. Pickoff and Dropoff also have two cost pools for support activities: maintenance and administration. The following table provides relevant data:

		Maintenance	Administration	Limo	Shuttle
Traced costs		$75,000	$30,000	$240,000	$324,000
Service consumption pattern					
			Services consumed by		
		Maintenance	Administration	Limo	Shuttle
Services	Maintenance		4,000 hours	2,000 hours	4,000 hours
provided	Administration	5 persons		20 persons	25 persons

The limousine expects to offer 10,000 hours of service, and the shuttle expects to provide 25,000 hours.

Required:

a. Allocate the costs of the support activities (departments) to the line activities (departments) using the direct method. Calculate the hourly cost rates for the limousine and shuttle services.

b. Allocate the costs of the support activities (departments) to the line activities (departments), using the step-down method. Rank support departments by size to determine the order of allocation.

c. Allocate the costs of the support activities (departments) to the line activities (departments), using the reciprocal method.

d. Which of the rates do you think is most accurate? Why?

16.33 Support department allocations (LO2). James and Quigley, LLC, is a CPA firm that offers both tax and audit services to its clients. The firm bills clients for cost plus 10%. It is straightforward to trace the direct costs associated with a particular client or engagement. However, the firm also incurs about $45,000 in support costs (or overhead) each month. Currently, the firm accumulates this overhead costs into three pools. The tax-related pool contains the cost of subscribing to tax journals, tax-related training, and so on. Likewise, the audit pool contains costs related to maintaining audit expertise. The final pool, administration, pertains to costs such as maintaining the office and secretarial support.

The firm wishes to explore alternative ways of allocating this overhead to clients so that each client is charged for its fair share of the CPA firm's overhead costs. The following table provides relevant data.

		Audit	Tax	Administration	Client 1	Client 2
Traced costs		$15,000	$7,500	$22,500		
	Audit				40%	60%
Services	Tax				70%	30%
provided by	Administration	10%	20%		40%	30%

Required:

a. Using the step-down method, what is the overhead cost allocated to each client? Allocate administration costs first.

b. Recall that there are three methods—the direct method, the step-down method, and the reciprocal method—for allocating support department costs. Would your answer to part (a) differ if you employed the direct method? Why or why not?

c. Would your answer to part (a) hold regardless of the order in which we allocated support activities for the step-down allocation?

d. Using logic rather than numbers, argue why your answer to part (a) would not differ if you employed the reciprocal method?

16.34 Dual-rate allocation (LO3, Advanced). The Consummate Consulting Company (CCC) offers a range of consulting services, grouped into Strategic, Technology, Cost, Marketing, and Personnel. The company allocates the cost of supporting personnel (e.g., the cost to process payroll, maintain HR policies, and so on) to user groups based on head count (i.e., the number of persons employed in the consulting group).The following data pertain to the most recent year.

Group	Strategic Management	Technology Management	Cost Management	Marketing Management	Personnel Management
Staffing	25	45	12	50	18

At the current staffing level of 150 employees, CCC estimates that providing staff services costs $12,250 per month. CCC expects personnel administration costs to increase to $12,875 if staff size increases to 175 persons; likewise, costs would decrease to $11,625 if employment were to drop to 125 persons only.

Required:

a. Allocate the current costs to the five consulting groups in proportion to their current staffing levels.

b. The Cost Management group recently lost a subgroup that focused on Business Process Outsourcing. The group previously had 20 persons instead of the 12 persons now employed. Compute the cost prior to the drop-off in staffing. Compute the costs allocated to the Strategic Management group (which had no change in staffing levels) before and after the change in staffing levels for the Cost Management group. (*Hint:* Use the high-low method to figure out the fixed and variable costs for staffing.)

c. How could CCC modify its allocation procedures to reduce the effect of actions in one group affecting the costs allocated to other groups?

16.35 Support department allocations and make or buy (LO2, Advanced). The Grand Mogul is a 5-star hotel in Mumbai, India. The hotel has installed its own electrical generators to supplement the normal power supply and to ensure uninterrupted power to its demanding clientele. The Power Department now generates 1,200,000 KWh of energy per year. The hotel also has a large Maintenance Department that keeps the hotel's facilities and equipment in excellent working condition. The following data are available (Rs. denotes Indian currency).

	Maintenance	Power Generation	All Other Hotel Operations
Traced costs	Rs. 1,750,000	Rs. 3,000,000	Not relevant

Service consumption pattern

		Maintenance	Power	Hotel Operations
Services	Maintenance		30%	70%
provided by	Power	20%		80%

A local firm, with independent power generation capabilities, approaches the Grand Mogul and offers to sell it all needed power for Rs.3.00 per KWh. If it chooses to buy needed power, the Grand Mogul would eliminate the power generation equipment and all associated staff, and put the freed space to other uses. Hotel management is confident of support quality, and so; the decision will turn on monetary considerations alone.

Required:

a. Evaluate the monetary benefits of outsourcing power generation to the local firm. Be sure to consider the effects of eliminating the Power Department on the costs incurred in the Maintenance Department.

b. What other information would you like in order to improve the confidence in your estimated monetary benefit? How will this information help improve your decision?

16.36 Dual-rate allocations (LO3). The Waterworks Department of the City of Pleasantville provides services to both the Parks and Recreation Department and the citizens of Pleasantville. Recently, a citizen has approached you to complain (nicely) about the wide variations in her water bills. The citizen's household had consumed exactly 2,500 gallons of water each month, but the actual bill varied quite a bit. Looking into the matter, you discover the following:

1. March: As per normal patterns, the residents consumed 1.75 million gallons of water, and the P&R Department consumed 0.25 million gallons.

2. May: The city filled several large outdoor swimming pools with water in preparation for the summer. Thus the P&R Department consumed 750,000 gallons of water, raising total consumption to 3 million gallons. Usage by residents was also higher than normal at 2.25 million. You know that maximum usage almost never exceeds these levels.

3. December: The P&R Department was mostly shut down, reducing its usage to only 0.10 million gallons of water. Overall use by residents also dipped to 1.4 million gallons, perhaps because they were traveling for the holidays.

You discover that the City's Water Department anticipates a periodic surge in demand (to fill pools, skating rinks, fight fires, and so on). Consequently, the City has installed capacity to process 3 million gallons of water per month. The City anticipates that residents would consume 1.75 million gallons on average, with a low of 1.4 million gallons and a high of 2.25 million gallons per month. Likewise, the P&R Department could consume anywhere from 0.1 to 0.8 million gallons per month.

The water treatment plant budgets for fixed costs of $30,000 per month and variable cost of 0.015 per gallon of water.

Required:

a. Calculate the resident's bill for March, May, and December using actual usage and budgeted costs.

b. Repeat requirement (a) using dual rates. That is, allocate fixed costs based on maximum usage and variable costs based on actual usage.

c. Comment on the costs and benefits of using dual rates to determine the water bill mailed out to individual residents.

16.37 Dual-rate allocations (LO3). Drs. Steven Wolf and Robert Brown are partners in an orthopedic clinic located in suburban Detroit. Recently, the clinic acquired an X-ray machine. The two physicians have approached you for help in equitably allocating the machine's cost between themselves. They provide the following data:

	Dr. Brown	Dr. Wolf
Expected use per month	300 exposures	200 exposures
Actual use for March	240 films	240 films

They also tell you that their actual variable cost of $10,720 was $1,120 higher than their expected cost of $9,600, or $20 per film. The expected fixed cost (machine, amortizing room modification, salary for technician, and so on) was $7,500 for the month. Actual cost was $8,000.

Required:

a. Determine the cost allocated to each physician under the following schemes:
   • Total actual cost allocated in proportion to actual use.
   • Total expected cost (per flexible budget) allocated in proportion to budgeted use.
   • Expected fixed cost allocated in proportion to expected use, expected variable cost allocated in proportion to actual use.

b. Which of the above allocations do you think is most equitable? Why?

16.38 Dual-rate allocations (LO3). Prestige U.'s world-renowned management school offers MBA programs to three audiences: daytime students, evening students, and executives. The school prides itself on student support, meaning that the students get numerous handouts each class. These handouts cover lecture outlines, assignments, suggested solutions, articles from the academic and practitioner press, and so on.

A different administrator operates each program. The administrator's charge is to reduce the costs of operating the program while maintaining adequate quality. The following dispute has arisen over the allocation of the costs of the copy center: $24,000 + 0.03 cents per copy.

The following data are available:

| | Program | | | |
---	Daytime	Evening	Executive	Total
Most recent quarter				
# of copies	600,000	500,000	400,000	1,500,000
# of students	300	600	100	1,000
Long-term average				
# of copies	720,000	450,000	330,000	1,500,000
# of students	400	500	100	1,000

Required:

a. Suppose all costs were allocated to the programs based on the actual number of students. Determine the cost allocated to each program.

b. Comment on the allocation in part (a). Suggest a superior driver, keeping in mind that the university wishes to use a single number (one rate) to charge out copy center costs.

c. How would you improve the allocation procedure to reflect the consumption of copy center resources by the various programs? Be sure to consider the drivers of fixed and variable costs in your answer.

16.39 **Dual-rate allocations (LO3, Advanced).** Kevin DenAdel is the chief executive officer of a biotechnology firm that specializes in developing disease- and drought-resistant strains of wheat, corn, and soybeans. The firm is organized into three divisions, with separate staff, facilities, and equipment. However, because the underlying science is similar, all three divisions use the same technology, albeit with differing intensity. The current debate centers on the cost of the DNA sequencing machine.

Wheat Division: We currently sequence about 1,000,000 base pairs each year at a cost of $0.45 per base pair. We looked into getting our own machine. We found one that has enough capacity. Its annual fixed cost is $400,000. As per industry standards, variable costs would be $0.10 per base pair, regardless of scale. So, we are still getting the sequencing done by a reliable vendor.

Corn Division: We are in the same boat, although our volume is only 500,000 base pairs a year. We can get a small machine, but it is not cost-effective. It will cost us close to $0.55 per pair when we can get it done outside for $0.45 per pair. When our volume increases, as we anticipate, we may revisit this issue.

Soybean Division: We are probably the least intensive users of sequencing. Maybe we make 100,000 pairs in a year, and it is simply not viable for us to get a machine. The smallest machine will give us five times the capacity we need.

Knowing that the firm is currently paying $720,000 for DNA sequencing, Kevin is looking into buying a machine to satisfy the needs of all three divisions. He has found a machine that has a capacity of 2 million base pairs a year. This machine will trigger annual fixed costs of $550,000.

Required:

a. Calculate the change in the firm's profit if Kevin decides to buy the machine and has all sequencing done internally.

b. What other factors should Kevin consider in his decision?

c. Suppose Kevin acquires the machine and instructs all divisions to do their sequencing in-house. How much cost should be allocated to each division?

d. The head of the Soybean Division argues that none of the fixed cost should be allocated to her division. She argues that the firm would have likely bought the machine whether her division wanted it or not, and that she is merely using the capacity that would otherwise go to waste. Evaluate the merits of this argument.

Glossary

Absorption costing A method whereby a product's inventoriable cost includes direct manufacturing costs, such as materials and direct labor, as well as indirect manufacturing costs such as machine depreciation and factory. Generally Accepted Accounting Principles (GAAP) requires absorption costing.

Account classification method A cost estimation technique that involves systematically classifying a company's list of cost accounts into fixed and variable categories.

Accounting rate of return (ARR) The average annual income from a project divided by the average annual investment in the project.

Activity The basic element of any business process.

Activity-based Costing (ABC) An allocation methodology used to estimate the controllable cost of capacity resources.

Activity-based management (ABM) Using information from ABC systems to improve profitability by managing products, customers, and resources.

Allocation basis Same as "cost driver."

Allocation rate The cost pool divided by the allocation volume.

Allocation rate Equals the costs in the cost pool divided by the allocation (denominator) volume.

Allocation volume The sum of the cost driver amounts across all cost objects.

Allowable cost The cost target we must meet to achieve profit targets.

Annuity A stream of cash flow with the property that the cash flows per period.

Applied overhead The amount of overhead allocated to products using a predetermined overhead rate.

Avoidable fixed costs Costs that need not be incurred if an option is not chosen. Same as controllable fixed costs.

Balanced scorecard (BSC) A tool for systematically choosing performance measures linked with the firm's overall strategy.

Batch-level activities Activities that pertain to a group of units.

Batch-level cost A cost that varies in proportion to the number of batches of units made (used synonymously with step cost).

Benchmarking Systematic evaluation of various activities and business processes relative to the best practices.

Bottom-up budgeting A process by which lower-level employees actively participate in setting budgets.

Breakeven revenues The sales volume in revenues at which profit equals zero.

Breakeven volume The sales volume in units at which profit equals zero.

Budget A plan for using limited resources.

Budget reconciliation report A report that uses variances to reconcile the difference between master budget profit and actual profit.

Burden Term frequently used to refer to "allocation rate."

Business process Converts a set of organizational inputs into a measurable output.

Capacity The maximum volume of activity that a company can sustain with available resources.

Capacity costs The sum of variable and fixed overhead costs.

Capital budgeting The collective term for the mechanisms and tools used to evaluate expenditures on long-lived resources.

Cash budget A budget that focuses on the inflow and outflow of cash.

Centralized decision making An organizational setting where a few top managers make all the decisions.

Chief executive officer (CEO) The highest ranking executive in an organization. The CEO is responsible for carrying out the policies of the board of directors on a day-to-day basis.

Chief financial officer (CFO) The person in an organization who oversees all accounting and finance functions.

Chief internal auditor (CIA) The person in an organization who oversees the internal audit function.

Contribution margin Revenues less variable costs.

Contribution margin ratio The unit contribution margin divided by the unit price. The contribution margin ratio represents the portion of each sales dollar that, after covering variable costs, goes toward covering fixed costs and, ultimately, profit.

Contribution margin statement An income statement that groups costs by their variability, reporting variable costs and fixed costs as separate line items.

Control account A temporary holding account for accumulating costs such as direct labor and overhead. We zero out a control account at the end of an accounting period.

Control decisions Decisions related to motivating, monitoring, and evaluating performance.

Controllable cost, controllable benefit A cost or benefit that a decision maker chooses to incur, relative to doing nothing.

Controllable performance measure A performance measure that reflects only the consequences of the actions taken by the decision maker.

Controller The person in an organization who manages the day-to-day accounting and issues guidance concerning corporate accounting policies.

Conversion costs The sum of direct labor and manufacturing overhead costs.

Core competency Skill set and expertise that characterize a firm and its employees.

Cost accounting Accounting systems for calculating the values of ending inventories and the cost of goods sold.

Cost allocation A procedure that distributes a common cost among the items giving rise to the cost.

Cost center Organizational unit that has control over and is accountable for costs incurred in offering products or services.

Cost driver Attributes that we can measure for each cost object that are used to distribute the cost pool among cost objects.

Cost gap The difference between the current cost and the allowable cost.

Cost hierarchy The classification of costs into unit-, batch-, product-, and facility-level.

Cost leadership A strategy of competing on the basis of cost advantages.

Cost objects The items, or entities, to which costs are to be allocated.

Cost of capital The opportunity cost of money in the form of returns from alternate investments.

Cost of goods manufactured (COGM) The cost of items finished and transferred from work in process inventory to finished goods inventory.

Cost of goods sold (COGS) The cost of products sold in a period. The cost of items transferred from finished goods inventory to the income statement.

Cost pool The total costs to be allocated.

Cost structure The proportion of total costs that are fixed and variable.

Critical success factors (CSF) Things that must "go right" for the organization to be successful.

Cross-subsidization Some cost allocation systems allocate systematically lower amounts to some products and higher amounts to allocate other products. In such instances, products receiving higher allocations are said to cross-subsidize products receiving lower allocations.

Current cost The cost of new product as per current configurations and production technologies.

Customer perspective One of the four perspectives in the balanced scorecard. This perspective ensures that the organization considers the customer's viewpoint.

Customer planning The set of decisions to assess the profitability of individual customers and customer segments, including the actions taken to improve their profitability.

Decentralization The practice of delegating authority to lower-level managers.

Decentralized decision making An organizational setting where decision-making authority is dispersed throughout the firm.

Decision Choosing an option from a set of options to achieve a goal.

Decision framework A four-step process that consists of specifying the decision goals, identifying available options, evaluating these options, and then selecting the option that best meets the decision maker's goals.

Denominator volume Same as "allocation volume."

Departmental rates The use of many rates, usually one per department, for allocating capacity (overhead) costs to products.

Direct cost, direct benefit A cost or benefit that is uniquely related to a decision option.

Direct costing Term frequently used to refer to "variable costing."

Direct labor Labor costs than can be traced to individual units of a product in a cost-effective manner.

Direct materials Materials costs than can be traced economically to individual units of a product.

Direct method An allocation procedure that ignores the relationship among support activities and focuses instead on the relationship between support and line activities.

Discount factor The amount by which a future cash flow is multiplied to obtain its present value.

Discount rate The rate of return employed to compute the present value of future cash flows.

Discounting The practice of expressing a future cash flow in terms of its present value.

Discretionary cost center A cost center for which there is no clear relation between inputs and outputs.

Dual-rate allocations A procedure that employs two separate drivers to allocate fixed and variable costs in a cost pool.

DuPont model A method for decomposing ROI into two component parts: profit margin and asset turnover.

Economic value added (EVA) A performance measure similar to residual income. The difference is that EVA has specific guidelines on how to compute income, investment, and the weighted average cost of capital.

Engineered cost centers Cost centers for which there is a clear relation between inputs and outputs.

Excess capacity/Excess supply A condition that obtains when available capacity exceeds realized demand.

Excess demand A condition that obtains when realized demand exceeds available capacity.

Facility-level activities Activities that are required to sustain the business.

Facility-level cost Cost that does not vary at the unit-, batch-, or product-level. Cost required to sustain the organization.

Favorable variance A difference between an actual result and a budgeted amount that leads to an *increase* in profit.

Financial accounting Accounting information system that aims to meet the needs of decision makers outside the organization.

Financial budgets Budgets quantifying the outcomes of operating budgets in summary financial statements.

Financial measures Metrics that rely on data recorded in a firm's accounting system.

Financial perspective One of the four perspectives in the balanced scorecard. This perspective ensures that the organization meets its ultimate goals.

Fixed cost A cost that does not change as the volume of activity changes.

Fixed manufacturing overhead Indirect manufacturing costs that do not vary with production volume.

Fixed overhead Indirect manufacturing costs that do not vary with production volume.

Flexible budget A budget made for the actual level of sales, retaining all other plan assumptions in the master budget.

Flexible budget variance The difference between actual profit and flexible budget profit.

Full costing Term frequently used to refer to "absorption costing."

Goals Objectives that decision makers try to achieve.

Gross margin Revenues less product costs.

High-low method A cost estimation technique that uses two observations pertaining to the highest and lowest activity levels to estimate fixed and variable costs.

Hurdle rate Minimum required rate of return chosen by management. Often exceeds the cost of capital.

Incremental (differential) approach An approach for framing and solving decisions that involves expressing the benefits and costs of the various decision options *relative* to one of the options.

Indirect cost, indirect benefit A cost or benefit that is not unique to a decision option—only a portion relates to a decision option.

Informativeness principle The notion that any metric that provides information about a manager's effort or skill could be a useful performance measure.

Initial outlay All costs connected with purchasing an asset and getting it ready for its intended use.

Innovation and learning perspective One of the four perspectives in the balanced scorecard. This perspective ensures that the organization does not stagnate and has mechanisms that allow it to grow and stay competitive.

Input price variance Profit effect associated with the difference between the budgeted and actual price of an input.

Input quantity variance Profit effect associated with the difference between the budgeted and actual input quantity used.

Internal business perspective One of the four perspectives in the balanced scorecard. This perspective ensures that the organization's processes are aligned with its customer and financial goals.

Internal rate of return (IRR) The discount rate at which a project's net present value is zero.

Inventoriable costs See Product costs.

Investment center Organizational unit that has control over and is accountable for revenues, costs, and long-term investment decisions.

Job shop Setting that involves discrete production of unique products.

Joint cost A cost that is common to two or more products. Costs of a joint process.

Joint product Products that are produced in a joint process. It is not possible to produce one joint product without producing the others as well.

Kaizen Philosophy of continuous improvement.

Labor efficiency variance See Input quantity variance.

Labor rate variance See Input price variance.

Lagging measures Measures that reflect past performance.

Leading measures Measures that capture the drivers of future performance.

Life-cycle analysis A technique that partitions a product's life into discrete stages and thereby guides efforts toward pricing and cost control.

Line activity An activity that is directly related to making and selling the firm's products and services.

Lumpy resource Resources for which it is difficult to match the demand for capacity with the supply.

Managerial accounting Accounting information system that aims to meet the needs of decision makers inside an organization.

Manufacturing firm A firm that uses labor and equipment to transform inputs such as materials and components into outputs.

Manufacturing overhead The sum of all indirect manufacturing costs.

Margin of safety The percentage by which current sales exceed breakeven sales.

Market share variance The profit effect due to differences between the actual and budgeted share of the market for a product.

Market size variance Profit effect due to differences between the actual and budgeted size of the market for a product.

Master budget Comprehensive set of operating and financial budgets.

Master budget The budget as prepared at the start of the accounting period.

Materials efficiency variance See Input quantity variance.

Materials price variance See Input price variance.

Merchandising firm A firm that resells essentially the same product it buys from suppliers.

Mixed cost A cost that contains both fixed and variable components.

Modified payback method/period The length of time it takes to recoup the initial investment using discounted cash flows.

Net present value (NPV) The present value of all of the cash flows associated with a resource.

Nonfinancial measures Measures that employ data not in the firm's accounting system.

Normal costing A product-costing system that uses predetermined overhead rates to apply overhead to products.

Operating budgets Budgets reflecting the collective expression of numerous short-term decisions that conform to the direction set by long-term plans.

Operating leverage The ratio of fixed costs to total costs (total costs = fixed costs plus variable costs).

Operations costing A combination of job costing and process costing.

Opportunity cost The value of the next-best option.

Organization A group of individuals engaged in a collectively beneficial mission.

Organization chart A graphical representation of the hierarchical relations among positions in an organization.

Overapplied overhead The difference between actual overhead and applied overhead. Arises when actual overhead is smaller than applied overhead.

Overhead The costs of capacity resources.

Overhead Same as manufacturing overhead.

Overhead costs Term frequently used to refer to "capacity costs."

Overhead rate Term frequently used to refer to "allocation rate."

Payback method/period The length of time it takes to recoup the initial investment using undiscounted cash flows.

Period costs A financial accounting concept under GAAP. Any cost that is not a product cost. A cost related to the selling of goods and the administration of the organization.

Planning decisions Decisions about acquiring and using resources to deliver products and services to customers.

Plant-wide rate The use of one rate for the entire company when allocating capacity costs (overhead) to products.

Practical capacity A realistic estimate of the maximum possible activity level.

Predetermined overhead rate Overhead rate computed using expected overhead costs and expected activity volumes at the start of a plan period, typically a year.

Present value The value today of a future cash flow.

Prime costs The sum of direct materials and direct labor costs, as these are the primary inputs into the production process.

Process shop Setting that involves continuous production of homogeneous products.

Product costs A financial accounting concept under GAAP. Any cost associated with getting products and services ready for sale.

Product mix The proportion, expressed in units, in which products are expected to be sold.

Product planning The set of decisions about which products to offer and their prices.

Product-/customer-level activities Activities that relate to a specific product or a specific customer.

Product-level cost A cost that varies in proportion to the number of products.

Profit center Organizational unit that has control over and is accountable for both revenues and costs.

Profit margin Contribution margin less allocated capacity costs.

Profit margin Contribution margin less the controllable cost of capacity resources.

Purchase price variance The difference between the budgeted and actual price of materials multiplied by the actual quantity of materials *purchased*.

Real option analysis A collection of mathematical techniques for valuing the flexibility associated with a project.

Reciprocal method An allocation procedure that fully accounts for the relationship among support activities.

Reciprocity in consumption A consumption pattern in which two departments provide services to each other.

Regression analysis A statistical method that uses all available observations to estimate fixed and variable costs.

Relative performance evaluation The practice of measuring a manager's or a division's performance against other managers or divisions.

Relevant cost analysis See Incremental (differential) approach.

Relevant cost, relevant benefit A cost or benefit that differs across decision options.

Relevant range A firm's normal range of operations. Over this range, we expect a stable relation between activity and cost.

Residual income (RI) The income that a division generates over and above the required rate of return on investment.

Resource planning Decisions that pertain to improving the efficiency and effectiveness of organizational processes.

Responsibility accounting Set of concepts pertaining to decision rights and performance evaluation in decentralized organizations.

Responsibility center An organizational subunit.

Responsibility center An organizational subunit with specified decision rights. There are three common forms of responsibility centers: cost centers, profit centers, and investment centers.

Return on investment (ROI) A measure of profit generated per dollar of investment—equals divisional operating income divided by divisional investment.

Sales mix variance Used in multiproduct firms, it captures the effect of changes in the sales mix from the budgeted level.

Sales price variance The difference between actual revenues and flexible budget revenues.

Sales quantity variance Used in multiproduct firms, it captures the effect of an aggregate change in sales quantity, holding the sales mix at the budgeted level.

Sales volume variance The difference in profit between the flexible budget and the master budget.

Salvage value The final one-time costs or benefits associated with disposing of a resource.

Segment (product) margin The contribution margin of a segment (e.g., product, customer, geographical region) less traceable fixed costs.

Self-consumption A support department consuming its own output.

Selling and administration costs Nonmanufacturing costs. A term frequently used to refer to "period costs."

Sequential allocation See Step-down method.

Service firm A firm whose product is neither tangible nor storable.

Shareholder value The long-run expected wealth potential of an organization to its shareholders.

Spending variance The difference between budgeted fixed costs and actual fixed costs.

Split-off point Step in a joint process after which we can identify and process the joint products separately.

Step cost A cost that increases in discrete steps as the volume of activity increases.

Step-down method An allocation procedure that partially accounts for the relationship among support activities.

Strategy Approach for creating and sustaining its value proposition.

Sunk cost A past expenditure that cannot be changed.

Support activity An activity that is not a line activity. These activities help the firm execute the line activity.

Target costing A technique for cost planning during product design and development.

Time value of money Phrase used to denote that a dollar today is worth more than a dollar tomorrow.

Top-down budgeting A process by which top management sets the budgets.

Total manufacturing costs charged to production The sum of materials, labor, and overhead added to the work-in-process account during the period.

Total profit variance The difference between actual profit and master budget profit.

Totals (gross) approach An approach that includes non-controllable costs and benefits to construct a contribution margin statement for each decision option.

Traceability The degree to which we can directly relate a cost or a revenue to a decision option.

Transfer price A notional price paid for an internal transfer of goods or services.

Treasurer The person in an organization who manages cash flows and serves as the contact point for banks, bondholders, and other creditors.

Two-factor allocation See Dual-rate allocation.

Underapplied overhead The difference between actual overhead and applied overhead. Arises when actual overhead is larger than applied overhead.

Unfavorable variance A difference between an actual result and a budgeted amount that leads to a *decrease* in profit.

Unit contribution margin The contribution margin per unit.

Unit-level activities Activities that are proportional to production volume.

Unit-level cost A cost that increases or decreases in direct proportion to the number of units produced (used synonymously with variable cost).

Value The benefits less the costs of a decision option.

Value chain Set of logically sequenced activities that together execute the chosen business strategy.

Value differentiation A strategy of competing on the basis of providing customer value through innovation and service.

Value proposition The key source of customer value provided by an organization.

Variability The relation between a cost or a benefit and an activity.

Variable cost A cost that is proportional to the volume of activity.

Variable costing A method that separates variable costs from fixed costs. Under this method, the cost of a unit of product in inventory includes only variable manufacturing costs, such as direct materials, direct labor, and variable manufacturing overhead.

Variable overhead Indirect manufacturing costs that vary with production volume.

Variance The difference between an actual result and a budgeted amount.

Variance analysis Technique for determining why actual revenues, costs, and profit differ from their budgeted amounts.

Weighted contribution margin ratio Contribution margin ratio averaged across multiple products, with each product's contribution margin ratio being weighted by its share of revenues (which is a function of both the product mix and prices).

Weighted unit contribution margin Unit contribution margin averaged across multiple products, with each product's unit contribution margin being weighted by the product mix (i.e., its share of total sales in units).

Whale curve A curve that plots customer profitability, after ranking customers in order of their profitability. Has the appearance of a "whale."

Index